THE CAMBRIDGE HISTORY OF
# FIFTEENTH-CENTURY MUSIC

Through forty-five creative and concise essays by an international team of authors, this *Cambridge History* brings the fifteenth century to life for both specialists and general readers. Combining the best qualities of survey texts and scholarly literature, the book offers authoritative overviews of central composers, genres, and musical institutions as well as new and provocative reassessments of the work concept, the boundaries between improvisation and composition, the practice of listening, humanism, musical borrowing, and other topics. Multidisciplinary studies of music and architecture, feasting, poetry, politics, liturgy, and religious devotion rub shoulders with studies of compositional techniques, musical notation, music manuscripts, and reception history. Generously illustrated with figures and examples, this volume paints a vibrant picture of musical life in a period characterized by extraordinary innovation and artistic achievement.

ANNA MARIA BUSSE BERGER is Professor of Medieval and Renaissance Music History and Theory at the University of California, Davis. She has published articles and books on notation, mensuration and proportion signs, mathematics and music, and music and memory. In 1997 she was awarded a Guggenheim Fellowship; in 2005–6 she was the Lehman Visiting Professor at Villa I Tatti, Florence. She won the Alfred Einstein Award for the best article by a young scholar in 1991, and, in 2006, the Wallace Berry Award for the best book from the Society for Music Theory and an ASCAP Deems Taylor Award for her book *Medieval Music and the Art of Memory* (2005; Italian translation, 2008). In 2014 she won the Colin Slim Award from the American Musicological Society and the Bruno Nettl Award from the Society for Ethnomusicology. In 2011–12 she was the Lise Meitner Fellow at the University of Vienna, where she worked on her current project on "Music in Mission Stations in East Africa." Currently she is a Fellow at Wissenschaftskolleg zu Berlin.

JESSE RODIN is Associate Professor of Music at Stanford University. He is the author of *Josquin's Rome: Hearing and Composing in the Sistine Chapel* (2012) and a volume of *L'homme armé* masses for the *New Josquin Edition* (2014). He directs the Josquin Research Project (josquin.stanford.edu), a digital search-and-analysis tool for exploring a large corpus of Renaissance music, and Cut Circle (cutcircle.org), a vocal ensemble performing fifteenth-century music. His work has been recognized with awards and fellowships by the American Musicological Society, the American Council of Learned Societies, and the American Society of Composers, Authors, and Publishers. Current projects include a monograph on "form" in fifteenth-century music (Cambridge), and a recording of the four late cyclic masses of Guillaume Du Fay (Cut Circle and Musique en Wallonie).

THE CAMBRIDGE HISTORY OF
## MUSIC

The Cambridge History of Music comprises a group of reference works concerned with significant strands of musical scholarship. The individual volumes are self-contained and include histories of music examined by century as well as the history of opera, music theory and American music. Each volume is written by a team of experts under a specialist editor and represents the latest musicological research.

*The Cambridge History of American Music*
Edited by David Nicholls

*The Cambridge History of Western Music Theory*
Edited by Thomas Christensen

*The Cambridge History of Musical Performance*
Edited by Colin Lawson and Robin Stowell

*The Cambridge History of World Music*
Edited by Philip V. Bohlman

*The Cambridge History of Fifteenth-Century Music*
Edited by Anna Maria Busse Berger and Jesse Rodin

*The Cambridge History of Seventeenth-Century Music*
Edited by Tim Carter and John Butt

*The Cambridge History of Eighteenth-Century Music*
Edited by Simon P. Keefe

*The Cambridge History of Nineteenth-Century Music*
Edited by Jim Samson

*The Cambridge History of Twentieth-Century Music*
Edited by Nicholas Cook and Anthony Pople

# THE CAMBRIDGE
## HISTORY OF
# FIFTEENTH-CENTURY
# MUSIC

*

EDITED BY
## ANNA MARIA BUSSE BERGER
AND
## JESSE RODIN

CAMBRIDGE
UNIVERSITY PRESS

# CAMBRIDGE
## UNIVERSITY PRESS

University Printing House, Cambridge CB2 8BS, United Kingdom

One Liberty Plaza, 20th Floor, New York, NY 10006, USA

477 Williamstown Road, Port Melbourne, VIC 3207, Australia

314-321, 3rd Floor, Plot 3, Splendor Forum, Jasola District Centre, New Delhi - 110025, India

79 Anson Road, #06-04/06, Singapore 079906

Cambridge University Press is part of the University of Cambridge.

It furthers the University's mission by disseminating knowledge in the pursuit of
education, learning and research at the highest international levels of excellence.

www.cambridge.org
Information on this title: www.cambridge.org/9781108791885

First published 2015
First paperback edition 2019

*A catalogue record for this publication is available from the British Library*

*Library of Congress Cataloging in Publication data*
The Cambridge history of fifteenth-century music / edited by Anna Maria Busse
Berger and Jesse Rodin.
pages    cm – (The Cambridge history of music)
Includes bibliographical references and index.
ISBN 978-1-107-01524-1
1. Music – 15th century – History and criticism.   I. Berger, Anna Maria
Busse.   II. Rodin, Jesse.
ML172.C33 2015
780.9´031–dc23
2014034794

ISBN 978-1-107-01524-1 Hardback
ISBN 978-1-108-79188-5 Paperback

*For Daphna and Karol*

# Contents

[vii]

# Figures

# Music examples

Unless specified otherwise, note values are unreduced.

# *Notes on contributors*

MARGARET BENT, FBA, is an emeritus Fellow of All Souls College, Oxford, having taught previously at Brandeis and Princeton Universities and served as President of the American Musicological Society. Her many publications range over English and Continental music, repertories, notation, and theory of the fourteenth to sixteenth centuries, including a study and facsimile of the early fifteenth-century Veneto manuscript Bologna Q.15 (2008), and a reconstructed Liber cantus from the Veneto (2012), a region in which she is exploring networks of musicians. Other current work relocates the origins of Jacobus, the author of the *Speculum musicae*, from Liège to Spain.

ANNA MARIA BUSSE BERGER is Professor of Medieval and Renaissance Music History and Theory at the University of California, Davis. She has published on notation, mathematics and music, music and memory, and music in mission stations in East Africa. Her books include *Mensuration and Proportion Signs: Origins and Evolution* (1993) and *Medieval Music and the Art of Memory* (2005, Italian translation, 2008), which won the Wallace Berry Award from the Society of Music Theory in 2005. In 2011–12 she was the Lise Meitner Fellow at the University of Vienna, Currently she is a Fellow at the Wissenschaftskolleg zu Berlin.

LAWRENCE F. BERNSTEIN is the Karen and Gary Rose Emeritus Term Professor of Music at the University of Pennsylvania. His areas of interest include the sixteenth-century chanson, the music of Ockeghem and Josquin, and – more recently – the symphonies of Joseph Haydn. He served as Editor-in-Chief of the *Journal of the American Musicological Society* from 1974 to 1976 and as founding editor of the AMS Studies in Music. In 2009 he was elected an honorary member of the American Musicological Society.

BONNIE J. BLACKBURN, FBA, is a Member of the Faculty of Music at Oxford University and affiliated with Wolfson College, Oxford. She specializes in music and music theory of the fifteenth and sixteenth centuries, with a particular interest in compositional practice, early printing, notation, and canons. She has edited the music of Johannes Lupi and two volumes for the New Josquin Edition. Together with Edward E. Lowinsky and Clement A. Miller she edited *A Correspondence of Renaissance Musicians* (1991).

M. JENNIFER BLOXAM is Herbert H. Lehman Professor of Music at Williams College and former Director of the Williams-in-Oxford Programme. She earned her B.Mus. from the University of Illinois (1979), and her Ph.D. from Yale University (1987). Her scholarship focuses on plainsong and polyphony in the decades around 1500, with particular emphasis on its ritual and cultural framework. In addition to her print publications, she collaborates with the Dutch vocal ensemble Cappella Pratensis to create film, recording, website, and concert projects devoted to the contextualization of this music. Recent fellowship awards include the National Endowment for the Humanities and the Yale Institute of Sacred Music.

PHILIPPE CANGUILHEM is Professor of Musicology at the University of Toulouse. His work focuses on Italian music in the sixteenth century, with special emphasis on Florentine musical life. He is also interested in improvised counterpoint in the Renaissance; he has published an edition and translation of Vicente Lusitano's counterpoint treatises (2013). In addition to articles in *Early Music History*, *Urban History*, *Revue de musicologie*, *Recercare*, etc., he has published two books, on Vincenzo Galilei (2001) and Andrea and Giovanni Gabrieli (2003).

JULIE E. CUMMING is Associate Dean of the Schulich School of Music, McGill University, and author of *The Motet in the Age of Du Fay* (1999). Recent publications include "From Two-Part Framework to Movable Module," in *Medieval Music in Practice: Studies in Honor of Richard Crocker*, ed. Judith Peraino (2013) and "Renaissance Improvisation and Musicology," *Music Theory Online* (2013). She was the principal investigator on the Digging into Data Challenge Grant, "Electronic Locator of Vertical Interval Successions (ELVIS): The first large datadriven research project on musical style" (2012–13).

ANTHONY M. CUMMINGS (M.F.A., Ph.D., historical musicology, Princeton University) is a specialist in the music of the Italian Renaissance and early jazz. He has authored, co-authored, or co-edited nine monographic publications and numerous journal articles in his fields of expertise. His intellectual biography of Nino Pirrotta won the John Frederick Lewis Award from the American Philosophical Society for the best book published by the Society in a particular calendar year. Cummings was formerly Professor of Music at Tulane University and is now Professor of Music and Coordinator of Italian Studies at Lafayette College in Pennsylvania.

DAVID FALLOWS, FBA, studied at Jesus College, Cambridge (B.A., 1967), King's College, London (M.Mus., 1968), and the University of California at Berkeley (Ph.D., 1977). From 1976 to 2010 he taught at the University of Manchester. His books include *Dufay* (1982), *A Catalogue of Polyphonic Songs, 1415–1480* (1999) and *Josquin* (2009); his other publications nearly all concern the "long" fifteenth century, ca. 1380–1520, with a focus on the songs. He was elected a Fellow of the British Academy in 1997 and was President of the International Musicological Society, 2002–7.

David Fiala is Associate Professor of Musicology at the Centre d'Études Supérieures de la Renaissance in Tours (CESR, UMR 7323). He served as editor of the *Revue de musicologie* from 2007 to 2013. His research interests focus on music patronage and musicians' careers in the late medieval and early modern periods. His main projects include an online "Prosopography of Renaissance Singers," a book on "The Musical Patronage of the Dukes of Burgundy and Princes of the Habsburg Household, 1467–1506," a complete edition of the works of Guillaume Costeley, and a co-edited volume on music and musicians in the Saintes-Chapelles, thirteenth–eighteenth centuries.

Alison K. Frazier, Associate Professor of History at the University of Texas at Austin, works on late medieval and Renaissance religious and intellectual history, with an emphasis on manuscript and early print. She has held fellowships from the American Academy in Rome, the Guggenheim Foundation, and Villa I Tatti Harvard University Center for Italian Renaissance Studies. Her current projects include studies of the execution of Pietro Paolo Boscoli (1513), of a humanist vita of Catherine of Siena (1501), and of fifteenth-century hexameral commentary.

James Hankins, Professor of History at Harvard University, is the author of numerous books and articles on Italian Renaissance subjects. He is the General Editor of the I Tatti Renaissance Library.

Leofranc Holford-Strevens retired in 2011 as Consultant Scholar-Editor at Oxford University Press. He is a classical scholar (the author of *Aulus Gellius: An Antonine Scholar and his Achievement*, 2003) with wide-ranging interests, particularly in calendrical studies (*The History of Time: A Very Short Introduction*, 2005) and musicology, in which he has written several articles on the Latinity of theorists and composers. Together with Bonnie J. Blackburn he has edited *Florentius de Faxolis: Book on Music* (2010).

Deborah Howard, FBA, is Professor Emerita of Architectural History and Director of Research in the Faculty of Architecture and History of Art in the University of Cambridge and a Fellow of St John's College, Cambridge. Her principal research interests are the art and architecture of Venice and the Veneto; music and architecture in the Renaissance; and the relationship between Italy and the Eastern Mediterranean. Her recent books include *Sound and Space in Renaissance Venice* (with Laura Moretti, 2009), *Venice Disputed* (2011); *The Music Room in Early Modern France and Italy* (ed. with Laura Moretti, 2012); and *Architecture and Pilgrimage* (ed. with Paul Davies and Wendy Pullan, 2013).

ANDREW KIRKMAN is Peyton and Barber Professor of Music at the University of Birmingham (UK), where he teaches on a broad range of historical topics. His research centers on sacred music of the fifteenth century, and he has published and lectured widely on English and Continental music of the period, including the music of Du Fay, Binchois, Ockeghem, and Josquin. He is also very active as a conductor of vocal and instrumental ensembles, including the award-winning Binchois Consort, with which he has recorded nine CDs on the Hyperion label.

MICHAEL LONG is Professor of Musicology at Indiana University. He has published articles on music of the fourteenth and fifteenth centuries and a book, *Beautiful Monsters: Imagining the Classic in Musical Media* (2008). His current projects include a study of Machaut reception and a book on music and the filmic visionary.

LAURENZ LÜTTEKEN is Professor of Musicology at the University of Zurich. He has published extensively on music between the fourteenth and twentieth centuries, including *Guillaume Dufay und die isorhythmische Motette*, *Musik der Renaissance*, and, most recently, *Richard Strauss: Musik der Moderne*. In 2013–14 he was a Fellow at the Wissenschaftskolleg zu Berlin. Since 2014 he has served as general editor of MGG-online.

EVAN A. MACCARTHY is Assistant Professor of Music History at West Virginia University. He earned his Ph.D. in historical musicology from Harvard University with a dissertation on music and intellectual life in fifteenth-century Ferrara, has published articles on late medieval music and music theory, and is currently writing a book on the intersections of music, pedagogy, and the revival of classical literature across the Italian peninsula in the fifteenth century. In 2012–13 he was the CRIA Fellow at the Villa I Tatti Harvard University Center for Italian Renaissance Studies in Florence, Italy.

PATRICK MACEY is Professor of Musicology at the Eastman School of Music, University of Rochester. His research focuses on music in Florence in the late fifteenth century, and his book, *Bonfire Songs: Savonarola's Musical Legacy* (1998), received the Phyllis Goodhart Gordan Award from the Renaissance Society of America. He has also published articles on the music of Josquin des Prez, and serves on the editorial board of the New Josquin Edition, for which he is editing the five- and six-voice chansons.

HONEY MECONI teaches at the University of Rochester, where she is Susan B. Anthony Professor of Gender and Women's Studies, Professor of Music in the College Music Department, and Professor of Musicology at the Eastman School of Music. Her publications include *Pierre de la Rue and Musical Life at the Habsburg-Burgundian Court*; *Early Musical Borrowing*; *Fortuna desperata: Thirty-Six Settings of an Italian Song*; and many shorter works. Her book on Hildegard of Bingen is forthcoming. Honors received include NEH, Mellon, and Fulbright Fellowships and the AMS Noah Greenberg Award for "distinguished contribution to the study and performance of early music."

JOHN MILSOM is Professorial Fellow in Music at Liverpool Hope University. He has published widely on sixteenth-century music, with particular emphasis on Tudor topics, Josquin des Prez, and the analysis of compositional method in vocal polyphony. He has also created the online Christ Church Library Music Catalogue, a major research resource relating to the contents and provenance history of the internationally important music collections at Christ Church, Oxford.

KLAUS PIETSCHMANN is Professor of Musicology at the Johannes Gutenberg University of Mainz. His principal research interests are the social, institutional, and theological aspects of sacred music in late medieval and early modern Italy and Germany, in particular the papal chapel in the sixteenth century; iconography; and eighteenth- and nineteenth-century Viennese opera. Recent publications include *Kirchenmusik zwischen Tradition und Reform: Die päpstliche Kapelle im Pontifikat Pauls III* (2007); *Musikalische Performanz und päpstliche Repräsentation der Renaissance* (ed., 2014); and *Der Kanon der Musik: Ein Handbuch* (ed. with Melanie Wald-Fuhrmann, 2013).

ALEJANDRO ENRIQUE PLANCHART is Emeritus Professor of Music at the University of California, Santa Barbara, where he taught music history, composition, and Latin paleography and conducted the early music ensembles. He has also taught at Brandeis, Yale, and Harvard Universities. He has published articles and books on Latin plainsong, Guillaume Du Fay and other Renaissance topics, Latin American music, and twentieth-century music, plus over one hundred musical compositions, including symphonies, songs, and chamber music. He is the recipient of a Guggenheim fellowship, the Howard Mayer Brown Award from Early Music America, and the medal of the city of Tours.

YOLANDA PLUMLEY is Professor of Historical Musicology at the University of Exeter. She is author of *The Art of Grafted Song: Citation and Allusion in the Age of Machaut* (2013), *The Grammar of Fourteenth-Century Melody* (1996), *Codex Chantilly, Bibliothèque du Château de Chantilly, MS 564* (2008, with Anne Stone), and (with R. Barton Palmer) is general editor of a new edition of the complete poetic and musical works of Guillaume de Machaut.

KEITH POLK has an M.M. from the University of Wisconsin, Madison, and a Ph.D. from the University of California, Berkeley. He has produced numerous articles and several books on instrumental music of the Renaissance. He is also a French hornist, having performed with the San Diego Symphony, the Amsterdam Concertgebouw Orchestra, the Boston Baroque, and the Smithsonian Chamber

Players, among others. He is Professor Emeritus, University of New Hampshire, and has also taught at Brandeis University, the New England Conservatory, and Regents College, London.

ANNE WALTERS ROBERTSON is the Claire Dux Swift Distinguished Service Professor of Music at the University of Chicago. Her publications include *Guillaume de Machaut and Reims: Context and Meaning in his Musical Works* (Cambridge, 2002); "The Savior, the Woman, and the Head of the Dragon in the Caput Masses and Motet," *JAMS* 59 (2006), which was awarded the H. Colin Slim Award of the American Musicological Society; and "The Man with the Pale Face, the Shroud, and Du Fay's Missa Se la face ay pale," *Journal of Musicology* 27 (2010).

JESSE RODIN is Associate Professor of Music at Stanford University. He is the author of *Josquin's Rome: Hearing and Composing in the Sistine Chapel* (2012) and a volume of *L'homme armé* masses for the New Josquin Edition (2014). He directs the Josquin Research Project (josquin.stanford.edu), a digital tool for exploring a large corpus of Renaissance music, and Cut Circle (cutcircle.org), a vocal ensemble performing fifteenth-century music. His work has been recognized with awards and fellow-ships by the AMS, ACLS, and ASCAP. Current projects include a monograph on "form" in fifteenth-century music.

DAVID J. ROTHENBERG is Associate Professor of Music at Case Western Reserve University. He is author of *The Flower of Paradise: Marian Devotion and Secular Song in Medieval and Renaissance Music* (2011) and co-editor, with Robert R. Holzer, of the *Oxford Anthology of Western Music*, 1: *The Earliest Notations to the Early Eighteenth Century* (2013).

THOMAS SCHMIDT-BESTE is Professor of Music at the University of Manchester. His research interests include vocal music and its sources in the fifteenth and sixteenth centuries, instrumental music of the late eighteenth and nineteenth centuries (Mozart and Mendelssohn in particular), music editing, and the history of musical genres (motet, string quintet, sonata). He is the author of the Cambridge Introduction, *The Sonata* (2011) and a collaborator of the *Leipziger Ausgabe der Werke von Felix Mendelssohn Bartholdy*, and currently leads a major research project on "Production and Reading of Music Sources, 1480–1530."

PETER SCHUBERT is Professor at McGill University's Schulich School of Music, where he participates in the ELVIS project with colleague Julie Cumming, and where he recently presented a workshop in Renaissance improvisation with Massimiliano Guido. He has written several articles on Renaissance music and two textbooks on counterpoint (one with Christoph Neidhöfer). In 1998 he founded VivaVoce, a vocal ensemble that has released four CDs, most recently "Scenes from the Gospels," a selection of Renaissance motets, on the ATMA label.

NICOLE SCHWINDT studied musicology and German language and literature (Ph.D., 1986, University of Heidelberg) and is currently Professor of Musicology in the Department for Early Music at the Staatliche Hochschule für Musik in Trossingen, Germany. She has been invited to teach at Bern University (2006–8) and at Stanford University (2015). Since 2001 she has served as the editor of *TroJa – Kolloquium und Jahrbuch für Renaissancemusik*. Her research focuses on secular music of the fifteenth and sixteenth centuries. A comprehensive survey on music and poetry in the Renaissance appeared in 2004 as part of the book *Musikalische Lyrik*.

RICHARD SHERR is the Caroline L. Wall '27 Professor of Music at Smith College. He is the author of *Papal Music Manuscripts in the Late Fifteenth and Early Sixteenth Centuries* (1996) and has published many articles on Renaissance subjects. He is also the editor of *The Josquin Companion* (2000), *Masses for the Sistine Chapel*, Monuments of Renaissance Music 13 (2009), and is the General Editor of the Sixteenth-Century Motet series (thirty volumes) of transcriptions of motets of the sixteenth century (1987–2000).

PAMELA F. STARR is Professor of Music History at the University of Nebraska-Lincoln and a Fellow of the American Academy in Rome, and has served three terms as Secretary of the American Musicological Society. Her publications on music and institutional patronage of the fifteenth centuries and early modern England have been supported by the NEH, ACLS, Folger and Huntington Libraries, among others, and have appeared in *Early Music History*, *Journal of Musicology*, *Early Music*, *JAMS*, and other journals.

ANNE STONE is Associate Professor of Musicology at the Graduate Center of the City University of New York. She is the author of *Modena, Biblioteca Estense Alpha.M.5.24: Commentary* (2005) and *Chantilly Codex, MS 564: Critical Study and Facsimile Edition* (2008), co-authored with Yolanda Plumley. Current projects include a new edition of the polyphonic songs of Guillaume de Machaut and a monograph whose working title is *Reading Late Medieval Song*.

REINHARD STROHM, FBA, has taught at King's College, London, and Yale University, and, from 1996 to 2007, he was Heather Professor of Music at Oxford University. In 2012 he received the Balzan Prize in Musicology. His books include *Music in Late Medieval Bruges* (1985); *The Rise of European Music* (Cambridge, 1993); and *Music as Concept and Practice in the Late Middle Ages* (ed. with Bonnie J. Blackburn, 2001).

RICHARD TARUSKIN briefly inhabited the fifteenth century during the twentieth, but has moved on, though he retains fond memories of the time he spent in the company of Ockeghem and Busnoys. His contribution to this volume reflects his overriding interest in the more recent past, as reflected in his monograph *Stravinsky and the Russian Traditions* and the *Oxford History of Western Music*, which devotes two of its five volumes to the twentieth century. He is Class of 1955 Professor Emeritus at the University of California at Berkeley, where he taught in the music department from 1987 to 2014.

BLAKE WILSON is Professor of Music at Dickinson College. He is a former Fellow of Villa I Tatti, where he returned as a visiting professor in spring 2011. He is the author of *Music and Merchants: The Laudesi Companies of Republican Florence* (1992), *Singing Poetry in Renaissance Florence: The Cantasi come Tradition c. 1375–1550* (2009), and articles in the *New Grove Dictionary*, *Journal of Musicology*, *Early Music History*, *Recercare*, *Rivista italiana di musicologia*, and I Tatti Studies. He is currently writing a book on oral poetry and improvisatory singing traditions in early modern Italy.

EMILY ZAZULIA is Assistant Professor of Music at the University of Pittsburgh. Her research focuses on the development of music notation, particularly the intersection of musical style, complex notation, and intellectual history, as well as the use of obscenity in early music. She has received fellowships from the National Endowment for the Humanities, the American Council of Learned Societies, and the American Musicological Society. She is currently working on a wide-ranging study of notational aesthetics in polyphonic music, ca. 1380–1520.

# Acknowledgments

A volume of this scope could not have been produced without the help of many colleagues and friends. We are grateful above all to our authors, not only for tailoring their contributions to the requirements of a book such as this, but also for putting up with myriad requests and tight deadlines.

Several people provided helpful feedback on the organization of the volume, the Introduction, or both: Daphna Davidson, Karol Berger, Lawrence F. Bernstein, David Fallows, Allen Grieco, Beatrice Kitzinger, Charles Kronengold, Birgit Lodes, Michael Long, Laurenz Lütteken, John Nádas, Christopher Reynolds, Joshua Rifkin, Richard Sherr, Reinhard Strohm, and Richard Taruskin.

We are grateful to several people at the University of California, Davis. Beverly Wilcox did excellent work on the article texts and bibliographies; Bryce Cannell created the beautiful musical examples. Thanks also to Jessie Ann Owens, who in her capacity as dean allocated funds to cover these costs, and to Stephen Bingham for technical support.

In 2011 Alison Frazier kindly organized a session at the Renaissance Society of America meeting in Montreal that was devoted to papers by contributors to this volume (Alison Frazier, Jennifer Bloxam, and David Rothenberg).

Special thanks are due to Joshua Walden, whose help with many aspects of this project was invaluable.

# *Abbreviations*

## Sigla of manuscripts

| | |
|---|---|
| Aosta 15 | Aosta, Seminario Maggiore, MS 15 (*olim* A 1° D 19) |
| Apel Codex | Leipzig, Universitätsbibliothek, MS 1494 ("Apel Codex") |
| Apt 16bis | Apt, Basilique Sainte-Anne, Trésor, 16bis |
| Barcelona 454 | Barcelona, Biblioteca Nacional de Catalunya, MS 454 |
| Berkeley 744 | Berkeley, University of California Music Library, MS 744 |
| Berlin 78.C.28 | Berlin-Dahlem, Staatliche Museen der Stiftung Preußischer Kulturbesitz, Kupferstichkabinett, 78.C.28 |
| Bologna 2216 | Bologna, Biblioteca Universitaria, MS 2216 |
| Bologna Q.15 | Museo Internazionale e Biblioteca della Musica di Bologna, MS Q.15 (*olim* Civico Museo Bibliografico Musicale, MS Q.15; *olim* Liceo Musicale 37) |
| Bologna Q.16 | Museo Internazionale e Biblioteca della Musica di Bologna, MS Q.16 |
| Bologna Q.17 | Museo Internazionale e Biblioteca della Musica di Bologna, MS Q.17 |
| Brussels 5557 | Brussels, Bibliothèque royale de Belgique/ Koninklijke Bibliotheek van België, MS 5557 |
| Brussels 9085 | Brussels, Bibliothèque royale de Belgique/ Koninklijke Bibliotheek van België, MS 9085 |
| Brussels 9126 | Brussels, Bibliothèque royale de Belgique/ Koninklijke Bibliotheek van België, MS 9126 |
| Buxheim Organ Book | Munich, Bayerische Staatsbibliothek, Cim. 352b (*olim* Mus. Ms. 3725) |

| | |
|---|---|
| Cambrai 6 | Cambrai, Mediathèque municipale, MS 6 |
| Cambrai 11 | Cambrai, Mediathèque municipale, MS 11 |
| Cambrai 1328 | Cambrai, Mediathèque municipale, MS B. 1328 (*olim* 1176) |
| Cambridge O.3.58 | Cambridge, Trinity College, O.3.58 (Trinity carol roll) |
| Cancionero de la Colombina | Seville, Catedral Metropolitana, Biblioteca Capitular y Colombina, MS 7-1-28 |
| Cancionero de Palacio | Madrid, Biblioteca de Palacio Real, MS II-1335 |
| Cape Town 3.b.12 | Cape Town, South African Public Library, MS Grey 3.b.12 |
| Chantilly 564 | Chantilly, Bibliothèque et Archives du Château, MS 564 (*olim* 1047) |
| Chigi Codex | Vatican City, Biblioteca Apostolica Vaticana, Chigi C.VIII.234 |
| Copenhagen 291 | Copenhagen, Det Kongelige Bibliotek, Thott 291.8° |
| Cordiforme Chansonnier | Paris, Bibliothèque nationale de France, Rothschild 2973 |
| Cortona fragment | Cortona, Archivio Storico del Comune, fragment without shelfmark no. 2 |
| Dijon 517 | Dijon, Bibliothèque municipale, MS 517 |
| El Escorial IV.a.24 (EscB) | El Escorial, Real Monasterio de San Lorenzo del Escorial, Biblioteca y Archivo de Música, IV.a.24 |
| El Escorial V.III.24 (EscA) | El Escorial, Real Monasterio de San Lorenzo del Escorial, Biblioteca y Archivo de Música, V.III.24 |
| Emmeram Codex | Munich, Bayerische Staatsbibliothek, Clm 14274 (*olim* Mus. 3232a; Cim. 352c) |
| Eton Choirbook | Winchester, Eton College, MS 178 |
| Faenza 117 | Faenza, Biblioteca Comunale, MS 117 ("Faenza Codex") |
| Florence 26 | Florence, Biblioteca Nazionale Centrale, Panciatichiano 26 |
| Florence 27 | Florence, Biblioteca Nazionale Centrale, Panciatichiano 27 |
| Florence 112bis | Florence, Biblioteca Nazionale Centrale, Mag. XIX, 112bis |

| | |
|---|---|
| Florence 121 | Florence, Biblioteca Nazionale Centrale, Magl. XIX, 121 |
| Florence 178 | Florence, Biblioteca Nazionale Centrale, Magl. XIX, 178 |
| Florence 229 | Florence, Biblioteca Nazionale Centrale, Banco rari 229 |
| Florence 230 | Florence, Biblioteca Nazionale Centrale, Banco rari 230 |
| Florence 2211 | Florence, Archivio Capitolare di San Lorenzo, MS 2211 |
| Florence 2794 | Florence, Biblioteca Riccardiana, MS 2794 |
| Foligno s.s. | Foligno, Biblioteca Comunale, MS s.s. |
| Fountains Fragment | London, British Library, Add. MS 40011B |
| Franus Cantionale | Hradec Králové, Krajské Muzeum, Knihovna, MS II A 6 |
| Glogauer Liederbuch | Kraków, Biblioteka Jagiellońska, Mus. 40098 |
| Laborde Chansonnier | Washington, Library of Congress, M.2.1 L25 Case |
| Leiden 2720 | Leiden, Bibliotheek der Rijksuniversiteit, B.P. L. 2720 |
| Leipzig 1084 | Leipzig, Universitätsbibliothek, MS 1084 |
| Leipzig 1236 | Leipzig, Universitätsbibliothek, MS 1236 |
| Lochamer Liederbuch | Berlin, Staatsbibliothek zu Berlin, Preußischer Kulturbesitz, Mus. ms. 40613 |
| London 20 A. xvi | London, British Library, MS Royal 20 A. xvi |
| London 3307 | London, British Library, MS Egerton 3307 |
| London 15224 | London, British Library, Add. MS 15224 |
| London 29987 | London, British Library, Add. MS 29987 |
| Lucca 184 | Lucca, Archivio di Stato, MS 184 |
| Lucca 238 | Lucca, Archivio di Stato, Biblioteca Manoscritti, MS 238 |
| Mellon Chansonnier | Yale University, Beinecke Rare Book and Manuscript Library, MS 91 |
| Milan 2266 | Milan, Archivio della Veneranda Fabbrica del Duomo, Sezione Musicale, Librone 4 |
| Milan 2267 | Milan, Archivio della Veneranda Fabbrica del Duomo, Sezione Musicale, Librone 3 |
| Milan 2268 | Milan, Archivio della Veneranda Fabbrica del Duomo, Sezione Musicale, Librone 2 |

| | |
|---|---|
| Milan 2269 | Milan, Archivio della Veneranda Fabbrica del Duomo, Sezione Musicale, Librone 1 |
| Modena α.F.9.9 | Modena, Biblioteca Estense e Universitaria, MS α.F.9.9 |
| Modena α.M.5.24 (ModA) | Modena, Biblioteca Estense e Universitaria, MS α.M.5.24 (*olim* lat. 568) |
| Modena α.M.11–12 | Modena, Biblioteca Estense e Universitaria, MSS α.M.11–12 |
| Modena α.X.1.11 (ModB) | Modena, Biblioteca Estense e Universitaria, MS α.X.1.11 (*olim* lat. 471) |
| Montecassino 871 | Montecassino, Biblioteca dell'Abbazia, MS 871 |
| Munich 3154 | Munich, Bayerische Staatsbibliothek, Mus. ms. 3154 ("Leopold Codex") |
| Munich 3224 | Munich, Bayerische Staatsbibliothek, Mus. ms. 3224 |
| Naples VI.E.40 | Naples, Biblioteca Nazionale di Napoli, MS VI.E.40 |
| Nivelle de la Chaussée Chansonnier | Paris, Bibliothèque nationale de France, Rés. Vmc 57 |
| Old Hall MS | London, British Library, Add. MS 57950 |
| Oxford 26 | Oxford, Bodleian Library, MS Arch. Selden B. 26 |
| Oxford 213 | Oxford, Bodleian Library, Canon. Misc. 213 |
| Paris 568 | Paris, Bibliothèque nationale de France, f. it. 568 (Pit) |
| Paris 676 | Paris, Bibliothèque nationale de France, Département de la Musique, Fonds du Conservatoire, MS Rés. Vm$^7$ 676 |
| Paris 1597 | Paris, Bibliothèque nationale de France, f. fr. 1597 ("Lorraine Chansonnier") |
| Paris 4379 | Paris, Bibliothèque nationale de France, n. a. fr. 4379 (4 independent components) |
| Paris 4917 | Paris, Bibliothèque nationale de France, n. a. fr. 4917 |
| Paris 6771 | Paris, Bibliothèque nationale de France, n. a. fr. 6771 ("Reina Codex") |
| Paris 15123 | Paris, Bibliothèque nationale de France, f. fr. 15123 ("Chansonnier Pixérécourt") |
| Perugia 431 | Perugia, Biblioteca Comunale Augusta, MS 431 (G 20) |

| | |
|---|---|
| Reina Codex | Paris, Bibliothèque nationale de France, n. a. fr. 6771 |
| Ritson MS | London, British Library, Add. MS 5665 |
| Rome 2856 | Rome, Biblioteca Casanatense, MS 2856 |
| Schedelsches Liederbuch | Munich, Bayerische Staatsbibliothek, Cgm 810 |
| Segovia s.s. | Segovia, Archivo Capitular de la Catedral, MS s.s. |
| Seville 5-1-43 | Seville, Catedral Metropolitana, Biblioteca Capitular y Colombina, MS 5-1-43 |
| Seville 5-5-20 | Seville, Catedral Metropolitana, Biblioteca Capitular y Colombina, MS 5-5-20 |
| Siena K.I.2 | Siena, Biblioteca Comunale degli Intronati, MS K.I.2 |
| Speciálník Codex | Prague, Hradec Králové, Krajske Muzeum, Knihov II.A.7 |
| Squarcialupi Codex | Florence, Biblioteca Medicea Laurenziana, Med. Palat. 87 |
| Strahov Codex | Prague, Památník Národního Pisemnictví, Strahovská Knihovna, MS D.G.IV.47 |
| Strasbourg 222 C.22 | Strasbourg, *olim* Bibliothèque de la Ville, MS 222 C.22 (lost) |
| Trent 87 | Trent, Castello del Buonconsiglio, Monumenti e Collezioni Provinciali, MS 1374 (*olim* 87) |
| Trent 88 | Trent, Castello del Buonconsiglio, Monumenti e Collezioni Provinciali, MS 1375 (*olim* 88) |
| Trent 89 | Trent, Castello del Buonconsiglio, Monumenti e Collezioni Provinciali, MS 1376 (*olim* 89) |
| Trent 90 | Trent, Castello del Buonconsiglio, Monumenti e Collezioni Provinciale, MS 1377 (*olim* 90) |
| Trent 91 | Trent, Castello del Buonconsiglio, Monumenti e Collezioni Provinciale, MS 1378 (*olim* 91) |
| Trent 92 | Trent, Castello del Buonconsiglio, Monumenti e Collezioni Provinciale, MS 1379 (*olim* 92) |
| Trent 93 | Trent, Biblioteca dell'Archivio Capitolare, MS 93* |
| Turin I.27 | Turin, Biblioteca Nazionale Universitaria, MS Riserva musicale I.27 |
| Turin J.II.9 | Turin, Biblioteca Nazionale Universitaria, MS J.II.9 |

| | |
|---|---|
| Turin T.III.2 | Turin, Biblioteca Nazionale Universitaria, MS T.III.2 (Codex Boverio) |
| Vatican CG XIII.27 | Vatican City, Biblioteca Apostolica Vaticana, Cappella Giulia MS XIII.27 |
| Vatican CS 13 | Vatican City, Biblioteca Apostolica Vaticana, MS Cappella Sistina 13 |
| Vatican CS 14 | Vatican City, Biblioteca Apostolica Vaticana, MS Cappella Sistina 14 |
| Vatican CS 15 | Vatican City, Biblioteca Apostolica Vaticana, MS Cappella Sistina 15 |
| Vatican CS 19 | Vatican City, Biblioteca Apostolica Vaticana, MS Cappella Sistina 19 |
| Vatican CS 23 | Vatican City, Biblioteca Apostolica Vaticana, MS Cappella Sistina 23 |
| Vatican CS 35 | Vatican City, Biblioteca Apostolica Vaticana, MS Cappella Sistina 35 |
| Vatican CS 41 | Vatican City, Biblioteca Apostolica Vaticana, MS Cappella Sistina 41 |
| Vatican CS 49 | Vatican City, Biblioteca Apostolica Vaticana, MS Cappella Sistina 49 |
| Vatican CS 51 | Vatican City, Biblioteca Apostolica Vaticana, MS Cappella Sistina 51 |
| Vatican CS 64 | Vatican City, Biblioteca Apostolica Vaticana, MS Cappella Sistina 64 |
| Vatican CS 197 | Vatican City, Biblioteca Apostolica Vaticana, MS Cappella Sistina 197 |
| Vatican Rossi 215 | Vatican City, Biblioteca Apostolica Vaticana, MS Rossi 215 |
| Vatican San Pietro B80 | Vatican City, Biblioteca Apostolica Vaticana, MS San Pietro B80 |
| Venice IX. 145 | Venice, Biblioteca Nazionale Marciana, MS It. IX. 145 (=7554) |
| Verona 690 | Verona, Biblioteca Capitolare, MS DCXC |
| Verona 755 | Verona, Biblioteca Capitolare, MS DCCLV |
| Verona 756 | Verona, Biblioteca Capitolare, MS DCCLVI |
| Verona 757 | Verona, Biblioteca Capitolare, MS DCCLVII |
| Verona 758 | Verona, Biblioteca Capitolare, MS DCCLVIII |
| Verona 759 | Verona, Biblioteca Capitolare, MS DCCLIX |
| Verona 761 | Verona, Biblioteca Capitolare, MS DCCLXI |

| | |
|---|---|
| Vienna 1783 | Vienna, Österreichische Nationalbibliothek, Handschriften- und Inkunabelsammlung, MS 1783 |
| Vienna 11778 | Vienna, Österreichische Nationalbibliothek, Handschriften- und Inkunabelsammlung, MS 11778 |
| Warsaw 5892 | Warsaw, Biblioteka Narodowa, MS RM 5892 (*olim* 2016) |
| Wolfenbüttel 287 | Wolfenbüttel, Herzog Albrecht Bibliothek, MS Guelferbytanus 287 Extravagantium |
| Wolkenstein Codex A | Vienna, Österreichische Nationalbibliothek, Codex vindob. 2777 |
| Wolkenstein Codex B | Innsbruck, Iniversitäts- und Landesbibliothek, Cod. s.s. (Wolkenstein-Handschrift B) |
| Zwettl | Zwettl, Zisterzienstift, MS without number |

## Journals

| | |
|---|---|
| *AcM* | *Acta Musicologica* |
| *AfMw* | *Archiv für Musikwissenschaft* |
| *BJhM* | *Basler Jahrbuch für historische Musikpraxis* |
| *EM* | *Early Music* |
| *EMH* | *Early Music History* |
| *JAF* | *Journal of the Alamire Foundation* |
| *JAMS* | *Journal of the American Musicological Society* |
| *JM* | *Journal of Musicology* |
| *JRMA* | *Journal of the Royal Musical Association* |
| *MD* | *Musica Disciplina* |
| *ML* | *Music & Letters* |
| *MQ* | *Musical Quarterly* |
| *PMM* | *Plainsong and Medieval Music* |
| *TVNM* | *Tijdschrift van de (Koninklijke) Vereniging voor Nederlandse Muziekgeschiedenis* |

## Reference works

| | |
|---|---|
| *Grove Music Online* | www.oxfordmusiconline.com/ |
| *MGG* | *Die Musik in Geschichte und Gegenwart*, ed. Friedrich Blume, 17 vols., Kassel, 1949–86 |

| MGG2 | *Die Musik in Geschichte und Gegenwart*, 2nd edn., ed. Ludwig Finscher, 29 vols., Kassel and Stuttgart, 1994–2007 |
| New Grove | *The New Grove Dictionary of Music and Musicians*, ed. Stanley Sadie, 20 vols., London, 1980 |
| NG2 | *The New Grove Dictionary of Music and Musicians*, 2nd edn., ed. Stanley Sadie, 29 vols., London, 2001 |
| OED Online | www.oed.com |

## Other

| ASV | Archivio Segreto Vaticano |
| BnF | Paris, Bibliothèque nationale de France |
| CMM | Corpus Mensurabilis Musicae |
| CSM | Corpus Scriptorum de Musica |
| DTÖ | Denkmäler der Tonkunst in Österreich |
| LU | *Liber Usualis* |
| MSD | Musicological Studies and Documents |
| NJE | New Josquin Edition, ed. Willem Elders *et al.* (Utrecht, 1987– ) |
| OO | *Opera Omnia* |
| PMFC | Polyphonic Music of the Fourteenth Century |
| RISM | Répertoire international des sources musicales |

# Introduction

ANNA MARIA BUSSE BERGER AND JESSE RODIN

At one time or another most students of early music encounter a problem: there is a wide gap between introductory texts, which after a certain point are no longer enough, and the scholarly literature, which, owing to a sea of unfamiliar terms and concepts and an understandable tendency toward heightened specificity, can seem impenetrable. This book aims to fill that gap – not by dumbing down a vibrant and long-standing scholarly tradition, but through creative and wide-ranging essays by leading scholars that treat a variety of topics in compact form. Our authors – thirty-eight in all, represented in no fewer than forty-five essays – have endeavored to reflect the most recent research while framing their contributions so as to invite specialist and non-specialist readers alike.

Histories of music typically address music students and music scholars. This volume is certainly intended for these audiences, but from the beginning we have also sought to engage the disciplines of art history, literature, social history, the history of ideas, and cultural studies. We have thought too of the general reader. This might be someone who has listened to a motet by Josquin des Prez or spent time in Florence's museums and is wondering how humanism might have manifested itself in music. Or it might be someone who, having heard echoes of "early music" in Stravinsky's *Mass*, is curious about where the composer got his ideas. Fifty years ago it would have been unthinkable to address a book of this kind to such a wide readership; fifteenth-century music was known only to specialists, and few pieces were recorded. Now for the first time we find ourselves in a historical moment when music from all periods is available online. If a reader wants to listen to one of the works discussed in this volume, chances are good that she can do so in a matter of seconds.

There are many other reasons a book such as this could not have been written fifty years ago. In the past few decades, the widespread availability of modern editions and recordings has facilitated an unprecedented depth of scholarly engagement with the repertory and theoretical literature; this change is reflected above all in Part II, which offers striking insights into improvisation and compositional process, and Part VII, which evinces a sophisticated understanding of music theory, in particular the discourses around and uses of musical notation. New work on humanism (Part III) has enriched our understanding of this important intellectual "movement," thanks in no small measure to contributions by scholars outside musicology (Hankins, Frazier). A multidisciplinary perspective also characterizes Part IV, which showcases the ever wider intellectual and aesthetic contexts scholars have discerned for fifteenth-century music. Our field is more attuned to questions of historiography and reception than ever before; it is not for nothing that we have chosen Part I and Part X, which explore how we confront the past, as bookends. Even those portions of the book that may at first blush seem commensurate with older writings reflect fundamentally new ways of thinking – about the central role played by genres in defining the musical landscape (Part IX), the complex interplay between institutions, urban environments, gender, and politics in shaping musical practices (Part V), relationships between music and sacred themes (Part VI), and the materiality and intellectual background of the musical sources upon which so much of our field depends (Part VIII).

Other changes are more explicitly historiographical. Take as one example the shifting fortunes of fifteenth-century composers. Whereas half a century ago the period was defined mainly by the trio Du Fay (then "Dufay"), Ockeghem, and Josquin, with a few others waiting in the wings, we now embrace a more pluralistic view that has benefited from work on Agricola, Bedyngham, Binchois, Busnoys, Compère, Dunstaple, Gaspar, Isaac, Morton, Obrecht, de Orto, Regis, and La Rue, among others.[1] In a similar vein, for our views of individual musicians we are no longer as reliant as we once were on the pronouncements of theorists. (Petrus de Domarto, whom Richard Taruskin aptly dubbed "Tinctoris's perennial whipping boy," is no longer considered a third-rate composer[2] – nor, for that matter, is Tinctoris himself.) If the handful of composer studies included here (Part I) continues to center upon the "big three," that is in part because their best works number among the most extraordinary aesthetic and intellectual achievements of the age. It is also because these composers have loomed so large in the scholarship and because the methodological questions that arise from their music are unusually rich.

---

1  See the relevant bibliographies in *NG2*. Further examples, with a focus on the most recent literature, include: Gallagher, *Johannes Regis*; special issues of the *Journal of the Alamire Foundation* (on Jacob Obrecht: vols. 2–3, 2010–11) and the *Journal of Musicology* (on Henricus Isaac: vol. 27, 2011); Rodin, *Josquin's Rome* (on Gaspar and de Orto); and Fitch, "'Virtual' Ascriptions in Ms. AugsS 142a."
2  See Taruskin, "Antoine Busnoys and the *L'homme armé* Tradition," 284, and Wegman, "Petrus de Domarto's *Missa Spiritus almus.*"

Still another change is geographical. It has long been known that a staggering percentage of fifteenth-century musicians originated in a tiny geographic area, a portion of the Burgundian territories bounded by Cambrai, Namur, Leuven, and Bruges (now northwestern Belgium and northernmost France). Trained in local schools (*maîtrises*) evidently characterized by overachievement, many of these musicians moved from place to place with dizzying frequency, traipsing not only across the Alps, to Italy, but also to and from England, Spain, Poland, Hungary, and Bohemia. In the fifteenth century such travel was by no means unique to musicians: one finds movement by merchants and bankers between the financial centers of Bruges, Florence, and Lübeck; a tendency of Italian courts to import from the North not only musicians, but also tapestries and oil paintings; and increasingly close political ties between East and West that owe in part to the Councils of Constance and Basel. The upshot, as concerns the history of music, was the development of an international musical style, with "international" now defined more broadly than ever before. As several essays in this volume attest, many so-called peripheral areas are turning out to have been important centers in their own right.[3]

## The fifteenth century – and periodization

There is a certain freedom in writing a history of Western music bound only by the chronological range 1400–1500. The ostensibly neutral dates, imposed benevolently by the organizers of this series, obviate the usual requirement to embrace (or repudiate) one or another received periodization. There need be no "Middle Ages," no "Renaissance" here – and indeed these terms, particularly the latter, will make few appearances in these pages.[4] Their absence is salutary in several respects. To give just one example: by concluding in the middle of the so-called "Josquin generation" we are able to avoid an unfortunate tendency to cast that era merely as the progenitor of sixteenth-century contrapuntal practice and the precursor of new, proto-madrigalistic ideals of word–tone relations. More generally, the lack of an assigned "thesis" has freed our authors to tell complex, nuanced, sometimes even contradictory stories. To our ears, this cacophony is all to the good.

---

3 See the contributions by Strohm, Pietschmann ("Institutions"), Berger ("Oswald"), Bent, Schmidt-Beste, and Schwindt. On the "international" style more generally, see above all Strohm, *The Rise of European Music*.
4 One caveat is that of all the volumes in this series organized by century, ours is the earliest. The *ars antiqua* and *ars nova*, not to mention the four or so centuries before them, have been herded into a single, "medieval" volume – which in turn puts pressure on our volume to be "non-medieval."

Still, escaping a monolithic title is not the same as escaping its resonances. Whether we speak of "late medieval," "Renaissance," or "early modern," these terms – Cellarian, Burckhardtian, Johnsonian – linger in our imaginations.[5] This remains true even when we reject such terms outright; doing so merely catches us in a reactive pose, as we define our subject *against* rather than *through* them. Put differently, we are more or less stuck.[6] But whereas some would lament this situation, we prefer to think that it is not so very dire. On the contrary, periodization can help us see patterns, which after all is a main task of the historian. Indeed the period designations we are in one sense so grateful to have avoided are in another sense useful for organizing our thinking. And the problems thrown up by the collision of periods and the values that attend them can guide us toward greater subtlety and away from the oversimplified views such labels are often said to impose.

This volume therefore grapples – continues to grapple – with a swirl of historical developments that caused earlier writers to see new periods beginning in the years 1380, 1400, 1420, 1450, 1480, and 1500. Ours is a long fifteenth century, one that takes account of historicizing trends around 1400 that look back to the end of the trecento, and that peers just far enough into the sixteenth century to witness the first flowering of polyphonic music printing.[7] Those who go in search of early modernity and "Renaissances" will find them: in the emergence of a strong work concept (Lütteken), in the new importance placed on the senses in experiencing music (Pietschmann), in stylistic ruptures with music of previous generations (Cumming/Schubert, Milsom, Rodin), and, perhaps above all, in unprecedentedly rich portraits of fifteenth-century humanism (Hankins, Strohm, Holford-Strevens, Wilson, Frazier). By contrast, anyone for whom the fifteenth century is "late medieval" will be drawn to essays that convey the ongoing importance of the memorial archive (Berger) and the manuscript tradition (Bent, Schmidt-Beste), continuities in notation and music theory (Stone, Zazulia, MacCarthy), and the enduring value placed on ritual, devotion, and ecclesiastical authority (Bloxam, Rothenberg, Robertson, Sherr, Starr) – though every one of these authors, we hasten to add, focuses on change at least as much as sameness, allowing the material, not an externally imposed label, to generate thematic coherence.

---

5  See Cellarius, *Historia universalis*; Burckhardt, *The Civilization of the Renaissance in Italy*; and Johnson, *Early Modern Europe*. With respect to the first of these terms the story is immensely complex; credit can by no means be given exclusively to Cellarius. See, for instance, Gordon, *Medium Aevum and the Middle Age*; and Robinson, "Medieval, the Middle Ages."

6  Cf. Strohm, "'Medieval Music' or 'Early European Music'?" Our thanks to Professor Strohm for sharing an advance copy of his text.

7  On the latter see above all, and with references to further literature, Boorman, *Ottaviano Petrucci*.

## Book overview

Historiography is all. The way we write history – the values we bring to bear, the decisions we make about what to include and what to leave out, even the terms we use – conditions our thinking at the most basic level. In conceiving this volume we have done our utmost to reflect the state of the field while also pushing at its edges. On the one hand, we have not shied away from soliciting overviews – creative and thoughtfully organized overviews, but overviews nonetheless – of topics we believe are nowhere else covered adequately at a commensurate length. On the other, we have invited essays by scholars outside musicology and allocated extra space to areas that strike us as particularly vibrant or promising. And we have sought to showcase a variety of perspectives and methodologies by assembling a large and international team of authors. We pray that you, dear reader, will forgive us for failing to deliver complete coverage: for reasons both conceptual and practical, we have (sometimes inadvertently) skipped over major areas of inquiry. Our essays on music in churches, courts, and cities, for instance (Part V), include precious little on Ferrara, Naples, Milan, St. Peter's in Rome, and Bruges, musical centers to which significant studies have been devoted;[8] this is in part for reasons of space, in part because several essays on music in other civic and courtly contexts give at least a sense of the relevant issues. Similarly, we have included only three essays on the history of music theory (Part VII), in this case because the *Cambridge History* series devotes an entire volume to the subject.[9]

Other omissions are subtler. The relatively little space we give to issues of gender and sexuality, for example (cf. Blackburn), reflects the slow rate at which these topics have found their way into musicological studies of this period;[10] this circumstance may, more than any ideologically driven aversion, reflect a perceived paucity of historical materials. We have also given relatively short shrift to performance practice (more on this below),[11] the institutions of music pedagogy,[12] and the practice of editing,[13] all worthy topics for which a substantial literature exists. As editors we recognize that any choice is a choice

---

8 See Lockwood, *Music in Renaissance Ferrara*; Atlas, *Music at the Aragonese Court of Naples*; Merkley and Merkley, *Music and Patronage in the Sforza Court*; Reynolds, *Papal Patronage and the Music of St. Peter's*; and Strohm, *Music in Late Medieval Bruges*.

9 *The Cambridge History of Western Music Theory*, ed. Christensen.

10 A notable exception is Higgins, "Parisian Nobles, a Scottish Princess, and the Woman's Voice."

11 Major studies include *Performance Practice*, ed. Brown and Sadie; and Leech-Wilkinson, *The Modern Invention of Medieval Music*.

12 On the *maîtrise* see Becker, "The Maîtrise in Northern France and Burgundy"; Wright, *Music and Ceremony at Notre Dame of Paris*, ch. 5; and Demouy, "Une source inédite de l'histoire des maîtrises." For England see Mould, *The English Chorister*. See also *Music Education in the Middle Ages and the Renaissance*, ed. Murray *et al.*

13 The standard studies are Caldwell, *Editing Early Music* and Grier, *The Critical Editing of Music*.

against – and though we did not frame our decisions about what to include in negative terms, we acknowledge that the contents and organization of this volume reflect our historiographical priorities.

Thus while this is not a book about the historiography of fifteenth-century music, it seems sensible to begin (Part I) with essays that address head-on some of the challenges posed by the study of this period. Michael Long asks what it means to "hear" and "listen to" music of the fifteenth century. In an analysis of the *hydraulis* (organ) mentioned at the outset of a famous motet by Antoine Busnoys and, arguably, echoed decades later in a mass by Josquin, he considers how, through cultural allusion and sheer sonic forcefulness, the sound of the cantus firmus might have created a "quasi-ritual cultural moment," illuminating "experiential modes located outside the hierarchical apparatuses of 'preparation' that inform our understanding of historical aural reception." Arguing from a very different perspective, Klaus Pietschmann approaches the practice of listening through an analysis of contemporary texts. Having identified several "essential modes of perception," he examines the "doctrine of the internal senses and their effect on music comprehension ... with a special focus on the spiritual efficacy of sacred polyphony" on the one hand, and the "justification of earthly sensual pleasure" on the other. Together these essays can help us hear fifteenth-century music with greater clarity, historical sensitivity, and self-awareness.

In recent decades scholars have struggled to reach consensus about the terms we use to describe pieces of music and the relationships between them. In this volume we have striven for some degree of terminological uniformity, but we have also chosen not to intervene in cases of substantive disagreement. Where one scholar speaks of "isorhythm" (Lütteken), others now avoid the term;[14] and where one essay uses "*fuga*" to identify certain kinds of melodic repetition (Milsom), another prefers "imitation" (Cumming/Schubert).[15] In some cases the choice of modern formulation carries especially significant implications. The terms "work" and "musical borrowing," for instance, are in one sense purely pragmatic, but as the contributions by Laurenz Lütteken and Jesse Rodin in Part I reveal, they carry immense weight. In an innovative essay that reasserts the importance of the "work" while grounding the work concept in a robust theoretical context, Lütteken pinpoints five "theoretical and practical premises upon which the musical work of art depends ...: notation and

---

14 See Bent, "What Is Isorhythm?," which can be fruitfully read alongside Emily Zazulia's essay in this volume.

15 Milsom lays out a proposed analytical terminology for fifteenth- and sixteenth-century music in "Crecquillon, Clemens, and Four-Voice *Fuga*." See also Cumming, "Text Setting and Imitative Technique."

written tradition, authorship and professionalization, historicity and historical memory, the position of music in emerging generic classifications of the arts, reproducibility, and 'aesthetics'." Rodin reassesses the famous tradition of polyphonic masses on the *L'homme armé* melody as well as the emphasis scholars have placed on "musical borrowing." Fifteenth-century polyphony is strikingly allusive: this was an age in which composers regularly based new works on older ones, choosing as models not only chant but also recent polyphonic compositions. Rodin begins by "propos[ing] a new way of parsing the musical connections that bind several [*L'homme armé* masses] together"; he then turns the "discussion on its head by questioning the terminological propriety and methodological value of musical borrowing all told."

Each of the composer-based studies in this section offers insight into a particular figure while also confronting poignant historiographical questions. In an impressive précis of Du Fay's life and works, Alejandro Planchart observes how, relative to other fifteenth-century composers, "the gaps in Du Fay's biography are comparatively small, the succession of his patrons and employers comparatively clear. Thus it is possible not merely to establish many basic facts, but also to bring these facts into conversation with broader cultural and political developments." Lawrence Bernstein focuses on questions that have beclouded the study of Jean d'Ockeghem. Using subtle analytical methods born of deep engagement with the music, Bernstein puts forward a new model for interpreting Ockeghem's compositions, grappling along the way with a fraught historiography. In an essay on Josquin that takes as its point of departure a famous article by Joshua Rifkin, Rodin suggests that the study of this composer poses unparalleled historiographical and epistemological challenges.[16] After identifying five central problems with which every student of Josquin must contend, Rodin makes an argument about how to move forward, asking us "to contextualize with respect to the evidence we have rather than the evidence we wish we had; to tell a richly textured story without falling into storytelling; and to maintain high evidentiary standards without neglecting our historical imaginations."

Composer-based discussions usually circle back, at one point or another, to that most traditional of musicological topics: the history of musical style. While out of fashion in certain quarters, style analysis is for this period a cutting-edge area of research, thanks both to our newfound intimacy with the music and the ever expanding range of techniques scholars are using to evaluate it. In recent years there has emerged an exciting literature on

---

16 See "Problems of Authorship in Josquin," in conjunction with several other significant contributions (e.g., "Munich, Milan, and a Marian Motet"; "A Black Hole?"; and "Musste Josquin Josquin werden?").

improvisation, composition, and the intersection between the two (Part II). Central to both these practices is the musical memory. In an essay on the memorial archive, Anna Maria Busse Berger highlights the degree to which the *memoria* served as a foundation for all fifteenth-century musicians, who were trained to memorize interval progressions and visualize polyphonic structures in the mind.[17] With this framework in place, readers can fruitfully approach Philippe Canguilhem's essay on the practice and intellectual context of improvisation. Canguilhem reframes the debate about the meaning of *cantare super librum* ("singing upon the book"), arguing that fifteenth-century thinkers understood "counterpoint" to embrace both written and improvised polyphony.[18] In doing so he corrects the modern misconception that improvisation is characterized by an absence of compositional planning. In a similar vein, Berger's study of Oswald von Wolkenstein interrogates the borders between oral and literate culture through the example of an almost certainly illiterate musician. Drawing on the work of the anthropologist Jack Goody, Berger posits a "secondary orality" that distinguishes "between oral culture, on the one hand, and oral plus written and printed culture, on the other" – a distinction that can help us understand how "the written page permitted different ways of memorizing material and texts."

Moving into the realm of so-called art music, two further essays examine the preserved repertory from sophisticated analytical vantage points. In a discussion of Josquin's famous *Ave Maria ... virgo serena*, John Milsom changes the state of play with respect to this hotly contested piece, using "forensic analysis" of Josquin's stretto *fuga* to distance the motet from Milan. In doing so he also asks what it means to approach polyphonic works of this period. Julie Cumming and Peter Schubert, by contrast, trace a single technique – imitation – across three successive generations of composers; their analysis lends unprecedented clarity to a procedure that developed in the fifteenth century and would come to dominate musical practice throughout much of the sixteenth.

This volume breaks ground in its treatment of the relationship between music and fifteenth-century humanism (Part III). As James Hankins explains, humanists "came to colonize a cultural space somewhere between theology ... and the professional studies of law and medicine" – that is, the "liberal arts, the arts worthy of a free man or woman, of people who did not (in theory) have to earn a living." In a persuasive multidisciplinary study, Hankins reasserts the importance of the Italian humanists, who "championed a new way of judging

---

17  A wider discussion of these issues appears in Berger, *Medieval Music and the Art of Memory*.
18  This argument resonates with one first made in Sachs, "Arten improvisierter Mehrstimmigkeit."

music according to its moral and civic purposes . . . and . . . created an audience of educated amateurs for 'classic' music."

In spite of mounting evidence to the contrary, humanism is often said to be a uniquely Italian phenomenon – which makes Reinhard Strohm's contribution particularly welcome. Tracing a common set of humanistic tendencies across a wide geographic area, Strohm argues that even if non-Italian humanists did not transform their local cultures, they viewed them through humanistic eyes. The impact of their ideas on musical composition can be seen in "the application of rhetorical figures (*colores rhetorici*) to the musical texture," the setting of "a greater variety of Latin poetic forms," their defense of "incorrect" (i.e., non-classical) Latin pronunciation, and the development of "the modern understanding of composed music as a 'completed and independent work'." Leofranc Holford-Strevens turns a spotlight on the second of these developments, examining the formal properties of Latin poetry set by fifteenth-century composers. Casting the fifteenth century as an era of possibility and change, Holford-Strevens expertly describes the "protracted process" by which Latin literature was remodeled "upon the grammar, style, and form of classical prose and poetry."

Humanism fostered an environment that, to quote Blake Wilson, "promoted the virtues of an active life of civic engagement, and an attendant focus on oral discourse in the vernacular in conjunction with the newly exalted disciplines of rhetoric and poetry." Wilson's essay demonstrates how the *canterino* and *improvvisatore* gave voice to the humanists' ideals.

Like Strohm's, Alison Frazier's essay is in one sense a corrective, this time to the notion that humanism is a uniquely secular phenomenon. Presenting exciting new research on Offices created for women saints, Frazier shows how fifteenth-century humanists undertook bold experiments in ritual, "colonizing" the sacred genres of the saint's Life, biblical exegesis, and the liturgical Office in an effort to enhance their impact on the faithful. Taken together these essays paint a dynamic, multifaceted image of humanism, one that serves as an invitation to further scholarly inquiry. They also draw seamlessly on recent work in other disciplines.

Nowhere is this multidisciplinary strategy more prevalent than in Part IV, which brings music into conversation with architecture, feasting, and poetry to convey the wide range of contexts in which it was experienced. In an insightful essay that unites acoustics, space, building practices, and institutional contexts, Deborah Howard describes "the intimate relationship between space and musical performance." She "chart[s] colliding waves of interaction, in which," for example, "northern polyphony attuned to flamboyant Gothic settings was grafted into Italian liturgy and ceremonial, to be framed within architectural settings increasingly tinged by the inspiration of ancient Rome." Anthony Cummings observes an important connection between music-making and dining: "both activities occur in 'real time' and are dynamic or kinetic in nature." Drawing on contemporary accounts of often lavish banquets, Cummings shows how combining these practices generated multi-media and multi-sensory aesthetic experiences. Such feasts often included sung lyric poetry, the genre at the center of Yolanda Plumley's rich account of New Year songs. Investigating a large corpus of poetic texts, Plumley discerns the generic and textual norms that bind this repertory, both musical and literary, together. She further illuminates how these songs participate in a culture of late medieval gift-giving, a "social transaction between author and patron, or lover and lady."

The fifteenth-century institutions that supported musical pursuits – church, court, city – held sway over practically every aspect of musical production: the types of music that were cultivated, performance contexts, the extent and means of dissemination, the economic status and daily schedule of professional musicians, even who was allowed to perform and listen. While a volume such as this can scarcely address all the subtleties that shaped the institutional media-tion of musical practices, Part V offers both a robust overview and a series of case studies that, taken together, give texture to the institutional politics of fifteenth-century music-making. Pietschmann's overview chapter defines the musical institution as "a group of musicians attached to a courtly, ecclesiastical, or civic entity that provided a foothold or financial support for musical production." Identifying the fifteenth century as a decisive period in the development of musical institutions, Pietschmann focuses on the court chapel, taking a comparative approach to the question of music's function and arguing that chapels tended "to project exclusivity and cachet . . . and foster internal stability and identity."

In the North, the most famous chapel of the period was that of the Valois dukes of Burgundy, who sought, in the words of David Fiala, "to immerse their courts in the most luxurious of sonic environments." Notwithstanding a piteous survival rate of polyphonic sources, Fiala is able to offer a sophisticated account of music at the Burgundian court, thanks in part to the extensive archival holdings of the Burgundian state.

Richard Sherr takes us behind the veil of the Sistine Chapel, certainly the most important site of polyphonic music-making in late fifteenth-century Italy. His study, which critically evaluates the writings of papal master of ceremonies Johannes Burckard, offers fresh insights about institutional hierarchy, the responsibilities and changing status of the singers, and matters of performance practice. The Vatican remains at the center of Pamela Starr's essay, which probes above all the economics of earning a living as a fifteenth-century singer. With extraordinary clarity, Starr describes the process by which singers navigated a labyrinthine papal bureaucracy to procure "benefices" – that is, remunerated posts held by ordained clergy. Starr further shows how the study of beneficial documents has yielded a gold mine of biographical and prosopographical information about fifteenth-century musicians.

Precious biographical details are sometimes also lurking in surviving letters, chronicles, and poems. Through two closely related case studies, Bonnie Blackburn uses evidence of this kind to illuminate the world of the female musician. These women were either anonymous singers and players or "high-born ladies, daughters or wives of courtiers and rulers"; they were not only "extremely talented but also confident entrepreneurs." Blackburn's essay relates significant discoveries about performance contexts and practice. It also alerts us to how issues of gender can inform the study of fifteenth-century music.

In late fifteenth-century Florence, the lauda stood at the meeting point between seemingly disparate but in fact deeply interconnected elements: religious fervor, Carnival celebrations, and political upheaval. Focusing on the influential figure of Girolamo Savonarola, Patrick Macey paints a nuanced picture of this tumultuous cultural moment, helping us understand how urban environments fostered a unique kind of music-making.

The lauda epitomizes something important: in an era that lacked a dividing line between realms that we today would characterize as "secular" and "sacred," the expression of religious values extended well beyond the walls of the church. Through three complementary studies, Part VI explores the importance to music of religious devotion and liturgy.

The tight link between music and religious ritual undergirds Jennifer Bloxam's essay. Drawing on six "basic genres of ritual action" defined by Catherine Bell, Bloxam offers an interpretive framework for the analysis of music and ritual, inviting us to "focus on music's function in relation to the different and overlapping purposes of ritual behavior." David Rothenberg reminds us that the veneration of the Virgin Mary was central to fifteenth-century music-making. Drawing on polyphonic works from across the century, he shows how Mary's dual status as "the exalted Queen of Heaven and a humble lady of this earth" conditioned devotional practices both public and private, with a concomitant heterogeneity of musical genres (e.g., mass and song-style motet) in which her veneration found expression.

Noting the prevalence of certain sacred themes in fifteenth-century music, Anne Walters Robertson asks: "What shared experiences helped drive the cultivation and circulation of beloved sacred motifs?" To answer this question

she explores the practice of reading "sacred affective literature," texts translated into the vernacular in the fifteenth century that "required the reader to
immerse herself in the details of Jesus' life and that of the Virgin." Robertson
uses these texts as an interpretive lens through which to evaluate both "sacred"
and "secular" polyphonic works; she even proposes that affective writings can
help us understand why composers of this era began to set text with newfound
sensitivity.

The past few decades have witnessed ever closer scholarly engagement with
the music-theoretical literature, on the one hand, and the notational worlds of
the preserved repertory, on the other. Part VII brings these subjects together.
In an essay distinguished by its clarity of presentation, Anne Stone presents an
overview of fifteenth-century musical notation. Taking as a guide the *Libellus
cantus mensurabilis*, a fourteenth-century treatise that was read and commented
on throughout the fifteenth century, Stone demystifies many complex features
of rhythmic and metrical notation as theorized by writers on music and put
into practice by composers.

Modern and late medieval musical notation are conceptually distinct in a
central respect: whereas for us the interpretation of note shapes is usually fixed,
in the fifteenth century these signs gained meaning only through contextual-
izing "metasigns." Taking this conceptual difference as a starting point, Emily
Zazulia introduces what she terms the "aesthetic of notational fixity," a novel
and important compositional paradigm within which singularly notated
musical lines could spawn manifold sonic realizations. Zazulia's impressive
study charts the development of this concept as both a theoretical idea and a
notational reality in the works of major composers of the period.

Turning to the theorists themselves, Evan MacCarthy considers the changing
content and organization of treatises on music. Filtering his discussion through
the lens of genre, MacCarthy contrasts treatises that fit squarely "into a larger
program of quadrivial studies" with those by writers such as Prosdocimus de
Beldemandis and, even more, Tinctoris, who "infused speculative ideas with a
keen awareness of musical practice and contemporary repertory."

For us moderns, of course, access to the repertory is almost entirely
dependent on the surviving sources. Part VIII is devoted to a pair of magisterial
studies by Margaret Bent and Thomas Schmidt-Beste that describe the extant
manuscripts of polyphonic music in the first and second halves of the century,
respectively. Far more than mere surveys, these essays contend with a range of
issues: geographical distribution, survival rates, types of sources, owners,
makers, and scribes, authorship, and the performing life of the repertory.
Bent and Schmidt-Beste also offer insight into the material qualities of the
books, including size, intended use, notation, page layout, texting practices,

compilation, and organization – qualities that in many cases are easy for readers to observe in action, thanks to the increasing number of digitized manuscript images now available online. While Schmidt-Beste's essay stops just short of the transition, beginning in 1501, from manuscript to print, he nonetheless reminds us that the so-called "great paradigm shift" effected by the introduction of print "did not by any means imply a decline in manuscript production and use." Indeed in many ways the vibrant manuscript culture of the sixteenth century can be interpreted as a continuation of older practices.

While many fifteenth-century sources are essentially miscellanies, even more betray one or another type of generic organization: one finds songbooks devoted almost exclusively to settings of *forme fixe* poetry, institutional manuscripts in which liturgical and paraliturgical music is organized according to local requirements, even private books that group masses separately from motets. Taken together this picture underscores the powerful role played by genres, the subject of Part IX, in disciplining musical practice. In fifteenth-century music one finds a fairly small number of genres, each encompassing a large and heterogeneous repertory. The closest we have to a contemporary account of musical genres is a statement by Tinctoris, who in his *Diffinitorium musices* (*Dictionary of Musical Terms*) adapts Cicero's threefold classification of oratory, characterizing the mass as great (*magnus*), the motet as middling (*mediocris*), and the song as small (*parvus*). We have followed Tinctoris's scheme to the extent that Part IX begins with these three genres – but we have also endeavored to reflect the range of the surviving repertory by commissioning chapters on instrumental music, sacred song, and chant.

Andrew Kirkman interprets the polyphonic mass as a genre "whose time had come: physical expression of eschatological concerns, responding to fear of purgatory, reached its peak at this time, as seen in expressions of devotion for intercession by the saints, and especially the Virgin, in church building, iconography of various kinds, ritual, and music." After tracing the origins of the mass in the fourteenth century, Kirkman uses a series of carefully chosen examples from across the century as the basis for an elegant discussion of developments in musical symbolism and style.

Of all fifteenth-century musical genres, the motet is surely the hardest to pin down. Lütteken observes how, relative to the previous century, contemporary "definitions . . . present fundamental interpretive challenges, insofar as they describe a genre that was no longer governed by any discrete set of normative features" but rather by "functional polysemy, itself an indicator of the transition to the modern age." Lütteken's analysis draws attention to "the development of new and intricate compositional norms in a highly diverse ritual-functional context."

Songs "are first and foremost actions – a practice," writes Nicole Schwindt. In a discussion that moves seamlessly between musical and cultural analysis, she characterizes the fifteenth century as "a decisive period for song as an artistic form: . . . songs . . . were set down as verbal and musical texts, composed in multi-voice structures with fixed rhythms, increasingly attributed to their creators by name, reproduced by performers, and inserted into complex inter-textual exchanges."

Keith Polk alerts us to innovations in instrumental music: new instruments, instrument combinations, and manuscript sources, the rise of patronage, and the advent of improvisation manuals. Polk casts the end of the century (ca. 1480–1500) as a watershed, arguing that changes in scoring, style, repertory, performance practice, and listening habits transformed the very fabric of instrumental music-making.

Strohm describes a vast and international corpus of non-liturgical sacred songs on poetic texts that emerged in the fifteenth century. These mostly anonymous songs "are serenely unaffected by distinctions such as 'Middle Ages vs. Renaissance,' or 'polyphony vs. monophony'." Taken together they reflect "the growing participation of lay people in the singing of God's praise." They have also filtered down to the present day, as many continue to be sung in church services of one kind or another.

That Gregorian chant was the daily bread of every late medieval church musician is a well-known fact of the period. Less clear today, in part because chant scholars have tended to focus on earlier sources, is the issue of how chant was performed in the fifteenth century. Drawing in part on the writings of Tinctoris, Sherr illuminates a surprisingly heterogeneous practice character-ized by regional chant "dialects" and a variety of approaches to rhythm. In a provocative twist, the author asks us to reevaluate the received wisdom that the place where a given polyphonic work was composed can be deduced from the version of the chant melody upon which it is based.

From the beginning, generic classification has impinged on the reception of fifteenth-century music, the subject of Part X. In an essay on the reception of the chanson, David Fallows "draw[s] a path through fifteenth-century song in terms of the pieces that survive in the largest number of sources." His discussion brims with insights about manuscript survival rates, repertorial longevity, canonicity, anonymity and attribution, popularity as a measure of the composer's (sometimes shifting) fame, and performance practice.

After 1500 the reception of fifteenth-century music took a curious turn: thanks in part to the sudden arrival of polyphonic music printing (1501), some works continued to be preserved and written about long after their first performances. In this respect Josquin was very much in the right place at the right time, as it was his music (and, to a much smaller extent, that of his contemporaries) that remained in the canon, largely to the exclusion of Binchois, Busnoys, and company. This highly skewed reception persisted until ca. 1600, after which fifteenth-century music largely faded from view, only to be taken up again during the next great age of history writing: the nineteenth century.

Crucially – and understandably, given the sources then available – nineteenth-century historians (e.g., Raphael Georg Kiesewetter and August Wilhelm Ambros) relied mainly on sixteenth-century sources, above all the writings of Henricus Glareanus, when discussing fifteenth-century music. Ambros, whose way of thinking was indebted to Hegelian dialectics, was really the first historian to lavish the music of this period with not only praise but also astonishing intellectual energy. Kirkman deftly shows how Ambros's philosophical orientation helps explain his decision to place the cyclic mass at the center of the inquiry, to privilege authored works over anonymous ones, and to raise the compositional technique of imitation to a position of central importance – all choices that continue to exert an influence on modern scholarship.

A web of influences accounts for the tortured reception of Johannes (Jean d') Ockeghem. Ockeghem reception began in earnest in the sixteenth century in theoretical treatises by Adrian Petit Coclico and Ambrosius Wilphlingseder, gained force in the eighteenth in the writings of Charles Burney, John Hawkins, and Johann Forkel, and pushed through not only to the nineteenth-century historians but on to Heinrich Besseler and his followers in the 1920s. Bernstein's elegant essay brings clarity to this history, revealing the forces that led to the vilification and, eventually, adulation of this extraordinary figure.

Such adulation – not just of Ockeghem, but of many contemporary composers – has persisted in part thanks to the advent of recording technology, which has allowed fifteenth-century music to be fixed in more or less infinitely reproducible sound. In an essay that brings together issues of performance practice with matters economic, generic, and reportorial, Honey Meconi traces recordings of fifteenth-century music from their beginnings in the 1930s up to the present day.

Even as performances and recordings of fifteenth-century music have proliferated, it must be acknowledged that the literature on performance practice has dwindled. In part this simply reflects the way the scholarly winds have been blowing: while the lively debates of the late twentieth century – about text underlay, tempo, the use of instruments, instrumentation, pitch standards, and so on – are hardly settled, in recent years a healthy pluralism has taken hold, with scholars increasingly inclined to embrace a range of historically informed performance practices. Such pluralism may in part reflect a collective sense that we lack the evidence, at least right now, to push these questions significantly further. But even if this volume addresses them only occasionally (Meconi, Schmidt-Beste), this is not in any way to debase such discussions. On the contrary, the field of performance practice seems ripe for a resurgence, thanks to a proliferation of conversations between historians of music, art, and architecture, and the advent of digital resources for reimagining timbre, tempo, and acoustical environments. It may yet be possible to say more about the performance forces for, and the sound of, a mass by Obrecht sung at St. Donatian's in Bruges, or the rondeau *Je ne vis oncques la pareille* as it was performed at the Feast of the Pheasant, with the tenor reportedly sung by a stag.

The project of recovering and indeed reconceiving that musical world can be detected in the music of many twentieth-century composers. Before the full flowering of the recording industry, some composers began not only to study fifteenth-century music, but also to edit and perform it. Casting the twentieth century as "an age of sonic archeology," Richard Taruskin describes the engagement of figures such as Schoenberg, Webern, Stravinsky, and Hindemith with Du Fay, Isaac, Josquin, and their contemporaries. These modernists were interested above all in "structural" features then prized by scholars (e.g., imitation canon, cantus-firmus procedure, and isorhythm) – and one should recall that Webern was himself a scholar who in 1909 published an edition of Isaac's *Choralis Constantinus*. One finds in this period a "confluence of musicology and advanced composition that made the twentieth century, the century of modernism, as if paradoxically more sympathetic to the distant musical past than any previous century had been." Even if, as Taruskin observes, interest in fifteenth-century compositional techniques has waned in recent decades, one still finds prominent echoes, such as a work by the scholar-composer Fabrice Fitch that takes not Josquin but Agricola as its point of departure (*Agricologies*, 2004–8). It seems only fitting to conclude with an essay that traces the reception of fifteenth-century music up to the present day – a reception that has shaped this book in myriad ways and that this book will inevitably and, we hope, helpfully play its own role in shaping for future generations.

## Bibliography

Atlas, Allan W., *Music at the Aragonese Court of Naples*, Cambridge, 1985
Becker, Frederick Otto, "The Maîtrise in Northern France and Burgundy during the Fifteenth Century," Ph.D. diss., Peabody College, 1967

Bent, Margaret, "What Is Isorhythm?," in *Quomodo cantabimus canticum: Studies in Honor of Edward H. Roesner*, ed. David Butler Cannata, Gabriela Ilnitchi Currie, Rena Charnin Mueller, and John Louis Nádas, Middleton, WI, 2008, 121–43

Berger, Anna Maria Busse, *Medieval Music and the Art of Memory*, Berkeley and Los Angeles, 2005

Boorman, Stanley, *Ottaviano Petrucci: Catalogue Raisonné*, New York, 2006

Brown, Howard Mayer, and Stanley Sadie, eds., *Performance Practice: Music before 1600*, New York, 1990

Burckhardt, Jacob, *The Civilization of the Renaissance in Italy*, London, 1995. Orig. pub. 1880 as *Die Kultur der Renaissance in Italien*

Caldwell, John, *Editing Early Music*, Oxford, 1985

Cellarius (Keller), Christoph, *Historia universalis ... in antiquam et medii aevi ac novam divisa (Universal History Divided into an Ancient, Medieval, and New Period)*, Jena, 1708. Orig. pub. 1685–96

Christensen, Thomas, ed., *The Cambridge History of Western Music Theory*, Cambridge, 2002

Cumming, Julie E., "Text Setting and Imitative Technique in Petrucci's First Five Motet Prints," in *The Motet around 1500: On the Relationship between Imitation and Text Treatment?*, ed. Thomas Schmidt-Beste, Turnhout, 2012, 83–110

Demouy, Patrick, "Une source inédite de l'histoire des maîtrises: Le règlement des enfants de choeur de Notre-Dame de Reims (XVIe s.)," in *Symphonies lorraines: Compositeurs, exécutants, destinataires. Actes du colloque de Lunéville (20 novembre 1998)*, ed. Yves Ferraton, Paris, 1998, 169–81

Fitch, Fabrice, "'Virtual' Ascriptions in Ms. AugsS 142a: A Window on Alexander Agricola's Late Style," *JAF* 4 (2012), 114–38

Gallagher, Sean, *Johannes Regis*, Turnhout, 2010

Gordon, George, *Medium Aevum and the Middle Age*, S.P.E. Tract 19, Oxford, 1925

Grier, James, *The Critical Editing of Music: History, Method, and Practice*, Cambridge, 1996

Higgins, Paula, "Parisian Nobles, a Scottish Princess, and the Woman's Voice in Late Medieval Song," *EMH* 10 (1991), 145–200

Johnson, William, *Early Modern Europe: An Introduction to a Course of Lectures on the Sixteenth Century*, Cambridge, 1869

Leech-Wilkinson, Daniel, *The Modern Invention of Medieval Music: Scholarship, Ideology, Performance*, Cambridge, 2002

Lockwood, Lewis, *Music in Renaissance Ferrara, 1400–1505: The Creation of a Musical Center in the Fifteenth Century*, Cambridge, MA, 1984

Merkley, Paul A., and Lora L. M. Merkley, *Music and Patronage in the Sforza Court*, Turnhout, 1999

Milsom, John, "Crecquillon, Clemens, and Four-Voice *Fuga*, " in *Beyond Contemporary Fame: Reassessing the Art of Clemens non Papa and Thomas Crecquillon. Colloquium Proceedings, Utrecht, April 24–26, 2003*, ed. Eric Jas, Turnhout, 2005, 293–345

Mould, Alan, *The English Chorister: A History*, London, 2007

Murray, Russell E., Jr., Susan Forscher Weiss, and Cynthia J. Cyrus, eds., *Music Education in the Middle Ages and the Renaissance*, Bloomington and Indianapolis, 2010

Reynolds, Christopher A., *Papal Patronage and the Music of St. Peter's, 1380–1513*, Berkeley, 1995

Rifkin, Joshua, "A Black Hole? Problems in the Motet around 1500," in *The Motet around 1500: On the Relationship between Imitation and Text Treatment?*, ed. Thomas Schmidt-Beste, Turnhout, 2012, 21–82

"Munich, Milan, and a Marian Motet: Dating Josquin's *Ave Maria . . . virgo serena*," *JAMS* 56 (2003), 239–350

"Musste Josquin Josquin werden? Zum Problem des Frühwerks," in *Josquin Desprez und seine Zeit*, ed. Michael Zywietz, forthcoming

"Problems of Authorship in Josquin: Some Impolitic Observations. With a Postscript on *Absalon, fili mi*," in *Proceedings of the International Josquin Symposium Utrecht 1986*, ed. Willem Elders and Frits de Haen, Utrecht, 1991, 45–52

Robinson, Fred C., "Medieval, the Middle Ages," *Speculum* 59 (1984), 745–56

Rodin, Jesse, *Josquin's Rome: Hearing and Composing in the Sistine Chapel*, New York and Oxford, 2012

Sachs, Klaus-Jürgen, "Arten improvisierter Mehrstimmigkeit nach Lehrtexten des 14. bis 16. Jahrhunderts," *BJhM* 7 (1983), 166–83

Strohm, Reinhard, "'Medieval Music' or 'Early European Music'?," in *The Cambridge History of Medieval Music*, ed. Mark Everist and Thomas Forrest Kelly, forthcoming

*Music in Late Medieval Bruges*, Oxford and New York, 1985; rev. edn. 1990

*The Rise of European Music*, Cambridge, 1993

Taruskin, Richard, "Antoine Busnoys and the *L'homme armé* Tradition," *JAMS* 39 (1986), 255–93

Wegman, Rob C., "Petrus de Domarto's *Missa Spiritus almus* and the Early History of the Four-Voice Mass in the Fifteenth Century," *EMH* 10 (1991), 235–303

Wright, Craig, *Music and Ceremony at Notre Dame of Paris, 500–1550*, Cambridge, 1989

· PART I HISTORIOGRAPHY ·

*LISTENING*

# 1

# Hearing Josquin hearing Busnoys

MICHAEL LONG

*For Lewis Lockwood*

"How was this composition heard in its own time?" Most twenty-first-century teachers and scholars of fifteenth-century music have approached a musical work by way of this interrogative formula. If art history's disciplinary task, as Donald Preziosi wrote, is "rendering the visible legible," we suppose by analogy that the work of musicology is to render the *audible* legible, a notion reflected in the now familiar question posed at the outset of this chapter.[1] Art historians have an advantage, of course: the visual is before them, open to view and review, while the historical audible is over and done (or "lost," as we often say, as if to seek comfort in the romance of bereftness). Yet our enthusiasm for asking historical questions about aural engagement with musical repertory remains undeterred, and we often frame what we say and write today in experiential terms, relying on powerful and seemingly straightforward words like "hearing" and "listening." Prevailing vocabularies of late medieval and Renaissance "aurality" are of fairly recent vintage, however, and it is worth reflecting upon what has brought us to the current position, and what precisely we are doing when we foreground aural experience within the historiography of musical reception.

Joseph Kerman's *Contemplating Music* and the new-musicological positions it catalyzed and nourished in the 1980s and 1990s posed a particular challenge to scholars of fifteenth-century music. Kerman's critique of music-historical positivism and its methodological inflections may have been directed mainly at Bach research, but there was sufficient bleeding over to early music scholarship in general (notably as cultivated at Princeton and in the UK) and enough targeting of scholars active in late medieval and Renaissance music research (including Margaret Bent and Arthur Mendel) to place most of the work being done on fifteenth-century topics through the 1980s smack in the crosshairs of an intensifying disciplinary salvo. Young scholars found themselves profoundly implicated, since "with depressing frequency" they were adhering faithfully to "the dominant tradition in doctoral dissertations" by engaging in "the

---

1 Preziosi, *Rethinking Art History*, 35.

preparation of editions and studies of a documentary, archival sort."[2] A path out of this dilemma of poor publicity (one that would lead toward some recuperation of viability and disciplinary impact) emerged in the tactical discourse of early music scholars by the end of the next decade. Without rejecting conventional ways of investigating and narrating the history of fifteenth-century musical practice through its artifacts, efforts were made to position these methods as vital to the understanding of fifteenth-century "music itself." A new, widely accepted rhetoric of the ear has since enlivened many of the stories we tell about historical music and the contexts in which it circulated.

## Hearing and historiography

A 1997 volume bearing the optimistic title *Hearing the Motet* was emblematic of this new turn, reflecting according to its introduction "an increasing concern among scholars and performers with bringing to light the diverse ways in which these works may have been *heard* in their own time."[3] The book's contents "expand on traditional musicological methods," and – if we look closely – reveal in retrospect the particularly text-critical (rather than sound-specific) trajectory of that expansion. Of the collection's six essays on fifteenth-century music, three featured the word "Reading" in their titles, while another advertised "Meaning and Understanding."[4] Hearing, as it entered mainstream historiographical discourse, was a metaphor for close reading in the absence of sound. As Margaret Bent has written of the late medieval isorhythmic motet: "We cannot recover the sounds of medieval music, but we can recover much of *its sense as a text*."[5] The texts associated with late medieval musical activity came to be seen as involving a particular mode of reception, one that Bent and others have termed "informed" listening or "adequate" hearing. This practice – it is argued – is available to modern scholars, even though the fourteenth- or fifteenth-century sounds once heard are now inaccessible. We can assume the role of a work's implied or ideal listener by contemplation of the work, especially in its manuscript traces. Indeed it is incumbent upon us to do so, for "we can only 'hear' these compositions *adequately* if we also do some 'listening' outside the real time of actual performance."[6] Suggesting that particular compositional and poetical

---

2 Kerman, *Contemplating Music*, 115.     3 Pesce, ed., *Hearing the Motet*, 3 (emphasis added).
4 Wegman, "For Whom the Bell Tolls"; Higgins, "Love and Death in the Fifteenth-Century Motet"; Bloxam, "Obrecht as Exegete"; Sherr, "Conflicting Levels of Meaning."
5 Bent, "The 'Harmony' of the Machaut Mass," 80.
6 Bent, "Polyphony of Texts and Music," 82. Bent refers here to a practice of "prepared" listening.

nuances were likely to have been *audible* to their core audience, and particularly to the "attentive" listeners among them, musicologists imbue specific ideologies of listening (to borrow a phrase coined by Simon Frith in a different context) with an aura of cultural (and even experiential) authenticity, situating deductions of interpretation and analysis within an imaginary construct of historical and implicitly sensory life-praxis.

When John Butt outlined a general "theory of listening" grounded in three categories, the second and third of them involved mapping music against the backdrop of time, but only as a linear sequence of coherent (or intelligible) events in the first case, and in the other as a field charted through post-aural contemplation and engagement with a "listening self" already implicit in the unique work. This is reminiscent of Bent's "adequate" listener.[7] In contrast to these musical quasi-narratives or networks of meaning, Butt's first category was what he called "a form of *hearing*," lacking the "intentionality or involvement suggested by listening." He links this practice especially with less "determinate" musics, particularly those of "the remote cultural world."[8] In suggesting that "a more engaged level of hearing is certainly not to be excluded, such as when music is used as an aspect of meditation or as part of a formal ritual," Butt appears to locate some "hearing" experiences mainly within the domains of cognition or the anthropology of music, respectively, as a mode of engagement with sound, but without the engagement of intellect.[9] Even if his theory – as it is fully elaborated – betrays a skew toward a tonal colonialism, Butt's apparatus underscores a critical point: that "hearing" and "listening" are terms requiring considerable qualification and attention no matter the musical repertory under consideration.

That there exists a spectrum of possible aural engagements with musical sound – an infinite range of hearing and listening experiences potentialized by any sounding musical environment – is a logical proposition. Yet it is not one much acknowledged by historical musicologists, whose business it is to elucidate both fundamental and nuanced distinctions between one musical object and another. Our approach to describing musical sound is axiom-based: what we learn to "listen for" in one or another kind of music is mainly circumscribed by our own specialist discourse and by our compulsion to "fix" items within it. "Informed" or "prepared" listening has led to deep and rich investigations of texts (an expansive category that includes relevant material not generated by

7 Butt, "Do Musical Works Contain an Implied Listener?," 8–9, 12. Butt's typology is reminiscent of Bent's notion of the "hierarchical" nature of "educated listening" ("The 'Harmony' of the Machaut Mass," 81).
8 Butt, "Do Musical Works Contain an Implied Listener?," 8.
9 On the "anthropology of music" in the sense of a prescribed ritual accompaniment vs. "musical anthropology," see below, p. 34 and n. 37.

"musical experience itself" including the sources of cantus firmi; theological, mathematical, and philosophical concepts; devotional conventions; musical notation; and even the modern score-referent markers of form and style).

Consider the musical work (or the historical listening experience) identified in our narratives as Josquin's *Missa Hercules dux Ferrarie*. Josquin's mass represents an expression and articulation of many musical practices that must have fundamentally informed musical hearing and listening around 1500, and even before.[10] The metaphorical language brought to bear on this musical entity since the middle of the last century offers a meaningful snapshot of stasis and change in early music historiography, configuring how we imagine fifteenth-century music to have realized its intended effects and how we prioritize the underlying fifteenth-century cultural axioms supporting them. In Edgar Sparks's classic *Cantus Firmus in Mass and Motet, 1420–1520*, the Hercules cantus firmus was first invoked in his discussion of two motets by Antoine Busnoys, *Anthoni usque limina* and *In hydraulis*, both composed – like the later Josquin mass – around a "contrived" tenor.[11] Josquin's famous *soggetto cavato* (*re ut re ut re fa mi re*), excavated from the vowels of the text phrase *Hercules dux Ferrarie*, markedly resembles the *re ut re* tenor of *In hydraulis* in its melodic incipit and unchanging long-note rhythmic profile. In the motet – which celebrates Johannes Ockeghem by naming him alongside the anchors of musical mythography, Pythagoras and Orpheus – Busnoys expanded the motive into a cantus firmus by threefold repetition of *re ut re* (beginning on *d*, *a*, and *d'* above), realizing in sound the Pythagorean intervallic ratios (tone, fifth, fourth, and octave). Josquin used the same outline in the mass, reiterating the Hercules *soggetto* on *d*, *a*, and *d'* for each cantus-firmus statement. There are additional commonalities. Busnoys employs a retrograde after every forward statement, and in the mass, the pitch position of each of the three units making up the cantus firmus is in retrograde twice, descending rather than ascending through the d octave (*d'*, *a*, *d*). Busnoys employed proportional signatures for each main section of the motet, which along with the esoteric Greek ratio names sung in the text have invited arithmetical "readings" of the motet score. Josquin twice invoked the spirit of arithmetical proportion through an energetic double diminution of the cantus firmus.

For Sparks in 1963, these tenor contrivances engineered by Busnoys and Josquin formed "scaffolding" for an increasingly apparent "rationalistic" architecture of polyphonic music. We can sense the concreteness of his

---

10 For a review of recent positions regarding the date of the mass see Fallows, *Josquin*, 259, 261–62; Reynolds, "Interpreting and Dating," 102–8.

11 Sparks, *Cantus Firmus*, 217. Alexander Blachly has also underscored the significance of *In hydraulis* as a model for Josquin's mass. See "The Cantus Firmus of Josquin's *Missa Hercules dux Ferrarie*," 379.

metaphorical model in that word: "scaffolding" pervades Sparks's text and is reiterated by other scholars in the same repertorial context to this day. That Josquin's mass manifests an exaggerated or extreme musical skeleton has been noted regularly. Two decades after Sparks, Lewis Lockwood stressed that the work is "exceptional for its strictness of organization and the *rigidity* of its treatment of the subject," and David Fallows amplified this assessment by gesturing toward the notion of specific intention, an intellectual self behind the edifice, describing the structure as "*ambitiously* rigid."[12]

Since the 1960s we have learned to be aware of the potential charge carried by metaphorical language, yet Sparks's general understanding of the work's compositional priorities is clearly still viable and in circulation as a general model for understanding it. Looking out for "structure" (a word we invoke more often than we ponder what we imply about music by doing so) is an attractive option for making "sense" of a cantus-firmus composition in terms that have been historiographically advantaged over cognitive or anthropological experiences of sound. Of course, in order to perceive an intentional, rationalist construct we must consume the work as a whole, the way we take in a building's architectural essentials all at once. The music must be assumed to possess an integrated identity, an architectonic self that is open to a modern, resonant intellect. A tacit understanding of the 1960s that engagement with the musical object need not take place "in real time" was, as cited above, re-inscribed overtly as a dictum of "listening" more than three decades later.

What has changed, however, is that the same architecture of polyphonic music, especially in a cantus-firmus composition, is now taken not so much for a concrete edifice as for a kind of *system*, with the system of a single coherent work understood as a microcosmic iteration of larger systems – usually linked to cultural "meaning" – that organized cultural existence in the past. Since the 1980s, fifteenth-century music has come to be taken as a kind of sonic *Weltanschauungsbild*, mirroring the emblematic content of late medieval culture. Craig Wright, for example, locates the crux of the *Missa Hercules* at the points of structural retrograde: "Statistics demonstrate intent: in the more than 150 compositions of Josquin Desprez, retrograde motion is found in only three works: this Mass for Hercules and his two Armed Man Masses. By means of musical symbolism, Josquin suggests that Hercules and the Armed Man are fellow knights in armor."[13] Wright's reading of the mass's architecture is enriched by literary and theological texts adduced to support his view that

12 Lockwood, *Music in Renaissance Ferrara*, 245; Fallows, *Josquin*, 257 (emphases added). Compare also Blackburn, "Masses," where the tenor is characterized as "peculiarly rigid" (83).
13 Wright, *The Maze and the Warrior*, 193.

the mass's Hercules theme is profoundly and essentially metaphorical or allegorical. The architectural frame of the whole, fitted with appropriate glossing, provides the key to what the Hercules tenor "means."

Musicologists now regularly set themselves the task of unearthing which other texts reside silently behind the activity of "informed" listening – i.e., listening for sense – and then making the case for that relevancy to a particular situation. The markers we now point to in these text- and score-based readings are finer than those emphasized in earlier analyses, and appear to resonate encouragingly with the accepted notion of "hearing" music "as if" in its own time. In the case of the *Missa Hercules*, Christopher Reynolds has suggested that Josquin's music should be heard as an act of musical rhetoric, an audible essay in sound that makes its points through topical or gestural allusion.[14] His study was included in a volume devoted to "new approaches" to the subject of musical borrowing. Editor Honey Meconi's introduction emphasized the project's focus on an updated agenda for early music analysis, one that was concerned with musical sound, taking account of what musical citation "meant," not only for composers but for "listeners," and highlighting the significance of reconstructing the parameters of "aural familiarity." Reynolds's analysis does not concern the architecture of the cantus firmus, but rather the Hercules subject's gestural identity in a systematic complex of allusive musical rhetoric. Busnoys's *In hydraulis* rates only a brief mention late in the essay, where Reynolds suggests that the "organizational parallel" between the works cannot bear witness to a particularly early date for Josquin's mass.

Now the congruence that provided the historiographical thread of coherence to Sparks's foundational work on cantus-firmus procedures and his understanding of "rationalist" compositional intention carries no "meaning" for hearing the mass's rhetoric, within which it turns out that paying attention to the cantus firmus remains key – but here in a very different way. For Reynolds, "re ut re ut re fa mi re" was a recognizable allusion not to Busnoys (and his remarkable architecture), but to similar motives that appeared in some works of the composer Walter Frye, especially a bit of contratenor melody in Frye's Marian *Missa Nobilis et pulchra*. The Marian implications of Frye's mass, specifically Frye's music for the phrase "ex Maria virgine," were carried over, Reynolds argued, into Josquin's new rhetorical essay on Ercole, Duke of Ferrara – a man renowned for his fervent and expensive devotions and even for specifically Marian tastes in devotional practice.[15]

14 Reynolds, "Interpreting and Dating."     15 Ibid., 100.

Whether or not the connections drawn by Reynolds are indeed relevant to the work is less important in the context of this chapter than how his argument operates with respect to new models of musical hearing. When Josquin's "Marian" intertext expands to six voices in the final Agnus Dei, it accommodates not only Walter Frye and the Virgin (in the cantus firmus) but an extra nod toward the music of Alexander Agricola's paraphrase chanson *Si dedero* and thus to the unsung Lenten chant text it implies: "[Josquin's] sung mass text [i.e., the third Agnus Dei] voices the liturgical prayer for mercy and peace, the textual allusions of the ostinato (both sacred and secular [Frye's Virgin and Josquin's Ercole]) identify the supplicant as Ercole and his willing intercessor as the Virgin Mary, and the contrapuntal chanson allusion [i.e., gestures found in Agricola's *Si dedero*] conveys [via the unsung text of the responsory verse] a message of rest that might well be interpreted as Ercole's wish for an end to his worldly life."[16]

No longer experientially constrained by the rigid girders of Sparksian structure, this implied listener – if he is to hear Josquin adequately – must apprehend and interpret a tremendous lot of explicit and implicit sound data on the fly. The music will be "heard" (in its textual and sonorous totality) as a complex but coherent utterance of diverse threads, like all the objects painted on a single canvas. However, the rich rhetorical dessert served up in this telling of Josquin's final Agnus Dei now pays little heed to the sonic effect of its predominant acoustical flavor: the simple, long-note, foursquare tune that by this point in the mass has been *heard* eleven times before. And that, of course, is the very feature that, over time, defined the architecture of Sparks's vision of the whole. Is the unusual character of this sparse, simplistic, determined tenor by the end of the mass merely a box into which Josquin dumped some extra sermonizing at the last instant? Dispiritingly, and this is how we let ourselves off the hook, to confront this aspect of the work's *real* sounding in time – i.e., how the blockish cantus firmus may have first struck a fifteenth-century eardrum (and then how it could have felt on the twelfth go-round) – would seem to depend on those unrecoverable and unmentionable elements our history avoids.

The scholarly discourse of late medieval and Renaissance listening has been borrowed primarily from other disciplines, and provides little encouragement for the contemplation of significant effects experienced when we hear other kinds of music in real time, particularly any that rely on acoustical prominence (e.g., Haydn's surprise chord) or contextual isolation (e.g., the arresting sonority that launches the Beatles' "A Hard Day's Night") to provoke a special kind of short-lived engagement or response in the musical ear. Listening in real time, rather than "listening" to the page, forces other issues. Cross-over musician Brian Eno's succinct definition of his composed, experimental "ambient music" of the 1970s as something "able to accommodate many levels of listening attention . . . as ignorable as it is interesting" points to the complex instability of aural experience: listening is indeed about intentionality (i.e., a decision whether or not to pay attention), but it is really less about a *single realization of intention* (i.e., to turn our "listening" function on or off) than about responses in each moment of continuous hearing that govern how much attention we bring to bear on what we hear.[17] Moreover, it is about calculating what we will get in return (the sense that it might be "interesting" to listen *now* but maybe not *now*). The apprehension of all musical sound in time is subject to a process, or a set of processes, that constitute the attentiveness spectrum; Eno's ambient music was an artifice designed to underscore the experience of that continuum.

It would be reasonable to say that not just ambient, but *all* music is open to all such positions while it is sounded within the range of hearing. Thus, when we tentatively venture into conversations about music that we can't in fact hear (for example, fifteenth-century polyphony as it was sounded in the fifteenth century), we might think a little more than we have done about the fragmentary moments of perception that add up to a continuous "listening event." All the notes (heard or read) add up to some conceptual totality, but they don't all play the same – or even much – part in how we hear and listen to music in real time, however committed we are to aural engagement. Yet, if we were to set about describing what sounds we thought (in our wildest imagination) were most significantly *heard* in centuries past, it would be virtually impossible for us to fill out the contextual nodes that determine a sensible, linear historiography in the conventional sense. These nodes are the points of cultural intersection in which items are fixed (stylistically, institutionally, socially, biographically, theologically, etc.) in historical writing. The model of the whole depends on a musical object's status as a resource for repeated, uniform, and non-contradictory reception "in its own time" against these organizing backgrounds, a *sense* (as Bent implies) of reception that is recoverable in ours.

Still, musical sound – we've maintained – is our business, and perhaps we should look to sound for a way to confront historical hearing, even if that sound is not five hundred years old. When presenting Josquin's *Missa Hercules dux Ferrarie* in the classroom I play (as a sonic foil to more recent recordings such as those by the New London Chamber Choir or the Hilliard Ensemble) a

---

17 Eno, *Ambient 1: Music for Airports.*

performance recorded in the late 1950s by the Société des Chanteurs de Saint-Eustache under the direction of Émile Martin.[18] Upon hearing the first Kyrie, most students (and even most academics) respond (immediately) not with groans or "knowing" academic chuckles, but with genuine surprise and laughter. At the opening of the mass, the *soggetto* is played (in an unabashedly forward and expressive manner) on modern instruments including a loud corps of trombones for the cantus firmus. The shock-and-awe extravagance – at least considered from the current disciplinary perspective – is if nothing else a useful reminder that hearing this music in the time when it was new could have been, as was Berlioz's *Tuba mirum* (which Martin's trombones recall) in his time, a "remarkable" hearing experience.[19] First, to feel the edges between artfully crafted musical sound and its absence – dramatically memorialized for us in the visual artifact of the tenor partbook by a series of sharply incised longa rests followed by a string of blockish breves, all looking the same – was more special at the turn of the sixteenth century than it is now. Thus, what *we* hear as an *exaggerated* modern performance might be taken instead as a cross-epochal acoustical analogy for the now unimaginable experience of hearing polyphonic music's being sounded in a universe not yet saturated by the noise of compositional technique and its electrically enhanced iterations. More significantly, by privileging the tenor's resonance – as a musical sound "effect" – the old recording exposes how the language of historiography in each generation has guided our attention away from what very well may have been crucial aspects of the work's profile as musical sound.

Josquin launched the mass with a signal, an attention-grabber: an announcement (or foreshadowing) of the solmization subject in the superius part. In the unreal time of musicology's structural listening, we'd call it, rather nonsensically, a "pre-imitation."[20] The *soggetto* is reiterated immediately by the tenor voice (an octave lower). Josquin designed a similar "special effect" of musical "spatializing" for the opening of the Sanctus and final Agnus as well. Modern performances of course prefer timbral blending of all voice parts, including the tenor (even if, as has been suggested, it sings the phrase "Hercules dux Ferrarie"), projecting through this now-familiar acoustical homogeneity the remarkable and intricate contrapuntal expertise of the Josquinian "score" more than anything else.[21] By contrast, the French rendition from the 1950s

---

18 Düsseldorf: Musica Sacra, ca. 1960.
19 For these reasons, I don't entirely concur with Christopher Page's representations of "advances" in musical performance practice for our understanding, and indeed our "hearing" of medieval music. See Page, *Discarding Images*, xxiii–xxiv.
20 See, for example, Fallows, *Josquin*, 257.
21 Concerning the possible texting of the *soggetto*, see Lockwood, *Music in Renaissance Ferrara*, 247 and Blachly, "The Cantus Firmus of Josquin's *Missa Hercules dux Ferrarie*," 383–86.

acoustically isolated the foreshadowing of the subject on a double reed instrument, *legato*, then blasted the tenor's entry, and every one of its clearly articulated breves, on *conservatoire* trombones, *fortissimo*. Leaving aside the (here) mainly irrelevant questions of historically informed performance practice in any general sense, could this in fact be how Josquin *experienced* the moment of the tenor's sounding at each, and maybe especially the first and last, occurrence in the mass? Is it even possible that the performers – whatever the vocal and/or instrumental forces may have been – were meant to exaggerate the sound of the cantus firmus in some way (and perhaps its foreshadowing in some other way)? Could that have been Josquin's expectation? Could the sound of a cantus firmus in performance have been significant to the hearing experience of fifteenth-century polyphony (at least in certain cases), as much so as the composer's technical industry regarding the structural disposition and contrapuntal ornamentation of the tune?

## Hearing history

If Busnoys's "contrived" tenor was in fact sounding in Josquin's memory as he undertook the *Missa Hercules* (and I think it was, as I will clarify presently), we might now consider the possibility that Josquin – whether he had ever actually heard *In hydraulis* or had only heard of it from others – was *hearing* (in his mind's ear) something extreme or exaggerated in his model, by which I mean not so much an architectural as an aural overload. Given recent scholarship's enthusiasm for interpreting details of texts, it's surprising that the rather exotic "hydraulis," the first image/word presented in Busnoys's motet, has figured so inconspicuously in discussions of the whole piece.[22]

> [Prima pars]
> In hydraulis quondam Pithagora
> Admirante melos phthongitates
> Malleorum, secutus equora
> Per ponderum inequalitates,
> Adinvenit muse quiditates.
>
> Epitritum ast hemioliam
> Epogdoum et duplam perducunt
> Nam tessaron penthe concordiam
> Nec non phthongum et pason adducunt
> Monocordi dum genus conducunt.

---

22 An exception is Benthem, "Text, Tone, and Symbol," 216. He suggests that the scribe of the manuscript Munich 3154 entered the text from memory, and imagined the word in its French-sounding form, *ydraulis*, accounting for the peculiarity of the Munich text, an observation particularly intriguing in light of the specifically French backdrop to the motet's creation I propose here.

[Secunda pars]
Hec, Oggeghen, cunctis qui precinis
Galliarium in regis latria,
O practicum tue propaginis
Arma cernens quondam per atria
Burgundie ducis in patria.

Per me, Busnois, illustris comitis
De Charulois Indignum musicum,
Saluteris tuis pro meritis
Tamquam summum Cephas tropicidum:
Vale, verum instar Orpheicum.[23]

On an occasion when Pythagoras was wondering at the tones in water organs [and] the tonalities of hammers, having followed with his eyes [or "gazed at" or "borne in mind"] the surfaces according to the inequalities of the weights, he discovered the essential natures of the muse [with play on "music" and "water"].

These produce [lit. "lead through to"] epitrite and hemiola, epogdous and duple, for they lead towards the harmony of fourth, fifth, and also tone and octave, while they connect [lit. "lead together"] the species of the monochord.

Ockeghem, you who sing before all in the service of the King of the Gauls, O strengthen the practice of your generation, examining these things on occasion in the halls of the Duke of Burgundy in your fatherland.

By me, Busnois, unworthy musician of the illustrious Count of Charolais, be greeted for your merits as the highest trope-uttering Cephas [i.e. Peter]; farewell, true image of Orpheus.

While the poem goes on to include mention of the percussive demonstrations of the Pythagorean musical ratios, more familiar to most students than those he deduced from organ pipes, the placement of the organ before even the name of Pythagoras himself was surely intended as a real and effective verbal hook, especially for the literate ear. Literate or not, musical listeners, of course, tend to pay particular attention to the very beginnings of things, which are also crucial in setting up the cognitive parameters of musical anticipation.[24] Anticipating the tenor must have been in general a sensual and sensory staple of listening practice, registered and felt strongly by listeners of all fifteenth-century polyphonic ceremonial music, significantly

---

23 The text is unique to a single manuscript (Munich 3154, fols. 47v–48r) and is notoriously problematic. The version given here is David Howlett's reconstruction and translation in "Busnois' Motet *In hydraulis*," 187–88. Howlett also provides a literal transcription of the manuscript text (185).

24 On phenomena of expectation in general, see Huron, *Sweet Anticipation*. From the perspective of what Huron termed "expectation" in time (see his ch. 10), *In hydraulis* provides an interesting case. The motet is on the one hand clearly periodic, which assists long-range predictability. But as with many early to mid-fifteenth-century "serious" compositions (motets and masses), the first duo is long enough that predictability of the tenor's eventual entry is mitigated, except in the case of a listener who has already heard the entire work.

so in *In hydraulis*.[25] Such expectations will have physiological relevance when they are satisfied, extending beyond the cognizance of sound to somatic responses triggered by it, including non-choreographic motion. Busnoys withholds his tenor for eighteen perfect *tempora*; its eventual manifestation is (in real time) a long-awaited moment. A listener's experience of that initial period must have included puzzling over what kind of tune Busnoys could make (or cite) that would reflect the grand, wordy musical mythography exposed in the opening duo of the motet. That would be a good reason to pay a particular sort of attention, at least until the tenor begins to sound – an Eno-esque position of partial engagement: "it might be interesting to listen (like this) for now."

As for the hydraulis, did Busnoys expect not just his text, but the motet's musical performance to somehow materialize his signal image? Reports of early church or palace organs (of the first millennium through about the twelfth century) regularly emphasize their acoustical prominence, likening their sound level to that of large bells, and their effect to "the crash of thunder."[26] That acoustical understanding of the early instrument – situated in the fifteenth-century musical imaginary – lends a special flavor to the possible experience of tenor entry in Busnoys's motet. A substantial machine sounding within a sufficiently grand, resonant space would have made for a remarkable experience, especially in the soundscape of the earlier Middle Ages. One such machine was a hydraulis that survived for centuries in the cathedral of Reims. While this organ burned along with most of the old cathedral well before the time of Busnoys and Ockeghem, it seems to have been one of the only extant instruments of its type in the West and famous among European musicians.[27] This instrument was probably heard in Reims for centuries during the cathedral's most singular ritual moments: the coronations of the French kings, in which the Princes of the Blood generally participated; among these, the Duke of Burgundy ranked in the top tier.[28] By the fifteenth century, though the hydraulis was gone, earwitness reports suggest that acoustical extravagance was central to the royal ritual. An account of Louis XI's coronation in 1461 stressed the sheer *sound* of that event, as "the whole world seemed to quiver and rock and all ears were deafened."[29] That the Reims organ was associated with the tenth-century scholar Gerbert d'Aurillac (later Pope Silvester II), author of a treatise on the measurement of organ pipes (versus

25 I have suggested elsewhere that the cognitive aspects of this phenomenon in fifteenth-century music are analogous to those encountered in modern rap songs that begin with sampled material. Long, *Beautiful Monsters*, 35.

26 Williams, *The Organ in Western Culture*, 217.    27 Ibid., 151, 216.

28 On the primacy of the Duke of Burgundy, see Menin, *An Historical and Chronological Treatise* (1723), 79–80.

29 Whitwell, *The Wind Band*, 186.

those governing the Boethian monochord) provides an additional layer to the identification of *In hydraulis* with the instrument.[30]

Writers on Busnoys have not only overlooked the Reims hydraulis and its royal resonance, but also that the very notion of the hydraulis as a mechanical emblem of dynasty enjoyed a famously royal and famously French pedigree, inscribed in a widely circulating medieval "history" that the Byzantine Emperor Constantine the Fifth gave one ("with great leaden pipes") as a prestigious gift to the first Frankish king, Pippin, in the year 757. It was reported that Charlemagne, too, insisted on acquiring a similar instrument.[31]

While scholarly analyses make much of Busnoys's tenor, it has been primarily as an architectural or mathematical entity, i.e., as a musical analogue of principles shared by any number of learned and aesthetic cultural products including visual art and literary or academic texts.[32] Yet in the new France, still nervously emerging from the institutional devastations and cultural interventions wrought by the English presence during the Hundred Years War, the tenor of *In hydraulis* was very likely intended to manifest *in more than just a metaphorical way* the mechanical noise heard both by Pythagoras the first musician *and* by Pippin the first king, and thereafter by *each generation* of their dynastic descendants in music and government. Those of the living world – the musicians Busnoys and Ockeghem, and the leaders of the houses of France and Burgundy – are recorded in the motet's *secunda pars*. I don't think it unreasonable to imagine Busnoys's motet tenor, as realized in the 1460s, somehow imitating (with vocal dynamics, an organ, or other instruments) what a twelfth-century writer had described as the "loud, ordered sounds" of the Reims hydraulic organ.[33] Indeed, perhaps that acoustical effect was part of the point of contriving this work – as opposed to some other work, which may have *sounded* different – in the first place. I'd suggest further that this apparition of the extraordinary and ancient musical sound of the hydraulis, never literally heard by a fifteenth-century ear, launched a sort of ritual moment at the instant of its apprehension by proxy, resonating with the musical imaginaries of court musicians in the Franco-Burgundian orbit.

---

30  The treatise (variously misattributed) survives in several manuscripts; Gerbert's position as a pedagogue of musical arithmetic enriches the profile of the work as a "musician's motet," resonating with pedagogical conventions (see below, p. 35).

31  See, for example, Bush and Kassel, eds., *The Organ*. For a detailed historical examination of reports concerning the Carolingian organs associated with Pippin, Charlemagne, and Louis the Pious, see Williams, *The Organ in Western Culture*, 137–46. While the actual sound (or "screech") produced by these instruments and the details of their technology cannot be determined with absolute certainty, it seems clear that the Byzantine organ had grand (and noisy) associations, including imperial processions and acclamations (Williams, 71).

32  *In hydraulis* is discussed in terms of its numerical structure or "disposition" by Brothers, "Vestiges of the Isorhythmic Tradition" and Busnoys, *Collected Works*, Pt. 3, ed. Taruskin, 74–80. Benthem, "Text, Tone, and Symbol," reads the numerical details for their symbolic implications.

33  Williams, *The Organ in Western Culture*, 216.

Moderns easily forget that not all histories require or presuppose literacy. Certain histories can only be heard. This is particularly true of musical histories, which belong to communities of musicians sharing a heritage and a sense of place in the world for themselves and for the music they make. When the court players of Techiman in Ghana – whose drums are famously understood to "talk" – participate in a royal funeral, the sound they make accomplishes a series of anthropologically significant tasks.[34] First, the music informs those in attendance that even though the chief has passed, the traditional lives of the Techiman people will continue as it has throughout history, *a history inscribed only acoustically* in the music of the drums and the memory of generations of specialist musicians. Drums must recite the *names* by which history is defined, taking care not to speak erroneously about (i.e., misname) any member of the lineage.[35] In addition, the drums remind other leaders within hearing of the responsibilities of their position: that a chief's role in society is always to step forward and never to fall back. They also speak of kinship and succession: within families, within political entities, and even among musicians. A drummer of the new generation will sometimes occupy a featured position alongside older, master musicians.[36] He makes a case for his expertise by making sound within this community of specialists, demonstrating that he has heard enough to begin "talking" in public, as the elders do, about the chief or other weighty matters.

Ritual prescriptions make up an important segment of the "anthropology of music." Beyond these prescriptive frames, though, when the drummer hits the skin and the drum is heard to speak with the voice of an ancestor (or when a singer in another culture begins to vocalize with specific cultural intent), that instant of music's sounding can initiate a ritual state, i.e., a sort of menu of understandings, in performer and hearer wherein musical information is processed in special ways in both directions. This experience is part of what Anthony Seeger called by contrast "musical anthropology."[37] Only at the moment of music's being sounded is the overarching ritual (which in the Techiman drumming provides a forum for the recitation of history) manifested as something beyond cultural prescription. Indeed, ritual moments are often launched by acoustical actions that occur outside the frame of prescribed

34 My synopsis of the Techiman funeral drumming is extracted from Christopher Roy's DVD, *Drums of Africa*.

35 On the name and naming as a distinct representation of the individual in African traditions involving musical and rhetorical practices, see Pasteur and Toldson, *Roots of Soul*, 230, cited in Kopano, "Rap Music as an Extension of the Black Rhetorical Tradition," 212.

36 The communication in performance between elder and younger drummers is documented in Roy's video. See also Chernoff, *African Rhythm and African Sensibility*, 9–21, where the author describes the dynamics of his apprenticeship among African musical cultures.

37 Seeger, *Why Suyá Sing*, xiii–xiv. See also below, n. 42.

structures. They provide aural signals that the community of listeners is entering the ritual mode.[38]

As accomplished in literate arts as Busnoys and Josquin were, it cannot be
assumed that their listeners relished only – or even mainly – texts and inter-
texts, structures, and technique. The pipes of the French hydraulis had
resounded with acoustical enactments of cultural continuity and dynastic
succession. They were vessels inhabited by the voices of the past, of courtly
and musical ancestors never seen, who, over centuries, were ritually freed to
speak and to be heard clearly and communally by the touch of a living musician's hand on the keys. Busnoys's text was meaningful beyond its antiquarian
elements as well. Linking the composer himself and Ockeghem with the houses
of the kings of France and dukes of Burgundy, the singers of *In hydraulis* retold
relevant and real histories by means of name-emblems. By reference to political
entities (and indeed not only the royal, but the Burgundian line through the
specific naming of the Count of Charolais, poised to assume the ducal title as
Charles the Bold) contemporary musicians are placed within larger associated
social aggregations. Paying attention only to the name pairs recited by the
singers (Pythagoras and Orpheus, Ockeghem and Busnoys, the King of France
and the Duke of Burgundy), a listener will take away three dramatic themes
from the words: music "in the abstract," the living representatives of the
musical tradition, and the political entities within which both music and
musicians are located. All of these themes are rendered audible in the boldly
simplistic "Pythagorean" dynastic tenor, *re ut re*, sounding around and within
the performers.

The anthropological outline is profoundly analogous to the talking skins of
Techiman's royal drums. Busnoys's tenor connects the piece to the cantus firmi
of other late medieval musicians' motets, and to the kinds of musical communities in which they circulated.[39] The sounds of musical teaching and learning
(solmization syllables, the Boethian divisions) embody the unending cyclic
repetitions comprising music history. They remember the beginning of a
musician's entry into the field, where he must sing before his elders.
Eventually they represent his taking on the responsibility of a shared history,
given shape in a public polyphonic matrix. In the case of *In hydraulis*, Busnoys's
acoustical conjuring of musical ancestry and progeny reflected a very specific

---

38 Ibid., 6–7.
39 Fallows, *Josquin* (48–55), discusses the relationship between *In hydraulis*, Josquin's *Illibata dei virgo
nutrix*, and Compère's *Omnium bonorum plena*. While not addressing *In hydraulis*, Rob Wegman has recently
sketched an intriguing and compelling scenario for these kinds of works in French musicians' meetings in
the fifteenth century, revealing documentary evidence for the participation of Josquin and Ockeghem in
such gatherings. See Wegman, "Ockeghem, Brumel, Josquin."

contemporary embodiment of the anthropology of professional social structures by emphasizing his relationship to the generational leader, music's "chef
d'oeuvre," Ockeghem, in whose presence (the motet suggests) Busnoys made
his case for admission to the top ranks.

*In hydraulis* could have provided hearers with cognitive and
anthropological experiences of considerable value. The mechanical noise of
the hydraulis – by the fifteenth century an acoustical emblem rather than a
literal "performing force" – along with these strains of a kind of unwritten
history-telling in Busnoys's piece were perhaps both sounding in Josquin's
imagination as he contemplated a cantus firmus for Ercole's mass. Josquin's
*soggetto* is comprised mainly of the ducal title. "Hercules dux Ferrarie"
sings – in a more direct fashion than any other cantus firmus could – of
Ercole's place among his ancestors and descendants, his role as a dynastic
placeholder. Lineage was a subject of considerable anxiety for the "new"
Estense dukes as the line sought legitimacy in the second half of the fifteenth
century.[40] In the ensuing decades, the Hercules tenor was borrowed for other
European dukes and kings, even though their names did not fit the *soggetto*,
suggesting an understanding that there was something inherent in the *sound
image* that was deemed appropriate for other occasions possessing similar
cultural intentions.

The overblown trombones on our fifty-year-old recording of Josquin's *Missa
Hercules* are heard after the *soggetto* has tentatively materialized in the superius
(suggesting an annunciatory and liminal pre-ritual space). Calling attention to
their own sound, savoring the acoustical shape of each note, letting each step
forward as a grand and articulated entity, and *forcing* a response (even if it is
one of surprise and laughter) that embraces cognitive and anthropological,
individual and communal engagements in a moment of aural reception: these
may tell us exactly how Josquin meant the work to sound – which is to say, as
the thunderous dynastic pipes of *In hydraulis* would have *sounded* to him. If so,
the sounding of either cantus firmus does not merely "symbolize." Busnoys,
Josquin, and the drums of Techiman *realize* the wholeness of community and
the wholeness of history as *moments of sounding* as did the organ of Reims
(which was believed by some medievals to be the very one given to Pippin). I
think it likely that both cantus firmi created a special sort of acoustical
space embracing a reiterated quasi-ritual cultural moment, an effect multiply

---

40 See, for example, Blachly, "The Cantus Firmus of Josquin's *Missa Hercules dux Ferrarie*," 388. If Josquin
envisioned a performance of the Hercules mass that "sounded" like – i.e., produced an effect like – *In hydraulis*,
Ercole d'Este had the forces available, including multiple trombones, in the ducal music contingent beginning
in the 1480s. See the musician lists published in Lockwood, *Music in Renaissance Ferrara*, 314–28.

anticipated and satisfied in the course of hearing each work.[41] Within the special environments projected by these simple but weighty, expressionistically "antique" cantus-firmus parts a host of absent figures (Greek musicians, Carolingian kings, and the long-defunct ancient lords of Ferrara) regained their voices, sang their names, and were *heard*.[42] And I see no reason this imaginary space would not have been carved out in an especially dramatic – even from our perspective melodramatic – way in performance.

What this could suggest about the general subject of fifteenth-century hearing, then, is that some of the most learned musical edifices or musical texts may have possessed the capacity to engage the ear in profound ways we haven't talked much about, experiential modes located outside the hierarchical apparatuses of "preparation" that inform our understanding of historical aural reception. To maintain that the score before us (original or editorial) provides a window on the musical experience of historical hearing might require contemplating its role as witness to a phenomenal past, representing not just a set of intentions but *something that once happened*.[43] Music, as it happened, may have been registered and appreciated in some way by fifteenth-century listeners who would find themselves below our cut-off point for retrospectively determined adequacy, and even by those who weren't paying very much attention. Perhaps it should be part of our task, as we render the audible legible, to consider these possibilities along with what they mean for the organization of history.

## Bibliography

Bent, Margaret, "The 'Harmony' of the Machaut Mass," in *Machaut's Music: New Interpretations*, ed. Elizabeth Eva Leach, Woodbridge, Suffolk, 2003, 75–94
"Polyphony of Texts and Music in the Fourteenth-Century Motet," in *Hearing the Motet*, ed. Pesce, 82–103
Benthem, Jaap van, "Text, Tone, and Symbol: Regarding Busnoys's Conception of *In hydraulis* and its Presumed Relationship to Ockeghem's *Ut heremita solus*," in *Antoine Busnoys: Method, Meaning, and Context in Late Medieval Music*, ed. Paula Higgins, Oxford, 1999, 215–53

41 In the case of the mass, the nature of cognitive anticipation would be inflected somewhat by whether the composition is received as a continuous entity or as constituent units in a liturgical ritual. In the latter (and most likely) case, the ritualizing of dynasty forms an embedded, implicit layer within the conventional ritual prescription of the liturgy.

42 The analogy with African drums is compelling: drums represent the "voice" of absent ancestors. Chernoff, *African Rhythm*, 150. Also compare John Blacking's discussion of Venda music in *How Musical is Man?* Blacking's book concludes with an interesting contemplation of the relationship between ethnomusicology and cognition, or "cognitive anthropology" (112–13).

43 As Edward Muir noted of the scholarly anxiety surrounding work on late medieval and early modern ritual, "The actual ritual moment is long gone and can never be recaptured, but that does not mean it never existed." See Muir, *Ritual in Early Modern Europe*, 9.

Blachly, Alexander, "The Cantus Firmus of Josquin's *Missa Hercules dux Ferrarie*," in *Liber amicorum Isabelle Cazeaux: Symbols, Parallels and Discoveries in her Honor*, ed. Paul-André Bempéchat, Hillsdale, NY, 2005, 377–94

Blackburn, Bonnie J., "Masses Based on Popular Songs and Solmization Syllables," in *The Josquin Companion*, ed. Richard Sherr, Oxford and New York, 2000, 51–87

Blacking, John, *How Musical is Man?*, Seattle, 1973

Bloxam, M. Jennifer, "Obrecht as Exegete: Reading *Factor orbis* as a Christmas Sermon," in *Hearing the Motet*, ed. Pesce, 169–92

Brothers, Thomas, "Vestiges of the Isorhythmic Tradition in Mass and Motet, ca. 1450–1475," *JAMS* 44 (1991), 1–56

Bush, Douglas E., and Richard Kassel, eds., *The Organ: An Encyclopedia*, New York, 2006

Busnoys, Antoine, *Collected Works*, Pt. 3, ed. Richard Taruskin, The Latin Texted Works: Commentary, New York, 1990

Butt, John, "Do Musical Works Contain an Implied Listener? Towards a Theory of Musical Listening," *JRMA* 135 (2010), 5–18

Chernoff, John Miller, *African Rhythm and African Sensibility: Aesthetics and Social Action in African Musical Idioms*, Chicago, 1979

Eno, Brian, *Ambient 1: Music for Airports* (Polydor 2310 647), 1978, liner notes

Fallows, David, *Josquin*, Turnhout, 2009

Higgins, Paula, "Love and Death in the Fifteenth-Century Motet: A Reading of Busnoys's *Anima mea liquefacta est/Stirps Jesse*," in *Hearing the Motet*, ed. Pesce, 142–68

Howlett, David, "Busnois' Motet *In hydraulis*: An Exercise in Textual Reconstruction and Analysis," *PMM* 4 (1995), 185–91

Huron, David, *Sweet Anticipation: Music and the Psychology of Expectation*, Cambridge, 2006

Kerman, Joseph, *Contemplating Music: Challenges to Musicology*, Cambridge, 1985

Kopano, Baruti, "Rap Music as an Extension of the Black Rhetorical Tradition: 'Keepin' it Real'," *Western Journal of Black Studies* 26 (2002), 204–13

Lockwood, Lewis, *Music in Renaissance Ferrara, 1400–1505: The Creation of a Musical Center in the Fifteenth Century*, Cambridge, 1984

Long, Michael, *Beautiful Monsters: Imagining the Classic in Musical Media*, Berkeley, 2008

Meconi, Honey, ed., *Early Musical Borrowing*, New York, 2004

Menin, M., *An Historical and Chronological Treatise of the Anointing and Coronation of the Kings and Queens of France*, London, 1723

Muir, Edward, *Ritual in Early Modern Europe*, Cambridge, 2005

Page, Christopher, *Discarding Images: Reflections on Music and Culture in Medieval France*, Oxford, 1993

Pasteur, Alfred B., and Ivory L. Toldson, *Roots of Soul: The Psychology of Black Expressiveness. An Unprecedented and Intensive Examination of Black Folk Expressions in the Enrichment of Life*, Garden City, NY, 1982

Pesce, Dolores, ed., *Hearing the Motet: Essays on the Motet of the Middle Ages and Renaissance*, New York and Oxford, 1997

Preziosi, Donald, *Rethinking Art History: Meditations on a Coy Science*, New Haven, 1989

Reynolds, Christopher, "Interpreting and Dating Josquin's *Missa Hercules dux Ferrariae*," in *Early Musical Borrowing*, ed. Meconi, 91–110

Roy, Christopher, *Drums of Africa: Talking Drums of Techiman*, DVD [on demand; produced by the filmmaker], African Art Video, no date

Seeger, Anthony, *Why Suyá Sing: A Musical Anthropology of an Amazonian People*, Cambridge, 1987

Sherr, Richard, "Conflicting Levels of Meaning and Understanding in Josquin's *O admirabile commercium* Motet Cycle," in *Hearing the Motet*, ed. Pesce, 193–212

Sparks, Edgar H., *Cantus Firmus in Mass and Motet, 1420–1520*, Berkeley, 1963

Wegman, Rob C., "For Whom the Bell Tolls: Reading and Hearing Busnoys's *Anthoni usque limina*," in *Hearing the Motet*, ed. Pesce, 122–41

"Ockeghem, Brumel, Josquin: New Documents in Troyes," *EM* 36 (2008), 203–17

Whitwell, David, *The Wind Band and Wind Ensemble before 1500*, Northridge, CA, 1982

Williams, Peter, *The Organ in Western Culture, 750–1250*, Cambridge, 1993

Wright, Craig, *The Maze and the Warrior: Symbols in Architecture, Theology, and Music*, Cambridge, 2001

# 2

# Religion and the senses in fifteenth-century Europe

KLAUS PIETSCHMANN

TRANSLATED BY JAMES STEICHEN

It has become easy to win over new students to the study of fifteenth-century music. The widespread availability of recordings of Du Fay, Josquin, and others puts the sonorous qualities of this music on full display. Indeed its sensuous appeal is able to effortlessly overcome the distance of the centuries, offering seemingly unmediated access to the technical structures and cultural conditions of this strange yet powerful sonic world. This phenomenon should perhaps also be credited to increasing scholarly interest, beginning in the 1990s, in questions that address the conditions and circumstances of musical hearing in the fifteenth century.[1] One fundamental obstacle to answering these questions lies in the paucity of contemporary accounts of specific musical listening experiences.[2] The quantity of those impressions of sacred music, in particular, that have come down to us is grossly incommensurate with the significance of these repertories, given their widespread transmission in manuscript sources and the immense financial resources that were required to maintain them in practice.

The following reflections draw together several strains of thought to show the modes of comprehension that structured the sensory experience of sacred polyphony. The point of departure is a passage from the autobiography of Johannes von Soest, one of the most loquacious witnesses to the listening experiences of fifteenth-century art music; this passage provides an encapsulation of the essential modes of perception of late medieval art music. The second section focuses on the doctrine of the internal senses and their effect on music comprehension – which in the late Middle Ages came into contact with the tradition of speculative music theory – with a special focus on the spiritual efficacy of sacred polyphony and the considerable critique that this music engendered. Finally, the discussion will turn to the justification of earthly sensual pleasure, including the "listening pleasure" of sacred music.

---

1 For an overview of this increasingly large body of scholarship see Michael Long's article in this volume (Ch. 1). For the present discussion a few central texts should be mentioned: Burnett, Fend, and Gouk, eds., *The Second Sense*; Wegman, ed., "Music as Heard"; "Listening Practice"; Albin, "Auralities."
2 See for example Strohm, "Musik erzählen."

Well before the shift, during the Counter-Reformation, to a rhetorically oriented conception of the listening experience, Italian humanists posited the existence of rarefied senses in the hereafter.

## Listening experience as musical epiphany: Johannes von Soest

By the time he wrote his verse autobiography around 1500, Johannes von Soest (1448–1506) had had a noteworthy career, including a stint as a singing master ("Sängermeister") in Heidelberg.[3] He later studied medicine in Padua and for unexplained reasons relinquished his musical career to become a doctor. The passage in question is, to be sure, a somewhat stylized account of an experience long past, but it is nevertheless portrayed as a decisive experience that would resonate for the rest of his life. The connotations of his description of the experience are all the more significant since they come from the perspective of a seasoned professional looking back on his life. Johannes is here described as arriving as a young teenager at court, having been "discovered" by the reigning Duke Johann I of Cleves, and hearing the court choir for the first time:

> Onwards I went until, behold!
> In Cleves I heard at last the throng
> Of ducal singers young and old –
> It struck me as angelic song.
> My heart began to leap for joy,
> So much that from delight I wept
> And thought "Good God, could I
> Such skill in art as these adepts, employ
> That I'd prefer to a duke's estate."[4]

The listening event is outlined very briefly: Johannes hears boys and adults singing together – surely a reference to elaborate polyphony. This singing at first prompts an association with angelic music, relating to a traditional

---

3 Pietschmann and Rozenski, "Singing the Self."
4 Da fur ich hyn bys das ich kam
　Gen Kleff da selbs ich dan vernam
　Des fursten sengher in gemeyn
　Dy songhen also grosz und kleyn
　Das mych ducht engelscher gesanck
　Myn hertz da von in frewden spranck
　So ser das ich vor frewden weynt
　Und docht ach Got werstu vereynt
　Mytt solcher konst so meysterlich
　Das nem ich fur al fursten rich.
　Pietschmann and Rozenski, "Singing the Self," 154.

Boethian conception that as early as Aurelianus Reomensis and the *Musica enchiriadis* saw polyphony as analogous to the harmonic conditions of *musica mundana* and put contrapuntal theory into a relation with the music of the angels.[5] Under the influence of Aristotelian reception among the Parisian arts community after 1300, specifically Jacobus Leodiensis, this theoretical, reason-oriented concept expanded, in turn occasioning a dispute over music and the sensuousness of the listening experience.[6] The music of the angels thus moved into a more immediate horizon of experience, which in the end created the premise by which Johannes could compare the court music of Cleves with "angelic song."

But this association leads Johannes to an emotional reaction: the music, having been heard, penetrates his heart, releasing immense joy and moving him to tears. This experience alludes to the theological discourse on the senses, with its origins in late antiquity and continuing through the entire medieval period, a discourse primarily concerned with the correspondence between external sense perception and an internal sensorium. In the third century, building upon Neoplatonic perception theory, Origen developed the theory of the five spiritual senses,[7] which resulted from quasi-sensuous moments of holy experience. In particular, the musically mediated transcendental prayer experiences of Augustine, described in the *Confessions*, acquired an enduring meaning: "How I wept during your hymns and songs! I was deeply moved by the music of the sweet chants of your Church. The sound flowed into my ears and the truth was distilled in my heart. This caused the feelings of devotion to overflow. Tears ran, and it was good for me to have that experience."[8] In Augustine's account it is the auditory perception of sacred music which, mediated by the internal senses, speaks to the heart and is then manifested as a real experience through the emotional reaction of tears. Johannes's account adheres closely to this Augustinian topos. This external and internal sense experience prompts a desire to become united with this "art," that is, to complete the experience through reasoned understanding and active participation. In another respect, this experience is exemplary of a professional musician in this era of cultural upheaval, insofar as this typically religious prototype of perception and hermeneutics is portrayed in more or less secular terms, focused on the enjoyment of music in and of itself: the experience is presented as first and foremost an aesthetic event and only secondarily as a

---

5  See Hammerstein, *Die Musik der Engel*.
6  Hentschel, *Sinnlichkeit und Vernunft*; Albin, "Auralities," 47 ff.
7  See the summary in Scheerer, "Sinne, die," cols. 837 ff.
8  "Quantum flevi in hymnis et canticis suave sonantis ecclesiae vocibus commotus acriter! Voces illae influebant auribus meis, et eliquabatur veritas in cor meum, et exaestuabat inde affectus pietatis, et currebant lacrimae, et bene mihi erat cum eis." *Confessions*, 9.6.14 (trans. in St. Augustine, *Confessions*, 164).

mystical, spiritual experience. The passage accordingly evinces a modern understanding of music as an autonomous art – prevalent in the music-theoretical discourse of humanism, to which Johannes von Soest would have been exposed in the course of his studies in Padua – that is closely correlated with the "professionalization of the composer" that occurred in the late fifteenth century.[9] This insight points to another fundamental problem, that is, how sacred polyphony became a thorny theological issue. In Johannes's description of the epiphanic experience in Cleves there is no mention of what text the musicians sang; his emotional response is produced purely by the sound's sensuous appeal.

## The spiritual senses: holy experience or lasciviousness?

The concept of a sensuously mediated encounter with God complementing a rational engagement with Christian doctrine was further elaborated by authors such as Bernard of Clairvaux and Bonaventure.[10] The doctrine of the spiritual senses made possible an unmediated affective access to God, distinct from representations of the angels in their multitude of merely intellectually perceptible music. In a reversal of the hierarchy of senses handed down from antiquity, according to which reason-oriented sight and hearing were paramount, the sense of touch rose to the top, since it made possible a complete union with the object of perception. There thus arose an array of pious practices that sought to integrate all of the senses, a trend that would intensify in the late Middle Ages:[11] for the eyes, there were increasingly colorful and realistic representations of biblical figures and saints' lives; descriptions of the smells ascribed to deceased saints and their relics steadily intensified in sweetness and stimulatory effect; amber rosary beads became wildly popular, since they added not just a tactile but also an olfactory dimension to the experience of prayer; and the cult of the body and blood of Christ (Corpus Christi) and communal Eucharist, when possible in both species, of bread and wine, became more widespread. Overall, the order of the day was, in the words of Pierre d'Ailly, "to go through the pleasures of the eternal rewards already in this life, and to taste their sweetness with delight."[12] In this manner, the pleasures of

---

9 Wegman, "From Maker to Composer," esp. 469 ff.
10 For a summary with a special focus on musical perception, see Wald-Fuhrmann, "Die Motette im 15. Jahrhundert," 69–73.
11 Largier, "Inner Senses – Outer Senses," 8.
12 "divinas aeternorum praemiorum delectationes jam quodammodo experimentaliter attingere, et eorum suavitatem delectabiliter sapere." See ibid. and Pierre d'Ailly, *Compendium contemplationis*, 3.11, in his *Opuscula spiritualia*, 134.

the senses – always prone to leading one astray through lascivious temptation, and thus regarded with great skepticism by the Church Fathers – acquired a disciplined corrective and a positive orientation toward God.

Along with this spiritual valorization of the human sensorium several meditative practices in the late Middle Ages arose that were closely aligned to the perception of art music. Increased attention to spiritual uplift came through the practice of *ruminatio*, wherein biblical texts or prayers were subjected to multiple affective permutations, whether through mumbled repetition, reversal and recombination, or ornamentation of individual words. The internalization of texts was thus heightened and addressed specifically to the internal senses, which could be intensified with a musical dimension. Compositional structures of sacred vocal music (e.g., text-setting, points of imitation, cantus-firmus treatment, and changes in mensuration) can thus be understood as musicalized *ruminatio*, actively executed by the singer and through active listening experienced simultaneously by the recipient.[13]

Medieval authors paid special attention to the *jubilus*, which was singled out as both the source and result of nearness to God. This wordless praise of the soul unified with God was often associated with the music of the angels or heavenly worship, placing it within a stone's throw of the music-theoretical tradition.[14] It was thus not a huge logical leap to bring sacred music and the Boethian concept of *musica mundana* into a closer relationship with the doctrine of the internal senses, and thus to treat the increasingly elaborate practice of vocal polyphony as a potential source of sensuously mediated spiritual experience. The most prominent proponent of this viewpoint in the fifteenth century is without a doubt Johannes Tinctoris, who in his *Complexus effectuum musices* describes how such spiritual musical perception combines sensuous and cognitive listening practices. This blurring of the boundaries between external and internal modes of reception most readily accounts for Tinctoris's frequent and varying uses of the category of musical *dulcedo*, an experience of spiritual glorification that, although arising from personal taste, is nevertheless applicable to all the senses, as Rob Wegman has demonstrated: "The sweetness of polyphony may represent the outwardly perceived nature of music to untutored ears, but it cannot be achieved without full control of music's inwardly perceived nature."[15]

In opposition to this *rapprochement* of the music of the angels and its perceptibility through external and internal senses, there was, to be sure, a recalcitrant skepticism regarding vocal polyphony's obfuscation of text and the

---

13 Wald-Fuhrmann, "Die Motette im 15. Jahrhundert," 74.
14 Fuhrmann, *Herz und Stimme*, 150 and index.   15 Wegman, "Sense and Sensibility," 306.

professionalization of sacred music in general. One result of this conflict was the complete internalization of the *jubilus*. This practice reached its peak in the context of the veneration of St. Cecilia, the patron of music, who "sang in her heart for God alone" and whose music was not meant to be perceived in earthly realms.[16] In this valorization of Cecilia we see a discontinuity between the music of the angels and actual sacred music, insofar as the mystical union of earthly and heavenly praise was completely internalized.

Indeed, in the context of the reformed mendicant orders, authors reacted with polemical vehemence against vocal polyphony, fiercely criticizing singers' lack of internal conviction and use of inappropriate vocal techniques as worldly and theatrical.[17] The sensuous response such music elicited was thus discredited as a harmful and forbidden pleasure, consigned to the category of the lascivious. This critique did not extend to traditional unison choral singing, which was singled out as the only practice capable of producing positive and beneficial effects while allowing for a reasoned comprehension of sung texts. In its most extreme manifestations, such opposition led to the complete elimination of vocal polyphony by reformers such as Girolamo Savonarola in Florence, Ulrich Zwingli in Zurich, and John Calvin in Geneva.

## The glorification of the senses in the heavenly hereafter

Until the advent of fifteenth-century Italian humanism, few writers had considered how earthly sensuous pleasures might be projected into the heavenly realm. This new perspective offers a key to understanding the affective and spiritual modes of perception of liturgical vocal polyphony above all (but not exclusively) among contemporary Italian elites; as such it allows us to view the immense growth of sacred polyphony during this period within a specific context of cultural and pious practices.

A key reference point for the integration of sensuous attraction into the Christian world-view (including the affective perception of art music) is Lorenzo Valla's dialogue *De voluptate* of 1431. Valla strives for a reconciliation of Epicurianism with Christianity: he compares restrained earthly pleasures with heavenly joy and declares that they are in fact compatible with a God-fearing and virtuous life.[18] The Christian belief in the resurrection of

---

16 Connolly, *Mourning into Joy*, 63.
17 On such critiques of polyphony in the fifteenth century, see, most notably, Wegman, *The Crisis of Music*.
18 Substantial portions of this discourse were first summarized in Tenenti, *Il senso della morte*, 176–79. On the music-specific aspects see also Pietschmann, "The Sense of Hearing Politicized" and "Musik für die Sinne."

the body made a comparison between the sensuous pleasures of this world and the next appear more consequential, such that an ascetic denial of earthly sensuality in and of itself could not be regarded as a Christian virtue. In his reflections on the senses and their pleasurable attractions, Valla ascribes an exalted role to music with regard to the sense of hearing, although he does not go into specifics.[19]

In a similar manner, other authors engage with the question of the sensuous pleasures of the blessed. Giannozzo Manetti leaves musical pleasure out of the discussion in his *De dignitate et excellentia hominis* (1452), although in his earlier and well-known *Oratio* for the dedication of the Florentine cathedral he had described his listening impressions as a premonition of heavenly song.[20] A change in perspective occurs for perhaps the first time with Bartolomeo Rimbertini.[21] His point of departure is not the usual stylized listening experience (which according to the topos serves as an analogy for the music of the angels), but rather the songs of the blessed themselves, which are directly related to earthly musical practices. In his *Tractatus de glorificatione sensuum in paradiso*, Rimbertini concerns himself with the transformation of the five senses in the hereafter. When representing the "sevenfold reform of the audible in the hereafter" ("septiformis reformatio audibilis in patria"), which concerns the removal of all limitations on hearing, speaking, and singing in paradise, Rimbertini also considers the "harmonic consonance" ("consonantia armonica"), about which he determines:

> The Blessed have a better command of the consonances, singing in small note values, coloraturas, etc. than Pythagoras, Boethius, and all musicians. Who could – given the bodily agility of the blessed, who freely develop their tongues and [vocal] organs; and given the optimal disposition of their [vocal] organs as well as their complete knowledge of the *ars musicae*; and given their great and intense enthusiasm in praise of God, encouraging each other – who could have any doubt that there a completely sweet harmony reigns?[22]

The word choice makes it clear that in Rimbertini's view, the song of the blessed is characterized by the most pleasing sounds and wealth of expertise; this suggests he was thinking of vocal polyphony in its most fully realized form.

---

19 Valla, *Von der Lust*, 72–75. See also Strohm, "Neue Aspekte von Musik und Humanismus," 139.
20 Žak, "Der Quellenwert von Giannozzo Manettis Oratio," 14–15. See also Zanovello, "Les Humanistes florentins."
21 On Rimbertini in general see Kaeppeli, "Bartholomaeus Lapaccius de Rimbertinis," as well as Pietschmann, "The Sense of Hearing" and Wald-Fuhrmann, "Die Motette im 15. Jahrhundert," 77–80.
22 "Unde [beati] scient melius quam pictagoras. Boetius: et omnes musici consonantias: fracturas vocum et coloraturas: et ista omnia. Unde data agilitate corporum beatorum que faciet linguam et organa expedita: et data organorum optima dispositione: et data perfecta scientia artis musice: et dato amore magno et intensissimo deum laudandi: et se invicem exorandi: quis dubitet armoniam ibi esse dulcissimam." Rimbertinus, *De deliciis sensibilibus paradisi*, fol. 33r.

Earlier he explicitly states that Christ himself praised God in heaven, in that he spoke and sang at the same time, "with great variety and diversity of the notes of discant or other polyphony."[23]

Celso Maffei, a canon at St. John Lateran, also expresses these sentiments, but goes one step further.[24] In his *Delitiosa explicatio de sensibilibus deliciis paradisi*, published in 1504 and dedicated to Pope Julius II, he determines that

> It should be acknowledged that the saints in the world to come will possess a better understanding of the proportions of song and sounds of the *ars musicae* than anyone in this world. Accordingly they will better execute breakings of the voices and have more suitable voices than any musician.[25]

Maffei's choice of words shows that, like Rimbertini, he sees in the song of the blessed nothing more than an improvement on earthly singing practices. Still evident, as before, is the Boethian conception of an *ars musicae*, consisting of an all-encompassing world harmony of which vocal polyphony is the sounding emanation. Thus the song of the blessed must consist of the most highly realized vocal polyphony. Furthermore, Maffei posits a hierarchy of the sensuous qualities of the blessed:

> Beyond any doubt, the sweetness of the voices and sounds that will sound in glory exceeds by five hundred times any sweetness of song in this life. For some saints, however, only by one hundred times, for some by a thousand times, etc. ... If a saint stands higher than another in his sense of hearing, he will also according to the sweetness of the acoustical object produced stand on a higher step of the hierarchy, and on a lower step if he produces a less edifying effect.[26]

Since God himself stands atop this hierarchy, a higher sensorial quality implies a closer proximity to the Creator. In view of the fundamental similarity between earthly and heavenly song, such a conception has far-reaching consequences for the spiritual qualities of sacred polyphony. A more deeply religious content results merely from the beauty of the sound: the greater the sensuous pleasure that flows from a composition in the context of worship, the

---

23 "cum multa varietate et diversitate notarum discantus vel alterius harmonie." Ibid.
24 On Celso Maffei see Widloecher, *La Congregazione dei canonici regolari lateranensi*; McDannell and Lang, *Heaven: A History*, 136; Tenenti, *Il senso della morte*, 180–82.
25 "Tenendum est quod sancti in futuro statu melius scient proportiones vocum et sonorum secundum artem musicae quam aliquis in hoc mundo. Similiter scient fractiones vocum optime peragere et habebunt organa aptiora quam aliqui musici." Maffei, *Delitiosam explicationem*, without fol.
26 "Suavitas vocum et sonorum quae erit in gloria excedet secundum grossam extimationem saltem quinquagesies omnem suavitatem cantus huius vitae. Sed in quibusdam sanctis erit centies tanta. Et in quibusdam milesies. Et in aliquibus plusque milesies tanta etc. ... Quia ergo unus sanctus secundum auditum magis meruit quam alter ideo secundum hoc suavitas obiecti audibilis erit in ordine ad ipsum maior: Et minor in alio qui minus meruit secundum effectum scilicet delectationis." Maffei, *Delitiosam explicationem*.

more similar it is to heavenly music. Moreover, the vigor of the listener's internal senses is also greater and causes a more intense union with God.

To be sure, most of these authors are not to be regarded as prominent spokesmen for the theological-humanistic discourse of the fifteenth century; nevertheless their statements can be deemed representative of a broadening of perspective within these circles. Now that compositional practice had been equated with the music of the angels, with even the heavenly praise of Christ himself, the compositional and performative abilities of elite composers achieved the highest conceivable status, and as a result made it possible to address the internal senses and the heart; this in turn occasioned the desired connection of the soul with God. Such a view is clearly of a piece with the musical perspectives of Marsilio Ficino, even if he did not directly address the effects of contemporary art music.

## Musical rhetoric

With this cognitive construct the traditional lines of argument followed by critics of polyphony were skillfully undermined: from the assumption that human senses were also present among the incorruptible saints – in optimized form, to be sure – it could be concluded that their worship was fundamentally similar to earthly singing practices and their effects. Such a construct did not go uncontested, however. The Dutch humanist Mattheus Herbenus, who spent time in Italy in the 1470s and could have come into contact with the musical perspective outlined above, took issue with precisely this equation of earthly polyphony with the music of the angels.[27] In his 1496 treatise *De natura cantus ac miraculis vocis*, he determines that

> The blessed spirits bring to God a proper song, although not with human voices but with spiritual ones, with heavenly instruments and songs; with the highest unity and perfection, in which the unified voices melodiously blend together without any deviation. Thus the tenor is indistinguishable from the contratenor, the high from the low, the octave from the fifth.[28]

Herbenus thus concludes that earthly song is directed toward earthly ears and allows words to unfold according to the principles of rhetoric. This was more successfully achieved, Herbenus maintains in a later passage, by the ancients

---

27 On Herbenus see Sachs, "Herbenus, Mattheus."
28 "Persolvunt itaque iustum Deo canticum beatissimi spiritus, non mortalibus quidem organis sed intellectualibus, sed divinis instrumentis ac modulis; summa unitate atque perfectione, ubi omnium voces communes omnibus sine ulla discrepantia melodissime consonant. Non enim illic alius Tonor a Contratonore est, non a gravi acutus cantus alius, non diapason a diapente dissidet." Cited according to Thesaurus Musicarum Latinarum, www.chmtl.indiana.edu/tml/start.html, accessed 3 August 2011.

and in time-honored *cantus planus* than by most contemporary composers of vocal polyphony. If he ascribes any spiritual efficacy to certain pieces – by Gaspar van Weerbeke or Jacob Obrecht, for instance – this is due to their rationally oriented composition, their texts, or the perceptibility of their cantus firmi; all of these can bring the spirit to pious contemplation, with neither external nor internal sensual appeal.[29]

This shift of musical perception – from a sensuously mediated mystical experience of sensuous pleasures by the blessed in paradise to a verbally oriented, rationalistic use of the sense of hearing – influenced later discussions of church music in the early years of the Counter-Reformation in Rome. In particular, Jacopo Sadoleto, an austere humanist who held a clear position on the need for church reforms, described music in 1533 as something that simply titillates the ears, similar to bird songs or animal noises, which mankind should by no means wish to imitate.[30]

Indicative of things to come is a well-known letter of Bernardino Cirillo, who in 1549 called for the new, sensuously oriented text-setting of the Italian madrigal, which "in certain harmonies and affective cadences lets words speak that don't communicate," to be pressed into the service of church music.[31] In 1564, at the height of the debates on church music, this letter was reprinted by Aldo Manuzio, incurring the displeasure of Pope Pius V (1566–72), with further publication subsequently suppressed.[32] But his call to use the sensuous capabilities of music to express that which words could not would become a founding principle for a new musical era.

## Bibliography

Albin, Andrew Justin, "Auralities: Sound Cultures and the Experience of Hearing in Late Medieval England," Ph.D. diss., Brandeis University, 2011

Augustine, St., *Confessions*, trans. Henry Chadwick, Oxford, 1991

Burnett, Charles, Michael Fend, and Penelope Gouk, eds., *The Second Sense: Studies in Hearing and Musical Judgement from Antiquity to the Seventeenth Century*, London, 1991

Connolly, Thomas, *Mourning into Joy: Music, Raphael, and Saint Cecilia*, New Haven and London, 1994

Fuhrmann, Wolfgang, *Herz und Stimme: Innerlichkeit, Affekt und Gesang im Mittelalter*, Musiksoziologie 13, Kassel, 2004

Hammerstein, Reinhold, *Die Musik der Engel: Untersuchungen zur Musikanschauung des Mittelalters*, Bern, 1962

29 Cited according to Thesaurus Musicarum Latinarum.    30 Palisca, *Humanism*, 14 ff.

31 "In certi numeri, e cadentie affetuose ... fa parlare a quelle parole, che non parlano." Palisca, "Bernardino Cirillo's Critique," 289 n. 33.

32 Pietschmann, *Kirchenmusik*, 101.

Hentschel, Frank, *Sinnlichkeit und Vernunft in der mittelalterlichen Musiktheorie: Strategien der Konsonanzwertung und der Gegenstand der Musica Sonora um 1300*, Beihefte zum Archiv für Musikwissenschaft 47, Stuttgart, 2000

Kaeppeli, Thomas, "Bartholomaeus Lapaccius de Rimbertinis 1404–1466," *Archivum Fratrum Praedicatorum* 9 (1939), 86–127

Largier, Niklaus, "Inner Senses – Outer Senses: The Practice of Emotions in Medieval Mysticism," in *Codierungen von Emotionen im Mittelalter*, ed. C. Stephen Jaeger and Ingrid Kasten, Trends in Medieval Philology 1, Berlin and New York, 2003, 3–15

"Listening Practice," colloquium in *Early Music* 25 (1997), 591–714

Maffei, Celso, *Delitiosam explicationem de sensibilibus deliciis paradisi*, Verona, 1504

McDannell, Colleen, and Bernhard Lang, *Heaven: A History*, New Haven, 2001

Palisca, Claude V., "Bernardino Cirillo's Critique of Polyphonic Church Music of 1549: Its Background and Resonance," in *Music in Renaissance Cities and Courts: Studies in Honor of Lewis Lockwood*, ed. J. A. Owens and A. M. Cummings, Warren, MI, 1997, 281–92

*Humanism in Italian Renaissance Musical Thought*, New Haven, 1985

Pierre d'Ailly, *Opuscula spiritualia*, Douai, 1634

Pietschmann, Klaus, *Kirchenmusik zwischen Tradition und Reform: Die päpstliche Kapelle und ihr Repertoire unter Pabst Paul III. (1534–1549)*, Capellae Apostolicae Sixtinaeque collectanea acta monumenta 11, Vatican City, 2007

"Musik für die Sinne: Zum Funktionsspektrum von Hohelied-Motetten des 15. Jahrhunderts," in *Normierung und Pluralisierung: Struktur und Funktion der Motette im 15. Jahrhundert*, ed. Laurenz Lütteken, Kassel, 2011, 87–112

"The Sense of Hearing Politicized: Liturgical Polyphony and Political Ambition in Fifteenth-Century Florence," in *Religion and the Senses in Early Modern Europe*, ed. Wietse De Boer and Christine Goettler, Leiden, 2013, 273–88

and Steven Rozenski, "Singing the Self: The Autobiography of the Fifteenth-Century German Singer and Composer Johannes von Soest," *EMH* 29 (2010), 119–59

Rimbertinus, Bartholomeus, *De deliciis sensibilibus paradisi*, Venice, 1498

Sachs, Klaus-Jürgen, "Herbenus, Mattheus," in *MGG2, Personenteil*, 8, Kassel, 2002, cols. 1359–61

Scheerer, E., "Sinne, die," in *Historisches Wörterbuch der Philosophie*, ed. Joachim Ritter and Karlfried Gründer, rev. edn. by Rudolf Eisler, 9, Basel, 1995, cols. 824–69

Strohm, Reinhard, "Musik erzählen: Texte und Bemerkungen zur musikalischen Mentalitätsgeschichte im Spätmittelalter," in *Kontinuität und Transformation in der italienischen Vokalmusik zwischen Due- und Quattrocento*, ed. Sandra Dieckmann *et al.*, Musica Mensurabilis 3, Hildesheim, 2007, 109–26

"Neue Aspekte von Musik und Humanismus im 15. Jahrhundert," *Acta musicologica* 76 (2004), 135–57

Tenenti, Alberto, *Il senso della morte e l'amore della vita nel Rinascimento (Francia e Italia)*, Turin, 1957, repr. 1989

Valla, Lorenzo, *Von der Lust, oder, Vom wahren Guten*, Latin–German edition translated with an introduction by Eckhard Kessle, Munich, 2004

Wald-Fuhrmann, Melanie, "Die Motette im 15. Jahrhundert, ihre Kontexte und das geistliche Hören: Forschungsüberblick und Perspektiven," in *Normierung und Pluralisierung: Struktur und Funktion der Motette im 15. Jahrhundert*, ed. Laurenz Lütteken, Kassel, 2011, 57–86

Wegman, Rob C., *The Crisis of Music in Early Modern Europe, 1470–1530*, New York, 2005

    "From Maker to Composer: Improvisation and Musical Authorship in the Low Countries, 1450–1500," *JAMS* 49 (1996), 409–79

    "Sense and Sensibility in Late-Medieval Music: Thoughts on Aesthetics and 'Authenticity'," *EM* 23 (1995), 299–312

    ed., "Music as Heard," special issue of *MQ* 82 (1998), 427–691

Widloecher, Nicola, *La Congregazione dei canonici regolari lateranensi: Periodo di formazione (1402–1483)*, Gubbio, 1929

Žak, Sabine, "Der Quellenwert von Giannozzo Manettis Oratio über die Domweihe von Florenz 1436 für die Musikgeschichte," *Die Musikforschung* 40 (1987), 2–32

Zanovello, Giovanni, "Les Humanistes florentins et la polyphonie liturgique," in *Poétiques de la Renaissance: Le modèle italien, le monde franco-bourguignon et leur héritage en France au XVIᵉ siècle*, ed. Perrine Galand-Hallyn and Fernand Hallyn, Geneva, 2001, 625–38 and 667–73

*TERMS AND CONCEPTS*

# 3

# The work concept

LAURENZ LÜTTEKEN

TRANSLATED BY JAMES STEICHEN

The concept of the musical "work" is based on the assumption that a composed piece of music is a work of art. Such an idea is neither conceptually self-evident nor factually verifiable, and in the fifteenth century – as in all time periods – it was manifested in a particular way. The term "work" implies activity, efficacy, and labor, but can also signify output, i.e., that which results from work. Following the Greek term "ergon" (ἔργον), the Latin "opus" retains this dual meaning, signifying both the process of creation and the created product, and has never been employed exclusively to refer to an end result. In this latter sense the more common term is *artificium* (composite), as in *res artificiosa* (artificial thing), *artis opus* (work of art), or *opus arte factum* (or *perfectum*, work made of art, or consummate work). This terminology has contributed to three fundamental problems for music history:

1. Since Latin was the dominant scholarly language until well into the modern age, it is difficult to determine at what point "opus" came to acquire the additional meaning of a musical work of art as a created product. Further complicating this issue is that "opus" continued to be used even after Latin's status as the scholarly *lingua franca* began to decline. In its strictly musical sense as a term to document and count a composer's works, "opus" was first employed in the early seventeenth century, during this time of transition for Latin, and has been in continuous use in this manner up to the present day.

2. The term "opus" (and its translations) has always retained a connotation of craftsmanship. There was thus an implicit emphasis on the creative activity inherent in a "work" (particularly in medicine), even with respect to the finished product (as in the German meaning of "Werk" as fortification). In the aesthetic discourses of the fifteenth century and later eras, however, works of art (including music) were considered successful to the degree that they eliminated all such traces of craftsmanship. Thus the question arises as to when exactly musical works of art began to be considered "created" in this artistic sense, as opposed to the more workmanlike sense of being "made."

3. More broadly: owing to the special disciplinary status that music has held over time, it is difficult to distinguish between the general concept of a "work of art" and more specific musical senses of the term. Music gradually retreated from this peculiar status, and was subsequently reintegrated into the larger classificatory systems of the arts, albeit in a contentious and often inconsistent manner.

These challenges point to a larger historical problem. The development of the concept of a musical work of art, however it is defined, cannot be systematically correlated with changes in terminology. On the contrary, the ancient status of music as a rational act of human beings – as *ars* (*techne*, τέχνη), which in the sense of *energeia* (ενέργεια) can simultaneously affect the human soul – guaranteed the *ars musicae* a privileged role in the Platonic systems of knowledge that led to the creation of the seven *artes liberales*. Music's status as a liberal art, however, was fundamentally opposed to any understanding of music as a material creation. To a degree, the conceptualization of music as *ars* did acknowledge its sensuous manifestations – in Boethius, for example, who makes reference to specific music from sixth-century Ravenna – but it was nevertheless not accorded any enduring material status. Even when music acquired its own material history as an art form (and thus became self-referential), it continued to be affected by this imponderable quality. The moment of this shift is difficult to identify with precision: it appears different depending upon the perspective from which it is viewed, and was the result of an imprecise convergence of various processes.

A musical work of art "is not the sum of its phenotypes, but is contained *in* them."[1] The possibilities implied by these premises do not necessarily relate to and involve each other, but there is one point in time at which they all began to be present simultaneously. Such a moment occurred in the fifteenth century, when all of the theoretical and practical premises upon which the musical work of art depends were present: notation and written tradition, authorship and professionalization, historicity and historical memory, the position of music in an emerging generic classification of the arts, reproducibility, and "aesthetics."[2] While all of these premises are interrelated, they cannot readily be superimposed nor organized in a linear trajectory or chronological timeline, and are thus best considered individually.[3]

---

1 Wiora, *Das musikalische Kunstwerk*, 15.    2 Strohm, "'Opus'."
3 Cf. Calella, *Musikalische Autorschaft*; Lütteken, *Musik der Renaissance*.

## Notation and the written tradition

Music does not need to be fixed or transmitted in written form to constitute a work.[4] Just as something may have the character of a work without being notated (for example, the keyboard music of Conrad Paumann), the fact of writing music down does not presuppose a "work character" (for example, in plainchant). Even so, the instantiation of music in its own system of significa-tion is central to almost every concept of "creation." The stability that music derives from notation is essential to the work concept, insofar as it constitutes a decisive materialization. Once fixed in notation, music no longer exists merely as aural perception. Since the invention of musical notation in the ninth century, there developed a twofold sense of the written. On the one hand, music came to be viewed as an independent body of literature; on the other, the development of neumatic notation initiated an emphasis on consciously shaped music, also emphasized in the canonization of Boethius's *De institutione musica*. This duality of the written sense caused music theory and music composition to develop in distinct, if not entirely different, directions. It was only much later, during the Enlightenment (with its unconditional turn toward aural experience), that a fundamentally different disposition toward musical writing would develop.

The history of polyphony is thus a history of written traditions and hence implicitly a history of work concepts. The moment compositional challenges came into play, music became at least partially released from the strictures of ritual context. To a certain extent this is already evident in early polyphony, as in the *clausulae* of the later edition of the *Magnus liber* (Florence, Biblioteca Medicea Laurenziana, Plut. 29.1 and Wolfenbüttel, Herzog August Bibliothek, Cod. Helmst. 628).[5] That multiple musical renderings could be fashioned from the same material signifies a disengagement from liturgical or ritual context. With the development of mensural notation in the late thirteenth century music history entered a new phase, as individual signs were equipped with the dual significance of pitch and duration. Against this background, work concepts are manifest in the repertory of the later fourteenth century, even in the absence of attributions (for example, in the anonymously transmitted motet *Inter densas/Imbribus irriguis/Admirabile*, which systematically explores every compositional possibility of *musica mensurabilis*).[6] At the same time, the changing formats of the sources themselves show a variety of work concepts in action: the abandonment of score notation, the development of music

---

4 See Berger, *A Theory of Art*, 28 ff.    5 Cf. Kaden, *Des Lebens wilder Kreis*, 125 ff.
6 Further on this motet, see Emily Zazulia's essay in this volume, Ch. 31.

manuscripts as an independent form of transmission, and the "work-like" arrangement of their components.

In the fifteenth century musical notation entered a new phase. In a group of northern Italian manuscripts from the first decades of the century, large repertories were for the first time written down soon after their composition, not with the intention of immediate reproduction but for archival purposes. This development granted the musical manuscript a new status; indeed this project of repertorial preservation is arguably the most idiosyncratic example of music writing in the history of the written tradition. Notated compositions were treated as "works" in that they record how the music existed in performance, not insofar as they serve as a prescriptive prompt for future presentation: the "work quality" inhered in the performance itself, not the written memento. (The same distinction applies, in a slightly different manner, to the short-lived and anachronistic Florentine notation that spanned several generations, preserved in the Squarcialupi Codex.) The indexes of the surviving sources, organized according to their textual incipits, provide significant evidence for this trend. In the first half of the fifteenth century, these textual incipits began to be accompanied first by additional internal information such as mensuration signs (Oxford 213) and, eventually, musical incipits (suggested in the Emmeram Codex; used systematically for the first time in Modena α. X.1.11). Setting aside the question of how normative it was to include such accompanying information, this apparent materialization of the text points to a concept of the musical work as something "created." Such additional resources are a prerequisite for printed musical works (e.g. Petrucci's *Odhecaton A* of 1501), which appeared later than literary texts printed with movable type owing to technical challenges, not the lack of a work quality. Indeed in Petrucci's earliest prints the ethos of a work quality extends not just to individual pieces but to the fixed notion of a complete "book," whose determinants include genre and, where applicable, authorship. Along with these practices, the explicit numbering of works emerged for the first time as an organizational tool (three numbered books of Josquin masses appeared in 1502, 1505, and 1514, eleven numbered books of frottole between 1504 and 1514). At the same time, the boundaries of the written word began to diminish in the fifteenth century, as exemplified by Leonardo Giustinian, whose poetry, in contrast to his music, was written down only after his death.

## Authorship and professionalization

The attribution of creations to an author is a precondition for every modern concept of the musical work, even in cases when authorship is ceded to a performer or exists by negation, i.e., is deliberately disavowed or assumed in a collective. From a historical perspective, however, authorship stands as a secondary and comparatively recent determinant of the work concept. Until well into the fifteenth century, authorial attribution was not a dominant feature of musical transmission but only one of several possibilities. By around 1500 it had acquired the normative character that has held fast in our cultural consciousness up to the present day. A significant number of celebrated compositions from the late fourteenth and fifteenth centuries clearly lay claim to a distinct work status, despite being transmitted without their authors' names (e.g., all the Chantilly motets, *Elizabet Zacharie* in Trent 87, and *In ultimo lucente Junii/Pacem Deus* in Trent 89, datable to June 1451). This is all the more remarkable since in other contexts, such as architecture, a model of authorial attribution had been present for some time. It is thus clear that only as a result of complicated historical processes did authorship become an essential condition for work character. It was neither necessary nor inevitable.

This ambiguity is particularly clear in situations where authorship was claimed *without* a clear notion of a work. The names provided by Anonymous IV (Leoninus and Perotinus), for instance, were apparently suggested not with the deliberate intention of identifying artistic personages and their significance with respect to "works," but for the purpose of classification. This practice of cipher-like authorization endured into the fifteenth century. It is in this manner that Johannes Tinctoris cites the names of composers – not to characterize the individuality of musical productions, but rather to distinguish between historical layers (e.g., generations) of composition. In literary transmission the names of authors were recorded from early on, as in troubadour and trouvère transmission (with ancillary impact on music history), or in the musical notation of Guillaume de Machaut's mostly literary oeuvre. By contrast, in musical contexts authorial attribution was used as a means of identification and distinction only in exceptional cases. Even the fictitious portraits in the Squarcialupi Codex, singular in the history of both musical manuscripts and musicians' portraits (which would also emerge in the fifteenth century), fail to reveal anything about the composers depicted – with the exception, perhaps, of information about the religious orders with which they were affiliated – and remain more or less inscrutable ciphers. Only in the repertory of the trecento do we first encounter the idea of correlating a work's individuality not just with names but also with specific compositional qualities.[7]

---

7 See Finscher, "Die Entstehung des Komponisten."

Even though authorship became a constitutive phenomenon of musical work concepts at a comparatively late stage, it quickly emerged as a central element. As in the discourses surrounding painting and poetry, in discussions of the composer as creator ca. 1500 "creatio" was increasingly considered to be work-like, encompassing the crucial attributes of reputation and posthumous fame. From the earliest such discussions there arose questions about the comparative value of individual works and composers. Such considerations had consequences in the social realm, for example in Henricus Isaac's contending with Josquin to gain a position at Ferrara in 1503. That in his *Book of the Courtier* of 1528 Baldessar Castiglione could treat such conceptions of authorial authenticity in an ironic manner shows how quickly they took root. In the late medieval period we thus see, albeit at first in isolated instances, the emergence of material equivalents for works, including remuneration for specific compositions. Documentation of this phenomenon is initially sparse, however: in 1378 Francesco Landini received payment for five motets, and in 1466 Nycasius de Clibano was honored for his polyphonic Marian antiphons.[8]

Indeed it is only in the fifteenth century that we first encounter figures in whom we can discern the modern criterion of the individual composer. This cannot be said of Machaut, who considered himself first and foremost a poet, nor of fourteenth-century composers, most of whom lack a "biography" and whose oeuvres often comprised only one or two genres. In the case of Johannes Ciconia (?–1412), by contrast, we not only know his name and the basic contours of his "biography" but also possess an oeuvre consisting of several contributions to each major genre, documented in contemporary sources. These works not only display an individual style but also contain distinctive idioms that match the expectations of each respective genre. The first musician in whom these criteria condense in a particularly meaningful way is Guillaume Du Fay (ca. 1400–74).[9] While his compositions are better documented in the first half of his life than in the second, he may nonetheless be regarded as a composer in the modern sense. The sources indicate that Du Fay worked consciously to shape his official employment as a cleric to serve his career as a musician; indeed on his gravestone he presented himself as a musician first and a canon second.

Compositional individualization posited a professionalization on two levels. First, composing became a craft, such that various problems could be addressed with recourse to a specific system of values. We can see that in certain situations Du Fay regarded a number of solutions as equivalent, as in his manner of

---

8 Documented in Pirrotta, "Landini," col. 165; Smijers, "De Illustre Lieve Vrouwe Broederschap," 73.
9 See Alejandro Planchart's contribution to this volume, Ch. 5.

treating chanson texts. When marking the end of a verse, for instance, Du Fay turned alternately to "instrumental" passages, to pauses, and to cadences – widely divergent techniques that together constitute a spectrum of possibilities. Though mutually exclusive, each of these potential solutions claims validity in its own right. In Quintilian's *Institutio oratoria*, rediscovered in 1416, this kind of practice was termed "antinomia." The internal musical discourse of the cantus-firmus mass, for instance, would be unthinkable without such a premise. This mode of thinking necessitated professional forms of organization for the production and reproduction of music. Although the "capella" as a specifically musical institution is a product of the fourteenth century, its proliferation throughout Europe as a means of cultural display and political distinction occurred only in the fifteenth. At this time we also find the first attempts by composers to renegotiate the terms of their clerical careers, whether by adding specific musical responsibilities (Du Fay and Johannes Ockeghem), leaving certain ecclesiastical duties behind (Josquin and Jacob Obrecht), or replacing such duties entirely (Isaac). Such changes are a precondition for the independent material recognition of compositional achievement – that is, the remuneration of the act of composing itself, as opposed to composition as an activity incidental or ancillary to employment.

## Historicity and historical memory

The concept and definition of a work depend first and foremost on an inherent musical and compositional memory, and by extension rely on a self-reflective sense of music history. A central but by no means exclusive vehicle for such consciousness is genre, which contains both implicit and explicit norms for works realized within its parameters. In the complex system of genres in existence since the fourteenth century, compositions enter into an internal dialogue that is a central prerequisite for the essence of a work quality. Only later did this dialogue come to be associated with the personality of individual composers, most clearly in the wide-ranging reception of Josquin in the sixteenth century, with its thorny problems of attribution.[10] Here for the first time we see the concept of music history as a long-term pattern of perception spanning several generations. The foundations for this concept were laid in the fifteenth century, in the remembrances of Ciconia and Du Fay long after their deaths, or in the Squarcialupi Codex, which spans the output of three generations. The concept of genre thus provided a genuinely musical mode of thinking that was not in evidence in such a comprehensive

---

10 See Rodin, "Josquin and Epistemology," in this volume, Ch. 7.

form in the other arts, and that shaped the contours of the nascent musical work.[11] This process began in the fourteenth century, particularly with the development of a complex system of secular songs, and acquired self-referential traits from an early stage (e.g., Machaut, *Ma fin est mon commencement*; J. Alanus, *Sub Arturo plebs/Fons citharizancium/In omnem terram*).

The significance of genres becomes apparent when their boundaries are made the object of discussion and when they have been transgressed or called into question. Several such examples appear in the first decades of the fifteenth century. Du Fay's motet *Supremum est mortalibus*, apparently composed in 1433 for the coronation of Emperor Sigismund in Rome, is striking not only because it reduces the by-then customary four-voice motet texture to three voices, but also because it interpolates fauxbourdon sections into an isorhythmic motet and thus contravenes the listener's expectations. Regardless of precisely why Du Fay composed the motet this way, the scale of his play with norms is remarkable. Similarly, Du Fay's rondeau *Bien veignés vous*, with its canon in the two outer voices, integrates a musical element from another genre (strict canon) into song, a genre that does not typically engage in contrapuntal play of this kind. If we understand the first decades of the fifteenth century as a time in which a modern awareness of musical genres was born, it is remarkable that the deliberate transgression of generic norms was systematically explored from the very beginning, and indeed was considered a mark of compositional distinction. Josquin's generic experiments beginning around 1500 (that is, his songs for five and six voices) show just how sophisticated such procedures would become within the space of a few decades.

After this short preliminary phase, the classification of musical genres quickly established itself as an implicit and highly effective cognitive structure with a great degree of differentiation. The ephemeral character of musical works of art had fostered a mode of thought intended above all to fulfill a commemorative function. It was not just individuals who were the object of this type of commemoration and re-envisioning (known as *memoria*), but also processes and facts; this phenomenon should thus be understood more broadly as a comprehensive social reality that affected everyone involved. *Memoria* as an act of remembrance promoted a kind of continuity with an implied exaltedness. Such a conceptualization is another decisive precondition for the concept of the musical work, which came to be understood as endowed with the ability to outlive its creator and exert a power beyond the creator's direct influence.

---

11 Finscher, "Werk und Gattung."

## Music's position in a nascent system of the arts

Imposing the concept of the work of art on music required the translation of the *ars musicae* from the context of the *artes liberales* into a more modern system of the arts. The underlying rationale for this shift was the belief that all human creations that affect the senses were interrelated and could thus be mastered systematically, in identical or at least similar ways. This transition, which in music was an inconsistent and indeed somewhat tortured process, began in the fifteenth century and would not come to a close until probably sometime in the eighteenth century.

Around 1400 a new musical realm of experience emerged, and with it the idea that composed music was first and foremost a presentation of text to listeners, a concept introduced emphatically by Ciconia. This development exacerbated an already problematic theoretical situation, since music-theoretical literature grounded in the *artes liberales* could provide no specific categories for such an experience. It was arguably not until introduction of the term *varietas* by Johannes Tinctoris in his *Liber de arte contrapuncti* (1477) that any rhetorical standardization was attempted to theorize this kind of compositional event. Even though the rules of composition presented by Tinctoris were grounded in practical considerations, and even though his discussions of specific works focus primarily on issues of notational technique, his concepts nevertheless indicate a turn to sounding, composed, perceptible music as a new experience of reality.[12]

In painting, Leon Battista Alberti introduced a similar concept of *varietas* that demonstrates the broad manner in which such changes were taking place across the arts. In his treatise *De hominis dignitate* (*Oration on the Dignity of Man*) of 1486, Giovanni Pico della Mirandola (a proponent of Florentine Neoplatonism) described *varietas* as one of the central characteristics of the protean nature of man, with significant consequences for an understanding of human cultural achievement. This attempt to arrive at a new definition of human dignity (a topic to which Giannozzo Manetti had devoted an essay as early as 1452) is clearly articulated at the very outset of his posthumously published treatise, in which he asserts that man is distinguished not by unity but by multiplicity: "varia ac multiformis et desultoria natura" (his multiple and multifaceted yet also mercurial nature).[13] In Castiglione's *Book of the Courtier* of 1528, the concept of *varietas* (including but not limited to musical

---

12 Wegman, "From Maker to Composer"; Luko, "Tinctoris on *Varietas*"; Strohm, "Werk – Performanz – Konsum," 348 ff.
13 Giovanni Pico della Mirandola, "Oratio. (De hominis dignitate)," 104.

matters) is elevated to serve as an underlying principle of courtly life in general, a precept that can lend coherence to its many expectations and realities.

By introducing a rhetorical term as a standard of composition and reception, music came into greater proximity with the other arts, whose essence no longer consisted primarily of demonstrating matters anagogically but in making an impression on the human senses. This process employed a certain logic and coercion. By means of rational theories, particularly in scholasticism, the soul had been segmented into individual "properties," each of which favored distinct sensory perceptions. By contrast, this new conception of man was characterized by an emphasis on the unity of the soul and its cognitive capacities, an idea first summarized in Pico della Mirandola's *Oratio*. In this way the impressions of the senses could be bundled, and with rhetoric as a controlling instrument furnished with a connective authority. Sensory perception thus entered into a competition between the arts, a *paragone* carried out aggressively in Leonardo da Vinci's famous treatise on painting (posthumously reconstructed from fragments). This granted immediate expression to an imaginary unity of the arts as those achievements of man capable of impressing his senses. With regard to painting such theoretical endeavors represented a remarkable success story. Beginning with Alberti, one finds a theory for an art that, as part of the *artes mechanicae*, had initially failed to be recognized as worthy of theoretical discourse.

With regard to music, this new orientation toward human perception did not unfold smoothly but was marked by disruption and unpredictability. Grounding composition in the discourse of craftsmanship implicitly dissolved music's status with respect to the *artes liberales*. Yet music theorists expressly clung to this idea; indeed this tension determined the direction of music theory. The potential conflict that presented itself is not opposed to the musical work concept, however, but rather has a constitutive function – and it was in the fifteenth century that this function first emerged and was acknowledged openly for the first time, with all of its consequences.

## Reproducibility and "aesthetics"

It is evident in writers as early as Johann Mattheson (1681–1764) that the creation of the work concept primarily through the dimension of sense perception was of enormous consequence for the aural realization of a score – that is, for performance in the modern sense of the word. Performance thus emerged from the shadow of imprecise reproduction to figure as a central component of the work in the theoretical writings of the Berlin school of the 1750s. When the history of interpretation came to a head in the nineteenth

century, it would assume a work-like character in its own right.[14] The earliest
origins of this process date back even further, however, to the time when the
system of the arts was established. In this early phase of instrumental music,
performance achieved its *virtus* – and the performer accordingly acquired the
status of virtuoso – precisely by divesting itself of the impression of producing
something through laborious toil, a change that had already been realized in
painting. Not surprisingly, in music this was first accomplished in the context
of keyboard and lute performance, in which written transmission had always
played a subordinate role.

With the rise of the *cappella*, the fifteenth century saw not only the establishment of a network of comparable institutions – in fact it was the relative
uniformity of these that enabled the astonishing mobility of musicians – but
also the creation of institutional repertories with their own modes of transmission. This gave rise to practices that were at once contradictory and complementary. On the one hand, works could be copied, performed, listened to,
and evaluated in multiple contexts and far from the site of their composition.
On the other, specific local conditions could give rise to specific "works" whose
validity operated within a localized framework. This juxtaposition of works
operating simultaneously at general and local levels points to another context
that was crucial for the work concept: the delineation of evaluative practices.

Although such practices might seem parochial and geographically and chronologically discrete, they are in fact indicative of a larger trend. A decisive
aspect of the work concept is its compatibility with aesthetic discourses, but
these phenomena are not synonymous. Rather, the work concept represented
one of the more significant components of an emergent aesthetics of music;
indeed the introduction of a work concept focused on created products first
gained clear contours in the fifteenth century. This sort of thinking was present
in the intellectual circle of Pope Eugene IV and left remarkable traces in his
composers.[15] Most revealingly, in the motet *Argi vices polyphemus/Tum pilemon*
by N. Frangens de Leodio (ca. 1410, Aosta 15) the poet and composer show
their hand with the remark "ut sit opus consummatum" ("so that the work
might be completed").[16] By transferring the concept of the created work (as
Nicholas of Cusa had defined it for the work of art in general) to a piece of
composed, polyphonic music, a precedent had been set for a discourse that
consolidated music and the other arts. The resulting convergence of rhetorical
and poetic categories has not been fully examined to this day. In 1549
Nicolaus Listenius described the nature of *musica poetica* as "opus perfectum

14  Cf. Hinrichsen, "Musikwissenschaft und musikalisches Kunstwerk."
15  See Cahn, "Zur Vorgeschichte des 'Opus perfectum et absolutum'."
16  Ed. in *Italian Sacred and Ceremonial Music*, ed. Gallo and von Fischer.

et absolutum."[17] Despite the different lines of tradition superimposed in such a formulation, his clear intention is to draw out the work-like character of composed music.

A prerequisite for aesthetic discourse is the regular availability of music – or put differently, the reproducibility of a notated text and its sound; and it was written traditions that enabled composers to refer to each other and compare works through both reading and listening. Writing also facilitated the reproduction of the same music in widely varying contexts. John Dunstaple's four-voice Pentecost motet *Veni sancte spiritus/Veni creator*, for example, is transmitted in five sources. Although this motet is a unique instance, it shows how, somewhat paradoxically, a stable written tradition enabled musical works to be reproduced in different contexts and in (presumably) varying styles of performance.

The corresponding aesthetic practice of commenting upon individual pieces is first encountered in Glareanus's *Dodekachordon* of 1547, which well into the sixteenth century would remain an isolated case. Nevertheless, the availability of a variety of works in different social contexts made possible a variety of aesthetic judgments. Such views were rarely put forth in writing, and even when they were it was not in the context of music-theoretical discourse but rather in poetry, for example in Martin Le Franc's *Champion des Dames* or Jean Molinet's "Nymphes des bois."[18] Still, a significant number of musical works themselves contain such aesthetic judgments. The choice of a model composer or work – whether for the purposes of imitation or citation – presupposed prior aesthetic evaluation. Such judgments were even more pronounced when patrons were involved. These cases were not necessarily limited to written sources: enthusiasm for the organists Conrad Paumann and Isaac Argyropoulos resulted from listening experiences alone, and judgments and opinions for or against a particular composition, composer, or singer often derived from the experience of a work in performance, not writing. Patrons aside, by the middle of the fifteenth century it had become common practice for members of a given chapel to compete with one another, a performance-based practice predicated on aesthetic value judgments of the most sophisticated kind.

Time and again and in many sources we find requests for specific works or information about the recruitment of qualified choirboys, singers, or chapel masters. Proof of the complexity of such transactions lies in the often unsatisfactory results of such searches. In any case, these processes were evidently invested with considerable financial means and expertise. Even "private" manuscripts such as the Emmeram Codex or the Schedelsches Liederbuch

17 Nicolaus Listenius, *Musica*, sig. a3v.    18 See Strohm, *Guillaume Du Fay*.

presuppose that collectors were capable of making clear decisions about what was to be included and what might be left out. Such decisions probably affected fourteenth-century Florentine music as well, albeit less overtly. Only in the fifteenth century did these practices become notable in and of themselves as aesthetic judgments reflecting specific social situations.

## Conclusion

In the fifteenth century the work concept and its underlying premises displayed considerable variation and dynamism, but such instability does not belie their existence. They were present in several distinct but interconnected planes, which this discussion has endeavored to present schematically. Larger conceptual ambiguities aside, these concepts are remarkably well defined; their modes of operation can be observed clearly. That these different levels are not entirely compatible is a clear portent of modernity, and although none of the processes involved shares the same vanishing point, they are nevertheless closely related both conceptually and chronologically. As the work concept gradually stabilized, a phenomenon was established within music history that well into the twenty-first century has yet to lose any of its fractious or dynamic potential.

## Bibliography

Berger, Karol, *A Theory of Art*, Oxford, 2000

Cahn, Peter, "Zur Vorgeschichte des 'Opus perfectum et absolutum' in der Musikauffassung um 1500," in *Zeichen und Struktur in der Musik der Renaissance: Ein Symposium aus Anlaß der Jahrestagung der Gesellschaft für Musikforschung Münster (Westfalen) 1987*, ed. Klaus Hortschansky, Musikwissenschaftliche Arbeiten 28, Kassel, 1989, 11–26

Calella, Michele, *Musikalische Autorschaft: Der Komponist zwischen Mittelalter und Neuzeit*, Habilitationsschrift Universität Zürich, 2003 (publication in preparation)

Finscher, Ludwig, "Die 'Entstehung des Komponisten': Zum Problem Komponisten-Individualität und Individualstil in der Musik des 14. Jahrhunderts," in *Report of the Second Symposium of the International Musicological Society, Zagreb, June 23rd–27th 1974*, ed. Ivo Supičić (= *International Review of the Aesthetics and Sociology of Music* 6, 1975), 29–45; repr. in Ludwig Finscher, *Geschichte und Geschichten: Ausgewählte Aufsätze zur Musikhistorie*, ed. Hermann Danuser, Mainz, 2003

"Werk und Gattung in der Musik als Träger kulturellen Gedächtnisses," in *Kultur und Gedächtnis*, ed. Jan Assmann and Tonio Hölscher, Frankfurt am Main, 1988, 293–310

Gallo, F. Alberto, and Kurt von Fischer, eds., *Italian Sacred and Ceremonial Music*, PMFC 13, Monaco, 1987

Hinrichsen, Hans-Joachim, "Musikwissenschaft und musikalisches Kunstwerk: Zum schwierigen Gegenstand der Musikgeschichtsschreibung," in *Musikwissenschaft: Eine Positionsbestimmung*, ed. Laurenz Lütteken, Kassel, 2007, 67–87

Kaden, Christian, *Des Lebens wilder Kreis: Musik im Zivilisationsprozeß*, Kassel, 1993

Listenius, Nicolaus, *Musica*, Wittenberg, 1537

Luko, Alexis, "Tinctoris on *Varietas*," *EMH* 27 (2008), 99–136

Lütteken, Laurenz, *Musik der Renaissance: Imagination und Wirklichkeit einer kulturellen Praxis*, Stuttgart and Weimar, 2011

Pico della Mirandola, Giovanni, "Oratio. (De hominis dignitate)," in *De hominis dignitate. Heptaplus. De ente et uno e scritti vari*, ed. Eugenio Garin, Milan, 2004, 101–65

Pirrotta, Nino, "Landini," in *MGG* 8, cols. 163–68

Smijers, Albert, "De Illustre Lieve Vrouwe Broederschap te 's-Hertogenbosch. IV. Rekeningen van Sint Jan 1450 tot Sint Jan 1475," *Tijdschrift der Vereeniging voor Noord-Nederlands Muziekgeschiedenis* 13 (1929), 46–100

Strohm, Reinhard, *Guillaume Du Fay, Martin Le Franc und die humanistische Legende der Musik*, Neujahrsblatt der Allgemeinen Musikgesellschaft Zürich 192, Winterthur, 2007

——— "'Opus': An Aspect of the Early History of the Musical Work-Concept," in *Complexus effectuum musicologiae: Studia Miroslao Perz septuagenario dedicata*, ed. Tomasz Jeż, Studia et dissertationes Instituti Musicologiae Universitatis Varsoviensis B 13, Kraków, 2003, 309–19

——— "Werk – Performanz – Konsum: Der musikalische Werk-Diskurs," in *Historische Musikwissenschaft: Grundlagen und Perspektiven*, ed. Michele Calella and Nikolaus Urbanek, Stuttgart and Weimar, 2013, 341–55.

Wegman, Rob C., "From Maker to Composer: Improvisation and Musical Authorship in the Low Countries, 1450–1500," *JAMS* 49 (1996), 409–79

Wiora, Walter, *Das musikalische Kunstwerk*, Tutzing, 1983

# 4

# The *L'homme armé* tradition – and the limits of musical borrowing

JESSE RODIN

If the concept of musical borrowing in the Renaissance had to be encapsulated by a single example, the best choice would almost certainly be the *L'homme armé* tradition. This group of approximately forty polyphonic mass cycles, composed between ca. 1460 and the late sixteenth century, is unique: no other cantus firmus served as the basis for so many new pieces or as the starting point for so rich a practice of compositional emulation and one-upmanship. The surviving corpus of *L'homme armé* masses abounds in technically sophisticated display so elaborate that it is often tempting to posit direct lines of musical engagement between one composer and another.

While much has been written about the origins of the tradition, it is still not – and may never be – possible to pinpoint why and for what occasions most *L'homme armé* masses were composed. The text of the parent chanson, known mainly from a Burgundian manuscript of the 1470s (Naples VI.E.40), speaks vaguely of an armed man:

| | |
|---|---|
| L'homme, l'homme, l'homme armé | The man, the man, the armed man |
| l'homme armé | the armed man |
| l'homme armé doibt on doubter | the armed man must be feared |
| doibt on doubter | must be feared |
| On a fait partout crier | It has been cried out everywhere |
| que chascun se viengne armer | that everyone must arm himself |
| d'un haubregon de fer | with an iron coat of mail |
| L'homme, l'homme . . . | The man, the man . . . |

Craig Wright and Andrew Kirkman have linked this *homme armé* with Christ, who wars with the devil on behalf of humanity; Flynn Warmington has even identified a fifteenth-century ceremony in which an armed man unsheathed a

I would like to express my gratitude to David Fallows, Sean Gallagher, and Lewis Lockwood for their helpful comments and corrections.

sword during Mass.[1] In a compatible interpretation, William Prizer, Michael
Long, Alejandro Enrique Planchart, and others have proposed that the earliest
*L'homme armé* masses can be associated with a planned crusade against the Turks by
Philip the Good and the Burgundian Order of the Golden Fleece.[2] More recently
Sean Gallagher has identified a specific context for the setting by Johannes Regis:
his *Missa Dum sacrum mysterium/L'homme armé* was almost certainly composed in
1462 for a foundation at Cambrai cathedral.[3] Regis's Armed Man is St. Michael
the archangel, who is often depicted slaying a dragon – indeed the mass was
composed as an addition to a special procession, originally endowed by the
canon Michel de Beringhen, that took place each year on the feast of St. Michael.

Frustratingly, Regis's is the only mass in the tradition that can be connected
unambiguously to a specific context and dated with precision.[4] The problem is
that the Armed Man rapidly acquired a multiplicity of cultural associations that
at more than 500 years' distance are hard to tease out. This issue points up the
futility, in most cases, of trying to link fifteenth-century sacred works with
specific contexts. Moreover, the musical tradition of *L'homme armé* masses soon
took on a life of its own, such that within a generation composers may have
bracketed, forgotten about, or been ignorant of the religious and political
forces behind the earliest settings.[5] This point underscores the degree to
which composerly devices were introduced for aesthetic and intellectual delec-
tation rather than as markers of specific social, religious, or political meanings.

In what follows I explore the musical life of the Armed Man, beginning with –
well, that's no easy matter – and extending up through settings by Josquin, Pierre
de La Rue, and others active at the turn of the sixteenth century. In the first part of
this essay I propose a new way of parsing the musical connections that bind several
fifteenth-century settings together. Next I consider several additional examples of
musical borrowing, with respect to both masses and secular *L'homme armé* settings.
In the final section I turn this discussion on its head by questioning the terminological propriety and methodological value of musical borrowing all told.

1 Warmington, "The Ceremony of the Armed Man"; Wright, *The Maze and the Warrior*, 159–205, 282–88,
and 328 n. 16; and Kirkman, *The Cultural Life*, 98–134. Further on the cultural contexts for the Armed Man,
see Kirkman's essay in this volume, Ch. 35. See also David Fallows, "*L'homme armé*," *Grove Music Online*.
2 Prizer, "Music and Ceremonial"; Long, "*Arma virumque cano*"; and Planchart, "The Origins." Geoffrey
Chew may have been the first to hint at this idea; see "The Early Cyclic Mass," 266–67.
3 Gallagher, *Johannes Regis*, 59–114.
4 Nonetheless see the arguments about the dating of Du Fay's and Ockeghem's masses in Planchart, "The
Origins." On the dating of Basiron's mass, see Lockwood, "Aspects," 111; Ercole d'Este called this mass
"new" (*noua*) in 1484. Circumstantial evidence can help with the dating of several other masses, but hard
facts are few and far between.
5 This is not to suggest that those forces had evaporated. To take but one example: as late as 1490, Pope
Innocent VIII held a congress in Rome, the goal of which was to launch a crusade against the Turks. As
usual this came to nothing, but it could have been an occasion for the composition of a work such as
Josquin's *Missa L'homme armé super voces musicales*.

## A new hypothesis: three fountainheads

The earliest surviving reference to a *L'homme armé* mass dates from 1462–63, when Regis's setting was copied in Cambrai. Taken in the context of Gallagher's recent findings, there is now good reason to believe that Regis's mass forms part of the tradition's earliest layer, one that, according to a growing consensus, also comprises the settings of Guillaume Du Fay and Johannes Ockeghem. Including Regis in this club not only makes good evidentiary sense; it also opens the door to a new way of understanding the musical connections among a much larger group of fifteenth-century *L'homme armé* masses.[6]

The settings by Du Fay, Ockeghem, and Regis are remarkably heterogeneous.[7] This jibes with the idea that ca. 1460 there was as yet no "tradition" in which these composers felt inclined to participate.[8] It might also indicate that settings 2 and 3 were composed without knowledge of setting 1, or at least without any more knowledge than that setting 1 existed.[9] All three masses introduce distinct "operations" on the cantus firmus, each of which, I will suggest, had a substantial afterlife. The most significant innovations are Du Fay's use of retrograde motion in his Agnus Dei III, Regis's almost pervasive treatment of the *L'homme armé* melody in quasi-canon at the lower fifth, and Ockeghem's notation of the tenor in semibreves and minims, under signs of major prolation (this usually produces mensural augmentation, whereby rhythms of a given duration are notated in the tenor in values half or even a quarter as large as in the other voices). Beyond these one can point to several other techniques that appear to have been noticed by later composers. Du Fay uses a signature of one flat in all voices but the discantus, which has none. He also introduces several verbal canons, including a whimsical instruction in the final section: "let the crab go out half but come back full."[10] Regis quotes sacred texts extraneous to the liturgy of the Mass and employs the mensuration sign O2 in the Agnus Dei III.[11] Ockeghem uses verbal canons to transpose the

---

6 This discussion builds on ideas put forth in Lockwood, "Aspects," 107–10; and Gallagher, *Johannes Regis*, 64 n. 20.

7 See Lockwood, "Aspects," 112–15. For editions of these masses and twelve others, see *Monumenta Polyphoniae Liturgicae*, ed. Feininger, Series I, Tomi I and III.

8 On this point see Wegman, "Mensural Intertextuality," 193–99.

9 Cf. Planchart, "The Origins," 332–33, who argues that Du Fay's mass served as a model for Ockeghem's; and Gallagher, *Johannes Regis*, 93–98, who suggests Du Fay's setting preceded that of Regis. Less convincingly, see Heide, "New Claims," who proposes that Regis's mass is the earliest. None of these interpretations is incompatible with mine.

10 *Cancer eat plenus sed redeat medius.* The tenor is to sing the melody backwards (like a crab) at half speed, then forwards at normal speed.

11 The Agnus Dei III is notated under ¢ in the mass's unique source, but was almost certainly notated originally in O2; see Gallagher, *Johannes Regis*, 98–113.

cantus firmus downward in the Credo (by a fifth) and Agnus Dei (by an octave). And in the Christe and Et resurrexit, he brings the tenor into metrical alignment with the other voices, effecting a lively "6/8" (these sections are notated uniformly under ₵).[12] This brief summary reveals not only a wide range of compositional procedures, but also how little overlap we find among these early masses. This point extends even to mode: whereas Du Fay casts his setting in G-Dorian, Ockeghem uses G-Mixolydian, Regis (mainly) D-Dorian.

Ockeghem, Regis, and Du Fay cannot possibly have foreseen that in the period ca. 1465–ca. 1500 composers would draw so heavily on precedents they established (see Table 4.1). Du Fay's use of retrograde motion, for instance, is echoed by several composers, including Antoine Busnoys, who in his Agnus Dei apparently ups the ante through the much rarer technique of inversion;[13] Jacob Obrecht, who ups the ante still further by employing retrograde inversion; and Philippe Basiron and Josquin (sexti toni), whose settings conclude with simultaneous forward-and-backward cantus-firmus statements. Ockeghem's mensural augmentation, meanwhile, was picked up most influentially in Busnoys's mass, which in turn provided a direct model for Obrecht's.[14] Mensural augmentation also appears in the settings by Johannes Tinctoris (albeit with verbal instructions that satisfy the theorist's sense of notational propriety), Josquin (super voces musicales), Bertrandus Vaqueras, and even Giovanni Pierluigi da Palestrina.[15] Regis's quasi-canonic presentation also had a ripple effect. This can be seen most directly throughout Guillaume Faugues's setting and the sixth Naples mass, in which a pair of cantus-firmus-carrying voices are governed by strict *fuga*, again at the lower fifth.[16] In all of this the point is not that these procedures – retrograde motion, mensural augmentation, and imitation canon – are unique to the *L'homme armé* tradition. Rather, what gives pause is that so many *L'homme armé* masses partake of these

---

12 There has been some debate about the interpretation of Ockeghem's notation in these sections. See Busnoys, *Collected Works*, 5 n. 16, 28–29 n. 61, and 30–31; Blachly, "Reading Tinctoris for Guidance on Tempo," 416–23; and Gallagher, "Ockeghem's Oronyms."

13 On inversion see Gallagher, *Johannes Regis*, 63–64 n. 17.

14 On the relationship between Busnoys's and Obrecht's masses, see Strunk, "Origins of the *L'homme armé* Mass," 25–26.

15 De Orto uses major prolation without mensural augmentation and mensural augmentation without major prolation. The latter practice also appears in Matthaeus Pipelare's mass.

16 Strict *fuga* on *L'homme armé* also appears in Pipelare's Agnus Dei III, which expands to five voices in order to present the preexisting melody in canon at the octave; Compère's Sanctus and Agnus Dei, which feature canons at the second, fifth, and ninth; Basiron's unison canons in the Kyrie II, Et unam sanctam, and Osanna II; Tinctoris's Et incarnatus est, in which the upper voices paraphrase *L'homme armé* in canon at the fourth; the Sanctus and Osanna of Josquin's *sexti toni* mass, with canons at the unison and fifth, respectively; and Vaqueras's five-voice setting, based throughout on canons at various intervals. The apotheosis of *fuga* on *L'homme armé* is Mathurin Forestier's pervasively canonic mass, the Agnus Dei III of which features a 7-out-of-1 stacked canon with starting pitches on every "ut" in the Gamut (that is, on *G*, *c*, *f*, *g*, *c'*, *f'*, and *g'*).

techniques, and that all of them are represented in the troika Regis, Ockeghem, and Du Fay.

There is a danger in overdrawing this conclusion. For one thing, several later composers introduced cantus-firmus manipulations that veer off in different directions (a characteristic example is Loyset Compère's Pleni, in which the tenor sings the first phrase of the tune beginning successively on *e*, *f*, *g*, and *a*). For another, there is ample evidence that some later masses injected new life into the tradition. Among these Busnoys's stands out, so much so that Richard Taruskin suggested – impossibly, it now seems clear – that his setting was the earliest.[17] Even so, Taruskin was right to note that Busnoys's mass had significant ramifications. Along with Obrecht's wholesale imitation of his cantus-firmus treatment, one finds later echoes of Busnoys's head motive (Faugues and Antoine Brumel), the striking pause he introduces in the middle of the Agnus Dei III (Tinctoris and Josquin), his metrically adventurous Confiteor (Tinctoris), even his setting's mensural and rhythmic structure (a *Missa De Sancto Johanne Baptista* probably by Obrecht).[18] Indeed there are several instances in which composers appear to have set their sights on more recent *L'homme armé* masses rather than look back to Du Fay, Ockeghem, and Regis. (To take but one further example, in La Rue's (first) setting a series of mensuration canons takes aim at Josquin's *super voces musicales* mass.)[19] Stepping back from these individual cases, we find composer after composer seeking to establish credentials in a dynamic tradition that reinvented itself over time. By the end of the fifteenth century composers were engaging in a dialogue with the most recent settings while also looking back to the three fountainheads.

## Traditional "borrowings"

The foregoing analysis depends on an expanded conception of musical borrowing that encompasses compositional techniques.[20] But there is also good reason to search for outright quotations of musical material, in line with the bulk of the literature on borrowing.[21] Musical quotation, after all, is

---

17 Taruskin, "Antoine Busnoys," 255–93. Cf. the responses by Fallows (*JAMS* 40, 146–48), Strohm (*JAMS* 40, 576–79), and Wegman (*JAMS* 42, 437–43). See also Wegman, *Born for the Muses*, 97–98 n. 10; Fitch, *Johannes Ockeghem: Masses and Models*, 62–64; and the literature cited in n. 9.

18 On Tinctoris's mass see Zazulia, "Tinctoris the Reader"; on the *Missa De Sancto Johanne Baptista* see Wegman, "Another Imitation," 189–202.

19 Glareanus was the first to notice this relationship; see *Dodecachordon*, 274.

20 As advocated in Rodin, "When in Rome," 358–64. See also Rodin, *Josquin's Rome*, 307–8. For this type of "borrowing" see Burkholder, "The Uses of Existing Music," 854.

21 A useful bibliography, curated by J. Peter Burkholder, appears at www.chmtl.indiana.edu/borrowing/.

Table 4.1 *Compositional techniques in twenty-four L'homme armé masses (listed in rough chronological order)*
Checkmarks in boxes indicate fairly clear cases of "borrowing." The smaller checkmark denotes a fleeting or ancillary example.

| | Du Fay | | | D+O | | Ockeghem | | | | Regis | | | | |
|---|---|---|---|---|---|---|---|---|---|---|---|---|---|---|
| | Retro-grade | Partial sigs. | G-Dor. | Verbal canons | Mens. aug. | Section in lilting triple | C.f. transp. | G-Mix.[a] | Fuga on L.A. | Multiple texts | C.f. on E | C.f. migration | O2 | D-Dor. |
| Caron | | ☑ | ✓ | | | | | ✓ | ✓ | | | | ✓ | |
| Faugues | | | ✓ | | | | | | ✓ | | | | | |
| Naples I–VI | ✓ | ✓[b] | | ✓ | ✓ | ✓ | ✓ | ✓ | | ✓ | | | | |
| Busnoys | ✓[c] | | ✓ | ✓ | ☑ | ✓ | ✓ | | | | | | ✓ | |
| Bologna Q16 | ✓ | | | ✓ | | ✓ | ✓[d] | ✓ | | | | | | |
| Tinctoris | | | ✓ | ✓ | ✓ | | | | ✓[e] | | | ✓ | | |
| Compère | | | | ✓ | | | | | ✓[f] | ✓ | | | | |
| Obrecht | ☑ | | | ☑ | ☑ | ☑ | ☑ | | | | ✓ | ✓ | | |
| Basiron | ✓ | | ✓ | ✓ | | ✓ | ✓ | ✓ | | | ✓ | ✓ | ✓ | |
| de Orto | ✓ | | | ✓ | ✓[g] | | ✓ | | | | ✓ | ✓ | ✓ | |
| Josquin *s.v.m.* | ✓ | | | ✓ | ☑ | ✓ | ✓ | | ✓[h] | | ✓ | ✓ | | ✓ |
| Brumel | ☑ | | ✓ | | | ✓ | | | | | | | ✓[i] | |
| Josquin *s.t.* | | | | ✓ | | | | | ✓ | | | | ✓ | |
| La Rue I | | | | | | | | | ✓ | | | ✓ | | ✓ |

| | | | | $\checkmark^{j}$ | | $\checkmark$ | | $\checkmark$ | | $\checkmark$ |
|---|---|---|---|---|---|---|---|---|---|---|
| Pipelare | | $\checkmark$ | $\checkmark$ | ☑ | $\checkmark$ | | | | $\checkmark$ | |
| Vaqueras | | | | | | | $\checkmark^{k}$ ☑ | | | | $\checkmark$ |

[a] In Ockeghem's mass the Agnus Dei III is exceptionally in G-Dorian.

[b] Masses III and IV.

[c] Inversion, which trumps retrograde (the same holds for the mass in Bologna Q.16).

[d] Agnus Dei III, phrase by phrase.

[e] Et incarnatus est only.

[f] Sanctus and Osanna only (the same holds true for Josquin's *sexti toni*).

[g] Mensural augmentation appears in the Agnus Dei III only; otherwise the cantus firmus is related to the other voices predominately by minim equivalence.

[h] Mensuration canons (the same holds true for La Rue I).

[i] Christe only.

[j] Agnus Dei III only (O against C2).

[k] Agnus Dei III only

central to late medieval ways of composing; without it the genre of the cantus-firmus mass would not exist.

Such a search must begin with *L'homme armé* itself. As Lewis Lockwood proposed in a foundational essay, this deceptively simple melody most likely began life as a composed monophonic song.[22] Elaborating this idea, Reinhard Strohm has interpreted *L'homme armé* as an "artistic imitation of [a mono-phonic *chanson rustique* that] originated in an urban, northern, French-speaking environment in the early fifteenth century." It "describes ... what [the com-poser] heard in a late medieval town: the warning sound of the watchman's horn from the tower, as a hostile army is approaching across the plains – *L'homme armé!*"[23] As for the melody's earliest uses, Planchart has argued that its first polyphonic appearance was in a secular context: the combinative chanson *Il sera/L'homme armé*, which apparently pokes fun at the Burgundian chaplain and singer Symon le Breton.[24] In *Il sera* the tune begins on G with no flat in the signature; this may represent the original form of the melody. Of course it's hard to be sure, since the earliest polyphonic settings present *L'homme armé* in so many different modal guises. At all events *Il sera* is not unique, but rather the first of six secular settings, four of which combine *L'homme armé* with another preexisting melody.[25] And there are still further fifteenth-century references, including an anonymous motet (*Ave rosa speciosa*) that quotes *L'homme armé* in a bass voice, and a pair of textual citations by the Burgundian court chronicler and poet Jean Molinet.[26] When considered in the context of twenty-five masses certain to have been composed by ca. 1508,[27] we have evidence of a rich tradition of musical echo, with each composer quoting, reshaping, and at times abandoning his preexisting material in the process of creating something (mostly) new.

The literature on *L'homme armé* has addressed still another category of borrowing: quotations of music extraneous to the cantus firmus. Leeman Perkins, for instance, has argued that Ockeghem's rondeau *L'autre d'antan* is modeled on *L'homme armé*, and that it, in turn, lies in the background of several passages in his and Busnoys's masses.[28] Christopher Reynolds has noted

---

22 Lockwood, "Aspects."
23 Strohm, *The Rise of European Music*, 465–67, and Strohm, *Music in Late Medieval Bruges*, 129–31. Planchart, "The Origins," 312 n. 21 suggests the song is by a court composer "who wrote it in the manner of an urban *chanson rustique*."
24 Symon was active 1431–64. Though the song's sole attribution is to one "Borton," Planchart proposes Du Fay as the composer. See Planchart, "The Origins," 323.
25 A list appears in Fallows, *Catalogue of Polyphonic Songs*, 259.
26 On *Ave rosa speciosa* see Houghton, "A New Motet." Cf. Gallagher, *Johannes Regis*, 202–5. For Molinet see Lemaire and Wangermée, "Le Rondeau *Il sera par vous combattu*," 155–57.
27 This tally includes the music in Table 4.1 plus Franchinus Gaffurius's mass, which is lost.
28 Perkins, "The *L'homme armé* Masses," 372 ff.

parallels between a song by Busnoys (*Ma tressouveraine princesse*) and an anonymous three-voice *L'homme armé* mass in the manuscript Bologna Q.16.[29] Taruskin has pointed to a short two-voice passage in the middle of Busnoys's Sanctus in which the B section of the tune is paired with a catchy bassus phrase; similar material appears in the Credo of Du Fay's mass and the Agnus Dei I of Basiron's.[30] Jaap van Benthem has suggested that the famous 3-out-of-1 mensuration canon in the Agnus Dei II of Josquin's *super voces musicales* mass begins by quoting the contratenor of Ockeghem's *Ma bouche rit*.[31] And, also with respect to *super voces musicales*, Paula Higgins and Michael Long have uncovered correspondences between Josquin's head motive and motets by Ockeghem (*Ut heremita solus*) and Busnoys (*In hydraulis*).[32] To accept these arguments is to imagine a rich tradition of compositional allusion and citation.

## The limits of borrowing

I'm about to get very worried about borrowing as a term and concept, so it seems only fair to begin, *mea culpa*, by acknowledging that I've used the word on several occasions to describe identities in compositional technique or musical material.[33] Upon reflection, "borrowing" strikes me as a strange way to describe acts of musical quotation, citation, and allusion. This is in part because the term implies a kind of exchange that does not occur in musical contexts.[34] Obrecht would not – could not – *return* Busnoys's cantus-firmus treatment, as if it were an umbrella. (A better parallel would be the always insincere "Can I borrow a piece of paper?") This definitional problem persists when one examines the history of the term. In its early uses, to borrow indicated "to take the temporary use of," as is familiar from modern contexts, but also a much wider range of meanings, including "to render oneself indebted for …; to adopt (thoughts, expressions, modes of conduct) … or (words, idioms, customs, etc.) from a foreign language or people"; and "to obtain (a temporary favor) by request."[35] In Shakespeare's *King John*, to borrow is in one instance to reflect something rather than possess it ("The borrow'd majesty, of England"), in another to emulate or learn ("inferior eyes, / That borrow their behaviours from the great"). In *King Lear* the main work of the

---

29 Reynolds, "The Counterpoint of Allusion," 240.     30 Taruskin, "Antoine Busnoys," 263–64.
31 Benthem, "Kompositorisches Verfahren," 9.
32 See Higgins, "In hydraulis," 77–79 (the reference to Long is at 78 n. 138). See also Rodin, *Josquin's Rome*, 234 and 237–41.
33 I back away from traditional notions of borrowing in Rodin, "A Most Laudable Competition," and *Josquin's Rome*, 307–8.
34 I am grateful to Charles Kronengold for sharing his thoughts on this topic.
35 "borrow, v.1," *OED Online*, accessed March 2012.

term is to imply impermanence or falseness ("If but as well I other accents borrow"); the same is true in Spenser's *The Faerie Queene* ("Whose borrowed beautie now appeareth plaine"). Such definitional heterogeneity is fascinating in its own right, but the central point is that these examples fail to provide a precedent for contemporary scholarly practice. Even early musicological uses are a poor match: beginning around the mid-nineteenth century music historians tended to use the term pejoratively, to indicate stealing musical material from oneself or another composer.[36]

But of course definitions change over time – so rather than place undue weight on semantics, let me move right away to a more significant, conceptual problem. We use borrowing to signal intentionality, the act of willfully taking something, and yet in many cases we can't be sure the borrower would acknowledge as much.[37] To understand the severity of this problem one need look no further than Table 4.1. Here checkmarks enclosed in boxes signal what I take to be fairly clear cases of self-conscious borrowing, whether from one of the fountainheads or a younger composer. Oliver Strunk was the first to notice that Obrecht's mass represents a full-scale homage to (or at least aping of) Busnoys. One can also feel confident that Basiron's simultaneous forward and retrograde cantus-firmus statement in the Agnus Dei III owes something to Du Fay's example, and that Josquin's use of this technique beneath a pair of stretto canons owes something at least to Basiron; that Firmin Caron's peculiar combination of staff signatures, with pervasive B♭s in all voices but the discantus, looks back to Du Fay; that notations of the *L'homme armé* melody using mensural augmentation follow Ockeghem's (or Busnoys's) example; and that Vaqueras's pervasive use of strict *fuga* most likely represents a response to Regis or Faugues.[38] One could tentatively posit further connections along these lines. Tinctoris's troped Mass text, for instance, was probably inspired by Regis.[39] And as I've argued elsewhere, Marbrianus de Orto's manner of transposing the cantus firmus almost surely represents a homage to Ockeghem, while Josquin's is best interpreted as an attempt to one-up both Ockeghem and de Orto.[40] For all of this, my sea of caveats – "fairly clear," "probably," and

36 In the *Musical Times and Singing Class Circular*, for instance; see Holmes, review of "Haydn's Masses No. III," 132; and Prout, "Handel's Chandos Anthems," 392.

37 Several points introduced here dovetail with John Milsom's important essay "*Imitatio*," 141–51. Though I read Milsom's piece only after completing this one, it must nonetheless count as a central intertext. In what follows I avoid "intertextuality" in part because, as Milsom describes, it has been appropriated unhelpfully by music historians. Moreover, even Kristeva's and Barthes's (original) uses of the term are not a perfect fit for what I have in mind here, insofar as they embrace so great a range of connections – for Kristeva *every* text is "constructed from a mosaic of quotations" – as to cast the net perhaps too widely.

38 Vaqueras doubtless sang both masses from Vatican CS 14.        39 See Gallagher, *Johannes Regis*, 78–79.
40 Rodin, "When in Rome," 323–31.

"almost surely" – points up how difficult it is to be certain that apparent instances of borrowing did not come about by chance or as the result of unconscious association. And that's just with respect to the most obvious examples: as a glance at all the checkmarks *not* enclosed in boxes reveals, there are rather few "fairly clear cases of self-conscious borrowing." This point holds true well beyond the *L'homme armé* tradition; leaving aside all the pieces based obviously (and, in most cases, explicitly) on preexisting material (e.g., a mass on the song *Le serviteur*), it is rarely possible to prove that a given musical echo is not fortuitous. That's no reason to stop looking, but it does suggest we ought to be cautious, especially when trying to decide whether a given "borrowing" constitutes emulation, competition, or homage.[41]

Equally worrying are examples in which the purported musical identity between two passages is open to question. It's easy enough to line up a pair of melodic lines that have a string of five or six notes in common, but we have as yet no agreed-upon criteria for assessing whether those melodies are similar enough to withstand scrutiny. Is it reasonable to posit musical borrowing, for instance, when two pieces are both cast in a lively triple meter and feature opening melodic lines that rise a sixth before falling? What if those passages line up hardly at all in terms of rhythm, metrical stress, phrase structure, contrapuntal context, and register?[42] Rather than search for often dubious hidden meanings, we might begin by assuming there's less, not more, than meets the eye.[43] My sense is that in the fifteenth century musical citations were confined largely to obvious, nearly exact correspondences that occur *at beginnings* of pieces and subsections thereof. When composers quoted one another's music, they wanted their fellow musicians to notice. Anything else is liable to be a false positive.

Still another limitation of borrowing concerns cases where musical identity can be established but for which it may be inappropriate to posit willful acts of citation. When two passages really do line up it may be tempting to propose that one composer was quoting the other, but in many instances the musical parallelism may have come about for other reasons. By using the language of borrowing to interpret such examples, we may be missing out on the importance of memory, convention, contrapuntal "grammar," and genre. As Anna Maria Busse Berger has argued, late medieval musicians built up often vast memory archives that they used in the act of composing.[44] If students memorized a common stock of melodic gestures and contrapuntal progressions, then

---

41 For these categories see Brown, "Emulation, Competition, and Homage." Cf. Wegman, "Another Imitation"; Meconi, "Does *Imitatio* Exist?"; and Burn, "'Nam erit'."
42 On this point see LaRue, "Significant and Coincidental Resemblance."
43 I owe this formulation to Joshua Rifkin.        44 Berger, *Medieval Music and the Art of Memory*.

we should not be surprised that these turn up in multiple pieces. Leaving aside the trained memory, it's clear that then, as now, grammatical and generic norms significantly restricted composers' choices.[45] John Milsom has shown how the constraints of stretto *fuga* could lead Du Fay and Josquin to compose passages united by shared material but unlikely to reflect intentional citation.[46] If, in a similar vein, we return to the example of two melodies that rise a sixth, then descend, it would probably be more convincing to use that correspondence as a springboard for a discussion of musical convention – how fifteenth-century melodies that begin on the first degree and favor conjunct motion have a habit of rising a fifth, then reaching one note higher to the unstable sixth degree, then falling to a cadence. Borrowing might seem the sexier interpretive tool, but the *lingua franca* is often more powerful.

There is one further issue. Borrowing limits us to situations involving overlap between at least two passages and (usually) at least two composers. There is nothing wrong with observing connections of this kind, but it doesn't follow that we should give preferential treatment to works that invite comparative analysis. A piece that borrows isn't necessarily more interesting than one that doesn't; nothing in the act of borrowing ensures a heightened degree of intellectual or aesthetic achievement.[47] By valorizing borrowing we risk forgetting to evaluate each piece on its own terms; we might also miss out on opportunities for immersive engagement with the music that goes beyond overlapping passages. Engagement of this sort can alert us to aesthetic decisions that *separate* pieces from one another, indeed that help define distinct compositional personalities. To undertake such analysis – to figure out how Ockeghem's *Missa L'homme armé* differs from his *Missa Caput*, not to mention how Ockeghem differs from Faugues – is to sidestep the author-to-author communication that animates Eliot, Bate, and Bloom.[48] Instead we might use close, even microscopic knowledge of musical surfaces to undertake comparative study of one compositional parameter, Morellian analysis of a seemingly insignificant detail, or computer-aided studies of large amounts of musical data.[49] Until recently it has been all but impossible to approach fifteenth-century music in this way; major impediments have included a dearth of performances, recordings, and easily comparable editions. But as several other essays in this volume attest, studies of surface-level musical features are already yielding fruit.

---

45 For the latter see Bent, "The Grammar of Early Music."    46 Milsom, "*Imitatio*," 146 ff.
47 An example might be the textless setting of *L'homme armé* attributed to Josquin.
48 Eliot, "Tradition and the Individual Talent"; Bate, *The Burden of the Past*; and Bloom, *The Anxiety of Influence*.
49 An eloquent defense of this approach appears in Ginzburg, "Clues," 96–125. See also Gallagher, "Models of *Varietas*," 162–63, and "Syntax and Style," and the Josquin Research Project (http://josquin.stanford.edu).

Lest all this seem like too harsh an indictment of borrowing, I'll conclude by noting a side benefit of what I want to call rigorous connoisseurship: it can help us detect genuine, meaningful instances of citation and allusion. For all the worries I've enumerated, "borrowing" remains an important avenue for understanding how composers engaged with the musical world around them. And the *L'homme armé* tradition, with its fountainheads and intertwining streams, remains an important site for such investigations, even if we can't always be sure which musical intersections are meaningful. Still, when confronting identities in compositional technique or musical material, perhaps it would make sense to shift our terminological and methodological center of gravity – from the intention-laden "borrow" to a more neutral term that has already made several appearances in these pages: "echo."[50] To echo is to transform, which is inevitable whenever existing material or techniques are put to new uses. Echoes embrace both intentional citations and fortuitous correspondences; they also encompass everything from precise quotations to vague reflections.[51] Heard in this way, the *L'homme armé* tradition is a resonant, indeed cacophonous echo chamber that challenges us to distinguish originary sounds from their reverberations.

## Bibliography

Bate, Walter Jackson, *The Burden of the Past and the English Poet*, Cambridge, MA, 1970

Bent, Margaret, "The Grammar of Early Music: Preconditions for Analysis," in *Tonal Structures in Early Music*, ed. Cristle Collins Judd, New York, 1998, 15–59

Benthem, Jaap van, "Kompositorisches Verfahren in Josquins Proportionskanon 'Agnus Dei': Antwort an Edward Stam," *TVNM* 26 (1976), 9–16

Berger, Anna Maria Busse, *Medieval Music and the Art of Memory*, Berkeley, 2005

Blachly, Alexander, "Reading Tinctoris for Guidance on Tempo," in *Antoine Busnoys*, ed. Higgins, 399–427

Bloom, Harold, *The Anxiety of Influence: A Theory of Poetry*, New York, 1973

Brown, Howard Mayer, "Emulation, Competition, and Homage: Imitation and Theories of Imitation in the Renaissance," *JAMS* 35 (1982), 1–48

Burkholder, J. Peter, "The Uses of Existing Music: Musical Borrowing as a Field," *Notes* 50 (1994), 851–70

Burn, David, "'Nam erit haec quoque laus eorum': Imitation, Competition, and the 'L'homme armé' Tradition," *Revue de musicologie* 87 (2001), 249–87

Busnoys, Antoine, *Collected Works*, ed. Richard Taruskin, Masters and Monuments of the Renaissance 5, New York, 1990

---

50 My source is Hollander, *The Figure of Echo*. Hollander writes (p. 64): "In contrast with literary allusion echo is a metaphor of, and for, alluding, and does not depend on conscious intention."
51 See the variety of definitions offered in "echo, v." and "echo, n.," *OED Online*, accessed March 2012.

Chew, Geoffrey, "The Early Cyclic Mass as an Expression of Royal and Papal Supremacy," *ML* 53 (1972), 254–69

Eliot, T. S., "Tradition and the Individual Talent," in *The Sacred Wood: Essays on Poetry and Criticism*, London, 1920, repr. 1932, 47–59

Fallows, David, *A Catalogue of Polyphonic Songs, 1415–1480*, Oxford, 1999

"*L'homme armé*," Grove Music Online

"Letter from David Fallows," *JAMS* 40 (1987), 146–48

Fitch, Fabrice, *Johannes Ockeghem: Masses and Models*, Paris, 1997

Gallagher, Sean, *Johannes Regis*, Turnhout, 2010

"Models of *Varietas*: Studies in Style and Attribution in the Motets of Johannes Regis and his Contemporaries," Ph.D. diss., Harvard University, 1998

"Ockeghem's Oronyms: Gesture and Tempo in the Missa L'homme armé," paper read on 23 April 2009 at Stanford University as part of the symposium *Reading and Hearing Johannes Ockeghem*

"Syntax and Style: Rhythmic Patterns in the Music of Ockeghem and his Contemporaries," in *Johannes Ockeghem: Actes du XL^e colloque international d'études humanistes. Tours, 3–8 février, 1997*, ed. Philippe Vendrix, Paris, 1998, 681–705

Ginzburg, Carlo, "Clues: Roots of an Evidential Paradigm," in Ginzburg, *Clues, Myths, and the Historical Method*, trans. John and Anne C. Tedeschi, Baltimore, 1992, 96–125

Glareanus, Henricus, *Dodecachordon: Translation, Transcription, and Commentary*, ed. Clement A. Miller, 2 vols., [Rome], 1965

Heide, Klaas van der, "New Claims for a Burgundian Origin of the *L'homme armé* Tradition, and a Different View on the Relative Positions of the Earliest Masses in the Tradition," *TVNM* 55 (2005), 3–33

Higgins, Paula, "In hydraulis Revisited: New Light on the Career of Antoine Busnois," *JAMS* 39 (1986), 36–86

ed., *Antoine Busnoys: Method, Meaning, and Context in Late Medieval Music*, Oxford, 1999

Hollander, John, *The Figure of Echo: A Mode of Allusion in Milton and After*, Berkeley, 1981

Holmes, E., Review of "Haydn's Masses No. III," *Musical Times and Singing Class Circular* 7 (1855), 131–40,

Houghton, Edward, "A 'New' Motet by Johannes Regis," *TVNM* 33 (1983), 49–74

Kirkman, Andrew, *The Cultural Life of the Early Polyphonic Mass: Medieval Context to Modern Revival*, Cambridge, 2010

LaRue, Jan, "Significant and Coincidental Resemblance between Classical Themes," *JAMS* 14 (1961), 224–34, repr. *JM* 18 (2001), 268–82,

Lemaire, Claudine, and Robert Wangermée, "Le Rondeau *Il sera par vous combattu/ L'homme armé*, poème de l'équivoque?," *Revue belge de musicologie* 56 (2002), 145–58

Lockwood, Lewis, "Aspects of the *L'homme armé* Tradition," *Proceedings of the Royal Music Association* 100 (1973–74), 97–122

Long, Michael, "*Arma virumque cano*: Echoes of a Golden Age," in *Antoine Busnoys*, ed. Higgins, 133–54

Meconi, Honey, "Does *Imitatio* Exist?," *JM* 12 (1994), 152–78

Milsom, John, "'*Imitatio*,' 'Intertextuality,' and Early Music," in *Citation and Authority in Medieval and Renaissance Musical Culture: Learning from the Learned*, ed. Suzannah Clark and Elizabeth Eva Leach, Woodbridge, 2005, 141–51

*Monumenta Polyphoniae Liturgicae Sanctae Ecclesiae Romane*, ed. Laurence Feininger, Series I, Tomi I and III, Rome, 1948/1957–66

Perkins, Leeman L., "The *L'homme armé* Masses of Busnoys and Okeghem: A Comparison," *JM* 3 (1984), 363–96

Planchart, Alejandro Enrique, "The Origins and Early History of *L'homme armé*," *JM* 20 (2003), 305–57

Prizer, William F., "Music and Ceremonial in the Low Countries: Philip the Fair and the Order of the Golden Fleece," *EMH* 5 (1985) 113–53

Prout, Ebenezer, "Handel's Chandos Anthems," *Musical Times and Singing Class Circular* 17 (1876), 391–94

Reynolds, Christopher A., "The Counterpoint of Allusion in Fifteenth-Century Masses," *JAMS* 45 (1992), 228–60

Rodin, Jesse, *Josquin's Rome: Hearing and Composing in the Sistine Chapel*, New York, 2012
  "A 'Most Laudable Competition'? Hearing and Composing the *Beata Virgine* Masses of Josquin and Brumel," *TVNM* 59 (2009), 3–24
  "'When in Rome . . .': What Josquin Learned in the Sistine Chapel," *JAMS* 61 (2008), 307–72

Sparks, Edgar H., *Cantus Firmus in Mass and Motet 1420–1520*, Berkeley, 1963, repr. New York, 1975

Strohm, Reinhard, "Letter from Reinhard Strohm," *JAMS* 40 (1987), 576–79
  *Music in Late Medieval Bruges*, New York, 1985, rev. edn. 1990
  *The Rise of European Music, 1380–1500*, Cambridge, 1993

Strunk, Oliver, "Origins of the *L'homme armé* Mass," *Bulletin of the American Musicological Society* 2 (1937), 25–26

Taruskin, Richard, "Antoine Busnoys and the *L'homme armé* Tradition," *JAMS* 39 (1986), 255–93, and the responses by David Fallows, Reinhard Strohm, and Rob C. Wegman, in *JAMS* 40 and 42

Warmington, Flynn, "The Ceremony of the Armed Man: The Sword, the Altar, and the L'homme armé Mass," in *Antoine Busnoys*, ed. Higgins, 88–130

Wegman, Rob C., "Another 'Imitation' of Busnoys's *Missa L'homme armé* – and Some Observations on *Imitatio* in Renaissance Music," *JRMA* 114 (1989), 189–202
  *Born for the Muses: The Life and Masses of Jacob Obrecht*, Oxford, 1994
  "Letter from Rob C. Wegman," *JAMS* 42 (1989), 437–43
  "Mensural Intertextuality in the Sacred Music of Antoine Busnoys," in *Antoine Busnoys*, ed. Higgins, 175–214

Wright, Craig, *The Maze and the Warrior: Symbols in Architecture, Theology, and Music*, Cambridge, MA, 2001

Zazulia, Emily, "Tinctoris the Reader," forthcoming

*COMPOSER STUDIES*

# 5

# Guillaume Du Fay: evidence and interpretation

ALEJANDRO ENRIQUE PLANCHART

*For Joshua Rifkin*

As Jesse Rodin observes in Chapter 7, Josquin des Prez presents music historians with a difficult case. Despite a spate of documentary discoveries in the last two decades, Josquin's biography is riddled with lacunae that are not always easy to fill even with reasonable hypotheses. If he was born ca. 1450, as most scholars now think, his compositions do not begin to appear in the sources with any regularity until he was in his forties; more generally, there is little hard information about the chronology of his music. By the 1530s Josquin's fame had attained mythical proportions, and music publishers released a flood of works that do not survive in sources from his lifetime. This phenomenon has given rise to a stylistic picture clouded by a large number of doubtful and inauthentic works.

The case of Guillaume Du Fay is almost the polar opposite. This is true not only because for long periods of his life he was associated with institutions – the cathedral of Cambrai, the church of Saint Géry (also in Cambrai), the papal chapel, and the church of St. Donatian in Bruges – that kept detailed and voluminous records, but also because those records are unusually well preserved. Very little is known about Du Fay's employment at the Malatesta court in Pesaro, the court of Louis Allemand in Bologna, and the church of Ste. Waudru in Mons, but we have substantial (if incomplete) documentation from the courts of Savoy and Burgundy. Moreover, Du Fay's personal and clerical career is considerably better documented than those of most of his contemporaries. Overall the gaps in Du Fay's biography are comparatively small, the succession of his patrons and employers comparatively clear.[1] Thus it is possible not merely to establish many basic facts, but also to bring these facts into conversation with broader cultural and political developments in order to tell a richly textured story about Du Fay's life and music.

---

1 A full biographical and musical study, complete with discussions of all the major documents, is Planchart, *Guillaume Du Fay*.

## Musical sources

The source situation for Du Fay's music, particularly in his early years, is quite good. Over a period of twenty-five years, ca. 1420–45, a series of manuscripts transmits Du Fay's music in consistently good versions and with solid attributions. Further, we know enough about the circumstances surrounding the copying of these sources to conclude that scribes had early and reliable access to Du Fay's music. In rough chronological order these are:[2]

1. Bologna Q.15. Transmits virtually all of Du Fay's sacred music composed before ca. 1433.
2. Oxford 213. The scribe had access to virtually all the secular music that we have from Du Fay until 1436 and a good deal of the sacred music, together with information about the date and place of composition of a number of works.
3. Modena α.X.1.11 (ModB). Contains music for Vespers followed by a collection of motets, including almost all the Vespers music we have from Du Fay as well as all of his isorhythmic motets from ca. 1433 to 1445.
4. Cambrai 6 and 11. Copied after October 1434 and after 1442, respectively.
5. Trent 92, part I (fols. 1–143). Copied ca. 1435–39 by Nicole Merques, most likely in Geneva and Basel.

These sources transmit Du Fay's works with reliable attributions and mostly in good readings over the period ca. 1414–45. Some misconceptions about Bologna Q.15 and ModB need clarification. Bologna Q.15 was a personal manuscript by a scribe who probably had ready access to Du Fay's music, but also felt little compunction in heavily editing the music he copied. This includes adding contratenors, some of them extremely clumsy, to works of Johannes Ciconia, Du Fay, and others;[3] largely eliminating the plainsong invocations in most of the Kyries and replacing them with threefold polyphonic repetitions that make a complete hash of the musical structure; and arranging Du Fay's hymns in a cycle according to his own predilections. The scribe of ModB treated Du Fay's hymns similarly.[4] This manuscript, copied

---

2  For detailed descriptions of these sources, see Margaret Bent's essay in this volume (Ch. 33). I omit a few early and reliable sources (e.g., Aosta 15, Bologna 2216, and Trent 87) because their connections to Du Fay are less immediately clear.

3  Du Fay's *Gaude virgo mater Christi* (*OO*, 01/19) is a case in point. (*OO* refers to the Du Fay *Opera Omnia*, ed. Planchart, online at www.diamm.ac.uk/resources/music-editions/du-fay-opera omnia/.)

4  See Anderson, "The Organization and Complexes." A comparable study of ModB has not been published. Ward, "The Polyphonic Office Hymn," 162–63, argues that because the last two hymns of the cycle use melodies not commonly found in Italian sources, the hymns were not intended for the papal chapel but rather for Savoy, a view echoed by Fallows in *Dufay*, 146. But these "non-Italian" melodies were also not in use in Savoy; see Planchart, "Music for the Papal Chapel," 114–18, and Du Fay, *OO*, 07.

largely when the papal chapel was in Florence, surely echoes some of the papal liturgy, but it was again a personal manuscript, and it is stretching things too far to say that it was "for" the papal chapel.[5]

After ca. 1445 the source situation for Du Fay's music changes drastically. From 1440 to his death he was at Cambrai except for two sojourns (1450–51 and 1452–58) in Savoy. At Cambrai he produced an enormous amount of liturgical music for the cathedral, the court of Burgundy, even the court of Savoy (despite the schism) – but not a single source from Cambrai has survived between 1445 and 1500, although the records of the fabric note the copying of an immense amount of polyphony. Similarly, no contemporary sources of liturgical music from Savoy have survived, and from Burgundy we have only a single choirbook, compiled ca. 1468–74 and containing two works by Du Fay (Brussels 5557). Otherwise we have only fragments, the only substantial one being a choirbook with at least one mass by Du Fay that was copied in Bruges ca. 1463.[6]

As such Du Fay's late music survives to a considerable extent in copies that are distant in place and time from his circle of activity and with varying degrees of corruption and completeness. The most important of these sources are the central Trent Codices, copied ca. 1453–65 by Hanns Wiser and several assistants in Munich (Trent 93) and Trento (Trent 90, 88, and 89). How Du Fay's music reached Wiser and in what state is not known, but a good deal of it apparently came from Cambrai itself.[7] Next to the Trent Codices, several Roman collections, connected with the papal chapel and the Basilica of San Pietro in Vaticano and copied ca. 1474–1513, transmit a number of the late works, perhaps from older copies then in Rome.[8] In one instance, the most extended version of Du Fay's hymn collection, which must have remained in the papal chapel since the 1430s, is incorporated anonymously in an elaborate polyphonic Roman hymnal of the 1490s (Vatican CS 15). Curiously, the Este court of Ferrara, with which Du Fay had an active connection in the 1430s and 1440s, preserves only one of the late masses in a heavily edited version in a manuscript copied ca. 1481, but nothing else.[9]

The secular music fared slightly better. Again there are virtually no northern French or Burgundian sources extant, but Du Fay was in contact with the French royal court in 1455, and it is clear from a letter he wrote to the Medici in 1456 that the court's poets and singers were interested in his music. He and

---

5 Cf. Phelps, "A Repertory in Exile."    6 Strohm, *The Lucca Choirbook*.
7 Strohm, "Quellenkritische Untersuchungen."    8 Fallows, *Dufay*, 223–24.
9 Modena, Biblioteca Estense, MS α.M.1.13 (*olim* lat. 456), fols. 159v–176r. Another Ferrarese manuscript, Rome 2856, probably copied ca. 1480, transmits the song *Il sera par vous – L'homme armé*, without text and in a marginally competent four-voice arrangement with an ascription to "Borton," probably the arranger, Pierre Bordon.

Johannes Ockeghem became friends and remained in contact probably until
the end of Du Fay's life. Accordingly his later songs show up in very good
readings in manuscripts from the Loire Valley, representing the interests of
patrons from the French Royal court, as well as in later manuscripts from
Savoy, where Du Fay's memory was kept alive.

## Du Fay as "composer"

Despite the loss of late sources, Du Fay's music survives in higher proportion
than that of his contemporaries and immediate successors. Du Fay was unusual
in defining himself *primarily* as what we call today a "composer" rather than as a
singer or even a clergyman.[10] His self-description in his epitaph is "musicus," a
term whose meaning had begun to change from "music theorist" to "composer." Moreover, the scribe of Oxford 213 uses the term "Guillermus Du Fay
composuit" for eleven works.[11]

Du Fay promoted his music and sought to disseminate it. One of his earliest
works, a Kyrie – Sanctus – Agnus cycle, is based on a plainsong that was sung at
Cambrai as part of the *Missa ad tollendum schismam*, which indicates he probably
composed it *sub spem* in 1414 when he realized that he would be going to
Constance with the Cambrai delegation and would thus have an opportunity to
present himself to the council chapel as a composer.[12] Similarly, the Sanctus
"Papale" (ca. 1426–27), which features an alternation between choirboys and
an adult choir, is probably also a "prospective" work: whereas Du Fay's then
patron (Louis Allemand) did not employ choirboys, the papal chapel did.[13]
During his years in the papal chapel, Du Fay embarked on two or perhaps three
large "compositional" projects of a scope not seen since the creation of the
*Magnus liber organi* at Notre Dame in the twelfth and thirteenth centuries: a
cycle of hymns *per circulum anni*; a cycle of plainsong-based Kyries and largely
plainsong-based Glorias that covered all the liturgical categories, from *duplex
maior* (including Easter) to *simplex minor*;[14] and a cycle of proses for the major
feasts of the year, probably begun in Rome and completed in Savoy.[15]

In 1439, when the impending schism between the Council of Basel and Pope
Eugene IV forced Du Fay to retreat strategically to Cambrai in order to

---

10  Cf. Wegman, "From Maker to Composer."
11  In Oxford 213 the name of the author is followed by the word *composuit* in twenty-two cases. The
proportions in the use of the term are interesting: nine composers have one ascription with *composuit* each,
Grenon has two, and Du Fay has 11. And whereas most *composuit* indications are restricted to fols. 114v–
139v, those added to ascriptions to Du Fay are found throughout the manuscript.
12  Planchart, "The Early Career," 350–60.
13  Fallows, *Dufay*, 179–81; and Planchart, "Institutional Politics," 136–39.
14  Kovarik, "The Performance." A fuller discussion will appear in Planchart, *Guillaume Du Fay*.
15  Planchart, "The Polyphonic Proses."

preserve his northern benefices, his first stop was the court of Burgundy. There Duke Philip engaged him in an enormous cyclic project: a series of six *missae communes*, in this case the Mass Propers for the weekly services of the Order of the Golden Fleece in Dijon.[16] Thus began a relationship with the dukes of Burgundy wherein Du Fay, though not a member of the Burgundian chapel, became a composer for the court of Burgundy, providing it with a remarkable number of major works over the years, including the motet *Moribus et genere* (1441) (*OO*, 02/13), the *Missa L'homme armé* (1460–61) (*OO*, 03/05), and almost certainly the *Missa Ecce ancilla – Beata es Maria* (1463) (*OO*, 03/06).[17] At the end of his life Du Fay left his entire collection of polyphony, some ten volumes in all, to the Duke of Burgundy;[18] indeed the court of Burgundy (or rather the Order of the Golden Fleece) continued to think of Du Fay as "its composer," and after his death appropriated his *Missa pro defunctis* and apparently a setting of the Office of the Dead for its annual commemoration of the departed chevaliers.[19]

During his long decade at Cambrai in the 1440s, Du Fay was working mostly as an "independent contractor" in musical composition, writing works for his own cathedral, the Burgundian chapel, the court of Ferrara, the court of Savoy, and the Franciscan Order. Indeed there is no comparable level of simultaneous activity that we know from any other composer before Henricus Isaac.[20] This happened because Du Fay was in an anomalous situation. Most clerical musicians returned at the end of their careers to the place where they had their major benefice, to retire from their court or chapel duties; Du Fay had to do this in mid-career on account of the political circumstances created by the schism. His relationship to the Duke of Burgundy, who apparently regarded Du Fay as part of his extended *familia*, provided him with a protective cover under which he remained in contact with the court of Savoy without fear of interdict from Eugene IV.[21] In Cambrai Du Fay engaged himself in a thorough revision and updating of the cathedral's liturgical books, including the copying of a new antiphoner, two volumes of polyphonic Mass Ordinaries, and two volumes of polyphonic Propers.[22] This latter project was especially significant:

---

16  Planchart, "Guillaume Du Fay's Benefices," 149–54. On his authorship see Planchart, "Connecting the Dots," 17–20. Doubts raised by Gerber in "Dufay's Style," and her *Sacred Music from the Cathedral at Trent*, 60–81 are based on a misunderstanding of the liturgical tradition and chant variants in Dijon and Cambrai and sometimes upon misreadings of the clefs in the chant books.

17  On these works see, respectively: Lütteken, *Guillaume Dufay*, 297–99 and Du Fay, *OO*, 02/13, with references to earlier literature; Planchart, "The Origins and Early History" and Planchart, "Ricercare and Variations," 52–54.

18  Wegman, "*Miserere supplicanti Dufay*," 18–19.

19  Prizer, "Music and Ceremonial," 133.      20  Cf. Wegman, "Isaac's Signature."

21  Cf. Planchart, "Connecting the Dots," 21–22.

22  Curtis, "Music Manuscripts," 155–66.

because very little music for the Propers existed at the time, Du Fay composed probably 23–25 cycles, only a fragment of which survives. Indeed Du Fay's "systematic" approach to hymns, Kyries and Glorias, and proses found its continuation in his music for Cambrai in the 1440s.

During the same decade Du Fay also composed for several other institutions. For the Burgundian chapel he wrote modest works for Vespers, such as *Hic vir despiciens* (*OO*, 01/08). For the Este court in Ferrara he composed the chanson-motet *Signeur Leon* (*OO*, 10/04/03), which Sean Gallagher has shown is connected with the papal gift of the Golden Sword to Leonello d'Este in 1448.[23] Du Fay's connections with Ferrara went back to 1433, with the ballade *C'est bien raison* for Niccolò III d'Este;[24] toward the end of the 1440s Du Fay brought to completion a Mass Ordinary cycle with two sets of alternate Propers, one for St. Francis of Assisi and one for St. Anthony of Padua, complete with a full set of polyphony for Vespers (antiphons, hymn, responsory, *Benedicamus domino*, and motet) that Fallows has argued were intended for the Basilica del Santo in Padua in connection with the dedication of Donatello's altar in 1450.[25] This pattern continues during Du Fay's later sojourns in Savoy. Fallows surmises, probably correctly, that his journey there in 1450 was connected with offering the Franciscan masses and vespers to the Basilica in Padua.[26] From his second sojourn a couple years later, we have pieces like the *Missa Se la face ay pale* (*OO*, 03/04) and the Italian rondeau *Dona gentile* (*OO*, 10/01/07), clearly written for his patron in Savoy,[27] but also songs that set texts by French court poets, which are probably the songs he refers to in a letter of February 1456 as "some chansons which, at the request of some gentlemen of the King's court, I composed when I was in France with Monseigneur de Savoye."[28] The songs were composed at the request of French courtiers, but in the letter Du Fay mentions he is sending them to the Medici, again, *sub spem*. The letter also mentions "four Lamentations for Constantinople . . . and the texts were sent to me from Naples."[29] This surely means they were sent to him with a request for his composition, and now in turn he is offering to send them to the Medici if they are interested.

After his final return to Cambrai Du Fay continued to compose for other patrons. Most prominently, we find the *Missa L'homme armé* and almost

---

23 Gallagher, "Seigneur Leon's Papal Sword."

24 Lockwood, *Music in Renaissance Ferrara*, 38–42, with citations of earlier literature; Fallows, *The Songs of Guillaume Dufay*, 70.

25 Fallows, *Dufay*, 66–68 and 182–88.

26 Ibid., 66–68.

27 See Robertson, "The Man with the Pale Face"; Fallows, *The Songs of Guillaume Dufay*, 46–49.

28 Florence, Archivio di Stato, Mediceo avanti il Principato, MS VI 765. See D'Accone, "The Singers of San Giovanni," 318–19, with earlier literature; Fortuna and Lunghetti, eds. *Autografi dell'archivio mediceo*, 38–39 and ill. 18.

29 D'Accone, "The Singers of San Giovanni."

certainly the *Missa Ecce ancilla – Beata es Maria*, for the Order of the Golden Fleece; probably most of the very late songs, including pieces that show Du Fay's awareness of the music of Busnoys, such as *Dieu gard la bone* (*OO*, 10/05/15), for the Burgundian court; a commission by Antonio Squarcialupi to set a poem by Lorenzo de' Medici (a request that for whatever reason Du Fay did not comply with);[30] and masses Du Fay apparently sent to Rome via Gilles Crépin, who had been a singer at St. Peter's in Rome and at the court of Savoy, and a petit vicaire at Cambrai from December 1464 to July 1468.[31]

Given this pattern, it should come as no surprise that at the very end of his life Du Fay apparently decided to use his *Missa Ave regina celorum* for the dedication of Cambrai cathedral in July of 1472, officiated by his close friend Pierre de Ranchicourt, then bishop of Arras.[32] As a *musicus*, that is, a creator of *res factae* for multiple patrons and occasions, Du Fay probably saw no reason not to rework his own last mass to suit this purpose.

## Du Fay's works as biographical documents

Apart from the extensive documentation presented in studies by Craig Wright and Fallows,[33] the pieces in themselves can often function as biographical documents. A few instances have already been noted, but by now all the isorhythmic motets and mass cycles can be dated, either to within a year or to an exact date. The songs and some of the cantilena motets are less easily datable, but a few songs have dates attached in Oxford 213, and others, like *He compaignons* (*OO*, 10/05/23), can be dated by such features as the mention, in the text, of musicians in the service of Malatesta di Pandolfo in 1423, whose "fellowship" was surely permanently dissolved by the fall of 1424.[34]

Three textual acrostics have yielded biographical fruit: "Isabette" (*J'ay mis mon cuer*, *OO*, 10/02/04), "Petrus de Castello Canta" (*Fulgens iubar ecclesie*, *OO*, 02/14), and "Robertus Auclou curatus Sancti Iacobi" (*Rite maiorem*, *OO*, 02/05). Fallows proposed that Isabette is Elizabetta di Galeazzo Malatesta (1407–77), an intellectual prodigy and the favorite niece of Du Fay's patron Archbishop Pandolfo di Malatesta.[35] Pierre du Castel was successively petit

---

30 Haar and Nádas, "Johannes de Anglia."
31 Bouquet, "La cappella musicale," 283; Reynolds, *Papal Patronage*, 44; Lille, Archives Départementales du Nord, 4G 7567, fol. 5v.
32 Cf. Wegman, "*Miserere supplicanti Dufay*," and Planchart, "Notes on Guillaume Du Fay's Last Works," 63–69.
33 Wright, "Dufay at Cambrai"; Fallows, *Dufay*.
34 Planchart, "Guillaume Du Fay's Benefices," 124–25, and Planchart, "Four Motets," 13–16. We have the least information about Du Fay's social circle during the late 1430s.
35 Fallows, *The Songs of Guillaume Dufay*, 65. Litta, *Famiglie celebri italiane*, X, 46 = dispensa 161, pl. vii.

vicaire in 1433, *magister puerorum* from 1434 to 1447, and a grand vicar from
1437 on at Cambrai. On his dismissal as *magister puerorum* he became a canon of
St. Géry. *Fulgens iubar* dates most likely from ca. 1445, when two silver
reliquaries given to the cathedral by canon Jehan Martin were refurbished
and provided with pallets for carrying during the procession of the
Purification; one of the reliquaries had an inscription with the last words in
Du Fay's tenor, *Quem genuit adoravit*.[36] Robert Auclou had been Louis
Allemand's secretary from 1419 to 1424, and after a year of law studies in
Paris was called by Allemand to Bologna. It is a virtual certainty that it was
Auclou who recruited Du Fay to join Allemand's court in 1426. The cantus
firmus of *Rite maiorem* comes from a Matins responsory for St. James that is an
*unicum* in the antiphoner of San Giacomo il Maggiore in Bologna, so the motet
must date from 1426–27, when Du Fay and Auclou were in Bologna.[37]

## Du Fay as stylistic innovator

Du Fay's beneficial career was relatively slow and difficult,[38] but his musical
career was both vertiginous and in many ways without precedent. His earliest
datable work, the Kyrie – Sanctus – Agnus of 1414, is a graceful work, but one
that could have been written by almost any well-trained northern composer at
the time. Four years later, with *Vasilissa ergo gaude* (*OO*, 02/01) and the series of
motets that follow, he had internalized the style of Johannes Ciconia, the most
important composer of the previous generation – and yet the sound and
texture of these works already reveals a distinctly personal voice. Another
work of those years, the *Missa Sine nomine*, belongs to an early flowering of
mass cycles not based on a cantus firmus, of which Du Fay's mass might be the
earliest example.[39] Du Fay unifies the mass through an immense variety of
procedures, including a common head motive in the Kyrie and Agnus that is
presented in an even more complex version at the start of an internal section in
the Gloria;[40] a succession of mensuration changes, analogous rhythmic textures at the ends of movements; and, most unusually, plainsong intonations
composed by him that tie the Sanctus and the Agnus together.[41] Du Fay's
earliest works also include experiments with what can be called "genre

---

36 Lütteken, *Guillaume Dufay*, 300–1; Nosow, *Ritual Meanings*, 183. (Nosow's chronology of Martin's
death is off by two years.)
37 Planchart, "Four Motets," 17–25.
38 See Planchart, "Guillaume Du Fay's Benefices," 130–38.
39 Strohm, *The Rise of European Music*, 170.
40 This motive, particularly the version used in the Gloria, serves also as the opening of the ballade
*Resvelliés vous* (*OO*, 10/02/09); cf. Fallows, *Dufay*, 165–68.
41 Cf. *OO*, 03/01, p. 35.

mixtures." *Vergene bella* (OO, 01/23), for instance, has the structure of a motet but a contrapuntal surface reminiscent of the songs, and shows Du Fay incorporating melodic gestures of late trecento secular music in his own style. Similarly, as Robert Nosow has shown, the early cantilena motet *Flos florum* (OO, 01/18), also characterized by an intermingling of song and motet styles, became a seminal work that spawned a series of imitations.[42]

In the mid-1420s Du Fay produced one of his few true "experiments," the *Missa Sancti Jacobi* (OO, 03/02). This setting grew almost as a coral reef, from a three-movement Ordinary, built on a complex cycle of alternating textures that expanded markedly on the kind of *divisi* writing one finds in Antonio Zachara,[43] to a five-movement Ordinary, where in the last two sections the *divisi* are written out as separate parts, to almost a plenary mass, with the addition first of two motet-like movements (introit and offertory), later with a motet-like alleluia, an introit *repetitio*, and a communion in chant-paraphrase style,[44] this last being one of the earliest if not the earliest example of fauxbourdon texture.[45]

Moving beyond the *Missa Sancti Jacobi*, the truly momentous change for Du Fay's music was the adoption of chant-paraphrase cantus firmi, usually in the cantus voice.[46] (Fauxbourdon was simply a subgenre of this procedure.) This allowed Du Fay to bring into his liturgical music techniques he had honed for several years in song composition, including tight control of tonal goals as well as motivic construction that ranged from free counterpoint to what Graeme Boone has aptly called "motivic reaction,"[47] that is, an exchange of motivic shapes that, if not actually imitative, fall just short of imitation. With these techniques Du Fay had an extremely efficient way of producing works that made use of the appropriate chants for a given liturgical occasion. Du Fay's ambitious projects of the 1430s (the hymn cycle, cycle of Kyrie eleison and Gloria settings, and cycle of proses) represent a considerable burst of creativity. To these we should add an impressive series of "papal" motets: *Balsamus et munda* (1431), *Ecclesie militantis* (ca. 1432), *Supremum est* (1433), *Salve flos Tusce* (1436), and *Nuper rosarum flores* (1436). In these works Du Fay

42 Nosow, "The Florid and Equal-Discantus Motet Styles," 152–90; see also Cumming, *The Motet in the Age of Du Fay*, 99–117.

43 Bent, "*Divisi* and *a versi*," 108–11.

44 For the genesis of the mass see Planchart, "Guillaume Dufay's Masses," 26–33; Bent, "Music and the Early Veneto Humanists."

45 The literature on fauxbourdon is both immense and vexed. The best survey of the topic with all the relevant bibliography remains Brian Trowell, "Fauxbourdon."

46 In a few works the chant paraphrase is in a second cantus or a lower voice. This happens only when the chant rises above $g''$ on account of having been transposed up an octave, as was Du Fay's common practice. See Planchart, "The Polyphonic Proses of Guillaume Du Fay," 94–95.

47 Boone, "Dufay's Early Chansons," 168.

crystallized his use of a tenor cantus firmus as well as the procedures of isomelism; the latter gave rise to the cyclic variation structure one finds in later works such as *Fulgens iubar ecclesie* (1445 or 1447)[48] and the *Missa Se la face ay pale* (1453).

Du Fay's turn toward paraphrased cantus firmi also led him to largely abandon the free cantilena style in liturgical and ceremonial works. His last cantilena works show this transition taking place. In *Mirandas parit* (ca. 1436) (*OO*, 01/25), we find a surface reminiscent of the tenor motet, with an introductory imitative duo, a delayed tenor entrance in the *prima pars*, and several internal duets in the *secunda pars*, with long notes in the tenor as it reenters; the incomplete *Iuvenis qui puellam* (*OO*, 01/24) is characterized by varied textures, patches of fauxbourdon (as in *Supremum est*), and massive declamation in divided breves with fermatas; and *O proles Hispanie* (ca. 1440?) (*OO*, 01/16) features a double text. This last piece is the densest of Du Fay's cantilena motets, with four-part writing virtually all the way through and textural references to earlier "cut-circle" motets with a florid cantus.[49] Du Fay's last extended essays in cantilena style formed part of a long-range project, probably from the middle or late 1440s, that included a mass Ordinary, mass Propers, and polyphonic vespers. Here, as in the Proper cycles for the Order of the Golden Fleece composed ca. 1439–49, Du Fay had to contend with longer chants that were less amenable to paraphrase. This precluded a cantus line that sounded like the cantus of a fifteenth-century cantilena, leading Du Fay instead to cultivate a more expansive melodic style lacking the chains of small motives one finds in his other freely composed cantus parts. This development, in turn, established a foundation for the melodic style of his late works.[50]

In the 1440s, when Du Fay was most likely working on cycles of mass Propers, the *Proprium missae*, a majority of which have not survived, he undoubtedly came upon what can be described as a "second wave" of English music – in particular, Ordinary cycles imported to Cambrai to expand the use of polyphony for the liturgy *in choro*.[51] Among these masses was surely the immensely influential *Missa Caput*, with its distinctive four-voice texture featuring a low and motivically integrated contratenor.[52] This texture, which Du Fay adopts in his last isorhythmic motet, *Fulgens iubar ecclesie* (*OO*, 02/14), became essentially the standard for all of Du Fay's surviving late sacred music.[53]

---

48  Brown, "New Evidence of Isomelic Design"; Fallows, *Dufay*, 117–23.
49  See Cumming, *The Motet in the Age of Du Fay*, 233–35.
50  An analysis of some of these settings appears in Planchart, "Guillaume Du Fay's Second Style," 318–40.
51  See above, p. 91.      52  See Wegman, "Petrus de Domarto."
53  Two lost late works, the *Requiem* and the mass for St. Anthony Abbot (which were copied together in a single book that Du Fay left to the chapel of St. Stephen at Cambrai), were three-voice pieces, probably

As Du Fay abandoned the isorhythmic motet and started composing cantus-firmus masses, beginning with the *Missa Se la face ay pale* (*OO*, 03/04), he not only used the four-voice texture of *Caput*, but also expanded the isomelic recurrences he had used in his last motets to tie the Gloria and Credo together and create motivic cross-references among all the five movements. In addition his choice of a secular rather than plainchant cantus firmus in both the masses *Se la face ay pale* and *L'homme armé*, while not entirely unprecedented, pointed in a new direction. In *L'homme armé*, isomelic procedures are less noticeable to the ear than in *Se la face ay pale*, largely because they are concentrated in the free melodic extensions of the tenor, specifically at the end of the Gloria and Credo.[54] Cantus-firmus motives begin to appear in the other voices, sometimes through imitation of a characteristic gesture (e.g., the D–D–D–G phrase), but also, toward the end of the mass, through extensive citation of the tune or its melodic outline in all the voices and at different pitch levels.[55] Moreover, the mass is organized through a network of motives.[56]

Du Fay retains this texture in his last two surviving motets. The *Salve regina* has the plainsong largely in the cantus (as in the Proper settings of the 1440s) and the nearly consistent four-voice scoring one finds in *O proles Hispanie*.[57] The later *Ave regina celorum* (*OO*, 01/06) is a Janus-faced work. It returns the cantus firmus to the tenor (as in the two masses that precede it), but subjects it to some of the paraphrase technique Du Fay had used in the plainsong-derived cantus settings of the 1440s and before. It also creates a "polytextual" texture in that the tenor performs only the liturgical text while the other voices also sing the tropes. Since the tenor (and the low contratenor) usually have delayed entrances at the start of each *pars* (as happens in the late isorhythmic motets), when the tenor enters with the liturgical text the other voices are already singing the trope. More than in any earlier work, however, the musical substance of the tenor permeates the entire polyphonic fabric through the use of imitation, so the piece sounds at times like a forerunner of the polyphonic paraphrase works of the late fifteenth century. While the extended use of duets

closer in style to the proper cycles of the 1440s and the mass for St. Anthony of Padua. In the case of the *Requiem* we have a reference to it being a three-voice work in a letter of Niccolò Friggio describing a performance in Brussels in 1501 (Prizer, "Music and Ceremonial," 133), and the structure of the lost mass for St. Anthony is reflected in an incompletely preserved plenary mass (Trent 89, fols. 59v–71r), that follows the liturgy for the saint used at Cambrai and incorporates a number of formal traits of Du Fay's late music, but is clearly the work of a modestly talented composer, probably one of the petits vicaires at Cambrai, following the pattern set by Du Fay's work (Planchart, "The Books," 204–12).

54 See *OO*, 03/05, 49–53.
55 Cf. *OO*, 03/05, Agnus, mm. 41–109.
56 A fine analysis of this aspect of the work appears in Treitler, "Dufay the Progressive."
57 Dèzes, "Das Dufay zugeschriebene 'Salve Regina'," doubted Du Fay's authorship, and his view was accepted by Besseler in "Von Dufay bis Josquin," but as Strohm notes, Dèzes's judgment was premature (Strohm, *The Rise of European Music*, 438 n. 198), and neither Dèzes nor Besseler knew of further sources that point to Du Fay's authorship (cf. *OO*, 01/07, 8).

makes the *Ave regina* sound far thinner than the *Salve regina*, its scoring lacks the almost schematic structure one finds in *Nuper rosarum flores* or *Fulgens iubar ecclesie*.

The polytextuality of the *Ave regina* becomes a main feature of the *Missa Ecce ancilla – Beata es Maria*, which is scored just as lightly, with an enormous amount of imitative writing in the duets. But in this mass the cantus firmus is virtually never reflected in the melodic structure of the other voices, which share among themselves a loose network of motives. M. Jennifer Bloxam has offered an intriguing argument for hearing the simultaneous sound of the cantus-firmus text and the mass text as a kind of Marian exegesis of the Mass itself.[58]

The *Missa Ave regina* summarizes all of these tendencies: it uses a plainsong tenor cantus firmus that is often paraphrased, not quite as elaborately as the cantus paraphrases of the Proper cycles, but more elaborately than in *Ecce ancilla*. The tenor's melodic substance is sometimes taken over by the other voices through extended imitation, and the *fuga* in the duets is often more elaborate than in the *Missa Ecce ancilla*, with the *dux* and the *comes* sometimes reversing places.[59] The mass retains the polytextual texture of the *Ecce ancilla*.[60] The head motive includes all four voices and is absolutely identical in all five movements;[61] an extended, identical coda ties together the Gloria and Credo, a procedure that harks back to the *Missa Sine nomine*.[62] Particularly innovative is the citation, in the Agnus Dei, of passages from the motet *Ave regina celorum*, most strikingly the entire "miserere supplicanti Du Fay" passage,[63] as well as references to distinctive textures in the motet, often in self-contained sections. More generally, *Ave regina* now and then cites features from all of Du Fay's mature masses, making it a *summa* of his late style, as Fallows has noted.[64] In all of this the work breaks new ground, pointing the way to the imitation mass of the next generation.

Thus at the very end of his life Du Fay is still exploring new directions, while at the same time summing up and consolidating aspects of his own stylistic journey. This journey is most immediately apparent when one considers his songs. These are Du Fay's most concentrated works, in which virtually every detail becomes immensely important. The progression noticeable in the iso-rhythmic motets, most of which are securely datable, can be seen in the songs as

---

58 Bloxam, "Dufay as Musical Theologian." This would be a different manifestation of the kind of Christological program present in the *Missa L'homme armé* (cf. Planchart, "The Origins and Early History," 329–32).

59 Cf. *OO*, 03/07, Credo, mm. 25–38.

60 But see Wegman, "*Miserere supplicanti Dufay*," 34–41, but also *OO*, 03/07, 40.

61 See *OO*, 03/05, 46.     62 *OO*, 03/07, Gloria, mm. 217–39, Credo, mm. 282–305.

63 *OO*, 03/07, Agnus, mm. 107–29; see also Wegman, "*Miserere supplicanti Dufay*," 33 and 48–49.

64 Fallows, *Dufay*, 212–13.

well, particularly at the beginning of his career. *Belle plaisant et gracieuse* (*OO*, 10/05/04), probably one of his earliest songs, written most likely at Cambrai,[65] is, like the Kyrie – Sanctus – Agnus cycle, a work that could have been written by any well-trained northern composer at the time. But by 1423 he is writing the ballade *Resvelliés vous* (*OO*, 10/02/09) and the rondeau *He compaignons* (*OO*, 10/05/23). At their time these works were unique: the ballade not so much for its virtuosic rhythmic surface, but because of the harmonic-contrapuntal language, where at the outset the octave $d''–d'$ of the cantus is divided with a tritone, $g\sharp'$, which remains essentially unresolved, and the rondeau with its expanded low range announced at the very beginning with the contratenor on *gamma-ut*.[66] One finds similar variety in songs from ca. 1425 in Laon, where in close proximity Du Fay can write a work as carefully contrived as *Adieu ces bon vins* (*OO*, 10/05/01)[67] and works that completely turn around all the usual relationships between the voices, such as *Je me complains* (*OO*, 10/02/05) and *Ma belle dame souveraine* (*OO*, 10/05/40). Taken together, the songs of the 1430s also reflect the expansion of the tonal world initiated in some of the late Malatesta works (e.g., the Gloria–Credo pair no. 3 (*OO*, 05/05), which includes signed D♭). *Craindre vous vueil* (*OO*, 10/05/13) is particularly telling because it is an extended revision of an earlier song, *Quel fronte signorille* (*OO*, 10/01/05); this reworking opens a window into Du Fay's compositional procedure, including his criteria for tonal-contrapuntal structure.[68]

The songs of the 1440s and 1450s show a return of the virelai, now as a bergerette, in works such as *Helas mon dueil* (*OO*, 10/02/02),[69] but also an abandonment of the whimsical texts and what could be called the "compaignons" songs of his early years in favor of texts closer to the traditions of the *amour courtois*. In this period we also find an increased use of structural imitation between cantus and tenor, sometimes with the further involvement of the contratenor (e.g., *Franc cuer gentil*, *OO*, 10/05/22). Fallows rightly emphasizes how the late songs become at the same time more "conventional"

---

65 Boone, "Dufay's Early Chansons," 158–60, with a perceptive analysis of the tonal structure of the piece, and how far beyond Loqueville's style it moves.

66 The date for the ballade is clear since it was intended for the celebrations surrounding the wedding of Carlo di Malatesta with Vittoria di Lorenzo Colonna on 18 July 1423. That of the rondeau is based on the persons named in the text, including Ernoul and Hughes de Lantins, Jehan Humblot, and Didier Thierry, chaplains of Malatesta di Pandolfo in 1423 (cf. Planchart, "Guillaume Du Fay's Benefices," 124–25). The possibility of a later date when this constellation of people might have been together again is made moot by the implications of new documentation concerning Du Fay in late 1424 and 1425; cf. Planchart, "The Liègeoise Diaspora."

67 See Fallows's perceptive discussion in *Dufay*, 86–88.

68 See Planchart, "Two Fifteenth-Century Songs," and *OO*, 10/05/13, notes.

69 Gallagher, "Seigneur Leon's Papal Sword," 20–27, places this song without commentary among the songs of the 1450s, but the geographical places mentioned in the text point to the area of Cambrai and thus to the 1440s; see Planchart, "Du Fay and the Style of Molinet," 65–67.

and extraordinarily expressive.[70] They also incorporate mensuration changes and melodic patterns that assimilate their texture to that found in the late masses, as in *Dieu gard la bone* (*OO*, 10/05/15).[71]

In the songs, as in other genres, Du Fay produced works that pushed generic limits or referred to other genres. The simplest cases are pieces like *Se la face ay pale* (*OO*, 10/02/08), an entirely *sui generis* ballade in terms of its poetry, which uses a five-syllable line and *rhyme equivoquée*. The unique Italian rondeau *Dona gentile* (*OO*, 10/01/07), a late work with echoes of Ciconia,[72] features a new approach to musical shape: it is complex, entirely through-composed, and, while not apparent at first sight, seems to be the result of Du Fay's having edited an Italian ballata by suppressing part of the *volta* to produce a pseudo-rondeau.[73]

We also find several hybrids, which in the work of later composers developed into definite subgenres. A central category is the chanson-motet or motet-chanson, depending on the balance of elements. Du Fay's earliest essay, not quite yet a new subgenre, is *Je ne puis plus – Unde veniet* (*OO*, 10/04/02), one of the few genuinely ironic pieces of the fifteenth century. This minuscule work apes the structure of an isorhythmic motet, with a text complaining of impotence or incompetence; it also features several deliberate formal and contrapuntal errors.[74] In *Seigneur Leon – Benedictus qui venit* (*OO*, 10/04/03), we are still aware that this is a "rondeau with a cantus firmus," but the surviving lamentation for Constantinople (*OO*, 01/21) is written in the shape of a new-style motet in the English manner, with a double-cursus cantus firmus and two sections, one in O and the other in C, that mirror the formal plan of the English *Missa Caput* and a number of mid-century English motets.

The other hybrids led eventually to the combinative chanson. Again, there is a very early example, *Resvelons nous, resvelons, amoureux – Alons en bien tos au may* (*OO*, 10/04/01), where a strophic song (only one stanza survives) is set above a simple canonic ostinato that sounds like an *ars antiqua* refrain. A second example, the attributed work *Il sera par vous – L'homme armé* (*OO*, 10/04/04), is a full-fledged combinative chanson, setting a full rondeau over two voices, one carrying most of the *L'homme armé* tune, the other a portion of the text and tune mixed with war calls.[75] Still another example, one of the few songs of Du Fay where one can hear engagement with Ockeghem, particularly in terms of tessitura, is *Je vous pri, mon tres doulx ami – Ma tres doulce amie – Tant que mon argent dura* (*OO*, 10/04/05). Here a rondeau refrain (presumably an entire

---

70 Fallows, *Dufay*, 162–64.
71 See Planchart, "Du Fay and the Style of Molinet," 68–71.
72 Ibid., 67.    73 Fallows, *The Songs of Guillaume Dufay*, 48, makes a convincing argument for this.
74 Planchart, "Du Fay and the Style of Molinet," 64.
75 The case for Du Fay's authorship and the reasons for the shifts of the cantus firmus from the tenor to the contratenor are given at length in Planchart, "The Origins and Early History."

rondeau in the original) is set above three voices, two of which quote fragments of at least two *chansons rustiques*. The piece is both extremely complex and very sophisticated, and some scholars have expressed doubts about its authorship since the only ascription is in a very late source.[76] What has not been noted is that both the formal plan and the tonal strategy of this song are nearly identical to those of Du Fay's very late rondeau *Dieu gard la bone* (*OO*, 10/05/15), to the point that both songs are structural twins.

Notwithstanding this last example, it is harder to hear Du Fay's engagement with other composers in the songs than in the masses and motets. This is in part because the early songs tend to be very idiosyncratic, while the late songs assimilate themselves to the common style of the third quarter of the fifteenth century, cleaving, as Fallows notes, "to the centre of the tradition."[77] It is this that makes Du Fay's clear reference to Ciconia's style in *Dona gentile* so startling. The same can be said for the very low tessitura of *Les douleurs* (*OO*, 10/05/38), which probably represents a reaction to having heard Ockeghem's voice.[78] In his late years, Du Fay most likely came to know the songs of the Burgundian composers Antoine Busnoys and Hayne van Ghizeghem, but their music appears not to have influenced Du Fay's a great deal. The most Busnoys-like of his late songs, *Vostre bruit* (*OO*, 10/05/59), probably precedes Du Fay's encounter with Busnoys's music.[79] A few songs look back to the topoi of Du Fay's early songs within the highly controlled language of his late style (e.g., *Puisque vous estez campieur* (*OO*, 10/05/53)), much as the *Missa Ave regina celorum* contains references that go back to the 1420s or 1430s. In the end Du Fay's style, despite its radical evolution over more than half a century, remained stubbornly his own.

## Bibliography

Anderson, Michael Alan, "The Organization and Complexes of the Q 15 Hymn Cycle," *Studi musicali* 35 (2006), 327–61

Bent, Margaret, "*Divisi* and *a versi* in Early Fifteenth-Century Mass Movements," in *Antonio Zachara da Teramo e il suo tempo*, ed. Francesco Zimei, Lucca, 2005, 91–134
  "Music and the Early Veneto Humanists," in *Proceedings of the British Academy* 101, ed. Francis Michael Longstreth Thompson, Oxford, 1999, 101–30

Besseler, Heinrich, "Von Dufay bis Josquin: Ein Literaturbericht," *Zeitschrift für Musikwissenschaft* 11 (1928–29), 1–22

---

76  Cf. Fallows, *The Songs of Guillaume Dufay*, 96; Maniates, *The Combinative Chanson*, xxxii–xxxiii, but see the notes in *OO*, 10/04/05.
77  Fallows, *Dufay*, 164.    78  Planchart, "Du Fay and the Style of Molinet," 68.
79  Cf. *OO*, 10/05/59, notes.

Bloxam, M. Jennifer, "Dufay as Musical Theologian: The Case of the Missa Ecce Ancilla Domini," in *Program and Abstracts of Papers Read at the American Musicological Society Seventy-first Annual Meeting, October 27–30, 2005, Philadelphia*, 2005, 124–25

Boone, Graeme, "Dufay's Early Chansons: Chronology and Style in the Manuscript Oxford, Bodleian Library, Canonici misc. 213," Ph.D. diss., Harvard University, 1987

Bouquet, Marie Thérèse, "La cappella musicale dei Duchi di Savoia dal 1450 al 1500," *Rivista italiana di musicologia* 3 (1968), 233–85

Brown, Samuel Emmons, Jr., "New Evidence of Isomelic Design in Dufay's Isorhythmic Motets," *JAMS* 10 (1957), 7–13

Cumming, Julie, *The Motet in the Age of Du Fay*, Cambridge, 1999

Curtis, Liane, "Music Manuscripts and their Production in Fifteenth Century Cambrai," Ph.D. diss., University of North Carolina at Chapel Hill, 1991

D'Accone, Frank, "The Singers of San Giovanni in Florence during the 15th Century," *JAMS* 14 (1961), 307–58

Dèzes, Karl, "Das Dufay zugeschriebene 'Salve Regina' eine deutsche Komposition: Stilkritische Studie," *Zeitschrift für Musikwissenschaft* 10 (1927–28), 327–62

Du Fay, Guillaume, *Opera Omnia*, ed. Alejandro Enrique Planchart, Santa Barbara, 2013, and online at www.diamm.ac.uk/resources/music-editions/du-fay-opera omnia/

Fallows, David, *Dufay*, rev. edn., London, 1987

  *The Songs of Guillaume Dufay: Critical Commentary to the Revision of Corpus Mensurabilis Musicae, ser. 1, vol. VI*, MSD 47, Stuttgart, 1995

Fortuna, Alberto Maria, and Cristina Lunghetti, eds., *Autografi dell'archivio mediceo avanti il principato*, Scriptorium Florentinum 1, Florence, 1977

Gallagher, Sean, "Seigneur Leon's Papal Sword: Ferrara, Du Fay, and his Songs of the 1440s," *TVNM* 57 (2007), 3–28

Gerber, Rebecca, "Dufay's Style and the Question of Cyclic Unity in the Trent 88 Mass Proper Cycles," in *I codici musicali trentini: Nuove scoperte e nuovi orientamenti della ricerca*, ed. Peter Wright, Trent, 1996, 107–19

  ed., *Sacred Music from the Cathedral at Trent: Trent, Museo Provinciale D'arte, Codex 1375 (olim 88)*, Monuments of Renaissance Music 12, Chicago, 2007

Haar, James, and John Nádas, "Johannes de Anglia (John Hothby): Notes on his Career in Italy," *Acta musicologica* 79 (2007), 291–358

Kovarik, Edward, "The Performance of Dufay's Paraphrase Kyries," *JAMS* 28 (1975), 230–43

Litta, Pompeo, *Famiglie celebri italiane*, 185 parts in 10 vols., Milan, 1819–1883

Lockwood, Lewis, *Music in Renaissance Ferrara 1400–1505: The Creation of a Musical Center in the Fifteenth Century*, rev. edn., New York and Oxford, 2009

Lütteken, Laurenz, *Guillaume Dufay und die isorhythmische Motette: Gattungstradition und Werkcharakter an der Schwelle zur Neuzeit*, Hamburg, 1993

Maniates, Maria Rika, *The Combinative Chanson: An Anthology*, Recent Researches in the Music of the Renaissance 77, Madison, WI, 1989

Nosow, Robert, "The Florid and Equal-Discantus Motet Styles of Fifteenth-Century Italy," Ph.D. diss., University of North Carolina at Chapel Hill, 1992

  *Ritual Meanings in the Fifteenth-Century Motet*, Cambridge, 2012

Phelps, Michael, "A Repertory in Exile: Pope Eugene IV and the MS Modena, Biblioteca Estense Universitaria, α. X.1.11," Ph.D. diss., New York University, 2008

Planchart, Alejandro Enrique, "The Books that Guillaume Du Fay Left to the Chapel of Saint Stephen," in *Sine musica nulla disciplina ... Studi in onore di Giulio Cattin*, ed. Franco Bernabei and Antonio Lovato, Padua, 2006, 175–212

"Connecting the Dots: Guillaume Du Fay and Savoy during the Schism," *PMM* 18 (2009), 11–32

"Du Fay and the Style of Molinet," *EM* 37 (2009), 61–72

"The Early Career of Guillaume Du Fay," *JAMS* 46 (1993), 341–68

"Four Motets of Guillaume Du Fay in Context," in *Sleuthing the Muse: Essays in Honor of William Prizer*, ed. Kristine K. Forney and Jeremy L. Smith, Hillsdale, NY, 2012, 13–30

*Guillaume Du Fay* (forthcoming)

"Guillaume Du Fay's Benefices and his Relationship to the Court of Burgundy," *EMH* 8 (1988), 117–71

"Guillaume Dufay's Masses: A View of the Manuscript Traditions," in *Papers Read at the Dufay Quincentenary Conference, Brooklyn College, December 6–7, 1974*, ed. Allan W. Atlas, Brooklyn, 1976, 26–60

"Guillaume Du Fay's Second Style," in *Music in Renaissance Cities and Courts: Studies in Honor of Lewis Lockwood*, ed. Jessie Ann Owens and Anthony M. Cummings, Warren, MI, 1997, 307–40

"Institutional Politics and Social Climbing through Music in Early Modern France," *Analecta musicologica* 43 (2009), 115–52

"The Liègeoise Diaspora in Italy in the Early Fifteenth Century" (forthcoming)

"Music for the Papal Chapel in the Early Fifteenth Century," in *Papal Music and Musicians in Medieval and Renaissance Rome*, ed. Richard Sherr, Oxford, 1998, 93–124

"Notes on Guillaume Du Fay's Last Works," *JM* 13 (1995), 55–72

"The Origins and Early History of *L'homme armé*," *JM* 20 (2003), 305–57

"The Polyphonic Proses of Guillaume Du Fay," in *Uno gentile et subtile ingenio: Studies in Renaissance Music in Honour of Bonnie J. Blackburn*, ed. M. Jennifer Bloxam, Gioia Filocamo, and Leofranc Holford-Strevens, Turnhout, 2009, 87–99

"Ricercare and Variations on Ockeghem, Du Fay, and Cambrai," in *"Hands-On" Musicology: Essays in Honor of Jeffery Kite-Powell*, ed. Allen Scott, Ann Arbor, 2012, 36–61

"Two Fifteenth-Century Songs and their Texts in a Close Reading," *BJhM* 14 (1990), 13–36

Prizer, William F., "Music and Ceremonial in the Low Countries: Philip the Fair and the Order of the Golden Fleece," *EMH* 5 (1985), 113–53

Reynolds, Christopher, *Papal Patronage and the Music of St. Peter's, 1380–1513*, Berkeley, 1995

Robertson, Anne Walters, "The Man with the Pale Face, the Shroud, and Du Fay's *Missa Se la face ay pale*," *JM* 27 (2010), 377–434

Strohm, Reinhard, ed., *The Lucca Choirbook*, Late Medieval and Early Renaissance Music in Facsimile 2, Chicago, 2008

"Quellenkritische Untersuchungen an der Missa 'Caput'," in *Quellenstudien zur Musik der Renaissance 2. Datierung und Filiation von Musikhandschriften der Josquin-Zeit*, ed. Ludwig Finscher, Wolfenbütteler Forschungen 26, Wiesbaden, 1984, 154–76

*The Rise of European Music 1380–1500*, Cambridge, 1993

Treitler, Leo, "Dufay the Progressive," in *Papers Read at the Dufay Quincentenary Conference, Brooklyn College, December 6–7, 1974*, ed. Allan W. Atlas, Brooklyn, 1976, 115–27

Trowell, Brian, "Fauxbourdon," *Oxford Music Online*

Ward, Tom, "The Polyphonic Office Hymn and the Liturgy of Fifteenth-Century Italy," *MD* 26 (1972), 161–88

Wegman, Rob C., "From Maker to Composer: Improvisation and Musical Authorship in the Low Countries, 1450–1500," *Music* 49 (1996), 409–79

"Isaac's Signature," *JM* 28 (2011), 9–33

"*Miserere supplicanti Dufay*: The Creation and Transmission of Guillaume Dufay's *Missa Ave regina celorum*," *JM* 13 (1995), 18–54

"Petrus de Domarto's *Missa Spiritus almus* and the Early History of the Four-Voice Mass in the Fifteenth Century," *EMH* 10 (1991), 235–303

Wright, Craig, "Dufay at Cambrai: Discoveries and Revisions," *JAMS* 28 (1975), 175–229

# 6

# Jean d'Ockeghem

LAWRENCE F. BERNSTEIN

His credentials are matchless. After his appointment, as a young man, to the distinguished chapel of Charles I, Duke of Bourbon, Jean d'Ockeghem moved to the royal court of France, probably in 1451, where, for nearly a half-century, he served as *premier chapelain* to three successive kings of France. He is praised widely for his graciousness, his Christian virtues, and his skill as a singer. Jean Molinet, who singles out the music of Gilles Binchois, Antoine Busnoys, Guillaume Du Fay, and Ockeghem as the best of its day, lists Ockeghem as the first among these masters. A retrospective assessment of Ockeghem's accomplishments made by the Italian humanist Cosimo Bartoli in 1567 characterizes them as having changed music much as Donatello's transformed sculpture: he credits Ockeghem with nothing less than providing the impetus for what came to be known as the musical Renaissance. And Johannes Tinctoris – not an easy man to please – ranks Ockeghem in his *Liber de arte contrapuncti* of 1477 "first among the most excellent composers of his generation."[1]

These are the attributes of a musician who had to have been the leading composer of his generation, which makes all the more inexplicable the number of enigmas that surround him and his music. In light of the composer's longevity and length of service, for example, it is difficult to explain the relatively small number of works that survive attributed to him: twenty chansons; fourteen masses or mass sections; the earliest known polyphonic Requiem; and only four motets; and one motet-chanson, whose authorship remain uncontested.[2] Did the apparent dearth of compositions result from a reallocation of priorities from composition to the administrative responsibilities associated with the post of Treasurer of St. Martin of Tours? Could the

---

1 For a concise summary of Ockeghem's reputation, see Perkins, "Jean de Ockeghem." The strength of Tinctoris's accolade, however, needs to be measured against the possibility that he offered it partly as a means of making amends for the sharp criticism he had leveled at a number of major composers, including Ockeghem, in the *Proportionale musices*. See Blackburn, "Did Ockeghem Listen to Tinctoris?" 631–34.

2 *Ut hermita solus* was attributed to Ockeghem in Guillaume Crétin's lament on the composer's death, and it is included among the compositions of undisputed authorship in the *Collected Works*. Its authenticity has been challenged on stylistic grounds, however, in Lindmayr-Brandl, "Ockeghem's Motets."

contrapuntal complexity of works like the *Missa Prolationum* or *Prenez sur moy* have demanded of their composer an inordinate amount of time for planning, conception, and execution alike? Or, did the fact that Ockeghem devoted nearly his entire career to the service of the French crown skew the representation of his works in the manuscripts? Not a single one of Ockeghem's masses comes down to us in a French source. What we have is transmitted essentially in manuscripts written outside France, chief among them the Chigi Codex, which is of Netherlandish provenance. One can only wonder if a greater number of works might have survived had their most likely repository, the Bibliothèque royale, not been subjected to systematic vandalism during the French Revolution, and had Ockeghem worked in Italy, thereby facilitating the preservation of an even greater number of works in Italian manuscripts.

Related to the inexplicable scarcity of Ockeghem's music is another conundrum: the extraordinary diversity inherent in the relatively few sacred works we have.[3] This is particularly notable in the masses, which Fabrice Fitch has characterized as differing from each other considerably in their approach to basic compositional technique, most notably in their handling of preexistent material.[4] Substantial diversity in a small pool of compositions inevitably impedes any attempt to formulate a generalized view of a composer's style.

Our understanding of Ockeghem's music is often complicated further by the lack of a clear appreciation of the destination for which it was intended. A didactic impetus appears to underlie a number of Ockeghem's works. The *Missae Cuiusvis toni* and *Prolationum* and *Prenez sur moy* seem designed, at least in part, for pedagogical purposes: to test the skill of an elite cadre of singers in their handling of the modal system, mensuration, and solmization, respectively.[5] Were other compositions destined primarily for the singers' edification, too?

Of all the paradoxes that arise in connection with Ockeghem's music, the most extraordinary is surely the precipitous decline in the composer's reputation that began in the middle of the sixteenth century. The nature of that decline and the reasons for it are discussed elsewhere in this volume.[6] Some of those reasons are practical and understandable (if regrettable). Of course, Charles Burney would recoil at the canonic *Prenez sur moy* given that his only source for the chanson was a transcription that misrepresented the interval of imitation and order of entries, producing what must have looked to him like an

---

3 The chansons, on the other hand, are far more consistent in the allegiance they demonstrate to the standard conventions of the *formes fixes* and discant–tenor style.
4 Fitch, *Johannes Ockeghem*, 3–4. In the eleven Ockeghem masses Fitch discusses in this study, for example, no two are alike with respect to the manner in which the cantus firmus is transformed or the extent to which the borrowed material is disposed in the free voices.
5 Perkins, "Ockeghem's *Prenez sur moi*," 155–56.
6 Bernstein, below, Ch. 43.

awkward accumulation of triads in first and second inversion. Forkel's railing at what he perceived to be the unwieldy notation of the *Missa Prolationum* must be read in light of his understandable ignorance of what a mensuration canon is. And in their ideological skirmishes with the proponents of *musica scholastica*, mid-sixteenth-century advocates of *musica practica* were bound to come down hard on Ockeghem for his emphasis on technical artifice. All they knew of his music, after all, were the few works that survived in theoretical treatises – technical *tours de force* like the *Missa Prolationum* that could only raise a red flag to opponents of *musica scholastica*.

Distortions of Ockeghem's music did not come to an end when its sources were brought under control and its notation understood. One of the most egregious examples is Heinrich Besseler's characterization of the complexity of Ockeghem's music as a vehicle for the expression of pietistic spirituality. Having privileged transparency and lucidity in the music of Du Fay, and in need of a way to account for the beauty of Ockeghem's music despite what he took to be the absence in it of these central qualities, Besseler linked the complexity of Ockeghem's works to a mystical agenda (doing so at the University of Heidelberg, where mysticism was widely studied in the 1920s and 1930s).[7] The underlying axiom in this characterization is that the levels of complexity in Ockeghem's music are so high that the music is, in essence, irrational, and therein resides the link to mysticism. Besseler's student at Heidelberg, Manfred Bukofzer, expanded on his mentor's approach to Ockeghem's music and intensified the argument for its pervasive lack of rational structure. Searching for the specific means whereby Ockeghem "managed to be 'mystical' in music," Bukofzer suggested that

> [H]e renounces with amazing consistency all customary means of articulating a composition: cadences, profiled motives, symmetrical phrase structure, lucid interrelation of parts, imitation, sequences, prominence of one voice over others ... His music avoids precisely those features that would enable the listener to grasp the details or the large structural units and to integrate them in his mind. We have here no less than a far-reaching renunciation of rational organization in music ...[8]

Leaving aside the absence of evidence for Ockeghem's contact with northern European pietism, it must be said that Bukofzer carried his correlation of Ockeghem's complex musical style and irrationality to an extreme. He left no room for relative gradations in the projection of complexity. Such flexibility

---

7 Further on Besseler's approach, see Bernstein, below, Ch. 43. See also Bernstein, "Ockeghem the Mystic."
8 Bukofzer, "*Caput*: A Liturgico-Musical Study," 291–92.

might have enabled him to address a critical problem in his argument. Bukofzer's renunciation of rational organization in music is so "far-reaching" that he seems to be describing a music that would strike the listener as inchoate – a quality no one associates with Ockeghem's music. Indeed, as we shall see, the subtlety of Ockeghem's style resides, to a considerable extent, in his ability to subvert the conventional properties of musical organization while – *at one and the same time* – imbuing his music with the means whereby it is prevented from collapsing into the chaotic world of irrationality. It is an approach I have described elsewhere as an aesthetic of concealment, a compositional strategy pursued widely in the Ockeghem masses and examined by Fabrice Fitch.[9]

Consider the opening of the Gloria of the *Missa Mi-mi* (Ex. 6.1).[10] We would hesitate, for fear of venturing into anachronism, to call the cadence with which this passage closes a deceptive cadence, but it functions exactly like one. This is so owing to the way in which it is contextualized both in the Gloria as a whole and within this passage in particular. The mass is in the Hypophrygian mode, in which cadences on both E and A may be expected, both of them implying stability, although not necessarily at the same level. Indeed, this polarity is spelled out unequivocally in the opening of the passage at hand, which uses clear homorhythmic texture and slow harmonic rhythm to attach equal emphasis to harmonies on E and A. Thus, when the superius melody begins to accelerate at the end of the example, settling into a cadential suspension formula on A, the listener has every reason to expect the cadence to resolve to a harmonic sonority on that scale degree. The harmonic resolution to F comes as a surprise, and the further inflection in that sonority with the addition of the D in the contratenor is even more destabilizing. This particular cadence has a strong impact on the listener. Its deceptive quality suggests continuation. Yet the avoidance of A after its arrival was so strongly signaled that it actually enhances its importance by promising the ultimate realization of that arrival. It is delayed for a long time, until the particularly strong perfect cadence on A (mm. 36–37) that is underscored by its rhythmic weight, clarity of articulation, and unique disposition as an under-third cadence. This sturdy cadence on A conveys a sense of a debt finally made good, and it gains a level of stability that is significantly augmented because the listener has been kept waiting for it for so long.

All of these implications inherent in our "deceptive" cadence are prospective; they look ahead in one way or another. But a cadential gesture is strongly articulatory, and this one, melodically, at least, fulfills the listener's expectation

---

9 Bernstein, "Ockeghem the Mystic," 840–41. Fitch, *Johannes Ockeghem*.
10 Musical examples and measure numbers follow Ockeghem, *Masses and Mass Sections*, ed. Benthem.

Example 6.1 Johannes Ockeghem, *Missa Mi-mi*, the opening of the Gloria (after the edition by Jaap van Benthem)

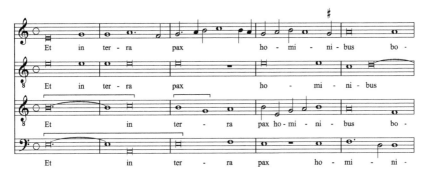

of arrival on A and serves, therefore, to divide the phrase (albeit less strongly than a conventional perfect cadence). Its deceptive quality and, more importantly, the manner in which Ockeghem uses that quality structurally enable this moment both to break the momentum of the phrase and simultaneously to drive it forward. From the perspective of the listener's perception of the passage, there is a quality of antithesis inherent in the Janus-faced nature of the gesture just described. That quality, moreover, as I hope to demonstrate, can serve as a paradigm for various ways in which Ockeghem's music achieves its unique measures of subtlety and concealment.

It stands to reason that the same principles that govern this "deceptive" cadence also operate in elided (or evaded) cadences, which appear in very great numbers in Ockeghem's music. That such devices were perceived by the Renaissance ear as simultaneously embodying a sense of articulation and an implication of continuation may be read in Zarlino's definition of an evaded cadence: "[A] cadence is evaded ... when the voices give the impression of leading to a perfect cadence, and turn instead in a different direction."[11] Ockeghem typically offers high levels of variety in the ways in which he achieves such elision, often overlaying them with substantial rhythmic complexity and embedding them in highly mutable textures. Nonetheless, a gesture that conveys the "impression of leading to a perfect cadence" goes a long way toward providing the listener with a sense of structural articulation, while serving simultaneously to propel the music onward.

Any composer capable of imbuing his music with meaningful vertical sonorities in the context of a double mensuration canon or a triple canon in which the outer voices imitate at the interval of a seventh must have been keenly

---

11 Zarlino, *The Art of Counterpoint*, 151.

astute about the vertical properties of his music. Ockeghem, in other words, had a firm grasp of what we call harmony. His focus on this dimension of music is demonstrable from instances in which he departs from the implications of his models. Not surprisingly, for example in *Alma Redemptoris mater*, he generally stays closely wedded to the Marian antiphon he paraphrases in the tenor of this motet, a chant that comes down to us in a highly stable transmission. This level of fidelity, in turn, underscores the importance of the few instances in which he departs from the cadential plan of the chant. In the second verse, Ockeghem alters two cadences from the antiphon – one on G, the other on E. In his polyphony, he represents the first of these with a weak G cadence that elides into a much stronger added cadence on E. For the second cadence on E from the chant, he substitutes an equally decisive cadence on C. His reason for the emendations seems clear. They enable the second verse of the polyphony to replicate exactly the harmonic goals of the first, enhancing thereby, as the motet progresses, the quality of contrast Ockeghem is about to invest in the following verse.[12] To cite two other examples of such alteration of preexistent material, in the Kyrie of the fragmentary *Missa Ma maistresse*, Ockeghem establishes a closed tonal form by adding a tone beyond the last note of the chanson tenor at the end of Kyrie II, and throughout the *Missa De plus en plus*, he fits the chant tenor to the Mixolydian context of the polyphony by changing the medial cadences in the tenor from D to G.[13]

The awareness of the structural properties of vertical sonorities reflected in these alterations is often translated by Ockeghem into the basis for long-range tonal designs. His brief motet *Ave Maria* offers an example.[14] If one turns first to the final cadence of the piece in pursuit of its mode, final, and tonal center, the work appears to be in the Hypophrygian mode transposed to A. The latter scale degree takes on the role of tonal center, given its use in cadences at important junctures earlier in the motet. And the emphasis on D at the opening of the work and several times thereafter is also consistent with Hypophrygian practice, in light of the tendency in that mode to lend special weight to both its final and cofinal. This "tonal" logic seems compelling, and it would appear to be of Ockeghem's own design, given the absence in the work of preexistent material. The motet opens with emphasis on the final and cofinal, quickly

---

12 See the transcription of the polyphony aligned with the chant and the accompanying discussion in Bernstein, "Ockeghem the Mystic," 814, 818–19.
13 Cf. Sparks, *Cantus Firmus*, 154–55, and Fitch, *Johannes Ockeghem*, 71. The most recent and most detailed study of Ockeghem's "alterations" in the *Missa De plus en plus* is Sherr, "Thoughts on Ockeghem's *Missa De plus en plus*: Anxiety and Proportion in the Late 15th Century." The "anxiety" to which Sherr refers in the title of his study is Harold Bloom's "anxiety of influence," a concept he most engagingly applies to Ockeghem's underlying motive for making these alterations.
14 See the edition in Ockeghem, *Collected Works*, 3: 6–7.

moving from the latter to the former. That juxtaposition is reiterated in the same order with the cadences at measures 7 and 11, respectively. Thereafter, the final is avoided for a long time, the cofinal and other scale degrees taking its place, and a need for the return of the final is thereby generated. That need is fulfilled near the end of the work (m. 33) and confirmed with the greatest clarity in the last measure of the piece. The tonal design seems particularly transparent.

However, the quality of antithesis we noted in connection with the "deceptive cadence" discussed above appears to enter into the tonal design of this motet, too, for there are aspects of it that are anything but clear. Normally, a work in the Hypophrygian mode once transposed will carry a B♭ in the signature. Not only is this absent in *Ave Maria*, but many of the B♮s that appear throughout the work are unavoidable. As a result, a good number of the cadences on A must be approached from the raised subsemitone, which strongly counters our sense of a Phrygian sound. Even near the end of the work, where signed B♭s begin to accrue in a way that clarifies the modality, some B♮s remain unalterable (as in the tenor at m. 41 and the bassus in the following measure).

Focusing on prominent harmonic sonorities in *Ave Maria* as a vehicle for mapping the tonal design of the piece greatly clarifies one's understanding of the structure of this motet. And doing so seems compatible with Ockeghem's approach, given the instances in which he presses changes in preexistent material into the service of precisely this objective. Nonetheless, the perception of harmonic sonority is inseparable from modality in works like this one, and, in the latter domain, the work is highly ambiguous. In part, that is endemic to the use of the Phrygian pair in polyphony, where the cofinal often competes with the final for prominence. As we have seen, moreover, Ockeghem does little to counter this ambiguity, opting, in fact, to expand upon it. Indeed, his choice of the Phrygian mode for works like this motet, the *Missa Mi-mi*, and the chanson *Presque transi* may be seen as a manifestation of his affinity for the high levels of ambiguity inherent in this mode.[15] Once again, Ockeghem manages to generate clarity and ambiguity concurrently, this time in the closely related spheres of tonal design and modality.

The role of imitation in Ockeghem's music has been the object of a great deal of commentary, much of it falling wide of the mark with respect to its accuracy. As is well known, Hugo Riemann went so far as to attribute to Ockeghem the invention of a pan-imitative style, for which, we now know, there is no

---

15 The matter of Ockeghem's choice of the Phrygian mode specifically in pursuit of the enhancement of modal ambiguity is discussed in Goldberg, "Text, Music, and Liturgy," 200. For additional aspects of ambiguity in Ockeghem's *Ave Maria*, see Bernstein, "Ockeghem's *Ave Maria*."

evidence at all.[16] Typically, when attempts were made to correct this view, the pendulum swung too far, and the composer's use of imitation was all but denied completely, as in Bukofzer's characterization of Ockeghem's style. The truth lies somewhere in between, as has been shown more recently – just where, however, is not always easy to pinpoint. Among the most valuable treatments of the issue is Irving Godt's essay on "hidden canon" in the *Missa Mi-mi*.[17] Godt builds upon a study by Reiner Zimmermann that distinguished between two types of obscured imitation in Ockeghem's music: one that preserves identities in pitch but not in rhythm, the other that maintains the rhythms but not the pitches.[18] In the *Missa Mi-mi*, Godt finds some examples of strict imitation, but more often he cites instances of free imitation, in which transposition, disguised entries, divergent pitches, and blurring of rhythmic identity obscure the imitative relationships. Those elements of camouflage are applied to a putative canonic excerpt in the Agnus of the *Missa Mi-mi*, where the lack of introductory rests and even a change in the interval of imitation *in medias res* blur the canonic imprint even more.

The question mark in the title of Godt's study ("Hidden Canon in the *Missa Mi-Mi?*") is telling, reflecting, as it does, the measure of ambivalence he associates with the listener's perception of Ockeghem's imitation. He depicts in the listener a struggle to ascertain the point to which a contrapuntal texture can take liberties of the sort described and still retain a sense of its being palpably imitative for that listener. The dichotomy inherent in this approach is familiar to us: with one hand, Ockeghem provides the clarifying sense of unity that arises from imitative relationships, while, with the other, he destabilizes the same textures by sowing seeds of doubt regarding their status as examples of genuine imitation. The dichotomy itself is hardly new in the realm of counterpoint. It is present even in strict imitative counterpoint, which projects substantive unity across the texture while complicating the cognitive process for the listener by virtue of the need to track competing independent lines. By weakening the substantive

---

16  Riemann, *Handbuch der Musikgeschichte*, 2/1: 229–30. Riemann's crediting Ockeghem with this achieve-ment, however, may now be seen as a part of an early hyperbolic effort to resuscitate the composer from the unwarranted negative reception described above. His approach took its impetus from a similarly mis-guided, if well-intended, move on the part of Raphael Kiesewetter nearly a century earlier to identify Ockeghem as the leader of the Netherlands School of Composition. In his prize-winning monograph, *Die Verdienste der Niederländer um die Tonkunst* (1829), Kiesewetter advanced this thesis on the foundation of the recently discovered evidence that Ockeghem was born in Hainaut, but he was unduly emboldened to amplify his argument by the attribution of Josquin's *Missa Gaudeamus* to Ockeghem in Vienna 11778. With no reason in 1829 to doubt the accuracy of this attribution, Kiesewetter's leap to acceptance of Josquin's imitative style as having been pioneered by Ockeghem can be readily understood. Further on Kiesewetter's characterization of Ockeghem and the role nationalism may have played in it, see Higgins, "Antoine Busnois," 216–21, and Perkins, "Toward a Typology," 422–23. However wrong-headed Kiesewetter's treatment of Ockeghem may have been in certain respects, he must be credited with having done much to reestablish the composer's centrality.

17  Godt, "An Ockeghem Observation."      18  Zimmermann, "Stilkritische Anmerkungen," 254.

identity among the members of an imitative frame to the extent that he does, Ockeghem shifts the balance of this dichotomy to one that is, in keeping with so many other aspects of his style, markedly less transparent.

Ockeghem's approach to melody appears to be among the most elusive aspects of his music, to judge from the level of subjectivity that permeates various attempts to describe his melodic design. Besseler began the trend when he referred to Ockeghem's music as "an endless, enraptured flow in torrents of sound."[19] Bukofzer saw in Ockeghem's melodies "[t]he desire to create a ceaselessly flowing style."[20] Later writers follow suit, suggesting that Ockeghem is "fond of melodies floating for a long time 'in suspense' before coming to rest on the final cadence,"[21] and that "the individual melodic lines are ample, intense, quasi improvisational."[22] In some ways, these characterizations of Ockeghem's melodic style seem apt. At the same time, they share an anti-rational bias in their common avoidance of any attempt to seek some sort of structural process that governs our composer's melodies.

Consider Example 6.2, a melodic excerpt from *Alma Redemptoris mater* that begins in the superius and is continued in the tenor. Almost any one of the foregoing subjective characterizations fits it. The line does flow circuitously and seemingly unpredictably over a long expanse of time. It changes direction often, randomly mixing stepwise motion and small leaps, and, save for one sequential gesture, it eschews obvious repetitive patterns. There are no internal caesuras. In keeping with the traditional view, there does seem to be something rhapsodic about this melody. Yet, it is not without its source of control: a structural foundation that consists in the simplest of abstract patterns, a descending scale that fills the E octave, carefully and systematically touching upon every scale degree as it winds its way inexorably downward.

Melodies like this one abound in Ockeghem's music. Example 6.3 offers another one, drawn from the opening of *Ave Maria*. At its onset, as we have seen, this motet in the transposed Hypophrygian mode plays with the ambiguities associated with the final and cofinal of the mode (A and D, respectively). Emphasis on A is inherent in the superius melody quoted in the example. In Section 1 of the example, the melody begins on A and moves systematically down the octave, but, significantly, it falls short of reaching the lower A by one scale degree. The foreshortened octave has important implications: it demands to be completed. Section 2 of the excerpt sharply undermines the latter implication by leaping upward. It compounds its failure to provide the implied goal by proceeding to change direction erratically (although it does touch upon

---

19  Besseler, *Altniederländische Motetten*, i: "ein endlos verzücktes Schweben in Klangfluten."
20  Bukofzer, "*Caput*: A Liturgico-Musical Study," 285.
21  Bridgman, "The Age of Ockeghem and Josquin," 256.     22  Reese, *Music in the Renaissance*, 132.

Example 6.2 A descending line in Ockeghem, *Alma Redemptoris mater* (mm. 13–19) that begins in the superius and continues in the tenor (after the edition by Wexler and Plamenac)

Example 6.3 The opening of Ockeghem, *Ave Maria* (after the edition by Wexler and Plamenac)

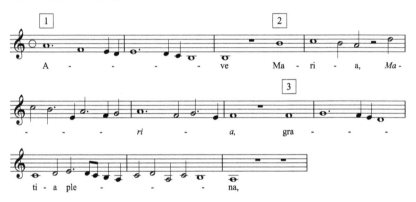

A – albeit in the higher octave – more than once). These multiple deviations intensify the need to fill the incomplete octave. In Section 3, downward motion resumes, suggesting an imminent return to the main business of the phrase: the completion of the foreshortened octave. That need is fulfilled with the emphatically embellished cadence on the low A. Thus, in the realm of melodic design, once again, Ockeghem mixes antithetical elements. The convoluted and circuitous shifts of direction in melodies such as these produce a high level of complexity, but that is reined in by the underlying pattern – so rudimentary in its structure that it will be readily recognized by any listener.

Even when he scales the heights of complexity, as in the double mensuration canons of the *Missa Prolationum*, Ockeghem is not averse to ameliorating the high levels of intricacy with touches of the utmost simplicity. In the opening of the mass, for example, as the members of the two canonic pairs begin together and immediately set about the knotty business of expanding the distance of imitation, the range of harmonic sonorities is highly limited and the harmonic rhythm very slow. The listener who struggles to confront the intricacy of a double mensuration canon can momentarily fall back on the stability inherent in the simplest array of harmonic sonorities (mainly on F). Only when the two canonic pairs stabilize the distance of imitation and thus simplify the texture just a bit does Ockeghem allow the harmony to become more active.

\* \* \*

Thus, with extraordinary consistency and across the gamut of musical style, Ockeghem opts, within a given parameter, to conjoin processes that result in clarity with those that impede that sense of transparency. The deceptive or evaded cadences to which he is so partial, for example, provide the lucidity that accompanies an articulatory gesture, but the quality of elision inherent in such cadences signals continuation, the very opposite of articulation. He laces his compositions with networks of long-range, predictable tonal goals. In the same works, however, he is apt to blur the modality upon which the predictability of the tonal design depends. (This is particularly true in works couched in the Phrygian mode, given its built-in propensity for ambiguity.) Ockeghem's textures gain clarity from the sense of unification provided by imitation, but the imprecise character of that imitation often leaves the listener wondering if it is adequately real to foster a genuine perception of such unity. Long, serpentine melodies abound in Ockeghem's music, inevitably resulting in a sense of unpredictable meandering. But that opaque quality is frequently kept in check when the circuitous melodic design is riveted to the most basic of abstract melodic patterns.

Sowing seeds of clarity into obscurely complex processes obviously introduces a measure of control – one that can serve to prevent the most impenetrable of them from toppling into the abyss of chaos. But the matter is more complicated, for inherent in the stark combination of antithetical processes – of the simple with the complex – is a marked potential for a different level of ambiguity. The listener who confronts this combination can readily wonder about the compositional intent underlying a passage that embodies it. Are the elements of simplicity meant to clarify an otherwise obscure passage, or are the devices of complexity designed to counteract the simpler processes precisely for the purpose of generating instability or tension?

This reaction may be taken as an aural equivalent of the high level of ambiguity we perceive in visual phenomena like reversible figures – the well-known "Duck or Rabbit," for example, generally said to have been introduced as a matter of scientific interest by the psychologist Joseph Jastrow in 1899

Figure 6.1 "Duck or Rabbit"

(Figure 6.1).[23] The analogy holds better if we regard the visual image to be a reversible figure rather than as an optical illusion, as it is often wrongly characterized. The distinction between the two resides in the capacity of expectation to affect our perception of reversible images, which is not true of optical illusions. In one study, the "Duck or Rabbit" figure was shown to two groups of subjects: one on Easter Sunday, the other in October. In October, the majority of subjects identified the drawing as a duck, but on Easter Sunday, the majority saw it as a rabbit. These results are taken to be demonstrative of the influence of motivational expectancy on visual perception.[24]

Looking at the "Duck or Rabbit" figure inevitably gives rise to a sense of instability as our perceptions shift erratically in ways that seem to be beyond our control. Much the same might be said about our reactions to places in Ockeghem's music where he does little to convey whether his conjoining of elements of complexity and clarity is meant to emphasize the one or the other. We do have recourse to our expectations, however. In the face of, say, a series of elided cadences that extends to very great length, we could remain ill at ease with the ambiguity that makes it so hard, on the face of it, to favor the capacity of such cadences either to arrest motion or to continue it. But if we feel that we *need* the articulatory power of a cadence – if we have been led to expect that – the expectation itself can color how we perceive the elided cadences and thereby help resolve the ambiguity inherent in Ockeghem's penchant for building antitheses of this sort into his music. If Ockeghem meant for his music to work in this manner, he would seem to be demanding a more active

23 Jastrow, *Fact and Fable*, 295.    24 Brugger and Brugger, "The Easter Bunny," 577–78.

role on the part of the listener than is characteristically required by the music of his generation, and, in turn, this would constitute an importantly unique attribute of his style and of the ways in which the listener relates to it.

Allusions to the subtlety of Ockeghem's music are made frequently, going all the way back to Guillaume Crétin, who attributes to our composer "tous les secrets de la subtilité."[25] Crétin's phrase admits to a variety of interpretations. If one focuses on *subtilité*, allusions to the *ars subtilior* spring to mind, and a model for understanding Ockeghem's music in light of its complexity emerges. On the other hand, if *secrets* is seen as the operative word in this phrase, then concealment – the ways in which Ockeghem hides his tracks – would appear to be an important key to understanding his music. Ambiguity, however, can also be a component of subtlety, and it results, in ample measure, from the frequency and consistency with which Ockeghem forces clarity and complexity to collide with one another in his music. As we attempt to gain a deeper understanding of the elusively unique style of this composer, probing the role ambiguity of this sort plays in it, along with the ways in which Ockeghem seems to press upon the listener responsibility for its management, would appear to be a promising avenue of approach.

## Bibliography

Bernstein, Lawrence F., "Ockeghem the Mystic: A German Interpretation of the 1920s," in *Johannes Ockeghem*, ed. Vendrix, 811–41

"Ockeghem's *Ave Maria*: Evidence of Structural Cogency," in *From Ciconia to Sweelinck: Donum natalicium Willem Elders*, ed. Albert Clement and Eric Jas, Chloe: Beihefte zum Daphnis 21, Amsterdam, 1994, 75–89

Besseler, Heinrich, ed., *Altniederländische Motetten*, Kassel, 1929

Blackburn, Bonnie J., "Did Ockeghem Listen to Tinctoris?," in *Johannes Ockeghem*, ed. Vendrix, 597–640

Bridgman, Nanie, "The Age of Ockeghem and Josquin," in *Ars Nova and the Renaissancce, 1300–1540*, New Oxford History of Music, 3, ed. Dom Anselm Hughes and Gerald Abraham, London, 1960, 239–302

Brugger, Peter, and Susanne Brugger, "The Easter Bunny in October: Is It Disguised as a Duck?," *Perceptual and Motor Skills* 76 (1993), 577–78

Bukofzer, Manfred F., "*Caput*: A Liturgico-Musical Study," in *Studies in Medieval and Renaissance Music*, New York, 1950, 217–310

Chesney, Kathleen, ed., *Oeuvres poétiques de Guillaume Crétin*, Paris, 1932

Fitch, Fabrice, *Johannes Ockeghem: Masses and Models*, Centre d'Études Supérieures de la Renaissance de Tours: Collection Ricercar 2, Paris, 1997

Godt, Irving, "An Ockeghem Observation: Hidden Canon in the *Missa Mi-Mi?*," *TVNM* 41 (1991), 79–85

25 Chesney, *Oeuvres poétiques de Guillaume Crétin*, 60–73.

Goldberg, Clemens, "Text, Music, and Liturgy in Johannes Ockeghem's Masses," *MD* 44 (1990), 185–231

Higgins, Paula Marie, "Antoine Busnois and Musical Culture in Late Fifteenth-Century France and Burgundy," Ph.D. diss., Princeton University, 1987

Jastrow, Joseph, *Fact and Fable in Psychology*, Boston and New York, 1900

Kiesewetter, Raphael Georg, *Die Verdienste der Niederländer um die Tonkunst*, Amsterdam, 1829

Lindmayr-Brandl, Andrea, "Ockeghem's Motets: Style as an Indicator of Authorship. The Case of *Ut heremita solus* Reconsidered," in *Johannes Ockeghem*, ed. Vendrix, 499–520

Ockeghem, Johannes, *Collected Works*, vol. 3: *Motets and Chansons*, ed. Richard Wexler and Dragan Plamenac, Boston, 1992

   *Masses and Mass Sections*, ed. Jaap van Benthem, Utrecht, 1994

Perkins, Leeman L., "Jean de Ockeghem." *Grove Music Online*, accessed 16 January 2013

   "Ockeghem's *Prenez sur moi*: Reflections on Canons, *Catholica*, and Solmization," *MD* 44 (1990), 119–83

   "Toward a Typology of the 'Renaissance' Chanson," *JM* 6 (1988), 421–47

Reese, Gustave, *Music in the Renaissance*, New York, 1959

Riemann, Hugo, *Handbuch der Musikgeschichte*, 2/1: *Das Zeitalter der Renaissance (bis 1600)*, Leipzig, 1907

Sherr, Richard, "Thoughts on Ockeghem's *Missa De plus en plus*: Anxiety and Proportion in the Late 15th Century," *EM* 38 (2010), 335–46

Sparks, Edgar H., *Cantus Firmus in Mass and Motet, 1420–1520*, Berkeley, 1963

Vendrix, Philippe, ed., *Johannes Ockeghem: Actes du XL^e colloque international d'études humanistes, Tours, 3–8 février 1997*, Paris, 1998

Zarlino, Gioseffo, *The Art of Counterpoint: Part Three of* Le Istitutioni harmoniche, *1558*, trans. Guy A. Marco and Claude V. Palisca, New Haven, 1976

Zimmermann, Reiner, "Stilkritische Anmerkungen zum Werk Ockeghems," *AfMw* 22 (1965), 248–71

# 7

# Josquin and epistemology

JESSE RODIN

*For Joshua Rifkin*

To study Josquin des Prez is to stand at the edge of an epistemological precipice. So much about his life and works eludes us that any attempt to characterize this composer must at some level contend with questions about how we know what we know – in particular, how we negotiate the often hazy lines between fact and fiction, deduction and conjecture, and certainty and belief. Since as long ago as the sixteenth century, writers on Josquin have had to confront basic questions at every turn: What pieces did he write? Where was he when? Who *was* Josquin?[1] In the past two decades a series of archival discoveries has reshaped our understanding of Josquin's career, in part by filling in some long-standing gaps. But these findings also ask us to take stock – to interrogate underlying assumptions by bringing epistemological questions to the surface. This isn't just a matter of revisiting older literature with an eye toward ideas that have been superseded; it's also about openly acknowledging all we don't know so as to make the most of what we do.

## Problems

I suggest that research on Josquin has been stymied by five fundamental problems:

### Biographical lacunae

Biographical information tends to be sparse whenever a fifteenth-century musician is concerned – but in all of Western music there is no composer as famous as Josquin about whom we possess so little hard evidence. Recently documents have to come to light that have clarified our picture of Josquin's biography, in part by uncoupling Josquin des Prez from several other contemporary musicians with similar names.[2] But while these new findings have brought us closer to the "real" Josquin, they haven't filled in every gap; in

---

1 For the latter question see Elders, "Who Was Josquin?," and Wegman, "Who Was Josquin?"
2 An immensely useful summary of the documentary evidence appears in Fallows, *Josquin*, 353–409. Cf. Osthoff, *Josquin Desprez* for the picture as it was understood in 1965.

Table 7.1 *Josquin's biography*

| ca. 1450 | Birth, possibly in or near St. Sauveur |
|---|---|
| ?–1466 | Choirboy at the church of St. Géry, Cambrai[a] |
| 1475–78 | In the employ of Duke René of Anjou (Aix-en-Provence; probably until 1480) |
| 1483 | In Condé-sur-l'Escaut to claim an inheritance |
| 1484–85 | In the employ of Cardinal Ascanio Sforza in Milan and Rome |
| 1489 | Ducal singer in Milan (Jan.–Feb.) |
| 1489–94 | Singer in the Sistine Chapel choir, Rome (possibly past 1494) |
| 1494 | Receives wine from chapter of St. Géry, Cambrai (Aug.–Sept.) |
| 1499, 1501 | Pair of visits to the city of Troyes (southeast of Paris) |
| 1503 | In Lyon with the Ferrarese singer Coglia (a.k.a. Girolamo da Sestola) |
| 1503–4 | "Maestro de capella" for Duke Ercole I d'Este in Ferrara |
| 1504–21 | Canon and provost at the collegiate church of Notre Dame, Condé-sur-l'Escaut |
| 1521 | Death, Condé-sur-l'Escaut |

[a] This assumes that "Gossequin de Condé" is indeed Josquin des Prez, which is very likely but not certain.

fact, they've created some new ones.[3] Taking a hard-nosed view of the evidence, the main facts of Josquin's biography are hardly plentiful (see Table 7.1).

Several lacunae remain, most notably in the periods 1480–83, 1485–89, and 1495–1503. These gaps fall smack in the middle of Josquin's career; they encompass most of the years between his thirtieth birthday, by which time one can surmise he had already done at least some composing, and his employment in Ferrara at around age 53. Not knowing where Josquin was during these years is an enormous impediment to telling a convincing story about his life and works. And while several hypotheses have been put forward – a sojourn in Hungary, employment in the French royal court during the reigns of Louis XI and/or Louis XII, and a trip to Spain with the Burgundian Duke Philip the Fair – a lack of documentation makes building an argument based on one of these possibilities a bit like trying to balance the Jack of Clubs on a pair of wobbly Sixes.

### Canonical conundrums

The best-known and most widely written about problem in Josquin research concerns his canon of works.[4] This issue has been on the scholarly radar since at

3  We now know that Josquin was not in Milan 1459–84, nor in Rome 1486–89.
4  The title of this section echoes Blackburn, "Canonic Conundrums."

least the 1960s and has been a matter of central concern for the past twenty-five years.[5] The main difficulties are that a large number of works attributed to Josquin also circulate with ascriptions to other composers, and that many works without conflicting attributions survive in sources that are untrustworthy or date from after the composer's death (or both). All told at least 340 pieces circulated with ascriptions to Josquin between ca. 1488 and the early seventeenth century.

Josquin scholars have rightly noted that publishers stood to gain financially by placing the composer's name on pieces of doubtful attribution – but this is just one of the reasons we find ourselves in the present mess. In many cases titular confusion may be to blame. The *Missa Une musque de Biscaye*, for instance, may have garnered an attribution to Josquin because someone mixed it up with the composer's securely attributed song of the same name.[6] Similarly, Josquin's fairly well attributed *De profundis clamavi* (NJE 15.13, *a 5*) may have misled scribes and printers into attributing three other settings of this text to him (NJE 15.11, 15.12, and 15.14).[7] In all likelihood a different sort of carelessness lies behind several other dubious attributions. To take but one example: in the Spanish keyboard tablature of Gonçalo de Vaena, *Arte novamente inventada* (Lisbon, 1540), a portion of Josquin's *Missa Sine nomine* is erroneously labeled *ercules* (as in the *Missa Hercules dux Ferrarie*), while the In nomine of the *Missa Gaudeamus* is titled "Pleni sunt"; this sort of mislabeling, rather than anything substantive, is probably also the best explanation for why the latter is attributed to "Obrec."[8] More interesting are situations in which, ca. 1520–60, music publishers may have been handed works circulating anonymously that looked to be in an older style. In some cases they may have observed musical features that reminded them of Josquin; in others Josquin may simply have been the only composer from that older generation whose music they knew; in still others, attaching Josquin's name may have been a way of raising a piece's status. In all such cases the ascriptions we find could well represent educated guesses. Misattributions might also have arisen as the result of hearsay, of the type "I heard Master Glareanus say this is a work by Josquin

---

5 See Kerman, "A Profile for American Musicology," 66, and Lowinsky, "Character and Purposes of American Musicology," 227–28. By the 1980s it made sense to hold an international conference on problems of attribution: see *Proceedings of the International Josquin Symposium Utrecht 1986*, ed. Elders and de Haen.

6 Bonnie Blackburn makes this suggestion in "Masses on Popular Songs," 72–73. Wegman, "Who Was Josquin?," 30–33, argues that the mass "is one of the most solidly attested in the Josquin canon." But cf. Benthem, "Une mousse de Biscaye," and Rifkin, "Masses and Evidence," both of whom show that the sources for this mass derive from a common parent – and, by extension, from a single attribution.

7 One of these (NJE 15.14) is almost surely by Senfl; another may be by Champion (NJE 15.12). On the latter see Macey, "Josquin and Champion."

8 See the NJE 11, Critical Commentary (Lewis Lockwood), 30–31.

des Prez." The likelihood of such situations arising would naturally be greater in places where Josquin's music had not been known during his lifetime; for this reason one finds a cluster of dubious attributions in German-speaking lands, where a kind of Josquin mania seems to have taken hold beginning around 1530.[9]

Part of the reason the source situation for Josquin's music is so dire is that precious few manuscripts of sacred music survive from late fifteenth-century France. This problem affects several composers, among them Pierre de La Rue and Jean Mouton; if we were to tell a history based on northern sources alone, we'd be forced to posit that all these composers burst onto the scene in the early sixteenth century. In Josquin's case we know for a fact that this isn't so – and yet, even taking into account Italian manuscripts, relatively few compositions bearing his name apparently circulated before 1500. Moreover, it is precisely in the years just after 1500 when, as a result of Josquin's rising status, we begin to find increasing numbers of questionable attributions. To put the problem too strongly: in the years before 1500 little music by Josquin survives; after 1500 much of what survives is questionable.

### A Swiss-cheese chronology

The problem of lost fifteenth-century northern sources for Josquin's music is double-edged. Not only does it make questions of authenticity harder to sort out; it also hampers our ability to construct a chronology of the composer's works. The earliest extant source for Josquin's music may date from as late as 1485.[10] Even ca. 1490, by which time Josquin was about forty years old, the surviving sources contain only a tiny handful of works. This makes it all but impossible to construct a convincing chronology for the early part of Josquin's career.[11] After 1490 the number of surviving sources increases to the point where a tentative chronology is possible, but even here matters are not straightforward, since the paucity of early manuscripts makes it tempting to date pieces earlier, sometimes much earlier, than their first appearance in the sources.[12] Few such arguments can withstand scrutiny – but neither can one simply assume that the surviving sources happen to present an accurate chronological picture.[13]

Making matters worse, there are hardly any works for which external evidence makes firm dates possible. Only a handful of pieces can be dated

---

9 On Josquin's German reception see Schlagel, "The *Liber selectarum cantionem*," and the literature cited there.
10 Rifkin, "Munich, Milan, and a Marian Motet," 313–32.
11 See Rodin, *Josquin's Rome*, ch. 1.
12 Joshua Rifkin wrestles with this problem in "Musste Josquin Josquin werden?"
13 This is true in part because of the unavoidable tendency to date the repertory on the basis of the sources and the sources on the basis of the repertory they contain.

with near certainty: *Miserere mei, Deus* and, in all likelihood, *Virgo salutiferi* date from Josquin's tenure in Ferrara (1503–4), while *Plus nulz regretz* can be tied to celebrations for the Treaty of Calais in 1508. Beyond this one can point to *Ave Maria … virgo serena*, which must have existed by 1485; about nine sacred pieces that can be associated with Josquin's tenure in the papal chapel; and the lament for Ockeghem's death (*Nymphes des bois/Requiem*), which has a *terminus post quem* of 1497. This is hardly enough evidence upon which to base a full-scale chronology.

## A sui generis *reception*

Ironically, one of the greatest impediments to accessing the historical Josquin is the extraordinary reception he enjoyed after his death. Thanks in large part to the novel technology of music printing, Josquin is the first composer whose reputation far outlasted his own lifetime.[14] And yet it is difficult to assess his contemporary fame, particularly in the years before 1500.[15] Not only did Josquin's music fail to achieve wide circulation before the turn of the sixteenth century, but until that time there is little reason to believe he was held in higher esteem than his contemporaries. The first unmistakable evidence of Josquin's preeminence is the 1502 publication of Ottaviano Petrucci's *Misse Josquin*.[16] This volume, containing five unquestionably authentic masses, constitutes the first-ever single-author music print. Petrucci also used a piece by Josquin to introduce each of his first three motet books (1502, 1503, and 1504), and subsequently devoted two additional volumes to Josquin's masses (1505 and 1514). More generally, the early decades of the sixteenth century witnessed an explosion in the circulation of Josquin's music, and a concomitant increase in references to Josquin's stature. Among the earliest and best known is a letter dated August 1502 in which Girolamo da Sestola ("il Coglia"), agent for Duke Ercole I d'Este, writes that "by having Josquin [rather than Isaac] in our chapel I want to place a crown upon this chapel of ours."[17]

It was only after 1521 that the composer's reputation reached its pinnacle. The ensuing decades witnessed dozens of new compositions based on Josquin's songs and motets, including a handful of *si placet* parts added as late as the early seventeenth century. Over the same period Josquin's best-known works continued to be copied, printed, and cited by theorists. Equally significant are the many anecdotes attesting to Josquin's talents that circulated

---

14 On Josquin's posthumous reception see principally Owens, "Music Historiography"; Owens, "How Josquin Became Josquin"; Wegman, "And Josquin Laughed"; and Kirkman, "From Humanism to Enlightenment." References to further literature appear in Kirkman's essay.
15 Rodin, "When Josquin Became Josquin."     16 See Fallows, *Josquin*, 1–7.
17 See Lewis Lockwood, "Josquin at Ferrara," 113.

Table 7.2 *Josquin's most widely disseminated music*

| Piece | Voices | MSS | Prints | Tablatures | Treatises | Total sources |
|---|---|---|---|---|---|---|
| *Missa De beata virgine* | 4–5 | 44 | 8 | 17 | 2 | 71 |
| *Benedicta es celorum regina* | 6 | 27 | 9 | 24 | 5 | 65 |
| *Stabat mater* | 5 | 26 | 8 | 19 | 1 | 54 |
| *Preter rerum seriem* | 6 | 33 | 7 | 9 | 2 | 51 |
| *Missa L'homme armé super voces musicales* | 4 | 18 | 7 | 6 | 12 | 43 |
| Other music surviving in eight or more printed books | | | | | | |
| *Inviolata, integra et casta es, Maria* | 5 | 15 | 8 | 5 | – | 28 |
| *Miserere mei, Deus* | 5 | 10 | 8 | 2 | – | 20 |

throughout the sixteenth century, the apotheosis of which is Glareanus's *Dodecachordon* of 1547. This abundance of evidence could seem like a treasure trove, but in fact it makes the project of describing the historical Josquin harder, not easier. As Rob Wegman has noted, none of the posthumous stories about Josquin can be taken at face value; while they certainly reflect the "force of opinion," they may not (and in several cases cannot) accurately describe Josquin's words and deeds.[18] As concerns the dissemination of Josquin's music the picture is equally murky. Not only were some of his most significant compositions largely forgotten, but many of the pieces that carried his name are now thought to be by other composers. Even among his securely attributed works, it is striking how the sixteenth century's view of Josquin concentrated around five- and six-voice sacred music, much of which would appear to date from late in his career, when these scorings became increasingly common. Josquin's biggest hit was his *Missa De beata virgine*, all or portions of which survive in no fewer than seventy-one sources. As Table 7.2 shows, the next most popular pieces were *Benedicta es celorum regina*, *Stabat mater*, *Preter rerum seriem*, and, thanks in part to citations by music theorists, the *Missa L'homme armé super voces musicales*. None of Josquin's songs apparently circulated as widely (his most popular songs are *Plus nulz regretz*, *Adieu mes amours*, and the perhaps dubious *Mille regretz*, which survive in twenty-nine, twenty-six, and twenty-five sources, respectively). Taking all of this together, the picture of the

18  Wegman, "Who Was Josquin?," 23 ff.

composer that emerges from his sixteenth-century reception is highly skewed, thanks both to stylized accounts of his genius and the idiosyncratic corpus of works that came to represent his output and style.

These problems persist right up to the present. Because eighteenth- and nineteenth-century music historians were forced to rely heavily on Glareanus and late printed sources, their accounts are littered with dubious claims about Josquin's personality and oriented toward works of questionable attribution. In the last fifty years scholars have begun to take a more critical approach to posthumous witnesses; even so, old habits of thought die hard.

### An ill-defined lingua franca

In a funny way this last problem is the hardest of all, though it has received by far the least attention. The literature includes many discussions of individual pieces and considerable praise of Josquin's compositional skill. But with a handful of exceptions, we have not yet figured out what makes Josquin's music different from that of Henricus Isaac, Pierre de La Rue, or Loyset Compère. More worrying still, only a handful of Josquin's contemporaries have benefited from studies that show what makes *their* music distinct. As such it is remarkably difficult to answer two central questions: With respect to the so-called Josquin generation, how ought one to characterize the musical *lingua franca*? And to what extent is Josquin unique?

One impediment to answering these questions is the tendency of writers since Ambros to highlight two features of Josquin's style: his development of a musical language closely tied to the meaning and structure of the text, in which syllabic motives project the words clearly and expressively; and a preference for fully imitative textures, with all voices accorded equal importance. While neither of these features is necessarily uncharacteristic of the composer, their significance has been overemphasized, in part because many of the pieces from which this view was developed have either been redated or deattributed.

*Ave Maria … virgo serena* illustrates the problem.[19] In its frequent use of imitation, paired homorhythmic duos, regular full-stop cadences, texture changes, and largely syllabic declamation, this early motet, with its *terminus ante quem* of 1485, already exhibits features heretofore associated with Josquin's mature style; it can thus reasonably be concluded that these techniques were part of Josquin's compositional toolbox from the beginning. And yet these very features are in fact relatively uncommon in Josquin's securely attributed output, particularly in pieces that probably date from the 1480s and 1490s. Beginning around the turn of the sixteenth century, moreover,

---

19 On *Ave Maria* see the essay by John Milsom in this volume (Ch. 11).

these techniques came to be used widely, suggesting that they are not an ideal yardstick with which to measure distinctive elements of Josquin's style. Indeed, looking across the whole of Josquin's securely attributed music, there are rather few pieces that show the kind of sensitivity to text-setting for which the composer is renowned. And pervasive imitation, really an innovation of Nicolas Gombert and his contemporaries, is nowhere to be found in Josquin's securely attributed output – save *Ave Maria . . . virgo serena*, that is.[20] As such there is a fair amount of ground-clearing that has to happen before it is possible even to begin defining Josquin's style against the *lingua franca*.

## Guilty until proven innocent

By now the reader may be ready to throw up her hands. With so many unknowns, is there any point in even trying to pursue the historical Josquin? Is this field not doomed to circle in a morass of conjecture and uncertainty? The severity of these problems has made it enormously difficult to look them squarely in the eye. Instead writings on Josquin are characterized by two prevailing approaches. The first and by far more common has been to do what we do when we write about Machaut, Mozart, or Mahler: tell as richly textured a story as possible. For the composers just mentioned this strategy works just fine, give or take; for Josquin, telling a richly textured story means massively underestimating uncertainty. This can be observed in myriad ways: the thoroughness with which scholars have sought to characterize Josquin's life and works; the tendency to let pieces into the canon on the basis of flimsy stylistic evidence and to exclude pieces on the basis of equally dubious criteria (e.g., the presence of parallel fifths); and the common practice of using pieces of doubtful authenticity as a yardstick against which to measure pieces of equally dubious authenticity.[21] The twin, mutually reinforcing dangers of circularity and overinterpretation loom large.

Recently several scholars have taken a different approach that is at once sensitive to these methodological dangers and critical of authenticity-centered scholarship. This argument suggests we can't know the historical Josquin – or that, in light of his unusually rich posthumous reception, the historical Josquin isn't worth knowing.[22] To the extent that they cause us to interrogate unexamined assumptions, these studies are invaluable. But they tend to conflate the issues of paltry source material and unsound methodologies; this, in turn, causes them to make more of the uncertainties surrounding Josquin's life and works

---

20 Cf. the contributions by Milsom and Cummings and Schubert in this volume (Ch. 11 and Ch. 12).
21 On these dangers see principally Rifkin, "Problems of Authorship" and "A Singer Named Josquin."
22 See Wegman, "And Josquin Laughed"; Wegman, "Who Was Josquin?"; Higgins, "The Apotheosis of Josquin des Prez"; and Wegman, "The Other Josquin."

than is reasonable. In a similar vein, it has become fashionable in some circles to spend more time disavowing questions of attribution – "not that it matters who wrote it" – than actually thinking about them. Just because our field has expanded fruitfully in new directions doesn't mean that "old" problems ought now to be framed as passé or uninteresting. The questions we ask must be conditioned by the nature of the material under consideration. In Josquin research, matters of basic historical fact, not least in the realm of attribution, have not been properly controlled. Imagine for a moment trying to write about the *Ring* cycle without knowing whether it was composed by Wagner or Verdi. That comparison may be a touch extreme – but while authorship will always be a metaphor, it's a remarkably powerful metaphor.[23] We ignore it at our peril.

How, then, to move forward? As concerns the historical Josquin, one need not choose between proceeding on shaky terrain and giving up entirely. There is a third option: to treat gaps in our knowledge as an opportunity to confront methodological, historiographical, and epistemological problems with candor. Only by airing our dirty laundry can we avoid fuzzy thinking, on the one hand, and spurious attacks, on the other. This means acknowledging with unprecedented openness the uncertainties that swirl around this composer while also bringing to bear the full force of our intellectual capacities in order to negotiate the line between what we know and what we don't know. In an essay with "epistemology" in the title, some might expect me to wax philosophical at this stage, but in fact I have a deeply practical sort of epistemology in mind. There are no "unassailable," "neutral," or "objective" facts of history – but when searching for information about a historical figure, there are varieties of evidence we ought to take more seriously than others. A pay record that clearly gives a composer's full name is as close to a smoking gun as we can hope for in this period; the same holds true for a legal document prepared according to strict standards of accuracy; a piece whose text names its dedicatee; a manuscript containing a work copied while its composer was in residence in that institution; or, where attribution is concerned, a source situation in which we find stemmatically independent ascriptions from within a composer's lifetime. The documentary evidence surrounding Josquin is not littered with such smoking guns, but we do have several.

More than a quarter-century ago, Joshua Rifkin challenged scholars to consider works by Josquin guilty until proven innocent.[24] I wish to propose that we approach all aspects of research on the historical Josquin with a guilty-until-proven-innocent epistemology. To do so is to apply ourselves, in

---

23 I owe this notion to Joshua Rifkin (personal communication).
24 Rifkin, "Problems of Authorship," 46.

Descartes's words, "sincerely and without reservation to the general demolition of [our former] opinions."[25] This means identifying a bedrock of material, however modest, about which we can be all but certain, and treating everything else with suspicion. Some might bristle at a mode of scholarly inquiry that resonates with the logic of the Spanish Inquisition – but as Rifkin noted, what "may make for humane justice . . . also makes for weak scholarship."[26]

## From an evidentiary bedrock to a stylistic picture

The biographical details sketched in Table 7.1 can serve as a starting point, as can the most fundamental sorts of information about the institutions in which Josquin worked, the musicians with whom he associated, and the broader social, cultural, and political developments of his age. Since evidence concerning Josquin's biography, his contemporary reputation, and the chronology of his works is thin on the ground, we stand to make the most headway by studying his securely attributed works. The only way to identify these is to approach all the roughly 340 pieces ascribed to him as if they were spurious, and to let pieces back into the canon only if they meet the most rigorous criteria of source-based evidence. (Style analysis can be useful, too, but because this methodology is inherently comparative, it can be engaged only once a core canon has been identified.) Adopting this approach yields, by my count, a laughable number of securely attributed works: fifty-one (see the Appendix). Laughable, perhaps, but nonetheless very useful, since this core group comprises quite a lot of music: twelve masses, one mass section, twenty-three motets, and fifteen songs. We might commune with these fifty-one works – sing them, listen to them, memorize them, study their sources and contexts, and analyze them against a backdrop of hundreds of other works by Josquin's contemporaries. In doing so we don't have to forget about the other 289 pieces that bear Josquin's name; we can keep the latter in play, as it were, by repeatedly testing how they fit with an emerging story about the core group (not to mention how they fit with other stories about other groups of works).[27]

    While this is not the place to attempt a full characterization of Josquin's compositional style, I would like to use these fifty-one extremely secure works – and no others – as the basis for a few thoughts about what makes his music special. In recent years scholars have begun to converge around the notion

25  See *The Philosophical Writings of Descartes*, 2:12.
26  Rifkin, "Problems of Authorship," 46–47. Cf. Kelly, "Inquisition and the Prosecution of Heresy," 444, 446, and 449–50.
27  On the basis of comparative analysis, I would suggest that in most cases it is in fact not so very difficult to tell genuine works from spurious ones. One attempt to keep the latter in play is the Josquin Research Project (josquin.stanford.edu), which makes fully searchable and browsable all the music attributed to Josquin as well as an ever-growing corpus of fifteenth- and sixteenth-century music.

that Josquin, more than anyone else of his generation, revels in repetition. He likes building musical surfaces out of short, catchy gestures piled on top of one another, an approach that has been described with terms like "motivicity," "interlocks," and "conspicuous repetition."[28] In some cases these surfaces reveal enormously sophisticated technical ability; in others they are dead simple. All such passages betray what I have called Josquin's obsessive compositional personality: an interest in reining in the potentially dizzying melodic heterogeneity afforded by several intertwining voices and, often, building energy through an intense concentration of contrapuntal resources. This extends to Josquin's interest in ostinato, exact canon, and stretto *fuga*. It even extends to his melodic manner: Josquin favors melodic lines that reach up to a high note, then attack that note several times in close succession before relaxing into a cadence.

The opening of the Agnus Dei from the *Missa La sol fa re mi*, while in certain respects an extreme example of Josquin's obsessiveness, is instructive (see Example 7.1).[29] This mass is famously based on a five-note ostinato that is stated about 250 times over the course of five movements. In the Agnus Dei Josquin begins by showing off his combinative powers. It's not simply that one finds eight statements of the motto in the opening eleven bars. It's also that (see Figure 7.1 and Example 7.1): (1) in measures 1–5 Josquin combines "la sol fa re mi" with itself in six different ways; (2) in measures 3–4 all voices but the bassus sing nothing but the ostinato; (3) in measures 6–9 the altus sings two slightly decorated retrograde statements of the motto that fit together with forward statements in the superius and tenor; and (4) in those same measures the bassus reiterates a motive related to the music of measures 2–3, contributing to a musical surface animated by subtle changes to repeating patterns. Equally extraordinary is that, over the course of this mass section, Josquin recapitulates every two-voice "interlock" (that is, every two-voice counterpointing of "la sol fa re mi" with itself) that has been presented throughout the mass while also adding two new ones, for a total of nine unique combinations.

This complexity is inaudible. Nonetheless Josquin gives us plenty we *can* hear. His endless riffing on "la sol fa re mi" – even discounting retrograde statements, there is an average of nearly one statement per measure – produces a densely packed musical surface, with motives and countermotives appearing in ever-changing combinations. We can also hear how Josquin builds up a whole that exceeds the sum of its parts. This is evident in a sophisticated registral plan,

---

28 See Rifkin, "Motivik – Konstruktivismus – Humanismus"; Rifkin, "Miracles, Motivicity, and Mannerism"; Milsom, "Crecquillon, Clemens, and Four-Voice *Fuga*"; Milsom, "Analyzing Josquin"; Milsom, "Josquin des Prez and the Combinative Impulse"; Rodin, "When in Rome," 343–53 and Rodin, *Josquin's Rome*, ch. 2. On Josquin's use of *fuga* see also Urquhart, "Canon, Partial Signatures, and 'Musica Ficta'."
29 See the discussion in Blackburn, "Masses on Popular Songs," 80–81.

Example 7.1 Ostinato statements in Josquin, *Missa La sol fa re mi*, Agnus Dei I/
III, mm. 1–9. Dashed boxes indicate retrograde statements

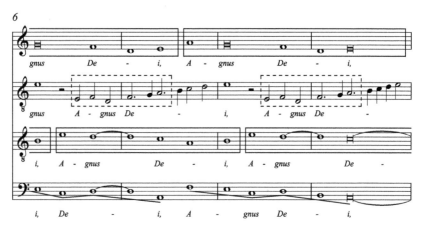

wherein the superius sings its highest note, *a′*, eleven times in measures 1–20 only
to exceed it in a stunning passage in measures 20–23 (similar processes govern the
altus and tenor). It is also evident in Josquin's approach to parameters like texture,
rhythmic activity, and cadential arrivals. To take just the last of these: while at the
beginning of this movement he prepares a series of "soft" arrivals to A, C, E, E,
and A, for a traditional cadence one must wait until the final measure.

Josquin's broad interest in repetitive structures and combinative procedures
can be seen in hundreds of other passages across his output. A few (less rigorous)
examples can be taken as representative: at the text "Zorobabel" in *Liber generationis*, a short, assertive duo, composed in invertible counterpoint, appears six

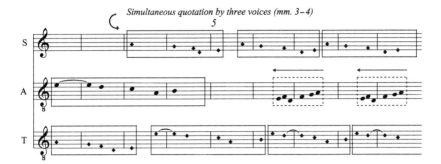

Figure 7.1 Ostinato statements in Josquin, *Missa La sol fa re mi*, Agnus Dei I/III, mm. 1–9. Dashed boxes indicate retrograde statements

times in a row in four different transpositions; at the opening of the canonic *Inviolata, integra et casta es, Maria* (*a 5*), the superius sweeps down a tenth in stepwise motion, then repeats the gesture twice in immediate succession with the bassus moving in parallel tenths; a simple cadential motive accounts for almost every note of the lighthearted (if single-minded) *Une musque de Biscaye*, based on a canon at the fourth between the upper voices; at the text "procedit" in the Credo of the *Missa Gaudeamus*, Josquin produces music of astonishing eloquence by causing a turning figure derived from the cantus firmus to flood a reduced texture of superius, altus, and tenor, all at the top of their respective ranges;[30] and the Agnus Dei III of the *Missa L'homme armé super voces musicales* incorporates a series of ostinato-like figures in the lower voices beneath the sustained pitches of the *L'homme armé* melody in the superius.[31] This contrapuntally virtuosic mass illustrates Josquin's tendency to set himself one challenge after another: it incorporates no fewer than seven mensuration canons and is based on a cantus firmus at modal odds with the other voices.[32]

One could fill a volume with discussions of the varied uses to which Josquin puts repetition. But rather than proceed in this vein, it might be worth mentioning several sides of his compositional personality that have surfaced only occasionally in the literature. Josquin now and then produces stunning harmonic shifts, such as the surprising turn near the end of *Faulte d'argent* (at the last statement of "pour argent se reveille").[33] He sometimes concocts elegant chains of syncopations, as in an extraordinary passage in *Gaude virgo*

---

30  See Planchart, "Masses on Plainsong Cantus Firmi," 103.
31  See Rodin, "Finishing Josquin's 'Unfinished' Mass," 438–41.
32  See Rodin, *Josquin's Rome*, ch. 6.
33  See Bernstein, "A Canonic Chanson" and "Chansons for Five and Six Voices," 396–400. Josquin also uses cross-relations to great effect. An extraordinary (if not uncontroversial) example is discussed in Urquhart, "An Accidental Flat." See also Macey, "An Expressive Detail."

featuring stretto *fuga* (beginning at the text "Gaude Christo ascendente"). In *Memor esto* he uses a fortuitous textual repetition (the opening words return at the end) as an excuse for a full-scale "recapitulation," complete with diminution of the piece's opening motive.[34] At times Josquin writes with great weight and intensity, as in the magisterial opening of *Preter rerum seriem*, built on stately chains of parallel thirds against cantus-firmus-derived drones.[35] Elsewhere he can be downright frivolous, as in the jumpy melodies of *Bergerette savoysienne*. He is capable of extraordinary conclusions, as in the Credos of the masses *La sol fa re mi, L'homme armé sexti toni, Gaudeamus, Malheur me bat, Faisant regretz,* and *Sine nomine,* each of which prepares its climax in a unique way.[36] Josquin at times introduces sudden pauses, as in an arrival on E♭ during the Christe of the *Missa Fortuna desperata* or, more subtly, at the words "dum videbat" in the five-voice *Stabat mater/Comme femme,* where the free voices fleetingly drop out, calling attention to the tenor's slow progress.[37] And one finds passages whose expressive aims apparently lack any precedent, as in the surprising use of musical interruption – strict quotations from Ockeghem's *D'ung aultre amer* are twice stopped dead in their tracks – in the *secunda pars* of *Tu solus*.[38] Lest all this seem like a puff piece, I'll add that Josquin also writes bad (some might say "less successful") pieces now and then. Among the securely attributed works a prominent example is the Credo *De tous biens playne,* in which Josquin's self-imposed task of quoting two preexisting melodies at the same time apparently taxed his creative energies.[39]

* * *

Stepping back from these examples, it is striking how rich a portrait of Josquin it is possible to paint from only fifty-one works. To do so is not to give up on the other 289; on the contrary, those 289 cry out for rigorous comparative analysis, as do hundreds of works by Josquin's contemporaries. One must begin by acknowledging, on the one hand, that fifty-one pieces represent less than what Josquin actually composed. On the other, to begin with fifty-one is to accept that "what Josquin actually composed" is and will always be out of reach – and that our task is to keep reaching. This extends in several directions: the cultural contexts of Josquin's music, the circumstances of his life, his relationships with other musicians, even his political views or religious beliefs. No matter which of these

---

34 See Macey, "Josquin as Classic," 32, and Fallows, *Josquin,* 94.
35 See Milsom, "Motets for Five or More Voices," 290–93, and Fallows, *Josquin,* 285–88.
36 All but two of these culminate in a striking post-cadential extension. On Josquin's use of this procedure, including a discussion of how his practice differs from that of his contemporaries, see Tuan, "Beyond the Cadence."
37 I owe this observation to Victoria Chang.    38 See Fallows, *Josquin,* 130–31.
39 See Sherr, "Mass Sections," 219–23, esp. 220 n. 25; and Rodin, *Josquin's Rome,* 85–93.

avenues we explore, we are certain to encounter fierce methodological resistance. Indeed this is the challenge Josquin poses, perhaps more acutely than any other figure in the history of Western music: to contextualize with respect to the evidence we have rather than the evidence we wish we had; to tell a richly textured story without falling into storytelling; and to maintain high evidentiary standards without neglecting our historical imaginations. All of this can be extremely frustrating. It can also be wonderful, since at every turn we are forced to think, compare, play devil's advocate, argue, and, if we've done our job, think again, with full knowledge that few questions are likely ever to be "settled." To approach Josquin in this rigorous, open-ended fashion is to embrace the Mishnaic proverb:

לא עליך המלאכה לגמור, ולא אתה בן חורין להבטל ממנה.

It is not incumbent upon you to finish the work, but neither are you free to desist from it.       –Rabbi Tarfon, *Pirkei Avot* (Ethics of the Fathers), 2:16

# Appendix
## Fifty-one works of extremely secure attribution

### Masses

*Ave maris stella, De beata virgine, Faisant regretz, Fortuna desperata, Gaudeamus, Hercules dux Ferrarie, L'homme armé sexti toni, L'homme armé super voces musicales, La sol fa re mi, Malheur me bat, Pange lingua, Sine nomine* [recte *Ad fugam*] (NJE 12.2)

### Mass movement

Credo *De tous biens plaine*

### Motets and other sacred works a 3–4

*Alma Redemptoris mater/Ave regina celorum, Ave Maria ... virgo serena, Monstra te esse matrem, Domine non secundum peccata nostra, Ecce tu pulchra es, Gaude virgo, Honor decus imperium, Liber generationis, Memor esto verbi tui, Missus est Gabriel angelus, O admirabile commercium, Tu solus qui facis mirabilia*

### Motets a 5–6

*Benedicta es celorum regina, Huc me sydereo/Plangent eum, Illibata Dei virgo nutrix/La mi la, Inviolata integra et casta, Miserere mei Deus, O virgo prudentissima/Beata mater, Pater noster, Salve regina* (NJE 25.5), *Preter rerum seriem, Stabat mater/Comme femme, Virgo salutiferi/Ave Maria*

*Songs* a 3–4

*Adieu mes amours, Bergerette savoysienne, Comment peult avoir joye, Entrée suis en grant pensée* (NJE 27.8), *Entré je suis* (NJE 28.14), *Ile fantazies de Joskin, Plus nulz regretz, Que vous madame/In pace, Scaramella, Une musque de Biscaye*

*Songs* a 5–6

*Faulte d'argent, Nymphes des bois/Requiem, Nimphes nappés/Circumdederunt me, Petite camusette, Se congié prens* (NJE 30.11)

# Bibliography

Benthem, Jaap van, "Was 'Une mousse de Biscaye' Really Appreciated by L'ami Baudichon?," *Muziek & Wetenschap* 1 (1991), 175–94

Bernstein, Lawrence F., "A Canonic Chanson in a German Manuscript: *Faulte d'argent* and Josquin's Approach to the Chanson for Five Voices," in *Von Isaac bis Bach: Studien zur älteren deutschen Musikgeschichte: Festschrift Martin Just zum 60. Geburtstag*, ed. Frank Heidlberger *et al.*, Kassel, 1991, 53–71

"Chansons for Five and Six Voices," in *The Josquin Companion*, ed. Sherr, 393–422

Blackburn, Bonnie J., "Canonic Conundrums: The Singer's Petrucci," *BJhM* 25 (2001), 53–69

"Masses on Popular Songs and Solmization Syllables," in *The Josquin Companion*, ed. Sherr, 51–87

Descartes, René, *The Philosophical Writings of Descartes*, trans. John Cottingham *et al.*, 3 vols., Cambridge, 1984–91

Elders, Willem, "Who Was Josquin?," in *Proceedings of the International Josquin Symposium Utrecht 1986*, ed. Elders and de Haen, 1–14

and Frits de Haen, eds. *Proceedings of the International Josquin Symposium Utrecht 1986*, Utrecht, 1991

Fallows, David, *Josquin*, Turnhout, 2009

Higgins, Paula, "The Apotheosis of Josquin des Prez and Other Mythologies of Musical Genius," *JAMS* 57 (2004), 443–510

Josquin des Prez, *New Edition of the Collected Works (New Josquin Edition)*, 30 vols., Utrecht, 1987–

Kelly, Henry Ansgar, "Inquisition and the Prosecution of Heresy: Misconceptions and Abuses," *Church History* 58 (1989), 439–51

Kerman, Joseph, "A Profile for American Musicology," *JAMS* 18 (1965), 61–69

Kirkman, Andrew, "From Humanism to Enlightenment: Reinventing Josquin," *JM* 17 (1999), 441–58

Lockwood, Lewis, "Josquin at Ferrara: New Documents and Letters," in *Josquin des Prez: Proceedings of the International Josquin Festival-Conference Held at the Juilliard School at Lincoln Center in New York City, 21–25 June 1971*, ed. Edward E. Lowinsky in collaboration with Bonnie J. Blackburn, London, 1976, 103–137

Lowinsky, Edward E., "Character and Purposes of American Musicology: A Reply to Joseph Kerman," *JAMS* 18 (1965), 222–34

Macey, Patrick, "An Expressive Detail in Josquin's *Nimphes, nappés*," *EM* 31 (2003), 400–411

"Josquin and Champion: Conflicting Attributions for the Psalm Motet *De profundis clamavi*," in *Uno gentile et subtile ingenio: Studies in Renaissance Music in Honour of Bonnie J. Blackburn*, ed. M. Jennifer Bloxam, Gioia Filocamo, and Leofranc Holford-Strevens, Turnhout, 2009, 453–68

"Josquin as Classic: *Qui habitat, Memor esto*, and Two Imitations Unmasked," *JRMA* 118 (1993), 1–43

Milsom, John, "Analyzing Josquin," in *The Josquin Companion*, ed. Sherr, 431–84

"Crecquillon, Clemens, and Four-Voice *Fuga*," in *Beyond Contemporary Fame: Reassessing the Art of Clemens non Papa and Thomas Crecquillon. Colloquium Proceedings, Utrecht, April 24–26, 2003*, ed. Eric Jas, Turnhout, 2005, 293–345

"Josquin des Prez and the Combinative Impulse," in *The Motet around 1500: On the Relationship of Imitation and Text Treatment?*, ed. Thomas Schmidt-Beste, Turnhout, 2012, 211–46

"Motets for Five or More Voices," in *The Josquin Companion*, ed. Sherr, 281–320

Osthoff, Helmuth, *Josquin Desprez*, 2 vols., Tutzing, 1962–65

Owens, Jessie Ann, "How Josquin Became Josquin: Reflections on Historiography and Reception," in *Music in Renaissance Cities and Courts: Studies in Honor of Lewis Lockwood*, ed. Jessie Ann Owens and Anthony M. Cummings, Warren, MI, 271–80

"Music Historiography and the Definition of 'Renaissance'," *Notes* 47 (1990), 305–30

Planchart, Alejandro Enrique, "Masses on Plainsong Cantus Firmi," in *The Josquin Companion*, ed. Sherr, 89–150

Rifkin, Joshua, "Masses and Evidence: Petrucci's Josquin," unpublished paper

"Miracles, Motivicity, and Mannerism: Adrian Willaert's *Videns Dominus flentes sorores Lazari* and Some Aspects of Motet Composition in the 1520s," in *Hearing the Motet: Essays on the Motet of the Middle Ages and Renaissance*, ed. Dolores Pesce, New York, 1997, 243–64

"Motivik – Konstruktivismus – Humanismus: Zu Josquins Motette *Huc me sydereo*," in *Die Motette: Beiträge zu ihrer Gattungsgeschichte*, ed. Herbert Schneider, Mainz, 1992, 105–34

"Munich, Milan, and a Marian Motet: Dating Josquin's *Ave Maria ... virgo serena*," *JAMS* 56 (2003), 239–350

"Musste Josquin Josquin werden? Zum Problem des Frühwerks," in *Josquin des Prez Und seine Zeit*, ed. Michael Zywietz, forthcoming

"Problems of Authorship in Josquin: Some Impolitic Observations. With a Postscript on *Absalon, fili mi*," in *Proceedings of the International Josquin Symposium Utrecht 1986*, ed. Elders and de Haen, 45–52

"A Singer Named Josquin and Josquin D'Ascanio: Some Problems in the Biography of Josquin des Prez," unpublished paper

Rodin, Jesse, "Finishing Josquin's 'Unfinished' Mass: A Case of Stylistic Imitation in the *Cappella Sistina*," *JM* 22 (2005), 412–53

*Josquin's Rome: Hearing and Composing in the Sistine Chapel*, New York, 2012

"'When in Rome ... ': What Josquin Learned in the Sistine Chapel," *JAMS* 61 (2008), 307–72

"When Josquin Became Josquin." *Acta musicologica*, 81 (2009), 23–38

Schlagel, Stephanie P., "The *Liber selectarum cantionem* and the 'German Josquin Renaissance'," *JM* 19 (2002), 564–615

Sherr, Richard, "Mass Sections," in *The Josquin Companion*, ed. Sherr, 211–38

   ed., *The Josquin Companion*, Oxford and New York, 2000

Tuan, Eric, "Beyond the Cadence: Post-Cadential Extensions and Josquin's Compositional Style," undergraduate thesis, Stanford University, 2012

Urquhart, Peter, "An Accidental Flat in Josquin's *Sine nomine* Mass," in *From Ciconia to Sweelinck: Donum natalicium Willem Elders*, ed. Albert Clement and Eric Jas, Amsterdam, 1994, 125–44

   "Canon, Partial Signatures, and 'Musica Ficta' in Works by Josquin Des Prez and his Contemporaries," Ph.D. diss., Harvard University, 1988

Wegman, Rob C., "'And Josquin Laughed . . . ': Josquin and the Composer's Anecdote in the Sixteenth Century," *JM* 17 (1999), 319–57

   "The Other Josquin," *TVNM* 58 (2008), 33–68

   "Who Was Josquin?," in *The Josquin Companion*, ed. Sherr, 21–50

## · PART II IMPROVISATION AND COMPOSITION ·

# 8

# Oral composition in fifteenth-century music

ANNA MARIA BUSSE BERGER

One of the most puzzling questions for scholars of fifteenth- and sixteenth-century music is how composers went about creating polyphonic compositions. In manuscripts the voices are notated separately on the page, as described in Margaret Bent's essay in this volume (Ch. 33). The earliest surviving scores date from the middle of the sixteenth century. And these scores are anthologies, not sketchbooks.[1] Does this mean that scores were not used in the process of composition? In the absence of any surviving scores scholars assumed until very recently that composers worked out polyphony on *cartelle*, that is, erasable tablets in score format, and then transferred each part from the score into partbooks. It is an assumption that makes eminently good sense to us today. Motets, masses, and chansons are for the most part complicated structures where dissonances are carefully prepared and resolved. All of us who learned counterpoint today did our exercises entirely in writing. We cannot conceive of polyphony for three or more voices without notating them in score.

And yet, in recent years, we have gradually learned to accept the disturbing fact that we cannot transfer our own mental processes to the Middle Ages. We now know that musicians in the fifteenth century did not rely on writing but were able to plan entire multi-part compositions in the mind.[2]

## Instruction in discant and counterpoint

What enabled medieval musicians to easily engage in such mental planning, an activity that is way beyond our reach? The obvious answer is that the education students received must have prepared them for these kinds of mental activities. In the last several years historians have demonstrated that students had to

---

1 Edward E. Lowinsky was the first to discuss this issue at length in two important articles: "On the Use of Scores" and "Early Scores in Manuscript."
2 The first to suggest that polyphonic composition was done in the mind was Leech-Wilkinson, "Machaut's '*Rose, Lis*'." Owens, in her groundbreaking book *Composers at Work*, makes a strong case that most pieces were worked out mentally.

memorize an extraordinary amount of material in all subjects from early childhood on.[3] Students first learned how to read by memorizing the psalter in
Latin; next they committed nouns and verbs to memory; then the nouns and
verbs were combined with adjectives; and finally entire Latin texts were
memorized. As a result, students had committed hundreds of word combinations to memory, which allowed them to speak and write competent Latin.
Teachers were less interested in original texts and more in well-stocked memories. Similarly, instruction in arithmetic began with memorization of basic
mathematical facts like multiplication and division tables (see Figure 8.1)
followed by entire word problems with their solutions. It is striking that all
of these word problems were memorized individually, even though they
differed little from each other. This is very different from our approach to
arithmetic: we consider mathematics to be a symbolic and logical system where
a few basic rules can be applied to many problems and situations. Thus, the
training in grammar and arithmetic was based on memorization. An accomplished student would be able to map out long speeches and texts in the mind
without recourse to paper, just as a merchant could transform currencies and
costs of merchandise in the mind.

   Training in music was based on exactly the same principles: students would
begin by learning the musical gamut through the Hand (see Philippe
Canguilhem, Ch. 9). Once they had committed all the available pitches to
memory, they would learn which intervals are consonant and which are dissonant, usually with the help of interval tables, which looked similar to multiplication tables (see Figure 8.2). The most important part of counterpoint
instruction consisted of the systematic memorization of interval progressions.[4]
These are already discussed at length in the *regula del grado* treatises of the late
fourteenth century and by the early fifteenth-century theorist Ugolino of
Orvieto. The most exhaustive treatment, however, can be found in Johannes
Tinctoris's *Liber de arte contrapuncti* of 1477. Tinctoris is generally recognized
for being the first music theorist to provide us with detailed rules for diminished counterpoint. When we look at his treatise in modern edition, it is 147
pages long (without the table of contents). And yet, more than one-half
(roughly eighty pages) is devoted to a listing of interval progressions.
Tinctoris is the most systematic and thorough theorist in the fifteenth century;
he does not shy away from reforming notational and contrapuntal practice.
Thus, it is typical of him to list *all* available interval progressions in a way
that to us may seem tedious. And yet in the fifteenth century, this pedagogical

---

3 Grendler, *Schooling in Renaissance Italy*, 175 f.; on memorization in arithmetic, see Egmond, "Commercial
Revolution."
4 Berger, *Medieval Music*, 130–50.

Figure 8.1 Multiplication table from Filippo Calandri, *Aritmetica*, Florence, Biblioteca Riccardiana, MS 2669

method was valued highly. Indeed, Tinctoris carefully organizes his text so as to help the student in the process of memorization (see Table 8.1).

Tinctoris describes these progressions in great detail both verbally and in music examples. That a theorist of Tinctoris's caliber spends so much space on interval progressions can only mean that he considered them the central element of counterpoint instruction. He must have known that once these progressions were memorized, it would be very easy to improvise or compose polyphony in the mind.

He ends his treatise with the following warning: "so, in our time, I have known not even one man who has achieved eminent or noble rank among musicians, if he began to compose or sing *super librum* at or above his twentieth year of age."[5] It seems likely that Tinctoris is here referring to the memorization of interval progressions and the facility such a training provided for both composition and improvisation. In other words, they functioned similarly to

5 *Liber de arte contrapuncti*, 156; trans. Seay, 141.

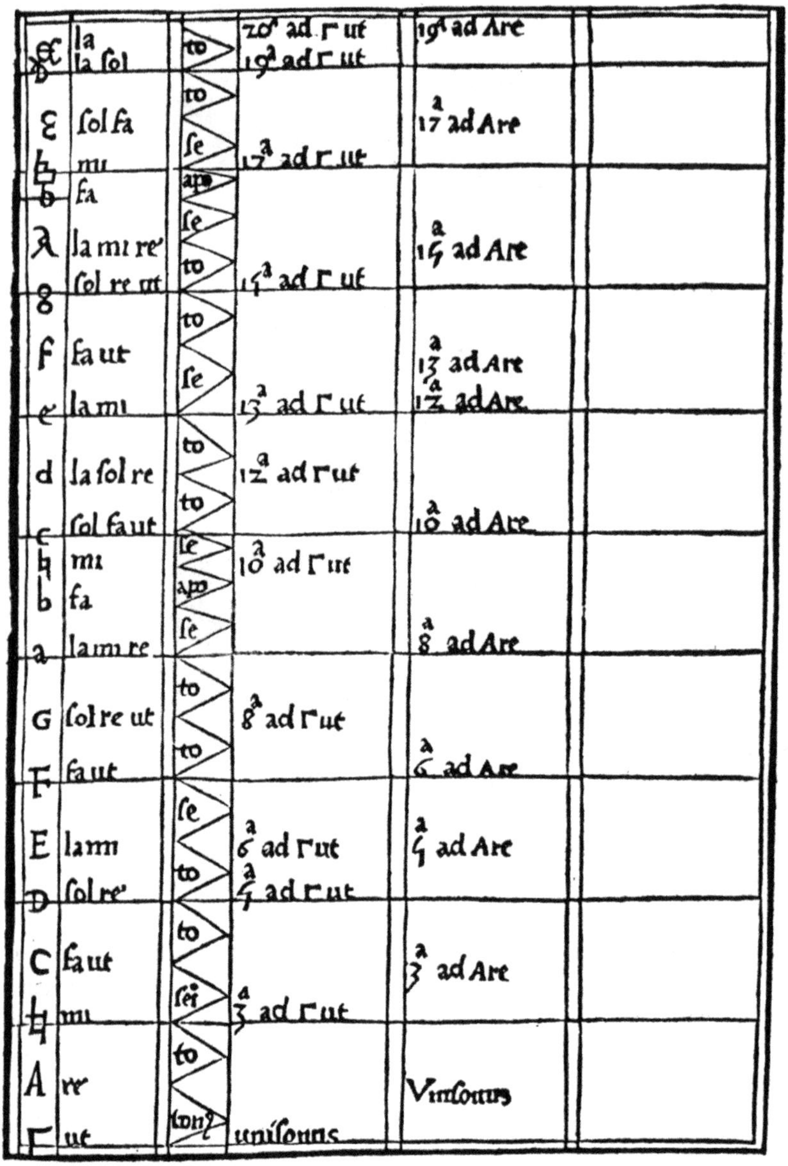

| | | | | | | |
|---|---|---|---|---|---|---|
| ee | la | to | 20a ad Γ ut | 19a ad A re | | |
| dd | la sol | to | 19a ad Γ ut | | | |
| cc | sol fa | to | | 17a ad A re | | |
| | | se | | | | |
| ♮♮ | mi | | 17a ad Γ ut | | | |
| bb | fa | apo | | | | |
| | | se | | | | |
| aa | la mi re | to | | 15a ad A re | | |
| gg | sol re ut | | 15a ad Γ ut | | | |
| | | to | | | | |
| ff | fa ut | se | | 13a ad A re | | |
| ee | la mi | | 13a ad Γ ut | 12a ad A re | | |
| dd | la sol re | to | 12a ad Γ ut | | | |
| | | to | | | | |
| c | sol fa ut | | | 10a ad A re | | |
| ♮ | mi | se | 10a ad Γ ut | | | |
| b | fa | apo | | | | |
| a | la mi re | se | | 8a ad A re | | |
| G | sol re ut | to | 8a ad Γ ut | | | |
| | | to | | | | |
| F | fa ut | | | 6a ad A re | | |
| E | la mi | se | 6a ad Γ ut | 5a ad A re | | |
| D | sol re | to | 5a ad Γ ut | | | |
| C | fa ut | to | | 3a ad A re | | |
| ♮ | mi | semi | 3a ad Γ ut | | | |
| A | re | to | | Unisonus | | |
| Γ | ut | tonus | unisonus | | | |

Figure 8.2 Consonance table from Franchinus Gaffurius, *Practica musice*, bk. 3, ch. 8

Table 8.1 *Interval progressions in Tinctoris,* Liber de arte contrapuncti

---

Ch. 3: 1–1, 1–3, 1–5, 1–6, 1–8 [a] (concentrates on the unison)

Ch. 4: 3–1, 3–5, 3–6, 3–8, 3–10 (with the tenor starting below the counterpoint, using both minor and major thirds)

3–1, 3–3, 3–5, 3–6, 3–8, 3–10 (with the tenor starting above the counterpoint)

Ch. 5: 4 (the fourth does not occur in two-part interval progressions)

Ch. 6: 5–3, 5–5, 5–6, 5–8, 5–10, 5–12 (tenor starting below)

  Then the whole series is repeated with the tenor above.

Ch. 7: 6–3, 6–5, 6–6, 6–8, 6–10, 6–12 (tenor below)

  Then the whole series is repeated with the tenor above.

Ch. 8: 8–3, 8–5, 8–6, 8–8, 8–10, 8–12, 8–13, 8–15 (tenor below)

  Then the whole series is repeated with the tenor above.

Ch. 9: 10–3, 10–5, 10–6, 10–8, 10–10, 10–12, 10–13, 10–15, 10–17 (tenor below)

  Then repeated with the tenor above.

Ch. 10: 11 (like ch. 5)

Ch. 11: 12–5, 12–6, 12–8, 12–10, 12–12, 12–13, 12–15, 12–17, 12–19 (tenor below, repeated with tenor above)

Ch. 12: 13–10, 13–12, 13–13, 13–15, 13–17, 13–19 (with tenor below, then repeated with tenor above)

Ch. 13: 15–10, 15–12, 15–13, 15–15, 15–17, 15–19, 15–20, 15–22 (with tenor below, then repeated with tenor above)

Ch. 14: 17–10, 17–12, 17–13, 17–15, 17–17, 17–19, 17–20, 17–22 (with tenor below, then repeated with tenor above)

Ch. 15: 18 (like ch. 4)

Ch. 16: 19–12, 19–13, 19–15, 19–17, 19–19, 19–20, 19–22 (with tenor below, then repeated with tenor above)

Ch. 17: 20–17, 20–19, 20–20, 20–22 (tenor below, then repeated with tenor above)

Ch. 18: 22–17, 22–19, 22–20, 22–22 (tenor below, then repeated with tenor above)

---

[a] The numbers refer to the interval size. Thus 1–1 is unison–unison, and 1–3 is unison–third.

the multiplication tables that allowed merchants to do complicated transactions in the mind.

It is striking that with the exception of Tinctoris, theorists are remarkably quiet as to how diminished counterpoint was learned.[6] It seems that students acquired these skills through three methods: first, and most importantly, they underwent rigorous training in improvisation as described by Canguilhem. Second, many students would probably also copy compositions, either for

---

6 Berger, "The Problem of Diminished Counterpoint."

themselves or the institution they worked for. And third, students were expected to sing and memorize a large number of polyphonic pieces. As Julie Cumming and Peter Schubert have shown (see Ch. 12), these pieces consist of many previously memorized formulas which could be reused and adapted in ever new ways. Thus, we can easily imagine how students were able to pull chunks from their memorial archive and adapt them to their particular needs – all without recourse to notation. They probably did this not much differently from visual artists who had also memorized lots of individual drawings through model books, which eventually made their way into their paintings.[7]

## Visualization

Now that we have explained how composers and singers memorized units from small formulas to larger polyphonic passages, we need to turn our attention to the question of how composers kept track of simultaneities of three or four parts without actually writing them down. I suggest we look at English sight and faburden treatises that describe how beginners would visualize the chant on a single staff with one or two added parts during performance (see Canguilhem, Ch. 9).[8] Pseudo-Chilston, writing in the early fifteenth century, expected his students to visualize consonant intervals for the entire tenor.[9] The central fact about visualization of sights is that the pitch on which the added part is visualized through a number is then transposed up by a fifth, an octave, or a twelfth. So for the "mene sight" it is transposed a fifth up, for the "treble sight" an octave, and for the "quatreble sight" up a twelfth. Let us look at the quatreble sight in some detail as visualized by the student and as realized in sound (see Example 8.1). In Example 8.1b, the number to the left or right or on top of the note indicates the interval above the plainchant which the student will sing: thus 12 next to $g$ becomes $d''$ above the $g$, 13 on top of the $b$ becomes $g''$ above the $b$, and so on. With the help of sights, the student sees all of the consonances in his mind's eye while he performs or writes them down. These visualizations often involve transpositions that appear cumbersome to us, yet they seem to have been considered easy for beginning students in the fourteenth and fifteenth centuries.[10] Now, if beginners were able to visualize two-part counterpoint, it seems reasonable to assume that accomplished composers could visualize entire polyphonic compositions. In short, it seems likely that composers of polyphony would have visualized

7 Berger, "Models for Composition."
8 For a detailed discussion of visualization and sights, see Berger, *Medieval Music*, 198–210.
9 See Georgiades, *Englische Diskanttraktate*, 23–27.
10 They are, moreover, mentioned by numerous other fifteenth-century theorists. Ibid., 209.

Example 8.1 Pseudo-Chilston, quatreble sight
(a) in sound
(b) as visualized

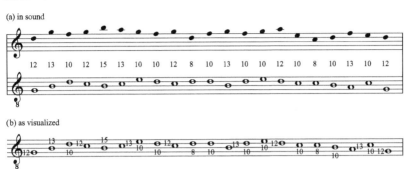

their polyphonic structures on the staff, either all parts on the same staff, or one after another, always keeping track of the consonant intervals.

## Orality in isorhythmic motets

Now that we have explained how simultaneities were visualized, we need to address the question how composers could work out entire structures such as isorhythmic motets in the mind. These are pieces that would not have come into existence without notation; moreover, they are compositions that need to be preserved intact in writing (see Lütteken, Ch. 3). If even a single note is altered, the entire structure might collapse. Composers' names are regularly attached to the manuscripts or mentioned by music theorists, and it is clear that they took pride in their authorship. Again, it seems to contradict all of our assumptions to suggest that orality might have played a role in the creation of these pieces. And yet, there is plenty of evidence that it did.

First of all, even though these pieces were transmitted in writing, a number of scholars have argued convincingly that they were sung by heart.[11] Now, if you want to commit a composition to memory, it must be structured in such a way that it can be easily memorized. What makes a piece memorable? As Walter Ong argued as early as 1982: "Think memorable thoughts."[12] Memorable thoughts can be anything from simple repetitive patterns to complicated structures. The author will take a diagram or take a particular building, say a church or a monastery, and locate part of the text in various rooms of this

---

11 Berger, *Medieval Music*, 212–14.
12 Ong, *Orality and Literacy*, 34.

building. When he wants to recover the text, he will retrieve each section of the text as he walks through the structure, always in the same order.

In recent years it has become clear that these memory structures were used not only to memorize old pieces, but also to help in the composition of new ones. They allow you to compose a text in the mind and place it into various parts of your structure during composition. Then, when you later want to retrieve the text, you retrace your steps and read from your imagined text in the diagram without ever writing down a word or a note.

How do we know that composers used memory techniques? First, numerous music theorists from the Middle Ages and Renaissance use terms familiar from memory treatises that describe visual activities. Franco and Jacques de Liège, for example, use the word *respicere* (to keep in mind) in their treatises when telling composers that if they want to construct a triplum (the top voice) they must always have the discant (middle voice) and tenor in mind.[13] The verb is typically found in memory treatises to describe visual memorization in contrast to *recordare* and *retinere*, which are more generalized. Similarly, Franco and Leonel Power use the verb *imaginare*, which means to visualize.

Second, a number of theorists compare motets to architectural structures with the tenor as the foundation, foremost among them Johannes de Grocheio. Surely, the most interesting discussion of isorhythmic motets is found in the treatise *Ars (musicae)* by the Dutch theorist Johannes Boen from the middle of the fourteenth century. Boen defines the term *color* as others define *talea*, that is, a group of notes with a repeated rhythmic pattern.[14] He goes on to describe how thirty tenor pitches are divided into 6×5 or 3×10 separate note-groups. And this division happens to "bring some badly needed order" to the piece. In other words, *color* was invented to structure the notes in a composition. Performers and composers therefore thought not in separate, individual notes, but in groups of notes; in doing so they were "chunking," as psychologists call it. And "chunking" is done in order to memorize. What this then implies is that the rhythmic (and, for that matter, also melodic) organization and structure enabled composers to work out pieces in their mind and performers to keep their place during performance. Boen's discussion shows clearly that the composer planned and visualized the piece before he wrote it down.

Third, the mid-fourteenth-century theorist Egidius de Murino also stresses the importance of *divisio* in motets: "When the music is made and ordered, then take the words which are to be in the motets and divide them into four parts,

---

13  Berger, *Medieval Music*, 220–21.
14  Ibid., 222–24.

and likewise divide the music into four parts."[15] While this passage was intended for the instruction of beginners, it makes clear that composers worked in sections.

Thus, I suggest that composers of isoryhthmic motets chose to organize their pieces in tightly organized structures because it allowed them to work out the pieces in their mind and make them memorable to performers. *Ars nova* notation allowed them to see the isorhythmic structure of the motet at a glance, like the mnemonic diagrams. The tenor is usually on the lowest left staff, the triplum on the top left, and the motetus on the facing right page. Unlike modern transcriptions, which take up many pages, the entire piece can here be seen on one folio or one manuscript opening. (See Figs. 33.1, 34.1, and 34.2 for various ways in which the voices are arranged on the folio.)

What happened to composition in the mind in the second half of the fifteenth century and later, when we find elaborately structured motivic "interlocks"? (See Rodin, Ch. 7, and Milsom, Ch. 11.) There is little doubt that oral composition continued throughout the sixteenth and seventeenth centuries. In 1607, Claudio Monteverdi describes composition in the mind as follows:

> I shall send your Lordship [Vincenzo, fourth Duke of Mantua] the other sonnet, set to music, as soon as possible – since it is already clearly shaped in my mind – but if I should spin out the other time even a little, in His Highness's opinion, please be good enough to let me know and I shall send it at once.[16]

As various treatises on improvisation show, training in the art of memory remained the same.[17] But it is also likely that beginning in the second half of the fifteenth century, some composers would, in addition, sketch motivic and imitative passages on *cartelle* or on paper. Thus writing did not replace oral composition, but could be used side by side with it.

## Bibliography

Berger, Anna Maria Busse, *Medieval Music and the Art of Memory*, Berkeley, 2005

"Models for Composition in the Fourteenth and Fifteenth Centuries," in *Memory and Invention: Medieval and Renaissance Literature, Art, and Music*, ed. A. M. Busse Berger and M. Rossi, Florence, 2009, 59–80

"The Problem of Diminished Counterpoint," in *Uno gentile et subtile ingenio: Studies in Renaissance Music in Honour of Bonnie J. Blackburn*, ed. M. Jennifer Bloxam, Gioia Filocamo, and Leofranc Holford-Strevens, Turnhout, 2009, 13–27

---

15  Leech-Wilkinson, *Compositional Techniques*, 19.

16  Monteverdi, *The Letters of Claudio Monteverdi*, 44. See also the discussion by Owens, *Composers at Work*, 65–66.

17  See, for example, Schubert, "From Improvisation to Composition" for a comparison of improvisation and counterpoint.

Egmond, Warren van, "The Commercial Revolution and the Beginning of Western Mathematics in Renaissance Florence, 1300–1500," Ph.D. diss., Indiana University, 1976

Georgiades, Thrasybulos, *Englische Diskanttraktate aus der ersten Hälfte des 15. Jahrhunderts*, Munich, 1937

Grendler, Paul, *Schooling in Renaissance Italy: Literacy and Learning, 1300–1600*, Baltimore, 1989

Leech-Wilkinson, Daniel, *Compositional Techniques in the Four-Part Isorhythmic Motets of Philippe de Vitry and his Contemporaries*, New York, 1989

"Machaut's 'Rose, Lis' and the Problem of Early Music Analysis," *Music Analysis* 3 (1984), 9–28

Lowinsky, Edward E., "Early Scores in Manuscript," *JAMS*, 13 (1960), 126–73, repr. in *Music in the Culture of the Renaissance and Other Essays*, Chicago, 1989, 803–40

"On the Use of Scores by Sixteenth-Century Musicians," *JAMS* 1 (1948), 17–23, repr. in *Music in the Culture of the Renaissance*, 797–800

Monteverdi, Claudio, *The Letters of Claudio Monteverdi*, trans. Denis Stevens, Oxford, 1995

Ong, Walter J., *Orality and Literacy: The Technologizing of the Word*, London, 1982

Owens, Jessie Ann, *Composers at Work: The Craft of Musical Composition, 1450–1600*, New York, 1997

Schubert, Peter, "From Improvisation to Composition: Three Sixteenth-Century Case Studies," *11th Publication of the Collected Writings of the Orpheus Instituut*, forthcoming from Leuven University Press

Tinctoris, Johannes, *Liber de arte contrapuncti*, in *Opera theoretica*, ed. Albert Seay, CSM 22, [Rome], 1975, 2: 11; trans. A. Seay as *The Art of Counterpoint*, MSD 5, [Rome], 1961

# 9

# Improvisation as concept and musical practice in the fifteenth century

PHILIPPE CANGUILHEM

> There is no greater folly than the rejection of the gifts of the moment.
>
> Quintilian, 10.6.6

Toward the end of the fifteenth century, several writers on music address the respective statuses of composed and improvised music. In his counterpoint treatise of 1477, the composer and theorist Johannes Tinctoris (ca. 1435–1511) considers musical creation as either a collective action in process (*cantare super librum*) or the fruit of an individual activity resulting in a written product (*res facta*, also referred to as *cantus compositus* in his glossary of musical terms published ca. 1495). To quote Karol Berger, Tinctoris

> found it entirely natural to distinguish "composers" (*compositores*) from "singers" (*cantores*) and to talk of musical "works" (*opera*) as something one not only "heard" (*audio*), but also "examined" (*considero*). For Tinctoris, the works of admired composers were worthy of being treated as models for imitation no less than the classical works of poetry.[1]

Thus during the fifteenth century we find the emergence of the notion that music, because of the fixed nature of its written form, could strive for the status associated with a literary work such as a poem. Not only can works be reproduced at will by different musicians for different audiences, but they also become comparable with other, similar works, and can serve as models for other composers. Tinctoris probably aimed to bestow the dignity of the poet upon those musicians writing a *cantus compositus*; indeed it is clear that his conception of the composer helped to structure a hierarchy that later came to impose itself on the Western musical world. As a majority of the contributions in the present volume attest, our history of music is a history of musical works and their composers.[2]

Numerous written accounts, however, testify to a fifteenth-century fascination with spontaneous creation and improvised performance, be it musical (vocal and/or instrumental), poetic (in Latin or in the vernacular), or a

---

1 Berger, *A Theory of Art*, 117.    2 See in particular Laurenz Lütteken's essay in this volume, Ch. 3.

combination of the two. Exploring this essential aspect of Renaissance musical practice is a difficult endeavor that demands much flexibility in its historical interpretation. This explains why the subject has been and continues to be problematic for music historians. The most outstanding problems can be approached through the following questions: What do we mean by "improvisation" in the fifteenth century? Can the difference between improvisation and composition be considered as grounded in the distinction between oral and written music? Or, more concretely, under what circumstances did musicians improvise and what were the techniques that allowed for such spontaneous musical creation?

## The concept of improvisation in the fifteenth century

Tinctoris is not the only author to have addressed the relationship between composition and improvisation in dialectical terms. Other examples exist from the same period, including a counterpoint treatise from southern Germany that will be considered below. These different accounts shed light on techniques and attitudes, and on a vocabulary of terms, but do not in themselves constitute a theoretical corpus on the subject. To consider the cultural background in an attempt to understand how the phenomenon of improvisation was perceived, we must look at the poetic and rhetorical theories of the period. We are encouraged to follow this path by the numerous references to poets and orators of antiquity that Tinctoris himself cites in his treatise on counterpoint, including Homer, Aristotle, Cicero, Horace, and Virgil. In the fifteenth century, we can highlight two models that fueled interest in spontaneous creation, both of which originated in Florentine humanist circles: the *furor poeticus* of Platonic ancestry as seen through the works of Marsilio Ficino, and Quintilian's *calor rhetoricus* as revisited by Angelo Poliziano.

   While the theory of inspiration could be thought of as being crystallized in the writings of Ficino and his followers, certain of his premises can be traced back to earlier sources. In his *Vita di Dante* (1436), Leonardo Bruni privileges the inspired poet to the detriment of those ensconced in science and academicism. The poet creates "thanks to a natural gift engaged and put into movement by a certain hidden internal force, that we call fury and occupation of the mind."[3] This reference to *furor poeticus* signals a preoccupation with this concept from as early as the middle of the fifteenth century. One of its more

---

3  "per ingegno proprio agitato e commosso da alcun vigore interno e nascoso, il quale si chiama furore ed occupazione della mente." Quoted in Chastel, *Marsile Ficin et l'art*, 142.

striking manifestations can be found in the description of one of Pietrobono del Chitarrino's musical improvisations in Ferrara in 1456. Ludovico Carboni depicts the lute player "afire like one inspired by a divine power," who is gradually driven out of himself ("he exulted to no small degree, he cavorted, he could not contain his joy") until the breaking point: "then sweat poured freely from his face; his strings could not take it, and broke from his excessive desire for praise."[4]

Only a year later, in 1457, Ficino wrote the epistle *De divino furore*, in which a conception of the four furies (amorous, poetic, mystic, and prophetic) appears for the first time. Drawing upon various Platonic dialogues, most notably *Ion*, Ficino elaborated a theory of enthusiasm that sees the inspired poet as possessed by the Muses, and whose spirit is mobilized through various songs and other poetic forms. Not only can poetic fury be expressed "thanks to musical tones and harmonic sweetness"; one of the characteristics of Ficinian inspiration lies in its abruptness and unpredictability, which helps explain why improvisation was held in such high esteem during the meetings of the Academia Platonica.[5]

Parallel to the emergence of a theory of inspiration that promoted spontaneity, the fifteenth century witnessed a renewed interest in classical rhetoric, which profited from immense prestige. Since its rediscovery by Poggio Bracciolini in 1416, Quintilian's *Institutio oratoria* was widely distributed among the Italian humanists before quickly imposing itself throughout Europe as a major cultural reference during the Renaissance. Quintilian considers improvisation the linchpin of the orator's art: "The crown of all our study and the highest reward of our long labours is the power of improvisation."[6] In the tenth book of his treatise, he advocates two improvisatory techniques in particular. The first consists of adopting a logical method for precisely ordering the various parts of a speech. Here Quintilian applies the principles of the art of memory, which figure in the treatise *Ad Herennium* (among others) that was attributed to Cicero. These principles were applied to musical pedagogy in various ways during the Middle Ages and the Renaissance.[7]

---

4 Gallo, *Music in the Castle*, 89–90. On Pietrobono, a major figure of fifteenth-century Italian music, Lewis Lockwood writes: "Although not a note of his music survives, no other musician in 15th-century Italy made such a profound impression on such a wide range of his contemporaries." See *Grove Music Online*, "Pietrobono de Burzellis."

5 On furor and spontaneity, see Lecointe, *L'Idéal et la différence*, 285–91; and Galand-Hallyn and Hallyn, *Poétiques de la Renaissance*, 109–21.

6 Quintilian, *Institutio oratoria*, 10.7.1; English edn., 133. For the influence of Quintilian's treatise on fifteenth-century theories of improvisation, see Lecointe, *L'Idéal et la différence*, 329–33, and Cave, *The Cornucopian Text*, ch. 4.

7 10.7.5–7; English edn., 135–7. See also Berger, *Medieval Music*.

Regarding the second technique, Quintilian explains that the improviser must mentally conceive the ideas that he will develop. In this process he is helped by *visiones* (*phantasiai* in Greek), "through which man is capable of imagining things that are not present, to such an extent that he has the impression of seeing them with his own eyes or of holding them out in front of him."[8] According to Quintilian, these *phantasiai* "must be kept clearly before our eyes and admitted to our hearts: for it is feeling and force of imagination that make us eloquent."[9] These remarks cannot help but remind us of the fifteenth-century contrapuntal technique, prevalent throughout Europe, that was referred to in England as "sight." A singer wishing to spontaneously add a voice to a plainchant melody imagined the note he wanted to sing within the range of a four-line staff, either above or below the chant line, by visualizing the consonance it would produce. This idea of improvising as "seeing" can be observed in Leonel Power's treatise on descant, which employs the term "ymaginations" to refer to counterpoint, and in a Catalan treatise on the same subject entitled *Regles de contrapunt al visu*.[10]

For Quintilian, however, a mastery of improvisatory techniques in oratory was insufficient. "If a speaker is swept away by warmth (*calor*) of feeling and genuine inspiration, it frequently happens that he attains a success from improvisation which would have been beyond the reach of careful preparation."[11] Improvisation is thus made possible by an impetus that emerges in an instant, allowing even for some to "write in the heat of the moment." And Quintilian is not the only authority evoked in the fifteenth century to justify *calor*. In fact, the expression *calor subitus* is employed by Statius to account for the immediate inspiration that led him to write his *Silvae*, a volume of poetry rediscovered by Poggio around the same time as the revival of Quintilian's work.[12]

Overlapping with those of *furor*, these theories of *calor* played an important role for Angelo Poliziano (1454–94), a student and friend of Ficino. There are many instances in his work that demonstrate a strong interest in improvised creation. In a letter to Lorenzo de' Medici of 5 June 1490 about Lorenzo's son Piero, he states: "Not two evenings ago I heard Piero sing *improviso*, for he

8 Schrÿvers, "Invention, imagination, et théorie des émotions," 49.      9 10.7.15; English edn., 141.
10 On this point, see Berger, *Medieval Music*, 200–10 and Fuller, "Organum – Discantus – Contrapunctus," 496–97. See also Butler, "The Fantasia as Musical Image." On Leonel Power, see Berger, *Medieval Music*, 209, where other examples are cited, such as John Hothby's "discantus visibilis." On the Catalan treatise, see Sachs, *Der Contrapunctus im 14. und 15. Jahrhundert*, 94. See also the chapter by Berger in this volume (Ch. 8).
11 10.7.13–14; English edn., 140–41. On the notion of *calor subitus*, see Galand-Hallyn and Hallyn, *Poétiques de la Renaissance*, 130–34. The following citation can be found in 10.3.17; English edn., 101.
12 On the influence of Statius's *Silvae* on Poliziano, see Mengelkoch, "The Mutability of Poetics." In the preface of his book, Statius says that his poems "mihi subito calore et quadam festinandi voluptate fluxerunt" ("poured out in a sudden heat and a particularly delightful rush"; Mengelkoch, 107).

came to assail me at home with all these improvisers. He satisfied me won-drously, *et praesertim* in the jokes and retorts, and his ease and pronunciation, so that I seemed to see and hear Your Magnificence in person."[13]

Poliziano's model is Homer, since unlike Virgil, who "composed but a few lines each day," the most beautiful of all the Homeric hymns "sprang forth from his mouth without effort, and in improvisatory fashion; it overflowed into a living source, so to speak." Poliziano speaks of divine influx and an impulse to define the improvised outpouring of Homer, whose poems "are not made on the anvil of a human forge." He even goes on to belittle the careful, meticulous work of literary creation: "too much craft pollutes our written works, and the file does not polish them, but rather wears them away."[14]

This pejorative image of the anvil is also found in a judgment asserted by humanist Matteo Bosso regarding the talents of poet and musician Aurelio Brandolini: "With regard to the *lyra* – let me speak quite boldly – Apollo and Amphion yield to him. By this one thing he is victorious over the famous poets: what they hammered out through long nights and by burning the midnight oil, he fashions and sings extemporaneously." This fascination with Brandolini's capacity for spontaneous creation is also found in the continuation of Matteo Bosso's description:

> his *lyra* was handed to him and right away he put together and sang metrical verses on whatever it was. Finally, when asked to speak of famous men of ancient glory whose native land was Verona, he, without any hesitation or taking time to think, [*nulla intercedente cogitatione vel haesitatione cum mora*], described at length Catullus, Cornelius Nepos, Pliny the Younger, the dignity of citizenship, and the splendor of the city with a very fine song that earned most splendid and well-deserved praise.[15]

With regard either to Latin verse or vernacular poetry, improvisers are often described as accompanying themselves on the lyra, a Latin term that indeter-minately refers to the lira da braccio and its bowed strings or instruments of the lute family. Music indeed helped to recall the metric structures and rhythmic utterances of poems created on the spot. But in such descriptions, all of the improviser's energies are concentrated on the text. Indeed at the end of the fifteenth century, Vincenzo Calmeta emphasizes that in this manner of singing, the text must be "accompanied by the music in the manner of masters

---

13 Poliziano, *Prose volgari*, 78; cited from Pirrotta and Povoledo, *Music and Theatre*, 23–24, with emenda-tions. On his wonder at the gifts of the eleven-year old improviser Fabio Orsini, see Abramov-van Rijk, *Parlar cantando*, 151–54.
14 Quoted in Lecointe, *L'Idéal et la différence*, 319–20.
15 Quoted in Gallo, *Music in the Castle*, 85.

accompanied by their servants, not making the thoughts and emotions sub-
servient to the music, but the music to the emotions and thoughts."[16]

A large number of striking accounts that reflect upon extempore creations
also stress the importance of the visual impact felt by audiences. Consider a
description by Brandolini of another improviser, the lutenist Pietrobono of
Ferrara. Brandolini was nearly blind, as his nickname Lippus indicates, for
which reason we can appreciate his essentially visual description all the more:
"Pay close attention, as his left hand runs along the entire cithara, as his hand
swiftly travels along the tuneful strings. You will marvel at how all his fingers
fly simultaneously, how one hand is in so many places at once."[17] Here,
Pietrobono's sonic performance is disassociated from the wonder procured
from his musical gestures. These phenomena contribute to the establishment
of a "production of presence" that was indispensable to the success of improvisation, and whose power is so clearly analyzed by the humanist Michele Verino
in his account of singer Antonio di Guido's talents.[18]

## Improvisation and writing

How can we integrate these accounts into a history of music so insistent on
recognizing the emergence of the composer as a central figure of musical life in the
fifteenth century? To resolve the problems posed by improvisation, the historiographical tradition has chosen to construct an explanatory system based on two
oppositions. First, composition and improvisation diverge with regard to premeditation: whereas composition is carefully planned, improvisation is characterized by the absence of premeditation. In other words, spontaneity cannot be
prepared. Second, written music, though an integral part of composition, is
considered foreign to the phenomenon of improvisation. Corollary to these
oppositions is that an absence of planning aligns itself with orality, while the
preparation of a composition necessarily involves writing. This interpretive model
was employed often throughout the twentieth century, notably by those who
have used the notion of the "unwritten tradition," as detailed by Nino Pirrotta, to
account for the activities of fifteenth-century Italian singer-improvisers.[19]
However, a close rereading of the salient sources in light of recent scholarship
makes it necessary to re-address this issue, and ultimately results in a much more
comprehensive approach to the process of musical creation in this period.

16 Pirrotta and Povoledo, *Music and Theatre*, 28.     17 Gallo, *Music in the Castle*, 123.
18 Cited by Blake Wilson in his essay in this volume, Ch. 16. On "presence culture," see Gumbrecht,
*Production of Presence*.
19 For a recent example of this historiographic tradition and a complete bibliography of Pirrotta's
writings on the "unwritten tradition," see Rossi, "*Vergine bella* e Dufay."

The association of improvisation with an absence of planning is a modern misconception. In fact, during this period improvisation should be understood only through the lens of *extemporaneitas*, the act of creating in a given moment.[20] This is only possible, however, after a period of long and patient preparation that Quintilian translates as *consuetudo* and *exercitatio*, habit and exercise. In particular, the author of *Institutio oratoria* places crucial importance on memory, deeming it necessary for both improvisation and composition, two activities that were ultimately considered equivalent: "the precepts which I laid down for premeditation apply to improvisation also."[21] The exercises that permitted one to achieve expertise in improvisation systematically involved writing: "our style must be formed by continuous and conscientious practice in writing, so that even our improvisations may reproduce the tone of our writing." And again: "as regards writing, this is certainly never more necessary than when we have frequently to speak extempore."[22]

Thus improvisation is by no means at odds with writing; on the contrary, it is profoundly dependent upon it. In this regard, several musical sources from the fifteenth century – thus by definition written – have come to document the connection between writing and improvisation, and can tell us how the latter was taught and practiced by musicians. The *Fundamenta* left by the German organists and keyboard players offer excellent examples. Some manuscripts copied in the mid-fifteenth century contain what is effectively a series of systematic formulas in German keyboard tablature sometimes referred to as *Fundamentum*, the most widely known being the *Fundamentum organisandi* (1452) by the blind organist and lutenist Conrad Paumann. Here these formulas are arranged into different types: cadences (*clausulae*), progressions with ascending or descending intervals while the tenor is played by the left hand (*ascensus et descensus*), ornamentations on a single repeated note in the tenor (*pausae* or *redeuntes*), and sequences of homophonic consonances (*concordantiae*).[23] Learning and memorizing these formulas allowed instrumentalists to spontaneously produce a right-hand part above a sacred or secular tenor. Once these formulas were memorized, musicians "were able," Berger writes, "to use them in unwritten performances as well as in written-out compositions."[24] Although Paumann and his German organist colleagues' improvisations have

---

20 This misconception is often expressed in scholarship dedicated to musical improvisation. "Our understanding of 'improvisation' includes the notion of spontaneous, unpremeditated music-making: 'The art of performing music spontaneously, without the aid of manuscript, sketches, or memory'." Bent, "*Resfacta* and *Cantare Super Librum*," 374, citing the definition of "improvisation" in the *Harvard Dictionary of Music*.
21 10.7.18; English edn., 143.    22 10.7.8–9; English edn., 137 and 10.7.28–29; English edn., 149.
23 Butt, "Germany and the Netherlands," 147–52. For an edition of multiple *Fundamenta*, see *Keyboard Music of the Fourteenth and Fifteenth Centuries*, ed. Apel.
24 Berger, *Medieval Music*, 128, regarding formulas from the Vatican organum treatise written in the thirteenth century. She offers a discussion of the formulaic technique on pp. 127–30.

not survived, the large majority of their written compositions that remain reflect this formulaic style present in the *Fundamenta*.

Other notated pieces reflect the practice of improvisation to varying degrees of fidelity as well. Guillaume Du Fay's well-known song *Vergine bella* relies on what the Italians called an *aere*, a musical formula or tune on which one could sing poetry.[25] An *aere* can be adapted with considerable flexibility and elasticity to fit verses of varying lengths, in much the same way as a chant recitation tone can be adapted to fit different psalm lengths. A number of *aeri* used to set Latin poetry or strophic Italian poems (*capitoli*, *sonetti*) have been transmitted through Petrucci's early sixteenth-century publications, giving us an idea of the musical materials used by improvisers. The *aere* used by Du Fay was copied in Trent 87 in two textless versions: one without ornamentation, the other more melodically developed. (The first resembles the examples printed by Petrucci, and simply serves as a melodic and rhythmic skeleton with a minimal contrapuntal schema.) We can also find this *aere* in the lauda *Padre del cielo* attributed to a certain Frater pauperculus, with a degree of musical elaboration less sophisticated than that of Du Fay.[26] In contrast to the *Fundamenta* that constitute preparatory documents for improvisation, *Vergine bella* and *Padre del cielo* show how improvisations were able to serve as stimuli for compositions of different natures; they appear as two individual and fixed extensions of a creative process based on the same musical model, one that could also have manifested itself as spontaneous song.

## Cantare super librum

In recent years improvised counterpoint has commanded more scholarly debate than any other practice of improvisation during the Renaissance. We owe these debates to counterpoint treatises, our main source for fifteenth-century discussions of the difference between improvisation and composition.[27] As early as 1412, the theorist Prosdocimus de Beldemandis proposes the following distinction: "It must be known, too, that counterpoint taken in the proper sense is twofold, vocal, and written: vocal, that which is uttered, and written, that which is notated." He adds: "Everything that will be said of counterpoint below is to be understood to pertain to both."[28] To understand the weight of this remark, we must remember that counterpoint pedagogy, as

---

25  Rossi, "*Vergine bella* e Dufay."
26  Venice, Biblioteca Nazionale Marciana, MS Ital. IX, 145, fol. 31r. See Rossi, "*Vergine bella* e Dufay."
27  On these historiographical debates, see Ferand, Bent, Blackburn, and Wegman cited in the bibliography.
28  Prosdocimus de Beldemandis, *Contrapunctus*, 33.

numerous contemporary treatises attest, was an oral practice that children studied along with plainchant and mensural music.[29] The high proportion of brief treatises written in vernacular languages points to oral instruction aimed at "ordinary singers who needed to learn elementary techniques and whose command of written (or even spoken) Latin was uncertain."[30]

Prosdocimus goes on to state that the everyday, oral practice of counterpoint can also be written down – but here he asserts unambiguously that whether written or sung, all counterpoint follows the same rules. Indeed all the authors who address this question speak of a unified contrapuntal practice. A particularly effective synthesis appears in an anonymous south German treatise written in 1476: "in re contrapunctus et modus componendi idem sunt" ("in substance, counterpoint and composition are identical").[31] Around the same time, Tinctoris reminds us that the rules of counterpoint can be broken either spontaneously or in the course of composition: "I have seen many composed melodies using the whole hand and even going outside it and I have heard many boys singing counterpoint extending to the triple diapason."[32]

Fifteenth-century counterpoint consisted in adding a voice – whether orally or in notation – to a preexisting melody, and hence was thought of above all as an individual exercise. But what happened when multiple singers or instrumentalists practiced counterpoint together on the same melody? Here the distinction between composition and improvisation cannot be limited to an opposition between written and oral practices, or between spontaneity and preparation. A process of collaborative creation is at work, whereas in the act of composition, multiple voices added to a chant would be invented by one and the same musician. Collective improvisation thus brings up the question of intention. How can I know what the other musicians will sing while I am singing myself, and how can I prepare for each individual situation?

Renaissance musicians were certainly conscious of the constraints associated with multi-voiced counterpoint, which they differentiated from individual contrapuntal practice. Already in 1434, Giorgio Anselmi highlighted the difference between *discantus*, an action performed by one singer, and *contrapunctus*, a term that implies the presence of a third singer.[33] Tinctoris's well-known expression *cantare super librum* (singing upon the book) refers to collective creation, and is derived from the French *chanter sur le livre*. Shortly after 1500, Spanish writers speak of *contrapunto concertado*, the Italians of *contrapunto alla mente*, while in Germany, theorists designate this collective practice using

---

29  See Wegman, "From Maker to Composer" and relevant bibliography.
30  Fuller, "Organum – Discantus – Contrapunctus," 495–96.
31  Sachs, *De modo componendi*, 150.     32  Tinctoris, *The Art of Counterpoint*, 18.
33  Anselmus, "*De musica*," ed. Massera, 200.

the term *sortisatio*. The aforementioned German treatise of 1476 states that *sortisare* is "aliquem cantum diversis melodiis inprovise ornare" ("to ornate an ordinary chant extempore with different melodies"). Following Ferand, music historians have read the term *sortisare* as a corrupted version of *sortitio* (a random draw), and thus a reference to the idea that chance shapes the character of collective counterpoint.[34] This explanation, in turn, has contributed to a picture of improvised counterpoint as inferior to composition in that its aesthetic result depends on chance. In fact the term more likely originates from the English "consort" or the French *assortir* (to match), hence an assemblage of that which goes well together.[35] *Sortisatio*, then, does not recall indeterminacy, but rather the notion of harmony, of an "assortment" of multiple voices.

It is in this regard that our modern conception of improvisation shows its limitations in describing the phenomenon of collectively performed counterpoint. If we associate improvisation with indeterminacy today, we do so only because we have wrongly considered this act as being neither premeditated nor prepared. By contrast, in fifteenth-century polyphonic improvisation, as in Quintilian's improvised discourse, everything was prepared in accordance with predictable circumstances. The instrumentalists who polyphonically ornamented basse danse tenors and the singers who sang "upon the book" on a plainsong melody were well-versed in these everyday exercises. The melodies that served as their point of departure were hardly unfamiliar to them. Singers who practiced *sortisatio* relied on given melodies from plainchant books, most notably from the Gradual. In fact, the sources attest to the practice of performed counterpoint based on Mass Proper chants such as the Introit and the Alleluia. Some manuscripts from the second half of the fifteenth century even contain written examples of Proper settings that imitate performed counterpoint on a plainchant melody (see Example 9.1 below).

In terms of instrumental practice, about fifty basse danse melodies are preserved in a manuscript of Burgundian provenance, Brussels 9085, and in a Parisian printed source dating from no later than 1496. A quick glance at these sources reveals the similarity of the notation and style of these pieces with the plainchant repertory.[36] The stylistic coherence of the parent melodies and the predictable recurrence of the occasions on which these melodies were used considerably reduces the role that indeterminacy played in performed counterpoint. Therefore, even if for the sake of convenience we today call this practice

---

34  Ferand, "'Sodaine and Unexpected' Music," 11: "from *sortior*, to cast lots, hence improvised music 'by chance'."
35  On this point, see Meyer, "*Sortisatio*," 199.
36  On this tradition, see Keith Polk's article in this volume, Ch. 38.

"improvisation," it is by no means "a leap into the unforeseen," to quote Terence Cave.[37]

How could musicians minimize indeterminacy while singing or playing multiple voices simultaneously? The treatises that evoke collective counterpoint techniques describe a common process that involves locking one voice into strict parallel motion with the preexisting tenor.[38] This allows one or multiple supplementary voices to add counterpoint to the tenor under the condition that they follow a certain number of rules. Fauxbourdon and its byproducts, first described in English treatises, constitute the most widespread example of this technique in the fifteenth century. According to an anonymous tract copied around 1430, the voice producing the counterpoint must sing only thirds or fifths below the plainsong. Under this condition, a third voice could be added, which would double the plainsong a fourth higher. Solmization technique enabled the third voice to pronounce the same syllables as if it were singing the plainsong, but at another pitch level. This is why the Spaniard Juan de Lucena affirmed in 1463 that when singing *fabordón*, "one sings with flats, while the other sings natural."[39] This remark, and the numerous Continental musical sources in which scribes copied hymns and psalms by imitating this technique in written form, with the tenor defined as "a faulx bourdon," show that the aesthetic result must have greatly interested European musicians in the mid-fifteenth century.

Shortly before 1500, a theorist calling himself Guilielmus Monachus detailed various techniques that singers were using to add two or three voices to a plainsong melody. Presenting fauxbourdon as an "English manner," he also proposes another technique that places the cantus firmus below rather than in between the two additional voices. He explains that an upper voice must sing in parallel sixths above the tenor while the third voice sings thirds above the same referential voice. The sounding result is nearly identical to the faburden described in English treatises, although here it is difficult to designate this practice as improvisation since the two added voices function in strict parallelism.[40]

Monachus proposes other methods of counterpointing a tenor, notably by adding three voices: a cantus locked by parallel upper sixths accompanies a contratenor bassus that alternates between thirds and fifths below the chant, while a contratenor altus sings thirds and fourths above the same melody.

---

37 Cave, *The Cornucopian Text*, 125.
38 A survey of these techniques appears in Janin, *Chanter sur le livre*.
39 Juan de Lucena, *Libro de vida beata* (Rome, 1463). See Paz y Meliá, *Opúsculos literarios*, 157.
40 On the first and last note of each phrase, the cantus must sing an octave above the tenor, and the contratenor a fifth above. See Monachus, *De preceptis artis musicae*, 38.

When the tenor progresses by conjunct movements in a "minor" mode, the resounding four-voiced sonorities are those that we find decades later in polyphonic arrangements of airs based on dances, such as *Guardame las vacas* or the *passamezzo antico*. The treatise concludes by describing a procedure that would soon become widely known: doubling the tenor in parallel motion a tenth above, leaving a third intermediary voice the space to create counterpoint as it wished, under the condition that it did not produce two identical consonances in a row. This parallel tenths technique became the procedure most commonly used by singers performing a *contrapunto concertado*, as later described by Vicente Lusitano.[41] This practice is confirmed by late fifteenth-century sources that imitate multi-voiced performed counterpoint on a plainsong or arrange basse danse tenors such as *La Spagna*. In Example 9.1, the outer voices move in parallel tenths in measures 2, 3, 4, and 9. In measure 7 we find one of the characteristics of collective improvisation of the period, as highlighted by Tinctoris in his counterpoint treatise: unlike composed works that must avoid dissonances between all pairs of voices, here each of the two added voices is consonant with the tenor, but can create dissonances with one another.

The conflicting opinions sparked by Tinctoris's chapter comparing performed counterpoint (*cantare super librum*) with written composition (*res facta*) have at times obscured the true value of this text for the history of improvisational techniques.[42] In fact, Tinctoris refers to performed counterpoint in many other passages in the treatise, and he gives examples that provide us with a fairly precise idea of the abilities attained by certain singers. He explains how singers transformed the plainchant into a measured melody of equal semibreves or breves (like the tenor of Example 9.1), a fixed rhythmic pattern, or even a measured melody where the value of the notes is variable. Indeed Tinctoris asserts that "the highest degree of art and skill" was attained by certain singers, albeit rarely, who were able to improvise counterpoint not only on a tenor, but also on a different voice of a polyphonic composition.[43] This statement shows that by the end of the fifteenth century, the most talented singers had transformed counterpoint from a utilitarian discipline, necessary for ornamenting plainsong, into an ostentatious exercise to showcase their virtuosity. Tinctoris adds: "if it be made knowledgeably and sweetly, the more praiseworthy it is for being the more difficult." With this

---

41 Canguilhem, "Singing upon the Book," 82–83.
42 Bk. 2, ch. 20.
43 Tinctoris, *The Art of Counterpoint*, 112. According to Bonnie Blackburn, this phrase indicated that "some are even able to sing over two voices from a *res facta*." See Blackburn, "On Compositional Process," 256. It is in fact ambiguous whether "non solum ... sed etiam" means over a tenor or over a different voice of the composition, or over two voices.

Example 9.1  Anon., *Alleluya Salve virgo* (first part) (Segovia s.s., fol. 151r)

last statement, the famed theorist reminds us that for fifteenth-century musicians, although recognition as an artist and creator equivalent to that of the poet was attained through the composition of *res facta*, the ability to produce a new melody instantaneously in spite of numerous constraints would earn a musician renown among connoisseurs. After all, what could be more precious for an artist than to be revered and respected by members of his own community?

## Bibliography

Abramov-van Rijk, Elena, *Parlar cantando: The Practice of Reciting Verses in Italy from 1300 to 1600*, Bern, 2009

Anselmus, Georgius, *Georgii Anselmi Parmensis "De musica,"* ed. Giuseppe Massera, Florence, 1961

Apel, Willi, ed., *Keyboard Music of the Fourteenth and Fifteenth Centuries*, Corpus of Early Keyboard Music 1, Rome, 1963

Bent, Margaret, "*Resfacta* and *Cantare Super Librum*," *JAMS* 36 (1983), 371–91

Berger, Anna Maria Busse, *Medieval Music and the Art of Memory*, Berkeley, 2005

Berger, Karol, *A Theory of Art*, New York and Oxford, 2000

Blackburn, Bonnie J., "On Compositional Process in the Fifteenth Century," *JAMS* 40 (1987), 210–84

Butler, Gregory G., "The Fantasia as Musical Image," *MQ* 60 (1974), 602–15

Butt, John, "Germany and the Netherlands," in *Keyboard Music before 1700*, ed. Alexander Silbiger, 2nd edn., New York, 2004, 147–234

Canguilhem, Philippe, "Singing upon the Book according to Vicente Lusitano," *EMH* 30 (2011), 55–103

Cave, Terence, *The Cornucopian Text: Problems of Writing in the French Renaissance*, Oxford, 1979

Chastel, André, *Marsile Ficin et l'art*, 3rd edn., Geneva, 1996

Ferand, Ernest, "'Sodaine and Unexpected' Music in the Renaissance," *MQ* 37 (1951), 10–27

Fuller, Sarah, "Organum – Discantus – Contrapunctus in the Middle Ages," in *The Cambridge History of Western Music Theory*, ed. Thomas Christensen, Cambridge, 2002, 477–502

Galand-Hallyn, Perrine, and Fernand Hallyn, eds., *Poétiques de la Renaissance: Le modèle italien, le monde franco-bourguignon et leur héritage en France au XVIe siècle*, Geneva, 2001

Gallo, F. Alberto, *Music in the Castle*, Chicago, 1995

Gumbrecht, Hans Ulrich, *Production of Presence: What Meaning Cannot Convey*, Stanford, 2004

Janin, Barnabé, *Chanter sur le livre: Manuel pratique d'improvisation polyphonique de la Renaissance, xve et xvie siècles*, 2nd edn., Lyon, 2014

Juan de Lucena, *Libro de vida beata*, Rome, 1463

Lecointe, Jean, *L'Idéal et la différence*, Geneva, 1993

Lockwood, Lewis, "Pietrobono [Petrus Bonus] de Burzellis [de Bruzellis, del Chitarino]," *Grove Music Online* (accessed 1 September 2013)

Mengelkoch, Dustin, "The Mutability of Poetics: Poliziano, Statius and the *Silvae*," *Modern Language Notes* 125 (2010), 84–116

Meyer, Christian, "*Sortisatio*: De l'improvisation collective dans les pays germaniques vers 1500," in *Polyphonies de tradition orale: Histoire et traditions vivantes*, ed. Christian Meyer, Paris, 1993, 183–200

Monachus, Guilielmus, *De preceptis artis musicae*, ed. Albert Seay, [Rome], 1965

Paz y Meliá, Antonio, *Opúsculos literarios de los siglos XIV á XVI*, Madrid, 1892

Pirrotta, Nino, and Elena Povoledo, *Music and Theatre from Poliziano to Monteverdi*, Cambridge, 1982

Poliziano, Angelo, *Prose volgari inedite e poesie latine e greche*, ed. Isidoro Del Lungo, Florence, 1867

Prosdocimus de Beldemandis, *Contrapunctus*, ed. and trans. Jan Herlinger, Lincoln, NE, 1984

Quintilian, *Institutio oratoria*, trans. H. E. Butler, vol. 4, London, 1922

Rossi, Francesco Rocco, "*Vergine bella* e Dufay: Dalla tradizione improvvisativa alla *res facta*," in *Petrarca in musica*, ed. Andrea Chegai and Cecilia Luzzi, Lucca, 2005, 83–99

Sachs, Klaus-Jürgen, "Arten improvisierter Mehrstimmigkeit nach Lehrtexten des 14. bis 16. Jahrhunderts," *BJhM* 7 (1983), 166–83

    *De modo componendi: Studien zu musikalischen Lehrtexten des späten 15. Jahrhunderts*, Hildesheim, 2002

    *Der Contrapunctus im 14. und 15. Jahrhundert: Untersuchungen zum Terminus, zur Lehre und zu den Quellen*, Wiesbaden, 1974

Schrÿvers, P. H., "Invention, imagination, et théorie des émotions chez Cicéron et Quintilien," in *Rhetoric Revalued*, ed. Brian Vickers, Binghamton, NY, 1982, 47–57

Tinctoris, Johannes, *The Art of Counterpoint*, trans. Albert Seay, [Rome], 1961

Toliver, Brooks, "Improvisation in the Madrigals of the *Rossi Codex*," *AcM* 64 (1992), 165–76

Treitler, Leo, *With Voice and Pen: Coming to Know Medieval Song and How It Was Made*, New York, 2003

Trumble, Ernest, *Fauxbourdon: An Historical Survey*, Brooklyn, 1959

Wegman, Rob C., "From Maker to Composer: Improvisation and Musical Authorship in the Low Countries, 1450–1500," *JAMS* 49 (1996), 409–79

# 10

# How did Oswald von Wolkenstein make his contrafacta?

ANNA MARIA BUSSE BERGER

The transition in music from orality to literacy is a much discussed topic. Let me begin by quickly summarizing what I believe is the current view of the matter. By the early fourteenth century, at the latest, most of the polyphonic music became the territory of specialists who underwent rigorous training in mensural notation.[1] Without their knowledge of notation, these composers would not have been able to create isorhythmic motets or polyphonic chansons. Mensural notation opened enormous possibilities: composers were now able to indicate intricate rhythms unambiguously, and it gradually became possible to formulate counterpoint rules that would have been unimaginable without writing. As a result, we now have compositions that needed to be preserved exactly, since the slightest change would ruin the entire structure; these pieces were not only listened to, but also studied. In short, notation changed the way composers thought about music. Anthropologists have shown that within a few years of the invention of writing systems, word and number games become common; we can observe something similar within a few years of the invention of mensural notation. Isorhythmic motets and polyphonic chansons show the composer's delight in experimenting with new rhythmic possibilities such as diminution, augmentation, and retrograde movement.[2]

In short, we can safely assume that all fourteenth- and fifteenth-century composers of polyphony were literate, and they knew their mensural notation well. There is one exception, however: the last great Minnesinger, Oswald von Wolkenstein.

Oswald was born around 1376 and died in 1445 in Meran in South Tyrol.[3] He is relatively unknown outside Germany and Austria, so it will come as a surprise that many Germanists consider him the most important German poet between Walther von der Vogelweide and Goethe.[4] His life is unusually well

My thanks to Julie Cumming, Nicole Schwindt, Reinhard Strohm, and Anne Stone for their helpful comments.

1 See Stone, below, Ch. 30.  2 Berger, *Medieval Music*, ch. 6.
3 Welker, "Oswald von Wolkenstein."  4 Kühn, *Ich Wolkenstein*.

documented. A member of a noble Tyrolean family, he traveled extensively throughout his life. He spent two years as a young man in East Prussia and Lithuania with the Teutonic knights, colonizing the territory and exterminating the native population. Subsequently, he was part of King Ruprecht's Italian campaign, and, more importantly, a councilor for King Sigismund of Hungary, whom he accompanied on trips to France, Navarre, Paris, England, and Rome.

Oswald's compositions are transmitted mainly in two manuscripts that were probably made during his lifetime, possibly under his supervision in the Augustinian priory at Novacella, close to his birthplace. The earlier one, MS A, now in Vienna, was copied around 1425, the later one, MS B, now in Innsbruck, around 1432.[5] Both include a portrait of Oswald. The one in Innsbruck is attributed to Pisanello and was probably painted in 1433 when he accompanied Sigismund to Rome for his coronation as emperor.

Altogether 131 lieder, fifty-seven monophonic melodies, and thirty-seven polyphonic settings from two to four voices are transmitted under Oswald's name.[6] Eleven of the monophonic melodies are used more than once. Most remarkable is that at this point sixteen of the thirty-seven polyphonic settings have been identified as contrafacta, and the general impression is that more will be found. Note that in all cases Oswald turns the tenor of an originally discant-dominated song into the main melody. Until recently it was generally assumed that all of the monophonic song melodies were composed by Oswald himself. This too no longer seems certain: in 2001, Rainer Böhm made the remarkable discovery that Oswald's monophonic song *O wunniklicher, wolgezierter mai* (Kl. 100) is derived from the tenor of Gilles Binchois's popular three-voice rondeau *Triste plaisir et douloureuse joye.*[7]

To be sure, it took scholars a long time to identify the models of Oswald's songs: as we will see, he often alters the original composition nearly beyond recognition. All the same, given that so many of his compositions are contrafacta, one has to ask to what extent Oswald was an original composer of polyphonic music.[8] Are any of the pieces really his? And, moreover, why would he always take the tenor and make it into the main melody?

---

5 Note, though, that Reinhard Strohm argues that Wolkenstein Codex A was copied in Vienna in "Native and Foreign Polyphony." See also Schwob, *Historische Realität*, 235 ff.

6 For a list of his songs, see Welker, "Oswald von Wolkenstein." The polyphonic songs have been edited by Pelnar in *Die mehrstimmigen Lieder*; see also Strohm, "Die vierstimmige Bearbeitung," and "Song Composition." See also Welker, "New Light," "Some Aspects," and "Mehrstimmige Sätze."

7 Böhm, "Entdeckung einer französischen Melodienvorlage." More recently, Isabel Kraft has also described the two pieces in "Rondeau oder Reigen." See also Strohm's discussion of how Oswald went about performing and transmitting his pieces in "Lied und Musik."

8 Göllner was the first to raise this question in "Landinis 'Questa fanciulla'." For an excellent study of citation in fourteenth-century song, see Plumley, *The Art of the Grafted Song.*

There is a vast amount of secondary literature on Oswald, particularly by Germanists. Since the 1970s we can observe a fundamental shift in the understanding of how his literary work came into existence. While earlier scholars considered Oswald a great poet who created his works in writing, it is now clear that knights did not attend schools, did not memorize chant, and usually did not learn Latin. Instead, they were placed as pages in the service of a lord whom they served and from whom they learned the codes of chivalry; their life centered around mastering knightly skills in the use of weapons, horsemanship, and warfare. In addition, some had legal and diplomatic training.

As a result, George Fenwick Jones argued more than thirty years ago that Oswald could not read or write.[9] Naturally, this claim did not go unchallenged; and while it is impossible to prove that Oswald did not know how to read, this skill would have been unusual for someone in his position. What we know for certain is that Oswald employed a scribe who is mentioned in one of his songs.[10]

It seems even less likely that Oswald was versed in mensural notation: in a brilliant but little-known article from 1974, the Germanist Erika Timm asked whether it would be possible for an amateur to learn how to compose polyphony in the Middle Ages outside church circles.[11] She first demonstrates that there is no evidence that mensural notation was part of Oswald's, or for that matter, any knight's education. Next, she employs simple statistics to make her point: there are 180 composers listed in fourteenth- and fifteenth-century manuscripts, of whom fifty-six are unknown. Of the remaining 124, 107 are clerics, and thirteen have titles like *magister* added to their names, which shows that they had a university education. None of the remaining composers has a title such as *dominus* or *miles* assigned to his compositions. In the end, there remain only two aristocratic composers, John of Aragon and Henry of England, both of whom had their own chapels with musicians who helped them compose and notate their music. In short, this evidence makes it very unlikely that Oswald knew mensural notation. Reinhard Strohm has similarly argued that Oswald was musically illiterate, memorized the songs when he heard them, and had them copied later.[12]

It is surprising that with a few exceptions, musicologists have shown so little interest in investigating further the implications of the fact that here we have a great poet and capable composer/singer who might have been musically illiterate. Instead, scholars have concentrated on demonstrating

9 Jones, *Oswald von Wolkenstein*.    10 See also Welker, "New Light."
11 Timm, "Ein Beitrag zur Frage" and *Die Überlieferung der Lieder*.
12 Strohm, *The Rise of European Music* and "Song Composition"; see also Welker, "New Light," "Some Aspects," and "Die Überlieferung."

Figure 10.1  Oswald von Wolkenstein, *Wol auf, wir wollen slafen*, MS A, fol. 45r

interrelationships between various manuscripts, and showing convincingly that there is a central European tradition of transmission of French and Italian polyphony from which most of Oswald's contrafacta were derived.[13] This concentration on the musical texts is both necessary and understandable. First, a comparison of the manuscripts shows without a doubt that Oswald's pieces were derived from their models. Second, polyphonic music, in particular, is for most of us intimately associated with notation. For us it seems counterintuitive that someone might have been a composer of polyphony without being musically literate.

Let us return to our main question: how did Oswald go about transforming polyphonic chansons into German lieder? And how would he have composed polyphonic songs for which there seems to be no model? Figure 10.1 shows the Vienna manuscript version of the two-voice song *Wol auf, wir wollen slafen*, which

13 See Timm, *Die Überlieferung der Lieder*; Strohm, "Native and Foreign Polyphony"; Welker, "New Light."

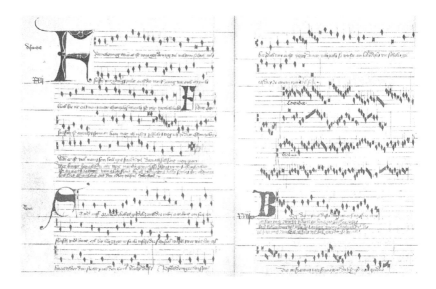

Figure 10.2  Oswald von Wolkenstein, *Stand auf, Maredel*, MS A, fols. 14v–15r

does not seem to be a contrafactum (MS A, fol. 45r). Could Oswald have composed it on his own? It is a very simple piece mainly in minims with a few semibreves; there are no complicated mensuration signs and no syncopations, and the counterpoint is so simple that it must have grown out of improvisation. I think it would be very difficult to argue with certainty that Oswald would not have been able to read this music. All you have to know is how a staff works, and that a minim is faster than a semibreve. The vast majority of two-voice compositions by Oswald for which no model has been found fall into this category. He could easily have notated them with the help of a scribe who had some rudimentary knowledge of notation. But the important point is that notation was not necessary for the composition of this piece, since it is a simple strophic song.

At the opposite end of the spectrum, we have the four-voice song *Stand auf, Maredel* (Figure 10.2), which is a contrafactum of the anonymous rondeau *Jour a jour la vie*, which circulated in eight different manuscripts and versions.[14] Timm has discovered that it was originally notated as a two-voice song in Vienna MS A, then erased and replaced later in the manuscript with the four-voice version.[15] The notation of the four-voice version requires thorough training in mensural notation. Yet the two-voice version, also found in MS B, could have easily been transmitted orally: it is strophic, the discant and tenor

---

14 Pelnar, *Die mehrstimmigen Lieder*, p. xv, where all concordances are listed.
15 Timm, "Ein Beitrag zur Frage," 321–22.

have different texts, making it easier to memorize the melodies, and they have rhymes in common. David Fallows has shown that in his multi-textual songs Oswald consistently uses the same rhyme in both voices at the same time.[16] None of the French composers whose songs Oswald transcribes uses rhymes in this way. In short, Oswald's was much easier to memorize.

Let us now take a closer look at a song by Oswald that lies somewhere in between these two extremes and compare it to its original version. *Frölich, zärtlich, lieplich und klärlich, lustlich, stille, leise* (see Figure 10.3) is based on the popular anonymous rondeau *En tes doulz flans* from the Reina Codex. The model is a three-voice chanson in rondeau form (see Example 10.1). It is obviously a piece transmitted in writing. This, however, does not mean that the song was not sung from memory by the singers when they performed it. Only the top voice is texted.

Oswald's lied is so transformed that it is no wonder it took scholars so long to identify the model (see Example 10.2). The differences are as follows:

1. The melody is transferred to the tenor, the only texted voice in the Innsbruck manuscript B. Oswald is generally credited with being the inventor of the *Tenorlied*. A comparison of the original tenor with Oswald's transformed tenor melody shows that he left the tenor essentially intact (see Example 10.3). (The only differences are that he dropped the breve *c′* in m. 8 of the chanson and shortened the *a* in m. 43 by one-half.) As is to be expected, both songs have a major cadence at the end of the first section (m. 24), but within the two sections Oswald adds a number of cadences that are of no importance in the model while disregarding others. (The cadences are indicated by a comma.) The discant is treated with considerably more freedom. In three phrases the passing notes are different.

2. Oswald is only interested in the tenor melody, and sings the *prima* and *secunda partes* in direct succession. In other words, he either does not understand how a French rondeau works, or consciously disregards the form, transforming the melody into a simple strophic song that can be reused for the three stanzas of his text.

3. As in all of his contrafacta, Oswald leaves out the countertenor.

4. As in his other songs, Oswald has divided the longer notes of the melody into many shorter ones. He has done this in both tenor and discant. In other words, he has removed all melismas and transformed the tenor into a syllabic song.

5. The original flat has been omitted from the key signature.

6. There are some clef mistakes in Oswald's song.

---

16 Fallows, "Two Equal Voices."

Figure 10.3 Oswald von Wolkenstein, *Frölich, zärtlich, lieplich und klärlich, lustlich, stille, leise*, MS A, fols. 32v–33r

So how did Oswald create his new text if he was unable to read mensural notation? Why did he transform the tenor into the main melody? And why did he transform a melismatic tenor into a syllabic melody? Obviously, we can only speculate, but some explanations seem more likely than others.

Example 10.1 Anon., *En tes douz flans*, Paris 6771 (Reina Codex), ed. W. Apel, PMFC 22, p. 55

There is general agreement among Oswald scholars that he was introduced to many of the models from which he made contrafacta at the Councils of Constance and Basel.[17] Or he could have learned the songs at other courts he visited during his frequent travels. If, as we believe, Oswald had no training in mensural notation and counterpoint, then the polyphonic performances he heard at these courts must have been a revelation to him.[18] I think it is unlikely

17 Planchart, "The Early Career," 354 and 359; see also Schuler, "Die Musik in Konstanz."
18 Staehelin has similarly suggested that German musicians made so many contrafacta because German polyphony was considerably simpler at this point. "The Constitution," 177.

Example 10.2 Oswald von Wolkenstein, *Frölich, zärtlich, lieplich und klärlich*

Example 10.2  (cont.)

that he immediately had copies made of the original chansons when he made his contrafacta, because then he would not have had the earlier mentioned four-voice song *Stand auf, Maredel* notated in a rudimentary two-voice version in the manuscript before he got his hands on the four-voice version.

So how, then, did he learn the tenor and discant parts? Could he have learned them by listening to them? Picking out the tenor by ear cannot have been easy for someone who was not trained to sing polyphony. I think it is most likely that he participated in performances of polyphonic chansons by singing and memorizing the tenor, which would have been in his voice range.[19] This would also provide us with an explanation for why he turned the tenor into the main melody. This was his part when he performed it, first with an ensemble, then alone.[20] In other words, the creation of the German tenor lied might be based on the simple fact that the tenor was in Oswald's range. This confirms Timm's

19 Similarly, Strohm has suggested that he learned and memorized the material with the help of other musicians in "Song Composition."
20 This adds also further support to the theory that fifteenth-century chansons were regularly performed by voices without instruments.

Example 10.3 Comparison of tenors of *En tes douz flans* and *Frölich, zärtlich, lieplich und klärlich*

point that Oswald was less interested in the polyphonic structure and more in the tenor voice, which he could adapt to his purposes.[21] The fact that he transformed a three-voice Binchois chanson into a monophonic lied, taking again only the tenor, adds further support to this hypothesis.

Moreover, the melodies and new texts were transmitted orally until he had access to someone who knew mensural notation and could put it all into writing. If our assumptions are correct, we would have to find characteristics in both melody and text that would make them memorable. The melody of *Frölich, zärtlich* (Example 10.2) is as simple as that of our first example, *Wol auf, wir wollen slafen*: even someone with little training could have understood the notation. Oswald must also have created the new text and memorized both it and the melody until he had access to someone who knew mensural notation and could put it all into writing.

Obviously, any text would have made the tune easier to memorize. There is general agreement among ancient and medieval scholars of memory that in societies that know writing, memorization of a written text or melody begins with committing the structure of the piece to memory. For example, an isorhythmic motet can be summarized in a simple formula such as 2×5×6, which would indicate the number of tenor *taleae* and *colores*.[22] Similarly, a *forme fixe* would be easy to memorize, because it consists of a sequence of sections repeated in a certain fixed order, such as ABaAabAB for a rondeau. In Oswald's case it is striking that he rejected the more complex structure of the rondeau in favor of a simple strophic form, probably because it was so much easier to memorize, even for someone who did not know how to read music. He did this in all of his contrafacta.

What makes a text memorable? Authors of medieval treatises on the art of memory stress particularly the effectiveness of imagery and sound patterns. In his treatise *De memoria artificiali* from ca. 1335, Thomas Bradwardine says the following about the images selected: "Their quality should be truly wondrous and intense, because such things are impressed in memory more deeply and are better retained."[23] He emphasizes the importance of using a truly striking image: "One places a very red bull to the right of the ram with his rear feet; standing erect, the ram then with his right foot kicks the bull above his large and super-swollen testicles, causing a copious infusion of blood."[24]

---

21  Timm, "Ein Beitrag zur Frage," 322.     22  Berger, *Medieval Music*, ch. 6.
23  Trans. Carruthers, *The Book of Memory*, 282–83.
24  Trans. ibid., 283–84.

Concerning sound patterns, putting material into verse was the most common method of memorization and was used for practically every subject. The twelfth and thirteenth centuries in particular saw an enormous growth in the use of verse for didactic purposes in nearly all fields, among them grammar, medicine, law, theology, arithmetic, and music theory.[25]

Similarly, cognitive psychologists describe multiple constraints that are central to memorization, including organization of meaning, imagery, and patterns of sound. The sound patterns listed in particular by David Rubin in his 1995 book *Memory in Oral Traditions* are poetic devices familiar to all of us, such as assonance, rhyme, alliteration, and rhythm.[26] Psychologists call these formal multiple constraints, which reduce the available possibilities. General constraints are set when the genre is chosen; for example, a sonnet sets up an expectation of fourteen lines, each line containing ten syllables in iambic meter. The particular constraints, as, for example, rhythm, should come at the beginning of the poem, rhyme at the end of the first line, and alliteration and assonance are employed throughout to provide cues for the remaining recall. To quote Rubin, "Both the general and specific constraints add cue-item discriminability, increasing the amount recalled and restricting the kinds of errors or variations made." Rubin stresses how difficult it is for the poet to change words "without reducing the amount and quality of poetic devices."[27]

Let us compare the first stanza of Oswald's poem (see Appendix) with the French text (Appendix):

Frölich, zärtlich, lieplich und
    klärlich, lustlich, stille, leise,
in senfter, süsser, keuscher, sainer weise
wach, du minnikliches, schönes weib,
reck, streck, breis dein zarten, stolzen
    leib!
Sleuss auf dein vil liechte öglin klar!

Taugenlich nim war,
wie sich verschart der sterne gart
inn der schönen, haittren, klaren sunne
    glanz.
wol auff zu dem tanz!
machen ainen schönen kranz

En tes doulz flans plains de la
    virginité
Et de excellence plus qu'on ne
    porait dire
Virgine pucelle, portas l'humanité
En tes doulz flans plains de la
    virginité
Bien doit trover cascuns ta
    dignité
Quant en tel volait herberge
    eslire.
En tes doulz flans plains de la
    virginité

---

25 Berger, *Medieval Music*, 180–88, which includes a list of secondary literature; see also Klopsch, *Einführungen in die Dichtungslehren*.
26 Rubin, *Memory in Oral Traditions*.    27 Ibid., 176 and 210.

| von schawnen, prawnen, plawen, grawen, | Et de excellence plus qu'on ne porait dire |
| gel, rot, weiss, | |
| viol plümlin spranz. | |

The text of the French song seems at first glance to be considerably more regular. All lines have approximately the same number of syllables and there are only two rhymes. And yet, when one listens to the music the text seems irrelevant – it recedes into the background. What you hear and remember is a three-voice composition with a dominating discant voice enlivened by the tension and resolution of frequent, irregular cadences. Oswald's song, on the other hand, is completely dominated by the text and the tenor melody. Indeed, both are so memorable that it just requires a few hearings to have both text and tenor melody firmly committed to memory. And this in spite of the fact that the syllable scheme is irregular (the first line of every strophe is considerably longer than the following).

Oswald is a virtuoso of poetic devices. All of his songs have memorable images, and our example *Frölich, zärtlich* is no exception: the first stanza describes the waking up of his lover in vivid colors; you can just visualize her stretching and moving her body: "reck, streck, breis dein zarten, stolzen leib!" This image is intensified by the internal rhyme of *reck* and *streck*, as well as the assonances of *breis*, *dein*, and *leib*. The second stanza focuses on the red mouth and all of the things the mouth can do: lisping, kissing, whispering, murmuring, again with rhymes and assonances. The words of the first line present a virtual tongue twister, and the mouth imitates the sounds made by the lovers: "Lünzlot, münzlot, klünzlot und zisplot, wisplot." Many of the words are Oswald's creations: for example, "münzlot" probably derives from *Münze* = coin, but here it is used figuratively for *küssen*, and alludes to *Mund* = mouth and/or *mutze* = vulva.[28] The last stanza describes what would happen if the physical longings were fulfilled, with striking images of meeting of the mouths, tongues, breasts, waists, etc.

Now to the form: the poem consists of three stanzas in trochaic meter; each stanza has two sections that follow the *prima* and *secunda partes* of the rondeau. The song consists of three closely linked strophes, each two lines rhyming; only the penultimate line stands alone. Instead, in all three strophes the penultimate lines rhyme with each other in at least two, if not three, syllables: "gel, rot, weiss," "hel zu vleiss," and "snel zu fleiss." In addition, the lines around the penultimate one in each stanza are similarly constructed, consisting

---

28 Marold and Robertshaw, *Kommentar zu den Liedern*, 170–71.

almost entirely of double assonances: "Frölich, zärtlich, lieplich und klärlich, lustlich, stille, leise," in the first stanza, "Lünzlot, münzlot, klünzlot und zisplot, wisplot freundlich sprachen," in the second; and "Wolt si, solt si, tät si und käm si, näm si meinem herzen," in the third. In short, Oswald's poetry certainly fulfills all the requirements of a memorable poem.

So how did this recomposition take place? I would suggest the following scenario: Oswald heard the chanson, learned and most likely performed the tenor melody with a group, transformed it into a strophic song, and composed his memorable text to fit the melody. Thus, it might not be a coincidence that all of the chansons on which his lieder are based were extremely popular and for the most part transmitted in several manuscripts. Oswald composed the text to garner applause and admiration for his performance. To quote Strohm, "his work was his singing."[29]

Let us now take stock. What we have here is an important poet and a competent composer who either could not write at all or had a rudimentary knowledge of writing and notation, but who used a written model for orally conceived compositions that he later had written down, perhaps first in a monophonic version, then in a polyphonic one, with the help of copies of the model piece. The composition began in writing, was memorized, and resulted in a new orally conceived composition that may have been performed at first without notation, but was eventually preserved by scribes under instruction from Oswald. In other words, even though Oswald might not have been able to write, he lived in a society that valued written texts. We could perhaps call this process secondary orality.

This fits well with a theoretical framework outlined by the anthropologist Jack Goody.[30] He has argued that it makes little sense to maintain a clear-cut distinction between oral and written culture. Instead, he suggests replacing this with a distinction between oral culture, on the one hand, and oral plus written and printed culture, on the other. The result is a considerable refinement of how compositions were put together in societies that have knowledge of writing, but still work out pieces in the mind. The adjustment Goody proposes might seem small, but it helps us to move away from the idea that once writing was invented, all features of an oral culture rapidly disappeared. It allows us, instead, to see in the musical culture of the Middle Ages a rich and complex interplay of oral and literate features. With regard to Oswald, we know that he could dictate his texts and melodies to his scribe and so preserve them intact. He could ask the scribe to read and sing them to him from the manuscript and would

29 Strohm, "Lied und Musik," who explains in fascinating detail that Oswald's pride was attached not to his melodies, but to his texts and the performance of the songs.
30 Goody, *The Interface between the Written and the Oral.*

be able to distinguish the correct from the incorrect version of his piece. In other words, writing did not eliminate memorization; quite the contrary, the written page permitted different ways of memorizing material and texts.

We have observed in this song that Oswald's text is more memorable than that of the original composition on which it is based. He continuously employs striking images, which he combines with rhymes, assonances, and alliterations. While we have to be careful not to overinterpret, I think these features of Oswald's poems may possibly be connected with the fact that he was an oral poet and an oral composer. For him the sound of the language must have been as important as the music itself.

# Appendix

Text and translation of Oswald's *Frölich, zärtlich, lieplich und klärlich*

I    Tenor
Frölich, zärtlich, lieplich und klärlich, lustlich, stille, leise,
in senfter, süsser, keuscher, sainer weise
wach, du minnikliches, schönes weib,
reck, streck, breis dein zarten, stolzen leib!
Sleuss auf dein vil liechte öglin klar!

Taugenlich nim war,
wie sich verschart der sterne gart
inn der schönen, haittren, klaren sunne glanz.
wol auff zu dem tanz!
machen ainen schönen kranz

von schawnen, prawnen, plawen, grawen,
gel, rot, weiss,
viol plümlin spranz.

II
Lünzlot, münzlot, klünzlot und zisplot, wisplot freuntlich sprachen
aufs waidelichen, güten, rainen sachen
sol dein pöschelochter, rotter mund,
der ser mein herz lieplich hat erzunt

Und mich fürwar tausent mal erweckt,
freuntlichen erschreckt
auss slauffes träm, so ich ergäm
ain so wolgezierte, rotte, enge spalt,
lächerlich gestalt,

zendlin weiss dorin gezalt,
trielisch, mielisch, vöslocht, röslocht,
hel zu vleiss
waidelich gemalt.

III
Wolt si, solt si, tät si und käm si, näm si meinem herzen
den senikleichen, grossen, herten smerzen,
und ain brüstlin weiss darauff gedruckt,
secht, slecht so wer mein trauren gar verruckt.

Wie möcht ain zart seuberliche diern
lustlicher geziern
das herze mein an argen pein
mit so wunniklichem, zarten, rainen lust?
mund mündlin gekusst,
zung an zünglin, brüstlin an brust,
bauch an beuchlin, rauch an reuchlin,
snel zu fleiss
allzeit frisch getusst.

Translation by Albrecht Classen, *The Poems of Oswald von Wolkenstein*: 136–37

1. Wake up happily, softly, gracefully, brilliantly, delightfully, calmly, and
   restfully in a pleasant, sweet, pure, and considerate manner,
   you delightful, beautiful woman:
   stretch, stand up, show your graceful, noble body proudly;
   open your bright, clear eyes!

   Observe carefully
   how the garden of stars
   fades away in the gleaming of the beautiful, bright, and brilliant sun.
   Let us go to the dance,
   let's make a beautiful wreath
   with a bouquet
   of yellow, brown, blue, grey
   yellow-red-white
   and violet flowers.

2. Your full red lips should lisp, whisper, speak silently, and chatter
   delightfully about delightful, charming, pleasant matters.
   These lips have truly awoken me a thousand times
   and tenderly,

and have rattled me out of the dream of my sleep, every time
when I observe such a tender, red, narrow gap between them,
formed into a smile,
framed by white, lined-up little teeth,
making her mouth smile, round and softly, in the color of roses,
really brightly,
like a wonderful picture.

3. If she wanted and she should – if she came, she would remove from my
heart this painful, heavy, bitter suffering!
Especially if she let rest a white little breast on me,
see, then my sadness would be simply swept away.

How could a delightful, graceful young woman
lift up my heart even further,
without causing pain,
granting only fantastic, lovely, pure happiness?
Lips on lips, they kiss!
Tongue to tongue, breast on breast,
belly on belly, hair on hair,
really fast,
and always pushing hard.

## Bibliography

Berger, Anna Maria Busse, *Medieval Music and the Art of Memory*, Berkeley, 2005

Böhm, Rainer, "Entdeckung einer französischen Melodienvorlage zum Lied *O wunni-klicher, wolgezierter mai* (Kl. 100) von Oswald von Wolkenstein," *Jahrbuch der Oswald von Wolkenstein-Gesellschaft* 13 (2001/2), 269–78

Carruthers, Mary, *The Book of Memory: A Study of Memory in Medieval Culture*, Cambridge, 1990

"Thomas Bradwardine, 'De memoria artificiale adquirenda'," *Journal of Medieval Latin* 2 (1992), 25–43

Classen, Albrecht, *The Poems of Oswald von Wolkenstein: An English Translation of the Complete Works (1376/77–1445)*. Basingstoke, 2008

Fallows, David, "Two Equal Voices: A French Song Repertory with Music for Two or More Works of Oswald von Wolkenstein," *EMH* 7 (1987), 227–41

Göllner, Theodor, "Landinis 'Questa fanciulla' bei Oswald von Wolkenstein," *Die Musikforschung* 17 (1964), 393–98

Goody, Jack, *The Interface between the Written and the Oral*, Cambridge: 1987

Jones, George Fenwick, *Oswald von Wolkenstein*, New York, 1973

Kraft, Isabel, "Rondeau oder Reigen: 'Triste plaisir' und ein Mailied Oswalds von Wolkenstein," in *"Ieglicher sang sein eigen ticht": Germanistische und musikwissen-schaftliche Beiträge zum deutschen Lied im Mittelalter*, Wiesbaden, 2011, 75–97

Klopsch, Paul, *Einführungen in die Dichtungslehren des lateinischen Mittelalters Verslehre*, Darmstadt, 1980

Kühn, Dieter, *Ich Wolkenstein: Biographie*, Frankfurt am Main, 1977; repr. 1996

Marold, Werner, and Alan Robertshaw, *Kommentar zu den Liedern Oswalds von Wolkenstein*, Innsbruck, 1995

Pelnar, Ivana, *Die mehrstimmigen Lieder Oswalds von Wolkenstein*, 2 vols., Tutzing, 1981–82

Planchart, Alejandro E., "The Early Career of Guillaume Du Fay," *JAMS* 46 (1993), 341–68

Plumley, Yolanda, *The Art of Grafted Song: Citation and Allusion in the Age of Machaut*, New York, 2013

Rubin, David C., *Memory in Oral Traditions: The Cognitive Psychology of Epic, Ballads, and Counting-Out Rhymes*, Oxford, 1995

Schuler, Manfred, "Die Musik in Konstanz während des Konzils 1414–1418," *AcM* 38 (1966), 150–68

Schwob, Anton, *Historische Realität und literarische Umsetzung: Beobachtungen zur Stilisierung der Gefangenschaft in den Liedern Oswalds von Wolkenstein*, Innsbruck, 1979

Staehelin, Martin, "The Constitution of the Fifteenth-Century German Tenor Lied: Drafting the History of a Musical Genre," in *Music in the German Renaissance: Sources, Styles, and Contexts*, ed. John Kmetz, Cambridge, 1994, 174–81

Strohm, Reinhard, "Lied und Musik," *Jahrbuch der Oswald von Wolkenstein-Gesellschaft* (forthcoming)

"Native and Foreign Polyphony in Late Medieval Austria," *MD* 38 (1984), 205–30

*The Rise of European Music, 1380–1500*, Cambridge, 1993

"Song Composition in the Fourteenth and Fifteenth Centuries: Old and New Questions," *Jahrbuch der Oswald von Wolkenstein-Gesellschaft* 9 (1996–97), 523–50

"Die vierstimmige Bearbeitung (um 1465) eines unbekannten Liedes von Oswald von Wolkenstein," *Jahrbuch der Oswald von Wolkenstein-Gesellschaft* 4 (1986–87), 163–74

Timm, Erika, "Ein Beitrag zur Frage: Wo und in welchem Umfang hat Oswald von Wolkenstein das Komponieren gelernt?," in *Oswald von Wolkenstein: Beiträge der philologisch-musikwissenschaftlichen Tagung in Neustift bei Brixen, 1973*, ed. Egon Kühebacher, Innsbrucker Beiträge zur Kulturwissenschaft, Germanistische Reihe 1, Innsbruck, 1974, 308–31

*Die Überlieferung der Lieder Oswalds von Wolkenstein*, Lübeck, 1972

Welker, Lorenz, "Mehrstimmige Sätze bei Oswald von Wolkenstein: Eine kommentierte Übersicht," *Jahrbuch der Oswald von Wolkenstein-Gesellschaft* 6 (1990–91), 255–66

"New Light on Oswald von Wolkenstein: Central European Traditions and Burgundian Polyphony," *EMH* 7 (1987), 187–226

"Oswald von Wolkenstein," in *Grove Music Online* (accessed 3 March 2012)

"Some Aspects of the Notation and Performance of German Song around 1400," *EM* 18 (1990), 235–46

"Die Überlieferung französischer Chansons in der Handschrift 2777 der Österreichischen Nationalbibliothek (Wolkenstein-Handschrift A)," in *Wiener Quellen der älteren Musikgeschichte zum Sprechen gebracht*, ed. Birgit Lodes, Tutzing, 2007, 311–30

# 11

# Making a motet: Josquin's
## *Ave Maria ... virgo serena*

JOHN MILSOM

The year is 2015, and two students have been given the task of sketching the early life history of a famous composition of their choice. One of them is working on Stravinsky's *Le sacre du printemps*, the other on what is probably the best-known motet of the fifteenth century, *Ave Maria ... virgo serena* by Josquin des Prez. They are a week into their researches; so how are they getting on?

The student busy with *Le sacre* has a desk laden with books, a mind full of facts, and a strong sense of how everything fits together. Here are documents about Diaghilev's *Ballets russes*, including writings by Stravinsky himself, showing how *Le sacre* was commissioned and conceived. Here is a facsimile of Stravinsky's sketchbook for the work, filled with traces of the creative process. Here is the music in its finished states – the full score and the two-piano version made for ballet rehearsals. Here is a dossier of press clippings telling how the work was received at its earliest performances. Here are historical recordings, including ones conducted by Stravinsky, revealing that his own interpretation was anything but fixed. And here are countless descriptions, analyses, and critiques of *Le sacre*, dealing with its musical pedigree, its innovations, and its impact. This student's essay can be built on a firm foundation of evidence.

At the desk next door, the student working on *Ave Maria* is in greater disarray, not because of a shortage of materials, but rather because of a shortage of facts. Nobody knows for sure when, where, or why this motet was composed, and the experts openly disagree with one another; one theory (David Fallows and others) tentatively places this work in France in the mid-1470s, another (Joshua Rifkin and others) tentatively in Milan a decade later, and there are other theories, now usually rejected.[1] No sketch material or autograph score survives, and the motet's earliest known source comes from

---

1 Fallows, *Josquin*, 60–65; Rifkin, "Munich, Milan, and a Marian Motet"; and other literature cited in those two studies. See also Taruskin, "Josquin and the Humanists," in *Oxford History*, 1:547–84.

Innsbruck, a city Josquin may never have visited.[2] Modern editions of the piece abound, but they differ subtly from one another, and the latest of them, in the seemingly authoritative New Josquin Edition, sidesteps a thorny editorial issue in measures 48–52, where according to one theory the music might spiral flatwards in a most disconcerting way.[3] There are recordings, but at best these only speculate about how the music might have sounded when Josquin was alive. As for the reception history of this piece, the most interesting documents date from the twentieth century, when this motet won especial favor. Relatively little is known about its reception in and immediately after Josquin's lifetime, beyond the fact that it became one of his more popular works and served as a model for other compositions. Clearly this essay must rely on theories and interpretations that could run through the fingers like so much dry sand.

It might be thought that the student of Stravinsky's *Sacre* has the more enviable task, but in reality the student of *Ave Maria* is fired by the challenges posed by this piece. Why are facts so thin on the ground? When solid evidence is scarce or non-existent, how do we contextualize and make sense of a musical work? Do we give up in despair, or instead come at it from new and untried angles? These are good questions, and they call for some tutorial guidance.

* * *

In answer to the question "Why are facts so thin on the ground?," the following points need to be made. First, before 1500 compositions seem not to have come into being by way of written contracts between commissioner and composer. There is nothing resembling the contracts that sometimes survive for the making of paintings, where a patron might specify the subject matter, medium, and size of the desired new piece, and the terms under which the artist should work and be rewarded.[4] This may be because a new composition could be made in a short time by a single person without significant expenditure on materials; but it might also be because fifteenth-century compositions were often written not to commission but rather at the composer's whim. The latter may be implied by the famous 1502 letter of Gian de Artiganova to Ercole d'Este, duke of Ferrara, concerning the relative merits of Henricus Isaac and Josquin des Prez as the duke's potential future employee. In Gian's view, "Josquin composes better, but he composes when he wants to," whereas Isaac "is very rapid in the art of composition," is "good-natured and easy to

2  Now Munich 3154; discussed most recently in Rifkin, "Munich, Milan, and a Marian Motet."
3  NJE 23.6, from which all quotations from the work in the present chapter have been drawn with permission. Arguments for and against the flatwards spiral in measures 48–52 are reviewed in Bent, "Diatonic *Ficta* Revisited."
4  Baxandall, *Painting and Experience*, ch. 1, "Conditions of Trade."

get along with," and "will compose new works [*cose nove*] more often," presumably on request.[5] This letter is open to more than one interpretation, but it could at least imply that a motet such as Josquin's *Ave Maria* need not have been made to order, or for a specific event.

Second, we can probably dismiss the hope of ever seeing Josquin's autograph notations for the work-in-progress, since none need ever have existed in durable form. Little is known about the physical processes involved in making a new fifteenth-century composition, but the near total absence of autograph notations on paper or parchment implies that composers either devised new pieces in their heads, with or without the aid of instruments, or drafted them on erasable surfaces that could be wiped clean once a set of performing parts had been made.[6] If Josquin sketched and drafted his ideas as he composed, no trace of this has come to light, and almost certainly never will. Instead, all we have is the finished work, preserved in copies some distance removed from his original.

This brings us to the sources of *Ave Maria* – initially manuscripts, and later also printed copies. It might be hoped that these, and especially the earliest manuscripts, would tell us something about the *when*, *where*, and *why* of this motet; but again we face a dead end. Although *Ave Maria* could have found its way to Innsbruck from Milan around 1484, the motet might have been composed and in circulation ten or more years before that, in which case its possible transmission from Milan to Innsbruck would not get us very far. Fifteenth-century music manuscripts sometimes yield vital information about the origins of the works they contain, but this is not always the case, and often the earliest witnesses have simply disappeared without trace – as seems to be the case with Josquin's *Ave Maria*. Very few extant manuscripts copied in the last three decades of the fifteenth century contain motets, and the ones we possess simply cannot answer all the questions we ask of them.

The quest for facts about *Ave Maria* now narrows down to study of the work itself – its words and its musical content. The words in particular demand attention, for a motet text will sometimes hint (or more than hint) at function, especially when aligned with known biographical, liturgical, political, or historical facts; read this way, a text may imply that its musical setting was composed for a specific function, event, person, or place. The text of *Ave Maria* is seemingly unique to this motet; no composer before Josquin is known to have set precisely these words, nor has the text as a whole been found in any independent literary source. This is a *cento* text made out of three

5 Most recently cited and discussed in Fallows, *Josquin*, 236–37. See also Lockwood, "'It's true that Josquin composes better'," and Wegman, "Isaac's Signature."
6 Owens, *Composers at Work*, and Milsom, "Notes from an Erasable Tablet."

independent parts, all of which address the Virgin Mary.[7] First comes the opening of a sequence that begins with words taken from the scene of the Annunciation (the angel Gabriel's salutation to Mary), but is in fact linked in some liturgical sources to the feast of the Assumption of the Virgin. Josquin's text continues with five stanzas of non-liturgical verse marking the Five Corporeal Joys of Our Lady – her Conception, Nativity, Annunciation, Purification, and Assumption. The earliest known sources of this prayer are almost exclusively fifteenth-century French books of hours, which sometimes link it with an Office or Mass of the Conception of the Virgin; the words reflect the increasing devotion in the fifteenth century to the Virgin, and the burgeoning cult of Mary's apocryphal mother, St. Anne. Josquin's text ends with a rhyming couplet of non-liturgical verse that was widely known and used in Josquin's lifetime; it occurs in donors' portraits and on gravestones as well as in books of hours and in music. This couplet is expressed in the first person singular: "O mother of God, remember me. Amen."

Where might a four-voice setting of this Marian *cento* text have been made or wanted? Again there are different views. On one hand, the text has been described as "exactly the kind of pastiche so often encountered in early Milanese motets" (Reinhard Strohm), one that reveals "the Milanese fondness for composite structures" (Rifkin), irrespective of the geographical origins of its component parts (which might indeed have been drawn from French books of hours imported into Italy).[8] This interpretation would allow Josquin's motet to be aligned with the Sforza court chapel in the mid-1480s. On the other hand, because each of the three text components "independently points towards northern Europe" as its place of origin (Fallows), in combination they logically suggest that the motet has its roots in France or the Low Countries, where these texts were definitely known and used.[9] Both theories are plausible; neither can be proved or easily dismissed.

Turning next to the music, two facts come into play that might seem key to understanding Josquin's *Ave Maria*. First, the motet starts by quoting the plainchant melody to which the "Ave Maria" sequence was sung liturgically – or rather, it quotes a version of that melody. Chant dialect is often specific to locality, and a quoted chant may therefore contain vital evidence about the region or place for which a composition was destined. Nobody disputes the fact that Josquin, by opening his motet with the interval of a rising fourth, is drawing on a state of the plainchant that has been located only in a few

---

7 For discussions of Josquin's text and its sources, see Fallows, *Josquin*, 62–65; the commentary to NJE 23.6; and Blackburn, "For Whom Do the Singers Sing?," 603–4 and endnotes 23–25.
8 Strohm, *The Rise of European Music*, 608; Rifkin, "Munich, Milan, and a Marian Motet," 277.
9 Fallows, *Josquin*, 64–65.

northern European sources; the chant melody was simply not sung that way in Milan.[10] This might seem to clinch the case – but again it has been challenged on the reasonable grounds that a composer born and brought up in northern Europe might have "simply quoted the chant in the form known to him from his upbringing or training" (Rifkin), even when writing in or for Milan, where the chant dialect differed.[11] Put another way, Josquin may have felt no obligation to draw on Milanese chant even when composing in or for Milan.

The second musical fact also concerns the motet's opening. Its first four breves are polyphonically identical (other than in transposition) to those of the five-voice *Ave Maria ... virgo serena* by Johannes Regis (ca. 1425–ca. 1496).[12] During the years of Josquin's childhood and early career, Regis was resident in Soignies, not far from places frequented by Josquin such as Tournai (60 km away), Condé-sur-l'Escaut (50 km), and Cambrai (90 km), and there is every reason to suspect that the young musician had access to the older man's work. It is therefore possible that Josquin's *Ave Maria* starts by citing Regis, in the same way that his combinative motet *Alma Redemptoris mater/Ave regina (a 4)* nods simultaneously to two other musical mentors, Guillaume Du Fay and Johannes Ockeghem.[13] Attractive as it is, though, this idea too can be challenged. The direction of flow might be the reverse; Regis could be quoting Josquin. The similarity may be coincidental; neither man need have known the other's work. And even if deliberate, Josquin could have cited Regis in a motet composed in or for Milan.[14]

Beyond this point, the only facts to be had about *Ave Maria* are ones that can be gleaned from Josquin's polyphony itself. Arguably, however, these are the facts that should matter most to us, since they are the ones that make this motet so interesting and important. Whether composed in France in the 1470s or in Milan in the 1480s, *Ave Maria* is a startlingly novel work by the standards of earlier fifteenth-century music, and it has often been viewed as a harbinger of things to come; in the words of Richard Taruskin, "The whole 'perfected art' of sixteenth-century sacred music, it sometimes seems, was formed on the example of this one supreme masterpiece."[15] Many descriptions exist of the work's highly distinctive musico-rhetorical manner. The following one by

---

10  For discussions of the chant and its sources, see Fallows, *Josquin*, 62–63, and the commentary to NJE 23.6. For the Milanese version of chant as set to polyphony by Compère, see Taruskin, *Oxford History*, 1:524–25.
11  Rifkin, "Munich, Milan, and a Marian Motet," 276–77.
12  One voice of Regis's setting is lost, but its first four breves were clearly identical to Josquin's; see Dumitrescu, "Reconstructing and Repositioning Regis's *Ave Maria*."
13  Fallows, *Josquin*, 37–39.
14  Rifkin, "A Black Hole?," 64–67 n. 155.
15  Taruskin, *Oxford History*, 1:565.

Jeremy Noble, written for the 1980 edition of *The New Grove* and retained in subsequent editions of the dictionary, is representative:[16]

> The basic texture is imitative, yet each section of the text is given a slightly different treatment. For the opening words of the angelic salutation [mm. 1–30] there is literal imitation at the octave or unison, working (no doubt with symbolic intent) from the highest voice to the lowest; each phrase overlaps its predecessor, but in such a way that all four voices are heard together only in the three measures before the first main cadence. For the first strophe of the rhyming votive antiphon that follows ["Ave cujus conceptio," mm. 30–54], a duet of upper voices is imitated by a trio of lower ones, leading more quickly this time into a longer full section whose denser texture is enlivened by sequence and close internal imitation; for the second strophe ["Ave cujus nativitas," mm. 54–77], duets of lower and upper voices, now imitating one another at the 5th, converge briefly to form a four-part texture, which then tapers away to the unrelieved duet of the third strophe ["Ave pia humilitas," mm. 78–93]. This temporary austerity enhances the effect of the crucial fourth strophe, "Ave vera virginitas" [mm. 94–110], whose four-part texture is given new rhythmic life by a change of metre; the close canon between superius and tenor may symbolize the Child within the Virgin's womb. After a fifth strophe ["Ave preclara omnibus," mm. 111–42] in which this almost purely harmonic texture is resolved into melodic imitation once more, the motet ends, after a whole bar's pause, with a chordal invocation of stark simplicity ["O mater dei, memento mei," mm. 143–52]. The musical form precisely mirrors that of the text, yet without any sense of constraint; articulation is achieved by subtle changes of procedure and texture, but with no loss of onward momentum in spite of the fact that every main cadence falls on C . . .

To this we should add that the motet is technically easy to perform; it is not a showpiece for virtuoso singers. A motet composed along these lines would be almost unthinkable in the works of Guillaume Du Fay, Johannes Ockeghem, Johannes Regis, or Antoine Busnoys. How, then, has Josquin arrived at this outcome? On what precedents could he have drawn?

It is here that the Milanese theory plays its trump cards. In the 1970s, Ludwig Finscher, Joshua Rifkin, and others independently noticed that some of the characteristics of *Ave Maria* are present or embryonic in a group of motets composed apparently for the court chapel of Galeazzo Maria Sforza, duke of Milan between 1466 and his assassination ten years later.[17] The composers of these motets, Gaspar van Weerbeke and Loyset Compère, had like Josquin been born and trained in the Low Countries, but were lured south by the prospects for employment offered by Sforza wealth and power. In Milan they pioneered a new motet style based on the principles of economy,

16 Macey *et al.*, "Josquin des Prez."      17 Rifkin, "Munich, Milan, and a Marian Motet," 241–42 n. 9.

repetition, and clear enunciation of the words. Why they should have done so is unknown, but audience expectation may have played a part in it; as Julie Cumming explains, "Italian princes such as the Dukes of Ferrara and Milan . . . sought to win people over, cultivate support, and make alliances. They may have wanted motets that were easy for courtiers and envoys to understand and enjoy . . . The 'dumbing down' of sacred music through the introduction of repetition may have appealed to these Italian patrons of the Josquin generation, out to impress their subjects and their competitors with music that was easy to appreciate, not difficult to understand."[18]

What is the chronological relationship between these Milanese motets and Josquin's *Ave Maria*? Back in the 1970s, *Ave Maria* could itself be claimed as a Milanese motet of the mid-1470s for two reasons. First, during the period 1474–76 a singer called "Juschino" or "Judoco de picardia" worked alongside Weerbeke and Compère in the Milanese ducal chapel; this man was surely the motet's composer. Second, watermark evidence in the Innsbruck manuscript implied that *Ave Maria* had reached that city by 1476, supporting the view that the motet itself must date from the mid-1470s or earlier. But these beliefs both proved to be false ones. First, the singer at Milan turned out to be not Josquin des Prez (d. 1521) but rather Juschinus de Kessalia (d. 1498), a musician to whom no compositions have yet been credited, let alone a gem so perfectly cut as *Ave Maria*.[19] Second, *Ave Maria* appears to be a late addition to the Innsbruck manuscript, copied not in the 1470s but rather on hitherto unused pages in the 1480s, and possibly as late as 1484–85.[20] As chance would have it, however, these are precisely the years when Josquin des Prez is now known to have been in Milan in the service of Cardinal Ascanio Sforza, the late duke's brother.[21] Thus *Ave Maria* might still be claimed as a "Milanese motet," though younger than those of Weerbeke and Compère by a decade.

This theory has a number of vulnerabilities. Most obviously, Josquin need not have been in Milan to know about the "Milanese style"; the Milanese motets of Weerbeke and Compère could have been transmitted northwards in manuscripts that no longer survive, providing models for composers outside Italy.[22] It might also be asked whether the so-called "Milanese style" was in any case cultivated solely in Milan, or even had its origins there; too few manuscripts survive from the 1470s and 1480s to prove the point.[23] But the Milanese

18 Cumming, "From Variety to Repetition," 43–44.
19 On Kessalia, see most recently Fallows, *Josquin*, 9–10, 328–29, and 450.
20 Adjustments to the date of copying of *Ave Maria* into the Innsbruck manuscript have been independently proposed by Jeffrey Dean, Elizabeth Cason, and Joshua Rifkin; see Rifkin, "Munich, Milan, and a Marian Motet," 294 ff.
21 For a summary of the documentary evidence for this, see Fallows, *Josquin*, 110–12.
22 Ibid., 61 n. 19.    23 Ibid., 118–19.

theory faces its stiffest challenge from the internal evidence of *Ave Maria* itself –
its musical style and ideas. On closer inspection, Josquin's motet turns out to be
an autonomous and idiosyncratic conception that need not have relied much if
at all on Milanese models; a one-to-one relationship is simply not required.
Moreover, *Ave Maria* makes use of an organizational principle that recurs
elsewhere in Josquin's music, and on that count it more obviously bears
Josquin's fingerprint than it does a hallmark from Milan. Thus the effort of
trying to relate this motet to precedent and place may have diverted us from
the fact that *Ave Maria* is first and foremost a creation of Josquin's mind –
equivalent to viewing *Le sacre du printemps* more as a product of Paris and
Diaghilev's *Ballets russes* than a work by Stravinsky.

In summary: though it may be hard or impossible to answer questions about
the *where*, *when*, and *why* of Josquin's motet, something of its early life history
might emerge if we were to address the matter of *how* it was composed. Thus
the tutorial leaves off its review of the existing literature, and instead comes at
*Ave Maria* from some new and untried angles.

* * *

There are good reasons for believing that Josquin began work on his motet by
pondering the opening of Regis's *Ave Maria*. Regis had discovered that the
first segment of the plainchant melody can be superimposed on itself to
generate *fuga* (imitation) that answers at the unison.[24] Example 11.1a
shows the first four phrases of the chant (A–D) as known to Regis and
Josquin; Example 11.1b gives the opening *fuga* of Regis's motet based on
chant phrase A, Example 11.1c the equivalent opening of Josquin's motet.
Fifteenth-century composers often developed ideas created by their peers;
the large family of *L'homme armé* masses surveyed by Jesse Rodin in Chapter 4
demonstrates this point; so it would seem logical that Josquin, by composing
unison and octave *fuga* not only out of phrase A but also from the next three
segments of the chant (phrases B, C, and D), has expanded Regis's seed idea.
Moreover, Josquin has made a discovery that draws his motet into fresh
intellectual territory. Not only will each of the first two phrases of chant (A
and B) interlock with itself to create unison/octave *fuga* (A+A, B+B). They will
also interlock with one another (A+B) to generate faultless counterpoint; see
Example 11.2, in which the three combinations are shown as complementary
musical ideas. Josquin will have found, too, that the ingenious fusion of A+B

---

24 Before 1600, most music theory and pedagogy written in Latin or Italian uses the term "fuga" for the
modern concept of "imitation." In English writings, the equivalent term is "fuge."

Example 11.1 (a) plainchant *Ave Maria . . . virgo serena*, opening four phrases (A–D); (b) Johannes Regis, *Ave Maria . . . virgo serena*, *fuga* based on chant phrase A (with editorial reconstruction of the missing voice); (c) Josquin des Prez, *Ave Maria . . . virgo serena*, *fuga* based on chant phrase A

is possible only if A lies below B – and this may explain why he passes the *fuga* downwards through the voices, so that the fourth statement of A can serve as a bass to the first statement of B. Thus the "literal imitation at the octave or unison, working (no doubt with symbolic intent) from the highest voice to the lowest" (Noble) may in fact arise from contrapuntal necessity, while also conveniently suggesting the descent of the Holy Spirit to the Virgin Mary at the scene of the Annunciation.

Example 11.2 Josquin, *Ave Maria . . . virgo serena*, interlocks made from chant phrases A and B: (a) A+A; (b) B+B; (c) A+B

What is the relationship of this opening to the Milanese motets of Compère and Weerbeke? It has been likened in the past to some similar-sounding passages by Compère that are also made from downwards-progressing *fuga* at the octave/unison.[25] But Josquin's *fuga* is chant-based where Compère's is freely composed, and the latter therefore possesses none of the combinative ingenuity found at the start of *Ave Maria*. Moreover, Josquin's opening *fuga* might as easily derive from Regis, and then possess a logic of its own in pursuit of the A+B counterpoint; so the resemblance to passages by Compère may in fact be nothing more than coincidence.

Turning next to the interior of Josquin's motet, there is one section of *Ave Maria* that has never been claimed as Milanese in style. For the fourth strophe of the sequence text, "Ave vera virginitas" (mm. 94–110), Josquin has

---

25  Rifkin, "Munich, Milan, and a Marian Motet," 271–74.

composed an extended span of strict *fuga* in which the melodic line of the superius is replicated by the tenor one semibreve unit later at the interval of a lower fifth. *Fuga* made in this way naturally observes a simple set of laws: provided the leading voice sings a melody made only from the intervals of rising seconds, falling thirds, rising fourths, falling fifths (and in theory larger intervals symmetrically arranged), or repeats the pitch on which it stands, a second voice can replicate it a fifth lower and a unit later, giving rise to flawless counterpoint; see Example 11.3, in which Josquin's polyphony is shown both in conventional score and in analytical reduction to first-species counterpoint. A few sixteenth-century books of music pedagogy make brief mention of this texture/technique, but they do not give it a name; recently it has come to be known as "stretto *fuga*."[26]

Josquin was not the first or only person to compose stretto *fuga*. On the contrary, it occurs in much fifteenth- and sixteenth-century music, from at least Du Fay to at least Monteverdi. But it is not part of the "Milanese style." For reasons unknown, barely a snatch of stretto *fuga* occurs in the Milanese motets of Weerbeke and Compère, an absence made all the more curious by the fact that music by Compère written before his move to Italy makes generous use of the texture/technique.[27] His encomium to Du Fay and his circle, *Omnium bonorum plena*, which securely dates from the early 1470s, is full of stretto *fuga*; Example 11.4 shows a typical passage, here used to set Compère's own name. Why he should have abandoned stretto *fuga* after his move to Italy is unknown, but his action has consequences for understanding *Ave Maria*: Josquin's use of it connects his motet to northern practices, not to Milan.

Why does Josquin use stretto *fuga* for the stanza "Ave vera virginitas?" Jeremy Noble suspects symbolic intent: "the close canon between superius and tenor may symbolize the Child within the Virgin's womb"; but a more structural and purely musical interpretation is also possible. The intervals from which stretto *fuga* is made – rising seconds, falling thirds, rising fourths – are also the intervals of plainchant phrase A ("Ave Maria"), used for Josquin's opening polyphony; see Example 11.5. Moreover, between these two passages

---

26 Milsom, "*Imitatio*"; Milsom, "Josquin des Prez and the Combinative Impulse," 218–22; and Milsom, "Style and Idea." The intervals of stretto *fuga* can be inverted, i.e., melodic lines made out of falling seconds, rising thirds, falling fourths, rising fifths, etc. will give rise to *fuga* at the upper fifth after one unit. The duration of a unit is irrelevant to the underlying laws of this kind of *fuga*; it could be a semibreve (as here), a minim, a breve, or indeed any other length of note. Further on the laws of stretto *fuga*, see the essay in this volume by Julie E. Cumming and Peter Schubert, Ch. 12.

27 The only instances of stretto *fuga* in Milanese motets by Weerbeke and Compère are listed in Milsom, "Josquin des Prez and the Combinative Impulse," 238 n. 55.

Example 11.3  Josquin, *Ave Maria . . . virgo serena*, stretto *fuga* at "Ave vera virginitas": (a) conventional score (equivalent to NJE 23.6, mm. 94–106); (b) analytical reduction into units

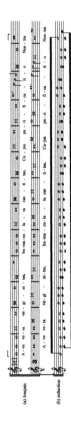

Example 11.4  Loyset Compère, *Omnium bonorum plena*, stretto *fuga* used to set the composer's own name: (a) conventional score (transcribed from Trent 91, fols. 34v–35r); (b) analytical reduction into units

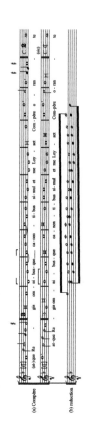

Example 11.5  Intervallic identity between (a) plainchant *Ave Maria . . . virgo serena*, opening phrase A; (b) Josquin, *Ave Maria . . . virgo serena*, stretto *fuga* at "Ave vera virginitas" (equivalent to NJE 23.6, mm. 94–106); (c) reduction of (b) to its essential intervals

most of the principal thematic content of Josquin's *Ave Maria* is also made from rising seconds, falling thirds, and rising fourths, often worked in *fuga*. A chain of intervallic connections derived from the opening chant therefore runs through this motet.[28] Why Josquin should have forged this chain can only be guessed, but perhaps he too sensed an alluring idea: that the intervals of Gabriel's salutation to Mary at the scene of the Annunciation gradually transmutate into the tight *fuga* of the fourth stanza symbolizing "the Child within the Virgin's womb."

It is worth examining parts of this chain in order to ponder Josquin's *fuga* choices. The extracts in Example 11.6 are all passages of *fuga* from *Ave Maria* made out of rising seconds, falling thirds, and sometimes rising fourths. Each is notated first in conventional notation, then in analytical reduction into units. Extract (a), from the start of the motet, makes *fuga* out of plainchant, with voices answering at the unison or lower octave. Extract (b), "Celestia, terrestria," is essentially stretto *fuga* at the lower fifth between tenor and bassus (unit = minim), with superius shadowing bassus at the upper tenth;[29] this is the passage where the polyphony might spiral flatwards if the bassus sings B♭s. Extract (c), "Ave cujus nativitas," is again in stretto *fuga* at the lower fifth (but unit now = semibreve), lightly decorated with lower returning notes and infilling.[30] Extract (d), "Ut lucifer lux oriens," works a zigzag melody in *fuga* initially after four semibreve units (A), then after two semibreve units (B), and finally in decorated stretto *fuga* at the lower twelfth in minim units (C). Extracts (b)–(d) therefore prefigure "Ave vera virginitas" (Example 11.3 above), which is an extended span of pure stretto *fuga* at the lower fifth worked in triple-meter semibreves.

What if anything is "Milanese" here? Not the configurations of *fuga* at the interval of the fifth; the Milanese motets of Compère and Weerbeke contain almost nothing equivalent to these. Nor is there anything Milanese about the chain of intervallic connections that runs through *Ave Maria*, a musical idea that is evidently Josquin's own, and one to which he returned at least once in later life, in a showpiece of tight intervallic integration.[31] The opening *fuga* at the

---

28 *Ave Maria* has been said to display "wholesale thematic integration" and "melodic unity"; see Godt, "Motivic Integration in Josquin's Motets," 274–83, and Judd, "Some Problems of Pre-Baroque Analysis," 219–22; but these do not consider the possibility that the motet might be underpinned instead by intervallic consistency drawn from the contours of a chant.

29 Later in life, Josquin used this same texture to set the names "Josquin, Perchon [de la Rue], Brumel, Compere" in his *déploration* for Ockeghem, *Nymphes des bois* (NJE 29.18).

30 The analytical reduction for Extract (c) draws on Thomas Morley's demonstration of how stretto *fuga* in its "plain" state can be "broken" with decoration and infilling; see Grimshaw, "Morley's Rule."

31 The six-voice *Nimphes, nappés/Circumdederunt me* (NJE 30.6), in which melodic material made from rising seconds, falling thirds, rising fourths, falling fifths, and rising octaves is worked in various configurations of two- and four-voice *fuga*, latterly in stretto against a chant-based canonic cantus firmus.

Example 11.6 Josquin, *Ave Maria . . . virgo serena*: passages of *fuga* made from rising seconds, falling thirds, and rising fourths: (a) opening (equivalent to NJE 23.6, mm. 1–6); (b) "Celestia, terrestria" (equivalent to NJE 23.6, mm. 44–50); (c) "Ave cujus nativitas" (equivalent to NJE 23.6, mm. 54–8); (d) "Ut lucifer lux oriens" (equivalent to NJE 23.6, mm. 64–71 and 73–76)

(cont.)

unison/octave does bear some surface resemblance to passages by Compère, but this could be coincidence; Josquin's solution may arise partly from Regis, partly from combinative necessity. None of these observations disproves the theory that *Ave Maria* was composed in or for Milan in the mid-1480s, but collectively they do create some real distance between *Ave Maria* and its putative Milanese precedents. By extension, they downplay the significance of pedigree, and instead emphasize the motet's idiosyncrasy.

✳ ✳ ✳

Example 11.6 (cont.)

We end where we began: with the two students researching *Le sacre du printemps* and *Ave Maria* respectively. *Le sacre* belongs to an age when tangible evidence of the work-in-progress and its early reception was likely both to have existed and to have been preserved, and the story of its genesis is indeed amply documented. The same is not true of *Ave Maria*, for which no significant written record of the work-in-progress may ever have existed, and none is known to survive. Whereas the historian of *Le sacre* can select from an abundance of materials, the historian of *Ave Maria* must search for new documents, interrogate known evidence in new ways, and try coming at the work from untried angles – though in the knowledge that this celebrated work may forever stay as enigmatic as the smile of the *Mona Lisa*.

What the student can productively do, though, is look yet more closely at the music itself. Even in the absence of sketches, drafts, recensions, and other forms of *avant-texte* that would make true genetic criticism of fifteenth-century music possible, rich research opportunities exist within the field of forensic analysis – which is to say, analysis that is concerned more with how compositions were made than with how they sound.[32] Help can be had from fifteenth-century theoretical writings, which usefully deal with fundamentals such as notation and counterpoint. But it is also possible to step beyond the theorists, who for reasons of their own do not always discuss (or discuss in detail) phenomena that are demonstrably present in the music of their day. When the theorists fall silent, forensic analysis can imply much about the mechanics of craft, and in turn about the mentality of invention. If discoveries can still be made about pieces as familiar as Josquin's *Ave Maria*, then vast possibilities surely remain for probing the inner workings of fifteenth-century polyphony at large.

## Bibliography

Baxandall, Michael, *Painting and Experience in Fifteenth-Century Italy: A Primer in the Social History of Pictorial Style*, Oxford, 1972

Bent, Margaret, "Diatonic *Ficta* Revisited: Josquin's Ave Maria in Context," in Bent, *Counterpoint, Composition, and Musica Ficta*, New York and London, 2002, 199–217 (with introductory remarks at 25–27)

"The Grammar of Early Music: Preconditions for Analysis," in *Tonal Structures in Early Music*, ed. Cristle Collins Judd, New York, 1998, 15–59

Blackburn, Bonnie J., "For Whom Do the Singers Sing?," *EM* 25 (1997), 593–609

Cumming, Julie, "From Variety to Repetition: The Birth of Imitative Polyphony," *Yearbook of the Alamire Foundation* 6 (2008), 21–44

Dumitrescu, Theodor, "Reconstructing and Repositioning Regis's Ave Maria . . . virgo serena," *EM* 37 (2009), 73–88

Fallows, David, *Josquin*, Turnhout, 2009

Godt, Irving, "Motivic Integration in Josquin's Motets," *Journal of Music Theory* 21 (1977), 264–92

Grimshaw, Julian, "Morley's Rule for First-Species Canon," *EM* 34 (2006), 661–66

Judd, Cristle Collins, "Some Problems of Pre-Baroque Analysis: An Examination of Josquin's *Ave Maria . . . virgo serena*," *Music Analysis* 4 (1985), 201–39

Lockwood, Lewis "'It's true that Josquin composes better . . . ': The Short Unhappy Life of Gian de Artiganova," in *Uno gentile et subtile ingenio: Studies in Renaissance Music in Honour of Bonnie J. Blackburn*, ed. M. Jennifer Bloxam, Gioia Filocamo, and Leofranc Holford-Strevens, Turnhout, 2009, 201–16

Macey, Patrick *et al.*, "Josquin des Prez," in *Grove Music Online*, accessed 12 June 2012

Milsom, John, "'*Imitatio*,' 'Intertextuality,' and Early Music," in *Citation and Authority in Medieval and Renaissance Musical Culture: Learning from the Learned*, ed. Suzannah Clark and Elizabeth Eva Leach, Woodbridge, 2005, 141–51

"Josquin des Prez and the Combinative Impulse," in *The Motet around 1500: On the Relationship of Imitation and Text Treatment?*, ed. Thomas Schmidt-Beste, Turnhout, 2012, 211–46

---

32  For some further examples of forensic analyses applied to music by Josquin, see Milsom, "Playing with Plainchant."

"Notes from an Erasable Tablet," in *"Recevez ce mien petit labeur": Studies in Renaissance Music in Honour of Ignace Bossuyt*, ed. Mark Delaere and Pieter Bergé, Leuven, 2008, 195–210

"Playing with Plainchant: Seven Motet Openings by Josquin and What We Can Learn from Them," in *Josquin and the Sublime: Proceedings of the International Josquin Symposium at Roosevelt Academy Middelburg, 12–15 July 2009*, ed. Albert Clement and Eric Jas, Turnhout, 2011, 23–47

"Style and Idea in Josquin's *Cueur langoreulx*," *JAF* (forthcoming, 2015)

Owens, Jessie Ann, *Composers at Work: The Craft of Musical Composition 1450–1600*, New York and Oxford, 1997

Rifkin, Joshua, "A Black Hole? Problems in the Motet around 1500," in *The Motet around 1500: On the Relationship of Imitation and Text Treatment?*, ed. Thomas Schmidt-Beste, Turnhout, 2012, 21–82

"Munich, Milan, and a Marian Motet: Dating Josquin's *Ave Maria . . . virgo serena*," *JAMS* 56 (2003), 239–350

Strohm, Reinhard, *The Rise of European Music, 1380–1500*, Cambridge, 1993

Taruskin, Richard, *The Oxford History of Western Music*, New York and Oxford, 2005

Wegman, Rob C., "Isaac's Signature," *JM* 28 (2011), 9–33

# 12

# The origins of pervasive imitation

JULIE E. CUMMING AND PETER SCHUBERT

Pervasive imitation became the dominant musical texture in sacred music of the late fifteenth and sixteenth centuries.[1] In pervasive imitation all of the voices are involved in repeating the same melodic material, and many or all of the phrases in the work begin with imitation. We will take a look at imitation in the early fifteenth century, and then focus on how pervasive imitation developed from the mid- to the late fifteenth century. Most of our examples are motets, since their position in the middle of the genre hierarchy, between chansons and masses, makes them resemble both, as Cumming has shown.[2] We will show how some patterns arise out of improvised practices, and tally imitative patterns in the section openings of the first five Petrucci motet prints, considering the contrapuntal constraints of imitative textures, with respect to both time and pitch intervals of imitation. Our conclusions reveal a surprising consistency of techniques in the late fifteenth century, and clear differences from imitation as used both earlier and later. This snapshot of an emerging musical style is of particular interest because this was a period when the aesthetic aims of variety and complexity were giving way to those of intelligibility and accessibility.[3]

Imitative music is different from free counterpoint in that the consequent voice has to do what the lead voice did some time interval earlier, and the lead voice, if it continues, has to accommodate the consequent voice (i.e., follow the rules of counterpoint). In looking for patterns of imitation, the elements that we must consider are the pitch interval of imitation between voices, the time interval of imitation between voices, and the continuation of the lead voice (whether or not this continuation is repeated in the second voice). While some

---

1 This chapter draws on Cumming and Schubert, "Patterns of Imitation, 1450–1508." Thanks to our students Dan Donnelly and Jacob Sagrans for their work on this chapter. We also recommend our other articles listed in the Bibliography. On imitation see also Beiche, "*Fuga*/Fuge," and Schubert, "Counterpoint Pedagogy," 511.

2 Cumming, *Motet*, 43, 288–303. See also Taruskin, *Oxford History*, 1: 501–46.

3 See Cumming, "From Variety to Repetition" and Luko, "Tinctoris on *Varietas*." See also Sparks, "Some Uses of Imitation," 269: he comments that in the early sixteenth century "consistency and simplicity of musical means were now preferred over complexity and variety."

scholars have discussed pitch level of entries and varied continuations of the repeated melody (*soggetto*), there has been little discussion of time intervals of imitation and how they interact with repeated contrapuntal combinations.[4] Our aim is to discuss the different procedures and types of imitation, and to show the gradual emergence of patterns of imitation over the course of the fifteenth century. By the end of the century some of these patterns become commonplaces.

## Imitation in the early fifteenth century

Imitation can be found in early fifteenth-century music, but usually in two voices and in restricted circumstances. Sometimes two-voice imitation is found against a preexistent cantus firmus, or against a freely composed tenor. The examples we find are very brief, at the unison or octave, and tend, not surprisingly, to outline a triad, as in Guillaume Du Fay's *Balsamus et munda cera* (Example 12.1).[5]

Johannes Ciconia sometimes writes a long line in one cantus voice that is then repeated in the other (as in Example 12.2, Ciconia's *O virum omnimoda*).[6] These two voices do not overlap (except for one note).[7]

More often imitation is found in free duos. We believe that the unaccompanied duo is the laboratory in which most experiments and advances in imitative technique were made. There are several types of imitation found in duos. In one type (as in Example 12.3, Ciconia's *Doctorum principem*),[8] the solo voices are non-overlapping or overlap for only one note.

Another widespread type is overlapping canon at the unison. In the case of *Vassilissa ergo gaude*, the canon continues for the whole introitus section,[9] but in the case of Example 12.4, *Ecclesie militantis*,[10] the imitation breaks off at the

---

4  For pitch level of entries see Rifkin, "Munich, Milan, and a Marian Motet," 278: "finally, imitation at the fourth or fifth itself occurs rarely not only in Milan, but pretty much everywhere before the last years of the century; among composers of the generation immediately preceding Josquin's, for example, only Caron appears to have employed it with any frequency"; see also 329–32 n. 21, and Rifkin, "Busnoys and Italy," 558, esp. n. 214. Rifkin discusses pitch interval of imitation more fully in "A Black Hole?," 24, 27–28, 31. David Fallows argues that Josquin and others used imitation at the fifth well before the end of the century: see *Josquin*, 62 n. 21, and 97. For the time interval of imitation see Schubert, "Hidden Forms" and "A Lesson from Lassus," 3–9.

5  Example from Dufay, *Opera*, 1, no. 13, pp. 54–58. Treatise discussions of canon over a cantus firmus can be found in, among other treatises: Zarlino, *Le istitutioni harmoniche* (1558), 256–58 and (1573), 302–17; Morley, *Plaine and Easie*, 98. See also Collins, "Zarlino and Berardi"; Schubert, *Modal Counterpoint*, 319–33; and Grimshaw, "Morley's Rule."

6  Example from Ciconia, *Works*, no. 15, pp. 81–84.

7  This is sometimes called "echo imitation"; see Cumming, *Motet*, 72–73, Table 4.2, 80, and 323 n. 37, for additional references. We will not consider global canons, as in Du Fay's *Inclita stella maris*.

8  Example from Ciconia, *Works*, no. 17, pp. 89–93.

9  For a modern edition of *Vassilissa* see Dufay, *Opera*, 1, no. 7, pp. 21–24.

10  Example from Dufay, *Opera*, 1, no. 12, pp. 46–53.

Example 12.1 Guillaume Du Fay, *Balsamus et munda cera/Isti sunt agni novelli*, mm. 4–6. Two-voice triadic imitation over a cantus firmus

entry of the second voice, so the continuation of the first voice (mm. 5–7) is not replicated in the second (mm. 8–10). "Incidental" imitation can also occur buried in the course of a free duo, as in Du Fay, *Magnanime*, measures 40–42.[11]

Another type of imitation at the unison is "triadic" imitation, which we have seen used against a cantus firmus in Du Fay's *Balsamus* (Example 12.1 above). It also can occur briefly in an unaccompanied duo, as in Du Fay's *Magnanime*, measures 11–12.

In the early fifteenth century we find two-voice imitation at the octave at the beginnings of phrases in some chansons.[12] There is even some three-voice imitation in chansons, often an enrichment of the two-voice triadic duo with little overlap, as in Du Fay's *Ce jour de l'an* (Example 12.5, mm. 1–4), or where the contratenor opportunistically anticipates the imitation between the structural voices, superius and tenor, during the long notes at the cadence (Example 12.5, mm. 6–8).[13] In general, imitation is fairly rare in Du Fay chansons, and very rare in those of Binchois; it is not an essential feature of the style.

We have found a few early fifteenth-century examples of imitation at the fifth. One type is imitation at the fifth after several beats, as in measures 145–47 of Du Fay's *Fulgens jubar* (ca. 1442) (Example 12.6 – the first and last notes of the imitative passage are indicated with dotted lines).[14] One possible reason for the movement from imitation at the unison to imitation at the fifth is the shift in mid-century away from two upper parts in the same range toward a single upper voice with a lower second cantus part.

11 For a modern edition of *Magnanime*, see Dufay, *Opera*, 1, no. 17, pp. 76–80.
12 Imitation at the unison is found in the two equal upper voices in motets of the period; since in the chanson imitation generally comes between superius and a lower tenor, it is normally at the octave.
13 Example from Dufay, *Opera*, 6, no. 38, p. 58.    14 Example from Dufay, *Opera*, 1, no. 18, pp. 80–88.

Example 12.2 Johannes Ciconia, *O virum omnimoda/O lux et decus/O beate Nichole*, mm. 1–17. Two-voice imitation with one-note overlap over free tenor

Another category of imitation at the fifth has a short time interval between entries, sometimes called *fuga ad minimam* or stretto *fuga*.[15] These imitative passages are often concealed in the middle of a passage of free counterpoint, as in Example 12.6, *Fulgens iubar*, measures 148–51, where the time interval of imitation shrinks from three semibreves to a minim. The best-known example

---

15 John Milsom discovered a simple rule for writing canons at the fifth after a very short time interval, which he dubbed "stretto *fuga*." The term stretto *fuga* is a concise way of saying that the time interval consists of one note (of whatever value) in note-against-note counterpoint. Since then Milsom, Schubert, and others have identified descriptions of the technique by several theorists: Montanos, *Arte de música*, "de compostura," fols. 9v and 10v; Sancta Maria, *Libro llamado el arte de tañer fantasía*, 2a parte, ch. 33, "Del modo de hazer fugas," fols. 66v and 67r; Morley, *Plaine and Easie*, 98; Rodio, *Regole di musica*, 27 and 29. See also Froebe, "Satzmodelle des 'Contrapunto alla mente'," where he refers to the fifteenth-century theorist Johannes Hothby. For modern discussions see Gauldin, "The Composition of Late Renaissance Stretto Canons," and Collins, "'So You Want to Write a Canon?'." On "fuga ad minimam" see also Beiche, "*Fuga*/Fuge," 8.

Example 12.3 Ciconia, *Doctorum principem/Melodia suavissima/Vir mitis*, mm. 8–12. Unaccompanied two-voice imitation with one-note overlap

Example 12.4 Du Fay, *Ecclesie militantis/Sanctorum arbitrio/Bella canunt gentes/Gabriel/Ecce nomen Domini*. Imitation breaks off at the entry of the second voice

from this period is Du Fay's *Nuper rosarum flores*, where two of the duos are dominated by stretto *fuga*.[16] The earliest place we have found stretto *fuga* at the fifth is in Du Fay's *Flos florum*, which must have been composed before 1425 (Example 12.7); here the stretto *fuga* occurs between the cantus and contratenor voices.[17]

---

16 Modern edition of *Nuper rosarum* found in Dufay, *Opera*, 1, no. 16, pp. 70–75. The passages in stretto *fuga* are mm. 15–17 and 113–23. Rifkin mentions the use of imitation at the fifth in this piece in "A Black Hole?," 27, but adds that "transposed imitation, like imitation itself, appears to have gone underground somewhere in mid-century, and it does not return to any substantial extent until imitation at the unison and octave had already re-established themselves."

17 See Bent, *Bologna Q15*, 1:20 and 219. Example from Dufay, *Opera*, 1, no. 2, pp. 6–7.

Example 12.5 Du Fay, *Ce jour de l'an*, mm. 1–9. Three-voice triadic imitation with minimal overlap

Example 12.6 Du Fay, *Fulgens iubar ecclesie/Puerpera pura parens/Virgo post partum*, mm. 145–50. Imitation at the fifth in upper two voices (tenor and contratenor have rests and are not shown)

Example 12.7 Du Fay, *Flos florum*, mm. 21–26, cantus and contratenor (the tenor rests). Stretto *fuga* at the fifth above

## Two-voice stretto *fuga*

The rules for stretto *fuga* at the fifth are found in Table 12.1.[18] For imitation at the fifth *above* the possible melodic intervals include the unison, ascending odd-numbered intervals (third and fifth), and descending even-numbered intervals (second and fourth). Melodic directions are reversed for stretto *fuga* at the fifth *below*. Any guide (or dux) melody made up of the melodic intervals shown here will produce a correct canon. It is often possible to recognize stretto *fuga* melodies by their use of these characteristic melodic interval patterns (especially common are sequential melodies with alternating thirds and fourths in opposite directions). Thus stretto *fuga* relates melodic interval choice to contrapuntal technique: it teaches us that many melodies are not freely composed, but must behave in restricted ways given the particular use to which they will be put.[19] We firmly believe that stretto *fuga* would have been a technique known to every choirboy, and therefore would have been part of the compositional arsenal of every composer.[20]

---

18  From Schubert, *Modal Counterpoint*, 157.

19  Stretto *fuga* can also be improvised at the fourth above or below and at the unison or octave above or below. Stretto *fuga* at the fourth has slightly different rules for unisons and seconds. Stretto *fuga* at the unison or octave can only use consonant melodic intervals (so seconds are outlawed, as are some fourths and fifths, unless there is an accompanying voice).

20  Hothby provides examples of stretto *fuga* in *De arte contrapuncti*, ed. Reaney, 88–91, examples 10–11. In "A Medieval Scholasticus" Brand describes how Hothby trained choirboys in improvised polyphony in Lucca. For the prevalence of improvised polyphony in the Renaissance see Canguilhem, "Singing upon the Book."

Table 12.1 *Melodic motions for stretto* fuga *at the fifth above and below*

| at the 5th above | unison | 3rd up | 5th up (once) | | 2nd down | 4th down (once) |
| --- | --- | --- | --- | --- | --- | --- |
| at the 5th below | unison | 3rd down | 5th down (once) | | | 4th up (once) |

Example 12.8 Johannes Puyllois, *Flos de spina*, contratenor primus and tenor, mm. 35–40. Stretto *fuga* at the fifth below

Imitation at the fifth, especially in stretto *fuga*, becomes increasingly important in the decades after *Nuper rosarum*, as the following examples from the 1450s, 1460s, and 1470s show. In the Puyllois example from the 1450s (Example 12.8), the duet is between the high contratenor and the tenor.[21] As is normal in the mid-fifteenth century, the canon is concealed, beginning in the middle of a phrase and ending before the cadence. Regis's *Clangat plebs* (from before 1477) works the same way (Example 12.9; notes in parentheses break out of stretto *fuga* momentarily).[22]

In a passage from a three-voice motet from the 1460s by Johannes Touront (Example 12.10), we see stretto *fuga* in the middle of the phrase (mm. 24–26), as

21 Example from Cumming, *Motet*, 241–43.
22 Example 12.9, *Clangat plebs*, is the first piece in Petrucci's *Motetti a cinque* (1508). All of the examples taken from the first five Petrucci motet prints (on which see below, n. 26) have been edited from those prints. Petrucci motets have been provided with a number indicating the book and the position in the book: 100s are *Motetti A*, 200s are *Motetti B*, etc. *Clangat plebs* is 501, the first piece in the fifth book. Decimals after the Petrucci number indicate *partes* after the *prima pars*, so Example 12.12 (206.3) is the *tertia pars* of the sixth piece in *Motetti B*. *Motetti a cinque* is missing the partbook for the contratenor secundus; that voice has been taken from Winkler, *Tenormotetten*, 2:180–94.

Example 12.9 Johannes Regis, *Clangat plebs flores/Sicut lilium* (501), superius and contratenor secundus, mm. 51–54. Stretto *fuga* at the fifth above (notes in parentheses break out of the pattern)

well as imitation at the fifth between tenor and superius after three semibreves in measures 28–29.[23]

In Compère's *Omnium bonorum plena* (probably early 1470s), seven of nine extended duos include stretto *fuga*. This piece, composed more than thirty years after *Nuper rosarum*, is dedicated to Du Fay; perhaps the prominent use of stretto *fuga* is a reference to the earlier work (Example 12.11).[24]

In Example 12.11a, the phrase begins in homorhythm, and the stretto *fuga* is not obvious. In Example 12.11b the canonic portion of the passage is marked. The time interval is one minim so the second voice is syncopated with respect to the first. The pitch interval is the fifth below (see Table 12.1), so the melodic intervals used are ascending second, descending third, ascending fourth, and unisons (shown as tied notes in Example 12.11c). The use of unisons makes mixed values (both minims and semibreves) possible.

Most mid-fifteenth-century examples, including those we have just seen (Examples 12.6, 12.8–11), use concealed stretto *fuga* at the minim. This may have to do with the aesthetic of *varietas*, where repetition is avoided or concealed. As the century progresses, the time interval becomes longer, and embellishments are inserted. A typical example of this new approach to stretto *fuga* is found in the *tertia pars* of Josquin's three-voice *Ave verum corpus* (Example 12.12). In contrast to Compère's concealed stretto *fuga* at the minim (Example 12.11), Josquin starts the stretto *fuga* at the very beginning of the phrase. His time interval is stretched out to the breve, and the melody includes embellishments (passing tones and neighbor tones).[25]

---

23 Example from Cumming, *Motet*, 203. Another famous example from the 1460s is Du Fay's *Ave regina celorum* III (1464), mm. 138–45, where the two-voice stretto *fuga* in the superius and altus is accompanied by a free bass line. See Dufay, *Opera*, 5, no. 51, pp. 124–30.
24 See Fallows, "Josquin and Trent 91." Example from Compère, *Opera omnia*, 4: 32–38.
25 Josquin's Example 12.12 contains the same melodic intervals (up two steps, down a third, up a fourth, and down another third) as those in a musical example by Montanos, showing how a simple note-against-note structure can be embellished. The Montanos example is reprinted by Schubert in *Modal Counterpoint*, 157–58 and "Counterpoint Pedagogy," 518.

Example 12.10 Johannes Touront, *Compangant omnes*, mm. 24–31. Stretto *fuga* at the fifth below, and imitation at the fifth after three semibreves

Stretto *fuga* determined the future of imitative texture in two ways. First, its most common pitch interval, the fifth, became a standard resource for composers, and came to govern entries at longer time intervals. Second, stretto *fuga* can be realized in more than two voices, so it can govern even an entire four-voice fabric for at least short stretches.

We examined the use of imitation in Petrucci's first five motet prints (published in Venice, 1502–8) as a way to understand style change in the late fifteenth century. These prints include music from all over western Europe, extending from the 1470s up to the dates of publication.[26] The repertory shows the motet at a time of experimentation and significant style change from the mid-fifteenth-century style of Regis and Tinctoris, up to works of Josquin and his contemporaries.[27] With a team of graduate students we compiled data on imitation at the beginning of each *pars* of every motet (174 pieces,

---

26 The five anthologies are described in Boorman, *Ottaviano Petrucci: Motetti A numero trentatre* (RISM 1502¹, Boorman no. 3); *Motetti De passione De cruce De sacramento De beata virgine et huiusmodi B* (RISM 1503¹, Boorman no. 7); *Motetti C* (RISM 1504¹, Boorman no. 15); *Motetti libro quarto* (RISM 1505², Boorman no. 21); and *Motetti a cinque Libro primo* (RISM 1508¹, Boorman no. 46). When we say "Petrucci motets" in this essay, we mean the motets in the first five books, not motets from the later *Motetti de la Corona* series.
27 On the breadth of repertory in the first five Petrucci motet prints, see Brown, "The Mirror of Man's Salvation," 746–47; and Blackburn, "Lorenzo de' Medici," 38–39.

Example 12.11 Loyset Compère, *Omnium bonorum plena*, superius and contratenor, mm. 43–47. Stretto *fuga* at the fifth below

Example 12.12 Josquin des Prez, *Ave verum corpus*, 3.p. (206.3). Stretto *fuga* at the fifth below, after a breve

356 *partes*).[28] Our analyses led us to expand the corpus of presentation types for imitative polyphony first described by Peter Schubert.[29] We also compiled data on the time and pitch interval of imitation (see Tables 12.3 and 12.4 below for an example of the kind of data we collected). We are therefore able to search the repertory for all of these features, including stretto *fuga*.

---

28 The students were Adalyat Issiyeva, Alison Kranias, Alexis Luko, Catherine Motuz, and Michel Vallières. Some of Cumming's findings are found in "Text Setting."
29 Schubert, "Hidden Forms."

As at the beginning of the fifteenth century, imitation at the unison or octave is still predominant in the Petrucci motet prints. Imitation at the fifth accounts for slightly less than a third of the two-voice imitative examples, of which around half use stretto *fuga*. The others have longer time intervals, from one semibreve to several measures. We call both of these "free imitation" (FI-2) as long as a contrapuntal combination is not repeated. This is a bit counterintuitive, since the second voice is bound to follow the first voice, but the duo is free in that it is not repeated. (The examples of stretto *fuga* we have seen so far are a subset of FI-2.)

There are two ways to extend the time interval between entries in FI-2: one is a slowed-down stretto *fuga*, as in Josquin's *Ave verum corpus* (Example 12.12); the structural notes are still related as the minims were, but the mensural unit separating the entries expands from the minim to the breve. Examples of two-voice stretto *fuga* in the Petrucci prints tend to use a longer time interval and more embellishment than in the mid-fifteenth century.

The other way is to provide a longer melody in the lead voice before the second entry; this is no longer stretto *fuga*. Examples include passages in Du Fay's *Fulgens iubar* (Example 12.6) and Touront's *Compangant* (Example 12.10), or in Josquin's *Ave Maria* (see Ex. 11.2, p. 192), and Obrecht's *Laudes Christo* (Example 12.20 below). Longer time intervals tend to make the *soggetto* more memorable, since more of it is heard before the second voice enters, and the reduction of overlap between the voices also makes it easier to understand the text.[30] This corresponds to our sense of changing musical style over the period.[31] Another development was to have more parts involved in imitation.

## Three-voice stretto *fuga*

Stretto *fuga* in three voices occurs rarely at beginnings of *partes* in Petrucci, and then mostly at the octave and unison. However, there is one type of three-voice stretto *fuga* that interests us because it prefigures a common sixteenth-century imitative pattern: a combination of stretto *fuga* at the fifth and octave (possible patterns are shown in Figure 12.1).[32]

"Pitch intervals" in Figure 12.1 refers to intervals between the voices in order of entry (see the box on the right: the tenor enters on G, the bass a fifth below,

---

30 We do not find imitation at the minim at the beginnings of *partes*, although it does occur in the middle parts of the Petrucci motets. One reason for this might be that short time intervals are metrically destabilizing, and thus inappropriate for beginnings. Two-voice imitation in general, and stretto *fuga* in particular, are also much more common in the middle of *partes*, where they are used in internal duos and trios.

31 Cumming, "From Variety to Repetition." Strict stretto *fuga ad minimam* never completely disappeared; see Milsom, "Absorbing Lassus," 312–13, Ex. 8.

32 Collins discusses Zarlino's treatment of three-voice stretto *fuga* in "Zarlino and Berardi" and Butler describes it in "The Fantasia as Musical Image." See also Schubert's demonstration: www.youtube.com/watch?v=eu_-OfAABHw.

| Pitch intervals | Scale degrees | Voices |
|---|---|---|
| −5; +8 | 511 | TBS |
| +5; −8 | 155 | TSB |
| +8; −5 | 551 | BST |
| −8; +5 | 115 | SBT |

Figure 12.1 Three-voice stretto *fuga*, invertible at the 12th

Example 12.13 Henricus Isaac, *O decus ecclesie* (506), superius, contratenor primus, and bassus, mm. 59–62. Three-voice invertible stretto *fuga*, scale degrees 511

and the superius an octave above the bass). "Scale degrees" are based on the interval combination at the beginning of the canon (the lowest note of the fifth is "1").[33] "Voices" indicates the relative ranges of the entries. The four combinations shown here are the only possible ways to use scale degrees 1 and 5 in stretto *fuga* (although twelfths can substitute for fifths and unisons or double octaves for octaves). Because the canon has to work at both the fifth and the octave after the same time interval, it is not possible to move the lead voice by step; all the other intervals for two-voice stretto *fuga* at the fifth are valid (see Table 12.1).[34]

Isaac uses three-voice stretto *fuga* in *O decus* (Example 12.13), where it is concealed in typical mid-fifteenth-century style (the actual canon begins on the

---

33 In entries a fourth apart, we have labeled the upper note as "1" and the lower note as "5." These scale degrees do not always correspond to the final of the piece.
34 The reader is reminded that the continuation of the first voice must accommodate the second voice's entry, and likewise, the continuation of the second voice must accommodate the beginning of the third. Therefore the pitch interval creates restrictions on the melodic intervals available. These limited choices, even more than in two parts, make improvisation even easier.

Example 12.14 Isaac, *O decus ecclesie* (506), superius, contratenor primus, and bassus, mm. 36–39. Three-voice invertible stretto *fuga*, scale degrees 115

second note in the bass and on the third note in the superius). This is an example of the more old-fashioned *fuga ad minimam* (as in Examples 12.6–11) with some basic passing-tone ornamentation (descending thirds are filled in).

Another passage of three-voice stretto *fuga* in the same piece (Example 12.14a) is closer in style to the (two-voice) *fuga* in Josquin's *Ave verum corpus* (Example 12.12): each entry begins after a rest, there is a longer time interval of imitation (a semibreve), and the *soggetto* is embellished with repeated notes and ties (Example 12.14b shows how this passage is an embellished version of note-against-note stretto *fuga*).

## Four-voice stretto *fuga*

Stretto *fuga* can also be improvised in four voices.[35] Whereas most of the Petrucci motets that begin with three-voice stretto *fuga* use imitation at the unison and octave, in four-voice examples imitation at the fifth and octave is more common.

---

35 The rules for melodic motions must again be modified slightly: the melodic unison can only be used once (repeating a second time will introduce a fourth), except when the fifth is replaced by the twelfth. Also, the fourth note of the lead voice cannot be dissonant with the fourth entry (this last rule is contextual and breaks out of the otherwise mechanical rule-following we expect from stretto *fuga*). In fact, in the

Table 12.2 *Four-voice stretto* fuga *with invertible counterpoint at the twelfth* (Table 12.3 lists the stretto *fuga* examples from the openings of the *partes* in Petrucci that are summarized here.)

| Scale degrees | Pitch intervals | Voices | No. of examples in Petrucci |
|---|---|---|---|
| a. | | | |
| 1155 | −8; +5; −8 | STAB | 1 |
| | −8; +12; −8 | ABST | 3 |
| b. | | | |
| 5511 | +8; −5; +8 | BATS | 0 |
| | +8; −12; +8 | TSBA | 7 |
| c. | | | |
| 5114 | −5; +8; −5 | ABST | 0 |
| | −12; +8; −5 | SBAT | 0 |
| d. | | | |
| 1552 | +5; −8; +5 | TSBA | 0 |
| | +12; −8; +5 | BSTA | 1 |

Here one often finds invertible counterpoint: the entry of each voice alternates between being below and above the previous entry – that is, a plus sign always alternates with a minus sign in the list of pitch intervals (see Table 12.2 and Table 12.3; the most common pattern is +8, −12, +8, with scale degrees 5511).[36] In fact, there are only four possible patterns of this type, shown in Table 12.2, a–d. (In the four-voice stretto *fuga* examples, the fifth is usually replaced by a twelfth.)

The anonymous *O claviger regni* (Example 12.15) features the most common four-voice pattern. It is slightly embellished, with an ornamental descending third in the second breve value of the *soggetto*, as well as passing tones for the final ascending fourth.

The anonymous *Sancta Maria, quesumus* (Example 12.16) begins with four-voice stretto *fuga* at a time interval of one semibreve. After the strict imitation at the beginning, the voices continue with a "stretto *fuga*" interval choice (an ascending third), but with free treatment of the rhythm. In both this example and the previous one, the imitation breaks off right after the entrance of the fourth voice, as shown by the second set of dotted lines.

examples we have found in the literature, the lead voice often fails to get to a fourth note. Thus four-voice stretto *fuga* is better for points of imitation where the voices continue freely after the *soggetto* than it is for sustained canons.

36 In the three-voice examples at the beginnings of *partes*, eleven use only unison and octave, while seven include imitation at the fifth. In the four-voice stretto *fuga* examples, nine use only unison and octave, while fifteen involve imitation at the fifth.

Table 12.3 *Four-voice stretto fuga in points of imitation at the beginnings of partes in the first five Petrucci motet prints (15 examples)*
Underlined scale-degree and pitch-interval patterns occur more than once; asterisk (*) indicates that the soggetto is slightly varied

| Scale degrees | Pitch interval of imitation | Voices in order of entry | Time interval in semibreves | Petrucci no. | Composer | Title |
|---|---|---|---|---|---|---|
| Conventional stretto *fuga* using invertible counterpoint at the 12th (13) | | | | | | |
| 5511 | +8; −12; +8 | T; S; B; A* | 2; 2; 2 | 104 | Pinarol | Surge propera amica mea |
| 5511 | +8; −12; +8 | Ctb; S; B; Cta | 1; 1; 1 | 509 | Obrecht | Laudemus nunc |
| 5511 | +8; −12; +8 | T; S*; T; B | 2; 2; 2 | 304.3 | Josquin | Factum est autem cum |
| 5511 | +8; −12; +8 | T; S; B; A | 2; 2; 2 | 304 | Josquin | Factum est autem cum |
| 5511 | +8; −12; +8 | T; S; B; A | 1; 1; 1 | 325 | Anon. | Confitemini domino |
| 5511 | +8; −12; +8 | T; S; B; A | 2; 2; 2 | 229 | Anon. | Hec est illa dulcis rosa |
| 5511 | +8; −12; +8 | T; S; B; A | 2; 2; 2 | 431 | Anon. | O claviger regni celorum (Ex. 12.15) |
| 1155 | −8; +12; −8 | A; B; S*; T* | 1; 1; 1 | 227 | Anon. | Sancta Maria (Ex. 12.16) |
| 1155 | −8; +12; −8 | A; B; S; T | 2; 2; 2 | 303.3 | Josquin | Liber generationis |
| 1155 | −8; +12; −8 | A; B; S; T | 4; 4; 4 | 439.5 | Josquin | Vultum tuum |
| 1155 | −8; +5; −8 | S; T; A; B | 3; 3; 3 | 436 | Brumel | Conceptus hodiernus |
| 1115 | +8; −8; +5 | B; S; T; A | 1; 1; 1 | 133.2 | Ghiselin | Anima mea liquefacta est |
| 1552 | +12; −8; +5 | B; S; T; A | 1; 1; 1 | 404.3 | La Rue | Salve regina (Ex. 12.19) |
| Unconventional stretto *fuga* using different intervals of inversion | | | | | | |
| 1155 | +8; −4; +8 | B; A; T; S | 1; 1; 1 | 427 | Clibano | Festivitatem dedicationis (Ex. 12.17) |
| 1515 | −4; +11; −4 | T; B; S; A | 2; 2; 2 | 120 | Craen | Ave Maria gratia plena (Ex. 12.18) |

Example 12.15 Anon., *O claviger regni* (431). Four-voice invertible stretto *fuga*, scale degrees 5 5 1 1

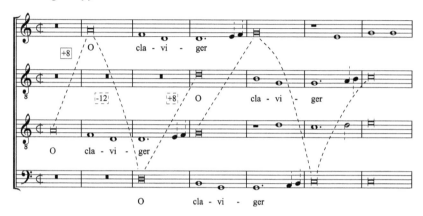

Example 12.16 Anon., *Sancta Maria, quesumus* (227). Four-voice invertible stretto *fuga*, scale degrees 1 1 5 5

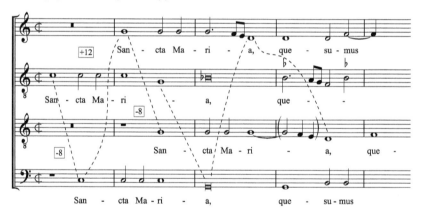

In four-voice stretto *fuga*, the most common pitch intervals of entry in Petrucci are +8, −12, +8 (occurring seven times in Table 12.3), with the order of voices most often TSBA. The imitation therefore begins with the tenor and superius voices. The prominence of these voices may reflect the tenorist's role as leader of improvisation, or derive from compositional norms, since the structural pairing of tenor and superius is fundamental to fifteenth-century music and continues throughout the sixteenth century.[37] This order of entries

---

37 See Wegman, "From Maker to Composer," 444–49. On the role of the tenorist, see Cumming, "From Two-Part Framework," and Schubert, "Musical Commonplaces."

Example 12.17 Jero. de Clibano, *Festivitatem dedicationis* (427). Scale degrees 1155, invertible counterpoint at the eleventh

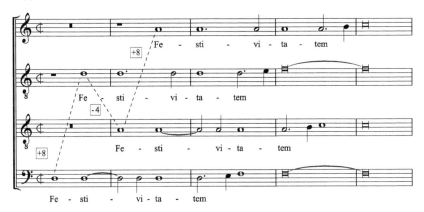

Example 12.18 Nicolaus Craen, *Ave Maria*. Scale degrees 1515, invertible counterpoint at the seventh

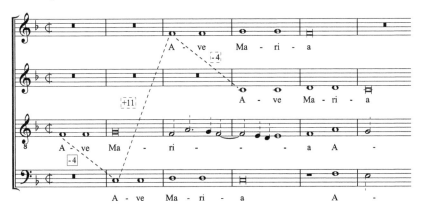

spaces the voices widely, as does the second most common arrangement, ABST (−8, +12, −8, occurring three times in Table 12.3). Examples 12.15 and 12.16 are characterized by slow, static, and widely spaced perfect intervals before the voices break off into shorter values and free counterpoint.

In the sixteenth century, by contrast, four-voice stretto *fuga* most commonly uses fifths rather than twelfths, so the entries separated by octave are filled in immediately (+8, −5, +8, rather than +8, −12, +8); thus they resemble three-voice stretto *fuga* (as shown in Figure 12.1 and Examples 12.13 and 12.14). The difference between the fifteenth- and sixteenth-century approaches is not a

Example 12.19  Pierre de La Rue, *Salve Regina* II, 3.p. (404.3). Stretto *fuga* with entries on three scale degrees: 1552

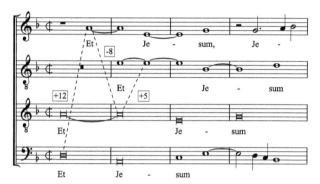

technical one, since stretto *fuga* still obtains, but the aesthetic has changed, favoring more closely spaced sonorities, with a fourth voice added at one extreme or the other. As Nicola Vicentino noted, "at the beginning of a composition, the voices should not enter at extreme ranges – for instance, a soprano very high and a bass very low. This kind of opening, heard in compositions that are not very modern, strikes the ear as crude."[38]

There is a single instance of stretto *fuga* at the octave and the fourth at the beginning of a *pars* in the Petrucci motets (Example 12.17). Although the scale degrees of the entry notes are 1 and 5, the intervals of imitation of fourth and octave result in invertible counterpoint at the eleventh, which offers very few melodic choices.[39] This example, like those using invertible counterpoint at the twelfth, uses many repeated notes and sits on the same sonority for the first three measures.

Nicolaus Craen's *Ave Maria* (Example 12.18) is the only example of four-voice stretto *fuga* in Petrucci that alternates scale degrees 1 and 5 (1515). The rarity of this procedure is unexpected, given how common the 1515 scale-degree pattern is in later points of imitation. There is, however, a good reason: alternation of scale degrees is not possible in "conventional" four-voice stretto *fuga* invertible at the twelfth, because there has to be an octave between two of the entries. It is only possible when a different, and difficult, type of contrapuntal inversion is used: invertible counterpoint at the seventh.[40] Craen thus chose a less familiar type of invertible counterpoint for the sake of the alternation.

---

38 Vicentino, *L'antica musica*, trans. Maniates, 246.
39 For the rules for stretto *fuga* at different pitch intervals see Collins, "'So You Want to Write a Canon?'"
40 The tenor–bass combination in measures 2–3 moves from a fifth to a third; this is inverted in the bass–superius combination in measures 3–4, which moves from a third to a fifth. Transformation of a fifth into a

Only one Petrucci motet opening uses the invertible stretto *fuga* pattern that results in entries on three different pitch classes (1552): Pierre de La Rue's *Salve Regina* II (Example 12.19). This modally unstable pattern makes more sense at the beginning of the *tertia pars* than at the beginning of the piece. The point of imitation is also obscured by the early entrances of the tenor and altus (dotted lines in the example show where the voices would enter after a time interval of a semibreve).[41]

Eleven of the fifteen examples in Table 12.3 use the conventional stretto *fuga* pattern with invertible counterpoint at the twelfth: seven begin with the ascending octave (5511) between the first two entries, four with the descending octave (1155). These patterns (shown in Examples 12.15 and 12.16), recur much more often than the others, each of which is unique (Examples 12.17–19).

In this period of experimentation, why might the stretto *fuga* patterns invertible at the twelfth have been so much more common than other intervallic combinations? Invertible stretto *fuga* has many features that must have been appealing to composers of the late fifteenth century:

- Regularity and repetition. The periodicity of entries more than a minim apart creates a clear sense of meter and emphasizes the identity of the repeated *soggetto*.
- The improvisatory tradition. These patterns would have been at the composers' fingertips (or at the tips of their tongues). Once the initial *soggetto* was constructed with the correct melodic intervals, the composer knew that the additional entries in the point of imitation were guaranteed to work. This can help us understand how musicians composed without a score, as Jessie Ann Owens describes.[42]
- Scale degrees 1 and 5. The use of these scale degrees in the two most common stretto-*fuga* patterns tends to reinforce the principal pitches of the mode.
- Repetition and variety. The repetition of the contrapuntal modules reinforces the memorability of the *soggetto*, while invertible counterpoint creates a variety of vertical intervals.

All these elements together make an irresistible package. Is it any wonder that composers experimenting with four-voice imitative polyphony chose stretto *fuga*?

---

third and vice versa only happens in invertible counterpoint at the seventh, as shown by this table of intervals and their inversions:

1234567
7654321

41 In Table 12.3, this passage is described as starting with the interval of a twelfth: +12, −8, +5. This seems to be quite extreme, but in fact the twelfth is filled in on account of the early entrances of the inner voices. For a detailed discussion of underlay in this piece, see Schubert and Cumming, "Text and Motif."
42 Owens, *Composers at Work*, 7.

Still, stretto *fuga* is not the only way to write equally spaced (or periodic) imitative entries. Table 12.4 lists the fifteen examples of four-voice Periodic Entries using pitch intervals other than the unison and octave in which the time interval of imitation is longer than one unit.[43] In these pieces, composers achieve various compositional goals through imitative techniques other than stretto *fuga*.

## Periodic imitation at longer time intervals

One of the attractions of longer time intervals is escaping the melodic restrictions imposed by stretto *fuga*. In order to understand how periodic imitation is structured, it is helpful to think of the segment of the *soggetto* sounded before the next entry of each voice as a "subject," and the continuation of the first

Table 12.4 *Four-voice Periodic Entries with longer time intervals (not stretto* fuga*) and including pitch intervals of imitation other than unison and octave in points of imitation at the beginnings of* partes *in the first five Petrucci motet prints (15 examples)* Asterisk (*) indicates that the soggetto is slightly varied.

| Scale degrees | Pitch interval of imitation | Voices in order of entry | Time interval in semibreves | Petrucci no. | Composer | Title |
|---|---|---|---|---|---|---|
| Combinations of 1s and 5s | | | | | | |
| 1115 | −8; −8; +12 | S; T; B; A* | 2; 2; 2 | 203.5 | Josquin | Qui velatus facie fuisti |
| 5551 | +8; −8; −5 | A; S; T; B | 4; 4; 4 | 319.2 | Anon. | Miles mire probitatis |
| 5551 | 1; +8; −12 | A; T*; S; B* | 4; 4; 4 | 321 | Anon. | Virgo precellens deitatis |
| 5551 | +8; −8; +4 | B; S; T; A* | 2; 2; 2 | 333 | Josquin | Planxit autem David |
| 5111 | −5; +8; +8 | T; B; A; S* | 2; 2; 2 | 445 | Anon. | Si bibero crathere pleno |
| 1151 | −8; +5; −5 | S; T*; A*; B* | 2; 2; 2 | 103 | Compere | O genetrix gloriosa |
| 1551 | +5; −8; −5 | A; S; T; B | 4; 4; 4 | 117 | Compere | Sile fragor ac verborum (Ex. 12.22) |

43 See Schubert, *Modal Counterpoint*, 227–42.

Table 12.4 (*cont.*)

| Scale degrees | Pitch interval of imitation | Voices in order of entry | Time interval in semibreves | Petrucci no. | Composer | Title |
|---|---|---|---|---|---|---|
| **Combinations of 1s and 5s** | | | | | | |
| **Stacked canons (2)** | | | | | | |
| 5147 | −5; −5; −5 | S; A; T*; B* | 4; 4; 4 | 326 | Anon. | Respice me infelicem |
| 5147 | −5; −5; −5 | S; A; T; B | 3; 3; 3 | 413 | Obrecht | Laudes Christo (Ex. 12.21) |
| **Partially stacked canon (the first pitch interval of imitation is different)** | | | | | | |
| 1152 | 1; +5; +5 | A; B; T; S | 4; 4; 4 | 221.9 | Compere | In nomine Jesu (Officium de Cruce) |
| **Other pitch intervals of imitation with three or more pitch classes** | | | | | | |
| 5114 | −5; +8; −5 | T; B; S; A | 3; 3; 3 | 201 | van Stappen | Non lotis manibus |
| 3151 | −10; +5; +4 | S; B; T; A | 1; 1; 1 | 325.2 | Anon. | Confitemini domino |
| 4511 | −7; +11; −8 | A; B; S; T | 2; 2; 4 | 424.7 | Brumel | Gloria laus et honor |
| 1135 | +8; +3; −6 | B; A; S; T | 2; 2; 2 | 413.2 | Obrecht | Laudes Christo |
| 1537 | +5; −10; +5 | A; S; B; T | 2; 2; 2 | 306.2 | Anon. | Davidica stirpe Maria |

voice that accompanies the subject in the second voice as the "countersubject" (see Figure 12.2).[44] Of course the beginning of the subject and the countersubject usually make a unified whole, and are understood as a complete melodic unit. The longer overlap between the new voice and the old voice creates a substantial contrapuntal combination, or module, that is repeated each time a new voice enters, as long as the beginning of each *soggetto*, or "subject" (S), is accompanied by the same "countersubject" (CS).[45] Figure 12.2 schematizes the

44 In *Libro llamado el arte de tañer fantasía*, ch. 33, Sancta Maria describes the continuation of the first voice after the second has entered: "and then the voice that has finished the *passo* must necessarily serve as accompaniment to the other voice."
45 For the term module, see Owens, "The Milan Partbooks," 284; on Periodic Entries, see Schubert, "Hidden Forms," 488–89 and 498–504, and Cumming, "Text Setting," 96–98.

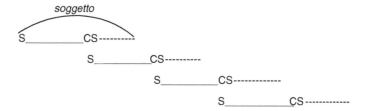

Figure 12.2 Periodic Entries (PEn)

vocal entries and the combinations created between them. Schubert has called this presentation type Periodic Entries (PEn), a category that includes both stretto *fuga* and imitation at longer time intervals.

Probably the most famous piece to begin with a set of Periodic Entries is the first work in Petrucci's *Motetti A*, Josquin's *Ave Maria*, which begins with four entries at the octave and unison.[46] This is not an instance of stretto *fuga* since the time interval is four semibreves and the module contains more than one consonance.[47] By using Periodic Entries at only the unison and octave, the composer sacrifices the use of two scale degrees but retains periodicity and modular repetition.

Another type of Periodic Entry is what Alan Gosman has called "stacked canon," in which the pitch distance is the same between all pairs of entries. In Example 12.20, Obrecht's *Laudes Christo*, each voice enters a fifth below the previous one, moving around the circle of fifths so that the *soggetto* begins on four different pitches (5147).[48] Obrecht sacrifices the stable use of only first and fifth degrees for the sake of exact modular repetition (shown in the example with numbers indicating the intervals between the voices), with no contrapuntal inversion. The long time interval also allows for clear text declamation. The periodic nature of this opening is emphasized by the rhythmic unisons (the dotted minim and *fusae*).

Some Periodic Entries sacrifice modular repetition, creating minimal overlap between each entry of the *soggetto*, as in Example 12.21, Loyset Compère's *Sile fragor*, where the overlap is only one note. The lack of a repeated countersubject allows more choice of melodic intervals (here the *soggetto* includes an ascending second and an ascending third), and permits the scale-degree pattern 1551. Neither of these features is possible in four-voice stretto *fuga* inverted at the twelfth.

46 For a musical example, see John Milsom's discussion of this piece in Ch. 11, Examples 11.1–2.
47 *Ave Maria* is not shown on Table 12.4 because it uses only pitch intervals of octave and unison.
48 Gosman, "Stacked Canon." Gosman's work was inspired by Urquhart; see "Calculated to Please the Ear," 95 n. 15. See also Burn, "Further Observations on Stacked Canon."

Example 12.20 Jacob Obrecht, *Laudes Christo* (413). Stacked canon, scale
degrees 5147

Example 12.21 Compère, *Sile fragor* (117). Periodic Entries, one-note overlap
(in boxes), scale degrees 1551

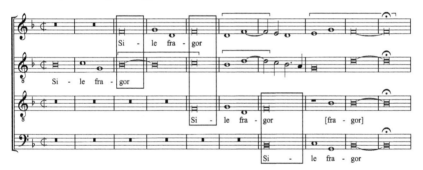

## Other presentation types

Among those Petrucci motets that use non-periodic presentation types, a relatively small number begin with what Schubert calls Imitative Duos, or IDs.[49]
(These do not appear in Table 12.4, since they are not periodic.) A prime example
is the *tertia pars* of Josquin's *Vultum tuum* (see Example 12.22). (The actual duo
begins with stretto *fuga* at the fifth above, at the breve; it switches to stretto *fuga*
at the semibreve starting on the second beat of m. 4.) By waiting to introduce the
second pair of voices, Josquin is able to use alternating entries on the first and

49 On Imitative Duos see Schubert, "Hidden Forms," 488 and 495–98, and Cumming, "Text Setting,"
95–96.

Example 12.22 Josquin, *Vultum tuum deprecabuntur*, 3.p. (439.3). Pair of Imitative Duos, scale degrees 1515

fifth degrees without getting involved in invertible counterpoint at the seventh, as in Example 12.18. Josquin thus sacrifices periodicity for a lengthy repeated module and alternation of first and fifth degrees.

Out of 356 total *partes* in the Petrucci prints, only twenty begin with Imitative Duos, and of those almost two-thirds use imitation at the fourth or fifth. IDs are thus considerably less common than the fifty-one examples of four-voice Periodic Entries (the thirty in Tables 12.3 and 12.4, plus twenty-one examples at the unison and octave). Shortly after the turn of the century, however, Imitative Duos became the most common presentation type for imitative polyphony.[50]

## Conclusion

Our study of imitation in the fifteenth century has provided insight into compositional techniques and led to a clearer understanding of how imitation developed. By examining a large body of repertory – selected early and mid-fifteenth-century motets as well as Petrucci's Venetian motet prints – we have been able to identify recurring patterns and changing practices. Imitation at both the octave and fifth had been in use for a long time. But during the second

50 Rifkin, "A Black Hole?," 27–29, 43, 45, 56–70, 82.

Table 12.5  *The changing face of imitation in the motet, ca. 1450–1508*

| Features | Imitation ca. 1450–ca. 1480 | Imitation ca. 1480 and after |
|---|---|---|
| No. of voices | in 2 voices only, in duet sections, or within a 3- or 4-voice texture | all voices in a piece or section (3- or 4-voice points of imitation) |
| Where in phrase | often appears in the middle of a phrase | each entry begins a phrase and is preceded by rests |
| Text-setting | melismatic; little coordination with text phrase | entries begin with syllabic declamation of the same text |
| Time interval of imitation (TI) | 2nd voice often follows after a semibreve or a minim; TI can conflict with the mensural structure (stretto *fuga*) | each voice enters after a time interval of imitation several beats long (embellished stretto *fuga*); TI conforms to mensural structure |
| Pitch interval of imitation (PI) | octave or fifth | octave or fifth OR octave and fifth (combinations of octave and fifth leading to mix of 1st and 5th scale degrees) |
| Repeated counterpoint | No: does not involve a repeated contrapuntal combination (module) | Yes: often involves a repeated contrapuntal combination (module) |

half of the century, new patterns emerged, in conjunction with a new preference for repetition. The mid-fifteenth-century style of imitation did not disappear, but became less common, as new approaches to imitation became more prominent at the end of the century. We can look at the changes over time in relation to a variety of features, summarized in Table 12.5.

The patterns of imitation that derive from improvisable stretto *fuga* provided a template for late fifteenth-century composers to create four-voice imitative polyphony. These patterns coincided with a new interest in exact repetition and contrapuntal modules, and an emphasis on the first and fifth scale degrees. Stretto *fuga* remained an essential feature for the rest of the sixteenth century, but the four-voice invertible stretto *fuga* resulting in Periodic Entries that was so common in the Petrucci prints would give way to imitative duos and other presentation types using more varied time intervals of imitation. Recognizing the relationship between improvisation and composition provides a clearer vision than ever before of how imitative texture developed.

The features of invertible stretto *fuga* described here also had longer-term implications for musical style. Modular repetition pointed toward the repetition of vertical blocks of music, or harmonic repetition. Periodicity reinforced a clear sense of regular duple meter, newly established as the norm in the late fifteenth century. Entries on the first and fifth scale degrees served to regularize modality just when theorists first began explicitly discussing mode and polyphony. Indeed, the patterns afforded by stretto *fuga* continued to function as fundamental building blocks of polyphonic music into the eighteenth century.

# Bibliography

Beiche, Michael, "*Fuga*/Fuge," in *Handwörterbuch der musikalischen Terminologie*, ed. Hans Heinrich Eggebrecht, Stuttgart, 1972–2006

Bent, Margaret, ed., *Bologna Q15: The Making and Remaking of a Musical Manuscript: Introductory Study and Facsimile Edition*, Lucca, 2008

Blackburn, Bonnie J., "Lorenzo de' Medici, a Lost Isaac Manuscript, and the Venetian Ambassador," in *Musica Franca: Essays in Honor of Frank A. D'Accone*, ed. Irene Alm, Alyson McLamore, and Colleen Reardon, Stuyvesant, NY, 1996, 19–44

Boorman, Stanley, *Ottaviano Petrucci: A Catalogue Raisonné*, New York, 2006

Brand, Benjamin, "A Medieval Scholasticus and Renaissance Choirmaster: A Portrait of John Hothby at Lucca," *Renaissance Quarterly* 63 (2010), 754–806

Brown, Howard Mayer, "The Mirror of Man's Salvation: Music in Devotional Life about 1500," *Renaissance Quarterly* 43 (1990), 744–73

Burn, David, "Further Observations on Stacked Canon and Renaissance Compositional Procedure: Gascongne's 'Ista Est Speciosa' and Forestier's 'Missa L'Homme Armé'," *Journal of Music Theory* 45 (2001), 73–118

Butler, Gregory G. "The Fantasia as Musical Image," *MQ* 60 (1974), 602–15

Canguilhem, Philippe (trans. Alexander Stalarow), "Singing upon the Book according to Vicente Lusitano," *EMH* 30 (2011), 55–103

Ciconia, Johannes, *The Works of Johannes Ciconia*, ed. Margaret Bent and Anne Hallmark, PMFC 24, Monaco, 1985

Collins, Denis, "'So You Want to Write a Canon?' An Historically-Informed New Approach for the Modern Theory Class," *College Music Symposium* 48 (2008), 108–23

"Zarlino and Berardi as Teachers of Canon," *Theoria* 7 (1993), 103–23

Compère, Loyset, *Opera omnia*, ed. Ludwig Finscher, 5 vols., CMM 15, n.p., 1958–72

Cumming, Julie E., "Composing Imitative Counterpoint around a Cantus Firmus: Two Motets by Heinrich Isaac," *JM* 28 (2011), 231–88

"From Two-Part Framework to Movable Module," in *Medieval Music in Practice: Essays in Honor of Richard Crocker*, ed. Judith Peraino, Münster, 2013

"From Variety to Repetition: The Birth of Imitative Polyphony," *Yearbook of the Alamire Foundation* 6, ed. Bruno Bouckaert and Eugeen Schreurs, Peer, 2008, 21–44

*The Motet in the Age of Du Fay*, Cambridge, 1999

"Text Setting and Imitative Technique in Petrucci's First Five Motet Prints," in *The Motet around 1500: On the Relationship of Imitation and Text Treatment?*, ed. Thomas Schmidt-Beste, Turnhout, 2012, 83–109 and Peter Schubert, "Patterns of Imitation, 1450–1508," paper presented at the conference on Medieval and Renaissance Music, Utrecht, 2009, and at the Annual Meeting of the American Musicological Society, Philadelphia, 2009

Dufay, Guillaume, *Opera omnia*, ed. Heinrich Besseler, 6 vols., CMM 1, Rome, 1951–66

Fallows, David, *Josquin*, Turnhout, 2009

"Josquin and Trent 91: Thoughts on *Omnium bonorum plena* and his Activities in the 1470s," in *Manoscritti di polifonia nel Quattrocento europeo: Atti del Convegno internazionale di studi, Trento – Castello del Buonconsiglio, 18–19 ottobre 2002*, ed. Marco Gozzi, Trent, 2004, 205–12

Froebe, Folker, "Satzmodelle des 'Contrapunto alla mente' und ihre Bedeutung für den Stilwandel um 1600," *Zeitschrift der Gesellschaft für Musiktheorie* 4 (2007), 13–55, www.gmth.de/zeitschrift/artikel/244.aspx

Gauldin, Robert, "The Composition of Late Renaissance Stretto Canons," *Theory and Practice* 21 (1996), 29–54

Glareanus, Henricus, *Dodecachordon*, Basel, 1547; facs. Hildesheim, 1969, and New York, 1967; trans. Clement A. Miller, [Rome], 1965

Gosman, Alan, "Stacked Canon and Renaissance Compositional Procedure," *Journal of Music Theory*, 41 (1997), 289–317

Grimshaw, Julian, "Morley's Rule for First-Species Canon," *EM* 34 (2006), 661–66

Heyden, Sebald, *De arte canendi*, Nuremburg, 1540; facs. New York, 1969; trans. Clement A. Miller, [Rome], 1972

Hothby, Johannes, *De arte contrapuncti*, ed. Gilbert Reaney, CSM 26, Neuhausen-Stuttgart, 1977

Luko, Alexis, "Tinctoris on *Varietas*, " *EMH* 27 (2008), 99–136

Milsom, John, "Absorbing Lassus," *EM* 33 (2005), 305–20

"'Imitatio,' 'Intertextuality,' and Early Music," in *Citation and Authority in Medieval and Renaissance Musical Culture: Learning from the Learned*, ed. Suzannah Clark and Elizabeth Eva Leach, Woodbridge, 2005, 141–51

"Josquin des Prez and the Combinative Impulse," in *The Motet around 1500: On the Relationship of Imitation and Text Treatment?*, ed. Thomas Schmidt-Beste, Turnhout, 2012, 211–46

Montanos, Francisco de, *Arte de musica theorica y pratica*, Valladolid, 1592. Trans. Dan M. Urquhart, "Francisco de Montanos's Arte de musica theorica y pratica: A Translation and Commentary," Ph.D. diss., Eastman School of Music, 1969

Morley, Thomas, *A Plaine and Easie Introduction to Practicall Musicke*, London, 1597; facs. Amsterdam, 1969. Ed. R. Alec Harman, New York, 1973

Owens, Jessie Ann, *Composers at Work: The Craft of Musical Composition, 1450–1600*, New York, 1997

"The Milan Partbooks: Evidence of Cipriano de Rore's Compositional Process," *JAMS* 37 (1984), 270–98

Rifkin, Joshua, "A Black Hole? Problems in the Motet around 1500," in *The Motet around 1500: On the Relationship of Imitation and Text Treatment?*, ed. Thomas Schmidt-Beste, Turnhout, 2012, 21–82

"Busnoys and Italy: The Evidence of Two Songs," in *Antoine Busnoys: Method, Meaning, and Context in Late Medieval Music*, ed. Paula Higgins, Oxford, 1999, 505–71

"Munich, Milan, and a Marian Motet: Dating Josquin's *Ave Maria … virgo serena*,"
     *JAMS* 56 (2003), 239–350

Rodio, Rocco, *Regole di musica*, Naples, 1609; facs. Bologna, 1981

Sancta Maria, Thomas de, *Libro llamado el arte de tañer fantasía*, Valladolid, 1565; facs.
     Geneva, 1973, Barcelona, 2007. Trans. Almonte Howell, Jr. and Warren
     E. Hultberg, Pittsburgh, 1991

Schubert, Peter, "Counterpoint Pedagogy in the Renaissance," in *The Cambridge History
     of Western Music Theory*, ed. Thomas Christensen, Cambridge, 2002, 503–33

     "From Improvisation to Composition: Three 16th-Century Case Studies," in
     *Improvising Early Music*, ed. Dirk Moelants, Collected Writings of the Orpheus
     Institute, Ghent, 2014, 93–130

     "Hidden Forms in Palestrina's First Book of Four-Voice Motets," *JAMS* 60 (2007),
     483–556. For a corrected version of the appendix see www.music.mcgill.ca/
     ~schubert

     "A Lesson from Lassus: Form in the Duos of 1577," *Music Theory Spectrum* 17 (1995),
     1–26

     *Modal Counterpoint, Renaissance Style*, 2nd edn., New York, 2008

     "Musical Commonplaces in the Renaissance," in *Music Education in the Middle Ages and
     the Renaissance*, ed. Russell E. Murray, Jr., Susan Forscher Weiss, and Cynthia
     J. Cyrus, Bloomington, IN, 2010, 161–92

     and Julie E. Cumming. "Text and Motif *c*. 1500: A New Approach to Text Underlay,"
     *EM* 40 (2012), 3–14

Sparks, Edgar H., "Some Uses of Imitation in Sacred Music of the 15th Century," *JAMS*
     5 (1952), 269

Taruskin, Richard, *The Oxford History of Western Music*, 6 vols., Oxford, 2005

Urquhart, Peter, "Calculated to Please the Ear: Ockeghem's Canonic Legacy," *TVNM* 47
     (1997), 72–98

Vicentino, Nicola, *L'antica musica ridotta alla moderna prattica*, Rome, 1555; facs. Kassel,
     1959. Trans. Maria Rika Maniates as *Ancient Music Adapted to Modern Practice*, New
     Haven, 1996

Wegman, Rob C., "From Maker to Composer: Improvisation and Musical Authorship in
     the Low Countries 1450–1500," *JAMS* 49 (1996), 409–79

Winkler, Heinz-Jürgen, *Die Tenormotetten von Johannes Regis in der Überlieferung des Chigi-
     Codex*, 2 vols., Capellae Apostolicae Sixtinaeque collectanea acta monumenta
     5, Vatican City, 1999

Zarlino, Gioseffo, *Le istitutioni harmoniche*, Venice, 1558, 1571, and 1573; facs. of 1558
     and 1573, New York, 1965; facs. of 1573, Ridgewood, NJ, 1966. Part 3 of 1558
     trans. Guy A. Marco and Claude V. Palisca, New Haven, 1968

# · PART III HUMANISM ·

# Humanism and music in Italy

JAMES HANKINS

Of all the varied strands woven into the cultural fabric of Renaissance Italy, the most vivid in the quattrocento was that associated with the study of ancient literature, the *studia humanitatis*, christened "humanism" by nineteenth-century scholars. Though study and imitation of the Latin classics as well as the "language arts" of grammar (correct speech) and rhetoric (persuasive speech) go back to antiquity,[1] literary studies were reorganized conceptually and reinvigorated in the second half of the fourteenth century, thanks mostly to the extraordinary influence of Petrarch. It was Petrarch who envisaged the humanities as a distinct form of culture and justified the study of pagan literature by demonstrating its compatibility with Christianity and its potential for the reform of contemporary societies.[2] The humanities came to colonize a cultural space somewhere between theology (understood by humanists as oriented to the next life and to the divine) and the professional studies of law and medicine. Humane studies were the studies appropriate to this life and this world. They distinguished themselves by insisting that they had nothing to do with the arts of getting and spending; they were *liberal* arts, the arts worthy of a free man or woman, of people who did not (in theory) have to earn a living. Such persons could pursue an active life of involvement in government or a life of scholarly retirement, but they had to have at least enough freedom and leisure to cultivate their souls through literary study. The liberal arts were also in this vision *bonae artes*, arts that gave the individual moral worth and dignity, arts that served the commonwealth by making its leaders virtuous and wise. The wisdom and virtue of princes and civic leaders, it was believed, would filter down to the

I would like to thank Margaret Bent, Bonnie Blackburn, Anna Maria Busse Berger, Leofranc Holford-Strevens, and Evan MacCarthy for helpful comments and bibliographical suggestions. Important general treatments of humanism and fifteenth-century music may be found in Palisca, *Humanism in Italian Renaissance Musical Thought*; Lowinsky, "Humanism in the Music of the Renaissance"; Kristeller, "Music and Learning"; Moyer, *Musica Scientia*; Pirrotta, *Music and Culture* and "Musica e umanesimo"; Bent, "Humanists and Music" and "Music and the Early Veneto Humanists"; Strohm, *The Rise of European Music*; "Music, Humanism"; and "Neue Aspekte"; and Haar, "Humanism." Vecce, *Gli umanisti e la musica* presents a collection of relevant texts.

1 Witt, *In the Footsteps of the Ancients*, ch. 6.  2 Hankins, ed., *The Cambridge Companion*, 39–45.

population at large via word and example. At school, students of the humanities would acquire the lost ancient art of eloquence, the art of persuading
others. This was a more useful study for future leaders than the logic of the
scholastics, as Petrarch argued: moral improvement required a teacher or a
political leader who could appeal to the passions with "the sharp, burning
barbs of his eloquence."[3] The young humanist would also study poetry,
history, and moral philosophy, deriving arguments for, and examples of,
good conduct from the best sources: the statesmen, warriors, poets, and
philosophers of ancient Greece and Rome.

Perhaps the humanists' most powerful idea, however, was the idea of the
Renaissance itself. This was a narrative that became a fixed background
assumption in European consciousness for centuries, until eventually replaced
by the Enlightenment idea of progress. It was this narrative that turned the
study of the humanities into a movement of ideas. We might define the
Renaissance movement as a set of cultural assumptions that included, mini-
mally, the following theses: that the language and culture inherited from the
immediate past was corrupt, thoroughly vitiated by the barbarians (sometimes
identified as Goths or Gauls) who had destroyed the Roman Empire; that this
Middle Age of barbarous culture continued into the present and was responsible for modern Italy's weakness, failure, and division; and that only a revival
or rebirth of ancient Roman virtue could restore the lost glories of Italy. These
assumptions were the premise for a movement that came to embrace nearly all
areas of quattrocento culture, including painting, sculpture, music, architecture, military science, and politics, as well as education and the traditional
liberal arts. And it was Petrarch's followers in the fifteenth century – notably
Leonardo Bruno and Flavio Biondo – who were the first to postulate that Italy
had at last succeeded in reviving something of the virtue and wisdom of old
Rome: it had begun to emerge from medieval darkness into a new Golden Age
that it was appropriate to describe as a rebirth of antiquity.

The key to humanism's influence in the quattrocento was its successful
transformation of traditional grammatical training in the Latin language. The
type of grammar schools found in most important Italian towns of the
Renaissance had arisen in the twelfth century as pre-professional schools to
train future notaries, lawyers, and doctors. But the humanists from the 1390s
onwards, while retaining traditional methods and texts,[4] found a new audience
and a new purpose for training young men and women in Latin language and
literature. The new students of the humanities included the nobility and
wealthy members of the upper classes in Italian city-states. The new purpose

3 Petrarca, *Invectives*, 317.    4 Black, *Humanism and Education*.

was providing these future leaders with eloquence and virtue, including practical wisdom or prudence. Education in the Latin language was thus transformed, from pre-professional training taught by grammarians into the
education of the ruling class, taught by *literati*, or what later in the quattrocento
came to be nicknamed *umanisti*. Both the teachers and the taught claimed
higher status on account of their studies, and won it. As in Confucian China,
the classical came to be associated in the minds of educated people with the
noble. At the same time humanists insisted that true nobility was not inherited
but earned through virtuous behavior. The best way to earn nobility, or at least
lay claim to it, was through the study of classical literature.[5]

The new humanist educators of the early fifteenth century – men such as
Guarino Veronese, Gasparino Barzizza, and Vittorino da Feltre – offered training
in the arts of grammar and rhetoric and an intensive grounding in a small group
of Latin classics: Cicero, Sallust, Virgil, Horace, and a few others. They also,
increasingly, insisted that the young men and women under their care should
learn to read ancient Greek. Moreover, humanist teachers, in their influential
treatises on education, defended the study of the other, traditional liberal arts
such as arithmetic, geometry, astronomy, and music; and from the 1420s
onwards there is evidence that music was actually taught in humanist schools.[6]
In making music part of liberal education, the *literae humaniores*, they appealed
especially to the authority of Quintilian's *Institutes*, the great handbook for the
new rhetorical education, whose use was championed by Valla. For Quintilian as
for Cicero, the ideal orator needed to learn more than rhetoric: to become a
master statesman he needed to frequent the company of the Muses and the
Graces; and music was of particular importance. Indeed Quintilian stated that
"without a knowledge of music there can be no perfect eloquence."[7] Hence
musical study in the humanist school became potentially a high-status activity,
even noble. Some humanists even championed the restoration of music to its
ancient status as a noble activity, making it a key goal of their movement.[8]

## Music in humanist education

The inclusion of music in elite education, however, was by no means free of
controversy. The controversy was unavoidable since Aristotle had devoted most
of Book 8 of his *Politics* to precisely the question of whether, what kind, and how

5 Rabil, *Knowledge, Goodness and Power*.
6 See Kallendorf, *Humanist Educational Treatises* for texts and translations of the most famous educational
treatises. Fenlon, "Music in Italian Renaissance Paintings," 197–98, finds evidence of music teaching in
Vittorino's school by 1424.
7 *Institutes*, 1.10.11, 20, trans. in Butler, *The Institutio Oratoria of Quintilian*.
8 Lorenzetti, *Musica e identità nobiliare*.

music should be taught in the best commonwealth. The *Politics* was a canonical text. It had been translated around 1260 by William of Moerbeke and was well known in Italy thereafter. The most influential political writer of the later Middle Ages, Egidio Colonna, raised the question of the musical education of the prince in his *De regimine principum* only to summarize Aristotle's views and send his readers to the *Politics* for further study.[9] The latter was translated anew around 1436/38 by Leonardo Bruni in what proved to be an immensely popular Latin version,[10] and Donato Acciaiuoli wrote a full commentary on Bruni's version which remained the most important humanist commentary well into the sixteenth century.[11] Hence the *Politics* remained a point of departure for humanist discussions of music throughout the fifteenth century and into the sixteenth century, as can be seen from works like Paolo Cortesi's *De cardinalatu* (1506) and Castiglione's popular *Book of the Courtier* (begun 1508, published 1528).[12]

Aristotle's analysis set the agenda for humanist debates about the role of music in elite education. All humanists agreed that music could and should be taught, but the agreement ended there; many questions remained open. Should students learn medieval musical theory in the Boethian tradition, as Pier Paolo Vergerio seemed to suggest in his famous educational tract?[13] Or did the study of such "barbarous" medieval writings threaten to spoil one's Latin style? Was musical taste learned by training the ear, did it require *aures eruditae*, or could music be appreciated by everyone?[14] Should students merely learn "music appreciation," as the Spartans were said to have done, or should they also learn to sing and play themselves, like the Athenians and other Greeks? Was musical performance a liberal or a mechanical art? Aristotle advised that gentlemen should perform music only when young, and only as amateurs; music was useful mainly to distract the young, like rattles given to babies to prevent their breaking the furniture.[15] To acquire professional competence and play in public was not, in his considered opinion, appropriate to members of the elite.[16] Aristotle also held that stringed instruments were nobler than wind instruments, a hierarchy that long survived in Western musical culture.[17]

---

9 *De regimine principum*, 2.8 (Rome, 1607, p. 307).
10 Hankins, "The Dates of Leonardo Bruni's Later Works."    11 Acciaiuoli, *Commentaria*.
12 See Sachs, "Zur Funktion der Berufungen," and Wegman, *The Crisis of Music*, 66–76.
13 Vergerio in Kallendorf, *Humanist Educational Treatises*, 43. Vittorino da Feltre is reported to have lectured on Boethius's musical theory; see Palisca, *Humanism in Italian Renaissance Musical Thought*, 7.
14 Wegman, "Johannes Tinctoris and the 'New Art'" and "Johannes Tinctoris and the Art of Listening."
15 *Politics*, 8.6, 1340$^{b}$27.
16 Ibid., 8.7, 1341$^{b}$9. The passage is paraphrased by Aeneas Silvius Piccolomini in his treatise on education; see Kallendorf, *Humanist Educational Treatises*, chs. 91–92, pp. 247–51; and Strohm, "Enea Silvio Piccolomini and Music."
17 Aristotle's views were amplified in Acciaiuoli's commentary (Acciaiuoli, *Commentaria*, ad loc.), who explained that the Stagirite's strictures on the flute and cithara were not really meant to condemn those

And how did one's age, sex, and social status affect whether, how, when, and what kind of music should be played? Should kings and princes play instruments, or was that inappropriate to their role? Should women play instruments, and if so, should they play in public or only in private? And what kind of music was appropriate for noblemen to play? Aristotle distinguished between "lascivious" and moral music, as well as between music that was good for character and music that was good for the mind, but what, concretely, did those distinctions refer to? What about musical settings of love poetry, for example – were they necessarily lascivious, as the more severe ancient authorities held? Aristotle also distinguished "vulgar" from noble music, implying a class distinction within music, and he identified some musical modes and rhythms as more adaptable to the noble ends of music than others.[18] But, given the humanists' almost complete ignorance of how ancient music sounded, how could his advice be applied to modern musical practice?

Humanist writers offered a wide range of answers to these questions. It was not always easy, however, to map Aristotle's standards of decorum onto Renaissance Italian society. Fortunately, Aristotle was not the humanists' only authority, and in the course of the fifteenth century a body of *exempla* was elaborated from numerous classical sources, Greek and Latin, that allowed them to argue both sides of the question as necessary.[19] For instance, on the question whether princes should play, sing, or display expertise in music, one could cite, in the negative, the examples of Augustus, Nero, Sardanapalus, or Philip of Macedon; but telling in favor of princely musicianship were the cases of Achilles, Themistocles (who had suffered social shame for his ignorance of music), Epaminondas, and, crucially, King David of Israel, the greatest musician of the Bible. Aristotle had restricted the study of music to the young, but Plato's *Phaedo* (60d) showed the aged Socrates, at the very end of his life, setting tales of Aesop to music.[20] Moreover, as the humanists became increasingly familiar with ancient Greek literature, they gained access to a world where music performance was prized as a noble accomplishment. The Romans, broadly speaking, regarded the practice of music as ungentlemanly, the task of professional entertainers, but Greek culture offered many examples of philosophers, statesmen, and even military leaders who were accomplished

---

instruments *tout court* but rather the kind of music associated with them in antiquity. The fullest discussion of the cultural origins of various instruments is in Tinctoris, *Libri quinque de inventione et usu musice*, in *Johannes Tinctoris: Complete Theoretical Works*, ed. Woodley, Dean, and Lewis.

18 The distinction was elaborated in Acciaiuoli's commentary, which distinguished the music of the freeborn (*ingenui*) and the ignorant (*imperiti*), who enjoy bagpipe music.

19 Castiglione, *The Book of the Courtier*, 55–56 provides, in effect, a compendium of humanist praises of music; see Haar, "The Courtier as Musician." The most exhaustive version of the *laus musicae* theme may be found in Brandolini, *On Music and Poetry*.

20 In the version of Valerius Maximus, 8.7.ext8, Socrates learns to play a stringed instrument in old age.

musicians.[21] As Quintilian reported, "the armies of Sparta were fired to martial ardor by the strains of music" and Lycurgus himself in his stern laws "approved of the training supplied by music" (1.10.14–15). Such exempla did much to discredit the view – still defended for example by Gasparo Pallavicino in the *Courtier* – that to play and sing music was effeminate and unworthy of the knightly classes.

As time went on, more and more modern examples of princely musicians could be cited alongside the ancient ones. Early in the century Leonardo Giustinian, in a famous funeral oration (1418), praised the Venetian admiral Carlo Zeno for surpassing his ancient counterpart Themistocles; unlike the *indoctus* Themistocles, Zeno had learned music and how to play the lyre.[22] It was known that Pius II, Ferdinand II of Naples, his daughter Beatrice d'Aragona, Queen of Hungary, Lorenzo de' Medici, his son Giovanni de' Medici (Leo X), Ercole d'Este, and Ascanio Sforza were capable musicians, even if they usually performed discreetly in private.[23] Still, Michael Marullus in his *Education of a Prince* (dedicated to Charles VIII of France) could write in 1495 that princes might listen to noble music but that they should not take up corrupting instruments like the lute, the cithara, or the flute, even at home with no one else present.[24] On the other hand, a number of humanists, following various ancient examples, themselves sang or played instruments: Giovanni Conversino of Ravenna,[25] Leonardo Giustinian,[26] Vittorino da Feltre,[27] Leon Battista Alberti,[28] Isotta Nogarola,[29] Benedetto Accolti,[30] Ludovico Carbone,[31] Angelo Poliziano,[32] Aurelio and Raffaele Brandolini, and Marsilio Ficino among others. Ficino, it was reported, taught how to perform music on the lyre, as did Guarino of Verona.[33]

---

21 Francesco Patrizi of Siena, *De institutione reipublicae*, 2.2, fol. XXIv: "The Greeks valued music much more than the Romans: even civic leaders were not only experienced at singing, but were even useful dancers." This assertion is in part based on Cicero, *Tusculan Disputations* 1.4.

22 McManamon, *Funeral Oratory*, 89.

23 Ferdinand II (Brandolini, *On Music and Poetry*, 18–21), Beatrice d'Aragona (MacCarthy, "Tinctoris and the Neapolitan *Eruditi*," 52), Ascanio Sforza (de Faxolis, *Book on Music*, xi), Pius II (Brandolini, *On Music and Poetry*, 16), Lorenzo de' Medici (Brandolini, *On Music and Poetry*, 16), Ercole d'Este (Lockwood, *Music in Renaissance Ferrara*, 125), Leo X (Brandolini, *On Music and Poetry*, 6).

24 Marullus, *Poems*, 395.

25 Mercer, *The Teaching of Gasparino Barzizza*, 22: "Giovanni Conversino composed *volgare* verses, put them to music himself, and then sang."

26 Wilson, "'Tranferring Tunes and Adjusting Lines'." Giustinian had been a student of Guarino of Verona. A type of vernacular song, the *giustiniana*, was named after him.

27 Sabbadini, "L'ortografia latina di Vittorino da Feltre," 214.

28 Alberti, according to Landino (*Poems*, 247) (*Xandra* 27.9–10) could "intone facile elegies on the Latin *cithara* and sport learnedly on the Tuscan lyre."

29 Bembo, *Lyric Poetry*, 145: "of glorious beauty, learnèd with the lyre, and skillful at singing."

30 In Cortesi, *De cardinalatu* (1510), quoted by Brancacci, "Musica, retorica e critica musicale," 425.

31 Gallo, *Music in the Castle*, 69 ff. Carbone claimed that he learned how to sing poetry to the lyre from Guarino.

32 Gallo, *Music in the Castle*, 81.   33 Ibid., 71–72.

Most humanists encouraged women to sing and play instruments, but indoors and not in public.[34] By the early sixteenth century, indeed, musical skill was almost required for noble women. In his dialogue *Notable Men and Women of Our Time* (1527/30), Paolo Giovio writes:

> Nothing in a noble girl can be more wholesome and pleasing than musical exercises. They drive out the pensive moods such as often occur in torpid leisure; they get rid of all objects of boredom and alleviate anxieties, and edify a mind calmed by the charm of rhythmic harmonies so as to attain moderation, temperance, and gentleness. Hence the Athenians supposed that out of the liberal disciplines, music alone was especially worthy of a freeborn woman – so much so that they supposed women who were unskilled or uninterested in it lacked nobility.[35]

Aside from women, it was generally agreed that neither Latin nor vernacular poets could be ignorant of music, as their métier required a sensitivity to sound, pitch, and rhythm.[36] Francesco Filelfo, court poet to the Sforza, claimed proudly that his odes were inspired by musical harmonies.[37] Ficino, the greatest quattrocento champion of Plato, believed that the divine poetic frenzy of which Plato had written was inspired by song, and that great poetry was best interpreted and performed by inspired musicians like the rhapsodes who performed the Homeric epics in ancient times to the sound of the lyre.[38] Orators, too, according to Cicero and Quintilian, needed musical training. It was not just useful as part of the general education of the ideal orator, his *enkyklios paideia*; it was an indispensable part of his calling, insofar as oratory was a branch of literature: numerous ancient authorities attested that the teaching of literature and music could not be separated. Music trained the ear in rhythm and melody, which helped the orator identify euphonious combinations of sound; and it trained his voice, showing him how to deploy various tones, tempos, and volumes so as to stir the emotions of his audience.[39] This was a view endorsed by numerous humanist authorities on rhetoric.

---

34 *Epigrams*, 4.4 (to Alessandra Scala), in Marullus, *Poems*, 149–51; in Alberti's play *Philodoxus*, written during the 1420s, prurient interest is aroused by the heroine singing, indoors, verses to the lyre in praise of Hercules and the gods; see Grund, *Humanist Comedies*, 107.

35 Giovio, *Notable Men and Women of Our Time*, 453.

36 Bruni, *On Literary Study*, in Kallendorf, *Humanist Educational Treatises*, 22–24; Gregorio Tifernate, cited in Gallo, *Music in the Castle*, 103; Brandolini, *On Music and Poetry*, 36.

37 Filelfo, letter 1280. I consulted this text in an unpublished transcription of Filelfo's letters based on MS 863 of the Biblioteca Trivulziana (Milan) by Jeroen De Keyser, whom I thank.

38 Ficino, *Commentaries on Plato*, 1: *Phaedrus and Ion*, xxxv–xxxvii, 195–207.

39 Quintilian, *Institutio Oratoria*, 1.10; Gaffurio, *The Theory of Music*, 24; Brandolini, *On Music and Poetry*, 36: music "perfects (*perficit*) the orator, since it furnishes him the rhythms of body and voice." On the application of rhetorical principles to the performance of music, see Bent, "Grammar and Rhetoric."

## The ends of music

Humanist educators thus helped turn music into a respected art appropriate for social elites and influenced how they practiced it. The elevation of music to the status of a noble art also helped revive the ancient debate about the broader purposes or ends of musical performance in society. Aristotle's *Politics*, again, was a point of departure. The Stagirite began from the traditional Greek view that there were three kinds of life: the pleasure-seeking life of ordinary men and women, the active (or civil) life of the statesman and soldier, and the contemplative life of the philosopher. Each of these produced a justification for the study of music: music in itself gave pleasure; music written in the proper modes and measures supported the states of soul needed for active virtue; other, more intellectual forms of music aided contemplation.

Aristotle's analysis was elaborated and debated by a number of humanist writers on music. Despite the hierarchy of ends implied by the *Politics*, most humanists accepted that pleasure and relaxation were reasonable goals for music; for the young it was an innocent diversion that kept them from wasting their restless minds on more vicious pursuits like gaming. A number of humanists such as Franchino Gaffurio, Donato Acciaiuoli, and Francesco Patrizi of Siena accepted Aristotle's view that good music – music that employed the right modes and rhythms and instrumentation – could help young men form habits of virtue by arousing the right affections in the soul.[40] Good music projected powerful "representations" (*homoiomata* in Greek, *similitudines* in Bruni's translation) of the virtues into the soul, and in this respect music was superior to the visual arts (*Politics* 1340[a]5–6). Music could help the young experience vicariously and therefore recognize what noble feelings were like; it would thus help guide them in hitting the mean of good actions.[41] That was the main reason why music was useful to troops going into battle: it infused martial valor into their hearts by means of vigorous, joyful, confident tunes and rhythms. These provided a kind of aural simulacrum of the emotional state of a courageous man.

Followers of Plato such as Ficino went further still. Since the very order of nature was created according to number and harmony,[42] good human music, the image of that divine music, had the power to heal both body and soul of the diseases inflicted on them by vices and a perverted will. While Aristotle had denied that music had any influence on health,[43] Ficino in his work on magic,

---

40 Gaffurio, *The Theory of Music*; Acciaiuoli, *Commentaria*; Patrizi, *De institutione reipublicae*, 2.2. That music should be *morata*, of good moral character, was an idea well known to medieval music theorists via Boethius.

41 See Acciaiuoli, *Commentaria*; Cortesi, *De cardinalatu*.

42 A Platonic doctrine most frequently cited from Boethius, *Cons.* 3, metrum 9.

43 *Politics*, 1.2, 1338[a]20.

the *De vita*, developed an elaborate theory based on Platonic sources about the role of music in maintaining bodily health and psychic harmony.[44] Once purged of disturbances, the soul would then be aroused from its slumber in the material world, able to hear the subtle harmonies of heaven and be pierced by desire for the final end of man, assimilation to God. This was because we human beings alone among the animals have a sense of rhythm and harmony, thanks to which we can order the unquiet motions of our nature; i.e., the passions. Music could help in this ordering insofar as it was itself an ordering of motion. The kind of music that had this power did not come from fortune or human art or practice but by divine inspiration from God:

> The duty [*officium*] of the musician is to imitate grace in sound, and elegance of speech in singing; he should also remember that motions of rational soul [*animus*] ought to be much more consonant than voices. For a musician whose contemplative soul [*mens*] is dissonant when the voice and lyre are sounding together is disorderly [*inconcinnus*] and a stranger to the Muses. David and Hermes Trismegistus bid us sing of God, given that our ability to sing is owed to the God who creates motion.[45]

Contemplation and the voice are intimately linked with music, and nowhere more so than in singing poetry to the lyre (a genre Ficino refers to as "Orphic music"). The musical interpretation of poetry, like poetry itself, is a divine gift, as is shown by the fact that even stupid, uneducated people can sing poetry in an inspired way. God "does this to prevent men from supposing that poetry is achieved by human subtlety and application – something that would happen were He to employ clever and prudent men for it."[46] The divine source of good music explained why the best religious music was successful in raising the human soul to heaven and conforming our hearts and minds to God. It also, for Ficino, meant that the best singer was a man with a purified soul: moral goodness enabled artistic goodness.

Both Plato in his *Republic* and *Laws* and Aristotle in the *Politics* had also stressed the importance of music to the stability and happiness of states. A number of humanists took up their arguments with enthusiasm. Gaffurio, for instance, wrote that good music had a role in preventing political as well as moral corruption; citing Plato, he stated that to change the laws of music was

---

44  Ficino, *Three Books on Life, passim*; see also Walker, *Spiritual and Demonic Magic*, ch. 1, and *Music, Spirit and Language*; Gaffurio, *The Theory of Music*, 15; Brandolini, *On Music and Poetry*, 38.

45  Ficino, *Opera omnia*, 1:744.

46  Ficino, *Commentaries on Plato*. The most influential text, because translated into Italian and Spanish, was the letter *De divino furore* in his *Lettere*, 25; an English translation may be found in *The Letters of Marsilio Ficino*, 1:18. Ficino's discussion of Plato's musical legislation in *Laws II* is found in Ficino, *Opera omnia*, 2:1492–94; see also Walker, *Spiritual and Demonic Magic*, ch. 1, and Allen, *The Platonism of Marsilio Ficino*, 55–57.

to change the laws of the state.[47] It was no accident that in ancient Greece, laws and decrees were recited to music, just as princes and senates in modern times were wont to publish laws and decrees to the sound of trumpets and horns. "Therefore, among the ancients, music was a discipline for use either in divine cult or in the teaching of youth or in maintaining the commonwealth and the state and without any apparatus of the theater, which did not yet exist."[48] Carlo Valgulio too, in his *Contra vituperatorem musicae*, spoke of the moral dangers of bad music, how it could render soft and indolent the souls of citizens, especially young ones. Or it could make good citizens, since good music creates a psychic motion that expels evil disturbances from the soul.[49] The political theorist Francesco Patrizi of Siena marched out a phalanx of ancient authorities who testified to the importance of music to the state: Socrates believed harmonious music was necessary for civic life; Lycurgus thought it was necessary to help men endure labor; the poet Tyrtaeus helped the Spartans defeat the Messenians in a battle by changing the rhythmic interval (*moduli*) of his trumpet, thus increasing their courage; Pythagoras brought *pudor* to seditious youths in Croton by having the flute-player change his rhythms; the Pythagoreans also made men more religious by playing certain songs while they were asleep and dreaming. Even the dour Romans had political uses for music: the demagogue Gaius Gracchus charmed the populace during his speeches by having a slave playing the syrinx in the background, using certain mollifying and lascivious rhythms; the Roman armies were made more terrifying by the *tubarum clangor* which accompanied them on the march.[50] Similarly, the humanist Roberto Valturio in his *De re militari* (written 1446/55, first published 1472), aimed to demonstrate to Sigismondo Malatesta, lord of Rimini and *condottiere*, that a prince with military ambitions could not be ignorant of a science that put the emotions of men under his control.[51]

All this went to show that knowledge of music was useful for a *vir civilis*: to foster *ingenium*, to make men readier and more eager, not only to fight, but also to undertake the highest civil business.[52] Good music was a civilizing influence, spreading harmony, checking barbarism, and promoting what would today be called the "soft power" of a sovereign by bringing glory to his court.[53] Fortunately, no Renaissance humanist went as far as Plato did in the *Laws*

47 Gaffurio, *The Theory of Music*, 23–24. This is a pun on the Greek word *nomoi*, which means "laws" but also refers to a fixed, traditional melody used by the ancient Greeks in festival performances. Another discussion of music's role in founding states and civilizing the human race is found in Brandolini, *On Music and Poetry*, 42.
48 Gaffurio, *The Theory of Music*, 24.      49 Valgulio, *Contra vituperatorem musicae*, 100.
50 Patrizi, *De institutione reipublicae*, fols. XXIr–XXIIv.
51 Valturio, *De re militari*, 2.4. See also Gaffurio, *The Theory of Music*, 16, on the military uses of music.
52 Patrizi, *De institutione reipublicae*, fol. XXIIv.
53 Gallo, *Music in the Castle*, 112, citing Francesco Bandini's praise of the court of Naples; see also Brandolini, *On Music and Poetry*, 16.

(653c–671a), calling for musical melodies and rhythms to be strictly regulated by the state in the interests of public morality.[54] Such regulations were generally left to the Church, which was usually ineffective at enforcing them.

## Musical scholarship

In addition to debating the true ends of music in their works on education, the humanists also introduced new kinds of writing about music: musical scholarship in the antiquarian tradition – including the historical reconstruction of ancient music – and music criticism.[55] The new genres grew naturally from the rich loam laid down by the Renaissance narrative: that Greco-Roman antiquity was exemplary; that the present was corrupted by barbarism; and that renewal depended on the recovery of what had been lost. The most straightforward response to these premises was basic musical scholarship: the discovery, editing, and translation of new ancient texts. Manuscript-hunting had been a key part of the humanists' activity since the time of Petrarch, and ancient musical texts were eventually included within its scope. The fifteenth century saw a dramatic increase in Western Christendom's knowledge of the theory and performance of ancient music.

In the medieval period, knowledge of Greek music theory (the Romans had no theoretical writings of their own) was derived from a small number of late ancient authors writing in Latin: chiefly Boethius, Martianus Capella, Macrobius, and Calcidius. Thanks to their knowledge of Greek, the humanists vastly enlarged this patrimony.[56] Humanist interest in new sources for Greek musical theory goes back to at least the 1430s, when an important codex containing Porphyry's commentary on Ptolemy's *Harmonics*, Aristides Quintilianus's *De musica*, and Bacchius Senior's *Introduction to the Art of Music* became known to humanists in the circles of Francesco Barbaro in Venice and Niccolò Niccoli in Florence. Most of the remaining unknown Greek texts on music theory were brought to Venice when Cardinal Bessarion donated his famous manuscript library to the city in 1468. Pietro d'Abano's late medieval translation of pseudo-Aristotle's *Problemata*, of which books 11 and 19 provide important treatments of musical theory and practice, were first printed in 1475 in Mantua. By that time, two rival translations, by George of Trebizond and Theodore Gaza, had been produced for Pope Nicholas V in the early 1450s. In 1484 Marsilio Ficino, himself an

---

54 Although such calls for musical censorship were not unknown from clerical quarters: see Wegman, *The Crisis of Music*. In his *argumentum* to Plato's *Laws* II (Ficino, *Opera omnia*, 2:1492–94), Ficino summarizes, without endorsing, Plato's *instituta* restricting the *licentia* of poets, musicians, and painters.
55 Moyer, *Musica Scientia*.
56 The fundamental study is Palisca, *Humanism in Italian Renaissance Musical Thought*, from which much of the material in this paragraph is taken.

accomplished musician, published his translations of the works of Plato (begun in 1469), which included the first complete translation of the *Timaeus* with Ficino's extensive commentary; this commentary, further enlarged in 1496, contained an influential treatment of Platonic musical theory. The *Laws* (653c–671a) provided a model for humanist musical criticism.

The first wave of humanist textual scholarship on Greek music theory reached its zenith at the end of the fifteenth century in the work of Giorgio Valla, whose *De expetendis et fugiendis rebus opus* (published 1501) "set out singlehandedly to resurrect Greek musical science."[57] Five (composed in 1491) of this work's forty-nine books provided a compendium of Greek musical theory based on translated extracts from original sources, principally pseudo-Plutarch's *De musica*, Ptolemy's *Harmonics*, Aristides Quintilianus, and Bryennius's *Harmonics*. Though the impact of the humanists' textual work on musical composition and performance lay mostly in the sixteenth century, the presence of the new sources begins to be felt already in the 1490s, in theoretical works by Gaffurio and Carlo Valgulio. Valgulio went so far as to call for the recently recovered Greek theory to replace the "corrupt" *musica theorica* inherited from the Middle Ages.[58] The move recalls contemporary efforts by Ermolao Barbaro and other humanists to use the ancient Greek commentators as a means of freeing Aristotle from his medieval interpreters. Barbaro himself, Angelo Poliziano, and later Paolo Cortesi were among those who tried to reform the "barbarous" language of medieval musical theory in accordance with humanist standards.[59]

In addition to reviving ancient Greek music theory, humanist scholars also directed their researches to finding out about the origins of music, how ancient music was performed, the various occasions on which it was performed, and what instruments were used.[60] The supreme example of this sort of research in the fifteenth century was written by the most important musical theorist of the fifteenth century, Johannes Tinctoris. His *De inventione et usu musice* (ca. 1481), originally in five books,[61] closely resembles other humanist syntheses of

57 Palisca, *Humanism in Italian Renaissance Musical Thought*, 67.

58 Possible predecessors of Valgulio in this regard are Bartolomé Ramos de Pareja and Johannes Gallicus, discussed in Strohm, "Music, Humanism," 360 and n. 50. For Gaffurio's applications of humanist musical scholarship to his theoretical work, see Gaffurio, *The Theory of Music*, and Kreyszig, "Franchino Gaffurio als Vermittler der Musiklehre."

59 Brancacci, "Musica, retorica e critica musicale"; Holford-Strevens, "Humanism and the Language of Music Treatises" and "Musical Humanism."

60 Humanist research on ancient instruments was also collected by Paolo Cortesi's colleague in the papal court, Raffaele Maffei; see his *Commentariorum urbanorum libri XXXVIII* (Basel, 1544) [first published 1506], cols. 814–15.

61 The full text has unfortunately been lost, but an ample selection of excerpts was printed in Naples, ca. 1481–83. See Strohm and Cullington, *Egidius Carlerius, Johannes Tinctoris: On the Dignity and the Effects of Music*.

historical research such as Valturio's *De re militari* or Francesco Patrizi's twin treatises on politics, the *De regno* and the *De institutione reipublicae*. A particularly close parallel is provided by Leon Battista Alberti's *De re aedificatoria* (1452; first published 1485), which collects and arranges by subject matter all available ancient sources on architecture, with a view to bringing the ancient art of building back to life. In similar fashion, Tinctoris's treatise discusses the Greek and Hebrew origins of music; musical practices in ancient times in Israel and among the Greeks and Romans; famous singers of antiquity and of modern times; the various types of instruments used in antiquity; what sort of repertory was considered appropriate for each; and their relationship to modern instruments. He shows particular interest in the "chapel" of King David, noting that, according to a passage in Ecclesiasticus 47:11, "he placed his singers before the altar, that by their voices they might produce sweet melody and daily sing praises in song."[62] Like Alberti his purpose was not to recommend slavish imitation of the ancients, which was hardly possible under contemporary conditions, but to reforge the links with the past that had been broken and to find justification and inspiration in antiquity for modern musical practices.

The Renaissance narrative of loss and rebirth led not only to the recovery of ancient musical theory and practice; it also began to shape perceptions of music's own history. By the time of Tinctoris, writers on music had begun to appropriate the Renaissance narrative in order to establish periods in the history of their own art.[63] That story too lies mostly in the sixteenth century, but Tinctoris's discussions of an *ars nova* of music that had emerged in his own time deserve some comment.[64] In the dedication of the *Proportionale musices* (1473–74) addressed to his patron King Ferdinand II of Naples, Tinctoris distinguished three periods: (1) a pre-Christian period, populated by musicians both pagan and Jewish who performed and composed brilliantly (*elegantissime*), but whose music had sadly all been lost; (2) a period of church music extending from the Church Fathers to at least Guido of Arezzo, which also was distinguished by "admirable musicians"; and (3) a recent period of chapel music, modeled on King David's chapel (*more Davidico*) and sponsored by Christian princes, in which church music had ascended to hitherto unknown heights,

---

62  See also Gaffurio, *The Theory of Music*, 19. The same passage was cited a half century later by Martin Luther, to defend the practice of polyphony in the Hofkapelle of Saxony; see Wegman, *The Crisis of Music*, 43.

63  Owens, "Music Historiography"; Strohm, "Music, Humanism"; Ficino's account of the revival of Orphic lute playing ibid., 355, 394–95; see also Gallo, *Music in the Castle*, 91–92, 101.

64  Woodley, "Renaissance Music Theory"; Strohm, "Music, Humanism"; Blackburn, "Music Theory"; Wegman, "Johannes Tinctoris and the 'New Art'"; MacCarthy, "Tinctoris and the Neapolitan *Eruditi*"; the Latin text can be found online at earlymusictheory.org/Tinctoris/texts/deinventioneetusumusice/.

enough to win the title of an *ars nova*.[65] The *ars nova* was divided into two generations, that of John Dunstaple, Guillaume Du Fay, and Gilles Binchois, who were followed by Johannes Ockeghem, Antoine Busnoys, Johannes Regis, and Firmin Caron; the second generation was said to be superior to the first in its powers of invention (a criterion of excellence taken from rhetoric). The passage chimes with the Renaissance narrative in a couple of ways: first, because the modern art is superior to that of the early Christian period (which is not, however, given the derogatory label "medieval"); and second, in that Ferdinand and other princes of his time are said to have revived the ancient chapel of King David. The (perhaps self-serving) implication is that princely generosity has raised musical excellence to a level that the support of the Church alone in earlier times had not achieved.

In the prologue to his *Liber de arte contrapuncti* (1477), Tinctoris strengthens his earlier suggestion that medieval Christian music was inferior to that of his own day by describing how he had examined "a few ancient songs" (*nonnulla vetusta carmina*) of unknown authorship and found them incompetent and tasteless. In fact, he adds, there is nothing worth hearing except what has been composed in the last forty years. In this period there has arisen "an endless number of composers" divided, again, into two generations, the latter more excellent and "divine" than the former. They are so excellent that (in the absence of surviving ancient music) they can stand as models for the composers of today. Here again the Renaissance master-narrative hovers behind Tinctoris's account of music history. In this passage, however, the credit for the renewed flourishing of the musical art is not given to princely patronage; instead, it is said to have come about either "through some heavenly influence or through assiduous practice," explanations that gesture towards those in the preface to Alberti's *De pictura* (1436) and other contemporary accounts of the Renaissance.[66]

Tinctoris's generational analysis of musical progress, later repeated and updated by a number of sixteenth-century writers on music,[67] runs parallel to accounts of the progress of literature found in contemporary humanist writers like Paolo Cortesi. Cortesi described a gradual improvement in Latin eloquence and prose style over the generations from Petrarch's to his own. A

---

65  The pre- and post-Christian periodization is repeated in *De inventione et usu musicae*, where Tinctoris's reconstruction of King David's musical practices is further developed. On Tinctoris, see also Evan MacCarthy's essay in this volume, Ch. 32.

66  Ferguson, *The Renaissance in Historical Thought*; Panofsky, *Renaissance and Renascences*. Tinctoris's phrase encapsulates two contemporary types of explanation for renewed cultural efflorescence: one that the age is favored by the stars; the other that remarkable men through their own powers and efforts have revived the sound culture of antiquity.

67  Owens, "Music Historiography."

similar analysis would later be adapted by Lilio Giraldi in his *Modern Poets* to describe the progress of modern Neo-Latin poetry, and by Giorgio Vasari to describe the revival of art from Giotto to Michelangelo.[68] This historical model, however, owes less to the Renaissance's tripartite periodization of history than to Cicero's accounts of the progress of oratory in his *Brutus* and *De oratore*. The Ciceronian model of cultural progress, however, unlike the later Enlightenment model, had an achievable end-point, namely the perfection of the art; the goal of artistic progress is ever closer approximation to an ideal. After that, there can only be corruption and decline.

## Musical criticism

The idea that the history of music could be represented as a narrative of progress from generation to generation is only one example of the ways in which rhetorical literature was to influence how humanists understood and analyzed music. Rhetorical concepts were also, eventually, employed in the humanists' various forays into music criticism, just as Alberti had earlier employed them for the analysis of painting.[69] However, among humanists, the elaboration of such standards was to emerge only toward the end of the quattrocento. The earliest humanist criticism arose in the mid-fifteenth century from efforts to establish moral criteria for distinguishing good and bad music. The discourse was overwhelmingly Aristotelian. In Valturio's *De re militari*, for example, we find a distinction introduced between the type of ancient music that could not be safely imitated and that which had the positive moral effects of which Aristotle had spoken.[70] For the soldier-prince, music was a powerful weapon that could change the hearts of men by arousing or sedating passions, so it needed to be deployed with care; in its corrupt forms, it might induce effeminacy, *laetitia inanis*, and *amatoria voluptas*; morally sound music, however, could sustain the virtues. Valturio turned to the ancient Church Fathers for guidance and found them divided. But after a careful sifting of passages in Jerome, Gregory, Athanasius, and Augustine he concluded that there was a licit form of music that could be used by the *condottiere* prince. One should avoid "effeminate music [such as was found] in theaters and on the stage," one should stay away from "shameless, rather mannered melodies, brutish and heterogeneous." Instead, one should prefer the type of ancient music that was "simple, moral, prudent, masculine and modest, [the type] in

68 Cortesi, *De hominibus doctis dialogus*; Baker, *Italian Renaissance Humanism*; Wegman, "Johannes Tinctoris and the 'New Art'," 174–76.
69 Baxandall, *Giotto and the Orators*, 121–39.
70 Valturio, *De re militari*, [unfoliated], bk. 2, ch. 4.

which the praises of brave men were sung, and which they themselves sang; and anyone who was ignorant of this type of music [like Themistocles] was held to be uneducated."

The simple, moral, and manly music of antiquity imagined by Valturio continued to be invoked as a standard of taste by humanist critics aiming to revive the storied power of ancient song. The same moral criteria, linked with the same classic[71] aesthetic values, can be found in other humanist writers on music such as Donato Acciaiuoli, Marsilio Ficino, Francesco Patrizi of Siena, Franchino Gaffurio, Marcus Marullus, and Paolo Cortesi. As late as the 1490s, Carlo Valgulio was still using classic standards to evaluate music, but now interpreted the older Aristotelian moralism through the lens of a Platonic psychology and ontology derived from his friend and master Ficino.[72] Valgulio gives us both a more precise idea of humanist aesthetic values and a theoretical framework for justifying them. In the preface to his translation of ps.-Plutarch's *De musica* (published in 1507) he attacks music that is too complex and overly variegated; music that is too soft and enticing, or, alternatively, too "brawling" (*clamistrata*) and exuberant; music that uses too many instruments and has too dense a texture. Such music makes citizens soft, lazy, and shameless; it corrupts morals; its practitioners are ignorant, vainglorious men. Good music by contrast is "strong, severe, decorous, and simple." As sung by ancient men it was learned, elegant, and constrained by regular meters; its rhythms, accents, and melodies were fitted to the human voice and able to express the subject matter and promote good morals. Up until the time of Cleopatra the subject matter of singers was primarily historical and mythical, and therefore required learning a great deal about antiquity (*priscae res*); Valgulio gives as an example the song describing the battle of Apollo and the Dragon Python performed at the Pythian Games in Delphi. After Cleopatra, decline set in and music was corrupted by ignorance and sensuality. That was why the Church Fathers had condemned the ancient music of their day and had sought to replace it with Christian music.

Just why classic music had good moral effects (and non-classic bad) Valgulio explains using Platonic and Pythagorean psychology. The human soul was like

---

71 I use the adjective "classic" here to indicate aesthetic values said to be those characteristic of morally sound music in antiquity: simplicity, restraint, educated taste (*doctrina*), elegance, decorum. "Corrupt" ancient music such as that condemned as effeminate or lascivious both by pagan philosophers and Church Fathers would not count as "classic" in this sense. The distinction was common in the quattrocento; see, for example, Guarino of Verona, *Epistolario*, 1:8, who specifies that his praise of ancient music excludes the intemperate sort.

72 Valgulio, *In Plutarchi Musicam, ad Titum Pyrrhinum* [preface to his translation of ps.-Plutarch, *De musica*] in *Plutarchi ... Opuscula (quae quidem extant) omnia* (Basel, 1530), fols. 244v–247v. Other humanist writers who invoke the Platonic theory of divine *furor* include Gaffurio (cited in Moyer, *Musica Scientia*, 90 = *De harmonia*, 4.17) and Brandolini, *On Music and Poetry*, 40–42.

a tetrachord, consisting of four faculties that needed to work in harmony, the higher directing the lower and the lower modeled on the higher. The four faculties were unmediated intuitive knowledge (*intellectus*), dialectical reasoning (*ratio*), image-making (*imaginatio*), and sense. The divine element in us, *intellectus*, is simple and pure and uniform. Imagination and sense are the mortal parts, interacting with the physical world, and therefore filled with mutation and variety. *Ratio* is in the middle, a faculty proper to mankind (analogous to soul in Ficino's philosophy[73]); it orients the soul either to things above, the *divina*, or to mortal things. If the *ratio* is oriented to higher things, it creates a soul that possesses "marvelous moral harmonies (*morum concentus*), namely, ones that are simple, grave, and beautiful"; if it consorts with the mortal world, the *ratio* becomes "heterogeneous, soft, and ugly" as a result. Classic music, in this fundamentally Plotinian analysis, supports the higher tendencies in reason and yields good morals by "driving out the evils brought into the soul by disturbances"; music attunes the soul to higher things by increasing its resemblance to their ordered simplicity. It supports the contemplative life.

In Valgulio's *Contra vituperatorem musicae*, printed in 1509, the Brescian humanist gives a somewhat different, though still Platonic, justification of classic aesthetic values.[74] In the soul, as in the universe, there are two kinds of motion. The higher motion, the circular motion of the starry sphere, is simple, direct, and unchanging: it is the motion of pure reason. The other motion is like that of the planets: variable, indirect, complex. It corresponds to the irrational motions of the passions in the soul. It is the motion that causes all conflicts and dissonances, all error and evil: "surges of mad desire, conflagrations of lust, terrible greed for money, pitiful striving for honors." To subordinate the lower to the higher motions, we need music, a gift of God, which has to be written in such a way as to reinforce the simple and eternal motions of reason:

> By its [music's] sweet entwinings [*suavissimis nexibus*] and sensuous spacings [*dulcissimis intervallis*] we shall be able to adjust the opposing and differently orientated motions of our minds like lyre strings and make them always concordant. The aim is that people who are inherently irrational should always obey reason and follow its lead gladly and willingly, rather than being dragged along protesting, and should never belittle its authority. Thus, with music's help and support, we shall always keep the motions of our minds in line with heavenly revolutions, maintain stability, and share the joy and bliss of heavenly beings.

---

73 Ficino's ontology has five substances, not four, but Valgulio has probably changed the metaphysics to fit his analogy of the tetrachord.

74 Valgulio, *Contra vituperatorem musicae*, 89. The argument is based on the Platonist Porphyry's commentary on Ptolemy's *Harmonics*.

In both works of Valgulio, as elsewhere in humanist writings on music, it is a key feature of classic music that it is linked with good morals and education. Since according to humanist doctrine morality and classical learning were tantamount to "true nobility," to prefer classic music was to claim elite status.[75] Classic music was superior to both popular and traditional clerical music as Latin was to the *volgare*. As Raffaele Brandolini put it in his *De musica* (1513), "The former is geared to the senatorial rank, the latter to the plebeian; the one is praised by those with powerful minds, the latter by bumpkins; the one by Romans, the other by barbarians; the one by the learned . . . the other by the unlearned."[76] Valgulio shared his low opinion of contemporary singers, who, he says, know only a few syllables of Latin (he means the solmization syllables) and are filled with envy and vulgarity; he would lament the music of modern times if the job had not already been well done by Gaffurio.[77]

Eventually these moral and metaphysical ways of conceptualizing musical values were supplemented by an analytical language that was to become ever more dominant in humanist circles in the sixteenth century, namely, that of classical rhetoric. Although there are hints of it in Tinctoris and Gaffurio, this type of analysis is most fully worked out in the *De cardinalatu* (1510) of Paolo Cortesi, the leader of the Roman academy of his day, and in the literary oration *De musica* of Raffaele Brandolini (1513), a former humanist singer. Rhetorical analysis of music made the expression of words and the affections they aroused the most important value; music should be subordinate to words.[78] Humanists here to some extent made common cause with the clerical critics of polyphony, who similarly complained about music that masked rather than enhanced texts as well as about music that was both luxurious and luxuriant rather than simple and restrained.[79] But the humanists did not long for a return to Christian antiquity and Gregorian chant; their taste in music rather reflects a wider shift of aesthetic values. The neoclassical culture of Renaissance Italy for almost a century had rejected florid, exuberant, complex, difficult, and mystifying tendencies in late medieval art in favor of what were believed to be the classical values of simplicity and restraint, power and weight, clarity and harmonious proportion. Humanists held that music's power to enhance the word, its expressivity, depended on matching musical rhythm with the natural rhythms of speech; effective text declamation was what brought about the *maxima*

75  Rabil, *Knowledge, Goodness and Power.*      76  Brandolini, *On Music and Poetry*, 97.
77  Valgulio, *In Plutarchi Musicam.*
78  Harrán, *Word–Tone Relations.* For an example of a theorist who took the opposite view, see the work of Le Munerat (Harrán, *In Defense of Music*).
79  Wegman, *The Crisis of Music.*

*permotio in audiendo.*[80] This meant that musicians and composers had to have knowledge of grammar and rhetoric so as to understand phonetics, pronunciation, prosody, scansion, and accentuation. In other words, they should ideally have a humanist education, though there were examples of untutored, natural talents. One such was Serafino Aquilano, the most famous singer of the age, of whom Cortesi wrote that his melodies were sweet because of the close connection of words and music.[81] Sweetness (*dulcedo* or *suavitas*) was only one of a variety of critical terms drawn from rhetoric: others were *subtilitas* (refinement), *concinnitas* (legible or audible order), *celeritas*, *varietas*: all virtues of style or *elocutio* according to the rhetorical manuals. The critical vocabulary elaborated by Brandolini to evaluate the performances of the humanist singer similarly reflected the traditional parts of rhetoric: invention, disposition, ornament, delivery, and memory.[82]

Cortesi's musical criticism in *De cardinalatu* is of crucial importance in that he attempts to bridge the gap between ancient, mostly Aristotelian, categories of analysis and modern practice. Earlier writers like Valturio had repeated what Aristotle had said about the effects of the various Greek modes on human passions, but they had not tried to relate them to modern performance traditions; and they did not know how to respond to Aristotle's critiques of certain instruments as tending to immorality. But Cortesi does precisely this. He discusses in detail the various forms (genera) of instrumental music and vocal music. He creates a hierarchy of instrumental genres suitable for cardinals: first organs, then viols (*lembi*) played with bows, and finally plucked lutes – a hierarchy that seems to be based on those instruments' relative resemblance to the sonorities of the human voice. The barbiton is ruled out and the flute ignored, presumably as associated with eroticism. Cortesi rates the organ-playing of Isaac, son of the philosopher John Argyropoulos, higher than that of Dominic of Venice or Daniel the German because the latter indulge "intemperately" in a style of playing marked by *effusa percursio*, presumably some kind of keyboard virtuosity, rather than distinguishing in a knowledgeable way among the *artificiosi modi*.

Then he turns to the traditional three modes of song mentioned by the ancients: the Phrygian, Lydian, and Dorian. The Phrygian mode he seems to identify with Franco-Flemish polyphony, a type of singing "by which the listeners' minds are wont to be estranged by the sharp contention among voices ... the mode which French musicians use canonically in the palatine

---

80 Cortesi, *De cardinalatu*, bk. 2, ch. 7, fols. LXXIIv–LXXIVr [irregular foliation]. On the importance of text declamation to the humanists, see Harrán, *Word–Tone Relations* and Abramov-van Rijk, *Parlar cantando*.
81 Cortesi, *De cardinalatu*.    82 Brandolini, *On Music and Poetry*, 84 ff.

chapel [i.e. the Sistine] on Christmas and Easter."[83] The Lydian mode is divided into two species: one is complex, the "lugubrious, tearful Spanish style" used for solemn papal liturgies and cardinals' funerals; the other is *simplex*, a kind of slow, controlled chanting "such as we saw inflect the verses of Virgil as they used to be sung by the poet Cariteo under the patronage of Ferdinand II [of Naples]." Finally, there is the Dorian *ratio*, "more temperate because of an equal mean,"[84] which some take to be "the fixed standard of singing instituted by Saint Gregory in his Litany," i.e. Gregorian chant.[85] We moderns, however, "distinguish this whole [Dorian] *ratio* of singing into masses, motets, and songs." Within the three species of Dorian, Josquin is the greatest composer of masses, Jacob Obrecht and Henricus Isaac of motets. Petrarch is said to be the founder of modern song, "who would sing to the lute the *carmina* he composed." Obrecht and Isaac are compared in terms drawn, again, from rhetoric: Obrecht is regarded as having great subtlety but his way of composing is rather repellant [*horridior*], and he pleases more those who prefer a dazzling and artificial interlacing [of voices] to sensory pleasure, like those who prefer vinegar to juice. Isaac is swifter in invention and has a more flowery style of ornament. Here rhetorical criticism seems to verge on an idea of taste.

But what Cortesi has done above all in this passage is to take Aristotle's scattered remarks on the emotional effects of the Greek modes and use them to typologize the music of his own time. There is also an implicit hierarchy, since for Aristotle the Dorian mode was the mode of reason and character, inherently ethical, temperate, and manly, and suitable to the philosophical life, while Phrygian melodies were more appropriate to stimulating action and Lydian songs were most closely associated with death, grief, and strong emotion; they served as medicines for one's cares. Cortesi's analysis does not map precisely on to Aristotle's, to be sure, but it does allow him to celebrate composers in the highest genus of music and to make distinctions between the best and the less accessible forms of polyphony.

Cortesi's discussion indeed reveals an ambivalent attitude to polyphony, and this is typical of humanists writing about music at the end of the

---

83  Cortesi, *De cardinalatu*. On the liturgical background see Dean, "Listening to Sacred Polyphony," 614, who also quotes passages from the papal *caeremonarii* that seem to share Cortesi's annoyance with polyphony.

84  I take "an equal mean" to refer to Aristotle's teaching in the *Ethics* where he distinguishes "equal means" from means that achieve balance by leaning more toward one extreme than another. This passage on the modes in particular, however, tracks *Politics* 8.340[b]4–5 and 8.1341[b]35 ff. See also Gaffurio's *De harmonia*, 3.8, where he compares three kinds of mean, arithmetic, geometric, and harmonic, to democratic, oligarchic, and aristocratic government (trans. Miller, 166).

85  For the meaning of Cortesi's language here see Holford-Strevens, "Humanism and the Language of Music Treatises," 435–37.

fifteenth century.[86] Earlier, there had been a tendency for humanists to dislike polyphony; some saw it as a foreign invention, medieval in origin, wedded to a tradition of theory and practice preserved in barbarous Latin.[87] A surprising number of humanists, even including Erasmus, aligned themselves in some measure with the traditionalists' assault on polyphony that intensified after 1470 and was only overcome in the early decades of the cinquecento.[88] The humanist insistence on the primacy of the word made them inclined to prefer monodic or simple homophonic musical forms. Yet there are other humanists like Ludovico Carbone, trained by Guarino, who show an appreciation for polyphony already in mid-century;[89] and by the end of the quattrocento some forms of polyphony seem to have been accepted as legitimate by important writers like Cortesi and Raffaele Brandolini.[90] The success of music theorists like Gaffurio, Florentius de Faxolis, and Tinctoris in adapting their theoretical works to humanist stylistic taste must also have helped break down prejudice.[91] Tinctoris's impressive musical scholarship probably played some role in winning acceptance for famous composers and singers as artists worthy of respect. Tinctoris also made the case that appreciation of polyphonic music required *aures eruditae*, a claim that must have had some snob-appeal for humanists. But it is likely that the decisive factor for most humanist *literati* was the highly competitive enthusiasm for polyphonic music shown by leading Renaissance princes. Dependent as they were on princely and ecclesiastical favor, it would have been difficult for humanists to mount a serious campaign against a form of music championed by patrons such as Borso d'Este, Ferdinand II of Naples, Lorenzo de' Medici, Galeazzo Maria and Ascanio Sforza, and Leo X. The form of music they themselves favored, improvised Latin verse sung to the lyre, also stood in need of princely patronage, to be sure; yet it was to prove far less successful.

86 Cortesi (as above) seems to distinguish between the polyphony of the Franco-Flemish singers in the papal chapel and the music of Josquin and Isaac, which he praises, while expressing doubts about Obrecht.
87 Pirrotta, "Music and Cultural Tendencies."
88 Wegman, in *The Crisis of Music*, documents further examples, not discussed by Pirrotta, of the humanists' distaste for polyphony.
89 Gallo, *Music in the Castle*, 99. Pirrotta's exaggerated view that humanists "despised" polyphony has rightly been criticized in passing in Strohm, *The Rise of European Music*, 542, and with more force in Bent, "Music and the Early Veneto Humanists." Bent shows that international art music written in the polyphonic style was fully integrated into the culture of Veneto humanists in the late trecento and early quattrocento. Here it seems useful to distinguish between music that humanists may have enjoyed and appropriated in the Veneto ca. 1400 and the "classic" music promoted by humanists as a more mature expression of their ideals in the second half of the fifteenth.
90 For Brandolini's appreciation of polyphony see Brandolini, *On Music and Poetry*, 18, where he praises Ferdinand II and Lorenzo for their support of chapel singers.
91 Florentius de Faxolis, *Book on Music*.

## The humanists' favorite musical genre: improvised monodic song to the lyre

In recent decades, some musicologists were puzzled by a phenomenon some-times referred to as "the secret of the quattrocento," namely, the strange lack of famous Italian composers and musicians in the fifteenth century. This seeming hiatus occurred between two other periods, the "long" trecento and the mid-cinquecento, when Italian musicians were recognized leaders in European musical life.[92] The mid-quattrocento was one of distinguished achievement for Italians in the visual arts, literature, and philosophy, so that the absence of important indigenous musicians amid the first flowering of the Renaissance was even more mysterious. Famous composers and performers lived and worked in Italy during the quattrocento, but they were foreigners trained abroad. Thanks above all to the work of Nino Pirrotta, however, scholars have come to understand that the musical energies of the Renaissance movement were simply invested elsewhere.[93] While northern musicians in England and the Low Countries were developing polyphony in brilliant ways, producing music that was preserved and valued for centuries, Italian musicians, modeling themselves on ancient sources, were reviving the extempore performance of Latin poetry to the lira da braccio. In a nice turn of historical irony, their attempts to revive the lost music of antiquity were themselves lost to posterity, owing to their ephemeral nature. Nevertheless, the humanist project to bring to life again the classical singer of tales has left many traces in historical and literary records.

As Blake Wilson shows elsewhere in this volume (Ch. 16), humanist art song was not created *ex nihilo*; it was built upon the solid tradition of the civic *canterino*. But just as the humanists ennobled the traditional study of grammar by turning it into the *studia humanitatis*, an elite form of education with a moral purpose, so too they tried to appropriate and transform the role of the *canterino* in Italian society. And despite their large debts to the *canterino* tradition, the humanists, as so often, claimed they were reviving an art which had been lost for centuries.[94] In fact their real goal was to reform and elevate the forms of entertainment used by civic and courtly elites. Such entertainments would no longer feature clowns, tumblers, mimes, and singers of love songs; there would henceforth be no drums and cymbals, trumpets and horns playing music of the

---

92 See Abramov-van Rijk, *Parlar cantando*, for a summary of this historiography; the expression "secret of the quattrocento" goes back to the Italian musicologist Fausto Torrefranca.
93 Pirrotta, "Music and Cultural Tendencies."
94 See Texts 9 and 10 in Strohm, "Music, Humanism," where Ficino and Pontano state that performing poetry to the lyre was an art that had been revived after having been lost for some unspecified intervening period.

hunt. These the humanists tried to stigmatize as vulgar or potentially immoral.[95] Instead, the leisure hours of the upper classes would be transformed into occasions for the celebration of classical virtue. When the tables were taken away after a banquet, a humanist singer would stand forth and perform extempore verses in Latin, accompanying himself with a lyre-like instrument, identified from coeval illustrations as the lira da braccio. He might chant verses from, or sing settings of Virgil, Horace, or Ovid,[96] but more typically, he sang verses he had composed himself, presumptively extempore and under divine inspiration.

Raffaele Brandolini, looking back in 1513 over a long career as singer of humanist songs, gives us the most complete account of the repertory. He sang, he tells us, historical verses about peace and war and, especially at cardinals' houses, verses about the deeds of saints and martyrs; he sang of matters sacred and profane, ancient and modern; his verses celebrated the councils and deeds of citizens as well as the sayings and doings of philosophers; he engaged in extemporaneous verse dialogues with learned diners in which were discussed questions of moral philosophy; these would highlight the vices of the moderns by comparing them with the virtues of the ancients. "Often I was supposed to repeat in verse a history that had been read or to explain a problem proposed on a certain subject, a task I carried out many times at the banquets of cardinals."[97]

The flavor of these occasions is preserved in a number of sources. Giovanni Pontano's dialogue *Antonius* describes an open-air meeting of Pontano's Neapolitan academy under a portico in the Piazza del Nilo during Carnival. The dramatic date is shortly after the death of Pontano's mentor, Antonio Beccadelli, in 1471; the date of composition is sometime in the 1490s.[98] Various passers-by engage the group in learned conversation and tell jokes. Then a stranger called the Lyre-Player (*Lyricen*) stops by the portico to sing songs, including some of Pontano's own amatory verse. The Lyre-Player is described as a man who "gets past the barbarous music of the past" and

---

95 Brandolini, *On Music and Poetry*, 29–37, censures such entertainments as unworthy of civic and ecclesiastical leaders; Brandolini's book was itself provoked by a critical remark of its dedicatee, Corradolo Stanga, who had attempted to equate Brandolini's art with that of vulgar court entertainers.

96 Virgil (Cortesi, *De cardinalatu*); Horace (Beroaldo, *Orationes et quamplures apendiculae versuum*, cited in Pirrotta, *Music and Culture*, 387 n. 35); Ovid's *Heroides* (Giovio, *Notable Men and Women*, 457). See also the essay by Philippe Canguilhem in this volume, Ch. 9. On the custom of reciting classical poetry to the lyre in Renaissance academies, see Hankins, "Humanist Academies."

97 Brandolini, *On Music and Poetry*, 106. Brandolini's own account of his performances is confirmed by the testimony of Matteo Bosso, cited in Gallo, *Music in the Castle*, 85 and Canguilhem, Ch. 9 n. 15 in this volume.

98 It is known that Pietrobono del Chitarrino came to Naples to perform in 1473, so Pontano may be giving us a portrait of the famous singer. On his career see Lockwood, *Music in Renaissance Ferrara*, ch. 10. A less likely candidate is Raffaele Brandolini's older brother Aurelio Brandolini, who performed in Naples as well during the 1470s; since he was nearly blind (a congenital condition he shared with his brother), it seems unlikely that he had the military experience of which the Lyre-Player boasts in ch. 104.

"revives an ancient art"; an interlocutor compliments him by saying, "posterity will have a much greater debt [to you] if you have any imitators. For we hope that, if you leave any like yourself, music will be restored to its ancient greatness and perfection." The Lyre-Player is about to leave for a wedding, where he will also sing, when a procession celebrating Carnival appears, including a trumpeter and a second bard (*vates*). They erect a platform and benches for a kind of theatrical performance. Then a short, ribald song is sung by a Masked Actor (*istrio*) in iambic senarii, modeled on that of Prologus in Roman comedy, intended to warm up the crowd. There follows the first part of a long Latin poem (216 lines) in hexameters sung or chanted by the second bard, who is called the Masked Poet (presumably because he is wearing a carnival mask); it takes the form of a mini-epic or epyllion about a battle of the Roman general Sertorius.[99] This work, based on Sallust's prose history, is described as an extemporaneous composition (though it is independently listed by Pontano as among his poetical works). The poem, despite its classical subject, is filled with veiled allusions to members of Pontano's academy. Then comes another comic interval of thirty-six Plautine lines from the Masked Actor as the Poet pauses for a drink – an act mocked by the actor, who also, however, encourages the audience to go on listening to the Masked Poet's military story. Then the Poet resumes his tale for another 414 lines, celebrating the courage and prudence of Sertorius that won him fame and glory. The end of the poem is also the conclusion of the dialogue.[100] The mixing of serious and comic elements is entirely typical of the way humanists, following the Socratic maxim *iocari serio*, tried to capture and channel in moralizing ways the leisure hours of educated elites.

A less carnivalesque and more contemplative mood and subject matter is implied by the various descriptions of Orphic singing by Ficino. A good example is the following passage of Ugolino Verino's Latin epic, the *Carlias*, of 1489, which presents the famous Platonist as performing in a Lydian mode:

> But once hunger has been driven away, the Etruscan poet Marsilius stands up and strikes his lyre. Then with a sonorous voice he harmonizes verses of the sort that Rhodopeian Orpheus sang mournfully on the lyre when he had lost Eurydice, weeping in vain in wicked Tartarus while the shades looked on: what is the boundary of the sea, the earth, and the sky; what are the causes of things, what is the spirit, whence and wherefore were men created, and whither fly the

---

99 It may be that the great popularity of the epyllion or short epic in the quattrocento is related to the requirements of after-dinner performance. The subject has not to my knowledge been investigated. For examples of humanist epyllia, see Maffeo Vegio, *Short Epics*, and Hankins, "Renaissance Crusaders," 375–83.
100 Pontano, *Dialogues*, 1: *Charon and Antonius*. The poem *Sertorius* has a loose structure and repetitions which give the impression of an extemporaneous composition, so should perhaps be regarded as a specimen of mixed orality.

swift souls that have departed the body, whether they seek the sky and the Stygian swamp; the Lydian was singing these things with his learned plectrum.[101]

In promoting extempore Latin poetry *ad lyram*, the humanists believed themselves to be reviving a lost ancient art. It was widely assumed by humanist scholars that lyric poetry, didactic poetry, and historical epics in antiquity were sung or intoned to the lyre or cithara rather than recited.[102] Brandolini even claimed that in antiquity, music and poetry were the same art.[103] Here the humanists' great authority was Virgil, whose *Aeneid* was the most widely read ancient text of the Renaissance. Not only did Virgil himself, in the very first lines of his epic, present himself as a singer of historical tales and a seeker of divine inspiration, but at the end of Book 1 he depicts Iopas, the court poet of Dido's Carthage, singing after a banquet a didactic poem about astronomy on his gilded lyre (*cithara*).[104] But there were other ancient authorities for improvised verse as well. Poliziano claimed that Homer's verses (unlike Virgil's) poured forth spontaneously.[105] Brandolini in the *De musica* also mentions Archias, a poet defended in a famous speech by Cicero; there Cicero praises his extempore poetic performances as "almost divinely inspired" (*quasi divino quodam spiritu inflari*):

> How many times have I seen this man Archias – with no written text – delivering *ex tempore* a vast number of the finest verses describing contemporary affairs! How many times, when called back [for an encore], did he speak on the same subject matter but in different words and sentences![106]

Cicero also described in his *De oratore* (3.194) the Greek poet Antipater Sidonius, who performed extempore verses: "his abilities were such that when he concentrated on it, he could express himself easily in verse." Ficino's translation of Plato's *Ion* into Latin (published 1484) added a philosophical and religious coloring to the notion of improvisational singing: Plato's

---

101 Ugolino Verino in *Carlias: Ein Epos des 15. Jahrhunderts*, ed. Thurn, 410–11 (= bk. 15, lines 282–91). See also Thurn's *Kommentar zur* Carlias *des Ugolino Verino*, 727–28. I owe the reference and the translation to James K. Coleman; see his "Orphic Poetics." It is likely that Ficino actually sang from the collection of 87 short religious poems known as the *Orphic Hymns* which he himself translated from the Greek; see Kristeller, *Marsilio Ficino*, 135.

102 This was a view often repeated among humanists; see, for example, Ludovico Carbone, cited in Gallo, *Music in the Castle*, 69; see also the essay of Blake Wilson in this volume on the *canterino*, Ch. 16, and Wilson, *Singing Poetry in Renaissance Florence*. See also Allen, *The Platonism of Marsilio Ficino*, 53–55, who remarks that Ficino's "conception of a poem was essentially musical."

103 Brandolini, *On Music and Poetry*, 13.

104 *Aeneid*, 1.740–47. See Quintilian, 1.10.10, who cites the authority of "the greatest of poets, in whose songs we read that the praise of heroes and of gods were sung to the music of the lyre (*cithara*) at the feasts of the gods."

105 See the essay of Canguilhem in this volume, Ch. 9, at n. 12.

106 Cicero, *Pro Archia poeta*, 18 (trans. JH).

picture of the ancient rhapsode, the inspired performer of Homeric verse, linked to the divine by a golden chain, drawn to its power like iron filings to a magnet, were turned into standard topoi for defending humanist art song.

The singing of extempore Latin verses to the lute or lira da braccio was necessarily a rare and specialized skill, and we know of only a few examples of humanists who could perform the feat (though there may well be others): Pietrobono del Chitarrino, the Brandolini brothers Aurelio and Raffaele, Marsilio Ficino, Angelo Poliziano, Angelo Maturanzio, Probo of Sulmona, Giles of Viterbo, and Andrea Marone.[107] These men found patrons among the leading princes of Italy, including Borso d'Este, Ferdinand II of Naples, Lorenzo de' Medici, Mattias Corvinus, and Popes Sixtus IV, Alexander VI, and Julius II. Clearly they were dazzling, sought-after entertainers. But it is hard to know just how extempore their performances were: whether and to what degree they relied on materials prepared ahead of time and memorized. That performances were improvised, however, was always insisted upon because it was inseparable from the idea of the poet's divine inspiration. It was the unpremeditated character of the poetry that guaranteed its divinity, the sense audiences had that they were in the presence of a supernatural phenomenon, a divine gift. It is a sense well captured in Raphael's famous fresco of Mount Parnassus in the Stanze (1510/11), which depicted an inspired Apollo lifting his eyes to heaven as he bowed a lira da braccio, surrounded by the nine Muses and all the most famous poets, ancient and modern.

A less familiar literary counterpart to this famous image can be found in a dialogue of Paolo Giovio, *Notable Men and Women of Our Time*. The passage shows, *inter alia*, that the art of improvisational singing was still being cultivated as late as the 1520s:

> These days the incredible, astonishing brilliance of Andrea Marone[108] of Brescia enjoys the utmost admiration of the learned, for he is accustomed to pour out Latin verses on the spot in a variety of meters and rhythms on whatever subject you name – a bold undertaking, to be sure, and an impudent and reckless occupation if wondrous success did not follow naturally and through a nearly divine impulse. He summons the Muses with lyre and song, and once he has set his mind to verse and inspired it with a heightened excitement, like a torrent he is carried along with such force that his poems, though composed on the spur of the moment and without premeditation, seem the result of long advance planning and prior reflection. As he recites, his fiery eyes

---

107 For this list see Brandolini, *On Music and Poetry*, 109; Richardson, "'Recitato e cantato'"; and the essays of Blake Wilson and Canguilhem in this volume, Ch. 16 and Ch. 9.
108 This account of Andrea Marone (1475–1528) complements Pierio Valeriano's description of Marone's gift for extemporaneous versification, in *Pierio Valeriano on the Ill Fortune of Learned Men*, 184–87. On Marone's career and the loss of most of his works in the Sack of Rome, see Gaisser's account ibid., 305.

are fixed, his sweat pours, his veins swell; and – what is wondrous – as the verses flow forth, his trained ears, as though not his own, intently and precisely regulate every beat.[109]

By the 1520s, however, extempore playing of Latin verses to the lyre was an art close to extinction, and had been mostly replaced by the singing of verses in the *volgare* to the lyre or lute. The performances of Serafino Aquilano (and his many imitators) of Petrarchan verse were wildly popular, and clearly a hard act to follow. Many amateur performers and even a few professional *citaredi* were now women, which made the insistence on Latin even more difficult to maintain.[110] The music being sung in courts, whether monodic, homophonic, or polyphonic, was increasingly written by professional composers and sung from printed books. One of the earliest such collections, printed by Ottaviano Petrucci in 1505, had a song in it labeled *aer di versi latini*, without a text and so, presumably, suitable for improvisation.[111] But it is the only such song for Latin verse listed in the eleven volumes of *frottole* and six volumes of music for the lute printed by Petrucci, a famously canny businessman, between 1501 and 1520. The conclusion seems inescapable that the singing of improvised Latin verses was not in great demand from the wider public created by the printing press.

## Conclusion

Before the end of the fifteenth century, the humanist movement in Italy had relatively little direct impact on wider European traditions of either *musica theorica* or *musica practica*. Its culture rarely intersected with the music of the early Renaissance that survives today and is most often associated with the quattrocento. The great series of polyphonists from Dunstaple and Du Fay to Isaac and Josquin would have written their masses, motets, and songs with or without the humanists. This situation would change in the sixteenth century, when humanism would have a much more profound impact on theory, style, and repertory, though it is true that the foundations for this change were laid in the fifteenth century. It is equally true that humanists had some considerable impact on the musical life of educated Italians, as it was experienced at the time, by promoting the extempore singing of verse to the lyre. But our

---

109 Giovio, *Notable Men and Women*, 227 (2.16).
110 For Castiglione's praise of Elisabetta Gonzaga's performance of a canzona based on bk. 4 of the *Aeneid*, the *Dulces exuviae*, of which there existed many settings by well-known composers, see Holford-Strevens in this volume, Ch. 15 at n. 36.
111 Ottaviano Petrucci, publisher, *Strambotti, Ode, Frottole, Sonetti, et modo de cantar versi latini e capituli, Libro Quarto* (Venice, 1505). On the history of Petrucci's collections see Fallows, "Petrucci's *Canti* Volumes: Scope and Repertory."

knowledge of the latter phenomenon is almost entirely literary, and the reconstruction of it as music performance remains difficult and speculative.

The humanists left a more pervasive mark on the musical culture of the early Renaissance, however, thanks to the wider shift they brought about in the moral and aesthetic values embraced by Italian elites.[112] They championed a new way of judging music according to its moral and civic purposes, using critical standards elaborated from the antiquarian study of music and the art of rhetoric. Even more important, via the humanist school, they created an audience of educated amateurs for "classic" music, secular music that was entertaining but still morally serious. They championed music that celebrated the virtues and wisdom of the ancients in poetry, enhanced by particular kinds of melody, harmony, and rhythm. In due course this humanist-trained audience found performers and composers to satisfy its tastes. Unlike clerical vocalists in churches and palatine chapels, who sang to God on behalf of the immortal souls of mankind, the humanist singer sang to men and women in courts and academies to entertain them, but also for their moral benefit in this life.[113] In this sense the humanists' encounter with music forms part of the larger Renaissance story of how European elites challenged the authority and disciplines of the medieval Church and created authorities and disciplines of their own.

## Bibliography

Abramov-van Rijk, Elena, *Parlar cantando: The Practice of Reciting Verses in Italy from 1300 to 1600*, Bern, 2009

Acciaiuoli, Donato, *Commentaria in Aristotelis Politicam*, Venice, 1566

Allen, Michael J. B., *The Platonism of Marsilio Ficino: A Study of his Phaedrus Commentary, its Sources and Genesis*, Berkeley, 1984

Baker, Patrick, *Italian Renaissance Humanism in the Mirror*, Cambridge, 2015

Baxandall, Michael, *Giotto and the Orators: Humanist Observers of Painting in Italy and the Discovery of Pictorial Composition, 1350–1450*, Oxford, 1971

Bembo, Pietro, *Lyric Poetry*, trans. Mary P. Chatfield, Cambridge, MA, 2005

Bent, Margaret, "Grammar and Rhetoric in Late Medieval Polyphony: Modern Metaphor or Old Simile?," in *Rhetoric beyond Words: Delight and Persuasion in the Arts of the Middle Ages*, ed. Mary Carruthers, Cambridge, 2010, 52–71

"Humanists and Music, Music and Humanities," in *Tendenze e metodi nella ricerca musicologica*, ed. Raffaele Pozzi, Florence, 1995, 29–38

"Music and the Early Veneto Humanists," *Proceedings of the British Academy* 101, Lectures and Memoirs, Oxford, 1999, 101–30

---

112  Haar, *Essays on Italian Poetry and Music*, 48: "the seemingly infertile native musical culture of the '400 had in fact brought about a revolution in taste and a new relationship between word and tone."

113  Dean, "Listening to Sacred Polyphony c. 1500"; Blackburn, "For Whom Do the Singers Sing?"

Beroaldo, Filippo, *Orationes et quamplures apendiculae versuum*, Bologna, 1491

Biondo, Flavio, *Italy Illuminated*, ed. and trans. Jeffrey A. White, Cambridge, MA, 2005

Black, Robert, *Humanism and Education in Medieval and Renaissance Italy: Tradition and Innovation in Latin Schools from the Twelfth to the Fifteenth Century*, Cambridge and New York, 2001

Blackburn, Bonnie J., "For Whom Do the Singers Sing?," *EM* 25 (1997), 593–609

"Music Theory and Musical Thinking after 1450," in *Music as Concept and Practice in the Late Middle Ages*, ed. Reinhard Strohm and Bonnie J. Blackburn, New Oxford History of Music 3/1, Oxford, 2001, 301–45

Brancacci, Fiorella, "Musica, retorica e critica musicale nel *De cardinalatu* di Paolo Cortesi," *Rinascimento* 39 (1999), 409–30

Brandolini, Raffaele Lippo, *On Music and Poetry (De Musica et Poetica: 1513)*, trans. Ann E. Moyer and Marc Laureys, Tempe, AZ, 2001

Castiglione, Baldesar, *The Book of the Courtier: The Singleton Translation: An Authoritative Text Criticism*, ed. Daniel Javitch, New York, 2002

Coleman, James K., "Orphic Poetics and the Intellectual Life of Lorenzo de' Medici's Circle," Ph.D. diss., Yale University, 2010

Colonna, Egidio, *De regimine principum*, Rome, 1607

Cortesi, Paolo, *De cardinalatu*, 1510. Section "De musica" edited in Nino Pirrotta, "Musica e orientamenti culturali nell'Italia del Quattrocento, Appendice II," in *Musica tra Medioevo e Rinascimento*, Turin, 1984, 234–49

*De hominibus doctis dialogus*, ed. Maria Teresa Graziosi, Rome, 1973

Dean, Jeffrey, "Listening to Sacred Polyphony c. 1500," *EM* 25 (1997), 611–36

Fallows, David, "Petrucci's *Canti* Volumes: Scope and Repertory," *BJhM* 25 (2001), 39–52

Faxolis, Florentius de, *Book on Music*, ed. and trans. Bonnie J. Blackburn and Leofranc Holford-Strevens, Cambridge, MA, 2010

Fenlon, Iain, "Music in Italian Renaissance Paintings," in *Companion to Medieval and Renaissance Music*, ed. Tess Knighton and David Fallows, Berkeley and London, 1992, repr. Berkeley and Oxford, 1997, 189–209

Ferguson, Wallace K., *The Renaissance in Historical Thought: Five Centuries of Interpretation*, Boston, 1948

Ficino, Marsilio, *Commentaries on Plato 1: Phaedrus and Ion*, ed. and trans. Michael J. B. Allen, Cambridge, MA, 2008

*Lettere*, ed. Sebastiano Gentile, Florence, 1990

*The Letters of Marsilio Ficino* (Book I), trans. members of the language department of the School of Economic Science, London, London, 1985

*Opera omnia*, Basel, 1576

*Three Books on Life*, ed. Carol V. Kaske and John R. Clark, Binghamton, NY, 1989

Gaffurio, Franchino, *De harmonia musicorum instrumentorum opus*, trans. Clement A. Miller, n.p., 1977

*The Theory of Music*, trans. Walter Kurt Kreyszig, ed. Claude V. Palisca, New Haven, 1993

Gallo, F. Alberto, *Music in the Castle*, trans. Anna Herklotz and Kathryn Krug, Chicago, 1995

Giovio, Paolo, *Notable Men and Women of Our Time*, trans. Kenneth S. Gouwens, Cambridge, MA, 2013

Grund, Gary R. *Humanist Comedies*, Cambridge, MA, 2005

Guarino of Verona, *Epistolario*, ed. Remigio Sabbadini, 3 vols., Venice, 1915–19

Haar, James, "The Courtier as Musician: Castiglione's View of the Science and Art of Music," in Haar, *The Science and Art of Renaissance Music*, ed. Paul Corneilson, Princeton, 1998, 20–37

*Essays on Italian Poetry and Music in the Renaissance, 1350–1600*, Berkeley, 1986

"Humanism," in *Grove Music Online*

Hankins, James, "The Dates of Leonardo Bruni's Later Works (1437–1443)," *Studi medievali e umanistici* 5–6 (2007–8), 11–50

"Humanist Academies and the 'Platonic Academy of Florence'," in *On Renaissance Academies: Proceedings of the International Conference "From the Roman Academy to the Danish Academy in Rome," 11–13 October 2006*, ed. Marianne Pade, Rome, 2011, 31–46

"Renaissance Crusaders: Humanist Crusade Literature in the Age of Mehmed II," *Dumbarton Oaks Papers* 49 (1995), 111–207; repr. in Hankins, *Humanism and Platonism in the Italian Renaissance*, Rome, 2003, 293–424

ed., *The Cambridge Companion to Renaissance Philosophy*, Cambridge, 2007

Harrán, Don, *In Defense of Music: The Case for Music as Argued by a Singer and Scholar of the Late Fifteenth Century*, Lincoln, NE, 1989

*Word–Tone Relations in Musical Thought: From Antiquity to the Seventeenth Century*, Neuhausen-Stuttgart, 1986

Holford-Strevens, Leofranc, "Humanism and the Language of Music Treatises," *Renaissance Studies* 15 (2001), 415–49

"Musical Humanism," *EM* 30 (2002), 481–82

Kallendorf, Craig W., ed., *Humanist Educational Treatises*, Cambridge, MA, 2002

Kreyszig, Walter Kurt, "Franchino Gaffurio als Vermittler der Musiklehre des Altertums und des Mittelalters: Zur Identifizierung griechischer und lateinischer Quellen in der Theorica musice," *AcM* 65 (1993), 134–50

"Franchino Gaffurio und seine Übersetzer der griechischen Musiktheorie in der Theorica musice (1492): Ermolao Barbaro, Giovanni Francesco Burana und Marsilio Ficino," in *Musik als Text: Bericht über den Internationalen Kongress der Gesellschaft für Musikforschung, Freiburg im Breisgau 1993*, ed. Hermann Danuser and Tobias Plebuch, Kassel, 1998, 164–71

Kristeller, Paul Oskar, *Marsilio Ficino and his Work after 500 Years*, Florence, 1987

"Music and Learning in the Early Italian Renaissance," in *Renaissance Thought and the Arts: Collected Essays*, expanded edn., with a new afterword, Princeton, 1990, 142–62

Landino, Cristoforo, *Poems*, trans. Mary P. Chatfield, Cambridge, MA, 2008

Lockwood, Lewis, *Music in Renaissance Ferrara, 1400–1505: The Creation of a Musical Center in the Fifteenth Century*, Oxford, 1984

Lorenzetti, Stefano, *Musica e identità nobiliare nell'Italia del Rinascimento: Educazione, mentalità, immaginario*, Florence, 2003

Lowinsky, Edward E., "Humanism in the Music of the Renaissance," in *Music in the Culture of the Renaissance and Other Essays*, ed. Bonnie J. Blackburn, 2 vols., Chicago, 1989, 1:154–218

MacCarthy, Evan A., "Tinctoris and the Neapolitan *Eruditi*," *JAF* 5 (2013), 41–67

Maffei, Raffaele, *Commentariorum urbanorum libri XXXVIII*, Basel, 1544

Marullus, Michael, *Poems*, trans. Charles Fantazzi, Cambridge, MA, 2012

McManamon, John M., S.J., *Funeral Oratory and the Cultural Ideals of Italian Humanism*, Chapel Hill, NC, 1989

Mercer, R. G. G., *The Teaching of Gasparino Barzizza with Special Reference to his Place in Paduan Humanism*, London, 1979

Moyer, Ann E., *Musica Scientia: Musical Scholarship in the Italian Renaissance 1480–1600*, Ithaca, 1992

Owens, Jessie Ann, "Music Historiography and the Definition of 'Renaissance'," *Notes* 47 (1990), 305–30

Palisca, Claude V., *Humanism in Italian Renaissance Musical Thought*, New Haven, 1985

Panofsky, Erwin, *Renaissance and Renascences in Western Art*, Stockholm, 1960

Patrizi, Francesco, of Siena, *De institutione reipublicae*, Paris, 1534

Petrarca, Francesco, *Invectives*, ed. and trans. David Marsh, Cambridge, MA, 2003

Petrucci, Ottaviano, publisher, *Strambotti, Ode, Frottole, Sonetti, et modo de cantar versi latini e capituli, Libro Quarto*, Venice, 1505

Pirrotta, Nino, "Music and Cultural Tendencies in 15th-Century Italy," *JAMS* 19 (1966), 127–61; repr. in Pirrotta, *Music and Culture*, 80–112

   *Music and Culture in Italy from the Middle Ages to the Baroque*, Cambridge, MA, 1984

   "Musica e umanesimo," in *Poesia e musica e altri saggi*, ed. Nino Pirrotta, Florence, 1994, 89–106

Pontano, Giovanni Gioviano, *Dialogues*, 1: *Charon and Antonius*, ed. and trans. Julia Haig Gaisser, Cambridge, MA, 2012

Quintilianus, Marcus Fabius, *Institutio Oratoria*, trans. Harold Edgeworth Butler, *The Institutio Oratoria of Quintilian*, Cambridge, MA, 1921–22

Rabil, Albert, Jr., *Knowledge, Goodness and Power: The Debate over Nobility among Quattrocento Italian Humanists*, Binghamton, NY, 1991

Richardson, Brian, "'Recitato e cantato': The Oral Diffusion of Lyric Poetry in Sixteenth-Century Italy," in *Theatre, Opera, and Performance in Italy from the Fifteenth Century to the Present: Essays in Honour of Richard Andrews*, ed. Simon Gilson and Catherine Keen, Leeds, 2004, 67–82

Sabbadini, Remigio, "L'ortografia latina di Vittorino da Feltre e la scuola padovana," *Rendiconti della R. Accademia Nazionale dei Lincei* 4 (1928), 209–21

Sachs, Klaus-Jürgen, "Zur Funktion der Berufungen auf das achte Buch von Aristoteles' 'Politik' in Musiktraktaten des 15. Jahrhunderts," in *Musik und die Geschichte der Philosophie und Naturwissenschaften im Mittelalter: Fragen zur Wechselwirkung von "Musica" und "Philosophia" im Mittelalter*, ed. Frank Hentschel, Studien und Texte zur Geistesgeschichte des Mittelalters 62, Leiden, 1998, 269–92

Strohm, Reinhard, "Enea Silvio Piccolomini and Music," in *Uno gentile et subtile ingenio: Studies in Renaissance Music in Honour of Bonnie J. Blackburn*, ed. M. Jennifer Bloxam, Gioia Filocamo, and Leofranc Holford-Strevens, Turnhout, 2009, 719–28

   "Music, Humanism, and the Idea of a 'Rebirth' of the Arts," in *Music as Concept and Practice in the Late Middle Ages*, ed. Reinhard Strohm and Bonnie J. Blackburn, New Oxford History of Music, 3/1, Oxford, 2001, 346–405

   "Neue Aspekte von Musik und Humanismus im 15. Jahrhundert," *AcMus* 76 (2004), 135–57

   *The Rise of European Music, 1380–1500*, Cambridge, 1993

   and Donald Cullington, eds., *Egidius Carlerius, Johannes Tinctoris: On the Dignity and the Effects of Music: Two Fifteenth-Century Treatises*, London, 1996

Thurn, Nikolaus, *Kommentar zur Carlias des Ugolino Verino*, Munich, 2002

Tinctoris, Johannes, *Libri quinque de inventione et usu musice*, in *Johannes Tinctoris: Complete Theoretical Works*, ed. Ronald Woodley, Jeffrey J. Dean, and David Lewis, online at earlymusictheory.org/Tinctoris/texts/deinventioneetusumusice/

Valeriano, Pierio, *Pierio Valeriano on the Ill Fortune of Learned Men: A Renaissance Humanist and his World*, trans. with an introduction by Julia Haig Gaisser, Ann Arbor, 1999

Valgulio, Carlo, *Contra vituperatorem musicae*, in *"That liberal and virtuous art": Three Humanist Treatises on Music: Egidius Carlerius, Johannes Tinctoris, Carlo Valgulio*, trans., annotated and ed. J. Donald Cullington; with an introduction by Reinhard Strohm and the editor, Newtownabbey, 2001

   *In Plutarchi Musicam, ad Titum Pyrrhinum* [preface to his translation of ps.-Plutarch, *De musica*] in *Plutarchi . . . Opuscula (quae quidem extant) omnia*, Basel, 1530, fols. 244v–247v

Valturio, Roberto, *De re militari*, Verona, 1483

Vecce, Carlo, *Gli umanisti e la musica: Un'antologia di testi umanistici sulla musica*, Milan, 1985

Vegio, Maffeo, *Short Epics*, trans. M. C. J. Putnam with James Hankins, Cambridge, MA, 2004

Verino, Ugolino, *Carlias: Ein Epos des 15. Jahrhunderts*, ed. Nikolaus Thurn, Munich, 1995

Walker, Daniel Pickering, *Music, Spirit and Language in the Renaissance*, ed. Penelope Gouk, London, 1985

   *Spiritual and Demonic Magic from Ficino to Campanella*, London, 1958

Wegman, Rob C., *The Crisis of Music in Early Modern Europe, 1470–1530*, New York, 2008

   "Johannes Tinctoris and the Art of Listening," in *"Recevez ce mien petit labeur": Studies in Renaissance Music in Honour of Ignace Bossuyt*, ed. Pieter Bergé and Marc Delaere, Leuven, 2008, 279–96

   "Johannes Tinctoris and the 'New Art'," *ML* 84 (2003), 171–88

Wilson, Blake, *Singing Poetry in Renaissance Florence: The "Cantasi come" Tradition (1375–1550)*, Florence, 2009

   "'Transferring Tunes and Adjusting Lines': Leonardo Giustinian and the Giustiniana in Quattrocento Florence," in *Uno gentile et subtile ingenio: Studies in Renaissance Music in Honour of Bonnie J. Blackburn*, ed. M. Jennifer Bloxam, Gioia Filocamo, and Leofranc Holford-Strevens, Turnhout, 2009, 547–67

Witt, Ronald G., *In the Footsteps of the Ancients: The Origins of Humanism from Lovato to Bruni*, Boston, 2003

Woodley, Ronald, "Renaissance Music Theory as Literature: On Reading the *Proportionale Musices* of Iohannes Tinctoris," *Renaissance Studies* 1 (1987), 209–20

# Fifteenth-century humanism and music outside Italy

REINHARD STROHM

## Humanism, Renaissance, music

"Humanism outside Italy" is a periphery without a center. A periphery does not have an identity of its own: it is only negatively defined as a non-center. Apart from their relationship with the center, do the manifestations of fifteenth-century humanism outside Italy have anything in common? Today they seem to share the fate that their humanist credentials are often scrutinized rather severely. A prevailing assumption is that the intellectual culture in the countries north of the Alps was characterized by scholasticism until the end of the fifteenth century, when the influence of Italian humanism had become paramount.[1]

Humanism is definable as the cultivation of classical antiquity in literary and related disciplines, a cultural trend occurring in various epochs and regions; Italian Renaissance humanism is the most outstanding example of this trend.[2] But there were other examples. The ecclesiastical and courtly humanism of medieval France, for example, from Walter of Châtillon to Philippe de Vitry, Jean Charlier de Gerson, and beyond, had older roots than the Renaissance and was an independent tradition until it came under strong Italian influence in the fifteenth century.[3]

The picture of Italian humanism radiating out to other countries and innovating their intellectual climates is an attractive one. It conforms to our historical image of the Italian Renaissance itself – an innovative, expansive, and persuasive cultural campaign. But as the example of the French tradition shows, humanism and Renaissance did not always coincide.

The situation of music was special, too. If a fifteenth-century musical "rebirth" or even "Renaissance" can be diagnosed outside Italy, it

---

1 For Paul Oskar Kristeller's concept of humanism and for the question of "vernacular humanism" – independent approaches in various countries – see Oberman, "Quoscunque tulit foecunda vetustas," esp. xvii; Dresden, "The Profile of the Reception"; Ijsewijn, "The Coming of Humanism"; Hay, "England and the Humanities"; and Spitz, "The Course of German Humanism."
2 Haar, "Humanism."
3 Simone, *Il rinascimento francese*; G. Ouy coined the term "humanisme des chancelleries." See his "Les Premiers Humanistes."

was originally unaided by humanism, let alone Italian humanism. Some sort of "contrary motion" happened between Italy and other countries:[4] the radiation of Italian Renaissance humanism to other regions of Europe did not include a strong musical component, whereas music from other regions was transferred to Italy without the component of humanism.

Therefore, our survey of "Fifteenth-century humanism and music outside Italy" concerns, above all, *the connections with music which humanism forged in other countries*. These connections between humanist precepts and non-Italian musical environments shed new light on these environments themselves and contributed to long-lasting changes in them.

## The challenge of practice

The French poet Martin Le Franc (1410–61) writes in his "Letter to the Savoy Secretaries," ca. 1439:

> Some people, we can see, know the ins and outs of many things, but if they have not steeped themselves in practice, they fail in the action as if they were inexperienced; as when they bring a great deal of judgment to the outlines and shapes of bodies, but unless they have not become used through frequent painting to externalize what they have internally envisaged, they will break down almost in the first attempt at drawing. Some others profusely debate dyapente, dyatesseron, and musical proportions – but if they have not familiarized their vocal chords with many sounds they will never be judged pleasing harmonists.[5]

The Sienese humanist Enea Silvio Piccolomini (later Pope Pius II, 1458–64) stated in a famous disputation at Vienna University, 1445:

> Perhaps someone will ask how it can happen that one who knows what is good does not carry it out. The answer is easy. There are very many people who teach music in the schools, who do not know how to sing the shortest versicle in church, like Themistocles among the Athenians, who was judged to be rather

---

4 Gustave Reese and Howard M. Brown, who emphasized the radiations of music from the North to the South, were criticized in Palisca, *Humanism*, 1. Panofsky, *Renaissance and Renascences*, 165–68, observed a strange "chiasm" in the fine arts: innovation in painting was strongest in the North, weakest in Italy, whereas in literature and architecture, the roles of North and South were reversed.

5 "Videmus enim quosdam multarum rerum racionem cognoscere sed usu non tritos tamquam inexpertis in agendo remitti quemadmodum de lineamentis corporumque figuris multam diiudicacionem parant, sed nisi crebro pingendo usu extra formarint quod intus effigiatum est, pene in prima protractione deficient. Nonnulli etiam de dyatessaron, de dyapente deque musicis proportionibus habunde disputant sed nisi vocales arterias multis sonis accommodarint numquam predicabuntur suaves harmonici" (trans. R. S.). See Strohm, "Music, Humanism," 402, 404.

uneducated when he refused to play the lyre at a banquet. Nor do all physicians, who teach medical practice, know how to heal ...[6]

The Netherlands musician and humanist Rudolph Agricola (1444–85) writes near the end of his acclaimed textbook *De inventione dialectica* (1479):

> Of no use are all those rules that are taught about making musical instruments or of what proportions the notes are generated; it is useless to know the prescribed pitch intervals, consonances, and dissonances; or which consonances are connected correctly to which others or to themselves, which time durations must be observed and which modes: unless a careful training has made them part of the habit, consolidated them, instilled them, and turned them almost into a person's nature.[7]

These are energetic pleas in support of practice and exercise in the arts, against theory. They belong to a humanist critique of scholastic teaching that challenges fundamental conventions of transmitting knowledge. Their common background is the study of eloquence: the writings on the training of the orator by Cicero (*De inventione*, *De oratore*, *Brutus*), in the pseudo-Ciceronian *Rhetorica ad Herennium*, and in Quintilian's *Institutio oratoria*. According to these authorities, the education of the orator should be based on natural talent (*natura*), technical know-how (*ars*), and exercise or practice (*usus*) – although Quintilian follows the *Rhetorica* in also recommending the imitation of models (*imitatio*) as an educational tool.

The authors cited above compare various arts and sciences. For Le Franc, music needs as much practice as oratory, painting, and drawing; Piccolomini compares it with the practice of the physician, Agricola with agriculture, politics, and warfare. This is a typically humanist motion of thought that begins with classical oratory (*eloquentia*) and moves its precepts to other fields of knowledge or skill, sidestepping the medieval system of the seven liberal arts, in which music is a theoretical pursuit close to arithmetic and astronomy. The three authors also valuate disciplines known as *artes mechanicae* (practical arts), and they move music closer to the emerging *studia humanitatis*: grammar, rhetoric, poetry, history, and moral philosophy. Music was otherwise rarely

---

6 "Querit fortasse aliquis, qui fieri potest, ut bonum sciens non operetur. Facilis responsio est. Plurimi sunt, qui in gignasiis musicam docent, qui cantare vel minimum versiculum in ecclesiis ignorent, sicut apud Atthenienses Themistocles, qui in convivio recusasset liram, habitus est indoctior. Nec omnes medici, qui practicam legunt, mederi sciunt" (trans. R.S.). See Lhotsky, *Die Wiener Artistenfakultät*, Beilage iii, 265; Strohm, "Enea Silvio Piccolomini and Music," 724.

7 "Nihil profuerint multa illa, quae de conficiendis musicorum praecipiuntur instrumentis, quibus proportionibus singulae nascantur: nihil quae de vocum intervallis, quae de consonantibus, et dissonantibus, et que quibus consonantiae recte, aut secus subnectantur, quae temporum spatia sint observanda, qui modi: si non omnia diligens meditatio assuefecerit, firmaverit, indiderit, et prope in naturam verterit" (trans. R.S.). See Agricola, *De inventione dialectica*, bk. 3, ch. 16, pp. 443–44. The *scholia* comments: "usage can do the most in all things" (usum omni in re plurimum posse).

chosen as an example of practical training in the arts and sciences; it is addressed here, I suggest, because our three authors had experienced musical practice in the areas of their activity north of the Alps.

## Musical humanists and humanist musicians

Musical humanists of the period working outside Italy had in common that they applied classical modes of thinking to musical practices around them, rather than advocating new types of music or exploring music theory, let alone ancient music theory. The latter interest was more typical for Italian humanism, because most ancient music theory and aesthetics was Greek, with few Latin translations (often from Arabic) being available, and the knowledge of Greek developed much faster in Italy than in the North. The recovery of ancient music theory was first attempted by literary scholars in Italy; musical specialists such as Franchino Gaffurio followed.[8] Of the many foreign musicians active in fifteenth-century Italy who were influenced by humanism, only Johannes Gallicus of Namur (ca. 1415–73) explored ancient musical systems.[9] Other musical foreigners in Italy, such as the Liégeois Johannes Ciconia (d. 1412), the Englishman John Hothby (d. 1487), the Walloon Johannes Tinctoris (d. 1511), and the Spaniard Bartolomé Ramos de Pareja (fl. 1460–90), were concerned with present practice and its medieval roots; they had only a marginal interest in classical sources of music.[10]

The musical writings of humanists in the North reflect their authors' diverse status, interests, and skills. Most of them discuss the contemporary practice of music, a few also its history or aesthetics. Some writers make only isolated, casual remarks on musical matters, merely demonstrating curiosity; some have a lasting personal but non-professional interest in music; some are responsible for music in their court or church positions; yet others are humanists at heart but earn a living as schoolmasters or singers. Trained musicians, on the other hand, are sometimes only tangentially linked to humanism, whether through expert friends, rivals, or patrons who stimulate their classical studies. Only a few academic humanists have enough musical expertise to practice the art themselves or even to integrate their music with their other studies.

8  Palisca, *Humanism*, 23–50; Blackburn, "Music Theory," 333–35.
9  On Gallicus, see Palisca, *Humanism*, 7 and 280–83; contradicted by Mengozzi, *The Renaissance Reform*, 141–63.
10  See Blackburn, "Music Theory" on Conrad von Zabern (306), Adam von Fulda (307), Hothby and Ramos (316–25), and Tinctoris (325–33); Mengozzi, *The Renaissance Reform*, on Ciconia (117–30); and Woodley, "Tinctoris, Johannes." Palisca, *Humanism*, 283, adds Erasmus of Höritz, who wrote shortly after 1500 in Vienna or in Italy.

An Italian humanist who spent decisive years in the North (1431–58) was Enea Silvio Piccolomini. He was an orator and secretary first at the Council of Basel, then at the court of King Frederick III. His musical interests were non-professional, but this very fact seems to have encouraged him to study the value of music-making within a general humanist education, as he shows in his *De institutione liberorum* (ca. 1451), written for the education of Prince Ladislaus Postumus of Habsburg. Piccolomini's treatise *De commendatione artium*, written for the University of Vienna, belongs to a widely known literary type: the academic oration held for the inauguration of academic terms. In both these writings Enea Silvio praises the usefulness of music among the arts and sciences.[11] More influential in their epoch were his historical, anecdotal, and critical letters and disputations. He makes a relevant humanist point when pouring ridicule on the inept psalm-singing of himself and other secretaries at a ceremony of the Council of Basel (1440): this is a counter-example to his statement cited above, supporting the importance of exercise in the arts.

The Italian humanist Gregorio da Città di Castello (called Tiphernas) also held an inaugural oration (*De affinitate et cognatione scientiarum*) on the arts in 1456, perhaps at Paris University: he expands his celebratory theme to identify contacts between music and rhetoric (see below). Comments on music and musicians also exist by Erasmus of Rotterdam (1469–1536), one of which is the poetic *déploration* (or *naenia*) "Ergone conticuit" on the death of Jean Ockeghem (d. 1497), which was later set to music by Lupus or Johannes Lupi.[12] Less well known are four short epitaphs for Ockeghem by the Aostan humanist Petrus Paulus Senilis (Vieillot, Viot), a secretary of King Louis XI of France, whose leading chapel musician was Ockeghem. These epitaphs were written ca. 1472, when the famous composer was still alive but could have been expecting to die soon. A fifth poem directly addresses the composer to console him over the death of a close friend.[13] What the epitaphs thematize is the dual achievement of Ockeghem's performances (the "marvelous songs he sang") and the honor acquired through the written compositions he left to posterity ("nova scripta reliquit"). Johannes Tinctoris attests to Ockeghem's and his colleague Antoine Busnoys's "competent Latinity," which may imply that he knew the two famous composers from humanist academic studies, perhaps at the Universities of Paris or Orléans.[14]

A personal relationship linked the composer Guillaume Du Fay (ca. 1395–1474) with the churchman, poet, and orator Martin Le Franc, mentioned above. The fact of their acquaintance has never been in much doubt, but Le

---

11 Piccolomini's writings on music are assembled in Strohm, "Enea Silvio Piccolomini."
12 See Dunning, "Erasmus, Desiderius."     13 Strohm, "Hic miros cecinit cantus."
14 See Woodley, "Renaissance Music Theory."

Franc's humanist credentials have only recently been acknowledged in musicology. When he was secretary of the Savoy court and of the Council of Basel (ca. 1439–43), he formulated what I call the "humanist legend of music": the idea that musical composition was subject to a similar work-creating process as the classical literatures themselves.[15] According to Le Franc, success in musical composition is achieved by imitating famous models (just as Virgil, Ovid, and Horace had imitated the Greeks), and musical creations can be transmitted to posterity in turn. Le Franc, a poet indebted to the French medieval tradition and influenced by Cicero, Horace, Petrarch, and Boccaccio, singles out the composers Du Fay and Binchois as examples of successful imitators. Their models cannot be found in antiquity but only in recent times: Le Franc selects the Englishman John Dunstaple as a model and the Parisian composers Tapissier, Carmen, and Césaris as superseded forerunners. Le Franc adds that the famous musical improvisers of the Burgundian court surpass even the composers; this comparison, too, implies imitation and emulation, as the ancients have practiced. These ideas are expressed in some famous lines of Le Franc's poem *Le Champion des Dames* (ca. 1442), which is otherwise unrelated to music, and in a Latin letter of ca. 1439 directed to the Savoy secretaries (see above). Le Franc, who also knew the composers Nicolas de Merques and Bartholomeus Poignare, was surely capable of advising Du Fay or other musicians on Latin texts for their compositions. Du Fay's testament mentions a book of "eclogues" by Martin Le Franc (see below).[16] The momentous discourse of music as a work-creating art was surely not Le Franc's idea alone. Piccolomini and Du Fay were two of his interlocutors who might have shared it: the former in the Basel conciliar context, the latter most probably at the court of Savoy.

The special situation of musical humanism in France is typified by three scholars connected with the Parisian Collège de Navarre. Jean Charlier de Gerson (1363–1429), the great theologian and man of letters, discussed music in his late writings *De canticorum originali ratione*, *De canticordo*, and *De canticis*. He took it as a spiritual metaphor;[17] but he also investigated the etymology of the term "canticum" and described many contemporary instruments. For church ritual he designed a handbook on the education of choirboys (*Doctrina pro pueris ecclesie parisiensis*, 1411), written in the spirit of church reform and education.[18]

Gerson's nephew, Gilles Charlier (Egidius Carlerius, ca. 1400–72), taught for many years at the Collège de Navarre, and from 1436 to his death was Dean of

---

15  Strohm, "Music, Humanism," and *Guillaume Du Fay*.      16  Fallows, *Dufay*, 251.
17  Irwin, "The Mystical Music."
18  For Gerson's influence on the Ockeghem circle, see Kirkwood, "Kings, Confessors, Cantors."

Cambrai cathedral. There he coincided with Du Fay, who composed the plain-songs for his texts of a Marian Office.[19] Carlerius shares the musical attitudes of his uncle; in his *Tractatus de duplici ritu cantus ecclesiastici in divinis officiis* (ca. 1470; printed Brussels, 1479) he defends a moderate form of polyphonic music (probably against radical monastic reformers) alongside an austere, penitential type of plainsong. His references to Greek, Hebrew, and Latin authorities are largely drawn from medieval sources and do not reveal an independent human-ist effort, but they address the history and aesthetics of musical traditions.[20] A third churchman teaching at the Collège de Navarre, Jean Le Munerat (ca. 1440–99), was also a church singer (*concentor*). He left editions of liturgical books and a treatise on plainsong, *De moderatione et concordia grammatice et musice* (printed Paris, 1490), which asserts the independent status of word delivery against the "grammarians" – humanists insisting on correct (classical) Latin pronunciation of the liturgical texts. This has been interpreted as a significant fifteenth-century debate.[21] Piccolomini apparently participated in it when criticizing local musicians for not knowing "how to sing the shortest versicle in church" (see above): they did not pronounce the Latin words correctly. Defenders of polyphony such as Carlerius, or of musical independ-ence from language such as Le Munerat, should not be equated with medieval scholastics: the French elite included widely educated Latinists who sought to use their classical knowledge in favor of a native artistic tradition.

Du Fay's association with Le Franc may recall the friendship between the composer Philippe de Vitry (1291–1361) and Petrarch, or the latter's friendship at Avignon with the Netherlands musician Ludovicus Sanctus de Beringhen, whom Petrarch addressed as "Socrates." Two extant music treatises by Sanctus demonstrate scholastic musical thought, however.[22] Petrarch's followers north of the Alps sometimes transmitted motet texts by Philippe de Vitry, without the music, alongside the works of the arch-humanist.[23]

That humanism was slow to reach the Low Countries may be true;[24] but its musical connections are not hard to find. Antoine Haneron (1400–90), a famous diplomat, humanist, and professor of Latin eloquence at the Burgundian University of Leuven (1431–39) also supported musical life at the church of Our Lady, Bruges, where he was provost.[25] A manuscript now at Trier (Seminarbibliothek, MS 44) but probably written at Leuven University

---

19  Haggh, "The Celebration of the 'Recollectio'."
20  *Egidius Carlerius*, ed. and trans. Strohm and Cullington; expanded as *"That liberal and virtuous art."*
21  Harrán, *In Defense of Music.*    22  Giger, "Ludovicus Sanctus (Ludwig van Kempen)."
23  Wathey, "The Motets of Philippe de Vitry." No musical interests seem documented for the most assiduous Netherlands follower of Petrarch, Arnoldus de Geilhoven (d. 1442).
24  Ijsewijn, "The Coming of Humanism."
25  Ibid., 215 and 218–20. On Our Lady's, Bruges, see Strohm, *Music in Late Medieval Bruges.*

(ca. 1470) reflects musical interests and the *studia humanitatis* in the Haneron circle. It contains literary texts including letters, *artes dictaminis*, and three music treatises: the third of them explains fifteenth-century mensural notation (fol. 342r).[26] The largest item is the correspondence (ca. 1463–66) of Johannes de Veris (Jan van de Veren), a schoolmaster and cantor in Oudenburg near Bruges.[27] This humbly employed musician was an ardent humanist; he was a friend of the Abbot of St. Bavo in Ghent, Raphael de Mercatellis, a patron of literature, music, and the arts, and of the Bruges canon Johannes Ondanc, a servant of the Burgundian court and an expert musician ("clericus, litteratus, musicus vocalis, et instrumentorum") (a clerk, educated in letters, and a musician of the voice and instruments). Another correspondent of Veris was the Carmelite Nicasius Weyts, a chaplain of Our Lady's at Bruges, who contributed much to singing in local churches and is the author of a treatise on mensural notation preserved in the Faenza Codex.[28] Weyts did not accept the classical Latin prescribed in Lorenzo Valla's *De elegantiis linguae latinae*, as Veris urged him to do. To another Bruges correspondent, Veris recommended the cantor position at Sint-Gertrude of Bergen-op-Zoom (where Obrecht was to be employed in 1480–84), claiming that he would be allowed to concentrate on Gregorian plainsong (although he also knows the "Boethian modes"), while another choirmaster would have to teach discant and notation.[29]

Rodolphus Agricola from the province of Groningen (Frisia) cultivated the *studia humanitatis*, wrote the period's major work on dialectics (see above), and was a professional musician, being employed as organist at the court of Ferrara (1476–77). His studies at Groningen, Leuven, Erfurt, Pavia, and Ferrara brought him in contact with northern and Italian humanists. He held the inaugural oration at the Ferrara *studio* in 1476, praising the musical abilities of Duke Ercole I.[30] When studying at Pavia in 1474, he had similarly praised the musical interests of the rector of the University of Pavia, Johannes de Erfordia. This person was the German nobleman and humanist Johann von Dalberg, previously a student at Erfurt like Agricola himself. When Dalberg had become bishop of Worms, he invited Agricola to enter the service of the Palatinate court at Heidelberg.[31]

---

26  Strohm, "Neue Aspekte."
27  Edited in Meersseman, "L'Épistolaire," 164–65; see also Arnould, "New Manuscripts," 318–20.
28  Faenza 117. Strohm, *Music in Late Medieval Bruges*, 43–44, 52, 66.
29  "neque aliud onus cantus nisi gregoriani tibi dabitur, tametsi boeticos modulos nosti. Discantui et coklibus docendis alius preest qui chorum sua arte decorat": Meersseman, "L'Épistolaire," 180.
30  Lockwood, *Music in Renaissance Ferrara*, 151–52 and "Agricola, Rudolph"; Rudolph Agricola, *Letters*, ed. van der Laan and Akkerman.
31  Strohm, "Neue Aspekte," 155–57, also concluding that three compositions attributed to "Johannes de Erfordia" in the 1470–75 section of the Faenza Codex are Dalberg's.

Agricola also befriended the Antwerp choirmaster and composer Jacob Barbireau (1455–91). In one of his letters to Barbireau (1 November 1482), Agricola regretfully declines an invitation from the City Magistrate of Antwerp – to a position not in music but as orator or secretary – and narrates his experiences at musical establishments in Heidelberg and Cologne. He praises the Heidelberg court chapel and its leader, Johannes von Soest.[32] Other letters deal with education, including that of Barbireau himself, who wishes to study with Agricola. Although Agricola's other writings touch upon music only rarely (as in the example given above), the distance between the academic orator and the professional musician seems to become negligible here. A similar dual platform was probably available to the humanist Rutgerus Sycamber de Venray in his *Dialogus de musica* (ca. 1500),[33] and certainly to Mattheus Herbenus (1451–1538), rector of the capitular school of St. Servatius, Maastricht, who has left several humanist writings and the treatise *De natura cantus ac miraculis vocis*.[34] The widely connected ecclesiastic was an expert musician and wrote on ritual practice in a spirit of educational reform, like Gerson two generations before him.

It seems much more difficult today to identify connections – which there may well have been – between music and fifteenth-century English humanism. The leading composer John Dunstaple (d. 1453) was a learned astronomer and friend of humanists: "Dunstaple must have been acquainted at St Albans with his obituarist, Abbot John of Wheathampstead, who in turn was closely associated with Duke Humfrey and Queen Joan, and with Italian humanist circles."[35] The humanist credentials of Abbot John are solid (they include his epitaph for the composer, "Clauditur hoc tumulo qui coelum pectore clausit / Dunstaple Joannes") (This tomb encloses Joannes Dunstaple, who enclosed the sky in his breast); those of the patron of both, Duke Humfrey of Gloucester, are beyond any doubt. Yet the texts set by Dunstaple are in medieval Latin, and no biographical detail connects him personally with humanists either in France or Italy, where his music was performed. The absence of such evidence for other English composers (Leonel Power, John Plummer, Walter Frye) is somewhat less surprising; the Londoner John Bedyngham (ca. 1422–59/60?), who perhaps studied at Oxford, later may have served foreign patrons, perhaps at Ferrara or in France, and thus came under the influence of secular humanist poetry. English humanist writings on music before 1500 are not known today.[36]

32 Kooiman, "The Letters of Rodolphus Agricola," 136–46; Rudolph Agricola, *Letters*. A musical comment in Johannes von Soest's autobiography is discussed in Klaus Pietschmann's essay in this volume (Ch. 2).
33 Ed. Soddemann.    34 Sachs, "Zu den Fassungen der Musikschrift."    35 Bent, "Dunstaple."
36 An attempt to connect the Continental appreciation of Dunstaple with humanism is made in Sandmeier, *Geistliche Vokalpolyphonie*.

Musical humanism was also rare on the Iberian peninsula, since humanism itself had only a tenuous foothold in the region before the Spanish "Golden Age." A tradition of writings on plainsong and, later, mensural practice, reaches from Fernand Estevan (1410) via Domingo Marcos Durán to Guillermo Despuig (de Podio) and Gonzalo Martínez de Bizcargui (1508), but was "largely untouched by humanism."[37] The music theory of Bartolomé Ramos de Pareja (ca. 1440–ca. 1490) was developed in Italy. In the secular field, however, there are conspicuous Iberian parallels with the performative and poetic practices of Italian courts: the outstanding poet-musician Juan del Encina (1468–1529/30) and many lesser-known courtiers imitated ancient theatrical and lyrical genres. Encina's *Arte de poesía castellana* (printed in 1496) invokes classical models for both the literary and the musical compo-nents of his practice.[38]

East-central European intellectuals with humanist leanings were active at the universities of Kraków, Prague, Leipzig, Vienna, and the courts of Poland, Bohemia, Austria, and Hungary, and the episcopal sees, for example of Kraków and Lemberg (today L'viv, Ukraine). The Kraków academic Nicholas de Radom (Mikołaj Radomski, fl. 1400–30) left manuscripts of polyphony where, for the first time in history, the term "opus" is applied to musical compositions. No wonder: the works in question are by Antonio Zacara da Teramo and Johannes Ciconia; Radomski seems to have studied in Italy, perhaps Padua.[39] The composer and Latin poet Petrus Wilhelmi from Grudziądz (Graudenz) in northern Poland (ca. 1400–ca. 1480) left numerous motets in a regional style; their texts, usually containing acrostics of the author's name, may reflect a "humanisme des chancelleries," as cultivated by one of the courts in the region.[40] The Czech theorist Paulus Paulirinus (1413–ca. 1471) describes instruments and musical practices in his encyclopedic *Liber viginti artium* (ca. 1440; fragment); while relatively unconcerned about the medieval system of the *artes*, he does not obviously refer to antiquity. Undeniable evidence of humanist experiments in the region, datable ca. 1470–80, are two neo-Latin polyphonic songs on the seasons in the so-called Glogauer Liederbuch (from Zagań, Lower Silesia), one of which is also in the Moravian (?) Strahov Codex. The anonymous poet adopts the style of an Anacreontic or Horatian ode to celebrate Christmas/Winter (*Viminibus cinge*) and Easter/Spring (*Alga iacet humilis*). The hexameter texts are set in such a way that the note values of the tenor exactly reproduce the quantities of the Latin

---

37  Blackburn, "Music Theory and Musical Thinking," 309–16.
38  See Stevenson, *Spanish Music*; Strohm, *The Rise of European Music*, 574–80.
39  Perz, "Il carattere internazionale"; Strohm, "'Opus'."
40  Awianowicz, "The Graeco-Latin Vocabulary," also doubts direct derivations from classical literature.

Example 14.1 Anon., *Viminibus cinge tristantem*, Glogauer Liederbuch, no. 142

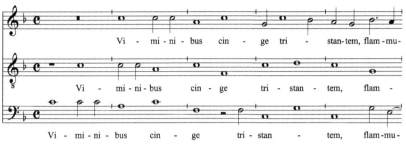

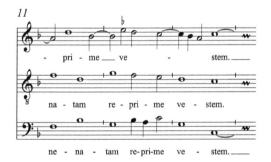

Translation:   With vine leaves crown the grieving one; warm him, small
flame. Rejecting the disease, take away his poisoned shirt.

verse (see Example 14.1).[41] The technique anticipates that of the "humanist
ode" of German-speaking university circles (see below).

The teaching of the *studia humanitatis* at Heidelberg University had been
initiated by Peter Luder in 1456. Conrad Celtis (1459–1508), later called the
German "arch-humanist," took a master's degree at Heidelberg in 1484, when
Agricola taught there; a few years later Celtis taught at Erfurt, where humanist

41  At the request of the author, note values in Example 14.1 are in 2:1 reduction [the editors].

tendencies had been in evidence for some time. Musical humanists also worked at the universities of Leipzig and later Cologne, but above all at Vienna, Freiburg, and Ingolstadt. Many visited Italy, for example the Nuremberg patrician Hartmann Schedel, who studied at Leipzig and Padua, ca. 1460. His music manuscript (the Schedelsches Liederbuch) has been described as a document of the musical discipline rather than a practical songbook.[42] In fact, Schedel practiced music – and had a love of German secular poetry, which the book documents – in his student years, but later focused on the more renowned arts of medicine and history. Those northern humanists who did not opt to relegate music to the library as did Schedel would either advertise their fondness for the art as an adjunct to the *studia humanitatis* (as did Agricola and Le Franc) or maintain contacts with practicing musicians as friends, advisors, or correspondents. In the early 1500s, musical humanists gathered at Nuremberg – Willibald Pirckheimer, Jacob Locher, and Johannes Cochlaeus – promoted the art in their writings and correspondence.

Music theory of a humanist orientation, although focused on compositional practice, is found in the *Musica* by the composer Adam von Fulda (ca. 1445–1505). He completed this comprehensive introduction to the art in 1490, dedicating it to the humanist poet Joachim Lüntaler, a lawyer at the episcopal court of Passau. Adam skillfully inserts classical citations (Cicero, Seneca, Caecilius, Balbus), quotes the *Carmen de laude musicae* by Jean Gerson, and thematizes the question of influence and progress by asserting his partial independence of the "antiqui," by whom he understands older medieval authorities. As regards the "moderni," his named models of composition are Du Fay and Busnoys, and he uses the fifteenth-century treatises of Conrad von Zabern and anonymous German authors.[43]

To integrate musical practice and humanist knowledge in new artistic creations, an idea comparable to Italian experiments with improvised Latin song, was the aim of Celtis, his friend Jacob Locher (1471–1528), called "Philomusus," and their musical allies. Their creation of the "humanist ode" relied on university education and courtly patronage. Locher and the Alsatian humanist Jakob Wimpheling (1450–1528) produced Latin dialogues or dramas in the 1490s, inserting choral odes in classical meters or styles into the prose text; performances took place at the Habsburg-founded university of Freiburg and at Worms in the circle of Johann von Dalberg, frequented by Celtis and the humanist poet Johannes Reuchlin. Locher's first drama, *Historia de rege Frantie* (Freiburg, 1495), was printed with the musical notation for the choruses. Although attacked by theologians, Locher was favored by Habsburg court

---

42 Kirnbauer, *Hartmann Schedel.*   43 Sachs, "... nec in processu."

circles and crowned *poeta laureatus* by Maximilian I in 1497.[44] Celtis's *Ludus Dianae*, a play in the same manner, was given in 1501 at the Habsburg court in Linz.

Latin lyrical poetry imitating Horace was also set to music independently of drama (although perhaps with later dramatic uses in mind). While at Ingolstadt University in the 1490s, Celtis commissioned settings of the nineteen different Horatian meters from the Tyrolean musician Petrus Tritonius (Traibenreiff, ca. 1465–ca. 1525); these were printed as *Melopoiae* in 1507. Other musicians of the Habsburg orbit followed the trend, notably Paul Hofhaimer, whose settings of original Horatian odes were published posthumously in 1539 as *Harmoniae poeticae*. Celtis's work for Maximilian I continued at Vienna University from 1501, in the context of a (later) so-called *Sodalitas Litteraria Danubiana*. Sixteenth-century ramifications of the humanist ode include uses of classical meters for German Protestant hymn texts and for French secular poetry, the so-called "vers mesurés à l'antique."

The court of Maximilian I absorbed humanist musical exploration, relying on several forerunners. One surely was the humanist circle at the court of Duke Siegmund of Tyrol. His chancellor, Johannes Fuchsmagen, was in touch with the Paduan professor of Croatian descent, Franciscus (Franjo) Niger, whose *Grammatica brevis* (Padua, 1480) demonstrated five different Latin meters with mensural music notation.[45] Fuchsmagen dedicated a collection of Latin poems in various meters to Duke Siegmund on his second wedding at Innsbruck in 1484, and Niger sent a book of *Epithalamia* in similar styles. It may be significant that Henricus Isaac, a composer much associated with neo-Latin lyrics, was present at Innsbruck in 1484 and received a gratification from Fuchsmagen.[46]

## Three major contributions of northern humanism

Some of the humanist engagements with music surveyed here may appear casual. But three topics have left a trail in music history.

The first was a so-called "musical rhetoric," meaning in this case not the art of oratory itself, nor education in it, but the application of rhetorical figures (*colores rhetorici*) to the musical texture. Historians conventionally date this phenomenon no earlier than ca. 1500, and musicological attempts to interpret compositions by Du Fay or Ciconia, for example, as rhetorically composed seem to lack explicit support in sources of the time.[47] But already in the

44 A comprehensive study is Dietl, *Die Dramen Jacob Lochers*.     45 Stipčević, "Glazba u Nigerovoj."
46 Strohm, *The Rise of European Music*, 538–39.
47 Elders, "Guillaume Dufay" and "Humanism and Early-Renaissance Music."

fourteenth century musicians may have imitated such literary artifice in their settings: Philippe de Vitry might have been one of them. Eustace Deschamps (ca. 1390) pairs music with poetry, calling them "musique artificielle" and "musique naturelle," respectively;[48] poetry was, in turn, the "seconde rhétorique" of the French tradition. There is some further evidence. In his inaugural oration of 1456 (for Paris?) mentioned above, Tiphernas discusses affinities between music and poetry, adding that – "although it may seem strange" – certain *colores* of music are comparable to *colores rhetorici*, "for example those of *repeticio* and *frequentatio*" (repetition, recapitulation of main points) "and several others."[49] A *color rhetoricus* in music is also mentioned in the eclectic treatise of the German scholar Gobelinus Person (1417), referring to emphatic deviations from harmony or mode that are allowable when considering the author's particular intention.[50] The tradition of such expressive figures was to last for centuries. Tiphernas's example of repetition and recapitulation as "rhetorical colors" seems also to connect with the older term "color" for melodic repetition in the motet: a humanist interpretation of a musical tradition?

Second, humanist influence encouraged musicians to set a greater variety of Latin poetic forms. Many of these were of classical origin: *encomium* (praise), *laus urbium* (praise of cities), *epithalamium* (wedding poem), *satira* (satire), *oda* (ode, chorus), *epitaphium* (tomb inscription), *naenia* (lament on the death), *elegy* (mourning song), and *ecloga* (bucolic or rustic song). Some of these had medieval forerunners, especially the large family of praise-poems in panegyric and epideictic styles. Petrarch wrote a Latin praise-poem to Italy, "Salve cara deo tellus," which was set to music in the 1430s. The *laus urbium*, "praise of cities," can be specifically anchored in Leonardo Bruni's *Laudatio* of Florence (ca. 1406), which followed classical models. Johannes Ciconia and other musicians in Italy had already set such texts since ca. 1406; Du Fay followed with his motets in praise of the cities of Florence and Bern. The latter (1438) marks a northern engagement with this species, which was to become the Renaissance *Staatsmotette*.[51] The *epithalamia* of the Innsbruck court in 1484 (we do not have musical settings for them) were inspired by Italian models. One of the latter might be *Perfunde celi rore* for Ferrara, ca. 1473, perhaps by Johannes Martini, who had some connection with the Innsbruck court. A *satira* set to music is quite possibly Du Fay's strange motet *Iuvenis qui puellam*, which arguably

48 As pointed out, for example, in Haar, "Humanism."
49 "Addamus etiam hoc, quod fortasse mirum videatur, colores in musica inveniri rhetoricis coloribus similes ut repetitionem, frequentationem et alios complures." *Gregorii Tiphernii de studiis litterarum oratio*, in *Reden und Briefe*, ed. Müllner, 190. Further details in Strohm, "Neue Aspekte."
50 Reckow, "Zwischen Ontologie und Rhetorik," 158.     51 Strohm, *Guillaume Du Fay*, 13–15.

mocks in parodistic legal language the relationship between Pope Eugene IV and the Council of Basel.[52] A four-voice setting of an ode by Horace (*Tu ne quaesieris*) is found in Trent 89, ca. 1466.[53] The musical realization of quantitative rhythms in the "humanist ode" was the next step, as shown above (see Example 14.1). Several settings of funeral laments (*déplorations, naeniae*) exist outside Italy, and Jacob Obrecht's "motet" on the death of his father (*Mille quingentis*, 1488) is an *epitaphium*. Isaac's motet (*naenia*) on the death of Lorenzo de' Medici (1492), *Quis dabit capiti meo aquam*, on a text by Angelo Poliziano, is paralleled by his setting of the mournful choral ode (or elegy) "Quis dabit pacem populo timenti" from Seneca's tragedy *Hercules Oetaeus*: the latter may be related to northern school drama performances. Humanists were fond of eclogues; Martin Le Franc was a specialized poet and teacher of this genre.[54] The subjects of such poems combined those of Virgil's *Georgica* and *Bucolica* (*Eclogae*): they were generally "pastoral," to use a later term. The performances of Latin poetry by Italian *improvvisatori* probably fall in this category. A conspicuous northern contribution was, I suggest, the vernacular poetry of *chansons rustiques*, polyphonic songs often based on popular ditties. To put it the other way around, the fashion of pastoral chansons in various vernaculars was imitated in humanist neo-Latin poems that would then qualify as *eclogae*: a typical case of a humanist connection with extant musical traditions.

Finally, northern humanism developed the modern understanding of composed music as a "completed and independent work" (*opus perfectum et absolutum*, in Nicolaus Listenius's phrase, 1537), whether by first applying the term "opus" to music, as seen in the manuscripts of Nicolaus of Radom, or by explicitly comparing musical composition with classical works of literature, as did Martin Le Franc, ca. 1439–42, followed by Tinctoris in his *Complexus effectuum musice*, ca. 1475.[55] The ideas of work character, authorship, transmission, and imitation are Ciceronian and, by osmosis, Italian; their emphatic application to music in the fifteenth century has co-determined the way we think of music today. That this "humanist legend" has also led us to belittle the performative, oral, and ephemeral aspects of music-making is a complaint often heard today. What may be said in its defense is that a good many of the musical compositions cherished today would not even exist without the challenge of the humanist work concept. This may already be true for the motets and masses of a Du Fay or an Ockeghem.

---

52 Ibid., 27.    53 Staehelin, "Trienter Codices und Humanismus."
54 Strohm, "Music, Humanism," 374.
55 Ibid., 397–98. See also Laurenz Lütteken, "The work concept," in this volume (Ch. 3).

# Bibliography

Agricola, Rudolph, *De inventione dialectica, cum scholiis Joannis Matthaei Phrissemii*, Paris, 1539
  *Letters*, ed. Andrie van der Laan and Fokke Akkerman, Tempe, AZ, 2002
Arnould, A. "New Manuscripts Related to Johannes de Veris," *Humanistica Lovanensia* 38 (1989), 318–20
Awianowicz, Bartosz, "The Graeco-Latin Vocabulary of Petrus Wilhelmi de Grudencz," in *The Musical Heritage of the Jagiellonian Era*, ed. Paweł Gancarczyk and Agnieszka Leszczyńska, Warsaw, 2012, 201–6
Bent, Margaret, "Dunstaple, John," in *Grove Music Online* (accessed 11 March 2013)
Blackburn, Bonnie J. "Music Theory and Musical Thinking after 1450," in *Music as Concept*, ed. Strohm and Blackburn, 301–45
Dietl, Cora, *Die Dramen Jacob Lochers und die frühe Humanistenbühne im süddeutschen Raum*, Berlin and New York, 2005
Dresden, Sem, "The Profile of the Reception of the Italian Renaissance in France," in *Itinerarium Italicum*, ed. Oberman and Brady, 119–89
Dunning, Albert, "Erasmus, Desiderius," in *Grove Music Online* (accessed 11 March 2013)
Elders, Willem, "Guillaume Dufay as Musical Orator," *TVNM* 31 (1981), 1–15
  "Humanism and Early-Renaissance Music: A Study of the Ceremonial Music by Ciconia and Dufay," *TVNM* 27 (1977), 65–101
Fallows, David, *Dufay*, London, 1982
Giger, Andreas, "Ludovicus Sanctus (Ludwig van Kempen)," in *Grove Music Online* (accessed 11 March 2013)
Haar, James, "Humanism," in *Grove Music Online* (accessed 10 March 2013)
Haggh, Barbara, "The Celebration of the 'Recollectio Festorum Beatae Mariae Virginis,' 1457–1987," in *Trasmissione e recezione delle forme di cultura musicale. Atti del XIV congresso della Società Internazionale di Musicologia, Bologna 1987*, ed. Angelo Pompilio *et al.*, Turin, 1990, 3:559–71
Harrán, Don, *In Defense of Music: The Case for Music as Argued by a Singer and Scholar of the Late Fifteenth Century*, Lincoln, NE and London, 1989
Hay, Denys, "England and the Humanities in the Fifteenth Century," in *Itinerarium Italicum*, ed. Oberman and Brady, 305–67
Ijsewijn, Jozef, "The Coming of Humanism to the Low Countries," in *Itinerarium Italicum*, ed. Oberman and Brady, 193–301
Irwin, Joyce L. "The Mystical Music of Jean Gerson," *EMH* 1 (1981), 187–201
Kirkwood, Gayle C., "Kings, Confessors, Cantors and Archipellano: Ockeghem and the Gerson Circle at St-Martin of Tours," in *Johannes Ockeghem*, ed. Vendrix, 101–37
Kirnbauer, Martin, *Hartmann Schedel und sein "Liederbuch": Studien zu einer spätmittelalterlichen Musikhandschrift (Bayerische Staatsbibliothek München, Cgm 810) und ihrem Kontext*, Bern, 2001
Kooiman, P., "The Letters of Rodolphus Agricola to Jacobus Barbirianus," in *Rodolphus Agricola Phrisius 1444–1485*, ed. F. Akkerman and A. J. Vanderjagt, Leiden, 1988, 136–46

Lhotsky, Alphons, ed., *Die Wiener Artistenfakultät 1365–1497: Festgabe der Österreichischen Akademie der Wissenschaften zur 600-Jahrfeier der Universität Wien*, Vienna, 1965

Lockwood, Lewis, "Agricola, Rudolph," in *Grove Music Online* (accessed 11 March 2013)
  *Music in Renaissance Ferrara, 1400–1505: The Creation of a Musical Center in the Fifteenth Century*, Cambridge, MA, 1984

Meersseman, Gilles G., O.P., "L'Épistolaire de Jean van den Veren et le début de l'humanisme en Flandre," *Humanistica Lovanensia* 19 (1970), 119–200

Mengozzi, Stefano, *The Renaissance Reform of Medieval Music Theory: Guido of Arezzo between Myth and History*, Cambridge, 2010

Müllner, Karl, ed., *Reden und Briefe italienischer Humanisten*, Vienna, 1899; new edn. by Barbara Gerl, Munich, 1970

Oberman, Heiko Augustinus, "Quoscunque tulit foecunda vetustas," in *Itinerarium Italicum*, ed. Oberman and Brady, ix–xxviii
  and Thomas A. Brady, Jr., eds., *Itinerarium Italicum: The Profile of the Italian Renaissance in the Mirror of its European Transformations, Dedicated to Paul Oskar Kristeller on the Occasion of his 70th Birthday*, Leiden, 1975

Ouy, Gilbert, "Les Premiers Humanistes français et l'Europe," in *La Conscience européenne au XVe et au XVIe siècles, actes du colloque international*, Paris, 1982, 280–95

Palisca, Claude V., *Humanism in Italian Renaissance Musical Thought*, New Haven and London, 1985

Panofsky, Erwin, *Renaissance and Renascences in Western Art*, Stockholm, 1960

Perz, Miroslaw, "Il carattere internazionale delle opere di Mikołaj Radomski," *MD* 41 (1987), 153–59

Reckow, Fritz, "Zwischen Ontologie und Rhetorik: Die Idee des *movere animos* und der Übergang vom Spätmittelalter zur frühen Neuzeit in der Musikgeschichte," in *Traditionswandel und Traditionsverhalten*, ed. Walter Haug and Burghart Wachinger, Tübingen, 1991, 145–78

Sachs, Klaus-Jürgen, "'… nec in processu cum antiquis concordaverim': Zur Musiktheorie des 15. Jahrhunderts in Deutschland," *Die Musikforschung* 62 (2009), 213–26
  "Zu den Fassungen der Musikschrift des Mattheus Herbenus (um 1495)," *Die Musikforschung* 55 (2002), 395–405

Sandmeier, Rebekka, *Geistliche Vokalpolyphonie und Frühhumanismus in England: Kulturtransfer im 15. Jahrhundert am Beispiel des Komponisten John Dunstaple*, Göttingen, 2012

Simone, Franco, *Il rinascimento francese: Studi e ricerche*, Turin, 1961

Spitz, Lewis W., "The Course of German Humanism," in *Itinerarium Italicum*, ed. Oberman and Brady, 371–436

Staehelin, Martin, "Trienter Codices und Humanismus," in *I codici musicali trentini a cento anni dalla loro riscoperta*, ed. Nino Pirrotta and Danilo Curti, Trent, 1986, 158–69

Stevenson, Robert, *Spanish Music in the Age of Columbus*, The Hague, 1960

Stipčević, Ennio, "Glazba u Nigerovoj *Grammatica* brevis (1480)," in his *Glazba, tekst, kontekst*, Zagreb, 2006, 21–40

Strohm, Reinhard, "Enea Silvio Piccolomini and Music," in *Uno gentile et subtile ingenio: Studies in Renaissance Music in Honour of Bonnie J. Blackburn*, ed. M. Jennifer Bloxam, Gioia Filocamo, and Leofranc Holford-Strevens, Turnhout, 2009, 719–27

*Guillaume Du Fay, Martin Le Franc und die humanistische Legende der Musik*, 192. Neujahrsblatt der Allgemeinen Musikgesellschaft Zürich auf das Jahr 2008, Winterthur, 2007

"Hic miros cecinit cantus, nova scripta reliquit," in *Johannes Ockeghem*, ed. Vendrix, 139–65

"Music, Humanism, and the Idea of a 'Rebirth' of the Arts," in *Music as Concept and Practice*, ed. Strohm and Blackburn, 346–405

*Music in Late Medieval Bruges*, Oxford, 1985; rev. edn., 1990

"Neue Aspekte von Musik und Humanismus im 15. Jahrhundert," *AcM* 76 (2004), 135–57

"'Opus': An Aspect of the Early History of the Musical Work-Concept," in *Complexus effectuum musicologiae: Studia Miroslao Perz septuagenario dedicate*, ed. Tomasz Jeż, Kraków, 2003, 309–19; rev. in *Musik des Mittelalters und der Renaissance: Festschrift für Klaus-Jürgen Sachs zum 80. Geburtstag*, ed. R. Kleinertz *et al.*, Hildesheim, 2010, 205–17

*The Rise of European Music, 1380–1500*, Cambridge, 1993

and Bonnie J. Blackburn, eds., *Music as Concept and Practice in the Late Middle Ages*, New Oxford History of Music, 3/1, new edn., Oxford, 2001

and J. D. Cullington, eds. and trans., *Egidius Carlerius, Johannes Tinctoris: On the Dignity and the Effects of Music: Two Fifteenth-Century Treatises*, London, 1996; expanded as *"That liberal and virtuous art"*: *Three Humanist Treatises on Music*, Newtownabbey, 2001

Sycamber de Venray, Rutgerus, *Dialogus de musica*, ed. Fritz Soddemann, Beiträge zur rheinischen Musikgeschichte, 54, Cologne, 1963

Vendrix, Philippe, ed., *Johannes Ockeghem: Actes du XL$^e$ Colloque international d'études humanistes, Tours. 3–8 février 1997*, Paris, 1998

Wathey, Andrew, "The Motets of Philippe de Vitry and the Fourteenth-Century Renaissance," *EMH* 12 (1993), 119–50

Woodley, Ronald, "Renaissance Music Theory as Literature: On Reading the *Proportionale musices* of Iohannes Tinctoris," *Renaissance Studies* 1 (1987), 209–20

"Tinctoris, Johannes," in *Grove Music Online* (accessed 10 March 2013)

# Poetic humanism and music in the fifteenth century

LEOFRANC HOLFORD-STREVENS

This chapter examines the effect of humanism on the Latin poetry set by fifteenth-century composers, primarily from the formal point of view. At the beginning of the century, there were three forms that Latin poems might take:[1]

(i) *Metra* (singular *metrum*), in the quantitative meters of classical verse (though not necessarily handled in the classical manner), which were regulated by syllabic length: a syllable was long (–) if it contained a long vowel,[2] or if (with some exceptions), although the vowel was short, there were at least two consonants after it; otherwise it was short (∪), except that the last syllable of a verse was always treated as long. In such verses a final vowel, or a final vowel followed by *m*, was elided before an initial vowel or *h*; composers, however, set the elided syllable like any other other. Rhyme was used only by poets who did not aspire to the classical style. Quantitative poetry exhibits a great number of *metra*, each given its own name by ancient or modern scholars.

(ii) *Rhythmi* (singular *rhythmus*, in the Middle Ages often spelled *ritimus*), always rhymed,[3] in which final -*m* was treated as a full consonant and the sequence of final and initial vowel, when not avoided, yielded a hiatus; the few elisions found are nearly always of same before same. There were two kinds:

  (*a*) Accentual, requiring word-stress in particular positions but taking no account of quantity. Some such *rhythmi* were related to classical *metra*, either by substitution of stress for length, or by retention of the characteristic stress-patterns that resulted from the quantitative structure.

  (*b*) Syllabic, ignoring both quantity and accent. Such verses were particularly congenial to speakers of French, who had given up attempting to reproduce the Latin accent as (for example) Italians did and simply, as

---

1 See for more detail Holford-Strevens, "Latin Poetry and Music."
2 Classically also a diphthong, but at this date all diphthongs had been reduced to simple vowels in speech and nearly always in writing; in what follows "vowel" includes classical diphthongs.
3 The rhymes may extend over one, two, or three syllables.

in their own language, emphasized the last syllable not of words but of phrases.

All these forms are to be found in texts set to music, whether written by the composers themselves or by others. Johannes Ciconia's oeuvre includes several motets on texts that speak in his name, of which none is in quantitative meter; of the rest, two are indeed *metra*, but both display a high degree of amateurishness.[4] Guillaume Du Fay's Latin motets have texts of varied styles and merit; the only one that speaks in his name is in elegiac couplets, and the quantitative poems likeliest to be his own work are by no means the worst.[5] In the course of the century, the expectation of quantitative meter grew stronger; it was attempted, with less than total success, by Johannes Regis,[6] and also by Jacob Obrecht.[7] More impressive is Johannes Ockeghem's *Intemerata Dei mater*,[8] which matches the best contemporary standards in versification and diction, even if its tone is that of a man expressing his feelings rather than demonstrating his skill.

Nevertheless, the triumph of quantity was not complete when Josquin des Prez, before the end of the century, composed his motet *Illibata Dei virgo nutrix*, of which both parts are syllabic *rhythmi*.[9] The *prima pars*, which he signs with an acrostic, is in decasyllables on the French pattern, with a caesura after the fourth syllable:[10]

| | |
|---|---|
| Illibata Dei virgo nutrix | Unsullied maiden, nurse of God, |
| Olympi tu regis o genitrix, | O thou mother of the king of Olympus [heaven], |
| Sola parens Verbi puerpera, | only parent-bearer of the Word, |
| Que fuisti Eve reparatrix, | who wast she that made good Eve's [harm], |
| Viri nephas tuta mediatrix – | sure mediatrix of the man's [Adam's] sin – |
| Illud clara luce dat scriptura – | Scripture presents that in a clear light – |
| Nata nati alma genitura, | daughter of thy Son by a life-giving engenderment, |
| Des ut leta Musarum factura | grant that the Muses' joyful creation |
| Prevaleat ymis,[11] et süave[12] | may prevail over the nether world, and that, sweetly |
| Roborando sonos ut guttura | strengthening their sounds, our throats |
| Efflagitent laude teque, pura, | may pray with praise, and on thee, pure one,[13] |
| Zelotica arte clament: Ave. | with zealous art call: Hail. |

4 Holford-Strevens, "The Latin Poetry of Johannes Ciconia and 'Guilhermus'."
5 Holford-Strevens, "Du Fay the Poet?," 107–16.
6 Holford-Strevens, "The Latin Texts of Regis's Motets."
7 Holford-Strevens, "The Latinity of Jacob Obrecht."
8 See Dean, "Okeghem's Valediction?"; cf. Winkler, "Zur Vertonung von Mariendichtung."
9 *De beata Maria virgine* 2, in *Motets on Non-Biblical Texts*, ed. Elders, no. 24.3.
10 Most French verse of the period is in lines of either eight syllables (*octosyllabes*) or ten (*décasyllabes*); in the latter the fourth syllable is regularly followed by a word-break, known as a caesura, though there may be a more important break after the sixth.
11 A common medieval spelling of *imis*.
12 In medieval Latin *suavis* generally has three syllables; classically it has only two.
13 *Pura* fits better as vocative, addressed to the Virgin, than as ablative, qualifying the singers' art.

The *secunda pars* is more complex; as laid out as in the New Josquin Edition,[14] which despite controversy seems to be the correct arrangement, it comprises six pentasyllables (lines of five syllables) followed by four hendecasyllables (lines of 11 syllables), divided respectively 4 + 7,[15] 5 + 6, 5 + 6, and 6 + 5, after which come another eight pentasyllables before the final extra-schematic *Amen*.

| | |
|---|---|
| Ave, virginum | Hail, virgins' |
| decus, hominum | glory, and human beings' |
| celique porta, | gate of heaven, |
| ave lilium, | hail, lily, |
| flos humilium, | flower of the humble, |
| virgo decora. | beauteous maiden. |
| | |
| Vale ergo, tota pulchra ut luna, | Be well therefore, all fair as the moon, |
| electa ut sol, clarissima, gaude. | elect as the sun,[16] most illustrious one, rejoice. |
| Salve tu sola, consola, amica, | Hail thou, our only love, console |
| "la mi la" canentes in tua laude. | those that sing *la mi la* in thy praise. |
| | |
| Ave Maria, | Hail Mary, |
| mater virtutum, | mother of virtues, |
| venie vena. | vein of mercy. |
| Ave Maria, | Hail Mary, |
| gratia plena, | full of grace, |
| Dominus tecum, | the Lord is with thee. |
| Ave Maria, | Hail Mary, |
| mater virtutum. | mother of virtues. |
| | |
| Amen. | Amen. |

The devotional pentasyllables are unremarkable, save for the postponed *-que* in *hominum celique porta*,[17] a device known from classical poetry; but the middle section, which clearly refers to the *La mi la* soggetto extracted from the vowels of *Maria*,[18] can hardly be anyone's work but the composer's.

If new *rhythmi* were thus still being written, it is no surprise that existing ones did not cease to be set; Josquin incorporated the widespread "Ave cuius conceptio" in his motet *Ave Maria ... virgo serena*.[19] The text consists of

14 Critical Commentary, 32–33; so too Fallows, *Josquin*, 52–53.
15 Music and syntax discourage 6 + 5 with caesura after *tota*.
16 Song of Songs 6:9 (Vulgate numeration).
17 "Gate of human beings and of heaven" would be far less natural an expression.
18 Sung throughout by the tenor, but at this point (mm. 131–35) also by all other voices except the superius; mostly on D–A–D (*la mi la* in the soft hexachord), though sometimes a fifth lower.
19 *De beata Maria virgine* 1, in *Motets on Non-Biblical Texts*, ed. Elders, no. 23.6. On the text see the Critical Commentary, 91–92.

octosyllables with a fixed stress on the sixth, designated 8pp ("pp" standing for "proparoxytone," accented on the last syllable but two) in couplet-rhymed quatrains, a favourite hymn measure adapted from St. Ambrose's unrhymed iambic dimeters (verses of the form $\cup-\cup-\underset{\cup}{}-\cup-$) by substituting length for quantity.[20] The first stanza runs:

| | |
|---|---|
| Aue cuius conceptio, | Hail, [thou] whose conception, |
| solemni plena gaudio, | full of sober joy, |
| celestia terrestria | fills [all] things heavenly and earthly |
| noua replet letitia. | with new happiness. |

Even the supreme humanist Politian, a scholar centuries in advance of his time and an author who repudiated slavish imitation of the classics, in his two Servite-commissioned hymns to the Virgin of 1491,[21] did not use Ambrosian meter, but blended the ancient and the medieval in 8pp lines that admitted elision and dispensed with rhyme.[22] One was set by Josquin,[23] and also by Robert Wilkinson:[24]

| | |
|---|---|
| O virgo prudentissima, | O most prudent virgin, |
| quam celo missus Gabriel, | whom Gabriel, sent from heaven |
| supremi regis nuntius, | as the supreme King's messenger, |
| plenam testatur gratia, | attests to be full of grace, |
| | |
| cuius devota humilitas, | whose devout humility, |
| gemmis ornata fulgidis | adorned with the gleaming gems |
| fidentis conscientiae, | of trusting conscience, |
| amore Deum rapuit. | seized God with love. |
| | |
| Te sponsam factor omnium, | Thee the maker of all (calls) his bride, |
| te matrem Dei filius, | thee the Son of God his mother, |
| te uocat habitaculum | thee the blessed Spirit |
| suum beatus spiritus. | calls his dwelling-place. |
| | |
| Per te de taetro carcere | Through thee from the foul prison |
| antiqui patres exeunt; | the ancient fathers come out; |

---

20 The symbol $\cup$ denotes a syllable that may be either long or short. (Ambrose sometimes fills these positions with two short syllables, equivalent to a long one; this is not permitted in the *rhythmus*).

21 "O virgo prudentissima" and "Ecce ancilla Domini"; in *Omnia opera Angeli Politiani*, sigs. [ii 4]v*[5]r, [5]r–v; see Del Lungo, *Florentia*, 201–3 (for the date 181), who notes the allusions to the Servite order (*tuos servulos*) and their Basilica della Santissima Annunziata.

22 His only failure to elide is in the first line of "Ecce ancilla Domini," for which he could hardly avoid the church pronunciation; however, he avoids placing final -*m* in an elidable position. The occasional rhymes (as in St. Ambrose) are not structural but accidental.

23 *Motets on Non-Biblical Texts*, no. 24.9; setting discussed and dated ca. 1503 by Brown, "Notes towards a Definition of Personal Style," 190–93.

24 See Williamson, *The Eton Choirbook*, facs. of sig. d8v, discussion p. 57, suggesting that the text may have reached Oxford before it was printed. Incipit only in *The Eton Choirbook* 3, 161.

| | |
|---|---|
| per te nobis astriferae | through thee for us the starry |
| panduntur aulae limina. | court's gates are thrown open. |
| | |
| Tu stellis comam cingeris,[25] | Thy hair is girt with stars, |
| tu lunam premis pedibus, | thou treadest the moon with thy feet, |
| te sole amictam candido | at thee clad in the gleaming sun |
| chori stupent angelici. | the choirs of angels wonder. |
| | |
| Tu stella maris diceris, | Thou art called the star of the sea, |
| quae nobis inter scopulos, | that amidst the rocks, |
| inter obscuros turbines, | amidst the dark whirlwinds, |
| portum salutis indicas. | showest us the haven of salvation. |
| | |
| Audi, virgo puerpera | Hear, virgin that borest a child |
| et sola mater integra, | and only inviolate mother, |
| audi precantes quaesimus | hear thy servants, we beg thee, |
| tuos Maria seruulos. | Mary, as they pray. |
| | |
| Repelle mentis tenebras, | Drive away the darkness of the mind, |
| disrumpe cordis glaciem. | break up the ice of the heart, |
| nos sub tuum praesidium | protect us as we take refuge |
| confugientes protege. | beneath thy ward. |
| | |
| Da nobis in proposito | Grant us perseverance |
| sancto perseverantiam | in our holy purpose, |
| ne noster adversarius | lest our Adversary |
| in te sperantes superet. | overcome those that hope in thee. |
| | |
| Sed et cunctis fidelibus | But even to all the faithful |
| qui tuum templum visitant, | that visit thy temple, |
| benigna mater, dexteram | kindly mother, proffer the (right) hand |
| da caelestis auxilii. | of heavenly assistance. |
| | |
| Amen. | Amen. |

Out of these ten stanzas, Josquin's *prima pars* sets the first, third, sixth, and fourth (in that order), the *secunda pars* the seventh and eighth; of Wilkinson's setting only the beginning survives, comprising the first four.

It was also Politian who wrote the lament for Lorenzo il Magnifico set by Henricus Isaac,[26] in unprecedentedly free verse with a da capo structure:

---

25  Literally: "thou are girt as to the hair with stars," a Greek-derived construction typical of classical Latin poetry.

26  *Opera omnia*, sig. [ii 6]r–v (headed "Intonata per Arrighum Isac"), [κκ 10]r (headed "Monodia in Laurentium Medicem"); no textual independence is shown by the transcript in MS Trieste, Biblioteca Civica A. Hortis, RP 2–53, fol. 74r. Music ed. Wolf in DTÖ 14, 1:45–8; see Picker, *Henricus Isaac*, 119.

| | |
|---|---|
| Quis dabit capiti meo | Who will give my head |
| aquam, quis oculis meis | water, who will give my eyes |
| fontem lachrymarum dabit, | a fountain of tears, |
| ut nocte fleam, | that I may weep by night, |
| ut luce fleam? | that I may weep by day?                        5 |
| | |
| Sic turtur viduus solet, | Thus the widowed turtledove is wont, |
| sic cygnus moriens solet, | thus the dying swan is wont, |
| sic luscinia conqueri. | thus the nightingale to complain. |
| Heu miser, miser. | Alas, wretched, wretched (am I). |
| O dolor, dolor. | O woe, woe.                                    10 |
| | |
| Laurus impetu fulminis | That, that laurel-tree |
| illa, illa iacet subito, | suddenly lies by the stroke of lightning, |
| laurus omnium celebris | the laurel-tree attended by |
| Musarum choris, | the choirs of all the Muses, |
| nympharum choris, | the choirs of (all) the nymphs,                15 |
| | |
| Sub cuius patula coma | under whose spreading leaves[27] |
| et Phoebi lyra blandius | both Phoebus's lyre sounds more enticingly |
| et vox dulcius insonat. | and his voice more sweetly. |
| Nunc muta omnia, | Now all things are silent, |
| nunc surda omnia. | now all things are deaf.                       20 |
| | |
| Quis dabit capiti meo | Who will give my head |
| aquam, quis oculis meis | water, who will give my eyes |
| fontem lachrymarum dabit, | a fountain of tears, |
| ut nocte fleam, | that I may weep by night, |
| ut luce fleam? | that I may weep by day?                        25 |
| | |
| Sic turtur viduus solet, | Thus the widowed turtledove is wont, |
| sic cygnus moriens solet, | thus the dying swan is wont, |
| sic luscinia conqueri. | thus the nightingale to complain. |
| Heu miser, miser. | Alas, wretched, wretched (am I). |
| O dolor, dolor. | O woe, woe.                                    30 |

This poem consists of six cinquains (five-line stanzas), of which last two are identical with the first two, each comprising three octosyllables (*ill(a) illa* exhibiting elision) and two pentasyllables. The repeated stanzas apart, six of the twelve octosyllables (lines 1, 6, 7, 16, 17, 18) are correct quantitative glyconics, $- \underline{\smile} - \smile \smile - \smile -$, though the first, with the second element short, has parallels in Catullus but only one in Horace; five match the meter in accentual pattern: 2 *áquam, quís óculis méis* corresponds to *pennis non homini*

---

27 Literally "hair," a standard poetic metaphor.

*datis* in Horace, *Odes* 1.3.35; 8 *síc luscínia cónqueri*, 11 *láurus ímpetu*[28] *fúlminis*, and 13 *láurus ómnium célebris* to *audax omnia perpeti* (v. 25 of the same poem); 12 *ílla, ílla iácet súbito* to *nequiquam deus abscidit* (v. 20);[29] only line 3 *fóntem lachrymárum dábit* has an accentual pattern impossible for a classical glyconic unless read with a secondary stress on *la-*, when it can be assimilated to the first line of the ode, *Sic te diva potens Cypri* or to 1.13.11 *rixae sive puer furens*. The pentasyllables in stanzas 1–3 are hypodochmiacs, – ∪ – ∪ – responding to a variety of dochmiac in stanza 4, – – – ∪ – .[30]

The first stanza is derived from Jeremiah 9: 1: *Quis dabit capiti meo aquam et oculis meis fontem lacrimarum? Et plorabo die et nocte interfectos filiae populi mei*, "Who will give water to my head, and to mine eyes a fountain of tears? And I will weep day and night for the slain of the daughter of my people."[31] In the second stanza, however, we are back in classical antiquity; the dying swan and the lamenting nightingale are commonplace, and the turtledove's coo was interpreted as a groan (Theocritus, *Idyll* 7.141; Virgil, *Bucolics* 1.58), but at Ovid, *Amores* 2.6.12–16, a turtledove is bidden to mourn for its best friend, a parrot. In stanza 3 the laurel of course represents Lorenzo, but the image is all the more shocking because the laurel was supposed in antiquity to be proof against lightning; for that very reason the emperor Tiberius, who was abnormally frightened of thunderstorms, always wore a laurel wreath when dark clouds appeared (Suetonius, *Tiberius* 69). In stanza 4, the association of both laurel and lyre with Phoebus Apollo needs no comment; the reference to spreading leaves suggests Lorenzo's protection of artists, but the adjective *patula* also recalls Virgil's *Bucolics*, eclogue 1, lines 1–2:

> Tityre, tu recubans patulae sub tegmine fagi
> siluestrem tenui Musam meditaris auena.

> Tityrus, you, lying back under the cover of the spreading beech,
> practice the woodland Muse on your slender oat-pipe.

However, the opening *Quis dabit* recalls another text, also set by Isaac on the same occasion,[32] taken from the ancient tragedy *Hercules Oetaeus*, then thought

---

28  Eduard Fraenkel, in *Renaissance Latin Verse*, ed. Perosa and Sparrow, 140, suggested substituting the poetic ablative *impete*, which would correct the meter; however, other verses remain incurable.
29  Or, with the chief stress on the first *illa*, to *non, si me satis audias* (*Odes* 1.13.13)
30  Paoli, "La trenodia del Polizano," 165–76, scans the entire poem quantitatively, matching every line with a meter found in Greek tragic choruses, but the whole does not make a plausible tragic ode.
31  So the Douay version of 1610 (spelling modernized), faithfully rendering the Latin text; the sense of the original (8:23 in Hebrew Bibles) is better given by the King James version, "Oh that my head were waters, and mine eyes a fountain of tears, that I might weep …".
32  Ed. Wolf in Isaac, *Weltliche Werke*, 1:49–52; see Picker, *Henricus Isaac*, 119–20. On the two poems see Leuker, *Bausteine eines Mythos*, 435–46, who suggests that *Dive … pacem* is the work of Aurelio Lippo Brandolini.

to be by Seneca (lines 1541–45, 1580–86),[33] in continuous Sapphic hendeca-syllables, $- \cup - - - \cup \cup - \cup - -$:

| | |
|---|---|
| Quis dabit pacem populo timenti | Who shall give peace to a fearful people, |
| si quid irati superi per urbes | if the angry gods bid something (evil) |
| iusserint nasci, iacet omnibus par | be born throughout the cities? He lies, like all others, |
| quem parem tellus genuit Tonanti. | whom the earth bore equal to Jove. |
| Planctus immenas resonet per urbes. | Let grief resound through the measureless cities. |
| Nulla te terris rapiet uetustas; | No old age shalt snatch thee from the earth; |
| tu comes Phoebi comes ibis astris. | thou wilt go to the stars in Phoebus's company. |
| Ante nascetur seges in profundo, | Sooner shall the harvest grow in the deep, |
| vel fretum dulci resonabit unda. | or the sea echo with sweet water, |
| ante discedet[34] glacialis ursae | sooner shall the star of the icy Bear |
| sidus et ponto vetito fruetur, | depart and enjoy the forbidden ocean, |
| quam tuas laudes populi quiescant. | than the nations cease from thy praises. |

This last line is in fact the opening of Isaac's *secunda pars*; it is followed by a new text in a well-known *rhythmus*, the accentual Sapphic, that ignores the quanti-ties of the *metrum* but preserves the regular stress-pattern of accents on the first or second syllable and the fourth, sixth and/or eighth, and tenth.[35] Only the penultimate line would pass quantitative muster; it is followed by a correct adonic, $- \cup \cup - -$.

| | |
|---|---|
| Diue, pax orbis, Medice, qui nostros | Holy Medici, peace of the world, who once |
| casus in terris miseratus olim, | tookest pity on our misfortunes upon earth, |
| maxima Phoebi soboles, ex alto | greatest son of Phoebus, from aloft |
| redde, Laurenti, cita mors ex orbe | restore, Lorenzo, what swift death took with her |
| quam tulit secum, miseri precamur, | from the world – we pray in our misery – |
| undique pacem. | everywhere peace. |

Although the versification is unclassical, there are two classical touches: the participle *miseratus* used for the finite verb *miseratus es*, and the word-order *cita mors ... quam tulit ... pacem* for *pacem quam cita mors tulit*. The suggestion that Lorenzo was a god on earth is barely concealed.

The setting of classical poetry revived a practice known from the tenth to the twelfth centuries, which would be much favored in the sixteenth, especially with passages from the fourth book of the *Aeneid* relating to Dido and

---

33 Scholars had not yet recognized that lines 1580 and 1581 are in reverse order.
34 So many manuscripts of the play; the correct reading is *descendet*, "shall descend."
35 The rules of Latin word-stress impose this pattern on any Sapphic hendecasyllable divided after the fifth syllable; there is a variation of the *metrum* in which the caesura falls after the sixth, but this is rarely found after Horace and is not reflected in the *rhythmus*.

Aeneas.[36] Another specimen is an anonymous motet that takes its text from the metrical portion of Boethius, *De consolatione philosophiae*, book 3, chapter 10, lines 1–6, 15–18, and once more 1–2; it is in an arbitrary mixture of Sapphic hendecasyllables with Phalaecian, $---\cup\cup-\cup-\cup--$.[37]

| | |
|---|---|
| Huc omnes pariter venite capti | Come hither together all that are in thrall, |
| quos fallax ligat improbis catenis | whom the deceitful lust that dwells |
| terrenas habitans libido mentes. | in earthly minds fetters in evil chains. |
| Haec[38] erit vobis requies laboris, | This shall be your rest from toil, |
| hic portus placida manens quiete, | this the harbor that endures in peaceful quiet; |
| hoc patens unum miseris asylum. | this is the one refuge open to the wretched. |
| Splendor quo regitur vigetque caelum | The splendor by which heaven is governed and thrives |
| vitat obscuras animae ruinas. | shuns the gloomy overthrow of the soul. |
| Hanc quisquis poterit notare lucem | Whosoever shall be able to mark this light |
| candidos Phoebi radios negabit. | will deny that Phoebus's rays are bright. |
| Huc omnes pariter venite capti | Come hither all together who are in thrall, |
| quos fallax ligat improbis catenis. | whom the deceiver fetters in evil chains.[39] |

To the Christian reader this poem would recall Matthew 11:28–29 *Venite ad me omnes qui laboratis et onerati estis … et invenietis requiem animabus vestris*, "Come unto me, all ye that labour and are heavy laden … and ye shall find rest for your souls"; it could therefore be accommodated within a volume of sacred compositions between *Gaudeamus omnes in Domino celebrantes* and *O dulcissima pulchra superni regis amica* (in continuous adonics).

Two other manifestations of classicism should be mentioned: the improvising of Latin verses to musical accompaniment, most famously by the brothers Aurelio and Raffaele Brandolini, of whom the former died in 1497, but the latter survived to defend the practice against the charge of indignity;[40] and humanists' demand that music, which had taken little heed of either accent or quantity, should conform to its text, with long and short syllables sung on breves and semibreves respectively, and elisions treated as single syllables. This first appears in Franciscus Niger's *Grammatica brevis* (Venice, 1480), though he fell short of the strictness that some composers would achieve after 1500.[41] Not all approved, as witness a statement made in the sixteenth century by a

---

36 See Ziolkowski, *Nota Bene*; Lowinsky, "Humanism in the Music of the Renaissance," 166–70, 179–92. Castiglione praised Elisabetta Gonzaga's performance of a *Dulces exuviae* setting to the lyre: *Carmina quinque*, 68.
37 Petrucci, *Motetti C*, fol. 30r (cantus); see Dean, "Josquin, Two Contrafacta," who notes places in which the music is at odds with the text, and suggests that the composer was either Josquin or one close to him.
38 Wrongly given in the source as *hic*, "here."
39 The severing of ll. 2 and 3 requires *fallax*, which properly qualifies *libido*, to be treated as a noun.
40 See Brandolini, *On Music and Poetry*. See also James Hankins's contribution to this volume, Ch. 13.
41 See Lowinsky, "Humanism in the Music of the Renaissance," 156–73; other settings are discussed by Holford-Strevens in "Musical Humanism." See also Reinhard Strohm's contribution to this volume, Ch. 14.

man whose heart lay in the fifteenth and who had not received a humanistic education: Giovanni Spataro expressed astonishment that Pietro Aaron (himself no Latinist) should wish to deprive composers of their free will and subject them to "grammatical accents";[42] eventually a moderate practice, which largely respected accentuation but treated quantity with freedom, would prevail.

By the early sixteenth century, humanism had made quantitative meters almost the only acceptable vehicle for Latin poetry, advanced the setting of ancient as well as modern poems, and encouraged the composition of music that at least to some extent respected the meter of the texts. But its work was not yet done; in particular, attempts at reviving ancient musical practice, and subjecting vernacular poetry to classical meter, had to wait some decades more.

Just as the recovery of classical works and even authors did not happen overnight, but took place over many years, so too was the remodeling of Latin literature upon the grammar, style, and form of classical prose and poetry a protracted process. In the fifteenth century we may still find poems, including those set to music, written in medieval *rhythmi*; we find others written in *metra*, not in themselves a new phenomenon but increasing in number and gradually becoming more classical in their diction. We also find hybrid and experimental poems such as are appropriate to an era of flux, when the old order is giving way but has not yet disappeared and the new has not yet taken its final form; anything seems possible.

## Bibliography

Blackburn, Bonnie J., Edward E. Lowinsky, and Clement A. Miller, eds., *A Correspondence of Renaissance Musicians*, Oxford, 1991

Brandolini, Raffaele, *On Music and Poetry (De musica et poetica, 1513)*, trans. Ann E. Moyer and Marc Laureys, Tempe, AZ, 2001

Brown, Howard Mayer, "Notes towards a Definition of Personal Style: Conflicting Attributions and the Six-Part Motets of Josquin and Mouton," in *Proceedings of the International Josquin Symposium Utrecht 1986*, ed. Willem Elders with Frits de Haen, Utrecht, 1991, 185–207

Castiglione, Baldassare, *Carmina quinque illustrium poetarum*, Venice, 1548

Dean, Jeffrey, "Josquin, Two Contrafacta, and the Lost Stanzas of 'Comment peult avoir joye'," in *Essays on Renaissance Music in Honour of David Fallows: Bon jour, bon mois et bonne estrenne*, ed. Fabrice Fitch and Jacobijn Kiel, Woodbridge, 2011, 279–85

---

42 "Et più ancora de vui sono maravegliato, vedendo che voleti tore el libero so arbitrio al musico et farlo subiecto a li accenti gramatici": letter of 27 November 1531, no. 36, §3, in Blackburn *et al.*, eds., *Correspondence of Renaissance Musicians*, 446. "Free will" was a hot topic at the time, Erasmus's *De libero arbitrio* having been answered by Luther's *De servo arbitrio*. "Accents," in ancient usage, included quantities.

"Okeghem's Valediction? The Meaning of *Intemerata Dei mater*," in *Johannes Ockeghem: Actes du XL^e Colloque international d'études humanistes, Tours, 3–8 février 1997*, ed. Philippe Vendrix, Paris, 1998, 521–70

Del Lungo, Isidoro, *Florentia: Uomini e cose del Quattrocento*, Florence, 1897

Erasmus, Desiderius, *De libero arbitrio diatribe sive collatio*, Basel, 1524

Fallows, David, *Josquin*, Turnhout, 2009

Holford-Strevens, Leofranc, "Du Fay the Poet? Problems in the Texts of his Motets," *EMH* 16 (1997), 97–165

"Latin Poetry and Music," in *The Cambridge Companion to Medieval Music*, ed. Mark Everist, Cambridge, 2010, 225–40

"The Latin Poetry of Johannes Ciconia and 'Guilhermus'," in *"Qui musicam in se habet": Essays in Honor of Alejandro Planchart*, ed. and Anna Zayaruznaya, forthcoming

"The Latin Texts of Regis's Motets," in *The Motet around 1500: On the Relationship of Imitation and Text Treatment?*, ed. Thomas Schmidt-Beste, Turnhout, 2012, 157–71

"The Latinity of Jacob Obrecht," *JAF* 2 (2010), 156–66

"Musical Humanism," *EM* 30 (2002), 481–82

Isaac, Heinrich, *Opera omnia*, [Rome], 1974–

*Weltliche Werke*, ed. Johannes Wolf, Denkmäler der Tonkunst in Österreich, 14/1 (28), Vienna, 1907; repr. Graz, 1959

Josquin des Prez, *Motets on Non-Biblical Texts*, NJE 21–24, Utrecht, 2003–9

Leuker, Tobias, *Bausteine eines Mythos: Die Medici in Dichtung und Kunst des 15. Jahrhunderts*, Cologne, 2007

Lowinsky, Edward E., "Humanism in the Music of the Renaissance," in *Music in the Culture of the Renaissance and Other Essays*, ed. Bonnie J. Blackburn, Chicago, 1989, 1:154–218

Luther, Martin, *De servo arbitrio*, Wittemberg, 1525

Paoli, Ugo Enrico, "La trenodia del Poliziano 'In Laurentium Medicum' [*sic*]," *Studi italiani di filologia classica*, N.S. 16 (1939), 166–76

Perosa, Alessandro, and John Sparrow, eds., *Renaissance Latin Verse: An Anthology*, London, 1979

Petrucci, Ottaviano, *Motetti C*, Venice, 1504

Picker, Martin, *Henricus Isaac: A Guide to Research*, New York, 1991

Poliziano, Angelo, *Omnia opera*, ed. Alessandro Sarzio, Venice, 1498

Williamson, Magnus, *The Eton Choirbook: Facsimile and Introductory Study*, Oxford, 2010

Winkler, Heinz-Jürgen, "Zur Vertonung von Mariendichtung in antiken Versmaßen bei Johannes Ockeghem und Johannes Regis," in *Johannes Ockeghem: Actes du XL^e Colloque international d'études humanistes, Tours, 3–8 février 1997*, ed. Philippe Vendrix, Paris, 1998, 571–93

Ziolkowski, Jan M., *Nota Bene: Reading Classics and Writing Melodies in the Early Middle Ages*, Turnhout, 2007

# Canterino and improvvisatore: oral poetry and performance

BLAKE WILSON

Fifteenth-century Italy witnessed a distinctive chapter in the ancient and global history of oral poetry. Aspects of Renaissance Italian poetic performance are clearly linked with oral practices of all times and places: the conception of poetry as a multivalent and nearly universal form of human discourse, a tendency for poetic voice to culminate in song (often instrumentally accompanied), and the inseparability of oral poetry from the agonistic environment of performance.[1] The interrelated operations of memory and improvisation, too, played essential roles: music was never notated and always improvised, while the poetry was sometimes improvised but may have been conditioned by writing. The capacity of a well-trained memory to engage in both recall and combinatorial invention meant that while "improvisation" of text or music almost always involved some element of composition in performance, it was rarely *ex nihilo*, but involved the refashioning (*rifacimento*) of preexistent materials.

Oral poetry in fifteenth-century Italy thrived in a dynamic environment created largely by the advent of humanism. Broadly speaking, the pervasive figure of the urban *canterino* (or *cantimpanca, cantastorie*), though typically not himself the recipient of a humanist education, nevertheless benefited from an environment strongly shaped by the cultural forces of humanism, which promoted the virtues of an active life of civic engagement, and an attendant focus on oral discourse in the vernacular in conjunction with the newly exalted disciplines of rhetoric and poetry.[2] The *canterino* (and his audiences) also displayed an unprecedented level of literacy, manifested in surviving autograph manuscript collections, the growing sophistication of his borrowed materials, and recourse to vernacular memory treatises.

While the fifteenth-century *canterino* was the successful descendant of the *joculatore* (*histrione, buffone*) who had worked the public spaces and private *palazzi*

---

1 Zumthor, *Oral Poetry: An Introduction.*
2 *Canterino* is the term most often seen in contemporary documents to refer to a broad range of improvising singer/poets who performed in a variety of public and private venues, often with the accompaniment of a lira da braccio; see Haar, *Essays on Italian Poetry and Music*, 76–99.

of Italian cities for several centuries, the humanist improvisers of the late fifteenth-century courts and academies were a more rarified breed: a transformation of the civic type in the direct light of ancient models of *cantare in sulla lira*, exemplified by the mythological figures of Apollo, Amphion, and especially Orpheus. The poetry and practices of both types were strongly shaped by the dynamic cultural forces of late fifteenth-century Italy, including the advent of print culture, the spread of polyphonic practice (and musical literacy), intensification of the debate on language (*questione della lingua*), and the spread of humanism to the courts, academies, and universities throughout the peninsula.

## The civic *canterino*

The natural habitats of the civic *canterino* were the republican city-states of central Italy. The humbler and more marginal ranks of oral poets (*cerretani, ciurmadori, ciarlatani*) had for several centuries traveled widely among Italian courts and cities, often combining verse and prose performance with other activities like juggling, acting, dancing, pulling teeth, and selling remedies (*histrioni, ioculatori, giullari*). By the fifteenth century, evidence in the form of letters, chronicles, surviving poetry, and communal records from cities like Florence, Siena, and Perugia suggests that the most successful *canterini* sustained professional lives by creating and singing poetry in designated public arenas (like Piazza San Martino in Florence), in the homes of wealthy citizens, and as employees of city governments (*araldo*).[3] During the early decades of the century, the blind *canterino* Niccolò cieco d'Arezzo had been commissioned to compose and perform encomiastic (*capitolo*) and didactic (*canzone morale*) verse for two popes, an emperor, the Signoria of Venice, and the priors of Siena and Perugia.[4] The Perugian communal contracts of 1432–33 describe him as *notabilissimus cantarinum et expertissimus in arte*, and as *citerista et cantore rimarum ... ac multiplicium ystoriarum* ("a most remarkable and expert *canterino* ... a lira-player and singer of poems ... and a great many stories") both at the meals of the priors and in public.[5] Magister Francischus Florentinus was expected *cotidie cum sono cantu docens optima exempla antiquorum romanarum et aliorum multorum* ("daily with his singing teach the best examples of the ancient Romans and many others") and his 1483 contract adds that these *cantilenas Romanorum* are to be sung *de inproviso* in Perugia's main piazza. In this context, the role of the *canterino* was not merely to entertain, but to instruct (*docens*) the priors on matters of morality and history and the Perugian public with regard to an

---

3 On the latter, see McGee, *The Ceremonial Musicians*, 69–104.
4 The poetry of Niccolò and other *canterini* is edited in Lanza, *Lirici toscani del Quattrocento*.
5 Rossi, "Memorie di musica civile in Perugia," 133–35.

appropriate civic ethos derived from the best ancient examplars. Without fail, the medium for this was improvisatory singing to the accompaniment of a string instrument variously described as a *citera/quitarra* or *viola*, probably a bowed instrument like the vielle, or an early version of what was soon to become the oral poet's instrument of choice, the lira da braccio.

During the fourteenth century, *canterini* had been active in most northern Italian courts and cities, and their pattern of ad hoc employment and itinerancy continued in the fifteenth century. The court of Ferrara, and to a lesser extent those of Mantua, Milan, and Bologna, showed a preference for the *canterino's* art, whose stock and trade, the *cantare* – a long narrative poem in ottava rima on heroic subjects drawn from ancient and medieval epic traditions – was readily accommodated to the neo-feudal posturing of ruling families like the Este. Blind *canterini* turn up with some frequency during the late fifteenth century. During 1468–78, Giovanni "orbo" da Parma served the Este court, where he performed *cose maravigliose de improviso* ("marvelous improvised things"), and was also described as a *maestro de' soneti*.[6] Francesco cieco da Ferrara (ca. 1460–1506) received payments from the Este to *canta in gesta* ("sing of great deeds"), but also from the courts of Bologna and Mantua, where the composition of his successful chivalric epic *Mambriano* (Ferrara, 1509) was closely followed by Isabella d'Este and Gianfrancesco Gonzaga during the early 1490s.[7]

Beginning with de facto Medici rule in the 1430s, several factors combined to make Florence fertile ground for *canterino* culture: a strong mercantile and political ethos of active public life, a vital tradition of vernacular poetry rooted in the legacy of the *tre corone* (Dante, Petrarch, and Boccaccio), and a thriving culture of civic humanism favorable to the practice of vernacular eloquence. For most of the century the Perugian priors had looked to Tuscany for its *canterini*; the majority of those came from Florence, where by the 1470s the priors were recruiting exclusively, for in that city "there are many qualified men who are expert in this practice."[8]

By 1435 Niccolò had moved to Florence. With the assistance of Michele del Giogante, a local accountant, poet, and impresario for the public performance of vernacular poetry in the city, Niccolò enjoyed commissions of sonnets from private citizens and contacts with the recently repatriated Medici family, quickly becoming a star performer at the primary venue for public perform-ance in the city, Piazza San Martino. A surviving account, transmitted by the

---

6 Ugolini, *I cantari d'argomento classico*, 18–19.
7 Everson, "Francesco Cieco da Ferrara."
8 Rossi, "Memorie di musica civile in Perugia," 141: "Et audientes quod in civitate florentie prout per literas cuiusdem dicte civitatis acceperunt sunt multi et ydonei homines et ad dictum exercitium intelligentes."

Neapolitan humanist Giovanni Pontano in his dialogue *De fortitudine*, captures Niccolò at a moment in the late 1430s when he was performing *sacras historias* in ottava rima for the churchmen who had filled the city after the relocation here of both the papal entourage of Eugene IV and the Council of Florence: "Good lord! What audiences have flocked to hear Niccolò cieco; on feast days, from the bench he sang sacred stories and the histories of ancient things, in Etruscan rhymes [i.e., ottava rima]. Here there were learned men, here a great many Florentines, all running to hear him perform."[9]

The very same performers who galvanized large, mixed audiences at San Martino were also favored in elite domestic settings, particularly those associated with the Medici, who were both patrons and practitioners of the *canterino*'s art. A letter addressed by Michele del Giogante to Piero de' Medici in 1454 recalls a dinner at the house of Lionardo Bartolini to honor Francesco Sforza's accession to the Milanese duchy in 1450, and a performance by a young protégé of Michele named Simone di Grazia for whom Michele sought patronage:

> [This] young boy [is] one of us Florentines, about 16 or 17 years old. And this boy, whom I already put to singing improvisations on the bench at San Martino, of fine intellect and imagination, really gifted by nature with this skill ... you already heard sing in Lionardo Bartolini's house, at a splendid dinner he gave for you, where I brought him, and he sang a few stanzas; you must remember it. I think you were also acquainted with his work when he brought with him a very pleasing little book I made for him, and he had sung a good part of the material written in it at San Martino, including a little work maestro Niccolò cieco performed as a motet at San Martino, which made hundreds of people there weep in sympathy ...[10]

Clearly a young professional like Simone pursued strategies that distinguished him from the *ciurmadori* (*ciarlatani*) who occupied the lower rungs of *canterino* practice: he must cultivate wealthy patrons, possess an aptitude (*fachultà*) for improvisatory singing (*cantare inproviso*) rooted in talent (*ingegnio*) and invention (*fantasia*), and undergo training in order to sing publicly *in panca* at San Martino. This passage also reveals the mixed orality of the practice; Michele had prepared a "little book" (*quadernuccio*) containing material directly related to what Simone sang in San Martino, which might refer either to finished works like the "motet" or, as *cantare inproviso* suggests, collections of material that formed that basis of improvised verse. That Niccolò performed a "little work" (*operetta*) also confirms that short, lyric works like the sonnet, and not only longer *cantari* and *capitoli*, were part of the *canterino*'s repertory.

---

9 *De fortitudine* (Naples, 1490), bk. 2.
10 Flamini, *La lirica toscana*, 600–601, 241–42; Kent, *Cosimo de' Medici and the Florentine Renaissance*, 47–48.

Perhaps the most detailed and candid description of a *canterino* performance was that recorded in 1459 by the young Galeazzo Maria Sforza at a dinner in his honor hosted by Cosimo de' Medici. The performer was Antonio di Guido (1418–86), who had begun his career at San Martino in 1437 and soon became the most famous *canterino* of his time:

> After dinner, I retired to a room with all the other guests. I heard a maestro Antonio sing, accompanying himself on the "citarra" [vielle/lira da braccio]. I think if your Excellency does not know him you must at least have heard him spoken of. He began from the first deeds carried out by your Excellency, and continued until the last ones . . . Not only that, but he went on to commend me, and he narrated everything with such dignity and style that the greatest poet or orator in the world, presented with such a task, would perhaps not have earned such praise for performing it . . .. from now on I will be singing his praises, for indeed, his performance was such that everyone showed their wonder and admiration, and especially those who were most learned: in his use of simile I don't believe even Lucan or Dante ever did anything more beautiful, and he combined so many ancient stories, the names of innumerable ancient Romans, fables, poets, and the names of all the muses . . . I must say that man made a very great impression.[11]

Antonio's performance was calculated not only to flatter the young Milanese duke, but to flaunt the Florence–Milan alliance before the assembled guests, which included the heads of Italy's most powerful ruling families. An equally significant aspect of this account is Antonio's evident capacity to recall and "combine" (*mescolare*) a prodigious array of stories and names, for it reveals that he possessed a well-trained memory.

## The *canterino* and the "arte della memoria"

Michele del Giogante recorded in one of his autograph anthologies "the principle of learning the art of memory, which was revealed to me by Maestro Niccolò cieco of Florence in December, 1435, when he came here."[12] Niccolò's treatise is one of four that can be directly linked to Florentine *canterini*; these were among dozens circulating in the city that had been variously translated or adapted from the ancient Roman rhetorical tradition to feed a growing demand for instruction in public speaking.

The "memorial archive," discussed earlier in this volume by Anna Maria Busse Berger with respect to composition (see Ch. 10), was perhaps even more readily applied to the *canterino*'s practice, since in the classical oratorical tradition

---

11 Ed. in Orvieto, *Pulci medievale*, 181.    12 Kent, "Michele del Giogante's House of Memory," 121.

memory was a strategic preparation for *pronuntiatio*, or performance. The technique transmitted in these treatises thus served something more creative than storage and rote recall; Mary Carruthers has described this memory as "the matrix of reminiscing cogitation, shuffling and collating 'things' stored in a random access memory scheme, or set of schemes, a memory architecture and a library built up during one's lifetime with the express intention that it be used inventively."[13] Niccolò's treatise concludes with a promise that brings to mind Galeazzo's description of Antonio's combinatorial facility with "stories" and "names": "these eight figures of artificial memory constitute every method and manner of being able to remember every name of a man or woman or other animal or other memorable thing … numbers, events, prose, allegories in sermons, the speeches of ambassadors, readings, each and every thing."[14]

There is no reason to assume that the *canterino*'s mnemonic skills with regard to texts did not extend to music as well. Though the long epic poems, like the ninety-four *cantari* (some 3,700 stanzas of ottava rima!) of Cristoforo l'Altissimo's *Il primo libro de' reali* sung at San Martino from June 1514 to July 1515, certainly relied on melodic formulas, even these must have varied during the performance, and at times veered between the poles of recitation and more fully-formed melody.[15] Some idea of the range of music available in the memorial archive of an oral poet is suggested by the Florentine "cantasi come" practice; it was common to copy devotional poetry (laude) with rubrics indicating the song to which the poem might be sung, and the musical sources ranged widely from formulas for rispetti (strambotti) to the polyphonic genres of French chanson, carnival song, and madrigal.[16]

## The humanist *improvvisatore*

Whereas the older vernacular practice of the *canterino* was conducted by professional singer-poets of modest, usually mercantile, origin and education, the new breed of improvisatory singers that emerged during the late fifteenth century typically were well-educated humanists who pursued their singing as they did their humanist scholarship, as an adjunct to such paid professions as notaries, diplomats, orators, and priests. The shift in perspective is illustrated in a letter written by the young Michele Verino, son of the famous humanist Ugolino Verino, while he was studying at the University of Florence. Michele was recalling a performance by the aging Antonio di Guido he had heard in San Martino sometime in the 1480s:

13 Carruthers, *The Book of Memory.*    14 Kent, "Michele del Gigante's House of Memory," 124.
15 Degl'Innocenti, *I "Reali" dell'Altissimo.*    16 Wilson, *Singing Poetry in Renaissance Florence.*

Concerning oratorical delivery, how esteemed is the witness of Demosthenes, to whom is attributed all the power of oratory. Once I heard Antonio singing the wars of Orlando in Piazza San Martino, and he sang with such eloquence that you seemed to be hearing Petrarch himself, and you would have believed yourself to be in the midst of the battle, not merely hearing a description of it. Later I read one of his own poems, so rough that he seemed like another person. Clearly, therefore, such works are best when delivered with eloquence, for this kind of practice benefits greatly from the diligent and judicious use of not only voice, but bodily gesture as well.[17]

Although Michele was clearly transported by Antonio's performance, his disciplined response was filtered through the lens of his *studia humanitatis*, especially his recent studies of Quintilian and Cicero. Antonio's improvised performance of a Carolingian epic in ottava rima (the "wars of Orlando") was for him a model demonstration of oratorical eloquence (in the vernacular, as signaled by his comparison with the exemplary vernacular poet Petrarch), including his appropriate use of *vox et gestus* (voice and gesture). Antonio's written poetry, on the other hand, is here subject to a different set of stylistic criteria, and fails to meet the young humanist's literary standards. Antonio was treated to a similar humanist makeover by Angelo Poliziano, who upon Antonio's death in 1486 eulogized the old *canterino* in a Latin epigram that likened him to Orpheus.

## Solo singing and the *studia humanitatis*

The recasting of solo singing to the lira da braccio as a humanist enterprise unfolded during the second half of the century in multiple centers, but especially where an older *canterino* practice coexisted with the flowering of humanist courts, academies, and universities: Milan, Ferrara, Mantua, Florence, Naples, and, through importation from these centers, Rome. One clear line of influence was through the *studia humanitatis*, as delineated in the pedagogical treatises of humanist scholar-teachers like Pier Paolo Vergerio (d. 1444), Vittorino da Feltre (d. 1446), and Guarino Veronese (d. 1460).[18] Vittorino trained his students to be sensitive to the aural qualities of written texts (especially poetic texts), and to "see ancient literature on the page as the script for an oral performance, one that required a trained memory and enunciation."[19] Singing verse to the accompaniment of a stringed instrument was promoted not only as a way to develop proper diction and an aid in the memorization of texts, but as a form of recreation, one with clear ancient

---

17  Verde, *Lo studio fiorentino*, 3/2:689.
18  Kallendorf, ed., *Humanist Educational Treatises*; Gallo, *Music in the Castle*, ch. 3.
19  Grafton, "The Humanist as Reader," 197.

precedent. As Guarino observed to his student Leonello d'Este in 1434, "what about Homer telling us that after the sweat of battle, [Achilles] took up his cithara and relaxed with song?"[20] Lodovico Carboni, orator of the Este court and teacher of rhetoric at the University of Ferrara, recalled that Guarino had taught all his students to compose Latin verses with musical accompaniment, by which means accompanied song became widely diffused in the university circles of the city. Michele Verino and his fellow students in Florence also embraced the practice; his surviving letters describe pleasant evenings spent among his fellow students singing verses *ad lyram*, or solitary moments of recreation spent singing *ad cytharam carmen extemporale* (extemporized songs to the cithara).[21]

The study of ancient texts fostered by the humanist curriculum led to even more expanded claims for the role of sung lyric poetry. Horace had famously declared that poetry *ad lyram* could guarantee the immortality of its authors and subjects, and Ficino's studies of Platonic and Neoplatonic philosophy led him to claims for the profound psychological and therapeutic benefits of music, especially the "Orphic singing to the lyre" he promoted in his immediate circles. The nearly magical power of music attributed to its exemplary ancient practitioners – principally Apollo, Amphion, Orpheus, Arion, and the biblical figure of David – were usually glossed by humanists as standing for the civilizing effect of rhetorically elevated discourse. It is small wonder, then, that many humanist-educated princes and prelates embraced the practice, both as patrons and, in some cases, as performers. According to the Florentine improviser Raffaele Brandolini, "Pope Pius II took such delight in metrical poetry accompanied by the lyre that he preferred this kind of enjoyment to all others. And not only did he enjoy hearing the lyre, but he was also not reluctant to play it very sweetly on occasion."[22]

## The *improvvisatori* in Medici circles

The particular vitality of humanist *cantare ad lyram* in Florence was nurtured by the sympathetic patronage of the Medici and the city's precocious humanism and widespread engagement with poetry, and it can be measured by the great number of individuals who practiced it (see Table 16.1).[23] Ficino's distinctive casting of this practice within a framework of medicine, theology, and

20 *Epistolario di Guarino*, 2:275; cited in Gallo, *Music in the Castle*, 73.
21 Verde, *Lo studio fiorentino*, 3/2:672–700.
22 Brandolini, *On Music and Poetry*, 19.
23 Table 16.1 is a provisional list of *improvvisatori* whose careers began in the fifteenth century and for whom there is evidence of sustained activity. Other evidence (for example, Vasari's biographies of Bramante, Verrocchio, Sodoma, *et al.*) suggests that improvisatory singing to the lira or lute was a widely cultivated avocation.

Table 16.1 *Provisional list of humanist improvvisatori, ca. 1450–1518*

| | Milan | Mantua | Ferrara | Naples | Rome | Other |
|---|---|---|---|---|---|---|
| I. Florentine | | | | | | |
| *A. Ficino and his correspondents* | | | | | | |
| Marsilio Ficino (1433–99) | | | | | | |
| Sebastiano d'Antonio Foresi (1424–88) | | | | | | |
| Cherubino di Bartolo Quarquagli | | | | | ca. 1469–77 | |
| Antonio d'Agostino da S. Miniato (ca. 1433–?) | | | | | | |
| Girolamo Benivieni (1453–1542) (see below) | | | | | | Pisa, 1479 |
| Baccio Ugolini (d. 1494) (see below) | | | | | | |
| *B. Lorenzo's circle* | | | | | | |
| Lorenzo de' Medici (1449–92) | | | | | | |
| Baccio Ugolini (d. 1494) | | 1459, 1480 | | 1488–93 | 1473 | |
| Girolamo Benivieni (1453–1542) | | | | | | |
| Angelo Poliziano (1454–94) | | 1480 | | | | |
| Il compare della viola [= lo Spagnuolo?] il Cardiere della viola | | | | | | |
| Filippo Lapaccini (ca. 1450–ca. 1512) | | 1482–, 1491–1512 | | | 1474 | |
| Bernardo Bellincioni (1452–92) | 1485 | | | | | |
| Piero di Lorenzo de' Medici (1472–1503) | | | | | | |

| | Milan | Mantua | Ferrara | Naples | Rome | Other |
|---|---|---|---|---|---|---|
| *C. Other Florentine improvisatori* | | | | | | |
| Leonardo da Vinci (1452–1519) | 1482– date unknown | | | | | |
| Jacopo Corsi (d. 1493) | | | | | 1493 | Venice |
| | | | | | | |
| Aurelio Brandolini (1454–97) | | | | 1466–80 | 1480–89, 1497 | Hungary, 1489; Verona |
| Bernardo Accolti, *L'Unico Aretino* (1458–1536) | date unknown | date unknown | | date unknown | 1489, 1494– | Urbino |
| Raffaele Brandolini (1465–1517) | | | | 1466–, 1493 | 1491–93, 1495–1517 | Venice |
| Atalante Migliorotti (1466–1532) | 1482/3 | | | | 1513–17 | Perugia, 1535 |
| Francesco Cei (1471–1505) | | | | | 1501–5 | |
| II. Non-Florentine | | | | | | |
| Pietrobono de Burzellis (ca. 1417–97) | 1456 | 1482–84/6 | 1441– | 1473 | 1471 | Hungary, 1487–ca. 1489 |
| Benedetto Gareth, *Il Cariteo* (ca. 1450–1515) | | | | 1468–1515 | 1501–3 | |
| Pamfilo Sasso (1455–1527) | | 1494–95, 1497 | | | | |
| Serafino Ciminelli "Aquilano" (1466–1500) | 1490, 1495–97 | | | 1478, 1493–94 | 1484, 1491–93, 1499–1500 | Urbino, 1494, 1498–99; Venice; Genoa |
| Andrea Cossa [Coscia] (fl. ca. 1490–1520) | 1491, 1518 | | | ? | | |

Neoplatonic cosmology was set forth as early as 1457.[24] In Ficino's thought, the sense of hearing is a direct channel for the kindling of divine frenzy within the soul, which occurs when the proper music, an "image of divine harmony," awakens within the soul its memory of a celestial harmony in which "our soul took part before it was imprisoned in our bodies." But not any music would do; some strive to "imitate the celestial music by harmony of voice and the sounds of various instruments [vocum numeris variorumque sonis instrumentorum], and these we call superficial and vulgar." Ficino here seems to be referring to some kind of measured music (vocum numeris), perhaps polyphonic song, which he would have had occasion to hear in Florence by this time. But those who "imitate the divine and heavenly harmony with deeper and sounder judgment render a sense of its inner reason and knowledge into verse, feet, and numbers," that is, into poetry intimately wedded to the "solemn music" of solo song accompanied by the lira da braccio.

Thereafter, Ficino's references to orphic singing with the lyre surface often in philosophical letters to his large network of patrons, friends, and students.[25] Ficino's mode is unflinchingly platonizing and can give the impression of a highly rarified activity, as when he describes how "on occasion I have heard our dear Lorenzo de' Medici, moved by divine frenzy, sing similar prayers to the lyre." But Ficino's music-making was also a serious activity rooted in a broadly shared Florentine cultural practice. Among his music-making correspondents and familiares, Antonio da San Miniato had been a canterino in his younger days, and Cherubino Quarquagli, Baccio Ugolini, and Bernardo Accolti were among the most famous improvisatory singers of secular strambotti and sonnets.[26] Ficino's musical soulmate appears to have been Sebastiano Foresi, a notary and accomplished musician who built lyres and played them well, and with whom Ficino spent many happy hours playing and singing.

The musical legacy of Ficino's writings can hardly be overestimated, for he bequeathed to a large, influential circle of humanist scholars an exalted conception and practice of sung poetry as a divine and almost magical aural experience. The many contemporary images of enraptured classical figures playing a lira da braccio, such as Raphael's Apollo in his Parnassus, owe something to this legacy, and Ficino's validation of the philosophical content of the Tuscan poetic tradition directly influenced the work of Angelo Poliziano and

---

24 Ficino, The Letters of Marsilio Ficino, 1:14–20. On Ficino and music, see also James Hankins's contribution to this volume, Ch. 13.
25 For Ficino's catalogus familiarum, in which he groups his friends according to these three categories, see his Opera Omnia, 1:936–37. On the complex matter of just what sort of "academy" these groups constituted at any time, see Hankins, "Humanist Academies."
26 Della Torre, Storia dell'Accademia Platonica, 788–800.

Lorenzo de' Medici, two of the most eloquent and ardent apologists for the exalted status of vernacular poetry.[27] The *improvvisatori* associated with vernacular poetry in Florence overlapped to some extent with Ficino's circle, but they constituted a looser, more worldly group united by the figure of Lorenzo, whose patronage most of them sought at some point.[28]

Lorenzo's documented involvement with *cantare in sulla lira all'improvviso* dates back to 1466, when Giuliano "Catellaccio" identified himself as Lorenzo's teacher on the viola (lira da braccio).[29] Lorenzo was rarely without access to a lira da braccio, especially during his country retreats, and fellow *improvvisatori* were often in his company throughout his life. An otherwise unnamed *compare della viola* was a part of Lorenzo's circles in the 1470s, and was the dedicatee in one redaction of Lorenzo's early *Uccellagione de starne*, a popularizing poem in forty-five stanzas of ottava rima, in effect a short *cantare*. Lorenzo's immersion in the performative *letteratura canterina*, both the longer forms of ottava rima and capitolo in terza rima as well as the shorter lyric forms of the sonnet, *canzone a ballo*, and barzelletta, laid the foundation for the later transformation of vernacular poetry by poets within Lorenzo's circle. Chief among these was Angelo Poliziano, whose vernacular poetry, particularly his *Stanze per la giostra* in ottava rima (1478) and many of his shorter poems (*Rime*), display a stylistic eclecticism in which Tuscan popular language is interwoven with erudite classical allusion, Neoplatonic thought, and a lexicon derived from Petrarch, Dante, and the poets of the *dolce stil novo*. Tuscan poetry, in other words, was transformed by humanist erudition without losing its traditional *cantabilità*.

There is slender evidence that Poliziano was himself a performer (Giovio reports that he died in a fit of passion for a noble youth induced by singing to the cithara), but he certainly knew the practice at first hand. In 1490 he wrote to Lorenzo regarding his patron's eldest son: "I heard our Piero sing *improvviso* the other night, when he came to assail me at home with all of these improvisers," among whom must have been the *il Cardiere della viola* who reportedly sang almost every evening in Piero's home after dinner.[30] Poliziano's most

---

27  Field, *The Origins of the Platonic Academy of Florence*, ch. 9, and more recently, Storey, "The Philosopher, the Poet, and the Fragment," 604–6.

28  Villoresi, "Panoramica sui poeti performativi." A poem by Antonio Cammelli datable to the late 1480s lists what might be construed as a Laurentian brigata of *poeti performativi*: Lorenzo, his son Piero, Poliziano, Girolamo Benivieni, Baccio Ugolini, Filippo Lapaccini, Matteo Franco, and Bernardo Bellincioni; ibid., 16.

29  D'Accone, "Lorenzo the Magnificent and Music," 276–78.

30  Ibid., 279 n. 54. Orvieto's argument that Poliziano was the mysterious "compare della viola" mentioned in documents beginning in the 1470s is not widely accepted; see his "Angelo Poliziano *Compare* della brigata laurenziana." On Poliziano's engagement with music, see Lovato, "Appunti sulle preferenze musicali di Angelo Poliziano."

famous monument to the art of the *improvvisatore* is his pastoral play *Orfeo*, written and performed at the Mantuan court around 1480 and featuring in its title role the most celebrated improvisatory singer of the day, Baccio Ugolini. Baccio was a priest and diplomat who traveled often and widely on behalf of Lorenzo, and his learning and charisma, combined with his consummate skills as a poet, singer, and lira player, made him welcome in courtly circles from Mantua to Naples. No one showed greater regard for Baccio's artistry than Poliziano, who created a role that featured Baccio playing his lyre and singing a classicizing sapphic ode in praise of the Gonzaga court. When a new production of *Orfeo* was attempted a decade later, the singing role was considered sufficiently demanding for the Gonzaga to actively (and unsuccessfully) recruit Atalante Migliorotti, a great Florentine *improvvisatore* of the next generation whom none other than Leonardo da Vinci had reportedly trained in the art.

## The *improvvisatori* in the Italian courts

As the information in Table 16.1 suggests, the activities of *improvvisatori* became increasingly peripatetic during the last third of the century. Florentines continued to outnumber singer-poets from other parts of Italy, but with the decline of Florence after the Medici expulsion in 1494, their careers, along with those of some extraordinary non-Florentines, shifted towards the new centers of humanist scholarship, the courts. Their skills as poets and performers made them natural participants in the vital literary cultures of the court-sponsored academies and gatherings (Bernardo Accolti and Benedetto Gareth, for example, were cast as interlocutors in Castiglione's *Il cortegiano* and Pontano's *Aegidius*, respectively), and their literary orientation often reflected the particular brands of humanism practiced at a given court.

### Ferrara

At Ferrara, the enduring ambition of the Este family to portray itself as descendants of French nobility nurtured a fascination with chivalric epic that culminated in the great epic poems of Boiardo (*Orlando innamorato*, 1483) and Ariosto (*Orlando furioso*, 1516). These were cast in the ottava rima that had long been a staple of *canterini*, and while there is naturally more evidence for the polyphonic settings of Ariosto after 1516, both poems were sung by *improvvisatori* at court and in the piazza.[31]

---

31 Haar, "Arie per cantar stanze ariosteche," 33–34; Salzberg, "In the Mouths of Charlatans," esp. 646–50.

## Naples

Thanks to the enlightened patronage of the Aragonese kings, Naples supported one of the most fertile humanist environments on the peninsula until its political collapse in the 1490s. The leading Neapolitan humanist, Giovanni Pontano (1429–1503), fostered in its court, university, and academic circles a particularly enthusiastic cultivation of Latin and vernacular poetry that attracted many of the leading *improvvisatori* of the day. The two Brandolini brothers, Aurelio and Raffaele, were born in Florence but reared and educated in Naples; they became famous *improvvisatori* as well as reputable humanist scholars. The court was strongly influenced by Florentine literary models, but particularly in the realm of vernacular poetry rejected Florentine eclecticism in favor of the emerging *petrarchismo* eventually to be codified in Pietro Bembo's *Prose della volgar lingua* (1525). The central figure of the Neapolitan court in this regard was Benedetto Gareth (Il Cariteo), a Catalan-born poet-singer who spent his entire career in service to the Aragonese kings.[32] He famously sang Virgil's poems at the request of Ferdinand II (ca. 1495–96), and his Petrarchan verse and manner of performing it were a significant influence, notably upon another Neapolitan, Andrea Coscia (or Cossa), who in turn exercised a decisive influence upon the most famous exponent of sung Petrarchan verse, Serafino Aquilano.

## Rome

Since at least the 1480s, *improvvisatori* had been drawn to the rich patronage environment of the Roman Curia, and after the French invasion of Italy in 1494, the intellectual center of humanism shifted decisively from Florence and Naples to Rome. Both Brandolini brothers left Naples for Rome, Aurelio in 1480, Raffaele in 1495, and entered successfully into the Latinate literary circles of the city's many curial institutions and households. The classicizing Latinity of the Roman environment is reflected in Raffaele Brandolini's treatise *De musica et poetica*, dedicated to Leo X in 1513, but drafted much earlier at the same patron's request when he was Cardinal Giovanni de' Medici. Brandolini mounted an elaborate defense of improvisatory performance of Latin verse as an essential humanist activity. It is from his account of his older brother Aurelio's career as a performer that we learn the most about the elite character and context of the practice he was advocating:

---

32 Kennedy, *The Site of Petrarchism*, 54–73.

He sang so often, so familiarly, and in so many different ways in the presence of the Pope himself [Sixtus IV, 1471–84], that every day in his private study he would expound in varied song the merits of the pontiffs at some times, serious questions of philosophy at others, or often sacred histories. He recited at many renowned banquets of both cardinals and bishops, and the most honorable assemblies of very learned men.[33]

In his treatise, Brandolini focused on the banquet as a primary venue for poetic performance in order to address what he perceived as an insufficiently revived aspect of ancient cultural life, the private social setting of the *symposium*, or *convivium*.[34] In fact, elaborate banquets had for some time been the occasion for the extempore singing of Latin verse, but the practice became especially fashionable in Leonine Rome.[35]

Vernacular verse was hardly ignored in Roman circles, however. The academy maintained by Paolo Cortesi (1465–1510) from the early 1490s until 1503 sponsored discussions and performances of vernacular poetry, in which the singer-lutenist Serafino Ciminelli Aquilano was a central figure. In Cortesi's *De cardinalatu libri tres* (1510), a guide to how cardinals should conduct themselves as "senators" of the church, he mentions *cantare ad lyram* among the kinds of music appropriate for performance after meals, and singles out a group of singers for special praise: Cariteo for his performances of Virgil in Naples, Serafino for the "controlled conjunction of word and song" in his strambotti, and three Florentines – Baccio Ugolini, Jacopo Corsi, and Bernardo Accolti – who had given him particular pleasure through their "singing *ex tempore* on the lyre in the vernacular tongue."[36]

Serafino figured prominently in the writings of two other academy members. Vincenzo Calmeta (1460–1508) was the singer's close friend and first biographer, and Angelo Colocci (1484–1549) saw Serafino's poetry into print in 1503 prefaced with an *Apologia delle rime di Serafino Aquilano*.[37]

---

33 Brandolini, *On Music and Poetry*, 111. On Aurelio, see Gallo, *Music in the Castle*, 74–97. Brandolini was familiar with a wide circle of improvisatory singer/poets, among whom he names Baccio Ugolini, Serafino Aquilano, Pietrobono (whose praises Brandolini literally sang at Naples in 1473; see Gallo, 90–97), Jacopo Sannazaro, and Benedetto Gareth at Naples, Bernardo Accolti, Angelo Poliziano, Antonio Maturazzo, Marco Probo Mariano of Sulmona, and Giles of Viterbo.
34 See the essay by Anthony Cummings on "Music and Feasts" in this volume, Ch. 19.
35 Falletti, "Le feste per Eleonora d'Aragona"; Pirrotta, "Music and Cultural Tendencies," in his *Music and Culture in Italy*, 89–90.
36 Pirrotta, "Music and Cultural Tendencies," 96–112.
37 Bologna, ed., *"Collettanee" in morte di Serafino Aquilano*, 72–80. See D'Amico, *Renaissance Humanism*, 102–7 on Cortesi's academy, and Rowland, *The Culture of the High Renaissance*, 92–105 on Calmeta and Collocci in relation to Serafino.

The reasons these two humanist scholars devoted unprecedented attention to a contemporary vernacular poet emerge in their writings: Serafino's strambotti and manner of performing them enthralled mixed audiences and spawned numerous imitators by virtue of his capacity to "express the passions of love in verse," and he was the exemplary figure in their arguments on behalf of a *lingua cortigiana*, a universal Italian vernacular that moved beyond regional Tuscan to include refinements from the best courtly language. For Colocci in particular, this *lingua comune* ideally drew on the best of supra-regional court usage to become the language of elevated social discourse of the courts, one that Castiglione promoted in *Il cortegiano* and that the well-traveled Serafino was positioned to exemplify. Serafino also emerges here as the first *improvvisatore* to elicit comments directed at the musical aspects of his performances. For Cortesi there was "nothing sweeter than the manner of his modes [of singing]." Calmeta claimed that Serafino brought to Rome a "smooth" (*stesa e piana*) and "refined" way of singing, based on the "musical form" of Andrea Coscia's singing to the lute, and Colocci praised his ability to unlock the emotions of his listeners through a rare conjoining of words and music. Serafino's melodies (*aeri*) were widely admired and occasionally transcribed, perhaps not unlike the popular *arie* for which the Venetian poet Leonardo Giustinian (a figure not otherwise associated with improvisation) was famous earlier in the century. Certainly the broader history of the strambotto at this time suggests a musical practice in transition from oral and improvised to written and fixed form.[38]

Serafino makes a fitting conclusion to a discussion of fifteenth-century *improvvisatori*, not just because he died in 1500, but because he is a Janus-faced figure at a critical juncture. As a professional and somewhat vagrant and multifaceted performer of modest education and social standing, there is much of the traditional *canterino* about him, but unlike most of his fifteenth-century predecessors, he moved in the fluid world of the humanist courts where new cultural forces came to bear on the performance practice of the oral poet. The traditional improvisatory art came into closer contact with polyphonic practice, as for example in the Florentine academies of the early sixteenth century, where Atalante Migliorotti and Bernardo Accolti rubbed shoulders with early madrigal composers.[39] The amorous and subjective modes of Petrarchan poetry favored more intimate performance venues and the

---

38 La Face Bianconi and Rossi, *Le rime di Serafino Aquilano in musica*, 6–7; Wilson, "Poliziano and the Language of Lament."
39 Cummings, *The Maecenas and the Madrigalist*, ch. 2.

presence of women as listeners and patrons. And far from eclipsing oral practice, the advent of print brought a new array of mixed oralities.[40] The continuing vitality of *canterino* culture in centers like Venice and the role of the humanist *improvvisatori* in the forging of new rhetorically driven genres like madrigal and monody are sixteenth-century stories with fifteenth-century roots.

## Bibliography

Bologna, Alessio, ed., *"Collettanee" in morte di Serafino Aquilano*, Lucca, 2009

Brandolini, Raffaele, *On Music and Poetry (De musica et poetica, 1513)*, trans. Ann E. Moyer and Mark Laureys, Tempe, AZ, 2001

Burke, Peter, "Oral Culture and Print Culture in Renaissance Italy," *ARV: Nordic Yearbook of Folklore* 54 (1998), 7–18

Carruthers, Mary, *The Book of Memory: A Study of Memory in Medieval Culture*, Cambridge, 1990

Cummings, Anthony, *The Maecenas and the Madrigalist: Patrons, Patronage, and the Origins of the Italian Madrigal*, Philadelphia, 2004

D'Accone, Frank A., "Lorenzo the Magnificent and Music," in *Lorenzo il Magnifico e il suo mondo: Convegno internazionale di studi (Firenze, 9–13 giugno 1992)*, ed. Gian Carlo Garfagnini, Florence, 1994, 259–90

D'Amico, John, *Renaissance Humanism in Papal Rome: Humanists and Churchmen on the Eve of the Reformation*, Baltimore and London, 1983

Degl'Innocenti, Luca, *I "Reali" dell'Altissimo: Un ciclo di cantari fra oralità e scrittura*, Florence, 2008

Della Torre, Arnaldo, *Storia dell'Accademia Platonica di Firenze*, Florence, 1902; repr. Turin, 1968

Everson, Jane E., "Francesco Cieco da Ferrara," in *Dizionario biografico degli italiani*, Rome, 1960–, 49:715–18

Falletti, Clelia, "Le feste per Eleonora d'Aragona da Napoli a Ferrara (1473)," in *Spettacoli conviviali dall'antichità classica alle corti italiane del '400: Atti del convegno di Viterbo 1982*, ed. Maria Chiabò and Federico Doglio, Viterbo, 1983, 269–89

Ficino, Marsilio, *The Letters of Marsilio Ficino*, trans. members of the Language Department of the School of Economic Science, London, 9 vols., London, 1975–2013

*Opera Omnia* (Basel, 1576; facs. edn. Turin, 1962)

Field, Arthur, *The Origins of the Platonic Academy of Florence*, Princeton, 1988

Flamini, Francesco, *La lirica toscana del Rinascimento anteriore ai tempi del Magnifico*, Pisa, 1891; repr. Florence, 1977

Gallo, F. Alberto, *Music in the Castle*, Chicago and London, 1995

---

40 Burke, "Oral Culture and Print Culture"; Richardson, *Manuscript Culture*, 226–58; Salzberg, "In the Mouths of Charlatans."

Grafton, Anthony, "The Humanist as Reader," in *A History of Reading in the West*, ed. Guglielmo Cavallo and Roger Chartier, Oxford, 1999, 179–212

Haar, James, "Arie per cantar stanze ariostesche," in *L'Ariosto: La musica, i musicisti. Quattro studi e sette madrigali ariosteschi*, ed. Maria Antonella Balsano, Florence, 1981, 31–46

*Essays on Italian Poetry and Music in the Renaissance, 1350–1600*, Berkeley, 1986

Hankins, James, "Humanist Academies and the 'Platonic Academy of Florence'," in *On Renaissance Academies: Proceedings of the International Conference "From the Roman Academy to the Danish Academy in Rome," Danish Academy in Rome, 11–13 October 2006*, ed. Marianne Pade, Rome, 2011, 31–46

Kallendorf, Craig, ed., *Humanist Educational Treatises*, Cambridge, MA, 2002

Kennedy, William J., *The Site of Petrarchism: Early Modern National Sentiment in Italy, France, and England*, Baltimore, 2003

Kent, Dale, *Cosimo de' Medici and the Florentine Renaissance: The Patron's Oeuvre*, New Haven, 2000

"Michele del Giogante's House of Memory," in *Society and Individual in Renaissance Florence*, ed. William J. Connell, Berkeley, 2002, 110–36

La Face Bianconi, Giuseppina, and Antonio Rossi, *Le rime di Serafino Aquilano in musica*, Florence, 1999

Lanza, Antonio, *Lirici toscani del Quattrocento*, 2 vols., Rome, 1973–75

Lovato, Antonio, "Appunti sulle preferenze musicali di Angelo Poliziano," in *Poliziano nel suo tempo: Atti del VI Convegno Internazionale, Chianciano-Montepulciano 18–21 luglio 1994*, ed. Luisa Rotondi Secchi Tarugi, Florence, 1996, 221–37

McGee, Timothy, *The Ceremonial Musicians of Late Medieval Florence*, Bloomington, IN, 2009

Orvieto, Paolo, "Angelo Poliziano *Compare* della brigata laurenziana," *Lettere italiane* 25 (1973), 301–18

*Pulci medievale: Studio sulla poesia volgare fiorentina del Quattrocento*, Rome, 1978

Pirrotta, Nino, *Music and Culture in Italy from the Middle Ages to the Baroque: A Collection of Essays*, Cambridge, MA, 1984

Pontano, Giovanni Giovano, *De fortitudine*, Naples, 1490

Richardson, Brian, *Manuscript Culture in Renaissance Italy*, Cambridge, 2009

Rossi, Adamo, "Memorie di musica civile in Perugia nei secoli XIV e XV," *Giornale di erudizione artistica* 3 (1874), 129–52

Rowland, Ingrid D., *The Culture of the High Renaissance: Ancients and Moderns in Sixteenth-Century Rome*, Cambridge, 1998

Salzberg, Rosa, "In the Mouths of Charlatans: Street Performers and the Dissemination of Pamphlets in Renaissance Italy," *Renaissance Studies* 24 (2010), 638–53

Storey, Christina, "The Philosopher, the Poet, and the Fragment: Ficino, Poliziano, and Le stanze per la giostra," *Modern Language Review* 98 (2003), 602–19

Ugolini, Francesco, *I cantari d'argomento classico*, Florence, 1933

Verde, Armando, *Lo studio fiorentino, 1473–1503: Ricerche e documenti*, 6 vols., Florence, 1973–2010

Villoresi, Marco, "Panoramica sui poeti performativi d'età laurenziana," *Rassegna europea di letteratura italiana* 34 (2009), 11–33

Wilson, Blake, "Poliziano and the Language of Lament from Isaac to Layolle," in *Sleuthing the Muse: Essays in Honor of William F. Prizer*, ed. Kristine K. Forney and Jeremy L. Smith, Hillsdale, NY, 2012, 85–114

    *Singing Poetry in Renaissance Florence: The "Cantasi Come" Tradition (1375–1550)*, Florence, 2009

Zumthor, Paul, *Oral Poetry: An Introduction*, Minneapolis, 1990

# Liturgical humanism: saints' Offices from the Italian peninsula in the fifteenth century

ALISON K. FRAZIER

Civic rituals that centered on saints constituted one of the most widely shared, reliably repeated, and generally positive experiences that humans could have in late medieval and Renaissance Europe. On these occasions, a person did not have to participate or even approve in order to observe the saint's ability to organize quantities of creativity and cash. In exchange for this salutary attention, the saint helped the proud and humble alike: local politics might designate favorites, but ritual promised a rough democracy of benefits. Our perception of this democracy, or catholicity, has contributed to making ritual an attractive area of historical research for the past thirty years. And although today's studies of early modern ritual seem most focused on state occasions such as royal entries and judicial punishments, ritual is also a significant way that Renaissance religion has been recuperated as a viable topic.[1]

To forward the recuperation, this essay looks at humanists' commemoration of saints in the official ritual of the liturgy. Because this subfield of music history is relatively new, what follows is not a definitive survey but a tentative overview.[2] After providing some background information, I offer four examples to demonstrate the variety and interest of the material. To encourage further research, I include a preliminary Appendix of authors and their saintly subjects.

## Introduction: humanists, Matins, breviaries

The Divine Office is the Church's daily, Psalm-based, cycle of prayer (in contrast to the Eucharistic service of the Mass).[3] For the humanists, as we

---

1 E.g. Trexler, *Public Life in Renaissance Florence*; Muir, *Civic Ritual in Renaissance Venice*; *Late Medieval and Early Modern Ritual*, ed. Cohn *et al.*

2 Of course, historians belonging to religious orders have long studied their orders' Offices, including those Offices written by humanists of the order. For a good example, see Delorme, "Un Second office rythmique de S. Bernardin," on humanist Pietro Ridolfi's Office of Bernardino of Siena.

3 For unfamiliar terms, see Harper, *Forms and Orders of Western Liturgy*; Hughes, *Medieval Manuscripts for Mass and Office*, and *Grove Music Online*. On saints, authors, and hagiographical texts mentioned in this essay, consult Frazier, *Possible Lives*, ad indicem. I will not mention these sources again.

shall see, the Office was also a form of public oratory, local history, rhetorical display, and civic education that stood to profit from their professional attention.[4] By humanists I mean people – in this case, men – whose education, patterns of cultural activity, epistolary networks, and patronage ties fostered the ideals of the *studia humanitatis* (a pedagogy, developed from the medieval *trivium* or language arts curriculum, that emphasized grammar, rhetoric, poetry, history, and moral philosophy, all ideally taught on the basis of classical primary sources).[5] The Italian peninsula is a logical place to look for the classicizers' efforts at liturgical revision. It is not just that the urban environment there nurtured the *studia humanitatis*; those cities also had a glut of saints needing commemoration. Thanks to the density of urbanization established in the classical period, the peninsula had more dioceses than the rest of Europe combined.[6] With dioceses came not only bishops, canons, and parishes with hierarchies of functionaries, but also panoplies of saintly founders and protectors in whom all that personnel was bound to take an interest.[7] Once the papacy had returned from Avignon, moreover, peninsular dioceses lay once again in relatively close proximity to the Curia. Proximity increased the opportunities for local humanists, lay and clerical, to win fame through new compositions, and encouraged humanist participation in liturgical aspects of Catholic reform. Equally important was the gradual, admittedly tense, seepage of humanist education into the religious orders, with the result that liturgies for order founders and heroes also came under rhetorical and historical scrutiny.[8]

The part of the Divine Office that especially attracted humanist attention was the day's first round of prayer, known as Matins. The longest of the seven liturgical hours, Matins offered the most scope for new composition. But Matins is also earliest of the hours: it begins after midnight and lasts until dawn brings round the Office of Lauds. Both length and lateness raise sharply the question of audience: for whom did the humanists compose, beyond the monks, canons, and friars professionally obligated to pray the hours?[9] Scholars argue that devout laypeople did attend the night Office celebrations,

---

4 Cf. Solvi, "Agiografi e agiografie," 111, on the saint as a civic figure for three levels of promotion: by *cantastorie*, by civic chroniclers, and by humanist purveyors of the *vir illustris* traditions. Thus Solvi surveys many genres, including liturgical ones.

5 See James Hankins's essay in this volume, Ch. 13.

6 Hay, *The Church in Italy*, 9–12, acknowledging problems of small size, poverty, and non-residency.

7 Webb, *Patrons and Defenders*.

8 See, e.g., the Offices for Sts. Catherine of Siena and Barbara of Nicomedia discussed below. Both were composed by Dominicans, the former for the order itself, and the latter for a layman.

9 Salmon, *L'Office divin au Moyen Âge*. On lay attendance, see Thompson, *Cities of God*, 242–45, drawing largely on saints' Lives, and Cattaneo, "La partecipazione," admitting the difficulty of using normative clerical writings as evidence.

encouraged by the extension of Vespers on the evening before the feast (First Vespers, *primae vesperae*). By the thirteenth and fourteenth centuries, some peninsular dioceses had developed specially lengthened Vespers services; these doubled Vespers or vigils incorporated textual material from the Matins Office, adding improvised polyphony, ritual processions, and even civic celebrations.[10] The Appendix provides evidence of fifteenth-century humanists' contributions to First Vespers, although what that meant in practice needs further study.

The basic set of ritual texts for Matins was complex and accordion-like, in that sections of it stretched or multiplied to suit the solemnity of the feast. At its simplest, Matins opened with two short versicles paired with responds to announce the start of the service. A hymn followed, and then an invitatory welcomed the lay participants (it was omitted in situations closed to the laity, such as papal or monastic observance). The Nocturns, which constituted the main body of the Matins Office, came next. A Nocturn consisted of at least three psalms, each with antiphons; then came at least three readings (*lectiones*, lessons, or lections), each with antiphons and responds. Offices for saints typically had three Nocturns (although just one was possible). The first and third featured relevant biblical and patristic lections, while the second Nocturn consisted of lections about the saint's life and virtues. Three lections in the second Nocturn was standard for the secular or cathedral Office; the monastic or papal Office usually offered four. If the saint was significant enough to be honored with a major feast, then the number of second Nocturn readings could rise to nine in secular settings, or twelve in monastic and papal settings.

Increasingly in the late Middle Ages and Renaissance, the hagiographic material of the second Nocturn readings might overwhelm lections in the first and third Nocturns as well. Moreover, readings could vary a great deal in length, from roughly 100 to several hundred words. To increase the coherence and impact of the Office, elements from the lections were repeated and elaborated in the antiphons; embedded quotations from authoritative, older Offices of celebrated saints might add to the effect.

The officiant could find the Matins texts gathered in the Sanctorale, a specially designated part of the breviary. By the late Middle Ages, a typical breviary included a Calendar of feasts; the Psalter; the Temporale (texts for the moveable, Christ-centered feasts of the Christian year); the Sanctorale (texts for the fixed feasts of the saints); and appended prayers and Offices, notably the Little Office of the Virgin and the Office of the Dead. Extensive instructions or

---

10 On the eleventh and twelfth centuries, Cattaneo, "La partecipazione," 416, 420; on the thirteenth and fourteenth centuries, Brand, "Vigils of Medieval Tuscany." To my knowledge, no study of the fifteenth-century situation exists.

rubrics (i.e., in red ink) appeared throughout. The Sanctorale had two parts: the Proper, that is, commemorations for the feast days of particular saints, such as John the Baptist, and the Common, which celebrated classes of saints, such as virgin martyrs. The Appendix below indicates that humanists wrote chiefly for the Proper. They tended to address, in other words, particular saints, the ones who mattered to patrons, urban congregations, and themselves. They worked especially on the lections, hymns, and antiphons of the second Nocturn, and were sometimes guilty of letting their texts spill over into the first and third Nocturns as well.

Humanists' Offices do not often appear in breviaries, however. Three factors may account for their absence. First, it can be hard to recognize humanists' contributions to the Sanctorale: service books rarely identify contemporary authors, and when they do, skepticism is in order, as in the case of the Office for Catherine of Siena (addressed below). Second, not all breviaries were small volumes favoring personal use, such as we tend to envision today. Many were large, expensive service books, of necessity kept in use for decades or centuries. Such volumes required updates in the form of manuscript or printed *libelli* (booklets).[11] As small, fragile, and often unique objects prepared for a local officiant, *libelli* had poor chances of survival unless bound into larger codices. Many have surely been lost. Those that survive, such as Raffaele Maffei's printed *Officium* (discussed below), are often unique exemplars. Third, out-of-date liturgical material was especially liable to destruction – in Europe as a whole because of the confessionalized environment of the sixteenth century, and across Italy in particular because that region bore the brunt of post-Tridentine efforts, quite unprecedented, to impose standardization – with the result that quattrocento liturgical imprints survive in relatively few copies.[12] These three problems may have combined to deform the evidence: at least in my experience, the majority of humanists' liturgical compositions are extant today only in drafts. This state of affairs guarantees that musical notation is rare, and thus, despite the centrality of music to the liturgical experience, this essay will not address it.[13]

---

11 Compare Gy, "The Different Forms of Liturgical Libelli" and Palazzo, "Le Role des *libelli*"; neither addresses the fifteenth century. The *libellus* format continued to serve a liturgical function well into the sixteenth century, e.g., Vatican City, Biblioteca Apostolica Vaticana (hereafter BAV), Vat. lat. 10774, where a *libellus* with musical notation for the text has been bound into a sixteenth-century breviary.

12 Green *et al.*, "The Shape of Incunable Survival," revising current estimates of incunable extinctions, emphasize the initial moment of market reception as the key to survival. Here, I suggest instead that post-market forces may be more important for liturgical survivals (for some high-end liturgical books, of course, the market hardly entered into the picture at all). Armstrong, "Nicolaus Jenson's *Breviarium romanum*," looks at a successful survival. On contemporaries' perception of Trent as a provincial council focused on peninsular practice, see Ditchfield, "Il papa come pastore?"

13 Cf. Zanovello, "Les Humanistes florentins"; Pirrotta, "Music and Cultural Tendencies." See further James Hankins in this volume, Ch. 13, and Patrick Macey's contribution, Ch. 26.

## The aims of humanist liturgical revisions

Fifteenth-century humanists' ideas about the liturgy are usually discussed in light of two early sixteenth-century texts, both composed by men trained in the *studia humanitatis*. The first, the *Libellus* on reforming the Church (1513), is a wide-ranging, prescriptive document.[14] After calling on Leo X de' Medici to convert Jews and conquer Muslims, after urging him to require Latin of all priests and to sponsor the translation of the Bible into vernaculars, Camaldolese authors Vincenzo Querini and Paolo Giustiniani complain about the "promiscuous reading" of untruthful Lives about saints and Church Fathers; argue that texts for Mass and Office must be presented worldwide in "maternal tongues"; decry the "superstitions" associated with "over-reaching observance of religious ceremonies" that lead the faithful to pray to saints rather than to God; and call for a single liturgy to be shared among all orders and dioceses.[15] Their program, in other words, aimed to downplay saints' cults altogether, while standardizing, historicizing, and vernacularizing the Sanctorale. Although the *Libellus* had a limited circulation, that group of proposals for liturgical reform remained of interest at the Council of Trent (1545–63).

In contrast to the *Libellus*, Cardinal Francisco Quiñones's Breviary (1535; 2nd edn. rev. 1536) was a service book, a pragmatic document.[16] At papal direction, Quiñones designed his Breviary for personal use by removing the choral element of chant. He also shortened the ritual texts, corrected factual errors, simplified the Latin, and reduced and rationalized the rubrics. The new Breviary was an enormous success, appearing in at least 110 editions between 1535 and 1558, when it was suppressed.[17] Together, the programmatic *Libellus* and standardized Breviary point to a fairly coherent humanist position on the liturgy. The key desiderata were brevity, accessibility (either through the vernacular or a simplified Latin), factual reliability, and a clarified, rationalized presentation.

Humanists' Matins Offices from the century preceding Quiñones's Breviary, however, indicate some divergences of opinion. By definition, of course, these texts were composed by men who were not simply critics of, but also contributors to, the cult of the saints. It's not surprising therefore that their loving attention to particular saints both played up that "superstitious" aspect of the liturgy decried by the *Libellus* and tended, in its very affections, to run counter to Quiñones's ideals of brevity and uniformity. The fifteenth-century humanists sought historical veracity but sometimes achieved it in ways hardly amenable to Tridentine tastes. Precisely as humanists, moreover, they tended to

14 Mittarelli and Costadoni, *Annales Camaldulenses*, 9, cols. 612–719.
15 Ibid., cols. 680, 683, 684, 686, 689.    16 Van Liere, "Catholic Reform of the Divine Office."
17 Jungmann, "Why Was Cardinal Quinonez' Reformed Breviary a Failure?"

favor not the vernacular, but a Latin ranging from reverently ornate to generously accessible. The four case studies below suggest other aims, too, such as recovering the sheer pleasure of the text, reflecting indirectly on socio-cultural issues, and of course seeking fame. Each author – in ways that reflected his education, his professional identity, the immediate context of composition, and his own relationship to the saint – took up the issues that seemed to him most pressing.

## Four Matins Offices by humanists

### Maffeo Vegio's Office for the feast of Monica of Thagaste (composed 1453–58)

Lombard humanist Maffeo Vegio (1407–58) served in the Curia under Eugene IV (d. 1447), Nicholas V (d. 1455), and Calixtus III (d. 1458). Friend and correspondent of many accomplished humanists, he is best known today for adding a thirteenth book to that premodern classroom staple, Virgil's *Aeneid*, and for writing the fifteenth-century's longest treatise on education, *De educatione liberorum* (based on his enthusiasm for the educational role of the family portrayed in Augustine's *Confessions*).[18] That same didactic impress also marks his short epic, the *Antonias*, which imagines the encounter between the originary desert hermit-saints, Paul and Anthony.[19] Such creative reconstructions were the stuff of classroom exercises (*progymnasmata*), which seem to have been a reliable wellspring for Vegio's authorial impulses.[20] Moreover, the *Antonias* was published almost exclusively in northern Europe (especially Deventer), a geographical focus that indicates classroom use in a proto-Erasmian situation. Thus, although we have no record of Vegio taking pupils, his status as an educator seems secure.

Vegio's pedagogical outlook extended to the liturgy as well. He composed extensive Lives and Offices for a contemporary, the Observant Franciscan Bernardino of Siena (d. 1444; canonized 1450); for two late medieval figures, Pope Celestine V (d. 1296; canonized 1313) and Augustinian Hermit Nicola da Tolentino (d. 1305/6; canonized 1446); and for two late antique saints, Augustine of Hippo (d. 430) and his mother Monica (d. 388). All these Offices have nine readings; most include hymns and the full complement of *historiae* (antiphons, responds, versicles, capitula); all represent a considered effort to increase the effectiveness of the liturgy.

---

18 Kallendorf, "The *Aeneid* Unfinished." *De educatione liberorum* has been edited by Sister Maria Fanning and Sister Anne Sullivan.
19 Vegio, *Short Epics*, trans. and ed. Putnam and Hankins.
20 On Vegio's attention to classroom material see also Della Schiava, "Le *Fabellae* esopoiche di Maffeo Vegio."

The Offices for Augustine and Monica stand out especially, for the lections in both cases derive from the writings of Augustine himself. This excerpting technique was not new. It had been tried already in a twelfth-century *vita s. Monicae* by Regular Canon Galter of Arrouaise (1155–93), a work Vegio clearly knew.[21] Galter had preserved Augustine's first-person voice in his *Life of Monica*, and Vegio followed this striking usage in his own *Life of Monica*. Vegio's novelty, however, was to move that first-person voice into the Matins readings of Monica's Office (as he also did in his Office for Augustine, not discussed here).[22] The first six of Vegio's nine lections derive verbatim from *Confessions* 2.2–3; 3.6 and 11–12; 5.7; and 6.1–2; the antiphons and responds echo the excerpts. Lection 7, Vegio's homily exploring an analogy in Luke 7 to Monica's maternal love, along with Vegio's epideictic lections 8 and 9 (largely rhetorical questions), guide further reflection on Augustine's celebration of his mother.

The resulting text had an immediacy that must have been electrifying for both celebrant and audience. With its opening words, the *Lectio prima* catapulted the audience into the all-too-physical being of an adolescent male with time on his hands:

> Where then was I, and how far from the delights of Your house, in that sixteenth year of my life in this world, when the madness of lust – needing no licence from human shamelessness, receiving no licence from Your laws – took complete control of me, and I surrendered wholly to it? . . . The briars of unclean lusts grew so that they towered over my head, and there was no hand to root them out . . . But in my mother's breast You had already laid the foundation of Your temple and begun Your holy habitation . . .[23]

And Vegio evidently expected people to understand all this, for he thought Augustine's Latin in the *Confessions* was relatively simple and accessible.[24]

Vegio's achievement deserves a moment's appreciation. On one hand, the use of the first person in a liturgical Office was unprecedented and thus shocking: Augustine's impassioned reminiscences emerged dramatically from the priest's mouth. That must have had implications for the priest as much as for his audience. On the other hand, such impersonations would have seemed

---

21 On Galter, see *Monumenta Arroasiensia*, ed. Tock and Milis, ad indicem, and Tock, "Galter of Arrouaise."

22 Szendrei, "On the Prose *Historia* of St. Augustine," does not discuss Galter, but masterfully analyzes the twelfth-century Office drawn "ex legenda eius" (437) and perhaps composed by Rupert of Deutz (434).

23 Augustine, *Confessions*, trans. Sheed, 26–27. Vegio's text in BAV, MS Ottob. lat. 1253 is consonant with the critical edition: Ubi eram et quam longe exulabam a deliciis domus tuae anno illo sextodecimo aetatis meae, quum accepit in me sceptrum (et totas munus ei dedi), vesania libidinis, licentiosae per dedecus humanum, illicitae autem per leges tuas? [*Conf.* 2.2.4]; Excesserunt caput meum vepres libidinum, et nulla erat eradicans manus . . . Sed in matris pectore iam inchoaveras templum tuum et exordium sanctae habitationis tuae . . . [*Conf.* 2.3.6].

24 Vegio, *De educatione*, ed. and trans. Fanning and Sullivan, 3.

perfectly familiar, for they, like Vegio's short epic, derived from classroom *prosopopoeia*. Rooted in the classical period and continued throughout the medieval one, these pedagogical, performative traditions were boosted in the Renaissance by the recovery of such works as Quintilian's *Institutes*.[25] Indeed, in *Confessions* 1.13.20 Augustine himself recalls a schoolboy exercise in impersonation (*ethopoeia*), linking it to his tears over Dido and his deep emotional engagement with the *Aeneid*.[26] Members of Vegio's audience who had experience of dramatic role-playing in the classroom would have found the priest's impersonation clever, especially if it was well performed, and they would have appreciated its visceral jolt. But that is not all. Such riveting use of the saint's *ipsissima verba* also ensured a historical accuracy achieved not through factual minutiae, but in the richly persuasive form of affective language and content.[27] In sum, Vegio made a compelling ritual performance of a schoolboy exercise. Augustine would have been delighted that his mother's tears and prayers had that effect for others besides himself.

### Tommaso Schifaldo's Office for the feast of Catherine of Siena (composed ca. 1461?)

When humanist Pope Pius II Piccolomini canonized Catherine of Siena (d. 1381) at Rome in 1461, a liturgy was sung.[28] The ambassador who reported it, however, failed to specify whether he heard the Common of One Virgin or a full Proper Office newly composed for the occasion. Two Proper Offices for Catherine exist: one rhymed, which is probably the earlier, and has a more traditional vocabulary; and one prose, which is clearly humanist.[29] Manuscripts and printed editions attribute the prose Office to Pius himself, but scholars have long known that the author was Dominican Tommaso Schifaldo of Marsala (ca. 1430–after 1497).[30] The "only notable Sicilian philologist . . . in the quattrocento," Schifaldo had studied at the University of Siena under Pius's friend Francesco Patrizi, epitomator of Quintilian, commentator on Petrarch, and expert in the verse form of sapphics.[31] Schifaldo himself was a teacher; he wrote biography, oratory, poetry, and an anti-Vallan grammar as well as commentaries on Juvenal, Persius, Ovid, and Horace. No doubt aware of Schifaldo's talents, his Dominican superior asked the grammarian, then at Rome, to compose an Office in Catherine's honor.

---

25 But see Ward, "Quintilian and the Rhetorical Revolution."     26 Woods, "Weeping for Dido."
27 Cf. Gibson, "Learning Greek History."
28 Further discussion in Frazier, "Humanist Lives of Catherine of Siena."
29 Brown, "Songs for the Saints of the Schism," 125, 130.
30 Mortier, *Histoire des maîtres généraux*, 366–67 and n. 1. Cf. Brown, "Songs for the Saints of the Schism," 109–17.
31 Zaggia, *Tra Mantova e la Sicilia nel Cinquecento*, 48 n. 48 (my translation).

Schifaldo reports with pride on the result, a "most elegant Office … fitted out with lyric hymns in sapphic, hendecasyllabic meter."[32] Rather than iambic dimeter, favored in the Middle Ages for hymns, Schifaldo chose the quantitative meter of Horace, Statius, and Prudentius.[33] The tunes that appear with these hymns are not borrowed from older Offices.[34] The prose text has neither rhythm nor rhyme, and its vocabulary avoids common Dominican tropes such as light, *lux*. And although Schifaldo was a Dominican, the Office nowhere mentions or alludes to Dominic or his order. Both Catherine and Pius were Sienese, but the prose Office mentions Siena hardly at all. Clearly Schifaldo intended to do something new.

The Office may well have had a political subtext (internal to the Dominicans, or to Sienese–papal relations, or both), but it was in the first place a statement of ambition. Schifaldo himself presented the Office to the pope, who praised it enthusiastically "above others" (evidently there were competitors) and signaled his approval by sending it to Santa Maria sopra Minerva, the Dominicans' church in Rome. No reports of performance are extant, but the composition was successful in objective terms, for it survives not as an author's draft or *libellus*, but in eight manuscript breviaries and more than half a dozen printed editions. In those codices, where the Office is, with a single exception, attributed to Pius, the text of the hymns remains fairly constant, but the text of the lections varies, offering now three lessons, now nine, now introducing misreadings, now rephrasing in an effort to improve. Thus only an approximate sense of Schifaldo's original composition is possible.

Even that approximate sense suggests that Schifaldo's novelties aimed not only at impact but also at a particular image of the saint. Rather than hewing closely to incidents from Raymond of Capua's *vita* of Catherine as the rhymed Office does, Schifaldo's prose Office in the Venice 1477/78 edition of the Dominican breviary ranges beyond Raymond to feature well-chosen anecdotes, linguistic play, and engaging specifics.[35] Although this edition does not include an antiphon about the controversial, invisible stigmata (only the 1476 imprint and earliest manuscript include that), its language is striking. The first lections chronicle the child's spiritual growth with charm: in "a not unlovely little speech," for example, young, blonde Catherine asks Mary for Christ as spouse. Mild stoic and epicurean echoes occur in lections that broach

---

32  See Schifaldo's *De viris illustribus eiusdem ordinis praedicatorum*, 93–94.
33  Charlet, "Aeneas Silvius hymnode," esp. 99–102. Note, however, that the rhymed Office for Catherine also has sapphic hymns.
34  The remainder of this paragraph relies on Brown, "Songs for the Saints of the Schism."
35  ISTC ibo113900 links to a facsimile. Brown, "Songs for the Saints of the Schism," ch. 4, does not discuss this imprint. On Raymond's *Life* of Catherine, see Nocentini, "The *Legenda maior* of Catherine of Siena."

the saint's charity and asceticism. Remarkably, the entire sixth reading is given over to the famous case of Catherine's 1374 ministry to Niccolò di Toldo, at whose execution the saint, enraptured, caught the prisoner's severed head in her arms – an incident not in Raymond's *vita*.[36] Lections 7 and 8 acclaim Catherine as spiritual doctor, celebrating her intellectual achievements. These emphases were gradually damped down in the subsequent revisions, as Catherine's *Life* was shaped to order norms.

### Pietro Ransano's Office for the Feast of Barbara of Nicomedia (composed in 1469)

Sicilian Dominican Pietro Ransano (1427–92) was not an educator but a rhetorician and Hellenist, an inquisitor and collector for the crusade and, toward the end of his life, a papal ambassador and bishop. He wrote epistles, panegyrics, histories, and funeral orations (including one for Maffeo Vegio).[37] As bishop of Lucera (1476–92), Ransano imposed the Dominican liturgy on his cathedral clergy.[38] But his liturgical activism apparently stopped there: Ransano didn't address Lucera's obscure first bishop or the Black Madonna associated with the expulsion of Lucera's medieval Muslim community.[39] Ransano's history of Hungary includes biographies of saintly royals, but these texts did not, it seems, migrate into the breviary. The *Annales*, Ransano's lengthy world history, includes hundreds of short notices derived from Usuard and Bede, but he did not contribute to reforming the martyrology. And although Ransano wrote an important account of fellow Dominican Anthony of Rivalto (d. 1460) for Pius II, he did not write an Office.

Ransano produced just two liturgical compositions. The best known is his 1455 Office for Vincent Ferrer (d. 1419) in nine readings with hymns and antiphons. Composed for the Dominicans at Bologna then guiding Vincent's canonization, this Office was successful in the sense that it entered print and was used by the order for centuries.[40] About a decade later, Ransano wrote a second Office. This time the subject was a saint he loved, the early fourth-century virgin martyr Barbara of Nicomedia.

Barbara was a challenging subject, for like many early saints her life – even her existence – is hard to document. Ransano followed an erudite Dominican liturgical tradition when he researched and wrote a lengthy *Life and Death of*

---

36 Catherine of Siena, *The Letters*, trans. Noffke, 1: 82–90 (letter T273).
37 Figliuolo, *Cultura a Napoli*, esp.149–200 on writings.
38 Alberti, *Descrittione di tutta Italia*, fol. 248r.    39 Taylor, *Muslims in Medieval Italy*.
40 Brown, "Songs for the Saints of the Schism," studies Ransano's Office for Vincent Ferrer; on Ransano's strategic retelling, see Smoller, *The Saint and the Chopped-Up Baby*, 171–73 with n. 32.

*Barbara* at the request of a lay friend.[41] A year later, in 1469, Ransano extracted from that *Life* an *Officium* for the friend's brother. This Office apparently did not enter print.[42] Any performances probably occurred in a private chapel at Palermo and drew upon a manuscript or printed *libellus*.

Ransano's *Officium* for Barbara differs from his *Vita Barbarae* in ways that suggest a considered approach to the task of liturgy. The *Vita* suits a Latinate elite appreciative of historical research; the *Officium* suits auditors still Latinate but less knowledgeable, and perhaps on that account more open to aspects of Barbara's story that had some contemporary relevance. In a dedicatory letter prefacing the *Officium*, Ransano warns the recipient not to be "amazed if the style of this little work seems very plain or rather insufficiently ornate and splendid," for "Offices of this sort ought indeed to be written in simple speech." Although the *Officium* does not always live up to this claim, it makes allowances for audience, simplifying content as well as style.

Space, of course, is at a premium in any Office. Ransano's *Officium* opens, for example, with Suetonian brevity and accuracy, identifying place, date, and family of birth; of necessity it dispenses with the *Life*'s extensive passages in direct address. The *Life* opens with two chapters exploring foundational topics drawn from Eusebius and Lactantius – early martyrs at Nicomedia, and biographies of the persecutors – and closes with brief notes on Barbara's posthumous cult.[43] The *Officium*, in contrast, commences with two lections that establish the uncomplicatedly loving relationship of the pagan father and his beautiful, virtuous, learned daughter, and ends with the heroine's death at her own father's hands. The aim of the *Officium*, at least as suggested by its narrative arc, is to create a compelling domestic drama about the abuse of patriarchal power.[44]

Marriage precipitates the drama. In the *Life* the father's plans for his daughter's marriage unfold at length and famously include locking Barbara in a tower to safeguard her chastity. In the *Officium* the tower nearly disappears, alongside the father's planning and the issue of chastity. The narrative fulcrum is Barbara's: she simply declares herself married to Christ. Thus, while both *Life* and *Office* emphasize the saint's agency, the very efficiency of the *Office* makes its depiction more forceful. Similarly, *Life* and *Officium* foreground Barbara's pagan philosophical learning, which leads to her facility with Scripture and

41 Figliuolo, *Cultura a Napoli*, 245–72, edits Ransano's *Vita et passio sancte Barbare*; on composition see 151–53. Dominican liturgical scholarship is explored in Boyle and Gy, eds., *Aux origines de la liturgie dominicaine*; see the treatment of the Sanctoral by Urfels-Capot, "Le Sanctoral du lectionnaire de l'office."
42 My discussion draws on Rome, Biblioteca Casanatense, MS 112.
43 Figliuolo, *Cultura a Napoli*, 245–47, 270–71.
44 Cf. Schutte, *By Force and Fear*, on the family drama of forced monachization. Ransano illustrates instead paternal opposition to the "bride of Christ," an illustration that Jacobus de Varagine, OP, thirteenth-century compiler-author of the *Golden Legend*, would have approved.

Origen's commentaries, but the miraculous self-baptism that results from all this scholarship stands out starkly in the laconic *Office*. And yet again: in the last, gruesome lections describing her tortures, the *Office* dispenses with the dilemma of impassibility (what is the martyr's physiological experience: pleasure? heroic extremes of pain? miraculous anesthetization?). The *Life* offers an awkward theological solution: Barbara prays that her pain convert to pleasure. The *Office* has no need of that miracle, for the martyr is majestically calm throughout, Christ's name ever on her lips. The earthly father's final, death-dealing blow is the blessing that seals Barbara's marriage to her heavenly spouse.

### Raffaele Maffei's Office for the feast of Actinea and Greciniana (composed 1518–19?)

In retirement, after decades of curial service, Raffaele Maffei wrote five Offices about patron saints dear to his hometown of Volterra. In contrast to the long, heartfelt Offices by Vegio, Schifaldo, and Ransano, Maffei's are plain-spoken, pointedly didactic, and brief – the early sixteenth-century program of liturgical reform had arrived. Commissioning the work, Volterra's cathedral canons explained that the old Offices were "neither easy for readers to understand, nor pleasing for audiences to hear," and gave Maffei license to correct them. He responded with restraint: although eloquence was important, he would not "offend against the integrity of history" or detract from the "real authority" of his "ancient sources." The results were good: his brother, Mario Maffei, sent a draft to Domenico Scribonio, the bishop of Imola then engaged in revising the breviary, and Scribonio offered high praise, sending drafts of his own for Raffaele to review. Leo X de' Medici approved Maffei's Offices in November 1519; they were printed in an octavo *libellus* of twenty-six leaves probably not long afterwards. One copy is extant; it has no colophon and Maffei's name does not appear in it.[45]

The "integrity of history" is the anxious theme of the Office for Actinea and Greciniana, sixth-century North Africans who had lived as hermits in Etruria. Almost everything about these saints is unknown.[46] Ransano responds to this challenge by scripting a ritual performance rather different from Vegio's Augustinian drama: now the priest must act the philologist. Thus the officiant declares right away that even the saints' *status* is unclear, *non satis exploratum.* Were the women virgins or matrons? In any event they were martyrs. They were rediscovered after a long time thanks to God, who will not long suffer his

---

45 Volterra, Biblioteca Guarnacci, shelfmark 1382 (XI 1 37) = CNCE 71446.
46 I draw on Maffei's drafts of this Office in BAV, MS Ottob. lat. 2377, fols. 254v–255v and Ottob. lat. 992, fol. 255r–v.

servants to abide unknown and inglorious: providence, the scholar-priest explains, can be counted on to rectify gaps in human historical memory.

Drawing on "an ancient codex," the celebrant retells the history of the martyrs' *inventio* (official finding). Unsure when the women's bodies were recovered, he conjectures that the discovery occurred under Innocent III, about 1200: as the monks dug in the foundations of their church, they found a stone affixed to the wall; it bore the women's names. Inscriptions are prime forms of authentication, but this one was so concise that it could hardly be deciphered. Although many clever men put their minds to the task, "they discovered nothing for sure." Meanwhile, a citizen received instructions in a dream: excavation near the marble inscription would reveal a treasure (*thesaurum*). Sure enough, right where the bodies lay close together, the monks found a lead *elogium* identifying the corpses and dating them: "These two most chaste women Actinia and Graeciniana died in the time of Diocletian and Maximian."

To this point the ventriloquist-priest has led his congregation to consider four types of proof: an ancient codex, a marble inscription, a dream, and a lead tablet. Lection 4 brings yet other forms of authentication to bear. The "ancient codex" reports a man at the scene seeking release from a demon, says the officiant. This demon, compelled by God, bore witness to the manner of the women's deaths, so that Christians might know that one was beheaded, the other transfixed by a spear. Demonic witness – on the face of it unreliable, as the officiant acknowledges – is quickly verified by careful examination of the women's bodies. A biblical analogy smoothes over the singularity of this evidence. The relics were placed in an altar in the church, as we know from their discovery during the *translatio* of St. Justus in our own day, avers Maffei through the officiant. Thus the priest claims authentication by contemporary events, those his auditors could remember because they had been eyewitnesses. All these things prove God's care for his saints. Note especially, the priest underlines, God's concern that the women's heroism be recorded both in marble and lead: if one inscription were lost, the other would remain to give notice of the martyrs' virtue and to be an occasion for imitation.

Maffei's original approach to the Matins readings represents a frontal assault on the abiding problem of identifying the early martyrs. In the fifteenth century, the problem preoccupied first-rank humanists, including Leon Battista Alberti and Giannozzo Manetti. It continued to occupy post-Tridentine scholars, and was made piquant by the renewal of martyrdom in confessionalized Europe. In Maffei's day the concern was that historical untruthfulness was spiritually and doctrinally damaging. In response, Maffei imports the internal dialogue of the critical historian explicitly into the liturgy.

In short, the Office for Actinea and Greciniana is a teaching document: codices, inscriptions, lead tablets, correct understanding of dreams and demons, inspection of corpses, and eyewitness memory of handling relics all enter the courtroom of the saints for evaluation. Humanist liturgical reform might make scholars of every priest and teach historical sophistication to every auditor.

## Conclusion

Ritual was central to Renaissance religion – not just the "world upside-down" ritual of the subalterns, but also the formal, Latinate ritual of the institutional Church. It is rare, however, that ritual is given license to experiment: comfortable though we may be with "invented tradition," experimental ritual remains an uneasy oxymoron. The fifteenth-century humanists, however, experimented boldly, with institutional approval; I have focused on their Offices for women saints to emphasize that fact. Their liturgical innovations, so often maligned in the scholarly literature, were in a sense the crowning labor of the Renaissance, at least if historian Ronald Witt is correct in positing a gradual humanist "colonization" of the medieval genres.[47] For what had started with the letter and oration, and continued into the dialogue, treatise, and philosophical commentary, concluded, I would argue, in humanist appropriation of the "churchy" genres: the saint's *Life*, biblical exegesis, and the liturgical Office. If we consider the last of these, it appears that the humanists could imagine new "forms and orders," and that we can observe them essaying a contribution to church reform, not to mention individual salvation. Vegio's resurrection of Augustine in the very act of extolling his mother; Schifaldo's ambitious presentation of Catherine as mystic, preacher, and author; Ransano's appreciation of the potential of the virgin martyr tale as domestic drama; and Maffei's determined importation of philological evaluation right into the Office – all aimed to increase the effect of the ritual on the audience. Every item in the Appendix below deserves similar attention, as we try to recover not just the words, but the music of liturgical humanism.

---

47  Witt, *'In the Footsteps of the Ancients'*.

# Appendix

## Humanist Offices for saints on the Italian peninsula ca. 1435–1535

*A preliminary listing (in alphabetical order by saint)*

| Saint (death date/canonization) | Author/editor | Composition | Notes[a] |
|---|---|---|---|
| Actinea & Greciniana (IX/*ab antiquo*) | Raffaele Maffei | by 1519 | 6 lections; extant in autograph MS draft, and print |
| Athanasius (IV/*ab antiquo*) | Egidius Sarteanensis, OFM | late 1455? | Office in primis vesperis; secundum morem monasticum; 3 nocturns each with 4 lectiones |
| | Ermolao Barbaro sr. | late 1455? | The third Nocturn of Egidius Sarteanensis' Office (above), consists of an *homilia* by Barbaro divided into 4 *lectiones*[b] |
| Augustine – *vita* (V/*ab antiquo*) – *conversion* | Maffeo Vegio | 1450 | 9 lections *ad vesperas*; extant in autograph MS |
| | Maffeo Vegio | 1450 | 9 lections; extant in autograph MS |
| Augustine, Nicolaus, Margarita, Theodora | Agostino Dati | by 1478 | antiphon and prayer for single Office (lost) celebrating the name-saints of each member of Dati's immediate family |
| Barbara (IV/*ab antiquo*) | Pietro Ransano, OP | by 1468 | 9 lections; extant in MS |
| Bernardino of Siena (1444/1450) | Maffeo Vegio | ca. 1453 | several Offices, each of 9 lections, imposed on a *vita*; one *ad vesperas* |
| | Pietro Ridolfi, OFM | by ca. 1479 | 9 readings; print[c] |
| | Agostino Dati | before 1478 | oration (homily); print (Siena 1503) |
| Bonaventure (XIII/1482) | Alessandro Ariosto, OFM | ca. 1482 | 9? 12? lections; for canonization? LOST |
| Catherine of Siena (XIV/1461) | Tommaso Schifaldo, OP | ca. 1461 | 3 and 9 lections; Pius II instigating; extant in MS and print |
| | François de Pins | by or in 1505 | Were readings ever imposed? extant in print |
| Celestinus papa (XIII/1313) | Maffeo Vegio | 1445 | 9 lections imposed on bk. 1 of Vegio's *vita Celestini* |

(cont.)

| Saint (death date/canonization) | Author/editor | Composition | Notes[a] |
|---|---|---|---|
| Guarinus ep. Palestrina (XII/Alexander III) | Agostino Novi, Lat. Can. | by 1511 | 5 lections *sic*; print (*Elucidarium*) and late MSS extant |
| Justus & Clemens (VI/*ab antiquo*) | Raffaele Maffei | 1507–19 | 9 lections; Volterra cathedral; extant in autograph MS and print |
| Linus papa (I/*ab antiquo*) | Raffaele Maffei | 1480?–1513? | 3 lections; Volterra cathedral; extant in MS and print |
| Marcus papa (IV/*ab antiquo*) | Francesco da Castiglione | by 1464 | 9 lections imposed on *sermo* for Florence, San Lorenzo |
| Maria, Immaculate Conception[d] | Leonardo Nogarola, OFM  Bernardino de' Busti, OFM | by Feb. 1477  by Oct. 1480 | Sixtus IV instigating  Sixtus IV instigating |
| Monica (IV/*ab antiquo*) – *translation* | Maffeo Vegio  Maffeo Vegio | 1453–58 | 9 readings; *In vigilia ad vesperam*; MSS extant  9 readings, of which 7–9 narrate translations; MSS extant |
| Nicolaus of Tolentino (XIV/1446) | Maffeo Vegio | 1454–58 | 9 readings; *In vigilia ad vesperam*; MSS extant |
| Octavianus (VI/*ab antiquo*) | Raffaele Maffei | by 1519 | 9 readings; Volterra cathedral; MS and print |
| Petronius (V/*ab antiquo*) | Zaccaria Enrichetti, notary | by ca. 1509 | Bologna, San Petronio *non vidi* |
| Theodosia (IV/*ab antiquo*) | Francesco Negri (?) | by 1498 | 12; print (Venice, 1498) |
| Thomas Aquinas (XIII/1323) | Antonio Pizamano, OP | by 1490 | 9 *ad vesperas*; print (Venice, 1490, 1498) |
| Victor Mauritanus (IV/*ab antiquo*) | Raffaele Maffei | by 1519 | 9; Volterra, cathedral; MS and print |
| Vincent Ferrer (1419/1455) | Pietro Ransano | ca. 1455 | 9; Bologna, OP; MS and print |

[a] In recording formats extant (that is, manuscript and/or print), I indicate only contemporary or near-contemporary sources.

[b] Venice, Biblioteca Correr, MS Cicogna 1143 (854), fols. 56v–60v; this appears to be the presentation manuscript to the women's convent of Santa Croce, where the headless body of Athanasius was honored.

[c] The Office, not all of it an original composition, is one of three bound into Vatican City, Biblioteca Apostolica Vaticana, MS Ottob. lat. 1982: see Delorme, "Un Second office."

[d] See Blackburn, "The Virgin in the Sun," for more information on these Offices.

# Bibliography

Alberti, Leandro, *Descrittione di tutta Italia*, Venice: presso Altobello Salicato, alla libraria della Fortezza, 1588

Armstrong, Lilian, "Nicolaus Jenson's *Breviarium romanum*, Venice, 1478: Decoration and Distribution," in *Incunabula: Studies in Fifteenth-Century Printed Books Presented to Lotte Hellinga*, ed. Martin Davies, London, 1999, 421–68

Augustine, St., *The Confessions of St. Augustine*, trans. F. J. Sheed, Indianapolis, 1992 (orig. published 1942)

Blackburn, Bonnie J., "The Virgin in the Sun: Music and Image for a Prayer Attributed to Sixtus IV," *JRMA* 124 (1999), 157–95

Boyle, Leonard E., and Pierre-Marie Gy, eds., *Aux origines de la liturgie dominicaine: Le manuscrit de Santa Sabina XIV L 1*, Rome, 2004

Brand, Benjamin, "The Vigils of Medieval Tuscany," *PMM* 17 (2008), 23–54

Brown, Terry David, "Songs for the Saints of the Schism: Liturgies for Vincent Ferrer and Catherine of Siena," Ph.D. diss., University of Toronto, 1995

Catherine of Siena, *The Letters of Catherine of Siena*, trans. and ed. Suzanne Noffke, 4 vols., Tempe, AZ, 2000–7

Cattaneo, Enrico, "La partecipazione dei laici alla liturgia," in *I laici nella "societas christiana" dei secoli XI e XII*, Milan, 1968, 396–427

Charlet, Jean-Louis, "Aeneas Silvius hymnode," in *Pio II e la cultura del suo tempo*, ed. Luisa Rotondi Secchi Tarugi, Milan, 1991, 95–104

Cohn, Samuel, Jr., Marcello Fantoni, Franco Franceschi, and Fabrizio Ricciardelli, eds., *Late Medieval and Early Modern Ritual: Studies in Italian Urban Culture*, Turnhout, 2013

Della Schiava, Fabio, "Le *Fabellae* esopoiche di Maffeo Vegio," in *Tradition et créativité dans les formes gnomiques en Italie et en Europe du Nord (XIVe–XVIIe siècles)*, ed. Perrine Galand, Turnhout, 2011, 133–64

Delorme, Ferdinand M., "Un second office rythmique de S. Bernardin," *Bullettino di studi bernardiniani* 2 (1936), 32–57

Ditchfield, Simon, "Il papa come pastore? Pio V e la liturgia," in *Pio V nella società e nella politica del suo tempo*, ed. Maurilio Guasco and Angelo Torre, Bologna, 2005, 159–78

Figliuolo, Bruno, *La cultura a Napoli nel secondo Quattrocento*, Udine, 1997

Frazier, Alison K., "Humanist Lives of Catherine of Siena," in *St. Catherine of Siena: The Creation of a Cult*, ed. Jeffrey Hamburger and Gabriella Signori, Turnhout, 2013, 109–34

*Possible Lives: Authors and Saints in Renaissance Italy*, New York, 2005

Gibson, Craig A., "Learning Greek History in the Ancient Classroom: The Evidence of the Treatises on Progymnasmata," *Classical Philology* 99 (2004), 103–29

Green, Jonathan, Frank McIntyre, and Paul Needham, "The Shape of Incunable Survival and Statistical Estimation of Lost Editions," *Papers of the Bibliographical Society of America* 105/2 (2011), 141–75

Gy, Pierre-Marie, "The Different Forms of Liturgical Libelli," in *Fountain of Life*, ed. Gerard Austin, Washington, DC, 1991, 23–34

Harper, John, *The Forms and Orders of Western Liturgy from the Tenth to the Eighteenth Century*, Oxford and New York, 1991

Hay, Denys, *The Church in Italy in the Fifteenth Century*, New York, 1977

Hughes, Andrew, *Medieval Manuscripts for Mass and Office*, Toronto, 1982

Jacobus de Voragine, *Legenda aurea*, ed. Giovanni Paolo Maggioni, 2nd edn. rev., Florence, 1998

Jungmann, J. A., "Why Was Cardinal Quinonez' Reformed Breviary a Failure?," in Jungmann, *Pastoral Liturgy*, London, 1962, 200–14

Kallendorf, Craig, "The *Aeneid* Unfinished: Praise and Blame in the Speeches of Maffeo Vegio's Book XIII," in Kallendorf, *In Praise of Aeneas: Virgil and Epideictic Rhetoric in the Early Italian Renaissance*, Hanover, NH, 1989, 100–28

Maffei, Raffaele, Office for Sts. Actinea and Greciniana, in draft. Vatican City, Biblioteca Apostolica Vaticana, MS Ottob. lat. 2377, fols. 254v–255v and Ottob. lat. 992, fol. 255r–v

Offices for saints of the Volterra diocese, Volterra, Biblioteca Guarnacciana, shelfmark 1382 (XI 1 37) = CNCE 71446, s.v. Volterra <diocese>, *Officium s. Victoris XIII Mai, s. Octauiani II Septembris, s. Iusti & Clementis II Pentecostes, s. Actiniae & Grecinianae XVI Iunii, s. Lini XXIII Septembris*. S.l., s.n., s.a. Not paginated or foliated

Mittarelli, Johannes Benedictus, and Anselmus Costadoni, *Annales Camaldulenses ordinis Sancti Benedicti*, Venice, 1755–72; repr. Farnborough, Hants., 1970

Mortier, Daniel Antonin, *Histoire des maîtres généraux de l'Ordre des Frères Prêcheurs*, 4: 1400–1486, Paris, 1909

Muir, Edward, *Civic Ritual in Renaissance Venice*, Princeton, 1981

Nocentini, Silvia, "The Legenda maior of Catherine of Siena," in *A Companion to Catherine of Siena*, ed. Carolyn Muessig *et al.*, Leiden, 2012, 339–58

Palazzo, Eric, "Le Role des *libelli* dans la pratique liturgique du haut moyen âge: Histoire et typologie," *Revue Mabillon*, n.s. 1 (= 62) (1990), 9–36

Pirrotta, Nino, "Music and Cultural Tendencies in 15th-Century Italy," *JAMS* 19 (1966), 127–61

Ransano, Pietro, Office for St. Barbara, Rome, Biblioteca Casanatense, MS 112, fols. 1–35v

Salmon, Pierre, *L'Office divin au Moyen Âge: Histoire de la formation du bréviaire du IX^e au XVI^e siècle*, Paris, 1967

Schifaldo, Tommaso, *De viris illustribus eiusdem ordinis praedicatorum*, ed. Giambattista Cozzucli in "Tommaso Schifaldo umanista del sec. XV," *Documenti per servire alla storia di Sicilia*, serie 4: *Cronache e scritti varii* 6, Palermo, 1897

[Schifaldo, Tommaso], Office for St. Catherine of Siena, in *Breviarium fratrum praedicatorum*, Venice [ca. 1477–78]. Online at http://daten.digitale-sammlungen.de/~db/0003/bsb00036179/image_1

Schutte, Anne J., *By Force and Fear: Taking and Breaking Monastic Vows in Early Modern Europe*, Ithaca, 2011

Smoller, Laura, *The Saint and the Chopped-Up Baby: The Cult of Vincent Ferrer in Medieval and Early Modern Europe*, Ithaca, NY, 2014

Solvi, Daniele, "Agiografi e agiografie dell'Osservanza minoritica cismontana," in *Biografia e agiografia di San Giacomo della Marca: Atti del Convegno internazionale di Studi (Monteprandone, 29 novembre 2008)*, ed. F. Serpico, Florence, 2009, 107–23

Szendrei, Janka, "On the Prose *Historia* of St. Augustine," in *The Divine Office in the Latin Middle Ages*, ed. Margot E. Fassler and Rebecca A. Baltzer, New York and Oxford, 2000, 430–43

Taylor, Julie, *Muslims in Medieval Italy: The Colony at Lucera*, Lanham, MD, 2003

Thompson, Augustine, *Cities of God: The Religion of the Italian Communes 1125–1325*, University Park, PA, 2005

Tock, Benoît, "Galter of Arrouaise," in *The Encyclopedia of the Medieval Chronicle*, ed. R. Graeme Dunphy, Leiden, 2010, 1:660

and Ludovico Milis, eds., *Monumenta Arroasiensia*, Turnhout, 2000

Trexler, Richard, *Public Life in Renaissance Florence*, New York, 1980

Urfels-Capot, Anne-Élisabeth, "Le Sanctoral du lectionnaire de l'office," in *Aux origines de la liturgie dominicaine: Le manuscrit Santa Sabina XIV L 1*, ed. Leonard E. Boyle and Pierre-Marie Gy, Rome, 2004, 319–53

Van Liere, Kate, "Catholic Reform of the Divine Office in the Sixteenth Century: The Breviary of Cardinal Francisco de Quiñones," in *Worship in Medieval and Early Modern Europe: Change and Continuity in Religious Practice*, ed. Karin Maag and John D. Witvliet, Notre Dame, IN, 2004, 152–99

Vegio, Maffeo, *De educatione liberorum*, ed. and trans. Sisters Maria Fanning and Anne Sullivan, Washington, DC, 1933–63

Lections for the Office of St. Monica, Vatican City, Biblioteca Apostolica Vaticana, MS Ottob. lat. 1253, fols. 63v–70

*Short Epics*, ed. and trans. Michael C. Putnam and James Hankins, Cambridge, MA, 2004

Ward, John O., "Quintilian and the Rhetorical Revolution of the Middle Ages," *Rhetorica* 13 (1995), 231–84

Webb, Diana, *Patrons and Defenders: The Saints in the Italian City-States*, London, 1996

Witt, Ronald G., *In the Footsteps of the Ancients: The Origins of Humanism from Lovato to Bruni*, Boston, 2000

Woods, Marjorie Curry, "Weeping for Dido: Epilogue on a Premodern Rhetorical Exercise in the Postmodern Classroom," in *Latin Grammar and Rhetoric: From Classical Theory to Medieval Practice*, ed. Carol Dana Lanham, London, 2002, 284–94

Zaggia, Massimo, *Tra Mantova e la Sicilia nel Cinquecento*, 1: *La Sicilia sotto Ferrante Gonzaga 1535–1546*, Florence, 2003

Zanovello, Giovanni, "Les Humanistes florentins et la polyphonie liturgique," in *Poétiques de la Renaissance: Le modèle italien, le monde franco-bourguignon et leur heritage en France au XVIe siècle*, ed. Perrine Galand-Hallyn and Fernand Hallyn, Geneva, 2001, 625–38

· PART IV MUSIC AND OTHER ARTS ·

# 18

# Architecture and music in fifteenth-century Italy

DEBORAH HOWARD

> Whenever he had composed a new song, he gave it to the singers to be sung, and meanwhile he walked around, listening attentively whether the concordant sound [*harmonia*] came together well.[1]

This anecdote about Josquin des Prez, recounted by Johannes Manlius in 1562, reminds us of the intimate relationship between space and musical performance: the composer "walked around" to hear the effect of his composition in its spatial context. Our language, too, underlines the close affinity between sound and space: "volume," for example, describes both the size of a room and the loudness of the music, while "choir" and "chapel" may refer to a group of singers, or to part of a church.[2] As every musician knows, the acoustic space forms an integral part of the sound, yet most studies of early Renaissance music pay little attention to architectural settings.[3]

Compositions in the quattrocento were rarely site-specific: even before the development of music printing around 1500, pieces were copied and transported across huge distances. It was not only churchmen and princes who sought new works from abroad: in the 1480s, for instance, two young Italian merchants exchanged musical compositions between Florence and Nantes.[4] Similarly, singers traveled around continually as patrons competed for their talents. Nevertheless, certain types of repertory suited particular types of building. The function of the music – devotional, ceremonial, recreational – usually determined the choice of performance space, but even within these categories there were numerous finer variations, depending on patronage, financial resources, the availability of musicians and repertory, and local tradition.

---

1 Wegman, "From Maker to Composer," 457, and "And Josquin Laughed," 330.
2 On the multiple definitions of "choir" see Cooper, "Singers and Setting," 185–86.
3 Recent attempts to bridge this gap include Zara, "Musica e architettura"; Howard and Moretti, *Architettura e musica* and *Sound and Space*; Baumann, *Music and Space*; Howard and Moretti, *The Music Room*; Zanovello, "'In the Church and in the Chapel'."
4 Wilson, "Heinrich Isaac among the Florentines."

More was known about acoustics than is generally realized. Already in the Middle Ages, experience reinforced the general principles laid out in antiquity by Vitruvius, especially in the context of worship. In his *De re aedificatoria* (1452) Leon Battista Alberti correctly asserted that a wooden ceiling was preferable to a vault for listening to speech.[5] Indeed the type of roofing plays a crucial role, but it is not the only variable. In its simplest terms, the resonance of an enclosed space varies according to its volume and the cladding materials, as Sabine's formula showed scientifically for the first time in 1898: the larger the volume and the harder the surfaces, the longer the reverberation. Some types of music benefit from resonant acoustics, while others are better suited to "drier" spaces. Similarly, the choice of instruments or the number and range of voices needs to take account of the acoustic qualities of the space.

Works of art such as paintings, manuscript illuminations, and, later in the period, engravings help to visualize past musical performances, although the small size of some images involved a simplification of the architecture and a reduction in the number of figures.[6] Likewise, surviving written documentation, though inevitably incomplete, can provide precious information on the names and numbers of musicians. These silent witnesses have to be integrated into an assessment of the acoustic characteristics of particular architectural spaces, based on experience and scientific knowledge. In this chapter, sacred and secular music will be considered separately, although inevitably there were overlaps – laude could be sung in domestic or urban spaces, while secular themes found their way into devotional music. Moreover, the same performers were often employed in both capacities and hired by the same patrons.

All over Europe, aesthetic choices by patrons, architects, and musicians ushered in remarkable stylistic and cultural transformations during the course of the fifteenth century, but in Italy the relationship between artistic and musical style was not an obvious one. Historians of art and architecture stress the gradual displacement of the Gothic by Roman-inspired classicism, whereas musicologists point to the dominance of northern European composers in quattrocento Italy.[7] While both perspectives are less simple than this dichotomy suggests, in what follows I will attempt to show that the two trajectories were far from independent.

---

5  Baumann and Haggh, "Musical Acoustics"; Howard and Moretti, *Sound and Space*, 6–8.
6  See McKinnon, "Representations of the Mass."
7  Belozerskaya has underlined the importance of northern, especially Burgundian, influence in a range of different media, including both music and the luxury arts, but with little consideration of architecture. See *Rethinking the Renaissance* and *Luxury Arts*.

# Sacred music

## Monasteries and friaries

Monks still led a secluded way of life, living mainly in silence, often in rural locations. Their days were punctuated by the regular sung recitation of the Divine Office in the choir of the church seven times each day (and night), not to mention the daily Mass. Sheltered by wooden stalls, often surmounted by canopies to reflect the sound back into their own space, the monks sang plainchant in a semi-enclosed volume. Within the choir the words could be clearly heard, while background resonance from the church as a whole sustained the uplifting spiritual meaning of their essentially private worship.

The major departure from Benedictine monasticism was the establishment of the urban mendicant friaries from the early thirteenth century onwards. No longer bound by silence and by the frequent recitation of the Divine Office, the friars were free to perform good works outside the walls of the convent. The mendicant orders built great Gothic churches around the perimeters of medieval cities, attracting generous donations and drawing vast crowds to their sermons. The huge volume of these churches, characterized by high Gothic vaults, masonry walls, and stone or marble floors, created very reverberant acoustics, poorly suited to the spoken word, although the presence of a large congregation could dramatically reduce the reverberation.[8]

As in the case of the rural monasteries, the choirstalls in mendicant churches offered more intimate conditions for the friars' own worship.[9] These were often located in front of the high altar, divided from the nave by a stone *tramezzo* or screen – an arrangement still to be seen in the Franciscan church of Santa Maria Gloriosa dei Frari in Venice (Figure 18.1).[10] The *tramezzi* typically supported pulpits and could also be used as raised platforms for religious drama. During the Counter-Reformation from the mid-sixteenth century onwards, many of these screens were removed and their choirstalls relocated behind the high altar, as for instance in the churches of Santa Croce and Santa Maria Novella in Florence.[11] It should not be forgotten, however, that the alternative tradition of locating the choir behind the high altar had already existed in Franciscan churches in Tuscany since the fourteenth century.[12]

---

8 As demonstrated in computer simulations by Braxton Boren regarding ceremonial in San Marco and the Redentore in Venice. See Boren, "Music, Architecture and Acoustics," 49–54, 84–91.

9 A remarkable interdisciplinary study of choirstalls – in terms of placement, decoration, ritual use, and music – is to be found in Allen, "Choir Stalls in Venice and Northern Italy."

10 Howard and Moretti, *Sound and Space*, 79–94.

11 Hall, *Renovation and Counter-Reformation*.    12 Cooper, "Franciscan Choir Enclosures."

Figure 18.1 Venice, Santa Maria Gloriosa dei Frari, view of the interior showing the *tramezzo*

Worship by the friars themselves was probably sung in plainchant for most of the quattrocento, perhaps with the addition of simple improvised harmonization. In the case of the Observant, or reformed, Franciscans and Dominicans, more elaborate choral polyphony was thought to be dangerously distracting. By the 1480s, however, many of the larger friaries in cities such as Venice and Florence had begun to employ trained singers and teach more elaborate polyphony or *cantus figuratus*. For instance, in the 1480s, Santa Maria Novella in Florence had "seven boys who sing the laude"; and in 1483, on his way to the Holy Land, the German pilgrim and Observant Dominican Felix Fabri was shocked by the polyphonic music at the Dominican church of Santi Giovanni e Paolo in Venice.[13]

Whereas plainchant or improvised polyphony could be sung from memory, performers of mensural polyphony and intricate counterpoint needed written music books, often huge in size. Thus trained singers could not occupy the choirstalls but had to gather around a free-standing lectern.[14] Moreover, most

13 D'Accone, "Sacred Music in Florence," 324: "sette fanciulli che cantano le laude"; Howard and Moretti, *Sound and Space*, 83.
14 See, for example, the predella of Orcagna's altarpiece, *Christ and Saints*, 1354–57, Florence, Santa Maria Novella, Strozzi Chapel (McKinnon, "Representations of the Mass," fig. 2c), and the manuscript illumination believed to represent Ockeghem and others in Fallows, "Johannes Ockeghem: The Changing Image," 218.

of the professional singers were not bound by religious vows, and it may have been felt inappropriate for them to share the stalls with the friars, except in designated seats.

Organs were to be found by the fifteenth century in most friary churches, and even in those of monasteries.[15] Indeed, many larger churches had two organs, including one smaller instrument. The distrust of polyphony did not extend to solo organ playing, since there was no danger of obscuring the words. The organ was often placed on the *tramezzo*, on the side wall of the choir, or high up on the nave wall in one of the nearby intercolumniations, allowing easy communication with the singers whenever a simple accompaniment was needed. The usual location of the organ in a raised position had the benefit of projecting the music more effectively down into the church through reflection from the ceiling. Illuminations showing trumpeting angels in organ galleries are unlikely to reflect real practice; there is limited evidence of the use of other instruments in churches in this period.[16] The placement of singers and/or instrumentalists in the organ loft did not become common practice until the sixteenth century.

While the Gothic architecture of the older mendicant churches delivered reverberant acoustics better suited to plainchant than to polyphony or preaching, the radical new architectural developments ushered in by Brunelleschi created less resonant spaces. For example, the flat, coffered, wooden ceiling of San Lorenzo in Florence was effective in reducing sound reflections; here the placing of the choirstalls behind the high altar helped to project the sung liturgy into the church. The canons of San Lorenzo already had a tradition of polyphonic singing dating back to the fourteenth century.[17] In Brunelleschi's church of Santo Spirito, as in the major friaries, the Augustinian canons began to employ northern teachers of polyphony in the late 1480s.[18]

The climax in the friars' musical life in late fifteenth-century Italy was reached in the Servite church of Santa Maria dell'Annunziata in Florence. Encouraged by Lorenzo de' Medici, the Annunziata shared the same singers as the cathedral of Florence, including the great Henricus Isaac. In the 1480s the friary employed as many as eighteen singers, including eleven musicians and seven friars.[19] Its great *tribuna* or domed presbytery, erected between 1444 and 1476 behind the high altar at the end of the existing rectangular nave, created a unique architectural setting (Figure 18.2).[20] Three architects in succession – Michelozzo Michelozzi, Antonio Manetti, and

---

15  Bowles, "A Preliminary Checklist"; Morelli, "Per ornamento e servicio."
16  Bowles, "A Preliminary Checklist," figs. 10, 12; Fallows, "The Performing Ensembles," 33–35.
17  D'Accone, "Una nuova fonte," 20–21.
18  D'Accone, "Sacred Music in Florence," 322–23.
19  D'Accone, "The Singers of San Giovanni," 337; Zanovello, "'In the Church and in the Chapel'."
20  Brown, "The Patronage and Building History."

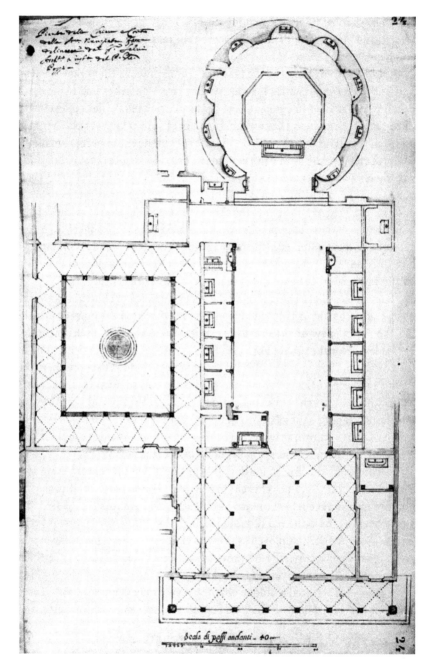

Figure 18.2  G. Salvi (attr.), Groundplan of SS. Annunziata, Florence, between 1690 and 1702. Archivio di Stato di Firenze

Figure 18.3 Michelozzi, Manetti, and Alberti, tribune of SS. Annunziata, Florence, 1444–76, interior showing choirstalls, lectern, and rear of high altar

Alberti – supervised its construction, with funding from local families and from Lodovico Gonzaga of Mantua. On its completion the friars' choir (originally placed at the head of the nave) was moved into the new choir in the centre of the domed tribune (Figure 18.3). The placing of octagonal stalls beneath a cupola echoed the new arrangement in Florence cathedral, to be discussed

below, but here the lower dome created more responsive performance conditions, projecting sound back to the singers. The lectern in the centre allowed
the musicians to sing their innovative, written polyphony while the rest of the
friars occupied the surrounding stalls. Nevertheless, the music's audibility
from the nave would have been limited, despite Alberti's enlargement of the
chancel arch, because of the screening effect of the high altar, which obstructed
the passage of direct sound.[21]

## Cathedrals

The cathedrals of Milan, Florence, and Siena all underwent dramatic transformations in their musical life over the course of the fifteenth century, in each
case against the background of huge Gothic interiors with very reverberant
acoustics. Although every cathedral was the center of a diocese and the seat
(*cathedra*) of the bishop, additional funding for both buildings and music might
be provided by local guilds or by a local prince or powerful citizen. Similarly,
extra singers could be supplied on special feast days by the city government. In
considering the role of architecture and music in the liturgy, the evidence must
be treated cautiously, for the arrangements of choirstalls and organs in Italian
cathedrals were substantially modified from the mid-sixteenth century under
the impact of the Counter-Reformation.

In the fourteenth century major cathedrals were already equipped with at
least one organ: for instance, an organ gallery or *palco* was installed in 1373 in
Siena cathedral in the new choir behind the high altar (Figure 18.4).[22] In 1387
two new organs were ordered for the nave of Florence cathedral, where the
crossing was still walled off awaiting the erection of the dome.[23]

In the early years of the quattrocento, most cathedrals employed no more
than two to four singers or cantors, usually ecclesiastics.[24] These cantors taught
plainchant and led the singing by the canons, chaplains, and clerk choristers in
the presbytery stalls, especially on feast days or at Vespers. Two cantors alone in
such huge spaces needed strong voices in order to make an impact. While
recruiting singers for Siena cathedral in 1447, the Sienese envoy in Genoa
remarked of one singer that "this tenor's voice seems too small for our
church."[25] By contrast, the numbers of canons, chaplains, and clerk choristers
who took part in the plainsong were much larger and might extend to fifty or

---

21 On the placing of the organs, see Morelli, "Per ornamento e servicio," 291–92.

22 Ibid., 285. On the furnishing of the new choir in Siena cathedral see van der Ploeg, *Art and Liturgy*, 118–20.

23 Poggi, *Il Duomo di Firenze*, cxxx; D'Accone, "Music and Musicians," 99; Waldman, "From the Middle Ages to the Counter-Reformation," 38–40.

24 McKinnon, "Representations of the Mass," 38; Pirrotta, "Music and Cultural Tendencies," 129; D'Accone, *The Civic Muse*, 144, and "Music and Musicians," 102.

25 D'Accone, *The Civic Muse*, 171–72.

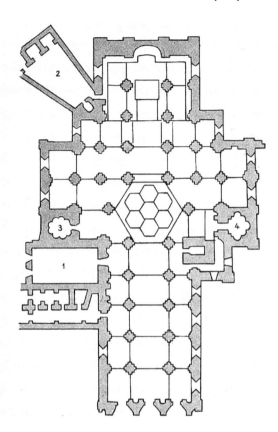

Figure 18.4 Siena cathedral, plan. 2 = sacristy, 3 = Cappella di San Giovanni Battista

sixty voices.[26] Long after the introduction of polyphony, traditional plain-chant, well suited to the reverberant acoustics, retained its central role in the liturgy because of its effectiveness in communicating religious texts and spiritual sustenance.

In 1431, shortly before the consecration of Florence cathedral, a new *pergamo* or projecting balcony was ordered from Luca della Robbia to house a new organ, and the instrument itself was commissioned from Matteo da Prato in the following year (Figures 18.5–6).[27] Soon afterwards, a second *pergamo* carved by Donatello was installed on the opposite wall, again for use as an organ loft; one of the smaller, older organs was installed there in 1457.

---

26 D'Accone, "Music and Musicians," 101–103, relating to Florence cathedral.
27 Poggi, *Il Duomo di Firenze*, cxxxvi; Janson, *The Sculpture of Donatello*, 119–23; Morelli, "Per ornamento e servizio," 285.

Figure 18.5 Luca della Robbia, "cantoria" (former organ gallery in Florence cathedral), 1431–38. Florence, Museo dell'Opera del Duomo

These raised galleries, later known as *cantorie* though not designed for singers, were placed high up on the diagonal walls of the crossing, over the doors to the sacristies, within which small spiral staircases gave access.[28] They were removed to the Museo dell'Opera del Duomo in the late nineteenth century. Reflecting the paired arrangement in Florence, a second organ was erected in Siena cathedral in 1453 over the door to the sacristy on the north side of the choir, probably opposite to the earlier instrument.[29]

The best-known claim for the consonance of music and architecture in quattrocento Italy concerns the motet *Nuper rosarum flores*, composed by Guillaume Du Fay for the consecration of Florence cathedral in 1436, following the completion of Brunelleschi's dome over the crossing (Figure 18.6). The work was probably performed by the visiting papal choir.[30] The connection of

28  The large organ was finally installed in the first gallery in 1448. For a study of the acoustic behavior of the space, see Baumann and Haggh, "Musical Acoustics," 201–8.

29  D'Accone, *The Civic Muse*, 19; Morelli, "Per ornamento e servicio," 290. A singing gallery was in this position in the mid-sixteenth century (ibid., 299).

30  D'Accone, "Music and Musicians," 116.

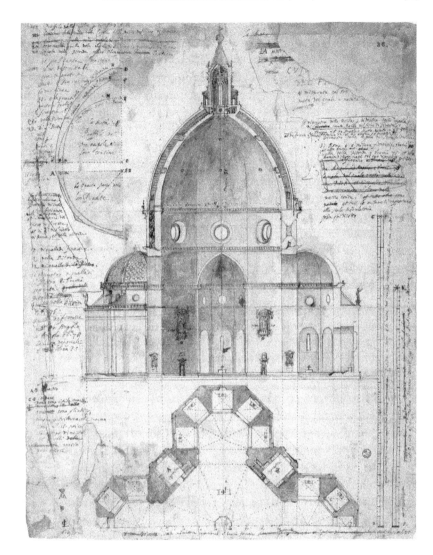

Figure 18.6 Ludovico Cardi, known as il Cigoli, plan and section of dome of Florence cathedral, by 1610. Gabinetto di disegni e delle stampe degli Uffizi

the motet with the dimensions of the church, first proposed by Charles Warren in 1973, was reformulated by Craig Wright in 1994 and, more recently, by Marvin Trachtenberg in 2001.[31] Their numerological analysis focuses on the

---

31 Warren, "Brunelleschi's Dome and Dufay's Motet"; Wright, "Dufay's *Nuper rosarum flores*"; and Trachtenberg, "Architecture and Music Reunited."

particular proportional series 6:4:2:3 found in the music, claimed to represent not only certain measurements in the cathedral itself, but also those of the biblical temple of Solomon. For example, the height of the dome and the length of the nave are both 144 braccia, the product of $6 \times 4 \times 2 \times 3$.[32]

In reality, such "perfect" numbers were commonly used in the proportions of medieval sacred buildings. Although these numbers in different combinations can generate a range of simple musical harmonies, harmonic ratios in the dimensions of a building have limited impact on the listening experience. Acoustic properties depend on size, materials, and ceiling type far more than on the incorporation of numerological relationships. In this case it is clear that the reverberant acoustics of the cathedral's interior can have done little to assist the listener, especially if the motet was performed in the low, wooden, octagonal choirstalls erected provisionally under the new dome to Brunelleschi's design.[33] More cautiously, one can at least draw on the Ciceronian ideal that musical harmony evoked the perfection of the city, as expressed by Leonardo Bruni in his *Laudatio*, a panegyric description of Florence, in 1403–1404:

> There is proportion in strings of a harp so that when they are tightened, a harmony results from the different tones; nothing could be sweeter or more pleasing to the ear than this. In the same way, this very prudent city is harmonized in all its parts, so there results a single great, harmonious constitution whose harmony pleases both the eyes and minds of men.[34]

A major change took place in Florence cathedral in 1439, three years after the consecration, with the establishment of the first polyphonic choir, to perform both in the cathedral and in the nearby Baptistry of San Giovanni, especially at Vespers and on feast days.[35] Initially just four singers were recruited in Ferrara in 1438 by Lorenzo de' Medici, Cosimo's brother. Because of the small numbers, the polyphonic psalms and motets must have been performed by solo voices, but the singing position of these four voices is uncertain. Given the size and reverberant character of the space, the newly built, wooden, octagonal enclosure under the dome would have offered minimal audibility, except to other listeners within these stalls. Subsequently more singers were recruited from both Italy and northern Europe, allowing musical experimentation using different positions and larger forces.[36]

32  Trachtenberg, "Architecture and Music Reunited," 755.
33  Baumann and Haggh, "Musical Acoustics," 206–207; Brown, "The Patronage and Building History," 81–83; Lavin, *Santa Maria del Fiore*, 23–24; Waldman, "From the Middle Ages to the Counter-Reformation," 42–54. Brunelleschi's choir survived with various modifications until a much higher, marble replacement was ordered from Bandinelli in 1546.
34  Translation from www.york.ac.uk/teaching/history/pjpg/bruni.pdf (last accessed 2 February 2012).
35  D'Accone, "Music and Musicians," 109–11; "The Singers of San Giovanni," 307–10.
36  D'Accone, "The Singers of San Giovanni," 315–19.

Meanwhile, in Siena, two of the singers hired in 1452 were specifically described as "per la cantoria," although its location was not specified.[37] Singers may have occupied some of the late fourteenth-century wooden stalls in the spacious choir behind the high altar.[38] As we have seen, the organs were also in this area. A screen enclosing the pulpit at the head of the nave is seen in the left background of a painted book cover of 1483, but it is uncertain whether stalls ever stood in this position (Figure 18.7).[39]

By the 1470s and 1480s the numbers of trained singers in Florence and Siena cathedrals reached unprecedented levels, reflecting both musical ambition and financial investment. By 1478 the chapel (or singing establishment) of Florence cathedral consisted of two tenors, two countertenors, the *magister capellae*, and four soprano choristers, and it continued to grow, reaching a maximum total of eighteen by 1493.[40] By 1482 Siena cathedral employed as many as seventeen singers – the largest number ever recorded there.[41] With such large numbers it was possible to employ more than one voice to a part when artistic or religious considerations warranted a stronger sound, audible from a greater distance. Finally, in the case of Milan cathedral, a letter of Beatrice d'Este of 1493 mentioned two raised balconies in the far corners of the choir – one for singers and the other for the wind band – all of whom performed at various points in the Mass.[42]

In all three cathedrals the long reverberation time would have challenged the singers, who had to adjust the tempo and volume to the conditions. The alternation of dissonances and consonances in the writing of counterpoint could not easily be detected if the long reverberation blurred the crucial harmonic shifts.[43] Suitable acoustic conditions for *cantus figuratus*, or mensural polyphony, could only be achieved within the great cathedrals in relatively self-contained spaces such as choirs, transepts, or chapels. For instance, choirstalls were installed in the self-contained, newly built Cappella di San Giovanni in Siena cathedral in 1482 (see Figure 18.4 above).[44] Otherwise, musicians, clergy, and visiting dignitaries had to gather closely together, as seen in the panel of 1483 (mentioned above), which depicts *The Presentation of the Keys of the City to the Virgin* in the

---

37 D'Accone, *The Civic Muse*, 213, Doc. 4.4.
38 Benton, "The Design of Siena and Florence Duomos," 143 and pl. 163; Norman, *Siena and the Virgin*, 27. John White's reconstruction with an octagonal choir in the crossing reflects the present sixteenth-century paving rather than the likely thirteenth-century arrangement. See van der Ploeg, *Art and Liturgy*, 83–91 and figs. 37–38.
39 Norman, *Siena and the Virgin*, 25.
40 D'Accone, "The Singers of San Giovanni," 346; "Lorenzo the Magnificent and Music," 283; "Sacred Music in Florence," 319.
41 D'Accone, *The Civic Muse*, 230.     42 Fallows, "The Performing Ensembles," 56 n. 10.
43 An explication of principles of counterpoint was published in 1496 by Gaffurius, *Practica Musicae*, bk. 3, trans. Young, 123–62. See also Blackburn, "On Compositional Process," 225.
44 D'Accone, *The Civic Muse*, 25.

Figure 18.7 Anonymous miniaturist, *Presentation of the Keys of the City to the Virgin*, biccherna (painted book cover on panel), 1483, Siena. Museo delle Tavolette di Biccherna

right aisle of Siena cathedral (Figure 18.7). By liturgical convention, musicians faced toward the altar, rather than toward the clergy or the congregation, for the sacred music was addressed to God rather than to the worshiper. The clergy and any other privileged listeners in the vicinity of the altar thus benefited from direct sound, but the singers were not easily audible to the lay congregation: instead the voices blended and diffused within the space around the altar before being reflected back into the nave.

In Florence the controversial status of *cantus figuratus* came to a head with the expulsion of the Medici in 1493 and the growing influence of the religious fanatic Girolamo Savonarola. In a sermon of 1496 he expressed his own preference for the familiar laude known to every worshiper.[45] By contrast, complex polyphony, in which the voices are only rarely coordinated rhythmically, tended to obscure the intelligibility of the text. In response to his disapproval, the entire musical chapel of the cathedral and baptistery in Florence – as in SS. Annunziata – was disbanded, only to be immediately reinstated on Savonarola's arrest five years later.

Despite the increasingly classical preoccupations of both humanists and artists, by the later years of the fifteenth century repertory by northern European musicians such as Du Fay, Jacob Obrecht, Henricus Isaac, Antoine Busnoys, Johannes Ockeghem, Josquin des Prez, Alexander Agricola, and Johannes Ghiselin was performed in all the major cathedrals on feast days, during Holy Week, and at Vespers – excepting the Savonarolan hiatus in Florence. The dangers of inferring close stylistic parallels between architecture and music are underlined by the observation that in Milan, the most flamboyantly Gothic cathedral in Italy, most of the musicians were Italian, despite the prevalence of northern musicians at court.[46] The musicians from the North were accustomed to lofty church interiors with Gothic vaulting, but *cantus figuratus* required a far greater acoustic clarity than plainchant or even *falsobordone*. Placing the singers in semi-enclosed choirstalls helped to improve the audibility for listeners in close proximity, but the background resonance of these huge interiors was ever present.

## Palatine chapels

All the palaces of Italian courts had chapels for the private worship of the household and courtiers, but there were two palatine chapels of far greater size and importance, both of them seats of musical and artistic investment. The first of these was the church of San Marco in Venice, and the second the Sistine Chapel in Rome.

---

45 D'Accone, "Sacred Music in Florence," 313 n. 3, and 327–28.
46 Sherr, "*Illibata dei virgo nutrix*," 453 n. 17, citing a verbal communication by Bonnie Blackburn.

San Marco was the burial place of St. Mark and the private chapel of the Doge of Venice. Its complex five-domed plan and relatively low mosaic domes created more favourable acoustics than the lofty Gothic cathedrals, for the rough surfaces of the mosaics helped to reduce disturbing sound reflections. In the fifteenth century the liturgy was still strongly influenced by Byzantine imperial ceremonial, well attuned to the character of the architecture; here the burst of musical innovation was to occur in the following century.[47] The Sistine Chapel, by contrast, was completely rebuilt and its musical life transformed in the last quarter of the fifteenth century.[48]

Unlike San Marco, the Sistine Chapel had little presence in the urban scene – it could only be entered through the Vatican Palace. The papal choir, known as the *schola cantorum*, had existed since the fourth century. The present chapel, begun in 1473 by Pope Sixtus IV and dedicated ten years later, replaced a late thirteenth-century predecessor in the same location.[49] Its plain rectangular form was very different from that of San Marco – the simple "shoe-box" is generally regarded as one of the optimum shapes for musical performance. About halfway along its length, a low marble wall surmounted by an open metalwork screen divided the lay area from that occupied by the papal court and high-profile visitors (Figure 18.8). The cosmatesque pattern on the floor indicates the former position of the cardinals' stalls, arranged around three sides of a rectangle facing towards the altar. A raised dais at the altar end formed a notional "presbytery," with the papal throne on the left side.

The singers' box, or *cantoria*, occupied the fourth bay (counting from the altar end) of the right wall on the lower level, straddling the screen so that it was visible from both sides. The space did not project into the room, but was set within the wall thickness. The position of the singers astride the sacred and lay areas of the chapel gave them a marginalized role in the liturgy, but also allowed them to communicate more directly with the lay congregation. They were relatively free from ritual requirements, being allowed to sit or stand at will.[50] In the later sixteenth century the screen was moved further from the altar wall to its present position to accommodate the growing number of cardinals (Figure 18.9).[51]

What were the acoustic implications of the unusual position of the *cantoria*? The main objective of its location astride the screen seems to have been to ensure visibility and audibility for religious and lay worshipers alike. The gallery was not raised high enough to benefit from reflected sound from the ceiling. On the other hand, the singers' voices would have been evenly diffused

47  Howard and Moretti, *Sound and Space*, 17–29, with further bibliography.
48  Rodin, *Josquin's Rome.*      49  Shearman, *Raphael's Cartoons*, 3–4, 21–30; Rodin, *Josquin's Rome*, 7–9.
50  Sherr, "The Singers of the Papal Chapel," 258.      51  Shearman, *Raphael's Cartoons*, 27.

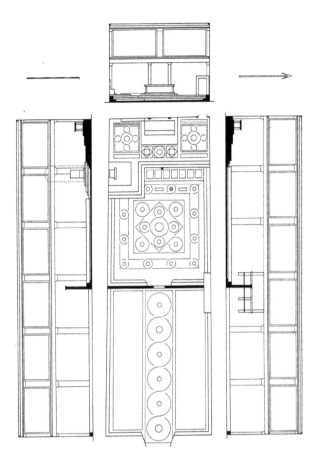

Figure 18.8  Rome, Sistine Chapel, begun 1473, reconstruction of plan as in ca. 1515. After Shearman, *Raphael's Cartoons*

through the simple "shoe-box" volume, for the screen was permeable and there were no ancillary spaces where sound could become trapped and cause later interference.[52] Given the large size of the lofty interior, the chapel is a resonant space, but when it was filled with people and hung with tapestries on ceremonial occasions, excessive reverberation would have been greatly reduced.[53] Textiles – both robes and hangings – not only dampened the sound but also added visual richness. A panegyric description of the Sistine Chapel, datable to 1482, asserted

52 On the acoustic properties of simple, rectangular sacred interiors, see Howard and Moretti, *Sound and Space*, 171–94.
53 For an analysis of the effects of crowds and draperies in church interiors, see Boren, "Music, Architecture and Acoustics," 49–51 and 84–89.

Figure 18.9  Étienne Dupérac, *Interior of the Sistine Chapel*, engraving 1578

that "viewers fall into wonderment before its interior walls draped in tapestries and gold."[54] In 1515 Leo X commissioned a new set of costly Flemish tapestries

54  Monfasoni, "A Description of the Sistine Chapel," 12.

from cartoons by Raphael, following the older festal tradition.[55] Sacred music within a ceremonial space cannot be evaluated as a purely auditory experience, removed from visual splendor and the solemnity of the ritual.

The role of music in the Sistine Chapel depended strictly on the needs of the liturgy, as codified by the masters of ceremonies. Of these, neither Johannes Burckard nor his successor Paris de Grassis seems to have had much interest in polyphonic music such as motets, which they considered mainly as time-fillers to occupy awkward intervals in the ritual.[56] In 1484–88 Burckard left a some-what scathing description of the singers in the papal chapel:

> *Item.* There are twelve singers [*cantores*], that is, two tenors, four countertenors and six high voices, who should have clear and melodious voices, and not hoarse or harsh ones; indeed, too many people singing distort melody and confuse hearing . . . And there have never been such inept and ugly voices in the chapel as there are today.[57]

Both Burckard and de Grassis took a dim view of *cantus figuratus*, which they felt made it harder to hear the words, especially in the case of the Credo, which required specific actions by the worshipers at certain points.[58] Although the singers had to be literate and able to sing plainchant, counter-point, and *cantus figuratus*, many of their duties involved simple monophonic recitation of readings and prophecies.[59] Daily attendance in the smaller private chapel of San Nicolò does not seem to have involved polyphony. Full forces and polyphonic singing were required only on important feast days or special occasions such as the funerals of cardinals.

While the wall frescoes – and later, of course, Michelangelo's ceiling and Raphael's tapestries – represented the vanguard of Italian pictorial art, the most innovative music was composed by northerners. Here Josquin des Prez reached his maturity alongside fellow northerners such as Marbrianus de Orto (Du Jardin).[60] It seems that they spurred each other on to ever greater inven-tiveness in their complex contrapuntal polyphony, involving repetitions at different pitches and speeds that gave impetus to the intricate harmonic and rhythmic structures – even if the masters of ceremony remained resolutely

---

55 Shearman, *Raphael's Cartoons*, 5–7 and 13.
56 Sherr, "*Illibata dei virgo nutrix*," 458 and 461; "Speculations on Repertory," 114–15.
57 Sherr, "Competence and Incompetence," 622–23.
58 Sherr, "*Illibata dei virgo nutrix*," 461; "The Singers of the Papal Chapel," 255; "Speculations on Repertory," 114–15.
59 Sherr, "The Singers of the Papal Chapel," 251–58.
60 Rodin, *Josquin's Rome*, Part III, 233–310. On the repertory of the papal chapel see *Papal Music and Musicians*, ed. Sherr.

unimpressed. This dazzling repertory was still in use in the Sistine Chapel in the later sixteenth century and its influence was felt all over Europe.[61]

## Secular music

### *The princely courts*

Northern culture permeated all the courts of the Italian peninsula during the fifteenth century. Music, art, and architecture – not to mention dancing, dress, and dining – fell under the spell of the glittering Burgundian court.[62] In the visual arts, this impact is often underrated, or dismissively labeled "International Gothic," but in music the inspiration from the North was paramount. Moreover, within Italy, the mobility of court life enhanced the transmission of culture. Not only artists, musicians, and ambassadors, but even the courts themselves, moved around from place to place.

The major Italian courts of the quattrocento employed as many musicians as the great cathedrals. In 1465, Naples had twenty-one singers and Savoy four-teen, and each employed an organist; in Milan Galeazzo Maria Sforza expanded his court chapel from four to thirty musicians in 1471–72 alone, and by 1481 twenty-seven singers were to be found at the court of Ercole d'Este in Ferrara.[63] Northern singers were preeminent, and the most innovative reper-tory was encouraged by intense competition between rulers. In the secular context, the perceived moral dangers of *cantus figuratus* were avoided, except perhaps at the daily Office and Mass in the palace chapels. Private chapels offered the opportunity for courtly display before elite visitors, underlined in the Palazzo Medici in Florence by the rich "International Gothic" character of Benozzo Gozzoli's frescoes. In Galeazzo Maria Sforza's case the extravagant expenditure on the decoration of his palace chapels in Milan and Pavia and the employment of famous musicians such as Jean Cordier and Agricola may have led indirectly to his assassination in 1476.[64]

The location of musical activity in princely palaces varied from place to place. While the Castel Nuovo in Naples had special rooms for music in the fifteenth century, at the courts of Ferrara and Mantua rooms of different sizes were used for music-making in various palaces and villas, depending on the occasion.[65] The *sala grande* was the setting for dancing and feasting at important

---

61 Dean, "The Repertory of the Cappella Giulia."
62 Belozerskaya, *Rethinking the Renaissance*, esp. 130–207, and *Luxury Arts*, esp. 186–226.
63 D'Accone, *Music in Renaissance Florence*, 337–38. D'Accone, *The Civic Muse*, 222; Welch, "Sight, Sound and Ceremony"; Lockwood, *Music in Renaissance Ferrara*, 134.
64 Welch, "Sight, Sound and Ceremony," 167 and *passim*; Belozerskaya, *Rethinking the Renaissance*, 194–200.
65 Knighton, "A Day in the Life," 81; Moretti, "Spaces for Musical Performance"; Fenlon, "Music Rooms."

ceremonies. On such occasions musicians occupied a dais at the edge of the room or even a raised tribune. A description of the *sala* at the wedding of Elisabetta Gonzaga and Guidobaldo da Montefeltro in 1489 refers to a *pozzo* (literally a well) on the entrance wall for the musicians – probably a circular enclosure rather than a sunken pit.[66] On this occasion, the velvet hangings helped to dampen the noise. Instruments as well as voices accompanied courtly feasts, as Johannes Tinctoris observed:

> Whenever important people hold glittering, stately banquets, what type of musicians do we not observe in attendance? There we find singers, there pipers, there drummers, there organists, there lutenists, there recorders, there trumpets, playing together so tunefully that it almost seems an actual picture of the joys above.[67]

Dancing played a major role in court festivities, and its spatial context can be inferred from dance manuals of the time, such as that of Giovanni Ambrogio.[68] The favorite dances at court were the *bassadanza* and the *ballo*, their slow sedate pace suggesting the ordered dignity of the realm.[69] Both men and women took part in pairs, and even when the dances involved small circular movements, the progressive sequences required long rectangular spaces. For instance, the main ceremonial *sala* at the Este palace of Belriguardo was eighty-three *passi* long and twenty-one *passi* wide.[70]

Music at court could also be more intimate. The *tarsie*, or wood inlays, that decorate the tiny *studiolo* of Federico da Montefeltro in Urbino show musical instruments in the feigned open cupboards, while a fictive clavichord lies on an illusionistic shelf (Figure 18.10).[71] Quieter instruments such as clavichords and lutes were ideal for the accompaniment of chansons, composed by the great northern composers such as Antoine Busnoys, Johannes Ockeghem, and Josquin for private music-making by the courtiers themselves.[72] To soothe his gout at the thermal baths, Lorenzo de' Medici took the cathedral organist and two cantors for entertainment, underlining the flexibility of performance sites. Though not officially a head of state, Lorenzo promoted court culture in the manner of a prince and even composed a dance manual himself.[73]

---

66 Nevile, *The Eloquent Body*, 35 and n. 98 on 197–98.
67 Strohm and Cullington, eds., *On the Dignity and the Effects of Music*, 60.
68 McGee, "Dancing Masters," 218–24.
69 D'Accone, *The Civic Muse*, 641; Belozerskaya, *Luxury Arts*, 214–19.
70 Nevile, *The Eloquent Body*, 28–32.
71 Fenlon, "Music in Italian Renaissance Paintings," 196–97.
72 Fallows, "Polyphonic Song in the Florence of Lorenzo's Youth"; D'Accone, "Lorenzo the Magnificent and Music."
73 D'Accone, "Lorenzo the Magnificent and Music," 271, 277–78. Images of dancing in art, such as Filippino's *Egyptian Dance*, were not necessarily realistic; see Fenlon, "Music in Italian Renaissance Paintings," 192–93.

Figure 18.10 Urbino, Palazzo Ducale, Studiolo of Federico da Montefeltro, *tarsie* (wood inlays) depicting illusionistic musical instruments, 1473–76

## Communal festivities

Many major open-air civic festivals involved musical accompaniment for dancing, feasting, or processions. Even in the hard landscape of an urban square, open-air acoustics are very different from those of enclosed churches or *sale*. Whereas there is less delayed reverberation, distinct echoes may be obtrusive. Most importantly, the initial sound needs to be much louder, and therefore the favorite instruments for open-air music in fifteenth-century Italy were wind bands, specially shawms, trombones, and trumpets, often accompanied by drums.[74] Trumpet fanfares from balconies were played by heralds, as elsewhere in Europe – major cities such as Siena, Lucca, Bologna, Florence, and Naples are all known to have employed trumpeters.[75] In Siena, the wind band, or *piffari*, included two shawms, a bombard, and a trombone, a group loud enough to take part in open-air celebrations such as the two-week lead-up to the Feast

74 D'Accone, "Lorenzo the Magnificent and Music," 260, 262; Welker, "Wind Ensembles."
75  D'Accone, *The Civic Muse*, 441.

of the Assumption. They also accompanied outdoor Masses in the cathedral square, and even university degree ceremonies.

The Campo in Siena must have been one of the best-suited open-air spaces acoustically, to judge by its theatrical arrangement and sloping paving. Indeed, the space was even an effective arena for preaching (Figure 18.11). Here balls were held on a temporary platform outside the Palazzo Pubblico at the lower end, for example to welcome the daughter of the Duke of Milan in 1465.[76] In Florence, the visit of the young Galeazzo Maria Sforza in 1459 was celebrated in the Mercato Nuovo with dancing and feasting, vividly described in an anonymous poem in praise of Cosimo de' Medici and his sons, from which we learn that shawms and trumpets accompanied the dances from a raised position, perhaps a high window or balcony.[77] Loud musical forces were needed to fill a space of this size. As many as twenty trumpet players heralded the entry of every lady and greeted the young count, and at the start of the dinner, trumpeters preceded the bearers of dishes.

Carnival offered scope for both musical and artistic invention in civic settings, often involving traditional, local *canti carnascialeschi*, performed by groups of young Florentines in costume rather than professional musicians. The rumbustious open-air setting seems to have been poorly suited to more elaborate compositions: for example, Isaac's *Alla Battaglia*, performed in 1488 on a carnival float or *trionfo*, was considered a failure, for it was too long and intricate for the purpose.[78]

## Conclusion

The intriguing intersections of musical and artistic life explored in this chapter have shown how the dynamics of cultural change – and exchange – do not conform to straightforward linear models. It is too simple to view the Italian Renaissance merely as a period of renewed interest in the antique, according to the schema bequeathed to posterity by Vasari. In parallel to the new classicism, the impact of courtly Gothic from northern Europe was felt in many different media – and perhaps most of all in musical life. This chapter has charted colliding waves of interaction, in which northern polyphony attuned to flamboyant Gothic settings was grafted into Italian liturgy and ceremonial, to be framed within architectural settings increasingly tinged by the inspiration of ancient Rome. Nonetheless, the most innovative music was often to be heard in old-fashioned architectural contexts such as Gothic cathedrals or medieval

76  Ibid., 643–44.
77  Nevile, *The Eloquent Body*, 146, 149, 153.
78  Wilson, "Heinrich Isaac among the Florentines," 108–10.

Figure 18.11  Sano di Pietro, *Bernardino Preaching on the Campo of Siena*, 1448, tempera and gold on panel, 162 × 101.5 cm. Museo dell'Opera del Duomo

castles. The constant peregrinations of musicians and the exchange of their compositions catalyzed the alchemy that combined these disparate elements. Princes, popes, and prelates alike recognized the power of this multi-sensory cultural experience.

# Bibliography

Allen, Joanne, "Choir Stalls in Venice and Northern Italy: Furniture, Ritual and Space in the Renaissance Church Interior," Ph.D. diss., University of Warwick, 2010

Baumann, Dorothea, *Music and Space: A Systematic and Historical Investigation into the Impact of Architectural Acoustics on Performance Practice Followed by a Study of Handel's Messiah*, Bern, 2011

and Barbara Haggh, "Musical Acoustics in the Middle Ages," *EM* 18 (1990), 199–210

Belozerskaya, Marina, *Luxury Arts of the Renaissance*, Los Angeles, 2005

*Rethinking the Renaissance: Burgundian Arts across Europe*, Cambridge, 2002

Benton, Tim, "The Design of Siena and Florence Duomos," in *Siena, Florence and Padua*, ed. Norman, New Haven, 1995, 2:129–43

Blackburn, Bonnie J., "On Compositional Process in the Fifteenth Century," *JAMS* 40 (1987), 210–84

Boren, Braxton, "Music, Architecture and Acoustics in Renaissance Venice: Recreating Lost Soundscapes," M.Phil. diss., Cavendish Laboratory, Cambridge University, 2010

Bowles, Edmund A., "A Preliminary Checklist of Fifteenth-Century Representations of Organs in Paintings and Manuscript Illuminations," *Organ Yearbook* 13 (1982), 5–30

Brown, Beverly Louise, "The Patronage and Building History of the Tribuna of SS. Annunziata in Florence: A Reappraisal in Light of New Documentation," *Mitteilungen des Kunsthistorischen Institutes in Florenz* 25 (1981), 59–146

Cooper, Donal, "Franciscan Choir Enclosures and the Function of Double-Sided Altarpieces in Pre-Tridentine Umbria," *Journal of the Warburg and Courtauld Institutes* 64 (2001), 1–54

Cooper, Tracy E., "Singers and Setting: Choir and Furnishing in an Age of Reform. The Example of San Giorgio Maggiore," in *Architettura e musica*, ed. Howard and Moretti, 183–200

D'Accone, Frank A., *The Civic Muse: Music and Musicians in Siena during the Middle Ages and the Renaissance*, Chicago, 1997

"Lorenzo the Magnificent and Music," in *Lorenzo il Magnifico e il suo mondo*, ed. Gian Carlo Garfagnini, Florence, 1994, 259–90; repr. in *Music in Renaissance Florence*, no. V

"Music and Musicians at Santa Maria del Fiore in the Early Quattrocento," in *Scritti in onore di Luigi Ronga*, Milan, 1973, 99–129; repr. in *Music in Renaissance Florence*, no. III

*Music in Renaissance Florence: Studies and Documents*, Aldershot, 2006

"Una nuova fonte dell'ars nova italiana: Il codice di San Lorenzo, 2211," *Studi musicali* 13 (1984), 3–31; repr. in *Music in Renaissance Florence*, no. II

"Sacred Music in Florence in Savonarola's Time," in *Una città e il suo profeta: Firenze di fronte al Savonarola*, ed. Gian Carlo Garfagnini, Florence, 2001, 311–45; repr. in *Music in Renaissance Florence*, no. VI

"The Singers of San Giovanni in Florence during the 15th Century," *JAMS* 14 (1961), 307–58; repr. in *Music in Renaissance Florence*, no. III

Dean, Jeffrey J., "The Repertory of the Cappella Giulia in the 1560s," *JAMS* 41 (1988), 465–90

Fallows, David, *Composers and their Songs, 1400–1521*, Aldershot, 2010

"Johannes Ockeghem: The Changing Image, the Songs and a New Source," *EM* 12 (1984), 218–30; repr. in *Composers and their Songs*, no. VII

"The Performing Ensembles in Josquin's Sacred Music," *TVNM* 35 (1985), 32–64; repr. in *Songs and Musicians*, no. XII

"Polyphonic Song in the Florence of Lorenzo's Youth, ossia: The Provenance of the Manuscript Berlin 78.C.28: Naples or Florence?," in *La musica a Firenze al tempo di Lorenzo il Magnifico*, ed. Piero Gargiulo, Florence, 1993, 47–61; repr. in *Songs and Musicians*, no. VIII

*Songs and Musicians in the Fifteenth Century*, Aldershot, 1996

Fenlon, Iain, "Music in Italian Renaissance Paintings," in *Companion*, ed. Knighton and Fallows, 189–209

"Music Rooms in the Ducal Palace in Mantua: From Andrea Mantegna to Giovan Battista Bertani," in *The Music Room*, ed. Howard and Moretti, 237–58

Gaffurius, Franchinus, *The Practica Musicae of Franchinus Gafurius*, trans. and ed. Irwin Young, Madison, WI, 1969

Hall, Marcia B., *Renovation and Counter-Reformation: Vasari and Duke Cosimo in Santa Maria Novella and Santa Croce 1565–77*, Oxford, 1979

Howard, Deborah, and Laura Moretti, *Sound and Space in Renaissance Venice: Architecture, Music, Acoustics*, New Haven, 2009

and Laura Moretti, eds., *Architettura e musica nella Venezia del Rinascimento*, Milan, 2006

and Laura Moretti, eds., *The Music Room in Early Modern France and Italy: Sound, Space, and Object*, Oxford, 2012

Janson, H. W., *The Sculpture of Donatello*, Princeton, 1963

Knighton, Tess, "A Day in the Life of Francisco de Peñalosa (*c.* 1470–1528)," in *Companion*, ed. Knighton and Fallows, 79–84

and David Fallows, eds., *Companion to Medieval and Renaissance Music*, Berkeley, 1992

Lavin, Irving, *Santa Maria del Fiore: Il Duomo di Firenze e la Vergine incinta*, trans. Silvia Panichi, Rome, 1999

Lockwood, Lewis, *Music in Renaissance Ferrara, 1400–1505: The Creation of a Musical Center in the Fifteenth Century*, Cambridge, MA, 1984; rev. edn. New York and Oxford, 2009

McGee, Timothy J., "Dancing Masters and the Medici Court in the 15th Century," *Studi musicali* 17 (1988), 201–24

McKinnon, James, "Representations of the Mass in Medieval and Renaissance Art," *JAMS* 31 (1978), 21–52

Monfasoni, John, "A Description of the Sistine Chapel under Pope Sixtus IV," *Artibus et Historiae* 4 (1983), 9–18

Morelli, Arnaldo, "Per ornamento e servicio: Organi e sistemazioni architettoniche nelle chiese toscane del Rinascimento," *I Tatti Studies: Essays in the Renaissance* 7 (1997), 279–303

Moretti, Laura, "Spaces for Musical Performance in the Este Court in Ferrara (c. 1440–1540)," in *The Music Room*, ed. Howard and Moretti, 213–36

Nevile, Jennifer, *The Eloquent Body: Dance and Humanist Culture in Fifteenth-Century Italy*, Bloomington, IN, 2004

Norman, Diana, *Siena and the Virgin: Art and Politics in a Late Medieval City State*, New Haven, 1999

Pirrotta, Nino, "Music and Cultural Tendencies in 15th-Century Italy," *JAMS* 19 (1966), 127–61

Poggi, Giovanni, *Il Duomo di Firenze: Documenti sulla decorazione della chiesa e del campanile tratti dall'archivio dell'opera*, Berlin, 1909

Rodin, Jesse, *Josquin's Rome: Hearing and Composing in the Sistine Chapel*, Oxford and New York, 2012

Shearman, John, *Raphael's Cartoons in the Collection of Her Majesty the Queen, and the Tapestries for the Sistine Chapel*, London, 1972

Sherr, Richard, "Competence and Incompetence in the Papal Choir in the Age of Palestrina," *EM* 22 (1994), 606–29; repr. in *Music and Musicians*, no. XIV

"*Illibata dei virgo nutrix* and Josquin's Roman Style," *JAMS* 41 (1987), 434–64; repr. in *Music and Musicians*, no. VIII

*Music and Musicians in Renaissance Rome and Other Courts*, Aldershot, 1999

"The Singers of the Papal Chapel and Liturgical Ceremonies in the Early Sixteenth Century: Some Documentary Evidence," in *Rome in the Renaissance: The City and the Myth*, ed. P. A. Ramsey, Binghamton, NY, 1982, 249–64; repr. in *Music and Musicians*, no. XI

"Speculations on Repertory, Performance Practice, and Ceremony in the Papal Chapel in the Early Sixteenth Century," in *Studien zur Geschichte der päpstlichen Kapelle: Tagungsbericht Heidelberg 1989*, Cappellae Apostolicae Sixtinaeque Collectanea Acta Monumenta, Collectanea II, ed. Bernhard Janz, Vatican City, 1996, 103–22; repr. in *Music and Musicians*, no. XII

ed., *Papal Music and Musicians in Late Medieval and Renaissance Rome*, Oxford, 1998

Strohm, Reinhard, and J. Donald Cullington, eds., *On the Dignity and the Effects of Music: Two Fifteenth-Century Treatises*, trans. J. D. Cullington, London, 1996

Trachtenberg, Marvin, "Architecture and Music Reunited: A New Reading of Dufay's 'Nuper Rosarum Flores' and the Cathedral of Florence," *Renaissance Quarterly* 54 (2001), 740–75

van der Ploeg, Kees, *Art, Architecture and Liturgy: Siena Cathedral in the Middle Ages*, Groningen, 1993

Waldman, Louis A., "From the Middle Ages to the Counter-Reformation: The Choirs of Santa Maria del Fiore," in *Sotto il cielo della cupola: Il coro di Santa Maria del Fiore dal Rinascimento al 2000*, ed. Timothy Verdon, Milan, 1997, 37–68

Warren, Charles W., "Brunelleschi's Dome and Dufay's Motet," *MQ* 59 (1973), 92–105

Wegman, Rob C., "'And Josquin Laughed . . . ': Josquin and the Composer's Anecdote in the Sixteenth Century," *JM* 17 (1999), 319–57

"From Maker to Composer: Improvisation and Musical Authorship in the Low Countries, 1450–1500," *JAMS* 49 (1996), 409–79

Welch, Evelyn S., "Sight, Sound, and Ceremony in the Chapel of Galeazzo Maria Sforza," *EMH* 12 (1993), 151–90

Welker, Lorenz, "Wind Ensembles in the Renaissance," in *Companion*, ed. Knighton and Fallows, 146–53

Wilson, Blake, "Heinrich Isaac among the Florentines," *JM* 23 (2006), 97–152

Wright, Craig, "Dufay's *Nuper rosarum flores*, King Solomon's Temple, and the Veneration of the Virgin," *JAMS* 47 (1994), 395–441

Zanovello, Giovanni, "'In the Church and in the Chapel': Music and Devotional
    Spaces in the Florentine Church of Santissima Annunziata," *JAMS* 67 (2014),
    379–428
Zara, Vasco, "Musica e architettura tra medio evo e età moderna: Storia critica di
    un'idea," *AcM* 77 (2005), 1–26

# 19

# Music and feasts in the fifteenth century

ANTHONY M. CUMMINGS

... after supper, in the garden of the Tadei, the famous Casolana sang divinely
to the lute.[1]

Maddalena Casolana's after-supper singing is a late Renaissance instance
of an ancient practice: the association of music and dining in Western
civilization is as old as Western civilization itself. In Homer's *Iliad*, book
9 – the famous "embassy book" – Achilleus is "delighting his heart in a
lyre, clear-sounding, / splendid and carefully wrought, with a bridge of
silver upon it" when the delegation arrives. He instructs Patroklos to
"'set up a mixing-bowl that is bigger, / and mix us stronger drink, and
make ready a cup for each man, / since these who have come beneath my
roof are the men I love best'."[2]

The association of music-making with dining is not difficult to understand:
both activities occur in "real time" and are dynamic or kinetic in nature.[3] In
that respect, they are like others of the arts involving movement – theater,
dance – where the substance of the work unfolds in time. In contrast, other art
forms – painting, sculpture, architecture – have a static materiality. The substance of the work is unchanging, although the viewer's experience of it
evolves, of course. And static works of art can also be featured in dynamic art
forms, such as processions, where a painting can figure in a dynamic *tableau
vivant*. These qualifications notwithstanding, music-making and dining share
the characteristic of kinesis, which makes them ideally suited to their concurrent use.

Indeed, before the advent of recording technology, one's experience of
music – as *sounding* music – was invariably of a live performance, and before
the establishment of the nineteenth-century concert tradition, musical performances typically accompanied other kinds of dynamic, real-time activity:
liturgical ceremonies, theatrical performances, public festivals organized
into a series of discrete phases, and so on. Because all such activities, like a

1 Fabretti, *Cronache*, 4:44.   2 Homer, *Iliad*, trans. Lattimore, 203–4.
3 Allen Grieco developed this interpretation in conversation with Margaret Bent; I am grateful to Dr.
Grieco for useful discussion of it.

musical performance, also unfolded in time, the concurrent use of several different media sharing this characteristic was logical. Liturgical ceremonies comprised complex ritual action interspersed with the recitation of texts and performance of musical settings thereof; theatrical performances accommodated entr'acte music; public festivals might feature a procession of floats, accompanied by instrumental playing or the singing of explanatory verse elucidating the metaphoric meanings intended by the festivals' organizers. In all such cases, a series of episodes occasioned the alternation of music with other kinds of activity or performative elements (or, in some instances, the simultaneous use of music and another performative element, such as at a banquet, where instrumental playing could accompany attendees' consumption of one of the courses). As we shall see, there were also contemporary theoretical justifications for associating music-making and dining, such as music's supposed aid in digestion.

Moreover, both banqueting and music-making involve similar creative processes. Both originate in raw material: undifferentiated pitches and pitch durations in the case of music-making; more or less undifferentiated foodstuffs in the case of banqueting. The creative act entails forging a dynamic artistic result from such materials.

## Sources

The relevant sources are varied in nature: textual, visual, musical. The textual material is of several types, of potentially varying historical value. On the one hand, there are treatises whose authors make theoretical arguments about the relationship of feasting and music-making, which demand careful interpretation and an evaluation of the authors' assumptions. On the other hand, there are eyewitness accounts of festive events where music-making and banqueting occurred. In some respects, the evidential status of these latter is less suspect, since their authors often had no other objective than reporting in a straightforward manner on the event witnessed.

## Fifteenth-century Franco-Burgundian practice

The fifteenth century inherited particulars of the practice of convivial music-making from the earlier Middle Ages. For example, in 1343, Clement VI was fêted by Cardinal Annibale di Ceccano on the outskirts of Avignon: "The meal consisted of nine courses (*vivande*) each having three dishes, that is a total of twenty-seven dishes ... A concert brought the main part of the feast to a close ... After dessert the master cook danced, together with his ...

assistants."[4] More than a century later (1454), a famous banquet attended by Philip of Burgundy and his son Charles the Bold had a similar structure, characterized by F. Alberto Gallo as "rigidly symmetrical": there were nine dramatic and nine musical performances, just as there were nine courses in 1343. The occasion for the 1454 banquet was a meeting of the Knights of the Golden Fleece, at the conclusion of which Philip announced a crusade to reclaim Constantinople from the Turks, who had taken the city the previous year.[5] (Featured prominently in the quasi-dramatic presentations was the mythological Jason, who – according to period convention – was the metaphoric representation of Europeans in confrontation with the non-European "Other."[6]) The contemporary descriptions of the banquet are uncommonly detailed, and – unusually – permit us to identify one of the actual compositions performed: "a marvelously large and beautiful stag entered," on whose back was

> a young boy, XII years of age ... And upon entering the hall the said child began the top voice of a song, very high and clear, and the said stag himself sang the tenor part without ... any other person, other than the child and the artifice of the stag, and the song they sang is entitled *Je ne vis onques la pareille*.[7]

A polyphonic setting of the text *Je ne vis oncques la pareille* is attributed in period manuscripts to either Binchois or Du Fay: a three-voice chanson, in the familiar fifteenth-century disposition of discantus, tenor, and contratenor.[8] I return to this composition at the conclusion, where I consider specific examples of the kind of music employed at fifteenth-century feasts.

The music-making on these occasions alternated with the food courses, affording variety in the succession of events and situating the courses within a contrasting, non-culinary frame. These non-culinary framing elements were quite varied in nature: "musical pieces, dances, masked processions, appearance of magical machines, live or artificial animals, minstrels, or acrobats between the courses of splendid courtly banquets."[9] In 1468, for example, a visitor to Ferrara reported that "[y]esterday ... while we were dining, we had

---

4 Mollat, *The Popes at Avignon*, 313–14. The detailed period description cited by Mollat is in Casanova, "Visita di un papa." Of course, the extravagance of such events at the papal court of Avignon elicited the (unfair) condemnation of figures like Petrarch: Robinson, *Readings in European History*, 1:502.

5 Gallo, *Music of the Middle Ages*, 102–107.

6 Cummings, *Lion's Ear*, 25–40; the more extended version of the material in Cummings, "Leo X and Roman Carnival"; and Cummings, "Dance and 'the Other'."

7 Fallows, "Specific Information on the Ensembles," 135; see also 134–36, 139. The contemporary description is open to some interpretation; I have been influenced by Fallows's. There is a recording on Dufay, *Guillaume Dufay c1400–1474, Missa "Ecce ancilla Domini." Le Banquet de vœu 1454*. Ensemble Gilles Binchois, 2 CDs, Virgin Veritas x2 7243 5 61818 2 3 (n.p., 2000), CD 2, track 7.

8 Dufay, *Opera omnia*, 6:109.

9 Pirrotta, "Intermedium." On the relationship of banqueting and dancing, see, for example, see Arena, "Rules of Dancing."

various amusements – of playing of harpsichords and lutes, and by jesters and by Master Giovanni Orbo, who recited in a marvelous manner, quite out of the ordinary."[10] The French word for such interpolations was "entremetz," the Italian word "intermedij" (or "intermezzi," or "intramesse"), terms that, despite their etymological differences, refer to the same phenomenon: between – or "intermediary to" – the discrete phases of a larger event, a different kind of performative activity was interpolated.

## Fifteenth-century Italian practice

Consistent with the larger program of the Italian Renaissance, convivial music-making in fifteenth-century Italy either imaginatively resuscitated ancient Greek and Roman tradition (insofar as it was recoverable) or reframed and reinterpreted medieval tradition, overlaying it with a classicizing veneer. In Phyllis Pray Bober's words, Plato's *Symposium* thus became "a poetic paradigm for future banquets."[11] Indeed, Italian Renaissance texts that describe banqueting at which there was music-making are often entitled "symposium" or "convivium," a self-conscious reference to the Platonic model.

A revealing example is provided by Giannozzo Manetti, "[e]lected ambassador to the Signoria of Venice by the *signoria* and colleges of Florence on the 23rd day of August, 1448."[12]

> On Tuesday morning [8 October] ... several Florentine youths ... came to eat with the Ambassador, and because they were all meritorious youths at the table ..., there were many different and beautiful discussions. That evening we again had supper with the ambassador, and there was varied instrumental playing and most delightful singing, so that we spent all that day and evening most playfully in dancing and song.[13]

Manetti left a detailed account of the actual discussions that took place at the banquet; its title expressly invokes the Platonistic term "symposium."[14] The banquet's attendees were from celebrated Florentine families: the Bardi, the Neri, the Portinari, the Strozzi. Precisely because their discussions proved so absorbing, Manetti invited the attendees to remain for supper. Two of them

---

10 Lockwood, *Music in Renaissance Ferrara*, 105 and n. 42, quoting Motta, *Musici alla corte degli Sforza*, 283.
11 Bober, "The *Coryciana*," esp. 231.    12 Della Torre, *Storia dell'Accademia platonica*, 276–77.
13 Ibid., 279.
14 "Jannotij manetti dialogus in domestico et familiari quorundam amicorum symposio venetijs habitus dum ibi florentini populi nomine legationis munere fungeretur ad donatum acciaiolum incipit feliciter"; ibid.

who had been appointed to judge the debate withdrew to Manetti's bedroom to deliberate:[15]

> while we were waiting impatiently for the forthcoming judgment of the above-mentioned judges, in order not to be affected by excessive tediousness of waiting, we, fortunately, joined with excellent masters of the lute and organ who had participated with us at the symposium, so that they might play some melodies. As they had been ordered, those men obeyed right away and made so great and sweet an effort with the melodies of the various instruments, until the judges – who had spent the long time of roughly three hours in the bedroom chamber – returned to us.[16]

Thus banqueting, learned discussion, and music-making all occurred on the same occasion.

Another celebrated quattrocento humanist furnishes similar information. In his *Convivia mediolanensia*, Francesco Filelfo reports on a (fictive?) convivial occasion featuring musical performances; there is an explicit appeal to custom (classical custom, certainly) as a guide to how such convivia ought to be structured. One of the guests, Francesco Landriano, suggests to his host, G. Antonio Rembaldo, that Rembaldo's sons sing to the accompaniment of (neoclassical) string instruments:[17]

> "so as not to seem to have ignored entirely the normal customs of a symposium, it may perhaps be timely to hear how capable in playing and singing your boys are, Rembaldo, both of whom I see ready, the one with the lyre, the other with the psaltery." "You admonish correctly," Rembaldo said, and – having turned to his boys – he ordered them to fulfill their tasks. And thus touching and gently strumming the strings, they – taking turns – accommodated the rhythms to these words: "Whoever wishes to see the beauty of the stars and the splendid unifications of the one who thunders, come here, happy, to rich meals under a benevolent star."[18]

A well-known poetic description of the wedding banquet for Francesco Sforza and Bianca Maria Visconti by Filelfo's contemporary Antonio Cornazano depicts a performance by the celebrated lutenist-singer Pietro Bono.[19] Here, too, there is an obvious attempt at classicization, since the language – though vernacular – "aims to recreate the flavor of Homeric times, probably known to the poet through Virgil's *Æneid*, or ... some snatch of

15 Ibid.	16 Ibid., 282 (trans. Claudia Wiener and Markus Dubischar).
17 Pirrotta, "Musica e umanesimo."
18 Filelfo, *Conuiuium*, c. 3 (trans. Claudia Wiener and Markus Dubischar). On Filelfo's text, see also Pirrotta, "Italien."
19 Cornazano, *Sforziade*, fols. 106v–107v, in Pirrotta, "Music and Cultural Tendencies," especially 139–41, 144–46.

Homeric translation provided to him by . . . Filelfo."[20] Although also fictive, Cornazano's account is useful in conveying a picture of the structure of such occasions and the place within them for music-making. In Nino Pirrotta's synopsis, [21]

> [t]he stage is Cremona, given to the bride as part of her dowry. The year is 1441. . . Cornazano . . . dismisses the banquet itself in a few lines and swiftly moves on to describe the mood of relaxation following the meal . . . [A]ll become silent while the protagonist himself, Sforza, tells of an episode of war and of mercy on the vanquished. After him one of his captains, whose name, Troilo, happens to have a classical ring, recalls past adventures and perils. Only when the pathos of reminiscence has reached its peak is the musician intro-duced, "whom the stars have endowed with the power of soothing and pacifying."

In many instances the tendency toward classicization extended to the icon-ography of the staged presentations. A 1495 supper in honor of the prince of Capua featured "Venus with Jupiter and Juno with fountains," who "came" after "the plates" had been "set on the tables"; the "float with Neptune led by ten silvered marine monsters" and "the fable of Neptune"; "three Sirens and Arion" who "sang verses"; and "Pan with an eclogue" and "Pomona with the same eclogue."[22]

At the 1475 wedding festivities of Costanzo Sforza and Camilla d'Aragona, "ORPHEO" sang verses to the accompaniment of what was described in the period account, classicistically, as "vna lyra d'oro,"[23] but to judge from the contemporary miniatures done as a record of the event, the instrument was some variety of viola da braccio. (The period miniatures are invaluable in our efforts to imagine these sumptuous occasions.[24]) Orpheus's particular role on that occasion was to offer dishes sent by Apollo.[25] In 1489, at the wedding festivities for Gian Galeazzo Maria Sforza and Isabella d'Aragona, Orpheus makes yet another appearance, on this occasion presenting the roasted game he had beguiled with his sing-ing.[26] At a 1473 banquet hosted by Cardinal Pietro Riario in his Palazzo della Cancelleria for Eleonora d'Aragona, who was in transit to Ferrara for her wedding to Ercole d'Este, Perseus, Andromeda, Ceres, Venus, Atalante,

---

20 Pirrotta, "Music and Cultural Tendencies," 139. Filelfo's translations of Homer remained unpub-lished; he was composing a Latin *Sfortias* at around the time when Cornazano was composing his *Sforziade*; Pirrotta, "Music and Cultural Tendencies," 139 n. 47. For assistance on Filelfo, I am grateful to Jeroen De Keyser and Luigi Silvano.
21 "Music and Cultural Tendencies," 139–40.
22 New York, Pierpont Morgan Library, MS Bühler 19*, fols. 85r–89r, ed. Scully in *The Neapolitan Recipe Collection*.
23 Marinis, ed., *Le nozze di Costanzo Sforza e Camilla d'Aragona*.   24 Ibid., pl. 10.   25 Ibid., 20–21.
26 Calco, "Nuptiæ Mediolanensium Ducum," 75–77.

Hercules, Bacchus, and other figures of classical mythology appeared. One course, which consisted of "five very large dishes of roast meats," featured "a young man ... with a garland and a viola in hand, and having arrived, he sang ... verses."[27] And amid the quasi-dramatic presentations were free-standing musical performances by the renowned solo singer Baccio Ugolini, among others.[28]

Such restitutions of antique tradition are attested by other kinds of sources, such as a 1424 letter to Vitaliano Faella from Guarino da Verona, who offers the classicizing justification that "you read about hardly any feasts of ancient times in which singers were not involved."[29]

## Theoretical arguments

Guarino's justification leads in turn to a fuller consideration of period rationales for convivial music-making. Famed Neapolitan humanist Giovanni Gioviano Pontano justified banqueting and accompanying music-making on grounds of their obvious effectiveness as means of rendering homage:

> Feasts organized to render homage / ... it is suitable that they be those ... demonstrated a short time ago in that feast ... offered to Charles, Duke of Burgundy ... Besides the great many courses of varied foods and great decorations, besides the sweetest musical compositions, after the second part of the dinner – which was truly splendid – mimes were introduced and a spectacle offered under the light of lamps.[30]

Another Neapolitan humanist, Johannes Tinctoris, similarly argued that music-making intensified the entire experience of a convivium: one of the effects of music enumerated in his treatise *Complexus effectuum musices* suggests that "[m]usic increases the joyfulness of banquets." (Here, too, there is a classicizing impulse, in that Tinctoris's objective was to identify past precedents for the habits of listening to music current among his contemporaries.)

Paolo Cortesi argued that music aided in digestion:

> How passions should be avoided, and music used after meals ... The same must be said about the kind of all other passions, against which an adverse position must be taken always by the senator [i.e., the cardinal] at other times, but more

27 The description is by "ELEONORA ... DUCISSA FERRARIE" herself. See Corvisieri, "Il trionfo romano di Eleonora d'Aragona," esp. 649. As Pirrotta, "Rom," suggested, the "jovene con una jorlanda" was Apollo. The account contains many other fascinating details about the music-making and theatrical effects.
28 Corvisieri, "Il trionfo romano di Eleonora d'Aragona," 680–81; Ferroni, "Appunti sulla politica festiva," esp. 61 and n. 44.
29 Gallo, *Music in the Castle*, 70–71, quoting Guarino da Verona, *Epistolario*, 1:405.
30 Pontano, *I trattati*, ed. Tateo, 102–107.

than ever at this time of recreation, lest his body be prevented from digesting the food by some intervening discomfort of his soul. Wherefore, since at this time those things must be sought after by which a cheerful mood is usually aroused, it may well be inquired whether the pleasure of music should be put to use particularly at this point, ... [W]e are convinced that music should be put to use at this time for the sake not only of merriment, but also of knowledge and morals.[31]

Musical *intermedij* thus enhanced attendees' experience of the banquets, articulated (and introduced substantial variety into) the sequence of elements of which convivia were composed, and supposedly aided in the digestive process.

## The music

Contemporary sources document an impressive variety of musical styles and genres deployed during banqueting. "[T]he *entrées* of convivial *entremets*" prominently featured "a custom": "the instrumentalist – almost always a tambourinist – who led the entrance of characters ... and then remained to provide a rhythmic background without participating in the action."[32] Further: depending upon their significance to the larger event, some of the phases of the convivium could be announced by instrumental fanfares.[33] When Eleonora d'Aragona was betrothed to Ercole d'Este,

[o]nce the ... publication of the marriage contract was finished ..., there came His Lordship and Madama ... Everything was ... in order in the great hall, ... Then began the festivities and dancing, ... and ... after the dancing went on for a while, it seemed suitable to His Excellency to announce the new kinship ... At the end of the speeches there began to sound trumpets and piffari to solemnize the announcements, then again there began the dancing ...; then there came the confections, with trumpets and piffari in the royal style.[34]

More elaborate instrumental playing, manifesting an appealing variety of instrumental colors, occurred during the courses themselves. In such cases, the performances were presumably of instrumental arrangements of vocal compositions, such as in the Casanatense chansonnier;[35] or of instrumental works conceived to accompany dancing, momentarily redeployed from their original purpose to a less functional role; or of more abstract instrumental genres

31 Cortese, quoted and translated in Pirrotta, "Music and Cultural Tendencies," 146–48, 152.
32 Pirrotta, "The Orchestra and Stage," esp. 210.
33 For other evidence, which suggests that instrumental fanfares could occur at the beginning and conclusion of the dinner proper, see Baroncini, "Zorzi *Trombetta*," esp. 61–62.
34 Lockwood, ed., *Ferrarese Chansonnier*, xxvii–xxviii and n. 25.
35 Rome 2856. Lockwood, *Ferrarese Chansonnier*.

altogether. A 1473 Roman banquet hosted by Cardinal Riario featured "[w]ind players and trumpet," "harp and small guitar," "*O rosa bella* ... sung to a small guitar," "recorders and viola," "two viols," "a harpsichord," "small guitar, harps[,] and viola together," and "a muted harp"; several "strambotti were sung."[36]

One could easily add to the references already cited that attest solo singing to string accompaniment,[37] itself a classicizing restitution of antique practice. The well-known Bolognese humanist Tommaso Tebaldi (called "Ergotele" by his contemporary Antonio Beccadelli, "il Panormita") was said to have sung to the accompaniment of the lyre,[38] and – more importantly for our purposes – to have done so specifically for Panormita's guests while they dined.[39] And in 1493, on the occasion of the nuptial benediction imparted by Alexander VI on his daughter Lucrezia Borgia and her husband Giovanni Sforza, the famed lutenist-singer Serafino Aquilano performed one of his pastoral eclogues at the conclusion of the supper that followed the ceremony.[40]

Given the vagueness of period accounts, what concrete particulars can be ascertained about the actual music performed? When the references are specific enough, one speculates more confidently. Thus one conjectures plausibly that the *Je ne vis oncques la pareille* performed in 1454 was the polyphonic setting attributed to Dufay or Binchois. The *O Rosa bella* "sung to a small guitar" in Rome in 1473 could well have been an adaptation for vocal soloist and string accompaniment of Johannes Bedyngham's famous polyphonic song.

But a great many of the references quoted here suggest that in fifteenth-century Italy, much of the music exemplified the tradition of quasi-improvised solo song, where the compositions typically were orally transmitted. Indeed, one reference to convivial music-making seems to document quattrocento humanism's potential equivocation about written vocal polyphony as a compositional practice. There were several vocal compositions performed on this occasion, some polyphonic – performed with "some ... experts" and dependent upon "those little signs of music" – and another, which apparently elicited far greater approval from the author of the account, the mythic Angelo Poliziano:

> No sooner were we seated at the table than [Fabio Orsini, the 11-year-old son of the host] was ordered to sing, together with some other experts, certain of those songs which are put into writing with those little signs of music, and immediately he filled our ears, or rather our hearts, with a voice so sweet that (I do not know about the others) as for myself, I was almost transported out of my senses, and was touched beyond doubt by the unspoken feeling of an altogether

36 [Tamassi], *Una cena carnevalesca del Cardinale Pietro Riario.*
37 For more on this tradition, see Blake Wilson's contribution in this volume, Ch. 16.
38 Barozzi and Sabbadini, *Studi sul Panormita*, 39.      39 Ibid., 40.      40 Aquilano, *Sonetti e altre rime*, 18.

divine pleasure. He then performed an heroic song which he had himself recently composed in praise of our own Piero dei Medici ... His voice was not entirely that of someone reading, nor entirely that of someone singing; both could be heard, and yet neither separated one from the other; it was, in any case, even or modulated, and changed as required by the passage ... You might have thought that an adolescent Roscius was acting on the stage.[41]

In such cases of oral transmission, we can only extrapolate from extant compositions that seem to reflect the unwritten tradition, however imperfectly. For example, around 1470, lutenist-singer Filippo Scarlatti copied the texts of "*Rispetti* to be sung to the lute" and "*stanze*" that "are declaimed to the lute at night as serenades."[42] (Although there is no mention of banqueting – the occasion for the performances is specified simply as "la sera" – the performance context is obviously related to that at issue here.) Scarlatti then copied two texts for which musical settings are extant (in the manuscript El Escorial IV.a.24), one of which – *Ora maj che fora sono* – is especially illustrative. In the Escorial manuscript, it is for solo voice and three lower instrumental "voices." But if one assumes a redaction – entirely typical of the time – where the singer performed only the cantus and tenor (the cantus sung, the tenor played on the lute or viola), "the necessary and sufficient nucleus of the composition" is preserved.[43] Works like *Ora maj* must have been typical of the provisions for many fifteenth-century Italian banquets,[44] as the accounts cited here suggest. The extant settings are precious testimony to unwritten practices that are now almost irretrievable.[45]

One final illustrative example. At the beginning of the sixteenth century, a repertory emerges that reflects fifteenth-century unwritten practice. Settings of Italian verse are identified as to text type, the implication being that any text in the poetic form identified could be substituted for the one provided with the musical setting. Thereafter, the setting is arranged for voice and lute. A lutenist-singer thus had readily available a repertory of model settings of sonnets, odes, and other verse forms.[46] Such model settings, like that in Example 19.1, suggest the kind of music performed by Orpheus, Apollo, and

41  Politianus, *Opera omnia*, 1:165–66, trans. Pirrotta and Povoledo, *Music and Theatre*, ch. 1, conclusion.
42  Pasquini, "Il codice di Filippo Scarlatti," esp. 428; Pirrotta, "Italien."
43  Pirrotta, "Su alcuni testi."
44  A qualification, however: Scarlatti describes *Ora maj* as a "Chanzona napoletana," and its text is irreverent (a nun escaping from the cloister). The documents quoted suggest instead that the texts set for these convivial occasions invoked classical material, and were often in Latin. Compositions like *Ora maj* would hardly have been deemed appropriate. It is, rather, the style of the setting that suggests something about the provisions for these banquets.
45  For an edition, see Pirrotta, "Su alcuni testi," 155–56. A recording – of the unredacted four-voice version – is on *Il cantar moderno*, Ensemble Daedalus. Accent ACC 9068D (Beert, n.d. [?1990]).
46  Cummings and Dean, "The 'Great Italian Songbook.'"

Example 19.1 Model setting for voice and instruments of the oda text *La dolce diva mia*. Vocal line from Petrucci, *Strambotti Ode Frottole Sonetti. Et modo de cantar versi latini e capituli. Libro quarto*, Venice, 1507, fol. 46v, with a period intabulation of the accompaniment for lute, from Paris, Bibliothèque nationale de France, Département de la Musique, Rés. Vmd. 27, fol. 47v

the other mythological figures who appeared at the sumptuous and atmospheric convivia reconstructed here.

Banqueting was a time-honored occasion for music-making during the fifteenth century. The fundamental structure of such an event was inherited from the earlier Middle Ages: the separate courses alternated with other kinds of intermediary activity, music prominent among them. In northern Europe, the music performed exemplified established compositional convention: the tradition of three-voice polyphonic settings of French secular texts, for example. The Italian Renaissance, perhaps predictably, classicized the activity inherited from the preceding centuries, so that convivial music-making was rationalized by reference to ancient precedent, the iconographic material was often classical in origin, and the kind of music-making privileged (solo singing to the accompaniment of one's own playing of a plucked or strummed string instrument) was understood as a classicizing restitution of ancient musical practice.

More generally, music's essential status as a kinetic phenomenon that unfolds in time afforded its simultaneous use with other kinds of performative activity, particularly where the larger activity was organized into such discrete phases, which furnished occasion for contrasting intermediary activity. During banqueting, there was an aesthetically satisfying concurrent appeal to various agents of human sense experience – the senses of smell, taste, sight, hearing, and even of touch – as the vivid contemporary accounts evocatively attest. They afford a reintegration into that world, an imagined reconstruction of the convivial activity of the medieval and early modern eras.

# Bibliography

Aquilano, Serafino, *Sonetti e altre rime*, ed. A. Rossi, Rome, 2005

Arena, Antonius, "Rules of Dancing," *Dance Research* 4 (1986), 3–53

Baroncini, Rodolfo, "Zorzi *Trombetta* and the Band of *Piffari* and Trombones of the *Serenissima*: New Documentary Evidence," *Historic Brass Society Journal* 14 (2002), 59–82

Barozzi, Luciano, and Remigio Sabbadini, *Studi sul Panormita e sul Valla*, Florence, 1891

Bober, Phyllis Pray, "The *Coryciana* and the Nymph Corycia," *Journal of the Warburg and Courtauld Institutes* 40 (1977), 223–39

Calco, Tristano, "Nuptiæ Mediolanensium Ducum sive Joannis Galeacij cum Isabella Aragona Ferdinandi Neapolitanorum Regis nepte," in *Tristani Calchi historiæ patriæ libri XX: [accedunt] . . . residua [i.e. historiæ patriæ libri XXI et XXII . . .]: e bibliotheca . . . Lucij Hadriani Cottæ. I-II*, 2 vols., Milan, 1627–44

Casanova, Eugenio, "Visita di un papa avignonese a suoi cardinali," *Archivio della Società Romana di storia patria* 22/3–4 (1899), 371–81

Cornazano, Antonio, *Sforziade*, Paris, Bibliothèque nationale de France, nouv. acq. 1472, fols. 106v–107v

Corvisieri, Costantino, "Il trionfo romano di Eleonora d'Aragona nel giugno del 1473," *Archivio della R. Società Romana di Storia Patria* 10 (1887), 629–87

Cummings, Anthony M., "Dance and 'the Other': The *Moresca*," in *Seventeenth Century Ballet: A Multi-Art Spectacle. An International Interdisciplinary Symposium*, ed. Barbara Grammeniati, Dartford, 2011, 39–60

"Leo X and Roman Carnival (1521)," *Studi musicali* 36 (2007), 289–341

*The Lion's Ear: Pope Leo X, the Renaissance Papacy, and Music*, Ann Arbor, 2012

and Alexander Dean, "The 'Great Italian Songbook' of the Early Cinquecento," *Studi musicali* n.s. 2 (2011), 25–48

Della Torre, Arnaldo, *Storia dell'Accademia platonica di Firenze*, Florence, 1902

Dufay, Guillaume, *Opera omnia*, ed. Heinrich Besseler, 6 vols., Rome, 1951–66

Fabretti, Ariodante, *Cronache della città di Perugia*, 4 vols., Turin, 1887–92

Fallows, David, "Specific Information on the Ensembles for Composed Polyphony, 1400–1474," in *Studies in the Performance of Late Mediaeval Music*, ed. Stanley Boorman, Cambridge, 1983, 109–59

Ferroni, Giulio, "Appunti sulla politica festiva di Pietro Riario," in *Umanesimo a Roma nel Quattrocento: Atti del Convegno*, New York and Rome, 1984, 47–65

Filelfo, Francesco, *Francisci Philelfi ad Thomam Thebaldum Mediolanense Conuiuium primum . . . Conuiuium Secundum*, [Milan], [1483]

Gallo, F. Alberto, *Music in the Castle: Troubadours, Books, and Orators in Italian Courts of the Thirteenth, Fourteenth, and Fifteenth Centuries*, Chicago and London, 1995

*Music of the Middle Ages II*, Cambridge, 1985

Guarino da Verona, *Epistolario*, ed. Remigio Sabbadini, 3 vols. Venice, 1915–16

Homer, *The Iliad*, trans. Richard Lattimore, Chicago, 1951

Lockwood, Lewis, *Music in Renaissance Ferrara, 1400–1505: The Creation of a Musical Center in the Fifteenth Century*, Cambridge, MA, 1984

ed., *A Ferrarese Chansonnier: Roma, Biblioteca Casanatense 2856*, Lucca, 2002

Marinis, Tammaro de, ed., *Le nozze di Costanzo Sforza e Camilla d'Aragona celebrate a Pesaro nel maggio 1475; Nozze Ricasoli-Firidolfi Ruffo di Guardialombarda*. Florence, n.d. [1946?]

Mollat, Guillaume, *The Popes at Avignon, 1305–1378*, New York and Evanston, IL, 1965

Motta, Emilio, *Musici alla corte degli Sforza: Ricerche e documenti milanesi*, Geneva, 1977 (repr. from *Archivio storico lombardo* 14 (1997), 29–64, 278–340, 514–61).

Pasquini, Emilio, "Il codice di Filippo Scarlatti: Firenze, Biblioteca Venturi Ginori Lisci, 3," *Studi di filologia italiana. Bullettino annuale dell'Accademia della Crusca* 22 (1964), 363–580

Pirrotta, Nino, "Intermedium," in *MGG*, 6:1310–26

"Italien B. 14.-16. Jahrhundert," in *MGG*, 6:1476–1500

"Music and Cultural Tendencies in 15th-Century Italy," *JAMS* 19 (1966), 127–61

"Musica e umanesimo," in his *Poesia e musica e altri saggi*, Scandicci, 1994, 89–106

"The Orchestra and Stage in Renaissance *Intermedi* and Early Opera," in his *Music and Culture in Italy from the Middle Ages to the Baroque*, Cambridge, MA, 1984, 210–16

"Rom. C. Spätmittelalter und Renaissance," in *MGG*, 11:695–702

"Su alcuni testi italiani di composizioni polifoniche quattrocentesche," *Quadrivium* 14 (1973), 133–57

and Elena Povoledo, *Music and Theatre from Poliziano to Monteverdi*, Cambridge, 1982

Politianus, Angelus, *Opera omnia*, ed. Ida Maïer, 3 vols., Turin, 1971

Pontano, Giovanni Gioviano, *I trattati delle virtù sociali*, ed. Francesco Tateo, Rome, 1965

Robinson, James Harvey, *Readings in European History*, 2 vols., Boston and New York, 1904–6

Scully, Terence, ed., *The Neapolitan Recipe Collection (New York, Pierpont Morgan Library, MS Bühler, 19): A Critical Edition and English Translation*, Ann Arbor, 2000

[Tamassi, Nino], ed., *Una cena carnevalesca del Cardinale Pietro Riario; Nozze Vigo-Magenta*, Rome, 1885

# 20

# French lyrics and songs for the New Year, ca. 1380–1420

YOLANDA PLUMLEY

Musicologists have long been aware of the ten New Year songs by Guillaume Du Fay, which mostly date from early in his career when he moved between Italy and the North. That Du Fay apparently penned more secular songs of this kind than any of his contemporaries or predecessors has led David Fallows to wonder about the catalyst for these works and their function, and how far the genre was already established by his time.[1] In fact, the French New Year genre was hardly new; as I explore here, Du Fay and his contemporaries were building on a lyric tradition that had flourished in France and other Francophone centers from at least 1380. In this essay, I examine aspects of the sizeable corpus of lyrics with and without music that survives in sources from the late fourteenth and early fifteenth centuries. I have discussed elsewhere how the new order of "fixed form" lyric and polyphonic chanson that crystallized ca. 1340 quickly became a locus for competitive demonstrations of lyric ingenuity and allusive play held at court and in urban contexts.[2] We will see here how the New Year repertory demonstrates a similarly strong sense of lyric community in its texts; although most of the intertextualities we encounter are generic markers rather than deliberate quotations, I suggest that some offer clues regarding points of contact or influence as the genre developed and migrated north and south from the great Valois courts. But what is especially fascinating about these works is the light they shed on the role of sonic artifacts – sung songs or recited lyrics – in New Year ritual ca. 1400. Not only did they serve to transmit seasonal greetings but often they embodied the New Year gift that formed the focal point of the social transaction between author and patron, or lover and lady.

Early versions of this essay were presented at the Medieval and Renaissance Music Conference in Tours in July 2005 and at interdisciplinary research seminars at the Universities of St Andrews and Olomouc in 2006–2007. I am grateful for the support of the Leverhulme Trust. At the Tours conference, Isabelle Ragnard informed me she, too, was investigating the New Year repertory and she kindly sent me her ensuing publication, "Les Chansons d'étrennes aux XIVe et XVe siècles." The corpus I consider here adds a few items to Ragnard's; Ragnard provides details for standard editions of these works. I am also grateful to Nicole Schwindt for sharing in advance of publication her study of fifteenth-century occasional songs, which includes discussion of New Year songs: "Amour courtois im Jahreslauf."

1 Fallows, *Dufay*, 54.    2 See Plumley, *The Art of Grafted Song*.

*＊*

Although largesse had long been considered an essential virtue of the high nobility, the Valois dynasty's concern to legitimize its claim to the French crown made it intensely conscious of the potential for gift-giving to underline its political authority. In his poem *La fonteinne amoureuse* of ca. 1360, Guillaume de Machaut (ca. 1300–77), who enjoyed the patronage of several Valois kings and princes during his long career, praises the liberality of the young noble protagonist, whom scholars have identified as Jehan, Duke of Berry, son of Jehan II of France; his song *Donnez signeurs* (Ballade 26), of similar date, advises the nobility to be open handed and emphasizes that this will earn them respect and loyalty. Gift-giving certainly played a significant role in court ceremony in Machaut's day, but it was after his death, during the turbulent reign of Charles VI (r. 1380–1422) that fêting the New Year at court assumed particular prominence. The political vacuum created by Charles's ascent to the throne as a minor and his subsequent mental illness was quickly filled by his uncles Jehan of Berry and Philippe of Burgundy, his brother Louis of Orléans, and his cousin Jehan of Burgundy. The resulting power struggle, which spilt into civil war in the early fifteenth century, was reflected in these princes' extravagant campaigns of cultural patronage and in their vigorous cultivation of the gift. By 1400, the practice of bestowing New Year gifts on the first of January had become a major court ceremony.[3] Recent studies of late medieval gift practice have highlighted the vast sums spent by French royalty on New Year gifts.[4] In 1404 alone, Louis d'Orléans spent the huge sum of 19,000 *livres* on items for this purpose, including gems and gold images for bestowal on those of the upper echelons, and a large number of drinking vessels and golden hats for his social inferiors.[5]

In turn, princes were courted by gifts from their equals and from others who sought their favor, protection, or financial support, including their householders and familiars. Inventories, manuscript illuminations, and textual accounts indicate that books were often given by those of lower ranks to their social superiors. Notable among such book donors to the royalty were the authors Jehan Froissart and Christine de Pizan. Musicians were similarly bound up in the court's gift culture. Whether in relatively secure employment as chapel singers or minstrels within the noble household, or in more precarious, itinerant careers, late medieval musicians depended on the favors of the

---

3  1 January was not at this time the official start of the year; on this and the development of New Year ceremony at the Valois courts, see Buettner, "Past Presents."
4  See also Hirschbiegel, *Étrennes*; Stratford, "The Goldenes Rössl"; Chattaway, "Looking a Medieval Gift Horse in the Mouth."
5  Buettner, "Past Presents," 604.

rich and powerful. But they were alert, too, to the potential of their art both to entertain and to bolster noble magnificence. The extant New Year song represents one genre through which poet-composers could usefully court their patrons' favor. As we will see, the addressees of most surviving works remain mysterious, but in a number of lyrics and songs the recipient is explicitly named or can be inferred. Whether these were commissioned works or opportunistic attempts to elicit reward at court is not known; but even where the work was composed for a lover to transmit seasonal greetings to his lady – as was probably true of the majority of works explored here – we are offered tantalizing glimpses of the role played by these occasional works in the celebration of New Year.

## The New Year repertory

The heyday of the New Year lyric tradition seems to have fallen between ca. 1380 and ca. 1440. Adam de La Halle's *Dame, vos hom vous estrine* from the late thirteenth century may be an early precedent: the narrator here bestows the song on a lady using the verb *estriner* (to reward, or bestow a gift), that was later closely associated with New Year gift-giving. Another early example is Jehan de Lescurel's *Belle et noble, a bonne estrainne*, written in the orbit of the French royal court ca. 1310,[6] which fêtes a lady with an *estrenne* and features vocabulary typical of New Year French lyrics ca. 1400. The lack of New Year songs or lyrics by Machaut, however, suggests the genre only began to flourish ca. 1380, as New Year ritual intensified at the French princely courts. Indeed, much of the extant repertory, especially the earlier portion, is connected in one way or another with that cultural milieu, although its sources indicate that many songs, along with the wider chanson repertory, were rapidly transplanted into francophone circles north and south.

Table 20.1 lists the extant song corpus, arranged into three chronological groups, and its sources (the tables appear at the end of the chapter). Group A lists works dating from before ca. 1415. The song from Berkeley 744 was copied into a compendium of music treatises dated 1375, while items described as *rondeaux* or *virelays chantés* in the unnotated chansonnier London 15224 attest to the circulation of French New Year songs before 1395 at the Francophile court of Giangaleazzo Visconti in Milan–Pavia; Leiden 2720 and the *Manière de language* of 1396 reflect their cultivation ca. 1400 at the court of

---

6 On Lescurel's likely activity within the royal circles that produced the interpolated *Roman de Fauvel* see Plumley, *The Art of Grafted Song*, ch. 2.

Holland and in England, respectively.[7] Chantilly 564, the Cortona fragment, and Modena α.M.5.24 (ModA) were all copied in Italy but transmit repertory from French royal circles and papal Avignon;[8] ModA, from Milan, also features some French songs by Antonello da Caserta and other Italian composers. Group B features songs from the early layers of Oxford 213 (Veneto, late 1420s),[9] including over twenty songs by composers who served Jehan of Berry[10] and works that intersect stylistically with the *ars subtilior* repertory of Chantilly 564 and ModA.[11] Chantilly 564 and Oxford 213 share several composers, including Baude Cordier, two of whose songs were added to the main corpus of Chantilly 564 after ca. 1418. Group C lists the New Year songs from the later layers of Oxford 213 and other sources from the 1430s and 1440s. Du Fay's contribution looms large here, but several songs are by his fellows at Cambrai Cathedral and the papal chapel in Rome, Arnold de Lantins (d. 1432), Guillaume Malbecque (d. 1465), and Nicolas Grenon (d. 1456), and by Gilles Binchois (d. 1460), who, like Grenon and other composers in Oxford 213, was connected with the Burgundian court.

An extant corpus of New Year lyrics without music from the same period provides a context for the songs and demonstrates that by ca. 1390 the New Year genre was thriving in French royal and related circles (Table 20.2–3). Eustache Deschamps's comment in his lyric "J'ay puis vint ans" that he had been writing New Year lyrics for twenty years suggests that the practice was well under way by 1380. Like him, Christine de Pizan, Jehan Garencières, and Alain Chartier were active in French royal circles; Deschamps and Garencières were in the service of Louis d'Orléans, father of Charles. Oton de Granson, whose works are transmitted in several sources alongside Chartier's, was a Vaudois noble, known to Deschamps and admired by Christine; he served the count of Savoy (who was married to a daughter of Jehan de Berry) and, later, the English king.[12] In addition to its New Year song texts, London 15224 transmits other New Year lyrics. This collection was compiled for Giangaleazzo Visconti, who was married to Isabelle of Valois, sister of Jehan de Berry and Philippe of Burgundy, and whose daughter Valentina in turn

---

7 See respectively: Wallis, *Anonymous French Verse* (allusions to Giangaleazzo as the Count of Vertus (Virtu) rather than Duke of Milan suggests the collection dates before 1395; one of the New Year *rondels chantés* cites his motto, "A bon droit"); Van Biezen and Gumbert, *Two Chansonniers from the Low Countries*; Leach, "Learning French by Singing" (which lists all the sources of the *Manière de langage*, a treatise teaching French to the English, certain of which also transmit the lyric of a late fourteenth-century song from Paris 6771 (Reina Codex); the full text of the New Year rondeau is at 266).
8 See, respectively, Plumley and Stone, *Codex Chantilly*; Di Bacco and Nádas, "The Papal Chapels," 82–86; Stone, *The Manuscript Modena*.
9 Fallows, *MS Canon. Misc. 213*.
10 Higgins, "Music and Musicians at the Sainte-Chapelle of the Bourges Palace."
11 Plumley and Stone, "Cordier's Picture-Songs."    12 See Grenier-Winther, *Oton de Granson*.

married Louis d'Orléans. The French royal embassies that Deschamps accompanied to the Pavian court in the 1390s provided opportunity for the transplantation of this French New Year tradition to Milan.

Certain of the lyrics without music by Christine and Deschamps are identified as New Year items in manuscript rubrics. Several address a specific patron, but the majority, like the songs, target an unidentified lady-love. Most celebrate the season but in "J'ay puis vint ans" Deschamps uses New Year as a context for a moralizing lament on the state of France, and in "Poux, puces, lantes et vermine" as a satirical wishing of ill-health on his companions. Even where manuscript rubrics are lacking, the New Year connection is generally made explicit in the body of the text. There is great unity in the textual vocabulary across the repertory, suggesting that by 1400 the New Year lyric had crystallized into a genre with its own conventions.

Some of the recurrent elements in the lyrics of Christine and Deschamps, which are typical across the lyric corpus, are shown in Table 20.2. One category of textual commonplace locates the time of year (see the second column): a fairly circumscribed set of idioms (highlighted by italics), usually located in the incipit or the refrain, identifies the context for the poem and its performance on the first day of the new year: "ce premier jour de l'an," "ce jour de l'an," "l'an nouvel," "ce bon jour de renouvellement," or even just "a ce bon jour." Other standard expressions transmit the New Year greetings (shown in the third column): these include "Bon jour, bon an," or even "bon jour, bon an, bon mois." The classic New Year greeting was "a bonne estraine," a catchphrase also documented on contemporary material objects designed as New Year gifts. Another conventional turn of phrase is the appeal to God to grant good things to the addressee: the standard formulation "Dieu vous doinst" is often followed by a choice of positive wishes. Sometimes the narrator does the bestowing ("[je] vous doing"), giving an "etrenne" (New Year gift) or simply a "don" (present); I shall return to the idea of the gift below.

Table 20.4 illustrates how songs selected from across the chronological groups conform to these conventions. Du Fay and his contemporaries were evidently building on a well-established tradition, but how, why, and exactly when the generic markers of New Year lyrics crystallized is unclear. The formal lyric competitions or *puys* staged throughout the fourteenth century in Paris and northern francophone towns may have played some part.[13] A poetry treatise by Baude Herenc from 1432 alludes to a practice of performing

---

13  See Plumley, *The Art of Grafted Song*, especially ch. 5.

*sottes chansons* (nonsense lyrics) on 1 January at the *puy* of Amiens,[14] although the example cited there does not feature the standard vocabulary witnessed in our New Year corpus. It seems equally possible that the New Year genre associated with the refrain forms (i.e., the ballade, rondeau, and virelai) developed within the court circles frequented by so many of the known authors.

Given the conventional nature of the textual content, it may seem perilous to read too much into the intertextualities that bind the repertory (see Table 20.5). Recurrent patterns of rhyme-words, for instance, may merely be by-products of the circumscribed vocabulary. Yet certain interrelationships invite reflection. Replicated phrases within the output of a single poet may seem banal, but in the case of songs they may imply the lyrics were penned by a single poet, perhaps the composer himself. Two songs by Arnold de Lantins, for instance, feature virtually the same line of text (see Table 20.5, e: "[vous] ay sur toute aultre choissy"); similarly, Du Fay's *Ce jour de l'an* and *Entre vous, gentils amoureux* share vocabulary and expressions with another of his occasional songs, *Ce moys de May*.[15] Recurrences linking works by different authors might suggest a shared origin or tell us something about the channels for transmission of works. Two of the lyrics by Charles d'Orléans (see Table 20.5, a) share the line "De cuer, de corps et quanque j'ay," a formulation also found in a lyric by Deschamps, who served Charles's parents; we know Charles inherited from them a book of Deschamps's poems. Two anonymous songs from ModA and one from Oxford 213 present two of the standard catchphrases in adjacent or near-adjacent position (see Table 20.5, d): "ce primier jour de l'an" and "a bone estrayne." This small textual resonance adds to certain musical correspondences linking *ars subtilior* songs from Chantilly 564 and early songs from Oxford 213 that led Anne Stone and me to propose that these repertories were probably closer chronogically than has generally been assumed.[16]

Several works in Table 20.5 feature similar incipits bearing the New Year greetings. Since quotations in late medieval lyrics traditionally occur in the incipit or refrain,[17] we might wonder whether these are deliberate allusions: "Bon an, bon jour, et bonne estraine" is the incipit of one of Deschamps's rondeaux, a formulation that appears (slightly rearranged) in the refrain of the anonymous lyric "La nuit de l'an" from Clermont Ferrand 249, a source that transmits lyrics from Deschamps's milieu (Table 20.5, c). The incipit of Du Fay's *Bon jour, bon mois, bon an et bonne estraine* echoes this, as does the opening of two lyrics by Christine, while his *Estrinez moy* echoes the opening of the

14  See the *Doctrinal de la second rhétorique*, 175; and Ragnard, "Les Chansons d'étrennes," 127.
15  See Boone, "Du Fay's Early Chansons," 173.
16  See Plumley and Stone, "Cordier's Picture-Songs."      17  See Plumley, *The Art of Grafted Song*.

rondeau from the *Manière de langage* of 1396. Another common opening, "Ce jour de l'an," links lyrics by Christine and Garencières with songs by Cordier, Lantins, and Du Fay (Table 20.5, b). Although this is clearly another New Year commonplace, intriguingly, a further correspondence links these items by Christine, Garencières, and Cordier (in their third, second, and fourth lines, respectively), strengthening this connection. Again, whether reflecting direct citation or use of a shared template, this tells us something about older lyric traditions (and even repertory) known to Du Fay and his contemporaries; in Cordier's case, it encourages us to wonder whether, like so many composers represented in Chantilly 564 and in the early layers of Oxford 213, he, too, was active in French princely circles.[18]

My discussion has focused on textual content even in the case of the songs since the musical settings generally reflect the diversity of musical styles, forms, and idioms of the time. Thus, some songs from Group A display elements of the *ars subtilior* style and feature the classic fourteenth-century scoring of texted cantus plus contratenor–tenor accompaniment. The more lyrical and transparent style that grew popular after ca. 1400 is reflected in the later songs (Groups B and C), which often feature more than one texted voice. Although chronology largely accounts for these stylistic differences, choice of form also influences style. In line with general trends, the ballades across the groups tend to be more elaborate and ambitious in style and scale than the virelais and rondeaux. *De quanqu'on peut* from Chantilly 564, for instance, features proportional rhythms, changes of mensuration, syncopation, and sequence typical of the *ars subtilior* generation. Elements of this *grande ballade* style persist in Cordier's ballade *Dame excellent* (Group B) alongside a more modern scoring of two texted cantus parts, while Lantins's *Tout mon desir* (Group C) combines classic ballade scoring with elements of the modern rondeau style, such as a triadic melody in contrary motion with the tenor, a transparent texture, and an oscillation between major and minor prolation. Although the ballade form was generally favored in the late fourteenth century, Group A is dominated by rondeaux and virelais, in contrast with the contemporary lyric-only corpus. These tend toward a greater simplicity than the ballades; only Antonello's virelai *Tres nouble dame* exhibits notable mensural and rhythmic complexities, and the rondeaux display a more heightened lyricism (*La grant beauté* provides a good example). In Groups B and C, unsurprisingly, the rondeau predominates; this form was generally favored by poets and composers after ca. 1410.

---

18  For an argument on stylistic grounds against Craig Wright's identification of Cordier with Burgundian harpist Baude Fresnel (d. 1397), see Plumley and Stone, "Cordier's Picture-Songs."

There is little to distinguish the New Year musical settings from the wider chanson repertory. Nevertheless, certain New Year songs demonstrate their composers' imaginative approaches to the seasonal content. In his *Estrinez moy*, for instance, Du Fay reflects the dialogue enacted in the lyric text by placing the lover's words in the cantus and his beloved's response in the tenor. Dialogue lyrics were not new: from ca. 1390, there is Deschamps's virelai without music "Et de quoy vous puis je estrener," which receives a response from his lady in matching form, and the dialogue song *J'aim. Qui?* by Paullet, who served Jehan of Berry and is represented in the early layer of Oxford 213. Seasonal greetings in New Year songs are often strategically placed for maximum impact: in the incipit, where they are heard prominently at the start or end of a musical section, or in the refrain, where they are sung repeatedly. Nicole Schwindt notes that in Lantins's *Tout mon desir* coloration highlights these words visually as well as aurally,[19] but there are no standard approaches to setting them. The virelai *Sans mal penser* from ModA is noteworthy for its emphasis on New Year catchphrases, which are concentrated at the end of the refrain (see Example 20.1). "Le primier jour" is set to a musical figure (phrase a) that returns at the opening of the *secunda pars*. This is followed by the setting of "De l'an vous presente m'amour" (phrase b), which is unusually triadic and features a motto-like series of semibreves that might flag a quotation. The ensuing setting of "A bone estrayne" (phrase c), the classic New Year greeting and punch line of this lover's address to his lady, provides a flourishing conclusion to the section that is heightened by melisma, syncopation, and sequential play.

## Lyrics, songs, and New Year ritual

Written records sometimes inform us about the nature and value of material objects exchanged, and manuscript illuminations may offer clues as to where such transactions took place at court. But evidence for *how* gifts were presented remains more elusive. The frontispieces of certain manuscripts portray a kneeling donor of lower rank presenting the book to a prestigious standing or seated recipient in a hall or private chamber of the court; a famous example is London, British Library, MS Harley 4431 (fol. 3), which shows Christine de Pizan kneeling before Queen Isabeau of France in the latter's private apartment in

---

19 Schwindt, "Amour courtois."

Example 20.1 Setting of New Year greetings in *Sans mal penser* (α.M.5.24; ModA)

the presence of ladies-in-waiting. Yet, as Brigitte Buettner stresses, such presentation scenes may be idealizations, since gifts were usually presented through the intermediary of court chamberlains.[20] The New Year lyric repertory offers tantalizing snapshots, albeit fictionalized ones, of the moment of contact between greeter and greeted. Christine's presentation of her ballade-gift to princess Marie of Berry, for instance, implies that author and patron share the same physical space. The New Year greeting "Bon jour, bon

20 Buettner, "Past Presents," 614.

an, bon mois" is contextualized twice by reference to the present moment: "*this* first day of the New Year" ("*ce* premier jour de l'an"). Of course, like the donor scenes in manuscripts, this may simply reflect wishful thinking on Christine's part rather than hard reality: we cannot know for sure that the author recited her lyric to the princess rather than simply submitting it in written form to an intermediary. On the other hand, as noted above, Du Fay's *Estrinez moy* provides an unusual lyric dramatization of the New Year encounter between two protagonists of similar status, a lover and his beloved, who agree to exchange their hearts as New Year gifts; although fictional, this offers an intriguing vignette of how one early fifteenth-century couple enacted the New Year ritual. We learn from Chartier's *Lay de Plaisance* that on New Year's day lovers honored their ladies, who dressed up for the occasion. Other songs indicate that dancing, making merry, and choosing a lady-love and offering her obedient service were further customs.

Most of the lyrics and songs serve not only to transmit New Year greetings but also to present a gift (see Tables 20.6 and 20.7). The most common kind of gift is immaterial, comprising a pledge of love, loyalty, or devotion. In *De quanqu'on peut* (Chantilly 564) (Table 20.7), the lover presents his lady with a thought (*pensament*), in *Or sus, mon cuer* (Oxford 213) a sweet sigh (*un doux souspir*), and in *Donés confort a vostre amy* (Oxford 213) the suffering lover turns the tables and asks for the lady's gift of her comfort. A promise of service is given in *La grant beauté* (ModA), which echoes the sentiment implicitly or explicitly expressed in those lyrics addressed to named patrons. In Deschamps's *Par mon desir* for Valentina Visconti this takes on a physical and metaphorical aspect, as the poet offers himself, body and soul (Table 20.6). The gift of love is, of course, a common trope. Sometimes the lover presents his abstract love, *amour*, but in most cases love is embodied and symbolized by the heart, body, and worldly goods of the lover. This features in lyrics by Christine, Deschamps, Charles d'Orléans, and Du Fay. In certain works, however, the gift is of a more tangible kind: in Christine's *Ce jour de l'an*, the lover also offers his lady a diamond. In Charles d'Orléans's *J'estraine de bien loing*, the lover presents a chaplet of marigolds (*soussies*). The same gift is given in Du Fay's *Je donne a tous*, suggesting a New Year custom now obscure to us. Perhaps this was linked to the crowning of winning entries at *puys*, where crowns, chaplets, and sometimes rings were bestowed on winning entries and runners-up;[21] Machaut's lyric *Se trestuit cil qui sont et ont esté* addresses the judges (*princes*) of a *puy*, and, intriguingly, asks them to crown him and his song

---

21 Plumley, *The Art of Grafted Song*, chs. 5 and 6.

with a chaplet of marigolds.[22] It also evokes the garlanding of courtiers at May Day celebrations.[23]

Especially interesting are cases where the work itself embodies the gift. Baude Herenc's poem *Le Parlement d'Amours* of 1432 (in *Jardin de plaisance*) suggests it was a custom on New Year's day for lovers to write lyrics for their ladies. In Deschamps's *Dame je vien paier ce que je doy* the narrator offers his heart, body, power, and all he can give, including the lyric itself (Table 20.6); he refers to his poem as a *chanson*, as if to evoke its performance. In three of Christine's lyrics, the author asks a patron to accept the ballade. In *Bon jour, bon an, bon mois* she invites Marie of Berry graciously to accept the ballade composed for her that very day ("prenez en gré ma ballade nouvelle ... Que j'ay faitte pour vous ceste journée"). This idea is echoed in certain of the songs (Table 20.7). In Antonello da Caserta's *Tres nouble dame*, the lover's gift to his lady is the song itself, again composed specially for the day ("un petit don par bon estrayne ... une canson de vray, faite pour vous"). Similarly, Arnold de Lantins's *Tout mon desir* is presented to the lady to transmit his New Year's greetings. In two of Christine's lyrics, the work-gift explicitly takes material form (Table 20.6). In *Bon jour, bon an et quanqu'il peut souffire*, the poet specifies that she presents the lyric in written form to her patron ("[je] vous presente / Cestui livret"); Christine added this ballade at the start of her *Débat de deux Amans* in a manuscript she presented to Charles d'Albret (Constable of France). Although *Des tous honneurs*, for Louis d'Orléans, lacks such a material context, here, too, the poet asks the prince to accept the fascicle bearing the lyric as a New Year gift ("ce livret que j'ay fait ... Ce jour de l'an soiez estrené").

This leads me to consider the most intriguing example of the New Year repertory, Baude Cordier's *Belle, bonne, sage*. It is presented in strikingly beautiful form, together with another picture-song by him, on a bifolio added after ca. 1418 to the existing corpus of Chantilly 564.[24] Cordier's song is magnificently self-referential. The lover-narrator states that his gift to his lady is this new song inscribed in his heart, which presents itself to her: this is depicted in the heart-shaped arrangement of the musical score. The narrator's comment suggests that the gift is the physical embodiment of the song, that is, the manuscript page. This leads me to wonder about the position of this remarkable work in

---

22  This is a *chant royal* (item 48 from Machaut's collected lyrics, *La Louange des Dames*), a form favored at these public competitions, which were popular in Paris and in the North.

23  A passage from Jean Renart's *Guillaume de Dole* describes how the best singer at a May gathering is awarded a diamond; see Schwindt, "Amour courtois." On Maying ritual in the French royal milieu in the late fourteenth century, see Crane, *The Performance of Self*, ch. 3.

24  For a full-size reproduction in color, see Plumley and Stone, *Codex Chantilly*, 2 (fol. 11v).

Chantilly 564. It was long assumed that the bifolio onto which it was copied was added to the main corpus *after* the addition of an index, since the latter omits the Cordier songs. However, in the course of our recent study of the manuscript, Anne Stone and I noticed that some hitherto unnoticed prick-marks used in the preparation of the index bifolio had left impressions on the Cordier bifolio.[25] This implies the two bifolios had a shared history: the Cordier songs were not added randomly at a later stage but were part of a process of rejigging the manuscript that involved its indexing, foliation, and possibly its binding. It seems the Cordier songs had already been copied when the index was made; the very small margins of these pages suggest that the bifolio was trimmed to fit the format of the manuscript's main corpus. An intriguing twist is that the scribe who copied the Cordier songs in a French or Burgundian hand also added some composer attributions in the main corpus, which was copied by an Italian with poor French: the Cordier scribe and the manuscript were thus together at the point when this preparation took place.

On the top page of the adjacent index bifolio, thus at the front of the whole manuscript, a title page was designed, probably years later by the Florentine merchant, banker, and poet Francesco d'Altobianco degli Alberti, who worked in Rome in papal circles in the late 1420s and early 1430s. Beneath the word "Musica," written in a humanistic hand, appear his initials, and beneath those the enigmatic words "Betise-Lisa." This may be a near anagram of "Elisabetta," one of the daughters of Alberti's colleague Tommaso Spinelli, to whom Alberti gave the manuscript in July 1461, according to a roughly added inscription in Spinelli's hand.

I am left wondering whether whoever masterminded the updating of the manuscript in the fifteenth century – possibly for Alberti or even an earlier owner – wasn't doing something akin to Christine de Pizan in using a song about gift-giving to preface and present a book to a patron. The visually stunning Cordier bifolio seems very fitting for this purpose: it provides a spectacular opening to the book while simultaneously celebrating the transaction of the gift. My suspicion that Cordier's *Belle, bonne, sage* relates to the gift of the manuscript is strengthened by its sister picture-song, *Tout par compas*, in which the poet declares: "J'ay fait ce rondel pour enoffre" ("I have made this rondeau as a gift"). If not pertaining to the gift of the codex to Spinelli's daughter in 1461, this might

---

25 Plumley and Stone, *Codex Chantilly*, 1:122–26.

relate to the acquisition of the manuscript by Alberti himself or by an earlier owner.[26]

* * *

There remains much more to discover about these occasional works and their function in late medieval court ceremony and in more informal contexts. While some information can be gleaned from rubrics and heraldic references, the recipients of the songs and the precise catalysts for the composition of these works currently remain obscure. Nevertheless, as I have endeavored to show here, study of these works and, in particular, the intricate interrelationships that bind them as a corpus, affords some insights into how they were conceptualized as well as possible influences and points of contact between the constituent repertories and their authors. These fascinating works also provide fascinating glimpses into late medieval New Year customs and traditions and the role of music and poetry therein.

Table 20.1 *New Year songs, ca. 1380–ca. 1440*
[R] = rondeau; [V] = virelai; [B] = ballade

---

A. Before ca. 1415
Berkeley 744 (1375)
    Anon., *Souviegne vous d'estriner vostre amant* [R]
London 15224 (before 1395; lyrics only)
    Anon., *Bone estreine en ce pleisant jour* [R]
    Anon., *De jour de l'an bien ait* [R]
    Anon., *Le primer jour que l'anee renoue* [V]
*Manière de language* (1396; lyrics only)
    Anon., *Estrainez moy de cuer joyous* [R]
Cortona fragment (ca. 1400)
    Anon. *Dame a qui bon an doner veuille* [V]
Chantilly 564 (main corpus, ca. 1418)
    Anon., *A mon pooir je garde et vueil garder* [V]
    Anon., *De quanqu'on peut belle et bonne estrener* [B]
ModA (ca. 1410)
    Antonello da Caserta, *Tres nouble dame souverayne* [V]
    Anon., *La grant beauté de vous, ma souverayne* [R]
    Anon., *Sans mal penser et sans folour* [V]

---

26 Ragnard proposed something similar but suggested the recipient was perhaps a Valois princess because of the fleurs-de-lys adorning Cordier's *Belle, bonne, sage* ("Les Chansons d'étrennes," 117); these might alternatively represent the *giglio* (lily), the symbol of Florence, home of the Alberti and Spinelli.

Table 20.1 (*cont.*)

Leiden 2720 (ca. 1400)
    Anon., *Au tamps que je soloye amer* [V]
    Anon., *Aux estrines cuers gracieulz* [R]
    Anon., *Sans jamais faire partement* [R]

B. 1410s–1420s
Chantilly 564 (added bifolio, after ca. 1418)
    Baude Cordier, *Belle, bonne, sage* [R]
Paris 4917 (before ca. 1425)
    Anon., *Vostre servant suy et seray* [R]
    Anon., *Ce primier jour que commanche l'annee* [R]
Oxford 213 (gatherings V, VI, VIII: late 1420s)
    Anon., *Or sus, mon cuer* [V] [gathering V]
    Cordier, *Ce jour de l'an* [R] [gathering VI]
    Cordier, *Je suy celuy qui veul toudis servir* [R] [gathering VII]
    Cordier, *Dame excellent* [B] [gathering VIII]

C. Ca. 1430–ca. 1450
Oxford 213 (gatherings II, III, IV)
    Du Fay, *Ce jour de l'an voudray joye mener* [R] [gathering II (unit IIx)]
    Du Fay, *Entre vous gentils amoureux* [R]
    Du Fay, *Estrinez moy, je vous estrineray* [R, dialogue]
    A. de Lantins, *Tout mon desir* [B] [gathering III, unit IIIx]
    A. de Lantins, *Amours servir et honourer* [R]
    Anon., *Donés confort a vostre amy* [R] [unit IIIz]
    Du Fay, *Belle, veulliés moy retenir* [R]
    Du Fay, *Bon jour, bon mois* [R]
    Malbecque, *Dieu vous doinst bon jour* [R]
    A. de Lantins, *Ce jour de l'an belle je vous supply* [R] [gathering IV]
    Du Fay, *Je requier a tous amoureux* [R]
    Du Fay, *Pouray je avoir vostre mercy?* [R]
    Du Fay, *Se ma dame je puis veir* [R]
    Du Fay, *Je donne a tous les amoureux* [R]
Paris 6771
    Nicholas Grenon, *La plus belle et doulce figure* [V]
El Escorial V.III.24
    Binchois, *La merchi ma dame et Amours* [R]
    Binchois, *Marguerite, fleur de valeur* [R]
    Anon., *Je cuidoye estre conforté* [R]
    Anon., *Bon jour, bon mois, bonne sepmaine* [R]
El Escorial IV.a.24
    Du Fay, *Mille bonjours je vous presente* [R]
Trent 87
    Anon., *Aux ce bon youre de la bon estren* [R]

Table 20.2 *Conventional vocabulary in Christine de Pizan's and Deschamps's New Year lyrics without music*

| Lyric | Identification of New Year | Greeting/wishes | Addressee |
| --- | --- | --- | --- |
| **Christine de Pizan (ca. 1364–ca. 1440)** | | | |
| Noble vaillant, chevalier [B] | Ce premier jour de l'an se renouvelle (refr.) | Dieu vous doinst tout soulaz delitable (l. 17, envoy) | Charles d'Albret (d.1415) |
| Bon jour, bon an et quanqu'il peut souffrir [B] | Ce jour de l'an que maint bon cuer resjoie (l. 5) | Bon jour, bon an (incipit) | Charles d'Albret |
| Haulte, excellent Royne couronnee [B] | Ce jour de l'an, ma redoubtee dame | Boneur, bon temps, tres agreeable annee (l. 9) | Isabeau de Bavière (d.1435) |
| De tous honneurs et de toutes querelles [B] | Ce jour de l'an vous soiez estrené | de chascun par communal jointure / Amé soiez (ll. 18–19) | Louis d'Orléans (d.1407) |
| Bon jour, bon an, bon mois, bonne nouvelle [B] | Ce premier jour de la presente annee (l. 2) | Bon jour, bon an, bon mois, bonne nouvelle (incipit) ... soiés estrenee / De toute joye (ll. 4–5) | Marie de Berry (d.1434) |
| | Ce plaisant jour de premier de l'an nouvel (refr.) | Si vous doint Dieux quanque pour moy voldraie | |
| | Ou jolis temps dont vient le renouvel (l. 16) | | |
| Ce jour de l'an que l'en doit estrenier [B] | Ce jour de l'an (incipit) | | [1399–1402] |
| **Eustache Deschamps (1346–ca. 1406)** | | | |
| J'ay puis vint ans au jour de l'an nouvel [B] | ... jour de l'an nouvel (incipit) | | dame |
| Du sens que Dieu donna a Salemon [B] | Ce jour de l'an | Dieux vous doint honour, force et renon (envoy) | Louis d'Orléans |

| | | | Valentina Visconti (d.1408) |
|---|---|---|---|
| Pour mon desir plus fort renouveller [B] | *A ce bon jour de renouvellement* | Vous veuil mon corps et ma vie ordener (l. 3)<br>Je ne vous say d'autre chose *estrener* (l. 9) | |
| Tant est cilz jours au joy d'uy solennez [B] | *... a ce bon jour*<br>Ce que je doy pour mes *estrenes* rendre (refr.) | | |
| Cuer, corps, penser, sens, maniere et avis [B] | *A ce bon jour ...* (l. 5) | a ce bon jour *vous doing* et veuil donner | dame |
| Mon cuer, mon corps, ma pensee et m'amour [B] | *A ce bon jour* ayez pitié de mi (refr.) | *vous doing* ... pour *estraine* ... *ce petit don* (ll. 2–3) | dame |
| Dame je vien paier ce que je doy [B] | *Ce jour de l'an* que vo debteur me voy (l. 3)<br>*A ce bon jour* | A ce bon jour ne veuillez refuser / ... *ce petit don* (ll. 9–10) | dame |
| Des sept vertus et des. VII. dons de grace [B] | *Ce jour de l'an* | *vous doing* cuer et pensee (envoy) | dame |
| Ce jour de l'an estener ne sçaroie [B] | *Ce jour de l'an estrener* (incipit) | | |
| Poux, puces, lantes et vermine [B] | | *Vous doint Dieux et senglante estraine* | Companions |
| Bon an, bon jour et bonne estraine [R] | *Bon an* (incipit/refr.) | *Bon an, bon jour et bonne estraine* (incipit)<br>Tout *vous doing* a cest journee (l. 9) | dame |
| Longue vie, joye, santé et paix [R] | Au commencement de *l'annee* (refr.) | Longue vie, joye, santé et paix / Grace et honour,<br>renommee et largesse / ... *vous doint Dieux* (ll. 1–3) | dame |
| Et de quoy vous puis je estrener [V] | *Ce jour de l'an* (l. 3)<br>Hui *a ce jour* | ... quel *don* vous puis je donner | |
| A ce bon jour que temps se renouvelle [V] | *A ce bon jour que temps se renouvelle* (incipit/refr.) | *Vous doing* mon cuer, corps et quanque j'ay (l. 3) | dame |

Table 20.3. *Other collections of New Year lyrics without music*

**Composed before ca. 1430**

London 15224 (before 1395)
A l'estreiner de ce bon jour [R]
Dame de trestout bien garnie [R]
Dieu vous estreine fleur sans per [R]
En ce bon jour trestout plein de liece [R]
San Gabriel qui tout diz boneur [R]
Ha jour a qui longuement sui donnee [B]

Oton de Granson (ca. 1345–97)
Belle, que j'aim plus qu'autre [B]
Ce premier jour que l'an se renouvelle [R]
Jadix m'evint que par merencolie [Complainte]
Joye, sainté, paix et honneur ['Estrainne']

Clermont Ferrand 249
Anon., La nuit de l'an, en dormant me sembla [B, ca. 1400?]

Jehan de Garencières (ca. 1371–1415)
Ce jour de l'an que l'on doit faire estraine [B]
Honneur, sancté, parfaicte joye [R]
Ce jour de l'an nouvel entré [R]
Ennuy, soucy, courrous et desplaisance [R]

Alain Chartier (1385–1430)
Lay de Plaisance [Lai, ca. 1410?]

Charles d'Orléans (1394–1465)
Je me souloye pourpenser [B]
J'estraine de bien loing m'amie [R]
Ad ce premier jour de l'annee [R]
Celle que je ne scay nommer [R]

Jehan Regnier (ca. 1392–ca. 1470)
Bon jour, bon an et bonne vie [R]
Or ay je veu le temps que je souloye [B]

**Later sources**

Rohan Chansonnier (ca. 1470)
Anon., Estrenez moy ou de dueil ou de joie [R]
Joye, soulas, honneur, liesse [R]

*Jardin de Plaisance* (1501)
A joye puissiez vous avoir [R]

Table 20.4 *Conventional vocabulary in New Year songs*

| Song | Identification of New Year | Greeting/wishes | Addressee |
|---|---|---|---|
| **London 15224** | | | |
| *Bone estreine en ce pleisant jour* [R] | Ce pleisant jour (incipit) | Bone estreine (incipit) Vous doint Diex (l. 2) | dame |
| *Ce jour de l'an bien ait* [R] | jour de l'an (incipit) | La veuille estreiner (l. 2) | Visconti ? |
| *Le primer jour que l'anee renoue* [V] | Le primer jour que l'anee renoue (incipit) | estreinee d'une pleisant douçour | Visconti (Valentina?) |
| **Chantilly 564** | | | |
| *A mon pooir je garde et veuil garder* [V] | le jour de l'an premier (l. 3) | bien estrené (l. 3) | dame |
| *De quanqu'on peut* [B] | belle et bonne estrener (incipit) | estrener (incipit) doner (l. 5) | dame |
| Cordier, *Belle, bonne, sage* [R] | A ce jour cy que l'an se renouvelle (l. 2) | don (l. 3) | |
| **Leiden 2720** | | | |
| *Au tamps que je soloye amer* [V] | Che novel an (l. 14) | — | audience |
| **ModA** | | | |
| *La grant beauté de vous* [R] | Ce primier jour de l'an (l. 5) | A bone estrayne (l. 5), ce don (l. 11) | dame |
| *Sans mal penser et sans folour* [V] | Le primier jour / De l'an (refr., ll. 5–6) | A bone estrayne (refr., end) | dame |
| Antonello da Caserta, *Tres nouble dame* [V] | — | un petit don par bon estrayne (refr., end) | dame |

Table 20.4 (*cont.*)

| Song | Identification of New Year | Greeting/wishes | Addressee |
|---|---|---|---|
| **Oxford 213** | | | |
| Cordier, *Ce jour de l'an que maint doist* [R] | ce jour de l'an (incipit) | estrenier (incipit) donner (l. 4) loer (l. 5) | dame |
| Cordier, *Dame excellent ou sont bonté* [B] | tres bon an (refr.) | tres bon an vos doint et tres bon jour (refr.) | dame |
| *Or sus, mon cuer* [V] | ce primier jour de l'an (l. 4) | a bonne estrinne (l. 4), dieux le doint bon jour (l. 7), don (l. 10) | dame |
| A. de Lantins, *Tout mon desir* [B] | Ce jour de l'an (l. 4) | Pour estriner ma doulche amye (refr.) | dame |
| A. de Lantins, *Amour servir et honourer* | De l'an ce premier jour (l. 2) | | dame |
| A. de Lantins, *Ce jour de l'an, belle* | Ce jour de l'an (incipit) | | dame |
| Du Fay, *Belle, veuillés moy retenir* | Ce jour de l'an (l. 6) | | dame |
| Du Fay, *Bon jour, bon mois, bon an* | Bon an (incipit) | Bon jour, bon mois, bon an et bonne estraine (incipit) Vous doinst | dame |
| Du Fay, *Ce jour de l'an* | Ce jour de l'an (incipit) | | |
| Du Fay, *Estrinez moy* | Ce jour de l'an nouvel (l. 3), a ce bon jour (l. 8) | Estrinez moy, je vous estrineray (incipit) | Lover/lady dialogue |
| Du Fay, *Je donne a tous les amoureux* | — | Je donne … pour estrines une soussye | amoureux |

| | | | |
|---|---|---|---|
| Du Fay, *Je requier a tous amoureux* | A ce jour de l'an gracieux (l. 5) | | dame |
| Du Fay, *Pourray je avoir vostre mercy?* | Ce jour de l'annee present (l. 3) | A l'estrinne vous presente | |
| Du Fay, *Se ma dame je puis veir* | Le primier jour de ceste annee (l. 2) | D'un bonjour sera estrinee (l. 3) | dame |
| Malbecque, *Dieux vous doinst bon jour* | Au commencement de l'annee (l. 2) | Dieux vous doinst bonjour et demy (incipit) | dame |
| Anon., *Bon jour, bon mois, bonne sepmaine* | | Bon moys, bonne sepmaine ossy (l. 4) | |
| | | Bon jour, bon mois, bonne sepmaine (incipit) | dame |
| Anon., *Donés confort a vostre amy* | Ce jour de l'an (l. 2) | | dame |

Table 20.5 *Close interrelationships between lyrics and song texts*

| Author | Related incipits | Related internal lines |
|---|---|---|
| **a.** | | |
| Eustache Deschamps | A ce bon jour que temps se renouvelle [V] | Vous doing mon cuer, mon corps et quanque j'ay (l. 3) |
| Charles d'Orléans | Ad ce premier jour de l'année [R] | De cuer, de corps et quanque j'ay (l. 2) |
| | J'estraine de bien loing m'amie [R] | De cuer, de corps et quanque j'ay (l. 2) |
| **b.** | | |
| Christine de Pizan | Ce jour de l'an que l'en doit estrenier [B] | Mon cuer, mon corps, quanque je puis finer (l. 3) |
| Baude Cordier | Ce jour de l'an que maint doist estrenier [R] | Mon cuer, mon corps, entierement donner (l. 4) |
| Jehan de Garencières | Ce jour de l'an que l'on doit faire estraine [B] | De cuer, de corps, de vouloir, de pensee (l. 2) |
| [Guillaume Du Fay] | Ce jour de l'an voudray joye mener [R] | |
| [Arnold de Lantins] | Ce jour de l'an belle je vous supply [R] | |
| **c.** | | |
| Eustache Deschamps | Bon an, bon jour, et bonne estraine [R] | |
| Anon., La nuit de l'an, en dormant | Avoir bon jour, bon an et bonne estraine (refr.) | |
| Christine de Pizan | Bon jour, bon an, et quanqu'il peut souffire [B] | |
| Christine de Pizan | Bon jour, bon an, bon mois, bonne nouvelle [B] | |
| Guillaume Du Fay | Bon jour, bon mois, bon an et bonne estraine [R] | |
| **d.** | | |
| Anon. (ModA) | La grant beauté de vous [R] | Ce primier jour de l'an / A bone estrayne (l. 5) |
| Anon. (ModA) | Sans mal penser et sans folour [V] | Le primier jour // De l'an a bone estrayne (refr., ll. 5, 7) |
| Anon. (Oxford 213) | Or sus, mon cuer [V] | Ce primier jour de l'an a bonne estrinne (l. 4) |
| **e.** | | |
| A. de Lantins | Ce jour de l'an belle je vous supply [R] | Car je vous ay sur toute aultre choissy (l. 9) |
| | Tout mom desir et mom voloir [B] | Et l'ay sur toute aultre choysie (l. 11) |

Table 20.6 *The gift in the lyrics*

| Lyrics without music | The gift | Formulation in the text |
|---|---|---|
| **Christine de Pizan** | | |
| Noble vaillant, chevalier | New ballade (to Charles d'Albret) | "Prenez en gré ma ballade nouvelle" |
| Bon jour, bon an et quanqu'il peut souffrire | This book (*livret = Débat de deux Amans*, to Charles d'Albret) | "Et vous presente / Cestui livret" |
| Haulte, excellent Royne couronnee | The ballade (to Queen Isabeau de Bavière) | "Ma balade pregne en gré vo sagece" |
| De tous honneurs et de toutes querelles | This book (*livret*, to Louis d'Orléans) | "De ce livret que j'ay fait … Ce jour de l'an soiez estrené" |
| Bon jour, bon an, bon mois, bonne nouvelle | New ballade (to Marie de Berry) | "Prenez en gré ma ballade nouvelle … Que j'ay faitte pour vous ceste journee" |
| Ce jour de l'an que l'en doit estrenier | Heart, body, himself, his goods and a diamond (to his lady) | "Mon cuer, corps … Moy, et mes biens vous ottroy … vous envoy ce petit dyamant" |
| **Eustache Deschamps** | | |
| Pour mon desir plus fort renouveller | Himself (to Valentina Visconti, duchess of Orléans) | "mon corps et ma vie … recevez noy, loial com torterelle" |
| Tant est cilz jours au joy d'uy solennez | Heart (to his lady) | "ymaginez / Mon povre cuer … Plus riche don n'ay; Pour Dieu recevez" |
| Cuer, corps, penser, sens, maniere et avis | Himself – heart, body, mind, and senses (to his lady) | "Cuer, corps, penser, sens, maniere et avis, Oir, veoir, sentir et odorer … vous doing" |
| Mon cuer, mon corps, ma pensee et m'amour | Heart, body, thought, and love (to his lady) | "Mon cuer, mon corps, ma pensee et m'amour / Vous baille et doing … et presente" |

Table 20.6 (*cont.*)

| Lyrics without music | The gift | Formulation in the text |
|---|---|---|
| Dame je vien paier ce que je doy | Heart, body, power, all can give and the song (to his lady) | "vous . . . de mon cuer estrener, Corps et pouoir et quanque j'ay donner . . . ma chanson" |
| Des sept vertus et des.VII. dons de grace | Heart, thought, and song (to his lady) | "vous doing cuer et pensee, Ceste chançon pour vo bien figuree" |
| Bon an, bon jour et bonne estraine | Heart, body (to his lady) | "De mon cuer et corps vous estraine, Tout vous doing a ceste journee" |
| Et de quoy vous puis je estrener | Heart, body, and love | "cuer, corps et amour / . . . je vous doing sans retourner" |
| A ce bon jour que temps se renouvelle | Heart, body, and all he has (to his lady) | "Vous doing mon cuer, mon corps et quanque j'ay" |
| **Charles d'Orléans** | | |
| Ad ce premier jour de l'annee [R] | Heart, body and all he has (to his lady) | "De cuer, corps et quanque j'ay / Privement estreneray" |
| J'estraine de bien loing m'amie [R] | Heart, body, and all he has, and circlet of marigolds (to his lady) | "Mon cuer de chapel de soussie . . . et a elle presenteray / Dez fleurs" |
| London 15224 | Service | |
| A l'estreiner de ce bon jour [R] | | |
| Dame de trestout bien garnier [R] | Promise of service | "Je vous promet . . . de vous servir" |
| Dieu vous estreine fleur sans per [R] | Love | "M'amour vous vodroie doner" |

Table 20.7 *The gift in the songs*

| Songs | The gift | Formulation in the text |
|---|---|---|
| **London 15224** | | |
| *Le primer jour que l'annee renoue* [V] | A pleasant "sweetness" | "Sui estreinee d'une pleasant dousour" (the lady speaks) |
| **Chantilly 564** | | |
| *A mon pooir* [V] | The lady's heart is received | "Le joli cuer . . . / duquel m'aviés le jour de l'an premier / Bien estrené" (the lady to the lover) |
| *De quanqu'on peut* [B] | Thought | "Je velle doner tal pensament" |
| Cordier, *Belle, bonne, sage* [R] | New song and heart | "vous fais le don d'une chanson nouvelle / Dedens mon cuer qui a vous se presente" |
| **ModA** | | |
| *La grant beauté de vous* [R] | Promise of service | "Je vous promet . . . de vous servir" |
| *Sans mal penser et sans folour* [V] | Love | "vous presente m'amour / A bone estrayne" |
| Antonello da Caserta, *Tres nouble dame* [V] | The song | "un petit don par bon estrayne . . . une canson de vray, fait' pour vous" |
| **Oxford 213** | | |
| Cordier, *Ce jour de l'an que maint doist* [R] | Heart and body | "Mon cuer, mon corps, entirement donner a ma dame" |
| *Or sus, mon cuer* [V] | A sigh | "un doux souspir" ["cuer" is the mediator to persuade the lady to accept] |

Table 20.7 (*cont.*)

| Songs | The gift | Formulation in the text |
|---|---|---|
| A. de Lantins, *Tout mon desir* | Song (commanded by Desire, Will, and Reason) | "chançon … Pour estriner ma doulche amye" |
| Du Fay, *Belle, veuillés moy retenir* | Heart | "Ce jour de l'an vous veul offrir / Mon cuer" |
| Du Fay, *Ce jour de l'an* | Heart, body, and goods | "a laquelle puisse presenter / Cuer, corps et biens" |
| Du Fay, *Estrinez moy* | (dialogue) Lover gives his heart to his lady | "je vous estrineray … Du cuer que j'ay pour vous donner" |
| Du Fay, *Je donne a tous les amoureux* | Gives marigold to all lovers (to cure hearts) | "Je donne a tous les amoureux / Pour estrinés une soussye" |
| Du Fay, *Pourray je avoir vostre mercy?* | Heart, body, and all his goods | "Que cuer, corps et tous biens aussy / A l'estrinne je vous presente" |
| Du Fay, *Se ma dame je puis veir* | Heart, body, and goods | "Cuer, corps et biens luy veuil offrir" |
| Malbecque, *Dieux vous doinst bon jour* [R] | Heart | "Je vous donne le cuer de mi / Pour estrene" |
| Anon., *Donés confort a vostre amy* | Asks lady to give comfort | "Donés confort a vostre amy" |

# Bibliography

Boone, Graeme MacDonald, "Dufay's Early Chansons: Chronology and Style in the Manuscript Oxford, Bodleian Library, Canonici misc. 213," Ph.D. diss., Harvard University, 1987 (Ann Arbor, 1987)

Buettner, Brigitte, "Past Presents: New Year's Gifts at the Valois Courts, ca. 1400," *Art Bulletin* 83 (2001), 598–625

Chattaway, Carol M., "Looking a Medieval Gift Horse in the Mouth: The Role of the Giving of Gift Objects in the Definition and Maintenance of the Power Networks of Philip the Bold," *BMGN: Low Countries Historical Review* 114 (1999), 1–15

Clermont Ferrand, Bibliothèque municipale, MS 249

Crane, Susan, *The Performance of Self: Ritual, Clothing, and Identity during the Hundred Years War*, Philadelphia, 2002

Di Bacco, Giuliano, and John Nádas, "The Papal Chapels and Italian Sources of Polyphony during the Great Schism," in *Papal Music and Musicians in Late Medieval and Renaissance Rome*, ed. Richard Sherr, Oxford, 1998, 44–92

Fallows, David, *Dufay*, London, 1982

  ed., *Oxford Bodleian Library, MS Canon. Misc. 213*, Chicago, 1995

Grenier-Winther, Joan, *Oton de Granson, Poésies*, Paris, 2010

Herenc, Baude, *Le Doctrinal de la seconde rhétorique*, in *Recueil d'arts de seconde rhétorique*, ed. Ernest Langlois, Paris, 1902; repr. Geneva 1974, 104–98

Higgins, Paula M., "Music and Musicians at the Sainte-Chapelle of the Bourges Palace, 1405–1515," in *Trasmissione e recezione delle forme di cultura musicale: Atti del XIV Congresso della Società Internazionale di Musicologia, Bologna 1997*, ed. Angelo Pompilio, Turin 1990, 3:689–701

Hirschbiegel, Jan, *Étrennes: Untersuchungen zum höfischen Geschenkverkehr im spätmittelalterlichen Frankreich der Zeit König Karls VI (1380–1422)*, Munich, 2003

*Le Jardin de plaisance et fleur de réthoricque*, Paris, 1501

Leach, Elizabeth Eva, "Learning French by Singing in 14th-Century England," *EM* 33 (2005), 253–70

*Manière de langage*, London, British Library, Harley MS 3988

Plumley, Yolanda, *The Art of Grafted Song: Citation and Allusion in the Age of Machaut*, New York and Oxford, 2013

  and Anne Stone, "Cordier's Picture-Songs and the Relationship between the Song Repertories of the Chantilly Codex and Oxford 213," in *A Late Medieval Song-Book and its Context: New Perspectives on the Chantilly Codex (Bibliothèque du château de Chantilly, Ms. 564)*, ed. Yolanda Plumley and Anne Stone, Turnhout, 2009, 303–28

  and Anne Stone, eds., *Codex Chantilly, Bibliothèque du Château de Chantilly, MS 564*, 2 vols., Turnhout, 2008

Ragnard, Isabelle, "Les Chansons d'étrennes aux XIVe et XVe siècles," in *Poètes et musiciens dans l'espace bourguignon: Les artistes et leurs mécènes*, Neuchâtel, 2005, 105–27

Rohan Chansonnier: Berlin, Staatliche Museen der Stiftung Preußischer Kulturbesitz, Kupferstichkabinett, MS 78.B.17

Schwindt, Nicole, "Amour courtois im Jahreslauf: Die Ritualisierung der Chanson im frühen 15. Jahrhundert," in *Amor docet musicam: Musik und Liebe in der Frühen*

*Neuzeit*, ed. Dietrich Helms und Sabine Meine, Studien und Materialien zur Musikwissenschaft 67, Hildesheim, 2012, 157–201

Stone, Anne, ed., *The Manuscript Modena, Biblioteca Estense, Alpha.M.5.24*, 2 vols., Lucca, 2003–5

Stratford, Jenny, "The Goldenes Rössl and the French Royal Collections," in *Treasure in the Medieval West*, ed. Elizabeth M. Tyler, Woodbridge, 2000, 109–33

Van Biezen, J., and J. P. Gumbert, eds., *Two Chansonniers from the Low Countries: French and Dutch Polyphonic Songs from the Leiden and Utrecht Fragments [Early 15th Century]*, Monumenta Musica Neerlandica 15, Amsterdam, 1985

Wallis, N. Hardy, *Anonymous French Verse: An Anthology of Fifteenth Century Poems Collected from Manuscripts from the British Museum*, London, 1929

· PART V MUSIC IN CHURCHES, COURTS, AND CITIES ·

# Musical institutions in the fifteenth century and their political contexts

KLAUS PIETSCHMANN

TRANSLATED BY JAMES STEICHEN

Apart from musical works, musical institutions have been the subject of musicological research for longer than any other subject. This reflects a consensus common to all historical disciplines, namely that institutions stand as a fundamental resource for understanding human social relations. Institutions reflect political, social, and religious structures as well as the societal prestige accorded to their activities. To their members, such entities offer discrete legal and economic parameters within which they can pursue their work more easily.

In musicology, the (long) fifteenth century has traditionally been considered a decisive period in the development of musical institutions.[1] The establishment of court chapels throughout Europe ensured that the cultivation of learned music (initially only sacred music) enjoyed a stable means of production and transmission well into the early twentieth century. Increased circulation of liturgical polyphony, the spread of new genres such as the mass, and the rise of the composer are all indebted to the growth of these institutions.

The character of such organizations was not primarily or exclusively that of a professional music ensemble. Rather, they served the larger purpose of performing regular, and often quite sophisticated, liturgical duties that included music. The establishment of polyphony as an integral element of such practices was the key musical novelty and coincided with the development of an author-centered understanding of the musical work and the figure of the composer as the locus of artistic achievement.[2] The extent to which this process was enabled by individual chapels depended on how much the leaders of such institutions recognized composition as distinct from or superior to traditional performative practices (choral singing and polyphonic ornamentation). From the courtly realm, this dynamic spread to other institutions: endowments began to use polyphonic

1 In the considerable literature on the subject, several more recent overviews are Schmidt-Beste, ed., *Institutions*; Lodes and Lütteken, eds., *Institutionalisierung*; Strohm, *The Rise of European Music*; Piperno et al., eds., *Cappelle musicali*; Marx *et al.*, eds., *Corti rinascimentali*.
2 See Laurenz Lütteken's essay in this volume, Ch. 3.

masses and devotions; brotherhoods began to augment or replace their performers with paid professionals; and many religious orders took up figural music, precipitating an increase in monastic regulations regarding music.[3]

For instrumental music, the dynamics were similar, with instrument building, technical proficiency, and artistic standards all experiencing noticeable growth from the mid-fourteenth century onward.[4] The fifteenth century witnessed the expansion of civic and courtly wind ensembles and increased mobility for individual musicians, but unlike sacred music, such changes do not correlate with changes to institutional structures, and were more likely manifestations of long-term developments. The same is true of *ménestrels* and players, who organized themselves into corporate guild-like entities, albeit without significant changes to musical practice.[5]

The process unfolded quite differently in the realm of secular vocal music. Many fifteenth-century manuscripts (such as the Loire Valley chansonniers) document a dynamic compositional discourse influenced by numerous innovations, but without institutional grounding. Composers of secular repertories – such as Guillaume Du Fay, Johannes Ockeghem, or Josquin des Prez – were officially employed and provided for through other means, often in chapels in which their primary responsibilities were liturgical performance, the training of young singers, and the composition of sacred music. Others held positions at court, as did Antoine Busnoys, who served as *valet du chambre* and *chantre* at the court of Charles the Bold; composers and performers were frequently employed in the church hierarchy in non-musical positions.[6]

Scholars commonly understand musical institutions in relation to their music-specific duties – as part of a system of musical patronage that fostered the creation and transmission of works of art and the improvement of performance practice. In other words, high-level musical practice would be impossible without patronage and institutionalization. This avenue of research consequently focuses on institutions and patronage systems whose musical output was especially prolific and has been preserved in written sources: the higher the artistic "value" of the surviving compositions, the greater their interest as research subjects. Only recently has attention been paid to institutions whose musical practices were of a lower quality or were not preserved. In these cases, research has focused on the structures and functions of musical practice within the institutional and broader social or political context, and less on musical repertories.

---

3 For an overview see Bryant and Quaranta, eds., *Produzione, circolazione e consumo.*
4 See the essay by Keith Polk in this volume, Ch. 38, and his *German Instrumental Music.*
5 For an overview see Hartung, *Die Spielleute im Mittelalter.*
6 See the essay by Pamela Starr in this volume, Ch. 24.

It is this latter perspective that is the premise of the following overview, in which institutional tendencies of courtly, ecclesiastical, and political contexts are foregrounded. Surviving musical repertories are given due consideration, but will not determine the focus of this study. In this context, a "musical institution" is considered to be a group of musicians attached to a courtly, ecclesiastical, or civic entity that provided a foothold or financial support for musical production. Although the discussion will focus on the establishment of musical chapels in European courts, the initial point of departure is an overview of types of musical functions in courtly, ecclesiastical, and civic contexts. These functions provided the institutional grounding for all musical practices, serving to project exclusivity and cachet to the outside world and foster internal stability and identity. Second is a survey of the development of representative court chapels in the fifteenth century. The final section posits a comparative view of this material with special emphasis on organizational structures.

## Functions of musical practice in courtly, ecclesiastical, and civic contexts

In the twenty-first century, replete with televisions and iPods, it can be difficult to comprehend music's role in the later Middle Ages. Its presence in everyday life was no less significant than today, but it always required active music-making, and the more ambitious or complex the music, the greater the demands on the musicians, the greater its social prestige, and thus the greater the cost. A mass by Du Fay or a fanfare for the entrance of a duke required highly specialized musicians, whose education and welfare were exceedingly costly, and unlike military or administrative expenses often were questioned by financial administrators. Thus the places in which art music could flourish also help to explain the processes and underlying rationales of its institutionalization.

These explanations are always a complex mix of the functional and symbolic. For every nobleman's court, participation in Christian worship was a constitutive element of governance, whose divinely ordained legitimacy was perpetuated by participation in the sacraments. Thus the maintenance of a private court chapel, whose core duties were to execute the liturgy, was virtually a requirement. Music played an essential role in major services, but fulfilled its liturgical function whether it was sung in simple chant or lavishly composed or improvised polyphony – the choice depended on the symbolic function the music had to fulfill in its particular context. When Ercole I d'Este began to increasingly embellish his court chapel, in part thanks to works such as Josquin's *Missa Hercules dux Ferrarie*, his goal was the symbolic elevation of the duke within the context of the liturgy, closely tied to his other efforts to lend his regime a sacred dimension.[7] That the chapel of Ferrara became one of the best in all of Europe can thus be interpreted in part by the drive to promote a pious image of the ruler (to the court, wider populace, and outside observers), at once ensuring internal stability and projecting external strength. Similarly, the creation of wind ensembles and the cultivation of virtuosic musical practices for the purposes of political representation, especially in the Holy Roman Empire, were closely tied to military readiness, which always held first priority. And as Laurenz Lütteken has argued, the subordinate role of vocal polyphony in these contexts should not be taken to mean that musical practices were necessarily backward or less developed.[8]

The question of political self-fashioning and the consolidation of symbolic capital, significant for all courts and states in the fifteenth century, was central to the organization of musical practice and the meaning of individual compositions. Even when criticism of liturgical polyphony gained steam in the course of the fifteenth century,[9] there was no doubt as to the mystical significance of music, which resonated with the music of the heavenly hosts and served as an audible means of political legitimation.[10]

This understanding of music would in turn affect the larger network of courtly institutions and other social fields in which musical practice in ritual contexts played a role. On one hand are the smaller chapels of princes, dukes, cardinals, and other nobles whose representational capabilities were circumscribed, and thus limited in the number of musicians they could employ; on the other are the pious lay brotherhoods that gained increasing prominence in the late Middle Ages. Initially the members of these organizations took primary responsibility for music-making, but the fifteenth century saw a marked increase in the employment of professional musicians. The most famous and well-researched examples are the polyphonic music of the so-called *Salve* brotherhoods of northwestern Europe, the *laudesi* of Florence, and the *scuole piccole* of Venice. A clear imitation of proceedings at court, these practices offered visual and audible manifestations, not only of an organization's piety, but also of its economic clout.[11] This focus on external representation marked a break with the original egalitarian conception of brotherly spirituality: the decline of congregational singing and its displacement by listening to spiritually uplifting art music signaled a shift toward individualized devotion, modeled on forms of courtly piety. In turn, the concept of an earthly

7 Lockwood, *Music in Renaissance Ferrara*, 133–42.
8 Lütteken, "Politische Zentren."      9 See the examples in Wegman, *The Crisis of Music*.
10 See the related essay by Klaus Pietschmann in this volume, Ch. 2.
11 Wilson, *Music and Merchants*; Quaranta, *Oltre San Marco*.

hierarchy mirroring that of heaven was transferred to a lay, primarily civic level. Indirectly, this tendency was reflected in the oppositional movements of *devotio moderna* and the mendicant orders, which promoted simple congregational singing and disavowed complex music.[12] Such expressions across all levels of society show increasing skepticism, on the eve of the Reformation, about earthly wealth and its symbolic display; such skepticism would turn a critical eye on musical institutions and their members.

These dynamics affected attitudes toward art music and its institutional role. Similar mechanisms are found in religious orders and civic environments where guilds or individuals financed the presentation of art music in the liturgy.[13] These institutionalized musical practices were arranged to achieve political or religious goals in a complex competition for distinction that more than justified considerable monetary investment.

## Court chapels in the fifteenth century

The institutional positioning of figural music in court chapels went hand in hand with the changing dynamics of political processes. At the start of the fifteenth century, distinct and largely independent fields of engagement, such as the Hundred Years War between France and England or the consolidation of the Holy Roman Empir, defined the political economy of Europe. New developments created a pan-European field of engagement, intensifying contacts and conflicts among political actors across the Continent. Of special note were the Councils of Constance and Basel, the meteoric rise and fall of Burgundy (which affected both France and the Holy Roman Empire), and Turkish attacks following the conquest of Byzantium in 1453, which created a united military front among the Christian powers to respond to this growing threat.

### The Councils of Constance and Basel

The trend of establishing musically sophisticated chapels had already begun at the start of the fifteenth century thanks to the Councils of Constance and Basel. These councils were made necessary by the Great Schism, which began in 1378. The 1417 election of Martin V (Odo Colonna) in Constance brought this conflict to an end, but the council agreed to convene further councils to rein in the powers of the papacy, with the next such gathering to take place in Basel

---

12  Hascher-Burger, *Gesungene Innigkeit*; Strohm, "Fragen zur Praxis."
13  On the *cantori di San Giovanni* in Florence see, for example, D'Accone, "The Singers of San Giovanni"; on the civic chapels of Cologne see Pietschmann, "Musikalische Institutionalisierung."

in 1431. This plan was ultimately unsuccessful, and following the 1439 election of the anti-pope Felix V (Amadeus VIII of Savoy) there was another schism.

The councils have been described as "occasions for the exchange of information and knowledge, new performance and compositional customs, and visual materials, whose worth cannot be reckoned."[14] Contemporary witnesses were impressed by its musical offerings, in particular those of the English delegations.[15] That musical ensembles were brought in as a means of representation is corroborated by the case of the chapel of the anti-pope John XXIII, which for the first time reveals the dominance of Franco-Flemish singers in Italy; John's legacy was assured by Martin V, who took over the personnel of the chapel, and by Eugene IV, who hired Guillaume Du Fay.[16]

Several manuscripts connected to these councils preserve the kind of polyphony that was performed during liturgical services:[17] the first part of Trent 92, the work of the Basel council singer Nicolas de Merques, as well as the manuscripts Aosta 15, Trent 87, and Zwettl. Margaret Bent has shown that parts of Bologna Q.15 were created in Basel and contain repertory that circulated during the council.[18] The appearance of English compositions in these sources corroborates the strong impression English singers left in Constance.

## England and France

The rivalry of France and England dominated the politics of the first half the fifteenth century. Both countries boasted court chapels with sophisticated liturgical music. In England, the legal independence of the nobility and the church gave rise to courtly structures that facilitated a high level of musical expertise, influenced by close political ties to France. These practices were relatively stable despite frequent political changes. The Hundred Years War (1337–1453), occasioned by competing claims to the throne by the houses of Valois and Plantagenet, was tremendously significant for the political and cultural development of both countries. After a period of peace at the end of the fourteenth century, hostilities resumed in 1415 and culminated in Henry V's defeat of the French at the Battle of Agincourt, securing his claim to the French throne. His death in 1422 forestalled the unification of France and England, however, and the peace treaty between Charles VII of France and Philip the Good of Burgundy in 1435 in Arras ended the conflict and resulted in a stronger sense of French national unity and the increasing insularity of English politics.

---

14 Hortschansky, "Musikleben," 37.      15 Schuler, "Die Musik in Konstanz während des Konzils."
16 Di Bacco and Nádas, "The Papal Chapels."
17 Ward, "The Structure of the Manuscript Trent 92–1."      18 Bent, *Bologna Q15.*

The expansion of the court chapel under Henry V was a direct result of wartime exigencies. The Chapel Royal, founded by Edward I (1272–1307) and Edward II (1307–27), was headed by a dean and consisted of not just liturgical personnel but also adult and boy singers.[19] Whereas in 1360 its members numbered sixteen men and four boys, under Henry V it doubled in size to thirty-two men and sixteen boys, a clear effort to demonstrate the king's piety. Henry's triumphant entry into London following the victory at Agincourt – replete with a sung *Benedictus* and other compositions probably composed by members of the Chapel Royal – was staged to draw parallels with Christ's triumphant entry into Jerusalem on Palm Sunday.[20] Despite the defeats that followed, the grandeur and artistic stature of the Chapel Royal continued to burnish the pious credentials of the English monarchy.

Chapels of the nobility could grow to a remarkable size, as in the case of Richard Beauchamp, the crown's representative in Normandy.[21] Other nobles had affiliations with the court and were thus attuned to its musical practices. The Old Hall manuscript, the most important document of English polyphony from the first half of the fifteenth century, provides evidence for these associations: it was originally compiled for the private chapel of Lionel, Duke of Clarence (1413–22, brother of Henry V), and turned over to the Chapel Royal after his death. Further removed from the seat of power were the cathedrals and college chapels of Winchester, Eton, Oxford, and Cambridge, all of which benefited from significant musical resources. Polyphonic repertory was performed as early as the close of the thirteenth century at Westminster Abbey in London, even though evidence of a choir school stems only from the late fifteenth century. While the source situation is sketchy, several manuscripts (in particular the Eton Choirbook, ca. 1500) attest to the high artistic accomplishments of these institutions. The extraordinary attractiveness of these institutions is corroborated by the small number of English musicians who sought positions on the Continent during the fifteenth century. Among the few who did were Robert Morton (active at the Burgundian court 1457–76) and John Hothby (active in Lucca 1467–87).[22]

The mobility of musicians from areas of French and Burgundian influence was higher, encouraged by unstable political conditions. Unlike England, in France the king and his nobles existed in a traditional feudal relationship that foreshadowed early modern centralism. The associated theocratic character of

19 Baldwin, *The Chapel Royal*; Wathey, *Music in the Royal and Noble Households.*
20 Bent, "Sources of the Old Hall Music," 23.
21 Wathey, *Music in the Royal and Noble Households*, 53 and *passim.*
22 There is no information about their education or reasons for leaving England. On the English in Ferrara, see Lockwood, *Music in Renaissance Ferrara*, 170.

the French monarchy was articulated most clearly in spectacular rituals of miraculous healing.[23] With respect to theological legitimation, the French monarchs thus held a distinct advantage over their English counterparts: the expansion of the Chapel Royal can be understood as an effort to close this representational gap.

Traditionally, France had enjoyed an elevated musical infrastructure, which had undergone significant enhancements since the late fourteenth century. In addition to the great cathedrals of Paris, Chartres, and Cambrai, which established vocal polyphonic practice in the thirteenth century and continued to house large permanent choirs, the courts of the kings and dukes retained immense chapels, whose members accompanied the rulers on their many journeys.

These high artistic standards were bolstered at the start of the fourteenth century by the establishment of the papal court at Avignon, which was politically and culturally tied to the French Crown. Beginning in 1384, just after the return of the papacy to Rome, the Burgundian court chapel expanded considerably.[24] This led to a musical-artistic consolidation in northwestern Europe around the turn of the century, accompanied by the systematic creation of top-flight educational institutions. The so-called *maîtrises*, financed by repurposed lucrative benefices and thus considerably better outfitted than traditional singing schools, arose rapidly in northern France and Burgundy, bringing to the fore an influential generation of fifteenth-century composers.[25] As a result, members of cathedral and abbey chapels achieved a considerable level of prestige and were put to use for the purposes of political representation and inter-city musical competitions such as those held in Bruges.[26] The Hundred Years War and rivalries among the French nobility affected, but apparently did not put a damper on, these developments.

France supported not only the Sainte-Chapelle, founded by Louis IX, but also a palace chapel at the royal residence on the Île-de-la-Cité, complete with its own *maîtrise* and staff of adult singers, who accompanied the king on his travels. (In the fifteenth century the monarchy spent little time in Paris.[27]) Sources are scarce, but the long association of Johannes Ockeghem as *premier chapelain* at the private chapel (1454–ca. 1487) speaks to its artistic renown. Few account ledgers have survived, but a report following the death of Charles VI in 1422 provides insight into the scale of music at court. There were sixteen singers and an organist, similar to the size of the ensemble at the end of the reign of Charles VII in 1461 (fifteen singers and an organist), though in the

---

23  Bloch, *Les Rois thaumaturges.*      24  See the related essay by David Fiala in this volume, Ch. 22.
25  Lütteken, "Maîtrise."      26  See, for example, Strohm, *Music in Late Medieval Bruges.*
27  Perkins, "Musical Patronage." The Île-de-la-Cité was also home to the Sainte-Chapelle; see above.

intervening years the number of musicians shrank owing to political instability.[28] Other members of the nobility affiliated with the royal household maintained their own chapels and ensembles, such as the Dauphin Louis, Duke of Guyenne (documented in 1414–15), and Marie d'Anjou, the wife of Charles VII, who maintained a chapel of around fifteen singers from 1452 until her death in 1463.[29]

The role of composition and polyphonic performance at the French court is less clear. While the presence of Gilles Binchois at the Burgundian court from ca. 1426 demonstrates the central role of art music there, at the French court no notable composer emerged before the arrival of Ockeghem in 1450 – a development doubtless connected with the resurgence of Charles VII shortly before the end of the war. Since no explicit evidence about the ceremonial orientation of sacred compositions survives, one can only speculate as to the role of these repertories in daily life and the symbolic functions of these chapels. There is much evidence, however, that the sacralizing efforts of the English and French monarchies occasioned a proliferation of mass settings in the first half of the fifteenth century. Recent scholarship has described the Christological symbolism of the *Caput* masses and the analogies created by representations of the triumphant entrances of the rulers of England, France, and Burgundy.[30] The long-term presence of the English in France occasioned further cultural exchange, musically evident in Continental enthusiasm for the so-called "contenance angloise."

Apart from the Burgundian chapel (treated in a separate essay in this volume; see Ch. 22), other courts in France maintained significant chapels, in particular the court of Savoy, whose dukes built a prestigious chapel in Chambéry, led for a time by Du Fay.[31] Sources for this institution are plentiful; account books and other sources allow us to reconstruct its personnel, and excerpts from the manuscripts Aosta 15 and Trent 87 and 92 document its repertory. By contrast, sources are scarce for the chapel of King René of Anjou (1409–80), who, after an unsuccessful attempt to assert his claim to Sicily and Aragon, lived as the Count of Provence in Aix-en-Provence, supporting a lively cultural atmosphere. Founded in 1449, René's chapel comprised six to eight singers, one of whom, from 1475, was Josquin des Prez. The chronicles of Jean Bourdigné describe this chapel as the best of his days. In 1480 King Louis XI called them to Paris to sing a Requiem for his uncle, and subsequently took them into his own service.[32]

28 Perkins, "Musical Patronage," 516.    29 Ibid., 519 and *passim*.    30 Kirkman, *Cultural Life*, 77–97.
31 Bouquet, "La cappella musicale"; Gentile, "Musica, musicisti e riti."
32 Quoted in Brenet, "La Musique à la cour du roi René," 157. See also Esquieu, "La Musique à la cour provençale du roi René."

## The Holy Roman Empire

It may come as a surprise that only with the Habsburg takeover of the vast Burgundian inheritance by Maximilian I a German king was for the first time in a position to become an important patron of music, but in fact this circumstance can be accounted for by political conditions. The Golden Bull of 1356 initiated a transformation of the Empire into a corporate legal union. Its constitution made the elected German king, the King of the Romans, accountable to the lords and cities that comprised the imperial estates; regular meetings beginning at the end of the fifteenth century established the so-called *Reichstage*. These forums contributed to a national "German" political consciousness. During the course of the fifteenth century, significant territorial powers emerged within the Empire: Austria, Bavaria, Württemberg, the Palatinate, Hesse, Saxony, Brandenburg, and Bohemia.

These powers modeled themselves on international standards, and in the process began to establish chapels in the western European mold. One of the first was the small but strategically important duchy of Cleves, ruled by the Brussels-born Johann I (1419–81), who in 1455 established a standing court chapel.[33] While no musical sources have survived, it appears that demanding liturgical polyphony was the core responsibility of the chapel's personnel.[34] The chapel consisted of three chaplains and six additional singers, half of whom were boys, augmented for special occasions by as many as nine extra boys.[35] These boys were trained at the abbey school of Cleves, itself modeled on the Franco-Flemish *maîtrises*.[36]

During the last third of the century, more chapels were founded at the Empire's main courts. A short-lived attempt by the Hessian Landgrave Ludwig II to establish a competitive chapel at his residence in Kassel in 1470 was forestalled by his untimely death the following year. Around the same time, chapel-like structures whose duties apparently included art music were established at the Saxon court, forming the basis for the creation of a court chapel in Torgau by Frederick the Wise.[37] In 1472, the Palatinate Count Frederick I established a chapel of singers, recruiting the chapel master, Johannes von Soest, from Kassel.[38] Frederick responded to criticism at court about the costs of this establishment by noting that the singers would support the liturgy and contribute to the welfare of the listeners.[39] This apologia

---

33  Pietzsch, "Zur Musikpflege," 22.        34  Wiens, *Musik und Musikpflege*, 49–50.
35  Pietzsch, *Archivalische Forschungen*, 96–100.
36  Wiens, *Musik und Musikpflege*, 42.
37  For a summary and accounts of additional literature see Steude, "Dresden, Höfische Musikpflege."
38  Žak, "Die Gründung der Hofkapelle." On Johannes von Soest see also above, Ch. 2.
39  Žak, "Die Gründung der Hofkapelle," 156–58.

squares with later comments by Emperor Maximilian in his autobiographical publication *Weißkunig* on his motives for establishing the court chapel.[40]

These circumstances can help explain why few other courts established polyphonic chapels of any importance. In Bavaria and Brandenburg there are traces of choirboys and adult singers, but little is known of their competence.[41] Shortly after his accession in 1496, Eberhard II of Württemberg – whose region had just been elevated to a duchy – created a chapel of five adults and six boys who sang four-voice music. As in Cleves, the duke's personal experiences shaped the character of the ensemble, since as a youth Eberhard had spent time at the Burgundian court in the 1450s. That no elite establishment was intended in Stuttgart is attested by an archival note explaining that boys whose voices had changed would be transitioned to theological studies or scribal duties.[42] Very little is known about the musical practices of the Empire's larger cathedrals or collegiate churches, except for Cologne cathedral, where beginning in 1454 a Marian mass was sung daily by six adults and six boys "in discantu et organo,"[43] and the abbey church of St. Maria im Kapitol (Cologne), where around 1466 there arose an unusual private chapel of a citizen whose obligations included a daily sung Mass with discant as well as the education and care of four boy singers.[44]

The German throne had undergone a period of long-term consolidation, since 1346–47 characterized by dynastic continuity. The decisive figure for the early fifteenth century was the Luxemburg Sigismund, who with his successors Albrecht II (elected in 1438) and Frederick III (crowned in 1440) ushered in a period of Habsburg dominance. Efforts to secure the Luxemburg and Habsburg territories led to a politics oriented to central and eastern Europe, which resulted in the addition of Austria and Hungary (as parts of the Luxemburg inheritance) to the Habsburg sphere of influence, while Poland and its vast Lithuanian territories fell to the Jagiellonian dynasty in 1386.

The Luxemburg-Habsburg kings had long employed court chapels with professional singers. Although the chapel of Sigismund has yet to be exhaustively researched, there is no doubt that it performed at a high level over a considerable time span. The earliest evidence stems from the time of the Council of Constance,[45] and the hiring of the renowned composer Johannes Brassart around 1434 indicates an expansion of the chapel, occasioned by Sigismund's journey to Rome and coronation as emperor by Eugene IV – a

---

40 Silver, *Marketing Maximilian*, 193.     41 Pietzsch, *Fürsten und fürstliche Musiker*.
42 Sittard, *Zur Geschichte der Musik und des Theaters*, 3.
43 Quoted in Leitmeir, "Musikpflege am Kölner Dom," 279.
44 Quoted in Pietschmann, "Musikalische Institutionalisierung," 241.
45 Király, "Die Musik am ungarischen Königshof," 34.

process that continued after Sigismund's death. *Romanorum rex*, a motet written for the death of King Albrecht (1439) and attributed to Johannes de Sarto, attests to the chapel's achievements, as does Brassart's motet *O rex Fridericus*, composed for the election (1440) and coronation (1442) of Frederick III. (Substantial portions of the chapel's repertory are preserved in the fourth part of the Aosta manuscript.[46]) These high standards were apparently maintained by Frederick III, who in 1466 established a group of German singers distinct from the Netherlanders.[47] After his takeover of the Burgundian court chapel in 1486 (and its transfer to Philip the Fair in 1494), Maximilian I structured his court music in a similar manner, maintaining a chapel dominated by German singers, which underwent a reorganization in 1498. In 1501 Maximilian hired the humanist (subsequently bishop of Vienna) Georg of Slatkonia to be its chapel master; already earlier he had added Henricus Isaac (1497) and Paul Hofhaimer (1489) to his ranks, demonstrating his reliance on other prominent chapels as models and his use of music as a means of display.[48] The cycle of Mass Propers *Choralis Constantinus* – begun by Isaac at the cathedral church of Constance, but nevertheless closely aligned with the court chapel's aesthetics – attests to these ambitions. The addition of polyphonic textures to even the Propers of the Mass represents an escalation of politico-religious self-fashioning competing with other European courts, where the practice of setting the Mass Ordinary was already established. Although the service books of Maximilian's chapel have not survived,[49] other sources attest to its character: the imposing Wolfenbüttel choirbook Cod. Guelf. A. Aug. 2, probably a gift of Maximilian to Wilhelm IV of Bavaria,[50] and the *Liber Selectarum Cantionum*, which was printed in 1520, shortly after Maximilian's death, were products of the court chapel's milieu.[51]

Among the primary opponents of the Luxemburg-Habsburg axis was the Hungarian King Matthias Corvinus (1458–90), who erected a costly Italian Renaissance-style court in Buda but failed to establish a national Hungarian dynasty for lack of a legitimate heir. Beginning with his second marriage in 1476 (to Beatrice of Aragon, daughter of King Ferrante I of Naples), his court appears to have been oriented to music of the highest Franco-Flemish and Italian standards. The addition of Johannes Stokem attests to the international ties of the chapel, strengthened if not initiated by the music-loving Beatrice.[52]

---

46 Wright, "Johannes Brassart"; Wright, "The Ownership of the Aosta Codex."
47 Pietzsch, *Fürsten und fürstliche Musiker*, 60.
48 Senn, *Musik und Theater am Hof zu Innsbruck*; Reimer, *Die Hofmusik in Deutschland*, 30–33.
49 Martin Bente's suggestion that these books formed the core collection of the Munich chapel has been refuted by Birgit Lodes in "Ludwig Senfl."
50 Becker, "Zum historischen Hintergrund."     51 Giselbrecht and Upper, "Glittering Woodcuts."
52 Fökövi, "Musik und musikalische Verhältnisse in Ungarn."

A 1483 report by the papal nuncio and *magister capellae* makes clear how well the Hungarian court was competing, at least from a Roman perspective: "He has a chapel of singers that surpasses everything I have seen before, similar to ours before it was devastated by the plague."[53] Perhaps it was this report that led Innocent VIII, in November of the same year, to increase the number of singers in the papal chapel by nine, to a total of twenty-four.[54]

## The Iberian peninsula

The rising importance of the Mediterranean sphere in fifteenth-century European politics is reflected in the dynastic relationships entered into by Philip the Good (1429) and Frederick III (1452) with Portugal, a formidable maritime and merchant power. This development in turn affected the portuguese court chapel, originally founded in 1299. After attaining independence with the support of the English under King John, Alfonso V and the Kingdom of Portugal achieved undisputed supremacy over the Iberian peninsula, and with the conquests of Prince Henry the Navigator extended their dominion to the west coast of Africa. The chapel was reorganized along Burgundian and English models, and from 1433 under King Duarte regulations for the court's polyphonic choral practice were set down.[55] During a trip to London around 1448, Duke Alvaro Vaz d'Almada asked William Say, Dean of the Chapel Royal, for a copy of its regulations on behalf of the newly crowned Alfonso V.[56] That Alfonso sent his chapel master Álvaro Alfonso to England in 1454 in search of repertory is also indicative of a plan to reorganize his chapel along English lines. (The compulsory use of the Sarum Rite in Portugal from the middle of the twelfth century surely played a role in these developments.[57]) The music of the chapel has unfortunately not been preserved.

Another center of power on the Iberian peninsula was created by the marriage in 1469 of Isabella, sister of the sonless Henry IV of Castile, to Ferdinand, heir to the throne of Aragon, creating the Kingdom of Castile and Aragon. The courtly apparatuses of both houses were maintained, including their well-established chapels. The development of the Aragonese chapel, founded in 1297, is especially well documented.[58] Beginning with the reigns of

---

53 "Habet enim cantorum capellam qua nulla, praestantiorem vidi, nostrae similem antequam pestis in ea grassaret." Haberl, *Die römische "Schola cantorum*," 242.
54 Ibid. See also Voci and Roth, "Anmerkungen zur Baugeschichte," 73.
55 Stevenson, "Iberian Musical Outreach," 96.
56 The edition *Liber Regie Capelle* (ed. Ullmann) is also based on this manuscript.
57 Stevenson, "Iberian Musical Outreach," 97.
58 Gómez Muntané, *La música medieval en España*, as well as her *Historia de la música en España*, 267–86.

Pedro IV and John I, both close allies of France, many French singers were recruited, and around 1400 there was an intensive exchange of personnel with the papal court at Avignon.[59] As in France and England, the court chapel was surrounded by a network of noble chapels. Supported by the so-called "Catholic Kings," prominent chapel masters produced a high level of compositional achievement: Francisco de Peñalosa in Aragon and Juan de Anchieta in Castile. Philip the Fair maintained the Castilian and Burgundian chapels into the next century (the latter inherited from Maximilian I), but the Aragonese chapel was dissolved upon the death of King Ferdinand in 1516.

By the middle of the fifteenth century the Aragonese had already expanded their territories to southern Italy. From Sicily, under Aragonese control since the thirteenth century, Alfonso V defeated King René of Anjou in Naples and in 1443 united the two kingdoms. The circle of humanists and the court chapel that Alfonso established in Naples were maintained after his death in 1458 by his illegitimate son Ferrante, while Sicily went to Alfonso's brother John II and was governed from Aragon. By 1451 the Naples chapel had grown to twenty-two singers, comparable to Burgundy and England, and remained stable under Ferrante's patronage.[60] In contrast to the French practices of his ancestors, Alfonso drew singers only from territories controlled by the Aragonese crown. But under Ferrante, Franco-Flemish singers were in evidence, including Johannes Tinctoris, who from the early 1470s shaped the court's musical culture as a chaplain, jurist, and teacher of music theory, and who remained close to Beatrice of Aragon after her marriage to Matthias Corvinus in 1476. The chapel's repertory incorporated international and local trends, as attested by the manuscripts Montecassino 871 and Perugia 431, prepared in Neapolitan Benedictine monasteries at the close of the fifteenth century.

## Italy

After Naples, the most important Italian centers of power were Milan, Venice, Florence, and the Papal States. The first half of the century was defined by ongoing internal and external conflicts: Venice's designs on the *terra firma* at the expense of Milan, and the efforts of the popes – recently returned from Avignon – to secure their position in Rome against the city's nobles. By contrast, the second half of the century witnessed a forty-year period of relative stability, thanks to the 1454 Peace of Lodi and an alliance of Italian states (Lega Italica); this created a secure environment in which humanistic and

59 Gómez Muntané, *La música medieval en España*, 232–37 and *passim*.
60 Atlas, *Music at the Aragonese Court*; D'Agostino, "La musica, la cappella."

artistic pursuits could flourish. At the same time, the traditional influence of the Empire in Italy restricted itself to the distribution of fiefdoms and legitimation of new dynasties: duchies for Giangaleazzo Visconti (1395) and Galeazzo Maria Sforza (1466) in Milan, and the elevations of Gianfrancesco Gonzaga to Margrave of Mantua (1432) and Borso d'Este to Duke of Modena (1452). The Medici, by contrast, were denied such opportunities for advancement until 1532; Cosimo "Il Vecchio" and Lorenzo "Il Magnifico" had to secure their leadership of prosperous Florence through tenuous comparisons to the nobility. In the second half of the century, the situation in Italy was defined on one hand by peaceful coexistence, but on the other by competition among the centers of power. Funded by lucrative trading relationships across Europe, the cultural-political ambitions of these rulers gave rise to extraordinary manifestations of humanism and the arts and transformed Italy into a central place in music history.

In the first half of the fifteenth century the papal chapel was the exemplary musical institution on the peninsula. Despite the papacy's unstable political position under Eugene IV, it experienced an artistic flourishing through the efforts of Du Fay, evident especially in his papal motets.[61] Within the orbit of the papal chapel, musical circles of great quality and renown were established in the households of the cardinals. Especially notable was the house of Philippe d'Alençon, a relative of the French royal family, whose *clerici capelle* in the 1390s included Johannes Ciconia.[62] Owing to the diverse backgrounds, influences, and career paths of the cardinals, different ways of establishing a musical retinue took shape. When Pietro Filargo of Crete was installed as archbishop of Milan in 1402, for instance, the Visconti hired Matteo da Perugia as first *biscantor* of the city's cathedral; upon Filargo's subsequent elevation to cardinal in 1407, however, the singer was transferred to his private household.[63]

Milan was exceptional for its early development of art music at its cathedral. Elsewhere in Italy, complex ecclesiastical-political circumstances had led to inadequate training and a decline in musical proficiency. Choir schools existed only in isolated centers (e.g., at Venice's St. Mark's beginning in 1403), and it was only with Johannes Ciconia in Venetian-controlled Padua between 1403 and 1411 that a prominent Franco-Flemish musician found himself at an Italian cathedral. In many places no such institutions existed. Pope Eugene IV, recognizing these deficiencies, laid a foundation for the development of Italian ecclesiastical music by establishing or improving the choir schools in many Italian cities: Tortona (1435), Pistoia (1436, 1439), Florence (1436, 1441),

---

61  See the essay by Richard Sherr in this volume (Ch. 40) as well as Nádas, "The Internationalization of the Italian Papal Chapels."
62  Di Bacco and Nádas, "Verso uno 'Stile internazionale'."     63  Brand, "*Viator ducens*."

Bologna (1436, 1439), Treviso (1437, 1438), Mileto (1438), Padua (1438), Castiglione Olona (1439), Urbino (1439), Verona (1440, 1442), Venice (1441), and Catania (1446).[64]

At the same time a new dynamic began to define Italian political rivalries, prompting the expansion of chapels and the acquisition of foreign, specifically Franco-Flemish, musicians. In Florence, the 1439 council and the international sympathies of the Medici family led to the creation of the *cantori di San Giovanni* for the Baptistry and Cathedral;[65] in Ferrara, the Este family's ambitions were the impetus for the creation in the early 1440s of a palace chapel, which according to a chronicler was outfitted by Leonello in a royal manner with singers from France, presumably in emulation of King Alfonso's chapel in Naples.[66] The repertory of the manuscript ModB (Modena α.X.1.11), probably used at the Ferrarese court, demonstrates that the level of the ensemble was formidable. The individual rulers determined the character of court music. Whereas Borso d'Este dissolved his chapel and retained only an instrumental ensemble, despite his elevation to Duke of Modena and Reggio (1452) and later Ferrara (1471), his successor Ercole I reorganized and expanded the chapel (to twenty-seven singers in 1481 and thirty-three in 1499), and hired distinguished Franco-Flemish musicians such as Johannes Martini, Jean Japart, Johannes Ghiselin, Josquin des Prez, Jacob Obrecht, and Antoine Brumel, transforming it into one of the most significant ensembles of its time.

The last third of the fifteenth century witnessed an unparalleled "arms race" among the Italian courts. Engaged in this competition were the Naples chapel of King Ferrante, the newly booming papal chapel of Sixtus IV, and the ambitious new chapel in Milan founded by Galeazzo Maria Sforza. Since the early 1450s, the Sforzas had expanded the cathedral's chapel, closely tied to the two court chapels (founded in 1473); among their forty singers were some of the most talented Franco-Flemish composers of the generation, including Gaspar van Weerbeke, Alexander Agricola, Johannes Martini, and Loyset Compère, as well as many Italian singers.[67] The court chapels were novel insofar as they were divided into two independent administrative entities, designated as *cappella* and *cappella di camera* (the chamber musicians). Their respective duties are not explicitly known, but they show similarities with French and English practice, in which several chapels existed side by side. No choral books have survived, although secondary sources such as the *libroni* of the Milan cathedral provide clues about repertory. The *motteti missales* (motet cycles that replaced settings of the Mass Ordinary) of Weerbeke or Compère

---

64 Gambassi, *"Pueri cantores."*     65 D'Accone, "The Singers of San Giovanni," 308–11 and *passim*.
66 Lockwood, *Music in Renaissance Ferrara*, 47.
67 Merkley and Merkley, *Music and Patronage in the Sforza Court*.

evince the Milanese ambition to secure a leadership role in compositional innovation by creating a new type of work closely related to the genre at the top of the musical hierarchy, the mass setting. Despite some emigration following the assassination of the duke in 1476, during the reign of Lodovico "il Moro" a respectable level was maintained; after he was deposed in 1499 the court chapel was dissolved. His wife Beatrice d'Este's preference for the frottola and the engagement of Franchino Gaffurio as the cathedral's chapel master in 1484 testify to a new interest in an indigenous profile (similar to contemporary tendencies in Mantua, Urbino, and Ferrara); this initiated a new arena of musical competition outside the chapel's institutional structure.

## Organizational models of European court chapels

When comparing the development of court chapels in fifteenth-century Europe, organizational structures and models most readily come into view. Chapels were autonomous corporate entities within the structure of their respective courts and were directly beholden to the sovereign. By contrast, personnel and leadership structures showed considerable variation as older traditions were superseded by new trends.

With respect to personnel, clerical status for chapel members remained the norm but became an increasingly marginal requirement. Johannes Ockeghem, for instance, waited some twenty years to be ordained a priest, despite having held the positions of *premier chapelain* in the private chapel of Louis XI and treasurer at Saint-Martin in Tours;[68] in the English Chapel Royal, by contrast, regulations dictated that at least half of the thirty singers should be priests.[69] The 1436 constitution of the Castilian court chapel did not require all chaplains and singers (considered as separate groups) to be ordained, but seating charts demonstrate a clear prioritization of priests (rather than a ranking according to seniority).[70] At the Burgundian court, the hierarchical offices of *clerc, sommelier*, and *chapelain* were decoupled from clerical status; the ordinances of 1469 base promotion on "the extant qualities of voice and good services."[71] The decidedly artistic orientation of the Burgundian chapel is further reflected in the prescribed minimal performing forces for polyphonic music (6/3/2/3).[72] King Duarte of Portugal similarly decreed in 1438 that his chaplains should be selected by virtue of voice type "to have one who sings altus, one contratenor,

68 On Ockeghem's biography and his positions at the French court see Magro, "Premièrement ma baronnie de Chasteauneuf."
69 Ullmann, ed., *Liber Regie Capelle*, 56.      70 Knighton, "Ritual and Regulations," 299.
71 "Les merites disponibles de voix et bons services." Fallows, "Specific Information," 146.
72 Ibid., 110 and 149.

and one tenor."[73] Boy singers and their teachers were usually part of a chapel's personnel, albeit with some exceptions: the private chapel of the French kings, for instance, did without boy singers, probably because their training was the responsibility of the Sainte-Chapelle.

Information on the status, selection, and duties of leadership offer further insights. At the Chapel Royal ultimate authority was granted to the dean, a cleric at the rank of bishop; this lent the institution both prestige and certain institutional capabilities. The papal *magister capellae* was a bishop, and in fourteenth-century Aragon the abbot of Santes Creus was the ex-officio *capellan mayor* of the chapel.[74] Maximilian I adopted this model, naming the imperial chapel master Georg of Slatkonia the bishop of Vienna in 1513. Such positions were almost always filled directly by the sovereign. The Sainte-Chapelle was one notable exception, with Charles VI decreeing in 1405 that the lead *cantor* should be elected for life by the members and canons of the palace chapel from within their own ranks.[75] This decidedly modern procedure, not adopted by the papal chapel until the late sixteenth century, had a practical motivation: to avoid lengthy vacancies since the court was so seldom resident in Paris. Some leadership roles were tied to specific duties. At the Aragonese chapel, for example, there was the *lugar teniente* (responsible in the absence of the *capellan mayor*), the *limosnero* (almoner), the *receptor* (receiver, in charge of collecting fines and distributing fees for special services), and the *sacrista* (who distributed salaries), to name but a few.[76] There is evidence of similar distribution of duties even in chapels for which no constitutions survive; Milanese payment records from the 1470s, for instance, list the offices of *abba* (abbot), *cardinale*, *prevosto*, and *sagristano* without defining the scope of their duties.[77] Examples such as Ockeghem's position as *premier chapelain* at the private chapel of the French king show that musical expertise played an increasingly important role, but with specifically musical positions are rarely named as such; an early example is the Portuguese *Leal Conselheiro*, which mentions a head chaplain, a musically knowledgeable chapel master ("meestre da capeella"), a tenor, and a master of the boys.[78]

---

73 "Qual he pera cantar alto, e qual pera contra, e qual pera tenor." Stevenson, "Iberian Musical Outreach," 97.

74 Knighton, "Ritual and Regulations," 297. Under Alfonso this tradition was broken, with at times two chapel masters mentioned. It is unclear whether they had musical duties in addition to administrative obligations. Atlas, *Music at the Aragonese Court*, 56.

75 Brenet, *Les Musiciens de la Sainte-Chapelle*, 25 ff.

76 Knighton, "Ritual and Regulations," 298–301. See also Atlas, *Music at the Aragonese Court*, 54.

77 Merkley and Merkley, *Music and Patronage in the Sforza Court*, 101.

78 Stevenson, "Iberian Musical Outreach," 96 ff.

Even more remarkable is the musically oriented organizational structure that Ercole I d'Este specified for his new chapel in Ferrara. Johannes Martini led the ensemble from 1473 to 1497 and was described as *cantadore composi- tore*.[79] This redefinition of the leadership role to encompass musical composi- tion marks a functional change in the court chapel as an institution. Indeed the new priority given to composition is evident in the choice of successors for Martini: Josquin, Obrecht, and Antoine Brumel. That these men were identi- fied as *maestro di cappella*, a title previously held by the teacher of the boys, shows how this title was transformed at the Ferrarese court around 1500 as well as in other locations.[80]

Hiring new chapel members generally fell to the leader of the ensemble, as prescribed in the constitution of the Chapel Royal, for example, or in con- sultation with senior members, as at the Castilian court.[81] The larger question is how the recruitment of new personnel proceeded in the context of increas- ingly internationalized standards. For kings and rulers who personally oversaw their ensembles, this could include sending out what we would today term headhunters and engaging in written correspondence. Early examples include the efforts of Alfonso V, who in 1419 sent Huguet to France and Germany, and later Pere Çabater "to the court of Rome and other places" to find singers; in 1424 he wrote personally to the singer Johan de Calamon from Barcelona.[82] Larger international networks also contributed to this process. The Medici family's financial holdings in the Netherlands were tied to their recruitment of singers, while Galeazzo Sforza employed his entire European diplomatic corps to assist in the founding of his chapel in the early 1470s.[83] In fact, Galeazzo's preparations – which included recruitment campaigns in Savoy, Naples, Rome, northern Italy, England, France, and Burgundy – sparked a political scandal in 1474, demonstrating the enormous symbolic capital ascribed to chapels. The Bruges-born singer Jean Cordier, who was in the service of King Ferrante of Aragon, was spirited away from Naples in secret by Galeazzo's agents. In response, Ferrante threatened to break off diplomatic relations with Milan, but Charles the Bold of Cordier's native Burgundy was recruited to broker a settlement and decided in favor of Milan.[84]

79 Lockwood, *Music in Renaissance Ferrara*, 171.
80 Ibid., 172. A "maestro de capilla" is not mentioned in the ordinances of the Castilian chapel, but existed in practice and was staffed by a prominent composer. Knighton, "Ritual and Regulations," 304. Similarly, in Cleves a chapel master is not mentioned in financial records, but a 1483 contract with one "Mesquin" indicates there was such a person. Wiens, *Musik und Musikpflege*, 73 n. 4.
81 Ullmann, ed., *Liber Regie Capelle*, 57; Knighton, "Ritual and Regulations," 294.
82 Gómez Muntané, *La música medieval en España*, 292 ff.
83 D'Accone, "The Singers of San Giovanni," 313–15; Merkley and Merkley, *Music and Patronage in the Sforza Court*, 33–86.
84 Merkley and Merkley, *Music and Patronage in the Sforza Court*, 41–64.

Talented boy singers were a coveted commodity, with numerous instances of poaching or even abduction;[85] especially spectacular was the attempt in 1470 by Duke Ludwig II of Hesse to obtain the release of a boy from the private chapel of Johann Hardenrath in Cologne through legal machinations, an effort blocked by the local government.[86] Demand for singers also led to voluntary emigration: in 1469 Johannes von Soest reports that he left Maastricht of his own volition to seek a position at the papal chapel.[87] Such decisions were partly occasioned by deteriorating economic conditions in the Netherlands during the wars with Burgundy. Thus in 1482 the singer Johannes de Vos, employed at St. Donatian's in Bruges, accepted an offer from Matthias Corvinus's court in Buda, since in Bruges, he claimed, he could scarcely survive on his salary.[88] That Vos remained in Bruges, presumably with a pay raise, shows that demand was becoming a negotiating tool for coveted singers.[89]

* * *

In conclusion, we return to the institutional dynamics of the chapel in the fifteenth century and their consequences for the history of composition. Several innovations attended the growth and professionalization of the musical apparatus of courtly liturgy: musical settings of the Ordinary in England, Burgundy, and France, their modification and expansion in the Milanese *motetti missales*, and settings of Mass Propers in the *Choralis Constantinus*, to name only a few. It might appear as if these innovations were merely the result of courts striving for political distinction, as in the visual arts, literature, and philosophy. But notwithstanding the clear connection between compositional accomplishments and other strategies of courtly artistic patronage, the question of their underlying relation to institutional structures is a thorny one. Although these courts conformed to the artistic standards of the day, promoting the production and reproduction of art music, they were nevertheless primarily structured according to the ceremonial demands of the liturgy. Because vocal polyphony was not an integral part of liturgical ceremony, its cultivation created a tension that could be glossed over but never done away with. More precisely, compositional innovation took place within the court chapels of the fifteenth century not because of, but rather despite, their institutional conditions.

---

85 One first-hand perspective on such an incident is the autobiography of Johannes von Soest. See Pietschmann and Rozenski, "Singing the Self."
86 Pietschmann, "Musikalische Institutionalisierung," 251.
87 Pietschmann and Rozenski, "Singing the Self," 157.      88 Strohm, *The Rise of European Music*, 605.
89 Strohm, *Music in Late Medieval Bruges*, 27.

# Bibliography

Atlas, Allan, *Music at the Aragonese Court of Naples*, Cambridge, 1985

Baldwin, David, *The Chapel Royal, Ancient and Modern*, London, 1990

Becker, Ursula, "Zum historischen Hintergrund des Wolfenbütteler Chorbuchs Cod. Guelf. A. Aug. 20: Beobachtungen zum Buchschmuck," in *Wolfenbütteler Beiträge: Aus den Schätzen der Herzog August Bibliothek* 15, Wiesbaden, 2009, 179–255

Bent, Margaret, *Bologna Q15: The Making and Remaking of a Musical Manuscript: Introductory Study and Facsimile Edition*, 2 vols., Lucca, 2008

"Sources of the Old Hall Music," *Proceedings of the Royal Musical Association* 94 (1967–68), 19–35

Bloch, Marc, *Les Rois thaumaturges: Étude sur le caractère surnaturel attribué à la puissance royale, particulièrement en France et en Angleterre*, Paris, 1924

Bouquet, Marie-Thérèse, "La cappella musicale dei Duchi di Savoia dal 1450 al 1500," *Rivista italiana di musicologia* 3 (1968), 233–85

Brand, Benjamin, "*Viator ducens ad celestia*: Eucharistic Piety, Papal Politics, and an Early Fifteenth-Century Motet," *JM* 20 (2003), 250–84

Brenet, Michel [Marie Bobillier], *Les Musiciens de la Sainte-Chapelle du palais*, Paris, 1910; repr. Geneva, 1973

"La Musique à la cour du roi René," *Le Ménestrel* 51 (1885), 148–49, 157

Bryant, David, and Elena Quaranta, eds., *Produzione, circolazione e consumo: Consuetudine e quotidianità della polifonia sacra nelle chiese monastiche e parrocchiali dal tardo Medioevo alla fine degli Antichi Regimi*, Bologna, 2006

D'Accone, Frank A., "The Singers of San Giovanni in Florence during the 15th Century," *JAMS* 14 (1961), 307–58

D'Agostino, Gianluca, "La musica, la cappella e il cerimoniale alla corte aragonese di Napoli," in *Cappelle musicali*, ed. Piperno *et al.*, 153–80; repr. in *Institutions and Patronage*, ed. Schmidt-Beste

Di Bacco, Giuliano, and John Nádas, "The Papal Chapels and Italian Sources of Polyphony during the Great Schism," in *Papal Music and Musicians in Late Medieval and Renaissance Rome*, ed. Richard Sherr, Oxford, 1998, 44–92

and John Nádas, "Verso uno 'stile internazionale' della musica nelle cappelle papali e cardinalizie durante il Grande Scisma (1378–1417): Il caso di Johannes Ciconia da Liège," in *Collectanea I*, ed. Adalbert Roth, Vatican City, 1994, 7–74

Esquieu, Yves, "La Musique à la cour provençale du roi René," *Provence historique* 31 (1981), 299–312

Fallows, David, "Specific Information on the Ensembles for Composed Polyphony, 1400–1474," in *Studies in the Performance of Late Mediaeval Music*, ed. Stanley Boorman, Cambridge, 1983, 109–59

Fökövi, Ludwig, "Musik und musikalische Verhältnisse in Ungarn am Hofe von Matthias Corvinus," *Kirchenmusikalische Jahrbuch* 15 (1900), 1–16

Gambassi, Osvaldo, *"Pueri cantores" nelle cattedrali d'Italia tra Medioevo e età moderna: Le scuole eugeniane. Scuole di canto annesse alle cappelle musicali*, Florence, 1997

Gentile, Luisa Clotilde, "Musica, musicisti e riti del potere principesco tra Savoia e Piemonte (fine XIV – inizio XVI secolo)," in *Cappelle musicali*, ed. Piperno *et al.*, 137–52

Giselbrecht, Elisabeth, and L. Elizabeth Upper, "Glittering Woodcuts and Moveable Music: Decoding the Elaborate Printing Techniques, Purpose, and Patronage of the *Liber Selectarum Cantionum*," in *Senfl-Studien I*, ed. Stefan Gasch, Birgit Lodes, and Sonja Tröster, Tutzing, 2012, 17–61

Gómez Muntané, María del Carmen, *Historia de la música en España e Hispanoamérica*, 1, Madrid, 2009

   *La música medieval en España*, Kassel, 2001

Haberl, Franz Xaver, *Die römische "Schola cantorum" und die päpstlichen Kapellsänger bis zur Mitte des 16. Jahrhunderts*, Leipzig, 1888 (= *Bausteine für Musikgeschichte 3*)

Hartung, Wolfgang, *Die Spielleute im Mittelalter: Gaukler, Dichter, Musikanten*, Düsseldorf and Zürich, 2003

Hascher-Burger, Ulrike, *Gesungene Innigkeit: Studien zu einer Musikhandschrift der Devotio moderna (Utrecht, Universiteitsbibliotheek, ms. 16 H 34, olim B 113)*, Leiden, 2002

Hortschansky, Klaus, "Musikleben," in *Die Musik des 15. und 16. Jahrhunderts*, ed. Ludwig Finscher, Neues Handbuch der Musikwissenschaft 3.1, Laaber, 1989, 23–128

Király, Péter, "Die Musik am ungarischen Königshof in der ersten Hälfte des 15. Jahrhunderts von der Zeit Sigismunds von Luxemburg bis zu Mathias Corvinus," *Studia Musicologica Academiae Scientiarum Hungaricae* 44 (2003), 29–45

Kirkman, Andrew, *The Cultural Life of the Early Polyphonic Mass: Medieval Context to Modern Revival*, Cambridge, 2010

Knighton, Tess, "Ritual and Regulations: The Organization of the Castilian Royal Chapel during the Reign of the Catholic Monarchs," in *De música hispana et aliis: Miscelánea en honor al Prof. Dr. José López-Calo, S.J., en su 65° Cumpleaños*, ed. Emilio Casares and Carlos Villanueva, Santiago de Compostela, 1990, 291–320; repr. in *Institutions*, ed. Schmidt-Beste

Leitmeir, Christian Thomas, "Musikpflege am Kölner Dom und dem erzbischöflichen Hof im 15. und 16. Jahrhundert," in *Erzbistum Köln*, ed. Pietschmann, 259–309

Lockwood, Lewis, *Music in Renaissance Ferrara, 1400–1505: The Creation of a Musical Center in the Fifteenth Century*, rev. edn., Oxford, 2009

Lodes, Birgit, "Ludwig Senfl and the Munich Choirbooks: The Emperor's or the Duke's?," in *Die Münchner Hofkapelle des 16. Jahrhunderts im europäischen Kontext*, ed. Theodor Göllner and Bernhold Schmid, Munich, 2006, 224–33

   and Laurenz Lütteken, eds., *Institutionalisierung als Prozess – Organisationsformen musikalischer Eliten im Europa des 15. und 16. Jahrhunderts*, Laaber, 2009 (= *Analecta Musicologica 43*)

Lütteken, Laurenz, "Maîtrise," in *MGG2, Sachteil* 5, cols. 1597–1602

   "Politische Zentren als musikalische Peripherie? Probleme einer musikhistorischen Topographie im deutschen Nordwesten des 15. und 16. Jahrhunderts," in *Das Erzbistum Köln*, ed. Pietschmann, 61–75

Magro, Agostino, "'Premièrement ma baronnie de Chasteauneuf': Jean de Ockeghem, Treasurer of St Martin's in Tours," *EMH* 18 (1999), 165–258

Marx, Barbara, *et al.*, eds., *Corti rinascimentali a confronto: Letteratura, musica, istituzioni*, Florence, 2003

Merkley, Paul A., and Lora L. M. Merkley, *Music and Patronage in the Sforza Court*, Turnhout, 1999

Nádas, John, "The Internationalization of the Italian Papal Chapels in the Early Quattrocento," in *Cappelle musicali*, ed. Piperno *et al.*, 247–69; repr. in *Institutions*, ed. Schmidt-Beste

Perkins, Leeman L., "Musical Patronage at the Royal Court of France under Charles VII and Louis XI (1422–83)," *JAMS* 37 (1984), 507–66

Pietschmann, Klaus, "Musikalische Institutionalisierung im Köln des 15. und 16. Jahrhunderts: Das Beispiel der Hardenrath-Kapelle," in *Das Erzbistum Köln*, ed. Pietschmann, 233–57

and Steven Rozenski, "Singing the Self: The Autobiography of the Fifteenth-Century German Singer and Composer Johannes von Soest," *EMH* 29 (2010), 119–59

ed., *Das Erzbistum Köln in der Musikgeschichte des 15. und 16. Jahrhunderts*, Kassel, 2008

Pietzsch, Gerhard, *Archivalische Forschungen zur Geschichte der Musik an den Höfen der Grafen und Herzöge von Kleve-Jülich-Berg (Ravensberg) bis zum Erlöschen der Linie Jülich-Kleve im Jahre 1609*, Cologne, 1971

*Fürsten und fürstliche Musiker im mittelalterlichen Köln: Quellen und Studien*, Cologne, 1966

"Zur Musikpflege an den Höfen von Kleve und Jülich," in *Studien zur klevischen Musik- und Liturgiegeschichte*, ed. Walter Gieseler, Cologne, 1968, 11–46

Piperno, Franco, *et al.*, eds., *Cappelle musicali fra corte, stato e chiesa nell'Italia del Rinascimento*, Florence, 2007

Polk, Keith, *German Instrumental Music of the Late Middle Ages: Players, Patrons and Performance Practice*, Cambridge, 1992

Quaranta, Elena, *Oltre San Marco: Organizzazione e prassi della musica nelle chiese di Venezia nel Rinascimento*, Florence, 1998

Reimer, Erich, *Die Hofmusik in Deutschland, 1500–1800*, Wilhelmshaven, 1991

Schmidt-Beste, Thomas, ed., *Institutions and Patronage in Renaissance Music*, Farnham, 2012

Schuler, Manfred, "Die Musik in Konstanz während des Konzils 1414–1418," *AcM* 38 (1966), 150–68

Senn, Walter, *Musik und Theater am Hof zu Innsbruck: Geschichte der Hofkapelle vom 15. Jahrhundert bis zu deren Auflösung im Jahre 1748*, Innsbruck, 1954

Silver, Larry, *Marketing Maximilian: The Visual Ideology of a Holy Roman Emperor*, Princeton, 2008

Sittard, Josef, *Zur Geschichte der Musik und des Theaters am Württembergischen Hofe*, 1, Stuttgart, 1890

Steude, Wolfram, "Dresden, Höfische Musikpflege," in *MGG2*, *Sachteil*, 2, cols. 1529–34

Stevenson, Robert, "Iberian Musical Outreach before Encounter with the New World: Portuguese Musical Contacts Abroad (before 1500)," *Inter-American Music Review* 8 (1987), 87–99

Strohm, Reinhard, "Fragen zur Praxis des spätmittelalterlichen Liedes," in *Musikalischer Alltag im 15. und 16. Jahrhundert*, ed. Nicole Schwindt, Kassel, 2001 (= *Trossinger Jahrbuch für Renaissancemusik* 1), 53–76

*Music in Late Medieval Bruges*, Oxford, 1985

*The Rise of European Music, 1380–1500*, Cambridge, 1993

Ullmann, Walter, ed., *Liber Regie Capelle: A Manuscript in the Biblioteca Publica, Evora*, London, 1961

Voci, Anna Maria, and Adalbert Roth, "Anmerkungen zur Baugeschichte der alten und der neuen *capella magna* des apostolischen Palastes bei Sankt Peter," in *Collectanea II: Studien zur Geschichte der päpstlichen Kapelle*, ed. Bernhard Janz, Vatican City, 1994, 13–102

Ward, Tom, "The Structure of the Manuscript Trent 92–1," *MD* 29 (1975), 127–47

Wathey, Andrew, *Music in the Royal and Noble Households in Late Medieval England: Studies of Sources and Patronage*, New York and London, 1989

Wegman, Rob C., *The Crisis of Music in Early Modern Europe, 1470–1530*, New York, 2008

Wiens, Heinrich, *Musik und Musikpflege am herzoglichen Hof zu Kleve*, Cologne, 1959

Wilson, Blake, *Music and Merchants: The Laudesi Companies of Republican Florence*, Oxford, 1992

Wright, Peter, "Johannes Brassart and Johannes de Sarto," *Plainsong and Medieval Music* 1 (1992), 41–61

"The Ownership of the Aosta Codex," in *Manoscritti di polifonia nel Quattrocento europeo*, Trento, 2004, 57–64

Žak, Sabine, "Die Gründung der Hofkapelle in Heidelberg," *AfMw* 50 (1993), 145–63

# Music and musicians at the Burgundian court in the fifteenth century

DAVID FIALA

The Valois dukes of Burgundy established a rich system of patronage that extended continuously from the end of the Middle Ages to the beginning of the modern era. Their wide-ranging cultural influence makes the primacy of the court's musical life of great interest to the history of music. Ruling over most of the territories where the Franco-Flemish singers and composers who dominated European art music from 1400 to 1550 were born and trained, the dukes of Burgundy supported the most distinguished musicians of their time.

The Burgundian state is singular for the richness of its archives, above all those of the ducal household, which remains among the best documented in Europe. Thanks to extremely well-preserved archival materials in Dijon, Lille, and Brussels, the number of musicians and the circumstances of their careers at court are accounted for without interruption from 1384 to 1506 and even beyond.[1] This documentary history comes to life, however, not through correspondence – as in other principalities, most notably in Italy – but from a particularly Burgundian practice. Officials dutifully recorded the daily comings and goings of all members of the court on strips of parchment, many of which have survived to this day.[2]

At our disposal then are myriad documents that showcase the sovereigns' desire to immerse their courts in the most luxurious of sonic environments. These sources, however, speak only of musical performance, almost completely ignoring musical creation, and thus rendering music an art of the moment, tangible only through a chronology of payments to musicians for *being present*. Investigation of the production of music books or musical works has only incompletely filled this gap.

---

1 Three monographs recount this history: Wright, *Music at the Court of Burgundy*; Marix, *Histoire de la musique et des musiciens*, and one forthcoming, Fiala, *Le Mécénat musical des ducs de Bourgogne*.
2 About 10% of these attendance records (*écrous de gages de l'hôtel*), or thirty to forty lists per year, have been conserved. Historian Werner Paravicini has done remarkable work on this documentation, notably his online database "Prosopographia Burgundica" of court accounting documents and some 6,000 attendance records.

The number of surviving musical manuscripts directly related to the court of Burgundy before 1500 can be counted on the fingers of one hand, in keeping with the general rarity of musical sources north of the Alps. While accounts of the Burgundian state's material assets thoroughly detail the production, purchase, and conservation of manufactured objects (notably of books), they offer limited information on music manuscripts. Before Philip the Fair established an atelier for the production of luxurious musical manuscripts, the copying, acquiring, and conserving of scores was the chapel's responsibility; if these activities involved official payments (which is far from certain), the archives hold only a few traces of them.

We might as well expect a number of musical works to contain textual references to historical events of the court. But while there are, for example, at least six pieces between 1430 and 1460 that praise the popes, only one fragmentary work from the entire fifteenth century references a Burgundian historical event: the motet *Nove cantum melodie* by Gilles Binchois, which celebrates the baptism of Philip the Good's first son, Antoine, on 18 January 1431.

Of course, the extant music produced by the dukes' employees and certain allusions in other repertories allow us to imagine the music that was fashionable at court. But because it is difficult to connect archival and narrative sources to musical works and musical sources, our understanding of the influence of Burgundian patronage on musical composition remains fragmented.

## Permanence and prestige of the musical organization of the court

The organization of musicians employed at the Burgundian court remained remarkably consistent over time, as attested by the similarity between accounting ledgers from the 1380s and the 1500s. Musicians were recruited into offices organized in four categories: (1) the domestic chapel of the household, which included twenty to thirty educated clerics, the majority of whom were priests; (2) the "trumpets of war" (*trompettes de guerre*), a protocol corps tightly linked to the heraldic officials whose numbers increased from four to twelve by the end of the century; (3) minstrels who played either *haut* or *bas* instruments; and (4) *valets de chambre*, the prince's personal servants. This group sometimes included a musician, generally a player of *bas* (soft) instruments (and, most often, a harpist).

Not only did the dukes maintain their own employees, but they also gave one-time payments to foreign musicians, servants of visiting noblemen, and the local musicians in regions to which they traveled. Music was an essential part of courtly politics in which the display of wealth was paramount.

While the administration formally accounted for these gifts, other sorts of transactions took place off the books. Guillaume Du Fay and Josquin des Prez, for example, served the Burgundian sovereigns but did not appear on the ledgers.[3] Similarly, the musical abilities of the courtiers are largely unaddressed in surviving documents, except for an ordinance from 19 April 1472 in which Charles the Bold asks to be surrounded by "sixteen gentlemen who know about music for his amusement and pastimes."[4] A few accounts reference their musical practices: at Cambrai in 1449, for instance, Philip the Good was entertained by "two altar boys who sang a little song, while one of his courtiers sang the tenor."[5] The dukes themselves received musical education. In 1372, the household of the one-year-old John the Fearless already included a minstrel; John himself was later able to play the flute and the bagpipe (*musette*). Similar stories exist for the majority of the dynasty's heirs; Charles the Bold was singled out as an accomplished musician.

The most important function of music at the courts was to showcase the princes' religious devotion. Olivier de La Marche begins his *Estat de la maison du Duc Charles de Bourgoingne dit le Hardy* with the following description of the chapel: "Let us begin with the state of the household, and with the service of God and his chapel, which must be the beginning of all things."[6]

### *"The best chapel in the world"*

The domestic chapel was an autonomous component of the household, responsible for singing the daily Mass, Vespers, and Compline. The chapel's members were organized into three categories: those responsible for the celebration at the altar, the prince's attendants, and the singers. Figure 22.1 clearly depicts this division of labor.

In this miniature, Philip the Good is kneeling in front of the small altar of his private oratory as the *sommelier de l'oratoire* holds the curtain open. To the right of the main altar we find one of the two *sommeliers de la chapelle*, whose duty it was to "care for the priest" (*administrer au prêtre*) and "bring the ornaments to the altar and take them back."[7] Seven of the nine singers, dressed in surplices in

3 For Du Fay's relationship with the Burgundian sovereigns from the late 1430s until his death, see Planchart, "Guillaume Du Fay's Benefices." For Josquin's probable participation in the Philip the Fair's trip to Spain in 1501–2, see Fallows, *Josquin*, 227–33.

4 "seize gentils hommes qui scavoient de la musicque pour son esbat et passe temps." Paravicini, "Charles le Téméraire," 342.

5 "petits des enfans d'autel [qui] canterent une canchonette de le quelle un de ses gentils homes tint le tenure." Marix, *Histoire*, 67.

6 "Et commencerons à l'estat de la maison, et au service de Dieu et de sa chapelle, qui doit estre commencement de toutes choses." La Marche, *Mémoires*, 4:1.

7 "present a porter les joyaulx sur l'autel et a les rapporter." Quotations are from the court ordinance, 1 January 1469. Passages relating to the chapel have been published by Fallows in "Specific Information on the Ensembles," 145–59.

Figure 22.1 Philip the Good attends a religious service celebrated by the
Burgundian chapel. *Traité sur l'oraison dominicale*, ca. 1457. Brussels,
Bibliothèque royale de Belgique/Koninklijke Bibliotheek van België, MS
9092, fol. 9r

the lower right-hand corner of the scene, surround a book with musical
notation placed on a stand. The courtiers behind the singers remind us that
these celebrations were a public affair, meant to display the princes' intense
devotion.

For 150 years the Burgundian musical chapel was more celebrated than any
other. In 1353, the king of France, John the Good, employed nine chaplains
and eight clerics under the head chaplain Gace de la Buigne, whose own
musical training is documented in two passages from his *Roman des deduiz de*

*la chasse*, a pedagogical poem dedicated to the young Philip the Bold.[8] With such an education, it is surprising that, as the first Valois Duke of Burgundy, he did not fund a chapel until gaining the title of Count of Flanders in 1384. The year before, his predecessor Louis de Male had four chaplains and four clerics who became the core group of Philip's chapel (which was at first a "chapel of Flanders"). By 1385 the group boasted eight chaplains and seven clerics, and its numbers continued to grow. The chronicler Michel Pintoin, known as the *religieux de Saint-Denis*, noted that Philip the Bold watched over the chapel "with utmost care to ensure that the divine service was royally celebrated day and night in his establishment. To enliven these ceremonies, he maintained in his chapel a much larger number of musicians than his ancestors; I would condemn such an excess of lavishness, were it not a particular sign of devotion to God."[9]

This lavishness indeed surpassed that both of his ancestors and of all of his contemporaries. Philip the Bold spent between 9,000 and 11,000 francs on his chapel every year. By comparison, Jean de Berry, who maintained a chapel from 1372 or earlier, spent between 5,500 and 6,000 francs for his chaplains' wages in 1400–1402, while the Avignon pope Benedict XIII spent 3,300 in 1404. In the same period, the livery of the royal chapel, which comprised in general twelve chaplains and six clerics, cost around 460 francs, while that of the Burgundian chapel mounted to 1,500 or even 1,700 francs. Philip's lavishness also resulted in his hiring more musicians than his contemporaries, for whom the number, more than any other criterion, was decisive. In 1401, the Burgundian chapel employed twenty chaplains, two clerics, and three stewards, while the chapels of Charles VI or Jean de Berry peaked at twenty members.[10]

After the death of his father, John the Fearless dismissed the *grande chapelle* on 16 June 1404, the very day of the funeral. Like Philip the Bold before 1384, John was content to have only a *petite chapelle* consisting of an older chaplain from his father's establishment and two chaplains from his time as Count of Nevers.[11] An ordinance of 5 November 1415 documents his reorganization of a musical chapel comprising fifteen chaplains and four clerics led by a head

---

8 See Wright, *Music at the Court of Burgundy*, 13–14.

9 "avec le plus grand soin à ce que le service divin fût célébré royalement nuit et jour en son hôtel. Il entretenait même dans sa chapelle, pour donner plus d'éclat aux cérémonies du culte, un nombre de musiciens beaucoup plus considérable qu'aucun de ses ancêtres; et je blâmerais en cela son excessive prodigalité, si ce n'était une marque particulière de dévotion envers Dieu." Cited by Schnerb, *Jean sans Peur*, 403.

10 Wright, *Music at the Court of Burgundy*, 79–83.

11 A payment given out to chaplains both in and out of the court's regular employ for the Christmas services in 1411 shows that major celebrations were enhanced.

chaplain.[12] This chapel may no longer have enjoyed its former splendor, but the quality of its singers certainly helped it regain its reputation. When Sigismund of Luxemburg met John the Fearless in Montbéliard in 1418, a member of his company, Antonio Tallander, proclaimed: "this is the richest chapel I have ever seen."[13]

As during the early reign of John the Fearless, Philip the Good's accession in 1419 led to another ten-year gap in the history of the chapel.[14] While no official ordinance points to the reestablishment of the chapel, Binchois's motet *Nove cantum melodie*, composed in January 1431, shows that it had indeed resumed its activities, despite a lack of payment records before 1436. The text of the second part of the motet refers to many of the names on the 1436 payroll and reveals a stronger desire for continuity than in 1415: at least seven of John the Fearless's chaplains who had found work elsewhere (mainly at the papal chapel) were reinstated.

The duke's marriage to Isabelle of Portugal on 10 January 1430 in Bruges was the first grand occasion that featured his musical chapel. An anonymous witness describes the wedding Mass as having been "grandly and solemnly sung by those of my Lord's chapel who were in great number and the most excellent in the art of music that one could hope to find."[15] This narrative shows the chapel to have been active at least one year before Binchois composed his motet.[16] Despite the lack of documented payments in these years, it appears that the chapel was reinstated for these 1430 celebrations; this is all the more noteworthy since it was on his wedding day that the Duke announced the creation of the Order of the Golden Fleece, an institution that would become a central patron of Burgundian sacred music.[17]

---

12 In 1416, twenty-nine robes were made from blue cloth for members of the prince's religious entourage. The accounting ledgers from 1419 reference sixteen chaplains (not including the first chaplain), five sommeliers, three choirboys (studying in Paris), and a quartermaster. See Wright, *Music at the Court of Burgundy*, 85–110.

13 Quoted in Wright, *Music at the Court of Burgundy*, 102.

14 During this period, the Duke continued to develop music in his territories by the establishment of two choir schools, one at the Sainte-Chapelle in Dijon in 1424, the other at the church of Saint-Pierre in Lille in 1425. See Marix, *Histoire*, 162–63.

15 "haultement et solemnellement chantée par ceulx de la chapelle de mondit seigneur qui estoient en grand nombre, des plus excellents en art de musique que l'on peust et seust eslire et trouver." Gachard, *Collection de documens inédits*, 2:86.

16 Two receipts identified by Sophie Jolivet confirm this. The first documents the purchase of "two chests to hold the ornaments of the chapel" on 19 February 1430 by "Nicaise du Puis, chapelain of the duke's chapel" (Archives départementales du Nord – hereafter ADN – B 1941/24, document no. 55979). The second, from 1 March 1432 from the local receiver of 8,249 francs and 5 sous, acknowledges the receipt of the receiver-general of finance of Artois for "chaplains and other members of the duke of Burgundy's chapel for their yearly wages and for the purchase of cloth to make robes" (ADN, B 1947, document no. 56368).

17 Prizer, "Brussels and the Ceremonies of the Order of the Golden Fleece," reframes earlier statements. The protocols of the Order do not provide details about the ceremonies, apart from one reference from the

Philip the Good's travels in the 1430s led to his chapel's international acclaim. About his stay at the court of Savoy in Chambéry in 1434, for example, Jean Le Fèvre wrote that the Mass on 8 February was "sung so melodiously by the Duke's chaplains that it was beautiful to hear, since at the time it was held to be the best chapel in the world, considering their numbers."[18] Similarly, in his account of the ceremonies of the Golden Fleece in Ghent in 1445, Olivier de La Marche refers to Vespers "sung by the musicians of the Duke's chapel, which was one of the best chapels, the most harmonious, and with the largest number of chaplains ever known."[19]

From the 1430s until the death of Mary of Burgundy in 1482, the chapel's history is entirely consistent. Of the dukes of this period, Charles the Bold was the most interested in music. In his depiction of the Duke, Jean Molinet stresses that he "filled his days not with vanity or worldly spectacle, but with holy Scriptures, approved stories of the most noble reputation, and above all, with the art of music, which he loved more than any other"; he "received the most famous singers in the world and maintained a chapel filled with such harmonious and delightful voices that, after celestial glory, there was no such jubilation."[20]

Even amid the tumult following the death of Mary of Burgundy in 1482, the chapel suffered only a brief period of inactivity. Maximilian of Austria re-instated it as soon as he reorganized his court in 1485, in preparation for his coronation as King of the Romans in Frankfurt. Molinet reports that the chapel was still the prince's first priority:

> Thus, to begin his preparations so that Our Lord God was honored, praised, and served, he reinstated the chapel to its condition in the time of Dukes Philip and Charles, when it had an excellent reputation around the world, but which strongly suffered and was almost entirely destroyed by the torments of the war, so that its chaplains were dispersed in many directions. Nevertheless, he sent for the most experienced musicians with the most con-sonant and proportionate voices that could be found, both those who had previously been in Burgundian service and others . . . altogether forming a very

account of the first chapter from Lille in 1431 that mentions that "the divine service and the grand ceremonies were nobly performed . . . by excellent musicians and organists." A decree from 1431, however, stipulates that the services are to be celebrated by "the chaplains and other members of the Duke's chapel."
18 "chantée par les chappelains du duc, tant mélodieusement que c'estoit belle chose à ouir; car pour l'eure, on tenoit la chappelle du duc la meilleure du monde, du nombre qu'ils estoient." Le Fèvre, *Chronique*, 2:293.
19 "chantées par les chantres de la chapelle du duc, qui fut une des meilleures chapelles, des mieux acordees et en plus grand nombre de chapellains que l'on sceust nulle part." La Marche, *Mémoires*, 2:87.
20 "employoit ses jours, non pas en fole vanité ou mondain spectacle, mais en saintes escriptures, hystoires approuvees et de haultes recommandation, souverainement en l'art de musicque dont il estoit amoureux que nul plus"; "recoeilloit les plus famez chantres du monde et entretenoit une chapelle estoffee de voix tant armonieuses et delitables que, apres la gloire celeste, il n'estoit autre leesse." Molinet, *Chroniques*, 1:62.

good chapel for which he [Maximilian] was greatly honored and praised by the princes of Germany.[21]

The regent Maximilian's Burgundian chapel functioned irregularly until 1491; the services of the Order of the Golden Fleece held that year in Mechelen (Malines) were performed by the choir of the church of Saint-Rombault. The chapel was finally reorganized in 1492. On 17 November, Philip the Fair took over the chapel and managed it according to his "excellent reputation," which was explicitly invoked in various edicts.[22] During two journeys to Spain in 1501 and 1506, the chapel achieved its apotheosis with over forty members, a half-dozen of which were already famous.

From 1430 to 1506 (and until the adulthood of Charles V in 1515), the Burgundian chapel never experienced more than a decade of inactivity, and retained its privileged place in the Burgundian household and the acclaim of chroniclers. Philip the Good's chapel had between twenty and twenty-five members, but Charles the Bold's had twenty-five to thirty, recalling the glory days of Philip the Bold.[23] With this in mind we can assert that the dukes of Burgundy maintained a performing force equivalent to and indeed often larger than those of their contemporaries.[24]

This notion of a continuous Burgundian patronage is further supported by the remarkable consistency of the chapel's budget. In 1469, the new Duke gave a special order that, to ensure regular payment of the chapel's wages, the head chaplain would receive 10,000 royal francs per annum directly from the Artois tax officer, exactly the amount Philip the Bold had spent on his chapel ca. 1400. From 1397 until the death of Charles the Bold, the chaplains' wages remained constant at 1 franc per day, by far the largest chapel salary at that time.[25] These comparisons are limited by the disparity of documentation

21 "Dont, pour commencement de ses preparatoires, affin que Nostre Seigneur Dieu fut honoré, loét et servi, il retint la chapelle en estat, laquelle, du tampz des ducz Philippe et Charles, avoit esté d'excellente renommée de par le monde universel, et fort amenrie et quasy du tout aneantie par torment de guerre, tellement que les chapelains d'icelle estoyent dispers et retenus en divers marches. Neantmoins, il fit cherchier et choisir les plus experimentez musiciens, ayans les plus consonantes et proporcionnées voix que possible estoit de trouver, tant de ceulx qui paravant y estoyent comme aultres . . . lesquelz, ensemble unis, estoffoyent une très bonne chapelle dont il fut grandement honouré et prisiét des princes d'Alemaigne." Ibid., 470.
22 This date can be deduced unequivocally from three official documents of 1495–96 that order retroactive payments to the chapel members for nearly three years of service.
23 The accuracy of these numbers depends on whether they include non-musical positions in the chapel (e.g., confessor, almoners). The distinction between the "petite" and "grande" (or music) chapels under the administration of Philip the Fair cleared up this ambiguity.
24 Charles d'Orléans employed about fifteen singers between 1455 and 1465, a few more than René of Anjou, who recruited twelve in 1449. The registry of the French royal chapel, by comparison, shows a maximum of twenty members.
25 The only two accounts that detail the French royal chapel members' wages indicate that between 1453 and 1461 the chaplains received "15 *livres tournois* per month," or half of the Burgundian salary. Réne of

between courts – but without question, the chapel of Burgundy boasted an "excellent reputation around the world." Whether it was *the* best in the world" is of course a matter of judgment. The two accounts of Leo de Rozmital's European voyages ca. 1465, for example, rave about the chapel of King Edward IV of England, but make no mention of that of Philip the Good.[26]

### The other court musicians

While much of the scholarly interest surrounding the chapel comes from the compositions attributed to its well-known musicians, the court heard many other musicians whose improvisational art has left little written testimony. Princely courts were spaces of social accession for the instrumentalists – and, to a lesser extent, singers – who animated banquets, parties, and balls and accompanied the prince at meals and in private. Recruited individually or in twos and threes, their number varied and was less clearly defined than the chapel or the *trompettes de guerre*. Four to six *haut* instruments performed dances and arrangements of popular songs, most often in trios. The duke and other lords and ladies of the court also employed drummers (*tambourins*) who spontaneously played dance melodies, though it is the *bas* instrumentalists who evoked the most notable accounts of their strong personalities.[27]

The earliest of these accounts – six stanzas from Martin Le Franc's *Champion des Dames*, a long poem dedicated to Philip the Good – is famous for its illustrated miniature of Du Fay and Binchois. This miniature, and a reference to the composers' "English countenance" (*contenance angloise*), are found within a debate between two allegorical characters on the decline of civilization.[28] Franc Vouloir uses music's "progression" since ancient times as a counter-argument to Lourt Entendement's assertion that civilization is in decline.[29] After exposing his progressivist theory in an introductory stanza, Franc Vouloir asserts that Du Fay and Binchois are finer composers than their predecessors (stanzas 2 and 3), and that contemporary instrumentalists have surpassed those who came before (stanzas 4 and 5). In the sixth stanza, he asks his interlocutor to draw his own conclusions from a confrontation between

Anjou's singers earned 6 *écus* per month in 1449. The 120 ducats offered by Ercole d'Este to the Milanese singers in the winter of 1479–80 was roughly a third less than the salary paid to the Burgundian chaplains until 1476.

26 "Musicians this joyful can be heard nowhere else … their choir is roughly sixty singers strong." Schmeller, *Des böhmischen Herrn Leo's Reise*, 42. The other account of this trip praises the talent of "more than forty-two of the king's singers," 155–57.

27 Further on *haut* and *bas* instruments, see Keith Polk's essay in this volume, Ch. 38.

28 Paris, Bibliothèque nationale de France, MS fr. 12476, fol. 98. The second manuscript of the poem dedicated to Philip the Good was copied in 1451 by a cleric who had sung at the papal chapel with Du Fay. See Avril, "Martin Le Franc, Barthélemy Poignare et l'illustrateur du 'Champion des dames'."

29 Le Franc, *Le Champion des Dames*, 4:67–69. See also Wegman, "New Music for a World Grown Old."

two groups of musicians: Du Fay and Binchois on one hand, and a duo of blind fiddle players from the Burgundian court on the other:[30]

| v. 16290 | – Tu as les avugles ouÿ | – You heard the blind men |
|---|---|---|
| | Jouer a la court de Bourgongne, | Play at the court of Burgundy, |
| | N'a pas? – Certainement, ouÿ. | Didn't you? – Certainly, yes. |
| | – Fust il jamais telle besongne? | – Was there ever such a creation? |
| | – J'ay veu Binchois avoir vergongne | – I saw Binchois feel ashamed, |
| | Et soy taire emprez leur rebelle, | And fall silent before their fiddle |
| v. 16295 | Et Dufay despité et frongne | And Du Fay disappointed and angry |
| | Qu'il n'a melodie si belle. | That he has no melody so beautiful. |

The rhetorical trajectory of these stanzas shows that for Martin Le Franc, the ultimate proof, in the field of music, that civilization was not in a state of decline was that even the most distinguished composers were moved by certain inspired improvisations.

Another account of Burgundian instrumentalists comes from Johannes Tinctoris's *De inventione et usu musicae*, which describes 1470s musical life in detail. The theorist recalls the effect two blind *vièle* players had on him in Bruges. The musicians were in fact the sons of one of the blind musicians from Le Franc's story, and served at the court between 1462 and 1470. Another passage describes Henri Bucquelin, Charles the Bold's lutenist, as the greatest improviser of his time, and perhaps the first to have mastered polyphonic techniques on the lute.[31]

These texts illustrate the exemplary musicianship of the Duke of Burgundy's instrumentalists, a tradition that continued under Philip the Fair, who hired as *valet de chambre* the lute and cornett virtuoso Augustine Schubinger; chroniclers have documented his participation at chapel services.

## Musical creation at the Burgundian court:
## boundaries and hypotheses

The Burgundian archives contain no documentation of payment for or commissioning of musical works. Four narratives refer to the performance of specific works, but the music for three of them does not survive.[32] Music historians must connect dense archival materials about performers with

30 These two fiddle players, Jean Fernandez and Jean de Cordoue, served the court from January 1435 until 1456. For information on their careers, see Fiala, "Les Musiciens étrangers." Chambéry in February 1434 is widely accepted as the setting of this scene because of the demonstrable presence of all of the main figures involved.

31 See Fiala, "Les Musiciens étrangers," 380–84 for more on the Fernandez brothers and Bucquelin.

32 La Marche, *Mémoires* refers to certain works performed at the banquet of 1454 (2:358), including *La sauvegarde de ma vie*, which is not found in any musical source, and the well-known *Je ne vis oncques,*

musical sources that reveal little about the creation or development of the repertories they transmit.

Although we know that the Burgundian chapel used the French royal family's liturgy, specific information about the services is rare. It is therefore difficult to assess the place of polyphony, all the more since the practice of "singing upon the book" (*chant sur le livre*) was probably frequent, if not mentioned directly. We may consider the musical corpus of the Burgundian court as falling into three categories marked by their relationships to the patronage system: works attributed to composers in the court's employ; works included in manuscripts produced or conserved by the court; and works containing textual or musical characteristics associated with courtly life.

## Composers at the court

The dukes of Burgundy employed fifteen musicians who are each credited with at least one work in contemporary musical sources. Strangely, not even one attributed composition remains of Philip the Bold's magnificent chapel. We know that the first Valois duke was in contact with Jean Tapissier and Jean Carmen, two of the three musicians who, according to Martin Le Franc, "astounded all of Paris" in the years before Binchois and Du Fay. Evaluation of the historical importance of his patronage, however, is hampered by the hypothetical nature of many attributions, including most notably the case of Baude Fresnel. Craig Wright has suggested identifying this *valet* and harpist, whose career at court is well documented from 1384 until his death in 1398, as the "maistre Baude Cordier" credited with several works in musical sources but otherwise completely unknown.[33] While an attractive hypothesis, it is problematic. Cordier's songs are so remarkable that if their composer was indeed in Burgundian service, he would have been by far the most important musical figure of the court.[34]

John the Fearless seems to have been particularly invested in the training of his choirboys; he entrusted their education to such renowned musicians as Tapissier and Nicolas Grenon. Although Grenon's presence at the court was

attributed to Binchois or Du Fay depending on the manuscript. In his account of the 1468 marriage ceremonies, he included the entire text of *Bien veignés la belle bergière* and *Faictes vous l'asne, ma maistress* (3:136 and 153; see also 4:110), though none of these figures in the songbooks of the period.

33  Wright (*Music at the Court of Burgundy*, 124–34) proposes two main arguments. Fresnel, like Cordier, was from Reims, and the reference to cordes (strings) in "cordier" could have been a nickname alluding to his job as a harpist. Apart from the lack of any reference to a "Baude Fresnel alias Cordier" despite rich documentation, two other considerations render this theory problematic. First, some of Cordier's chansons seem stylistically to postdate Fresnel's death. Also, though all of Cordier's attributions record his title as "master," the Burgundian documentation (notably fastidious in this regard) never refers to Fresnel as such. Plumley and Stone, "Cordier's Picture-Songs," indirectly suggest the implausible chronology of a Fresnel–Cordier assimilation.

34  Wright's designation of composers François de Gemblaco and Briquet also raises issues. See the articles by David Fallows in *New Grove* and in Fallows, *Catalogue of Polyphonic Songs*.

probably sporadic, his works could have been performed there. Pierre Fontaine, who had one of the longest careers of any musician at court, was the first member of the domestic chapel whose compositions have been preserved; a cleric since 1403, Fontaine appears on all extant chapel lists (during its active periods) until 1447. The recruitment of Jacques Vide as a *valet* in 1423 and as the tutor of two choirboys starting from 1426 fills in the chapel's inactive period at the beginning of Philip the Good's reign. Although promoted to secretary and given a portative organ by the duke in 1428, Vide no longer belonged to the household in 1433; he had instead taken – with much fuss – the position of provost at Sainte-Gertrude in Nivelles.[35]

Nevertheless, the employment of court composers was consistent until about 1430. With the exception of Fontaine, all served outside the chapel and produced little in terms of sacred music. They instead won renown for their chansons, written in a simple style with a melodic and formal elegance that set the standard for decades to come.[36]

The recruitment of Gilles Binchois in 1430 marks a turning point in the history of Burgundian musical patronage. His vast compositional output and privileged place in the chapel make him the first "court composer," well before the appearance of such a title, at the Burgundian court and perhaps everywhere else. Since he is the only leading composer who spent his entire career in the chapel, his oeuvre represents the court's aesthetic choices (as does that of Pierre de La Rue for the period 1490–1515).[37]

Continuing in the tradition of Fontaine and Vide, Binchois was the most brilliant chanson composer of his time. He also wrote a great deal of sacred music, the majority of which – most notably his mass movements – features simple, three-voice counterpoint and shows borrowings from Parisian plainchant, the basis of the chapel's daily offices. David Fallows deems his *Magnificat* "frankly ascetic" and notes that even his slightly more developed pieces hardly go beyond "strictly functional" counterpoint.[38] Fallows concludes: "The Burgundian court that employed Binchois was by all accounts a home of tradition; and Binchois wrote traditional music for it . . . a body of music that keeps fairly closely to a middle road, with nothing outrageous or startling; and from a distance this can look both unadventurous and drab."

For Fallows, Binchois's oeuvre supports a reading of the Burgundian chapel as a prestigious institution with limited artistic ambitions. But this view must

---

35 For the most complete biography, see Planchart, "Vide." One can add that in September 1434, Vide was sent to Eugenius IV in Florence (Toussaint, *Les Relations diplomatiques de Philippe le Bon*, 148).
36 See Strohm, *The Rise of European Music*, 141–49.
37 Considered a young man ("jovene homme") in 1419, he served until February 1453, when he retired to the church of Saint-Vincent in Soignies. See Kirkman and Slavin, *Binchois Studies*.
38 "Binchois," *New Grove*.

be refined because of two circumstances of the chapel. First, singers practiced their art in contexts outside religious ceremony and became accomplished chanson composers in their own right. Second, Philip the Good's lack of interest in music and his promotion of ceremonial austerity may further explain the limited output of his musicians.[39] Employing the most refined song composer of the era, he simply upheld the chapel's status in his thirty-seven-year reign without a single notable innovation. After 1430, the musicians' ranks were not replenished by any substantial recruitment. Jean Pullois (Johannes Puyllois), who was to become the main composer of the papal chapel, was refused a job after his 1446 audition, and no major composer replaced Binchois after his retirement in 1453. Many of the musicians during this period are known to us only through one work, confirming that although quite capable, they were hardly encouraged to compose.[40]

Philip the Good's inadequacies as a music patron are even more conspicuous when compared to his son, the music-lover and amateur musician Charles the Bold.[41] An account register of his household from 1457, when he was still Count of Charolais but ruled temporarily during the long absence of his father, presages his influence on the system of musical patronage.[42] He may have played a role in the recruitment of Robert Morton,[43] and was definitely responsible for a payment to a chaplain "for ceremonial vestments and other needs of a young man named Hayne de Ghizeghem."[44] It was for this lutenist and composer of *De tous biens pleine*, the most popular rondeau of the fifteenth century, and also for Adrien Basin, the composer of at least three surviving chansons, that Charles the Bold renewed the practice of hiring musicians as private *valets*. These two *valets* were certainly important to the duke; they were the last musicians he kept constantly with him until the end of his disastrous military campaign in 1476.

39 The biographies of Bonnenfant and Vaughan support this notion, though Graeme Small's introduction to the new edition of Vaughan's book highlights the lack of information on the duke's piety (Vaughan, *Philip the Good*, xx). Marix (*Histoire de la musique*, 93) is surprised that the duke did not employ any *bas* instrument players before 1430. One could consider the hiring of the two blind lutenists as Isabelle of Portugal's doing; moreover, Jacques Vide, the duke's musical *valet de chambre* during the 1420s, was never replaced.

40 This is the case for Clément Liebert, Richard de Bellengues alias Cardot, Robert le Pele, Constant de Languebrouc, and Simon Le Breton. Gilles Joye's four chansons may have been composed before he was hired in 1462.

41 A Milanese ambassador reported that during the siege of Neuss (1474), Charles often listened to new works and sometimes sang with his musicians. Olivier de La Marche states that he "loved music, even though he had a bad voice" and that he composed "a number of chansons that were well crafted and notated well," two of which would have been preserved. The duke heard a performance of one of his motets at Cambrai cathedral in 1460.

42 ADN B 3661 is the only extant register for Charles before his accession.

43 Morton, who was paid "to live with the chapel singers" ("pour soy entretenir avec les chantres de la chapelle") before being integrated into the ducal chapel, was periodically permitted to leave the duke's service in order to serve Charles of Charolais in the 1460s.

44 "pour le vestement et necessitez d'un jeusne filz appelé Hayne de Ghizeghem."

Morton, Hayne, and Basin are the first evidence of the count's musical interests. After his accession to the dukedom in June 1467, Charles privileged the "merits of the voice" above all other criteria, ecclesiastical concerns included, in a landmark provision found in an edict from January 1469 that details the hierarchy and daily functioning of the chapel.[45] This precision can be understood in the context of the duke's modifications to the chapel, including notably the recruitment of Antoine Busnoys. As with the majority of changes made at this time, Charles was personally invested in this hiring, bringing Busnoys up from Poitiers in the fall of 1466, paying him outside the chapel with the unprecedented title "the Duke's singer" (*chantre de mondit seigneur*), as was the case with another apparently talented musician, Pasquin Louis. It took more than two and a half years, during which time Busnoys obtained a university degree, and the creation of a "half-chaplain" ("demi-chapelain") position, for the duke to officially integrate the singers he wanted to hear into the chapel.

Busnoys came to the chapel with a full career behind him. Among other things, he had already completed a good number of the nearly sixty chansons attributed to him. Nonetheless, his sacred compositional output, characterized by greater inventiveness than we find in Binchois, was composed at least in part for the chapel of Burgundy,[46] and copied during this period in the only pre-served manuscript that can be described as a "choirbook of the Burgundian chapel" (Brussels 5557). It may be significant that this sole direct witness to the written repertory sung by the chapel dates from the years in which a major composer of sacred music was active there.

### Music manuscripts and repertory

All that has been said about the musical patronage of the dukes is to some extent undermined by the small number of surviving musical sources. With so few witnesses it is often difficult to confirm even which court musicians were "composers," let alone evaluate their works. In the case of Binchois, for instance, the composer's works are transmitted almost solely in four manu-scripts copied far from Burgundian territories, in northern Italy.[47]

Not only are musical sources produced at or for the court before 1470 practically non-existent, but the archives only partially fill in the gap. Details about the inventory and accounting of musical manuscripts can easily be summarized. In 1384, Philip the Bold bought a "book of motets" from a chaplain of the Paris Sainte-Chapelle and paid Jean Carmen in 1403 as a "scribe

---

45  Fallows, "Specific Information on the Ensembles," 146 n. 5.
46  See Gallagher, "Busnoys, Burgundy, and the Song of Songs."      47  See "Binchois," *New Grove*.

and notator of music, for having notated in the book of notes of the chapel certain hymns, Glorias, and Patrems newly made."[48] Under Philip the Good, three payments attest to the production of books for the chapel during the 1430s.[49] In 1446, we find mention of a "great book bought at Malines full of new vocal music like masses, motets, and several other things," and then in 1465, evidence of the copying of a "new mass in music."[50] As previously noted, only Charles of Charolais's register in 1457 provides evidence for an intense period of musical copying.[51]

The limited number of references to the copying of music shows that before the appearance of Petrus Alamire's atelier, there was no passion for collecting music books at the court of Burgundy.[52] Scores were utilitarian objects whose production was hardly ever paid for, leaving few traces of their existence. Once a repertory passed out of fashion, the scores were destroyed, or at best recycled. The cover of a 1512 ledger from the Duke of La Trémoïlle that was rediscovered in the 1920s, for example, was recognized as the index of a large manuscript copied in 1376, which had been used by the French royal chapel and the chapel of Philip the Bold.[53] Other such manuscripts are recorded alongside the invaluable volumes of Machaut in the later fifteenth-century inventories of the ducal library. None of these, however, is likely to have been used in the chapel, which took care of its own books containing up-to-date music. The chapel made its own inventories, mentioned in the margins of the ducal library, but none has been preserved.

Accounting ledgers and inventories of manuscripts provide no information about the creation and circulation of musical repertories. While this might seem consistent with the notion of a conservative and simple liturgical court repertory, such is not the case for the chanson, which was the most creative genre in courtly life. As it turns out, the five songbooks once categorized as

48 Wright's translation. See *Music at the Court of Burgundy*, 139–60.
49 Chaplain Guillaume Ruby was paid in 1431 "as compensation for two songbooks that he made for the chapel" and in 1434 "for having written, notated, and illuminated a book with the script of the Passion"; in 1438, Binchois was paid for "a book he had made and composed by order of the duke that contains the Passion in a new manner." See Marix, *Histoire de la musique*, 174 and 180.
50 Ibid., 20 and 130.
51 This register (already mentioned in n. 42) records payment for the binding of "two songbooks that my said lord had caused to be written" and for gifts to "a poor Dutch priest who brought songbooks to my lord" and a "poor Scottish cleric who had previously brought music." It also accounts for the painter Jean Hennekart's payment for illuminating "a large roll of parchment with a motet that was done at the birth of my Lady of Burgundy" or the making of "a lute in parchment with illuminations and music of a motet to the Virgin." In addition, it identifies three gifts to a chaplain from Tournai named Waghe Feustrier, who may have played an integral role in the compilation of an important manuscript (see Strohm, *The Lucca Choirbook*, 31–34).
52 Kellman, *The Treasury of Petrus Alamire*.
53 This manuscript may have been the one purchased in 1384. See Wright, *Music at the Court of Burgundy*, 147–58.

"Burgundian," a coherent collection from the last quarter of the fifteenth century, are now thought to have originated in the Loire Valley.[54] Their inclusion of songs by composers in Philip the Good and Charles the Bold's employ link these collections only indirectly to the court. The "real" Burgundian chanson collections – produced directly by colleagues of Binchois or Hayne – have disappeared, along with the chapel's other manuscripts that predate 1470.

Written traces of the court's musical life begin with the reign of Charles the Bold and the arrival of Busnoys. Accounting ledgers from as early as 1468–69 show unprecedented activity: copying three masses "in the chapel books," binding two masses and a motet, and copying a mass and a Magnificat "in one of the chapel's books." Two manuscripts produced by the same copyist bear witness to the musical repertory under Charles the Bold.[55] In the first (Brussels 5557), begun for the celebrations of the 1468 marriage, in Bruges, between the duke and Margaret of York, the copyist notated five English masses that were then bound with gatherings containing masses by Ockeghem and Du Fay, among others. The remaining blank pages were later filled with motets by Busnoys, probably in the composer's own hand. The second manuscript (Naples VI.E.40), a gift for Beatrice d'Aragona, contains a cycle of six anonymous *L'homme armé* masses, whose exceptional structural elaboration has in some instances been attributed to Busnoys. A verse of the dedicatory poem found at the end of the manuscript refers to a "prince Charles who used to enjoy this [music] very much," evidently Charles the Bold ("Charolus hoc princeps quondam gaudere solebat.") This manuscript forms part of the basis of a striking hypothesis concerning the influence of the court on musical composition: the possibility of a Burgundian origin for the *L'homme armé* mass tradition.[56]

Some works contain references that overtly allude to courtly life, such as the rondeau *Nul ne s'y frotte a ma maistresse* (No one touches my mistress) that quotes the motto of Antoine, nicknamed the *grand bâtard* of Burgundy: "Nul ne s'y frotte" (No one touches him).[57] Found in a Neapolitan manuscript from the 1490s (Perugia 431), it is attributed to "Magister Simon," who was probably the Burgundian chaplain Simon Le Breton. Master Simon is mentioned in

---

54  See Alden, *Songs, Scribes, and Society*. See also Thomas Schmidt-Beste in this volume, Ch. 34.
55  The recognition of the copyist is thanks to Klaas van der Heide; see "New Claims." The copyist was probably a member of the chapel.
56  See Jesse Rodin's contribution in this volume, Ch. 4.
57  Fallows, *Catalogue of Polyphonic Songs*, 298. A work by Johannes Ghiselin copied in the 1480s with the incipit text "Je l'ay emprins," Charles the Bold's motto, also appears as the Christe of his *Missa De les armes*, whose heraldic title has yet to be thoroughly explained (Fallows, ibid., 201). The rondeaux *Plus n'en aray* by Ghizeghem and *N'aray-je jamais mieux que j'ai?* by Morton could also refer to Philip the Good's motto: "Aultre n'aray."

the text of a well-known chanson, whose attribution is still in dispute, which combines the rondeau *Il sera pour vous conbatu* with the *L'homme armé* melody. However the song is understood, it at least provides evidence for this melody's place in Burgundian culture.[58] The link between the court and the emergence of *L'homme armé* masses around 1460 remains hypothetical, although Charles the Bold's profile, that of a warrior who spent almost all his reign on campaign, a music patron, and a musician par excellence, provides strong support for it.

The theory of a Burgundian origin for the *L'homme armé* tradition originated with the discovery, in Italian archives, of a diplomatic report of a meeting of the Order of the Golden Fleece in Brussels in 1501, recording that the Order had by then "taken for its own use" a Requiem composed by a Cambrai canon.[59] This reference to Du Fay's now-lost *Requiem* has encouraged much research on the ceremonies of this Order. One notable study describes the process by which six polyphonic Propers by Du Fay were probably commissioned by the duke around 1440 for six newly founded weekly votive services at the Sainte-Chapelle in Dijon and in the main chapters of the Order.[60] These six services also provide a context for the cycle of *L'homme armé* masses.[61] Research has suggested many other connections between the *L'homme armé* masses and the Order of the Golden Fleece, including a fascinating numerological study: the durations of the sections of Busnoys's *L'homme armé* mass are related to each other by simple proportions (1:2, 2:3, or 3:4), except for one middle section of thirty-one breves, which may be read as an allusion to the number of knights in the Order.[62] While these hypotheses cannot be proven, they urge us to consider the Burgundian court not only as a sponsor of chansons, but also as a decisive force in the history of sacred music.

## Conclusion

Born out of the French crown at the end of the fourteenth century, the court of Burgundy and its historical continuity left a substantial mark on the following century. The first and last Valois dukes (the two "Bolds," Philip and Charles) left the most lasting historical impression on music. Philip established a significant patronage system, fueled by a large number of talented and innovative musicians, which was to function nearly without change for almost a century. In the fifteenth century it was Charles who appears as the true musical Maecenas of the dynasty. He was the only duke to develop personal

---

58 Planchart, "The Origins and Early History," 317.     59 See n. 17 above.
60 Planchart, "Guillaume Du Fay's Benefices," 118 n. 3.
61 This hypothesis is put forth in van der Heide, "New Claims."
62 Taruskin, "Antoine Busnoys and the *L'Homme Armé* Tradition."

relationships with musicians, the most potent symbols of which were the recruitment of Busnoys and the clause in Du Fay's will leaving the duke six of his music books. Moreover, Charles's decision to hire Jean Molinet, the most musical poet of his time, as a historiographer, shows the extent to which the duke privileged music.

Maximilian of Austria may have sought to follow Charles's example as he reorganized his chapel beginning in 1485, though it was only after becoming emperor that he had the means to hire the necessary talent. It was in fact Philip the Fair who became the worthy successor to Charles the Bold, completing his model of musical patronage by organizing the most remarkable *scriptorium* in the history of music. Building on the organization of music at the courts of his predecessors, Philip enriched his chapel with an impressive number of composers: Pierre de La Rue, Gaspar van Weerbeke (1495–98), Jean Braconnier (1497–1506), Alexander Agricola (from 1500 until his death in 1506), Nicolas Champion (starting in 1501), Antoine Divitis (1505–6), and, finally, Marbrianus de Orto, the first composer of the chapel to receive the title of head chaplain, in 1505.

Taken as a whole, the Burgundian court's fifteenth-century musical culture is beyond comparison. Its influence was widespread and permanent, its limitations temporary. For many reasons, this was not the case at most rival courts: Savoy, Anjou, Orléans, Milan, Naples, Ferrara, Florence, and Venice. Only the courts of France and England and the papal chapel came close. Historical circumstances and the unique facets of the Burgundian musical patronage system described above – including, most notably, the richness of its archival materials – provide, perhaps, a partial explanation. But the lack of music manuscripts produced in the Low Countries before 1500 is so complete that the only real proof of Burgundy's profound musical influence is the presence of works by its court composers in every manuscript collection in Europe.

# Bibliography

Alden, Jane, *Songs, Scribes, and Society: The History and Reception of the Loire Valley Chansonniers*, New York and Oxford, 2010

Avril, François, "Martin Le Franc, Barthélemy Poignare et l'illustrateur du 'Champion des dames'," *Art de l'enluminure* 40 (2012), 2–59

Fallows, David, *A Catalogue of Polyphonic Songs, 1415–1480*, Oxford, 1999
    *Josquin*, Turnhout, 2009
    "Specific Information on the Ensembles for Composed Polyphony, 1400–1474," in *Studies in the Performance of Late Mediaeval Music*, ed. Stanley Boorman, Cambridge, 1983, 109–59

Fiala, David, *Le Mécénat musical des ducs de Bourgogne et des princes de la maison de Habsbourg, 1467–1506*, Turnhout, forthcoming

"Les Musiciens étrangers de la cour de Bourgogne à la fin du XVe siècle," *Revue du Nord* 84 (2002), 367–87

Gachard, Louis-Prosper, *Collection de documens inédits concernant l'histoire de la Belgique*, Brussels, 1833–35

Gallagher, Sean, "Busnoys, Burgundy, and the Song of Songs," in *Uno gentile et subtile ingenio: Studies in Renaissance Music in Honour of Bonnie J. Blackburn*, ed. M. Jennifer Bloxam, Gioia Filocamo, and Leofranc Holford-Strevens, Turnhout, 2009, 413–29

Kellman, Herbert, ed., *The Treasury of Petrus Alamire: Music and Art in Flemish Court Manuscripts, 1500–1535*, Ghent, 1999

Kirkman, Andrew, and Denis Slavin, eds., *Binchois Studies*, Oxford, 2000

La Marche, Olivier de, *Mémoires*, ed. Henri Beaune and Jules d'Arbaumont, Paris, 1888

Le Fèvre, Jean, *Chronique*, ed. François Morand, Paris, 1881

Le Franc, Martin, *Le Champion des Dames*, ed. Robert Deschaux, Paris, 1999

Marix, Jeanne, *Histoire de la musique et des musiciens de la cour de Bourgogne sous le règne de Philippe le Bon (1420–1465)*, Strasbourg, 1939; repr. Geneva, 1972

Molinet, Jean, *Chroniques*, ed. Georges Doutrepont and Omer Jodogne, Brussels, 1935

Paravicini, Werner, "Ordre et règle: Charles le Téméraire en ses ordonnances de l'hôtel," *Comptes rendus des séances de l'Académie des Inscriptions et Belles-Lettres* 143 (1999), 311–59

"Prosopographia Burgundica (1407–1477)," www.prosopographia-burgundica.org

Planchart, Alejandro Enrique, "Guillaume Du Fay's Benefices and his Relationship to the Court of Burgundy," *EMH* 8 (1988), 117–71

"The Origins and Early History of *L'homme armé*," *JM* 20 (2003), 305–57

"Vide, Jacques, Jacobus," in *MGG2, Personenteil*, 6:1561–62

Plumley, Yolanda, and Anne Stone, "Cordier's Picture-Songs and the Relationship between the Song Repertories of the Chantilly Codex and Oxford 213," in Plumley and Stone, *A Late Medieval Songbook and its Context*, Turnhout, 2009, 303–28

Prizer, William F., "Brussels and the Ceremonies of the Order of the Golden Fleece," *Revue belge de musicologie* 55 (2001), 69–90

Schmeller, Johann Andreas, ed., *Des böhmischen Herrn Leo's von Rožmital Ritter-, Hof- und Pilger- Reise durch die Abendlande, 1465–1467*, Stuttgart, 1844

Schnerb, Bertrand, *Jean sans Peur*, Paris, 2005

Strohm, Reinhard, ed., *The Lucca Choirbook*, Chicago, 2008

*The Rise of European Music, 1380–1500*, Cambridge, 1993

Taruskin, Richard, "Antoine Busnois and the *L'Homme Armé* Tradition," *JAMS* 39 (1986), 255–93

Toussaint, Joseph, *Les Relations diplomatiques de Philippe le Bon avec le Concile de Bâle (1431–1449)*, Louvain, 1942

van der Heide, Klaas, "New Claims for a Burgundian Origin of the *L'homme armé* Tradition, and a Different View on the Relative Positions of the Earliest Masses in the Tradition," *TVNM* 55 (2005), 3–33

Vaughan, Richard, *Philip the Good: The Apogee of Burgundy*, Woodbridge, 2002

Wegman, Rob C., "New Music for a World Grown Old: Martin Le Franc and the 'Contenance angloise'," *AcM* 75 (2003), 201–41

Wright, Craig, *Music at the Court of Burgundy, 1364–1419: A Documentary History*, Henryville, PA, 1979

# The papal chapel in the late fifteenth century

RICHARD SHERR

The term "papal chapel" (*capella papalis*) designated a number of things in the fifteenth century:

- The physical space where papal ceremonies occurred (there were several spaces in the Vatican Palace, the largest called the *capella maior*, which Pope Sixtus IV rebuilt and decorated in the late 1470s and early 1480s and which has since taken his name).[1]
- The personnel who participated in those ceremonies (the choir of singers was only a part of this personnel, and it is inaccurate to use "papal chapel" to designate the choir only).
- Any ceremony that was attended (or was supposed to be attended) by the pope.[2]

While we can place the origins of the papal chapel very early in the history of the papacy, for the purposes of this chapter, its history begins with the end of the Great Schism in 1417, as the institution developed for the popes in Avignon was adapted to the new circumstances of life in the Vatican. The chapter will also concentrate on the institution as it existed at the end of the fifteenth century. Table 23.1 lists the popes and their pontificates from 1417 to 1503.

Study of the papal chapel as an institution in the fifteenth century is hampered by the loss of all the internal documents of the chapel for that period.[3] Some information can be gleaned from other sources, however. Sometime in the late fifteenth century or the early sixteenth, the papal master of ceremonies, Johannes Burckard, made two sets of notes about the organization and personnel of the papal chapel; these notes (whose originals

---

1 The other chapels were the *Capella Sancti Nicolai* across from the Sistine, and the chapel of Nicholas V, which was near the papal bedroom. As far as I know, the Sistine Chapel was never called that in the fifteenth century.
2 See Schimmelpfennig, "Die Funktion der Cappella Sistina."
3 For the sixteenth century, on the other hand, there are almost too many documents.

Table 23.1 *Papacies from the Council of Constance to the end of the fifteenth century*

---

Martin V (21 November 1417–20 February 1431)
Eugene IV (3 March 1431–23 February 1447)
Nicholas V (6 March 1447–24 March 1455)
Calixtus III (8 April 1455–8 August 1458)
Pius II (27 August 1458–15 August 1464)
Paul II (31 August 1464–28 July 1471)
Sixtus IV (9 August 1471–12 August 1484)
Innocent VIII (29 August 1484–25 July 1492)
Alexander VI (11 August 1492–18 August 1503)

---

have not been found) were copied in the sixteenth century and are preserved in a volume in the Archivio Segreto Vaticano.[4] However, it is not clear what the notes represent. They seem not in fact to describe the chapel as Burckard knew it (he was a member from December 1483 until his death in May 1506), but to represent an older state of the institution, and perhaps even Burckard's ideal view of what the chapel should be like. Indications of this begin with the order in which he presents the personnel of the chapel in his notes, entitled *The manner in which the papal chapel is usually to be regulated and ordered for the honor of God and Our Lord the Pope* (see Appendix, B.1). This is followed by a list of the personnel of the chapel, with a short summary of their duties in the following order (see Appendix, A.1 and B.2–7):

*Sacrista* [Sacristan]

First there is one sacristan, who is usually a bishop and is a permanent official and directly subject to the pope. He oversees all the furniture of the private and public chapels, as well as all the books, the chalices of both chapels, and other ornaments, and whatever service the bell-ringers do, they do for the sacristan.[5]

*Magister capellae* [*Maestro di Cappella*][6]

Item. There is one *maestro di cappella* directly subject to the pope, who should diligently see to it that the singers sing the canonical hours nocturnal and diurnal at the due times and with due reverence and silence. This *maestro di cappella* retains his office during the lifetime of the pope [who appointed him], or else at the pope's pleasure, and he is appointed and changed only by the pope.

---

4 See the Appendix for a transcription.
5 Thanks to Leofranc Holford-Strevens for help with the translations.
6 I will use the Italian term to designate this position.

The *maestro di cappella* is usually appointed by the pope at his discretion, also called the chaplain or private chamberlain, who must be prudent with a good reputation, whose job is to govern the singers.[7]

### *Clerici ceremoniarum* [Clerks (Masters) of Ceremonies]

Item. There are two clerks of the ceremonies, who serve in alternate weeks in Masses and make sure that the ceremonial is followed. These are permanent officials, like the sacristan, and are appointed only by the pope.

### *Capellani missarum* [Mass Chaplains]

Item. There are two chaplains who celebrate the daily Mass in alternate weeks, who should be honest men with decent voices, who can read and pronounce well and who know Gregorian chant well.[8] These are not officials but are simple servants to be changed at will, and can be appointed and changed by the *maestro di cappella*.

### *Cantores* [Singers]

Item. There are twelve singers, that is, two tenorists, four contratenors, and six high voices, which should be clear and melodious, not hoarse or harsh: for an excessive number of voices destroys the melody and confuses the ear. These are not officials but simple servants, and the *maestro di cappella* always has the right to hire, fire, and change [the singers] whenever he thinks it necessary for the honor or necessity of the chapel or for its peace and quiet.

### *Clerici campanarum* [Clerks of the Bells]

Item. There are two bell-ringers who should be humble young men and apt for serving the chapel and they should obey the chapel officials, only in the things concerning the Divine Office. These are simple servants to be dismissed at will.

Burckard thus describes a complement of twenty individuals, of which the singers comprise 60 percent. But neither the order nor the total number is reflected in any of the lists of the chapel that are extant from the period in which he served, where the total number was closer to thirty, with the singers as a much higher percentage of the total, and which all present the personnel in the following order:

*Magister capellae*
*Sacrista*
*Cantores*
*Capellani missarum*
*Clerici ceremoniarum*
*Clerici campanarum*

---

7 Appendix A.1.     8 In papal masses, the *capellani missarum* served as deacon and subdeacon.

The mixture of history and wishful thinking is to be seen in Burckard's placing the sacristan above the *maestro di cappella* and his placement of the masters of ceremonies immediately after the *maestro*. As Pamela Starr has shown, the fifteenth-century papal chapel in Rome had been led solely by the sacristan until Calixtus III reinstated the office of *maestro di cappella* in 1455. It was also in Calixtus's pontificate that the payments to all the members of the chapel, from sacristan to bell-ringers, appear as one entry in the payment records of the Camera Apostolica known as the *mandati camerali* (Rome, Archivio di Stato, Camerale I), now, as then, the best source of lists of names of the personnel of the papal chapel.[9] The *maestro di cappella* is listed after the sacristan from 1457 until 1480, when the two switch places and remain that way in every list after that.[10] Burckard's order thus reflects the order established in 1457. Naturally, Burckard would think that his job would be next in importance after the two prelates, something the lists never indicate. His low opinion of the singers is reflected in his placing them second to last, only above the ringers of the bells.

Burckard had clearly done some research, consulting ceremonials in the papal library and also the *mandati*. For instance, his description of the changes in the salaries of the members of the chapel, particularly the singers, must have come from consulting the *mandati* lists (as he in fact admits; see Appendix, A.3):

> Everyone in the chapel should have the monthly salary which follows. First, the Sacristan, 10 ducats; *Maestro di Cappella*, 10; Sub-Sacristan, 4;[11] the Clerks of the Ceremonies always had 10 ducats each, until the troubles of Eugene IV; after that it was reduced to 5 – on this see the Ceremoniale which is in the papal library. The singers never had more than 5 ducats until [the pontificate of] Nicholas V, who gave singers with good voices 8 ducats [and] gave others 3, 4, [or] 5 ducats as they more or less merited. And all of them never had 8 until the time of Calixtus III. See the records of the Apostolic Chamber of those pontificates.

The salaries of the singers had in fact been set at 5 gold cameral ducats a month in the pontificate of Eugene IV and they were raised to 8 in the pontificates of Nicholas V and Calixtus III, remaining at that level until 1540.[12] A later document gives the reason for the raise:

---

9 They had been paid separately in the *mandati*. They are listed as a group for the first time in March 1457. See Starr, "Music and Music Patronage." For Roth, this is when the chapel really became an institution. See Roth, "La storia della Cappella Pontificia."

10 Starr, "Music and Music Patronage" and Roth, "La storia della Cappella Pontificia."

11 According to Roth, the position of sub-sacristan disappeared in 1459. See Roth, "La storia della Cappella Pontificia," 448 n. 92. This, then, is another indication that Burckard was describing an older institution.

12 Nicholas V, Calixtus III, and Sixtus IV all occasionally paid individual singers less than 8 ducats, but this was a relatively rare occurrence.

> VatS 702, fol. 3r. Memorandum without date [1551]
>
> Most Holy Father. From the time of Martin V and Eugene IV the singers of
> Your Holiness's chapel had 5 gold cameral ducats and the *spese in tinello*.
> Nicholas V of blessed memory gave the singers 3 more ducats for expenses
> and thus they remained with a salary of 8 gold cameral ducats.[13]

The increase of 3 ducats was related to the loss of the privilege of *spese in tinello*, technically the right of papal familiars to take their meals in the papal dining room, but probably meaning here what it meant in the sixteenth century: the daily distribution of loaves of bread and flasks of wine to all the members of the *familia*. The document implies that the salaries were increased in order to compensate the singers for the expense of having to buy their own bread and wine.[14] The singers were to spend most of the sixteenth century attempting to get back the *spese in tinello*.[15]

The *mandati camerali* were also the only documents where Burckard could have found the information about the changes in the size of the choir that he reports (with some editorial comment; see Appendix, A.2):

> The singers should be honest and moderate, expert musicians with voices
> suitable for service in the chapel and well practiced; and those who are not
> competent should be expelled and replaced with others who are better qualified.
> As to the number, it is true that never did any pope have more than twelve, and
> sometimes (they had) some eight or nine, except for Nicolas V, who had a large
> number, for no reason, from which confusion arises and the melody is ruined, as
> daily experience proves. And there have never been more incompetent and
> worthless voices in the chapel than today; let the *maestro di cappella* consider
> how he should act for the honor of the pope and himself.

It is possible that Burckard got the number twelve from consulting old ceremonials, especially the one that now has the call number Vat. Lat. 4763 in the Vatican Library, which contains an early fifteenth-century description of the papal choir as consisting normally of twelve singers plus a *maestro di cappella*.[16] But his statement that no pope had had more than twelve until Nicholas V increased the number could only have come from consulting the lists in the *mandati camerali*, provided he had not gone further back than the pontificate of Eugene IV.

---

13 "Pater B.me. Dal tempo de Martino V et Eugenio IV li cantori de capella de V.S. habeano cinque ducati de oro de camera et le expense in tinello. La fe.re. de Nico. V dette a deti cantori tre ducati più per le spese et cossi sonno restati con il salario di otto ducati de oro de camera."
14 One can only assume that it was considered cheaper to give them the 3 ducats a month than to include them in the *spese in tinello*. Thus, the raise was not exactly an act of munificence on the part of Nicholas V.
15 In fact, the memorandam quoted above is part of a concentrated and failed effort to get the *spese* reinstated.
16 Starr, "Music and Music Patronage," 75–76; Günther, "Zur Biographie einiger Komponisten der Ars subtilior," 180–81.

Thanks to the work of Alejandro Enrique Planchart, Pamela Starr, and myself, we know the exact number of singers in the choir in every month for which there is an extant list for the pontificates of Martin V to Pius II (1417–64) and the pontificates of Sixtus IV to Alexander VI (1471–1503), and can further estimate what the number was in months where there are no extant lists.[17] The one gap is the pontificate of Paul II (1464–71), for which I have relied on Starr's summaries and Franz Xaver Haberl.[18] While the number of singers was at one point as high as sixteen in the pontificate of Martin V, the *mandati camerali* for the pontificate of Eugene IV show that the number of singers never exceeded twelve, was occasionally as low as five, and stood at eight at the end of the pontificate.[19] On the election of Nicholas V in 1447, the number of singers began to increase, rising quickly from nine to fifteen by the end of 1447 and reaching the until then unheard of number of twenty-one for a few months in 1451. At the end of Nicholas's pontificate the number stood at eighteen singers. It was reduced to an average of sixteen by the end of the pontificate of Pius II. In the pontificate of Paul II the number remained about the same; it stood at fifteen at the end of the pontificate. Things changed radically in the pontificate of Sixtus IV. For most of the pontificate, the numbers range from fifteen to twenty (occasionally going below fifteen, but not for long and most often being above fifteen). It was fifteen in October 1483. Then suddenly, in November 1483 the number shoots to twenty-four, the result of the addition of nine singers at one swoop. As far as I can see this was an unprecedented event in the history of the chapel and it is reasonable to suppose that someone in a position of authority must have agreed to the great increase in expense (nine singers meant an increase of 72 gold cameral ducats a month to the budget of the chapel). This is also so close to the inauguration of Sixtus's newly decorated major palace chapel that it is not hard to agree with Adalbert Roth that the pope wanted to fill the *cantoria* of his newly built chapel with singers, as a living ornament to the liturgy to match the magnificent frescoes ornamenting the walls of the chapel (whether he also wanted to ornament the liturgy with the *sound* of all these singers singing at the same time is another question).[20] The response of the singers, by the way, was to incise their names into the walls

17 Starr, "Music and Music Patronage" and Sherr, "The Papal Chapel." I also consulted the lists for the pontificate of Sixtus IV but did not publish them. I am grateful to Prof. Planchart for sharing with me his unpublished work on the chapel in the pontificates of Martin V and Eugene IV.
18 Haberl, *Die römische "Schola Cantorum."*
19 These numbers do not include the choirboys who were members of the chapel from 1437 to 1441. Eugene IV had a particularly troubled pontificate.
20 Roth, "Primus in Petri aede." The first ceremony in the newly constructed and decorated chapel took place on 9 August 1483. Roth points out that a number of singers had become newly available through the dissolution of the chapels of the dukes of Milan and Ferrara and also through the death of Cardinal Ferry de Cluny.

of their newly frescoed *cantoria*, beginning a tradition that was to last until the eighteenth century. Chief among these singers was Josquin, who probably added his name when he joined the chapel in 1489, a mere six years after the completion of the decoration.[21] There were twenty-four singers when Burckard joined the chapel in December 1483, representing 72 percent of a complement of thirty-three individuals, and the number had increased to twenty-five by the last month of Sixtus's pontificate (August 1484). It was reduced to twenty-one at the beginning of the pontificate of Innocent VIII, inaugurating a new "base level" of about twenty, which is where it stayed more or less until the end of the pontificate of Alexander VI.

But Burckard seems fixated on the number twelve. He mentions it twice as an "ideal number" and even gives specific information about the disposition of the voice parts in such a choir (see above). It is not clear where he got this disposition, which seems to overshadow the tenors and also corresponds more or less to other fifteenth-century descriptions of voice parts.[22] Possibly he had found it in an old ceremonial. In any case, it confirms that the papal choir was expected to perform polyphony (there would have been no need to specify voice parts otherwise). But that was then. Burckard leaves no doubt about his opinion of the papal choir of his day. They numbered much more than twelve and therefore ruined the "melody" (Burckard makes this point twice) and further are terrible singers with "incompetent and worthless voices."

What on earth can he mean by these statements? Why should more than twelve people singing have any effect on "melody"? What does he mean by "melody"? That would seem to be a word for plainsong, not polyphony, but it is hard to see how an increase in the number of people singing could negatively affect the performance of plainsong. If he means polyphony, this would seem to say that all the singers performed it (otherwise the total number of singers in the choir would not matter), which runs counter to what seems to have been the case in the sixteenth century. And what does he mean by "today"? Burckard served in the chapel for twenty-two years, covering the end of the fifteenth century and the beginning of the sixteenth, and we do not know when in this period these notes were written. During that period, the papal choir, from our point of view, reached its highest level of excellence. It is true, however, that we judge excellence on the basis of the quality of the composers who were members of the chapel, not on the quality of the voices, about which we know nothing (during Burckard's tenure, the chapel employed Josquin, Gaspar van Weerbeke, Marbrianus de Orto, Bertrand Vacqueras, Johannes Hillanis,

21 Pietschmann, "Die Graffiti auf der Sängerkanzel."
22 Fallows, "Specific Information on the Ensembles."

Johannes Stockhem alias de Prato, and no doubt other composers whose works have not come down to us). Later evidence indicates that being a great composer did not necessarily mean that you were a strong singer (Palestrina was dismissed from the chapel in 1555 partly because of the "weakness" of his voice).[23]

A further indication that Burckard was perhaps indulging in wishful thinking and not describing his contemporary reality comes in his statement that the singers were mere "servants" who had no tenure of office and could be hired and fired at the will of the *maestro di cappella*, whose main job was to "govern the singers."[24] This certainly was not the case in the sixteenth century, when the extant constitutions of the chapel state that the singers were to be selected by audition and a vote of the other singers, had tenure of office, and governed themselves. In the mid-sixteenth century, the singers vigorously defended these privileges to the point of engineering the dismissal of a *maestro di cappella* who had tried to subvert them, and who had actually attempted to "govern the singers."[25] It is not clear when this became the norm, but it should be noted that as early as 1498, the singers were called a "College" in a papal bull, and Colleges had certain privileges, among them the right to select their own membership (as do Colleges today).[26] This also suggests that the choir already had the internal structure that we know it had in the sixteenth century. The order of names in the lists of the fifteenth century confirms that singers were always ranked by seniority.[27] They may even have had a constitution that was later lost.[28] It seems unlikely that the situation described by Burckard existed in the late fifteenth century, although it is possible. He certainly wanted it to be the case; it would have been an easy way of getting rid of the "worthless" voices.

Despite Burckard, there is no evidence that the popes of the fifteenth century were in any way displeased with their singers (this in stark contrast to the popes of the mid to late sixteenth century). There is also very little specific evidence that they were pleased with them. It is true that every pope in the period under discussion promulgated bulls granting the singers and other

23 See Sherr, "Competence and Incompetence."    24 See Appendix.
25 Sherr, "A Curious Incident."
26 In the bull "Debita consideratione" of 31 July 1498, Alexander VI refers to the singers "et eorum collegio." In a copy of the bull in Vatican CS 703, there is a marginal comment at this point: "Nota quod dicit collegio nam collegium esse declarat" ("Note that he says "collegio" and now declares [the singers] to be a College.").
27 In the sixteenth century, the College of Singers was led by the *maestro di cappella*, appointed by the pope, a dean, the singer with most seniority, and two elective offices: the *punctator* who assigned fines and the *abbas* who dealt with the finances of the College. According to Roth, the entire personnel of the chapel also constituted a College; see Roth, "Liturgical (and Paraliturgical) Music."
28 The official reason for the promulgation of the Constitution of 1545 was that earlier constitutions had been destroyed or lost in the Sack of Rome in 1527. See Sherr, "A Curious Incident."

members of the chapel various privileges with regard to the assecution of benefices, but this is no indication of special interest, as it was standard bureaucratic procedure to grant such privileges to groups of papal servants.[29] It is true that individual papal singers were provided with hosts of benefices, but this also was largely a bureaucratic procedure that depended more on the initiative of individual singers than the will of the pope. And popes were not really personally responsible for the specific language of their bulls, most of which was of the boilerplate variety. For instance, both Innocent VIII in 1488 and Alexander VI in 1498 promulgated bulls beginning with the words "Debita consideratione," which renewed all the privileges of their predecessors. The opening words of these bulls, promulgated ten years apart, are virtually identical.[30]

As Roth has pointed out, Sixtus IV, who is sometimes credited with "founding" the papal choir, did no more than confirm and extend privileges that had been granted by his predecessors going back to Eugene IV.[31] A better indication of the pope's interest, as Roth also pointed out, was his willingness, at the end of his pontificate, to spend more money on the choir than ever before.[32] But it was in fact Innocent VIII who gave the singers a really new privilege. In the bull *Etsi Romanus pontifex* promulgated on 20 July 1492 (five days before his death) the pope reserved to the *maestro di cappella* in perpetuity the right to present current singers in the chapel for all benefices made vacant by the death of singers and members of the chapel in or out of Rome.[33] This was a major privilege, overriding the rights of local collators; countless supplications from

---

29 Chief among these was the designation "familiaris continuus commensalis," which gave the singers special rights of preference with regard to expectatives and to the lawsuits that inevitably arose when they claimed benefices. Privileges granted by one pope had to be officially confirmed by his successor. The apostolic scriptors had similar privileges, as the singers found out in the sixteenth century.

30 Bull of Innocent VIII dated 4 October 1488 (Haberl, *Die römische "Schola Cantorum,"* 57): "Debita consideratione pensantes qualiter dilecti filii cantores capellani nostri et alii in capella nostra in divinis officiis deservientes in persolvendis altissimo continue laudibus sonoris vocibus elaborant ita ut non solum Domino in vocis exultatione complaceant sed etiam illius domum devota jucunditate illustrant dignum imo debitum reputamus . . ."

Bull of Alexander VI dated 31 July 1498 (Vatican CS 701): "Debita consideratione pensantes quantum dilecti filii cantores capellani nostri ac alii in cappella nostra divinis officiis deserviendi in persolvendis altissimo continue laudibus sonoris vocibus elaborans ita ut non solum domino in vocis exaltacione complaceant sed etiam illius domum devota jocunditate illustrent dignum quin potius debitum reputamus . . ."

The same language can be seen at the opening of the bull *Debita considerationes* promulgated by Clement VII on 27 May 1529 (Vatican CS 703, no. 11).

31 Haberl, *Die römische "Schola Cantorum,"* 54: "Aus den hier zum ersten Mal vorgelelgten Archivbeweisen lässt sich ersehen dass dieser Papst als der eigentliche Begründer der *capella palatina* betrachtet werden kann und dass durch ihn das goldene Zeitalter dieses Kunstinstitutes eingeleitet wurde." (From the archival material presented here for the first time, it can be seen that this pope can be considered to be the true founder of the *capella palatina* and that it was through him that the golden age of this artistic institution was initiated.) For the opposing view see Roth, "Zur 'Reform' der päpstlichen Kapelle."

32 Roth, "Liturgical (and Paraliturgical) Music."   33 Transcribed in Sherr, "A Curious Incident."

the late fifteenth and sixteenth centuries testify to the singers' use of it to claim benefices on the death of retired members of the chapel, some of whom had been absent from Rome for as many as twenty years. It does perhaps indicate a particularly benevolent attitude on the part of Innocent VIII toward his chapel.

What exactly did the singers do? We are much better informed about what they did in the sixteenth century; nonetheless, Burckard's notes do contain a description of their daily duties (see Appendix, B.8):

> Item: all members of the chapel are required to attend the Divine Office every day: that is, one clerk of ceremonies and one chaplain at Masses; however, the singers and bell-ringers [must attend] at Masses and all the hours; and those who are absent should be fined or punished according to the old regulations. However, the fines or punishments of the deficient should go to the Treasurer; for if they were to be given to the personnel of the chapel, they could easily collude among themselves.[34]

Haberl provides a similar description of duties from a bull promulgated by Sixtus IV:

> We command that in the apostolic palace the singers should be of a sufficient number so that every day, in the presence of the pope or not, they may sing Mass and the canonical hours in a public chapel so that those who come there recognize it as a place of prayer and are incited to devotion.[35]

These descriptions in fact concur with the list of the duties of the singers in the chapel in their Constitution of 1545, which specifies that they were to attend all the canonical hours and Mass every day of the week, apparently meaning that they worked from dawn until dusk.[36] Further, while Burckard states that one of the chaplains of the Mass was required to be present to celebrate the daily Mass, nothing is said about who should preside in the hours. The only conclusion is that in the fifteenth century as in the sixteenth, the singers themselves, acting like a cathedral chapter, were to celebrate the Offices in the Vatican Palace. Their official title, after all, was *cantores capellani*. The venue would have been the smaller chapel on the second floor of the Vatican Palace called the *Capella Sancti Nicolai*, destroyed in the sixteenth century on the construction of the *Cappella Paolina*, which took over the same function. Here, the singers were to gather every day to celebrate the daily liturgy of the Vatican Palace for anybody who cared to attend. That they also had to be

---

34 See the last paragraph of the Appendix.
35 Haberl, *Die römische "Schola Cantorum,"* 54: "Ordiniamus quod in palatio apostolico cantores in competenti numero esse debeant qui omnibus diebus sive exeat papa sive non Missam et horas canoncas in capella publice cantent ut qui illuc ingrediuntur domum illam orationis esse cognoscant et ad devotionem merito incitentur."
36 Chapters 43–49. The Constitution is transcribed in Haberl, *Die römische "Schola Cantorum,"* 96–108.

present at all papal Masses and Vespers celebrated in the Sistine Chapel was so obvious that Burckard did not need to mention it.[37] This was a very heavy workload. In the sixteenth century it also became a fiction (the full complement of Offices was only celebrated during Lent; on most days, the singers were finished after Mass [ca. 11 a.m.]), but it is possible that things were different in the fifteenth century. Burckard was also aware that singers would try to weasel out of their onerous duties on occasion, hence the mention of fines, which suggests that documents like the *Diarii Sistini* existed already in the fifteenth century.[38] The mention of the "old regulations" also implies the existence of early constitutions of the chapel.

What did they sing? If they really celebrated all the hours, then the majority of what they sang consisted of plainsong and psalm recitation. The occasions for composed polyphony were restricted largely to Vespers and Mass. The extant fifteenth-century repertory of the papal singers, preserved in the *fondo* Cappella Sistina of the Vatican Library, in fact consists entirely of polyphony for those ceremonies. But there is a problem. This repertory exists only in sources from the last decades of the fifteenth century; there are no manuscripts of polyphony in the *fondo* Cappella Sistina that predate ca. 1480. Further, it has been argued that the earliest manuscripts of polyphony in the library of the papal singers (Vatican CS14 and 51) did not originate in the papal chapel, even though they were in the library by ca. 1487 at the very latest.[39] This would leave Vatican CS 35 (compiled, according to Roth, ca. 1486–ca. 1491) as the earliest extant manuscript of polyphony copied specifically for the use of the papal singers.[40] This state of affairs led Roth to argue that the papal singers did not regularly sing composed polyphony until the end of the pontificate of Sixtus IV.[41] On the face of it this does not seem likely, especially for the beginning of the fifteenth century, considering the music that Du Fay seems to have composed for the papal chapel, although things could have changed after Du Fay left. But emphasis on plainsong did not necessarily mean the absence of polyphony. Consider, for instance, the report sent by Francesco Ariosto to Ercole d'Este describing the ceremony on Easter Sunday, 14 April 1471, when Paul II created Borso d'Este Duke of Ferrara in St. Peter's. When the High Mass started, Ariosto reported on the singing of the papal choir:

> Notwithstanding, you would have heard, Most Magnanimous divine Lord Hercules, proceeding from this chorus of most excellent singers a *concerto* of

37 In the sixteenth century, Paris de Grassis put the number of such ceremonies at five Matins, ten Vespers, and thirty-five Masses; see Sherr, "The Singers of the Papal Chapel."
38 The extant *Diarii Sistini* begin in 1535 and record precisely the fines that Burckard mentions.
39 Where is still a matter of dispute. See Sherr, ed., *Masses for the Sistine Chapel*.
40 Roth, "Die Entstehung des ältesten Chorbuches."      41 Roth, "Liturgical (and Paraliturgical) Music."

so many melodies at the beginning of the Holy Introit, receiving with marvelous signs of joy [the entrance of] His Holiness.[42]

A "concerto" of many melodies would seem to refer to polyphony, but its association with an introit also indicates that this polyphony was most likely created by complicated *contrapunctus*, improvising in many voices over plainsong. Most professional singers of the period were required to be expert in *contrapunctus*; in the sixteenth century *contrapunctus* was part of the audition of candidates for the papal choir. As Rob Wegman has argued, this kind of *contrapunctus* might have sounded no different from composed and written polyphony, yet it literally was not the same thing.[43] *Contrapunctus* was in fact a way for an emphasis on plainsong and the sound of polyphony to coexist.[44]

What does seem certain is that there was no desire to create a permanent library of polyphonic sources until the end of the fifteenth century.[45] We can only assume that sources used before then were either destroyed or considered to be the personal property of those who copied them who took them away when they left the papal chapel. The extant fifteenth-century repertory, preserved in Vatican CS 14, 51, 35, 15, and also bound into manuscripts compiled in the sixteenth century, amounts to 222 items, consisting of masses, mass sections, hymns, Magnificats, and motets by all the major composers of the fifteenth century, and there were undoubtedly more works in sources that have been lost.[46] By the end of the pontificate of Julius II in 1513, the extant repertory numbered 278 works, including 112 masses and mass sections, 110 motets, twenty-eight hymns, and twenty-eight Magnificats. If the decision to ornament papal ceremonies with composed polyphony really was taken as late as the late 1470s, then the idea certainly caught on with a vengeance. If Roth is correct, it represented a major change in the function of the choir.

I mentioned earlier that we know nothing about the sound of the papal choir. This is not strictly true. Papal bulls in favor of the chapel consistently use the phrase *sonoris/canoris vocibus* (with sonorous/melodious voices) in describing the singers, and even though this is boilerplate language, ritually repeated in bull after bull, it still may mean something real as an indication of the vocal quality that was expected of papal singers, and it is reinforced by Burckard's desire that the voices be "clear and melodious." The singers were expected to produce a loud, focused sound that would resound in the fairly large space of

---

42 "Non altramente haresti sentido, magnanime signore divo Hercole, ussire di quel choro de più excellentissimi cantori un concerto de tante melodie nello intonar quello sancto introito ricevendo cum maravigliosi signi de letitia la S. Sanctita." Quoted in Pastor, *The History of the Popes*, 4:186.
43 See Ch. 8 and Ch. 40 in this volume.    44 And this was a very special occasion.
45 A scribe was added to the chapel lists in 1497.
46 See Llorens, *Capellae Sixtinae Codices*, and Sherr, *Papal Music Manuscripts*.

the Sistine Chapel. Burckard thought the sound was terrible, but he is a prejudiced witness.

Even more interesting is the phrase that appears in the first bull in favor of the chapel promulgated by Sixtus IV on 20 June 1473, where the singers are described as "Those who delight the hearts of the audience with a certain sweet chant [melodia] and for the rest of us as we celebrate the divine service, render our acts of worship more pleasing and joyful."[47] This seems to be a rare direct reference to the real effect (or affect) of singing in the papal liturgy and why it was necessary. Roth pointed out that this does not seem to be boilerplate language (I have found it in no other papal bulls, although the word "joyful" or "with joy" (jocunditate) also turns up in the Debita consideratione bulls), and he suggested that it represents the real opinion of Sixtus IV concerning the importance of his singers to him.[48] Roth takes melodia to mean plainsong, the regular use of composed polyphony not yet having been established in the chapel in his opinion; this view might even be supported by the bull Etsi Romanus pontifex which, twenty years later, adds to the usual sonoris vocibus the words et dulcibus organis, which can only mean polyphony,[49] since there was no organ in the Sistine Chapel. Indeed, it is hard to imagine Josquin des Prez, who joined the chapel in the pontificate of Innocent VIII, wishing to be a member of an organization that would never sing his music. We will never know, of course, whether his was also one of Burckard's "worthless voices."

The papal chapel was not a static institution in the fifteenth century. Its organizational structure evolved over time, reaching the form that it was to have for centuries to come only in the 1480s. The singers were an ever-increasing portion of the total personnel (which clearly bothered Burckard) and probably had by the end of the century solidified into the College of Singers that we meet in the sixteenth century, a corporate entity fiercely jealous of its own privileges and its own financial security, and also with an inordinately high opinion of itself. The chapel attracted, if not the best singers, then certainly some of the best composers of the late fifteenth century. But the seeds of decadence had been sown. In the 1550s, the papal singer Ghiselin Danckerts proudly proclaimed the singers of the papal chapel to be superior to all other choirs in scientia (musical knowledge). At about the same time, Pope Julius III declared that most of the singers were "quite useless." In 1565,

---

47 "Illi quadam suavi melodia audientium corda letificant ac ceteris gratiora et iocundiora osequia celebrando divina officia nobis impedunt." See Roth, "Liturgical (and Paraliturgical) Music," 125. I use Roth's translation. Also quoted in Haberl, Die römische "Schola Cantorum," 54.
48 Roth, "Liturgical (and Paraliturgical) Music."     49 Sherr, "A Curious Incident."

thirteen singers were summarily dismissed, most for vocal incompetence.[50] Burckard would have approved.

## Appendix Archivio Segreto Vaticano, Miscellanea
## Arm. XI, vol. 93, fols. 133r–134r

A. Insuper inter annotationes et scripturas praefati Jo. Burchardi collegi sparsim infrascripta, que ad materiam de qua agere pertinere videntur licet sint admodum antiqua.

1. Magister Cappellae consuevit deputari a pontifice suo arbitrio sive cappellanus, seu cubicularius secretus, qui debet esse prudens, et magne reputationis, cuius officium est gubernare cantores.

2. Cantores debent esse honesti, et moderati, in musica experti, habentes voces idoneas ad serviendum cappellae et practicam bonam, et qui tales non sunt debent expelli, et alii bene qualificati subrogari. Quo ad numerum verum est quod nunquam aliquis papa habuit ultra xii et aliquando viii et ix praeter D. Nicolam papam Vtum qui habuit magnum numerum sine causa ex quo generatur confusio, et tollitur melodia, experientia quotidiana hoc probat: Et nunquam fuerunt ita ineptae et viles voces in cappella sicut hodie; provideat magister cappelle qua de honore pape et ipsius magistri cappelle agere.

3. Omnes de cappella debent omni mense habere summam quae sequitur. Primo Dominus sacrista ducati x, Magister Cappellae x, subsacrista iiii, clerici cerimoniarum semper habuerunt x ducati pro quolibet, usque ad tribulationem Eugenii iiii, postea fuerunt reducti ad v, super hoc videatur ceremoniale quod est in libreria pape. Cantores nunquam habuerunt nisi quinque ducati usque ad Nicolam papam Vtum qui cantoribus doctis et aptas voces habentibus dabat viii ducati, aliis dabat iii, iiii, v, similes quod plus aut minus merebantur, et nunquam habuerunt omnes simul octo nisi tempore Calisti papae iii. Videatur libri camere de tempore dictorum pontificum.

B. Ex alio folio sumpta sunt infrascipta videlicet

1. Modus quo cappella D.N. Pape regulari et ordinari consuevit ad laudem Dei et honorem prefati D.N. Papae

2. In primis est unus sacrista, qui consuevit esse episcopus, estque officialis perptuus, et papae immediate subiectus. Cui quidem cura est de omnibus paramentis cappellae tam secretae quam comunis et de omnibus libris utrius- que cappelle calicibus, et aliis ornamentis, et quidquid minestrant campanarii, ministrant pro sacrista.

50 Sherr, "The Counter-Reformation and the Singers of the Papal Chapel."

3. Item est unus magister cappellae immediate subiectus papae, qui debet diligenter attendere, ut per cantores horis debitis, debitaque cum reverentia, et silentio, horae canonicae nocturnae pariter et diurnae cantentur. Iste magister cappellae est officialis ad vitam papae alias ad beneplacitum papae, et per solum papam ponitur et mutatur.

4. Item sunt duo clerici cerimoniarum, qui missas habent ordinarium et alternis ebdomadis servire, cerimoniasque facere ab omnibus observati. Isti sunt officiales perpetui, ut sacrista, et per solum papam creantur.

5. Item sunt suo cappellani alternis septimanis missas quotidianas celebrantes, qui debent esse viri honesti, habentes voces mediocres, bene legentes, et pronuntiantes, et bene scientes cantum Gregorianum. Isti non sunt officiales, sed simplices servitores ad nutum mutabiles, et per magistrum cappelle possunt institui et mutari.

6. Item sunt xii cantores videlicet duo tenoristae, 4.or contratenores, et sex voices altae, quae debent esse clarae et melodiosae non raucae, nec asperae: Nimia enim multitudo vocum melodiam tollit, et confundit auditum. Isti non sunt officiales sed simplices servitores; et istos sempre consuevit magister cappellae ponere, et deponere, et mutare; quotiens visum est esse expediens honori, aut necessitati cappellae aut paci vel quieti.

7. Item sunt duo campanarii qui debent esse iuvenes humiles, et apti ad serviendum cappellae, et debent obedire officialibus cappellae in his solum, quae concernunt divinum officium. Isti sunt simplices servitores, et ad nutum revocabiles.

8. Item omnes de cappella tenentur omni die venire ad officium divinum, videlicet unus clericus cerimoniarum et unus cappellanus ad missas tamen; cantores, et campanarii ad missas, et omnes horas: et qui defuerint debent mulctari, seu puniri secundum ordinationes olim factas. Mulctae autem, seu poene deficientium debent ad thesaurarium venire; si enim applicarentur personis cappellae, facile possent inter se colludere.[51]

# Bibliography

Bölling, Jörg, *Das Papstzeremoniell der Renaissance: Texte, Musik, Performanz*, Tradition–Reform–Innovation 12, Frankfurt am Main, 2006

Fallows, David, "Specific Information on the Ensembles for Composed Polyphony, 1400–1474," in *Studies in the Performance of Late Medieval Music*, ed. Stanley Boorman, Cambridge, 1983, 109–59

---

51 The Latin text has been published in Sherr, "Competence and Incompetence" and earlier in Llorens, "Los Maestros de la Capilla Apostolica."

Günther, Ursula, "Zur Biographie einiger Komponisten der Ars subtilior," *AfMw* 21 (1964), 172–99

Haberl, Franz Xaver, *Die römische "Schola Cantorum" und die päpstlichen Kapellsänger bis zur Mitte des 16. Jahrhunderts*, Bausteine für Musikgeschichte 3, Leipzig, 1888

Janz, Bernhard, ed., *Collectanea II: Studien zur Geschichte der Päpstlichen Kapelle: Tagungsbericht Heidelberg 1989*, Capellae Apostolicae Sixtinaeque Collectanea Acta Monumenta 4, Vatican City, 1994

Llorens, José, *Capellae Sixtinae Codices musicis notis instructi sive manu scripti sive praelo excussi*, Studi e testi 202, Vatican City, 1960

"Los Maestros de la Capilla Apostolica hasta el Pontificado de Sixto V (1585–1590)," *Anuario musical* 43 (1988), 35–65

Pastor, Ludwig von, *The History of the Popes from the Close of the Middle Ages, Drawn from the Secret Archives of the Vatican and Other Original Sources*, trans. Frederick Ignatius Antrobus, Ralph Francis Kerr, *et al.*, St. Louis, MO, 1898–1953

Picker, Martin, "The Career of Marbriano de Orto (ca. 1450–1529)," in *Collectanea II*, ed. Janz, 529–58

Pietschmann, Klaus, "Die Graffiti auf der Sängerkanzel der Cappella Sistina: Vollständiger Katalog und Dokumentation," in *Institutionalisierung als Prozess: Organisationsformen musikalischer Eliten im Europa des 15. und 16. Jahrhunderts. Beiträge des internationalen Arbeitsgespräches im Istituto Svizzero di Roma in Verbindung mit dem Deutschen Historischen Institut in Rom, 9.–11. Dezember 2005*, ed. Birgit Lodes and Laurenz Lütteken = *Analecta Musicologica* 43 (2009), 225–73 (+ CD ROM)

Planchart, Alejandro Enrique, "Guillaume Du Fay's Benefices and his Relationship to the Court of Burgundy," *EMH* 8 (1988), 117–71

"Relations between Cambrai and the Papal Chapel from 1417 to 1447," in *Collectanea II*, ed. Janz, 559–74

Roth, Adalbert, "Die Entstehung des ältesten Chorbuches mit polyphoner Musik der päpstlichen Kapelle: Città del Vaticano, Biblioteca Apostolica Vaticana, Fondo Cappella Sistina, Ms. 35," in *Gestalt und Enstehung musikalischer Quellen im 15. und 16. Jahrhundert*, ed. Martin Staehelin, Wolfenbüttler Forschungen 83, Wiesbaden, 1998, 43–64

"Liturgical (and Paraliturgical) Music in the Papal Chapel towards the End of the Fifteenth Century: A Repertory in Embryo," in *Papal Music and Musicians*, ed. Sherr, 125–37

"'Primus in Petri aede Sixtus perpetuae harmoniae cantores introduxit': Alcune osservazioni sul patronato musicale di Sisto IV," in *Un pontificato ed una città: Sisto IV (1471–1484). Atti del convegno Roma 3–7 dicembre 1984*, ed. Massimo Miglio *et al.*, Rome, 1986, 217–41

"La storia della Cappella Pontificia nel Quattrocento rispecchiata nel Fondo Camerale I dell'Archivio di Stato di Roma," in *La musica a Roma attraverso le fonti d'archivio*, ed. Bianca Maria Antolini, Arnaldo Morelli, and Vita Vera Spagnuolo, Lucca, 1994, 433–55

*Studien zum frühen Repertoire der päpstlichen Kapelle unter dem Pontifikat Sixtus IV (1471–1484): Die Chorbücher 14 und 51 des Fondo Cappella Sistina der Biblioteca Apostolica Vaticana*, Capellae Apostolicae Sixtinaeque Collectanea Acta Monumenta 1, Vatican City, 1991

"Zur 'Reform' der päpstlichen Kapelle unter dem Pontifikat Sixtus' IV. (1471–1484)," in *Zusammenhänge, Einflüsse, Wirkungen: Kongressakten zum ersten*

*Symposium der Mediävisten in Tübingen 1984*, ed. Jörg O. Fichte *et al.*, Berlin, 1984, 168–95

Schimmelpfennig, Bernhard, "Die Funktion der Cappella Sistina im Zeremoniell der Renaissancepäpste," in *Collectanea II*, ed. Janz, 123–74

Sherr, Richard, "Competence and Incompetence in the Papal Choir in the Age of Palestrina," *EM* 22 (1994), 606–29

"The Counter-Reformation and the Singers of the Papal Chapel," in *La Papauté à la Renaissance: Actes du colloque tenu en juillet 2003 au Centre d'Études Supérieures de la Renaissance à Tours*, ed. Florence Alazard and Frank La Brasca, Savoir de Mantice 12, Paris, 2007, 711–28

"A Curious Incident in the Institutional History of the Papal Choir," in *Papal Music and Musicians*, ed. Sherr, 187–210

"The Papal Chapel ca. 1492–1513 and its Polyphonic Sources," Ph.D. diss., Princeton University, 1975

*Papal Music Manuscripts in the Late Fifteenth and Early Sixteenth Centuries*, Renaissance Manuscript Studies 5, Neuhausen, 1996

"The Singers of the Papal Chapel and Liturgical Ceremonies in the Early Sixteenth Century: Some Documentary Evidence," in *Rome in the Renaissance, the City and the Myth*, ed. Paul A. Ramsey, Binghamton, NY, 1982, 249–64

ed., *Masses for the Sistine Chapel: Vatican City, Biblioteca Apostolica Vaticana, Cappella Sistina, MS 14*, Monuments of Renaissance Music 13, Chicago, 2009

ed., *Papal Music and Musicians in Late Medieval and Renaissance Rome*, Oxford, 1998

Starr, Pamela, "Music and Music Patronage at the Papal Court 1447–1464," Ph.D. diss., Yale University, 1987

"Rome as the Centre of the Universe: Papal Grace and Music Patronage," *EMH* 11 (1992), 223–62

"Strange Obituaries: The Historical Uses of the *per obitum* Supplication," in *Papal Music and Musicians*, ed. Sherr, 177–86

"Towards the Cappella Sistina: A Profile of the Cappella Pontificia during the Pontificates of Nicholas V, Calixtus III, Pius II, and Paul II (1447–1471)," in *Collectanea II*, ed. Janz, 451–76

# The beneficial system and fifteenth-century polyphony

PAMELA F. STARR

Early Catholic and Protestant reformers weighed in heavily against abuses by the clergy, and by those appointing the clergy to an ecclesiastical office, or benefice. Succinctly put by papal historian Geoffrey Barraclough:

> Throughout the later Middle Ages, the propensity of the curia to turn its administration of provisions into a money-making apparatus, the conferment of benefices on foreigners, the unsuitability of providees, and the attendant evils of pluralism, non-residence, and the burdening of churches with expectancies to non-vacant benefices continued to be the main practical charges in the indictment which was gradually formulated against the centralized papal administration of the Beneficial System of the Church.[1]

The critique was put even more sharply by the Dutch reformer Erasmus: "Now the general run of priests ... good Lord, how stoutly they fight for their right to tithes, with sword, spear, stones, with every imaginable armed force"; by the Basel Protestant theologian and reformer Lampadius:

> If you want to know what embitters Christian hearts, it is this: that they recognize the true worship of God and God's righteousness and then see that this is hindered by the false prophets, and all sorts of abuses continue to be practiced, although they are a great abomination before God, such as simony, priests who do nothing (i.e. who don't work), fornication, drunkenness, *possessing many benefices*, etc.

[italics mine]; and by the deeply cynical author Rabelais in his *Pantagruel*:

> "I'd be glad," said Epistemon, "to pay for a bucket of tripes, if we could collate some of those horrific chapters with their originals – *Execrabilis, De multa, Si plures, De annatis per totum, Nisi essent, Cum ad monasterium, Quod dilecti,*

---

1 Barraclough, *Papal Provisions*, 14.

*Mandatum* and a few others, which take four hundred thousand ducats a year, and maybe more, out of France and send it off to Rome."[2]

Not coincidentally, the abuses alluded to above reached their high-water mark during the century preceding the Protestant Reformation, as clergy in the tens of thousands lodged their requests to the Holy See for the provision of ecclesiastical benefices by the fifteenth-century popes. These provisions, and the abuses that resulted, certainly played their part in the Protestant Reformation, as well as in the reforms promulgated during the Council of Trent. The eventual phasing out of the so-called "beneficial system" (more usually termed the system of papal provision of ecclesiastical benefices), was viewed by Reformation historians as one of the signal achievements of religious reform during this period. What has been less well appreciated – at least until a few decades ago – was the enormous gift to the history of fifteenth-century sacred polyphony provided by this same beneficial system, within which composers, performers, and music institutions flourished. It is safe to say that had music patrons of the late Middle Ages been denied the benefits of a system that supplemented the comparatively small salaries they could provide their musicians, the history of music in that century might have turned out quite differently. In this chapter I shall discuss the evolution of the medieval beneficial system and its culmination in the fifteenth century; demonstrate briefly how the system worked; and, finally, discuss the salutary effects of the system upon musicians, patrons, rulers, and the papacy, as well as on our understanding of music and musicians of that century.

## On benefices and how the "system" developed

An ecclesiastical benefice was defined officially in Canon Law as "a juridical entity established or constituted in perpetuity by competent ecclesiastical authority, consisting of a sacred office and with the right of collecting the revenues from the endowment attached to the office."[3] Put more simply, it was a position held by an ordained clergyman, together with the income that permitted him to function in that capacity. The medieval church further defined benefices in a number of ways: by the body granting the benefice ("major," or consistorial benefices were granted by the Consistory, the popes' advisory council of Cardinals; "minor" benefices of all types were

---

2 Erasmus, *The Praise of Folly*, 114; Oecolampadius, *Widerlegung der falsche gründt*, sigs. A4v–B1r (I thank my colleague Professor Amy Burnett for assistance with the translation of this quotation), and Rabelais, *Pantagruel*, bk. 4, ch. 53, in *Gargantua and Pantagruel*, 401–2. The speaker in *Pantagruel* is complaining about the papal edicts that reserved benefices in France (and everywhere) to the collation of the pope.
3 Canon 1409, *Corpus juris canonici*, Rome, 1917.

those granted by another agency, including the pope himself); by the type of clergy designated, either "regular" (i.e., member of a religious order) or "secular"; and by the nature of the duties and functions of the holder of the benefice. The vast majority of benefices conferred on the musical clergy during this period were "minor," "secular," and either with "cure of souls" (i.e., a priesthood of a parish church) or without "cure of souls" (the offices of chantry priest and canon and other officials serving in a cathedral or collegiate church). The latter were by far the preferred type of benefice, because they could be accumulated and held without recourse to papal dispensation.

Each of these benefices came with its own stipend. Some, for example the priesthoods serving wealthy parish churches, and canonries in well-endowed collegiate churches and cathedrals, were generous, yielding as much as 24 florins per annum, the florin being the standard unit of currency at the papal court and in its documents.[4] The incomes from several benefices could be held simultaneously by one clergyman, and – minus a small amount to reimburse the delegated replacements – the clergyman could retain the incomes for himself. It made a comfortable supplement to the salaries of those serving court establishments, and, in particular, those serving at the papal court. Because of their early training in the *maîtrises* of northern France and the Low Countries, and their duties in the chapels of secular rulers, many – indeed, most – fifteenth-century musicians were ordained clergy, and equipped, therefore, to partake fully and enthusiastically of the beneficial system. As will be shown, the musicians serving the pope were in a particularly advantageous position in this regard.

The medieval period saw an arresting change in the manner in which benefices were conferred.[5] At the end of the eleventh century, collation, or appointment to a benefice, was in the hands of the official in control of the territory or institution where the benefice was situated. It could be the Ordinary (Bishop) of a diocese, the chapter of a cathedral or collegiate church, or even a lay patron who had the collation (or "gift") of a particular benefice. Over the two centuries that followed, collation came to be largely concentrated in the hands of the popes. During the fourteenth century one would imagine the papacy to have been weakened, first by its transfer away from Rome to the French city of Avignon, and then by the Schism, when two, then three rival popes contended for supremacy. But in fact, the popes of this

4 10 florins would purchase a good suit of clothes in the mid-fifteenth century; a horse would cost 25 florins or more. Starr, "Music and Music Patronage," 93–94.
5 What follows is a brief summary of information presented in Starr, "Music and Music Patronage," 24–31, which in turn relies on Barraclough, *Papal Provisions*; Mollat, *La Collation des bénéfices*; and a number of specialized studies indicated in Starr, "Music and Music Patronage."

century were hugely successful in accumulating extraordinary powers, in particular over the provision of benefices to clergy. They accomplished this through three broad strategies: the use of mandates of provision, reservations, and expectative graces, or expectatives. The details of papal strategy in these arenas are convoluted and complex, and probably of more interest to historical scholars of the fourteenth century. In this chapter I can only briefly summarize this history.

The least controversial strategy, mandates, simply involved a request to the Ordinary with power of collation over a benefice to confer it on the papal choice of clergy. Eventually these requests became peremptory directives, as the pope co-opted benefices throughout the dioceses of western Europe. Through general reservation, the popes transferred large categories of benefices en masse from various dioceses to the control of the Apostolic See. Expectatives involved control over benefices when they were released by their incumbents at death. As with the other types, expectative benefices increasingly came under the control of the popes. By the end of the papal Schism, the popes in Rome were empowered to bestow most of the benefices aspired to by clergy, including musicians and their employers. Moreover, it was the sole prerogative of the popes to issue the dispensations that would enable clergy to hold benefices when otherwise rendered ineligible, as for example when suffering from the defect of illegitimate birth or trying to accumulate offices forbidden by canon law, such as parish priesthoods, or to hold multiple benefices in absentia. The desire for benefices, and for the enabling legislation to hold them, promulgated many thousands of official documents lodged at the papal court, including petitions from musician clergy and from their secular employers, kings, princes, dukes, and the popes themselves.

## How the beneficial system operated

In the course of the later Middle Ages, a substantial bureaucracy established itself at the papal Curia specifically to process the massive number of requests for benefices lodged from all dioceses in western Europe. The Chancery offices that dealt with such petitions, or supplications, were staffed with legal experts, scribes, and other functionaries, many of whom became part of the circle of elite humanists in Renaissance Rome.[6]

A petition to the pope followed a labyrinthine course of documents submitted, corrected, copied, and distributed. As with most government

---

6 On humanists at the papal Curia, see especially D'Amico, *Renaissance Humanism*; O'Malley, *Praise and Blame in Renaissance Rome*; and Partner, *The Pope's Men*.

bureaucracies, no document was discarded until it had been copied meticulously into registers, the majority of which survive to this day in the storage shelves of the Archivio Segreto Vaticano (ASV), or Vatican Archives. The ASV is the repository of most of the documents that pertained to clergy from the Middle Ages and subsequent historical periods. So, while mastering the minutiae of the process of acquiring a benefice and of the formularies that guided the process would probably have only interested officials in the papal Chancery, understanding the broad lines of the process and the diplomatics of the documents was essential to the petitioners and their representatives at the papal Curia. These details continue to occupy historians hoping to glean information about the petitioners represented there.[7]

A request for the provision of a benefice by the pope usually began its journey somewhere other than Rome, at the residence of the petitioner.[8] Vital information about the benefice and the petitioner would be sent on to his procurator, a representative in Rome with the expertise to inaugurate and see the process through to its hopefully successful conclusion.[9] The procurator would deliver his information – the raw material that would be drafted into a supplication – to a scribe in the office of supplications, the first legal document of the process. The formulary for supplications, as for all subsequent documents in the process, was precise and exacting. The information it presented was presumed to be correct. Misinformation, even as trivial as the spelling of a proper name, could invalidate the benefice.[10] In the Appendix the reader will see a transcription of a comparatively simple supplication, with its formula of chancery legalese.[11] This is a supplication from two musicians, Florentius Alexandry and Benedictus Sirede (also called Benoit) – colleagues originally from Ferrara – who were beginning their appointments in the papal chapel. The document employs the customary formula, language, and scribal abbreviations, and presents the names of the two petitioners, their clerical status

7 The best English-language guide to the documents emanating from the papal Curia and housed in the Vatican Archives remains Boyle's *A Survey of the Vatican Archives*. See also Boyle, "The Papal Chancery," xv–xxiv. A detailed discussion in English of the various curial offices and the documents produced there as they concerned papal musicians can be found in Sherr, "The Papal Chapel," 2–19, and Starr, "Music and Music Patronage," 36–62.

8 The major exceptions were, of course, the members of the papal chapel, who, because of their continuous residence at the papal court, and for other reasons mentioned below, submitted their petitions by the hundreds over the course of the century.

9 I have detailed the procuratorial process using the papal musician Johannes Puyllois, one of the few known – and indubitably most successful – musician procurators, as he negotiated the curial offices on behalf of a colleague, Johannes Okeghem. See Starr, "Music and Music Patronage," 36–62; and idem, "Rome as the Centre of the Universe," 228–34.

10 Hence, the versions "Okeghem" and "Du Fay" in this chapter. These versions appear consistently in the documents preserved at the ASV, and are presumed to be the correct spellings of their names.

11 This document also appears in Starr, "The 'Ferrara Connection'," with a transcription and discussion of its implications.

(priest and cleric, respectively), the diocese of affiliation (Therouanne and Sens), the professional position held (members of the papal chapel and therefore *continuans commensales* of the pope), the title and location, and status of the benefice requested (in this case, any and all benefices becoming vacant through the death of the incumbent or expected to be vacant in the future), closing with the papal "fiat" of concession and the official date that the petition was granted.[12]

As the foundational document for the paper trail that continued and completed the beneficial process through its conferral and collation, the papal supplication contained the fullest statement of information about the benefice and the clergy involved.[13] It went on to the office of the Datary, where the official date of conferral was registered;[14] to the Bullarium, where the letter of provision would be drafted that would be sent to the institution housing the benefice (the *bulla*, or lead seal, gave its name to the document, the papal bull); and to the office where the Annates, or fees surrounding the provision, were assessed and then paid by the procurator.

One might assume that at this final stage, the benefice was well and truly collated to the petitioner. But many documents housed at the Vatican Archives attest to difficulties experienced in actually taking possession of the benefice, especially if it was contested by a rival supplicant or the officials of the church where it was housed. So we cannot always determine if a musician actually succeeded to the benefice until his death, which was also duly registered – once again in registers housed at the papal Curia, in documents from other clergy requesting the benefices released by the death of their incumbent.[15]

I have produced this severely abbreviated description of the process of acquiring a benefice from the papal Curia for two reasons. First, to demonstrate the complexity of the process, and therefore the remarkable persistence of musician clergy, both those serving in the papal chapel and those far from Rome, in the acquisition of benefices that could provide a lucrative supplement to their income as performers, and after retirement. And second, to suggest

---

12 The reader will also observe the phrase at the beginning of the document, "motu proprio," implying an action taken at the instigation of the pope himself. Comparatively few supplications carry this phrase, as it was reserved for servants and honored associates. It carried a distinct priority in the case of multiple petitions for the same benefice. It should also be realized that the pope did not actually lodge such a petition: it very likely came from someone in the papal household, in this case probably from the *magister capellae* on behalf of the two chapel musicians. There is a healthy literature on the papal supplication. In addition to the works cited above, one might usefully conssult Katterbach, *Specimina supplicationum*.

13  This is undoubtedly why many historians have focused their attention on the supplications, extracting published calendars of the documents relating to specific countries and periods from the thousands of *Registri supplicationum*, which remain unindexed to this day.

14  The official date on which the supplication was granted by the pope was crucial. It established priority over the benefice, if requested or contested by other clergy. See Celier, *Les Dataires du XV^e siècle*, 73–74.

15  See Starr, "Strange Obituaries," 177–86.

how uniquely powerful the Vatican Archives are as a source of information about the thousands of musicians seeking benefices in the later Middle Ages.[16]

## Who benefited from the beneficial system?

As in any historical process, history records both winners and losers, and so it was with the beneficial system. The clear "losers" were the parishes who offered up their tithes and received priests who were either unqualified or absent, with pastoral care provided by a paid stipendiary chosen by the incumbent. Certainly no musician clergy in possession of such an office was known actually to perform the pastoral duties required. Cathedrals and collegiate churches, too, suffered when seats in the choirstalls were vacant, their occupants far away serving in a secular chapel of a prince or pope. (These churches eventually might benefit from the return from court service of their wayward canons in retirement, for example, as with Du Fay's return to the cathedral of Cambrai at the end of his career.)

In the column of "winners" were those same princes and popes. The beneficial system had its risks and rewards in the delicate dance of fifteenth-century politics.[17] In one well-studied example, popes of the mid-fifteenth century negotiated considerable pushback by the French Crown in the matter of benefices, resulting in the promulgation of the Pragmatic Sanction of Bourges, which accorded power over many benefices in France to the king, and bound pope and king in alliance (frequently an uneasy one).[18]

The fifteenth century saw the flowering of secular princely chapels, staffed with musicians adept at the performance, and frequently the composition, of sacred polyphony. The chapel served as the most visible (and audible) emblem of political power and authority, impressing visiting diplomats, courtiers, and nobility with courtly civility and wealth represented by a sacred establishment highlighted by the performance of polyphony. Courtiers were charged

---

16 Thanks to the dedicated and protracted labor at the ASV of a few scholars, Alejandro Enrique Planchart, Adalbert Roth, Richard Sherr, and the present author, the documents pertaining to musicians, and especially musicians serving the popes, have been retrieved from the vast and mostly unindexed repository of volumes emanating from the Curia and now housed at the ASV. Although various projects to digitize this information have been launched, to this date no complete database of all information drawn from the Vatican documents concerning musicians has been produced. However, I will take this opportunity to mention that I have been, and remain, ready to supply such information from my own personal, non-electronic files upon request to any scholar.

17 See Thomson, *Popes and Princes*, 145–66, for an elegant analysis of the politics of benefices during this century.

18 Ibid., 159–65. Among the individual studies of the Pragmatic Sanction, classics include Valois, *Histoire de la Pragmatique Sanction*, and Bourdon, "L'Abrogation de la Pragmatique." On the impact of the Pragmatic Sanction on a benefice concerning Okeghem, see Wexler, "The Politics of Ockeghem's Canonicate."

with the recruitment of skilled musicians, and were themselves skilled at manipulating the beneficial system to lure prospects to the court of their employer.[19] One of the more dazzling displays of this manipulation centered on the late fifteenth-century *tenorista* Jean Cordier, who by all testimony was one of the most gifted performers of the century. The competition for his services included the courts of Milan, Naples, Burgundy, and Rome.[20] On the other hand, sometimes recruitment per se was not needed. The papal chapel took its place among the most illustrious music chapels of the fifteenth century in large part because its members automatically had privileged access to benefices, as *capellani continuans commensales* of their employer, the pope.[21]

Whether or not they were being recruited for their gifts as performers or composers, musicians of this period took full advantage of the system in order to obtain one or more benefices to supplement their monthly salary as chapel musicians. They frequently used that status as a persuasive element in the language of the supplication for a benefice, as for example Guillaume Du Fay did in 1454 when he described himself as *primum capellanum*, first chaplain, or master of the chapel of the Duke of Savoy.[22]

But it was not the great composers of this era – *inter alia* Johannes Okeghem, Du Fay, Jacob Obrecht, and Josquin des Prez – who worked hardest and most successfully at the accumulation of ecclesiastical benefices. Many lesser lights did better than these great figures. Among these, the gold would have to go to Johannes Puyllois, a *Kleinmeister* by all accounts as a composer, and a performer of – apparently – ordinary abilities, who nonetheless in the course of his career obtained twelve benefices in the dioceses of Cambrai and Utrecht – this, in addition to his assistance in obtaining a benefice for Okeghem, as mentioned above. The income from Puyllois's benefices yielded a considerable estate which he passed on to his family at his death.[23] It seems clear that Puyllois's success in acquiring benefices owed much to his longevity in the papal chapel, and to his mastery of chancery procedures while serving at the papal court.

The possession of one or more benefices also served musicians as comfortable retirement plans, when it was time to end active service as a salaried member of a

---

19 Early studies of this phenomenon include Noble, "New Light on Josquin's Benefices"; Sherr, "The Papal Chapel"; Lockwood, *Music in Renaissance Ferrara*, 173–95; Reynolds, "Musical Careers, Ecclesiastical Benefices"; and Perkins, "Musical Patronage at the Royal Court of France."

20 A conspectus of the known facts of Cordier's life and career is set out in Starr, "Musical Entrepreneurship," 124–26. There, the reader will find a comprehensive listing of the studies on Cordier, including useful treatments on the use of benefices by the Sforza family in Milan by Paul Merkley, Lora Matthews, and Patrick Macey.

21 Starr, "Music and Music Patronage," 208–11.

22 Starr, "Rome as the Centre of the Universe," 234–38 and 258–59; Planchart, "Guillaume Du Fay's Benefices," 139.

23 See Starr, "Music and Music Patronage," 171–75, and "Musical Entrepreneurship" for a list and locations of his benefices, and for a facsimile of his will.

music chapel. The goal was to secure a benefice at a church near one's place of birth or early education, which for most was a diocese in northern France or the Low Countries. There, the possessor would occupy the canon's stall that he previously held *in absentia*. He might serve in a musical capacity, perhaps, like Du Fay, training choirboys at the cathedral of Cambrai and assisting with the copying of music books, or by contributing administrative expertise to the daily conduct of the chapter.[24] Even in death the beneficial system was exploited by musicians, who lodged frequently successful petitions for the accumulated benefices relinquished by their deceased colleagues.[25]

In sum, many among the fifteenth-century elite benefited from this system. But perhaps even greater benefits have accrued to scholars of our own century, who have made skillful use of the documents promulgated by this beneficial system. A fairly recent and quite spectacular example has been the discoveries by music historians Lora Matthews and Paul Merkley. Their work with documents from the ASV, among others, resulted in a thoroughgoing revision of Josquin's biography, in particular his name, date of birth, and early career. This, in turn, has cast wide ripples in our previous understanding of dating, provenance, and even ascription of some of Josquin's greatest works.[26] Not only Josquin's, but the biographies of nearly all the musical luminaries of the fifteenth century – Du Fay, Okeghem, Antoine Busnoys, Johannes Regis, and Obrecht, to cite just the pinnacle group – have, in the last three decades or so, been significantly revised and expanded through the use of documents produced by the beneficial process.[27]

As useful as the beneficial system has been for revising the details of career and biography of individual composers, of greater or lesser status, a far more significant use of the beneficial documents, in the opinion of this author, has been in establishing the prosopography of the musicians of this period. Beginning with the pioneering article by Christopher Reynolds in 1984, a number of scholars have focused on strategies to sharpen and deepen the profile of the fifteenth-century musician – where he came from, where he trained, where he worked, whom he knew, and where and when he retired and died.[28] For one example, we had always suspected that the typical musicians came from the Low Countries and France, without, in many cases,

24 On Du Fay's final years in Cambrai see Wright, "Dufay at Cambrai," 194–99, and Fallows, *Dufay*, 73–80.
25 Starr, "Strange Obituaries."
26 Matthews and Merkley, "Iudochus de Picardia and Jossequin Lebloitte dit Desprez"; Matthews and Merkley, "Josquin Desprez, Singer of King René d'Anjou"; Matthews, "Josquin Desprez and Ascanio Sforza"; Fallows, *Josquin*.
27 See, for just a few examples, Planchart, "Guillaume Du Fay's Benefices"; Wexler, "The Politics of Ockeghem's Canonicate"; Wegman, *Born for the Muses*; Gallagher, *Johannes Regis*; and Merkley, "Josquin Desprez in Ferrara."
28 Reynolds, "Musical Careers, Ecclesiastical Benefices."

strongly supporting documentation. Now, documents from the papal court, supplementing sometimes fragmentary information from local archives, have supplied much more precise data about the dioceses of origin of these musicians.[29] The preponderance of fifteenth-century musicians did, in fact, derive from Normandy, the Île-de-France, Picardy, Artois, Flanders, Hainaut, Brabant, and the bishoprics of Liège and Utrecht, as historians had suspected. But we also know authoritatively that some hailed from unsuspected locations in southern France, Spain, Italy, and even eastern Europe.[30]

From these documents scholars have also refined and expanded the profiles of the institutions in which these musicians spent their careers. *Rotuli* (extended supplications presented as a *rotulus*, or scroll) were submitted by the patrons of music chapels at the courts of Burgundy, France, Spain, Naples, Anjou, Savoy, and the Empire, requesting benefices or related privileges for their chaplains and musical personnel. These documents can supplement often imprecise or non-existent court records, permitting a more detailed understanding of the constituency of music chapels during this period.[31] One of the most interesting revelations from these documents has been the clear confirmation of the notion of musician itinerancy during this period: the tendency to wander from court to court and church to church, serving briefly before moving on.[32]

The beneficial system and the documents it created have thus played a significant role in enhancing the understanding of the musicians and musical institutions of this period – so much so that musicology students of the period are encouraged to acquire the skills to read and interpret these documents. But in contemplating the bottom line, the principal beneficiaries of the system of papal provisions would have to be all of us who have succumbed to the ravishing sonorities, constructive complexity and elegance, and expressive power of fifteenth-century polyphony, sacred and secular, through the centuries of its existence. Let me invoke, at the conclusion of this chapter, another early Protestant reformer, Martin Luther. He had, to be sure, the same antipathy to abuses of the clergy as his reforming colleagues. But he also had some experience and expertise in the polyphonic music of his age, the music that came into being in part because of the patronage of papal

---

29 Many of these studies center on a specific geographic region or city, for example, Strohm, *Music in Late Medieval Bruges*; D'Accone, *The Civic Muse*; and Kisby, ed., *Music and Musicians in Renaissance Cities and Towns*.

30 Starr, "Music and Music Patronage," 198–222.

31 See, among numerous studies centering on fifteenth-century chapels, Wright, *Music at the Court of Burgundy*; Lockwood, *Music in Renaissance Ferrara*; Atlas, *Music at the Aragonese Court*; and Merkley and Merkley, *Music and Patronage in the Sforza Court*.

32 See Reynolds, *Papal Patronage*, 33–59.

provisions. In his writings he would declare this music as "the excellent gift of God," and further: "I place music next to theology and give it highest praise."[33] Fifteenth-century polyphony also stands as the cornerstone for musical style of subsequent centuries. Let *that* be the enduring legacy of the beneficial system.

## Appendix Archivio Segreto Vaticano, Registra Supplicationum 447, fol. 231r

Motu proprio volumus et mandamus dilectos filios Florentium Alexandri, presbyterum Morinensis diocesis ac Benedictum Syrede, clericum Senonensis diocesis, familiares continuos commensales nostros ac in capella nostra capellanos numero et consortio aliorum cantorum et capellanorum aliorumque etiam familiarium nostrum continuorum commensalium in certo libro cancellarie apostolice ut quibusdam prerogativis, antelationibus, declarationibus, favoribus, concessionibus, et indultis assecutione beneficiorum ecclesiasticorum que vigor gratiarum suarum expectativarum per nos eis concessarum et concedendarum expectant gaudere debeant descriptoris agregari et pro talibus in eadem cancellaria ac in ipso libro describi, ita pro ipsi et eorum quilibet in simili assecutione beneficiorum que vigor gratiarum eis factarum et faciendarum omnibus et singulis prerogativis, antelationibus, exceptionibus, declarationibus, favoribus, et indultis eisdem descriptis concessis et concedendis per ... et absque differentia in omnibus et per Omnia uti frui et gaudere possint et debeant etiam perinde ac si a principio in ipso libro quo adhoc descripti fuissent. Fiat quod describantur. Datum Rome apud Sanctum Petrum decimo nono kalendis februarii Anno quarto [14 January 1451].

## Bibliography

Atlas, Allan, *Music at the Aragonese Court of Naples*, Cambridge, 1985

Barraclough, Geoffrey, *Papal Provisions: Aspects of Church History, Constitutional, Legal and Administrative, in the Later Middle Ages*, Oxford, 1935

Bourdon, Pierre, "L'Abrogation de la Pragmatique et les règles de la chancellerie de Pie II," *Mélanges d'archéologie et d'histoire* 28 (1908), 207–24

Boyle, Leonard, "The Papal Chancery at the End of the Fifteenth Century," in *Calendar of Entries in the Papal Registers Relating to Great Britain and Ireland: Papal Letters, 1484–1492*, 15, ed. Michael J. Haren, Dublin, 1978, xv–xxiv

*A Survey of the Vatican Archives and its Medieval Holdings*, Toronto, 1972

---

33   Quoted in Robin Leaver, "Luther, Martin," in *Grove Music Online* (accessed 7 October 2012).

Celier, Léonce, *Les Dataires du XV<sup>e</sup> siècle et les origines de la Daterie Apostolique*, Bibliothèque des Écoles Françaises d'Athènes et de Rome 103, Paris, 1910

D'Accone, Frank A., *The Civic Muse: Music and Musicians in Siena during the Middle Ages and the Renaissance*, Chicago, 1997

D'Amico, John, *Renaissance Humanism in Papal Rome: Humanists and Churchmen on the Eve of the Reformation*, Baltimore, 1983

Erasmus Roterodamus, Desiderius, *The Praise of Folly*, trans. Clarence H. Miller, New Haven, 1979

Fallows, David, *Dufay*, 2nd edn., New York, 1988

*Josquin*, Turnhout, 2009

Gallagher, Sean, *Johannes Regis*, Turnhout, 2010

Katterbach, Bruno, *Specimina supplicationum ex registris vaticanis*, Rome, 1927

Kisby, Fiona, ed., *Music and Musicians in Renaissance Cities and Towns*, Cambridge, 2001

Lockwood, Lewis, *Music in Renaissance Ferrara, 1400–1505: The Creation of a Musical Center in the Italian Renaissance*, Cambridge, MA, 1984

Matthews, Lora, "Josquin Desprez and Ascanio Sforza: A Singer in the Cardinal's Retinue," in *Chant and its Peripheries: Essays in Honour of Terence Bailey*, ed. Bryan Gillingham and Paul Merkley, Ottawa, 1998, 359–69

and Paul Merkley, "Josquin Desprez, Singer of King René d'Anjou," paper delivered at the annual meeting of the American Musicological Society, Toronto, 2000

and Paul Merkley, "Iudochus de Picardia and Jossequin Lebloitte dit Desprez: The Names of the Singer(s)," *JM* 16 (1998), 200–26

Merkley, Paul, "Josquin Desprez in Ferrara," *JM* 18 (2001), 544–83

and Lora Merkley, *Music and Patronage in the Sforza Court*, Turnhout, 1999

Mollat, Guillaume, *La Collation des bénéfices ecclésiastiques sous les papes d'Avignon (1305–1378)*, Bibliothèque de l'Institut de Droit Canonique, Université de Strasbourg, Paris, 1921

Noble, Jeremy, "New Light on Josquin's Benefices," in *Josquin des Prez: Proceedings of the International Josquin Festival-Conference Held at the Juilliard School at Lincoln Center in New York City 21–25 June 1971*, ed. Edward Lowinsky and Bonnie J. Blackburn, London, 1976, 76–102

Oecolampadius, Johannes, *Widerlegung der falsche gründt/ so Augustinus Marius Thuomb predicant zu Basel/ zu verwenen das die Meß ein Opffer sey*, Basel, 1528

O'Malley, John, *Praise and Blame in Renaissance Rome: Rhetoric, Doctrine, and Reform in the Sacred Orators of the Papal Court, c. 1450–1521*, Durham, NC, 1979

Partner, Peter, *The Pope's Men: The Papal Civil Service in the Renaissance*, Oxford, 1990

Perkins, Leeman L., "Musical Patronage at the Royal Court of France under Charles VII and Louis XI (1422–83)," *JAMS* 37 (1984), 507–66

Planchart, Alejandro E., "Guillaume Du Fay's Benefices and his Relationship to the Court of Burgundy," *EMH* 8 (1988), 117–71

Rabelais, François, *Gargantua and Pantagruel*, trans. Burton Raffel, New York, 1990

Reynolds, Christopher, "Musical Careers, Ecclesiastical Benefices, and the Example of Johannes Brunet," *JAMS* 37 (1984), 49–97

*Papal Patronage and the Music of St. Peter's, 1380–1513*, Berkeley, 1995

Sherr, Richard, "The Papal Chapel ca. 1492–1513 and its Polyphonic Sources," Ph.D. diss, Princeton University, 1975

The beneficial system and fifteenth-century polyphony 475

Starr, Pamela F., "The 'Ferrara Connection': A Case Study of Musical Recruitment in the Renaissance," *Studi Musicali* 18 (1989), 3–17

"Music and Music Patronage at the Papal Court, 1447–1464," Ph.D. diss., Yale University, 1987

"Musical Entrepreneurship in 15th-Century Europe," *EM* 32 (2004), 119–33

"Rome as the Centre of the Universe: Papal Grace and Music Patronage," *EMH* 11 (1992), 223–62

"Southern Exposure: Roman Light on Johannes Regis," *Revue belge de musicologie* 49 (1995), 27–38

"Strange Obituaries: The Historical Uses of the *per obitum* Supplication," in *Papal Music and Musicians in Late Medieval and Renaissance Rome*, ed. Richard Sherr, Oxford, 1998, 177–86

Strohm, Reinhard, *Music in Late Medieval Bruges*, rev. edn., Oxford, 1990

Thomson, John A. F., *Popes and Princes, 1417–1517: Politics and Polity in the Late Medieval Church*, London, 1980

Valois, Noël, *Histoire de la Pragmatique Sanction de Bourges sous Charles VII*, Archives de l'Histoire Religieuse de la France 4, Paris, 1906

Wegman, Rob C., *Born for the Muses: The Life and Masses of Jacob Obrecht*, Oxford and New York, 1994

Wexler, Richard, "The Politics of Ockeghem's Canonicate," in *Johannes Ockeghem: Actes du XL<sup>e</sup> Colloque International d'études humanistes, Tours, 3–8 février 1997*, ed. Philippe Vendrix, Paris, 1998, 65–78

Wright, Craig, "Dufay at Cambrai: Discoveries and Revisions," *JAMS* 28 (1975), 175–229

*Music at the Court of Burgundy (1364–1419)*, Henryville, PA, and Ottawa, 1979

# Professional women singers in the fifteenth century: a tale of two Annas

BONNIE J. BLACKBURN

We know very little about professional women musicians of the fifteenth century, and thus it would seem overly optimistic to write a chapter about them. Women are mentioned infrequently and only incidentally in chronicles and payment records, and are hardly ever identified. In two cases, however, we have substantial information about two women musicians, one English but working in Italy, and the other German, and it is to these impressive performers that this chapter is devoted.

Music filled the streets, homes, churches, and courts of the fifteenth century, but except for those serving the churches and courts the musicians themselves are largely anonymous. They generally come from the lower social classes. Some were clearly professionals, hired as town musicians.[1] Others were casual entertainers, who discovered that they could receive tips by playing or singing before visiting dignitaries. Occasionally we find women mentioned: for example, the city council of Fribourg paid "a singer with her brother" 58s. in 1442, and two viol players with a woman singer who came from Zurich received £7. 5s. in 1500.[2] Three young women sang before the King of the Romans in Augsburg in 1500.[3] In exceptional cases the woman is named: "the Roman King's three singers, Utz, Adam, and Margreth Haydelin" were paid in Nördlingen in 1490.[4] When women do appear, they are mostly named in conjunction with a relative; music was often a family profession.

Sometimes a letter will yield surprising information. For example, in Venice in November 1455 the eleven-year-old Count Galeazzo Maria Sforza, future duke of Milan, was entertained at a banquet by some "very notable" singers, "among

---

The first part of this essay draws on my article "Anna Inglese." My warmest thanks to Keith Polk and Katelijne Schiltz for help with secondary sources.

1 For urban musicians see *Music and Musicians in Renaissance Cities and Towns*, ed. Kisby. Those named in surviving payment records are all male.

2 Fellerer, *Mittelalterliches Musikleben*, 69 and 75. Polk, "Voices and Instruments," lists numerous references to performances with various forces, including these two. Women are listed on pp. 192–95, one of them in the Bishop of Mainz's service in 1430 (p. 193).

3 Polk, "Voices and Instruments," 193.    4 Ibid., 194.

whom was an English damsel, who sang so sweetly and suavely, that the voice appeared to be not human but divine."[5] While this description of the female voice, especially as angelic, is not at all unusual in medieval sources, the presence of a English woman singer in Venice in 1455 comes as a distinct surprise. The appellation "damisela" implies that she was young, and certainly unmarried. What could she have been doing in Venice? Possibly she was the daughter of an English merchant or was going on pilgrimage to the Holy Land together with her family. This may be the first sighting of the English singer Anna, whose career spanned nearly the whole second half of the fifteenth century. But not in England. All our information about Anna comes from Italian sources, and it is in Italy where she made her career. I shall return to her below.

We know much more about music performed by high-born ladies, daughters or wives of courtiers and rulers.[6] For such women, expertise in music was highly desirable as a social grace, along with dancing. The king of Naples "had no other pleasure nor could paradise be better than when he sees her [his daughter-in-law, Ippolita Sforza, duchess of Calabria] dancing and also singing. And when His Majesty wants to honour some great lord or great master he has her dance and sing privately." Moreover, Ippolita "has invented two new dances based on French chansons." Thus wrote the dancing-master Guglielmo Ebreo da Pesaro in a letter of 15 July 1466 to Ippolita's mother, Bianca Maria Sforza, the duchess of Milan.[7]

"Secretamente" was Guglielmo's word for the manner of Ippolita's performance; it refers to the place where she danced and sang, within the king's private chambers, accessible by invitation only. Ippolita's teenage brother Galeazzo Maria was similarly favored when he visited Florence in 1459, where he was entertained by Cosimo de' Medici. He stresses the intimacy of the surroundings:

> After dinner I went to visit the Magnificent Cosimo, who had a daughter of Piero, his son [Bianca de' Medici], play a pipe organ that was a delightful thing to hear, which in fact she has done every day since I have been here, and he also arranged for some of his singers to sing, all these things with singular pleasure. But more important, he treats me like one of the family, and lets his womenfolk be where I am, which means that he loves me with all his heart.[8]

---

5  Blackburn, "Anna Inglese," 243. The report comes from the young count's minders in a letter to his father, Duke Francesco Sforza. I drew it to the attention of Howard Mayer Brown, who cited it in his pioneering article "Women Singers and Women's Songs."
6  On the participation of noble ladies, see Higgins, "Parisian Nobles, a Scottish Princess," especially 191–95 and the literature cited there.
7  Motta, *Musici alla Corte degli Sforza*, 61–62. Guglielmo helped organize the dancing at many noble weddings; see *Guglielmo Ebreo of Pesaro*, ed. Sparti, 248–54. On dancing at court see also Bryce, "Performing for Strangers."
8  Galeazzo to his father; Blackburn, "Anna Inglese," Doc. 3.

More public events at court might also involve performance by court ladies, but not as soloists. These were typically weddings and banquets, with music and dancing as *intermezzi* between the courses. Guglielmo recalls a banquet hosted by Ippolita's husband, Duke Alfonso of Calabria, in honor of the Burgundian ambassador at Naples in 1474:

> in the middle of the repast the Duke of Calabria and Don Federico [Alfonso's brother] came with a mummery of maskers dressed in the French fashion ... And French dances were performed there during the repast itself with Lady [Ippolita Sforza,] Duchess [of Calabria], and with Lady [E]Leonora [of Aragon, her sister-in-law].[9]

The tradition of courtiers performing in masques was very long-lived. Some of these *intermezzi* must have involved elaborate choreography and long hours of rehearsal; Guglielmo was never short of requests for his services, which on one occasion involved partnering Eleonora in a dance.[10]

"I was also present at the nuptials of Duke Galeazzo [Maria Sforza], who took [to wife Bona of Savoy,] the Duchess who came from France," wrote Guglielmo in his autobiography.[11] So was an English singer called Anna Inglese. Unfortunately, she has left no autobiography or letters, but her career can be traced through court documents from Ferrara in 1465 to Naples in 1499.

On 4 June 1468 Galeazzo Maria, duke of Milan since 1466, ordered his treasurer to pay 100 gold ducats to "la Inglese cantarina" as a gift so she could travel home.[12] No women ever appear on the few lists of singers from the Milanese court, nor are any mentioned in extant payment records. Who was this Englishwoman, and what was she doing in Milan? A hundred ducats is a huge payment, so she must have been at the court for some time. It seems strange for her to leave at this point, for her presence at the wedding festivities in July would surely have been highly desirable. She did indeed leave Milan, but went to nearby Casale in Monferrato, where she obtained a credential letter on 24 June 1468 from Marquis Guglielmo Paleologo VIII recommending her to Galeazzo:

> Anna the singer, bearer of the present letter, has decided to come to your illustrious lordship to honor you at your marriage in the near future, and to perform various pleasant games and entertainments, which we think will please your aforesaid illustrious lordship. For which reason, because we understand

9 *Guglielmo Ebreo of Pesaro*, ed. Sparti, 253. The ambassador had brought the regalia of the Order of the Golden Fleece to confer on the King of Naples, Ferrante I; hence the decision to entertain in the French fashion.
10 Ibid., 32.    11 Ibid., 251.
12 Merkley and Merkley, *Music and Patronage in the Sforza Court*, xxvi n. 47.

the said Anna is an honorable person and very apt and sufficient for such games and festivities, we beg your illustrious lordship to accept her as recommended among her equals, as we believe your aforesaid lordship does.[13]

It is not clear whether Guglielmo knew that Anna had just been in Milan. However, it appears that it was Anna herself who decided to return. She comes across as very much of an entrepreneur. No mention is made of a husband or companion. That a woman – and a foreigner at that – should be able to travel and work on her own in quattrocento Italy is astonishing. This letter is one of the rare fifteenth-century documents concerning independent professional women musicians. The situation is quite different in the sixteenth century: with the flourishing of courtesan culture, women who made their living at least partly through music come into their own, and the madrigal demanded women's voices.

Anna, in fact, was not alone. She had her own ensemble, which included a *tenorista*, and she had been in Milan for some time before the farewell payment of June: on 24 May 1468 the Milanese singer Donato Cagnola complained to Galeazzo that, having lodged Anna and her "brigata" for about four months at the duke's request, he had been partially reimbursed only with great difficulty. Anna was indeed invited to stay: in June Galeazzo ordered his treasurer to give the *tenorista* of "la Inglese" cloth for a suit and a jacket.[14]

We gain some knowledge of Anna's skills, which were not restricted to singing, as well as her first name from Guglielmo's letter, but we know nothing more about her personally. The trajectory of her career, however, confirms that she was an independent woman with considerable initiative, and that she was completely at home in Italy. Before Milan she was in Ferrara: in 1465 the name "Anna cantarina Anglica" appears once in court records.[15] As in Milan, she is the only woman singer known to have been paid at the Este court in the fifteenth century.

After Milan and Monferrato Anna next turns up in Naples in 1471. In the "musica del S[enyor] R[ey]" a payment to "madama Agna Anglesa" is registered in the treasury on two occasions.[16] Further payments to "madama Anna" were made in 1476, 1480, and as late as 1499, when she received the very high

---

13 Blackburn, "Anna Inglese," Doc. 1, transcribed from Milan, Archivio di Stato, Potenze sovrane 124 (also in Motta, *Musici alla Corte degli Sforza*, 299–300, and Merkley and Merkley, *Music and Patronage*, xxvi n. 47).

14 Blackburn, "Anna Inglese," 239. The size and composition of the "brigata" is not mentioned. The presence of a *tenorista* suggests that Anna performed intricately ornamented lines over the accompaniment provided by her *tenorista* on the lute or lira da braccio; she may well have learned this skill from the most highly regarded improviser of the time, Pietrobono, whom she must have known in Ferrara. On Pietrobono, see also the essay by Philippe Canguilhem in this volume, Ch. 9.

15 Lockwood, *Music in Renaissance Ferrara*, 317. In "Anna Inglese" I speculate whether Anna was related to an English musician at the Ferrarese court or to an English student at the university.

16 Compagna Perrone Capano, *Frammenti di cedole della Tesoreria*, 63.

sum of 150 ducats. Following next on the list is "Galderi de Madamma Anna," who is paid 34 ducats.[17] If he is her son (Walter?), as Allan Atlas speculates, he is not mentioned in any other documents surviving from Naples.[18] It is difficult to tell how old Anna was; if she was about twenty years old in 1465, she would have been fifty-four in 1499 and could have had a teenage son. Alternatively, Galderi could have been her *tenorista*.

As Guglielmo of Monferrato's letter indicated, Anna could entertain as well as sing. To be an entertainer requires a certain type of personality, and this fits in well with Anna's ability to pursue an independent professional career. She might therefore have devised games, or told stories, or danced. A letter from the Milanese ambassador to Naples to Galeazzo Maria of 20 March 1472 provides a charming vignette of Anna among august company:

> The English woman singer who used to be at your court, and is very affection-ately disposed to you, is here in the service of Madona Leonora. She told Ippolita that finding herself recently in the garden with Madona Leonora, and jumping about and dancing with her, she said to her: "Well, Madona, when will the day come when I accompany you to Milan to your husband?" To which Madona Leonora responded in a low voice: "My husband is not at Milan, but elsewhere. And he is 40 years old."[19]

This was the time when Eleonora's marriage by proxy to Galeazzo's younger brother, Sforza Maria Sforza, was in the process of being dissolved, since it had been decided to marry her to the duke of Ferrara, Ercole d'Este, instead. It was rather unkind of Anna to mention accompanying Eleonora to *Milan*, alluding to the long-expected formal wedding to Sforza Maria. Clearly Eleonora did know that she was being wooed by Ercole, with her father's approval. Seven months after marrying Ercole by proxy, she was conducted to Ferrara. The Ferrarese delegation sent to accompany her included Pietrobono and other instrumentalists,[20] but we do not know if Anna was part of the Naples contingent on the long trip to Ferrara. She might well have been: at this point, as this letter shows, she was a companion, not merely a hired singer, and one on such familiar terms with the princess that she could tease her, using the semifamiliar "voi" rather than "Your Ladyship."

Naples was apparently the only court where Anna was on the regular payroll. She may very well have traveled to other courts as she did to Milan, to enliven social festivities. Such notices will be hard to find, however, because they will be of occasional payments, and may not have been preserved.

17 Blackburn, "Anna Inglese," 242.    18 Atlas, *Music at the Aragonese Court*, 106.
19 Blackburn, "Anna Inglese," Doc. 2, transcribed from Milan, Archivio di Stato, Sforzesco 221.
20 Corvisieri, "Il trionfo romano di Eleonora d'Aragona," 480 n. 1. See also the essay by Anthony M. Cummings in this volume, Ch. 19.

It was surprising enough to find a professional singer named Anna in the fifteenth century, but even more surprising was to discover a second one, this time German. She appears not to have been a freelance entrepreneur, as Anna Inglese was, but an employee in the household of Maximilian, Archduke of Austria. In 1486 Maximilian traveled with an enormous retinue to Frankfurt, where he was elected King of the Romans. The journey was described in detail by the Burgundian court chronicler Jean Molinet. At dinner in Frankfurt on the evening of 26 January 1486 Maximilian entertained the marquis Christophe de Baude. Present was

> a young woman, twenty years old, who sang and played musical instruments the best seen or heard in ages. To please the archduke, she sang songs and motets alone and also accompanied herself on the lute, harp, rebec, and clavichord, so melodiously and artfully and in perfect rhythm that she seemed more a demi-angel than a human creature.[21]

Although we have no similar reports of Anna Inglese's music-making, I suspect that she was equally talented, playing instruments as well as singing. Molinet's depiction is particularly interesting for confirming the possibility of singing not only songs but also motets solo (and Molinet, a composer himself, is to be trusted in his description). Fifteenth-century music was performed in many ways: solo, with voices on all parts, with an instrumental ensemble, and with voice and instruments.[22]

In Molinet's chronicle the young woman is not named, but other documents confirm that she was in Maximilian's employ for some years: in Augsburg in 1490 a payment was made to "des Romischen Kunigs Singerin" and in the same year in Nördlingen to "des Kunigs Singerin."[23] "Anna Nicodemi Cithareda Germana" died before 6 May 1491, as we learn from the Memorialbuch of Sebald Schreyer, churchwarden of St. Sebaldus in Nuremberg. He credits the poetic epitaph "Jupiter ut coeli concentum surgere terris," placed over her tomb on that day, to the German humanist Conrad Celtis and himself.[24] (For the epitaph see below.) The notice of her death

21 "Auquel souper survint une juesne fille de l'eage de .xx. ans, le mieulx chantant et jouant des instrumens qui piecha fut veue ne oye. Dont, pour conjoyr l'archiduc, elle chantoit seule chansons et motèz et juoit en chantant de lutz, harpe, rebelles et clavechimbalon, tant melodieusement, artificielement et de vraye mesure qu'elle sambloit mieulx estre demy angel que creature humaine." Molinet, *Chroniques de Jean Molinet*, 1:481.

22 All amply documented in Polk, "Voices and Instruments."

23 Ibid., 193. I am assuming that all these payments are to the same person, but may be wrong. Margreth Haydelin was one of Maximilian's singers in 1490; see above at n. 4.

24 Caesar, "Sebald Schreyer," 128. Schreyer describes her as "[kunstreichen fraun Anna genannt, so einen, Nicodemus genannt, zu eelichen mann gehabt hatt, die auch] mit guten sitten, zuchten, tugenden und schon des leibs wol gezirt und zu der kunst, musica, auch mancherley seytenspil hochberumbt und geubt

appears in the necrology of St. Sebaldus, where she is called "Anna Nuserin," therefore the wife of Nicodemus Nuser.[25]

Anna Nuserin created an enormous impression on her contemporaries, to judge by her posthumous fame: in addition to the epitaph mentioned above she is the subject of three poetic epigrams, one by Conrad Celtis and two anonymous. The "German arch-humanist" Conrad Celtis (1459–1508) was crowned Poet Laureate by the emperor Frederick III in 1487. He collaborated with the composer Petrus Tritonius in the musical setting of Horatian odes (1507) and was himself a musician: he sang and played the lute, harp, and viol.[26] The two epigrams are nos. 68 and 69 in Book II:[27]

### De Anna citharoeda Germana

Inflat ubi calamos et dulci carmine nervos
Temperat et pariter voxque manusque sonat:
Non homines te audisse putas sed Apollinis ora,
Dum movet ad placidam plectra sonora lyram.

On Anna, the German singer to the lute. When she blows on the reeds and mingles the strings with sweet song and voice and hand sound together, you do not think you have heard human beings but the voice of Apollo as he moves his sounding plectrum to the peaceful lyre.

### De eadem.

Iuppiter ut coeli concentum surgere terris
Vidit et arcanos tendere in arte modos,
Non tulit atque animam rapuit super aethera nostram,
Ut canat, ambrosias dum capit ille dapes.
Exuvias sepelit mons Noricus: umbra superstes
Evolat et decimam se canit esse deam.[28]

When Jupiter saw that the harmony of heaven was rising from the earth and extending its secret melodies in art, he did not endure it; he has snatched our darling away above the ether, that it may sing while he consumes his feasts of ambrosia. The Norican mountain [Nuremberg] buries the remains; the surviving shade flies away and sings that it is the tenth goddess [i.e. Muse].

[gewesen], so daß weder in deutscher noch welscher nacion von nymant gehort noch erfaren ist." The bracketed words come from the fuller quotation in the Nachlaß of Gerhard Pietzsch, 4:568 (copy in the Bayerische Staatsbibliothek, which Katelijne Schiltz kindly obtained for me).

25 *St. Sebald*, ed. Burger, 122.

26 Caesar, "Sebald Schreyer," 128. On Celtis see also the essay by Reinhard Strohm, Ch. 14 in this volume.

27 *Fünf Bücher Epigramme*, ed. Hartfelder, 38. I am grateful to Leofranc Holford-Strevens for translations of all four poems on Anna.

28 This is the epitaph placed over the tomb. There the last two lines differ: "Illius exuvias mons Moricus accipit: illa / Evolat: et decimam se probat esse deam," and "crescere" replaces "tendere" in line 2 (Caesar, "Sebald Schreyer," 128). The plaque also specifies that she lived twenty-two years and seven months.

As befits a humanist, Celtis compares Anna with a Muse, not an angel, and her skill in singing and playing instruments is likened to Apollo's.

Two anonymous epitaphs survive in Innsbruck, Universitätsbibliothek 664, a collection of verses by German humanists.[29]

### Epitaphium Annae Musicae

Perlege quisquis ades Germanis incola terris,
Perlege nec lacrima parce madere genas:
Anna iacet, iacet Anna, tuae praeconia gentis,
Musica cui facili tam bene nota manu!
Haec quotiens citharam plectro pulsavit eburno,
Credidimus cithara mille volasse manus,
Seu calamos inflare leves, seu psallere iuvit,
Pieridas dixti concinuisse deas.
Orphea iam tacuit vatem longaeva vetustas,
Amphionem Dirce non tulit ulla suum.
Magna ruunt, magnis mors invidet ipsa; quid ergo
Ingenio prodest praevaluisse deos?

Epitaph on Anna the Musician. Read, anyone present who dwells in German lands. Read, and spare not to wet your cheeks with a tear. Anna lies dead, Anna lies dead, the fame of your nation, to whom music was so well known by her skillful hand. Whenever she struck her cithara with the ivory plectrum we thought that a thousand hands had flown over the cithara. Whether it pleased her to blow into the light reeds, or to sing, you said that the Muses had performed with her. Now long-lived antiquity has fallen silent about the bard Orpheus, no Dirce bore her Amphion. Great things collapse, death himself envies the great; what then does it avail to have outstripped the gods in talent?

### Aliud Epitaphium De Eadem.

Ingemat Aonidum coetus, date carmina vates
Et tumulo aeternas spargite ubique rosas!
Anna iacet viridi nimium praerepta iuventa,
Quae fuerat vestri lausque decusque chori.
Quicquid ab antiquo Thamyras, Terpander et Orpheus
Excoluit docta concinuitque lyra,
Quicquid et in nostro finxit sibi musica saeclo,

---

29 *De carminibus Latinis*, ed. Zingerle, 123–24. The first epigram is also found in Besançon, Bibliothèque municipale, MS 1219, fol. 69, with a slightly different title: "Epitaphium Annae Alemaniae rei Musicalis peritissimae." A variant in l. 6, "Credidimus Cytharae mille fuisse manus," changes the meaning to "that the cithara had a thousand hands." Regarding line 10, Leofranc Holford-Strevens observes: "Dirce was not the mother of Amphion, who built the walls of Thebes with his lyre, but a careless reading of Vergil, *Bucolics* 2. 24 *Amphion Dircaeus*, 'Theban Amphion.' What he was trying to say seems to be that Amphion was nothing to Anna."

Sive manus, placidum seu fuit oris opus,
Noverat et geminas pariter ruit Anna per artes
Et calamis mixtos plectra dedere sonos:
Cesserunt veteres, cessit nova temporis aetas,
Crede, aderat toto clarius orbe nihil.

Another Epitaph on the same. Let the assembly of the Muses groan; give your songs, ye bards, and scatter everlasting roses all over her tomb! Anna lies dead, snatched away all too soon in her flowering youth, she who was the praise and glory of your choir. Whatever of old Thamyras, Terpander, and Orpheus nurtured and performed on their well-trained lyre, whatever too music has invented for herself in our age, whether it was the peaceful work of hand or voice, Anna knew, and rushed equally through twin arts, and the plectra gave forth sounds mingled with the reeds. The ancients gave way, the new age of time has given way; I believe there was nothing more glorious present in the whole world.

All four epigrams stress that Anna sang and played the lute and wind instruments. Although musicians usually specialized, some were adept at both wind and string instruments, and Anna appears to be exceptional in this regard, since she was a singer as well. Her death at the age of twenty-two struck her admirers as a cruel fate.

\* \* \*

We know all too little personally about fifteenth-century musicians, and next to nothing about women performers. From the few surviving mentions, we might have thought that all women musicians in this period were adjuncts to husbands and brothers and remained in the background. The two Annas discussed here open an unexpected window on the existence of professional women performers who were not only extremely talented but also confident entrepreneurs. The German Anna was in the service of the emperor. The English Anna was more independent: she had many patrons, and evidently moved around Italy as she pleased, accompanied by her professional ensemble. If the payment records of courts and cities yield very little information on women musicians, the richer sources are chronicles, letters, and poetry, which reveal the social context in which they performed.

## Bibliography

Atlas, Allan W., *Music at the Aragonese Court of Naples*, Cambridge, 1985
Blackburn, Bonnie J., "Anna Inglese and Other Women Singers in the Fifteenth Century: Gleanings from the Sforza Archives," in *Sleuthing the Muse: Essays in*

*Honor of William F. Prizer*, ed. Kristine K. Forney and Jeremy L. Smith, Hillsdale, NY, 2012, 237–52

Brown, Howard Mayer, "Women Singers and Women's Songs in Fifteenth-Century Italy," in *Women Making Music: The Western Art Tradition, 1150–1950*, ed. Jane Bowers and Judith Tick, Urbana and Chicago, 1986, 62–89

Bryce, Judith, "Performing for Strangers: Women, Dance, and Music in Quattrocento Florence," *Renaissance Quarterly* 54 (2001), 1074–1107

Burger, Helene, ed., *Nürnberger Totengeläutbücher*, 1: *St. Sebald 1439–1517*, Neustadt an der Aisch, 1961

Caesar, Elisabeth, "Sebald Schreyer, ein Lebensbild aus dem vorreformatorischen Nürnberg," *Mitteilungen des Vereins für Geschichte der Stadt Nürnberg* 56 (1969), 1–213

Compagna Perrone Capano, Anna Maria, *Frammenti di cedole della Tesoreria (1438–1474)*, Naples, 1979

Celtes, Konrad, *Fünf Bücher Epigramme von Konrad Celtes*, ed. Karl Hartfelder, Berlin, 1881; repr. Hildesheim, 1963

Corvisieri, Costantino, "Il trionfo romano di Eleonora d'Aragona nel giugno del 1473," *Archivio della Società Romana di Storia Patria* 1 (1878), 475–91

Fellerer, Karl Gustav, *Mittelalterliches Musikleben der Stadt Freiburg im Uechtland*, Regensburg, 1935

Higgins, Paula M., "Parisian Nobles, a Scottish Princess, and the Woman's Voice in Late Medieval Song," *EMH* 10 (1991), 145–200

Kisby, Fiona, ed., *Music and Musicians in Renaissance Cities and Towns*, Cambridge, 2001

Lockwood, Lewis, *Music in Renaissance Ferrara 1400–1505: The Creation of a Musical Center in the Fifteenth Century*, Cambridge, MA, 1984

Merkley, Paul A., and Lora L. M. Merkley, *Music and Patronage in the Sforza Court*, Turnhout, 1999

Molinet, Jean, *Chroniques de Jean Molinet*, ed. Georges Doutrepont and Omer Jodogne, 3 vols., Brussels, 1935–37

Motta, Emilio, *Musici alla Corte degli Sforza: Ricerche e documenti milanesi*, Milan, 1887; repr. Geneva, 1977

Polk, Keith, "Voices and Instruments: Soloists and Ensembles in the 15th Century," *EM* 18 (1990), 179–98

Salmen, Walter, *Spielfrauen im Mittelalter*, Hildesheim, 2000

Sparti, Barbara, ed. and trans., *Guglielmo Ebreo of Pesaro, De pratica seu arte tripudii/On the Practice of or Art of Dancing*, Oxford, 1993

Zingerle, Antonius, ed., *De carminibus Latinis saeculi XV. et XVI. ineditis*, Innsbruck, 1880

# Savonarola and the boys of Florence: songs and politics

PATRICK MACEY

With the death of Lorenzo de' Medici "il Magnifico" in April 1492, Italy faced a gaping political void. The fractious Italian states lost a unifying figure, and soon the floodgates opened to the French army of King Charles VIII, who held hereditary claim to the kingdom of Naples. In October 1494 the French swept through Alpine passes, across Lombardy, and into Tuscany. Piero de' Medici, the twenty-two-year-old son of Lorenzo, proved an inexperienced successor as strongman of Florence, and he surrendered to the French – without negotiation – crucial fortresses that guarded Florentine territory. The outraged citizens drove him from the city on 9 November 1494. Into this new leadership vacuum stepped the Dominican friar Girolamo Savonarola, a fiery preacher who had held Florentines spellbound since 1490 with his prophecies about the coming of a New Charlemagne from the North, one who would open Italy to the scourge of God's tribulations, but then reform the Church and usher in an age of renewal when infidels (the Turks) would be converted and universal peace would prevail. City leaders sent Savonarola as one of five representatives to negotiate with Charles, the New Charlemagne, and the friar's skillful diplomacy helped avert a sack of the city. Savonarola's star was in the ascendant, as his prophecies appeared to be finding fulfillment: Charles had invaded Italy, and he was expected to proceed to scourge Rome and renew the Church. The friar earned the confidence of Florentines, who watched with relief as the French troops finally set off for Naples on 28 November, leaving the city unscathed.[1]

How did a lowly friar rise to this august position? Savonarola (1452–98), born in Ferrara as the grandson of the noted ducal physician Michele Savonarola, abruptly left home in 1472 to join the Dominican order in Bologna. He moved to the monastery of San Marco in Florence in 1482 to teach theology, and there he found himself in an institution with strong ties to

This chapter draws on material more fully explored in my book, *Bonfire Songs*, with accompanying CD. The Savonarolan music discussed in the book is available in Macey, ed., *Savonarolan Laude*.
1 The literature on Savonarola is vast. For the most recent account of these events, see Weinstein, *Savonarola*, 105–19. For a summary of Savonarola's career and writings see Brown, "Introduction," xv–xxxv.

Medici patronage. His lukewarm preaching initially met with little success, but by delivering cycles of Lenten sermons in smaller towns in Tuscany in the late 1480s he honed his oratorical skills, and in 1490 Lorenzo de' Medici requested that he return to San Marco. He is today largely remembered as the spell-binding orator who attacked the corrupt ways of Pope Alexander VI (Borgia) and defied the pontiff's orders to stop preaching. The pope responded to the friar's disobedience with an order of excommunication in 1497, and in spring 1498 he was arrested, tried for heresy, hanged, and then burned in the Piazza della Signoria. The execution took place on 23 May, just a little over two years after his spectacular achievement in 1496 and 1497 at reforming the morals of at least a portion of the citizens of Florence. For a short time in the 1490s all eyes in Europe focused on his actions, but his downfall came quickly.

Savonarola's three-pronged program focused on political, social, and reli-gious reforms. In the period after the death of Lorenzo he proclaimed in his sermons a dire warning: "Lo, the sword of the Lord, soon and swiftly" ("Ecce gladius domini cito et velociter").[2] God would soon scourge the world, and the Church would face great tribulations. Christ would battle Antichrist and emerge as the victorious king.[3] To prepare for these events, the friar worked tirelessly in the political realm in late 1494 and 1495 with leaders of the city to establish a new constitution that would restore the republic after decades of Medici tyranny; he also promoted amnesty for former Medici supporters in order to ensure peace in the city.[4]

Savonarola turned his attention to the social realm, to the reform of public morals, and he organized the boys of Florence to enforce these reforms. Music played a central role in promoting social bonding of the youths, and the texts of newly composed songs helped spread the message of change, as we shall see. In his sermon of 10 December 1494, the friar launched an auspicious threefold prophecy for the city, telling the listeners packed into the cathedral that if they dedicated themselves to reform, then Florence would be "more glorious, richer, more powerful than ever before."[5] This marks a notable shift of tone from his former sermons, filled with threats of God's imminent scourging of Italy, to a new attitude of blazing optimism. Florence would be able to avoid the scourge and enjoy a glorious future, but only if the citizens reformed their lives.[6] This new prophecy took a sensational turn when, in his "renovatio" sermon of 1 April 1495, he announced a vision in which he traveled to the throne of the Blessed Virgin Mary in heaven and asked her to pray for Florence to the Holy Trinity. Mary then turned to the friar and declared that Florence

---

2 Weinstein, *Savonarola*, 90–91.
3 Ibid., 88.     4 Ibid., 130.     5 Ibid., 122.
6 Polizzotto, "Savonarola and the Florentine Oligarchy," 60.

would be "more glorious, more powerful, and richer than ever," but she stipulated that Florentines must live righteously, and punish sinners.[7] The friar subsequently spelled out the details of his vision in the *Compendium of Revelations*, published in August 1495 and distributed widely in Italy and in the North, including France and the Empire. To ensure Florence's favor in God's eyes, Savonarola pushed for legislation that would reform the morals of the citizenry. He inveighed against gambling, blasphemy, and prostitution, among other vices, and on the last day of 1494 he was successful in having city leaders enact harsh new penalties for sodomy.[8]

Regarding music, the friar's auspicious prophecies about the coming glory, riches, and power of Florence were directly incorporated into new sacred laude composed for the reformed Carnival celebration of 1496. The lauda is a sacred song in the vernacular, and the genre had been cultivated in Florence as early as the fourteenth century. The texts generally focus on praise of God and the Blessed Virgin Mary, or they express general penitence for sins. What is unusual in 1496 is the creation of new laude with topical and politically inspired texts. These new themes, along with the friar's extraordinary mobilization of the boys of Florence to carry out his social reforms, will be explored below.

Finally, Savonarola preached for religious reform by exhorting Florentines to return to the simplicity of the early Church. Here the elaborate polyphonic music (Latin motets and masses) performed in the cathedral and other Florentine churches came under attack. He argued that such music appealed to the senses and not to the spirit, and that it obscured the essential comprehension of the sacred words. It constituted nothing more than fleeting vanity, and distracted the worshiper from true religious contemplation.[9] In his Lenten sermon of 3 April 1495 he declared: "divine worship today involves too … much polyphonic music [*canti figurati*]. These are the honors that they carry out in divine worship: to cultivate things that delight the sense and the exterior; but interior worship appears to be regarded with no respect at all."[10] He returned to the abuses of polyphonic music many times in his sermons, and perhaps his most famous pronouncement came in the next year, in his Lenten sermon of 5 March 1496:

> The Lord doesn't want these things [elaborate music on feast days]; rather He says: "Remove from me the uproar of your songs; I will not listen to the songs of your lyre." God says: "take away your beautiful polyphonic songs." These

---

7 Weinstein, *Savonarola*, 149.     8 Ibid., 154–57.

9 Savonarola made these points repeatedly, and especially clearly in the Advent sermon on Haggai from 30 November 1494. Cited in Macey, *Bonfire Songs*, 93.

10 Savonarola, *Prediche sopra Giobbe*, 2:131. Cited in Macey, *Bonfire Songs*, 96. For a fuller account of Savonarola's attitudes toward music, see ibid., 91–98.

wealthy men have chapels of singers who appear to be in a regular uproar (as the prophet says here), because there stands a singer with a big voice who appears to be a calf and the others cry out around him like dogs, and one can't make out a word they are saying.[11]

The friar's point is clear: elaborate polyphony made it impossible to hear the words and it merely delighted the senses; it was pure vanity, and harmful to the spirit. Already in March 1493, the Signoria had disbanded the cathedral choir, probably at the urging of the friar. The favorite composer of Lorenzo de' Medici, Henricus Isaac, had worked at the cathedral since July 1485, and he was apparently sacked along with the others.[12]

Not all music merited condemnation. The friar did approve of sacred plain-chant and he showed a special fondness for simple laude. These had sacred texts in the vernacular, with clearly audible words; Savonarola himself wrote texts for some half a dozen laude for which music survives (see below).

## Lorenzo de' Medici and Carnival: musical sources for the lauda

Before examining Savonarola's transformation of civic life. we can gain a better understanding of Florentine traditions that roused his ire by taking a brief look at Carnival and its music during the 1470s and 1480s. During this period Lorenzo de' Medici directed the political life of the city from behind the scenes. Cherished republican traditions of Florence demanded that Lorenzo maintain his appearance as a citizen among equals, although he in fact ruled the city by ensuring the election of Medici partisans to government posts. Lorenzo turned Carnival to his own purposes as a communal festival, and he suppressed traditional festive rituals that were cherished by the leading families of the city. Through Carnival festivities he channeled the energy of the *giovani*, young men in their twenties who were neither eligible to vote nor financially able to marry (the legal age for adulthood was thirty), while de-emphasizing courtly rituals such as jousting, which had allowed patrician families to parade their honor and wealth.[13] Carnival was a licentious festival, when normal customs of restraint were turned on their head. As is well known, the season emphasized the appetites: excessive partying, feasting, and sexual activity, all of which would be abruptly curtailed with the arrival of Lent, the penitential season leading up to Easter.

---

11  Savonarola, *Prediche sopra Amos e Zaccaria*, 2:23. Cited in Macey, *Bonfire Songs*, 97–98.
12  D'Accone, "The Singers of San Giovanni," 346.
13  Trexler, *Public Life in Renaissance Florence*, 414–15. Orvieto, "Carnevale e feste fiorentine," 116–18.

Carnival songs played a central role in the urban festival, and they served as an outlet for sexual energy and innuendo, with texts that positively reveled in double meanings. The masked singers, young men and boys who most likely belonged to brigades of patrician youths associated with Lorenzo, gathered in small ensembles of about five performers and positioned themselves under the windows of the young women of Florence, who watched and listened from behind thin curtains.[14] The songs from this period are simple and tuneful; the scoring for three voice parts in chordal texture allows the voices to pronounce the words simultaneously, thus ensuring that listeners catch the erotic metaphors.

Table 26.1 provides a list of Lorenzo's Carnival songs. Many feature activities of artisans (bakers, perfume makers, etc.) and directly address the women in their opening lines, for example: *Berricuocoli, donne* (Carnival pastries, ladies, ... we offer), *O donne, noi siam giovani fornai* (O ladies, we are young bakers). The singers boast about their great prowess in the practice of their trades (thinly veiled references to their sexual skill), and they brandish their symbols, such as long cylindrical pastries filled with cream (Canto de' cialdoni).[15] The songs, at least in part, constitute an exhortation to pursue fertility and reproduction, and Florentines, men and women alike, delighted in the double meanings of the texts.[16]

Lorenzo also wrote texts for nine laude (Table 26.2), and many of these adopt music of preexisting Carnival songs. With the shift from Carnival to Lent on Ash Wednesday, it was a simple matter to insert the texts of sacred laude to

14 Trexler (ibid., 415), assumes that the singers were plebeian and that their songs referred to their own trades, but it seems more likely that they were patrician members of Lorenzo's brigade; see Orvieto, "Carnevale e feste fiorentine," 107. The ritual of Carnival under Lorenzo is described some seventy years after the fact by Anton Francesco Grazzini (Il Lasca), in his publication of carnival song texts, *Tutti i trionfi.* Grazzini's description is translated in Prizer, "Petrucci and the Carnival Song," 216–17.

15 For commentaries that explicate the double meanings of Lorenzo's Carnival songs, see Lorenzo de' Medici, *Canti carnascialeschi.* See also Prizer, "The Music Savonarola Burned," and Holford-Strevens, "Lorenzo de' Medici and the Carnal in the Carnival." The most important source of music for Carnival songs, Florence 230, was copied around 1515, more than fifteen years after Savonarola's execution, and so escaped the flames of the bonfires of vanities. The closing fascicle is a retrospective collection of Carnival songs, including many by Lorenzo, although all of them are missing one or two voice parts. Complete three-voice musical settings do survive for two of the songs by Lorenzo, with new texts that turn them into sacred laude in the printed anthology edited by Razzi, *Libro primo* (1563); thus Razzi's print preserves the complete musical setting for two of Lorenzo's Carnival songs, the *Canto de' profumi* and the *Trionfo di Bacco* (see Table 26.1). On the importance of Razzi's anthology as a repository of late fifteenth-century Florentine song, see Macey, *Bonfire Songs,* 49–58. The application of new texts to the music of an existing song is called a contrafact, and many laude are contrafacts based on the music of a preexisting Carnival song. With regard to Lorenzo's Carnival songs, complete musical settings for seven of these can be reconstructed. Furthermore, the musical style of these Carnival songs matches particular turns of phrase in other secular songs by Henricus Isaac, so he appears to be the composer of the seven recoverable Carnival songs by Lorenzo. See Macey, "Henricus Isaac and Carnival Songs."

16 On Florentine social rituals and erotics, especially the importance for issues of reproduction and the continuity of the commune, see Bryce, "Performing for Strangers," 1085–86.

Table 26.1  *Carnival songs of Lorenzo de' Medici (eleven in total)*

| | Music in Florence 230 | Music in Razzi, *Laudi* (1563) |
|---|---|---|
| Canto de' confortini (carnival pastries) | — | ?SATB, *Madre de' peccatori*, fol. 21v |
| *Berricuocoli, donne, e confortini* | | |
| Canto de' cialdoni (long carnival pastry) | TB, fol. 145r | |
| *Giovani siam, maestri molto buoni* | | |
| Canto degli innestatori (vine grafters) | S, fol. 149v | |
| *Donne, noi siamo maestri* | | |
| Canto dello zibetto (civet, for perfume) | | |
| *Donne, quest'è un animal perfetto* | ?TB, fol. 143r, textless[a] | |
| Canto de' fornai (bakers) | ?TB, fol. 149r, textless[a] | |
| *O donne, noi siam giovani fornai* | | |
| Canto delle forese (cucumber harvesters) | — | |
| *Lasse, in questo carnasciale* | | |
| Canto de' profumi (perfume makers) | S, fol. 144v | STB, fol. 68v |
| *Sian galanti di Valenza* | | |
| Canto delle cicale (gossipers) | — | |
| *Donne, siam, come vedete* | | |
| Canto de' sette pianeti (7 planets) | — | |
| *Sette pianeti siam, che l'alte sede* | | |
| Trionfo di Bacco (Bacchus and Ariadne) | TB, fol. 150r | STB, fol. 10v |
| *Quant'è bella giovinezza* | | |
| Canto de' visi addrieto (faces turned back) | S, fol. 151v | |
| *Le cose al contradio vanno* | | |

[a] Textless song, missing the soprano; the prosody of Lorenzo's text fits the music in Florence 230.

S = soprano, A = alto, T = tenor, B = bass

the well-known tunes of Carnival songs. When the text of a lauda is marked "cantasi come" this directs the singer to use the music of a preexisting secular song, or the music from another lauda (e.g., *cantasi come il canto de' profumi* means "sing this to the music for the Canto de' profumi"). In five cases Lorenzo draws music for his laude from his own Carnival songs. The lauda in Florence in this period mainly relied on the oral tradition and did not employ written-out music, so it leaned heavily on the *cantasi come* instruction.

Table 26.2 *Laude of Lorenzo de' Medici (nine in total)*

| Incipit[a] | Cantasi come (cc) (sing to the music of) | Music |
|---|---|---|
| *Ben arà duro core* | — | — |
| *Poi che io gustai,* | *Tanta pietà mi tira* | Razzi, *Laudi* (1563), |
| *Gesù, la tua dolcezza* | (lauda: Feo Belcari) | *Levati su omai*, fol. 37v[b] cc: *Tanta pietà mi tira*[c] |
| *O Dio, o sommo bene* | La canzona del fagiano | cc: carnival song, not by Lorenzo |
| *Quant'è grande la bellezza* | La canzona delle forese [recte: Trionfo di Bacco] | lauda: Razzi (1563), fol. 10v cc: carnival song by Lorenzo |
| *O maligno e duro core* | La canzona de' Valenziani [i.e., profumi] | lauda: Razzi, (1563), fol. 68v cc: carnival song by Lorenzo |
| *Peccator', su tutti quanti* | La canzona de' visi addrieto | cc: carnival song by Lorenzo |
| *O peccator, io sono Dio* | La canzona dei fornai | cc: carnival song by Lorenzo |
| *Io son quel misero* | La canzone delle cicale | cc: carnival song by Lorenzo, music lost |
| *Vieni a me, peccatore* | Cantasi come *Amore io vo fuggendo*; et anchora a uno modo proprio composto per Isac. Alternate cc: *Tu m'hai legato, amore* | cc: love song:[d] Florence 121, fol. 22v and Modena α.F.9.9, fol. 7v |

[a] The order as in Lorenzo de' Medici, *Laude.*
[b] The music of the concluding section of *Levati su omai*, on fols. 38v–39r of Razzi, is superfluous for Lorenzo's lauda, and should be omitted. Repeat signs should be added to the section after the first fermata on fols. 37v–38r (*S'el sonno*), so that the music of Lorenzo's first *piede* (rhyme: ABA) is repeated for the second *piede* (BAB). The *volta* (CcX) can then be sung to the music of the opening *ripresa* (XxY).
[c] Wilson, *Singing Poetry*, 189–95, gives the contents of *Laude facte e composte da più persone spirituali* (Florence, 1485/1486), an anthology of lauda texts. For *Levati su omai* by Gherardo d'Astore the *cantasi come* is *Tanta pietà*; see Wilson, 194, no. 161.
[d] The text of *Amor io vo fuggendo* is by Serafino Aquilano. See Blackburn, "Two 'Carnival Songs'," 126–27 and 174–75.

## Savonarola and the boys of Florence

After Lorenzo's death, Savonarola mobilized the boys of Florence to perform laude written by the friar himself and his followers. Before turning to the musical activities of the boys, we will take a brief look at their place in

Florentine society. Historians emphasize the aggressive behavior of children and adolescents against the background of a generally high level of adult violence in Italian cities during the fifteenth century.[17] Richard Trexler paints a vivid picture of unsupervised children who thronged the urban byways almost as soon as they had learned to walk: "Scarcely on their feet … Florentine brats appeared in the streets, beating balls against nunnery walls, burning mannequins of old women, stoning passersby, and mocking visitors: [these were] fitter victims of Herod, said one dour versifier, than the helpless Innocents whose murder had ruined that king's reputation."[18] In an attempt to harness the destructive energies of the city's youth, Florence fostered confraternities for adolescents. These were designed to socialize boys aged thirteen to twenty-four; on Sundays and feast days they met to sing psalms and hymns. The confraternities also marched in processions on feast days, and youths, dressed in white as "little angels," sang laude. They served as symbols of civic purity that would elicit God's favor, and in the 1490s Savonarola took this tradition to new levels of political intensity.[19]

Part of Savonarola's success lay in his ability to recruit young boys, aged six to sixteen, to help carry out his moral reform. While he built on the model of the confraternal structures, what is new is that he was able to turn the activities from religious to political ends.[20] In September 1495, shortly after the publication of Savonarola's *Compendium of Revelations*, Pope Alexander VI ordered the friar to stop preaching. Savonarola's sermons were the primary means by which he advocated reforms, but his enforced absence from the pulpit caused him to rely on the boys of Florence to carry these reforms forward. The boys, accompanied by an armed guard, were deputized by the communal authorities to chase gamblers and prostitutes from the streets, and they also collected alms for the poor during Lent.[21] For Carnival and Palm Sunday in 1496 they staged large processions through the city, and here they sang laude as they marched; they also performed laude in the cathedral. In the following years, during Carnival of 1497 and 1498, they went door to door collecting items such as worldly paintings, books of love poetry, dice, and musical instruments, which they piled onto a pyre in preparation for the bonfire of vanities in the Piazza della Signoria. The success of the youth brigades in cleansing the city of morally objectionable

---

17 Niccoli, "I bambini del Savonarola," 280 ff.
18 Trexler, *Public Life in Renaissance Florence*, 368; the grumbling commentator is Franco Sacchetti, who was active in Florence in the late fourteenth century.
19 Richard Trexler, "Ritual in Florence," 200–64, esp. 223 and 245. Reprinted in Trexler, *Dependence in Context*, 259–325, esp. 282–83 and 305–6. Trexler cites the youths in a procession from 1455 and notes the lack of further accounts about youths marching in processions until the Savonarolan period in the 1490s.
20 Trexler, *Public Life*, 474–82; Niccoli, "I bambini del Savonarola," 283–84.
21 Polizzotto, *Children of the Promise*, 110–23, esp. 118.

activities created a sharp divide in public opinion; some praised their actions while others severely criticized their aggression. Because the commune authorized the youth brigades, citizens complained that they lived in a city governed by boys and that they were "the laughing-stock of Christendom."[22]

## Music in the cause of reform

Music played a strong role in the friar's implementation of social and religious renewal. In the 1480s, when he was newly arrived in Florence and before he had conceived his program for reforming the city, Savonarola wrote texts for about a dozen laude; musical settings have come down to us for five of these (see Table 26.3). By composing his own laude, the friar responded to the thriving production and performance of laude in his newly adopted city. A good example of the sweet-sounding music of the lauda is his *Che fai qui, core* (What are you doing here, heart). He copied his lyric into a collection of sermon notes, the Codice Borromeo, which he wrote from 1483 to 1484 during his first period in Florence.[23] Significantly, he modeled the unusual textual form of the verse for his lauda on *Ecco 'l Messia*, by the recently deceased Lucrezia Tornabuoni (d. 1482), mother of Lorenzo de' Medici.[24] In fact, he placed the text of Lucrezia's lauda directly above his own in the Codice Borromeo. In turn, Lucrezia appears to have modeled her lauda on *Ben venga amore*, a work by the foremost poet of laude in Florence, Feo Belcari (d. 1484).[25] The secular model for all three laude is Poliziano's song for the celebration of May Day, *Ben venga Maggio*.[26] We find Savonarola, soon after his arrival in Florence, already modeling a lauda on a series of preexisting texts and a musical setting associated with some of the city's most prominent figures.

The text of the refrain and the first of ten stanzas are as follows:

| | |
|---|---|
| Che fai qui, core? | What are you doing here, heart? |
| Che fai qui, core? | What are you doing here, heart? |
| Vane al tuo dolce amore. | Go to your sweet love. |
| L'amor è Jesù Cristo, | Love is Jesus Christ, |

---

22  Polizzotto, *The Elect Nation*, 39. The Florentines cited are Piero Parenti and Bartolomeo Cerretani.
23  Cattin, ed., *Il primo Savonarola*, 191–95.
24  The textual form is unusual for two reasons: the first line consists of five syllables instead of the usual seven or eleven, and this opening line is immediately repeated. The music of the soprano is copied into a late sixteenth-century manuscript biography of the friar by one of his adherents, Fra Serafino Razzi (Biblioteca Medicea Laurenziana, MS S. Marco 429), and the melody is identical to the one used by Lucrezia Tornabuoni, whose lauda was printed in Razzi's *Libro primo*, fol. 15v. See Macey, *Bonfire Songs*, 104–6.
25  On the sources and musical styles of the Florentine lauda, see Wilson, *Singing Poetry in Renaissance Florence*.
26  Francesco Luisi, "*Ben venga Maggio*."

Table 26.3 *Laude by Savonarola with musical settings*
Preexisting poetic and musical models are in the left and middle columns; cc = *cantasi come.*

| Original secular song or lauda | Laude in Razzi, 1563[a] | Savonarola |
|---|---|---|
| cc: *Angela tu mi fai* (song) ← | *Jesù sommo conforto* | *Jesù sommo conforto* |
| cc: *Vergine tu mi fai* (lauda)[b] | F. Girolamo | (ca. 1483) |
| Ser Michele Chelli prete | Savonarola da Ferrara | |
| cc: *Ben venga Maggio*, | ← cc: *Ecco 'l Messia* (1st ← | *Che fai qui, core* |
| Poliziano | setting) | (ca. 1483) |
| (song) | Madonna Lucrezia | |
| | [Tornabuoni] de' | |
| | Medici | |
| cc: *In su quell' monte chiara* ← | cc: *In su quell'alto monte* ← | *In su quell'aspro monte* |
| (song) | di Authore incerto | (ca. 1483) |
| | [Bianco Gesuato] | |
| cc: *Leggiadra damigella*, or ← | cc: *Jesù sommo diletto e* ← | *Jesù dolce conforto e sommo* |
| *Molto m'annoia dello mio* | *vero* | (1484) |
| *messire* | d'Autore incerto [Feo | |
| (songs) | Belcari] | |
| | *Deh dolce redentore* | |
| | Lorenzo Tornabuoni[c] | |
| cc: *O benigno signore*, or ← | cc: *Alma che sì gentile / ti* ← | *Alma che sì gentile / tu che* |
| cc: *O rosa mia gentile* | *fe' per* | *sei* |
| (songs) | Gherardo d'Astore | (after 1484) |
| — | — | *Jesù splendor del cielo* |
| | | Original music |
| | | composed by Ser |
| | | Firenze (lost) |

[a] The musical settings for Savonarola's laude in the far right column are preserved in the retrospective collection Razzi, *Libro primo.* Exceptionally, the only actual text by Savonarola to appear in the 1563 print is *Jesù sommo conforto*, where it is attributed to the friar; the texts of his other laude do not appear in the print, but the music for singing them is preserved there.
[b] Savonarola copied this lauda on fol. 32r of the Codice Borromeo. His own lauda, *Jesù sommo conforto*, appears on fol. 53r of the same codex, and its poetic form is directly modeled on *Vergine tu mi fai*. See Savonarola, *Poesie*, ed. Martelli, 199, and Cattin, *Il primo Savonarola*, 193. The laudario Vatican City, Biblioteca Apostolica Vaticana, Rossi 424 includes *Jesù sommo conforto* with the instruction "cantasi come Vergine tu mi fai"; see the partial list of contents and this *cantasi come* instruction in Macey, *Bonfire Songs*, 312. For the secular song *Angela tu mi fai*, and the lauda by Michele Chelli, *Vergine tu mi fai*, modeled on it, see Wilson, *Singing Poetry*, 180–81 and the literature cited there.
[c] The musical setting of *Deh dolce redentore* in 1563 probably also served for singing d'Astore's lauda *Alma che sì gentile*, and thus Savonarola's lauda with the same incipit, *Alma che sì gentile*. See Macey, *Bonfire Songs*, 112–15.

| | |
|---|---|
| Che dolcemente infiamma, | which sweetly inflames, [and] |
| Fa lieto ogne cor tristo, | makes every sorrowful heart happy |
| Che a Lui sospira e brama. | that sighs for and desires Him. |
| Chi puramente l'ama | Whoever loves Him chastely |
| Si spoglia d'ogne errore. | rids himself of every error. |
| Che fai qui, core? (ecc.) | What are you doing here, heart? (etc.) |

The music is shown in Example 26.1 (for a recording, see www.cambridge. org/9781107015241).[27] While the original secular song celebrates the return of spring and the amorous coupling of lovers, Savonarola's own model, the lauda by Lucrezia Tornabuoni, was already twice removed from the secular source. In any case, Florentines expressed no qualms about singing laude to music from secular songs.

The text of Savonarola's lauda follows a simple poetic outline called a ballata, the most common textual form for both laude and Carnival songs in the fifteenth century. The rhyme scheme clarifies the formal pattern, and helps the singers remember the words of successive stanzas, especially important in a largely oral tradition that relied on memory rather than written music for performance. The song begins with three lines for the refrain (ripresa); the stanzas have six lines, here divided evenly into couplets. The stanza is made up of two feet (piedi) and a closing couplet (volta). The letters for the rhyme scheme of the ripresa are x and y, while the stanza is assigned the letters a and b; the complete rhyme scheme for ripresa and first stanza is: xxx ababbx.

After singing the refrain, the performers repeat the music of the first piede (ab) for the second piede (ab). The ripresa is represented musically with a capital letter, A, because it repeats both the words and the music between each stanza; lowercase letters indicate new music for the stanza, where new text appears when the music returns each time:

A b b c A

The musical form helps to articulate the poetic form and the rhyme scheme; the two elements can be shown as follows:

| formal unit: | ripresa | piedi | volta | ripresa (etc.) |
|---|---|---|---|---|
| rhyme: | xxx | ab ab | bx | xxx |
| music: | A | b  b | c | A |

The last line of the volta typically has the same rhyme as the first line of the ripresa, so the volta (meaning to "turn") guides the singers back to the ripresa.

---

27 The performance of laude appears to have relied on learning them by ear, so this oral tradition probably did not require that they be written down. The music survives thanks to the initiative of Fra Serafino Razzi, who gathered music in Florence for some ninety laude and published them in the *Libro primo*. Many of his musical settings clearly go back to the late fifteenth century, based on their musical style.

Example 26.1 *Che fai qui, core*; text: Girolamo Savonarola; music: Razzi (1563), fol. 15v (original text "Ecco 'l Messia," by Lucrezia Tornabuoni)

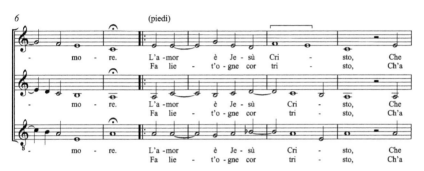

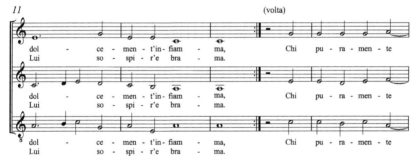

The music for *Che fai qui, core* is simple. The main melody, the soprano, happens to be placed in the middle voice, while the tenor supplies a simple harmonization below. The altus adds particular sweetness by providing a kind of discant above the soprano, mainly in parallel thirds. The extreme simplicity of the music that accompanies the soprano melody in the tenor and alto could easily have been improvised in an oral tradition, and the boys would have had no need of written notation when they performed the lauda.[28] Only in the mid-sixteenth century, when the oral tradition was dying out, was it necessary to collect and preserve all the parts of the music in written notation, as in Serafino Razzi's anthology, the *Libro primo delle laudi spirituali*, published in 1563.

## New laude for a new political order

A Florentine who went out to celebrate the last day of Carnival on Tuesday, 16 February 1496 would have been astonished to find thousands of boys processing through the streets carrying olive branches and singing laude that united their voices in angelic harmony. The shift to bright political optimism noted in Savonarola's sermons of 1496 ("Florence will be more glorious, richer, more powerful than ever before") had its parallel in a fresh departure for the lauda. The new lauda texts composed for this occasion echoed the friar's prophetic optimism by incorporating his exact words, as well as acclamations of "Long live Christ our king."

A signal change had swept through the city. In the past, Carnival was a period when boys gathered into gangs (*brigate*) and blocked off city squares, where they built huts of sticks; citizens were not allowed to enter unless they paid a toll, used by the boys to buy Carnival sweets. The gangs fought pitched battles in the dangerous game of stones; they hurled stones, and each year several boys would be badly injured or even killed. Now their harried parents marveled at the transformation in the boys' behavior, and pointed to Savonarola as the agent of such beneficial change.

Piero Parenti, a prosperous Florentine who had married into the Strozzi family, recounts how the boys now spent the Carnival days in February 1496 collecting alms for the poor, and on the last day (*Martedì grasso*, Fat Tuesday) he remarked that they gathered for solemn high Mass in the morning in the cathedral, where they sat in the choir and sang laude specially written and tailored to the occasion.[29] Luca Landucci, a Florentine pharmacist and father of some of the boys, noted their totally changed behavior:

---

28  See the essay on improvisation in this volume by Philippe Canguilhem, Ch. 9.

29  Parenti, *Storia fiorentina*, 1:311. Parenti recorded his impressions in the section marked February 1495 (new style 1496).

16 February 1496 . . . the boys sang laude to heaven, crying: "Long live Christ our king and the Virgin Mary, our queen!" They all carried olive branches in their hands, so that good and thoughtful people were moved to tears, saying: "Truly this change is the work of God . . ." And observe that there were said to be six thousand boys or more, all of them between five or six and sixteen years of age . . . I have written these things which are true, and which I saw with my own eyes, and felt with so much emotion; and some of my sons were among those blessed and pure-minded troops of boys.[30]

Landucci's mention of tearful onlookers explains why Savonarola's followers were derisively dubbed *Piagnoni*, or Snivellers.

Landucci goes on to describe the scene in the cathedral on the day after Carnival, Ash Wednesday:

17 February 1496. This was the first day of Lent, and an immense number of boys came to hear Fra Girolamo's sermon in Santa Maria del Fiore. Certain risers were erected for these boys along the walls opposite the chancel and behind the women; and there were also many boys among the women; and all those who stood on the steps sang sweet laude to God before the sermon began. And then the clergy came into the chancel and sang Litanies and the children responded. It was so beautiful that everyone wept, and mostly healthy-minded men, saying: "This is a thing of the Lord's."

And this went on each morning of Lent, before the friar came [to deliver his sermon]. And note this wonder: not a boy could be kept in bed in the morning, but all ran to church before their mothers.[31]

Again Landucci draws attention to the sweet singing of the boys, and the powerful emotional effect of their unified voices on those present. In Figure 26.1, a woodcut shows Savonarola preaching to the throng who crowded into the cathedral to hear his sermons. A curtain runs down the center of the nave, parting the women on the friar's right from the men on his left. The risers on which the boys stood are not shown, but they would have been placed behind the pulpit, and against the walls on either side of the nave.

Landucci fills in the picture of the singing in the cathedral with a further account of an accident on 15 August 1496, the feast of the Assumption of the Virgin Mary into heaven:

Fra Girolamo preached in Santa Maria del Fiore, and on account of the great crowd, one of the sets of wooden risers for the boys, towards the door of San Giovanni [the main entrance on the west], collapsed, but no one was injured. It was taken to be a miracle . . . And observe that during this time there was such a feeling of grace in that church, and such sweetness in hearing those boys sing,

30  Adapted from Landucci, *A Florentine Diary*, 102–103. For the original Italian, see *Diario fiorentino*, 122–25.
31  Landucci, *A Florentine Diary*, 102–103. Translation adapted. Original Italian, ed. Del Badia, 125–26.

Figure 26.1 Savonarola preaching in Florence cathedral. Girolamo Savonarola, *Compendio di revelatione* (Florence, 1495)

now above, now below, now from the side, all singing each in turn, quite modestly and in silence, that it did not appear to be something done by boys. I write this because I was present, and saw it many times, and experienced much spiritual comfort. Truly the church was full of angels.[32]

Several elements emerge in these accounts, and they take on strong symbolic and political significance. The singing of laude by the boys as they marched in procession through the city, and during their attendance at services in the cathedral, was compared by the citizens to the heavenly sounds of angels, and

32  Landucci, *A Florentine Diary*, 110–11. Original Italian, ed. Del Badia, 136–37.

the boys took on symbolic value as harbingers of an age of renewal, when Christ would descend to earth and be crowned king of Florence.

Savonarola himself noted the acclamations of the boys in his sermon in the cathedral on Ash Wednesday of 1496, which marked his triumphant return to the pulpit for his cycle of Lenten sermons, after having been silenced by the pope since September 1495:

> Your boys, who used to play the game of stones and sticks and many other crazy things, now have turned to divine laude and have made a procession on the day of Carnival … You know how many tears were shed when you heard those young voices sing the laude of our Savior Jesus Christ and of his mother Mary, often shouting in a loud voice all together with great jubilation: "Long live the Lord Jesus Christ, our King, and our Queen his mother the Virgin Mary!"[33]

At least four laude appear to have been created especially for this sacralized Carnival. All of them prominently feature the acclamation "Viva Cristo" in their opening lines, and the accounts of Landucci and Savonarola confirm that the boys sang these words at the Carnival of 1496, and during the subsequent observances of Palm Sunday. These laude are:

| Title | Text author |
|---|---|
| *Viva Cristo e chi li crede* | Filippo Cioni |
| *Viva, viva in nostro core* | Anonymous |
| *Viva ne nostri cuori, viva o Florentia* | Girolamo Benivieni |
| *Viva Cristo re nostro et la felice* | Anonymous |

All of the texts can be found in manuscripts and printed pamphlets containing other Savonarolan laude and tracts. Space permits only a brief discussion of the first two laude and their proposed musical settings.[34] Because the Catholic Church suppressed the cult of Savonarola after his death, much of the material related to his movement was destroyed; there are no contemporaneous sources containing musical settings for any of the above laude. Serafino Razzi's printed anthology from 1563 does contain musical settings for five of Savonarola's own laude as well as four other laude by his followers, yet the texts have been bowdlerized to omit mention of the friar, because the ecclesiastical authorities would have withheld printing permission if Savonarola had been explicitly represented in the anthology.[35] Razzi's collection is the logical place to seek musical settings for the laude on *Viva Cristo*.

---

33 Savonarola, *Prediche sopra Amos e Zaccaria*, 1:37–39. Cited in Macey, *Bonfire Songs*, 62–63.
34 See Macey, *Bonfire Songs*, 61–73 for further comment on these laude.
35 The Dominican Inquisitor General in Venice, Tommaso da Vicenza, added a notice to the reader after the colophon, in which he stated that Razzi's collection of laude contained nothing against religion and it was worthy to be published. For a discussion of these laude and their musical settings, see Macey, *Bonfire Songs*, 98–139. The exception is Razzi's ascription of *Jesù sommo conforto* to the friar.

Filippo Cioni, a follower of Savonarola and author of the first work, prominently headlines the acclamation to Christ:

| | |
|---|---|
| Viva Cristo e chi li crede: | Long live Christ and he who believes in Him: |
| Su, Fiorenza, all'operare, | Arise, Florence, to the task, |
| Ché Jesù vuol coronare | because Jesus wants to crown |
| Chi morrà per questa fede. | those who will die for this faith. |

The subsequent stanzas of the lauda call upon Florentines to cleanse their hearts and be transformed through living faith. The verse form is significant because it consists solely of short stanzas of four lines; only one musical setting of a lauda in Razzi's collection has this text form, and it is Lucrezia Tornabuoni's *Deh venitene pastori*.[36] The musical setting presented by Razzi possibly stems from the 1470s, and Filippo Cioni probably adopted it for his own lauda. (See Example 26.2. www.cambridge.org/9781107015241) Like the music for Savonarola's *Che fai qui, core*, this setting features the tune in the middle of the three-part texture, with a simple harmonizing tenor and an alto that functions as a discant above the tune in smooth parallel motion. The range of the tune covers only five notes, a fifth from $c'$ to $g'$, and the melody would be easy to memorize because the first three phrases are almost identical and they are open-ended harmonically. The fourth phrase provides strong closure for each stanza with ascent to the peak pitch, followed by a jaunty syncopated cadence. The lauda has the character of a march, with regular duple time and repeated notes, and the extremely simple texture and phrase structure guarantee that it would make a fine effect outdoors, as it most likely did in the vast procession of the Savonarolan boys for Carnival on 16 February 1496.

One other lauda, the anonymous *Viva, viva in nostro core*, has a variation on the acclamation "Viva Cristo," and its text incipit and music are clearly based on a preexisting Carnival song.[37] As mentioned earlier, Lorenzo de' Medici also drew the music for five of his laude from his own Carnival songs, so this was a well-established practice in Florence. The text is a ballata similar in form to Savonarola's *Che fai qui, core*: a recurring refrain (*ripresa*) and a stanza consisting of two *piedi* (two couplets, rhyming -etto -ate) followed by the four-line *volta*, with a rhyme that connects it to the preceding *piede* (-ate), and a concluding rhyme that links to the *ripresa* (-ore).

---

36 On the secular model for Lucrezia's lauda and a discussion of the music, see Wilson, *Singing Poetry in Renaissance Florence*, 134–36.

37 A book of Carnival song texts, *Canzone per andare in maschera*, published around 1515 but preserving songs by Lorenzo de' Medici and his contemporaries from around 1490, includes three songs with a similar opening line: *Viva, viva la potenza*; *Viva, viva el gran signore*; and *Viva, viva la ragione*. See Macey, *Bonfire Songs*, 64.

Example 26.2 *Viva Cristo e chi li crede*; text: Filippo Cioni; music proposed: Razzi (1563), fol. 36r (original text: "Deh venitene pastori," by Lucrezia Tornabuoni)

| | |
|---|---|
| Viva, viva in nostro core | Long live, live in our hearts |
| Cristo re, duce e signore. | Christ the king, leader and lord. |
| Ciascun purghi l'intelletto, | Let everyone purge his mind, |
| La memoria e voluntate | memory, and will |
| Dal terrestre e vano affetto: | of earthly and vain affections. |
| Arda tutto in caritate, | Let all burn in charity, |
| Contemplando la bontate | contemplating the goodness |
| Di Jesù, re di Fiorenza; | of Jesus, king of Florence. |
| Con digiuni e penitenza | Through fasting and penitence |
| Si reformi dentro e fore. | we reform ourselves inside and out. |

Razzi transmits another lauda with a similar text incipit, *Viva, viva in oratione*, and its music very likely served for singing the Savonarolan lauda. (See Example 26.3. www.cambridge.org/9781107015241) Several stylistic features are typical of Lorenzo de' Medici's Carnival songs: the lively melodic extensions at the ends of phrases, the open scoring with relatively wide spacing between the top two voices, and the closing section in triple time. The rather more complex musical style of this lauda is best suited for performance by a limited number of boys standing still in a piazza or in the cathedral, not while marching in a procession.

The other two laude listed above go further in their texts and include Savonarola's auspicious prophecy for Florence in his sermon of December 1494. Savonarola had helped avert the sack of the city by French troops in November of that year, and in the wake of this fortunate outcome, it appeared that Florence would be spared the wrath of God's avenging sword. The friar changed his tone of gloom and prophesied a bright future for Florence if the citizens reformed their ways: the city would be more rich, more powerful and more glorious than ever. Both laude quote the exact words of Savonarola's prophecy.

Savonarola and his followers attempted to maintain their high spirits of brotherly love and Christian joy in the ensuing years, especially through singing laude. They drew their central motto from the opening verse of Psalm 132 (Vulgate): "Behold how good and pleasant it is for brethren to dwell together in unity" ("Ecce quam bonum et quam iocundum habitare fratres in unum"). Savonarola quoted this verse frequently in his sermons, especially in 1497 and 1498, as the movement came under increasing attack from the pope and from Florentines themselves.[38] His followers joined hands and sang this verse while they danced in a circle in the piazza in front of the monastery of San Marco after the last bonfire of vanities on 27 February 1498. The tune appears to survive in Razzi's anthology of 1563, but with the text *Ecco 'l Messia* (a second

---

38  See Macey, *Bonfire Songs*, 23–28.

Example 26.3 *Viva, viva in nostro core*; text: anonymous; music: Razzi (1563), fol. 136v (original text "Viva, viva in oratione," anon.)

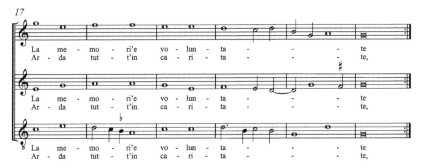

Example 26.3 (cont.)

setting of Lucrezia Tornabuoni's lauda). In May 1497 the pope excommunicated Savonarola, and in early 1498 he threatened to place the entire city under interdict if the authorities did not silence him. The end began in April, on Ascension Day, when Florentines attacked the monastery of San Marco and the friar was arrested. Under interrogation with torture he confessed that his prophecies had not been sent from God. He was condemned by the Church as a heretic, and executed on 23 May in the Piazza della Signoria, in front of the palace of the civic government (the Palazzo del Popolo, now Palazzo Vecchio). In the aftermath of the execution many of his followers were disillusioned, but others worked to sustain the spirit of brotherly love and looked forward to the promised material prosperity for the city. They collected the friar's sermons and tracts and continued to have them printed, and the music for Savonarolan laude was preserved and made available to a wider public in the retrospective anthology printed by the Dominican Serafino Razzi in 1563 (although, as mentioned, with texts largely bowdlerized, their Savonarolan origins disguised). Music in the form of laude by Savonarola and his followers was to play a major role in buoying the spirits of reformers in the sixteenth century as they worked not only for the preservation of Florence as a republic, but also for the spiritual renewal of the city.

## Bibliography

Blackburn, Bonnie J., "Two 'Carnival Songs' Unmasked: A Commentary on MS Florence Magl. XIX. 121," *MD* 35 (1981), 121–78

Brown, Alison, "Introduction," in *Selected Writings of Girolamo Savonarola: Religion and Politics, 1490–1498*, ed. Donald Beebe (New Haven and London, 2006), xv–xxxv

Bryce, Judith, "Performing for Strangers: Women, Dance and Music in Quattrocento Florence," *Renaissance Quarterly* 54 (2001), 1074–1107

Cattin, Giulio, ed., *Il primo Savonarola: Poesie e prediche autografe dal Codice Borromeo*, Florence, 1973

D'Accone, Frank A., "The Singers of San Giovanni in Florence during the 15th Century," *JAMS* 14 (1961), 307–58

   ed., *Florence, Biblioteca Nazionale Centrale, MS Banco Rari 230* (New York, 1986) (introduction and facsimile)

Grazzini, Anton Francesco ("Il Lasca"), ed., *Tutti i trionfi, carri, mascheaate* [sic] *ò canti carnascialeschi andati per Firenze dal tempo del Magnifico Lorenzo vecchio de' Medici*, Florence, 1559

Holford-Strevens, Leofranc, "Lorenzo de' Medici and the Carnal in the Carnival," in *Sleuthing the Muse: Essays in Honor of William F. Prizer*, ed. Kristine Forney and Jeremy L. Smith, Hillsdale, NY, 2012, 117–32

Landucci, Luca, *Diario fiorentino dal 1450 al 1516*, ed. Iodoco Del Badia, Florence, 1883, trans. Alice De Rosen Jervis as *A Florentine Diary from 1450 to 1516*, London, 1927

Luisi, Francesco, "*Ben venga Maggio*: Dalla canzone a ballo alla Commedia di Maggio," in *La musica a Firenze al tempo di Lorenzo il Magnifico*, ed. Piero Gargiulo, Florence, 1993, 195–218

Macey, Patrick, *Bonfire Songs: Savonarola's Musical Legacy*, Oxford, 1998
   "Henricus Isaac and Carnival Songs on Texts by Lorenzo de' Medici" (forthcoming) ed., *Savonarolan Laude, Motets, and Anthems*, Recent Researches in the Music of the Renaissance 116, Madison, WI, 1999

Medici, Lorenzo de', *Canti carnascialeschi*, ed. Paolo Orvieto, Rome, 1991
   *Laude*, ed. Bernard Toscani, Florence, 1990

Niccoli, Ottavia, "I bambini del Savonarola," in *Studi savonaroliani: Verso il V centenario*, ed. Gian Carlo Garfagnini, Florence, 1996, 279–88

Orvieto, Paolo, "Carnevale e feste fiorentine del tempo di Lorenzo de' Medici," in *Lorenzo il Magnifico e il suo tempo*, ed. Gian Carlo Garfagnini, Florence, 1992, 103–24

Parenti, Piero, *Storia fiorentina*, 1: *1476–78, 1492–96*; 2: *1496–1502*, ed. Andrea Matucci, Florence, 1994–2005

Polizzotto, Lorenzo, *Children of the Promise: The Confraternity of the Purification and the Socialization of Youths in Florence 1427–1785*, Oxford, 2004
   *The Elect Nation: The Savonarolan Movement in Florence 1494–1545*, Oxford, 1994
   "Savonarola and the Florentine Oligarchy," in *The World of Savonarola: Italian Élites and Perceptions of Crisis*, ed. Stella Fletcher and Christine Shaw, Aldershot, 2000, 55–64

Prizer, William F., "The Music Savonarola Burned: The Florentine Carnival Song in the Late 15th Century," *Musica e storia*, 9 (2001), 5–33
   "Petrucci and the Carnival Song: On the Origins and Dissemination of a Genre," in *Venice 1501: Petrucci, Music, Print and Publishing*, ed. Giulio Cattin and Patrizia Dalla Vecchia, Venice, 2005, 215–51

Razzi, Serafino, *Libro primo delle laudi spirituali*, Venice, 1563; facs. Bibliotheca musica bononiensis, sez. IV, n. 37, Bologna, 1969

Savonarola, Girolamo, *Poesie*, ed. Mario Martelli, in *Edizione nazionale delle opere di Girolamo Savonarola*, Rome, 1968
   *Prediche sopra Amos e Zaccaria*, ed. Paolo Ghiglieri, Rome, 1971–72
   *Prediche sopra Giobbe*, ed. Roberto Ridolfi, Rome, 1957

Trexler, Richard C., *Public Life in Renaissance Florence*, New York, 1980
   "Ritual in Florence: Adolescence and Salvation in the Renaissance," in *The Pursuit of Holiness in Late Medieval and Renaissance Religion*, ed. Charles Trinkaus, Leiden, 1974, 200–64; repr. in Trexler, *Dependence in Context in Renaissance Florence*, Binghamton, NY, 1994, 259–325

Weinstein, Donald, *Savonarola: The Rise and Fall of a Renaissance Prophet*, New Haven and London, 2011

Wilson, Blake, *Singing Poetry in Renaissance Florence: The Cantasi Come Tradition (1375–1550)*, Florence, 2009

· PART VI RELIGIOUS DEVOTION AND LITURGY ·

# Music and ritual

M . J E N N I F E R  B L O X A M

## Introduction: matters of definition and discovery

The topic of music and ritual is fundamentally anthropological, concerned with how people have used music within a ritual context, from prehistory to the present, all across the world. "Ritual" itself is a slippery concept whose definitional breadth reflects the various concerns and priorities of the disciplines that engage it: anthropology, religion, psychology, the arts. The term can be understood to encompass everything from personal habits invested with significance by one individual, to formalized social practices of a purely secular nature, to a broad array of private and communal activities based on religious beliefs.[1] This brief consideration of music and ritual in the fifteenth century will focus on the ways in which music functioned in rites based on the Roman Catholic religious beliefs that prevailed in the West at this time (rites understood here as purposeful communal ceremonies whose basic actions are meant to be repeated).[2]

Plainsong was the sonic glue of ritual in the fifteenth century, as it had been for more than a millennium. Most polyphonic musical genres of this period also served a ritual purpose, whether settings of the Mass Ordinary or Proper; settings of Office texts such as the Magnificat, Te Deum, antiphons, hymns, and psalms; or even that most functionally polysemous of genres, the motet. While much ritual music, both monophonic and polyphonic, was heard in a liturgical context, performed within the official and obligatory calendrical services of the Church such as daily Mass *in choro* and the canonical Hours, much also served extra-liturgical purposes (also known as paraliturgical, super-numerary, or votive functions). Examples of extra-liturgical ritual include processions both inside and outside the church, special votive Masses and Offices, devotions supported by lay confraternities such as Salve or *laudesi*

---

1 Bell, *Ritual*, 3–89; Muir, *Ritual in Early Modern Europe*, 1–19.
2 The ritual music of the beleaguered Jewish people in fifteenth-century Europe, centered primarily in Italy and Spain, is almost completely lost to us. A single extant polyphonic work – a three-voice motet setting a praise text in Hebrew, whose musical fabric is infused with what seem to be shofar signals used during Rosh Hashana – dates from mid-century. Harrán, "Another Look."

services, and commemorations for the dead endowed by individuals or confraternities. In other words, all liturgical music is ritual music, but not all ritual music is liturgical.[3]

Scholars have mined a wide variety of documents (ordinances and statutes, legal and financial records, liturgical books, etc.), sifting for nuggets of information about the musical life of urban centers, churches, courts, and confraternities; it is from these studies that a picture of music and ritual in this period emerges.[4] Images too, especially illuminations in service books and chronicles, provide snapshots of music-making in ritual contexts.[5] Rarely, however, can a particular polyphonic work be firmly situated in a specific ritual context, or specific ritual requirements demonstrably associated with particular repertories or composers' compositional decisions.[6]

The music of Guillaume Du Fay will serve as our primary reference point: not only does his production span the central fifty years of the century and encompass a broader array of ritual functions than any other single composer of the period, but scholars have grappled longer and harder with questions of ritual in Du Fay's music (and music thought to be by him) than with that of any other fifteenth-century composer.[7] What is more, he composed for a variety of ritual contexts, for institutions as diverse as the papal chapel, Cambrai cathedral, and the Burgundian and Savoyard courts.

## Ritual monophony, ritual polyphony

Most composers of polyphony for ritual use in the fifteenth century were, like Du Fay, clerical men immersed from boyhood in the daily performance of plainsong. Even at this late stage in its development, chant remained a vibrant repertory whose melodies, texts, and performance practices varied according to the needs and traditions of the different worship communities it served.[8] Service books from Florence and Cambrai, for example, reveal that composition of new texts and tunes continued, and existing repertories were revised in response to various needs and pressures: practical, personal, civic, political,

---

3 Flanigan *et al.*, "Liturgy as Social Performance"; also Petersen, "Liturgy and Ritual in the Middle Ages."
4 For a marvelous synthesis of documentary studies prior to ca. 1990 that reveals the myriad ways in which music served the needs of individuals and institutions in this period, see Strohm, *The Rise of European Music*, 269–319. The continuing depth and breadth of such investigation is demonstrated in the essays contained in Kisby, ed., *Music and Musicians in Renaissance Cities and Towns.*
5 Bowles, *Musikleben im 15. Jahrhundert.*
6 Richard Sherr has discovered such precious specific examples in his work on the papal chapel; see in particular "The Singers of the Papal Chapel," "Speculations on Repertory," and *"Illibata Dei Virgo Nutrix."*
7 The foundational introductions to Du Fay's life and music are Fallows, *Dufay*, and Planchart, "Du Fay, Guillaume."
8 See the essay by Richard Sherr, Ch. 40.

institutional, and aesthetic.[9] In Cambrai, for example, Du Fay supervised the updating of the liturgical books of the cathedral and composed new plainsong melodies for a Marian feast founded by a fellow canon.[10] For another great church, Santa Maria del Fiore in Florence, he very likely composed the poetry and music for a unique sequence sung at the cathedral's consecration Mass celebrated by Pope Eugene IV on the feast of the Annunciation in 1436.[11]

Plainsong remained integral to votive ritual as well, but other types of simple sacred song proliferate in this period, existing at the interstices between religious and popular, liturgical and votive, monophonic and polyphonic, improvised and notated.[12] The efflorescence of such genres as the Italian lauda, English carol, German Leise, Spanish villancico, and French *noël* signals the increasing involvement of laymen in devotional life.[13]

Much polyphony of the period, whether simple or complex, written down or not, originated as sonic ornament intended to intensify the experience of ritual, akin to opening an altarpiece, displaying a choir tapestry, and donning special vestments. The theologian Gilles Carlier (ca. 1390–1472), Dean of Cambrai cathedral and Du Fay's close colleague, evokes sacred polyphony's affective power in the strongest possible terms:

> This music wrings from the breast sighs and groans of devotion, instills heavenly love, and brings forgetfulness of earthly things, so that the mind – if not bound by the heavy chains of sin – seems to partake of heavenly joys, most of all when holy words combine with a tuneful voice to pierce the heart.[14]

Polyphony could enhance, supplement, and even replace ritual monophony. Du Fay's polyphonic settings of chant tunes, encompassing Proper and Ordinary plainsongs from the Mass as well as hymn, antiphon, responsory, Magnificat, and *Benedicamus domino* melodies, exemplify the most straightforward approach in which the plainsong, usually situated in the cantus, is draped in counterpoint. Polyphony could also supplement ritual ceremony, amplifying the grandeur of a special occasion by incorporating music where none was required, often using flowery and occasion-specific texts and emblematic plainsong cantus firmi to craft a kind of ritual embassy. Du Fay's great isorhythmic motet *Nuper rosarum flores* may have functioned in this way

---

9  Tacconi, *Cathedral and Civic Ritual*, and Haggh, "Guillaume Du Fay and the Evolution of the Liturgy." See also the essay by Alison K. Frazier in this volume, Ch. 17.
10  Haggh, "Guillaume Du Fay and the Evolution of the Liturgy."
11  Wright, "A Sequence for the Dedication of the Cathedral of Florence."
12  See the essay by Reinhard Strohm in this volume, Ch. 39.
13  For considerations of simple sacred song from a ritual perspective, see Østrem and Petersen, *Medieval Ritual and Early Modern Music*, 15–42, and Knighton, "Song Migrations."
14  Cullington, ed. and trans., *"That liberal and virtuous art,"* 34, 50. The treatise is thought to date from the last years of Carlier's life.

to open the consecration ceremony for the cathedral of Florence on 25 March 1436, presenting praise and petition to the Blessed Virgin on behalf of the people of Florence and honoring the presiding pope.[15] Finally, polyphony might on occasion even replace ritual plainsong. To bring Vespers services on special feasts to an impressive close, for example, a motet could serve in place of the *Benedicamus domino*, a practice supported by canons' foundations in Cambrai and elsewhere. Following immediately after the concluding prayers offered on behalf of the community by the celebrant, such motets served a contemplative function, inviting individual reflection.[16] The recurrent and communal nature of such motets encouraged the use of familiar preexisting texts, as witnessed by Du Fay's Vespers motet for St. Anthony of Padua, *O proles Hyspanie/O sidus Hyspanie*, a four-voice cantilena motet based on two antiphons for the saint.[17]

Composers' awareness of the ritual context of the music they created played a fundamental role in their compositional decisions. Just as the style of sacred monophony was shaped by its purpose within the ritual it helped enact, so the style of ritual polyphony was shaped by its ritual function. The solemnity and scale of the event, the forms and conventions of liturgical and votive genre, as well as the audience for the occasion were important factors in determining the compositional approach.

Du Fay's musical production, for example, reveals three broad rhetorical registers of ritually attuned style distinctions. His most elaborate structures and most complicated treatments of preexisting material, rhythm, counterpoint, and text are reserved primarily for large-scale works created for especially solemn ritual events, notably the Mass Ordinary cycles and isorhythmic motets for special occasions. Settings of Mass Propers and proses as well as individual Mass Ordinary sections tend to take a middle ground, while music for the Office usually adopts a simple, even austere style that extends in some cases to the use of fauxbourdon.[18]

Polyphony was most firmly tethered to its ritual context through the inclusion of plainsong; what chant was incorporated and how it was treated depended in large part on the work's ritual purpose. Local traditions of liturgy and plainsong, which shaped the content of sacred polyphony from its inception, continued to inform the composition of ritual polyphony in the fifteenth

---

15 On the motet as ritual embassy and *Nuper rosarum flores* in particular, see Nosow, *Ritual Meanings*, 84–104.
16 On the contemplative function of motets, see ibid., 122–24 and 135–80.
17 This motet was apparently intended for the dedication of Donatello's altar in Padua's basilica, though it reflected Cambrai's Vespers motet tradition and was subsequently used there. See Planchart, "Four Motets of Guillaume Du Fay," 27–28; and Nosow, *Ritual Meanings*, 187–94.
18 Planchart, "Du Fay's Plainsong Paraphrase Settings."

century. Composers' selection of particular chants for use within polyphony was often intimately connected to the specifics of place and purpose, and the discovery of these connections can help clarify matters of context and function, chronology, and even attribution. Thus a comparison of mass formularies reveals that Du Fay intended some of his Mass Proper settings for Cambrai cathedral while others were destined for the Sainte-Chapelle in Dijon in honor of Philip the Good's Burgundian Order of the Golden Fleece.[19] Similarly, investigation of the details of the papal Vespers liturgy demonstrates that Du Fay composed a cycle of hymn settings expressly for the papal chapel.[20] The eventual removal of the *Missa Caput* from Du Fay's canon began with the discovery that its cantus firmus was drawn from the English Sarum rite.[21]

Du Fay's compositional projects on behalf of particular institutions bear witness to the fact that polyphonic encrustation to liturgical and votive ritual observance escalated dramatically over the course of the century. Powered by improving economic conditions, demand for polyphony increased as polyphonic music became, like altarpieces, a measure of devotion as well as social or institutional prestige.[22] With the increasing appetite for ritual polyphony came growth in the number and size of church, court chapel, and confraternity choirs. Even church architecture changed over the course of the century in response to the increasing demand for votive ritual endowed by lay confraternities as well as lay and clerical individuals: railings and choir screens were installed to mark the sacred space within which the regular liturgy was enacted, with the concomitant construction of side chapels and the installation of private altars within the church where extra-liturgical devotions occurred. With the multiplication of spaces serving ritual purposes came a multiplication of images to enhance them; altarpieces and statues of Mary and the saints were particularly popular. These images served as visual foci for ritual singing: music and image combine to stimulate the interior devotional imagination of those attending religious rites, whether liturgical or votive.[23]

## Polyphony for genres of ritual action

Although most musical genres of the period served a ritual purpose, musical genre by itself does not always dictate a specific ritual function. A mass for

19 Planchart, "Guillaume Du Fay's Benefices."    20 Phelps, "Du Fay's Hymn Cycle."

21 The case for the deattribution was made by Planchart, "Guillaume Dufay's Masses," 1–13.

22 Haggh, "The Meeting of Sacred Ritual and Secular Piety."

23 Wilson, *Music and Merchants*, 183–211, details the intense symbiotic relationship of the devotional laude sung by Florentine confraternities and the images they commissioned; foundations for Vespers polyphony established by canons at the cathedral of Cambrai provide for candles to illuminate painted or sculpted images of the Virgin and the saints (Nosow, *Ritual Meanings*, 170–74).

Christmas, for example, serves a different purpose than a Requiem mass, and the motet genre in particular exhibits a remarkable functional polysemy.[24] Genres of ritual action proposed by scholars of ritual studies offer more nuanced categories for considering music and ritual than do musical genres. The six "basic genres of ritual action" proposed by Catherine Bell are especially useful because they invite us to focus on music's function in relation to the different and overlapping purposes of ritual behavior: calendrical and commemorative rites, including rites of feasting, fasting, and festivals; rites of exchange and communion; rites of passage, including political rites; and rites of affliction.[25]

## Calendrical and commemorative rites

Most rituals are about remembering, and much fifteenth-century polyphony was created for rites of remembrance conducted at regular intervals, whether annual, seasonal, weekly, or daily.[26] Central events in the lives of Christ, his mother, and the saints were marked by annual calendrical celebration; powerful intercessory agents such as the Virgin Mary and the Holy Spirit received weekly votive recollection; and the dead were memorialized through obit foundations.

Thus composers created and institutions collected polyphony to ornament major feast days and seasons of the liturgical year. Du Fay, for example, apparently undertook several discrete compositional projects in the 1420s and 1430s to provide proses, Kyries, and especially hymn settings tailored to the liturgical needs of the papal chapel.[27] He crafted a set of polyphonic Propers for the weekly cycle of votive Masses established in 1432 for the Order of the Golden Fleece by Duke Philip the Good of Burgundy at the Sainte-Chapelle in Dijon, which began with a Requiem Mass in plainsong every Monday and continued through the week with polyphonic masses for the angels, St. Andrew, the Holy Spirit, the Holy Cross, the Blessed Virgin, and the Trinity.[28] In 1470 the composer instituted his own obit Mass foundation on 5 August, the feast of Our Lady of the Snows, for which he composed his mass Ordinary setting based on the beloved Marian antiphon *Ave regina celorum*.[29] Du Fay's emphasis on ritual music designed for calendrical and commemorative use is typical of fifteenth-century composers, most of whom practiced their craft in the context of church and court chapel.

---

24 See the essay by Klaus Pietschmann, Ch. 2.      25 Bell, *Ritual*, 91–137.
26 On calendrical ritual more generally, see Bell, *Ritual*, 102–108, and Muir, *Ritual in Early Modern Europe*, 62–88.
27 Planchart, "Music for the Papal Chapel."
28 Planchart, "Guillaume Du Fay's Benefices," 142–69 and "Guillaume Du Fay's Second Style."
29 Strohm, *The Rise of European Music*, 284–87.

## Feasting, fasting, and festivals

Christian rites focused on feasting, fasting, and festivals tend to be calendrical in nature, associated particularly with the time immediately surrounding and including the penitential season of Lent.[30] Unlike the solemn commemorative orientation of the liturgical and votive occasions that inspired ambitious polyphonic responses on the part of composers like Du Fay, these rites relied primarily on monophony or simple polyphony, and often involved public processions or other group activities that encouraged public display of excessive behaviors both playful and punishing. The exuberance of Carnival season, held on the brink of Lent's austerity, is captured in the Florentine *canti carnascialeschi*, boisterous strophic poems set to simple chordal music and sung in rowdy procession through city streets.[31] On the other end of the spectrum were rites of penance concentrated in Holy Week, the most extreme being the ritual self-scourging practiced by *disciplinati* companies in Tuscany and Umbria as part of devotional services adapted from the Divine Office that mingled prayers, plainchant, and laude.[32]

The intensity of the Lenten season also encouraged ritual theater in which music played an important part, as people from all social strata enacted or observed dramatic presentations of key elements of the Passion story.[33] In England, for example, Brigittine nuns carried a bier and palms in procession on Palm Sunday, washed the altars and one another's feet on Maundy Thursday, symbolically buried the Cross on Good Friday and resurrected it on Easter morning, and finally performed the *Visitatio supulchri* before Easter Mass, all accomplished with special plainsongs.[34] In Ferrara, the chapel singers of Duke Ercole I d'Este (r. 1471–1505) sang as he bathed the feet of the poor on Maundy Thursday, and performed as well in spectacular Passion dramas on Good Friday. In one such drama presented in 1481, fourteen white-robed men emerged singing from the jaws of a large wooden serpent's head at the command of an actor representing Christ.[35] Such popular reenactments of Christ's triumph over Satan, common in Passion plays and Rogation processions across Europe, seem to resonate in three Mass Ordinary settings of the fifteenth century, the enormously influential anonymous English *Missa Caput* (once thought to be by Du Fay) and the *Caput* masses by Ockeghem and Obrecht based upon it. Taking as their cantus firmus a melisma on the word "caput" ("head") from an antiphon that accompanied the *Mandatum* ceremony,

30 On rites of feasting, fasting, and festival more generally, see Bell, *Ritual*, 120–28, and Muir, *Ritual in Early Modern Europe*, 89–124.

31 Prizer, "Reading Carnival."    32 Barr, *The Monophonic Lauda*, 131–50.

33 Fischer-Lichte, "The Medieval Religious Plays."    34 Yardley, *Performing Piety*, 124–55.

35 Lockwood, "Music and Popular Religious Spectacle at Ferrara," 575–77.

these masses appear to enact Christ's crushing of the serpent's head through musical manipulations of the chant melody, and would have been especially appropriate for use during the Eastertide season.[36] These masses thus suggest the porous boundary between rituals inside and outside the church, and invite us to consider the Mass ceremony itself as a site of ritual theater.

### Rites of exchange and communion

The Mass ritual, during which the priest offers the sacrificial gifts of bread and wine on behalf of the community in exchange for Christ's real presence in the communion gifts, was the ceremonial apex of every day regardless of festal rank.[37] Christians of the period experienced the Mass as an elaborate drama in which all present participated in a rememorative allegory tracing the life, passion, death, and resurrection of Christ in word, music, movement, gesture, and ceremonial trappings.[38] The ritual climax of the ceremony occurred as the celebrant declared Jesus' Words of Institution at the Last Supper, then elevated the consecrated Host for all to see.[39]

Music, whether chant or polyphony, provided the sonic underpinning of this ritual drama: it accompanied action, gave voice to praise and plea, confirmed belief, and conveyed the sacred stories contained in the ceremony.[40] Decisions regarding structure, style, pacing, and declamation of both chant and polyphony for the Mass hinged, to a greater or lesser degree, on practical, symbolic, and affective ritual considerations. This is especially so in the Sanctus, whose function it was to provide the aural setting within which the miracle of transubstantiation took place.[41]

Composition of polyphony for this central sacramental rite exploded over the course of the fifteenth century, as Du Fay's voluminous production of mass music attests. Its creation spanned his entire career, encompassed music for the Ordinary and the Proper, and originated for cathedral, papal, and secular court contexts.[42] He provided for a broad spectrum of

---

36 On this symbolic reading of the *Caput* masses, see Robertson, "The Savior, the Woman, and the Head of the Dragon." The multivalent nature of the enigmatic cantus firmus certainly allows for multiple interpretations of the *Caput* masses: Strohm, *Mass Settings*, 34, maintains that the original meaning of the word in its parent chant (referring to St. Peter's head) holds the key to its significance, while Kirkman, *Cultural Life*, 77–97, offers a Christological reading and proposes a link to festivities on the feast of Corpus Christi.
37 On rites of exchange and communion in general, see Bell, *Ritual*, 108–14.
38 Hardison, "The Mass as Sacred Drama."       39 Rubin, *Corpus Christi*, 1–82.
40 A vivid sense of how plainsong and polyphony functioned within a fifteenth-century mass ceremony can be heard and seen on the DVD *Missa de Sancto Donatiano (Bruges 1487) by Jacob Obrecht*, Cappella Pratensis, dir. Stratton Bull and Peter Van Heyghen, Fineline Classical FL 72414 (2009), and the complementary website: http://obrechtmass.com/home.php.
41 See the groundbreaking analysis by Long, "Symbol and Ritual"; see also Kirkman, *Cultural Life*, 183–207.
42 Fallows, *Dufay*, 146–50, 165–214.

calendrical and commemorative Mass ritual both liturgical and votive: Ordinary movements for feasts of different ranks, plenary and Proper settings for major feasts of the Temporale and select feasts of the Sanctorale, Proper and Ordinary music for the Blessed Virgin, and Propers for a weekly votive cycle.[43]

That Du Fay's last composition for the Mass ritual (the *Missa Ave regina celorum* from ca. 1470) was a complete setting of the Ordinary intended for his own obit service, based on a Marian antiphon and incorporating material from the highly personal motet he wrote to be sung as he lay dying, signals new emphases in mass music in the latter half of the century. First, Marian devotion became an increasingly important impetus to the composition of sacred polyphony, as did obit foundations.[44] Second, composers increasingly reached beyond the liturgy for materials to personalize and particularize their ritual music, drawing on polyphonic as well as monophonic models both sacred and secular.[45] Finally, a complex set of social, doctrinal, and aesthetic considerations coalesced to concentrate composers' attention on the complete setting of the Mass Ordinary.[46]

Indeed, Du Fay's four complete Mass Ordinary settings, all from the last two decades of his life, exemplify broad ritual contexts and approaches that shaped the composition of mass music in the decades around 1500. He surely composed the *Missa Se la face ay pale*, one of the earliest complete Ordinary settings based on a chanson, in connection with the Savoy court's veneration of the Shroud relic in 1453, casting the pale-faced lover of his earlier song as the suffering Christ.[47] Enthusiasm for masses based on vernacular love songs, however, soon transcended any specific courtly or historical context; as a more general affective devotional impulse focused on Christ's humanity and the loving maternity of the Virgin grew, song masses could serve a broad range of Christological and Marian ritual purposes both liturgical and votive.[48] Similarly, Du Fay's *Missa L'homme armé* may well have been meant to bring the crusader's spirit into the Mass ritual for Burgundian court chevaliers.[49] However, the multivalent symbolism of the militant song on which it is based – the "armed man" representing warriors from Christ Militant to every Christian protected by the armor of faith – generated a

43 See the Works List in Planchart, "Du Fay, Guillaume."
44 See the essay by David Rothenberg, Ch. 28, and Haggh, "The Meeting of Sacred Ritual and Secular Piety."
45 Kirkman, *Cultural Life*, 39–164.
46 Ibid., 167–214.
47 Robertson, "The Man with the Pale Face," 431–33.
48 See the essay by Anne Walters Robertson, Ch. 29.   49 Planchart, "The Origins and Early History."

long tradition of Armed Man masses appropriate to virtually any Mass celebration.[50]

In Du Fay's *Missa Ecce ancilla Domini/Beata es Maria* ("Behold the handmaid of the Lord"/"Blessed are you, Mary"), the melody and texts of two antiphons from the Annunciation liturgy unfold in the tenor, creating a dialogic structure designed to foreground the Virgin's reply to the angel Gabriel that precipitated the miracle of the Incarnation. Du Fay here places ritual drama front and center, affirming the power of plainsong cantus firmi to declare and dramatize a specific ritual association. Composers would continue to do the same for generations to come, even as they devised new approaches to creating music for the Mass ritual.

## Rites of passage

From the early Christian period on, special rites of passage punctuated major milestones in an individual's life, regardless of his or her station.[51] The sacraments of Baptism, Confirmation, Matrimony, and Extreme Unction in particular marked the fundamental beginning-of-life, coming-of-age, commitment, and end-of-life stages recognized in cultures past and present across the world. For men and women making the transition to holy orders, there were rites of ordination and consecration performed by a bishop, and, for a select few, elevations in rank were also ritually celebrated in special ceremonies of installation reserved for abbots and abbesses, bishops, cardinals, and popes.

Polyphony might on occasion serve to celebrate rites of passage in the lives of powerful people, both in the ecclesiastical and secular realms. The baptism of Prince Antoine of Burgundy, first-born son of Philip the Good and Isabella of Portugal, in Brussels on 18 January 1431, inspired court composer Gilles Binchois to create *Nove cantum melodie*, his only extant isorhythmic motet.[52] Although we do not know at what juncture in the festivities surrounding this happy occasion the motet was heard, its strikingly pervasive structural use of the number 3 (found in the mensural and isorhythmic plan) resonates with the baptism ritual's multiple thrice-performed actions (threefold exorcism blessings, threefold pouring or dipping of water) and multiple references to the Trinity. Ritual gesture and its symbolic content here appear to inform the deep structure of a musical composition made expressly for the occasion.

Elevations in ecclesiastical rank apparently inspired the creation of a number of ceremonial motets in the first decades of the century by northerners active in Italy, including Ciconia, Brassart, and Du Fay, but while their laudatory texts

50 Wright, *The Maze and the Warrior*, 159–205.
51 On rites of passage more generally, see Bell, *Ritual*, 94–102.
52 Weller, "Rites of Passage."

may enable identification of the individuals involved, the precise function of most of these works remains elusive. For example, Du Fay's grand five-voice isorhythmic motet *Ecclesie militantis/Sanctorum arbitrio/Bella canunt gentes/ Gabriel/Ecce nomen Domini* refers to the papal election of Pope Eugene IV and conjures ritual pageantry with mention of "a song of the clergy" and a "well-advised assembly," but whether it was sung during the coronation ceremony is unknown.[53]

Marriage celebrations with political implications for ruling houses would seem to invite special musical elaboration, so it is surprising that no fifteenth-century mass polyphony can be firmly associated with a wedding.[54] The ceremonial motet with its occasion-specific text would seem a likely genre to enhance nuptial celebrations, and indeed a few possible examples survive: Du Fay's four-voice isorhythmic motet *Vasilissa ergo gaude/Concupivit rex*, for example, celebrates the marriage of Cleofe Malatesta to the Greek despot Theodore II Palaiologos, but whether such wedding motets were sung as part of the nuptial rituals is unclear.[55]

For the somber rituals surrounding the final rite of passage, plainsong prevailed regardless of the status of the deceased.[56] Both vernacular devotional song and polyphony, however, could serve to comfort both the dying and the mourning community. Thus a young nun, expiring in the mid-1450s at the Convent of Santa Brigida al Paradiso outside Florence, sang and asked the sisters attending her to sing laude after she received the final sacraments; in Cambrai, Du Fay requested that his motet *Ave regina celorum*, composed in 1464 in anticipation of his death, be sung at his bedside after the administration of the last rites.[57] To Du Fay's own desire to be remembered in polyphony may be attributed the composition of the first polyphonic Requiem, a ritual whose music had resisted such elaboration for centuries: his three-voice setting, now lost, was apparently written for his own obsequies and annual obit service.[58] An earwitness who experienced the piece at the 1501 chapter meeting of the Burgundian Order of the Golden Fleece, by which time it had replaced the Order's votive plainsong Requiem Mass, judged it "mournful, sad and very exquisite" – testimony to the continuing affective power of ritual polyphony affirmed by his colleague Gilles Carlier decades earlier.[59]

53 Bent, "Early Papal Motets," 24–40.
54 On polyphony for weddings, see Robertson, "The Man with the Pale Face," 380–88.
55 Fallows, *Dufay*, 21, 104–10.
56 Haggh, "Singing for the Most Noble Souls."
57 On these rituals of separation, see Nosow, "Song and the Art of Dying."
58 Strohm, *The Rise of European Music*, 284–87.
59 Prizer, "Music and Ceremonial," 133–35, 142.

Processions, whether for carnival, a royal entry, or a feast day such as Palm Sunday, also functioned as rites of passage, marking the transition from one place, activity, or social dynamic to another. In outdoor processions, wind players might herald the progress of important individuals or relics through the urban landscape just as certain chants marked the geographic terrain traversed, and stations during processions, both outside and within the church environs, provided opportunity for polyphonic music.[60] Du Fay's isorhythmic motet *Fulgens iubar/Puerpera pura parens/Virgo post partum* was probably intended for just such a stational performance during the procession following the Office of Nones on the feast of the Purification of the Virgin in Cambrai, established in 1445–46. Ritual action is vividly reflected in the motet's materials: not only does the text refer to the candles carried by the processioners, but the last three words of the cantus firmus, "quem genuit adoravit" ("she worshipped the one she bore") match the inscription on the focal point of the ceremony, a silver reliquary displaying a painting of Mary in childbed with the newborn baby before her.[61]

## Political rites

The ceremonial pomp designed to affirm or transfer secular political power in the fifteenth century harnessed elaborate religious ritual to confirm rulers' God-given authority. Coronation and funeral rites of royalty as well as the processional royal entries of new sovereigns functioned as both secular and sacred rites of passage, involving the participation of political and ecclesiastical authority alike. Despite the opulent trappings of such occasions, plainsong nevertheless formed their musical bedrock, as witnessed by the extraordinary coronation ceremony of the English claimant to the French throne, Henry VI of England, at the cathedral of Notre Dame in Paris on 16 December 1437. The *ordo* detailing this ritual makes no mention of polyphony, though Dunstaple may have composed his *Missa Da gaudiorum premia* expressly for it, so perfectly tailored is his selection of cantus firmus and Kyrie trope.[62]

Because their texts could be fitted to the specific occasion, ceremonial motets were especially well suited to political ritual. Du Fay contributed his isorhythmic motet in praise of peace, *Supremum est mortalibus bonum*, to celebrate the arrival of emperor-elect King Sigismund in Rome prior to his coronation by Pope Eugene IV on 31 May 1433.[63] Precisely when during the pageantry the motet was sung is unknown, but the dramatic closing fermata chords proclaiming "Eugenius et rex Sigismundus" suggest its use at the

60 Reynolds, "The Drama of Medieval Liturgical Processions."     61 Nosow, *Ritual Meanings*, 180–87.
62 Wright, *Music and Ceremony*, 206–17.
63 Fallows, *Dufay*, 34–35.

culmination of the entry procession, when the two men first greeted each other on the steps of St. Peter's, or during the Mass that followed.[64]

## Rites of affliction

Rites of affliction "attempt to rectify a state of affairs that has been disturbed or disordered; they heal, exorcise, protect, and purify."[65] Prayers for intercession did of course permeate the daily ritual of the Catholic Church; they are embedded in every Mass and Office. Most substantial were the petitions to powerful intercessors concentrated in the call-and-response structure of the Litany of the Saints and various Marian litanies, mantric texts sung to sturdy recitation tones. These served as processional music during the Eastertide Rogation days, and by the fifteenth century had found a place in processions before Mass and after Compline as well.

Polyphony too could convey intense appeals for assistance through text and cantus-firmus choices. Du Fay's two motets imploring St. Sebastian for protection against the plague suggest the spectrum of ritual occasions such supplicatory music might serve. His intricate four-voice isorhythmic motet *O sancte Sebastiane/O martyr Sebastiane/O quam mira refulsit gratia/Gloria et honore* may have been composed for the Malatestas of Rimini in the early 1420s, when plague was rampant in Lombardy; its scale and complexity evoke a special communal occasion, perhaps sung in station during a pestilential procession.[66] The modest cantilena motet *O beate Sebastiane*, by contrast, seems perfectly suited for performance before the candlelit image of the saint at close of Vespers on the feast of St. Sebastian in Cambrai, as stipulated in an endowment established in 1454–55 by one of Du Fay's fellow canons.[67]

The most extraordinary rite of affliction known to have inspired complex polyphony is the papal ceremony of the Agnus Dei, a unique ritual conducted on the Saturday after Easter by every pontiff in the first year of his reign and every seven years thereafter. A dramatic addition to the liturgy took place at the close of that day's pontifical Mass: small waxen talismans stamped with the image of the Lamb of God and blessed by the pope to combat evil and protect the bearer were ceremoniously distributed to members of the Curia. For the first such occasion presided over by his patron Pope Eugene IV, held on 7 April 1431 in the Roman church of Santa Maria in Trastevere, Du Fay provided not only the intricate isorhythmic motet *Balsamus et munda cera/Isti sunt agni novelli* but probably also a troped Sanctus–Agnus Dei pair. Du Fay binds his polyphony to the ritual through both text (the motet employs a poem penned ca.

---

64 For a vivid contextual analysis of a contemporaneous motet whose materials make explicit the analogy between Christ's advent into Jerusalem and a royal entry, see Saucier, "Acclaiming Advent."
65 Bell, *Ritual*, 115.    66 Fallows, *Dufay*, 28.    67 Nosow, *Ritual Meanings*, 171–72, 245.

1365 by Pope Urban V specific to the occasion) and cantus firmus (based on an Easter responsory thrice intoned by the subdeacon bearing the amulets to the pope for distribution). Musical structure too captures the meaning of the ceremony: both the Agnus Dei and the motet present their chant tenors first forward and then in retrograde motion, a device widely used in fifteenth-century sacred music to symbolize Christ's descent into Hell, his victory over Satan, and his triumphant return.[68]

## Conclusion

In the decades after Du Fay's death in 1474 the production of polyphony for ritual purposes continued to increase all across Europe, with the number of composers growing in response to the burgeoning desire to accompany a wide range of ritual activities with the latest polyphonic music. Local traditions of chant and liturgy remain an important factor shaping music for ritual purposes, as seen in Jacob Obrecht's *Missa de Sancto Donatiano* from 1487, a work whose cantus firmi place it firmly within the unique liturgy of the patron saint of Bruges.[69] Henricus Isaac's ambitious projects to furnish chant-based Mass Proper cycles tailored to the rites of Constance cathedral and the Imperial court likewise confirm composers' continuing attention to the requirements of local liturgical practices.[70]

Yet the trend in the decades around 1500 is in the direction of music with more general rather than specific ritual utility. Motets for unique ritual occasions decline in number as Marian motets suitable for a broad array of ritual purposes multiply. Masses based on cycles of Ordinary chants appropriate for Marian celebrations (the *Missae de Beata Virgine* by composers such as Antoine Brumel, Josquin des Prez, Pierre de La Rue, and Isaac) as well as masses based on ferial plainsong (the *Missae de feria* by Matthaeus Pipelare and La Rue) attest to an increasing appetite for chant-based polyphony appropriate for less specific and more frequent ritual use. At the same time, masses based on secular songs, on solmization syllables, or on no preexisting material at all seem intended for performance at any Mass celebration.

The broad geographic diffusion of masses and motets in manuscripts around 1500 testifies to the ritual generalization of the repertory, a development furthered by their transformation into commercial products by the printer Ottaviano Petrucci in the first decade of the sixteenth century. His publications of masses and motets in partbook format helped make the repertory more

---

68 Wright, "Dufay's Motet *Balsamus*."    69 Bloxam, "Text and Context."
70 Burn, "What Did Isaac Write for Constance?"

readily available, both for performance in ritual contexts and for study and performance outside its original ritual function.[71] The separation of ritual music from its ritual context thus begins in earnest at the turn of the century, sowing the seeds of its modern status as independent art music.

# Bibliography

Barr, Cyrilla, *The Monophonic Lauda and the Lay Religious Confraternities of Tuscany and Umbria in the Late Middle Ages*, Early Drama, Art, and Music Monograph Series 10, Kalamazoo, MI, 1988

Bell, Catherine, *Ritual: Perspectives and Dimensions*, Oxford, 1997

Bent, Margaret, "Early Papal Motets," in *Papal Music and Musicians in Medieval and Renaissance Rome*, ed. Richard Sherr, Oxford, 1998, 24–40

Bloxam, M. Jennifer, "Text and Context: Obrecht's *Missa de Sancto Donatiano* in its Social and Ritual Landscape," *JAF* 3 (2011), 11–36

Bowles, Edmund A., *Musikleben im 15. Jahrhundert*, Musikgeschichte in Bildern 3:8, Leipzig, 1977

Brown, Howard Mayer, "Music and Ritual at Charles the Bold's Court: The Function of Liturgical Music by Busnoys and his Contemporaries," in *Antoine Busnoys: Method, Meaning, and Context in Late Medieval Music*, ed. Paula Higgins, Oxford, 1999, 53–70

Burn, David J., "What Did Isaac Write for Constance?," *JM* 20 (2003), 45–72

Cullington, J. Donald, ed. and trans., *"That liberal and virtuous art": Three Humanist Treatises on Music: Ægidius Carlerius, Johannes Tinctoris, Carlo Valgulio*, Newtownabbey, 2001

Fallows, David, *Dufay*, rev. edn., London, 1987

Fischer-Lichte, Erika, "The Medieval Religious Plays – Ritual or Theater?," in *Visualizing Medieval Performance: Perspectives, Histories, Contexts*, ed. Elina Gertsman, Aldershot, 2008, 249–61

Flanigan, C. Clifford, Kathleen Ashley, and Pamela Sheingorn, "Liturgy as Social Performance: Expanding the Definitions," in *The Liturgy of the Medieval Church*, ed. Thomas J. Heffernan and E. Ann Matter, Kalamazoo, MI, 2001, 695–714

Haggh, Barbara, "Guillaume Du Fay and the Evolution of the Liturgy at Cambrai Cathedral in the Fifteenth Century," in *International Musicological Society, Study Group Cantus Planus: Papers Read at the Fourth Meeting, Pécs, Hungary, 3–8 September 1990*, Budapest, 1992, 549–69

"The Meeting of Sacred Ritual and Secular Piety: Endowments for Music," on *Companion to Medieval and Renaissance Music*, ed. Tess Knighton and David Fallows, New York, 1992, 60–68

"Singing for the Most Noble Souls: Funerals and Memorials for the Burgundian and Habsburg Dynasties in Dijon and Brussels as Models for the Funeral of Philip the Fair in 1507," in *Tod in Musik und Kultur zum 500. Todestag Philipps des Schönen*, ed. Stefan Gasch and Birgit Lodes, Wiener Forum für ältere Musikgeschichte 2, Tutzing, 2007, 57–85

---

71 Staehelin, "Zur Rezeptions- und Wirkungsgeschichte."

Hardison, O. B., Jr., "The Mass as Sacred Drama," in O. B. Hardison, *Christian Rite and Christian Drama in the Middle Ages: Essays in the Origin and Early History of Modern Drama*, Baltimore, 1965; repr. Westport, CT, 1983, 35–79

Harrán, Don, "Another Look at the Curious Fifteenth-Century Hebrew-Worded Motet *Cados cados*," *MQ* 94 (2011), 481–517

Kirkman, Andrew, *The Cultural Life of the Early Polyphonic Mass: Medieval Context to Modern Revival*, Cambridge, 2010

Kisby, Fiona, ed., *Music and Musicians in Renaissance Cities and Towns*, Cambridge, 2001

Knighton, Tess, "Song Migrations: The Case of *Adorámoste, Señor*," in *Devotional Music in the Iberian World (1450–1800): The Villancico and Related Genres*, ed. Tess Knighton and Álvaro Torrente, Aldershot, 2007, 53–76

Lockwood, Lewis, "Music and Popular Religious Spectacle at Ferrara under Ercole I d'Este," in *Il teatro italiano del Rinascimento*, ed. Maristella de Panizza Lorch, Saggi di cultura contemporanea 134, Milan, 1980, 571–82

Long, Michael, "Symbol and Ritual in Josquin's 'Missa Di Dadi'," *JAMS* 42 (1989), 1–22

*Missa de Sancto Donatiano (Bruges 1487) by Jacob Obrecht*, Cappella Pratensis, dir. Stratton Bull and Peter Van Heyghen, Fineline Classical FL 72414, 2009

Muir, Edward, *Ritual in Early Modern Europe*, 2nd edn., Cambridge, 2005

Nosow, Robert, *Ritual Meanings in the Fifteenth-Century Motet*, Cambridge, 2012
　"Song and the Art of Dying," *MQ* 82 (1998), 537–50

Østrem, Eyolf, and Nils Holger Petersen, *Medieval Ritual and Early Modern Music: The Devotional Practice of Lauda Singing in Late-Renaissance Italy*, Turnhout, 2008

Petersen, Nils Holger, "Liturgy and Ritual in the Middle Ages," in *Cantus Planus: Papers Read at the 12th Meeting of the IMS Study Group, Lillafüred/Hungary, 2004. Aug. 23–28*, Budapest, 2006, 845–55

Phelps, Michael K., "Du Fay's Hymn Cycle and Papal Liturgy during the Pontificate of Eugene IV," *MD* 54 (2009), 75–117

Planchart, Alejandro Enrique, "Du Fay, Guillaume," in *Grove Music Online* (accessed 20 June 2013)
　"Du Fay's Plainsong Paraphrase Settings," in *Essays on Renaissance Music in Honour of David Fallows: Bon jour, bon mois et bonne estrenne*, ed. Fabrice Fitch and Jacobijn Kiel, Woodbridge, 2011, 103–13
　"Four Motets of Guillaume Du Fay in Context," in *Sleuthing the Muse: Essays in Honor of William F. Prizer*, ed. Kristine K. Forney and Jeremy L. Smith, Hillsdale, NY, 2012, 13–30
　"Guillaume Du Fay's Benefices and his Relationship to the Court of Burgundy," *EMH* 8 (1988), 117–71
　"Guillaume Dufay's Masses: Notes and Revisions," *MQ* 58 (1972), 1–23
　"Guillaume Du Fay's Second Style," in *Music in Renaissance Cities and Courts: Studies in Honor of Lewis Lockwood*, ed. Jessie Ann Owens and Anthony M. Cummings, Warren, MI, 1997, 307–40
　"Music for the Papal Chapel in the Early Fifteenth Century," in *Papal Music and Musicians in Medieval and Renaissance Rome*, ed. Richard Sherr, Oxford, 1998, 93–124
　"The Origins and Early History of *L'homme armé*," *JM* 20 (2003), 305–57

Prizer, William F., "Music and Ceremonial in the Low Countries: Philip the Fair and the Order of the Golden Fleece," *EMH* 5 (1985), 113–53

"Reading Carnival: The Creation of a Florentine Carnival Song," *EMH* 23 (2004), 185–252

Reynolds, Roger E., "The Drama of Medieval Liturgical Processions," *Revue de musicologie* 86 (2000), 127–42

Robertson, Anne Walters, "The Man with the Pale Face, the Shroud, and Du Fay's *Missa Se la face ay pale,*" *JM* 27 (2010), 377–434

"The Savior, the Woman, and the Head of the Dragon in the *Caput* Masses and Motet," *JAMS* 59 (2006), 537–630

Rubin, Miri, *Corpus Christi: The Eucharist in Late Medieval Culture*, Cambridge, 1991

Saucier, Catherine, "Acclaiming Advent and *Adventus* in Johannes Brassart's Motet for Frederick III," *EMH* 27 (2008), 137–79

Sherr, Richard, "*Illibata Dei Virgo Nutrix* and Josquin's Roman Style," *JAMS* 41 (1988), 434–64

"The Singers of the Papal Chapel and Liturgical Ceremonies in the Early Sixteenth Century: Some Documentary Evidence," In *Rome in the Renaissance: The City and the Myth*, ed. P. A. Ramsey, Medieval and Renaissance Texts & Studies 18, Binghamton, NY, 1982, 249–64

"Speculations on Repertory, Performance Practice, and Ceremony in the Papal Chapel in the Early Sixteenth Century," in *Collectanea II: Studien zur Geschichte der päpstlichen Kapelle. Tagungsbericht, Heidelberg, 1989*, Vatican City, 1994, 103–22

Staehelin, Martin, "Zur Rezeptions- und Wirkungsgeschichte der Petrucci-Drucke," *BJhM* 25 (2001), 13–21

Strohm, Reinhard, *Music in Late Medieval Bruges*, rev. edn., Oxford, 1990

*The Rise of European Music, 1380–1500*, Cambridge, 1993

ed., *Mass Settings from the Lucca Choirbook*, Early English Church Music 49, London, 2007

Tacconi, Marica S. *Cathedral and Civic Ritual in Late Medieval and Renaissance Florence: The Service Books of Santa Maria del Fiore*, Cambridge, 2005

Weller, Philip, "Rites of Passage: *Nove cantum melodie*, the Burgundian Court, and Binchois's Early Career," in *Binchois Studies*, ed. Andrew Kirkman and Dennis Slavin, Oxford, 2000, 49–83

Wilson, Blake, *Music and Merchants: The Laudesi Companies of Republican Florence*, Oxford, 1992

Wright, Craig, "Dufay's Motet *Balsamus et munda cera* and the Papal Ceremony of the Agnus Dei," in *Music and Medieval Manuscripts: Paleography and Performance: Essays Dedicated to Andrew Hughes*, ed. John Haines and Randall Rosenfeld, Aldershot, 2004, 325–48

*The Maze and the Warrior: Symbols in Architecture, Theology, and Music*, Cambridge, MA, 2001

*Music and Ceremony at Notre Dame of Paris, 500–1550*, Cambridge, 1989

"A Sequence for the Dedication of the Cathedral of Florence: Dufay's(?) *Nuper almos rose flores,*" in *Atti del VII Centenario del Duomo di Firenze*, ed. Timothy Verdon and Annalisa Innocenti, Florence, 2001, 3:55–67

Yardley, Anne Bagnall, *Performing Piety: Musical Culture in Medieval English Nunneries*, New York, 2006

# 28

# Marian devotion in the fifteenth century

DAVID J. ROTHENBERG

In the fifteenth century the Virgin Mary was viewed, perhaps more than at any other time in history, as "the woman for all seasons – and all reasons."[1] The veneration of saints was an obsession of fifteenth-century culture, and Mary stood at the forefront of the saintly community as its most favored member and thus the one who could recommend mortals most forcefully and effectively to Christ.[2] Her sanctity was not celebrated on a single feast day, as with most saints, but on five or six (and sometimes even more) different days, and the votive celebrations and private devotions that sprang up around these feast days made Marian devotion a constant of daily life.[3] In fifteenth-century music, too, Mary was a constant presence, as anyone with even a passing familiarity with the repertory cannot help but notice. Marian texts, devotional themes, and symbolism were prominent in all the major genres of fifteenth-century sacred music, and even secular genres sounded symbolic echoes of the Virgin.[4] Fifteenth-century musicians sang and composed to Mary on behalf of themselves and others, producing a corpus of Marian music so vast and varied that easy generalization is impossible. Nevertheless, a review of the basic elements of Marian devotion and their musical manifestations can give a sense of Mary's central place in fifteenth-century music.

The principal Marian feasts were those of the Virgin's [Immaculate] Conception (8 December),[5] Purification (2 February), Annunciation (25 March), Visitation (2 July),[6] Assumption (15 August), and Nativity (8 September). These feast days served, along with Christmas, Easter, and

---

1 Pelikan, *Mary through the Centuries*, 215–23.
2 For a useful general discussion of Marian devotion in the fifteenth century, see Rubin, *Mother of God*, 283–351; on the development of Marian doctrine in theological writings, see Graef, *Mary*, vol. 1, *passim*.
3 For discussion of the Marian liturgy and devotion as they pertained to fifteenth-century music, with extensive literature, see Rothenberg, *Flower of Paradise*, 13–19.
4 On Marian symbolism in fifteenth- and sixteenth-century music, see Elders, *Symbolic Scores*, 151–84.
5 The doctrine of the Immaculate Conception, which holds that Mary was conceived free of sin in St. Anne's womb, remained a subject of intense theological dispute in the fifteenth century. See Rubin, *Mother of God*, 173–76; Pelikan, *Mary through the Centuries*, 189–200; and Graef, *Mary*, 1:250–53 and 298–311.
6 The feast of the Visitation became widespread only in the late fourteenth century and was still not universally celebrated in the fifteenth. On the history of the Marian feasts, see Jounel, "The Veneration of Mary."

the complex of movable celebrations built around them (collectively called the Temporale), as the calendrical pillars of an unending cycle of Marian devotion. A Marian votive Mass, usually beginning with the Introit *Salve sancta parens*, was often celebrated on Saturday, the day of the week traditionally devoted to the Virgin. But votive Masses were not limited to Saturdays; they could be added to the proper liturgy of the day whenever devotion to the Virgin was desired.[7] The conclusion of the evening service of Compline, moreover, brought each liturgical day to a close with the singing of a Marian antiphon. For most of the year this was the *Salve regina*, but during Eastertide it was the *Regina caeli*, from Advent to the feast of the Purification it was the *Alma Redemptoris mater*, and from Purification to Easter it was the *Ave regina celorum*. The Marian votive Mass, too, featured seasonal variants that followed a similar schedule, with a Mass that opened with the Introit *Rorate caeli* supplanting the *Salve sancta parens* Mass during Advent, and one that opened with *Vultum tuum* replacing it from Christmas to Purification. Mary was thus venerated liturgically on virtually every day of the year, with the Marian feasts providing especially splendid celebrations and demarcating, along with the central feasts of the Temporale, seasonal variations in the daily routine of worship.

Mary was venerated in the private sphere as well, where personal prayer books, especially books of hours, abounded. Often called the "best-sellers" of the century, books of hours boiled down the liturgy into a simplified form for personal use.[8] Their centerpiece was the Hours of the Virgin, a full set of Marian votive offices (Matins, Lauds, Prime, Terce, Sext, None, Vespers, and Compline) that were sometimes found in breviaries and other liturgical books, but which by the fifteenth century were most often recited privately. The Hours of the Virgin had seasonal variants that lined up calendrically with the variants in the votive Mass and the Marian antiphons, which themselves were often included in books of hours as well. Other materials that appeared in these books were a calendar listing saints' days, selected Gospel readings from each of the four Evangelists, the Office of the Dead, the Hours of the Cross or of the Holy Spirit, several long Marian prayers (including the "Obsecro te," the "O, intemerata," and the "Stabat mater"), the Litany of the Saints, and short devotions to specific saints known as suffrages.

The most obvious sign of the importance that books of hours held in the fifteenth century is the care and lavishness with which they were decorated. There are, to be sure, modest exemplars that were owned by the urban

---

7 On the proliferation of votive masses in the twelfth through sixteenth centuries, see Jungmann, *The Mass of the Roman Rite*, 1:129–36.
8 For a useful discussion of books of hours and their role in fifteenth-century culture, see Wieck, *Time Sanctified*.

Figure 28.1 The Annunciation, Hours of the Virgin (Matins), *Très riches heures* of Jean, Duke of Berry, fol. 26r

bourgeoisie, but the most splendid examples, such as the famous *Très riches heures* of Jean, Duke of Berry from ca. 1410 (Figure 28.1), are some of the finest jewels of fifteenth-century manuscript illumination. In these books the Marian votive Mass often begins with an illumination of the Madonna, the Mass for the Dead with a funeral or burial scene, and the suffrages with depictions of their specific saints. Each of the Hours of the Virgin, moreover, became paired by convention with one of the common scenes of Marian visual iconography: Matins with the Annuncation (Figure 28.1), Lauds with the Visitation, Prime with Christ's Nativity, Terce with the Annunciation to the Shepherds, Sext with the Adoration of the Magi, None with the Presentation of Christ in the Temple, Vespers with the Flight into Egypt, and Compline with the Assumption or Coronation of the Virgin. Many of the devotional texts set to music in the fifteenth century can be found in books of hours among these rich visual depictions.

Fifteenth-century Christians spent so much time and effort praising the Virgin largely because they expected to spend a very long time in Purgatory after they died, and they wanted her help in reducing that time.[9] When they prayed, celebrated the liturgy, or sang to her, they hoped that she, the great Mediatrix or Intercessor, might reward them by interceding with Christ that he shorten their stay. An unwritten rule was that the greater the amount of Marian devotion, and the more splendid that devotion, the more likely she was to grant her favor. This is why so many major churches were dedicated to the Virgin and why wealthy institutions and citizens hired singers to sing Marian antiphons and Marian votive Masses on their behalf. It is also why many civic churches turned the nightly singing of the Marian antiphon into a lavish performance of polyphonic music and moved it to the nave, where the public could see and hear it. These nightly performances, called *Salve* services after the *Salve regina*, were widespread, but they were only one part of a collective effort to provide musical praise of the Virgin whenever and wherever possible.

Musicians in the fifteenth century spent considerable time singing and composing Marian music on behalf of others, but this did not stop them from seeking her intercession for themselves as well.[10] Already in the fourteenth century Guillaume de Machaut had composed his *Messe de Nostre Dame* and endowed the singing of it in perpetuity as part of a Saturday Marian votive Mass in honor of himself and his brother.[11] A century later, in the 1460s, the aging Guillaume Du Fay wrote his four-voice *Ave regina celorum* in which he quotes the Marian antiphon *Ave regina celorum* and tropes its text, asking Mary specifically to "have mercy on your dying Du Fay" ("Miserere tui labentis Dufay").[12] Josquin's *Illibata Dei virgo nutrix*, which was most likely composed in the 1490s, presents an acrostic of the composer's name and is built on a very

---

9 On the rise of the doctrine of Purgatory in the late Middle Ages, see Le Goff, *The Birth of Purgatory*.
10 See Blackburn, "For Whom Do the Singers Sing?"
11 Robertson, *Guillaume de Machaut and Reims*, 257–75.
12 He also composed the *Missa Ave regina celorum* based on this motet. See Planchart, "Notes on Guillaume Du Fay's Last Works."

simple cantus firmus consisting of the solmization syllables "la-mi-la," a
*soggetto cavato* of the three syllables in Mary's name (Ma-ri-a).[13] The motet
asks Mary to "console those singing 'la-mi-la' in your praise" ("consola ...
la-mi-la canentes in tua laude"), that is, to intercede on behalf of the composer
and those singing his motet.

Over the course of the century, Mary was praised with high church polyphony, simple plainchant, and music in the style of secular song. This stylistic
range reflects a central paradox of Marian devotion, namely, that she was
simultaneously both the exalted Queen of Heaven and a humble lady of this
earth. The musical genre most closely aligned with Marian devotion in the early
fifteenth century, which we can call the "cantilena motet," points more to her
humility than to her exaltedness.[14] A cantilena motet is a votive composition in
three voices featuring the same contrapuntal texture as the fifteenth-century
chanson – a cantus and tenor that form a structural pair, plus a non-essential
contratenor. The most famous cantilena motet is John Dunstaple's *Quam
pulchra es* from ca. 1420, which praises Mary with verses drawn from the
Song of Songs, the most erotic and sensual book of the Bible. Marian devotion
drew heavily on the Song of Songs because its verses – an amorous dialogue
between a male lover and female beloved – could be interpreted allegorically to
represent commonly held beliefs about the Virgin, such as her bodily
Assumption into heaven or her Immaculate Conception in St. Anne's womb,
that have no literal basis in Scripture.[15] Moreover, Marian appropriation of the
Song of Songs pointed to a linguistic and devotional resonance between secular
love songs and devotion to the Virgin that musicians had been underscoring
since the thirteenth century. If Mary could be praised allegorically with love
lyrics from the Bible, their logic went, she could be praised similarly with
secular love lyrics that venerated an earthly beloved in language appropriate to
the Virgin.

Early fifteenth-century musicians began exploring the resonance between
Marian devotion and secular song in the cantilena motet, as we see in Du Fay's
*Vergene bella* from the 1420s, a cantilena motet in all regards except for the
language of its text.[16] Rather than a Latin prayer, it sets a stanza in Italian from
Petrarch's "Vergine bella," the devotional *canzone* that concludes the poet's
*Canzoniere* (a collection of 366 poems in which secular verses about his beloved
Laura culminate in this prayer to the Virgin). Du Fay's musical setting

---

13 For further discussion of this piece, with extensive literature, see Fallows, *Josquin*, 48–55 and Rodin,
*Josquin's Rome*, 35–39.
14 See Rothenberg, *Flower of Paradise*, 97–105, and the literature cited there.
15 On the Song of Songs and Marian devotion see Matter, *The Voice of My Beloved*, esp. 151–77.
16 For further discussion and literature, see Rothenberg, *Flower of Paradise*, 92–122.

Example 28.1 Walter Frye, *Ave regina celorum* (opening)

resembles his French chansons from the 1420s much more closely than his sacred music from the period, but it is grouped in all its manuscript sources with Latin cantilena motets. It is thus a sacred composition with a secular style that reflects Mary's humility and a text that emphasizes the ability of vernacular language to praise Mary with more immediacy than the elevated language of Latin prayer.

No composition demonstrates more effectively the ways in which Mary bridged the gap between sacred and secular music over the course of the fifteenth century than Walter Frye's *Ave regina celorum*, a cantilena motet written ca. 1450 (Example 28.1).[17] Although probably composed in Frye's native England, it made its biggest splash on the Continent, where most who encountered it were unaware of its authorship. The numerous manuscripts that transmit it are predominantly chansonniers – collections of French songs – from the 1470s and 1480s, in which it appears anonymously. Users of these books, therefore, would have experienced it as a Latin Marian work in the style of a chanson that pointed toward a spiritual interpretation of the chansons that appeared alongside it. Frye's work was so well known that it

17 The text Frye sets ("Ave regina celorum, mater regis angelorum … ") is different from the great Marian antiphon with the same incipit ("Ave regina celorum, ave domina angelorum … "). For further discussion, with extensive literature, see Rothenberg, *Flower of Paradise*, 123–58.

Figure 28.2  Master of the Embroidered Foliage, *Madonna and Child Surrounded by Angels*, with music from Frye's *Ave regina celorum*

was incorporated into several works of visual art, all of which place the Virgin Mary in a setting that resembles an earthly court. One of these is an anonymous Flemish Madonna from the 1480s, attributed to the Master of the Embroidered Foliage, that now hangs in the Louvre (Figure 28.2). It shows Mary sitting on a throne with the Christ Child in her lap while two angels place a crown on her head. The trees in the upper corners indicate that she sits in a garden, an allusion to the Song of Songs 4:2 ("My sister, my spouse, is a garden enclosed, a fountain sealed up"), which was understood allegorically to describe Mary's virginity. The child reaches toward a chansonnier-size book from which three angels sing the clearly legible music of Frye's *Ave regina celorum* – its cantus voice on the verso folio, its tenor on the recto. The instrumentalist angels on the other side of the scene, meanwhile, play a recorder, a vielle, and a lute, all *bas* (soft) instruments that were appropriate for accompanying voices in the performance of French chansons.[18] In this scene, then, the Virgin is depicted as a courtly lady, serenaded by angels depicted as courtly musicians who perform Frye's *Ave regina celorum* as if it were a courtly song.

Mary figured just as prominently in the learned, cantus-firmus-based genres of sacred composition that were performed in more public or liturgical contexts. Du Fay's *Nuper rosarum flores*, for example, is an isorhythmic motet to the Virgin with an exceptionally complex symbolic program that was composed for the consecration in 1436 of the Duomo in Florence, a building dedicated to the Virgin as Santa Maria del Fiore (St. Mary of the Flower).[19] Around the same time, the emerging cyclic mass routinely used Marian cantus firmi that inflected the unchanging text of the Mass Ordinary toward devotion to the Virgin. Leonel Power's *Missa Alma Redemptoris mater*, an early English example built on the great Marian antiphon, treats its model isorhythmically, repeating it in identical form in all of its movements and thereby making the mass Marian. The single most influential English mass of the century, the anonymous *Missa Caput* from ca. 1440, has a cantus firmus that, although not drawn from the Marian liturgy, has recently been shown to have a Marian devotional component.[20] And Petrus de Domarto's *Missa Spiritus almus*, a widely disseminated and influential mass from ca. 1450 that subjected its cantus firmus to processes of mensural transformation, was built upon a melisma from the responsory *Stirps Jesse*, which was sung on the feasts of the Assumption, Nativity, and Annunciation.[21] In the second half of the century there was a proliferation of Marian cyclic masses, none more splendid than Jacob Obrecht's *Missa Sub tuum presidium* from around the turn of the sixteenth century, in which the final Agnus Dei has seven voices – a number often associated symbolically with the Virgin – that quote five different

---

18  See Fallows, "Secular Polyphony in the 15th Century" and Keith Polk's essay in this volume, Ch. 38.
19  See Wright, "Dufay's *Nuper rosarum flores*," and Trachtenberg, "Architecture and Music Reunited."
20  Robertson, "The Savior, the Woman, and the Head of the Dragon."
21  On the mass, see Wegman, "Petrus de Domarto's *Missa Spiritus almus*"; on the history of the responsory, see Fassler, "Mary's Nativity."

Marian cantus firmi, including the votive antiphon *Sub tuum presidium* for which the mass is named and portions of the *Salve regina* and *Regina celi*.[22]

The *Ecce ancilla Domini* masses by Du Fay, Johannes Regis, and Johannes Ockeghem all celebrate the Annunciation and illustrate the emulative play in which composers could engage when approaching a common devotional theme.[23] In the early 1460s Ockeghem and Regis both visited Cambrai, where Du Fay was a canon of the cathedral; the three masses were probably composed around this time.[24] The story of the Annunciation is told in Luke 1:26–38, which was read as the Gospel lesson at Mass on the feast of the Annunciation and on Ember Wednesday during the third week of Advent, as well as in the Marian votive Mass for Advent. In this passage the archangel Gabriel famously says to Mary, "Hail, full of grace [*Ave gratia plena*], the Lord is with thee: blessed art thou among women . . . Behold thou shalt conceive in thy womb, and shalt bring forth a son; and thou shalt call his name Jesus" (Luke 1:28 and 31). Mary is at first frightened, but she chooses to submit to the angel's announcement, saying, "Behold the handmaid of the Lord [*Ecce ancilla Domini*]; be it done to me according to thy word" (Luke 1:38). Often in depictions of the Annunciation Gabriel is shown saying "Ave gratia plena" (in Figure 28.1 these words are written on the banderole that represents his utterance), and Mary is sometimes shown responding with "Ecce ancilla Domini." On Ember Wednesday the Annunciation Gospel was often enacted dramatically, with choirboys playing the parts of Gabriel and the Virgin, in a ceremony known as the *Missa aurea* (Golden Mass); this may have provided the occasion for performance of the *Missae Ecce ancilla Domini*.

Du Fay's mass, probably the earliest,[25] incorporates two chants as cantus firmi: the antiphons *Ecce ancilla Domini* and *Beata es, Maria*, both of which were sung on the feast of the Annunciation and in various services during Advent. *Ecce ancilla Domini* sets Mary's words from Luke 1:38, and *Beata es, Maria* says that Mary is blessed because she believed what the Lord told her (through Gabriel's message). The entry of the cantus-firmus-bearing tenor is preceded in all five movements by an identical introductory motto in the upper voices (Example 28.2a). Regis's mass strives to surpass Du Fay's in its construction,

---

22  On this mass as well as Obrecht's *Missa Sicut spina rosam*, see Bloxam, "Plainsong and Polyphony."

23  On Du Fay's and Regis's masses, see Gallagher, *Johannes Regis*, 116–40; and Bloxam, "A Survey of Late Medieval Service Books," 132–52. On Ockeghem's mass, see Fitch, *Johannes Ockeghem: Masses and Models*, 78–90.

24  Wright, "Dufay at Cambrai."

25  Reinhard Strohm argues alternatively that Ockeghem's mass was composed first; see *The Rise of European Music*, 472–73. There is wide agreement, however, that Du Fay's mass was composed before Regis's.

Example 28.2  Mottos from the *Missae Ecce ancilla domini* by Guillaume Du Fay and Johannes Ockeghem

(a) Du Fay

(b) Ockeghem

Example 28.3  Cantus-firmus melodies in the *Missae Ecce ancilla domini* by Du Fay and Ockeghem

(a) Du Fay (from office antiphon *Ecce ancilla Domini*)

Ec  -  ce __  an  -  cil  -  la  Do  -  mi - ni  *etc.*

(b) Ockeghem (from processional antiphon *Missus est Gabriel angelus*)

Ec - ce  an - cil - la  Do  -  mi  -  ni___  *etc.*

using the same two cantus firmi plus five others (for a total of seven), all drawn from antiphons for the feast of the Annunciation or for Advent, and all either quoting the Annunciation Gospel directly or praising Mary for her submission to God's will. Ockeghem's setting is related to Du Fay's in an entirely different manner. All of its movements quote a single cantus firmus on the words "Ecce ancilla Domini . . ." in the tenor voice, but this is not the same melody that Du Fay uses (see Example 28.3). Instead, Ockeghem quotes the closing melisma of the processional antiphon *Missus est Gabriel angelus* for the first and second

Example 28.4  Hayne van Ghizeghem, *De tous biens plaine* (opening)

Sundays in Advent. Where he tips his hat to Du Fay (or vice versa) is in his use, in all movements except the Credo, of an introductory motto whose first bar is identical to Du Fay's (see Example 28.2). Regis also shared Du Fay's title and Annunciation theme, but whereas Regis took Du Fay's two cantus firmi and added five more, Ockeghem used a similar motto to Du Fay but quoted a different cantus firmus.

All the strands of Marian musical devotion discussed thus far converge in a group of late fifteenth-century masses and motets that draw their cantus firmi from well-known French chansons.[26] The number of sacred works that quote secular chansons is large, but let us take as representative examples a pair of motets built on two of the most widely disseminated chansons of the later fifteenth century: Loyset Compère's *Omnium bonorum plena*, which quotes the tenor of *De tous biens plaine* by the Burgundian court musician Hayne van Ghizeghem, and Josquin's *Stabat mater*, which is built upon the tenor of *Comme femme desconfortée*, attributed to Gilles Binchois. *De tous biens plaine* (Example 28.4) and *Comme femme desconfortée* (Example 28.5) are both rondeaux that lend themselves well to Marian appropriation, but they express very

26 On the use of secular cantus firmi in fifteenth-century Marian polyphony, see Bloxam, "A Cultural Context"; Bloxam, "'I have never seen your equal'"; and Rothenberg, *Flower of Paradise*, esp. 159–239. Most compositions based on secular songs are listed in Fallows, *Catalogue of Polyphonic Songs*.

Example 28.5 *Comme femme desconfortée* (opening)

different sentiments.[27] The former is a classic courtly love song that praises its beloved as "Full of all goodness," and "as worthy of praise as ever was any goddess." The latter is a love lament in which the narrator, "As a disconsolate woman, more than all others distraught," can be taken as either a disconsolate woman singing for herself or a man comparing himself to a disconsolate woman.

Compère composed *Omnium bonorum plena* in the 1470s for a gathering of singers.[28] Both its *prima* and *secunda partes* quote *De tous biens plaine*, and both sections of its Latin text begin with the words "Omnium bonorum plena," a direct translation into Latin of the French words "De tous biens plaine." In whichever language, these words cannot help but remind one of the "Ave gratia plena" that Gabriel uttered to Mary during the Annunciation, and indeed, the motet text plays upon this resonance in the *prima pars*, saying, "Nullus tibi comparari / potest certe nec aequari, / cui voce angelica / dictus est 'Ave Maria'" ("Nothing can be compared to you or equal you, to whom the angelic voice said 'Ave Maria'"). The *secunda pars* begins with an introductory duet in which the tenor voice paraphrases the tenor of *De tous biens plaine* while declaiming the words "Omnium bonorum plena" (Example 28.6); the most striking moment of the piece comes soon thereafter, when the tenor reenters

27 Both are discussed as well in Robertson's essay in this volume, Ch. 29.
28 See most recently Rothenberg, *Flower of Paradise*, 163–78, and the literature cited there.

Example 28.6 Loyset Compère, *Omnium bonorum plena* (beginning of 2.p.)

carrying the *De tous biens plaine* tenor as a strict cantus firmus (Example 28.7). At this moment the texture expands to the full four voices while the text begins "Funde preces ad Filium / pro salute canentium / et primo pro G[uillaume] Dufay" ("Offer prayers to your Son for the salvation of singers: first for Guillaume Du Fay") and then continues through a long list of other prominent singers and composers of the day, among them Antoine Busnoys, Johannes Tinctoris, Ockeghem, Regis, and Compère himself. Compère thus invokes both Gabriel's salutation and Hayne's chanson in a musical prayer to the Virgin on behalf of some of the most accomplished musicians of his day.

Josquin's *Stabat mater*, composed sometime from the late 1480s to ca. 1500, is a veritable *summa* of fifteenth-century musical devotion to the Virgin, incorporating both older techniques that look back through the fifteenth century and newer ones that look forward to the sixteenth.[29] The "Stabat

---

29 On the dating of this piece and for literature, see Fallows, *Josquin*, 213–15 and Rothenberg, *Flower of Paradise*, 198–211.

Example 28.7 Compère, *Omnium bonorum plena* (entry of cantus firmus in 2.p.)

mater" text, a rhymed prayer attributed insecurely to Jacopone da Todi (ca. 1230–1306), was sometimes included in the liturgy proper but in the fifteenth century was more often encountered as a supplemental prayer in books of hours. It is a meditation upon Mary's sorrow as she stood at the foot of the Cross and seeks in the most vivid terms to empathize with the Virgin: "Make my heart burn with the love of Christ, God, that I may please him … Let me weep with you [Mary]; let me carry Christ's death, the fate of his passion, and contemplate his wounds … Inflamed and incited by you, O Virgin, let me be defended on the day of judgment." Josquin's setting is conservative in that it quotes the tenor of *Comme femme desconfortée* as a strict long-note cantus firmus (Example 28.8), but is entirely novel in its text-setting, which gives the words of the "Stabat mater" a degree of aural clarity

Example 28.8 Josquin des Prez, *Stabat mater* (opening)

and emotional immediacy not encountered earlier in the century. The plaintive French text of *Comme femme desconfortée* already resonates with the sorrowful affect of the "Stabat mater" prayer, but Josquin's harmonic and rhythmic inflections at key moments heighten it further. We see this in his setting of "Fac me tecum plangere" ("Let me weep with you"), where a signed E♭ creates a sonority that darkens the already intensely sorrowful text, declaimed simultaneously by all voices with rhythm that emphasizes especially the word "plangere" ("weep") (Example 28.9). At moments like this, those singing or hearing Josquin's motet are invited not just to

Example 28.9  Josquin, *Stabat mater* (setting of "Fac me tecum plangere")

contemplate Mary's sorrow but to feel it, and through it to experience the redemptive power of the Crucifixion.

In Josquin's *Stabat mater*, as in countless works of fifteenth-century music, Mary is both exalted with the learned composition due a monarch and praised with more accessible secular music befitting a noble lady. The range of musical styles and registers that are employed to sing her praises reflects the diversity of Marian devotion that one encountered in fifteenth-century life, from elaborate festal liturgies celebrated by cathedral clergy to simple prayers recited at home by the laity. As both the Queen of Heaven and a lady of this world, Mary was, more even than Christ, the devotional figure who brought together the diverse strata of fifteenth-century society – and of fifteenth-century music.

## Bibliography

Blackburn, Bonnie J., "For Whom Do the Singers Sing?," *EM* 25 (1997), 593–609

Bloxam, M. Jennifer, "A Cultural Context for the Chanson Mass," in *Early Musical Borrowing*, ed. Honey Meconi, New York, 2004, 7–35

"'I have never seen your equal': Agricola, the Virgin, and the Creed," *EM* 34 (2006), 391–407

"Plainsong and Polyphony for the Blessed Virgin: Notes on Two Masses by Jacob Obrecht," *JM* 12 (1994), 51–75

"A Survey of Late Medieval Service Books from the Low Countries: Implications for Sacred Polyphony, 1460–1520," Ph.D. diss., Yale University, 1987

Elders, Willem, *Symbolic Scores: Studies in the Music of the Renaissance*, Leiden, 1994

Fallows, David, *A Catalogue of Polyphonic Songs, 1415–80*, Oxford, 1999

*Josquin*, Turnhout, 2009

"Secular Polyphony in the 15th Century," in *Performance Practice: Music before 1600*, ed. Howard Mayer Brown and Stanley Sadie, New York, 1989, 201–21

Fassler, Margot, "Mary's Nativity, Fulbert of Chartres, and the Stirps Jesse: Liturgical Innovation circa 1000 and its Afterlife," *Speculum* 75 (2000), 389–434

Fitch, Fabrice, *Johannes Ockeghem: Masses and Models*, Paris, 1997

Gallagher, Sean, *Johannes Regis*, Turnhout, 2010

Graef, Hilda, *Mary: A History of Doctrine and Devotion*, 2 vols., New York, 1963–65

Jounel, Pierre, "The Veneration of Mary," in *The Church at Prayer: An Introduction to the Liturgy*, ed. Aimé Georges Martimort *et al.*, 4: *The Liturgy and Time*, ed. Irénée Henri Dalmais *et al.*, trans. Matthew J. O'Connell, Collegeville, MN, 1986, 130–50

Jungmann, Josef A., *The Mass of the Roman Rite: Its Origins and Development*, 2 vols., trans. Francis A. Brunner, New York, 1951–55

Le Goff, Jacques, *The Birth of Purgatory*, trans. Arthur Goldhammer, Chicago, 1984

Matter, E. Ann., *The Voice of My Beloved: The Song of Songs in Western Medieval Christianity*, Philadelphia, 1990

Pelikan, Jaroslav, *Mary through the Centuries: Her Place in the History of Culture*, New Haven, 1996

Planchart, Alejandro Enrique, "Notes on Guillaume Du Fay's Last Works," *JM* 13 (1995), 55–72

Robertson, Anne Walters, *Guillaume de Machaut and Reims: Context and Meaning in his Musical Works*, Cambridge, 2002

"The Savior, the Woman, and the Head of the Dragon in the Caput Masses and Motet," *JAMS* 59 (2006), 537–630

Rodin, Jesse, *Josquin's Rome: Hearing and Composing in the Sistine Chapel*, New York and Oxford, 2012

Rothenberg, David J., *The Flower of Paradise: Marian Devotion and Secular Song in Medieval and Renaissance Music*, New York and Oxford, 2011

Rubin, Miri, *Mother of God: A History of the Virgin Mary*, New Haven, 2009

Strohm, Reinhard, *The Rise of European Music, 1380–1500*, Cambridge, 1993

Trachtenberg, Marvin, "Architecture and Music Reunited: A New Reading of Dufay's 'Nuper Rosarum Flores' and the Cathedral of Florence," *Renaissance Quarterly* 54 (2001), 740–75

Wegman, Rob C., "Petrus de Domarto's *Missa Spiritus almus* and the Early History of the Four-Voice Mass in the Fifteenth Century," *EMH* 10 (1991), 235–303

Wieck, Roger S., *Time Sanctified: The Book of Hours in Medieval Art and Life*, New York, 1988

Wright, Craig, "Dufay at Cambrai: Discoveries and Revisions," *JAMS* 28 (1975), 175–229

"Dufay's *Nuper rosarum flores*, King Solomon's Temple, and the Veneration of the Virgin," *JAMS* 47 (1994), 395–441

# 29

# Affective literature and sacred themes in fifteenth-century music

ANNE WALTERS ROBERTSON

One of the intriguing aspects of fifteenth-century sacred music is its tendency to recycle familiar, and often highly moving, themes. This sometimes leaves the impression that there was a consensus of sorts about which motifs, typically involving the Virgin Mary, Christ, and the saints, were to be venerated across the culture. The touching episodes of Jesus' Nativity were memorialized visually in illuminated books of hours, in paintings of the Virgin Mary nursing her newborn, in sculptures of the scene in the stable in Bethlehem, in the architecture of countless churches dedicated to the Mother of God, and in the mystery plays that elaborated the details of Christ's birth, just as it was celebrated aurally in music composed on the Christmas antiphon *Nesciens mater*. Similarly, the image of Mary weeping at the foot of the Cross was captured both in the visual and dramatic arts and in music based on songs in Latin (*Stabat mater*) and the vernacular (*Comme femme desconfortée*). Even the newer genres of sacred music sometimes conceived without cantus firmus – from the declamation-style pieces of John Dunstaple's generation to the early compositions of Josquin des Prez, Loyset Compère, and others who sought to imitate text directly – delighted in developing themes drawn from the Song of Songs, the Passion of Christ, the Psalms, and other emotional texts.

These subjects reinvented and perpetuated themselves in music throughout the late Middle Ages for many reasons. This period saw the rise of an international style, in part because composers had opportunities to exchange ideas.[1] They moved freely between church and court, they encountered one another at the great councils, and their music circulated widely in large repertory manuscripts. Yet sociological circumstances alone cannot explain the universality of recurring themes in sacred music and the cross-fertilization of these ideas among the arts in this period. Surely other stimuli, reflecting basic habits of mind and educations of composers and patrons, lie in the background. What

---

1 Strohm, *The Rise of European Music*.

shared experiences helped drive the cultivation and circulation of beloved sacred motifs in the fifteenth century?

One experience that was common to all was the reading of sacred affective literature. This writing, much of it in Latin and dating from the late fourteenth century, became more accessible to every level of society in the fifteenth century when translated into the vernacular. Its style differed starkly from the rigorous methodology of scholastic theology, in which tightly woven arguments scrutinized doctrines great and small. Affective treatises required the reader to immerse herself in the details of Jesus' life and that of the Virgin. Doing so, along with reciting foundational texts such as the Creed, the Lord's Prayer, and the *Ave Maria*, was touted as a key to salvation. Eminent Parisian theologian Jean Gerson (1363–1429) disparages scholarly study, writing: "However much advanced scholarship and great learning in God's law may be quite suitable for the person who wishes to come to the height of contemplation, nevertheless sometimes such knowledge blocks this pursuit."[2] Instead, as Englishman Nicholas Love (died ca. 1424) explains, "devout meditations on Christ's life are clearer in some places than the Gospels," and because of this, "contemplation of the humanity of Christ is more pleasant and more profitable and more successful than is contemplation of the Godhead."[3] Knowing the *vita* of Christ well, the *literati* might delve into lofty doctrine, but the *sine qua non* for the educated and uneducated alike was an unshakable grasp of the Savior's story.

## Affective devotional treatises and music based on sacred cantus firmi

A single treatise of affective devotion from the fourteenth century served as the basis for almost every aspect of devotional piety in the late Middle Ages.[4] This tract, the *Meditationes Vitae Christi* (*Meditations on the Life of Christ*), once attributed to St. Bonaventure, was actually penned by an Italian Franciscan monk named Johannes de Caulibus. The *Meditationes* presents much more than basic biblical accounts, consistently adding material that reaches well beyond the Gospels.[5] But its novel mode of communication sets it apart from previous discussions of Christ's life, for it appeals to the emotions. The reader is urged to situate himself in the events of Christ's life and exhorted through imperative verbs and the present tense to "behold" and "contemplate" its scenes.

---

2 Gerson, "The Mountain of Contemplation," 76; translation of French text found in Gerson, *Oeuvres complètes*, 7:16.
3 Sargent, ed., *Nicholas Love's Mirror*, 10.    4 Stallings-Taney, ed., *Iohannis de Caulibus Meditaciones*.
5 Ibid., ix–x; see also Karnes, *Imagination*, 144–46, 166–78.

This new model of devotion influenced late medieval spirituality in countless ways. Hundreds of manuscripts of the *Meditationes* survive, and the work was translated into French, Provençal, English, Italian, German, Dutch, Gaelic, Swedish, Spanish, Catalan, and Bulgarian throughout the fifteenth century.[6] The *Meditationes* stands among the earliest works to be published, beginning in 1470, and it was one of the first illustrated books.

Encapsulating the affective core of fifteenth-century devotion, the *Meditationes* likewise helped shape the arts of the late Middle Ages. Under its influence, the story of the Passion grew into a mega-genre of its own, the mystery plays, which often took several days to perform. Devotional vernacular poetry, including dialogues between the Virgin Mary and Jesus, laments of Mary at the foot of the Cross, passionate prayers to the Virgin, and copious poetry for the Passion, also draws on the *Meditationes*. Fifteenth-century iconography owes a massive debt to this work, from its description of the Nativity with the ox and ass laying their heads on the crèche and breathing on the infant Jesus to keep him warm, to its portrayal of the pathos of the Crucifixion in excruciating, drawn-out passages.[7] Like earlier Passion treatises and contemporaneous books of hours, moreover, the *Meditationes* organized the events of Christ's life for readers by ordering important scenes into dynamic sequences. In its discussion of the Passion, for example, the *Meditationes* correlates the episodes with the canonical Hours to promote effective, and affective, study.

Two highly admired lives of Christ were derived from the *Meditationes*, reworking it in different ways. The *Vita Christi* by the Carthusian monk Ludolph of Saxony from the 1370s was a true *summa*.[8] Considerably larger than the *Meditationes*, the *Vita Christi* includes the basic narrative plus a commentary incorporating hundreds of patristic references, meditations, and prayers. Ludolph's *Vita* was translated into German, French, Catalan, Castilian, Portuguese, English, and Italian, and was published repeatedly until the late nineteenth century. It was a favorite book of St. Ignatius of Loyola (1491–1556) and of the movement known as the *Devotio Moderna*. The *Mirror of the Blessed Life of Christ* (ca. 1410), a translation of the *Meditationes* by Carthusian prior Nicholas Love, abbreviated Johannes de Caulibus's work. Surviving in sixty-four manuscripts, Love's *Mirror* was published ten times between 1484 and 1606.[9]

---

6 On the increasing importance of French as a language of prayer in the fifteenth century, see Reinburg, *French Books of Hours*, 84–128, esp. 88, where the author writes: "religion was lived in a mixture of Latin and the vernacular."

7 Stallings-Taney, ed., *Iohannis de Caulibus Meditaciones*, 31, 270–80 (ch. 7, lines 34–37; chs. 78–79).

8 Ludolf von Sachsen, *Vita Christi*; French translation in Broquin, trans., *La Grande Vie de Jésus-Christ*.

9 Karnes, *Imagination*, 212–13; Sargent, ed., *Nicholas Love's* Mirror, ix–cxlii.

The *Meditationes* and its offshoots were widely read and their narratives painstakingly absorbed. Because traces of their stories are found everywhere in fifteenth-century arts, including motets and masses, we can assume that the customary scriptural and spiritual formation of composers and patrons involved close study of these works.

The development of affective motifs related to the Nativity offers a good example of the effect of these treatises. The biblical account of Jesus' birth, derived from Luke 1:26–38 and 2:7, tells us that his mother was a virgin and that she gave birth in a sinless state, having conceived Christ without the seed of man. Most earlier medieval discussions preserve these ideas. The immensely popular *Golden Legend* from the thirteenth century, for instance, reports simply: "In that night our Blessed Lady and Mother of God was delivered of our Blessed Saviour upon the hay that lay in the rack."[10]

The Church Fathers had nonetheless elaborated the basic doctrines of the Nativity with other tenets early on, popularized in works such as the *Meditationes*. Here we notice two non-biblical, affective details: that Mary delivered the infant without the pains of childbirth, and that she openly nursed the child as she had been taught to do by the Holy Spirit. In addition, the *Meditationes* focuses on the dynamic, emotional, graphic, and maternal aspects of the story:

> Cum autem venisset hora partus, scilicet media nocte Dominice diei, surgens Virgo appodiavit se ad quondam columnam que ibi erat ... Tunc Filius Dei exiens de matris utero, *sine aliqua molestia vel lesione*, in momento sicut erat in utero sic fuit extra uterum super fenum ad pedes matris sue. Et mater incontinenti se inclinans, recolligens eum et diligenter amplexans, posuit in suo gremio. *Et ubere de celo pleno, a Spiritu Sancto edocta, cepit lavare sive linire ipsum per totum cum lacte suo.*[11]

Nicholas Love's *Mirror* translates this passage as follows:

> When time of that blessed birth was come, that is to say the Sunday at midnight, God's Son of heaven as he was conceived in his mother's womb by the Holy Ghost, without seed of man, so going out of that womb *without travail or sorrow*, suddenly was upon hay at his mother's feet, and anon she, devoutly leaning over, with sovereign joy took him in her arms and sweetly embracing and kissing, laid him in her lap, *and with a full breast, as she was taught by the Holy Ghost, washed him all about with her sweet milk.*[12]

---

10  Caxton, *The Golden Legend*.
11  Stallings-Taney, ed., *Iohannis de Caulibus Meditaciones*, 31 (ch. 7, lines 22–32).
12  Sargent, ed., *Nicholas Love's* Mirror, 37 (ch. 6; my translation from Middle English).

In fifteenth-century mystery plays, moreover, the third-person narrator disappears and Mary unselfconsciously assures Joseph, and later the infant Jesus himself, that giving birth caused her no discomfort:

> Pour crainte j'ay asseurement
> certain de non estre grevee
> par virginité conservee
> dont l'enfantement se fera
> qui en riens ne me grevera;
> pour pesance ay ligereté,
> pour foiblesse pleine santé,
> car mon corps et mon ame ensamble
> sont bien disposés, ce me samble,
> et ne sens chose qui me grieve . . .
> Mon chere enffant, ma tres chere portee . . .
> Virginalment en mes flans te conceus,
> virginalment ton corps humain receus,
> virginalment t'ay enffanté sans peine.[13]

> For fear I am assuredly
> Certain not to be harmed
> By being a virgin
> And giving birth
> Which will in no way harm me;
> Instead of heaviness I feel lightness,
> Instead of feebleness, full health,
> For my body and my soul together
> Are well disposed, it seems to me,
> And I sense nothing that could harm me . . .
> My dear son, my very dear one that I have carried . . .
> As a virgin I conceived you in my body,
> As a virgin I received your human form,
> As a virgin I have given birth to you without pain.

These accretions are commonly seen in late medieval art in the vivid depictions of such themes as the *Maria lactans*,[14] which illustrates Mary, with one breast bared, nursing her infant, signaling a new sensuality that was motivated in part by the unabashed frankness of works like the *Meditationes*.

Fifteenth-century composers, like artists, were moved by the story of the Nativity. To undergird their polyphonic compositions, they often turned to an

---

13 Paris and Raynaud, eds., *Le Mystère de la passion d'Arnould Gréban*, 62–65 (lines 4885–94, 5068, 5072–74).
14 See the discussion of *Maria lactans* images in Bloxam, "A Cultural Context," 16–22. A useful collection of these depictions can be seen online at www.fisheaters.com/marialactans.html.

ancient Marian chant for Christmas and its octave, *Nesciens mater*, no doubt because its text incorporated both orthodox and more colorful doctrines:

> Nesciens mater virgo virum peperit sine dolore Salvatorem seculorum, ipsum regem angelorum, sola virgo lactabat ubere de celo plena.

> Knowing no man, the Virgin mother gave birth without pain to the Savior of the world; alone the Virgin nursed the very king of the angels with her breast filled from heaven.

English composers set these words in different ways, reflecting the evolving musical style of the fifteenth century. Byttering (fl. 1410–20) used homorhythm and a highly decorated chant that migrates among the three voices,[15] and John Trouluffe and other Englishmen followed suit. *Nesciens mater* also inspired a Kyrie and Gloria by John Plummer, both of which survive fragmentarily.[16] Not long after the turn of the century, the antiphon had captured the imagination of a Continental composer: the eight-voice motet *Nesciens mater* by Johannes Mouton (ca. 1459–1522) is a stately fourfold canon yielding eight voices. In the Medici Codex, the piece is copied in four voices only, with notational signs showing how to derive the others, producing the effect of "a body of four voices giving birth to another body of four voices."[17] The use of canon, as well as its notation, seems to point to the idea of Christ issuing from the Virgin's womb. And the somberness of the piece, along with its overall consonance, especially at the words "sine dolore," reflect the Virgin's painless delivery.

Clearly, *Nesciens mater* provided a particularly useful text and melody for composers wishing to commemorate the treasured Nativity narrative. The more carnal aspects of the story also turn up in music composed without a cantus firmus. The text of Josquin des Prez's "little" *Ave Maria* follows the famous *Ave* prayer at first, then takes a sudden turn in the second half of the piece:[18]

> Ave Maria, gratia plena,
> Dominus tecum.
> Benedicta tu in mulieribus
> et benedictus fructus

---

15  Hughes and Bent, eds., *The Old Hall Manuscript*, 139–40 (no. 50).

16  For these and other English fifteenth-century settings, see Curtis and Wathey, "Fifteenth-Century English Liturgical Music," 50, 60–61. Thomas Morley discusses a lost four-part motet on *Nesciens mater* by Dunstaple.

17  Lowinsky, ed., *The Medici Codex of 1518*, 171, 207–14 (no. 30). In the sixteenth century, the text was also set by Walter Lambe in the *Eton Choirbook*, by Johannes Frosch in a theory treatise, and by Ludwig Senfl, Andreas de Silva, and others.

18  Josquin, ed. Elders, NJE 23:16–19 (no. 4). On early settings of the *Ave* prayer, see Anderson, "Enhancing the *Ave Maria*." The Antiphon *Ave Maria* is quoted only in the first thirteen measures.

ventris tui:
Jesus Christus,
Filius Dei vivi.
Et benedicta sint
beata ubera tua,
que lactaverunt regem regum
et Dominum Deum nostrum.

Hail Mary, full of grace,
The Lord is with you.
Blessed are you among women
And blessed is the fruit
Of your womb,
Jesus Christ
Son of the living God.
And blessed be
Your beautiful breasts,
Which nourished the king of kings
And the Lord our God.

The phrase "Mary's beautiful breasts" is especially conspicuous because it is equated syntactically with the words "fruit of [Mary's] womb," heard earlier.[19] Josquin likewise emphasizes the "mammary" lines by introducing the words "Et benedicta sint beata ubera tua" with the first full-stop cadence in the piece and by changing the meter from duple to stately triple. This moment reminds us of the homorhythmic passages set in long notes that appear in other motets from Josquin's oeuvre, for instance his *Vultum tuum* cycle and the end of *Ave Maria ... virgo serena*. More generally, it recalls the earlier English tradition exemplified by Dunstaple's *Quam pulchra es*, in which the famous line "Come, my beloved" ("Veni, dilecte me") begins in extended note values following rests. As composers strayed from cantus firmi, they were often inspired to highlight the emotional content of the text.

## Affective poetry and music based on vernacular songs

Another category of affective writing that helped mold sacred music in the fifteenth century is important because of its early date and the special relationship it bears to mass and motet. Scores of dramatic works composed in the

---

19 On this piece, see Macey, "Josquin's 'Little' *Ave Maria*."

vernacular helped make the lives and attributes of Christ and the Virgin more comprehensible while also facilitating the flow of ideas between the sacred and secular spheres. Although these dramas are well known, many other devotional writings remain unedited, possibly because they come down to us in rather ordinary manuscripts that were apparently not copied for wealthy patrons. Typically in poetic form, these works, dating from as early as the fourteenth century, bear a striking resemblance to the texts of secular chansons on which masses and motets were based beginning several decades later.

Possibly because of their haphazard survival, these poems often bear generic designations, as seen in the title of this snippet from an unpublished collection of "Louenges" ("Praises") to the Virgin:

> Quant dieu vous feist sur toutes souveraine
> De tous ruisseaux vous estes la fontaine
> Ou loyaulx cuers se doyuent resiouyr,
> Et pour *les biens dont vous estes tant plaine*
> Mere de dieu a vous me viens offrir.[20]

> When God made you sovereign over all things,
> Of all streams you are the fountain
> Where loyal hearts may rejoice,
> And for *the good things of which you are full*,
> Mother of God, I come to offer [thanks] to you.

The description of Mary as "full of all goodness" brings to mind Hayne van Ghizeghem's (ca. 1445–1476/97) popular courtly song, *De tous biens plaine est ma maistresse* ("My mistress is full of all goodness"). Later in this poem, the Virgin is also addressed as "Ma maistresse tres exellente,"[21] echoing Hayne's words as well as those of Johannes Ockeghem (1410/25–1497) in his song *Ma maistresse* and the mass based on it. The polyvalence of both phrases illustrates how readily they might move from the earthly to the sacred realm, and vice versa, as several excellent studies have recently shown.[22]

Indeed, the idea that the Virgin Mary, like her earthly counterparts, was "filled with all goodness" is so ubiquitous in French devotional poetry that it becomes an affective metaphor. A fourteenth-century poem illustrates the manifold ways in which "de tous biens plaine" might be playfully varied, even alluding to Mary's pregnancy as "the goodness of which she is full," namely, her son:

---

20  Paris, Bibliothèque nationale de France (hereinafter "BnF"), fr. 2225, fol. 19v.    21  Ibid., fol. 25.
22  Bloxam, "I have never seen your equal"; Bloxam, "A Cultural Context"; Rothenberg, *Flower of Paradise*, and Rothenberg's contribution to this volume, Ch. 28. Reinburg notes a similar trend in the veneration of saints: "saints were called 'mistress,' 'master,' 'lady,' and 'lord'" in late medieval prayer; *French Books of Hours*, 240.

La dame *de tous biens fontaine*
vierge plesant et gracieuse
Dame de toute grace plaine
Ne peut *les biens dont elle est plaine,*
Le filz dieu ...
Vierge tant honnouree
*Qui de tous biens est plaine.*[23]

The Lady [who is the] *fount of all goodness,*
Pleasant and gracious Virgin,
Lady full of all grace,
Not to mention the *goodness of which she is full,*
The Son of God ...
Virgin so honored
Who is full of all goodness.

Apparently, The Virgin was referred to as "de tous biens plaine" almost as often as she was described in Latin as "omnium bonorum plena."[24] Little mental transformation would have been necessary to understand the purpose of Compère, Josquin, and others in using Hayne's song *De tous biens plaine* in sacred polyphony.[25] These words already evoked the image of Mary in the abundant semi-sacred poetry of the late Middle Ages.[26]

More emotional depictions of the lamenting Virgin in late medieval drama recall the empathy-inducing song *Comme femme desconfortée* ("As a disconsolate woman"). In the *Passion de Sémur* from the beginning of the fifteenth century, Mary herself uses the words "desconffort" and "desconfforter" while standing at the foot of the Cross:[27]

| | |
|---|---|
| Voy qu'il le veullent mectre a mort | Look how he wants to be put to death |
| *Dont je suis en grant desconffort.* | Because of which I am in great *discomfort.* |
| Quant je vous voy en ce tourmant, | When I see you in this torment |
| Je me doix bien *desconfforter* | I have to be greatly *discomforted.* |

The later passions, including the *Passion d'Arras* (before 1440) and Gréban's *Mystère*, use almost identical expressions.[28] In sacred music by Alexander

---

23 BnF, fr. 25418, fols. 125, 132v, 138r.    24 Rothenberg, *Flower of Paradise*, 163–64.
25 Many of these pieces are described in Rothenberg, *Flower of Paradise*, 159–92. See also the "Benediction of the Virgin's Limbs," mentioned in Bloxam, "A Cultural Context," 25.
26 Other examples of sacred texts that refer to Mary as "de tous biens plaine" are found in Rothenberg, *Flower of Paradise*, 162–63.
27 The *Passion de Sémur* is edited in Roy, *Le Mystère de la Passion en France*, 148, 152 (lines 7554–55, 7579–80).
28 The *Passion d'Arras*, attributed to Eustache Mercadé (*Le Mystère de la passion*, 213), records: "Hé! Filz, a droit me desconfort" (l. 18441), and "Je te tieng mort je te tieng mort, / Dont mon cuer est en desconfort" (ll. 18444–45). In Gréban's play, Mary uses the word three times while standing at the foot of the Cross immediately following Jesus' death: "O mon filz, trop me desconforte" ("O my son, you discomfort me too

Agricola, Johannes Ghiselin, Henricus Isaac, Josquin, and others that builds on the song *Comme femme desconfortée*, then, the hearer hardly needed to analogize an abandoned earthly lover and the Virgin: the *femme desconfortée* might well be the woman portraying the Virgin Mary in the *mystère* that was being performed in the town square.[29]

In some devotional poems, Christ himself speaks. An unpublished *Dialogue, en vers, entre Marie, l'âme, l'hôtesse et Jésus Christ* from the fifteenth century includes four characters – Mary, the Soul, the Guide, and Jesus – who weave in and out of intensely emotional conversations. At one point, Christ offers to throw himself into the sea ("Et me suis plongé en la mer") for the sake of the Soul, and he entreats her to look squarely upon his suffering face ("Regarde mo[i] face a face").[30] These highly charged sentiments bring to mind analogous ideas in Guillaume Du Fay's song *Se la face ay pale*, where the protagonist grows pale because of his love for a lady ("If the face is pale, the cause is love"). This song served as the basis for the first complete mass constructed over a secular cantus firmus, which most likely commemorated the arrival and subsequent veneration of the Holy Shroud in Duke Louis of Savoy's Sainte-Chapelle in 1453.[31] The ostensible theme of the song echoes many Passion texts that point out the pale face of Christ dying on the Cross, including Love's *Mirror* ("our Lord Jesus ... waxed all pale"), along with the *Meditationes* and Ludolph's *Vita Christi* (Jesus was "pale in death").[32]

Teaching spiritual precepts through affective verse, vernacular devotional poetry, and drama helped readers meditate on the distraught Virgin or the crucified Jesus in familiar language. It is easy to see why the songs *De tous biens plaine*, *Comme femme desconfortée*, and *Se la face ay pale*, whose texts recall this poetry, were deemed fit for service as vernacular cantus firmi in sacred masses and motets.[33] What is difficult to discern – and probably unknowable because of the interpenetration of registers – is which genre, vernacular sacred poem, or secular song lyric borrowed from the other. Given the early dates of the Marian poem featuring the expression "de tous biens plaine," and the *Passion de Sémur* highlighting "desconforter," however, it is noteworthy that these words were

---

much"); and later, "mon cueur plain de desconfort" ("my heart full of discomfort"); and finally, "tu me laisses desconffortee" ("you leave me disconsolate"); Paris and Raynaud, eds., *Le Mystère de la passion d'Arnould Gréban*, 339, 354 (lines 26026, 27067, 27079).

29 For a list of sacred pieces using this cantus firmus, see Rothenberg, *Flower of Paradise*, 195–96. See also his contribution to the present volume, Ch. 28.

30 BnF, n.a.f. 10032, fols. 69v, 70v; see Robertson, "The Man with the Pale Face," 407–9.

31 Robertson, "The Man with the Pale Face," esp. 402–5 and n. 49.

32 Sargent, ed., *Nicholas Love's Mirror*, 180 (line 18); Stallings-Taney, ed., *Iohannis de Caulibus Meditaciones* (l. 171); Broquin, trans., *La Grande Vie de Jésus-Christ*, 6:461.

33 The fifteenth-century chanson *Je ne vis onques la pareille* seems to equate a courtly lady and the Virgin: "I have never seen your equal, my gracious lady ... Upon seeing you I marvel / And say: could this be Our Lady?"; see Bloxam, "'I have never seen your equal'," 393.

being applied to the Virgin in poetry long before Hayne van Ghizighem and others penned their "secular" songs. Indeed, so great is the semantic and linguistic overlap between the two genres that we should wonder if fifteenth-century composers wrote these and other chansons for use in both spiritual and mundane contexts from the start.

## Filling the gaps? Affective writing and freely constructed music

In some ways, Marian music built on vernacular songs only added richness to a repertory already replete with opportunities for devotion through music with affective words. The four expressive antiphons in her honor (*Alma Redemptoris mater*, *Ave regina celorum*, *Regina celi*, and *Salve regina*), along with the angelic salutation *Ave Maria*, inspired polyphony for the Virgin well before the fifteenth century.[34] And as Josquin's "little" *Ave Maria* illustrates, some of the earliest music that sought to mimic key ideas in the text through specific musical strategies – changing textures, use of homorhythm, incipient word-painting – was composed around these same texts, beginning in the last quarter of the century.

The *Missa Se la face ay pale*, with its preexisting music based on Du Fay's chanson, however, suggests a somewhat different trajectory for devotional music for Christ. Paradoxically, there was little affective plainsong comparable to the great Marian antiphons for composers to use in honoring Jesus. In the fourteenth century, the English cultivated many sacred motets for saints and the Virgin, but only a handful that can be assigned to the Godhead, based on their texts.[35] Similarly, the earliest complete settings of the polyphonic Ordinary from this same time, the Mass of Tournai and Machaut's *Messe de Nostre Dame*, are intended for Mary rather than Christ. This lacuna is even more conspicuous because of the prolific corpus of late medieval art for the Passion that included exceptionally graphic representations of the Crucifixion, many drawn from the *Meditationes*. As Émile Mâle observed, not only was the Passion "the chief concern of the Christian soul," but "Christians [seemingly] wished to see their God suffer and die."[36]

To be sure, Christocentric fervor increased astonishingly during the fifteenth century. Every royal and princely *sainte chapelle* that sprang up in France in the thirteenth through early sixteenth centuries, imitating the

---

34 Anderson, "Enhancing the *Ave Maria*."
35 See Lefferts, *The Motet in England*, 173, and Robertson, *Guillaume de Machaut and Reims*, 192–206 (Machaut's Motet 21 for Christ and the Holy Spirit).
36 *Religious Art in France in the Late Middle Ages*, 82–83.

Sainte-Chapelle of Louis IX (Saint Louis) in Paris, housed at least one major Christological relic, typically a spine from the Crown of Thorns or a fragment of the Cross.[37] The Sainte-Chapelle of Duke Louis of Savoy in Chambéry possessed images of the Holy Face (the Veronica, or "vera icon") and famously guarded the Holy Shroud. This proliferation of "Jesus relics" throughout Europe accompanied a flowering of ritual and private devotion, adding new feasts such as the Holy Name of Jesus, and devotions to the Host, the Holy Face, and the Five Wounds. These occasioned the creation of Christological side altars, paintings, and confraternities. Music had to keep pace with affective Christological devotion. The use of vernacular songs in sacred polyphony such as *Se la face ay pale*, along with the occasional sequence or hymn from the Temporale, could only begin to fill the gap.

In part because of the paucity of affective plainchant for Christ, beginning in the last quarter of the fifteenth century composers such as Josquin, Compère, and others sometimes eschewed cantus firmi altogether or mingled freely composed passages with a sequence melody or a hymn from the Temporale, forging a new kind of motet in which the text is clearly expressed through syllabic setting and homophony. Many of these works reveal the inspiration for their texts in the prayers found in books of hours, especially in the lengthy passages in the hours of the Cross devoted to the suffering of Christ.[38] Although the origins of this novel musical style have often been related to nascent Italian humanism and the lauda, we should not overlook the impact of devotional treatises. As primers on how to "behold" and "contemplate" sacred mysteries, these writings must also have suggested to composers how they might "hear" the emotion of the Passion and other stories. In addition to the *Meditationes* and its associated works, production of which shifted from manuscript to print precisely at this time, composers drew on the poignant writings of saintly and papal authors, including Gregory the Great (540–604), the Franciscans Bonaventure (1221–74) and Bernardino of Siena (d. 1444), and Pope Sixtus IV (r. 1471–84). In the presence of this wellspring of affective influences, working alongside the stylistic changes and shifting needs and tastes of patrons in the later fifteenth century,[39] it is hardly surprising that a musical vocabulary corresponding to that of the emotional texts developed in this music.

In addition to Josquin's "little" *Ave Maria* and other Marian works, then, Christological compositions such as Josquin's *O bone et dulcissime Jesu*, his cycles on *O domine Jesu Christe* and *Qui velatus*, Compère's *motetti missales* cycle

---

37  Billot, *Les Saintes-Chapelles royales et princières*, 1–15.
38  Drake, ed., *Ottaviano Petrucci, Motetti B*, 8–18.
39  See Cumming, "From Variety to Repetition."

*Ave domine Jesu Christe*, and the anonymous *Salve sancta facies* once attributed to Josquin[40] have loose, intermittent, or no connection to Christological plainchant. To some degree, they seem to be creative additions to the contemporaneous sacred polyphony for the Savior based on preexisting music, such as Compère's motet *Ad honorem tuum Christe*. As the incipits of all of these pieces suggest, the goal was to pray directly to Jesus. This practice finds precedent not only in books of hours, but also, for instance, in the orations in meditative treatises, notably at the end of each chapter of Ludolph's *Vita Christi*.[41] The prayers that these composers chose are not surprising, since several were indulgenced, offering to those who recited them, and perhaps also to those who heard them, release from time in Purgatory.[42]

Much of the music in Petrucci's *Motetti B* (1503) is representative of this embryonic affective movement. Josquin's loosely unified motet cycle *Qui velatus* draws on the fervent language of St. Bonaventure, who penned the Office of the Passion from which the words of the composition were derived.[43] Irregularities in the presentation of the cycle, however, may point to the transmission of Christ's Passion in the *Meditationes* and its progeny. Just as Josquin declined to compose a motet for every hour of the Passion, omitting those for Matins and None and transposing the one for Lauds to the end, so the *Meditationes* combines accounts of the crucifixion and death of Christ into a single chapter encompassing both Sext and None.[44] Josquin's cycle, moreover, begins not with the expected texts from Matins and Lauds, but with that for Prime, a decision that may reflect his desire to focus on the Passion events of Good Friday. In the same way, the *Meditationes* and Love's *Mirror* distinguish between what happens to Jesus before and after his arrest, establishing the divide at dawn on Friday, corresponding to the hour of Prime.[45]

These similarities are suggestive, not definitive, nor is the connection between the meditative treatises, vernacular sacred poetry, and mystery plays and the newer musical style of Josquin always unequivocal.[46] But composers' penchant for subjects that parallel these writings is telling, and the instances

---

40  Ibid.; see also Macey, "Josquin, Good King René"; Fallows, *Josquin*, 74–77; Brown, "On Veronica and Josquin"; Blackburn, "The Virgin in the Sun," 182. Cf. Joshua Rifkin's discussion of the attribution of *O bone et dulcissime Jesu* in "Munich, Milan, and a Marian Motet," 328–30.

41  See, for instance, Broquin, trans., *La Grande Vie de Jésus-Christ*, 1:220, 6:362. All of Ludolph's prayers are edited in Bodenstedt, *Praying the Life of Christ*.

42  Blackburn, "For Whom Do the Singers Sing?"

43  Drake, ed., *Ottaviano Petrucci, Motetti B*, 8–18, 36–40 (discussion), 88–113 (no. 3; music of *Qui velatus* cycle).

44  Stallings-Taney, ed., *Iohannis de Caulibus Meditaciones*, 270 (ch. 78).

45  Sargent, ed., *Nicholas Love's* Mirror, 169.

46  The new polyphonic passions of the fifteenth century call for scrutiny in light of the *Meditationes* and its related works. Similarly, the many musical settings based on the Song of Songs and on the Psalms owe much to the extravagant commentaries on these books of the Bible that appeared at this time.

of expressivity that appear at this time touch on the very nature of musical art. As the ancients taught, music projected both "harmonia" – notes and counterpoint – and "ethos" – the passions. Johannes Tinctoris (1430 or 1435–1511) restricts his discussion to the former; indeed, treatments of the "ethical" role of music do not appear until the mid-sixteenth century in treatises of Nicola Vicentino (1511–75 or 1576) and others.[47] All the while, music by Mouton, Josquin, Compère, and their cohort contains hints of emotion, and the declamation-style settings of Dunstaple, Byttering, and their contemporaries date back even further.[48] Were compositional attitudes toward text habituated to some degree by composers' exposure to the newly translated lives of Christ and analogous writings that fundamentally molded the fifteenth-century mentality? At the very least, teasing out vestiges of the *Meditationes* and its kindred works in this music reminds us how composers, singers, and hearers would have learned to contemplate the memorable scenes of Christ's life, from his Nativity to the Crucifixion. Predating humanistic disquisitions on *imitatio* and mimesis by several decades, these affective writings provide a glimpse into the fifteenth-century mindset, one that may help account for how music was conceived, including the new sensitivity to text that composers pioneered.

# Bibliography

Anderson, Michael Alan, "Enhancing the *Ave Maria* in the Ars Antiqua," *PMM* 19 (2010), 35–65

Berger, Karol, *A Theory of Art*, New York and Oxford, 2000

Billot, Claudine, *Les Saintes-Chapelles royales et princières*, Paris, 1998

Blackburn, Bonnie J., "For Whom Do the Singers Sing?," *EM* 25 (1997), 593–609

"The Virgin in the Sun: Music and Image for a Prayer Attributed to Sixtus IV," *JRMA* 124 (1999), 157–95

Bloxam, M. Jennifer, "A Cultural Context for the Chanson Mass," in *Early Musical Borrowing*, ed. Honey Meconi, New York and London, 2004, 7–35

"'I have never seen your equal': Agricola, the Virgin, and the Creed," *EM* 34 (2006), 391–407

Bodenstedt, Sister Mary Immaculate, *Praying the Life of Christ: First English Translation of the Prayers Concluding the 181 Chapters of the Vita Christi of Ludolphus the Carthusian: The Quintessence of his Devout Meditations on the Life of Christ*, Analecta Cartusiana 15, Salzburg, 1973

---

47  Berger, *A Theory of Art*, 115–33.
48  As Cumming writes about a composition by Arnold de Lantins (d. before 1432): "The pacing of the text declamation and the coordination of the voices are carefully controlled for expressive effect"; Cumming, *The Motet in the Age of Du Fay*, 129.

Broquin, Dom Florent, trans., *La Grande Vie de Jésus-Christ par Ludolphe le Chartreux*, 2nd edn., 7 vols., Paris, 1870–83

Brown, Howard Mayer, "On Veronica and Josquin," in *New Perspectives on Music: Essays in Honor of Eileen Southern*, ed. Josephine Wright with Samuel A. Floyd, Jr., Warren, MI, 1992, 49–61

Caxton, William, *The Golden Legend*, in *Medieval Sourcebook: The Golden Legend (Aurea Legenda), Compiled by Jacobus de Voragine, 1275, Englished by William Caxton, 1483*, 1: "The Nativity of our Lord," www.fordham.edu/halsall/basis/goldenlegend/index. asp (accessed 19 September 2012)

Cumming, Julie, "From Variety to Repetition: The Birth of Imitative Polyphony," *Yearbook of the Alamire Foundation* 6 (2008), 21–44

*The Motet in the Age of Du Fay*, Cambridge, 1999

Curtis, Gareth, and Andrew Wathey, "Fifteenth-Century English Liturgical Music: A List of the Surviving Repertory," *RMA Research Chronicle* 27 (1994), 1–69

Drake, Warren, ed., *Ottaviano Petrucci, Motetti de Passione, de Cruce, de Sacramento, de Beata Virgine et Huiusmodi B, Venice, 1503*, Monuments of Renaissance Music 11, Chicago and London, 2002

Fallows, David, *Josquin*, Turnhout, 2009

Gerson, Jean, "The Mountain of Contemplation," in *Jean Gerson: Early Works*, trans. Brian Patrick McGuire, Classics of Western Spirituality 92, New York, 1998, 75–127

*Oeuvres complètes*, ed. Palémon Glorieux, Paris and New York, 1960–73

Hughes, Andrew, and Margaret Bent, eds., *The Old Hall Manuscript*, vol. 1/1, CMM 46, n.p., 1969

Josquin, *Motets on Non-Biblical Texts*, 3: *De beata Maria virgine 1*, ed. Willem Elders, NJE 23, Utrecht, 2006

Karnes, Michelle, *Imagination, Meditation, and Cognition in the Middle Ages*, Chicago, 2011

Lefferts, Peter M. *The Motet in England in the Fourteenth Century*, Ann Arbor, 1986

Lowinsky, Edward E. ed., *The Medici Codex of 1518: A Choirbook of Motets Dedicated to Lorenzo de' Medici, Duke of Urbino: Historical Introduction and Commentary*, Monuments of Renaissance Music 3, Chicago and London, 1968

Ludolf von Sachsen, *Vita Christi*, 5 vols., Salzburg, 1865; repr. 2001 (orig. pub. Strasbourg and Cologne, 1474)

Macey, Patrick, "Josquin, Good King René, and *O bone et dulcissime Jesu,*" in *Hearing the Motet: Essays on the Motet of the Middle Ages and Renaissance*, ed. Dolores Pesce, New York, 1997, 213–42

"Josquin's 'Little' *Ave Maria*: A Misplaced Motet from the *Vultum tuum* Cycle?," *TVNM* 39 (1989), 38–53

Mâle, Émile, *Religious Art in France in the Late Middle Ages: A Study of Medieval Iconography and its Sources*, Bollingen Series 90/3, Princeton, 1986

Mercadé, Eustache, *Le Mystère de la passion. Texte du manuscrit 697 de la bibliothèque d'Arras*, ed. Jules-Marie Richard, Arras, 1891

Paris, Gaston, and Gaston Raynaud, eds., *Le Mystère de la passion d'Arnould Gréban*, Paris, 1878

Reinburg, Virginia, *French Books of Hours: Making an Archive of Prayer, c. 1400–1600*, Cambridge, 2012

Rifkin, Joshua, "Munich, Milan, and a Marian Motet: Dating Josquin's *Ave Maria . . . virgo serena*," *JAMS* 56 (2003), 239–350

Robertson, Anne Walters, *Guillaume de Machaut and Reims: Context and Meaning in his Musical Works*, Cambridge, 2002

"The Man with the Pale Face, the Shroud, and Du Fay's *Missa Se la face ay pale*," *JM* 27 (2010), 377–434

Rothenberg, David J., *The Flower of Paradise: Marian Devotion and Secular Song in Medieval and Renaissance Music*, New York and Oxford, 2011

Roy, Émile, *Le Mystère de la Passion en France du XIVe au XVIe siècle: Étude sur les sources et le classement des mystères de la passion*, Geneva, 1974

Sargent, Michael G., ed., *Nicholas Love's* Mirror of the Blessed Life of Jesus Christ: *A Critical Edition, Based on Cambridge University Library Additional MSS 6578 and 6686*, Garland Medieval Texts 18, New York and London, 1992

Stallings-Taney, M., ed., *Iohannis de Caulibus Meditaciones Vite Christi olim S. Bonaventuro attributae*, Corpus Christianorum Continuatio Mediaevalis 153, Turnhout, 1997

Strohm, Reinhard, *The Rise of European Music, 1380–1500*, Cambridge, 1993; repr. 2005

· PART VII THEORY AND PRACTICE ·

# Measuring measurable music in the fifteenth century

ANNE STONE

## Introduction

The experience of singing or playing fifteenth-century music from manuscript facsimiles is exhilarating: the notation is similar enough to our own that it is relatively easy to do, but there are enough differences, in the domains of both rhythm and pitch, to inspire a kind of thrill in the recognition of historical and cultural difference. There is a sense that one is glimpsing a different way to conceptualize pitch and temporal relationships from those we have taken for granted in modern practice, a glimpse that can offer us insight into the music that is masked when we use modern editions.

The mensural system of rhythmic notation used in the fifteenth century, *musica mensurabilis*, was largely inherited from earlier centuries: its foundation was laid by Franco of Cologne and other theorists in the second half of the thirteenth century, and the theoretical innovations of the fourteenth-century *Ars nova* established all of the system's rules and procedures.[1] Nevertheless, composers of the fifteenth century used the notational system in important new ways in comparison with their fourteenth-century predecessors, expanding some features while de-emphasizing others. It is not an exaggeration to say that the fifteenth century was the golden age of *musica mensurabilis*, in which spectacular compositions were conceived that took advantage of the system's special properties. By the early sixteenth century, musical style and notational usage had changed. Notation was simpler, and closer to the modern system, and the metric play that characterized the motets and masses of the fifteenth century had largely disappeared.

After summarizing the principal rules of *musica mensurabilis*, this essay will focus upon aspects of the system that led to the most interesting features of fifteenth-century rhythmic style. It will also describe current scholarly arguments about aspects of fifteenth-century notation that are still not fully understood.

---

1 Franco of Cologne, *Ars cantus mensurabilis*. For a recent survey of medieval notation through the end of the fourteenth century, see Earp, "Notation."

## Fifteenth-century notation manuals

Students who learned mensural notation in the fifteenth century most likely did so from a textbook that was a century old, the *Libellus cantus mensurabilis* attributed to Johannes de Muris (ca. 1290–95 to after 1344), or a reworking of the same.[2] From Prosdocimus de Beldemandis (d. 1428), who made a commentary on this treatise as his graduation exercise from university in 1404, to Franchino Gaffurio (1451–1522), who used it as the basis of the second book of his *Practica musicae*, published in 1496, the majority of fifteenth-century theorists used the *Libellus* as a template for teaching notation. Yet fifteenth-century practice differed significantly from that of the fourteenth century, as we can see if we take a tour through the chapters of the *Libellus*, focusing on those areas where fifteenth-century notation expanded upon fourteenth-century norms.

The treatise begins by introducing the five note shapes, or *figurae*: maxima, longa, brevis, semibrevis, and minima.[3] A sixth shape, the semiminima, was not recognized by Muris but was found in musical sources beginning in the later fourteenth century. (See Figure 30.1.)

Theorists described the durational relationship between the shapes using the terms *modus* (governing the relationship between long and breve), *tempus* (breve and semibreve), and *prolatio* (semibreve and minim). Each of these rhythmic relationships could be either duple or triple; that is, each note shape other than the minim could be worth either two or three of the next lowest note. Notes worth three of the next smallest notes are "perfect" and those worth two are "imperfect." Music was thus organized metrically using combinations of perfect and imperfect relationships at different temporal levels. Tempus and prolation were the most commonly employed levels, and the four possible combinations of these were often referred to as the "four prolations" (see Figure 30.2). The *Libellus* prescribed signs that indicated the mensuration of the four prolations, and those signs were retained, with minor graphic variation, throughout the fifteenth century and beyond. The note

|  Maxima | Longa | Brevis | Semibrevis | Minima | Semiminima |

Figure 30.1 The mensural note shapes

---

2 Muris, *Libellus cantus mensurabilis*.

3 This cursory overview can be supplemented by Apel, *The Notation of Polyphonic Music*. A concise and informative summary of white mensural notation by Theodor Dumitrescu can be found online at www. cmme.org/misc/refsheet.pdf.

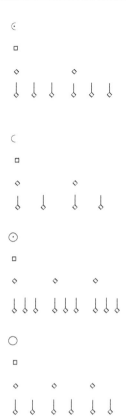

Figure 30.2  The four prolations

shape that took the beat (the "mensura," sometimes called "tactus" in the fifteenth century) was by default the semibreve, but could also be the breve or the minim in certain situations discussed below.

For the modern musician reading fifteenth-century notation, imperfect notes are very close to modern note shapes, since they are the origin of our binary system. Reading perfect note shapes is more complicated, for the following reason: if a breve is perfect, and worth three semibreves, how is a duration lasting two semibreves to be notated? In modern notation we distinguish between a half note and a dotted half note to represent these durations. But in the mensural system the two durations were represented by the same figure, and an extensive series of rules was developed over centuries to direct the interpretation of the note shapes, so that depending upon their context, perfect note shapes could be worth either two or three of the next smaller duration. The rules for perfect mensuration can be boiled down to three essential precepts:

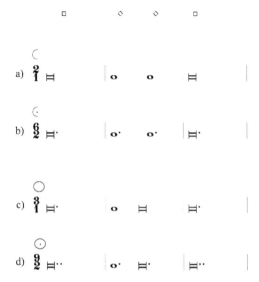

Figure 30.3  A rhythmic figure realized in the four prolations

(1) a perfect duration must be "imperfected," reducing its value by one-third, when, as very often happens, the duration in question is preceded or followed by a single note of the lesser value, or followed by more than three such notes; (2) if there are not enough notes in a given passage to form a complete perfection, a note shape must be "altered" by doubling its value to make up a complete time-unit of three beats; (3) in perfect mensurations if two note shapes of the same type follow in succession, the first is always perfect (according to the rule "like before like is always perfect"). Figure 30.3 compares the rhythmic result of perfect versus imperfect mensurations applied to a simple series of notes.

   The rules of imperfection and alteration date to the late thirteenth century, when they were established for the long and the breve; they were then extended in the fourteenth century to the semibreve and the maxima. These rules are often perplexing to a modern user because they stem from a conceptual starting point very different from our own. In the Franconian system time-units were always ternary, and were represented by the figures longa and brevis. Since there was only one possible meter to be expressed, it did not need to be stipulated in the notation; the performer supplied the metrical background against which the music was measured, providing mentally what the barline provides visually in a modern score. Beginning in the fourteenth century the longa and brevis time-units could be either duple or triple. As these units were populated by increasingly smaller and more varied durations, the performer was required to retain the time-unit map in his head and interpret this growing arsenal of figures in the correct metrical context. Thus between the thirteenth and sixteenth centuries the temporal span of a musical composition was considered to be made up of time-units mentally marked off by the performer, into which he organized the rhythms of specific compositions.

The absence of barlines coexisted with a rhythmic and metric elasticity that is a hallmark of fifteenth-century polyphonic style. This is not to say that performance was elastic or rhythmically imprecise. Rather, the rhythmic style of the music was one in which motives that by necessity imply "strong" and "weak" beats often had a syncopated relationship to the gridlike disposition of beats that regular barlines imply (and that performers clearly had in their heads). Syncopation as defined by fifteenth-century theorists was not merely the displacement of a series of notes from strong-beat positions (though that rhythmic gesture was included in fifteenth-century definitions of syncopation). In the definition of Johannes de Muris transmitted throughout the fifteenth century, syncopation was "a division of any figure into separate parts, which are brought back together by numbering perfections."[4]

Thus fifteenth-century syncopation was not understood against the fixed pattern of regularly occurring hierarchy of strong and week beats that a barline implies. Rather, it most often resulted from a scrambling of note values so that strong and weak beats were disposed in an irregular way. Figure 30.4 shows such a scrambling effect in the opening of the Christe from Guillaume Du Fay's *Missa Se la face ay pale* of ca. 1450. The mensuration is perfect modus with imperfect tempus, so a background pulse of imperfect breves is grouped in triple units.[5] The upper staves of Figure 30.4 show how the syncopations in the cantus voice are organized as a splitting up of implied breve groupings. Although the passage can be understood mensurally as spanning three perfect long units, at a lower level it is organized in unequal chunks of 1+3+2+2+1 breve units – that is, those units of time are the boundaries of the syncopated scrambling of smaller note shapes, as indicated by the highest stave of the example. Figure 30.4b shows three alternatives for barring the cantus line in modern notation.

The feeling of metric freedom that is possible to achieve using the mensural system has led editors in the twentieth century to adopt various strategies of transcription in their attempts to avoid imposing regular barlines as they translate fifteenth-century rhythms into modern notation.[6] Among the most

---

4 "sincopa est divisio circumquaque figure per partes separatas, que numerando perfectiones ad invicem reducuntur" (Muris, *Libellus cantus mensurabilis*, 66).

5 The two sources of the mass convey two different mensuration signs here: ¢ is found in the reading of Vatican CS 14, while Trent 88 transmits C. It is clear, nevertheless, that the mensura is on the breve rather than the semibreve, and the breves are grouped in threes. See the critical commentary in the complete works edition, Du Fay, *Opera omnia*, ed. Besseler, 3, p. iv.

6 For the idea that transcription is a kind of translation, see Bent, "Editing Early Music."

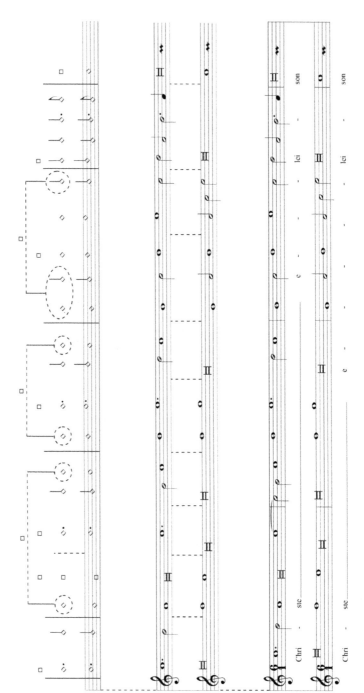

Figure 30.4a  Du Fay, *Missa Se la face ay pale*, Christe, opening duet

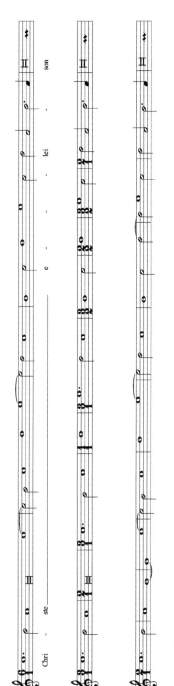

Figure 30.4b  Alternate transcription possibilities for cantus

frequently found solutions is the *Mensurstrich*, a line drawn in between bars rather than through them, a practice initiated by the German early music scholar Heinrich Besseler in editions he made beginning in the 1920s.[7] Other editors have explored unequal barring, using mensural note shapes or close modern analogues, or using tick marks rather than barlines, in an effort to represent the rhythmic sound-world of fifteenth-century polyphony.[8] None of these alternatives, of course, fully translates the ability of mensural notation to simultaneously project and disrupt metric regularity.

The particularity of the perfect/imperfect system, and the fact that the same figures can be interpreted to be either duple or triple, led to impressive feats of mensural architecture in the fourteenth and fifteenth centuries, particularly in the tenors of isorhythmic motets and later in cantus-firmus masses. Perhaps the *ne plus ultra* of this kind of manipulation was Johannes Ockeghem's *Missa Prolationum*, composed entirely as a double canon in which two musical lines were set against themselves canonically in a different mensuration, juxtaposing perfect and imperfect, so that the four resulting voices each proceed in a different mensural combination.[9]

But for all its contrapuntal and temporal ingenuity, the durations in the *Missa Prolationum* are organized by the unchanging minim of the *Ars nova* system. A different kind of mensural complexity was achieved when composers used various devices to override minim equivalence: mensuration signs and numbers, verbal and symbolic canons, and the concepts of diminution and proportion that underpinned them. Starting at the end of the fourteenth century and continuing through the end of the fifteenth, composers employed a dizzying array of these devices. Few terms and symbols were codified with any degree of universality until the later fifteenth century; practice was chaotic and variegated, and theorists from Prosdocimus de Beldemandis at the beginning of the century to Johannes Tinctoris near its end tried to establish rules in the face of an enormous diversity of practice.[10]

---

7  See, for example, vols. 3–5 of Du Fay, *Opera omnia*, ed. Besseler.

8  For a defense of unequal barring see Kohn, "The Renotation of Polyphonic Music." For a different kind of attempt to replicate the syncopated rhythmic style of fifteenth-century music, see Peter Maxwell Davies, *Missa super l'homme armé*, between rehearsal letters A and B, where a partial transcription of a fifteenth-century mass is carefully annotated with articulation marks to ensure that the performers stress the correct notes when they are not on the beat.

9  For further discussion see Emily Zazulia's contribution to this volume, Ch. 31, Figure 31.3. For a modern edition see Ockeghem, *Masses and Mass Sections*, ed. van Benthem, 3/4. To the mensural puzzle Ockgehem adds one more constraint: in each successive section between the Kyrie and the Osanna the canonic interval is increased by one. So in Kyrie I the canon is at the unison, in the Christe canon at the second, in Kyrie II at the third, and so forth.

10  For Prosdocimus's attempts to limit diminution to that described by Johannes de Muris see Bent, "The Myth of *Tempus perfectum diminutum*," 209–14.

## Mensuration and proportion signs

The mensuration signs described in the *Libellus* (see above, Figure 30.2) were not found in surviving musical sources until the very end of the fourteenth century, presumably because the mensuration of a piece of music was easily determined by context; the *Libellus* also gives instructions for determining the mensuration without an external sign.[11] By the early fifteenth century, however, the codified signs, together with a large arsenal of offshoots, began to be used to indicate not only mensuration, but also wholesale changes of duration, specifically those that required a change in the duration of the minim.[12] The sign Ɔ, for example, was widely used in Italian and northern sources beginning at the turn of the fifteenth century to indicate a 4:3 proportion, usually of the minim, indicating that four notes had to be performed in the time of three. Other signs, such as numbers, the combination of numbers and signs, and reversed signs were used with little systematization in the notationally experimental repertory of the *Ars subtilior*.[13]

By the second quarter of the fifteenth century a new crop of signs began to appear, and with them a new set of purposes. Signs in the *Ars subtilior* repertory were used primarily in the cantus and contratenor voices of songs to facilitate elaborate rhythmic ornamentation of a simpler contrapuntal framework, with the tenor generally keeping time with a steady and unelaborated melody. A high degree of artful self-reflexivity was involved; songs simultaneously presented and playfully commented upon their notation and the problems of its interpretation. After around 1420, the uses of mensuration and proportion signs seemed to shift. While there was a continuous tradition of self-referential play throughout the century, mensuration signs were now employed for two principal new purposes: the articulation of musical structure through proportional change and diminution, and the manipulation of tempo. They most frequently appeared, moreover, in the genre of the motet and the new cyclic Mass Ordinary, both larger-scale musical forms than the song, and whose structures could be underscored by manipulations of meter and tempo to great effect.

The earliest and most common of the new signs were the stroked (or "cut") circle and half-circle, Ø, ¢, which are first seen in music manuscripts copied in

---

11  See Johannes de Muris, *Libellus cantus mensurabilis*, ed. Berktold, ch. 6, and for a comprehensive history of these signs see Berger, *Mensuration and Proportion Signs*.
12  See Emily Zazulia's contribution to this volume, Ch. 31.
13  See Stone, "Ars subtilior." The earliest theorist to describe Ɔ and proportional numbers was Prosdocimus de Beldomandis in his commentary on the *Libellus* of 1304, *Expositiones tractatus*, 141–42.

the 1420s. The interpretation of these signs has been a source of controversy in recent scholarship in part because it has been impossible to establish a consistent interpretation for them that holds for the entire century. When a cut sign is placed in temporal simultaneity with an uncut sign in a different voice, the temporal relationship between the two can be determined from the counterpoint. In many cases, though, a cut sign appears simultaneously in all voices, and different interpretations are possible. The debates are not idle, for the sound of the music we hear will change depending on the interpretation given to the signs.[14] At the root of the controversy is the question of what kind of indication the cut sign is. Scholars relying on fifteenth-century theorists and the surviving repertory have variously interpreted the vertical stroke as a proportion sign, an indication of tempo change, a sign of diminution or proportional change, and a sign that has no temporal meaning at all. These meanings, moreover, can overlap in a musical context: for instance, an increase of tempo up to double the original speed has the same aural effect as a 2:1 proportion, but a different conception at its root. In other cases, a stroked sign appears in junctures in the music where a doubling of the speed seems implausible, but a less drastic increase in tempo – or no increase – makes better musical sense.

Reading fifteenth-century theorists does not clarify matters because their accounts are as inconsistent as the musical sources themselves.[15] Johannes Tinctoris's *Proportionale musices* (early 1470s) states unequivocally that a speeding up of the beat (*acceleratio mensurae*) "is proper to" the $\Phi$ – but this does not exclude the possibility of a speeding up of the beat to twice its original tempo, so that in the new tempo the breve has the duration of the old semibreve, and thereby constitutes a de facto diminution.[16] Meanwhile the slightly earlier fifteenth-century theorist Anonymous XI states that $\mathbb{C}$ is a sign of diminution *per semi* (by one-half), while $\Phi$ is a sign of diminution by one-third. He further equates $\Phi$ with $O2$, a modus-cum-tempore sign (see below).[17] Gaffurio first describes the stroke as a sign of diminution, which he defines as a removal of a certain amount of value from a note shape, rather than by the standard definition of the *Libellus* (see below, "diminution"). Later in the same passage,

14 For a variety of approaches to the topic, and leads to further bibliography, see Berger, *Mensuration and Proportion Signs*; Berger, "Cut Signs in Fifteenth-Century Musical Practice"; Blachly, "Mensuration and Tempo"; Cox, "'Pseudo-Augmentation'"; Cumming, *The Motet in the Age of Du Fay*; Bent, "The Early Use of the Sign $\Phi$"; DeFord, "The *Mensura* of $\Phi$ in the Works of Du Fay"; Schroeder, "The Stroke Comes Full Circle"; Wegman, "Different Strokes for Different Folks?."
15 See Berger, *Mensuration and Proportion Signs*, 125–39, and Schroeder, "The Stroke Comes Full Circle," for a summary of theorists' viewpoints. Schroeder includes a detailed summary of the scholarly literature prior to 1982.
16 Tinctoris, *Proportionale musices*, bk. 1, ch. 3. For varying interpretations of this passage see Wegman, "What is 'acceleratio mensurae'?"; Blackburn, "Did Ockeghem Listen to Tinctoris?"; Berger, "The Myth of *diminutio per tertiam partem*."
17 Wingell, "Anonymous XI," 155; the theorist adds that $O2$ is used by "modernissimos cantores."

however, he clarifies the meaning of the stroke signifying diminution, saying that "this [stroke] properly applies to the measurement of time, not to the note shapes, for with such a sign the mensura is diminished but not the value of the notes" ("Haec propriae temporali competit mensurae, non ipsius figuris; namque tali signo ipsa minuitur mensura non notularum numerus").[18] None of the theorists who discuss the stroked signs, however, distinguishes between their use in simultaneous as opposed to successive relationships, and it is difficult to know how to interpret this absence of distinction. Does it mean that theorists assumed the sign was used the same way in the two contexts? Or that the differences between the two contexts were so glaringly obvious (since simultaneous use had no accompanying ambiguity of interpretation) that it didn't need to be stated?

It also appears from a survey of the repertory, especially from the earlier part of the century, that ¢ and Φ had somewhat different, if overlapping, meanings: while ¢ seems more often to indicate a 2:1 proportion in note values (if only because it was more commonly used simultaneously with an uncut mensuration so that its meaning was unambiguous), Φ seems to mean different things at different times, and only sometimes results in a doubling of note values.[19]

The following four examples, all from the first half of the fifteenth century, and all of which have been amply discussed in recent scholarship, show the range of possibilities for the interpretation of Φ and the difficulty in establishing a single rule to explain its meaning.

### Baude Cordier, Belle, bonne, sage and Tout par compas

Two songs attributed to Baude Cordier found in Chantilly 564 transmit the earliest known use of Φ.[20] In both songs the function of Φ is to create a relationship with ℂ such that a minim under ℂ equals a semibreve under Φ, as shown in in Figure 30.5a. Both songs contain a number of different proportional changes signaled with proportional numbers, coloration, and hollow notes, another early fifteenth-century device that could signal proportional changes in duration, and the text of *Tout par compas* explicitly takes playing with mensuration signs as one of its themes. A number of songs in the earliest

18 Gaffurio, *Practica musicae*, bk. 2, ch. 14, quoted in Schroeder, "The Stroke Comes Full Circle," 151–52; translation modified.

19 See Blackburn, "Did Ockeghem Listen to Tinctoris?" for a discussion of his use of Φ followed by O, and for the insight that Ockeghem probably used O3 to mean *acceleratio mensurae*; for a discussion of ¢ in Busnoys that concludes that he intended 2:1 proportion by it, see Berger, "Cut Signs in Fifteenth-Century Musical Practice." In later practice ¢ came to be the preferred sign for duple meter.

20 These songs are appended to the Chantilly manuscript, whose main corpus contains mostly older repertory. For a discussion of its possible date see Plumley and Stone, *Codex Chantilly*, and "Cordier's Picture-Songs."

Figure 30.5a ₵ and Φ compared

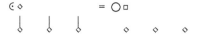

Figure 30.5b ₵ and O compared

layer of Oxford 213 employ similar combinations of mensuration signs, demonstrating that for one group of composers probably working in similar environments, this unequal relationship between ₵ and Φ was standard.[21]

This relationship seems to foreshadow a slightly different formulation in the second half of the fifteenth century, when the sign ₵ again took on an implied meaning of inequality with respect to O, in which the minim of ₵ was equivalent to the semibreve of O (see Figure 30.5b). In both cases, a semibreve under one sign is made equal to a minim under another sign. While in the earlier formulation it would seem that the minim under ₵ represented the note shapes in their normative state (*integer valor* in fifteenth-century parlance) and Φ was "diminished" with respect to it, in the later formulation, the semibreve of O represented *integer valor* and the minim of ₵ was understood to be "augmented" with respect to it.

While at the beginning of the century the most common mensuration was imperfect tempus with major prolation (₵), sometime in the second quarter of the century this was replaced by perfect tempus with minor prolation (O). By the second half of the century, ₵ was used extremely rarely, and virtually always in the tenors of cantus-firmus masses, where they had an unequal relationship to O, as described above, such that the minim of ₵ was equivalent to the semibreve of O when placed in music simultaneously.[22]

---

21  See "Cordier's Picture-Songs" and Bent, "The Myth of *Tempus perfectum diminutum*."
22  Richard Taruskin suggests that equating of the minim of ₵ to the semibreve of O was first done in three works in the Old Hall manuscript, and first seen in a Continental source in a mass pair by Lymburgia in Bologna Q15; see "Antoine Busnoys and the *L'homme armé* Tradition," 261 n. 16. Bonnie Blackburn suggests the shift occurred sometime between the 1440s, when Du Fay wrote *Missa Se la face ay pale*, and the 1470s, when Tinctoris "was fighting a lone battle for minim equivalence." See "Did Ockeghem Listen to Tinctoris?," 618. The use of the term "augmentation" to describe this relationship has been challenged by Margaret Bent, who argues that that term implies a norm against which the "augmented" notes are understood to be divergent, and that it is not always clear which note level is "normal." See "The Myth of *Tempus perfectum diminutum*." The term "inequality" here highlights the equivalence of minim to semibreve without stipulating which is the norm.

## *Guillaume Du Fay*, Vergene bella

In other cases, Φ is found simultaneously in all voices in a "horizontal" relationship to the previous mensuration, so that an exact proportional relationship is not clearly demanded by the music. Du Fay's much-discussed song-motet *Vergene bella*, based on a text by Petrarch, is one such example; it survives in Oxford 213 and probably dates to the 1430s.[23] The work is divided into three sections that are clearly articulated by strong cadences and changes in mensuration. The opening of the song is unsigned, the second section is signed O in all parts, and the final section is signed Φ. It is likely that the unsigned opening is also to be understood as Φ; it is clearly in *tempus perfectum* and organized into groups of three semibreves. The relationship between the rhythmic material under Φ and O is not markedly different. The openings of the first two sections are rhythmically identical, starting with three semibreves and continuing in a way that emphasizes the perfect breve as the organizing metric unit. It is clear that the Φ section has not been transcribed "up one level" from O, so that a performance at twice the speed is not indicated. The only difference between the rhythmic profiles of the two sections is that in the O section the minims are text-bearing, while in the Φ sections minims are ornamental; syllables are carried by semibreves as the lowest level, as shown in Figure 30.6. This difference encourages some scholars to suggest that the two signs indicate different rhythmic organizations that result in a somewhat slower tempo for O – slow enough so that syllables can be declaimed at the minim level.[24]

## *Du Fay*, Nuper rosarum flores

This celebrated motet by Du Fay was composed for the consecration of the dome of S. Maria del Fiore, the cathedral of Florence, in 1436, and its highly particular mensural structure is related symbolically to the architectural structure of the cathedral.[25] The two tenors repeat four times and each repetition is governed by a different mensuration sign: O, C, ₵, Φ (see Figure 30.7a). That these mensural changes correlate to the numerical ratios 6:4:2:3 is well established in the extensive literature about the motet, and therefore the sign Φ

---

23  This work's mensural plan has been discussed by a number of scholars; see DeFord, "The *Mensura* of Φ in the Works of Du Fay," 121–23; Planchart, "The Relative Speed of 'Tempora'," 36–38. For the date see Bent, "Petrarch, Padua, the Malatestas."

24  Cumming, *The Motet in the Age of Du Fay*, identifies thirty motets in the manuscript Bologna Q15 that share rhythmic features of the section in Φ in this song, and she dubs them the "cut circle motet"; see pp. 99–124, with a table listing the works on pp. 110–11.

25  The most persuasive account of the relationship is Wright, "Dufay's *Nuper rosarum flores*," who discusses further bibliography. See also Deborah Howard's essay in this volume, Ch. 18.

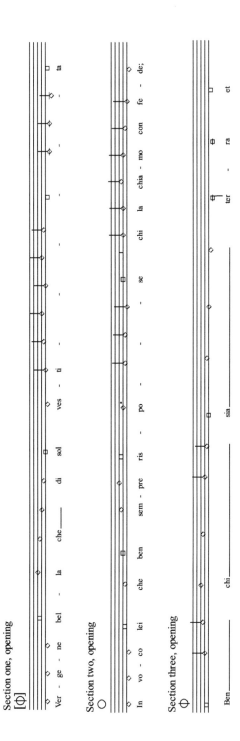

Figure 30.6 Du Fay, *Vergene bella*: openings of each section

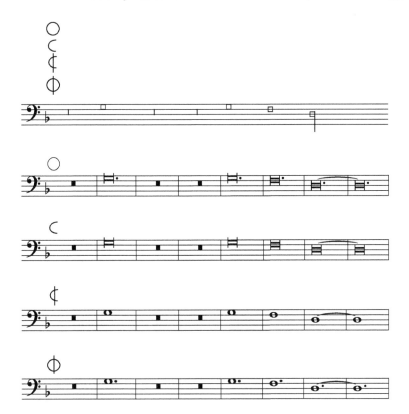

Figure 30.7a Du Fay, *Nuper rosarum flores*, tenor 1, opening, in four mensurations

clearly is established to signify one-half of O, just as ¢ signifies one-half of C (see Figure 30.7b).[26]

## *Binchois*, Asperges me

This polyphonic antiphon setting is found in five sources of the mid-fifteenth century, and each source presents a different array of mensuration signs governing its various sections.[27] Trent 87 presents a configuration that is

---

26  See Wright, "Dufay's *Nuper rosarum flores*." This is true at least in theory; however, in practice, as Ruth DeFord points out, in the final section of the motet all four voices are signed Φ simultaneously, raising the possibility that the performance of the last section does not have to be perfectly proportional. Regardless of the performance options, the symbolic intention of the signs renders Φ one-half as long as O. See DeFord, "The Mensura of Φ in the Works of Du Fay," 124–27.

27  Aosta 15, Trent 87, 90, 92, and 93. Modern edition in Binchois, *The Sacred Music*, ed. Kaye, 174–77. Discussed by Blachly, "Mensuration and Tempo," 26–27, who conflates source information about two different *Asperges me* settings by Binchois that are adjacent in some sources.

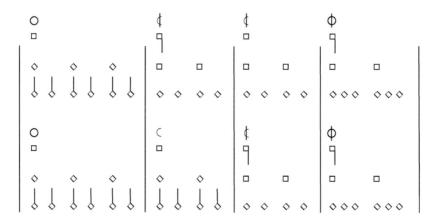

Figure 30.7b Schema of mensurations of *Nuper rosarum flores* (upper section represents upper voices, lower section represents tenors)

rather common in this repertory: a O stacked over a Φ, indicating that the first section of the antiphon is to be sung twice, once under O and once under Φ.[28] In this configuration it is impossible to determine whether the repetition under Φ should be performed twice as fast, at a faster tempo of indefinite relationship, or at exactly the same tempo, the stroke indicating only the fact of the repetition.[29] While this ambiguity is unlikely to be resolved definitively, it is worth noting that the sign also has the important, and unambiguous, function of articulating structure.

## Tinctoris on modus-cum-tempore signs

Another related class of signs that emerged toward the middle of the century was that in which numbers and mensuration signs were combined in one sign (thus O2, O3, Ө2, Ө3). These "modus-cum-tempore" signs indicated a combination of modus and tempus rather than tempus and prolation, and therefore indicated a de facto unequal relationship with traditional signs.[30] As with the stroked signs, their interpretation is not consistent. Anonymous XII lists and names them but does not indicate their proportional relationship to regular signs or *integer valor*; a graphic showing the relationship between Ө3, O3, C, and C seems merely to indicate that the modus-cum-tempore signs include modus, not that under those signs the longa equals the breve in normal

28 A facsimile is available at trentinocultura.net.
29 See Blachly, "Mensuration and Tempo," 27, and Bent, "The Early Use of the Sign Φ."
30 See Berger, *Mensuration and Proportion Signs*, 148–63.

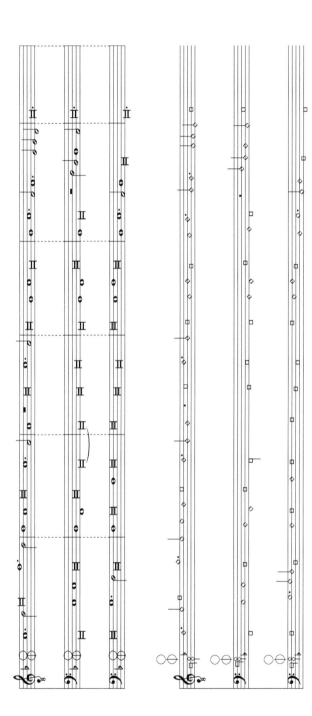

Figure 30.8 Opening of *Asperges me* in Trent 87, showing stacked signs

signs.[31] Tinctoris chastises composers for using the sign O2 as a sign of perfect modus and imperfect tempus, since, he says, the circle should be reserved for perfect tempus.[32] John Hothby expanded the signs by adding two numbers to the mensuration sign (thus, ⊙33) in order to indicate both the relationship of the maxima to the long (major modus) and that of the long to the breve (minor modus).[33]

Johannes Tinctoris's highly polemical remarks about improper use of proportion signs in *Proportionale musices* (early 1470s) are both entertaining and enlightening for the modern reader. Tinctoris scolds several eminent composers, including Ockeghem, for errors in the notation of proportional relationships. Tinctoris's concern about the practice of his contemporaries is twofold: first, he maintains that proportions must only be made between like elements – so perfect breves can be made proportional to other perfect breves and so on; second, he criticizes composers for failing to distinguish between proportions of equality (1:1) and proportions of inequality (2:1 and so forth). This results in proportion signs being used in all parts at the beginnings of works, where they have nothing to be proportional with, and leads to his famous chiding of Ockeghem for signing the "rustic chanson" *L'autre d'antan* with O3 in all parts.[34] The inexpert, Tinctoris rails, will look at the sign and say "let's sing it quickly; it's sesquialtera." What puerile ignorance, he exclaims, to call a proportion of equality (O3 in all voices) a proportion of inequality, namely sesquialtera! This diatribe indicates that at the time there was a lack of clarity about whether a given sign caused a proportion or governed tempo, and it's easy to see how a sign could migrate in practice from one to the other. If a sign has as its codified meaning a sesquialtera proportion, so that, for example, under the sign three semibreves are sung against two, then the de facto effect of the sign is to speed up the absolute duration of the semibreve, thereby lessening its value. A performance practice could easily have arisen in which the sign was divorced from its original meaning and was used as a kind of shorthand to indicate a slightly faster tempo akin to that achieved through sesquialtera proportion.

In the face of this inconsistency of musical practice, theoretical writing, and modern editorial practice, a would-be performer of music in which cut signs

---

31 Anonymous XII, *Tractatus et compendium cantus figurati*, ed. Palmer, 86–87.

32 *Proportionale*, bk. 3, ch. 5. For careful discussions of modus-cum-tempore signs used by specific composers, see Wegman, "Another Mass by Busnoys," 2–5, and "Petrus de Domarto's *Missa Spiritus et alma*," 252–58, and Gallagher, *Johannes Regis*, 98–114.

33 See Hothby, *Opera omnia*, ed. Reaney, 21 and 28. In a reworking of Hothby's treatise by John Tucke, the modus-cum-tempore signs are expanded further in a very idiosyncratic way, with concentric circles indicating the mensural levels from maxima to semibreve; see Reaney, ed., 53–58, and Woodley, *John Tucke*. Neither Hothby's or Tucke's signs appear to have been adopted by composers, however.

34 See Berger, "Cut Signs in Fifteenth-Century Musical Practice," 108–12, with references to further bibliography.

and modus-cum-tempore signs appear will have to make his or her own decisions in cases, such as the four discussed above, where the interpretation of the signs cannot be determined with security.

## Diminution

The last topic defined in the *Libellus* and transformed in fifteenth-century practice was diminution; as explained in the *Libellus*, "in diminution a long is placed for a maxima, a brevis for a long, a semibrevis for a breve, a minim for a semibreve, and a semiminim for a minim." There follows a short explanation of how diminution works in different mensurations. When both notes involved in the substitution are imperfect, it is straightforward, but in certain combinations of perfect and imperfect values, the diminution is more complicated. For example, "when the tenor is in perfect modus and perfect tempus, the diminution is made to one-third [*per tertium*] and not one-half."[35] This stipulation (diminution "per tertiam" rather than "per medium") caused some confusion both in the fifteenth century and among modern scholars, some understanding it to mean "reduced by one-third," but it is clear that "reduced to one-third" is the intended meaning.[36]

In the fourteenth century, diminution was virtually always confined to the tenors of motets, which commonly were structured so that a second statement of the *color*, the tenor's melody, was notated one level faster, with breves substituting for longs, and so on, just as the *Libellus* describes.[37] Thus the melody was written out first at a slower mensuration, say in longs and breves, then again using breves and semibreves. The effect of the diminution in these cases was a palpable increase in perceived speed, as the tenor melody that had been moving in slow notes was repeated at a faster rate as shorter notes replaced longer ones. Although Muris's rules proscribed the possibility of the substituted notes being of a different mensuration, the audible effect could include a perceptible metric shift as well as an acceleration of the perceived rate of speed.[38]

By the early fifteenth century, successive diminution of a tenor line was generally not written out but signaled by a verbal canon (a written instruction). Thus what was formerly written explicitly with note shapes had to be

---

35  For the Latin text, see Muris, *Libellus*, ed. Berktold, 120.

36  See Berger, "The Myth of *diminutio per tertiam partem*."

37  A number of works in the fourteenth century appear to be notated entirely up one level, as if the entire work were "in diminution" against a perceived norm. For a critical overview of this idea in the French tradition see Bent, "The Myth of *Tempus perfectum diminutum*."

38  See DeFord, "Diminution in the Theory of Johannes de Muris." I am grateful to Prof. DeFord for access to a pre-publication copy of this paper.

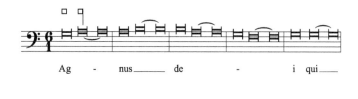

Figure 30.9 The diminution scheme in the tenor of *Ave sancta mundi salus/ Agnus dei*

realized mentally by the performer: one series of durations had to be performed two or more different ways according to the stipulation of the canon or mensuration signs.[39] The early fifteenth-century motet *Ave sancta mundi salus/Agnus Dei* by Matteo da Perugia offers a straightforward example, containing a threefold repetition of the Agnus Dei melody under a canon that reads: "Tenor dicitur de secundo modo 1° postea gradatim 2° et 3° diminuitur" (the tenor is performed in second mode first, then gradually diminished the second and third [times]). The upper voices remain in imperfect tempus with minor prolation throughout the motet, and the ternary grouping of the tenor is metrically at odds with them in three different ways (see Figure 30.9).

Once liberated from the limitations of rewriting the tenor in faster note values, the practice of diminution grew in scope and complexity. Both written canons and mensuration signs could be employed to effect diminution and its opposite, augmentation; typically a canon would stipulate that notes be performed "per semi" (by one-half) when diminution was called for. The signs used for diminution, as we have already seen, ranged from ⏀ and ¢ to modus-cum-tempore signs, all of which could also have different meanings.

---

39 See Zazulia, below, Ch. 31, for a discussion of this phenomenon, which she calls the "aesthetics of notational fixity."

The combination of canon and diminution and the metric play they made possible was exploited throughout the fifteenth century, perhaps most adventurously in the century's new genre, the polyphonic mass Ordinary. The cantus-firmus mass juxtaposed preexistent with newly composed music in the manner of the motet, and part of the expectation of the genre was manipulation of the cantus firmus using the resources of the mensural system. This manipulation routinely included augmentation and diminution, proportional changes, and even in some exceptional cases the elimination of note stems or the instruction to sing the opposite note value to that written.[40] The cyclic structure, in which the five parts of the Ordinary are based on the same preexistent material, further offered opportunities for mensural play in the service of extra-musical significance.[41] The cluster of cyclic mass Ordinaries based on the *L'homme armé* tune, for example, is a particularly well-studied group that exhibits all these features and shows how mensural schemes in the manipulation of the cantus firmus were imitated from one work to the next.[42]

## Conclusion: the end of *musica mensurabilis*

The mensural play that permeated the masses and motets of the fifteenth century was composed to be performed for an elite audience by well-compensated professional singers. At the risk of reductionist generalization, the many technological and social changes that accompanied the turn of the sixteenth century – foremost among them the development of music printing and its attendant new, larger, and less musically proficient audience – conspired to move musical style away from this kind of complexity. The important new genres of the sixteenth century, the madrigal and eventually the solo song, were text-driven, and their complexity derived from the interplay of music and textual rhetoric more than music-architectural means.

Thus while the mensural system was still technically in use in the sixteenth century, even into the turn of the seventeenth, in practice, notators gradually stopped using alteration, placed dots to indicate perfection, and generally used "imperfect" mensurations much more often than perfect ones. The joys of diminution and augmentation, and of grand mensural schemes, were less central to the musical landscape of the sixteenth century than they had been to that of the fifteenth century.

40 For these last procedures see Wegman, "Another Mass by Busnoys?"
41 For some representative examples of proportional diminution bound up in symbolic play, see Long, "Symbol and Ritual in Josquin's *Missa di Dadi*"; Zayaruznaya, "What Fortune Can Do to a Minim."
42 See Jesse Rodin's essay in this volume on the *L'homme armé* tradition, Ch. 4.

In recent years, mensural music has made a comeback, and it is safe to say that more people alive today have engaged with the magnificent manuscript sources of this music than ever did in the fifteenth century. This is due, of course, to the remarkable technological developments that have allowed us to pore over beautifully reproduced manuscript facsimiles of the most important sources of mensural music, and more recently to call up manuscript images on our computer and tablet screens, so that we may flip through these books as we sip our morning coffee.[43]

## Bibliography

Anonymous XII, *Tractatus et compendium cantus figurati*, ed. Jill Palmer, CSM 35, Neuhausen-Stuttgart, 1990

Apel, Willi, *The Notation of Polyphonic Music 900–1600*, Cambridge, MA, 1942

Bank, Joseph A. *Tactus, Tempo and Notation in Mensural Music from the 13th to the 17th Century*, Amsterdam, 1972

Bent, Margaret, *Bologna Q15: The Making and Remaking of a Musical Manuscript*, 2 vols., Lucca, 2008

"The Early Use of Cut Signatures in Sacred Music by Ockeghem and his Contemporaries," in *Johannes Ockeghem: Actes du XLᵉ Colloque international d'études humanistes. Tours, 3–8 février 1997*, ed. Philippe Vendrix, Paris, 1998, 641–80

"The Early Use of the Sign Ø," *EM* 24 (1996), 199–225

"Editing Early Music: The Dilemma of Translation," *EM* 22 (1994), 373–92

"The Myth of *Tempus perfectum diminutum* in the Chantilly Manuscript," in *A Late Medieval Songbook and its Context: New Perspectives on the Chantilly Codex (Bibliothèque du Château de Chantilly, Ms. 564)*, ed. Yolanda Plumley and Anne Stone, Turnhout, 2009, 203–27

"Petrarch, Padua, the Malatestas, Du Fay, and *Vergene Bella*," in *Essays on Renaissance Music in Honor of David Fallows: Bon jour, bon mois, et bonne estrenne*, ed. Fabrice Fitch and Jacobijn Kiel, Woodbridge, 2011, 86–96

"The Use of Cut Signatures in Sacred Music by Binchois," in *Binchois Studies*, ed. Andrew Kirkman and Dennis Slavin, New York, 2000, 277–312

Berger, Anna Maria Busse, "Cut Signs in Fifteenth-Century Musical Practice," in *Music in Renaissance Cities and Courts: Studies in Honor of Lewis Lockwood*, ed. Jessie Ann Owens and Anthony M. Cummings, Warren, MI, 1997, 101–12

"The Evolution of Rhythmic Notation," in *Cambridge History of Western Music Theory*, ed. Thomas Christensen, Cambridge, 2002, 628–56

*Mensuration and Proportion Signs: Origins and Evolution*, Oxford, 1993

"The Myth of *diminutio per tertiam partem*," *JM* 8 (1990), 398–426

"The Origin and Early History of Proportion Signs," *JAMS* 41 (1988), 403–33

---

43 Only a few representative samples of what is clearly a rapidly growing inventory may be mentioned here: the multi-volume black-and-white series Renaissance Music in Facsimile; color facsimiles such as Bent, *Bologna Q15*; online sources such as the seven enormous *Trent Codices Online*; Christofferson, *The Copenhagen Chansonnier and the "Loire Valley" Chansonniers*; Dumitrescu, *Computerized Mensural Music Editing* (which provides scored editions in mensural notation). The British Library, the Vatican Library, and many others have manuscript digitizing projects underway as of this writing.

"The Relationship of Perfect and Imperfect Time in Italian Theory of the Renaissance," *EMH* 5 (1985), 1–28

Binchois, Gilles, *The Sacred Music of Gilles Binchois*, ed. Philip Kaye, Oxford, 1992

Blachly, Alexander, "Mensuration and Tempo in 15th-Century Music: Cut Signatures in Theory and Practice," Ph.D. diss., Columbia University, 1995

    "Reading Tinctoris for Guidance on Tempo," in *Antoine Busnoys: Method, Meaning and Context in Late Medieval Music*, ed. Paula Higgins, Oxford, 1999, 399–427

Blackburn, Bonnie J. "Did Ockeghem Listen to Tinctoris?," in *Johannes Ockeghem: Actes du XL^e Colloque international d'études humanistes. Tours, 3–8 février 1997*, ed. Philippe Vendrix, Paris, 1998, 597–640

Christofferson, Peter Woetmann, *The Copenhagen Chansonnier and the "Loire Valley" Chansonniers: An Open Access Project*, http://chansonniers.pwch.dk

Cohen, Judith, *The Six Anonymous L'Homme Armé Masses in Naples Biblioteca Nazionale, MS VI E 40*, MSD 21, [Rome], 1968

Cox, Bobby Wayne, "'Pseudo-Augmentation' in the Manuscript Bologna, Civico Museo Bibliografico Musicale Q15 (BL)," *JM* 1 (1982), 419–48

Cumming, Julie, *The Motet in the Age of Du Fay*, Cambridge, 1999

DeFord, Ruth, "The *Mensura* of Φ in the Works of Du Fay," *EM* 34 (2006), 111–36

    "On Diminution and Proportion in Fifteenth-Century Music Theory," *JAMS* 58 (2005), 1–67

    "Diminution in the Theory of Johannes de Muris and his Followers," *Music Theory Spectrum* 38.1 (2016), forthcoming

Du Fay, Guillaume, *Opera omnia*, ed. Heinrich Besseler, CMM 1, 6 vols., Rome, 1951–66

Dumitrescu, Theodor, *The CMME Project: Computerized Mensural Music Editing*, www.cmme.org

Earp, Lawrence, "Notation," in *The Cambridge History of Medieval Music*, ed. Mark Everist and Tom Forrest Kelly, Cambridge, forthcoming.

Franco of Cologne, *Ars cantus mensurabilis*, ed. Gilbert Reaney and André Gilles, CSM 18, [Rome], 1974

Gaffurio, Franchino, *Practica Musicae* (1496), trans. Clement Miller, MSD 20, n.p., 1968

Gallagher, Sean, *Johannes Regis*, Turnhout, 2010

Gallo, F. Alberto, "Die Notationslehre im 14. und 15. Jahrhundert," in Frieder Zaminer, ed., *Geschichte der Musiktheorie* 5: *Die mittelalterliche Lehre von der Mehrstimmigkeit*, Darmstadt, 1984, 259–356

Hamm, Charles, *A Chronology of the Works of Guillaume Dufay Based on a Study of Mensural Practice*, Princeton, 1964

Hothby, Johannes, *Opera omnia de musica mensurabili*, ed. Gilbert Reaney, CSM 31, n.p., 1983

Hughes, Andrew, "Mensuration and Proportion in Early Fifteenth-Century English Music," *AcM* 37 (1965), 48–61

Katz, Daniel, "The Earliest Sources for the Libellus cantus mensurabilis secundum Johannem de Muris," Ph.D. diss., Duke University, 1989

Kohn, Karl, "The Renotation of Polyphonic Music," *MQ* 67 (1981), 29–49

Long, Michael, "Symbol and Ritual in Josquin's *Missa di Dadi*," *JAMS* 42 (1989), 1–22

Muris, Johannes de, *Libellus cantus mensurabilis*, ed. Christian Berktold, in *Ars practica mensurabilis cantus secundum Iohannem de Muris: Die Recensio maior des sogenannten "Libellus practice cantus mensurabilis,"* Munich, 1999

Ockeghem, Johannes, *Masses and Mass Sections*, ed. Jaap van Benthem, 3/4, Utrecht, 1996

Planchart, Alejandro Enrique, "The Origins and Early History of *L'homme armé*," *JM* 20 (2003), 305–57

"The Relative Speed of 'Tempora' in the Period of Dufay," *Royal Musical Association Research Chronicle* 17 (1981), 33–51

Plumley, Yolanda, and Anne Stone, "Cordier's Picture-Songs and the Relationship between the Song Repertories of the Chantilly Codex and Oxford 213," in *A Late Medieval Song-Book and its Context: New Perspectives on the Chantilly Codex (Bibliothèque du château de Chantilly, Ms. 564)*, ed. Yolanda Plumley and Anne Stone, Turnhout, 2009, 303–28

eds., *Codex Chantilly: Bibliothèque du Château de Chantilly, Ms. 564*, Turnhout, 2008

Prosdocimus de Beldemandis, *Expositiones tractatus practice cantus mensurabilis magistri Johannis de Muris*, ed. F. Alberto Gallo, Antiquae Musicae Italicae Scriptores 3, Bologna, 1966

*Renaissance Music in Facsimile: Sources Central to the Music of the Late Fifteenth and Sixteenth Centuries*, 25 vols., New York, 1986–88

Rodin, Jesse, "Unresolved," *ML* 90 (2009), 535–54

Schroeder, Eunice, "The Stroke Comes Full Circle: $\Phi$ and $\mathcal{C}$ in Writings on Music ca. 1450–1540," *MD* 36 (1982), 119–66

Sherr, Richard, "The Performance of Josquin's *L'homme armé* Masses," *EM* 19 (1991), 261–68

Stone, Anne, "Ars subtilior," in *The Cambridge History of Medieval Music*, ed. Mark Everist and Tom Kelly, Cambridge, forthcoming

Taruskin, Richard, "Antoine Busnoys and the *L'Homme armé* Tradition," *JAMS* 39 (1986), 255–93

Tinctoris, Johannes, *Proportionale musices*, in *Opera theoretica*, vol. iia, ed. Albert Seay, CSM 22, Rome, 1978. English trans. Albert Seay, *Proportions in Music*, Colorado Springs, CO, 1979. Italian trans. Gianluca D'Agostino, *Proportionale musices; Liber de arte contrapuncti*, Florence, 2008

*Trent Codices Online*, www1.trentinocultura.net/portal/server.pt?open=514&objID=226 52&mode=2

Wegman, Rob C., "Another Mass by Busnoys?," *ML* 71 (1990), 1–19

"Concerning Tempo in the English Polyphonic Mass, c. 1420–1470," *AcM* 61 (1989), 40–65

"Different Strokes for Different Folks? On Tempo and Diminution in Fifteenth-Century Music," *JAMS* 53 (2000), 461–505

"Petrus de Domarto's *Missa Spiritus almus* and the Early History of the Four-Voice Mass in the Fifteenth Century," *EMH* 10 (1991), 235–303

"What is 'acceleratio mensurae'?," *ML* 73 (1992), 515–24

Wingell, Richard, "Anonymous XI (CS III): An Edition, Translation and Commentary," 3 vols., Ph.D. diss., University of Southern California, 1973

Woodley, Ronald, *John Tucke: A Case Study in Early Tudor Music Theory*, Oxford, 1993

Wright, Craig, "Dufay's *Nuper rosarum flores*, King Solomon's Temple, and the Veneration of the Virgin," *JAMS* 47 (1994), 395–441

Zayaruznaya, Anna, "What Fortune Can Do to a Minim," *JAMS* 65 (2012), 313–81

Zazulia, Emily, "Verbal Canons and Notational Complexity in Fifteenth-Century Music," Ph.D. diss., University of Pennsylvania, 2012

# The transformative impulse

EMILY ZAZULIA

The *Missa Dixerunt discipuli*, a work by the little-known fifteenth-century composer Éloy d'Amerval, seems designed to demonstrate the unstable value of the maxima (⊐), the longest note value in use at this time. In the Gloria the maxima swells to the equivalent of eighty-one minims; in the Agnus Dei it shrinks to only sixteen. The appearance of the maxima itself is fixed – throughout the mass it retains its elongated head and downward-reaching tail – but the context in which it is interpreted changes significantly.

The maxima is not alone: the semibreve, breve, and longa are all at the mercy of context. This is because a note itself is only a rhythmic placeholder; its sung duration depends on the mensuration sign (akin to a modern time signature) under which it is interpreted.[1] A single series of note shapes may therefore give rise to multiple rhythmic permutations. The breve (◻), for instance, divides into two semibreves (◊) if it is read under *tempus imperfectum* (C), three if read under *tempus perfectum* (O). That same breve may be worth from four ($=2^2$) to nine ($=3^2$) minims (♪) depending both on how many semibreves it contains and whether each of those semibreves divides into two or three minims. Indeed the possibility for duple or triple divisions exists at all levels: prolation (◊), tempus (◻), minor modus (⊦), and major modus (⊐). As such the maxima can contain anywhere from sixteen ($=2^4$) to eighty-one ($=3^4$) minims – as it does in Éloy's mass.[2] Figure 31.1 illustrates the maximum values each note shape can assume. The *Missa Dixerunt discipuli* drives home the message that by themselves, notes convey no specific information – only the potential for information.

Éloy manipulates these relative durations by changing the mensuration sign under which the tenor performs the cantus firmus. Over the course of the mass, the composer uses all sixteen species of mensuration identified by Johannes Tinctoris. In other words, Éloy systematically explores every possible array of subdivisions, with maximas, longas, breves, and semibreves

---

1 This issue is discussed with exceptional clarity in Wegman, "Petrus de Domarto," 267–71. The classic study of the fifteenth-century mensural system is Berger, *Mensuration and Proportion Signs*.
2 Major modus is rare in the fifteenth century, as are maximas; it is discussed by Tinctoris in his *Liber imperfectionum notarum musicalium*. See Woodley, "At the Limits of Mensural Theory."

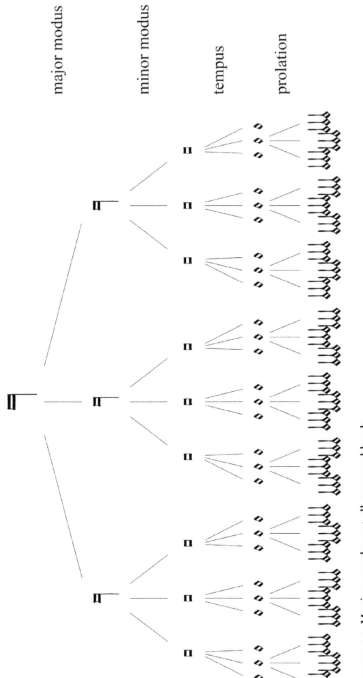

Figure 31.1 Maximum values at all mensural levels

alternately dividing into two or three of the next-smaller value.[3] Éloy is similarly comprehensive in selecting note shapes: his seven-note rhythmicization of the chant features all five principal shapes. See Figure 31.2, which shows the tenor as it appears in the Crucifixus.[4] As the figure illustrates, this tenor presentation gives rise to three cantus-firmus statements, each governed by a different mensuration. Crucially, the appearance of this brief cantus firmus remains constant throughout every movement of the mass, even though the organizing mensuration changes continually. The result is a process that showcases the highly contingent nature of fifteenth-century note values.

While Éloy's mass represents a zealous application of mensural reinterpretation, many of his contemporaries use this technique to a more moderate and yet still fundamental service, building elaborate mensural edifices by repeating singly notated lines under multiple mensuration signs. The most extreme examples are mensuration canons such as those in Johannes Ockeghem's *Missa Prolationum* and Josquin's *Missa L'homme armé super voces musicales*, in which multiple voices simultaneously read the same line under different mensuration signs, causing the voices to unfold at different speeds. In Figure 31.3, taken from Ockeghem's *Missa Prolationum*, the top voice (reading in C) sings imperfect breves while the altus's breves (reading in O) are perfect, causing the latter to progress through the line more slowly. Because both voices are in minor prolation, their semibreves are the same length. Far more common than mensuration canons are tenor motets and cantus-firmus masses that use mensural reinterpretation to produce variant versions of a given line in different sections of the mass; Éloy's mass is an example of this type. Though the mechanisms at work in these examples differ, they all rely on the same principle: that rhythmic value is not an intrinsic property of notes.

Mensural rereading was the first but by no means the only type of transformation practiced by late medieval musicians. Composers also explored pitch-based transformations such as transposition, inversion, and retrograde, and toward the end of the fifteenth century they introduced even more imaginative transformations. Though these procedures differ in execution, they all require a singer (usually a tenor) to apply a *process* to a notated line of

3 Wegman provides an overview of Éloy's mass in "Petrus de Domarto," 251 (see in particular Example 4). See also the helpful table in Sherr, *Masses for the Sistine Chapel*, 33.
4 For reasons of clarity I have removed thin lines separating sets of longa rests that appear in the manuscript. The stroke through the third Ȼ indicates that this statement is read in diminution; this affects only the way it relates to the prevailing O, not the overall mensuration.

(a) The numeral to the right indicates that the c.f. is sung three times

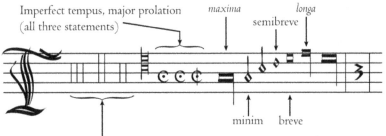

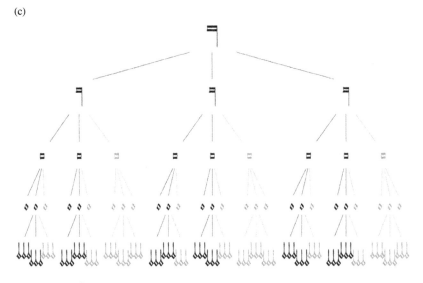

Figure 31.2 Éloy d'Amerval, *Missa Dixerunt discipuli*: (a) Tenor as it appears in the Crucifixus (Vatican CS 14, fol. 61r); (b) Divisions for all three c.f. statements; (c) Mensural values in the Crucifixus, tenor, statement 1 (gray values are inactive)

Figure 31.3 Johannes Ockeghem, *Missa Prolationum*, opening of the Kyrie, upper voices (diplomatic "facsimile" and score realization)

music. These processes, in turn, are only possible because of how notes assume specific meaning in late medieval notational practice.

## From fourteenth-century words to fifteenth-century signs

Mensural reinterpretation was not a fifteenth-century invention; many fourteenth-century motets, often referred to under the umbrella of "isorhythm," feature tenors that must be reread in different ways. While mensural reinterpretation has its roots in these motets, the sort of notationally based reinterpretation they exhibit exists alongside other types of repeating structures, including repetition of either pitch or rhythm as well as combinations of the two.[5] In the fourteenth century transformations are more often written out, and thus point less strongly to the process of metamorphosis itself. In the fifteenth century, by contrast, tenors are often read in different mensurations than the other voices, such that transformation is staged not as a by-product of other factors, but as an end unto itself.

Before about 1430, composers had written out series of intended mensurations in sometimes lengthy verbal instructions; thereafter they began to indicate mensural reinterpretation by using a different mensuration sign for each iteration. A late fourteenth-century example makes this distinction clear. The anonymous motet *Inter densas/Imbribus irriguis/Admirabile est* appears to be a precursor to Éloy's mass in that it also employs all five basic note shapes, which the singer must read under eight successive mensurations.[6] But unlike Éloy,

5 Bent, "What is Isorhythm?"
6 The motet is preserved in the Chantilly Codex, Chantilly 564. See Wegman, "Petrus de Domarto," 248–51.

who consistently uses mensuration signs, the composer of *Inter densas* provides the tenor with this instruction:[7]

> The tenor is to be sung eight times: first in major modus and perfect tempus, second in major modus and imperfect tempus, third in minor modus and perfect tempus, fourth in minor modus and imperfect tempus, fifth in major modus and minor perfect tempus, sixth in major modus and minor imperfect tempus, seventh in minor modus and major perfect tempus, [and] eighth in imperfect minor modus and major perfect mode, observing a rest when the mode is perfect.

These instructions read almost like a theoretical treatise.[8] The shift from inscriptions to signs reflects the broader trend of using mensuration signs more frequently.

## Intrinsic vs. extrinsic signification and the role of metasigns

Even in the fourteenth century, verbal instructions of this sort were rare; mensuration was more often signaled intrinsically, through coloration, the grouping of note shapes, and dots of division and perfection, rather than a dedicated mensuration sign.[9] How and why mensuration signs came to be used consistently is as shadowy as why mensuration was generally *not* made explicit earlier. Questions of causation aside, a survey of manuscript sources demonstrates that by 1440 a decisive shift had taken place.

In their discussions of the contingent nature of note shapes, music theorists attest to this shift in modes of signification. Prosdocimus de Beldemandis describes the semiotics of note shapes according to properties that are intrinsic and extrinsic to musical notes, adapting concepts from Aristotelian metaphysics.[10] He explains that a note's shape is an intrinsic property of the note – in Aristotle's terms, it is "essential." The specific value a note takes on is an accidental quality, signaled extrinsically. Prosdocimus's view follows from

---

7 Someone apparently anticipated the difficulty this tenor would pose to singers, since the motet's only source includes a solus tenor – a version that spells out the tenor transformations in notation that can be read exactly as written. Furthermore, the solus tenor occupies a more prominent place on the page than the canonic tenor. See Allsen, "Tenores ad longum," 46–49.

8 Well past 1430 composers continued to use verbal canons to signal augmentation and diminution, often in conjunction with a mensuration sign. Indeed the correct way of notating augmentation and diminution remained a hotly debated subject for decades. The motets in the final layer of Bologna Q15, which Margaret Bent dates to ca. 1433, are among the earliest to signal mensural reinterpretation with mensuration signs, though even among these works the use of multiple mensuration signs is exceptional. Bent, *Bologna Q15*, 22.

9 Stoessel, "The Captive Scribe," 190–91.

10 This discussion appears in Prosdocimus's *Expositiones tractatus practice cantus mensurabilis*. See Stoessel, "The Interpretation of Unusual Mensuration Signs," 182–83.

the writings of Johannes de Muris, who declared that the "figure" (i.e., the note) and its attendant signification are related but distinct.[11]

Prosdocimus's Aristotelian musings take on particular significance in pieces that feature mensural reinterpretation. These works highlight the distinction between the essential and accidental qualities of note shapes: the essential quality of a series of shapes, as in Éloy's maxima, remains intact even as the mensuration governing these shapes changes their accidental quality (i.e., specific values). Shifting the onus of determining value to a mensuration sign frees the composer to write a series of note shapes that may imply one mensuration but are in fact realized under another. The move from intrinsic to extrinsic signification of mensuration thus changes the role of mensuration itself: from an attribute of the melodic line to something imposed externally.

Because mensuration signs determine how the notes they govern are interpreted, they have a fundamentally different semiotic status than the notes themselves. Two distinct classes of notational symbols emerge: notes and the context-defining figures that award notes specific meaning. The first of these categories is simple enough, comprising note shapes and rests, as well as their placement on the staff. The second category, which includes clefs, verbal canons, and mensuration signs, establishes the circumstances under which notes and rests are to be interpreted. Because this latter group features signs that work on other signs, I refer to these context-defining symbols as metasigns. Notes rely on metasigns to activate their meaning. A simple change of metasign has the potential to recast the pitch or rhythm of every note it governs.

## Unsung texts

This brings us to the other major element that helped initiate what I want to call the transformative impulse: composers increasingly went out of their way to preserve the visual appearance of their cantus firmi. In doing so they showed a preference for an aesthetic I call notational fixity, which depends on a certain reverence for borrowed material.[12] The composer maintains most or all notational details from the cantus firmus's original source, creating a literal "fixed song," manipulated only by changing metasigns that may be seen to exist outside the song itself. The aesthetics of notational fixity fueled the

---

11 As Dorit Tanay shows, Muris recognizes that notes have two forms: their written *figura* and their musical signification. Tanay, *Noting Music, Marking Culture*, ch. 2.
12 For a fuller discussion of notational fixity, see Zazulia, "Verbal Canons and Notational Complexity," ch. 3.

transformative impulse, evincing a fifteenth-century interest in things sounding other than what they seem. Schematic transformation of the sort I've
described (as opposed to a looser, theme-and-variation type) thereby creates
an ontological paradox: the borrowed song remains constant in writing even as
it is varied in performance. This paradox draws attention to music's simultaneous existence in both script and sound.

Once again we find the roots of this aesthetic in the fourteenth century,
when written-out instructions were used to indicate various types of schematic transformation. In their earliest uses, verbal canons were used to clarify
aspects of notation that might otherwise be ambiguous.[13] Canons specified
the meaning of red notation (coloration), indicated mensural reinterpretation
(as in *Inter densas*), and clarified individual signs. The latter usage was especially common with the unusual mensuration and proportion signs of the
*ars subtilior*. In the first decades of the fifteenth century, verbal instructions
were used to indicate transformations such as retrograde and, rarely, transposition and inversion.[14] Verbal canons thus afforded a flexibility that proved
foundational for fifteenth-century cantus-firmus treatment. By the second
half of the fifteenth century, verbal canons take on the role for which they
are best known today – cryptic inscriptions whose meaning must be puzzled
out. Almost by accident, then, fourteenth-century composers introduced the
idea of transformation by using simple, clear instructions. Fifteenth-century
composers took this idea and ran with it.

Bonnie Blackburn has recently provided an overview of the enigmatic uses of
verbal canons.[15] She outlines fourteen categories of musical transformation:
augmentation, diminution, transposition, interval canon, mensural reinterpretation, retrograde, inversion, omission, substitution, rearrangement, ostinato,
extraction, addition, and *tacet* indications. The first five of these procedures
could have been (and sometimes were) achieved with a mensuration sign
instead of a canon. The rest, including idiosyncratic procedures such as rearrangement (i.e., performing the notated symbols in a different order), left no
other notational option. Above all, this collection of procedures is a testament
to the fantastic variety fifteenth-century composers explored in their schematic
notational manipulations.

Verbal canons stand apart from other metasigns in that they are not a
necessary notational element. Whereas a singer needed a clef and mensuration
sign to make sense of the notes before him, verbal canons were entirely

---

13 Ibid., ch. 1.
14 Charles Turner assembles a taxonomy of the early use of verbal canons in "*Sub obscuritate quadam
ostendens.*"
15 See Blackburn, "The Corruption of One."

supplementary. They are also entirely optional: virtually every line sung as the result of transformation by a verbal canon could have been written out in a more straightforward notation. Indeed canonic lines were sometimes written out as "resolutions," which function like an answer key to canonic notation. Resolutions often appear side-by-side with the canonic notation, though at times they replace it altogether.[16]

Why would a composer choose canonic notation over a straightforward presentation? Sometimes it was to flaunt their ingenuity at having been able to devise such clever canons. Other times, it was to maintain the integrity of borrowed material. Indeed, while resolved notation is clearer, this clarity comes at the expense of notational fixity. Verbal canons allowed the composer to notate his music in a way that highlighted schematic transformation. They remind us that in this period notation did much more than record sound.

## Setting the stage for an aesthetics of transformation

The expanded scope of schematic manipulations cannot be attributed to a single factor, but crucially coincided with changes on several fronts: the shift of cantus-firmus usage from single-section motet to multi-movement mass cycle, the use of chanson tenors as cantus firmi, the rise of four-voice texture with a low contratenor, and the developing aesthetic of notational fixity.

One can identify three principal stages: first, systematic transformations in some fourteenth-century motets; second, longer cantus firmi in the expanded dimensions of the early fifteenth-century motet; and third, the cyclic mass of the mid-fifteenth century and beyond. This last stage ultimately emerges as the most significant in terms of musical transformation. Indeed it is difficult to overstate the importance of the cyclic mass for both the increased prevalence of systematic transformations and the establishment of notational fixity as an aesthetic goal. Through all these stages, enlarged dimensions and complexity of procedure go hand in hand.

The opportunities and constraints presented by the almost unprecedented length, fixed text, and standard sectional divisions of the mass cycle shaped notational conventions. In a cantus-firmus mass, the borrowed material is stated at least five times – once in each movement – but can appear as many as twelve. Unlike motets in one or two *partes*, mass cycles require many page-turns, which cause the cantus firmus to be rewritten on each manuscript opening. These written-out repeats, ultimately a function of the larger

---

16 On the use of resolutions – or lack thereof – see Rodin, "Unresolved."

dimensions of these works, can be seen to have established the single graphical archetype. The mass cycle thus presented composers with a twofold opportunity: to increase the variety of cantus-firmus manipulations while also strengthening the tendency toward notational fixity.

The desire to preserve the notational identity of borrowed material, which began in earnest around 1450, was surely related to the increased use of chanson tenors as cantus firmi and the expanded length of the cited material. Unlike chant tenors, which had to be rhythmicized by the composer, chansons possess a rhythmic profile – and, by extension, a notational profile, which can be preserved even as it is manipulated. Thus while composers sometimes maintained notational fixity for fixity's sake, they usually did so in order to preserve a *res facta*.

The cyclic mass is also distinguished from other fifteenth-century genres by virtue of its text. Unlike motets and chansons, which are governed only by textual conventions, the Mass Ordinary comprises a set of basically static texts. Because composers set the same words over and over, it is not surprising that they expended greater effort on technical matters, perhaps in an effort to create variety among mass settings. Moreover transformative procedures were associated with the highest stylistic register, which by the 1440s the mass cycle had taken over from the motet.

The four-voice texture of most mass cycles facilitated cantus-firmus reinterpretation; indeed several of the earliest Continental four-voice masses feature schematic transformation, among them Petrus de Domarto's *Missa Spiritus almus* and Guillaume Du Fay's *Missa Se la face ay pale*. Rob Wegman and Julie Cumming have credited the anonymous English *Missa Caput* with introducing a four-voice texture featuring a low contratenor (contratenor bassus) that quickly became the standard texture in sacred music after about 1450.[17] The innovation of the *Caput* mass lies not so much in the expanded number of voices as in the new contrapuntal function of the low contratenor. This voice "was free to assume total control over the harmonic progressions, a task that had not previously been associated with any single, freely composed voice."[18] I suggest that the low contratenor also had a crucial impact on cantus-firmus treatment: it could accommodate the demands of a schematic tenor, easing difficulties that might otherwise arise from rule-based melodic transformation by serving as a kind of harmonic anchor.[19]

---

17 Cumming, *The Motet in the Age of Du Fay*; Wegman, "Petrus de Domarto," 297–302.
18 Wegman, "Petrus de Domarto," 296.
19 This textural development also represented a departure from the dominant four-voice texture of early fifteenth-century motets, such as Du Fay's *Nuper rosarum flores*, which featured two equal-range tenors, often both subject to schematic transformation.

With the rise of four-voice writing also came the convention of notating each voice in a separate quadrant of a manuscript opening. Choirbook format, with voices written individually rather than vertically aligned in score, carries implications that set fifteenth-century transformations apart from those of later composers such as Johann Sebastian Bach and Anton Webern, who are also famous for using procedures such as augmentation, retrograde, and inversion.[20] The chief difference is that whereas in later periods transformations had to be written out in order to vertically align the voices in score, fifteenth-century composers took as a given that each voice would be notated separately. While it is difficult to determine whether these coincident developments set the stage for notational transformation or were themselves products of it, we can be sure that the development of the mass cycle and its attendant conventions shaped how transformations were envisaged and achieved.

## Shared functions

Mensuration signs, clefs, and verbal canons each typically indicated a distinct set of transformations, though these occasionally overlapped. While augmentation was usually indicated by mensuration signs, for instance, verbal canons could do so instead (or in addition); all three metasigns were used to signal transposition. At times composers used different types of metasigns simultaneously to effect multiple transformations. By the mid-fifteenth century, the novel technique of mensural reinterpretation was being signaled by mensuration signs; augmentation and diminution, by contrast, were expressed with verbal canons as often as with mensuration signs.[21] For signaling pitch-based transformations, verbal canons were far more common than other means, which could include clef change or placement. Thus while a change of clef would seem to be the most expedient way to indicate transposition, composers used several techniques when calling for an adjustment of pitch space.

Most examples of imitation canon from the fifteenth century are signaled with a verbal canon that specifies the interval of transposition, often in conjunction with a *signum congruentiae* to show when the second voice should enter. A *signum congruentiae* could also be used on its own, without specifying the transposition interval of the *comes* voice, which presumably would have

---

20 Several pieces by Bach, including the *Musical Offering* and the Goldberg Variations, do use enigmatic notation in line with fifteenth-century practices. Some retrograde canons are written as single lines with a reversed clef at the end; elsewhere Latin inscriptions point to the canon's resolution. Still these works existed – if prominently – on the fringes of Bach's output; their fifteenth-century counterparts were more mainstream.

21 When composers use verbal canons to communicate augmentation or diminution, there is the potential for confusion as to whether it should be proportional or mensural.

forced the singers to test out several intervals of imitation to see which would work. Perhaps composers used clef changes less often because clefs, which must always sit on a line rather than a space, cannot indicate transposition at the fourth or octave.[22]

Despite this limitation, clefs were an essential metasign. The empty staff is like a graph with unlabeled axes in that it conveys only the *potential* for pitch information. Without a clef, contour is still perceptible, since the relationship between adjacent lines and spaces is limited to a tone or a semitone. But the distinction between tone and semitone is important. Another complicating factor is that each line and space was not associated with a specific pitch, as they often are today. Whereas modern notation relies mainly on three clefs (treble, octave-treble, and bass), thus enabling a musician to determine pitch content with relative ease even if the clef is missing, fifteenth-century notation regularly uses C1, C2, C3, C4, C5/F3, F4, F5, and G2 clefs, plus the occasional use of a Gamma (Γ) clef for music in an exceptionally low range. Mid-line clef changes, often used instead of ledger lines, seem not to have fazed singers. In rare cases we even find no clefs at all, only key signatures that indicate the placement of *fa*. The abundance and flexible interchangeability of clefs further highlights their importance for defining melodic space. Just as note shapes needed mensuration signs to fix their absolute durations, notes placed on the staff relied on clefs to bind them – if sometimes fleetingly – to specific pitches.

In a few pieces transposition is indicated not with clefs or verbal canons, but by the placement of mensuration signs. A striking example appears in the Sanctus of Marbrianus de Orto's *Missa L'homme armé* (see Figure 31.4), which combines mensural reinterpretation with transposition. To achieve these transformations, de Orto uses five different signs to indicate the successive mensurations under which the short tenor segment is to be

Figure 31.4 Marbrianus de Orto, *Missa L'homme armé*, Sanctus, tenor (Vatican CS 64, fol. 9v)

---

22 Though the technique remains rare, in the sixteenth century there are more examples of composers using multiple clefs to produce transformation. After 1500 two-voice canons, often at the fifth, became increasingly popular in pieces scored for five and six voices.

Figure 31.5  Johannes Ockeghem, *Missa Cuiusvis toni*, opening of the discantus (Chigi Codex)

sung. The placement of these signs on the staff further indicates the starting pitch of each repetition, which ingeniously follows the opening phrase of the *L'homme armé* melody. This parallelism leads to a striking visual presentation. The C3 clef assigns pitches not to the notes themselves, but to the mensuration signs, which in turn anchor the first note of each cantus-firmus repetition.

In Ockeghem's *Missa Cuiusvis toni*, the most famous clefless piece ever composed, a lack of clefs highlights the flexibility of the staff. This mass is at least theoretically performable "in any mode."[23] In lieu of a clef Ockeghem uses a symbol to designate the modal final in each voice. This symbol usually takes the form of either three or four dots or a dotted circle beneath a looping vertical flourish (see Figure 31.5). Ockeghem's invented sign allows the performers to coordinate their parts without fixing the final on a specific pitch – just a specific place on the staff. Without clefs, the singers select a final before settling on clefs and the placement of *mi* and *fa*, which allows them to read in the chosen mode. We have seen that not just any series of note shapes will come out squarely in more than one mensuration. The same is true for melodic lines, which are not guaranteed to be idiomatic in every mode – at least not without excessive editorial accidentals. By permitting multiple modal dispositions, the clefless notation of the *Missa Cuiusvis toni* highlights the distinction fifteenth-century musicians made between relative and fixed pitch. The notes and rests of Ockeghem's mass hold the potential for multiple musical results only by virtue of their combination with different sets of clefs.

The *Missa Cuiusvis toni* is unusual among examples that exploit the note–metasign distinction in that it does not feature a cantus firmus. Instead this piece might in a sense be considered "all cantus firmus": unlike the majority of strict cantus-firmus masses, in which transformation is limited to a single voice,

23 The precise number of possible modal dispositions remains a matter of debate. See Houle, "Ockeghem's *Missa Cuiusvis Toni*"; Perkins, "Modal Strategies"; Dean, "Okeghem's Attitude towards Modality"; Goldberg, "Cuiusvis toni."

here all voices are subject to pitch reinterpretation. The glue that holds the five movements together is not preexisting material but rather the principle of *finalis* variability.

This split between notes and metasigns, on the one hand, and composers' interest in their relationship, on the other, underpins the rise of the transformative impulse. More precisely, the establishment of metasigns as a separate semiotic category allowed for notational fixity, which in turn served as a precondition for the more elaborate schematic transformations used later in the century. The examples discussed here represent heightened instances of these techniques, but in practice their use was both widespread and varied.

Although schematic transformations were an important arrow in the compositional quiver, they almost never appear simultaneously in every voice. For reasons practical as much as aesthetic, composers retained significant freedom in shaping their musical surfaces. More work is needed before we can properly understand how rule-bound, schematic structures affect surface elements. For while generated voices undoubtedly constrain the musical surface, it is often hard to tell when aesthetic values are straining against rather than working in parallel with structural constraints.

If we are to understand fifteenth-century sacred music empathetically, we must begin by recognizing that its aesthetic world is not limited to sound. Schematic transformations are staged as part of the performative process; they draw notation into an aesthetic realm. Virtually all notated music requires that musicians realize it in performance, but the canonic manipulations of the late fifteenth century take this truism a step further by asking singers to change the way they engage with the notation before them; the singer acts as a filter or prism through which the music is refracted to reveal potentials that were implicit from the beginning. Canonic notation demands that the singer breathe life into it – but even as it enjoys such realization, the borrowed song remains untouched on the page. Rooted in musical language itself, the transformative impulse emanates from a drive to explore the semiotic potential of written song.

# Bibliography

Allsen, J. Michael, "Tenores ad longum and Rhythmic Cues in the Early Fifteenth-Century Motet," *PMM* 12 (2003), 43–69

Bent, Margaret, *Bologna Q15: The Making and Remaking of a Musical Manuscript*, Ars nova: Nuova serie II, Lucca, 2008

   "What is Isorhythm?," in *Quomodo cantabimus canticum? Studies in Honor of Edward H. Roesner*, ed. David Butler Cannata, *et al.*, Middleton, WI, 2008, 121–43

Berger, Anna Maria Busse, *Mensuration and Proportion Signs: Origins and Evolution*, Oxford, 1993

Blackburn, Bonnie J., "The Corruption of One is the Generation of the Other: Interpreting Canonic Riddles," *JAF* 4 (2012), 182–203

Cumming, Julie, *The Motet in the Age of Du Fay*, Cambridge, 1999

Dean, Jeffrey J., "Okeghem's Attitude towards Modality," in *Modality in the Music of the Fourteenth and Fifteenth Centuries*, ed. Ursula Günther, Ludwig Finscher, and Jeffrey J. Dean, Neuhausen-Stuttgart, 1996, 203–46

Goldberg, Clemens, "Cuiusvis toni: Ansätze zur Analyse einer Messe Johannes Ockeghems," *TVNM* 42 (1992), 3–35

Houle, George, ed., *Ockeghem's Missa Cuiusvis Toni: In its Original Notation and Edited in all the Modes*, Bloomington, IN, 1992

Perkins, Leeman L. "Modal Strategies in Okeghem's Missa Cuiusvis Toni," in *Music Theory and the Exploration of the Past*, ed. Christopher Hatch and David W. Bernstein, Chicago, 1993, 59–71

Prosdocimus de Beldemandis, *Expositiones tractatus practice cantus mensurabilis magistri Johannis de Muris*, ed. Alberto Gallo, Bologna, 1966

Rodin, Jesse, "Unresolved," *ML* 90 (2009), 535–54

Sherr, Richard, ed., *Masses for the Sistine Chapel: Vatican City, Biblioteca Apostolica Vaticana, Cappella Sistina, MS 14*, Monuments of Renaissance Music 13, Chicago, 2009

Stoessel, Jason, "The Captive Scribe: The Context and Culture of Scribal and Notational Process in the Music of the *Ars subtilior*," Ph.D. diss., University of New England, 2002

   "The Interpretation of Unusual Mensuration Signs in the Notation of the Ars sub-tilior," in *A Late Medieval Songbook and its Context: New Perspectives on the Chantilly Codex (Bibliothèque du Château de Chantilly, Ms. 564)*, ed. Yolanda Plumley and Anne Stone, Turnhout, 2009, 179–202

Tanay, Dorit, *Noting Music, Marking Culture: The Intellectual Context of Rhythmic Notation, 1250–1400*, Holzgerlingen, 1999

Tinctoris, Johannes, *Liber imperfectionum notarum musicalium*, in *Opera theoretica* 1, ed. Albert Seay, [Rome], 1975

Turner, Charles, "*Sub obscuritate quadam ostendens*: Latin Canon in the Early Renaissance Motet," *EM* 30 (2002), 165–87

Wegman, Rob C. "Petrus de Domarto's *Missa Spiritus almus* and the Early History of the Four-Voice Mass in the Fifteenth Century," *EMH* 10 (1991), 235–303

Woodley, Ronald, "At the Limits of Mensural Theory: Tinctoris on Imperfection, Alteration and the Punctus," in *Le notazioni della polifonia vocale dei secoli IX–XVII: Antologia – part seconda*, ed. Maria Caraci Vela, Daniele Sabaino, and Stefano Aresi, Pisa, forthcoming

Zazulia, Emily, "Verbal Canons and Notational Complexity in Fifteenth-Century Music," Ph.D. diss., University of Pennsylvania, 2012

# Transformations in music theory and music treatises

EVAN A. MACCARTHY

Around the year 1430, Ugolino of Orvieto (ca. 1380–1452) reiterated an age-old distinction between *musicus* and *cantor*. Advocating a middle road between a pure practical method and a speculative one, he argues that "those who desire to be trained a little in the background to such practice require a measure of speculation."[1] In writings on music, this balance between *musica practica* and *musica speculativa* underwent critical shifts in the fifteenth century, with an enduring effect on the form and genre of the music theory treatise. The evolution of the music treatise itself is our object of study here.

Matters of solmization, mode, mensural rhythm and notation, and counterpoint received many theoretical treatments over the course of the fifteenth century, often as part of ardent polemics. Irreconcilable debates arose over defining consonances, establishing agreeable tuning systems, and determining the proper use of *musica ficta*; these debates fomented yet further invective.[2] Simultaneously, theorists summarized and challenged texts both by recent writers (Marchetto da Padova, fl. 1305–19 and Johannes de Muris, ca. 1290–after 1344) and the looming authorities of Boethius and Guido of Arezzo, as theorists sought to reconcile ancient pedagogical texts with

---

1 Ugolino, *Declaratio musicae disciplinae*, bk. 3, prologue (ed. Seay, 2:60–61); adapted from the translation in Gallo, *Music of the Middle Ages II*, 111–12. Whereas the theorist "understands and demonstrates mode, time and prolation, alteration, imperfection and perfection, and the rest by means of speculation, the practical musician only reports these things from his experience." "Mediocriter affectare hanc musicam praticam mensuratam est eius secundum viam praticam et non speculativam, quae ad theoricum spectat notitiam habere. Ipse enim theoricus modum, tempus et prolationem, alterationem, imperfectionem et perfectionem, et cetera, via speculationis intelligit et demonstrat quae praticus solum exercitio suo pronuntiat. Vel mediocriter affectare est inter puram praticam, quae orationis est expers, et speculativa, quae omnis ratio est particeps, huius mensuratae musicae notitiam via quadam media velle ratione comprehendere ... Indigent enim speculatione quadam qui in huiusmodi pratica plenius desiderant edoceri." There are echoes here of the fourteenth-century *Speculum musicae* of Jacobus: "Si quis autem musicam theoricam simul et practicam possideret, perfectior esset musicus eo qui solum haberet alteram, dum tamen perfecte ambas possideret, ut alteram alter possidet" (bk. 1, ch. 3.12).

2 Two excellent surveys that trace the treatment of the major concepts of music theory in the fifteenth century are Herlinger, "Music Theory of the Fourteenth and Early Fifteenth Centuries," and Blackburn, "Music Theory and Musical Thinking." On notation, see the contributions by Anne Stone and Emily Zazulia in this volume, Ch. 30 and Ch. 31.

current musical practice.[3] The ideas of composition and the work concept continued to crystallize during the fifteenth century.[4] As musical styles and genres evolved, so too did the manner in which theorists explained musical phenomena.

These transformations of emphasis and new modes of thinking about music and its place in the arts surface in fifteenth-century treatises. One can trace significant changes in which topics were treated and how they were divided and organized within a single treatise or between multiple texts by a single author. Several subgenres of the music theory treatise emerged: we find encyclopedic approaches as well as topic-by-topic organization, and summaries of and commentaries on earlier theoretical traditions as well as cutting-edge responses to modern musical practice. In some cases the collected treatises of one theorist appear to serve as a pedagogical program for music students (e.g., John Hothby and Johannes Tinctoris); in others, the exhaustive treatment of all musical knowledge in one text gives the appearance of a reference work (Ugolino's *Declaratio*).

This essay explores how this spectrum of subgenres impacted the treatment of a common set of music-theoretical subjects. To consider this question, I will survey several Italian treatise subgenres, including the encyclopedic *summa*, the notebook and compendium, the dialogue, the *laus musicae*, and the focused treatment of notation, counterpoint, and mode. I will also consider how authors demonstrated their understanding of earlier music theory while also responding to contemporary musical practice. I conclude by pondering the readership of these theoretical writings.

## Genre and form

Most fifteenth-century music theorists approached their topic with strong backgrounds in the Quadrivium, having trained as theologians, speculative philosophers, physicians, or mathematicians. This circumstance produced texts rooted in the Pythagorean and Boethian traditions, highlighting music's relationship with mathematics and tethering music to arithmetic, geometry, and astronomy. In his *Nova musica* (first decade of the fifteenth century), for instance, the singer and composer Johannes Ciconia strung together citations and paraphrases of late antique and early medieval "auctores" in order to summarize their teachings on consonances, the modes, intervals, species, and proportions. The more innovative fourth and final book of the treatise does

---

3  See Mengozzi, *The Renaissance Reform*.
4  See Blackburn, "On Compositional Process," 246–78 and the essays by Laurenz Lütteken and Anna Maria Busse Berger in this volume, Ch. 3 and Ch. 8.

delve into connections with the arts of the Trivium, as well as the possibility of classifying musical works according to how they use elements introduced in the first three books. Indeed Stefano Mengozzi has recently suggested that with its call for a *renovatio* in music education, Ciconia's treatise is more humanistically inclined than was previously thought, and as a result is more directly concerned with practical matters than it might at first appear.[5] Overall the *Nova musica* reflects a trend toward an intermingling of ancient authorities with practical and humanistic discussions.

Some writings on music fit into a larger program of quadrivial studies, with a neat division between speculative and practical treatises. In the case of the physician Prosdocimus de Beldemandis (d. 1428), his oeuvre constitutes a complete study of music's practice and nature. According to the mathematician and Franciscan friar Luca Pacioli (1445–1517), Prosdocimus's treatises on subjects like music, astrology, and arithmetic earned him a place among universal authorities such as Euclid and Boethius.[6] Like Ciconia, Prosdocimus drew upon the writings of earlier authorities – but he also engaged with fourteenth-century theorists like Muris and Marchetto on matters of mode, mensural notation, even improvised polyphony, and was not always in agreement with them.[7] While at times hinged to the writings of Boethius, especially in his *Brevis summula proportionum* (1409) and his treatise on the monochord (*Parvus tractatulus de modo monacordum dividendi*, 1412), Prosdocimus infused speculative ideas with a keen awareness of musical practice and contemporary repertory, such as his proposal for a seventeen-note octave encompassing all the known chromatic pitches; his distilled observations on contrapuntal practice found in the six rules in his *Contrapunctus* (1412) that seem aimed at his academic audience at the University of Padua; and his rejection of Marchetto's division of the whole tone into five equal parts in his *Musica speculativa* (1425).

Prosdocimus is one of several fifteenth-century theorists who we know obtained university degrees or held university posts; others include Bartolomé Ramos de Pareja (ca. 1440–after 1491), Nicolò Burzio (1453–1528), Franchino Gaffurio (1451–1522), and Johannes Tinctoris (ca. 1435–1511).[8] Indeed even as a concern to address musical practice crept into theoretical writings, the academic roots of many theorists ensured the continued relevance of a quadrivial foundation for musical thought.

5 Mengozzi, *The Renaissance Reform*, 117–30.
6 Prosdocimus, *Plana musica, Musica speculativa*, 5–6; Newsome, "Quadrivial Pursuits," 167–236.
7 In his *Musica speculativa*, Prosdocimus sought to correct Marchetto's *Lucidarium* after finding "evils, lies, and mistakes concerning music" (ed. Herlinger, Preface, 158–59).
8 Moyer, "Music, Mathematics, and Aesthetics," 119.

The *Declaratio musicae disciplinae* (ca. 1430–35) of the composer and theorist Ugolino of Orvieto demonstrates a concerted attempt to convey both types of *musica* in one systematic and encyclopedic text, divided into five books. The first two books summarize the Guidonian curriculum: the first book treats pitches, intervals, mutations, mode, and *differentiae*, while the second covers note-against-note counterpoint (N.B., before any discussion of mensuration) within the hexachordal system, including a passage on using *musica ficta* to achieve a "delectabiliorem harmoniam" ("more delightful harmony").[9] The third book moves to mensural matters, wherein Ugolino continues the commentary tradition on the French *Ars nova* treatise *Libellus cantus mensurabilis*.[10] The remaining two books turn from practical matters to a comprehensive, speculative treatment of all *musica*. With significant reliance on an anonymous set of *Questiones* attributed to the circle of the Italian philosopher, astrologer, and mathematician Biagio Pelacani, the fourth book offers a mathematical consideration of proportions as the foundation of intervals.[11] The concluding fifth book considers the nature of sound and the traditional tripartite division of *musica instrumentalis*, *musica humana*, and *musica mundana* through a Boethian lens. A handful of manuscripts of Ugolino's *Declaratio* also carry an accompanying *Tractatus monochordi* that relies heavily on Prosdocimus's monochord treatise.[12] On the whole Ugolino's treatise is notable for the way it integrates writings by a host of ancient and recent theorists into a single, encyclopedic tome.

This preference for a large curriculum treating both the nature and practice of music continued throughout the century, but with a return to topic-specific treatises. This trend can be observed in the writings of John Hothby, an English theorist, composer, and Carmelite monk based in Lucca for much of his career. Well known as a teacher, Hothby covered the major subjects of counterpoint, mensuration, proportions, and plainchant theory. Many of his writings survive in manuscript copies of what appear to be circulated lecture notes, in either Latin or Italian and in various states of completeness and quality. (This circumstance has led to some questions of attribution.) Considering all of these writings together reveals a systematic, if at times confusing, approach to both speculative and practical music, including both chant and polyphony.

Hothby's intellectual ties to older theorists, namely Marchetto, Guido, and Boethius, stimulated intense, personal debates with his contemporary Ramos. One treatise resulting from this debate came in the form of a dialogue,

9 Ugolino, *Declaratio musicae disciplinae*, bk. 2, ch. 162 (ed. Seay, 1:229).
10 On Muris, see the essay by Anne Stone in this volume, Ch. 30.
11 Panti, "Una fonte della *Declaratio musicae disciplinae*."      12 See *Declaratio*, ed. Seay, 3:227–53.

Hothby's *Dialogus in arte musica*, a relatively rare subgenre up until this point.[13] Precedents for this are Pseudo-Odo's *Dialogus de musica* (early eleventh century), a text probably taught by Hothby, and Georgius Anselmi's *De musica* of 1434. In the latter, Anselmi presents three dialogues between himself and Pietro dei Rossi of Parma, set at the Bagni di Lucca over three days in September 1433, that treat both celestial and human harmony with a level of detail not seen since ancient times (e.g., Macrobius and Martianus Capella).[14] The dialogue's conversational, accessible tone enabled Anselmi to propose reforms to the Boethian model without the vitriol of other theorists' *ad hominem* attacks.

Traditionally minded theorists like Hothby responded to such calls for reform, reinforcing the defenses of Boethius, Pythagoras, and Guido. Johannes Gallicus (ca. 1415–73) is a unique case. Employing humanistic methods developed by contemporary scholars, he maintained the primacy of Boethius's *De institutione musica* as a textbook for learning music, having learned himself from the humanist educator Vittorino da Feltre with Boethius as his guide. Johannes's *Ritus canendi* (ca. 1458–64) is divided into two parts: first, a survey of Greek ratios, tetrachords, and the monochord; second, a treatment of notation, intervals, and modes of chant theory. Another important defender of earlier theoretical systems was Nicolò Burzio, whose *Musices opusculum* (also entitled *Florum libellus*) was printed in Bologna in 1487. Citing classical authorities like Pliny, Cicero, Martial, and Valerius Maximus, he combated Ramos (attacked here as "worthless," "arrogant," and "impudent") and Ramos's student Giovanni Spataro with apologetic defenses of Boethius ("the monarch of musicians"), Pythagoras, and the established practices of Guidonian solmization and hexachordal mutation. This precipitated a vituperative response from Spataro in 1491, the *Honesta defensio*, aimed directly at Burzio, cataloging what Spataro considered to be numerous errors.

## Tinctoris

Many sixteenth-century musicians engaged with Ramos's theories, so much so that a case could be made that he was the most influential theorist of his time. Still, this distinction must ultimately go to the Brabantine singer, composer, theorist, and teacher Johannes Tinctoris.[15] Both theorists

---

13  In *Tres tractatuli*, 61–76; trans. Seay in "The *Dialogus Johannis Ottobi*."
14  Tomlinson, *Music in Renaissance Magic*, 74–77. It is worth noting that this text only survives in a manuscript owned and annotated by Gaffurio.
15  On Tinctoris, see also James Hankins's essay in this volume, Ch. 13.

contributed to an increased reliance on the judgment of the ear, furthering the tug of *musica speculativa* into a more practical realm. But it was Tinctoris who, despite his rootedness in earlier theoretical traditions, promoted an empirical approach to music theory, composition, and performance that changed the face of music theory.

Tinctoris certainly participated in a widespread fifteenth-century tradition of prescriptive responses to current musical practice. But he also broke new ground by regularly citing contemporary composers and critically analyzing their works. To do this, he had to search through and closely examine works by various composers ("diversorum compositorum opera perscrutans") in order to render critical judgments. According to his own testimony, some of these critical observations earned him rather severe rebuttals.[16] Tinctoris's comments as well as those of other fifteenth-century writers have received much scholarly attention; these valuable remarks both offer evidence of the relative reception of different composers and shed light on changes in musical style and practice. At times Tinctoris's meaning is opaque. His discussion of *res facta* and *cantare super librum*, for instance, hints at contemporary practice but is frustratingly short.[17] Further insight on such issues can be gleaned from the counterpoint and mensuration treatises. These, together with short treatises on other notational issues, modernized earlier theoretical traditions (by such writers as Marchetto) by inserting polyphonic examples from the contemporary repertory, creating specially composed didactic examples, and citing the titles of works that the reader might have been expected to know or possess.

In Tinctoris's writings we can begin to observe moments of interaction between theorists and leading composers. These can alert us to an active discourse, as in Tinctoris's dedication, in 1476, of his treatise on the modes to Johannes Ockeghem and Antoine Busnoys, asking for their approval or rejection.[18] This same treatise features a model conversation between theorist and listener in which Tinctoris inserts a brief dialogue that employs direct speech between himself and a fictive inquirer to demonstrate how to accurately describe a modally complex song, in this case the treatise's sole mention of a polyphonic example: Du Fay's *Le serviteur*.[19]

---

16 Tinctoris, *Tractatus de punctis*, Prologue (earlymusictheory.org/Tinctoris/texts/depunctis); Tinctoris, *Liber de natura et proprietate tonorum*, Prologue, in *Opera theoretica*, ed. Seay, 1:65–67.

17 Bk. 2, ch. 20. A summary of this debate, with bibliography, is found in Judd, *Musical Theory in the Renaissance*, xviii–xix. See also the essays in this volume by Anna Maria Busse Berger (Ch. 8) and Philippe Canguilhem (Ch. 9).

18 Tinctoris, *Liber de natura et proprietate tonorum*, prologue (Seay, 1:65). On this interaction, see Blackburn, "Did Ockeghem Listen to Tinctoris?" Tinctoris ends by requesting their criticism of his own works – whether musical or theoretical is unclear.

19 Tinctoris, *Liber de natura et proprietate tonorum*, ch. 24 (Seay, 1:85–86).

Tinctoris can also be credited with helping advance new subgenres in music theory treatises. His *Terminorum musicae diffinitorium*, for instance, composed amid a new interest in lexicographic texts, was one of the first dictionaries of musical terms, written in the 1470s and later printed in the early 1490s in Treviso.[20] For all of its usefulness, the *Terminorum* offers exasperatingly brief definitions of musical concepts for the layman, here Tinctoris's dedicatee Beatrice d'Aragona. He also admits his passion for fields other than music, for "achieving knowledge in various subjects, not being satisfied with a single art."[21]

Texts aimed at enumerating the power and effects of music, or more generally heaping upon it words of praise, flourished in the fifteenth century.[22] Again, Tinctoris played an important role in this development, as can be seen in his *Complexus effectuum musices* (Treatise on the Effects of Music). An early version appeared in the early 1460s, before his journey to Italy; a revised and shortened version, naming just twenty of the many effects of music, circulated after about 1475.[23] In his dedication to Beatrice d'Aragona, Tinctoris admits that creating such a compilation is "beyond the ability of a *cantor*" since it draws on theology, philosophy, and poetry; with this statement he seems to signal that, even though he was also a singer and composer, he wishes to be considered a *musicus*, a title he gives himself in his sole surviving letter written almost twenty years later.[24] A much larger project Tinctoris set for himself but ultimately never completed was his *De inventione et usu musicae* (On the Invention and Use of Music), which sought to trace the origins and history of music from mythological legends up to his day. From surviving manuscript and print fragments, we encounter Tinctoris remarking on instrumental music and praising modern-day musicians including Ockeghem and Pietrobono in an informal tone that gives the impression he was trying to reach a wider audience.[25]

## *Musica theorica* versus *musica practica*

Two theorists from the second half of the fifteenth century distinguished between *musica theorica* and *musica practica* with unprecedented clarity:

---

20 Tinctoris, *Diffinitorium musice*, ed. Panti. See also MacCarthy, "Tinctoris and the Neapolitan *Eruditi*," 57–60.
21 Tinctoris, *Diffinitorium musice*, 4.
22 Holford-Strevens, "The *Laudes musicae* in Renaissance Music Treatises."
23 See Woodley, "The Printing and Scope." For two other humanist treatises on music, see *Tractatus de duplici ritu cantus* of Gilles Carlier and *Contra vituperatorem musicae* of Carlo Valgulio, trans. and ed. Cullington. On the latter, see the essay by James Hankins in this volume, Ch. 13.
24 See Woodley, "Tinctoris's Italian Translation," 194–202 and 236–44.
25 Allan Atlas describes Tinctoris here as "journalistic" (*Renaissance Music*, 234). See also MacCarthy, "Tinctoris and the Neapolitan *Eruditi*," 55–57.

Ramos and Gaffurio. In stark contrast to Tinctoris and Hothby, Ramos needed only one book to convey his theoretical precepts. His *Musica practica* of 1482 treats the theory of music as a performing art. Dividing his treatise into three parts, covering pitch, chant, and mensuration, Ramos provoked contemporary theorists with challenges to the authorities of Boethius and Guido. The first part of *Musica practica* is ironically dedicated to *musica theorica*, but is grounded in empirical conclusions in place of a reliance on older authorities. Ramos usually reserves citations for points of disagreement.

On the matter of tuning, Ramos challenges the speculative monochord proposed by Boethius, whose divisions are grounded in precise numerical measurements, complaining that "although this division is useful and pleasant to theorists, to singers it is laborious and difficult to understand."[26] In response to the increased use of imperfect consonances in fifteenth-century music, Ramos proposes a system of just intonation, favoring the purity of thirds and sixths in his division of the monochord (e.g., replacing the Boethian ratios of 81:64 and 32:27 for the major and minor third respectively with pure thirds of 5:4 and 6:5). Ramos also attacks Guido's hexachordal solmization system (*ut, re, mi, fa, sol, la*) as impractical, offering instead an eight-step sequence of syllables (*psal-li-tur per vo-ces is-tas*) that begins on C below gamma-ut and permits mutation on notes an octave apart by replacing any syllable with *psal*. These attacks provoked fiery responses from Hothby, Burzio, and Gaffurio, which in turn inspired a defense from Giovanni Spataro, who had studied with Ramos in Bologna.[27] These debates persisted for the next four decades, laying the ground for many conceptual discussions in the sixteenth century.

The theorist, choirmaster, and composer Gaffurio stands as one of the first theorists to achieve an earnest integration of the campaign of humanistic endeavors that had already begun to blossom early in the fifteenth century in other liberal and mechanical arts.[28] During an exciting period in which scholars circulated rediscovered or newly translated ancient texts, Gaffurio sought to elevate music theory to the position of the other arts like sculpture, architecture, and poetry, which had more direct links to their antique heritage, by collecting, copying, and commissioning translations of Greek music theory and attempting to explicate their contents. He composed a range of treatises, with the titles *Theoricum opus musice discipline* (Theory of the Discipline of Music, 1480), *Theorica musice*

---

26  Strunk, *Source Readings*, 201.
27  These debates are considered in detail in Mengozzi, *The Renaissance Reform*.
28  Adam of Fulda's *Musica* (1490) is also strongly influenced by his humanistic training.

(The Theory of Music, 1492), and *De harmonia musicorum instrumentorum opus* (On the Harmony of Musical Elements, 1518), following in the tradition of earlier theorists by treating intervals, proportions, consonances, and modes while also enlarging discussions of celestial, earthly, and human harmonies. Direct and indirect quotations in Gaffurio's writings confirm that he had read Ugolino, Prosdocimus, and Tinctoris, among others, even though he treated many topics very differently, especially dissonance treatment and proportions. These citations of contemporary theorists contrast strikingly with the *Liber musices* of Florentius de Faxolis, written probably in the late 1480s, which only cites ancient Greek and Roman authors, as well as early medieval theorists.[29] Gaffurio's greatest renown came from the *Practica musicae* (The Practice of Music, 1496; repr. 1497, 1502, 1512), with its dozens of polyphonic examples. Although Gaffurio's attempts to reconcile the ancient Greek modes with the more modern system did not pan out, his efforts spurred succeeding generations to pursue study of ancient Greek music, as seen in the writings of Henricus Glareanus, Nicola Vicentino, Gioseffo Zarlino, and Vincenzo Galilei.

## Reading audiences

The corpus of fifteenth-century music theory treatises prompts questions about their intent, function, and readership. Why were these treatises written? Who was the intended audience? How widely did they circulate? Even if hundreds of manuscripts were copied, how many treatises were actually read? In a period of evolving structures of music education and training, there is good reason to consider the audiences for these important texts.

Beyond named dedicatees, it is hard to determine how widely treatises circulated. As is often the case, dedications signify gratitude for patronage or other support in completing or publishing the text. Tinctoris dedicated several treatises to two members of the Aragonese court in Naples, King Ferrante and his daughter Beatrice. Gaffurio dedicated his *Theoricum opus musice discipline* to Giovanni Arcimboldi, the Cardinal of Novara (1480), his *Theorica musice* and *Practica musicae* to Lodovico Maria Sforza, the first as Duke of Bari (1492), the second as Duke of Milan (1496), and his *De harmonia musicorum instrumentorum opus* to Jean Grolier, who finally supported the text's publication in 1518.

---

29 Florentius de Faxolis, *Book on Music*.

Several treatises are dedicated to fellow musicians, clerics, or scholars, often local to the author. Ciconia dedicated his *De proportionibus* (1411) to the singer Giovanni Gasparo da Castelgomberto. Prosdocimus dedicated several books to colleagues and fellow scholars: his treatise on the monochord to a colleague at Padua, Nicholas de Collo of Conegliano; his *Musica speculativa* to Lucas de Lendenaria, Ciconia's successor at the cathedral of Padua; and his *Plana musica* to Antonio de Pontevico from Brixen. Tinctoris offered treatises to singers (Johannes de Lotinis, Jacob Frontin, Guglielmo Guignandi, and Martin Hanard) as well as composers (Ockeghem and Busnoys). Gaffurio extended his *Extractus parvus musicae* to the priest Filippo Tresseni, while Adam of Fulda presented his *Musica* to the lawyer Joachim Lüntaler.

Beyond dedications to individuals, it is clear that many treatises were written for other theorists, in dialogue with existing scholarship. Whether in response to earlier writings or to contemporary ones, theorists made use of direct and indirect citation, wholesale borrowing, commentary, and line-by-line critical invective. Such engagement denotes a circle of readership comprised of well-informed and invested scholars.

For all of this, there is considerable evidence that a much wider audience read and studied music theory in the fifteenth century. We find references to copying, collecting, and reading manuscripts of treatises in surviving correspondence and archival documents; citations of and reference to ancient and modern music theory by poets and scholars in non-musical texts; library inventories at courts, cathedrals, and monasteries holding music theory volumes; the maintenance and establishment of new choir schools across Europe; the hiring of music teachers and dancing masters; and the circulation of lecture notes and the compilation of commonplace books and *zibaldone* (notebooks), as encouraged in humanistic pedagogical treatises. Such treatises probably contributed to the production of miscellanea of music theory containing summaries, redactions, and compendia of older and contemporary theoretical writings. Perhaps the ultimate aim of all of this scholarship and study was the greatest skill developed by Tinctoris's student Beatrice d'Aragona: her ability to "proffer the most correct judgment of all types of musicians."[30]

## Bibliography

Bibliographic information for editions and translations of fifteenth-century theoretical writings can be found in David Russell Williams and C. Matthew

30  Tinctoris, *Liber de natura et proprietate tonorum*, ch. 1 (Seay, 1:69).

Balensuela, *Music Theory from Boethius to Zarlino: A Bibliography and Guide*, Hillsdale, NY, Pendragon Press, 2007. Online editions of many treatises may also be found at *Thesaurus Musicarum Latinarum*, www.chmtl.indiana.edu/tml. A new digital edition of the complete theoretical writings of Johannes Tinctoris is appearing online, under the direction of Ronald Woodley, at earlymusictheory.org.

Adam of Fulda, *Musica*, in *Scriptores ecclesiastici de musica sacra*, ed. Martin Gerbert, 3 vols., Saint-Blaise, 1784; repr. Milan, 1931, 3:329–81
Anselmi, Georgius, *De musica*, ed. Giuseppe Massera, Florence, 1961
Atlas, Allan, *Renaissance Music: Music in Western Europe 1400–1600*, New York, 1998
Bernhard, Michael, ed., *Quellen und Studien zur Musiktheorie des Mittelalters* 3, Veröffentlichungen der Musikhistorischen Kommission 15, Munich, 2001
Blackburn, Bonnie J., "Did Ockeghem Listen to Tinctoris?," in *Johannes Ockeghem: Actes du XL^e colloque international d'études humanistes, Tours, 3–8 février 1997*, ed. Philippe Vendrix, Paris, 1998, 597–640
　　"Music Theory and Musical Thinking after 1450," in *Music as Concept and Practice*, ed. Strohm and Blackburn, 301–45
　　"On Compositional Process in the Fifteenth Century," *JAMS* 40 (1987), 210–84
Burzio, Nicolò, *Florum libellus*, ed. Giuseppe Massera, Florence, 1975; trans. Clement A. Miller as *Musices opusculum*, MSD 37, Neuhausen, 1983
Carlier, Gilles, *Tractatus de duplici ritu cantus ecclesiastici in divinis officiis*, in *"That liberal and virtuous art"*, trans. and ed. Cullington, 31–57
Ciconia, Johannes, *Nova musica and De proportionibus*, ed. and trans. Oliver B. Ellsworth, Lincoln, NE and London, 1993
Cullington, J. Donald, trans. and ed., *"That liberal and virtuous art": Three Humanist Treatises on Music*, Newtownabbey, 2001
Faxolis, Florentius de, *Book on Music*, ed. and trans. Bonnie J. Blackburn and Leofranc Holford-Strevens, I Tatti Renaissance Library 43, Cambridge, MA, 2010
Gaffurio, Franchino, *De harmonia musicorum instrumentorum opus*, trans. Clement A. Miller, MSD 33, n.p., 1977
　　*Extractus parvus musicae*, ed. F. Alberto Gallo, Bologna, 1969
　　*Practica musicae*, trans. Clement A. Miller, MSD 20, n.p., 1968
　　*Theorica musice*, trans. Walter Kurt Kreyszig, ed. Claude V. Palisca, New Haven, 1993
Gallicus, Johannes, *Ritus canendi*, ed. Albert Seay, Colorado Springs, CO, 1981
Gallo, F. Alberto, *Music of the Middle Ages II*, trans. Karen Eales, Cambridge, 1985
Herlinger, Jan, "Music Theory of the Fourteenth and Early Fifteenth Centuries," in *Music as Concept and Practice*, ed. Strohm and Blackburn, 244–300
Holford-Strevens, Leofranc, "The *Laudes musicae* in Renaissance Music Treatises," in *Essays on Renaissance Music in Honour of David Fallows: Bon Jour, Bon Mois et Bonne Estrenne*, ed. Fabrice Fitch and Jacobijn Kiel, Woodbridge, 2011, 338–48
Hothby, Johannes, *La Calliopea legale*, ed. and trans. Timothy L. McDonald, CSM 42, Neuhausen, 1997
　　*De arte contrapuncti*, ed. Gilbert Reaney, CSM 26, Neuhausen, 1977

*Opera omnia de musica mensurabili*, ed. Gilbert Reaney, CSM 31, Neuhausen, 1983

*Opera omnia de proportionibus*, ed. Gilbert Reaney, CSM 39, Neuhausen, 1997

*Tres tractatuli contra Bartholomeum Ramum*, ed. Albert Seay, CSM 10, Rome, 1964

Jacobus Leodiensis, *Speculum musicae*, ed. Roger Bragard, 7 vols., CSM 3, Rome, 1955–73

Judd, Cristle Collins, ed., *Musical Theory in the Renaissance*, Farnham, 2013

MacCarthy, Evan A., "Tinctoris and the Neapolitan *Eruditi*," *JAF* 5 (2013), 41–67

Mengozzi, Stefano, *The Renaissance Reform of Medieval Music Theory: Guido of Arezzo between Myth and History*, Cambridge, 2010

Moyer, Ann, "Music, Mathematics, and Aesthetics: The Case of the Visual Arts in the Renaissance," in *Music and Mathematics in Late Medieval and Early Modern Europe*, ed. Philippe Vendrix, Turnhout, 2008, 111–46

Newsome, Daniel, "Quadrivial Pursuits: Case Studies in the Conceptual Foundation of the Mathematical Arts in the Late Middle Ages," Ph.D. diss., The City University of New York, 2012

Panti, Cecilia, "Una fonte della *Declaratio musicae disciplinae* di Ugolino da Orvieto: Quattro anonime 'Questiones' della tarda Scolastica," *Rivista italiana di musicologia*, 24 (1989), 3–47

Prosdocimus de Beldemandis, *Brevis summula proportionum quantum ad musicam pertinet and Parvus tractatulus de modo monacordum dividendi*, ed. and trans. Jan Herlinger, Lincoln, NE and London, 1987

   *Contrapunctus*, ed. and trans. Jan Herlinger, Lincoln, NE and London, 1984

   *Plana musica, Musica speculativa*, ed. and trans. Jan Herlinger, Urbana and Chicago, 2008

Ramos de Pareja, Bartolomé, *Musica practica*, ed. Johannes Wolf, Leipzig, 1901; trans. Clement A. Miller, MSD 44, Neuhausen, 1993

Seay, Albert, "The *Dialogus Johannis Ottobi Anglici in arte musica*," *JAMS* 8 (1955), 86–100

Spataro, Giovanni, *Honesta defensio in Nicolai Burtii parmensis opusculum*, Bologna, 1491

Strohm, Reinhard, and Bonnie J. Blackburn, eds., *Music as Concept and Practice in the Late Middle Ages*, The New Oxford History of Music 3/1, Oxford, 2001

Strunk, Oliver, *Source Readings in Music History*, New York, 1965

Tinctoris, Johannes, *Complexus effectuum musices*, in *"That liberal and virtuous art,"* trans. and ed. J. Donald Cullington, 58–86

   *De inventione et usu musicae*, excerpts ed. Jeffrey Palenik in "The Early Career of Johannes Tinctoris: An Examination of the Music Theorist's Northern Education and Development," Ph.D. diss, Duke University, 2008

   *Dictionary of Musical Terms (Terminorum Musicae Diffinitorium)*, ed. and trans. Carl Parrish, New York and London, 1963

   *Diffinitorium musice*, ed. Cecilia Panti, Florence, 2004

   *Opera theoretica*, ed. Albert Seay, 2 vols. in 3, n.p., 1975–78

Tomlinson, Gary, *Music in Renaissance Magic: Toward a Historiography of Others*, Chicago, 1993

Ugolino of Orvieto, *Declaratio musicae disciplinae*, ed. Albert Seay, 3 vols., CSM 7, Rome, 1959–62

Valgulio, Carlo, *Contra vituperatorem musicae*, in *"That liberal and virtuous art"*, ed. and trans. Cullington, 87–101

Woodley, Ronald, "The Printing and Scope of Tinctoris's Fragmentary Treatise *De inventione et usu musice*," *EMH* 5 (1985), 239–68

"Tinctoris's Italian Translation of the Golden Fleece Statutes: A Text and a (Possible) Context," *EMH* 8 (1988), 173–244

· PART VIII SOURCES ·

# Polyphonic sources, ca. 1400–1450

MARGARET BENT

The cultivation of high-art polyphony has always been the preserve of a cultured elite minority who could write, read, and sing it. In the early fifteenth century, the number of surviving books significantly increases, facilitating insights into the geographical spread and longevity of the repertory, how and for whom books of music were made, even matters of authorship and performance.

Whereas the contents of a liturgical manuscript can usually be predicted, nearly all polyphonic manuscripts are unique anthologies. There are almost no surviving cases of all or most of one such book being copied largely in the same order to form another,[1] even though at least two copies of a piece must have lain side by side for copying purposes. Close correspondences between different copies of the same piece are rarely reflected in order of copying or appearance.[2]

The number of more or less complete manuscripts surviving from before 1450 is small compared to the following period. There are as yet no series of institutional or commissioned choirbooks, such as we have from the late fifteenth century onwards for Ferrara (Modena), Milan, and the papal chapel, and from the Alamire workshop. There is, however, exceptional documentation for one case of serial copying: Simon Mellet was paid from 1444 to 1480 as the main music scribe of Cambrai cathedral, latterly with detailed specification of repertory by Du Fay and others; but only one polyphonic manuscript copied by him survives, and that is earlier, predating the archival record.[3] The printing of polyphonic music dates only from 1501; all fifteenth-century sources are handwritten. Most are notated in "choirbook" format, with the parts separately placed across an opening of two facing pages, or below each other on a single page to be read simultaneously by three, four, or more singers grouped around the book (see Figure 33.1).

---

1 A notable exception is the copying of most of Trent 93 into Trent 90 in the 1450s. See Bent, "Trent 93 and Trent 90," and the essay in this volume by Thomas Schmidt-Beste, Ch. 34.
2 Wright, "The Aosta–Trent Relationship Reconsidered."
3 See Curtis, "Simon Mellet" and Curtis, ed., *Cambrai Cathedral Choirbook*.

Figure 33.1 Old Hall manuscript (British Library, Additional MS 57950), fols. 30v–31r

Where pieces occupy more than one opening, they are (with minor exceptions) organized so that all turn the page at the same time although reading from different places on the opening. Some relatively homorhythmic English pieces, however, were copied in a kind of score notation, one part under the

Figure 33.1 (cont.)

other with the text below the lowest voice only; the notes are aligned more
for textual than for musical simultaneity: in other words, for singers reading
their own parts and not for a keyboard or armchair score-reader. Partbook

status has been claimed for a few individual manuscripts and fragments, all rather special cases; but no sets of partbooks survive until the Glogauer Liederbuch of the 1470s, and then few before 1500. Often depicted in paintings, rolls (scrolls) were probably more common than the small surviving number suggests; hard to store, they were vulnerable to loss and destruction. Some may have contained individual performing parts.

## Geographical survey

The majority of musical sources surviving from the first half of the fifteenth century are from northern Italy and the axis of the church councils of Constance and Basel, melting pots for international contacts between musicians in the retinues of prelates. From the 1420s onwards there is an extraordinary harvest of manuscripts of contemporary repertory from northern Italy and the southern Germanic lands. After the late fourteenth-century French repertory contained in the Ivrea and Apt manuscripts and the fragments of Cambrai 1328, very little survives from France until the manuscripts Cambrai 6 and 11 of the early 1440s,[4] apart from the luxurious Chantilly manuscript (Chantilly 564), compiled probably in the 1410s, but containing mostly older repertory. From Spain, there are almost no survivals from this period, though Chantilly and other manuscripts contain a few pieces by Spanish composers. Eastern Europe is not well represented, though a number of manuscripts from Poland contain music by local composers as well as by figures such as Johannes Ciconia and Zacara da Teramo that may have been acquired by Polish university students in Padua.[5]

Turin J.II.9, known as the Cyprus manuscript, is one of the largest, most beautifully written, and musically sophisticated sources of the period, but it is exceptional as an isolated collection. With no named composers and, puzzlingly, no concordances with other manuscripts for its 229 polyphonic compositions, it has proved hard to place. Among its rare features is the inclusion of a significant body of monophonic liturgical chant, with clear Cypriot associations, followed by sections devoted to polyphonic mass movements (Gloria–Credo pairs), motets, ballades, rondeaux, and virelais. The filled black notation, red coloration, and complex rhythmic style strongly reflect French style of around 1400, which was distinctly old-fashioned by the time of this compilation in the 1430s; its motets are not quite like anything else but show more influence of the post-Ciconian Italian motet than of French construction, and other features also point to northern Italy.

---

4 See Lerch, *Fragmente aus Cambrai*, and Fallows, "L'Origine du MS. 1328."
5 See Perz, ed., *Sources of Polyphony up to c. 1500.*

A strong connection with saints and liturgy of Cyprus had led to the conclusion that it originated at the Lusignan court there and was brought to Savoy by Anne of Lusignan on her marriage to Louis of Savoy in 1434. On the strength of the heraldic evidence, recent research has located it with the Avogadro family of Brescia.[6]

English music, by contrast, has many threads linking it to other collections within England and on the Continent. After centuries of only fragmentary survivals, the fifteenth century brings us several more or less complete English manuscripts along with a rich harvest of fragments. Continental manuscripts – notably Modena α.X.1.11 (ModB), the Trent codices, and Aosta 15 – often provide complete copies of pieces preserved fragmentarily or not at all in England; English music of the generation led by Dunstaple was in high demand abroad in the second quarter of the century. Relatively small insular sources include the elegant Egerton MS (London 3307), the more modest Selden ms (Oxford 26), both collections of liturgical items and carols, and the Trinity carol roll (Cambridge o.3.58), all of parchment. But of dominant importance is the "Old Hall" manuscript, a parchment book of high status and large format, compiled mostly in the 1410s, with initials of alternating gold leaf and blue lapis lazuli, some of which were later removed. 112 folios survive and at least twenty-five more are lost;[7] the 147 compositions comprise mass movements, antiphon settings, and motets. Although some repertory dates back to the 1390s, it also includes the latest compositions by Leonel Power, Pycard, and their contemporaries, replete with dazzlingly virtuosic mensuration canons and notational sophistries. The Fountains Fragment of around 1400 is an informally written void-notation paper manuscript of six well-filled leaves containing several concordances with older and less complex compositions. The contents of Old Hall seem to have been determined by the musicians who used it, at first in the chapel of King Henry V's brother and heir apparent, Thomas Duke of Clarence. Later additions, partly autograph, were made in the early 1420s by members of the Chapel Royal who served the infant King Henry VI. A now-fragmentary younger cousin of Old Hall was a royal manuscript of similar facture, of which some fifteen folios and fragments have now come to light.[8] Some of the older repertory is repeated, and some later additions to Old Hall by royal chaplains are now within the main body of the younger manuscript. In turn, there are new additions, attesting a process of overlapping

6  Data and Kügle, eds., *Il Codice J.II.9*; Kügle, "Glorious Sounds for a Holy Warrior."
7  See Bent, "The Old Hall Manuscript."
8  See Bent, "A Lost Choirbook," "The Progeny of Old Hall," and "A New Canonic Gloria."

generational renewal, as old repertory is gradually superseded. Dunstaple was not present in the main corpus of Old Hall, but now that a piece by him has turned up in pride of place in these fragments, heading the Gloria section, it seems less likely (as originally suggested) that this younger manuscript was compiled for Henry VI, who was not among Dunstaple's known royal patrons, but rather for one of his uncles, the Dukes of Bedford or Gloucester.

Such repertorial renewal within a user community is even more dramatically demonstrated from the Veneto manuscript Bologna Q.15, a vast collection of 324 pieces, mostly mass music and motets, extensively worked over and updated by its compiler, who was in the *familia* of bishop Pietro Emiliani of Vicenza.[9] Bologna Q.15 originated in this circle in the 1420s, but was its compiler's personal project over a fifteen-year period which saw massive revision: he discarded two-thirds of what he had painstakingly copied, and reinflated the manuscript to its original size, in the version we now have, with recopied pieces (sometimes with revisions) and new repertory. In no sense was it commissioned "for" the bishop's chapel, nor for the cathedral, as some have inferred. It is the largest and earliest of the *tre corone* of Veneto manuscripts; Oxford 213 and the larger-format Bologna 2216 date from the 1430s.[10] All three, to different degrees, mix sacred and secular repertory, much of it shared, and survive more or less in the state of completeness in which they ended their active lives. Oxford 213 and Bologna Q.15 were exclusively personal projects until relinquished by their scribes; Bologna 2216 has some additions by others. A fourth, fragmentary manuscript comes from the same region and has a similar repertorial mix.[11] All four represent a real crossroads, reaching back to 1400, with compositions by Ciconia and Hymbert de Salinis, while at the same time presenting the very newest music by the young Guillaume Du Fay and his contemporaries, and the first wave of the English music that was so sought-after for much of the fifteenth century.

## The life of the repertory

The performing life of composed polyphony was normally short; so, often, was the shelf-life of books containing it. In the 1470s Johannes Tinctoris famously decried old written music, and deemed music older than forty years not worth hearing. Martin Le Franc, ca. 1440, compared contemporary music

9 Bent, *Bologna Q15*.
10 Fallows, ed., *Oxford, Bodleian Library MS. Canon. Misc. 213*; Gallo, *Il codice musicale 2216*.
11 See Bent and Klugseder, *A Veneto Liber cantus (c. 1440)*.

favorably with that of forty years earlier. Musical styles changed almost as rapidly as in pop music today, and even new pieces were often adapted, with added or removed voices or changed text. Old music books were regarded as expendable, sometimes dismembered within half a century; parchment was recycled for miscellaneous purposes, paper usually discarded. The gaps in our knowledge are only partly filled by fragments that have survived in book bindings, mostly parchment, which – literally – flesh out what we know from the few manuscripts that have survived largely intact. Given the confluence of so many trends, conservative and avant-garde, often side by side, the *terminus post quem* for dating a manuscript often depends on known dates of composition, but the compilation may be considerably later than the contents suggest.

The pattern of rapid repertory renewal and discarding inferred from Old Hall and Bologna Q.15 has suggested a linear evolution of musical style, at least in "central" repertories, and to early datings of manuscripts containing "early" repertory. Despite the frequently short life of a piece of music, counterexamples exist in some notable instances of retrospective collections, and not only in cultural backwaters: luxury presentation manuscripts sometimes follow a more conservative pattern than personal anthologies, in repertory, format, and notation, and may embody reception of a style or repertory outside the milieu in which it was produced. Examples are three exceptionally sumptuous large-format parchment manuscripts: one is the Cyprus manuscript already described (1430s); the others are Chantilly 564 (1410s) and the Squarcialupi Codex (1420s).

Chantilly contains a preeminently French repertory of late fourteenth-century secular works and motets, but copied in an Italian hand; the earliest repertories of fifteenth-century French song are also north Italian.[12] The date of copying has not been definitively fixed, but it does seem to be a retrospective collection, compiled later than much of its contents. It is remarkable for its extensive notational and rhythmic complexity, and is prefaced by two of the most famous graphically notated pieces, by Baude Cordier, in the shape of a heart and a circle respectively.[13] Aspects of its contents and organization will be further discussed below. The nearly contemporary manuscript Modena α.M.5.24 (ModA, ca. 1410) presents a mostly secular repertory that may reflect institutional initiation, like Chantilly, with which it shares some repertory.[14] Although much smaller in content and format, it is finely written on parchment with expensive decorated capitals, but its core

---

12 Plumley and Stone, eds., *Codex Chantilly.*      13 See the essay by Anne Stone in this volume, Ch. 30.
14 Facsimile edition: *Il codice α.M.5.24 (ModA).*

original gatherings (fascicles II–IV) do not seem to have been planned, or the pieces grouped, in any discernible order, which is quite surprising given that the manuscript is of the status to have illuminated initials. It came into private hands for the added flanking gatherings of the 1420s, which are closely associated with Matteo da Perugia, but probably not autograph. Dedicated small-format "presentation" chansonniers are a feature only of later decades.

The Italian trecento repertory is known almost exclusively from six anthologies, usually discussed in the context of their fourteenth-century repertory: Vatican Rossi 215,[15] Florence 26 (FP), London 29987, Paris 568 (Pit), Paris 6771 (Reina), fascicle I, and the most famous of them all, the sumptuous Squarcialupi Codex. However, all but Rossi were retrospective compilations dating from the first quarter of the new century, old-fashioned at their time of compilation, again going against the generally short period for which musical repertory was in vogue. They were being compiled in Florence, northern Italy, and the Veneto at precisely the same time that music by the young Du Fay and his contemporaries, differently conceived and notated, was coming into circulation, along with the first wave of exported English music that soon became famously sought-after. Italy thus hosted a confluence of multiple currents. So, while the new international repertory was undergoing rapid renewal and revision, and absorbing new styles and influences, there was little or no interaction with these retrospective anthologies that were being copied and presumably used in different circles at precisely the same time or even in the same city.[16]

The Squarcialupi Codex is the latest and largest of these anthologies of trecento music, and by far the most lavishly illuminated polyphonic manuscript of the period.[17] It is organized by sections devoted to composers (as is the paper manuscript Florence 26), each headed by a miniature with an image representing that composer; the Landini page is the most elaborate of all. The plan was not entirely completed, as there are ruled openings with illumination but without music. The Italian repertory is extended into the new century by further fragmentary or palimpsest manuscripts containing some younger works, still with a tendency to composer groupings: Lucca 184 (ca. fifty folios from an original manuscript of over 100, a fragmentary but crucial source for the Italian-texted secular works of the Ciconia generation),[18] Turin T.III.2 (Boverio Codex) (fifteen folios with thirty-nine

15  With Ostiglia, Opera Pia G. Greggiati, Biblioteca Musicale, s.s.
16  Bent, "Continuity and Transformation."
17  Gallo, ed., *Il codice Squarcialupi*. See Nádas, "The Transmission of Trecento Secular Polyphony."
18  Nádas and Ziino, *The Lucca Codex*.

pieces),[19] and Florence 2211 (111 palimpsest folios with over 100 pieces). Despite an active papal chapel in Rome following the end of the Schism, no Roman manuscripts survive from this period, but an increasing number of fragments has come to light, and more are regularly being found, mostly in book bindings.[20]

## Survival rates

Hundreds of such isolated leaves, singly or in small groups, testify to massive losses. Some groups of leaves can be linked to the same original manuscript; each leaf or group may be the sole survivor of a lost manuscript, in some cases demonstrably of more than 100 folios. At a very rough estimate, what survives in book form represents no more than about 5 percent of the total number of manuscripts represented by fragments, and a much lower percentage still of the manuscripts that no longer exist, a small handful of which are documented in wills and inventories, while most have left no trace. This sorry loss must stand as a background to our evaluation of the music books that have chanced to survive. What we think of as the "most important" sources are complete or nearly complete books; but fragments can provide equally important testimony, adumbrating a fuller but lost context for those books.

Fragments also help to circumscribe the repertory by documenting different copies of the same piece; even where concordances survive incomplete, they may inform us about what happened to that piece in transmission, musically, chronologically, and geographically. An isolated leaf might have one or two voices on each side, from perhaps two different pieces, giving the full extent of those pieces but an incomplete texture. Pieces that were once present in more than one manuscript can sometimes be reconstructed by combining the contents of disparate fragments. In the case of English pieces in score, on the other hand, one leaf might contain the complete texture of a section, but not the full extent of the piece. Between the Winchester Troper of ca. 1000 and the Old Hall Manuscript of ca. 1412–25 no English manuscripts have survived in book form, only fragments recycled in book bindings. Many fragments have been lost, even within the last century, as libraries rebound books and sometimes discarded materials that may have included precious musical remains and information about provenance. The recycled fragments that found more

---

19 Facsimile and inventory in Ziino, ed., *Il codice T.III.2*.
20 For a survey of Italian fragments and papal connections, see Di Bacco and Nádas, "The Papal Chapels," and Cuthbert, "Trecento Fragments and Polyphony."

transient uses, such as for repairing artifacts, are lost forever, though a few strips have been found inside musical instruments and in building repairs.

Most of what is said here applies to music that was notated. We do not have unwritten music, which includes most purely instrumental music. Such music was not necessarily unprepared or "improvised."[21] Idiomatic instrumental music has left a rare trace in the exceptional and partly palimpsest Faenza manuscript of 1400–1425, which is a treasure trove of fifty-one instrumental diminutions on mostly known existing compositions.[22] It seems to be an accumulation by many arrangers, therefore more a communal manuscript than a personal copy, possibly of ecclesiastical or even monastic origin, and perhaps from the Veneto.

## Authorship

Most fourteenth-century music is presented anonymously; this is still true for some manuscripts up to about 1440 – all or most of Turin J.II.9, Paris 6771, and Cambrai 6 and 11. It is not until some early fifteenth-century manuscripts like Old Hall (most) and Chantilly (two-thirds) that a majority of pieces are attributed, as they are also in the coeval manuscripts containing Italian tre-cento repertory. Manuscripts dating from the 1420s onwards (notably Bologna Q.15, and Oxford 213 in the 1430s) include international repertory and its famous composers (Du Fay often appears in pride of place at the head of a collection) alongside local composers of limited circulation, all mostly named. Indeed, for some composers we are entirely dependent on a single manuscript; the local and obscure Johannes Lymburgia is only known for one piece outside Bologna Q.15, which contains forty-six to fifty works by or probably by him. A majority of lesser composers are known for only one or very few compositions. It is hardly likely that these lone works constituted the entire output of those musicians, and we must assume in most cases that much more has been lost in manuscripts of limited local circulation. Popularity then as now was partly self-perpetuating. In the fourteenth century, Guillaume de Machaut promoted his own poetical and musical works in de luxe manuscripts for his patrons, with a strong authorial stamp, but he remains an isolated case without precedent or consequent. There is no easy or single explanation for the increasing interest in authorial names in the early fifteenth century.[23] The appeal to us of named

---

21 On this see the essays in this volume by Anna Maria Busse Berger (Ch. 8) and Philippe Canguilhem (Ch. 9).
22 See now Memelsdorff, *The Codex Faenza 117*.
23 Cf. Schmidt-Beste's essay, Ch. 34, where this development is dated to the mid-fifteenth century.

composers has shaped how these repertories are studied and evaluated, to the detriment of anonymous music.

## Notation, page layout, and texting

Fourteenth-century notation uses filled ("full") black notes, with mensural or proportional differences shown as void or red notes towards 1400. In the fifteenth century, especially with a general shift from parchment to paper (except for some high-grade manuscripts), the functions are reversed, with filled notes gradually giving way to void, and red becoming less common, while black filled notes do service for what was previously void or red. Oxford 213 is one of the earliest Continental sources to use void notation, attested earlier in England (Fountains Fragment), and dramatically reflected in a change of personal usage from filled to void notation during the 1430s by Hermann Poetzlinger, the owner and main copyist of the Emmeram Codex.[24] Black full notation with all its accoutrements survives alongside void notation until 1500 or later, especially in conservative or luxurious sources, and notably English ones. Paper often suffered bleed-through from the density of ink resulting from filled-in black notes, and its ridged writing surface was better suited to the penmanship of void or outlined note shapes.

Fourteenth-century notations reflected three distinct national strands, French, Italian, and English. In the early fifteenth century these national styles gradually converged into an international style; French notation became the vehicle for the new generation of Du Fay in north Italian manuscripts, still with a residue of obsolescent Italian features in some sources. There are detectable cases of notational revision, and some pieces originally conceived in Italian notation were translated into French notation; this is how Ciconia's motets are presented in Bologna Q.15. Some manuscripts, like Old Hall in England and Bologna Q.15 in Italy, seem deliberately to have purged their notation of the older regional characteristics still evident in some sources concordant with them.

The distinction between choirbook format and the much less common score notation has been mentioned above. Three-part writing, the norm, may take the form of two texted, active, often equal-range upper parts, copied on facing pages, accompanied by or built upon a tenor, as in motets, or a cantus part accompanied by a grammatically essential tenor and inessential contratenor. In that case, the two lower parts, similar in range and movement, are written either lower on the page, or on the right-hand (recto) page

---

24 Rumbold with Wright, *Kommentar und Inventar.*

opposite the cantus part on the left. Most four-part pieces add a contratenor to the first compositional type. These contratenors are often but not always optional, sometimes demonstrably added later by the same or another composer. There are even five-part pieces in the Old Hall manuscript, most of them canonic.[25] Markings of "solo–chorus" in manuscripts of this period do not necessarily mean that multiple voices were required. In pieces with alternating scorings, "chorus" usually simply signals a three-part section as opposed to a duet.[26]

The uppermost voices are usually fully texted, likewise the second cantus in a motet or mass composition when it is equally active (though the second text is sometimes dropped in transmission). Upper parts of motets may have the same or two different texts. In mass compositions the texts will usually be the same unless the setting is "telescoped," for example, a setting in which the latter part of a Credo text is notated under the second voice, starting from the beginning of the music, so that it is sung simultaneously with the first part of the Credo. Omission of the second-voice text in some manuscripts gives the appearance of a textual omission. Lower voices may have partial text or only incipits identifying the start of each section. In syllabic or nearly syllabic settings, the verbal text took up more lateral space than the musical notes, and therefore tended to be written out before the music was copied. Problems of spacing are often evident in pieces that alternate melismatic and texted portions; to discern which was written first often gives a better sense of the intended fit of note to syllable than taking the alignment literally.[27]

## Owners and scribes

Because manuscripts of the later fifteenth century, or even series of manuscripts, are much more likely to have been compiled for a patron, church, or court, there has been a tendency to seek patrons or institutional pegs on which to hang manuscripts of the earlier part of the century, seeing their compilers as obedient scribes or copyists who were following orders, with only a passive role in the compilation. For expensively produced manuscripts this may sometimes be the case. But for others, there is growing evidence that many were personal projects. Some were owned and compiled over many years by a single expert musician, who selected and adapted

---

25  A few other exceptional pieces require more voices: Gemblaco, *Ave virgo/Sancta Maria*, Bologna Q 15, no. 236, has eight separately notated parts but is mostly performable by five singers.
26  Bent, "*Divisi* and *a versi*."
27  King, "Texting in Early Fifteenth-Century Sacred Polyphony," and Bent, "Text Setting in Sacred Music."

repertory and often took compositional initiatives. It is inconceivable that the compiler of Bologna Q 15 was following anyone else's detailed instructions throughout his manuscript's protracted vicissitudes. He probably had encouragement from his bishop in the form of materials for the book, and hospitality for the musicians who sang from it; but it would be misleading to imply that a patron had in any way commissioned it for his court or chapel, or prescribed its contents. The avocations of many musicians and singers are hidden from us by their day jobs, which almost never at this time specify that they are musicians. They may be cathedral canons, or chaplains, or even chamberlains or butlers in the service of a prince or prelate who might have taken pains to fill these domestic offices with talented musicians who could provide, together with singers from the cathedral, the pious private out-of-hours entertainment he relished. Even if the content of these music anthologies reflected or formed his tastes, it was the musicians who took charge of the repertorial choices and performance, no doubt enjoying indirect if not direct compensation.[28] The presence of such books in humanist circles undermines Nino Pirrotta's claim that such men would not have cultivated contrapuntally-based polyphony; at this time the agenda of the *studia humanitatis* was purely literary and cannot be extended to music.[29]

We sometimes know the identity of scribes, both institutional and personal compilers. In the first decade of the century, the Paduan monk Rolandus de Casale appended scribal signatures to his work, which now survives only in fragmentary form.[30] There are very few identified instances of holograph copies at this period. Some of the later additions to the Old Hall manuscript may have been entered by their composers, who were members of Henry VI's Chapel Royal. Some of the scribe-compilers of the Trent codices have been identified: Johannes Lupi (ca. 1410–67), who came from Bolzano in the South Tyrol, matriculated at the University of Vienna in 1428–29 and was beneficed as a priest in and around Trent from the late 1440s. The handwriting of his will of ca. 1455 identifies him as the copyist-compiler of Trent 87[1] and Trent 92[2], which he amalgamated with the independent manuscripts Trent 87[2] and Trent 92[1], all copied in the period 1433–45, to form the earlier Trent codices as we know them today.[31] If the composer Nicolas de Merques was indeed the scribe

---

28  Schmidt-Beste makes a similar point in Ch. 34.
29  Pirrotta, "Music and Cultural Tendencies." Pirrotta also assumes that Italian cathedral music was poorly developed because few *biscantori* are specified; but the health of a musical establishment at this time cannot be read from the surface documents, only between the cracks and by reconstructing networks that are only indirectly documented. See also Strohm, *The Rise of European Music*, 269–87.
30  See, most recently, Cuthbert, "Groups and Projects."
31  Wright, "On the Origins of Trent 87₁ and 92₁," hypothesizes an association of Lupi with Wiser from the time Wiser became succentor in Trent ca. 1455, later the cathedral schoolmaster (like Poetzlinger), and

of Trent 92[1], then we have autograph copies of all his known works, mostly unique to that MS.[32] Two gatherings of Trent 87[2] form a *libellus* compiled in the 1430s in the diocese of Namur by H. Battre, who seems to have been a schoolmaster or choirmaster, annotating copies for the *pueri* and *mutate voces* of his ensemble. Hermann Poetzlinger (d. 1469) was the main copyist of the Emmeram Codex, Wolfgang Chranekker of its third layer. A growing number of fragments has been shown to originate in Vienna,[33] where university circles may also be a source for repertory copied by graduates such as Lupi and Poetzlinger, who studied in Vienna and finally became schoolmaster of the Regensburg monastery of St. Emmeram in the 1440s.[34]

## Size and performance issues

Manuscripts fall roughly into two categories defined by size and status, but with considerable overlap: on the one hand, formally written books, probably commissioned by an institution or patron, usually of large format (40 cm or more) and often on parchment and professionally illuminated; and on the other, personal anthologies, mainly for private use, usually in quarto format (ca. 25–30 cm), often on paper and only in rare cases illuminated, varying in extent from one or a few fascicles to large books.[35] Either category can survive as complete or nearly complete volumes, or in fragmentary form.[36] The distinction between institutional or commissioned manuscripts and personal compilations corresponds closely to dimensions, discounting different sizes of writing block within a manuscript. The rounded measurements given in Table 33.1 serve to allocate a selection of manuscripts and fragments to these categories by height (measurements to within 2 cm).

Some manuscripts moved to different ownership or locations. Apt 16bis may have been brought from the papal chapel at Avignon to the cathedral of Apt by Richardus de Bozonvilla, a singer in the papal service at Avignon from 1379 to 1405 and provost of Apt cathedral. It has been proposed that the French singer and composer Benoît (Benotto) was the scribe-compiler of

---

possibly the bequest to him of his music books, superseding the will. He also copied the now fragmentary large-format paper choirbook Zwettl (ca. 40 cm), yielding both a personal anthology and an institutional manuscript by the same hand.

32  A comment by Tom Ward has been authoritatively developed by Wright, "Trent 87 and 92," and with more definitive evidence in "Nuove scoperte sulla carriera."

33  Strohm, "Native and Foreign Polyphony," and Strohm, *The Rise of European Music*. See now his project at www.musikleben.wordpress.com.

34  Rumbold with Wright, *Hermann Pötzlinger's Music Book*.

35  Excluded here are rough jottings or isolated parts on flyleaves or loose sheets, sketches, didactic notes, supplementary performing materials, and so on. Most such materials have perished; where they do survive, they are often *in situ* and in context.

36  Schmidt-Beste, "Private or Institutional – Small or Big?"

Table 33.1 *Formats of fifteenth-century manuscripts, ca. 1400–1450*

A. Large-format books (parchment unless specified)[a]
ca. 50 cm
   Cambrai 6 and 11
ca. 40 cm
   Squarcialupi
   Chantilly
   Old Hall
   Turin J.II.9
   Bologna 2216 (paper)
   ModB (paper)
   Zwettl (fragmentary; paper)

B. "Quarto" manuscripts, ca. 25–30 cm
Probably "institutional"[b]
   Apt 16bis (institutional, Avignon papal chapel, Apt cathedral)
   Modena α.M.5.24 (ModA, main corpus)
   London 3307 (Egerton)
   Oxford 26 (Selden)

Probably or certainly personal anthologies, paper unless specified
   London 29987 (parchment)
   Lucca 184 (parchment)
   Modena α.M.5.24, fascicles I and V (parchment)
   Paris 568 (parchment)
   Panciatichi 26
   Paris 6771 (Reina Codex)
   Fountains Fragment
   Strasbourg 222 C.22 (destroyed 1870)
   Emmeram Codex
   Trent 87, Trent 92
   Aosta 15 (mostly paper)
   Bologna Q.15 (mostly paper)
   Oxford 213
   Turin T.III.2 (Boverio Codex)
   Munich 3224 (parchment)

[a] For most of these an institutional or commissioned status is likely, with the possible exceptions of the less luxurious paper MSS Bologna 2216 and ModB.

[b] Mostly parchment, professionally written; ModA and Egerton illuminated.

ModB in the period 1435–48, first for the Duomo in Florence, where he was a singer, and that he then took it to Ferrara.[37] Although an Italian manuscript, it is the main source for motets by the English composers Dunstaple and Power. We have seen above that Old Hall was apparently compiled for Thomas Duke of Clarence, but passed on his death to the infant King Henry VI, and that Johannes Lupi evidently acquired the manuscripts he amalgamated with his own collections to form the books we know as Trent 87 and Trent 92. A number of personally owned manuscripts in the Veneto and elsewhere (documented but not extant) passed from individual to communal ownership, sold or bequeathed to cathedral sacristies, where they could continue in use by the same singing community.

The presence or dominance of settings of the Mass Ordinary and other sacred texts does not necessarily mean that these personal quarto books were primarily designed for liturgical use in church, and not only because most such collections mix sacred and secular repertory. A majority of texts in our manuscripts are sacred, if not necessarily liturgical, but so are the subjects of most fifteenth-century painting. The sacred–secular boundaries that apply to some later repertories have often been drawn too sharply for earlier periods, even for institutions: princes also had chapels and bishops had courts. Sacred or merely pious texts are not necessarily liturgical; musical settings of liturgical texts were not necessarily confined to church rituals, but had a much wider reach into daily life and into circumstances we would consider "secular." Polyphony was rarely required by the statutes of cathedral chapters (the copying program at Cambrai was exceptional) or specified in wills for memorial Masses; it was doubtless worked into services electively by individual initiatives in musical chapters such as Vicenza and Padua, whose members regularly complained about the scarcity of excellent singers, and took some pains to elect competent polyphonists to benefices in their control. Equally, cathedral musicians had every opportunity to make recreational highbrow chamber music together with members of the bishop's *familia* in his house and in the cathedral sacristy, where known musicians are often present, though not so specified, as witnesses to notarial documents. They must have been attracted to circles where such connoisseurship flourished. Semi-private music-making is altogether a more likely use of these books than anything resembling concert performance as we understand it. Oxford 213 contains predominantly secular songs, but also mass music, liturgical settings, and motets.

Smaller-format manuscripts compiled by expert singers or schoolmasters would have been used within their own community for performance or

---

37 Haar and Nádas, "The Medici, the Signoria, the Pope."

pedagogy. The size of the page and its notation has prompted the absurd but widely-held proposition that they couldn't and didn't sing from their own manuscripts, but no plausible alternative explanation for these huge efforts in copying has been forthcoming.[38] An archival function may sometimes have been in play, especially when music had to be copied at speed from a traveler passing through, and this may apply, together with some concerns about size and legibility, to the admittedly less user-friendly later Trent codices. Inaccuracy has also been invoked as an impediment to the use of manuscripts for performance. But if inaccuracies disqualify these manuscripts for use, they would also disqualify performance copies made from them. Small self-evident errors can be corrected during the learning of a piece without necessarily requiring written correction. Relatively few pieces are disabled by errors that cannot be so corrected, and personal manuscripts are often more accurate than their larger and more easily read cousins. The sumptuous Squarcialupi Codex is notably less accurate than some of the more modest copies of that repertory. And the more worked-over personal manuscripts in our period show signs of performance-related use and revision.

What is meant by "to sing from" can range between sight-reading and some degree of memorization.[39] The active role that a singer needed to bring to a performance, resolving mensural and contrapuntal choices in context, means that only a provisional memorization of a polyphonic part would have been possible until fitting it into a heard context with other singers. By the time a piece had been read a sufficient number of times to allow singers to resolve ambiguities, diagnose copying errors, optimize choices of inflections, and refine text placement, the performers would have had a close and partly memorized knowledge of it, with less dependence on reading. Sight-singing is quite possible for experienced readers, but repeated attempts would gradually result in a half-memorized piece, for which the written book would serve as a reminder and point of reference. So, something between the extremes of sight-reading and complete memorization would still leave a credible role for the book, as is also reflected in numerous pictures of singers showing varying degrees of concentration on the book around which they stand. Memory must indeed have played a role within the active repertories of this time, which were much more confined in size and stylistic range than anything we can imagine now; but this does not exclude reading.

Sometimes copies would have been made with, and informed by, direct knowledge of the piece in performance, sometimes not. Some copies were

---

38 See, for example, Hamm, "Manuscript Structure in the Dufay Era"; Staehelin, "Trienter Codices und Humanismus"; Lütteken, "Padua und die Entstehung des musikalischen Textes."
39 Berger, *Medieval Music.*

deliberately adapted to different performance situations, often adjusted to local needs. For example, many compositions in the Emmeram Codex appear there for two voices, without the grammatically inessential contratenor parts known from elsewhere, and many secular French songs in the same manuscript are provided with sacred Latin substitute texts. Venice It. IX. 145 contains two-part versions of music known elsewhere with three, as well as a collection of laude. Documentation of larger vocal ensembles for Burgundian polyphony comes only from later in the century,[40] when the Cambrai books were copied in duplicate (perhaps exceptionally), one for each side of the choir; judging from Cambrai 6 and 11, which have major repertorial overlap, both the format and the notation would have been exceptionally large and legible for choir as opposed to chamber use. Mostly, however, choirs sang plainsong, leaving polyphony as the preserve of specialist soloists. The folio-format manuscripts are unquestionably legible by a small choir; but the personal quarto books, ill suited to such use on a lectern in church in poor light, can easily be sung from by three or four singers, one to a part. Some may have been used by choirmasters as a point of reference for teaching boys to sing mensural music by rote; but at least partial memorization would have played a role in repeated performances by adult readers. The non-standard nature of individual anthologies, and of versions of pieces they contain, argue against multiple copies being the norm for performance.

## Compilation and organization

Charles Hamm's theory of "fascicle manuscripts" has been widely embraced as a kind of universal panacea that can be invoked to explain manuscript structures on a "mix and match" basis.[41] No one has ever doubted that a wide variety of informal or preparatory copies must have been in existence, some of them as fascicles, bifolios, or single sheets, a perfectly normal way of preserving and sending music. But despite the generalized dimensions given above, formats and page sizes were not standardized and interchangeable, and each case must be decided on its merits, not by resort to a single model, or indeed "theory."[42] It is all the more striking, given an apparent incompatibility between the overall dimensions of the Aosta manuscript and the earlier Trent codices, and the considerable variety of ruling patterns

---

40 Fallows, "Specific Information on the Ensembles."
41 Hamm, "Manuscript Structure in the Dufay Era," 169, and Hamm, "Interrelationships between Manuscript and Printed Sources." Cf. Schmidt-Beste's essay, Ch. 34, which sees this procedure at work in a number of sources from the second half of the century.
42 I challenged some of Hamm's specific examples in "Some Criteria for Establishing Relationships," 300 ff.

between sections of those manuscripts, that the overall format within the Trent group is so relatively stable, permitting the combining of the separate sections of Trent 87 and 92, and of the separate sections of Aosta 15; such a procedure would not, however, have been possible between Trent and Aosta.[43] Many larger personal anthologies were works in progress throughout their period of active compilation and use and must have been used unbound as separate fascicles, although intended for a single collection, before being combined and bound as we now have them. Some may never have been finally bound, which may account for their low survival. But to pit fascicle manuscripts as a general concept versus whole books is too sharp a division. There are a few cases of such incorporation, notably the "Battre" fascicles in Trent 87. In some cases, newer fascicles were placed at the beginning of a manuscript, in front of older fascicles, notably in Oxford 213, ModA, Aosta 15, the Emmeram Codex, and Chantilly, but this is not the same as combining independently compiled fascicles. Each situation is different and demands analysis from inside, not the application of an external "theory."

Most quarto manuscripts start with an orderly organization, but the original plan may be strained by adding pieces as they become available. Aosta 15, for example, starts with an ordering by genre and a corresponding table of contents, which was converted to a classified index when the copying order broke down. This voluminous quarto manuscript has all the characteristics of a personal assemblage, except that it was compiled in various stages during the 1430s by a relatively large number of scribes. This could be explained by changes of owner or institution, or the compilation of fascicles separately copied. Shorter compositions may be interpolated by the same scribe (as in Bologna Q.15) or by a later hand, to save space, on blank staves following a longer composition. When contents are now reported in a single consecutive listing, this may give the impression of random ordering, such as when a song or a lauda appears to interrupt a succession of mass movements.

We have seen that some sources of Italian trecento music (notably the Squarcialupi Codex and Florence 26) are arranged by composer groupings, but this is not found in other repertories at this time. A more common grouping is by genre (Chantilly, Turin J.II.9), or by settings of the same text, especially Mass Ordinary movements. The Old Hall manuscript presents sections devoted to each movement of the Mass Ordinary, first settings in score, then in choirbook layout, with a group of antiphons in score following the

---

43 The measurements given in Hamm and Kellman, eds., *Census-Catalogue of Manuscript Sources* are misleadingly approximate for the Trent codices overall.

Glorias, and a group of structured motets at the end, the last two being *Deo gratias* substitutes. It may lack a gathering of Kyries at the beginning. Such groupings of like-texted mass movements persisted long after unified cycles were being composed, thus separating musically related movements (Aosta 15, Trent 87[1] and 92[2], Cambrai 11). Apart from four cyclic presentations in Bologna Q.15 (all but one of which are composite), and the compilation there of Du Fay's *Missa Sancti Jacobi*, Trent 92[1] was one of the first manuscripts to group mass movements in cycles. Some manuscripts (Bologna Q.15 and Turin J.II.9) systematically pair Glorias and Credos, not always relating to compositional unity nor necessarily to the evolution of the cyclic mass.

The large-format manuscripts Chantilly, Squarcialupi, Old Hall, ModB, and Turin J.II.9 are all conspicuously well organized, and follow a pre-determined plan. Of these, only Chantilly and ModB have a table of contents. Some manuscripts have, or had, tables of contents in manuscript order, or classified indexes.[44] A prescriptive table of contents may precede the copying. Chantilly, for example, is copied in the order of a table of contents arranged by genre, with an unheaded first column implying three-voice ballades, then headings for *balades a iiij chans*, and *motes*. Foliation in the manuscript and correspondingly in the contents table was added later, starting at fol. 13, and it is from this later anomaly that it has been inferred that an original first gathering is lacking. A remarkable feature of ModB is a table of contents with musically notated incipits. The contents, size, and formality of this paper manuscript clearly make it suitable for liturgical use. It contains a large Vespers repertory of Magnificats, hymns, and antiphons, but also settings of non-liturgical motets, some of them occasional or ceremonial pieces.[45]

When present, a classified index may have been made either after the copying was complete, or progressively during compilation. If the latter, its recognizable stages may help to establish a chronological layering and copy-ing order, as in Oxford 213 and Paris 568. Despite the ordering by composer of some Italian anthologies, composer names were never the criterion for classified indexes. Composers are generally identified in indexes only to distinguish settings of the same text, an interesting contrast to the growing interest in adding their names to pieces in the body of a manuscript. Classified indexes are usually alphabetical by title (but not sorted beyond the first letter), as in Oxford 213, Paris 568, and Trent 92; or by genre (mass move-ment title), as in Aosta 15 and the partial index of Bologna Q.15. Of the Trent

---

44 See Lütteken, "Wege zur Musik"; Bent, "Indexes in Late Medieval Polyphonic Music Manuscripts"; and Bent, "The Trent 92 and Aosta Indexes in Context."
45 Inventory in Hamm and Scott, "A Study and Inventory of the Manuscript Modena."

codices, only Trent 92 has an index, and it has two. Trent 92[1] was indexed as a separate collection by its scribe (Nicolas de Merques). Lupi, the scribe of Trent 92[2], brought the two parts of the manuscript together and compiled a two-page index of the resulting composite book. Foliations were only needed when there was an index for them to relate to. Many manuscripts apparently without contemporary foliation may also not have had indexes. Although universally called foliations, the numbers often denote openings rather than folios, the unit of content rather than the physical object.

* * *

The first half of the fifteenth century is characterized by a wide range of types of sources, many of which have unique features, discouraging generalizations. Although some manuscripts were presumably commissioned by individuals or institutions, many, often with mixed sacred and secular repertory, seem to have been compiled by individual musicians at their own initiative and for their own pleasure and use within their musical communities. The surviving manuscripts attest a rich range of origins, purposes, and procedures, repertorial, regional, institutional, or personal. There was doubtless even greater variety in what is lost.

# Bibliography

Bent, Margaret, *Bologna Q15: The Making and Remaking of a Musical Manuscript*, Ars nova: Nuova serie II, Lucca, 2008

"Continuity and Transformation of Repertory and Transmission in Early 15th-Century Italy: The Two Cultures," in *Kontinuität und Transformation in der italienischen Vokalmusik zwischen Due- und Quattrocento*, ed. Sandra Dieckmann *et al.*, Hildesheim, 2007, 225–46

"*Divisi* and *a versi* in Early Fifteenth-Century Mass Movements," in *Antonio Zacara da Teramo e il suo tempo*, ed. Francesco Zimei, Lucca, 2005, 91–134

"Indexes in Late Medieval Polyphonic Music Manuscripts: A Brief Tour," in *The Medieval Book: Glosses from Friends and Colleagues of Christopher de Hamel*, ed. James H. Marrow *et al.*, Houten, 2010, 196–207

"A Lost English Choirbook of the 15th Century," in *International Musicological Society: Report of the Eleventh Congress, Copenhagen 1972*, ed. Henrik Glahn, Søren Sørensen, and Peter Ryom, 2 vols., Copenhagen, 1974, 1:257–62

"A New Canonic Gloria and the Changing Profile of Dunstaple," *PMM* 5 (1996), 45–67

"The Old Hall Manuscript: A Paleographical Study', Ph.D. diss., Cambridge University, 1968. Available on www.diamm.ac.uk/resources/doctoral-dissertations/

"The Progeny of Old Hall: More Leaves from a Royal English Choirbook," in *Gordon Athol Anderson (1929–1981) in Memoriam*, Musicological Studies 49, 2 vols., Henryville, Ottawa, and Binningen, 1984, 1:1–54

"Some Criteria for Establishing Relationships between Sources of Late-Medieval Polyphony," in *Music in Medieval and Early Modern Europe: Patronage, Sources and Texts*, ed. Iain Fenlon, Cambridge, 1981, 295–317

"Text Setting in Sacred Music of the Early 15th Century: Evidence and Implications," in *Musik und Text in der Mehrstimmigkeit des 14. und 15. Jahrhunderts*, ed. Ursula Günther and Ludwig Finscher, Kassel, 1984, 291–326

"The Trent 92 and Aosta Indexes in Context", in *I codici musicali trentini del Quattrocento: Nuove scoperte, nuove edizioni e nuovi strumenti informatici: Atti del convegno internazionale di studi, Trento, Castello del Buonconsiglio, 28–29 novembre 2009*, ed. Danilo Curti-Feininger and Marco Gozzi, Trento and Lucca, 2013, 63–81

"Trent 93 and Trent 90: Johannes Wiser at Work," in *I codici musicali trentini a cento anni dalla loro riscoperta: Atti del Convegno "Laurence Feininger, la musicologia come missione,"* ed. Nino Pirrotta and Danilo Curti, Trento, 1986, 84–111

and Robert Klugseder, *A Veneto Liber cantus (c. 1440): Fragments in the Bayerische Staatsbibliothek, Munich, and the Österreichische Nationalbibliothek, Vienna*, Wiesbaden, 2012

Berger, Anna Maria Busse, *Medieval Music and the Art of Memory*, Berkeley, 2005

Curtis, Liane, "Simon Mellet, Scribe of Cambrai Cathedral," *PMM* 8 (1999), 133–66

  ed., *Cambrai Cathedral Choirbook: Cambrai, Bibliothèque Municipale, MS 11*, Peer, 1992

Cuthbert, Michael Scott, "Groups and Projects among the Paduan Polyphonic Sources," in *I frammenti musicali padovani tra Santa Giustina e la diffusione della musica in Europa*, ed. Francesco Facchin and Pietro Gnan, Padua, 2011, 183–214

  "Trecento Fragments and Polyphony beyond the Codex," Ph.D. diss., Harvard University, 2006, online at www.trecento.com/dissertation/

Data, Isabella, and Karl Kügle, eds., *Il Codice J.II.9, Torino, Biblioteca Nazionale Universitaria*, Ars Nova 4, Lucca, 1999

Di Bacco, Giuliano, and John Nádas, "The Papal Chapels and Italian Sources of Polyphony during the Great Schism," in *Papal Music and Musicians in Late Medieval and Renaissance Rome*, ed. Richard Sherr, Oxford, 1998, 44–92

Fallows, David, "L'Origine du MS. 1328 de Cambrai: Note au sujet de quelques nouveaux feuillets, et de quelques informations supplémentaires," *Revue de musicologie* 62 (1976), 275–80

  "Specific Information on the Ensembles for Composed Polyphony, 1400–1474," in *Studies in the Performance of Late Medieval Music*, ed. Stanley Boorman, Cambridge, 1983, 109–59

  ed., *Oxford, Bodleian Library MS. Canon. Misc. 213*, Late Medieval and Early Renaissance Music in Facsimile 1, Chicago, 1995

Gallo, F. Alberto, *Il codice musicale 2216 della Biblioteca Universitaria di Bologna*, Monumenta Lyrica Medii Aevi Italica, 3.3, Bologna, 1968, 1970

  ed. *Il codice Squarcialupi: Ms. mediceo palatino 87, Biblioteca Laurenziana di Firenze*, Florence, 1992

  *Il codice α.M.5.24 (ModA)*, facs. edn., Lucca, 2003

Haar, James, and John Nádas, "The Medici, the Signoria, the Pope: Sacred Polyphony in Florence, 1432–1448," *Recercare* 20 (2008), 25–93

Hamm, Charles, "Interrelationships between Manuscript and Printed Sources of Polyphonic Music in the Early Sixteenth Century – an Overview," in *Datierung und Filiation von Musikhandschriften der Josquin-Zeit*, ed. Ludwig Finscher, Wiesbaden, 1983, 1–13

"Manuscript Structure in the Dufay Era," *AcM* 34 (1962), 166–84

and Herbert Kellman, *Census-Catalogue of Manuscript Sources of Polyphonic Music 1400–1550*, 5 vols., Renaissance Manuscript Studies 1, Neuhausen, 1979–88

and Ann Besser Scott, "A Study and Inventory of the Manuscript Modena, Biblioteca Estense, α.X.1.11 (ModB)," *MD* 26 (1972), 101–43

King, Jonathan, "Texting in Early Fifteenth-Century Sacred Polyphony," D.Phil. thesis, University of Oxford, 1996

Kügle, Karl, "Glorious Sounds for a Holy Warrior: New Light on Codex Turin J.II.9," *JAMS* 65 (2012), 637–90

Lerch, Irmgard, *Fragmente aus Cambrai: Ein Beitrag zur Rekonstruktion einer Handschrift mit spätmittelalterlicher Polyphonie*, Kassel, 1987

Lütteken, Laurenz, "Padua und die Entstehung des musikalischen Textes," *Marburger Jahrbuch für Kunstwissenschaft* 24 (1997), 25–39

"Wege zur Musik: Überlegungen zu Indices oberitalienischer Handschriften der ersten Hälfte des 15. Jahrhunderts," in *Studien zur italienischen Musikgeschichte*, ed. Friedrich Lippmann, 15 (1998) [= *Analecta musicologica 30*], 1:15–40

Memelsdorff, Pedro, *The Codex Faenza 117: Instrumental Polyphony in Late Medieval Italy*, 2 vols., Ars nova: Nuova serie III, Lucca, 2013

Nádas, John, "The Transmission of Trecento Secular Polyphony: Manuscript Production and Scribal Practices in Italy at the End of the Middle Ages," Ph.D. diss., New York University, 1985

and Agostino Ziino, *The Lucca Codex (Codice Mancini): Introductory Study and Facsimile Edition*, Ars Nova 1, Lucca, 1990

Perz, Mirosław, ed., *Sources of Polyphony up to c. 1500*, Antiquitates Musicae in Polonia 13–14, Graz, 1973–76

Pirrotta, Nino, "Music and Cultural Tendencies in 15th-Century Italy," *JAMS* 19 (1966), 127–61

Plumley, Yolanda, and Anne Stone, *Codex Chantilly: Bibliothèque du château de Chantilly, Ms. 564*, Turnhout, 2008

Rumbold, Ian, with Peter Wright, *Hermann Pötzlinger's Music Book: The St Emmeram Codex and its Contexts*, Woodbridge, 2009

*Kommentar und Inventar*, vol. 2 of Bayerische Staatsbibliothek and Lorenz Welker, eds., *Der Mensuralcodex St. Emmeram: Faksimile der Handschrift Clm 14274 der Bayerischen Staatsbibliothek München*, Wiesbaden, 2006

Schmidt-Beste, Thomas, "Private or Institutional – Small or Big? Towards a Typology of Polyphonic Sources of Renaissance Music," *JAF* 1 (2009), 13–26

Staehelin, Martin, "Trienter Codices und Humanismus," in *I codici musicali trentini a cento anni dalla loro riscoperta: Atti del Convegno "Laurence Feininger, la musicologia come missione*," ed. Nino Pirrotta and Danilo Curti, Trento, 1986, 158–69

Strohm, Reinhard, "Native and Foreign Polyphony in Late Medieval Austria," *MD* 38 (1984), 205–30

*The Rise of European Music 1380–1500*, Cambridge, 1993

Wright, Peter, "The Aosta-Trent Relationship Reconsidered," in *I codici musicali trentini a cento anni dalla loro riscoperta: Atti del Convegno "Laurence Feininger, la musicologia come missione*," ed. Nino Pirrotta and Danilo Curti, Trento, 1986, 138–57

"Nuove scoperte sulla carriera di Nicolas de Merques," *in L'Ars nova italiana del Trecento* 8, ed. Marco Gozzi, Agostino Ziino, and Francesco Zimei, Lucca, 2014, 483–88

"On the Origins of Trent $87_1$ and $92_2$," *EMH* 6 (1986), 245–70

"Trent 87 and 92: Questions of Origin, Repertory and Physical Make-Up," in *Music and Culture in the Age of the Council of Basel*, ed. Matteo Nanni, Turnhout, 2013, 111–33

Ziino, Agostino, ed., *Il codice T.III.2: Torino, Biblioteca nazionale universitaria*, Lucca, 1994

# Polyphonic sources, ca. 1450–1500

THOMAS SCHMIDT-BESTE

The great paradigm shift in the written transmission of polyphonic music in the early modern era remains, in the eyes of many, the "revolution of the printing press":[1] the invention of printing from movable type pioneered by Ottaviano Petrucci in 1501. But this view has rightly come under some scrutiny in recent years, with scholars pointing out that the "age of print" did not by any means imply a decline in manuscript production and use; manuscripts remained the medium of choice in many contexts on account of their size and flexibility of repertory selection, as well as physical appearance and beauty. Indeed, purely in terms of numbers and dissemination, the sixteenth century is the heyday of manuscript culture – alongside or in some contexts instead of print culture.

This development was set in motion in the second half of the fifteenth century, when conditions became prevalent that made the enormous prolifer-ation of polyphonic music after 1500 possible. As Margaret Bent notes in her contribution to this volume (Ch. 33), polyphonic music manuscripts before the middle of the fifteenth century tended (with exceptions) to be private collec-tions rather than – as was thought for a long time – sources documenting the repertory and practice of musical institutions. This does not mean that these sources could not have been *used* in an institutional context – but they were almost certainly not created for this purpose.

Even taking into account the probable loss of the majority of sources, the practice of singing polyphony from notation must have been relatively rare. The number of institutions and individuals cultivating this practice (regard-less of whether they read from the page or used it as an aide-mémoire[2]) was limited, as were the occasions for which the books were used; institutions employed singers in their chapels, but their repertory was primarily chant and *contrapunctus* (polyphony improvised on plainchant *super librum*).[3] Likewise, the number of private collectors or patrons of notated polyphonic music was

---

1 Eisenstein, *The Printing Press.*   2 See Berger, *Medieval Music.*
3 See Philippe Canguilhem's contribution in this volume, Ch. 9; also Bent, "*Resfacta* and *Cantare Super Librum*"; Wegman, "From Maker to Composer."

limited; interest in such items was restricted to the few who had the requisite training (or acquired a taste for it) in the locations where this art was practiced.

This begins to change after mid-century. For reasons not yet fully understood, but surely underpinned by a surge in literacy coinciding with the advent of printing, singing composed polyphony "from the page" becomes increasingly widespread and is commonplace by around 1500. It is accompanied by a proliferation of institutions employing personnel for the practice of *cantus figuratus* in France, the Low Countries, and England, and, slightly later, in Italy, Spain, and central Europe. Famous examples are the chapels of the French kings and the dukes of Burgundy, where polyphony was prescribed in daily services already before mid-century;[4] by its end, even lowly parish churches had permanent or casual personnel to sing composed polyphony at least on Sundays and high feasts (alongside the still standard practice of *contrapunctus*).

This change of institutional practice is underpinned by two developments. For one, training choirboys to read polyphonic notation became more and more the norm (again in the Low Countries and in England at first), who once grown up would provide an increasingly steady and readily available supply of singers capable of singing notated polyphony. For another, while the art of improvised *contrapunctus* remained widespread, the art of composing *cantus figuratus* attained an elevated status as a creative art in its own right. It is hardly by accident that both Rob Wegman and Jessie Ann Owens situate the birth of the "composer" in the modern, emphatic sense in the years following 1450,[5] and that composer ascriptions in the sources, while appearing with increasing frequency from ca. 1400 onwards, become ever more common after mid-century, corresponding to (as Laurenz Lütteken argues in his contribution to this volume, Ch. 3) an increasing sense of "musical authorship" that appears consolidated by ca. 1500.[6]

These developments implied, indeed necessitated a supply of written music to sing from; clearly, the number of notated sources of polyphony greatly increased in the decades in question – in sacred, secular, courtly, and civic institutions and in the private sphere. Even taking into account massive losses, the sample of extant sources, both geographically and chronologically, is sufficient to allow, for the first time, an attempt at a typology of sources of polyphonic music – differentiated by type, size, appearance, layout, use, function etc. – and the mutual relationships of these factors. Attempts at such a

---

4 Strohm, *The Rise of European Music*, 275–79.
5 Wegman, "From Maker to Composer"; Owens, *Composers at Work*.
6 Cf. Margaret Bent's essay in this section, Ch. 33.

typology have been rare up to now; while there are innumerable studies of individual sources and institutions, very few – beyond general overviews[7] – are comparable in scope to those done for chant sources,[8] much less late medieval books in general.

## Types, places, and makers

The most important effect of the increasing production of polyphonic sources is a tendency toward repertorial and functional specialization. While multi-genre miscellanies retain their place and purpose, we begin to see greater numbers of books containing liturgical or paraliturgical repertory specific to the ritual requirements of sacred institutions, often compiled according to genre and occasionally even internally ordered by liturgical function. By the end of the century, the functional collection of sacred polyphony clearly out-numbered the second principal type: the polyphonic songbook containing secular repertory in the vernacular.

The context of the institutional music book is usually that of the chapel – which increasingly implied an ensemble of singers charged with the perform-ance of polyphony – and the sacred ritual; the repertory is consequently associated with the local liturgy. The standard book type for this function is the choirbook: a manuscript large enough that all the singers could see and read the notation, with the voice parts arranged in *cantus collateralis*, that is in blocks across an opening of two pages. This corresponds with a repertory that tends to privilege the horizontal (linear) aspect of the texture over its vertical (har-monic) one; it visually emphasizes this horizontal coherence and ensures efficient use of the available space, especially in compositions with voices moving at very different speeds, thus requiring substantially different amounts of lateral space.

The arrangement of voices, which had allowed for a substantial amount of variation, is now standardized. In the normal four-part texture, the voices are usually arranged across the opening in long lines, the superius and tenor one below the other on the left-hand (verso) side, altus and bassus on the right (recto) side (see Figure 34.1). In central Europe, the disposition super-ius–bassus on the verso and altus–tenor on the recto is also common (see Figure 34.2). Three-part textures normally present the two upper voices on either side of the opening and the lowest voice either across the bottom of both sides or in its entirety on the side where the upper voice occupies less

---

7  Schwindt, "Quellen"; and Boorman, "Sources, MS. I. Introduction." A more recent attempt at system-atization is Schmidt-Beste, "Private or Institutional – Small or Big?"
8  E.g., Huglo, *Les Livres de chant liturgique.*

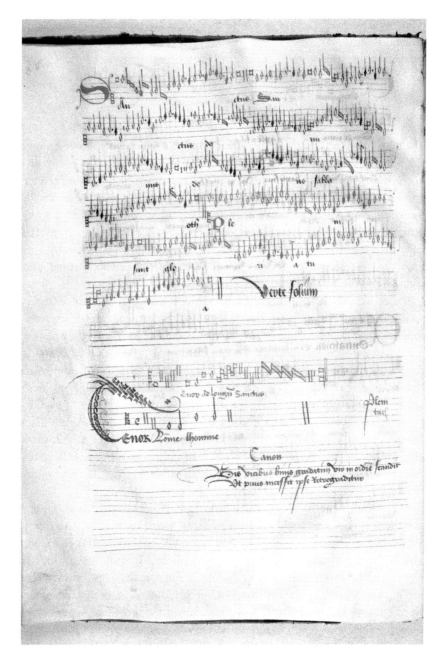

Figure 34.1 Naples, Biblioteca Nazionale di Napoli, VI.E.40, fols. 6v–7r

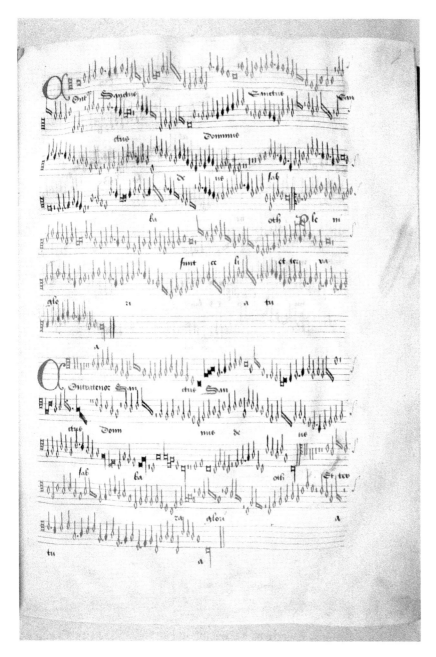

Figure 34.1 (cont.)

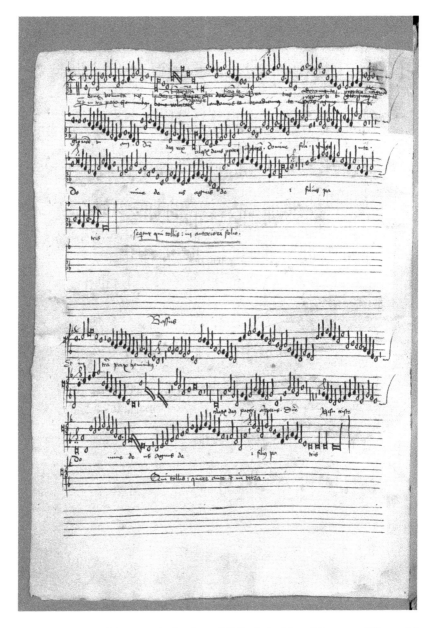

Figure 34.2 Munich, Bayerische Staatsbibliothek, Mus. Ms. 3154 ("Leopold Codex"), fols. 371v–372r

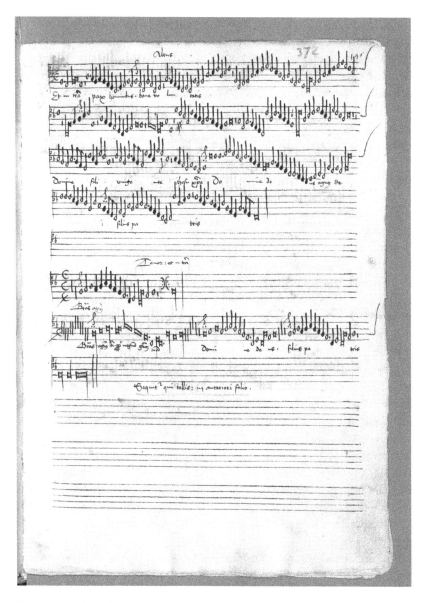

Figure 34.2 (cont.)

space. For five or more voices, the default layout was extended either by
fitting additional parts on either side, or by having one voice cross over from
one page to the other. Other layouts exist – for example, all voices on a single
page, or all voices notated in succession across pages or even page-turns, but

these are more prevalent in personal repositories than in institutional choirbooks.

In addition to making optimum use of space by using the opening rather than the page as a frame of reference, manuscripts were produced in ever growing sizes. By the end of the century, the larger institutions boasted manuscripts measuring 50 cm in height or more, and 70 cm or more in the sixteenth century.[9] Physical size, for these sources, is primarily determined by pragmatic considerations, not a desire to impress; a direct correlation is discernible between ensemble sizes and the size of the books from which they sang.[10] These books are not normally lavishly decorated or elaborately produced; instead, they reflect the everyday nature of both the repertory and the object. As *Gebrauchshandschriften* – manuscripts for use – they provide repertory whose shelf-life was limited and which was replaced on a regular basis. They are usually copied on cheaper and less durable paper, in contrast to the often ornate chant books copied on parchment, which (at least notionally) contained a "timeless" repertory. The function of decoration is pragmatic rather than aesthetic; illumination is rare, and the initials executed by the scribes – penned initials (cadels) or simple capitals – point the singers toward the place where their parts begin. Tellingly, in many sources the initial is not the first letter of the first word (as is almost invariably the case in contemporary textual sources), but the first letter of the voice designation – *B* for Bassus, etc. – and thus technically part of the rubric, not the sung text. The text itself is usually fully underlaid in most or all of the voices, meaning that these voices were presumably to be sung fully texted even though the (to modern eyes) casual underlay in words and phrases implies, depending on repertory and style, either a certain flexibility as to the precise allocation of syllables to notes or the existence of "unwritten rules" of declamation.[11] Scholars are still grappling with the question how to perform cantus-firmus voices in masses and motets, which can be untexted, supplied with incipits, partly texted, or fully texted with either the cantus-firmus text or the text of the other voices or both.

This utiliarian approach to manuscript production is similarly reflected in how, where, and by whom these sources were produced. They were not procured from professional *scriptoria* (like Bibles, missals, or chant books) or bought from a stationer like university texts; the majority were apparently compiled in-house. The copyists were, with few exceptions, not professional scribes, but singers in the chapels. Their most important task was to

---

9 For a discussion of manuscript sizes before 1450, see Bent's contribution in this volume, Ch. 33.
10 Schmidt-Beste, "Über Quantität und Qualität."
11 See Schmidt-Beste, *Textdeklamation*; Schubert and Cumming, "Text and Motif."

ensure the correctness of the notation and layout, a task which required a singer's expertise. Even Simon Mellet, a scribe responsible for a vast amount of music copying in Cambrai between 1444 and 1480, was primarily employed as a singer; Jean Orceau and Claudius Gellandi, the first two named scribes of the Cappella Sistina around the turn of the sixteenth century, were music scribes in the chapel, not the apostolic *camera*. As the sixteenth century progressed, the Cappella Sistina even employed separate scribes for chant and polyphony; Gellandi's successor, Johannes Parvus, was again a singer. The "semi-professional" character of polyphonic music scribes meant that their skill in notating music often surpassed that of copying text; in this they were competent but rarely more, in comparison with text scribes of the same period.

## Repertories and sources of sacred music

As long as liturgical requirements and local traditions were observed, it was apparently up to the compiler or singers to decide what compositions the books were to contain, taking into account the preferences of their employer or patron. Even institutional choirbooks are in this sense one-offs, the contents composed or collected by the chapel members themselves. This process of collection could take the form of what Charles Hamm has called "fascicle manuscripts," a term more obviously applicable here in fact than for the collections of the early fifteenth century which Hamm discusses:[12] rather than produce entire books from the outset that would have been unwieldy and impractical in service, ensembles might sing from single-quire booklets that, given the limited lifespan of the repertory, might later be discarded or bound into volumes to put on the shelf for archiving. The nature of the polyphonic choirbook layout encouraged the creation of self-contained booklets: because the notation had to begin on a verso and end on a recto, the first and the last pages often had to be left blank, serving as a kind of wrapper. When such booklets (each containing one or more compositions) were later bound into a volume, the resulting blank openings between quires could be used for "filler-pieces," and the outsides for title pages, indexes, or other liminary items. This also explains why many of these manuscripts contain music composed and copied over a substantial period of time, often decades. The evidence for this is substantial; not only were scribes often paid for copying fascicles rather than books,[13] but many extant manuscripts show

---

12 Hamm, "Manuscript Structure in the Dufay Era." Bent's essay in this volume sounds a cautionary note against applying Hamm's "theory" too simplistically.
13 See, for example, Curtis, "Simon Mellet."

their piecemeal genesis. In the Sistine Chapel, where this practice is particularly apparent, some of these booklets survive (e.g., Vatican CS 197 from the early 1490s, a single mass by Josquin; or the final quires of Vatican CS 35, with works by Marbrianus de Orto, and the first quire of Vatican CS 64, the *Missa L'homme armé* by the same composer, later bound with much younger repertory).[14]

The ephemeral nature of the repertory, along with the limited aesthetic appeal and material value of the books and their often piecemeal creation, all combine with political and religious vicissitudes to result in a highly limited survival rate, given the vast numbers of books that must have existed. From two of the most important chapels of the second half of the century with amply documented production of polyphonic music – the courts of France and England – not a shred survives. The third major courtly establishment of northwestern Europe, Burgundy, is represented by a single choirbook, Brussels 5557 (compiled ca. 1464–80), primarily containing mass settings; but as an object it asks as many questions as it answers. The heraldic devices on the first pages leave little doubt that it was produced for the Burgundian chapel, and at 37.5 × 28 cm, it is somewhat larger than the miscellanies of the same period. But it is hardly of sufficient scope to allow the fourteen singers required by Burgundian court ordinances to actually read from it; and even by the standards of the late fifteenth-century *Gebrauchshandschrift*, it is a singularly unimpressive book for such a grand institution. The contrast is particularly vivid when compared to a contemporary manuscript with Burgundian links (but without any indication that it was intended to be used in the liturgy at its destination): the lavishly illuminated parchment codex Naples VI.E.40 with the six *L'homme armé* masses that Charles the Bold gave to Beatrice of Aragon following her marriage to Matthias Corvinus of Hungary in 1476 in Naples. The situation is hardly better in nearby cities: Brussels, Antwerp, Bruges, Bergen op Zoom, and 's-Hertogenbosch all boasted substantial musical institutions in their cathedrals, parish churches, and confraternities, with rich documentation of the practice and copying of polyphony – but with nothing to show for it today. In Cambrai, two slim volumes are extant from the earlier part of the century, but the bulk of Simon Mellet's activity beginning in 1445/46 is lost. The same applies to English cathedrals and parish churches ravaged by Henry VIII's reformation, leaving only scattered fragments;[15] from before the century mark, only the lavish Eton Choirbook survives as a

14  Roth, "Die Entstehung des ältesten Chorbuches."
15  Wathey, "Lost Books of Polyphony in England"; Curtis and Wathey, "Fifteenth-Century English Liturgical Music"; Williamson, "Liturgical Polyphony in the Pre-Reformation English Parish Church."

complete witness to large-scale Tudor polyphony, alongside the less impressive but more repertorially varied "Ritson" manuscript, containing smaller liturgical works and carols.

In Italy, the two courtly institutions that pioneered the practice of polyphony are Naples and Ferrara. In the former, the Aragonese monarchy was firmly established by 1442–43, and King Alfonso immediately set about establishing a grand musical establishment. A substantial body of music manuscripts (many polyphonic) was either acquired or produced *in situ*, but hardly anything survives.[16] Allan Atlas has argued that the two manuscripts Montecassino 871 and Perugia 431, containing mixed liturgical and secular repertory and copied in the 1480s, preserve the music sung in the Neapolitan court chapel, but they were produced for monasteries in or near the city rather than for the court. The masses sung by the chapel in the 1470s might be contained in the two large and sumptuous choirbooks Vatican CS 14 and 51, if Adalbert Roth's hypothesis that they were presented by King Ferrante I of Aragon to Pope Sixtus IV in 1475 is correct.[17] The other extant books from the period that are probably associated with the city and the court contain secular repertory, on which more below.

Polyphonic music took off in Ferrara in the 1440s when Leonello d'Este had a new private chapel constructed and started recruiting singers. Until recently, it was thought that the large paper choirbook Modena B (Modena α. X.1.11) containing liturgical and paraliturgical polyphony was produced for the Este chapel around the middle of the century; but this has been questioned by John Nádas, James Haar, and Michael Phelps, who argue that the book was copied in Florence in the 1430s by the French singer Benoît ("Benotto"), who then took it to Ferrara with him.[18] In any case, the chapel reached the height of its splendor under Ercole I d'Este (1471–1505), with up to twenty-seven singers by the later 1470s and a set of lavish books, all – unusually – in parchment. Shortly thereafter, Duke Galeazzo Maria Sforza of Milan followed suit and from 1472 richly endowed his own chapel of singers. The four massive *Libroni* (Milan 2266–2269) of the Milanese Duomo, however, are another puzzle. Much of the repertory they contain (most notably the *motetti missales* cycles) is liturgically appropriate only to the court, where

---

16 Atlas, *Music at the Aragonese Court*, 114–25.

17 Adalbert Roth argues for a Neapolitan origin; see his *Studien zum frühen Repertoire der päpstlichen Kapelle*. In a series of unpublished papers, Flynn Warmington has argued for a Florentine or Venetian origin, and Emilia Anna Talamo for Ferrara in *Codices Cantorum*, 23–39. Most recently, Richard Sherr (*Masses for the Sistine Chapel*, 10–18) favors the hypothesis that the manuscripts were copied for Cardinal Giovanni d'Aragona (1456–85), the youngest son of the Neapolitan King Ferrante, who frequently visited Ferrara, Naples, and Rome.

18 Haar and Nádas, "The Medici, the Signoria, the Pope"; Phelps, "A Repertory in Exile."

Gaspar van Weerbeke and Loyset Compère were employed, rather than the cathedral – but archival evidence indicates that they were produced at the expense of the latter institution by its choirmaster, Franchino Gaffurio.[19] At the same time, Sixtus IV reorganized and expanded the papal chapel, establishing an archive of polyphonic music that was without peer until the end of the sixteenth century. After a precursor volume of uncertain function and provenance – Vatican San Pietro B80, either produced in the 1470s at St. Peter's itself or brought there later[20] – and the equally controversial mass books Vatican CS 14 and 51 (see above), the chapel boasts no fewer than seven large extant choirbooks completed or begun before 1500, apparently preserving a much larger proportion of the repertory than is extant from any other institution of the time.[21] These are nicely separated by liturgical function (barring some later additions): settings of the Mass Ordinary in Vatican CS 23, 35, 41, 49, and 197, and polyphony for Vespers in Vatican CS 15. Only Vatican CS 63 mixes the genres.

The survival rate of books from cathedrals, parish churches, monasteries, and confraternities is even worse than that for large courts. A single choirbook survives from Siena cathedral (Siena K.I.2) from the late fifteenth century, produced over a period of time: this is an excellent example of an unpretentious collection of polyphony for regular use. Reinhard Strohm has pieced together the loose leaves of the more elaborate but still utilitarian codex Lucca 238, containing masses and Marian repertory; this book was probably copied in the 1470s (with additions until the end of the century) for a confraternity in Bruges and subsequently used by John Hothby at Lucca cathedral.[22] Verona cathedral holds no fewer than six codices copied in the late fifteenth and early sixteenth centuries with mostly sacred/liturgical repertory – of which, however, probably only three were copied for the cathedral itself (Verona 757, 758, 759). The others are: Verona 756, from the Habsburg-Burgundian workshop; Verona 761, copied apparently in Rome for a yet-to-be-determined institution or occasion in Verona;[23] Verona 755, of uncertain provenance, either from Naples or a northern Italian religious institution;[24] and Verona 690, of entirely unknown origin.

---

19 Rolsma, "De onthullingen van het missal"; Rifkin, "Munich, Milan, and a Marian Motet," 245–64.
20 Reynolds, *Papal Patronage*, who argues for a Roman origin; but see against that Roth, *Studien zum frühen Repertoire*, 567–77.
21 Sherr, *Papal Music Manuscripts*; Rodin, *Josquin's Rome*, 117–31.
22 Strohm, ed., *The Lucca Choirbook*, 28–34.
23 According to Howard Mayer Brown, the codex was compiled for a nuns' convent in Verona; see his "Music for the Nuns of Verona." But Joshua Rifkin and others have convincingly argued for a Roman origin; see his "A Scriptor, a Singer, and a Mother Superior."
24 Roth (*Studien zum frühen Repertoire*, 556–66), argues for a Neapolitan connection, Dean for a northern Italian origin in "Verona 755 and the *Incomprehensibilia* Composer."

Polyphonic practice in monasteries and confraternities, especially in northern Italy, is further documented by miscellanies of liturgical or devotional polyphony (motets, laude), often combined with texts and monophonic music, and containing repertory similar to the Montecassino and Perugia manuscripts. Their small format documents a practice of individual or small-group devotion. Examples include the mid-century miscellany Venice IX. 145, later also the "Codex Grey" (Cape Town 3.b.12), as well as probably Turin I.27, Florence 112bis, and Florence 27.[25]

In Spain, while polyphonic practice became widespread at courts and other large centers, sources from before 1500 are again scarce; what little repertory survives is in cathedrals, monasteries, and religious orders, in the form of unpretentious miscellanies that could be put to a variety of uses.[26] Indeed, the mixed-repertory manuscripts from the turn of the century, such as the Cancionero de la Colombina, Paris 4379/IV, Segovia s.s., Barcelona 454, and Seville 5-5-20 stubbornly resist precise categorization or identification of origin and function.

The main focus in German-speaking lands is on the Trent codices, containing about 1,300 pieces, by far the richest source of polyphonic music from the period. Trent 87 and 92 are in several parts that were copied outside the city in the 1430s and 1440s and brought there by Johannes Lupi (see Ch. 33); Trent 93 was copied locally in the early 1450s and subsequently came into the possession of Johannes Wiser, from 1458 master of the cathedral choir school, who added to Trent 93 and was apparently responsible for the compilation of all the later codices. Peter Wright and others have painted a vivid picture of Lupi, Wiser, and their assistants working in an important ecclesiastical institution at one of the crossroads of Europe and amassing far more from all corners of the Continent than they could ever use.[27] To be sure, the seemingly random variety of the repertory in Trent 87 and 92 is explained by their piecemeal origin. A more functional emphasis occurs in the volumes compiled in and for Trent itself: Trent 93 (ca. 1450–55) contains mostly liturgical works for the Ordinary and Proper of the Mass, as does Trent 90, which is largely a copy of Trent 93 from the mid-1450s.[28] However, Trent 93 also contains an incongruous appendix of mostly earlier repertory, some English and some secular; and Trent 90, while leaving out this appendix, adds a vast, seemingly haphazard repertory covering all kinds of genres, functions, and regions. Trent 88 and 89, from the late 1450s and early 1460s, respectively, focus more on the liturgy

25 Filocamo, ed., *Florence, BNC, Panciatichi 27.*
26 Kreitner, *The Church Music of Fifteenth-Century Spain.*
27 Wright, "On the Origins"; Strohm, "Trienter Codices."　　28 See Bent, "Trent 93 and Trent 90."

(Trent 88 famously with a series of Mass Proper cycles attributed to Du Fay[29]), while the proportion of mixed repertory increases in the youngest of the seven codices, Trent 91, from the 1470s.[30] The only way in which these seven quarto volumes make sense is as a multi-purpose repository, combining the utilitarian with the collector's urge: their smallish format, perfunctory presentation, incomplete text underlay, and sometimes impractical layout, while not pre-cluding performance by a small group of singers, make it appear unlikely that they were designed with performance in the liturgy as their primary purpose – but individual pieces or groups of pieces could have been copied into larger fascicles for use by the Trent cathedral chapel or its school.[31]

Further to the north and east, a fair number of similar sources survive from the last decades of the century. They again contain a mixed repertory, combining sacred and secular as well as liturgical and non-liturgical pieces, from tiny textless (instrumental?) works to full-scale Mass Ordinary and plenary mass cycles. These are the (probably Silesian or Moravian) Strahov Codex from around 1470, which as Paweł Gancarczyk has shown is linked to the Habsburg court and the Trent codices;[32] the Wrocław Codex (Warsaw 5892 [olim 2016], again Silesia?); the manuscript Berlin 40021 (Saxony?);[33] and the Speciálník Codex copied in Prague, possibly for use in a school.[34] An exception in terms of format is the collection long known as the "Glogauer Liederbuch," which is neither from Glogau nor a Liederbuch (songbook), but another miscellany, from the Abbey of St. Augustine in Żagań (Silesia): it is the earliest extant complete source in partbooks rather than choirbook format.[35]

Through its inclusion of regional Bohemian repertory in a distinctive nota-tional style, Speciálník forges a link with the books of the Utraquist literary brotherhoods or *literati*. One such book, albeit of a more functional type, is the Franus Cantionale, which provides liturgical chant, texts, and monophonic and polyphonic motets and sacred songs for their services; books for the wealthier confraternities are larger and more lavishly decorated. The more modest liturgical/devotional "songbooks" were widespread from Bohemia and Poland to the Netherlands: they are really prayerbooks containing musical notation, the monophonic songs or chants occasionally expanded to simple two- or three-part polyphony. Examples are Munich, Bayerische

---

29 This attribution was first proposed by Laurence Feininger, but long considered fanciful, until shown to by correct by Alejandro Planchart; see Planchart, "Guillaume Du Fay's Benefices," 142–62.
30 Gerber, ed., *Sacred Music from the Cathedral at Trent.*    31 Strohm, "Trienter Codices."
32 Gancarczyk, "The Dating and Chronology of the Strahov Codex."
33 Berlin, Staatsbibliothek zu Berlin, Preußischer Kulturbesitz, MS Mus. 40021. Just, ed., *Der Mensuralkodex Mus. ms. 40021.*
34 Mráčková, "Behind the Stage."    35 Gancarczyk, "Abbot Martin Rinkenberg."

Staatsbibliothek, Clm 5023 (written at the abbey of Benediktbeuren in 1495) and a series of books in the tradition of the *Devotio moderna* in northwestern Germany and the Low Countries, such as Berlin 190, Berlin 280 (the Songbook of Anna of Cologne), and Brussels II.270.[36]

As the skills of reading and singing polyphony proliferated in the private sphere, those who received such training as part of their education but did not enter the singing profession were increasingly likely to own, collect, and practice polyphonic music "from the page." Musical amateurs such as the university professors Nikolaus Apel (Apel Codex) and Johannes Klein (Leipzig 1084 and Leipzig 1236), the schoolteacher Nikolaus Leopold (Munich 3154), and the collector and polymath Hartmann Schedel (Schedelsches Liederbuch) copied, compiled, or owned collections that are often indistinguishable – in size, elaboration, and choice of repertory – from other small folio or quarto manuscripts; we are simply lucky to know the names of the collectors. The Schedelsches Liederbuch is an exception of sorts: its very small format (ca. 15 × 10 cm), sense of internal order, and choice of repertory (short, originally vocal pieces without text, masking their diverse origins) mark it as the idiosyncratic collection of a true bibliophile.[37]

## The songbook: chansonniers and beyond

Even though it is a miscellany of various genres, Schedel's pocketbook size and focus on private "chamber music" brings us to another type of book that becomes common in the second half of the century: the songbook. With the exception of the Italian trecento manuscripts, up until this time polyphonic settings of vernacular poems had been transmitted in miscellanies rather than custom-made books – in marked contrast to monophonic or text-only songbooks like the troubadour/trouvère and Minnesang books or the Italian laudari. Starting around 1450, however, the polyphonic songbook or chansonnier comes into its own. These books share a number of general characteristics:

(a) They tend to be small, pocket-size books, no more than 10–20 cm in height.
(b) Their content tends to be homogeneous, predominantly or wholly containing repertory in only one language, genre, and musical style.

---

36 Berlin, Staatsbibliothek zu Berlin, Preußischer Kulturbesitz, MSS Germ. 8° 190 and 8° 280, and Brussels, Bibliothèque royale de Belgique/Koninklijke Bibliotheek van België, MS II.270. Hascher-Burger, *Gesungene Innigkeit*; also her website www.musicadevota.com/.
37 Kirnbauer, *Hartmann Schedel und sein "Liederbuch."*

(c) Depending on function, ownership, and context, their external appearance ranges from the scruffy to the gorgeous. Still, the proportion of lavish "coffee-table books" that are carefully laid out, beautifully written, and richly illuminated on the finest parchment is higher than in any other type of music book of the period. They could serve as valuable gifts or collectibles, and their visual appeal was generally as important as their musical content, accounting for their relatively high rate of survival.

(d) Their primary function does not appear to have been performance; while possible, reading from such small books would have been a struggle, even with one singer to a part. Their main purpose seems to have been to be owned, to be beheld, or perhaps to read along during performances by others, whether by collectors, bibliophiles, or patrons.[38] Unsurprisingly, these books have remained treasured collectors' items up to the present day.

(e) Usually, only the voice that carries the melody (normally the discantus) is underlaid with text. Additional strophes, if supplied, are added separately; one assumes these could be matched to the music at sight or from memory, as in a modern-day hymnal. The question of whether the lower voices were to be performed instrumentally, to be vocalized, or to be sung to the text of the top voice is still controversial – different practices may have prevailed at different times and in different contexts. As mentioned, performance from the page may not have been the principal intended function in any case.

(f) Even where these books were produced for or ended up at a court, they were ultimately private objects, belonging to an individual – dedicatee, ruler, patron – rather than an institution; the circumstances and tastes of that person and his or her immediate circle are often reflected in the books. This makes them easier to place and date than sacred collections or miscellanies: they tend to contain more specific repertory and paratextual hints, providing clues about patrons, owners, or dedicatees.

The largest category of songbooks is French chansonniers. Like the poetry on which they are based, chansonniers are widespread not only in France and the Low Countries, but across Europe, particularly in Italy. The most famous and spectacular are the so-called Loire Valley Chansonniers, a series of precious small choirbooks copied in the 1460s and 1470s, connected by repertory and scribal concordances, and containing works predominantly from the mid-century Franco-Burgundian courtly milieu: Dijon 517, Copenhagen

---

38 Alden, *Songs, Scribes, and Society.*

291, the Laborde Chansonnier (Washington M2.1. L25 Case), and the Wolfenbüttel Chansonnier (Wolfenbüttel 287). These books were long held to be "courtly" in the specific sense – produced for the itinerant court of Burgundy – but as Paula Higgins has shown, the evidence for a "French connection" is stronger.[39] What is more, Jane Alden has recently argued that they were not the result of courtly patronage at all, but instead produced for the wealthy, and intellectually and socially ambitious, administrative elite of notaries and secretaries associated with the French court – with Étienne Petit II (1449–1523) as the individual for whom Wolfenbüttel was written, and Adam Fumée (ca. 1416–94) as a possible sponsor of Laborde.[40] Less immediately connected to this group are the Chansonnier "Nivelle de la Chaussée" (Paris 57), which has links to the Burgundian court, and the slightly later Lorraine Chansonnier (Paris 1597), as well as Florence 2794 and London 20 A. xvi. The heart-shaped Cordiforme Chansonnier was copied further to the south, for Jean Montchenu of Savoy.

In Italy, French chansonniers were usually copied *in situ*, with only the repertory imported; they are widespread particularly around Florence and the Aragonese court at Naples; French repertory, while still in the majority, is mixed with Italian songs and even some in other languages. French compositions often appear with corrupt texts or are texted only with incipits, which again raises questions about performance and performability. Naples is most famously represented by the Mellon Chansonnier (New Haven 91) of the mid-1470s, probably compiled by Johannes Tinctoris for Beatrice of Aragon, Queen of Hungary; other extant books from the period that are likely to be associated with the city and the court are Bologna Q.16, El Escorial IV.a.24, Seville 5-1-43/Paris 4379[I], and the Foligno fragments (Foligno s.s.).[41] Their Florentine counterparts are Berlin 78.C.28, the Medici Chansonnier (Vatican CG XII.27), Florence 229, Florence 178, Bologna Q.17, and the Pixérécourt Chansonnier (Paris 15123). A direct link to the Este court of Ferrara can be established for the Casanatense chansonnier (Rome 2856), an ornate and unusually large (27 cm) parchment codex.

Books containing primarily Italian secular polyphony are rare before the end of the century: the resurgence of the madrigal is still a few decades away, and the surviving repertory is limited to frottole, strambotti, and canti. However, the popularity of these genres in northern Italian courtly, aristocratic, and humanistic circles produced fascinating unica, such as the tiny parchment codex Modena α.F.9.9, copied in Padua in 1496, which opens with a series of

---

39 Higgins, "Antoine Busnois," 213–308.
40 Alden, *Songs, Scribes, and Society*, 188–212.
41 Atlas, *Music at the Aragonese Court*, 118–25.

learned humanist paratexts before adorning the simple strambotti with a wealth of figurative, multicolored illuminations (birds, insects, flowers, plants, etc.). Larger and simpler, but nevertheless crucial for our understanding of the genre, are the Florentine book Florence 230 and Paris 676 from Mantua, which contains additional miscellaneous repertory. North of the Alps, where monophonic song collections survive in reasonable numbers, polyphony makes a somewhat delayed appearance; after the Wolkenstein Codex B of the 1430s – a large (49 cm) parchment manuscript dedicated to the works of one man that is in every way exceptional – the repertory is mostly transmitted through fragments and in miscellanies like the Glogauer and Schedelsches Liederbücher. Only the Lochamer Liederbuch, copied in the 1450s in Nuremberg, contains polyphonic songs alongside mostly monophonic repertory.

## Identifying makers and origins

As will have become clear, it is often difficult or impossible to state by whom, for whom, and for what purpose a fifteenth-century manuscript of polyphonic music was created. As both personal and institutional copies were made by insiders for their own use, paratexts such as colophons, dedications, dates, and titles are almost invariably lacking.[42] The choice of repertory is often particular to the person or institution, rendering composer ascriptions unnecessary: those who saw the book did not have to be told. Absent specific institutional requirements or traditions that shaped the choice and arrangement of the music, or internal or contextual clues about the occasion and time of production, one must rely on the nature of the liturgical or devotional repertory, the language and style of vernacular repertory (if present), the notation, and sometimes the format or material to even place a source within a region or period. These difficulties are compounded for fascicle manuscripts, which were sometimes copied or assembled over an extended period of time by several scribes or owners. Even where a number of sources survive in a library or archive connected with a particular institution, the evidence is often less than clear. Closer to 1500, increasing archival evidence for the "official" institutional copying of polyphony can shed light on the origins of specific books, as can heraldic and other evidence. For the simpler miscellanies, however, that information remains elusive.

Many sources are of course no longer in the place in which they originated, owing to the vicissitudes of history. When music traveled – because musicians themselves traveled, or because people elsewhere were interested in a particular style (e.g., the Italians in the French chanson) or in certain composers – it

---

42  Schmidt-Beste, "Dedicating Music Manuscripts."

was usually recopied at its destination: we find Spanish songs copied in French and Italian manuscripts, Flemish motets in central European miscellanies, and French chansons all over Europe. However, there is one type of book that did travel as a complete object: the gift. It could serve as a token of friendship, a present for an important occasion, or a gesture designed to impress. Such "presentation codices" had been common for centuries, but only now were books of polyphony considered interesting or valuable enough to serve this purpose. These were usually objects of high material value and visual appeal, such as Naples VI.E.40, with its six *L'homme armé* masses, or the Mellon Chansonnier – both gifts to Beatrice of Aragon.

The most important source of polyphonic presentation codices was the workshop of Petrus Alamire at the Habsburg-Burgundian court of Margaret of Austria (and, from ca. 1508 onwards, Charles V).[43] This was the nearest any workshop producing polyphonic music ever came to a proper *scriptorium*, even though the vast variety of sizes, level of calligraphy and illumination, and repertory indicates that Alamire worked on commission. He drew on a succession of musicians from the court chapel as scribes and made books to order, rather than pre-producing books of a standardized content and uniform "look" to serve a market as did the professional *scriptoria* of the time.[44] The pre-Alamire volumes produced by "Scribe B" at the same court around the turn of the century are largely luxury productions as well, either produced on commission or indeed to be used as gifts of state. In this early group, heraldics and miniatures indicate that the Chigi Codex for Philippe Bouton (ca. 1500), Vienna 1783 for Emanuel and Maria of Spain (1500), and Brussels 9126 for Philip the Fair and Juana of Spain (1504–5) were intended as presents for important dynastic events. While these books, lavish as they are, simulate the external appearance and content of the large-scale institutional choirbooks that emerged at the same time (collections of Mass Ordinary cycles and motets in a large format), there is little indication that their primary purpose was for use in performance at their destination, even where they were handed over to the chapel and not kept in the recipient's private possession.

\* \* \*

In short, the second half of the fifteenth century is the period in which the production of polyphonic music manuscripts diversifies and proliferates. While the multifunctional miscellany does not disappear, very different types of books also evolve for very different purposes. Editors, compilers, and scribes

43 Kellman, ed., *The Treasury of Petrus Alamire*, 10–14.
44 Saurma-Jeltsch, *Spätformen mittelalterlicher Buchherstellung*, 1:85–88 and 167 ff.

were able to customize books to meet specific purposes (as had been the case for other types of books for a long time), with all production parameters – size, material, level of calligraphy, amount and accuracy of text underlay, and decoration – corresponding to repertory, function, and context. This does not mean that a manuscript could not serve multiple or changing functions, or that a given source type could not simulate the external aspects of another: as we have seen with the presentation codices, physical size can be useful for performance by a large ensemble *as well as* visually impressive. But it is only the growing diversity of source types that allows us to draw such conclusions. Even so, the sources – produced by insiders for insiders – usually remain silent about many pressing issues: dates and places of origin, owners, and sponsors. It is unlikely that any amount of research will ever provide final answers to these questions.

## Bibliography

The principal reference tools for manuscript sources from this period are RISM, the *Census-Catalogue of Manuscript Sources of Polyphonic Music, 1400–1550*, ed. Charles Hamm and Herbert Kellman, 5 vols., Neuhausen-Stuttgart, 1979–88, and the Digital Image Archive of Medieval Music (www.diamm.ac.uk), the latter of which also holds digital reproductions of a growing number of sources as well as providing references to external image sources, editions, and secondary literature. The facsimile and source editions of the relevant repertory are too numerous to list here.

Alden, Jane, *Songs, Scribes, and Society: The History and Reception of the Loire Valley Chansonniers*, New York and Oxford, 2010

Atlas, Allan W. *Music at the Aragonese Court of Naples*, Cambridge, 1985

Bent, Margaret, "*Resfacta* and *Cantare Super Librum*," *JAMS* 36 (1983), 371–91

"Trent 93 and Trent 90: Johannes Wiser at Work," in *I codici musicali trentini a cento anni dalla loro riscoperta: Atti del Convegno "Laurence Feininger, la musicologia come missione,"* ed. Nino Pirrotta and Danilo Curti, Trento, 1986, 84–111

Berger, Anna Maria Busse, *Medieval Music and the Art of Memory*, Berkeley, 2005

Boorman, Stanley, "Sources, MS. I. Introduction," *Grove Music Online* (accessed 3 September 2012)

Brown, Howard Mayer, "Music for the Nuns of Verona: A Story about MS DCCLXI of the Biblioteca capitolare in Verona," in *Gestalt und Entstehung musikalischer Quellen*, ed. Staehelin, 111–24

Curtis, Gareth, and Andrew Wathey, "Fifteenth-Century English Liturgical Music: A List of the Surviving Repertory," *RMA Research Chronicle* 27 (1994), 1–69

Curtis, Liane, "Simon Mellet, Scribe of Cambrai Cathedral," *PMM* 8 (1999), 133–66

Dean, Jeffrey J., "Verona 755 and the *Incomprehensibilia* Composer," in *Manoscritti di polifonia nel Quattrocento europeo: Atti del Convegno internazionale di studi*, ed. Marco Gozzi, Trento, 2004, 93–108

Eisenstein, Elizabeth, *The Printing Press as an Agent of Change*, Cambridge, 1979

Filocamo, Gioia, ed., *Florence, BNC, Panciatichi 27: Text and Context*, Turnhout, 2010

Finscher, Ludwig, ed., *Datierung und Filiation von Musikhandschriften der Josquin-Zeit*, Quellenstudien zur Musik der Renaissance 2, Wiesbaden, 1983

Gancarczyk, Paweł, "Abbot Martin Rinkenberg and the Origins of the *Glogauer Liederbuch*," *EM* 37 (2009), 27–36

"The Dating and Chronology of the Strahov Codex," *Hudební Věda* 43 (2006), 135–46

Gerber, Rebecca L., ed. *Sacred Music from the Cathedral at Trent: Trent, Museo Provinciale d'Arte, Codex 1375 (olim 88)*, Monuments of Renaissance Music 12, Chicago, 2007

Haar, James, and John Nádas, "The Medici, the Signoria, the Pope: Sacred Polyphony in Florence, 1432–1448," *Recercare* 20 (2008), 25–93

Hamm, Charles, "Manuscript Structure in the Dufay Era," *AcM* 34 (1962), 166–84

Hascher-Burger, Ulrike, *Gesungene Innigkeit: Studien zu einer Musikhandschrift der Devotio Moderna (Utrecht, Universiteitsbibliotheek, ms. 16 H 34, olim B 113). Mit einer Edition der Gesänge*, Leiden, 2002

Higgins, Paula Marie, "Antoine Busnois and Musical Culture in Late Fifteenth-Century France and Burgundy," Ph.D. diss., Princeton University, 1987

Huglo, Michel, *Les Livres de chant liturgique*, Typologie des sources du moyen âge occidental 52, Turnhout, 1988

Just, Martin, ed., *Der Mensuralkodex Mus. ms. 40021 der Staatsbibliothek Preußischer Kulturbesitz Berlin*, 2 vols., Tutzing, 1975

Kellman, Herbert, ed., *The Treasury of Petrus Alamire: Music and Art in Flemish Court Manuscripts, 1500–1535*, Ghent and Amsterdam, 1999

Kirnbauer, Martin, *Hartmann Schedel und sein "Liederbuch": Studien zu einer spätmittelalterlichen Musikhandschrift (Bayerische Staatsbibliothek München, Cgm 810) und ihrem Kontext*, Bern, 2001

Kreitner, Kenneth, *The Church Music of Fifteenth-Century Spain*, Woodbridge, 2004

Mráčková, Lenka, "Behind the Stage: Some Thoughts on the Codex Speciálník and the Reception of Polyphony in Late 15th-Century Prague," *EM* 37 (2009), 37–48

Owens, Jessie Ann, *Composers at Work: The Craft of Musical Composition 1450–1600*, New York, 1997

Phelps, Michael, "A Repertory in Exile: Pope Eugene IV and the MS Modena, Biblioteca Estense Universitaria, Alpha. X.1.11," Ph.D. diss., New York University, 2008

Planchart, Alejandro Enrique, "Guillaume Du Fay's Benefices and his Relationship to the Court of Burgundy," *EMH* 8 (1988), 117–71

Reynolds, Christopher A., *Papal Patronage and the Music of St. Peter's, 1380–1513*, Berkeley, 1995

Rifkin, Joshua, "Munich, Milan, and a Marian Motet: Dating Josquin's *Ave Maria . . . virgo serena*," *JAMS* 56 (2003), 239–350

"A Scriptor, a Singer, and a Mother Superior: Another Story about MS DCCLXI of the Biblioteca Capitolare in Verona," in *Uno gentile et subtile ingenio: Studies in Renaissance Music in Honour of Bonnie J. Blackburn*, ed. M. Jennifer Bloxam, Gioia Filocamo, and Leofranc Holford-Strevens, Turnhout, 2009, 309–17

Rodin, Jesse, *Josquin's Rome: Hearing and Composing in the Papal Chapel*, New York, 2012

Rolsma, Saskia, "De onthullingen van het missaal: Een onderzoek naar de functie van Motetti missales," in *Meer dan muziek alleen: In memoriam Kees Vellekoop*, ed. R. E. V. Stuip, Hilversum, 2004, 291–305

Roth, Adalbert, "Die Entstehung des ältesten Chorbuches mit polyphoner Musik der päpstlichen Kapelle: Città del Vaticano, Biblioteca Apostolica Vaticana, Fondo Cappella Sistina, ms. 35," in *Gestalt und Entstehung musikalischer Quellen*, ed. Staehelin, 43–63

*Studien zum frühen Repertoire der päpstlichen Kapelle unter dem Pontificat Sixtus IV (1471–1484): Die Chorbücher 14 und 51 des Fondo Cappella Sistina der Biblioteca Apostolica Vaticana*, Vatican City, 1991

Saurma-Jeltsch, Liselotte E., *Spätformen mittelalterlicher Buchherstellung: Bilderhandschriften aus der Werkstatt Diebold Laubers in Hagenau*, 2 vols., Wiesbaden, 2001

Schmidt-Beste, Thomas, "Dedicating Music Manuscripts: On Function and Form of Paratexts in Fifteenth- and Sixteenth-Century Sources," in *"Cui Dono Lepidum Novum Libellum?": Dedicating Latin Works and Motets in the Sixteenth Century*, ed. Ignace Bossuyt *et al.*, Leuven, 2008, 81–108

"Private or Institutional – Small or Big? Towards a Typology of Polyphonic Sources of Renaissance Music," *JAF* 1 (2009), 13–26

*Textdeklamation in der Motette des 15. Jahrhunderts*, Turnhout, 2003

"Über Quantität und Qualität von Musikhandschriften des 16. Jahrhunderts," in *Die Münchner Hofkapelle des 16. Jahrhunderts im europäischen Kontext*, ed. Theodor Göllner and Bernhold Schmid, Munich, 2006, 191–211

Schubert, Peter, and Julie E. Cumming, "Text and Motif c. 1500: A New Approach to Text Underlay," *EM* 40 (2012), 3–14

Schwindt, Nicole, "Quellen," in *MGG*2, Sachteil 7, 1946–86

Sherr, Richard, ed., *Masses for the Sistine Chapel: Vatican City, Biblioteca Apostolica Vaticana, Cappella Sistina, MS 14*, Monuments of Renaissance Music 13, Chicago, 2009

*Papal Music Manuscripts in the Late Fifteenth and Early Sixteenth Centuries*, Neuhausen, 1996

Staehelin, Martin, ed., *Gestalt und Entstehung musikalischer Quellen im 15. und 16. Jahrhundert*, Quellenstudien zur Musik der Renaissance 3, Wiesbaden, 1998

Strohm, Reinhard, *The Rise of European Music, 1380–1500*, Cambridge, 1993

"Trienter Codices," in *MGG*2, Sachteil 9, 801–12

ed., *The Lucca Choirbook*, Late Medieval and Early Renaissance Music in Facsimile 2, Chicago and London, 2008

Talamo, Emilia Anna, *Codices Cantorum: Miniature e disegni nei codici della Cappella Sistina*, Florence, 1997

Wathey, Andrew, "Lost Books of Polyphony in England: A List to 1500," *RMA Research Chronicle* 21 (1988), 1–19

Wegman, Rob C., "From Maker to Composer: Improvisation and Musical Authorship in the Low Countries, 1450–1500," *JAMS* 49 (1996), 409–79

Williamson, Magnus, "Liturgical Polyphony in the Pre-Reformation English Parish Church: A Provisional List and Commentary," *RMA Research Chronicle* 38 (2005), 1–43

Wright, Peter, "On the Origins of Trent 87$_1$ and 92$_2$," *EMH* 6 (1986), 245–70

· PART IX GENRES ·

# The polyphonic mass in the fifteenth century

ANDREW KIRKMAN

While not quite its beginning and far from its end, the fifteenth century was certainly the polyphonic mass's heyday. The genre owes its historical importance to a combination of cultural and artistic factors, a productive concurrence whose impact has been felt in different – if likewise powerful – ways in its own time and ours. For clear cultural-historical reasons, it was an idea whose time had come: physical expression of eschatological concerns, responding to fear of purgatory, reached its peak at this time, as seen in expressions of devotion for intercession by the saints, and especially the Virgin, in church building, iconography of various kinds, ritual, and music. In its reuse of a preexisting melody, the cantus-firmus mass – the genre's predominant type and the primary focus of this chapter – embodied and expressed the key needs of its patrons, in terms of both spiritual welfare and public show, personal and political.[1] It typically involved the emblematic use of a melody, borrowed from outside the Mass liturgy and set in each of its five sections, and hence spanning very nearly the entire eucharistic rite within which it was embedded. The borrowed melody, which could be either sacred or secular in origin, thus inserted the proxy presence of the mass's endower and his or her particularized message into the central rite of the church and, crucially, its sacramental core: the elevation of the host, the location of the musical Sanctus.

This potential of the cantus-firmus mass to bring its donor into communion with Christ or one of the saints seems further to have fueled, in particular cases, the enrichment of cultural and political association connected with its usage and, in turn, musical borrowing and interquotation between pieces. A signal instance is the long dynasty of masses on *L'homme armé*, a phenomenon within which symbolic conflation of the spiritual battle of the priest at the altar with the bellicose self-image as soldiers of Christ of those secular lords who paid for

---

1 For a thorough treatment of this phenomenon see Kirkman, *Cultural Life*.

the melody's polyphonic settings created its own momentum in terms of courtly magnificence and musical dialogue between its composers.[2]

It is thus easy to see how the polyphonic mass became a forum for high musical invention on an unprecedentedly lavish scale. Like the great musical showpieces of any culture, it attracted the best talents, drawn by its technical and expressive possibilities and, whether directly or indirectly, its attendant opportunities for career and pecuniary advantage. Like their colleagues throughout the ages, composers of masses inevitably exercised their musical invention in the context of the possibilities – formal, textural, social, religious, political, and so on – made available and fostered by their particular social and institutional surroundings. In the case of the cantus-firmus principle, inventive musical minds were presented with a remarkable field of opportunity: the demand for particularity, coupled with the contrapuntal and general technical fields of possibility, was endless and endlessly challenging. The point bears emphasis: admittance of "composerly" possibilities to be explored within the format of a given musical structure is not incompatible with acknowledgment of the cultural forces that allowed that structure to emerge and flourish; indeed, as for musical expression more generally, the two are inextricably intertwined.

In the case of the mass, the particular nature of that expression, involving the overarching, multi-movement enfolding of a single melody within a rich and vastly extended polyphonic fabric, gained a particular purchase in a post-Enlightenment age concerned with a more "internally"-focused sense of unity. Situated as we are in a world still pervaded by such priorities, we should certainly be wary of ascribing similar motivations to composers writing in a world for which a unifying focus of that nature had no meaning. On the other hand, to fail to acknowledge the "unity" (or whatever we may choose to call it) encompassed by the repeated use of a cantus firmus throughout most poly-phonic masses of the fifteenth century simply on the grounds of the very different perspective on that selfsame feature in a later age would be equally misguided. While the cantus-firmus mass does not owe its format to the purely structural and "organic" unitary motivations familiar to our own age, it undeniably embraces a type of "unity" expressive of fifteenth-century con-cerns, one that, furthermore, composers took up and cultivated with great ingenuity. The central and perhaps most culturally absorbing point in this connection concerns the potential for a phenomenon fashioned according to particular societal needs to acquire very different meaning when viewed

---

2 Ibid., 98–134. See also Jesse Rodin's contribution to the present volume, Ch. 4. On dialogue, see Taruskin, "Antoine Busnoys," 262–65 and Burn, "Nam erit."

according to the criteria of another age. One might say indeed that this is a potentiality indispensable for any cultural artifact to accrue meaningfulness beyond the world that gave it birth.

It is impossible in the present context to give a comprehensive history of polyphonic mass compositions in the fifteenth century, and to attempt to do so would in any case be redundant: more comprehensive treatments of the genre and its composers are available in the *New Grove* and – with respect to some of its major contributors – in individual monographs.[3] Rob Wegman's website *Renaissance Masses, 1440–1520* (www.robcwegman.org/mass.htm) lists 689 Mass Ordinary cycles, a fair proportion of which is accessible on the site in the form of sound files. A significant minority (129) falls into the category of "sine nomine" Masses: those that lack known musical antecedents. Unsurprisingly, a preponderance of the most neglected works lies in this group: scholarship has traditionally found easier purchase on pieces with describable and measurable antecedents. That group, and especially its anonymous members, still holds considerable scope for stylistic study, especially in relating its members to masses by the more familiar composers and those written using more easily definable techniques.

The more nebulous end of musical interrelationships brings us up against the question of agency: as late as the mid-fifteenth-century corpus of Trent 88 we encounter series of mass movements that apparently owe their grouping to scribal rather than to compositional initiative.[4] Margaret Bent reminds us that our view of the extent of early mass pairs and three-movement partial cycles may, to a larger degree than we might imagine, be colored by the predilections of the scribe of Bologna Q.15: on the one hand he seems to have paired movements that were originally separate; on the other, examples of what appear to us to be fragmentary three-movement groupings may be erstwhile complete mass settings cut down by him for his own idiosyncratic reasons, for example to present "cycles" by associated pairs of composers.[5]

The polyphonic setting – dating back to the earliest stages of polyphony – of liturgical chants also continues throughout the fifteenth century and beyond. This practice is most characteristic of Mass Proper settings, and of two "hybrid" Ordinary/Proper genres: the surviving handful of plenary masses[6]

---

3 Some well-known and useful examples are Fallows, *Dufay*; Fallows, *Josquin*; Wegman, *Born for the Muses*; and Fitch, *Johannes Ockeghem: Masses and Models*.

4 See, for example, the "composite" cycle in Trent 88, fols. 54v–61v, copied in the late 1450s.

5 Bent, *Bologna Q15*, 1:153–57. Thus a "cycle" comprising Kyrie, Sanctus, and Agnus by Du Fay and Gloria and Credo by Zacara da Teramo appears in Besseler's edition of Du Fay's works as a *fragmentum tripartitum* comprising Kyrie, Sanctus, and Agnus (Dufay, *Opera omnia*, 4:8–14).

6 At least two examples – the *Missa Sancti Jacobi* and Mass for St. Anthony of Padua – are by Du Fay; it seems hard to ignore the possibility, as argued by Philip Weller in the sleeve notes for the recording of the mass by the Binchois Consort (Hyperion, CDA 67474), that a plenary cycle for St. Anthony Abbot surviving

and the Requiem mass, a genre that seems to have emerged only in the later fifteenth century in works by Guillaume Du Fay (lost), Johannes Ockeghem, Antoine Brumel, Pierre de La Rue, and Dionysius Prioris.

A series of (interconnecting) histories could be written to address each of these subgenres; however, this brief chapter will focus on complete, five-movement masses, in most cases based on a single preexisting model. This is the defining, and by far the numerically predominant, type of the era, and one that permits the following of a continuous thread through the period. While the importance of the cyclic mass clearly persists way beyond the fifteenth century, the tenor mass gives way increasingly in subsequent years to the "parody" or "imitation" type based on polyphonic antecedents, and it is surely fair to say that the balance of importance generally tilts in favor of the motet.

Clearly myriad narratives could be charted even through the cantus-firmus corpus; what I shall attempt here is to trace a path through a series of particularly significant, and by at least some criteria representative, examples which, *in toto*, give a powerful sense of the stylistic sweep of the genre in this, its richest period. However, the focus here will be less on the behavior of cantus firmi per se (a topic richly served in the past) than on the contrapuntal interactions that weave together musical fabric and character, and also – to some extent – on the original cultural meanings that they expressed.

## The beginnings of the "cyclic" mass

The structural principle of the "cyclic" mass based on a given cantus firmus clearly grew out of the motet-based practice of isorhythm, with its similar repetition – albeit within the frame of a single "movement" – of a preexistent melody.[7] Such borrowing, a practice with a clear affinity to the widespread late medieval procedure of "glossing" on Scripture, opened up limitless possibilities for the particularizing of the Ordinary sections of the Mass that in their bare textual form were the common property of every celebration of the rite. Indeed there are good grounds for suggesting that five-section cyclic masses – comprising the usual succession of Kyrie, Gloria, Credo, Sanctus, and Agnus Dei – were conceptualized by their early composers and users as successions of five "motets."[8] That viewpoint is easy to grasp in the context of the fourteenth-century mass groupings – including the Tournai, Barcelona, Toulouse,

in Trent 89 is in fact Du Fay's documented cycle for that saint. A further, Marian, plenary mass ascribed to Reginaldus Libert has likewise been ascribed to a composer associated with Cambrai, the "Reginaldus" documented there as master of the boys in 1424. See Ward, "Libert, Reginaldus."
7 As Bukofzer noted, "[the cantus firmus] is ... an isorhythmic tenor the *taleae* of which have grown to gigantic proportions, namely an entire movement." *Studies in Medieval and Renaissance Music*, 263.
8 Kirkman, *Cultural Life*, 30–31.

Besançon, and even Machaut mass – whose contiguity seems motivated in the first place by liturgical and performance/practical concerns rather than "internal" musical ones. But it is clear too in the context of the many early fifteenth-century settings of single movements and Gloria–Credo and Sanctus–Agnus Dei pairs.

From a purely musical viewpoint, such pairs would clearly seem to constitute the "incubation chamber" for the idea of purely *musical* linkage between settings of Mass Ordinary sections that are liturgically separated in time and function. From there it was presumably a small step to the notion of musical linkage across all five sections and the consequent possibility to particularize any given instantiation of the ritual in which the (multi-)piece was embedded. While it can be difficult, or even impossible, to differentiate compositional from scribal intentionality among this subset of pieces, clearly compositional pairs are demonstrable in manuscripts from the early decades of the fifteenth century, particularly Bologna Q.15, the Old Hall Manuscript, and the early Trent codices 87 and 92. Frequently the linkages seem to be limited to ranges, modes, and scoring; in other words, they are apparently motivated, as in the cases of the fourteenth-century "cycles" mentioned above, more by exigencies of performance than by an interest in a cogent system of interquotation.

A few mass pairs do, however, clearly make that leap, albeit in multifarious stylistic and technical ways. Among them are the two Gloria–Credo pairs by Johannes Ciconia that form the opening items of the *Collected Works* volume.[9] The second of these is among the few pairs whose movements (though not contiguous in any source) show similarities of tenor profile, though not in any formulaic fashion. Another is a Gloria–Credo pair in Bologna Q.15 by Hugo de Lantins whose movements are bound together by a repeated tenor pattern and its rhythmic imitations in the superius, but which similarly lacks the formulaic repetitions characteristic of isorhythm and full cantus-firmus practice.[10]

Incorporation of an outside melody that could carry emblematic significance was clearly the other staple of the cantus-firmus procedure. A group of early fifteenth-century mass movements by Zacara da Teramo and Bartolomeo da Bologna that each draw more or less extensively on the polyphonic substance of a song provide early examples,[11] as – on the sacred side – do Johannes Franchois de Gemblaco's Credo based on the Marian antiphon *Alma Redemptoris mater* and Rentius de Ponte Curvo's Gloria on the responsory *Descendit angelus* for the Nativity of St John the Baptist.[12]

9 Ciconia, *Works*, 1–24; discussed in the Introduction, xi–xii; critical commentary on 198–200.
10 Discussed in Gossett, "Techniques," 218–22.
11 Editions in *Early Fifteenth-Century Music*, ed. Reaney.    12 See Gossett, "Techniques," 222.

Where and when the two phenomena of outside borrowing and common quotation from movement to movement first came together is unclear. Whether, for example, the repeated tenor material in the aforementioned mass pairs by Ciconia and Lantins is preexistent or original is impossible to say; similarly, the origins of the iambic tenor melody (or melodies) that – in direct and varied repetitions – underpin the unique and enigmatic mass cycle that was copied as a late addition in the Cypriot Turin Codex (Turin J.II.9) are likely to remain obscure.[13] While these examples offer interesting points of comparison with the fully-fledged cantus-firmus masses emerging in England around the same time or slightly later, there seems no reason to postulate any linkage between the scattered emergences of these related ideas beyond common and widespread societal and ecclesiastical needs. Whatever the connection – or lack of it – between these pieces, it at any rate seems beyond dispute that the most consistent, and certainly the most influential, early experiments of this nature took place in England.

## England and the early cantus-firmus mass

The emergence and proliferation of polyphonic cyclic masses in England in the early fifteenth century constitutes one of a wide range of contemporary English outpourings of personal and corporate piety. The effect of this is still clearly visible today in the enormous contemporary expansion in the rebuilding, extension, and elaboration of churches that occurred at the time. A. H. Thompson noted that

> There is no period at which money was lavished so freely on English parish churches as in the fifteenth century ... In church after church ... the stonemason provided the framework for the exhibition of the full powers of artists and craftsmen in wood-carving and stained glass, in painting and in tomb-making.[14]

A similar point could be made of the cantus firmus, its larger armature likewise providing the frame for, and interacting harmoniously with, small-scale filigree work rather as local detail is subsumed within the constraining lines of perpendicular architecture.

Such architectural elegance is fundamental to what by common consent is one of the earliest cantus-firmus cycles: Leonel Power's *Missa Alma redemptoris mater*, composed – to judge from its source tradition – during or before the

---

13 Edition in *The Cypriot-French Repertory*, ed. Hoppin, 84–95. The mass lacks an Agnus Dei.
14 Thompson, *The English Clergy*, 128. See also Duffy, *The Stripping of the Altars*, 132.

1430s.[15] In three voices rather than the four that became customary beginning, a decade or so later, with the anonymous English cycles *Caput* and *Veterem hominem*, the mass is underpinned by statements of the first half of the eponymous antiphon, repeated "isorhythmically" from movement to movement. The cantus firmus, drawn from one of the four great Marian antiphons that, sung at the end of the Office of Compline, divide up the seasons of the church year, is laid out, typically for its time, in long note values and divided up by rests without apparent regard for any phrase structure implied by its original text. The fact that the mass survives only in Continental sources surely explains its lack of a Kyrie: following English festal tradition, that movement was most likely, in the piece's original state, to be an elaborate setting of a prosula text that was unusable in Continental contexts.

Typically of its milieu in general and its composer in particular, the mass offers a tableau of elegant gestures and motifs, interwoven with great lucidity and poise. Seldom directly responsive to the meaning of its texts in ways one might be given to expect from later practices, its texture is formed rather from an endlessly varied interweaving of dialogues: between musical and textual phrases, between chant and its elaboration, and between its freely interweaving superius and contratenor lines.

The tenor line, monolithically repeating in contour and rhythm from movement to movement, provides melodic material for the other voices and a rhythmic check on their progress in fully-scored sections. By contrast, its absence when resting permits the unconstrained superius and contratenor to cut loose in freely intertwining arabesques, now sharing each other's pace, now contrasting freely flowing soliloquies against more static underpinning. The superius more often traces a conjunctly undulating, "melodic" path, and seldom, unlike the contratenor, shares its rhythmic profile with the tenor. At points of cadence, though, it hands over to the contratenor – typically for its time – the responsibility for rhythmic vitality. Imitation, seldom at this period a thoroughgoing technique as it was to become in the next century, nonetheless adds its thread here and there to the larger tapestry, articulating the texture by its singularity rather than saturating it.

The concluding passage of the Credo (Example 35.1) will suffice to demonstrate the range, density, and freedom of contrapuntal interchange. At "Confiteor unum baptisma" ("I acknowledge one baptism") the superius, its original coloration indicating triple relationships against the continuing duplets of the other voices, branches out on its own rhythmic and metrical

---

15  See Bibliography for edition and recording.

Example 35.1 Leonel Power, *Missa Alma Redemptoris mater*, Credo, mm. 126–46

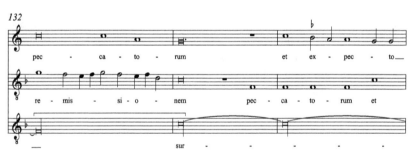

Example 35.1 (cont.)

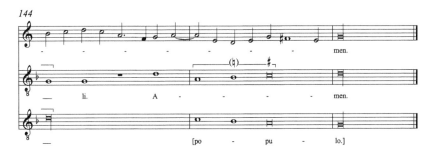

path before, at "in remissionem" ("in remission [of sins]"), joining with the contratenor in strict imitation. Over a long held C in the tenor, at "[et expecto] resurrectionem" ("I await the resurrection") the superius takes off on another flight of rhythmical fancy while the contratenor stamps out a syllabic passage firmly underscoring the basic pulse. The beginning of the last phrase, "Et vitam," emerges clearly from the texture via a simple homorhythmic gesture in parallel motion in the superius and contratenor, while with the final Amen the upper voice winds up the proceedings typically with a melismatic flourish.

Although – especially in this period of variable transmission of text underlay – notions of text delineation are typically open to dispute, these final phrases of the Credo are sculpted with distinctiveness and at least putative reference to meaning. The singular nature of the baptism seems acknowledged by the strongly individualized departure, in coloration, of the superius;[16] conversely, the plurality of sins receives similarly plural motivic statement in the two upper voices; the resurrection awaited attracts a more hubristic response in the melismatic upper voice, while the life to come is underscored by homophony, with the same line rising to its highest note, heard on only five prior occasions in the Credo. This last observation with regard to range acquires added point in the closing bars of the Agnus Dei, where, on "dona nobis pacem" ("grant us peace"), the contratenor soars up, for the first and only time, to inhabit its highest realm, topped by C on the modern treble stave.

That the cyclic mass was indeed an idea that articulated the needs of its time with particular precision is clear from the rapid transmission of English cycles onto Continental Europe, and, in short order, its takeup by Continental composers. Known, like so many English pieces of the time, only from Continental transmission, the Power mass was joined in the same range of manuscripts by a wide range of English mass settings and other intercessory pieces. As has often been noted, English music, and especially sacred music, enjoyed an international vogue at this time unequaled before the twentieth century. Yet one mass in particular reveals a tone and style that, in retrospect at least, seem the very quintessence of mass writing in the middle years of the fifteenth century: the anonymous *Missa Caput*.[17]

To judge from its transmission, the English *Missa Caput* was one of the most revered compositions of the fifteenth century: it survives in no fewer than seven manuscripts, more than for any other mass written before the 1480s. But its importance is measurable in far more than just the number of copies that have escaped destruction. At least two composers – Johannes Ockeghem and Jacob Obrecht – used it as a model for masses of their own, copying its cantus firmus exactly in profile, rhythm, and even the minutest notational detail; but its impact may well have gone a lot further than this: it seems to have been a key work in spawning a whole range of masses by Continental composers constructed on similar lines, and one of the earliest pieces to have added a fourth, low contratenor part in the bass range to the three-voice texture that was standard around the time it was composed (probably in the 1440s). This four-voice idiom, a forerunner of our standard SATB, spread rapidly through

---

16 Conversely, as Jesse Rodin points out to me, in later settings this passage is sometimes singled out for homorhythmic treatment, perhaps referring to the unitary bonding of the whole church in the taking of this sacrament.
17 See Bibliography for edition (ed. Planchart) and recording.

western Europe, and within about thirty years it had largely taken over as the standard texture for art music.[18]

A fifteenth-century mass cycle was typically identified in manuscript copies by the first word or words originally set to the melody borrowed for its tenor. In the case of the *Caput* mass this was the clue that more than half a century ago led Manfred Bukofzer to identify its structural melody (and that of its imitators) as a long melisma on the word "caput" drawn from an antiphon, *Venit ad Petrum*, found in various English and French liturgical uses.[19] The originating chant came from a ritual for the Washing of the Feet held on Maundy Thursday. The text comprises a dialogue between Jesus and Peter in which Jesus states: "If I wash thee not, thou hast no part with me." Peter replies: "Lord, not my feet only, but also my hands and my *head*."

Identification of the antecedent chant did not, however, provide an unambiguous reason for its choice as the basis for the anonymous mass and, subsequently, those of Ockeghem and Obrecht. No definitive answer to this question has ever been found (and none is likely to be). But, in explaining the extended life of a cantus firmus beyond its originary application, it would seem reasonable to look for a widely applicable, "exemplary" meaning that had the potential to be enriched and deepened by additional meanings in a broader range of contexts. With this in mind I proposed that the original, fundamental reference of the "caput" melisma was to the Pauline characterization – still deeply embedded in modern Christian theology – of Christ as head of the church that is his body.[20] As in the case of *L'homme armé*, probably used as a cantus firmus first and foremost in reference to Christ, the ultimate "Christian soldier," such a potent putative image would undoubtedly have made it attractive to endowers of masses as the potential bearer of a range of references to further, earthly figures – in both sacred and secular realms – seeking to affirm an authority, grounded in that of Christ, as "head" of his body here on earth.[21]

Whatever its origins, the grand scale and enhanced texture of this mass surely bespeak a lofty purpose. They also make for illuminating comparison with Power's *Missa Alma Redemptoris mater*, its senior by perhaps only a decade or so. In contrast to the single cantus-firmus statement in each movement of Power's mass, the anonymous *Caput* mass provides an early, and perhaps originating, example of the so-called "double-cursus" format

18 Wegman, "Petrus de Domarto," 295–97.
19 Bukofzer, *Studies in Medieval and Renaissance Music*, 226–30.
20 *Cultural Life*, 77–97.
21 For a very different interpretation see Robertson, "The Savior, the Woman, and the Head of the Dragon."

whereby each movement embraces two statements of the cantus firmus in distinct rhythmicizations, respectively in triple and duple meter. Also making an early appearance here is the so-called "head motif," a repeated aural tag that served, at the opening of each movement, to draw attention to the linkage between the liturgically dispersed sections of a cyclic mass. In so doing the repeated openings immediately announced the diverse movements' linkage and their shared role in embracing, and particularizing, a single overarching symbolic message.

But the most fundamental stylistic shift exemplified in this mass concerns its four-voice scoring. The fourth voice, at the bottom of the texture and variously described in the sources as "contra secundus" or "tenor secundus," adds far more than simply a textural augmentation: in shifting the borrowed tenor from an outer to an inner position in the texture, it permits a degree of flexibility and expressive freedom far beyond what was possible in the three-voice idiom evinced by Power's mass. The resulting impression, compared to the comparatively short-breathed Power mass, is of a more leisurely musical argument, its pace less obviously predetermined by its borrowed tune.

Part of that impression derives also from the broadening of the contrapuntal roles of the four voices of *Caput* compared with those of the three-voice style evinced by the Power mass. From the perspective of contrapuntal orthodoxy, the standard three-voice texture essentially comprises "2 plus 1": on the one hand a tenor/superius pair forming the basic contrapuntal framework with its cadence-articulating octaves; and on the other the "ancillary" contratenor part, filling out the texture, weaving the fabric together, and keeping things moving at cadences. The textural hierarchy of the Power mass is underscored also – in a link to the practice of isorhythm – by the almost consistent movement of the tenor in longer notes than those of the other voices.

The rhythmicization of the *Caput* tenor likewise begins in each statement with long note values, allowing for the conventional stately unfurling of sound, following an introductory duo, that typifies the movements of mid-century cantus-firmus masses. But for the most part (and especially at the ends of sections) it is less obviously differentiated from the profiles of its companions. This is especially noticeable in the second, duple-meter section of each movement, in which the rhythmic pace of the tenor approximates more closely and consistently that of the other voices. This relative rhythmic parity in each duple section serves also to support another feature typical of later fifteenth-century masses: a sense of rhythmic acceleration toward the conclusion of each movement. While the superius is undoubtedly the "busiest" part overall, the weaving together of all available combinations of duo and trio texture into a vigorous interchange makes for an exhilarating and constantly variegated work from the first notes of the Kyrie to the stately conclusion of the Agnus Dei, ushered in by a rare, if brief, moment of rhythmic imitation in all four voices.

This mass (or at least the idiom it exemplifies) marks a key moment in fifteenth-century mass composition, one whose stylistic implications continue to play out over the following several decades. While our picture of sacred music of the time is surely skewed by the serious lack of manuscripts from northern Europe, it appears from the southern European sources that do survive that aspects of the *Caput* idiom must have rippled out quickly beyond its native land, and perhaps nowhere more significantly than in our next witness, the *Missa Spiritus almus* by Petrus de Domarto.[22]

## Northern Europe at mid-century:
## Domarto and Du Fay

Though not entirely unrecognized hitherto, Domarto's stock has in recent years been assured by a seminal article by Rob Wegman. Wegman contextualized *Spiritus almus* as a linchpin historical work both in terms of its advocacy of the four-voice "*Caput*" texture with low contratenor, and in its radical and influential application of mensural cantus-firmus manipulation. While this latter development culminated (as we shall see) in the masses of Obrecht, it also embraced one and perhaps two cycles by Domarto's apparently younger contemporary Antoine Busnoys: the *Missa O crux lignum* and (if it is, as Wegman has argued, by Busnoys) the *Missa L'Ardant desir*.[23] All three of these masses share the characteristic of basing each section on a tune in the same written form that, under the aegis of various mensuration signs, assumes different rhythmic shapes in performance.[24]

As in the case of the *Caput* mass, the structural melody is a melismatic phrase, in this instance one set to the words "spiritus almus" ("nourishing spirit"), that concludes the Marian responsory *Stirps Jesse*. The allusion in the text is to the tree of Jesse: the Holy "family tree," familiar from depictions in stained-glass windows, linking Jesse, the father of David, with the Virgin and Christ. The spirit in question is the Holy Spirit, as underscored by the mass's head motif, drawn from the Introit trope for the Mass of the Holy Spirit, *Spiritus almus adest*. Robert Nosow has associated the mass, and a linked motet, with a Holy Spirit mass and motet endowed by Philip the Good, Duke of Burgundy to be

---

22 See Bibliography for edition and recording.    23 Wegman, "Another Mass by Busnoys?"
24 For more on this procedure see Emily Zazulia's essay in the present volume, Ch. 31.

performed annually on 16 August for his soul in the Church of Our Lady in Bruges from 1451 until 1466, the last occurrence of the feast before the duke's death.[25] *Spiritus almus* is thus apparently a witness, like some of the early masses on *L'homme armé*, to the lavish image creation of the Valois Court of Burgundy under its two last and most illustrious dukes.

Although no more than a few years can separate the *Missa Spiritus almus*, probably composed around 1450, from the *Missa Caput* whose textural layout it shares, the aural impression of the two masses is quite different. The constantly varying interactions and registral shifts of the earlier work are contrasted here with a stratified texture more frequently pitting slowly-moving lower parts against busier upper ones, a generally low tessitura, short-breathed rhythmic and melodic ideas, and motivic interplay residing predominantly in the exchange of brief motifs between the top two voices. To modern ears accustomed to more obvious "hook" this is a harder nut to crack. But after a few hearings attentive listeners will start to perceive that the idiom here, though of a different kind, is equally absorbing. Shifts of texture – full and sedate to reduced and more active – shape the larger contours, while playful interactions between the upper voices and artful interjections from the bass drape the scaffolding tune with a tissue of great, if more local, interest and finesse.

As is typically the case with cantus-firmus masses, the role of the borrowed melody is much more pervasive and influential on the fabric as a whole than appears at first blush to be the case. In this connection it is perhaps too infrequently borne in mind how much our perception of texture can be influenced by performance and listening conventions. For example, a tendency to vocal homogeneity in modern performances and the top-down listening encouraged by modern score format engender types of perception that may be more characteristic of the twenty-first century than the fifteenth. A step back from modern listening habits can begin to suggest the extent to which a composer like Domarto could harness the conventions and possibilities available to him to bring out details to which we as modern listeners may be less well attuned.

A series of cases in point is offered by statements of the "B" section of the structural chant.[26] Although beginning only a third higher than the melody's opening, the higher tessitura of this chant section's opening, coupled with its movement in regular breves, allows it to emerge resoundingly from the

---

25  Nosow, *Ritual Meanings*, 106–18.
26  See the layout of the chant as given in Wegman, "Petrus de Domarto," 245.

Example 35.2  Petrus de Domarto, *Missa Spiritus almus*, Kyrie, mm. 40–48

predominantly low-range texture, a potentiality exploited in various ways. An artful instance can be seen in the Christe, where the tenor 2 (the lowest voice) drops out to allow the long notes of the cantus firmus entry to intertwine with the more active other voices before, through supporting it in a duo, showcasing it as the higher of the two sounding parts (see Example 35.2).

Elsewhere it stands out hieratically against the quicker pace of its companion voices. This can be seen in Example 35.3, the opening statement of the tune in the Gloria, where, under the aegis of the ¢ mensuration, it moves in augmentation vis-à-vis the other voices (Tinctoris's "error of the English").[27]

---

27 On Tinctoris's reprimands of Domarto's mensural usage, including this one, see Wegman, "Petrus de Domarto," 238 and 252.

Example 35.3 Domarto, *Missa Spiritus almus*, Gloria, mm. 7–15

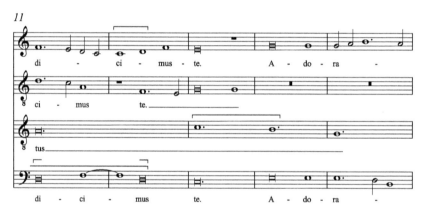

Conversely, in other instances its role as the driving engine of the structure emerges clearly, especially when, at the ends of the Gloria and Credo, its assumption of C3 mensuration forces a gear change that pulls the other voices into a triplet-based drive to the cadence (see Example 35.4).

As in *Caput*, a brief head motif signals the common origin of the movements and, in their original context, the particularization and personalization of the ritual event to whose message they gave voice. That message is played out with increasing insistence from movement to movement, with the introductory duo extending from just over two measures (Kyrie), to six (Gloria), to nine (Credo), to twelve (Sanctus), before contracting again to three measures in the Agnus, its sense of restored sobriety underscored by the transposition down an octave into the lowest voice of the line sung in prior movements by the contratenor altus.

Example 35.4 Domarto, *Missa Spiritus almus*, Credo, mm. 147–52

One senses in the larger shape of the work a great arch, which must have lent a satisfying sense of unity to the ritual in which it was embedded. Conversely, at the opposite end of the scale the action of the mass is marked locally by elegantly sculpted phrases and subtle interactions, making it a grateful and engrossing work for attentive singers and listeners alike.

While conceivably a direct contemporary of *Spiritus almus*, our next witness, Guillaume Du Fay's *Missa Se la face ay pale*, offers a radical stylistic contrast, emphasizing once more the remarkable diversity embraced by the genre even in its early days. Two contrasting hypotheses have been advanced to explain its genesis. Responding to its bright, celebratory tone and amorous lyric, Alejandro Planchart suggested that it might have been composed to celebrate the consummation, in 1452, of the marriage between the Dauphin Amadeus (later Amadeus IX) of Savoy and Yolande, daughter of Charles VII of France.[28] A recent hypothesis by Anne Walters Robertson has by contrast linked it to the arrival there of the Holy (later "Turin") Shroud in 1453.[29] At any rate, all commentators have concurred in placing the mass in the 1450s during Du Fay's second stint of employment at the Court of Savoy, and hence coinciding with the first copy of the mass, made in the late 1450s, in Trent 88. Such an origin receives further support from the likely composition of Du Fay's ballade, on whose tenor it is based, during his earlier phases of employment at the same court in the 1430s.[30]

The *Missa Se la face ay pale* is part of the first flowering, from the middle of the century, of mass cycles based on secular antecedents.[31] This new trend is combined with a more retrospective one in the foundation of the Gloria and Credo on the structural principles of isorhythm, with the rhythms of the model song appearing in each movement in a series of three proportionally diminishing statements – creating a strong "drive" to the conclusion in each case – and an identical layout producing movements of precisely equal length.[32] In its combination of obvious structural pairings between Gloria and Credo, on the one hand, and Sanctus and Agnus, on the other, with an outlying Kyrie, the cycle also harks back to the single movements and mass pairs that mark out the prehistory of the full polyphonic cycle. Yet for all that, the amalgamation of characteristics brought together in the mass makes for a structural approach that is radically new.[33] The same is true of its sound: contemporary hearers must have been struck by the mass's remarkable lucidity, a quality that has made it, to modern listeners and students, perhaps the most familiar and approachable cantus-firmus cycle of the mid-fifteenth century.

As in the *Caput* and Domarto masses, the opening of the polyphony in each movement is heralded by a head motif, presented consistently in duo texture in all movements except the Kyrie (see Example 35.5). Having announced itself as the opening phrase, however, the motif is followed in each movement by a phrase that is entirely distinctive, almost like a series of different answers to the same gently posed question. The cadences to each answer alternate between C and G (although the final of each movement is on F): the Kyrie on C; the Gloria

---

28  Planchart, "Fifteenth-Century Masses," 5–7.
29  Robertson, "The Man with the Pale Face."        30  Fallows, *Dufay*, 70.
31  Mass movements based on songs by Zacara da Teramo and Bartolomeo da Bologna push back the origins of the notion at least to the early fifteenth century, though in contrast to later cantus-firmus practice these are essentially modified song contrafacta.
32  For a useful chart of the layout of the cantus firmus across the course of the mass see Brown and Stein, *Music in the Renaissance*, 46.
33  The novelty was noted by Strohm: "The combination of the two elements ... – a cantus firmus of secular origin but treated in a strictly motet-like, four-part format – is about the only solution which the English had not attempted by then." (*The Rise of European Music*, 416.)

Example 35.5 Guillaume Du Fay, *Missa Se la face ay pale*, opening of each movement

on G (with the third in the superius); the Credo with a newly confident surge through a tenth and again ending on C; the Sanctus back to G; and finally the Agnus again on C.

Each response seems to set a tone that is then played out in the ensuing polyphony. In reality, however, the dialogue is always controlled and tempered by the tenor that, emerging at strategic points from the texture, reminds us repeatedly of its presence with greater or lesser insistence. Its role would have been even more prominent if, as seems at least possible, it was played by a trumpeter, perhaps the one who, along with singers and organist, was employed as part of the Savoy Chapel at least from 1449 until 1455 and probably (though earlier chapel accounts are lost) from 1428 or earlier.[34] This is most obvious in the case of the systematic alternations between full scoring and reduced (particularly duo) texture, which in the Gloria and Credo follow the same systematic pattern.

Yet the tenor's role in the contrapuntal gamesmanship goes much further than this. First, Du Fay makes endlessly varied play of the distinction or similarity of rhythmic profile between the tenor and the other voices. As an example, in the triple-time sections of the Gloria and Credo the faster-moving passages of the tenor, moving three times more slowly than in the model song, set up jazzy hemiolas. This can be seen to fine effect in Example 35.6 from the Gloria, where the effect is exposed by setting the tenor as the lower voice of a duo.

Much play is also made of the contrasting tessituras of different parts of the model tune, with its fanfare-like passages centered on high G piping clearly out of the texture and setting off a variety of contrapuntal ripples. This is nowhere more powerful and climactic than in the closing measures of the Gloria and Credo. In these two movements the progression between the three statements of the scaffold tune, in, respectively, threefold augmentation, double augmentation, and finally at the original pace, creates a strong sense of build across the contrapuntal canvas. With the profile of the melody – announcing itself in the highest range of the tenor part and moving at the same pace as its companion parts – emerging with clarity at the end of each movement, moreover, the last clutch of high heralding notes in the tenor sets a powerful scene for the closing quotation of the exuberant triadic pattern that had also concluded the song (see Example 35.7).

Far from being mere handmaids of the tenor, however, each of the other voices adds its own sculptured contribution to the elegant amalgam. Growing acquaintance serves only to augment admiration of the judiciousness of Du Fay's

---

34 Bouquet, "La cappella musicale," 251–52.

Example 35.6  Du Fay, *Missa Se la face ay pale*, Gloria, mm. 43–46

balance between melodic consistency and variety. In terms of the former, listeners cannot fail to absorb, even if only subliminally, the repeated returns to the rhythmic pattern of the superius in the first bar of the head motif, in its original or inverted form. For another example see Example 35.8, three statements of the same dovetailed falling figure in its different guises in, respectively, Gloria, Credo, and Agnus Dei, in each case leading to the same conclusion on C. The fact that one can listen to, or perform, this lovely work many times over without necessarily being directly conscious of its subtle repetitions and rhythmic interplays seems an important key to its remarkable achievement.

The focus on a mass based on a secular antecedent raises the question, which has long been a vexed one in musical scholarship, concerning the role of secular music in the most sacred and defining ritual of the Christian church. As is now widely recognized, many of these songs must have been chosen for their potential to give voice to veneration of the Virgin Mary, prime intercessor for human souls at the Court of Heaven.[35] Here composers built on a musical and textual tradition extending back to the thirteenth-century motet in which the expression, in the poems of courtly love, of devotion for an unattainable lady could also be understood as directed, on a spiritual plane, toward the Virgin.[36] In this context the plea to Christ's mother – directly via a Marian chant or in the substitute form of a courtly love song – would, it was hoped,

35 See Bloxam, "A Cultural Context," *passim*, and Brown, "Music and Ritual"; Rothenberg's discussion of a series of applications of secular polyphonic settings in "Marian Feasts," plus his contribution to this volume, Ch. 28; Kirkman, *Cultural Life*, 43–50.

36 For this aspect of the thirteenth-century motet see particularly Huot, *Allegorical Play*. Maniates outlined the same parallel in the context of a group of late fifteenth- and early sixteenth-century motets that draw on preexistent courtly songs (see "Combinative Techniques," 188–93). See also Bloxam, "A Cultural Context," 13–15. Rothenberg ("Marian Feasts") analyzes the nature and foci of Marian symbolism in the late Middle Ages and addresses them in a series of case studies from the thirteenth to the sixteenth century.

Example 35.7  Du Fay, *Missa Se la face ay pale*, Credo, mm. 271–80

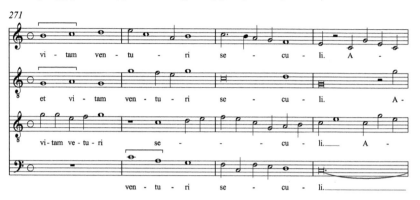

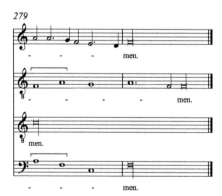

Example 35.8  Du Fay, *Missa Se la face ay pale*: (a) Gloria, mm. 49–52; (b) Credo, mm. 169–72; (c) Agnus Dei, mm. 27–29

(a)
*49*

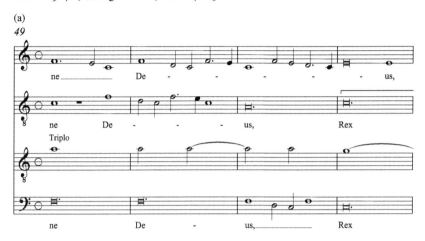

(b)
*169*

activate her desired grace at the one moment on earth (the transubstantiation at Mass) when her son, the judge of earthly souls, would become physically present. It is this powerful sense of advocacy that surely explains the advent and sudden spread of chanson-based masses in the later fifteenth century.

Viewed in this light, the congruence between the poetic register of the courtly love lyric and the rhetoric of Marian devotion was a highly propitious one. By contrast, the typically male gendering of the narrator of the love lyric would seem, at first sight, to have precluded in many cases the reuse of secular material to carry Christological significance. However, the ungendered status of the narrator in a few songs may have led to their application in settings

Example 35.8 (cont.)

(c)

fashioned to express devotion to Christ.[37] In some instances, moreover, a song may be susceptible to either interpretation, as in the case of *Se la face ay pale*, more traditionally seen as bearing Marian resonances but recently interpreted by Anne Walters Robertson as Christological. Here the female object of the narrative is accounted for by the feminine gender of the noun "anima," the soul addressed, in this interpretation, by the Redeemer himself.[38]

## Antoine Busnoys and *L'homme armé*

The most prominent example of a secular melody seemingly adopted to carry reference to Christ is the cantus firmus of our next example: *L'homme armé*. Embracing some forty masses spanning more than a century, this song was by far the most popular and probably the most ingeniously adapted cantus firmus of the fifteenth and early sixteenth century. Thus it is unsurprising that the family of masses that it spawned has engendered more explanatory effort than any other. Contexts have been proposed for individual masses and groups of them, and the eponymous armed man who is to be feared has been identified with a variety of figures, most prominently the Dukes of Burgundy Charles the Bold and Philip the Good.[39]

Yet however persuasive such hypotheses may have appeared on a local level, their explanatory power was limited to the piece, or pieces, to which they were addressed. A broader context was vaunted by Craig Wright, who proposed that

37 Kirkman, *Cultural Life*, 50–53.
38 "The Man with the Pale Face," 399–400.
39 Prizer, "Music and Ceremonial in the Low Countries"; and Planchart, "The Origins and Early History of *L'homme armé*." See also Jesse Rodin's contribution to the present volume, Ch. 4.

the first and foremost "armed man" was Christ himself, the good soldier who had redeemed humanity through his victory over evil on the Cross, doing daily battle for the souls of the faithful through his reappearance in the transubstantiated host of the Mass.[40] This primary identification would strongly have encouraged further associations with the central figure of the cantus firmus: for a princely magnate paying for the production and performance of such a mass, a metaphorical link with a martial cantus firmus could only add luster to his self-image as a soldier of Christ. The claims of a secular lord to the status of Christian soldier could find no more compelling forum than through being entwined in the mass with the musical embodiment of Christ himself.

This model is given a powerful added dimension by direct association between the notion of Christ as foremost Christian soldier and the rite of Mass itself: here, according to allegories laid out in late medieval Mass commentaries, the priest assumed the role of Christ himself, doing battle with the forces of evil, with his vestments characterized as the garments and "instruments" of the Passion. These were the "arma Christi" venerated with such fervor in the fifteenth century, most vividly via such devotional images as the Man of Sorrows and the Mass of St. Gregory.[41]

Such associations add a much deeper dimension to our perspective on the cultivation of *L'homme armé* masses at the Court of Burgundy. While the Valois dukes presided over the most powerful court in western Europe, their lack of regal and sacred legitimacy – particularly in relation to the neighboring French royal court with its "most Christian king" – was surely a strong motivating factor behind their chivalric and military posturings. Most prominent of these was the Order of the Golden Fleece and its material accoutrements, including – as scholars have come to believe – *L'homme armé* masses.[42]

Most of the conceits mentioned above – and many more besides – are encapsulated by a remarkable series of *L'homme armé* masses preserved anonymously in a Naples manuscript and apparently originating in the court of the last Valois Duke, Charles the Bold.[43] But in terms purely of musical fabric none of the earlier masses based on the melody seems to have been more admired than that by Antoine Busnoys, employed at the Burgundian court from the mid- to late 1460s.[44] While the chronological implications of shared musical materials can clearly be equivocal, Du Fay, Philippe Basiron, and Guillaume Faugues all share materials with Busnoys's mass in their own settings based on

40 Wright, *The Maze and the Warrior*, 159–205.
41 Kirkman, *Cultural Life*, 98–134.
42 Proposed in Prizer, "The Order"; see also Planchart, "Guillaume Du Fay's Benefices," 159–60.
43 For detailed discussion of this series of masses and further bibliography see Wright, *The Maze and the Warrior*, 184–88 and Kirkman, *Cultural Life*, 122–33.
44 See Bibliography for edition and recording.

the tune, and two masses, both apparently by Jacob Obrecht – his *Missa L'homme armé* and the anonymously surviving *Missa de Sancto Johanne Baptista* – even adopt the entire rhythmic organization of Busnoys's setting of the melody as their structural underpinning.[45] As Richard Taruskin has shown, the disposition of the tenor in Busnoys's mass also embraces a numeric program that relates it to the anonymous (possibly Busnoys) Naples masses and probably also to the Order of the Golden Fleece itself. Its status is confirmed by its survival today in no fewer than seven manuscripts, an unequaled number for the time of its composition (probably in the 1460s); and its influence seems further to be implied by the suggestion of two later theorists that Busnoys may even have composed the model song.[46]

While not all musical tastes could span half a millennium, no one who knows Busnoys's *Missa L'homme armé* will have any difficulty understanding its status in the eyes of its composer's contemporaries. First of all, it is beyond doubt one of the most mesmerizing and exhilarating pieces of the fifteenth century. Legendary for the virtuoso idiom of his sacred works, Busnoys is nowhere more pyrotechnic than here: it would have been fascinating to hear how the original singers of this work – its composer most likely included – would have approached such gestures as the famous bass surge through a tenth up to top F in the second part of the Gloria,[47] and the same part's even more challenging (at least to modern voices) climb up to top G in the previous section (Example 35.9). This is music that not only bespeaks confidence: it demands it, in ample measure, from its performers.

But there is much more here than just gymnastics: Busnoys has (to modern sensibilities anyway) an uncanny sense of timing, with everything seeming to fall felicitously, suavely sculpted components building into a masterly overall design. Thus points of repose are just as absorbing as points of tension, the brilliant pacing and manipulation of rhythm, pitch, and counterpoint seeming to draw the listener irresistibly inward, as well as onward. A stellar example is the moment of extraordinary stasis in the Agnus Dei where the tune, here presented in inversion, bottoms out on a low F in a moment of otherworldly beauty where time seems to stand still.[48] Everything seems calculated to entice the ear into Busnoys's often subtle and nuanced sound-world, and to listen intently to the gracefully arching and gently climaxing melodic lines in such reduced-voice passages as the Christe section of the Kyrie is to receive an impression of profound feeling and sincerity of utterance.

45  See Taruskin, "Antoine Busnoys" for the historical importance of Busnoys's mass; on Obrecht and the anonymous mass see Wegman, "Another Imitation" and *Born for the Muses*, 213–17.
46  Taruskin "Antoine Busnoys."      47  "Qui tollis," mm. 10–12 (Busnoys, *Collected Works*, 13).
48  Agnus Dei III, mm. 4–7 (Busnoys, *Collected Works*, 46).

Example 35.9 Antoine Busnoys, *Missa L'homme armé*, Gloria, mm. 35–38

## The scent of another world: Johannes Ockeghem and the freeing of the cantus firmus

While cantus-firmus procedure of one kind or another encapsulates the majority of fifteenth-century masses, a substantial minority shows a range of approaches that are both more individualistic and less internally consistent. A mass may refer simultaneously (in a foreshadowing of the later "parody" or "imitation" method more characteristic of sixteenth-century practice) to multiple voices of its model, quote from outside material only sporadically, or enter a twilight zone in which external reference melds into general or accidental reference, or (apparently) free counterpoint. All these features are characteristic, for example, of John Bedyngham's *Missa Dueil angoisseux*, a work whose external reference would, without the aid of its manuscript nomenclature, probably have escaped scholars for some considerable time, and would clearly – had the song been lost – have eluded them altogether. In such circumstances it would have joined the serried ranks of *Missae Sine nomine*, where it would have rubbed shoulders with many masses that show much greater internal consistency, whether or not such consistency was derived from unknown preexistent pieces.[49]

The wide fluctuation in this mass of density of external reference is a feature shared by numerous other cycles, both with and without known antecedents.[50] In some cases a single movement may make strong reference to a cantus prius factus that is more or less absent in the other four. Such is the case of the

---

49 A striking case in point is the anonymous mass in Trent 89 dubbed by Louis Gottlieb the *Missa Prolatio perfecta*, which shows strong parallels between movements, particularly between the beginnings of their respective subdivisions. For an edition see Gottlieb, "The Cyclic Masses of Trent Codex 89," 2:382–99, and see the discussion in Kirkman, "Innovation," 162–63.
50 On this phenomenon and its representatives see ibid., 159–66.

anonymous so-called *Missa O2* in Trent 89, its Sanctus based unambiguously on Du Fay's *Adieu m'amour*, a piece notable by its absence in most of the remainder of the cycle.[51] A similar preponderance of reference characterizes the Kyrie of an anonymous *Missa Le serviteur* in the same manuscript, and the *Missa Au travail suis* of our next witness, Johannes Ockeghem.

A seemingly gentler, if equally individualistic, spirit in comparison to the more Dionysiac Busnoys, Ockeghem seems to have reinvented his approach to the Ordinary of the Mass with each setting. Our focus here will be on a cycle that, while probably his best known, is at the same time perhaps his most enigmatic: the *Missa Mi-mi*.[52] Long thought to be freely composed, in 1985 it was linked to the same composer's song *Presque transi*. While the relationship between these two pieces is undeniable, the nature of that relationship continues to generate debate. How one views the links between mass and song depends on one's point of comparison, and more generally on one's perspective on the nature of inter-piece quotation in the later fifteenth century. For Jesse Rodin, the two works belong in a group of pieces that witness Ockeghem (with echoes in works by Obrecht, Matthaeus Pipelare, Marbrianus de Orto, and an anonymous composer) dialoguing on the challenges involved in composing in the Phrygian mode.[53] Fabrice Fitch, on the other hand, notes the similarity between the mass's external quotations and those of Ockeghem's masses on *Ma maistresse*, *Au travail suis*, and possibly – he argues – *Quinti toni*, practices expressive of the composer's quintessential "aesthetics of concealment."[54] Certainly the nature of the mass's apparent song references is not out of kilter with what can be observed in many other musical interrelationships of the period; but the varied scholarly perspectives on them bear testimony to how much still remains obscure concerning the nature and motivation of musical quotation in this period.[55]

Progress in that understanding is sure to involve enhanced engagement with the kinds of cultural forces that motivated composers to make such quotations in the first place. If such motivations could be uncovered in this case it seems reasonable to surmise that they would resonate with the mass's *Mi-mi*

51 A quotation identified by Robert Mitchell ("The Paleography and Repertory," 89). See the discussion in Kirkman, *Cultural Life*, 55–58.
52 See the Bibliography for edition and recording.
53 "*Mi mi.*" My thanks to Professor Rodin for providing me with a copy of his paper.
54 *Johannes Ockeghem: Masses and Models*, 161–71.
55 For further consideration of this issue see my *The Cultural Life*, 58–61. For another take on the possible meanings (or lack of them) of instances of inter-piece musical common ground, see the closing section of Jesse Rodin's essay in this collection, Ch. 4.

sobriquet.[56] While there is some disagreement concerning the focus of the appellation, all agree in associating it in some way with solmization syllables. That being so, Gayle Kirkwood's attempt to explain it – in light of the philosophy of Jean Gerson concerning the meanings of solmization syllables – as a reference to Christ the "most piteous" seems plausible.[57] Certainly such a hypothesis could neatly embrace the pleas of *Presque transi* for a turn to "that end free of suffering," and would make sense of the (apparently) high density of quotations in the Benedictus, the point in the rite of Mass at which Christ would be made flesh in the form of the transubstantiated host. If such questions are ultimately unanswerable they should certainly be posed, in the process enhancing our penetration of the world whose needs such compositions were shaped to express.

One point on which we would be unlikely to differ from our fifteenth-century forebears, however, is that the *Missa Mi-mi* is a work of surpassing beauty. Individual though it undoubtedly is even in the context of its composer's works – in its approach to Phrygian modality and in whatever it may have to say about practices of external borrowing, to name but two of its aspects – it would be fair to say that in many ways it distills the essence of Ockeghem's style.

There can be no more obvious demonstration of this than its approach to imitation, of which Fitch's examples offer eloquent demonstration.[58] Just one aspect of Ockeghem's contrapuntal language, imitation is most typically deployed by him in obscured and shifting patterns: contours and rhythms may assume subtly varied forms; imitative points may be buried in continuing lines rather than set off by rests; lines may start differently only to assume the same contour after a few notes; a single imitative point may be deployed in varied forms across its various voice parts; and so on.[59] Ockeghem's contrapuntal approach has surely tended to be viewed too much in light of later norms, whereas the reality of his time is a much more fluid approach to contrapuntal structuring than became customary in the sixteenth century. Denser and less lucid than in its later manifestations, his imitation

---

56 The traditional association of the title with the falling fifth motif in the bass has not gone unchallenged, not least because the low "A," if solmized as "mi," would imply an "Ut" outside the Guidonian Hand, and because of the lack anyway of a need for a B♭ (implying "mi" on the pitch A) in a Phrygian piece. For an alternative explanation, suggesting rather that the sobriquet refers to the setting of the mass in mode 4, see Duffin, "*Mi chiamano Mimi.*" On the other hand, Rodin's examples that seem to refer to Ockeghem's bass motif are not restricted to Phrygian pieces. It bears comment that Duffin's interpretation would not in any case affect the force of Kirkwood's hypothesis (see below) one way or the other.

57 Kirkwood, "*My my.*"     58 *Johannes Ockeghem: Masses and Models*, 171–76.

59 On this aspect of imitation, see the essay by Julie E. Cumming and Peter Schubert in this volume, Ch. 12.

nonetheless creates a texture combining great cohesion and interest with great variety, and as a consequence one unusually rewarding to repeated hearing.

## Epilogue: Obrecht and Josquin

The final part of this chapter draws the fifteenth century to a close via two masses by the acknowledged masters of the *fin de siècle*: the *Missae Malheur me bat* by Obrecht and Josquin. Both masses are based on a song, apparently by the shadowy Malcort, which has survived – bar the opening incipit – without words. Although the two composers have long been thought to have been working more or less coevally, recent revisions in Josquin chronology have by contrast seemed to confirm trends in their respective source traditions: namely that Obrecht's masses began to circulate in the late 1480s, a decade or so earlier than Josquin's. A corollary, Rob Wegman proposes, is that features of Josquin's masses once thought to be original may in fact have derived from the influence of Obrecht.[60]

Whatever he bequeathed in his turn, Obrecht shows clear debts to his major predecessors. His esteem for Ockeghem is strongly witnessed by the *Missa de Sancto Donatiano*, "a faithful imitation," in Wegman's words, of the older man's *Missa Ecce ancilla domini*, and by the *Missa Sicut spina rosam*, with its direct quotations of the *Missa Mi-mi*. Generally, though, a more obvious musical lineage extends back to Busnoys, and through him to Domarto, whose practice of mensural transformation remains a preoccupation of Obrecht. If, as Wegman suggests, the kind of restless forward drive inherited from Busnoys takes a back seat after the younger composer's (presumably) early masses, it never entirely disappears, and Busnoys's grandly architectural schemes surely find their inheritance in Obrecht's carefully controlled sense of overall structure, albeit in manifestations of rather different character.

Indeed originality of approach to structure is surely the most striking feature of Obrecht's mature mass writing, with each mass working out a predetermined schema that draws all five movements into one compelling statement. With such scaffolds, Wegman observes, Obrecht makes a decisive move away from the old dichotomy of full (cantus firmus) and reduced (mostly free) composition toward structures that are both more varied and more individualized, "a fundamentally new conception of the nature of the musical work."[61]

---

60 Wegman, "Obrecht [Hobrecht], Jacob."    61 Ibid.

The most characteristic means by which he achieves this is via his technique of cantus-firmus segmentation, a procedure that underpins the *Missa Malheur me bat*.[62] Here Obrecht takes the discantus of his model song and divides it into a series of arbitrarily determined sections which then become the scaffold, likewise set in the discantus, for the mass as a whole. Successive sections of the melody are each heard three times (four times in the second section of the Credo) in each section of the mass up to the first Agnus Dei. The fact that in each case, moreover, the three statements are geared, via a series of different mensurations, to accelerate up to a statement moving at the original speed builds a feeling of climax into each section.

What this model lacks, of course, is cyclic *musical* repetition across the various movements. Obrecht makes up for this via a scattering of quotations from the song tenor across the spread of the mass, mostly in sections in which the discantus, bearer of the main structural statements, is *tacet*. Finally, in the Agnus Dei he quotes the entire tenor of the song as the bassus of Agnus II,[63] and then reprises the entire discantus as the discantus of Agnus III. Besides this culminating gesture, one echoed in a number of masses by Obrecht, Josquin, and others, the effect of the schema is to impose a common structure on each movement that leads to a recurring sense of expectation.

A number of writers have commented that this formulaic method of construction smacks of archaic, isorhythmic approaches. Yet, as Wegman has eloquently demonstrated, in Obrecht's case the effect is very different. Rather like Bach, he seems to have thrived on the challenge of such restriction, lending each prearranged quotation an air of purely musical inevitability and enveloping it in a succession of ideas that lacks nothing in purely sensual beauty. Indeed, Obrecht's idiom is a model of a kind of lucidity that, compared with the earlier masses we have examined, sounds distinctly modern. It is rooted in a battery of easily audible textural markers: a large preponderance of imitation, whether involving all voices or in extended passages *a 2*; moments of chordal stasis; frequent use of passages in fauxbourdon; plus Obrecht's signature sequences, ostinati, and parallel motion in tenths.

Almost any section would suffice to show these processes in action, and the opening of the Gloria will serve that purpose here (see the cited edition). The section opens with an imitative point involving at first two and then all three lower voices, on the third phrase of the song's discantus that will duly appear in

---

62 See the Bibliography for edition and recording.
63 This is one of rather few aspects of Obrecht's mass that links it to Agricola's on the same model, where, as Fabrice Fitch reminds me, the entire tenor of the song is quoted in the bass of the Agnus III. Besides this it is hard to see much commonality of approach between the greatly rationalized Obrecht mass and that by Agricola, whose highly diverse approach to its model seems comparatively – and, for him, typically – whimsical.

the discantus, in extremely long notes and crowning the texture, at measure 31. The abrupt change of pace ushered in by that statement is underpinned by an idea in thirds in the middle voices and a very deliberate extended rising sequence in the bass. The statement's extended final G is undergirded by a similarly held E in the bass, while the inner voices expatiate on the "E minor" sonority in an obsessive stretto descending idea. There follows a statement in the bass of the passage from the tenor of the song that formed the original counterpoint to this section's discantus phrase, but this is swept away – in a device often used to "clear the palate" between statements of the cantus prius factus – by a passage in fauxbourdon, before the song discantus resumes its course.

While Obrecht's *Missa Malheur me bat* first appears in the surviving sources in 1497, Josquin's mass on the same song makes its debut in 1505. Such milestones are clearly crude guides in themselves to the dating of the actual works; nonetheless, stylistically based suppositions have tended to support the notion that the two masses were composed a decade or so apart from one another, and that Josquin's dates from the first years of the sixteenth century.[64] Certainly the Josquin mass distills, with profundity and brilliance, the legacy of the preceding decades while also developing trends that have come to be seen as more characteristic of the new century.

Though clearly based on a different reading of the song, the compositional approach of Josquin's mass bears similarities to Obrecht's, or at least to the mature style of which the latter is an expression.[65] Like Obrecht, he dissects his model song and deploys it in segments, but unlike Obrecht he makes more or less equal use of all three antecedent voices, albeit usually separately: while the Kyrie and Gloria set the song tenor in the mass tenor, the analogous procedure shifts to the discantus in the Credo and altus in the Sanctus. Like Obrecht, Josquin – at least in his Gloria and Credo – chops his model into segments, in this case of wildly disparate length, each of them (except the last one in the Credo) repeated. By contrast, the three sections of the Kyrie lay out the complete tenor as a conventional cantus firmus in three sections, the third of them recasting the duple-meter original into triple. The Sanctus adopts still another approach, with the cantus firmus passing thrice through the altus in contrasting mensurations before reverting, in the Benedictus, to just its first eleven measures, but each time beginning on a different pitch.[66]

---

64 For a hypothesis on the date of the Josquin see Fallows, *Josquin*, 262–63. For Obrecht, see Wegman, *Born for the Muses*, 281–84.
65 See the Bibliography for edition and recording.
66 For the layout of the parts of the song see Josquin, *Collected Works*, 9; *Critical Commentary*, 29, and Sparks, *Cantus Firmus*, 346–51.

I have left mention of the Agnus Dei, a very Josquinian tour de force, until last. Here the composer enters into a dialogue not only with Obrecht, but also with the brilliant, and probably contemporary, summatory finales in others of his own masses. Agnus I, in retrospect a kind of scene-setter, lays out the borrowed tenor in its tenor but, in a nod to more archaic approaches and probably directly to Obrecht, omits – via a verbal canon – all note values smaller than a semibreve. The composer then dresses up the resulting long-note cantus firmus with a series of ostinato gestures, repeated on different pitches in all three remaining voices. Agnus II entirely comprises a canon at the second, an extended prelude to the Agnus III that, like the same section of the *Missae Hercules dux Ferrarie* and *L'homme armé sexti toni*, is a canonic masterpiece *a 6*. Like the latter of these – with which, as Fallows notes, it shares some half a dozen sources – the Agnus III of *Malheur me bat* combines cantus-firmus statement with two tightly knit canons at the unison. If both the canonic armature and segmentation of the borrowed parts in the Agnus III gesture to the past, Josquin points in the opposite direction in his simultaneous deployment of two voices (superius and tenor) of his model, and in his alternation between spare, two-voice song quotations and lush, six-voice writing. He embraces the burgeoning practice of "parody" or "imitation" quotation more directly at the opening of the Sanctus, whose first eleven measures reprise all three voices of the song in their original configuration.

Perhaps needless to say, the above details delineate only the bare bones of this rich work. Those bones are fleshed out by a tissue of further quotation and motivic consistency that bind the whole together more tightly than had been the case with the Obrecht. But in both masses the important thing for the hearer is less the (technical) means than the audibly engrossing end: both speak directly and easily to a modern audience accustomed to textural clarity and periodic phrase structure; and in that very lucidity they simultaneously open perhaps the easiest (retrograde) path to an engagement with those earlier works out of whose idioms they grew.

# Bibliography

Bent, Margaret, ed., *Bologna Q15: The Making and Remaking of a Musical Manuscript*, Lucca, 2008

Bloxam, M. Jennifer, "A Cultural Context for the Chanson Mass," in *Early Musical Borrowing*, ed. Honey Meconi, New York, 2004, 7–35

Bouquet, Marie-Thérèse, "La cappella musicale dei duchi di Savoia dal 1450 al 1500," *Rivista italiana di musicologia* 3 (1968), 233–85

Brown, Howard Mayer, "Music and Ritual at Charles the Bold's Court: The Function of Liturgical Music by Busnoys and his Contemporaries," in *Antoine Busnoys: Method, Meaning, and Context in Late Medieval Music*, ed. Paula Higgins, Oxford, 1999, 53–70

and Louise Stein, *Music in the Renaissance*, 2nd edn., Upper Saddle River, NJ, 1999

Bukofzer, Manfred, *Studies in Medieval and Renaissance Music*, New York, 1950

Burn, David, "'Nam erit haec quoque laus eorum': Imitation, Competition and the *L'homme armé* Tradition," *Revue de musicologie* 87 (2001), 251–87

Busnoys, Antoine, *Collected Works*, ed. Richard Taruskin, New York, 1990

Ciconia, Johannes, *The Works of Johannes Ciconia*, ed. Margaret Bent and Anne Hallmark, Polyphonic Music of the Fourteenth Century 24, Monaco, 1985

Domarto, Petrus de, *Complete Works*, 2: *Missa Spiritus almus*, ed. David Kidger, Newton Abbot, Devon, 2005

Dufay, Guillaume, *Opera Omnia*, 2: *Missarum pars prior*; and 4: *Fragmenta Missarum*, ed. Heinrich Besseler, CMM 1, Rome, 1960, 1962

Duffin, Ross, "*Mi chiamano Mimi* ... but My Name is *Quarti toni*: Solmization and Ockeghem's Famous Mass," *EM* 29 (2001), 165–84

Duffy, Eamon, *The Stripping of the Altars: Traditional Religion in England, c.1400–c.1580*, New Haven, 1992

Fallows, David, *Dufay*, 2nd rev. edn., London, 1987

*Josquin*, Turnhout, 2009

Fitch, Fabrice, *Johannes Ockeghem: Masses and Models*, Paris, 1997

Gossett, Philip, "Techniques of Unification in Early Cyclic Masses and Mass Pairs," *JAMS* 19 (1966), 205–31

Gottlieb, Louis, "The Cyclic Masses of Trent Codex 89," 2 vols., Ph.D. diss., University of California at Berkeley, 1958

Hoppin, Richard, ed., *The Cypriot-French Repertory of the Manuscript Torino, Biblioteca Nazionale, J. II. 9*, 1: *Polyphonic Mass Movements*, CMM 21, Rome, 1960

Huot, Sylvia, *Allegorical Play in the Old French Motet: The Sacred and the Profane in Thirteenth-Century Polyphony*, Stanford, 1997

Josquin des Prez, *The Collected Works of Josquin des Prez*, 9: *Masses Based on Secular Polyphonic Songs 3*, ed. Barton Hudson, NJE 9, Utrecht, 1994; and *Critical Commentary*, Utrecht, 1995

Kirkman, Andrew, *The Cultural Life of the Early Polyphonic Mass: Medieval Context to Modern Revival*, Cambridge, 2010

"Innovation, Stylistic Patterns and the Writing of History: The Case of Bedyngham's Mass *Dueil angoisseux*," in *I codici musicali trentini: Nuove scoperte e nuovi orientamenti della ricerca*, ed. Peter Wright and Marco Gozzi, Trento, 1996, 149–75

Kirkwood, Gayle C., "*My my* as Theological Allegory," in Ockeghem, *Masses and Mass Sections*, 3, ed. van Benthem, xiii–xv

Maniates, Maria Rika, "Combinative Techniques in Franco-Flemish Polyphony: A Study of Mannerism in Music from 1450–1530," Ph.D. diss., Columbia University, 1965

Mitchell, Robert J., "The Paleography and Repertory of Trent Codices 89 and 91, together with Analyses and Editions of Six Mass Cycles by Franco-Flemish Composers from Trent Codex 89," Ph.D. thesis, University of Exeter, 1989

Nosow, Robert, *Ritual Meanings in the Fifteenth-Century Motet*, Cambridge, 2012

Obrecht, Jacob, *Collected Works*, 7: *Missa Malheur me bat; Missa Maria zart*, ed. Barton Hudson, Utrecht, 1987

Ockeghem, Johannes, *Masses and Mass Sections*, 3: *Masses Based on Freely Invented and Unspecified Material*, fascicle 2: *Missa My My*, ed. Jaap van Benthem, Utrecht, 1998

Planchart, Alejandro Enrique, "Fifteenth-Century Masses: Notes on Performance and Chronology," *Studi musicali* 10 (1981), 3–29

"Guillaume Du Fay's Benefices and his Relationship to the Court of Burgundy," *EMH* 8 (1988), 117–71

"The Origins and Early History of *L'homme armé*," *JM* 20 (2003), 305–57

ed., *Missae Caput*, New Haven, 1964

Power, Lionel, *Mass Alma redemptoris mater*, ed. Gareth Curtis, Newton Abbot, Devon, 1982

Prizer, William F., "Music and Ceremonial in the Low Countries: Philip the Fair and the Order of the Golden Fleece," *EMH* 5 (1985), 113–53

"The Order of the Golden Fleece and Music," paper read at the annual meeting of the American Musicological Society, Vancouver, 1985

Reaney, Gilbert, ed., *Early Fifteenth-Century Music*, CMM 11, vols. 5 and 6, n.p., 1975 and Neuhausen-Stuttgart, 1977

Robertson, Anne Walters, "The Man with the Pale Face, the Shroud, and Du Fay's *Missa Se la face ay pale*," *JM* 27 (2010), 377–434

"The Savior, the Woman, and the Head of the Dragon in the *Caput* Masses and Motet," *JAMS* 59 (2006), 537–630

Rodin, Jesse, "*Mi mi*, de Orto, and Ockeghem's Shadow," paper read at the annual meeting of the American Musicological Society, Philadelphia, 2009

Rothenberg, David, "Marian Feasts, Seasons, and Songs in Medieval Polyphony: Studies in Musical Symbolism," Ph.D. diss., Yale University, 2004

Sparks, Edgar H., *Cantus Firmus in Mass and Motet, 1420–1520*, Berkeley, 1963

Strohm, Reinhard, *Music in Late Medieval Bruges*, 2nd rev. edn., Oxford, 1990

*The Rise of European Music, 1380–1500*, Cambridge, 1993

Taruskin, Richard, "Antoine Busnoys and the *L'homme armé* Tradition," *JAMS* 39 (1986), 255–93

Thompson, A. Hamilton, *The English Clergy and their Organization in the Later Middle Ages*, Oxford, 1947

Ward, Tom R., "Libert, Reginaldus [Liebert]," in *Grove Music Online* (accessed 5 October 2014)

Wegman, Rob C., "Another 'Imitation' of Busnoys's *Missa L'homme armé* and Some Observations on *Imitatio* in Renaissance Music," *JRMA* 114 (1989), 189–202

"Another Mass by Busnoys?," *M&L* 71 (1990), 1–19

*Born for the Muses: The Life and Masses of Jacob Obrecht*, Oxford, 1994

"Obrecht [Hobrecht], Jacob," in *Grove Music Online* (accessed 5 October 2014)

"Petrus de Domarto's *Missa Spiritus almus* and the Early History of the Four-Voice Mass in the Fifteenth Century," *EMH* 10 (1991), 235–303

Wright, Craig, *The Maze and the Warrior: Symbols in Architecture, Theology, and Music*, Cambridge, MA, 2001

## Recordings

The Binchois Consort, conducted by Andrew Kirkman, "Busnois, *Missa L'homme armé* and Domarto, *Missa Spiritus almus*" (Hyperion, CDA67319)

The Binchois Consort, conducted by Andrew Kirkman, "Dufay and the Court of Savoy" (Hyperion, CDA 67715)

The Clerks' Group, directed by Edward Wickham, "Jacob Obrecht, *Missa Malheur me bat* and Motets by Obrecht and Martini" (ASV Gaudeamus, CD GAU 171)

The Clerks' Group, directed by Edward Wickham, "Ockeghem, *Missa Mi-mi, Salve regina* and *Alma redemptoris mater*" (ASV Gaudeamus, CD GAU 139)

Gothic Voices, directed by Christopher Page, "Missa Caput and the Story of the Salve Regina," The Spirits of England and France 4 (Hyperion, CDA66857)

The Hilliard Ensemble, "Leonel Power, Masses and Motets" (EMI, CDM 7630642)

The Tallis Scholars, directed by Peter Philips, "Josquin, *Missa Malheur me bat* and *Missa Fortuna desperata*" (Gimell, CD GIM042)

# The fifteenth-century motet

LAURENZ LÜTTEKEN

TRANSLATED BY JAMES STEICHEN

## Terminology and problems of definition

In the fourteenth century the motet was governed by a comparatively small set of compositional norms. These factors concerned not just the motet's technical aspects – tenors, polytextual structures, mensural notation, and isorhythmic disposition – but also its standing as the genre of the highest aesthetic rank and its social status as the music of the clerical elite. In this context, Pietro Capuano da Amalfi could easily define the motet in the second half of the fourteenth century: "tocius nove artis motectorum difficultas circa temporum varietatem et semibrevium figuracionem acceditur" (the difficulty of new motet composition therefore lies in the variety of the use of *tempora* and semibreves).[1] His treatise on mensural music quite naturally focused on the motet, but *musica mensurabilis* and the motet nonetheless comprised parts of a larger unity; the genre is part of the concept. At the start of the fifteenth century, this configuration became less distinct. It was not that there was no longer a consensus about what a motet was, but rather that these underlying norms had been strained to the breaking point. Indeed in the aftermath of developments ca. 1420–30, the motet entered a phase of considerable unpredictability. Nonetheless the term itself was never called into question. In the index of manuscript Modena α.X.1.11 (ModB, from the 1440s), for example, the term "motteti" is used for contributions to the genre in its narrowest sense, an indication of new generic problems.

Definitions of the term "motet" can be found in fifteenth-century writings. These definitions, however, present fundamental interpretive challenges, insofar as they describe a genre that was no longer governed by any discrete set of normative features. With the emergence of the polyphonic secular song and the mass setting, the congruence of notation and genre became increasingly obsolete. Even in the late fourteenth century, the theorist Anonymous V, probably of French origin and apparently closely associated

---

1 Pietro Capuano da Amalfi, *Mensurabilis musicae tractatuli*, 1:43.

with Johannes de Muris, describes the intricacies of mensural notation using examples from not just motets, but also mass settings and the latest *cantilenae*, such as the rondeau and madrigal.[2] Thus the motet stood in need of a new theoretical foundation distinct from the structures of *musica mensurabilis*.

A new theoretical clarity for the motet arose not from its musical-compositional features, but rather from its textual dimension. In the early fifteenth century, an author of probably German origin attempted to define the motet as a "cantus ecclesiasticus" (song of the church) based solely on the status of its texts.[3] The Jewish scholar Paulus Paulirinus (ca. 1413–after 1470), trained in Padua and later active in Pilsen, wrote around 1463 that the motet consisted of "uterque textus" (two texts) and a tenor, i.e., its essential features are polytextuality and a preexisting melody.[4] In Johannes Tinctoris's *Dictionary of Musical Terms*, written in 1472–73 but not printed until ca. 1494, the author arranges his entries according to an implicit hierarchy of mass, motet, and chanson. These genres correspond to the three *genera dicendi* of classical rhetoric, that is, *grande* (large), *mediocris* (medium), and *humilis* (small), with the motet ranking as "cantus mediocris."[5] But Tinctoris is also guided in his classification of musical compositions by the type, length, and stylistic classification of the respective texts. Although indexes of musical manuscripts do make distinctions between genres, up to around 1440 they are organized almost exclusively according to text incipits. For the motet – based on Latin texts, and not on formally standardized poems like the chanson – this creates considerable problems. Unlike mass settings, the shape of motet texts was subject to constant change, and unlike the chanson, the text affected the formal disposition of a piece (for example, its strophic layout or refrain structure) in only a tangential manner.

Faced with such a complex problem, fifteenth-century authors were somewhat perplexed. This difficulty was not inherent to the motet or music in general, but was part of a larger problem, since it was only in the fifteenth century that modern systems of generic classification began to be formulated, first in poetics and then in the other arts, in particular painting. Relying upon Aristotelian premises, genre theory even within poetics was rife with conflict, between overly general definitions often formulated by rules of exclusion, and self-serving guidelines designed to dovetail with authors' own works.[6] Thus in

---

2 Anonymous V, *Ars cantus mensurabilis*, ed. and trans. Balensuela.
3 Staehelin, "Beschreibungen und Beispiele," 239.
4 Paulus Paulirinus, *Liber viginti artium*, in Reiss, "Pauli Paulirini," 261.
5 The term is documented already in a library inventory from Milan from the year 1426, in connection with a (now lost) motet manuscript; the context is somewhat uncertain, however. See Pellegrin, *La Bibliothèque des Visconti*, 91.
6 See Colie, *The Resources of Kind*.

the fifteenth century, normative structures established in the fourteenth century (tenor, Latin, polytextual tendencies) were juxtaposed with new distinctions arising from the character of the compositions themselves. These differences center on social, ritual, and liturgical aspects, that is, the function of a particular work.

A motet's "function" is largely determined by the circumstances of its commissioning: the institution, occasion, performance conditions, ritual context, and compositional standards (not necessarily identical to the composer's own standards). These factors comprise the so-called "complex of expectations" of a particular work.[7] The compositional pluralization of the motet in the fifteenth century was initially focused on this complex of expectations, and was the result of both intentional adaptation to market conditions and an increasing degree of individuation: a functional pluralization in the broadest sense. Conversely, the character of these differentiations in turn determined the specific qualities of a composition. In fact, these factors influenced the contours of the music much more than scholars have allowed. This lack of compositional autonomy represents not a loss, but rather a rich diversification of the genre, and is best understood by attending less to theoretical accounts than the works themselves, which would give rise to new traditions. It is in fact this functional polysemy, itself an indicator of the transition to the modern age, that constitutes the defining characteristic of the motet. In this respect, moreover, the motet differs from the chanson and the mass, whose functions were much more narrowly defined.

Completed in 1476, the *studiolo* of Duke Federico III da Montefeltro in Urbino is exemplary of this typology of the motet. Lying in the partially opened trompe-l'oeil cupboards are two manuscripts with legible musical notation: the three-part chanson *J'ay pris amour* is found among other books in the library, whereas the four-part celebratory motet *Bella gerit musasque colit* appears in an ornate cabinet. The motet is evidently categorized as a precious object, distinguished from the chanson by its function – above and beyond any compositional or textual differences. This functional distinction is relevant not just to the production and reproduction of motets, but also to their preservation in manuscripts and other contexts (of which Federico's *studiolo* provides an inkling). In Gentile Bellini's monumental painting of a procession in front of San Marco (Venice, Galleria dell'Accademia, 1496) we see members of the Scuola di San Giovanni Evangelista – in all likelihood singing a motet – holding separate sheets of music in their hands. It is not clear how these sheets were produced and where they were preserved. It is thus owing to the motet's

7 For the definition of this term see Warnke, *Bau und Überbau*, 13 ff.

wide-ranging influence in the fifteenth century that Peter Gülke has suggested that we consider this genre as not just a musical phenomenon, but rather as the manifestation of a broader "motetic consciousness."[8]

## Functional diversity as pluralization

### Isorhythmics

Fifteenth-century musicians were already aware of the problem of creating order within a diffuse genre. In the index of the highly organized manuscript Modena α.X.1.11 (ModB), probably connected to the humanistic circle of Pope Eugene IV (1431–43), the term "motetti" is applied in a narrow sense that explicitly excludes antiphons, hymns, and Magnificat settings. Additionally, the manuscript's notation allows for distinctions between "isorhythmic" and "non-isorhythmic" works (in the isorhythmic motet texts the start of a new *talea* is marked by rubrication). Although this source is unique in its organizational precision, it nevertheless shows that this new pluralization had not gone unnoticed and had prompted attempts at classification.

The early fifteenth century saw a late flourishing of the isorhythmic motet. This technique was no longer a normative element of the genre (as it had been in the fourteenth century) but was one of many compositional possibilities. In fact, isorhythmic technique could be used in a variety of ways, even to the point of so-called "pan-isorhythm," that is, the isorhythmic organization of all the voices. Two additional trends emerged: a clear politicization of the motet (the external occasion expressed in the text) juxtaposed with the liturgical context in which the occasion was embedded. Even in the case of apparently liturgical motets we must assume that there was an additional impetus for composition, although such information is difficult to glean from the text. In other words, when a motet was created for a specific external occasion it is more readily identifiable; when created for a ritual or liturgical function it is more difficult to connect it to a specific date or place. The majority of the some ninety isorhythmic motets from the first half of the century originated in northern Italian city-states (the forty works in the manuscript Turin J.II.9 being a special case, as they are without attribution).[9] In the humanist-oriented republics of Padua and Venice, the need for public representation gave rise to political-ceremonial congratulatory motets on original Latin texts. Following August Wilhelm Ambros, these works have often been misleadingly called "state motets."[10] In particular, Johannes Ciconia developed the three-voice type

---

8 Gülke, *Guillaume Du Fay*, 412 ff.      9 Cf. the synopsis in Allsen, "Style and Intertextuality," 327.
10 Ambros called these motets "political editorials set to music"; see *Geschichte der Musik* 3:50.

with two equal upper voices and a supporting tenor not based on chant; the contratenor parts in the manuscript Bologna Q.15 are later additions. In his works we find a strange indifference to compositional techniques: the distinction between isorhythmic and non-isorhythmic motets is blurred beyond recognition. The works are so similar in their structure and formal disposition that the underlying compositional technique is not easy to discern. Accordingly, the freely invented tenor is often equipped with a text incipit, just as if it were a chant quotation.

Ciconia's motets were emulated by a small group of followers from his immediate circle – Antonius Romanus, Antonius de Civitate, Beltrame Feragut, Hugo de Lantins, Johannes de Lymburgia, and Cristoforus de Monte.[11] All were active in the same geographic region and conceived their works in a similar way; most of their pieces are assembled in a single manuscript (Bologna Q.15) whose compiler, in the service of the bishop of Vicenza, Pietro Emiliani, had close ties to this same region.[12] Most of the other surviving motet manuscripts from the first half of the fifteenth century are also associated with this region, especially Oxford 213 (ca. 1436, Venice), Bologna 2216 (ca. 1440), and Modena α.X.1.11 (ModB, ca. 1440, Ferrara, possibly under the auspices of the papal court). In the direct line of this tradition are the isorhythmic motets of Guillaume Du Fay, which, except for his last four works, were composed in Italy, mostly for the papal court. Particularly under Pope Eugene IV – a Venetian who during the first half of his pontificate commissioned motets for nearly every important official occasion – the politicizing tendency as understood by Ciconia was further intensified through the motet's integration into papal ritual.[13] By contrast, Du Fay's motets are clearly isorhythmic, written for four rather than three voices, and based again on preexisting and particularly meaningful tenors. The tenors are treated individually such that a different isorhythmic pattern results in each work. Along with this individualization there arose a number of compositional experiments – the expansion of the opening imitative duo in the upper voices (as in *Ecclesie militantis*, the five-part coronation motet for Eugene), for instance, or the superimposition of two tenors (as in *Salve flos Tusce*, composed in 1436 for the papal court at Florence). *Supremum est mortalibus*, composed for the coronation of Emperor Sigismund in Rome in 1433, is unique in using the structurally significant and probably symbolic technique of fauxbourdon. Du Fay's panegyrical motets thus enter into a complex union with papal ritual, conforming directly to the requirements of the ceremonial

11 See Kreutziger-Herr, *Johannes Ciconia*, 136.
12 Cf. Bent, *Bologna Q15*, 1:3 f. and *passim*. See also her essay in this volume, Ch. 33.
13 See Cumming, *The Motet*; Lütteken, *Guillaume Dufay*.

books, a strategy he also apparently pursued in his compositions for the Savoyard and Burgundian courts. Other compositions in this vein are the isorhythmic motets of the imperial Kapellmeister Johannes Brassart (?–1455), and arguably the fragmentary *Nove cantum melodie*, composed by Gilles Binchois for the baptism of the oldest son of Philip the Good, Antoine.

Concurrent with this politicization of the motet in northern Italy, in France the genre came to be integrated into liturgical contexts rather than serving a panegyric function. Among the most important composers are Johannes Carmen, Johannes Cesaris, Nicolas Grenon, Étienne Grossin, Richard Locqueville, and Johannes Tapissier, along with several anonymous musicians whose works have survived without attribution. Mostly set in four voices, these works are based on Latin texts and follow the hymnic tradition, with texts often collated using centonization (i.e., the construction of a new poem from preexisting components). Although these works are isorhythmic, their tenors, almost invariably drawn from chant, display comparatively simple proportions. (Carmen's motet for St. Nicholas, *Pontifici decori*, is typical, with its four identical *taleae*, in the proportions 1:1:1:1.) Directly associated with this trend are the isorhythmic motets of John Dunstaple. Unlike Du Fay's motets, these works display a strict pattern: they mostly adhere to a three-voice texture, lack an opening duet, and only employ the diminution types 3:2:1 and 6:4:3 (the only exceptions are the three-voice *Veni sancte spiritus* and *Specialis virgo*). All these motets are associated with saints' days; thus the particular occasions for which they were ostensibly composed are revealed only indirectly through their texts. The small number of surviving isorhythmic motets from the first half of the century by English composers (above all John Benet, Forest, Nicholas Sturgeon, and Thomas Damett) also follows this French tradition.

The isorhythmic motets of Du Fay and Dunstaple make up almost one-third of the entire transmitted repertory of the first half of the fifteenth century; in the history of composition these are the first series of works within a single genre in which we can trace the development of different techniques by two authors. Thus the isorhythmic motet does not represent a throwback to an earlier era; rather, it provides a crucial means for the realization of a modern way of engaging with genres and their norms. These trends find common cause in the use of Latin (always employed in at least two different texts simultaneously), and, above all, the ritual embeddedness of the works, more easily deduced in the case of Du Fay than Dunstaple, owing to more complete sources and explicit historical references. Through a dichotomy between occasion and ritual, this increasingly self-conscious ritualization became more readily apparent and beginning around 1500 led to more direct liturgical localization. In this sense, the trend can be understood as a more general cognitive marker of the incipient modern age: ritual contexts become apparent, ironically, to the same degree that they become questionable or begin to dissolve. Moreover, these conflicting contexts are thematized within the compositions themselves. Hence the sudden disappearance of the isorhythmic motet soon after 1440 constitutes only a caesura; the genre's complex of expectations is immediately transferred to the tenor motet.

### The tenor motet

The relationship between the isorhythmic motet and the tenor motet is difficult to trace, even though the general chronology suggests a connection: tenor motets first appeared when isorhythmic motets were on the wane. The few exemplary non-isorhythmic motets of the first half of the century (with the exception of the special case of Ciconia and some of his contemporaries) can thus not be regarded as intermediaries, since by then fundamentally different procedures had been established. The structure of Brassart's St. Lambert motet *Cristi nutu sublimato*, for example, grows out of contrasting two- and four-voice sections; it is thus not based on the tenor principle, but develops a compositional strategy completely irrelevant to the tenor motet. The tenor motet and isorhythmic motet are related in terms of their complex of expectations – an obligation to a solemn occasion – and for this reason evince similar qualities. Overtly political statements are suppressed in deference to paraliturgical demands. The use of original texts is favored, however, with bitextuality largely abandoned. Similarly, any compositional differences can be understood within a functional continuum. The one true novelty is the establishment of five-voice texture, which had previously been employed only in exceptional cases (in works by Du Fay and Johannes Franchois). The motet is no longer based on the tenor; instead this voice, still derived from chant, provides the composition's middle axis. Moreover, its contours still conform to isorhythmic principles: whereas in isorhythmic motets (excluding the few pieces with augmentation patterns, mainly in the Turin works) proportional diminution had led to a kind of acceleration, this new technique ultimately produces the same effect: the tenor is set first in long note values against the other voices, then speeds up to match their pace. Such acceleration is facilitated by the bipartite mensural scheme – O–¢ – that typically governs successive sections; this scheme is reminiscent of the diminishing *talea* principle.

Johannes Regis and Loyset Compère number among the most significant composers (setting aside composers of anonymous works) who composed tenor motets on an extremely large scale. (By way of example, the duration of Regis's Pentecostal motet *Lux solemnis/Repleti sunt* is 315 breves.) That such large compositional constructs could be organized without the backbone of isorhythmic patterns is clearly the most significant characteristic of the tenor motet. (This trend continues until around 1500, when Josquin, Jacob Obrecht, and Pierre de La Rue began to compose large-scale works in more than two sections.) For the next several decades the tenor motet stood as the most demanding type of motet setting, reaching its zenith in the time of Josquin. In the mere four motets that can be securely attributed to Johannes Ockeghem (two of them tenor motets)[14] – in particular in the five-voice *Intemerata Dei mater* – we can already discern remarkable developments peculiar to the genre: avoidance of the long-note tenor, expansion to a tripartite structure, organization through precisely balanced, often homorhythmic sonorities in various combinations of voices, and an extended final climax. Obrecht's large-scale motets draw directly on these predecessors and in a way constitute the culmination of the northern French–Burgundian complex of traditions.

This development reached its peak in the four- and six-voice motets of Josquin, many of which were composed in Italy and thus establish a link, both compositional and functional, to the political isorhythmic motet. Even though Josquin's large-scale tenor motets employ mostly Marian texts, their representational function is clearly discernible. Despite an uncertain chronology, some of these works also appear to be associated with the papal court: they use a single text, are occasionally expanded to encompass six voices (e.g., *Benedicta es celorum regina*), are characterized by intricately proportioned cantus-firmus treatment, and, similar to Du Fay's works, establish complex semantic relationships between the tenor and the other voices. The breadth of his output and the studiousness with which Josquin engaged with this genre can be observed in two pieces that by 1500 had already earned him considerable renown. In the sequence *Stabat mater dolorosa*, Josquin turns the content of the tenor on its head by using the secular tenor *Comme femme desconfortée* (borrowed from Binchois), juxtaposing a preexisting text with a quasi-newly-invented tenor.[15] Similarly, in the monumental tripartite penitential psalm *Miserere mei, Deus*, composed for Ercole I d'Este, the techniques of the tenor motet are reined in through the unification of all the voices and the use of a single, liturgically motivated text. Yet despite these moves toward simplification, the piece is raised to an extreme measure of structural and affective intensity, with twenty-one interjections of "miserere mei, Deus" and an intricate vocal dramaturgy by which the voices are combined in every possible permutation. These disparate qualities are brought together through the

14 On the sources and their transmission see Lindmayr, *Quellenstudien*.
15 See Rothenberg, *Flower of Paradise*.

work's association with Savonarola's psalm meditations.[16] Both works would prove enormously influential in the sixteenth century.

In the same period of 1450–1550, the isorhythmic motet had its own kind of afterlife, an observation first made by Rolf Dammann.[17] This took the form not of an independent tradition, but rather a self-reflexive use of established techniques, as in the *prima pars* of Obrecht's *Salve crux* or in Antoine Busnoys's multifaceted homage to Ockeghem (*In hydraulis*), which plays with every possible compositional parameter. That isorhythmic technique could be readily and even ironically employed argues for its continued availability as a compositional resource. In the motet *Probitate eminentem/Ploditando* by Petrus Wilhelmi von Grudencz (transmitted in the Glogauer Liederbuch), the isorhythmic treatment of the bi-textual structure gives rise to a new, third text in which the ostensible semantic level (a panegyric on an Augustinian canon) is reversed, turning the text into a satirical poem.[18]

## Sacralization and trivialization

The terminology currently used to describe motets is itself indicative of the difficulties inherent to the genre. Between "isorhythmic motet," coined by Friedrich Ludwig, and "tenor motet," introduced by Wolfgang Stephan, a third, somewhat makeshift term has been posited: the "non-isorhythmic motet." This term is quite literally a definition *ex negativo*, and like all such terms has little to say about the properties of the pieces in their own right. It seeks to describe a contentious period during the first half of the fifteenth century during which almost all normative compositional techniques were abandoned. At the same time, however, it points to developments through which not only were the last vestiges of a compositional consensus – the tenor structure – ultimately forsaken, but which in turn showed the way to new functions (e.g., in devotion). With the appearance of these works a homogeneous tradition was irreversibly disrupted, giving rise to the problematic term "song motet."[19]

The defining quality of these so-called "song motets" is their unambiguous connection to liturgical contexts. These compositions no longer refer to any special occasion but rather to repeatable liturgical rites. They are often private in their functional character, evident in the preference for Marian texts and passages from the Song of Songs. Such texts were central to the blossoming of

16 Cf. Macey, "Josquin's *Miserere*."
17 Dammann, "Spätformen der isorhythmischen Motette"; see Emily Zazulia's essay in this volume, Ch. 31.
18 Cf. Staehelin, *Neues zu Werk und Leben*.    19 See Leichtentritt, *Geschichte der Motette*, 31.

devotional culture and larger changes in the phenomenology of piety in the fifteenth century. Song motets are thus a response to the same demand for sacred intimacy that led to the production of elaborate books of hours. Their style accords with these needs: the pieces are as a rule set in three voices, following the pattern of the secular repertory and eschewing any special emphasis on the tenor. Such works achieved considerable fame, for example John Dunstaple's three-voice *Quam pulchra es* and Walter Frye's *Ave regina celorum*; it is no coincidence that these are both English compositions, the latter one of the most popular motets in the entire history of the genre, so famous that it was commemorated in paintings.

These works are by no means schematic in their compositional technique, whether in the disposition of voices, texture, or treatment of the tenor. Yet through their marked display of elements characteristic of the motet (above all the cantus firmus) they remain connected to art song, showing their dual roles that bridged official liturgy and private worship. This is also emphasized by the tendency of this kind of (Marian) motet to appear at the beginning of chansonniers (for example in Wolfenbüttel 287 or the Laborde Chansonnier, both beginning with Frye's *Ave regina*). This practice is analogous to the earlier practice in Spanish *cancioneros* of placing a Marian poem at the beginning of literary anthologies. As with the heyday of devotional books, the song motet is primarily a northern French–Burgundian tradition. There is a whole series of such works by Antoine Brumel that show a decidedly free treatment of text, which appears in a different arrangement on each repetition (this makes it unlikely that they were put to immediate liturgical use). Because of the status of the sources and the almost exclusively Continental transmission of such works, it is difficult to gauge what significance these pieces had for English composers (e.g., John Plummer) at mid-century.

Closely related to the "song motet" with respect to textual sources and, by extension, function are four-voice motets that for the first time treat all the voices equally, as either chant settings or even works without preexisting material (e.g., works by Alexander Agricola, Antoine Busnoys, and Johannes Martini). Included in this group are turn-of-the-century English composers such as John Browne and William Cornysh, represented in the Eton Choirbook, a manuscript dedicated primarily to iconic Marian devotion. In this extensive repertory one finds a wide range of practices, including imitative relationships between individual voices, the use of contrasting pairs, entirely free composition, and paraphrase cantus-firmus technique (as in a four-part *Regina celi* by Busnoys in which tenor and "Altertenor" perform a free antiphonal paraphrase in strict imitation at the fourth). In these "free" motets the equal treatment of the four voices presents a new compositional paradigm, anticipating the eventual turning away from tenor-focused textures.

That these works display compositional demands demonstrably more modest than those of the solemn isorhythmic and tenor motet does not necessarily imply a simplification. And yet with the establishment of this repertory – and to the degree that the polyphonic mass advanced in the hierarchy of musical genres – we can observe a compositional "trivialization." An increasingly large number of places of worship all over Europe now called for simple and easy to perform works for the daily liturgy. Characteristic examples are the Milanese *motetti missales* (Compère, Gaspar van Weerbeke, Franchinus Gaffurius), which may have replaced parts of the Ordinary in the Ambrosian rite, though opinions on this vary.[20] Their markedly simple structures apparently served as a model. These works feature an extremely limited four-voice setting following the strict syntactic layout of the text along with imitative writing mostly without cantus firmus, albeit with emblematic illustrations in the series of long-held chords with fermatas in the *O salutaris hostia* sections. The model revealed in these examples is similar to the technique of summarizing each syntactic unit of text in an imitative section (demonstrated almost didactically in Josquin's four-voice *Ave Maria . . . virgo serena*).

To be sure, the same types of text could be significantly enhanced when employing the tenor structure, but in this case it always resonated with the intimate moment of personal piety. This is evident most clearly in Du Fay's *Ave regina celorum* III, probably composed in 1464 and fitted with personal tropes. Self-assured and yet devout, the composer intended this piece for the hour of his own death and subsequent memorial services. The two traditions – the tenor motet based on a cantus firmus using newly written poetry and the devotional motet based on preexisting texts and obligated to the principle of imitation – are connected by the genre's now clearly defined liturgical context and are historically anchored in the figure of Josquin, who around 1500 set out to unite them with astonishing confidence.

The late fifteenth century also saw the development of polyphonic Propers, which had an unambiguous liturgical function, given their role in the Mass. These settings are related to the devotional motet and could also be arranged in cycles, yet they never developed a tradition of their own. Early examples are found in the anonymous Proper cycles in Trent 88 for the Sainte-Chapelle in Dijon, some of which were written by Du Fay.[21] The development culminated in the highly imaginative but still strictly chant-based Propers by Henricus Isaac around 1500 for the court of Maximilian I in Vienna (Weimar, Bibliothek

20 See Rolsma, "De onthullingen."    21 Cf. Planchart, "Guillaume Du Fay's Benefices."

der Evangelisch-Lutherischen Kirchengemeinde, MS A), which appeared in
1550 and 1555 – considerably altered – as part of the *Choralis Constantinus*.[22]

## Liturgical functions before and around
## 1500: psalm, antiphon, hymn

With the motet increasingly integrated into liturgical contexts, toward the end
of the fifteenth century a predictable but no less disconcerting trend emerges:
the delineation of clearly separable subgenres based on function, which in turn
form their own lines of tradition. This new taxonomy was based only on clearly
defined textual genres, however, not on compositional qualities, such that the
motet's orderly context remained ultimately intact. At first these subgenres
relied on simpler compositional techniques (primarily fauxbourdon), since
they were needed for immediate liturgical use, but soon after they began to
adopt the higher stylistic standards of the motet. Beginning around 1500 at the
latest, we can observe the parallel development of two complexly interrelated
compositional procedures: "functional polyphony" and motet.

First among these subgenres are psalms, which as a core element of the
monastic Office had always been central to solemn prayer, and which in the
devotional culture of the fifteenth century assumed new prominence in private
worship, especially in books of hours. Two developments in psalm composition
correspond to the dichotomy outlined above: on the one hand "free" settings
such as the psalm motet, which were not integral to the Office and therefore
could have recourse to paraphrase, and on the other functional polyphony,
which figured in the liturgy of Vespers. Whereas the former addressed the
need for private devotion, the latter met an increasing demand for a suitably
solemn yet manageable form of the Divine Office; both were unified by a
changing devotional conception of the psalms. Significant almost exclusively in
the context of the Italian cathedral repertory, so-called "Vesper psalms" have
their roots in early three-voice fauxbourdon settings in which the cantus firmus
is placed in the cantus (or discantus; e.g., Binchois, *In exitu Israel*, Trent 90,
Modena α.M.1.11 and 12, Verona 759); they are thus closely associated with the
earliest hymn settings, above all the cycle written by Du Fay for the court of
Pope Eugene IV. (In Martini's compositions the two forms are combined.) The
fauxbourdon settings point to a larger challenge: to create a musical rendering of
a long text with a point of departure provided by the chant, which because of the
comparative simplicity of the psalm tone is not very appealing. At the same time,
antiphonal psalm practices promoted the use of double-choir textures.

22 On the genesis and philology see Heidrich, *Die deutschen Chorbücher*, 209 ff.

By contrast, the psalm motet is not only directly connected to the history of the motet, but in the era of Josquin became the primary locus of text-setting innovations in the genre more generally. The first such pieces appeared suddenly around 1500, again in Italy (an anonymous mid-fifteenth-century setting of Psalm 120 in Trent 89 being the only known exception), and immediately Josquin moved to the forefront of this trend, with at least seven securely attributable works. His most elaborate settings, which generally tend to avoid the psalm tone (such as *Memor esto verbi tui* from Ps. 118, *Domine ne in furore tuo* from Ps. 37, or *De profundis*, Ps. 129),[23] exemplify the seemingly paradoxical goals of the new genre: on the one hand, extremely sophisticated artifice (in the *Miserere* (Ps. 50), for example, the tenor motet model is taken to its limits), and on the other a hitherto unknown private functionality (in some cases associated with the French court). In this sense, these psalm settings were compositional testimonials: commissioned for highly individual occasions (as may be assumed for the freely compiled excerpts from six psalms in the tripartite *Misericordias Domini*, scored for four voices) and realized by the composer with every artistic means at his disposal. In Du Fay's *Ave regina celorum* III, too, we have conclusive proof of a composer creating a work for his own personal use; similarly, Thomas Stoltzer in 1526 set a Latin psalm, as he wrote himself, "for especial enjoyment of these most beautiful words."[24] This highly artistic and increasingly individualistic rendering of the psalms, noticeable beginning around 1500, appears to correspond with the realistic mode of representation in the elaborate books of hours created at the end of the century. In either case, the end result is similar: a lavish instantiation of a sacred text for personal use in everyday life.

Against this background the psalm motet – contrary to developments in France – became a central compositional medium of the Reformation; even Luther himself contributed a modest, "autobiographically" motivated example (*Non moriar*; Ps. 117:17). On the one hand the motet could be employed programmatically in religious disputes; on the other it constituted, particularly in its use of the vernacular, a significant part of the newly defined pietistic practices.[25] With Luther as a steadfast champion, Josquin became a key point of reference, exerting a somewhat archaizing influence.

Psalm composition is inextricably tied to the antiphon, even though this tradition derives from non-psalmic Marian antiphons of the mid-fifteenth century. Despite this apparent disjunction, elaborately composed antiphons helped promote distinct liturgical functions for psalms in the era of Josquin (e.g.

---

23 Concerning questions of authenticity, see Rodin, *Josquin's Rome*, and the literature cited there.
24 Thomas Stoltzer, letter to Duke Albrecht of Prussia, 23 February 1526; facsimile in *MGG* 12, pl. 63.
25 See the essay by Reinhard Strohm in this volume, Ch. 39.

Compère, Antoine de Févin, and Henricus Isaac), while the free antiphon helped address the compositional problem posed by monotonous psalm tones. In this respect the antiphons are closely related to Mass Propers, which themselves contain antiphons and as such could also be set individually. The composition of antiphons and other specific liturgical forms appears to have been of particular significance at the chapel of the French court, for example in the works of Jean Mouton, whose well-wrought melodies were particularly admired by Glareanus.

Psalm settings were characterized by disparate but equally prized stylistic registers. At the same time there emerged more specialized liturgical types that differed substantially from the motet. This is clearest in the hymn, which in Du Fay's early cycle was structured as an *alternatim* setting: on one side fauxbourdon, on the other a cantilena with the chant in the highest voice. Composed either for the Savoyard court or, more likely, for Eugene IV and then copied and arranged for the papal chapel shortly before 1500, this hymn cycle would prove extremely consequential. Particularly striking is how it enhances otherwise simple textures: the artistic concept comes to encompass the whole of the work. (Du Fay was apparently the first to realize the cyclic concept in this form, in both hymns and propers.) The adherence of the hymns to the papal liturgy is notable, and in the Roman environment the genre came into closer contact with the motet (e.g., in Vatican CS 15) without regard to local repertories. From this development a whole string of individual hymn collections emerged (e.g., a now-lost hymn book by Martini, published by Petrucci in 1507) that illuminate the position of the new genre. The extent to which a "motetic awareness" permeates all these liturgical functional genres has not yet been examined systematically.

## Special types

The motet's pluralization in the fifteenth century made possible the emergence of independent types that, while based on the textual genres of the Office, constituted individual subgenres with increasingly tenuous relationships to the motet. The lines of tradition are ultimately independent, responding to a desire for functionally consistent texts – a tendency also evident in the hymn. Among these types is the Magnificat, whose significance as the Virgin's hymn of praise highlights the importance of Marian devotion in the polyphonic forms of the fifteenth century. Even its early examples (Dunstaple, Binchois, Du Fay) introduce what Ludwig Finscher has called "varied strophic form" – a type of functional polyphony comparable to the hymn.[26] Remarkably, the two oldest

---

26  See Finscher, "Zum Verhältnis."

surviving Italian Magnificat settings – including perhaps the oldest polyphonic Magnificat altogether, probably composed in the 1430s by the cantor of San Marco Johannes de Quadris – provide an isolated case of a through-composed, free setting. Similarly, Lamentations and Passion settings at first employed rather simple models: a quasi-strophic two-voice texture in the Lamentations by de Quadris, and a simple three-voice English treble setting in the earliest responsory Passions (London 3307). Whereas in the Lamentations we can discern a sudden incorporation of aspects of the psalm motet (e.g., Févin and Pierre de La Rue), Passion settings remained conservative and backward-looking in character, perhaps owing to their Lenten liturgical context. Regarding their texts, however, the two phenomena can be easily connected to the development of the motet: the Lamentations settings showing the poetic force of "individualized" psalm exegesis, the rise of the Passion demonstrating a shift from fifteenth-century Marian devotion toward a focus on the death of Christ.

This mutual permeation of forms is also found in a small subset of mass settings. After the appearance of Du Fay's spectacular *Missa S. Jacobi* (although its intentional cyclic unity has been called into question), the plenary mass played only a subordinate role in the history of the genre.[27] It is in this context that settings of the Ordinary and "motetic" propers came into direct contact; this blurring of boundaries appears occasionally to have been taken up as a challenge. This phenomenon is particularly pertinent to early Requiem settings, whose heterogeneity was overtly thematized (as can be seen, regardless of any philological difficulties, in Ockeghem's Requiem).

In addition to these distinct liturgical types and special forms associated only indirectly with the motet, including two settings of the text *Liber generationis* (anonymous in Trent 91; Josquin), within the motet more narrowly defined there developed certain forms that were at once functionally independent and still fully integrated within the genre. Settings of humanistic poetry, which in the first half of the century were still isorhythmic (e.g. Du Fay's *Salve flos Tusce*), acquired great significance toward the end of the fifteenth century, particularly in Florentine circles. In Isaac's *Quis dabit* settings of texts by Poliziano and Seneca an entirely new style is realized. These are mostly homorhythmic, strictly declamatory motets that mourn the death of Lorenzo de' Medici. The small number of motets using ancient texts represents another special case. In Josquin's *Dulces exuvie* the Virgilian text is deliberately coupled with a modern style, creating a complex musical ekphrasis (in contrast to the metric odes,

---

27  See Bent, "Introductory Study," in *Bologna Q15*.

which are not associated with the motet).[28] Another special case is the "motet chanson," with French texts on a Latin tenor, that appears in the last third of the fifteenth century.[29] In a way this is an abstract motetic "form of thought," executed in the manner of an elaborate secular song, notable examples being works by Du Fay (*O tres piteulx/Omnes amici*) and Ockeghem (*Mort tu as navré/ Miserere* on the death of Binchois). The genre reached its prime with Agricola, Compère, and eventually Josquin, with topoi of lamenting and mourning as its "functional" focus. A considerable number of these works are motets written by composers on the deaths of other composers, Josquin's lament on the death of Ockeghem (*Nymphes des bois/Requiem*) being a prime example. In this practice the composer's *memoria* emerges for the first time. In fact the "composer's motet" need not always be mournful in character (e.g., Compère, *Omnium bonorum/De tous bien plaine*, or Busnoys, *In hydraulis*).

The motet's modes of transmission underscore the independence to which the genre laid claim during the period under discussion. In the mixed manuscripts of the first half of the century, in particular in codices from northern Italy, the motet is always singled out for separate and privileged treatment; as the genre becomes increasingly diversified we see the emergence of independent motet manuscripts, similar to chansonniers and mass collections (Florence 112bis is an early example). The growing number of collections that combine Ordinary cycles and motets in the second half of the century (e.g., Vatican San Pietro B80 and the Chigi Codex) testifies to an increasing sacralization of the genre. This type of "choirbook" survived into the sixteenth century (e.g., Vatican CS 13 and CS 19) and is also found in England (London, Lambeth Palace Library, MS 1). Parallel to this, the motet collection emerged as an independent type of publication with the the first Petrucci prints (*Motetti A*, 1502[1], *Motetti de Passione* . . ., 1503[1]); over the course of the sixteenth century these would acquire a greater commercial significance.

The diverse proliferation of the motet in the fifteenth century can be regarded as a defining characteristic of the era, and indeed of the nascent modern age. The development of new and intricate compositional norms in a highly diverse ritual-functional context put a complex dynamic into motion. This wide-ranging character of the motet would affect the course of composition in the century to come, though the sixteenth century would witness no further diversification. By 1600 the dynamic produced during the fifteenth

---

28  See the essay by Leofranc Holford-Strevens in this volume, Ch. 15.
29  This term as well (first used by Stephan, *Die burgundisch-niederländische Motette*, 51) is quite problematic, but is generally accepted today. See Meconi, "Ockeghem and the Motet-Chanson," which includes a catalogue.

century had itself become historical, leaving the motet to be regarded in retrospect as an exclusively sacred genre.

# Bibliography

Allsen, Jon Michael, "Style and Intertextuality in the Isorhythmic Motet 1400–1440," Ph.D. diss., University of Wisconsin, Madison, 1992

Ambros, August Wilhelm, *Geschichte der Musik im Zeitalter der Renaissance bis zu Palestrina*, Breslau, 1868 (= *Geschichte der Musik* 3)

[Anonymous V], *Ars cantus mensurabilis mensurata per modos iuris*, ed. and trans. C. Matthew Balensuela, Lincoln, NE and London, 1994

Bent, Margaret, *Bologna Q15: The Making and Remaking of a Musical Manuscript*, Ars Nova: Nuova Serie II, Lucca, 2008

Capuano da Amalfi, Pietro, *Mensurabilis musicae tractatuli 1*, ed. F. Alberto Gallo, Bologna, 1966

Colie, Rosalie L., *The Resources of Kind: Genre and Theory in the Renaissance*, ed. Barbara Kiefer Lewalski, Una's Lectures 1, Berkeley, 1973

Cumming, Julie E., *The Motet in the Age of Dufay*, Cambridge, 1999

Dammann, Rolf, "Spätformen der isorhythmischen Motette im 16. Jahrhundert," *AfMw* 10 (1953), 16–40

Finscher, Ludwig, "Zum Verhältnis von Imitationstechnik und Textbehandlung im Zeitalter Josquins," in *Geschichte und Geschichten: Ausgewählte Aufsätze zur Musikhistorie*, ed. Hermann Danuser, Mainz, 2003, 109–22 (first edn. 1979)

Gülke, Peter, *Guillaume Du Fay, Musik des 15. Jahrhunderts*, Stuttgart and Kassel, 2003

Heidrich, Jürgen, *Die deutschen Chorbücher aus der Hofkapelle Friedrichs des Weisen: Ein Beitrag zur mitteldeutschen geistlichen Musikpraxis um 1500*, Sammlung musikwissenschaftlicher Abhandlungen 84, Baden-Baden, 1993

Kreutziger-Herr, Annette, *Johannes Ciconia (ca. 1370–1412): Komponieren in einer Kultur des Wortes*, Hamburger Beiträge zur Musikwissenschaft 39, Hamburg and Eisenach, 1991

Leichtentritt, Hugo, *Geschichte der Motette*, Kleine Handbücher der Musikgeschichte nach Gattungen 2, Leipzig, 1908

Lindmayr, Andrea, *Quellenstudien zu den Motetten von Johannes Ockeghem*, Neue Heidelberger Studien zur Musikwissenschaft 16, Laaber, 1990

Lütteken, Laurenz, *Guillaume Dufay und die isorhythmische Motette: Gattungstradition und Werkcharakter an der Schwelle zur Neuzeit*, Schriften zur Musikwissenschaft aus Münster 4, Eisenach, 1993

Macey, Patrick P., "Josquin's *Miserere mei Deus*: Context, Structure, and Influence," Ph.D. diss., University of California, Berkeley, 1985

Meconi, Honey, "Ockeghem and the Motet-Chanson in Fifteenth-Century France," in *Johannes Ockeghem: Actes du XL^e Colloque international d'études humanistes, Tours, 3–8 février 1997*, ed. Philippe Vendrix, Paris, 1998, 381–402

Paulirinus, Paulus, *Liber viginti artium* (Kraków, Biblioteka Jagiellońska, Cod. 267; ca. 1463); partially published in Josef Reiss, "Pauli Paulirini de Praga Tractatus de Musica (etwa 1460)," *Zeitschrift für Musikwissenschaft* 7 (1924/25), 259–264 (online at www.chmtl.indiana.edu/tml/15th/PAUTRA_TEXT.html)

Pellegrin, Élisabeth, *La Bibliothèque des Visconti et des Sforza ducs de Milan, aux XVe siècle*, Publications de l'Institut de Recherche et d'Histoire de Textes 5, Paris, 1955

Planchart, Alejandro Enrique, "Guillaume Du Fay's Benefices and his Relationship to the Court of Burgundy," *EMH* 8 (1988), 117–71

Rodin, Jesse, *Josquin's Rome: Hearing and Composing in the Sistine Chapel*, New York and Oxford, 2012

Rolsma, Saskia, "De onthullingen van het missaal: Een onderzoek naar de functie van *Motetti missales*," in *Meer dan muziek alleen: In memoriam Kees Vellekoop*, ed. René Ernst Victor Stuio, Hilversum, 2004, 291–306

Rothenberg, David C., *The Flower of Paradise: Marian Devotion and Secular Song in Medieval and Renaissance Music*, New York, 2011

Staehelin, Martin, "Beschreibungen und Beispiele musikalischer Formen in einem unbeachteten Traktat des frühen 15. Jahrhunderts," *AfMw* 31 (1974), 237–42

*Neues zu Werk und Leben von Petrus Wilhelmi: Fragmente des mittleren 15. Jahrhunderts mit Mensuralmusik*, Nachrichten der Akademie der Wissenschaften in Göttingen 2, Göttingen, 2001

Stephan, Wolfgang, *Die burgundisch-niederländische Motette zur Zeit Ockeghems*, Kassel, 1937; repr. Kassel, 1973

Warnke, Martin, *Bau und Überbau: Soziologie der mittelalterlichen Architektur nach den Schriftquellen*, Frankfurt am Main, 1984

# Fifteenth-century song

NICOLE SCHWINDT

TRANSLATED BY JAMES STEICHEN

Unlike motets, songs are not a genre in the conventional sense but a universal phenomenon: there have been songs at all times in history, for every conceivable occasion, in countless manifestations. People have always sung songs, and in this sense they are first and foremost actions – a practice. Only after the fact do they become objects, that is, works that can be fixed, changed, perceived, and reflected upon. It is in this reified form that song has emerged as a genre and come to figure in the history of art and culture.

The long fifteenth century was a decisive period for song as an artistic form: songs began to attain equal footing with and distinguish themselves from masses and motets. They were set down as verbal and musical texts, composed in multi-voice structures with fixed rhythms, increasingly attributed to their creators by name, reproduced by performers, and inserted into complex intertextual exchanges. Both descriptive and prescriptive norms were formulated for their creation and reception.

The definitions of Johannes Tinctoris[1] – according to which the mass is the great, the motet the middle, and the *cantilena* the small song (*cantus magnus, mediocris, parvus*) – are difficult to evaluate, since it is not clear whether he meant them as a hierarchical taxonomy of genres, and, even if so, whether such a hierarchy was based on the relative dimensions of these works, social or functional demands, or aesthetic value. What is clear is that for Tinctoris these three genres represented the core of fixed musical forms. Just a few years later he would label them as genres with hierarchical levels of *varietas*: "and there are not so many and such varieties in a chanson as in a motet, nor are there so many and such varieties in a motet as in a mass."[2] By 1500 these three terms had gained currency even among individuals with no particular knowledge of music, so that Paolo Cortesi could laconically recapitulate them – "MISSE: / MOTETI / CANTILENE" – in the margins when describing the various "canendi rationes"

---

1 Tinctoris, *Terminorum musicae diffinitorium* (1472/73, printed ca. 1495).
2 Tinctoris, *Liber de arte contrapuncti* (1477), bk. 3, ch. 8, in *Opera theoretica*, 2:155.

("the types of singing").[3] Song had become a constitutive element of an increasingly large complex of individuated genres understood as art music.

While masses and motets stand as discrete artistic products whose origins can often be traced to liturgical song, composed songs are open to the limitless field of universal practice. Through the strategic role of documentation and transmission we can uncover how song became a distinctive concept as a genre.

## Song – song tune – song setting

In the fifteenth century the history of song was predicated on a concept developed in the fourteenth: songs were conceived not as monophonic melodies to be subsequently adorned with added voices, but as multi-voice pieces from the start. Thus the complex of all previous types of song, at least those that have survived, was enlarged through this new paradigm, with far-reaching consequences. The musical rationality of polyphony – based on a systematic organization of intervals, durations, and harmonies developed by learned professionals affiliated with religious institutions – migrated to the realm of secular music, which was for the most part courtly in origin. Lyrics that had previously been treated monophonically – the love songs of troubadours, trouvères, and *Minnesänger* – acquired rule-based multi-voice textures. About one thousand surviving songs from the French *Ars nova* and the Italian trecento document this new conception, providing the basis for the flourishing of a variety of song types in the years to come.

With the development of mensural polyphony, the conditions for performance and composition also changed: author and performer became separated. The social aspect of performance – collaboration between several people in the presentation of a song, often without an audience – became more important, with a new role for connoisseurs. The level of musical competence required of both composer and performer was considerably greater, and "music" as a sounding phenomenon acquired new significance. The figure of the poet-singer was displaced by the collaboration of specialists. While key figures in the fourteenth century embodied the poet-musician as a creator of songs – Jacopo da Bologna earned fame as a poet and Guillaume de Machaut acquired his artistic authority in literary circles – the dominant paradigm now became the professional musician, responsible for the composition of the music, who would seldom (Antoine Busnoys is an exception) be regarded as a literary figure.

Most fifteenth-century songs have been transmitted anonymously, so we cannot be certain how the duties of musical and textual creation were parceled

---

3 Cortesi, *De cardinalatu* (1510), fol. 73v; facs. in Pirrotta, "Music and Cultural Tendencies," 150. On Cortesi, see the essay by James Hankins in this volume, Ch. 13.

out. Still, two tendencies are evident. Alongside a body of work by singers who were first and foremost writers, there developed a newer model, in which a written song text was set to music by a composer. Among the older generation of literary musicians, Leonardo Giustinian, Benedetto Gareth, and Pietrobono achieved particular renown, thanks to the literary climate and the dense network of courts on the Italian peninsula. In the classicizing spirit of humanism, they were regarded as modern Orpheuses. To be sure, there is a great gap between what we can appreciate of their musicianship and how it was prized by their contemporaries. Of Serafino Aquilano it was said that in the composition of songs ("componere canti") he carried away the palm from every other Italian musician.[4] "Composition" in this instance should be understood in its most literal sense as "putting together" – including the putting together of words and tones. A poet like Serafino, highly skilled in extemporizing a melody plus accompaniment on a lute or lira da braccio, could be considered a musician. Nonetheless, only poetic texts attributed to him have survived. The songs that have been transmitted – in manuscript and in print, such as Petrucci's sixth frottola book of 1506 – provide only vague hints as to the original state of the music, since for a given text many tunes might be transmitted (especially given the standard eight-line format of the strambotto, his favored form), and since the notated musical material had to be adapted for a realization in four-voice polyphony. A few key traits can be identified from these examples, however, and these are also present in other sources relating to the art of song-singers (see Example 37.1). First, the voice that carries the text is heavily ornamented, with melismas treated in an almost "instrumental" manner and little expressive cantabile; they often begin on a high note and continue steadily downward, corresponding to a relaxation of the vocal chords. Second, the logic of the phrase structure comes entirely from the human voice, which gives shape to the melody through a descending line that begins energetically before relaxing. Third, in accordance with the structure of the verses, the melodic material is repeated several times in identical or only slightly varying form. And fourth, the role of the music is to give voice to the text in a more powerful manner than could be achieved by speech alone.

This older concept of song is itself indebted to vernacular song. The stages of its development are not easy to trace in a strictly chronological manner, since it was itself based on an even more archaic model. Very little is known about the extemporaneous performance of songs in French-speaking lands in the fifteenth century, save some circumstances of their historical context. The traditional "Puys d'amour," or civic poetry competitions in Amiens, Douai,

---

4 "a ciascuno altro musico italiano nel componere canti tolse la palma"; Calmeta, "Vita del facondo poeta vulgare Serafino Aquilano," 60.

Example 37.1 Anon., *Non te stimar*, Milan, Biblioteca Trivulziana, MS 55, fols. 18v–19r

Valenciennes, Arras, and other cities near Cambrai, were an important locus of this practice. Musical realizations of conventional love poetry can be roughly reconstructed through the eyes of learned composers: Guillaume Du Fay, for one, could have composed songs for this purpose even while abroad. In *Ce jour le doibt* (Example 37.2) he mentions the Maas and Oise rivers, as well as the

Example 37.2  Guillaume Du Fay, *Ce jour le doibt*, Oxford 213, fol. 79r

official call to order by the head of the jury, the "prince d'amour." Among the surviving sources for this three-voice ballade are two rhythmically and harmonically integrated accompanying voices, both quite simple, that could be played on a harp by the singer. The vocal part, which presents the text in a predictable, syllabic manner, could have been improvised as written or even more simply.

The increasingly literate transmission of song, foreign to this older concept, made it necessary to settle upon a primary voice that would always sing the text. It is hard to say whether some regions preferred certain registers for the primary voice. Neapolitan lute singers perhaps sang the highest voice in falsetto. In German lands the natural male tenor range was preferred, which favored syllabic text-setting with little decoration and assigned the agile accompanying part to a higher register, unencumbered by polyphonic constraints.[5] The two-voice *alba Wach auf mein Hort* by the Tyrolean poet Oswald von Wolkenstein (Example 37.3) shows this tendency in the lower voice: the irregular and quasi-improvised melodic contours repeatedly descend from $a'$ to $d'$, then from $d'$ to $a$. Likewise, so-called "popular tune settings," that is, chansons with French texts from after mid-century that are peripheral to the art-song tradition, such as Gilles Binchois's *Files a marier*, favor the tenor as the carrier of the melody. This model remained in place in German-speaking regions well into the sixteenth century; indeed since 1930 German polyphonic songs have been referred to simply as *Tenorlieder*.

These few examples show how difficult it is, on the one hand, to have any real sense of non-notated song practice – a fundamental problem for the historiography of song – and on the other, how important it is to understand the interactions of these non-notated songs with the realm of art song. Music that was originally unwritten was forced into the formats of composed song; in return composed songs took on elements of the oral tradition. The oeuvre of a "singer-songwriter" such as Oswald shows the breadth of the concept of song at this time. In the first half of the century he came into contact with song types from all over Europe and adapted them for his own use: texts such as calendar poems that could be described by the words "spoken" or "sung" and songs transmitted with a single tune for use with multiple poems. Some melodies have been transmitted, making it possible to reconstruct the rarefied art of German *Übersingen*, i.e., improvised discant (such as *Wach auf mein Hort*) as well as the parallel structures reminiscent of organum, voice-crossing, and dissonances, as in examples from the Monk of Salzburg in the Mondsee-Wiener Liederhandschrift.[6] Oswald even applied the Germanic practice of a texted tenor to polyphonic chansons, replacing Binchois's three-voice *Triste plaisir* with his formally and semantically unrelated poem "O wunniklicher wolgezierter mai," a contrafactum that drastically

---

5 In Example 37.3, see the dissonant ninths in mm. 5, 11, 16/17, and 23, and the parallel fifths in mm. 8/9, 12–13, and 20/21.
6 Vienna, Österreichische Nationalbibliothek, Cod. 2856, fols. 166r–284v (copied 1452–69). On other compositions by Oswald, see Anna Maria Busse Berger's Ch. 10 in this volume.

Example 37.3 Oswald von Wolkenstein, *Wach auf mein Hort*, Kl. 101

alters the musical structure and the contour of the tenor voice. Some songs are preserved in single-voice and multi-voice monodic and polyphonic versions, making it impossible to tell which was authoritative. Oswald's output is merely a well-documented case, with simple and complex song materials, including completions and reductions, that survived because, as a poet, he consciously compiled his lyrical works in two large manuscripts.

This lack of definitive versions shows how monophony and polyphony co-existed, and, more importantly, that flexibility in the number of voices was characteristic of polyphonic songs. Thus, of the surviving works of such late trecento composers as Paolo da Firenze, Bartolino da Padova, Johannes Ciconia, and Zacara da Teramo, substantially more are transmitted as both two- and three-voice settings than as settings for three voices only. Elaborating the contra-puntally indispensable duo of cantus and tenor with a third voice was a valuable goal, but only in the rarest cases a *sine qua non*, and decidedly not a criterion of strict stylistic development. Simone Prudenzani's verse novel *Il Saporetto*, from the beginning of the fifteenth century, describes how the three singers Sollazzo, Frate Agostino, and Pier de Iovanale sang a whole series of songs as "principal" (main voice), "tenor," and "contra";[7] the songs he names, however, have been handed down mainly in two-voice versions without a contra, so we can only speculate as to whether there was ever a notated or improvised third voice.

As important and decisive as polyphony was in fifteenth-century song, its textural fabric is also characterized by profound instability. By the time of Machaut the three-voice chanson had become a normative model, even if the number of voices could be augmented by a triplum above or beneath the cantus. Based on a concept termed *Kantilenensatz* by Heinrich Besseler, this composi-tional model remained dominant until 1460.[8] The easily audible cantus is comprised of a singable, melismatic melodic line that carries the text and does not overwhelm it; the gently arched melody is driven by the words, but elevated declamation is not its central aim; the *raison d'être* of this voice is singability, musicality, beauty, and expressivity. The tenor, proceeding more quietly, com-plements the cantus through reasoned and logical counterpoint. The contra-tenor supplements these voices, not claiming a tonal space of its own, but instead taking an angular and occasionally nervous path, sometimes closer to the cantus, but mostly closer to the tenor. It is superfluous in a contrapuntal sense, offering a commentary on the main musical events.

A "twin ballad" with two texts written by Machaut's student Eustache Deschamps on the death of his teacher was set to music by one "F. Andrieu"

7 Prudenzani, *Il "Sollazzo" e il "Saporetto,"* sonnets 47 and 48, pp. 116 ff.
8 Besseler, *Bourdon und Fauxbourdon.*

Example 37.4 F. Andrieu, *Armes amours/O flour des flours*, Chantilly 564, fol. 52r (beginning)

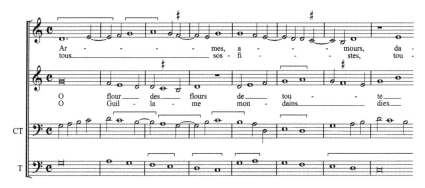

ca. 1400 (see Example 37.4). Though scored for four voices, it clearly demonstrates this distribution of voices already in the first few measures. Both poems sound simultaneously. While the tenor rhythms and intervals bring out the simple musical structure of the hexachord, the cantilena voice moves in a supple, wave-like fashion. Through voice exchange (see mm. 1–4 and 5–8), the second cantus sings the same melody as the first. Indeed the same music would occur twice were it not for the contratenor's varied "commentary," in one instance in a higher range and in the other in a lower.

While the structure of this example appears simple, it demonstrates an interest in sophisticated contrapuntal procedures that extended even to less prominent song composers. This chanson is transmitted in the Chantilly Codex, which contains several examples of exceedingly complex notation.[9] Indeed, song had both qualitatively and quantitatively outstripped the prestigious motet, which also concerned itself with lyrical texts, but song suddenly found itself at the extremes of elite artificiality.

Although such heightened artistic standards generated considerable momentum in the history of song, the simple, or at least simpler, song remained significant. These less pretentious pieces have survived from a variety of cultural contexts (the Reina Codex, purportedly from Padua, or in the Dutch fragment in Leiden, Leiden 2720), revealing that osmosis between the two spheres was decisive for the development of song. Thus in polyphonic pieces the flexibility (or even instability) of the number of voices evinces the relatively weak textual status of individual compositions as well as opportunities for new stylistic developments. This compositional openness found its counterpart in performance:

9 Chantilly 564, presumably Italian ca. 1400.

how to sing songs was considerably less prescribed than in other genres, whether in terms of singers – men, women, or children – or the use of loud or soft instruments.

This simpler type of piece was the dominant model for the generation of composers that had been active since the 1420s, even after having gradually exchanged the challenges of the *ars subtilior* style for more flowing and sensuous writing in *tempus perfectum*. In Savoy, at the courts of the Burgundian dukes, and at northern Italian centers in the papal court's sphere of influence, three-part structures with individual profiles for each voice remained the norm in chansons by Du Fay, Gilles Binchois, and their colleagues. The primary sources for this period (Oxford 213, completed in the Veneto in 1436, and the Burgundian chansonnier El Escorial V.III.24 (EscA), assembled about ten years later) confirm that this concept was also the norm in written documentation – though the contratenor was still unstable. Deviations in the written transmission of chansons, which could reflect a practice of doubling the sung parts heterophonically by a lute or harp, are most evident in this voice, which was often exchanged for a different, "substitute" contratenor. Binchois's *Deuil angoisseus* represents an extreme but by no means isolated example. This ballade circulated with no fewer than four different contratenors, two of which appear in a distinct four-voice version. Moreover, in one of the surviving three-voice versions the contratenor is by and large a conflation of the two contratenors of the four-voice version; the result is a "solus contratenor." What is notable is not that the piece was provided with different contratenors in different places, but rather that several sources present alternatives, thereby facilitating multiple realizations.[10] Such experimentation contributed to another compositional development from around 1450: the creation of a low contratenor. This was an important step toward the development of conventional four-voice textures and the shift from successive to simultaneous conception.

In Antoine Busnoys's *Ce n'est pas moy* (Example 37.5), composed perhaps before his move from France to the Burgundian court in 1467, voice-crossing between the tenor and contratenor is evident only in sporadic single notes (indicated with *).[11] A typical octave-leap cadence in the contratenor, measures 19–20, contributes a fifth ($c'$) between the $f$ and $f'$ of the primary voices; by contrast, in the medial and final cadences the contra shifts to a "modern" descent of a fifth. Indeed the contratenor's function has already become what

---

10  El Escorial V.III.24 with II, III, IV ("Solus"); Trent 88 (before 1460) with CT I, II, III; El Escorial IV.a.4 (after 1460): with CT I. See the synopsis in *Die Chansons von Gilles Binchois*, ed. Rehm, 46 and 73.

11  The bergerette form suggests a French provenance, but the song's transmission in exclusively in Italian sources (the Pixérécourt chansonnier, Paris 15123, partially from the middle of the 1480s; and Bologna Q.16, first part from 1487) also makes a Burgundian provenance possible.

Example 37.5 Antoine Busnoys, *Ce n'est pas moy*, Paris 15123, fols. 172v–173r

would be termed by the 1470s "contratenor bassus" (or, more commonly in sacred music, simply "bassus," together with a higher "contratenor altus"). This new type of contratenor is much more central to the composition than in the layered arrangements of the first half of the century, in which each voice

Example 37.5 (cont.)

had a specific physiognomy and function throughout. With these different contrapuntal requirements, the possibilities for how voices could unfold in the course of a song also changed. In principle the demand for an arch-shaped cantilena melody remained – but as Busnoys's chanson shows, the focus is now on expressive motifs that react with one other. Thus the text gives rise to two types of motivic figures (see Example 37.5): openings with an upward leap of a fourth and those with repeated notes. These correspond mostly to the poetic form, but at the beginning Busnoys uses the motivic contrast to break up the formal structure of the verse and shape the content of the text: "It is not I – it is you, Madame." He further emphasizes this turn with an emphatic change in register for the cantus, which leaps upward by an octave.

Busnoys distinguishes phrases of the text through clearly shaped motives and a consistent use of imitation that always involves the contratenor. (Indeed the song begins with a concise motive in that voice.) His interest in marking structural divisions in the text is especially clear at the beginning of the B section, where he introduces a new mensuration sign and a shift to homorhythmic texture.

These developments affect how one hears the music: the chanson is now a process moving forward in time, whose individual stages are marked by distinct musical gestures. By the close of the century, composers focused even more on the swift unfolding of motivic phrases, above all in four-voice settings such as Jacob Obrecht's Flemish song *Ic draghe de mutse clutse*.[12] More often than not such settings are transmitted with only a textual incipit, suggesting that from the start these were intended as "Lieder ohne Worte" or songs without words.

Four-voice writing had risen to prominence after Machaut, but until 1480 constituted a small minority in secular polyphony. Indeed owing to the flexibility of compositional structures, a fourth voice was at best incidental – except in the large *si placet* repertory, which usually supplied three-voice songs with an optional fourth voice.[13] Even once four-voice writing became standard in secular music, three-voice textures remained a legitimate format, as documented in the immense Braccesi chansonnier (Florence 229, ca. 1490). Indeed in the 1490s *tricinia* gained a specific profile: lighter and more transparent, less complex in character, closer to improvised models, and intellectually slighter. Representative of this trend are chansons by Antoine de Févin and Josquin, written in the circle of the French court in the last decade of the century, that are scored for fewer than four voices (e.g., Josquin's *A l'ombre d'un buissonet*). Beginning around 1500, the indication of prestige by means of the number of voices would proceed in the opposite direction – toward weighty five- and six-voice songs by Josquin and Pierre de La Rue at the court of Margaret of Austria in Malines. The number of voices emerged as a subcategory useful not only as a stylistic marker but also for the purposes of classification: in the Lorraine Chansonnier (Paris 1597, before or ca. 1500) three-voice pieces are followed by

12 Segovia s.s. (?1502), fols. 131v–132r.
13 See Self, ed., *The* Si placet *Repertory*.

four-voice works, in traditional fashion; by contrast, in Petrucci's *Canti B* and *Canti C* (Venice, 1502 and 1504) and in the Basevi Codex, chansons *a 4* precede those *a 3*.

In contrast to other genres, songs require a singable tune, so it is perhaps not surprising that even at the end of the fifteenth century, lavish sources sometimes transmit songs monophonically. Two chansonniers that circulated at the French court around 1500 contain song tunes that are either unique or elsewhere transmitted monophonically, or that are nearly identical to voices of polyphonic settings by Josquin, Loyset Compère, Henricus Isaac, and others.[14]

The flexibility of the chanson with respect to its number of voices facilitated new combinative techniques, wherein a song could be overlaid with a preexisting melody. (In such cases it is not always clear that both texts were intended to be sung.) In the so-called "combinative chanson," a subcategory of the "chanson rustique," a preexisting song tune (real or imagined) characterized by a free form, syllabic text-setting, a straightforward style, and a popular feel is surrounded by similarly uncomplicated voices (e.g., Binchois's *Files a marier/Se tu t'en marias*, in which both texts warn girls about marriage). Free and fixed forms could be layered (e.g., Johannes Ockeghem's rondeau *S'elle m'amera*, superimposed on the lighthearted ditty *Petite camusette*). Alternatively, one of the elaborated voices could embed a reference to a courtly chanson (Philippe Basiron, for instance, joins the cantus from Ockeghem's *D'ung autre amer* with the low-style martial tune of *L'homme armé*). In the "motet-chanson" from the 1470s and 1480s, a Latin cantus firmus is integrated into a lively song setting (e.g., Josquin's love assurances in the bergerette *Que vous madame* are combined with *In pace*, a psalm about sleep). In each case, contrasting forms and aesthetic registers are juxtaposed, resulting in a new meaning or witty verbal play. An instructive variation on this technique from around 1500 is found in Alexander Agricola's "art-song reworkings," in which one or more voices from a recognizable chanson such as Hayne van Ghizeghem's *De tous biens plaine* are replaced by voices that sound like virtuosic instrumental variations. In such works the poetic dimension recedes, as the composer is inspired by a musical model to create something new – indeed the polyphonic chanson realizes its full potential as a musically autonomous art object.

## Poems and their settings: form, content, language

Although a specifically musical impulse is the central force behind the history of song in the Renaissance, this development occurred through fruitful interactions between the two partners of a song, text and music. A key

---

14 Paris, Bibliothèque nationale de France, f. fr. 12744 and f. fr. 9346 ("Manuscrit de Bayeux").

witness to the increasing autonomy of these two disciplines is the treatise *L'art de dictier et de fere chançons, ballades, virelais et rondeaux*, completed in 1392 by Eustache Deschamps. Unlike his teacher Machaut, Deschamps embodies the increasingly common division between poet and composer; the poet writes for spoken rather than sung performance, or even perhaps for the act of reading, where one might only imagine a musical dimension. For Deschamps, a verbal text has its own aural dimension; he calls this sonic level of speech, uniquely and artistically connected to rhyme, "musique naturele." Insofar as he distinguishes "musique naturele" from the pitches, durations, and harmonies of composed songs, this verbal sensorium represents a radical innovation: both types of songs are music, but they pursue their goals in different ways. It is telling that the creators of the lyrics for polyphonic chansons are almost completely unknown, and that the immense corpus of poetry by major authors such as Christine de Pizan, Charles d'Orléans, and Alain Chartier was almost never used for polyphonic settings.

Deschamps is one of the first theorists of poetry to comprehensively treat the so-called *formes fixes*, which underpinned chansons from Machaut until around 1500, with parallels in other Romance song traditions. This term has been used in literary studies since 1872, but is not completely accepted because it does not take into account the full range of poetic forms. Nonetheless, its use is reasonable in music because almost all French songs up to the middle of the fifteenth century, and a significant number thereafter, show the influence of the *formes fixes*. Their importance lies not only in the invariable arrangement of strophes, but also in the way all three types – ballade, rondeau, and virelai – center on the structure of the refrain. In the time of the troubadours and trouvères, a lack of repetition was central to the prestigious *grand chant*; by contrast, repetition was part of the bodily action of a dancing song and the social practice of call-and-response, and thus characteristic for the less precious little song; now, in the poetic doctrines of the *seconde rhétorique*, the artful treatment of the refrain becomes an occasion for refined strategies of form and content.

The adoption of a clearly delineated repertory of poetic forms was enormously consequential for music. Songs became lyrical "small forms," with texts limited to at most three short stanzas. (Narrative songs are rare in the polyphonic repertory.) Whereas in virelais, bergerettes, rondeaux, and ballades the refrain was a staged moment for the return of familiar material, repetition now became something to be avoided in the musical progress of the piece. In its place elegant variety was cultivated as an aesthetic ideal: in *forme fixe* songs, text is rarely repeated. Since expansiveness was a goal, a preference for melismatic passages arose. Indeed melismas were no longer confined to textless preludes, interludes, or postludes. Three models of text declamation developed, of which Oxford 213 offers many examples: portions of verses could be set with a long melisma, especially at the opening (this practice was favored by Du Fay but not Binchois), but more common are verses that end with a long melisma; and smaller melismas could be distributed over the words. This legacy of the fourteenth century, evident in several *ars subtilior* ballades, lost ground in the 1420s and 1430s in favor of syllabic text declamation within the verse. The result was a musicalized presentation of poetic verse, whose words nevertheless followed a strict order without being cluttered or disturbed by repetition; this, in turn, threw the important and almost magical end-rhymes into relief. The polyphonic setting, with caesuras and cadences, clearly parallels the formal structure of the verse, even though it was primarily determined by the rhythmic movements of the cantilena. (There is no reason that melismas should be performed only as instrumental preludes, interludes, or postludes.)

The structure of the virelai demonstrates most clearly the basic Provençal poetic type of the high Middle Ages, which lived on in the Italian and Spanish ballata and villancico: a divided refrain (AB) is followed by a section designed as a pair of similarly structured lines (Cc). The third section of the stanza (*tierce*) is identical in meter and rhyme, and thus musically, with the refrain, albeit with new text (ab). The stanza is rounded off by the literal repetition of the refrain (AB).[15] Further stanzas repeat the pattern. By contrast, the structure of the ballade strophe is much simpler: an opening arranged in pairs (Aa) is followed by a middle section (B), which is rounded off with a short refrain (R). One finds an inverse relationship between the complexity of a song form and its prestige: even though the ballade is formally simpler than the rondeau, it was the genre of choice for socially significant occasions. The virelai never quite cast off its origins in dancing songs and was preferred for lighter subjects. From 1420 on it lost its appeal, after being cultivated by composers connected to Burgundian or French musical centers such as Cambrai and Bourges (e.g., Nicolas Grenon, Guillame Legrant, and composers at the Lusignan court on Cyprus).[16] The ballade followed an only slightly different path, having been elevated by Machaut to the *genus sublime* of the chanson. By 1420 it, too, had peaked in popularity, but thanks to its distinguished position in the hierarchy of genres, the ballade was occasionally chosen for serious texts (e.g., Binchois's *Deuil angoisseus*, on a poem by Christine de Pizan) or celebratory occasions (e.g., Du Fay's *Se la face ay pale*, probably for the marriage of the heir to the

15 Capital letters indicate identical music and text, lowercase letters indicate identical music and different text, albeit with identical meter and rhyme scheme.
16 Turin J.II.9 (repertory up to 1420, written before 1434); large parts of the repertory have tentatively been ascribed to Gilles Velut and Jean Hanelle in French exile.

Savoyard throne, although Anne Walters Robertson has suggested that it was written for the reception of the Holy Shroud[17]).

Without question, the most favored *forme fixe* in the fifteenth century was the rondeau. Already in Oxford 213 there are 187 rondeaux, as compared to only thirty-eight ballades and ten virelais. The rondeau proved practical in many different contexts, since its form could be appreciated as both simple and sophisticated; it functioned as both a trifle and an expansive and meaningful creation.[18] A refrain of either two-plus-two (*rondeau quatrain*) or three-plus-two (*rondeau cinquain*) lines, with enclosed rhyme (abba), provides the music for the whole piece:[19] A extends up to the (typically suspended) middle caesura and B until the end. In these ways the refrain alone ensures linguistic and musical sense. Accordingly, the poets often heightened the coherence of the two sections of the rondeau through enjambment. For a half-strophe with new text, half the refrain would follow (aA), which would continue necessarily into a full strophe (ab). This *tierce* is rounded out by a return to the refrain. For example, an eight-line rondeau has the following form: ABaAabAB. Thanks to its asymmetry, the structure is at once economical and open to rhetorical maneuvering. Owing to its inward-circling arrangement, the rondeau was also suited for lyrics of pleasant or melancholic self-reflection.

From the middle of the century the rhetorical potential of the refrain began to coalesce. New process-oriented thought, manifested in a formalism built on (often imitative) excerpts, proved incompatible with refrain structures. Consequently rondeaux were often composed as a refrain – that is, from only two strophes in the form AB; and the by now unfashionable virelai – reactivated in the circle of Ockeghem and Busnoys as the bergerette – was reduced to one strophe (AbbaA). Thus the virelai could be understood as an alternative to the rondeau; the counter-strophe (Cc) took the place of the half-strophe or half-refrain (aA) in the rondeau and used it as a contrasting excerpt.

Despite their dominance, rondeaux were not immune to adaptation. In the last quarter of the century, there was a tendency to suppress parts of the text in the repeating sections and insert newly composed music, so that in many rondeaux of Agricola's generation one sees through-composition with motto-like reprises of the refrain.

Toward the end of the century, ballades experienced a resurgence, although in different circumstances. They became the preferred mode for the lower stylistic

---

17 Robertson, "The Man with the Pale Face."
18 At ninety-five breves, the anonymous rondeau *Plus voy mon mignon* from the Nivelle de la Chaussée Chansonnier (Loire Valley, after ca. 1470) is one of the longest pieces in the fifteenth-century chanson repertory.
19 The typical rhyme scheme is abba or aabba.

register, whose rhetorical powers of persuasion relied less on intricacy than on forthright utterances. Instead of complicated recollections, material is simply stated twice. Indeed ballades often lost their refrains, changing into linear works. Similar to a bar form, they have a *frons* (*Aufgesang*) consisting of two musically identical *pedes* (*Stollen*), and a *cauda* (*Abgesang*) which can also be divided into two sections, preferably employing literal or almost literal repetition.[20] Josquin's three-voice *Si j'ay perdu mon amy*[21] illustrates this play with formal allusions:

| Music | Text |
|-------|------|
| A | Si j'ay perdu mon amy |
| B | Je n'ay point cause de rire; |
| A | Je l'avoye sur tous choisy, |
| B | Vray Dieu qu'en voulez vous dire? |
| C | Il m'avoyt juré sa foy |
| C' | De n'aymer aultre que moy |
| C'' | De n'aymer aultre que moy |
| D | Tout au long du moy de may |
| E | Qu'en voulez vous dire? |
| D' | Morte suys si je ne l'ay! |
| E' | Et qu'en voulez vous donc dire de moy?[22] |

The text is a travesty of the rondeaux and ballades of the first third of the century, with the joy of lovers in May as the antidote to unhappiness; but while in earlier poems the refrain cements the hopelessness of a sad situation, now textual echoes serve as comic punch lines.

The tendency of composers in the second half of the century to treat their material in a rational and economical manner – manifested in the systematic use of imitation – affected forms as well. Immediate repetition of textual or musical units and simple, symmetrical forms such as ABA became increasingly prevalent, especially from the 1470s on. These techniques were evident not just in simple strophic songs classified under the rubric of "popular song," but also in refrain forms. In his satirical rondeau *L'autre d'antan*, for instance, Ockeghem cites the opening measures at the end in a deliberately humorous gesture. Together with regular phrase divisions, quick triple meters, and syllabic declamation, the underlying form here is part of a song practice that Tinctoris labeled with the humanistic term "carmen Bucolicum."[23]

---

20  Typically in rhyming pairs (abab) or double rhyming pairs (ababcdcd).

21  Edition: NJE 27.34; early transmission from ca. 1500 in the Lorraine Chansonnier (Paris 1597) and in the monophonic Paris chansonnier 12744 with repeat signs after the fourth line.

22  "Now that I have lost my friend, / I have no more reason to laugh. / I chose him from among all others. / Good God, what do you say to this? / He pledged his loyalty to me, / that he would love no other / for the whole month of May. / What do you say to this? / I am dead if I can't have him. / And what will you then say of me?"

23  Tinctoris, *Proportionale musices* (ca. 1472–75), bk. 1, ch. 3.

The immense growth in chanson production in the fifteenth century led to greater diversity and differentiation of subjects. At first the "fin' amors" of the troubadours and trouvères was dominant, since the demands of polyphonic song continued the tradition of the *grand chant courtois*. The concept of "courtly love" (*amour courtois*, a term coined by Gaston Paris in 1883) made available a network of ideals, terms, images, and imagined behaviors, in part enacted by the high aristocracy through ceremonies and rituals. The feudal structure of society – predicated upon the relationship between lord and vassal – carried over into the relationship between the lover and the beloved, such that loyalty and service became central concepts and fueled an appropriate vocabulary. Love was understood as an ethical and pedagogical value and as a process of prolonged rapprochement. The woman – whether accessible or, more typically, inaccessible – is portrayed with a beauty that accords with spiritual and moral qualities; the persistent and ever-hopeful man vacillates between euphoria and despair, and must perfect himself psychically and mentally. Courtly love poems display a vast range of affective dispositions, from immense joy and aggressive optimism to desperate longing for death. This emotional diversity made possible a wide array of musical moods, especially evident in the chansons of Du Fay, who in his early years had an almost inexhaustible interest in them as textual material. Even if by this time the system of *amour courtois* was practically speaking merely a relic, it was nonetheless still present in the spiritual imagination of the European aristocracy of the fifteenth century. The poet could instantly summon up such topoi, whether through abstract terminology (honor, virtue), concrete images (glances), metaphors (sweet servitude), or allegorical personifications (mostly courtesy of the figural arsenal of the *Roman de la rose*, as in the compliant "Bel accueil" or the slanderous "Malebouche").

In German lyrics the intricate and dialectical concept of *amour courtois* faded after 1400 in favor of a linear concept of love, in which the mutual attraction of lovers goes smoothly or, at the worst, is thwarted by internal or external impediments such as unfaithfulness or envy (in the Lochamer Liederbuch, for example).[24] In chanson repertories the dissolution of *amour courtois* proceeded more slowly – earlier in the circles of the French crown than in the Burgundian duchy – and the range of themes multiplied. The physical body and the erotic had typically been peripheral to courtly love poetry and confined to marginal poetic forms such as the rarely set pastourelle; in the second half of the century, subjects encompassing everyday life and amusing or sentimental incidents gained new purchase, including those devoted to the more problematic, frivolous, and obscene aspects of love. The large song outputs of

24 Nuremberg, 1452–60.

Ockeghem, Loyset Compère, and Josquin offer a range of such thematically dissimilar materials. In one and the same social and intellectual environment, *amour courtois* was simultaneously perpetuated as an ideal while also being ironized and trivialized. Courtly "popular songs" derived their literary and musical appeal from the breaking of taboos, from an otherness that makes sense only in relation to established norms as an amusing outlet.

This distance between the artistic and popular spheres is most evident in the "combinative chanson," transmitted mainly in the Dijon and second Escorial chansonniers,[25] discussed above with respect to the layering of free and pre-existing voices. In this type of song, texts from the stylistic register of *amour courtois* were sung simultaneously with those from the popular sphere.[26]

This pluralization of material did not consist of just simpler, bolder, or more naïve themes, but even included the crass and nonsensical. At the other end of the spectrum, serious themes far removed from the language of love were available. Political subjects, however, remained decidedly in the margins, as did sacred ones – apart from Latin contrafacta of the German and eastern European region and vernacular contrafacta in the repertory of the Italian lauda, both of which were practically non-existent in French-speaking lands. Dirges for rulers or colleagues, beginning with Ockeghem's chanson of mourning for Binchois (*Mort tu as navré de ton dart*, after 1460) comprise a small but characteristic corpus. Such *déplorations* combine the French chanson text with a Latin liturgical cantus firmus. In such instances, song explores an intimate and personal dimension of mourning, articulated in the mother tongue, while chant represents a more "official" side.

How did actual speech influence the creation and use of polyphonic song? It is unmistakable that individual linguistic cultures developed their own poetic forms. The French virelai, Italian ballata, and Spanish villancico derive from the same genetic roots, but differ significantly in their details. The same is true of the "canzona-strophe" (or bar form), which was received and developed differently in Italy and Germany; there are fundamental differences at the level of declamation and in its language-dependent verse structure. Thus the flexible, syllable-counting prosody of the Romance languages stands in opposition to the versification of Germanic languages, with their alternation of stressed and unstressed syllables. (Attempts to restore the quantitative meters of antiquity gained currency only at the turn of the century, in conjunction with the rise of the "humanistic ode" cultivated at

---

25  El Escorial IV.a.24 (EscB, after 1460), fol. 4r (fol. 3v missing).
26  The chanson *O rosa bella / O dolce anima mia / No mi lassar morire / In cortesia, in cortesia*, preserved in EscB, is a radical example.

German courts and universities.[27]) We must assume that different underlying principles of the linguistic material led to typological permutations, and that this would make it possible to identify the origin of a song reliably. But what was possible with syllabic declamation often did not hold up to a style oriented toward melismatic writing and independent voice-leading.

Chansons derived from settings in languages other than French stand as the litmus test for the linguistic independence of the "chanson system." A small number come from Italy (e.g., Du Fay's *Quel fronte signorille*) or England (e.g., Bedyngham's rondeau *Mon seul plaisir*, probably originally sung as *Mi verry joy*). More common are songs that are chansons in style and compositional technique, but that linguistically and formally rely on indigenous traditions. Sources beginning around 1460 provide evidence that French chansons coexisted peaceably with chansons in other vernaculars, especially in places where Franco-Flemish musicians were present. An especially productive melting pot was the Aragonese court at Naples, in whose multilingual atmosphere poems in chanson form were created and transmitted in French as well as occasionally in English, Italian, Spanish, and even Flemish. Cultural relationships such as those between the Aragonese satellite courts in southern Italy and the Iberian Aragon courts gave rise to their own offshoot: the Spanish song form known today as canción. The names and biographies of composers connected to this genre – Juan Cornago, Enrique Foxer "de Paris," Juan de Urrede/Johannes Wreede – demonstrate that the native language of a composer was not a determining factor. The polyphonic chanson constituted a pan-European aesthetic that was unified for a while before being infiltrated or expanded upon by regional idiosyncrasies.

New stylistic formats began to appear in those moments when new literary movements in the vernacular took shape. Discussions of the *questione della lingua*, focusing on the privileged Tuscan dialect, raised awareness of an exemplary *volgare*, after which, beginning in the late 1460s, more poems were written in Italian; not coincidentally, there subsequently appeared a greater number of canzoni in polyphonic compositions. This alternative to the chanson was developed from simple declamation. With easily sung melodies in a six-note range, a mostly homorhythmic texture, and text carried in any voice, such pieces are characterized by a homogeneous, almost sensuous sound-world. Neapolitan sources of the 1460s began to incorporate isolated Italian songs in chanson contexts; a decade later, the Cordiforme Chansonnier (from Savoy) shows French and Italian exemplars side by side. The iconic example of the new sensuous appeal was the Florentine song *Fortuna desperata* from ca.

---

27 See the essay by Reinhard Strohm in this volume, Ch. 14.

Example 37.6 Anon., *Fortuna desperata*, Paris 4379, fols. 40v–41r (beginning)

1470 (Example 37.6).[28] Its paradigmatic quality is evident in its ubiquity: four dozen surviving compositions engaged creatively with this song.[29]

In a different time, place, and context, the frottola arose beginning around 1490 under the patronage of Isabella d'Este at the Mantuan court. The frottola took up the songs of the *improvvisatori*. When Bartolomeo Tromboncino and Marchetto Cara – typically enough, both not of Franco-Flemish origin –

28  Paris 4379 (Naples or Rome, ca. 1470–85), fols. 40v–41r.
29  See Meconi, "Poliziano, *Primavera*, and Perugia 431," esp. the chronogical list in App. A.

adapted this style of improvised singing for four-voice, written compositions, they allowed themselves contrapuntal progressions that are avoided in most composed chansons of the period. Syllabic text dominates, but much less important than what was sung was that something was sung at all – and, tellingly, in the vernacular. These polyphonic songs seldom function as elaborate art works; they are more a form of musical communication.

In Spain a literary figure was responsible for the emergence of the villancico, an offshoot of the canción. Juan del Encina, a student of Antonio de Nebrija, who had praised the vernacular in his *Gramática de la lengua castellana* (Salamanca, 1492), created not just the textual structure of the new genre, but also its musical physiognomy. He left the polyphonic conception of the canción behind to develop a new Spanish idiom.

A corresponding movement of linguistic and poetic renewal occurred in German lands, although it focused less on the propagation of (still copious) vernacular lyric production than on a canonization of new Latin poetry. In the large repertory of *Tenorlieder* that arose after 1490, the new concept of the *contrapunctus simplex* occurs as an experiment, stemming not from a Franco-Flemish composer, but rather from a vernacular artist: Paul Hofhaimer.

## Songs as cultural media

The concept of *natio* emerged during the course of the fifteenth century. Vernacular song genres were part of this process, which made the concept of a fixed "national" unity, fostered by a common language, more concrete. The tendency of song genres to correlate with a specific language is unmistakable by the end of the century, and is sometimes connected to political movements (e.g., the founding of the Spanish state by the "reyes católicos" or the Imperial Idea of Maximilian I in German lands). But it would be wrong to call the earlier decades of the century "international," despite the extensive migration of composers and the dispersal of various repertories. They are in fact "pre-national." With respect to their distribution and reception, language was only to a limited extent a determining factor.

That the chanson – a song based on a French text – could be spread and valued across Europe was a result of larger cultural-political networks. The economic and political power of the Burgundian court, with its resources in northeastern France and in Flemish regions, played an important role. The intensive cultivation of the polyphonic song by singer-composers trained in ecclesiastical *maîtrises* had a lasting effect on the conception of the genre: songs were secular *Kleinformen* ("small forms"), but in difficulty and composition they were equal to their sacred counterparts. This emphasis on musical content gave chansons a value that allowed them to circulate alongside their peripatetic authors both with and without music, and often together with sacred works.

The sources reflect both of these trends: Oxford 213, created ca. 1420–36 in the Veneto, contains many chansons by Du Fay and his colleagues, all of whom were employed in Italy (e.g., the brothers Hugo and Arnold de Lantins, Gualterius Libert, and Guillaume Malbecque); but it contains just as many chansons by musicians who took up residence in central and northeastern France, Burgundy, and other diocesan seats – artists who, like Binchois, presumably did not venture farther south than the Savoyard court (Nicolas Grenon, Franchois Lebertoul, Guillaume and Johannes Legrant, Richard Loqueville). This pattern holds true elsewhere. A half-century later, the Mellon Chansonnier, from the Aragonese court in Naples, contains a repertory almost entirely from north of the Alps (Busnoys, Ockeghem, and late Du Fay), which was probably transmitted by Franco-Flemish composers (Tinctoris, Vincenet). Without such powerful support a large amount of Franco-Flemish music, including chansons, made its way by 1470 to the bilingual culture at the southern frontier of the Germanic Empire at the diocesan court of Trent. The song repertory of the Trent codices (Trent 87–92 and 93), produced in an area where the vernacular was German and Italian and where French was not spoken, makes it clear that the genre was valued on account of its musical qualities, since the song texts are either corrupted, changed into Latin, or omitted entirely.

To cultivate chansons outside French-speaking regions was a mark of distinction in the fifteenth century. In the British Isles, French was not just the language of jurisprudence, but also the language in which one learned courtly manners. Apart from a fatal loss of sources, this is perhaps the reason for the small number of English-language polyphonic songs from the period. In Italian courts and the city-states, chansons were considered an esteemed parallel to indigenous forms. The humanist Giannozzo Manetti reports how at a Venetian soirée the guests, all young Florentine patricians, sang French chansons after dining ("ad gallicas cantilenas et melodias conversi") before performing "little" Italian ditties with instrumental accompaniment ("cantiunculis et symponiis").[30] That Florence was the center of chanson culture is evident from the nine surviving chansonniers from that city, compiled ca. 1440–90. But the chanson had begun to come into its own as a musical "product" and prestige object, for after 1450 the reliability of foreign texts in the Florentine sources began to decline. Ercole d'Este supported a thoroughly French musical culture in Ferrara;[31] tellingly, his very musical

---

30 Florence, Biblioteca Medicea Laurenziana, MS Plut. xc sup. 29 (*Jannotii manetti*), fol. 42v.
31 The manuscript Rome 2856 (Ferrara, ca. 1480) is one of the best sources of secular music by older Burgundian composers – though, as with the Mellon Chansonnier, the Neapolitan *genius loci* shows through, if faintly.

daughter Isabella, who did not speak French, introduced the prime genre for women in the vernacular, the frottola. One of the most beautiful frottola manuscripts presumably ended up in her library;[32] its quarto format represented an alternative to the typical chansonniers, but richly ornamented initials and lavish illuminations gave it the same level of visual appeal.

The sources that transmitted songs in the fifteenth century differ significantly in format, content, and function. The context in which they appear reveals the status that the song had in a particular culture. German sources from the clerical milieu (the Trent Codices, the Glogau partbooks of around 1480[33]) show from their unornamented presentation and irregular script that private music-making in official, sacred circles could be fulfilled by musically trained people through polyphony. While in German lands until 1500 the mixing of genres was characteristic, collections of French and Italian provenance show a separation of book types, a rule broken only in exceptional cases.

We are confronted with the historiographical conundrum that the flood of mostly anonymous French chansons is preserved mainly in foreign sources. This could be attributed to a massive loss of song collections, or to hitherto-unknown practices of preservation in French and Burgundian circles. The writer Jean Molinet, who was active first in the service of Duke Charles the Bold, and later at his successors' Habsburg-Burgundian courts, cites forty-one song titles in his *Debat du viel gendarme et du viel amoureux*, out of which the titles of only four are not known today. From this it may be possible to presume that the loss of works has not been severe.

The Loire Valley chansonniers illuminate how songs served as a means of forming a cultural identity. These five collections (Laborde, Wolfenbüttel, Dijon, Nivelle, and Copenhagen) were mostly prepared between 1465 and the 1480s in the regions controlled by the French Crown; they overlap in content, scribes, illuminators, and even the chronology of their assembly.[34] Their physical appearance is intriguing: although they are in choirbook format, they have charming small layouts, the poems appear in full, the notes are artfully presented; rich and almost continual decorations include ornamental borders, small pictures, portraits, and humorous *drôleries* in the initials. Everything about them invites contemplation, much like a book of hours. Several pictorial and verbal traces provide a way into the social milieu of the high-ranking notaries and secretaries of the king who enriched their libraries

32  Modena α.F.9.9 (?Padua, ca. 1496).
33  Silesia, 1475–85.
34  Chansonnier Laborde: Washington M.2.1.L25 Case (after ca. 1465); Wolfenbüttel 287 (after ca. 1465); Dijon 517 (early to mid-1470s); Nivelle de la Chaussée Chansonnier: Paris 57 (after ca. 1470); Copenhagen 291 (by the 1470s). See Alden, *Songs, Scribes, and Society*.

with these precious objects. To sing, play, hear, contemplate, and own art songs was to participate in strategies of self-fashioning adopted by the cultural elite. These strategies extended not least to aristocratic women, who regularly participated in this cultural sphere. Often the recipients of chansonniers as wedding gifts, these women acted as cultural ambassadors to regions with different native languages.

# Bibliography

Alden, Jane, *Songs, Scribes and Society: The History and Reception of the Loire Valley Chansonniers*, New York and Oxford, 2010

Besseler, Heinrich, *Bourdon und Fauxbourdon: Studien zum Ursprung der niederländischen Musik*, Leipzig, 1950

Binchois, Gilles, *Die Chansons von Gilles Binchois*, ed. Wolfgang Rehm, Musikalische Denkmäler 2; Mainz, 1957

Calmeta, Vincenzo, "Vita del facondo poeta vulgare Serafino Aquilano," in *Prose e lettere edite e inedite*, ed. Cecil Grayson, Bologna, 1959, 60–77

Cortesi, Paolo, *De cardinalatu libri tres*, Castro Cortesii, 1510; for a facsimile of the passage on music see Nino Pirrotta, "Music and Cultural Tendencies in 15th-Century Italy," *JAMS* 19 (1966), 127–61

Deschamps, Eustache, *L'Art de dictier*, ed. Deborah M. Sinnreich-Levi, East Lansing, MI, 1994

Josquin des Prez, *The Collected Works*, new edition, 30 vols., Utrecht, 1987–

Maniates, Maria Rika, ed., *The Combinative Chanson: An Anthology*, Madison, WI, 1989

Meconi, Honey, "Poliziano, *Primavera*, and Perugia 431: New Light on *Fortuna desperata*," in *Antoine Busnoys: Method, Meaning, and Context in Late Medieval Music*, ed. Paula Higgins, Oxford, 1999, 465–503

Prudenzani, Simone, *Il "Sollazzo" e il "Saporetto" con altre rime*, ed. Santorre Debenedetti, Turin, 1913

Robertson, Anne Walters, "The Man with the Pale Face, the Shroud, and Du Fay's *Missa Se la face ay pale*," *JM* 27 (2010), 377–434

Self, Stephen, ed., *The* Si placet *Repertory of 1480–1530*, Recent Researches in the Music of the Renaissance 106, Madison, WI, 1996

Tinctoris, Johannes, *Liber de arte contrapuncti*, in *Opera theoretica*, 2, ed. Albert Seay, CSM 22, Rome, 1975–78

*Proportionale musices*, in *Opera theoretica*, 2a, ed. Seay

*Terminorum musicae diffinitorium*, Treviso, ca. 1495; repr. Kassel, 1983

# 38

# Instrumental music in the fifteenth century

KEITH POLK

Between the late Middle Ages and the end of the Renaissance the mentality of the Europeans, the way they weighed the world around them, changed. Inventions and improvements on inventions tumbled on the scene at a dizzying pace. Guns, clocks, navigational aids, and the printing press are a sampling, and music, too, was swept along in an overwhelming tide of change. Instrumental music was especially affected, with such developments as keyed mechanisms for wind instruments and the sliding tubes of the trombone making their first appearance. Tracing the impact of invention on actual music played by instruments, however, has been difficult due to a central fact of instrumental performance: throughout the fifteenth century, players, especially the professionals, performed without music in front of them.[1] They either played from memory or improvised, with two important consequences. First, surviving manuscripts are extremely scanty, especially for ensemble music before about 1480. Second, and as a direct result of the paucity of sources, modern attention has been largely focused on music written apparently with vocal forces in mind – a focus that would have seemed quite peculiar to musicians and their audiences in the Renaissance. Instrumental music was considered an essential ingredient in almost all ceremonies and celebrations. Banquets, processions, weddings, dances, and so forth all demanded the presence of instruments. The following then will have two main goals: first, to trace the very rapid evolution of instrumental music as a reflection of the general drive for innovation of the time; and second, to convey some idea of the role instruments played in contemporary artistic life.

## 1400–1440

At about 1400 the late medieval tradition of dividing instruments into two groups by timbre, as loud and soft (*haut* and *bas* in French) was in full force.[2]

---

1 This is verified by numerous illustrations of the time; see Polk, "Ensemble Performance in Dufay's Time." On the reliability of fifteenth-century illustrations reflecting the realities of contemporary performances see Brown, "Instruments and Voices," 91–93.
2 For more detail on what follows see Polk, *German Instrumental Music*, 13–44 (on soft instruments) and 45–86 (on loud ones).

The soft group included instruments of gentler timbre, most importantly the fiddle, lute, harp, and keyboard instruments.[3] Trumpets (often combined with small kettledrums) and shawms were the most prominent among the loud instruments. Each category had its distinctive features. Soft instruments could be combined in a great variety of ways, though ca. 1400 the fiddle was the preeminent member of the group. The players of these instruments were both soloists and ensemble musicians. Those in the loud category were more exclusively ensemble players. Moreover, trumpets and shawms, which had been combined in the previous century, were embarking on their separate paths, the trumpets as a symbol of authority, the shawms more connected to musical rather than ceremonial functions. Both trumpet and shawm ensembles were also distinguished from the more flexible combinations of soft instruments in that their internal makeup was more rigid.

Innovations in instrument making were moving in several directions. Contemporary illustrations for the first time illustrate keyboard instruments of a harpsichord or clavichord type (the illustrations are not detailed enough to know whether the strings were plucked or struck). In the loud category, the addition of a key mechanism was becoming general on the bombard, permitting the development of a large size of shawm, and the shawm ensemble was now capable of both discant and tenor ranges, i.e. of counterpoint. The "tenor" shawm thus produced was still at a very high pitch (in later times it would have been considered an alto), and the even larger sizes of shawm produced in the sixteenth and seventeenth centuries were not yet available. To play with the shawms, a brass instrument with increased melodic capabilities was invented. Makers of trumpets had developed (again for the first time) the ability to bend tubing, producing instruments first in something resembling an S-shape. This was followed by bending the tubing into a folded shape, rather like the modern bugle. Subsequently came the much more intricate innovation, that of one tube sliding within another, which allowed a player to fill in some of the gaps in the bugle-call-like scale of the "natural" trumpet. Evidence suggests that this slide was first applied to a single tube, producing an instrument that has been termed the slide trumpet. It was this instrument that was taken over into the shawm ensemble to play the contratenor. Hints of this advance appear in documents from around 1400, but in any case the three-part ensemble of shawm, bombard, and slide instrument was well established by the 1420s. Note that all of these developments – the keyed stringed instruments, the addition of the key to the

---

3 Space restrictions make it impossible to discuss the characteristics of individual instruments; for detail see the articles in Duffin, ed., *A Performer's Guide.*

shawm, and the new slide mechanism – were unique to Europe, with no precedents either elsewhere at the time, or in antiquity.

Key to innovation was the support by patronage networks. Among courts, that of the duke of Burgundy provided a kind of model, with the support of a group of chamber players on soft instruments (including by the 1430s the brilliant duo of Cordoval and Fernandez playing lutes and fiddles), a trumpet band for ceremonial fanfares, and a wind ensemble to provide music for dancing, banquets, and other high occasions. Cities everywhere began to institute civic wind ensembles, though only Italian cities such as Bologna, Florence, and Venice supported trumpets. Those of Germany were particularly noteworthy, producing a surplus of artistic talent that was recruited vigorously by the courts and cities of Italy (the Florentine ensemble in the 1440s was entirely German). Civic support of soft ensembles was distinctly unusual, though Nuremberg was an important exception.[4]

Musical sources for this era are extremely scanty, with one splendid exception, the Faenza Codex (ca. 1420).[5] The value of this codex is that it provides a unique view of the repertory as well as the performance techniques that would have been expected of a contemporary chamber player. Included are items from the Mass designed evidently for performance with an organ alternating with a choir, i.e., probably for a large organ inside a church. But included as well are dances and intabulations of French and Italian songs. These would certainly not have been played in church, but on a smaller organ or perhaps a harpsichord – or perhaps, as has been argued, in a performance that included a lute (competence on both keyboard and lute was a standard expectation of chamber musicians then).[6] The textures of the pieces are almost exclusively for two parts, even when the originals upon which the Faenza versions were based were for three voices. The soprano is always retained intact, but in some pieces when the tenor of the original would rest, creating a potential break in the Faenza texture, the contratenor of the original was taken over – i.e., the desire in performance was to maintain the full two-part sonority. The lines in the soprano are often highly ornamented, with some ornamentation in the lower part as well, which provides a veritable catalogue of early fifteenth-century decoration technique.

4 On courtly and civic patronage see Polk, *German Instrumental Music*, 87–131.
5 For an edition see Plamenac, ed., *Keyboard Music of the Late Middle Ages*. For a revised ordering of the manuscript, see Memelsdorff, "Motti a motti." For a facsimile see Memelsdorff, *The Codex Faenza 117*.
6 See McGee, "Instruments and the Faenza Codex." His views have been hotly disputed by other scholars; for a compromise suggestion see Brown and Polk, "Instrumental Music," 120–22.

## 1440–1480

At mid-century the soft/loud tradition remained in place, but the barriers
between the two categories were steadily weakening. The soft instruments
remained much the same, though by about 1440 the duo of two lutes
emerged, quickly becoming the preeminent combination for chamber musicians.[7] In the loud category trumpet ensembles expanded significantly and by
about 1450 leading noble patrons consistently had six or more trumpets in
their stables. Wind ensembles, too, expanded, and by about 1450 prominent
courts and larger cities consistently supported at least four players: two
discant shawms, one bombard, and a slide instrument. The trumpet bands
were sharply distinct from the other winds, however, and remained restricted
to their traditional role of heraldic instruments. Their expansion into more
musical functions was a development of a later era.

In this era instrument makers seem to have focused most of their attention
on improvements to existing instruments. The treatise of Arnaut of Zwolle
reveals that by about 1440 both harpsichord and clavichord were entering into
mainstream practice.[8] A large lute, capable of true bass function, was now
available, and a small size of the instrument gradually replaced the quintern in
the lute duo. Perhaps the most distinctive innovation at mid-century was that
of the double slide applied to a brass instrument, i.e., an instrument essentially
the same as the modern trombone, and one capable of playing bass to the
shawms.

The momentum toward ever-increasing levels of patronage continued.
The Burgundian establishment probably reached its peak about 1450, with
the basic three-part framework of chamber players (with Cordoval and
Fernandez still present), ceremonial trumpets, and a wind band of four or
five. Intense international competition characterized the era. The duke of
Bavaria in Munich supported a stable analogous to that of Burgundy; among
his chamber musicians was the brilliant blind organist and lutenist Conrad
Paumann, at that time probably the most renowned German-speaking musician of any kind. Equally ambitious, the duke of Ferrara supported almost
exactly the same framework of ensembles. The dazzling star of his chamber
players was the spectacularly talented lutenist Pietrobono, whose stature in
Italy matched that of Paumann in Germany. Cities, too, viewed the support
of civic ensembles (almost always wind bands) as essential in promoting their

---

7 The organ was undergoing far-reaching changes at this time, but large organs were primarily associated
with vocal music and will not be considered here.
8  See Koster, "Arnaut de Zwolle."

image of stature and independence. Large towns such as Bologna, Florence, and Venice in Italy, Augsburg and Nuremberg in Germany, and Bruges and Ghent in the Low Countries all now maintained bands that included distinguished players. Moreover, the prominent cities were connected to an expansive network of other centers, and much smaller cities such as Dendermonde in Flanders and Windsheim in Bavaria devoted significant portions of their yearly budgets to the support of their ensembles.[9]

At mid-century the impulse for innovation was perhaps reflected most powerfully in the areas of repertory and performance practice. The extant manuscripts, if still scanty in relation to those for vocal performance, yield a distinctly wider-ranging picture. The Buxheim Organ Book from ca. 1465 is the major surviving keyboard source.[10] In some ways it follows the outlines of the earlier Faenza Codex in that it contains sacred items, songs both local (in this case German rather than Italian) and international (particularly settings of French chansons), as well as arrangements of dance tunes. But it transmits a greater range of styles, including some pieces with elaborate embellishments, and some with none at all. Moreover, the textures are now primarily three-part, matching the current model in vocal music, as heard in the French chanson. Much more modest in size, but every bit as significant, is the so-called Zorzi Trombetta manuscript, a collection assembled by a working instrumentalist who was part of a Venetian galley crew on the route between Italy, Flanders, and England. Zorzi (actually Giorgio da Modon, later a prominent member of the civic ensemble in Venice) included in his manuscript a number of his own contrapuntal sketches based on tenors of contemporary popular chansons.[11] The results of his efforts are sometimes rather raw but nonetheless reveal that this more or less everyday musician was obviously musically literate, had a command of counterpoint, and was plugged into the current popular art repertory.

The theorist Johannes Tinctoris stressed that Conrad Paumann was capable of polyphonic performance on the lute, something unusual among Italian lutenists, even for someone as brilliant as Pietrobono. In fact the instruction manuals in the Buxheim Organ Book that illustrate his keyboard teaching (termed *fundamenta*) demonstrate the way Paumann taught younger musicians

---

9 On Burgundy the classic work remains Marix, *Histoire* (see pp. 264–75). For Ferrara in this era see Lockwood, *Music in Renaissance Ferrara*, 95–108; on Bologna see Gambassi, *Il Concerto Palatino della Signoria di Bologna*; for Florence see McGee, *The Ceremonial Musicians*. On the Bavarian court see Polk, *German Instrumental Music*, 99–100 (for the cities mentioned see 126–31). Concerning patronage in Flanders, see Polk, "Minstrels and Music in the Low Countries."

10 Munich, Bayerische Staatsbibliothek, Cim. 352b.

11 Leech-Wilkinson, "Il libro di appunti di un suonatore di tromba" and Baroncini, "'Se canta dalli cantori'."

to master polyphonic skills.[12] The *fundamenta* did not simply teach embellish-ment techniques and written counterpoint, but were designed to show stu-dents how to create improvisations, i.e., not written, but on-the-spot, spontaneous counterpoint. These, taken along with the contrapuntal exercises of Zorzi Trombetta, suggest that instrumental musicians from mid-century onward were entering into an era that represented a kind of artistic high point. The predominant musical texture both in composed music and in improvisa-tion was one of layers, with the tenor being the fundamental voice, with which the discant formed a structural framework. To this a third voice, the contra-tenor, could be added. For skilled and well-trained instrumentalists, improv-isations of this kind were relatively straightforward in three and even, though probably more rarely, four parts. Scores of contemporary illustrations are emphatic in showing that instrumentalists performed without music in front of them. It is now clear that these players were not only performing from memory, but were also expected to generate completely new music whenever the occasion demanded.

At a remarkable banquet held by the duke of Burgundy in 1454, two of his chamber musicians (almost certainly Cordoval and Fernandez) performed a chanson with a solo female singer.[13] This and related sources demonstrate that one option for performance of chansons included solo voices and soft instru-ments. (Another was with voices alone. There is no evidence at this time that loud instruments participated in such performances.) It may also be observed that at mid-century, wind instruments occasionally performed in church – but they were present to add a kind of aural decoration; they did not yet play a role in the liturgy itself.

## 1480–1500

Up to about 1480 innovations had proceeded at a firm but moderate pace, but after that date, and very rapidly, came a kind of creative explosion, with changes sparking off in all directions. An astonishing number of new instru-ments and instrumental combinations suddenly appeared. Among the soft instruments the most dramatic new arrival was the viol consort. Yet the lute remained a premier instrument, both as a solo instrument and in ensembles. Among the loud group, trumpet ensembles expanded to the point that for the highest nobility a minimum was a dozen or so, now combined more consis-tently with large kettledrums. Expansion in the wind band was more modest,

---

12  See Polk, *German Instrumental Music*, 182–90.
13  Marix, *Histoire*, 40.

but highly significant for musical reasons, as the high nobility and the largest cities now supported five or six players (often two discant and two "tenor" shawms, with two trombones filling in the lower registers). Highly significant were a cluster of instruments that lay somewhere between the loud and soft classification. The cornett, which had evidently lurked in a kind of shadowed and secondary role previously, suddenly emerged as the discant instrument of choice in many performance contexts. Crumhorns, usually in the form of complete consorts, became available as a color option. Recorders had had some favor earlier in the century, but now became another alternative color for wind players. Note that from at least 1490, if not earlier, both crumhorns and recorders were standard doubles for professional wind players, and both were consistently used in whole consorts. The sixteenth century is sometimes described as the century in which instruments were characteristically played in consorts – but the consort principle was well established by the late fifteenth century.

Obviously the traditional barriers between the categories of loud and soft utterly shattered. Augustine Schubinger, to cite one example, was recruited as a trombonist for the civic ensemble in Florence in 1489. At some point thereafter he shifted focus to the cornett, and by about 1500 was performing not only with the sacred choir at the Habsburg court, but also within the liturgy of the Mass.[14]

The musicians supported by Emperor Maximilian I vividly illustrate the expanded patronage now in vogue. His "military" contingent included not only about twelve trumpets with their kettledrums, but a small group of flutes and drums. His court wind band was usually comprised of five parts, with Schubinger on cornett and Hans Neuschel on trombone (Neuschel, a native of Nuremberg, was the premier maker of brass instruments of his time), as well as a soft contingent featuring two or three lutes and the organist Paul Hofhaimer. Shortly after 1500 a group of four viols was added. The numbers fluctuated from year to year, but in general Maximilian maintained about double what had been the case at the Burgundian court two or three decades earlier.[15] Only the highest nobility could sustain patronage at this level, but support at other courts could have significant impact. Support of viol ensembles had come earlier at the court of Ferrara, for example, and indeed, the vogue for the viol may well have received definitive stimulus from the stature of that court in cultural matters. The Ferrara court was also one of the first to include a harpsichordist on the payroll, as in 1494.[16] Civic patronage, while far more

14 See Polk, *German Instrumental Music*, 77 and 85.    15 Ibid., 91–94.
16 Lockwood, *Music in Renaissance Ferrara*, 325.

modest, nonetheless reflected the same trend to growth. Larger cities such as Venice, Bruges, and Nuremberg now had five or six musicians in their civic bands, and most cities, even some of the smaller centers, now attempted to maintain a minimum of four.

The impact of the arrival of new instruments was matched by changes in repertory and performance practice. Concerning repertory, a striking change was signaled by a group of manuscripts assembled shortly after 1480, primarily in northern Italy, but containing secular music by northern composers. Previously such collections containing predominantly French chansons (in one of the late medieval fixed forms) had been provided with texts in one or more voices. The post-1480 manuscripts, by contrast, were either mostly or even entirely without texts. Moreover, the composers Johannes Martini (in his *La martinella* and *Tout joyeux*) and Henricus Isaac (with *La mora* and Helas) seem to have spearheaded the development of a different compositional approach. In the primary manuscripts that contain such pieces they are given without texts (the more popular pieces, such as *La mora*, sometimes occur with texts in secondary sources, but these are obvious contrafacta and do not convey the original intent of the composers). The pieces are three-part and highly imitative, with phrases based on short, profiled motives. The overall forms are such that none of the common poetic forms of the time provide a comfortable fit. It would appear almost certain that instrumental performance was envisioned for these pieces from their inception. The rapid pace of change so characteristic of the century was in place here as well, for imitation quickly became the predominant approach, replacing the layered textures based on a foundation tenor and discant duet. Just as critical in terms of the transformation of compositional style, after 1490 Isaac (and other composers as well) quickly shifted to favoring four or more parts.[17]

The shift to imitation in four and more parts dealt a devastating blow to the standard improvisational framework that had been in place for decades. Improvisation in three parts based on a tenor was relatively straightforward for skilled performers, but the range of options in imitation with four and more parts approached the infinite, posing almost insuperable problems. Improvisational skills were still required of professional instrumentalists, especially in dance music, but performers increasingly turned to written compositions. Another momentous change in performance practice concerned a transformed relationship with singers and sacred music. Previously

---

17 For a list of the relevant manuscripts and discussion of stylistic changes, see Polk, "Heinrich Isaac and Innovations in Musical Style."

the divide had been firmly marked off, with instruments other than organ almost never associated with performances by choirs in sacred music. A progression is especially clear in records in Bruges. In the late 1470s into the 1480s, civic wind players there became more and more involved in support of sacred services, such as the late afternoon service termed the *Salve* (*Lof* in Flemish). At first the players evidently performed from the church tower, i.e., outside, but at some point they moved inside the church. Moreover, a book of motets was written for the town band, probably primarily for use in these services.[18] The directional momentum was clear – by 1500 we have clear evidence of instrumental participation with singers within the liturgy itself.

One element that ran through the entire fifteenth century was a demand for instrumental music at almost every ceremony or celebration, a demand that provided constant employment opportunities for working musicians. Starting in about 1470, however, we can discern a new ingredient in the mix. In cities civic ensembles began to present regular performances in the late afternoon or early evening. These are well recorded in the Low Countries, with contracts indicating that the musicians were to play both secular songs and motets. These regular performances are doubly intriguing. On the one hand, they are perhaps the first example we have of concert performances, i.e., of music being presented to be heard for its own sake and not serving in some functional role (e.g., to accompany dancing). On the other, it was at precisely this time that a new compositional approach appeared that involved imitative textures; in pieces incorporating this approach a kind of musical logic comes to the fore where the listener can perceive melodic fragments as they move from voice to voice. Not only were there concerts, but there was now a repertory that lay listeners could understand with relative ease – yet more landmark contributions of this remarkable era.

## Bibliography

Baroncini, Rodolfo, "'Se canta dalli cantori overo se sona dalli sonadori': Voci e strumenti tra Quattro e Cinquecento," *Rivista italiana di musicologia* 32 (1997), 327–59

Brown, Howard Mayer, "Instruments and Voices in the Fifteenth-Century Chanson," in *Current Thought in Musicology*, ed. John W. Grubbs, Austin, TX, 1976, 89–137

    and Keith Polk, "Instrumental Music, c.1300–c.1520," in *Music as Concept and Practice in the Late Middle Ages*, The New Oxford History of Music 3/1, ed. Reinhard Strohm and Bonnie J. Blackburn, Oxford, 2001, 97–161

Duffin, Ross, ed., *A Performer's Guide to Medieval Music*, Bloomington, IN, 2000

---

18 On developments in Bruges see Polk, "Patronage of Instrumental Music in Bruges."

Gambassi, Osvaldo, *Il Concerto Palatino della Signoria di Bologna: Cinque secoli di vita musicale a corte (1250–1797)*, Florence, 1989

Koster, John, "Arnaut de Zwolle, Henri," in *Grove Music Online* (accessed 23 February 2012)

Leech-Wilkinson, Daniel, "Il libro di appunti di un suonatore di tromba del quindicesimo secolo," *Rivista italiana di musicologia* 16 (1981), 16–39

Lockwood, Lewis, *Music in Renaissance Ferrara 1400–1505: The Creation of a Musical Center in the Fifteenth Century*, Cambridge, MA, 1984

Marix, Jeanne, *Histoire de la musique et des musiciens de la Cour de Bourgogne sous le règne de Philippe le Bon (1420–1465)*, Strasbourg, 1939; repr. Geneva, 1972

McGee, Timothy, *The Ceremonial Musicians of Late Medieval Florence*, Bloomington, IN, 2009

"Instruments and the Faenza Codex," *EM* 14 (1986), 480–90

Memelsdorff, Pedro, *The Codex Faenza 117: Instrumental Polyphony in Late Medieval Italy; Introductory Study and Facsimile Edition*, Lucca, 2012/1013), vol. 1, Introductory Study; vol. 2, Facsimile Edition

"Motti a motti: Reflections on a Motet Intabulation of the Early Quattrocento," *Recercare* 10 (1998), 39–68

Plamenac, Dragan, ed., *Keyboard Music of the Late Middle Ages in Codex Faenza 117*, n.p., 1972

Polk, Keith, "Ensemble Performance in Dufay's Time," in *Dufay Quincentenary Conference: Papers Read at the Dufay Quincentenary Conference: Brooklyn College, December 6–7, 1974*, ed. Allan W. Atlas, Brooklyn, 1976, 61–75

*German Instrumental Music of the Late Middle Ages: Players, Patrons, and Performance Practice*, Cambridge, 1992

"Heinrich Isaac and Innovations in Musical Style ca. 1490," in *Sleuthing the Muse: Essays in Honor of William F. Prizer*, ed. Kristine K. Forney and Jeremy L. Smith, Hillsdale, NY, 2012, 349–64

"Minstrels and Music in the Low Countries in the Fifteenth Century," in *Musicology and Archival Research: Colloquium Proceedings Brussels 22–23.4.1993*, ed. B. Haggh et al., Brussels, 1994, 392–410

"Patronage of Instrumental Music in Bruges in the Late Middle Ages," *Yearbook of the Alamire Foundation* 7 (2008), 243–52

# 39

# Sacred song in the fifteenth century: cantio, carol, lauda, Kirchenlied

REINHARD STROHM

## A different repertory

This chapter describes a cluster of musico-poetic repertories under the generic title of "sacred song": repertories distinct from plainchant (*cantus planus*) on the one hand, and from secular song on the other. By "song" we shall here understand a melody with a poetic text in a strophic or patterned form, a piece that can be isolated, transferred, and reworked. This is a narrower definition than the generic term "song" for all that is sung or for the act of singing.[1] Plainchant is of course "song" in this wider sense of the term, and it also contains "songs" in the narrower sense (such as Office hymns and antiphons), but it subjects any song to a ritual placement and propriety. Ritual plainchant was indeed the main ancestor of fifteenth-century sacred song. It offered models for adaptation, paraphrase, troping, or translation, and it provided performative occasions: clerical feast, procession, pilgrimage, sacred drama. By contrast, the sacred songs discussed here were supernumerary to church ritual and increasingly regarded as independent in performance, function, and style.[2] Late medieval sacred songs have been described as an "expansion of the plainchant repertory," or as tropes or epigonal conductus.[3] Although valid as a general historical localization, such labels downplay the novelty and the separate artistic status of paraliturgical sacred song in the fourteenth to sixteenth centuries. Since medieval sacred music is conventionally divided into plainchant and polyphony, these repertories present an embarrassment to the historical narrative because they do not fully belong to either plainchant or polyphony. They participated in both.

1 In English the same word is used for the former, wider definition and the latter, narrower one. Two different words are available in Latin (*cantus*/*cantio*), German (*Gesang*/*Lied*), and Slavic languages (for example, Czech *zpěv*/*píseň*). Romance languages also offer this distinction (It. *canto*/*canzone*, Span. *canto*/*canción*, Fr. *chant*/*chanson*), but in ordinary use it is often blurred. On song see also Nicole Schwindt's essay in this volume, Ch. 37.
2 See, for example, the justification of a collection of "cantiones" in the Moosburg Gradual of 1360: Hiley, ed., *Moosburger Graduale*, fol. 230v.
3 Specialists of chant and Notre Dame polyphony have significantly contributed to these "late" repertories: see Haug, ed., *Troparia tardiva*; Anderson, ed., *Notre-Dame and Related Conductus*.

Their gradual separation from plainchant also implied a significant cultural development: the growing participation of laypeople in the singing of God's praise.[4]

Sacred song was flowering almost everywhere in fifteenth-century Europe. The varied repertories of devotional and ritual song – if we could ever draw them all together – would form a major component of that century's artistic heritage. They use many languages – Latin, German, Italian, English, Czech, Spanish, Dutch, Polish, Danish, and yet others – and they are serenely unaffected by distinctions such as "Middle Ages vs. Renaissance," or "polyphony vs. monophony." Most of the songs are authorless creations whose individual origins elude us. It is possible to distinguish national or regional repertories, using the evidence of numerous written sources. Yet somehow all these repertories seem connected, whether by musical or poetic material, formal traditions, modes of transmission, or ritual functions.[5] Recurrent practices were translation, troping, and the so-called contrafactum procedure, the creation of new words for known melodies. These practices enabled the migration of musical material between languages and repertories. Sacred songs were often written down polyphonically, whether as cantus firmi of complex mensural settings or in a form of simple counterpoint that could be improvised or adapted to local usages.

## Historical overview

In traditional genres such as these, history advances slowly. The tradition of adding sequences, tropes, versus, and conductus to the plainchant repertories had begun in the ninth century. It was mostly at home in monasteries, cathedrals, and their schools. In the thirteenth and fourteenth centuries collegiate schools, civic brotherhoods, and lay communities not only adopted the practice but also created new repertories for congregational singing. Franciscan and other mendicant orders acted as promoters. The fifteenth century witnessed the greatest contribution of parishes, grammar schools, lay devotions, and religious reform communities to the creation and cultivation of sacred songs. Schoolchildren performed them for public receptions and celebrations. The vernacular lyrics, often translations and paraphrases of plainchant texts, encouraged participation of the laity. Most repertories also included macaronic (mixed Latin and vernacular) texts, which were characteristic of the school environment. In Czech-texted cantiones, the use of the vernacular came to articulate religious and national aspirations.

4 Janota, *Studien zu Funktion und Typus*.    5 Salmen, "European Song (1300–1530)."

The status of sacred song was only partly transformed in the course of the sixteenth century. Printing expanded demand and distribution of the repertories, and especially helped the reception of German Kirchenlieder and French vernacular psalm settings. Whereas the Reformation of course changed theological aspects of the repertories, their institutional anchorage in city, parish, and school remained remarkably stable.[6] Congregational singing was particularly valued by the Lutheran and Bohemian Protestant communities. Catholic, Calvinist, and Anglican reforms led to temporary restrictions on the opportunities for lay singing, although this trend was later reversed. The fifteenth-century heritage of congregational singing has in fact survived and is now universal in religious practice.

## Forms, genres, and styles

The forms and genres of fifteenth-century sacred song often match those of other repertories. Strophic songs without refrains may resemble the Latin Office hymn. The great Provençal and French repertories of secular solo song provided models for sacred songs, for example the strophic form of the lai (Leich) for the Marian lament (*planctus Mariae*). The refrain forms of the ballata, virelai, Reigen, and carole are most often found; such collective dance-songs served as models for contrafacta. In the Anglo-Irish "Red Book of Ossory" (mid-fourteenth century), sacred contrafacta are specifically referred to their original secular song texts; the Catalan "Llibre Vermell" (ca. 1400) recommends sacred versions to replace secular dance-songs.[7] Minnesinger and early Meistersinger *Töne*, which are not cast in the dance and refrain forms, were also used as models, whether or not their texts themselves were sacred. In Italy the contrafactum procedure made much secular polyphony in the French *formes fixes* available to the sacred lauda.[8] Latin rhymed prayers, whose multi-strophic texts had originally been written for recitation only, were later sung to simple melodic schemes, as in the case of *Patris sapientia* (see below).

Polyphonic settings, predominantly in simple styles, are frequently found from ca. 1400. An early central European cantio, the Benedicamus trope *Procedentem sponsum de thalamo* (early fourteenth century), is transmitted by all its sources in the same two-part setting in a voice-crossing style. Other songs

6 Sternfeld, "Music in the Schools of the Reformation."
7 See Strohm, *The Rise of European Music*, 62–63, with further literature; Gómez y Muntané, ed., *El Llibre vermell de Montserrat*.
8 Cattin, "'Contrafacta' internazionali."

are found in both monophonic and polyphonic versions. The fifteenth-century English carol is mostly polyphonic in its written transmission, and a few composer names are transmitted (Richard Smert, John Troulouffe).[9] But the increasing use of polyphony in all regions, whether written or extemporized, did not lead to greater individualization of the songs as musical art-works. It was rather the reverse: simple two-part settings were increasingly written by non-specialized people. The best-known authors of sacred songs were poet-singers who created both secular and sacred monophony for their solo performances. Among them were the Monk of Salzburg (fl. 1390–1400), Oswald von Wolkenstein (1377/78–1445), Heinrich von Laufenberg (ca. 1390–1460), Leonardo Giustinian (ca. 1383–1446), and Feo Belcari (1410–84). Many other authors' names are known for the sacred poems, whereas composers' names for the melodies are rare. Some songs are traditionally ascribed to leading reformers and theologians such as Johannes Tauler, Johannes Hus, Thomas à Kempis, and Girolamo Savonarola.

## Liturgical origins

In the mid-fourteenth century, new sacred song collections suddenly appear almost simultaneously in central European sources, typically monastic or collegiate manuscripts for Mass, Office, and processions: Seckau (Styria), Prague, Moosburg (Bavaria), Aosta (N. Italy), Engelberg (Switzerland). The songs are at first embedded in the Latin liturgy of Easter and Christmas and linked to established liturgical performances, often of the *Benedicamus domino*. They are untitled, or called "versus," "trop(h)i," or "cantiones," occasionally "carmina" or "cantilene." The term "cantiones," explicitly given to song collections in the Moosburg gradual (1360) and in plainsong books from Prague, would be retained until at least the late sixteenth century. A genealogy of the fourteenth-century cantio as a late form of conductus, usually with the ritual function of a *Benedicamus domino* trope, has been proposed by Frank Ll. Harrison.[10] His hypothesis, based on the evidence of a fourteenth-century gradual from Aosta, seems corroborated by other sources as far as the Benedicamus is concerned. Other liturgical assignations are of course also found. The "Liber Cantionarius" of Seckau (Graz, Universitätsbibliothek, MS 756), dated 1345, exhibits a series of introit tropes in strophic form: the *Missa in galli cantu* on Christmas day is

---

9 Stevens, ed., *Mediaeval Carols*.     10 Harrison, "Benedicamus, Conductus, Carol."

Example 39.1 Benedicamus trope *Exultemus et letemur hodie*, from Plocek, *Zwei Studien zur ältesten geistlichen Musik in Böhmen*, 2:21–28, no. 16

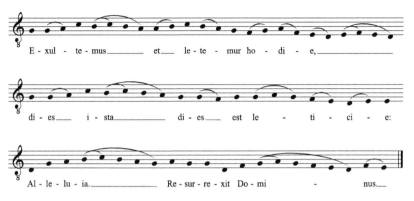

Translation: Let us rejoice and be merry today,
this day is a day of merriment:

Alleluia. The Lord has risen.

introduced by the "tropus" *Flos de spina procreatur*.[11] The Benedicamus trope *Exultemus et letemur hodie* is found in the same manuscript as "Benedicamus pascale" for the end of Mass (fols. 188v–189r), whereas in a processional from the Benedictine nunnery of St. George's, on Hradčany castle, Prague (Prague, Národní Knihovna, Hudební Oddělení, MS VI G 3b), it is assigned to Vespers (see Example 39.1). The text of *Exultemus* is woven together from references to other Easter chants, for example the *Alleluia* V. *Pascha nostrum*; its repeticio (refrain) is "Alleluia. Resurrexit dominus." The melody, however, is a close relative of the *Praeconium pascale*, maintaining its third mode. The two first lines are the versus (stanza), the third the refrain, usually called "repeticio":

V. Exultemus et letemur hodie,
Dies ista dies est leticie.
R. Alleluia. Resurrexit dominus.

## Central European repertories

Manuscripts from Bohemia and Moravia provide an almost unbroken over-view of the development of the cantio in that area until the late sixteenth

11 Irtenkauf, "Das Seckauer Cantionarium"; Brewer, "In Search of Lost Melodies"; Strohm, "Gesänge zu Weihnachten."

century.[12] A consistent song production began well before the Hussite reforms, as attested by monastic sources, for example the choirbooks from the nunnery of St. George's, Prague, or the Cistercian Hohenfurt/Vyšší Brod gradual of 1410. The Hussite endeavor to involve the congregation in singing generated many new Czech hymns as well as translations, for example in the so-called Jistebnický hymnal (a Gradual and Kyriale, ca. 1450).[13] The conciliatory attitude toward the Roman ritual in Utraquist circles, and from ca. 1480 the development of civic "Rorate" brotherhoods, stimulated musical and poetic creativity in both Latin and Czech. Bohemian "Cantionalia" transmit texts and melodies shared with manuscripts from Silesia, Moravia, Austria, Bavaria, and Saxony, but also with more distant collections from Trier, Rostock, Utrecht, and Denmark.[14] Major Bohemian collections compiled around 1480–1540 (Speciálník Codex, Franus Cantionale) contain polyphonic motets and mass sections from the Franco-Netherlands repertory alongside native Latin motets in a traditional style, chorale settings, and monophonic sacred songs.[15] Repertorial overlaps and stylistic parallels with the Lutheran Kirchenlied appear in the German-texted repertory of the Bohemian Brethren (later the Moravian Church), beginning with Michael Weisse's *New Gesang-Buchlen* of 1531.[16] Kirchenlieder derived from medieval Bohemian originals include *Gottes Sohn ist kommen* (*Ave yerarchia*; see Example 39.2), *Christus, der uns selig macht* (*Patris sapientia*), *Jesus Christus, unser Heiland* (*Ihesus Christus nostra salus*), and possibly *Ach Gott, vom Himmel sieh darein* (*Gaude mater in gaudio*) and *Gott der Vater wohn' uns bei* (*Pane bože bud přzinás*).[17]

In the diversified central European repertory, some songs never lost their original texts, for example the twelfth-century German Leise *Christ ist erstanden*, which had been modeled on the sequence *Victimae paschali laudes*; or the Benedicamus trope *Ad cantus leticie*. But frequently recorded texts do not have to be the original ones. The Latin text of the cantio *Ave pulcherrima regina* seems ubiquitous, yet it has a melodic precedent in the secular Minnesinger *Ton Sô vrô stent bluomen ander vesten*.[18] Secular songs for round dances (Reigen, *choreae*) were adapted for religious festivities with particular

---

12  Important source publications: Plocek, ibid.; Böse and Schäfer, *Geistliche Lieder und Gesänge in Böhmen*; Rothe, ed., *Die Hohenfurther Liederhandschrift*.
13  Brewer, "The Jistebnický Cantional and Corpus Christi."
14  Bergsagel, "The Practice of *Cantus planus binatim*."
15  Brewer, "Cantiones et moteti populi"; Černý, "Vícehlasé písňe konduktového."
16  Weisse, *Gesangbuch der Böhmischen Brüder*; Strohm, "Michael Weisse Transmitting Medieval Melodies to Bach."
17  The Bohemian origin of the two last-named songs is still a hypothesis: see Strohm, "Polyphonie und Liedforschung."
18  Kornrumpf, "'Ave pulcherrima regina'"; see also Strohm, *The Rise of European Music*, 332–33.

Example 39.2a The Bohemian cantio *Ave yerarchia, celestis et pia*, from the Hohenfurther Liederhandschrift (Vyšší Brod, Klašterní Knihovna, MS 42), fol. 145r. After Rothe, *Die Hohenfurther Liederhandschrift*, 366

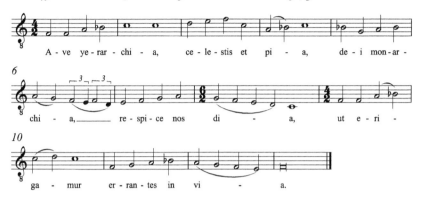

Translation:   Hail, heavenly and pious hierarchy,
              God's monarchy,
              regard us, godly one,
              so that we are straightened,
              as we err on our way.

Example 39.2b Michael Weisse, *Menschenkynd merck eben*, from Weisse, *Gesangbuch der Böhmischen Brüder*, sig. A 4v

Translation:   Humanfolk, now consider,
              what life is about,
              why God has sent his son
              from the highest throne,
              and made him a human.

Example 39.2c Johann Sebastian Bach, *Gott durch deine Güte* or *Gottes Sohn ist kommen*, BWV 600 (chorale setting in Orgelbüchlein). Text: Bohemian Brethren, 1544

ease; the Christmas carols *In dulci jubilo* and *Resonet in laudibus*, so popular today, were used for *Kindelwiegen* (child-rocking) dances in medieval churches. *Resonet* originated as a complex derivation from the antiphon *Magnum nomen domini Emanuel*, and then was widely distributed, involving various languages and semi-dramatic functions ("Joseph, dearest Joseph mine").[19] The oldest known sources of the rhymed prayer "Patris sapientia" and the Leise *In Gottes Namen fahren wir* are found as cantus-firmus settings in polyphony: of the original monophonic songs no earlier written trace has hitherto been found.

In addition to contrafactum procedures – which mostly functioned orally, by having new words sung to known melodies – further research is also needed on the opposite procedure, new melodies for known texts, and the compound adaptation procedure of drawing together known texts and known melodies. The Kirchenlied *In dich hab ich gehoffet, Herr*, for example, uses a fifteenth-century melody sometimes sung to the words "Christus ist erstanden von des Todes Banden," but the new words are a translation of Psalm 31, "In te, domine, speravi." Sometimes there were competing vernacular versions of Latin models,

19 Ameln, "'Resonet in laudibus'."

leading to a diffraction of texts. The processional antiphon *Laus tibi Christe, qui pateris*, itself derived from the hymn *Rex Christe, factor omnium*, had by ca. 1500 spawned at least three different German versions, all well known in the same region (*O, du armer Judas; Eya der großen Liebe; Ehre sei dir, Christe*).[20]

## The Netherlands

The religious movement of the *devotio moderna* in the northern Netherlands and parallel reform initiatives in the general area along the Lower Rhine and in north Germany, all beginning around 1400, inaugurated a song production of which we have countless written sources. The manuscripts come partly from the Augustinian houses of the Windesheim congregation, partly from mendicant friaries and nunneries of the "third order," partly from lay communities such as the Beguines. The manuscripts often resemble liturgical books, containing many older hymns, sequences, and tropes alongside the new Latin and Dutch songs. Both varieties, however, seem to have served more often for solitary praying and meditation, even when the notated version was polyphonic.[21] An influential modern edition of the repertory distorts the general picture by prioritizing the vernacular texts – understandably so in an attempt to recover a national heritage.[22] Despite the emphasis laid by these communities on collective life and worship in the choir, individual prayer was essential; thus many texts are cast in the first person singular and show individual devotion and mysticism. An example is the sequence *O dulcissime iesu*, transmitted in a dozen contemporary manuscripts and occasionally ascribed to Thomas à Kempis (see Example 39.3):

> O dulcissime iesu, qui de celo descendisti et vitam mundo contulisti,
> Legam de te, scribam de te, queram te, cantem de te, laudem te,
>   iesu puer dulcissime,
> Nam suavis es et mitis, humilis plenusque virtutibus, fili dei altissimi . . .

> O sweetest Jesus, who descended from heaven and gave life to the world,
> Let me read of you, write of you, seek you, sing of you, praise you,
>   Jesus sweetest boy,
> For you are gentle and mild, humble and rich in goodness, son
>   of the highest . . .[23]

---

20  *O du armer Judas* and *Ehre sei dir, Christe*: see Stalmann *et al.*, eds., *Das deutsche Kirchenlied* III, no. Ef7; *Eya der grossen Liebe*: see Lütolf *et al.*, eds., *Das deutsche Kirchenlied* II, no. 227.
21  Hascher-Burger, *Gesungene Innigkeit*.
22  Bruning *et al.*, eds., *Het geestelijk Lied van Noord-Nederland*.
23  Hascher-Burger, *Gesungene Innigkeit*, 251.

Example 39.3 "De dulcedine iesu et de plenitudine gratiarum et omnium virtutum quas habuit sequentia" (sequence of the sweetness of Jesus and of the fullness of mercy and all virtue which he had), from Hascher-Burger, *Gesungene Innigkeit,* 251

Many of these songs are set in a simple two-part style, sometimes in non-mensural notation. The two texted voices are usually kept in a narrow total range and notated in the tenor register (which women would sing an octave higher, transposed at sight). The rhythm, if notated, is the same for both voices. A widely disseminated Christmas song, the Benedicamus trope *Puer nobis nascitur,* can be shown to achieve polyphonic texture through a very simple rondellus technique of displacing simple melodic phrases both vertically and horizontally. Monophonic melodies of the songs were occasionally derived from two-part versions by assembling fragments of both voices in a single line.[24]

24 Strohm, "Song Composition in the Fourteenth and Fifteenth Centuries"; on rondellus technique, see also Bergsagel, "The Practice of *Cantus planus binatim.*"

## The Italian lauda

The documented history of the Italian lauda begins in the thirteenth century with the foundation of urban lauda companies (*compagnie de' laudesi*) – lay congregations for common prayer and singing. In its main sources before ca. 1400, the lauda was monophonic and often in strophic form. In the fifteenth century, the lauda repertory became as multifaceted as that of any secular musical genre, although the form of the songs was usually strophic with a refrain, comparable to the virelai/ballata pattern.[25] The genre was mainly practiced by urban lay communities, usually of the merchant and artisan classes in Tuscany and the Veneto; the devotees also had professional musicians to sing for them, or they participated in monastic cultivation. Polyphony was gradually accepted, although standards of function and style varied from community to community; the Benedictines, for example, preferred Latin texts set in a simple style. From the late fourteenth century onwards, new lauda texts were often created as contrafacta of secular songs, for example by the composers of the Florentine *Ars nova* polyphony and later by Franco-Netherlandish composers. Native poet-musicians such as Leonardo Giustinian and Feo Belcari assembled large collections of contrafacta with cues indicating "cantasi come ... " ("to be sung to the tune of ... ").[26] Belcari and other poets also used laude in vernacular sacred plays (*sacre rappresentazioni*).

A number of poems attributed to Giustinian ("O Jesu dolce, o infinito amore") or Bianco da Siena ("Cum desiderio io vo cercando") promote the imagery and feelings of love of Jesus and mysticism. Local priests (Johannes de Quadris, Petrus Haedus/Capretto) encouraged the creation of new songs; foreign composers (Arnold de Lantins, Johannes de Lymburgia) contributed polyphonic settings.[27] European influences may have stretched as far as the English carol.[28] The Latin lauda *Ave mater, o Maria*, the text of which was also set by the Liégeois composer Johannes de Sarto, was adapted into German by Oswald von Wolkenstein. Of the Christmas lauda *In natali domini laudant omnes angeli* polyphonic settings exist in Italy, Germany, Bohemia, and the Netherlands; later it became a Kirchenlied (*Da Jesus geboren war*), with changes in the melody. It is no coincidence that the lauda was the earliest sacred song repertory distributed in musical

---

25 Generally, see Wilson, "Lauda"; Cattin, *Studi sulla lauda*.
26 Luisi, ed., *Laudario Giustinianeo*.    27 Diederichs, *Die Anfänge der mehrstimmigen Lauda*.
28 Zec, "The Relationship of the Carol."

print;[29] it had a large middle-class following and maintained its dual appeal to collective singing and individual domestic devotion.

## The English carol

The English fifteenth-century carol differs from all other repertories in being consistently polyphonic; its few monophonic specimens may be survivors of a fourteenth-century practice. The assured two- or three-part counterpoint and mensural rhythm of many settings resemble other English mensural music of the Dunstaple era.[30] Verse and refrain ("burden" in John Stevens's edition) are regularly separated and often musically differentiated, almost suggesting a solo–tutti performance divided between specialized singers and a general choir. This points to a cultivation in colleges and Latin schools attached to monasteries and collegiate churches; one collection, the Ritson manuscript (ca. 1480), can specifically be linked to school and parish environments around Exeter cathedral.[31] The performative functions of the carols were to some extent analogous to those of the Continental cantiones: Christmas ceremonies including "child-rocking" (songs incorporating the words "Lullay, lullay"), processions, sacred drama (including the *Sponsus* and Epiphany plays), and school songs for daily prayers and meals.[32] The use of Latin lines, usually quoting liturgical chants, is more widespread than in Continental repertories. The vernacular poetry draws on popular traditions but often reveals literary ambitions and inspired lyricism, for example in the songs about visions of saints or the Virgin and the origins of plainsongs (as in the ballad-like "Alma redemptoris – as I lay upon a nyth"). Although some texts have an intense devotional or mystic flavor, the element of radical religious reform is lacking. Public and secular performance uses, however, are not only implied in some of the texts but also documented. It is known that schoolchildren sang carols in the streets for public events; the famous "Agincourt carol" (*Deo gratias, Anglia*) is believed to have been sung for the London reception of Henry V and his victorious army in 1415. Strictly liturgical functions of the carols are, by contrast, hardly demonstrable: to call them a "processional genre" (Greene, Stevens) seems as far as we can go.

29 Jeppesen and Brøndal, eds., *Die mehrstimmige italienische Laude*; Dammonis, *Laude libro primo*.
30 Stevens, ed., *Mediaeval Carols*.    31 Strohm, *The Rise of European Music*, 206–7 and 382–83.
32 On the texts and their functions, see especially Greene, *The Early English Carols*.

## The intercultural carol

Changes, revivals, continuities, and reforms of the repertories have been at work in almost every generation from the Middle Ages until today. Some of the melodies have inspired the most celebrated music Western civilization knows: this might not have happened without the impetus of the musical lay devotions of the fifteenth century. Today, carols are the oldest music known to virtually everyone in Western society: not only their practical use, but also their scholarly study involves more than just "reception." The researcher is faced with an environmental phenomenon, not only a distant object.[33] In fact, Christmas carols are a very popular pastime and have become a commodity of our consumer society. Popular religious songs connect people nostalgically with their past, with imaginations of childhood and belonging. The apparent innocence and integrative appeal of such songs may hide the divisiveness and bigotry that has sometimes been attached to them. But there is another side to this tradition. The early cantio, lauda, and carol overstepped the boundaries of the Catholic liturgy; in a later phase the songs became multidenominational; in the nineteenth century they reached other continents, and in the twentieth their peaceful message could become intercultural, secular, and political. One example is John Lennon's and Yoko Ono's *Happy Xmas (War Is Over)*, a protest song against the Vietnam war, which contains the line "war is over (if you want it)."

## Bibliography

Ameln, Konrad, "'Resonet in laudibus' – 'Joseph, lieber Joseph mein'," *Jahrbuch für Liturgik und Hymnologie* 15 (1970), 52–112

Anderson, Gordon Athol, ed., *Notre-Dame and Related Conductus: Opera Omnia*, 9 vols., Henryville, PA, 1979–88

Bergsagel, John, "The Practice of *Cantus planus binatim* in Scandinavia in the 12th to 16th Centuries," in *Le polifonie primitive in Friuli e in Europa*, ed. Cesare Corsi and Pierluigi Petrobelli, Rome, 1989, 63–82

and Niels Martin Jensen, "A Reconsideration of the Manuscript Copenhagen A.M.76, 8º: Its Significance for Danish Cultural History in the 15th Century," in *Festskrift Henrik Glahn 1919–29 maj.-1979*, Copenhagen, 1979, 19–33

Böse, Brigitte, and Franz Schäfer, *Geistliche Lieder und Gesänge in Böhmen*, 2/1: *Tropen und Cantiones aus böhmischen Handschriften der vorhussitischen Zeit 1300–1420*, Bausteine zur Geschichte der Literatur bei den Slawen 29/II, 1, Cologne and Vienna, 1988

Brewer, Charles E., "'Cantiones et moteti populi': Towards a Definition of Popular Song and Polyphony in Central and East Central Europe," in *Laborare fratres in*

---

33 Strohm, "Late-Medieval Sacred Songs."

*unum: Festschrift László Dobszay zum 60. Geburtstag*, ed. Janka Szendrei and David Hiley, Hildesheim, 1995, 25–36

"In Search of Lost Melodies: The Latin Songs of Graz 756," in *Dies est leticie: Essays on Chant in Honour of Janka Szendrei*, ed. David Hiley and Gábor Kiss, Ottawa, 2008, 93–109

"The Jistebnický Cantional and Corpus Christi: Aspects of the Hussite Liturgical Reform," in *Chant and its Peripheries: Essays in Honour of Terence Bailey*, ed. Bryan Gillingham and Paul Merkley, Ottawa, 1998, 320–37

Bruning, Eliseus, Marie Veldhuyzen, and Hélène Wagenaar-Nolthenius, eds., *Het geestelijk Lied van Noord-Nederland in de vijftiende eeuw*, Monumenta Musica Neerlandica 7, Amsterdam, 1963

Cattin, Giulio, "'Contrafacta' internazionali: Musiche europee per laude italiane," in Cattin, *Studi sulla lauda*, 401–24

*Studi sulla lauda offerti all'autore da F. A. Gallo e F. Luisi*, Rome, 2003

ed., *Italian Laude and Latin Unica in the MS Capetown, Grey 3.b.12*, CMM 76, Stuttgart, 1977

Černý, Jaromír, "Vícehlasé písně konduktového typu v českých pramenech 15. století" [Polyphonic songs of the conductus type in fifteenth-century Bohemian sources], in *Miscellanea Musicologica* (Czech Republic) 31 (1984), 39–142

Corsi, Cesare, and Pierluigi Petrobelli, eds., *Le polifonie primitive in Friuli e in Europa: Atti del congresso internazionale, Cividale del Friuli, 22–24 agosto 1980*, Rome, 1989

Dammonis, Innocentius, *Laude libro primo. Venezia 1508*, repr. with introductions by Giulio Cattin and Francesco Luisi, Venice, 2001

Diederichs, Elisabeth, *Die Anfänge der mehrstimmigen Lauda vom Ende des 14. bis zur Mitte des 15. Jahrhunderts*, Tutzing, 1986

Dreves, Guido Maria, Clemens Blume, and Henry Marriott Bannister, eds., *Analecta hymnica medii aevi*, 55 vols., Leipzig, 1886–1922

Gómez y Muntané, María, ed., *El Llibre vermell de Montserrat: Cantos y danzas s. XIV*, Sant Cugat de Vallès, 1990

Greene, Richard Leighton, *The Early English Carols*, Oxford, 1935, 2nd edn., 1977

Harrison, Frank Llewellyn, "Benedicamus, Conductus, Carol: A Newly-Discovered Source," *AcM* 37 (1965), 35–48

Hascher-Burger, Ulrike, *Gesungene Innigkeit: Studien zu einer Musikhandschrift der Devotio Moderna (Utrecht, Universiteitsbibliotheek, ms. 16 H 34, olim B 113)*, Leiden, 2002

Haug, Andreas, ed., *Troparia tardiva: Repertorium später Tropenquellen aus dem deutsch-sprachigen Raum*, Kassel, 1995

Hiley, David, ed., *Moosburger Graduale: München, Universitätsbibliothek, 2°Cod. ms. 156*, Tutzing, 1996

Irtenkauf, Wolfgang, "Das Seckauer Cantionarium vom Jahre 1345 (Hs. Graz 756)," *AfMw* 13 (1956), 116–41

Janota, Johannes, *Studien zu Funktion und Typus des deutschen geistlichen Liedes im Mittelalter*, Munich, 1968

Jeppesen, Knud, and V. Brøndal, eds., *Die mehrstimmige italienische Laude um 1500*, Leipzig, 1935

Kornrumpf, Gisela, "'Ave pulcherrima regina': Zur Verbreitung und Herkunft der Melodie einer Marien-Cantio im Rostocker Liederbuch," in *Musik in Mecklenburg:*

*Beiträge eines Kolloquiums zur mecklenburgischen Musikgeschichte*, ed. Karl Heller, Hildesheim, 2000, 157–72

Lodes, Birgit, Reinhard Strohm, and Marc Lewon, eds., *Musical Life of the Late Middle Ages in the Austrian Region (c.1340–c.1520)*, FWF online project, University of Vienna, forthcoming

Luisi, Francesco, ed., *Laudario Giustinianeo: Musiche a modo proprio, ricostruzioni e "cantasi come" nella tradizione musicale dei secoli XV–XVI–XVII per le fonti delle laude attribuite a Leonardo Giustinian*, 2 vols., Venice, 1983

Lütolf, Max, *et al.*, eds., *Das deutsche Kirchenlied: Kritische Gesamtausgabe der Melodien.* Abteilung II: *Geistliche Gesänge des deutschen Mittelalters. Melodien und Texte handschriftlicher Überlieferung bis um 1530*, 6 vols., Kassel, 2003–4

Petri, Theodoric, ed., *Piae Cantiones ecclesiasticae et scholasticae*, Greifswald, 1582; repr. London, 1910

Plocek, Václav, *Zwei Studien zur ältesten geistlichen Musik in Böhmen*, in co-operation with Andreas Traub, 2 vols., Bausteine zur Geschichte der Literatur bei den Slawen, 27/1 and 27/2, Giessen and Cologne, 1985

Rothe, Hans, ed., *Die Hohenfurther Liederhandschrift (H 42) von 1410*, Cologne, 1984

Salmen, Walter, "European Song (1300–1530)," in *Ars Nova and the Renaissance 1300–1549*, ed. Anselm Hughes and Gerald Abraham, The New Oxford History of Music 3, Oxford, 1960, 349–80

Stalmann, Joachim, *et al.*, eds., *Das deutsche Kirchenlied: Kritische Gesamtausgabe der Melodien.* Abteilung III: *Die Melodien aus gedruckten Quellen bis 1680*, 8 vols., Kassel, 1993–2010

Sternfeld, Frederick W., "Music in the Schools of the Reformation," *MD* 2 (1948), 99–122

Stevens, John E., ed., *Mediaeval Carols*, Musica Britannica 4, London, 1952; rev. edn. 1958

Strohm, Reinhard, "Gesänge zu Weihnachten im Stift Seckau," in *Musical Life*, ed. Lodes, Strohm, and Lewon, ch. A.2

"Late-Medieval Sacred Songs: Tradition, Memory and History," in *Identity and Locality in Early European Music, 1028–1740*, ed. Jason Stoessel, Farnham, 2009, 129–48

"Michael Weisse Transmitting Medieval Songs to Bach," in *Understanding Bach, Web Journal of Bach Network UK*, www.bachnetwork.co.uk/publications, 6 (2011), 56–60

"Das Orationale Kaiser Friedrichs III. und das europäische geistliche Lied," in *Wiener Quellen der älteren Musikgeschichte zum Sprechen gebracht: Eine Ringvorlesung*, ed. Birgit Lodes, Wiener Forum für ältere Musikgeschichte 1, Tutzing, 2007, 229–56

"Polyphonie und Liedforschung," in *Einstimmig – Mehrstimmig: Deutungsperspektiven zur Musik des 15. und 16. Jahrhunderts*, ed. Birgit Lodes = *MusikTheorie: Zeitschrift für Musikwissenschaft* 27 (2012), 162–75

*The Rise of European Music 1380–1500*, Cambridge, 1993

"Song Composition in the Fourteenth and Fifteenth Centuries: Old and New Questions," *Jahrbuch der Oswald-von-Wolkenstein-Gesellschaft* 9 (1996/97), 523–50

Weisse, Michael, *Gesangbuch der Böhmischen Brüder 1531*, facs., ed. Konrad Ameln, Kassel, 1957

Wilson, Blake, "Lauda," in *Grove Music Online* (accessed 17 February 2012)

  *Music and Merchants: The Laudesi Companies of Republican Florence*, Oxford, 1992

Zec, John J., "The Relationship of the Carol, the Processional, and the Rhymed Office of the Nativity Cycle as Influenced by the Mendicant Orders in the Late Middle Ages in England," Ph.D. diss., Catholic University of America, 1997 (UMI dissertations 9726485)

# 40

# Plainsong in the age of polyphony

RICHARD SHERR

If you asked any church musician of the fifteenth century what type of music was most important in the Catholic rite, he almost certainly would have said that it was Gregorian chant (*cantus planus* or plainsong). He would have said that even if he didn't really believe it because he would have known that this was the "right" answer to give to the question. If he were a curmudgeon, and there were a number of these, he would have added that plainsong, having its origins in divine inspiration and ancient practice, should be the only music in the liturgy; none of that newfangled polyphonic stuff.[1] There can be no doubt that the majority of what was sung during the liturgy was plainsong, just as plainsong was the basis of all musical education. The structure of the Catholic rite, with its many Offices, its thousands of antiphons, responds, etc., its hundreds of Propers of the Mass – far too many to be set to polyphony even if it had been desired – virtually dictated the preponderance of plainsong in all venues where the Catholic rite was celebrated with music. Weighty parchment tomes of plainsong produced in the fifteenth and later centuries, some with spectacular illuminations, are sitting in libraries and in the museums of cathedrals and churches all over Europe. And plainsongs continued to be composed for new Offices and for items of the Ordinary of the Mass. It would be interesting to know Guillaume Du Fay's reaction if he were told that of all the music he had produced during his lifetime, the only works that would be sung with regularity for nearly a century after his death would be the plainsongs he wrote in 1457 for the *Recollectio Festorum Beatae Mariae Virginis*, and further that no one would know that he had composed them.[2] He might have been pleased that he would have thus joined the ranks of the unknown composers of the Gregorian repertory and that his music had achieved the same status as theirs. On the other hand, he might have been disappointed.

---

1 Wegman, *The Crisis of Music in Early Modern Europe*.
2 Haggh, "The Celebration of the 'Recollectio Festorum Beatae Mariae Virginis'." The musical sources of the plainsongs have no attribution; the authorship is known only from an archival document. Du Fay's plainsongs were replaced in many localities after the Council of Trent.

Of course, it had occurred to some in the fifteenth century that the situation was a bit chaotic. There was an awareness that the sources of plainsong did not agree in all their melodic details. There was an awareness that not all of the melodies obeyed the "rules" of modal construction so laboriously learned in school. There was particularly an awareness in the fifteenth and later centuries that the plainsong melodies preserved in the written record did not obey the rules of Latin grammar and put melismas on weak syllables of the text. If we are to believe Jean Le Munerat, a singer and scholar active in Paris ca. 1465–99, there were attempts in the late fifteenth century to fix this by altering the placement of the text (which, he contended, also altered the melodies). Yet Le Munerat basically advises people to "live with it." Music is music and grammar is grammar, he says, and in plainsong, music holds sway over grammar and thus, the melodies as preserved in the ancient sources should remain untouched.[3] The extent to which he was successful in persuading people of his opinion is not clear, but I would venture to guess that the extant sources of the fifteenth century (unlike those of the late sixteenth) do not show much evidence of tampering with the melodies or with text placement. Newly composed plainsong of the period does show attention to long and short syllables, as well as to the correct exposition of the mode. Take, for example, one of Du Fay's newly composed antiphons for the *Recollectio* (see Example 40.1).[4] Even though there is a slight hint of the "French stress" in Latin declamation (*Chri-stûm*, for instance), care has been taken to place melismas over the strong syllables of the words. And Mode 5 is clearly delineated by outlining its defining fifth, fourth, and octave, just as Johannes Tinctoris and other theorists said it should be. The "Gregorian arch," which anybody who had spent his life singing plainsongs must have internalized, is also present in the melody.

In the late sixteenth century, the forces that Le Munerat was opposing clearly had won the day, but it depended where you were. The reforms of plainsong commissioned by people like Pope Gregory XIII essentially created a new plainsong dialect (represented by publications like the Roman *Editio Medicea*) in which the melodies were "corrected." But there was no attempt to impose this dialect on all Catholic dioceses and institutions.[5] The popes refused to mandate the use of the melodies of the Medicean edition; churches and institutions were free to continue to sing the old plainsongs or to change them as they saw fit.[6]

Where you were determined everything about the plainsong you sang. Calendars differed from place to place and even within the same city. Chants,

---

3 Harrán, *In Defense of Music*.
4 Transcription taken from Haggh, "The Celebration of the 'Recollectio Festorum Beatae Mariae Virginis'." Neumes indicated in her transcription have been omitted.
5 Karp, *An Introduction to the Post-Tridentine Mass Proper*.    6 And change them they did; see Karp, ibid.

Example 40.1 Guillaume Du Fay, *Ave virgo speciosa*

even of stable feasts of the Temporale, could also be different to greater and lesser degrees. This must have posed a problem for itinerant singers who traveled from church to church and court to court (that is, almost all the major composers of the period). Having carefully learned and probably memorized the plainsong repertory of one institution, they would find themselves having to learn a different repertory. If this bothered them we have no evidence of it. It had been the case for centuries.

So was plainsong in "the age of polyphony" much different from plainsong in the "age of monophony"? It was in certain respects much more stable. The repertory might have been subject to regional variation, but the stage of creation was long over and the melodies of the important plainsongs were largely the same all over Europe. Further, they were legible, written in the quadratic notation (punctus, virga, neumes) that was basically the same (even allowing for the German notation known as Hufnagelschrift) all over Europe. The same modal theory, developed for plainsong, was dutifully transmitted from treatise to treatise and learned by everyone all over Europe. This is boring. It is why chant scholars have generally been uninterested in plainsong in the age of polyphony.[7]

## The sources

The majority of sources of plainsong are manuscripts, and there is evidence of wholesale recopying of the plainsong repertory in various institutions in the fifteenth century. Printed sources of plainsong also appear in the fifteenth century, considerably earlier than they do for polyphonic music. There is no comprehensive catalogue of all the manuscript sources, although more and more individual collections are being catalogued and there are a number of ongoing database collections of plainsong manuscripts.[8] The situation is different for printed sources: the RELICS database now has nearly 14,000 entries of worship books printed before 1601.[9] Similarly, there are studies of the melodies of specific genres (Kyries, Credos, etc.) that include melodies produced in the fifteenth century and later.[10] Facsimiles of manuscripts and prints of late sources of plainsong are being produced. Scholars interested in particular polyphonic settings of plainsongs have also searched out the relevant contemporary sources of the melodies.[11] But it is all rather haphazard, and it does not look as if we will ever have the bibliographical control that we have for the oldest sources of plainsong. In fact, that might be an impossible goal.

## Rhythmicizing plainchant

The main question of the historical performance of plainsong is one of rhythm. The performance practice of the eighth to tenth centuries is the subject of much debate today. In the "age of polyphony" there was no debate, only an

---

7 There have always been exceptions to this (see the work of Mary Berry and Bruno Stäblein, for example) and the situation may be changing.

8 For the plainsong sources in the Cappella Sistina collection, for instance, see Llorens, *Cappellae Sixtinae Codices* and Talamo, *Codices cantorum*. On the massive collection of plainsong choirbooks in the cathedral of Toledo, see Noone and Skinner, "Toledo Cathedral's Collection." Some fifteenth-century manuscripts are included in the ongoing CANTUS database of chants of the liturgical office: cantusdatabase.org. More databases, including manuscript plainsong sources of the fifteenth century, are linked on the web page of the Regensburg ANTIPHONARIA project: www.uni-regensburg.de/Fakultaeten/phil_Fak_I/ Musikwissenschaft/cantus/Antiphonaria/. The downloadable Excel database file from gregofacsimil: http://gregofacsimil.free.fr/03-MANUSCRITS/INTERNET-ET-LES-MANUSCRITS/manuscrits_internet.html (2,328 items when last consulted on 1 February 2014) provides links to manuscripts of many types and dates available on the internet, including some chant manuscripts of the fifteenth century.

9 Renaissance Liturgical Imprints: A Census: quod.lib.umich.edu/r/relics/.

10 For example, Landwehr-Melnicki, *Das einstimmigen Kyrie*, and Miazga, *Die Melodien des einstimmigen Credo*.

11 See the items by Bloxam in the Bibliography.

apparent agreement that there were any number of ways of singing plainsong. Chief among these was the so-called "equal-note" performance practice, where every pitch received the same rhythmic value, but this was hardly the only practice. In fact, there is plenty of evidence that the procedures of mensural music had greatly confused the issue and had made inroads into the performance of plainsong. But just as there was no desire to create one standard set of melodies, there does not seem to have been any desire to create one standard performance practice.

There was general agreement that quadratic notation by itself conveyed little information beyond the pitches. It was of course noticed that the shapes of plainsong notation were similar to the shapes used in mensural notation (longs, breves, semibreves), but the choice of how to interpret this was seemingly left up to individuals and institutions. In his *Tractatus de notis et pausis*, Johannes Tinctoris has this to say about plainsong notation:

> Notes of uncertain value are those which are not limited to any regular value. Such are those we use in plainchant whose shape is sometimes similar to the long, breve, and semibreve, and sometimes dissimilar ... And these notes are sung now with measure, now without measure, now under perfect quantity, now under imperfect according to the rite of churches or the will of those singing.[12]

This description, which may represent the state of affairs in the 1460s and 1470s, seems to leave everything up in the air. Other theorists argue for the equal-note performance of plainsong, but even they admit that not everybody used this practice all the time.[13]

In his *Liber de arte contrapuncti*, Tinctoris may give us more concrete examples of what the performance of plainsong might have been like in his day. Chapter 21 of book 2 of the *Liber* is concerned with *contrapunctus super librum* (improvised polyphony over a preexistent melody) created over plainsong. Tinctoris gives a number of examples of how this could be done over cantus firmi drawn from the plainsong repertory: the first a verse from the sequence *Victimae paschali laudes*, the others labeled *Alleluia*. The first examples are of *contrapuncti* created when "at the will of those singing" every note of the plainsong is the same length, be it semibreves of major or minor prolation (used for the sequence) or breves of minor prolation (equal-note performance). Example 40.2 shows the plainsong *Alleluia* with every pitch expressed as a breve.[14] Over this, Tinctoris constructs a complicated contrapuntal voice,

---

12 Sherr, "The Performance of Chant," 180.   13 Ibid., 179–81.
14 This is also discussed in Berry, "The Performance of Plainsong." It should be noted in this case that Tinctoris presents the entire Respond including the jubilus, that is, the section that would have been sung by the chorus.

Example 40.2 *Alleluia* [Respond of the *Alleluia Dulce lignum*, *LU* 1456], tenor only, from bk. 2, ch. 21 of Tinctoris, *Liber de arte contrapuncti*

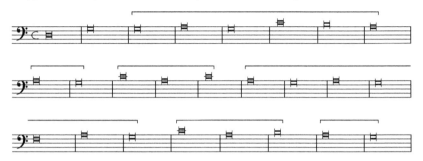

presumably as an example of what might be done.[15] The point was obviously that the contrapuntist(s) had to be able to predict when the pitches would change. Equal-note performance of the underlying plainsong makes this easy.

Tinctoris then presents two more ways a plainsong could be organized (see Example 40.3 and Example 40.4). Both of these create small repeating rhythmic cells (numbered in the example), another way of being able to predict when the pitches would change.[16] Above these he constructs ever more complicated contrapuntal voices.

These examples raise a question: is Tinctoris giving the manner in which plainsong would have been performed even if there were no *contrapunctus*, or is he describing decisions made in order to create *contrapunctus*? One might think that the latter is the case and that this has no bearing on the performance of plainsong. But then we have an observation about *contrapunctus* that is not accompanied by a music example:

> In many churches this plainchant is sung without measure, above which a most suave harmony is made by the learned [singers], and, in this, a good ear is necessary for those harmonizing, in order that they may notice most attentively the line sung by the tenors, lest, while these are singing one note, they harmonize upon another.[17]

---

15 Complete transcriptions of the contrapuntal voices in Johannes Tinctoris, *Opera Theoretica*, ed. Seay (from which the present examples are taken, doubling the note values), and Tinctoris, *The Art of Counterpoint*, trans. Seay. See also Philippe Canguilhem's essay in this volume, Ch. 9.

16 Tinctoris probably did not know that this technique was in fact the origin of all mensural polyphony.

17 "In pluribus etiam ecclesiis cantus ipse planus absque mensura canitur, super quem suavissimus concentus ab eruditis efficitur. Et in hoc auris bona concinentibus necessaria est ut attentissime cursum tenoristarum animadvertant ne istis unam notam canentibus illi super aliam concinant." Tinctoris, *Liber de arte contrapuncti*, bk. 2, ch. 21, in *Opera Theoretica*, ed. Seay, 2:117; *The Art of Counterpoint*, ed. Seay, 110. Tinctoris is echoing here comments by earlier writers on the performance of plainsong. See Berry, "The Performance of Plainsong."

Example 40.3 *Alleluia*, tenor only, from bk. 2, ch. 21 of Tinctoris, *Liber de arte contrapuncti*

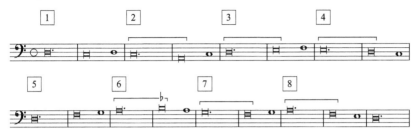

Example 40.4 *Alleluia*, tenor only, from bk. 2, ch. 21 of Tinctoris, *Liber de arte contrapuncti*

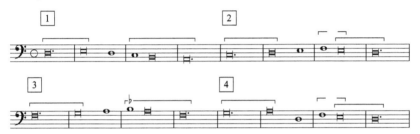

This is about as close to a fifteenth-century description of the "oratorical rhythm" of the Monks of Solesmes (the flowing style based on the accentuation of Latin words which has dominated chant performance from the late nineteenth century to the present) as we are likely to get (Tinctoris obviously did not consider it to be the same as equal-note performance, which is in fact "measured"). Here, the timing of the change in pitches cannot be predicted, so the contrapuntist really has to be on his toes. But this in turn suggests that the other rhythmic examples were chosen because, like unmeasured performance, they were an accepted way of singing plainchant, no matter how strange that might appear to us. But perhaps this should not be pressed too far. Examples of *contrapunctus* in the sixteenth century consistently present plainsong tenors as equal notes, and it is possible that Tinctoris merely made up his rhythmically organized plainsongs for demonstration purposes.[18]

18 On sixteenth-century *contrapunctus* see Canguilhem, "Singing upon the Book."

## Mensural plainsong

Chapter 22 of book 2 of the *Liber de arte contrapuncti* concerns *contrapunctus super figuratum cantum* (counterpoint over melodies expressed in free mensural notation as in polyphonic compositions). Amazingly, one of these is also a plainsong *Alleluia* (see Example 40.5). Tinctoris reserves it for this chapter because here the figures and neumes of plainsong notation are in fact to be read literally as if they were the figures and ligatures of mensural notation (once again making it possible to predict when the pitches would change). Can this also have been an option for the performance of plainsong?

In fact there is plenty of evidence for the intrusion of mensural notation into plainsong, although it seems to have been restricted to particular examples of particular genres. This is now generally called *cantus fractus* and refers to plainsong that is written either in clear mensural notation or in a mixture of quadratic and mensural notation.[19]

The main genres in the fifteenth century that were subject to *cantus fractus* were Credos, sequences, and hymns. That certain examples of these (not all, however) were written in mensural or quasi-mensural notation was admitted by everybody, even those who advocated equal-note performance of plainsong. The prime example is the Credo called *Cardinalis* or *Maior* (*LU*, Credo IV), probably composed in the thirteenth century, which is transmitted in almost all sources in a mixture of quadratic and mensural notation (using virgae [= breves], semibreves, minims, and c.o.p. ligatures, often including the mensuration sign ¢).[20] See Example 40.6.[21] Here the rhythm approximates the declamation of the words and is somewhat irregular. The same sort of rhythm was also applied to the much older Credo melody, known as Credo I, which was rarely written as a *cantus fractus*.[22]

On the other hand, the hymn *Conditor alme siderum* is often transmitted in clear mensural notation in which trochaic rhythms seem to have been imposed

---

19 *Cantus fractus* is the subject of a number of modern studies, conferences, and a database (Progetto RAPHAEL (Rhythmic and Proportional Hidden or Actual Elements in Plainchant), www.cantusfractus.org).
20 See Sherr, "The Performance of Chant"; Besutti, "Il Credo *Cardinalis* nei testimoni di area lombarda"; and other publications. It may be that the melody was originally composed to be accompanied by another voice in two-part polyphony (the Credo is sometimes transmitted that way) and was mensural for that reason. See Gozzi, "Il canto fratto: Prima classificazione." A performance of a two-voice version is included on the CD accompanying *Il canto fratto: L'altro gregoriano*. "C.o.p. ligatures" are two semibreves in ligature, *cum opposita proprietate*.
21 A complete transcription is in Sherr, "The Performance of Chant."
22 Sherr, "The Performance of Chant."

Example 40.5 *Alleluia* [begins like the *Alleluia Concaluit cor meum*, LU 1473], tenor only from bk. 2, ch. 21 of Tinctoris, *Liber de arte contrapuncti*

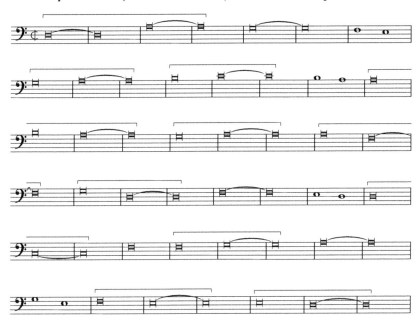

Example 40.6 Credo *Cardinalis*, beginning, from the *Graduale Romanum* (Venice, 1515)

Pa - trem     om - ni - po - ten -     tem.

on the words, causing a misplaced accent in the beginning (see Example 40.7).[23]

There are many other examples of *cantus fractus* Credos, sequences, and hymns in sources of the fifteenth to the eighteenth centuries.[24] They exist side by side with Credos, sequences, and hymns written in quadratic notation. Franchinus Gaffurius even suggests that some singers imposed a mensural reading on the quadratic notation of Credos, sequences, and hymns.[25] Singers must have had no problem changing the manner of plainsong

---

23  Transcribed from ModB. See Gozzi, "Il canto fratto," 9, figure 2. Of course in terms of the melody the setting is correct, since the melisma occurs on a strong syllable. The melody is also transmitted without mensural notation.

24  See the items on *canto fratto* in the Bibliography.     25  Sherr, "The Performance of Chant," 184.

Example 40.7 *Conditor alme siderum* written as *cantus fractus*

Con - di - tor al - me si - de - rum

performance depending on what was being sung. Whether they also chose to interpret the quadratic notation of the entire plainsong repertory as mensural notation as in the Tinctoris example above cannot be proven at present, but it might have been a viable option.

## Plainsong and polyphony

How much of the performance of plainsong in the fifteenth century was actually monophonic? Again it depended where you were. In the cathedral of Notre Dame in Paris, where polyphony had been banned, monophony reigned.[26] There were undoubtedly many other similar conservative institutions. But in the cathedral of Bourges, where the canons were very concerned that there always be singers of "organum" present in the choir (that is during all the Offices that were celebrated there), it would seem that some sort of polyphony was expected in the normal performance of plainsong.[27] After all, even Pope John XXII in his notorious bull *Docta sanctorum* had sanctioned simple polyphonic embellishment of plainsong.[28] English faburden, widely practiced in the fifteenth century, produced precisely this kind of simple polyphony and could be applied to any type of plainsong. Tinctoris, in the examples quoted earlier, clearly assumed much more elaborate embellishment of plainsong, and it has even been posited that the sound of sophisticated multi-voice *contrapunctus super librum* in the fifteenth century was not that much different from so-called *res facta* or written music.[29] But perhaps the more elaborate kinds were reserved for specific genres of plainsong; it may not be a coincidence that Tinctoris's plainsongs quoted above are *Alleluias*, for instance. Since the skill of *contrapunctus* was required of singers in the major musical institutions of the time, there is a distinct possibility that a good deal of what should have been monophonic renditions of plainsong in the age of

---

26 Wright, *Music and Ceremony at Notre Dame of Paris*.
27 Sherr, "Music at the Cathedral of Bourges."
28 Klaper, "Verbindliches kirchenmusikalisches Gesetz" and countless other studies.
29 Wegman, "From Maker to Composer." Tinctoris was also aware of simple note-against-note polyphonic embellishment of plainsong, but he considered it to be ridiculous (*Liber de arte contrapuncti*, bk. 2, ch. 22). See also Canguilhem's essay, Ch. 9.

polyphony was in fact polyphonic in those places. And it should not be forgotten that plainsong was often performed alternating with polyphonic elaborations played on the organ.

In short, plainsong resounded in a number of different ways in the fifteenth century. There was variety in the melodies, which were not exactly the same in all sources, and some were newly written. Plainsong melodies were performed as equal notes, or were perhaps organized in repeating rhythmic cells, or sung as if they were mensural, or in a free manner. Some were conceived as *cantus fractus*. And plainsong could always serve as the basis of polyphonic embellishments of greater and lesser sophistication. The different methods of performance could even have alternated during the celebration of any single liturgical event. This state of *varietas* continued well beyond the fifteenth century until it was obliterated in the early twentieth.

## Plainsong in polyphony

Finally, we must consider plainsong in composed and notated polyphony (*res facta*). It continued to play its historical role as cantus firmus, although now it had to share the stage with secular melodies. Modern scholarship has been increasingly concerned with identifying the exact plainsongs that underlie polyphonic compositions. The operating assumption is that when a composer composed a work based on a plainsong cantus firmus, he chose a version of the melody that was current in the institution where he happened to be working at the time. Finding these versions is not always easy; it requires among other things a sophisticated knowledge of plainsong sources and liturgical traditions that many Renaissance musicologists do not have.[30] When it can be done important insights follow. M. Jennifer Bloxam has uncovered a rich tradition of symbolic associations in masses composed in the Low Countries in the fifteenth century with multiple plainsong cantus firmi whose texts were meant to be sung along with that of the Ordinary.[31] Alejandro Planchart has been able to place and date a number of the works by Du Fay on the basis of specific liturgies and plainsong traditions, as has Bloxam with masses by Jacob Obrecht.[32] Sometimes, the smallest of details can lead to significant conclusions. On the basis of one melodic variant in the plainsong Introit *Gaudeamus omnes*, Planchart was able to posit that Josquin's *Missa Gaudeamus* was

---

30 And it requires precisely the kind of bibliographical control that we do not have at present.
31 Bloxam, "Sacred Polyphony and Local Traditions"; Bloxam, "Dufay as Musical Theologian"; and other studies.
32 Planchart, "Guillaume Du Fay's Benefices" and many other studies; Bloxam, "Sacred Polyphony and Local Traditions."

composed in northern Italy, which is the only place this melodic variant appears to have been current.[33] Of course, such conclusions are possible only when the composer quotes the plainsong strictly without embellishment (which is usually not the case). And the basic assumption itself perhaps needs to be tested. For instance, Josquin ignored the plainsong tradition of the hymn *Ave maris stella* current in the papal chapel in his polyphonic setting composed for the papal chapel itself, preserved in a manuscript in which the plainsong is written out multiple times.[34] Perhaps some melodies simply could or would not be unlearned. The force of memory and of the oral performance tradition has also been observed in polyphonic settings based on the Credo *Cardinalis* and Credo I and in certain hymns and sequences where the *cantus fractus* rhythms which were generally sung, even if not always notated, are clearly present.[35] The effect on polyphony of the internalization of the melodic procedures of plainsong in composers who sang it every day still needs to be studied.

# Bibliography

Baroffio, Giacomo, and Michele Manganelli, eds., *Il canto fratto: Un repertorio da conservare e da studiare. Atti dei convegni tenuti a Radda in Chianti dal 1999 al 2004*, Radda in Chianti, 2005

Berry, Mary (Sister Thomas More), "The Performance of Plainsong in the Later Middle Ages and the Sixteenth Century," Ph.D. thesis, Cambridge University, 1969

Besutti, Paola, "Il Credo *Cardinalis* nei testimoni di area lombarda: Ipercorrettismo o diverse tradizioni?," in *Il canto fratto: L'altro gregoriano*, ed. Gozzi and Luisi, 69–84

Bloxam, M. Jennifer, "Dufay as Musical Theologian: The Case of the Missa Ecce ancilla Domini," unpublished paper read at the Seventy-First Annual Meeting of the American Musicological Society, Washington, DC, November 2005

"On the Origins, Contexts, and Implications of Busnoys's Plainsong Cantus Firmi: Some Preliminary Remarks," in *Antoine Busnoys: Method, Meaning, and Context in Late Medieval Music*, ed. Paula Higgins, Oxford, 1999, 71–88

"Sacred Polyphony and Local Traditions of Liturgy and Plainsong: Reflections on Music by Jacob Obrecht," in *Plainsong in the Age of Polyphony*, ed. Kelly, 140–77

"A Survey of Late Medieval Service Books from the Low Countries: Implications for Sacred Polyphony, 1460–1520," Ph.D. diss., Yale University, 1987

---

33 Planchart, "Masses on Plainsong Cantus Firmi," 93–101 (on the *Missa Gaudeamus*). The pitch in question fills in a third on the word "diem" in plainsong sources of the north Italian tradition (it is *g* in the sources, which becomes *d'* in the transposed version of the melody used by Josquin). In the sections of Josquin's mass where this part of the plainsong is the cantus firmus, Josquin uses this *d'* and does so in long notes that are unmistakably structural (see p. 98, Ex. 5.3).

34 Sherr, "Two Hymns and Three Magnificats." The plainsong preserved in Vatican CS 15 clearly ends its first phrase on *g*, while Josquin's setting copied in the same manuscript clearly ends on *a*, as do most plainsong sources of the melody.

35 Sherr, "The Performance of Chant."

Caldwell, John, "Plainsong and Polyphony 1250–1550," in *Plainsong in the Age of Polyphony*, ed. Kelly, 6–31

Canguilhem, Philippe, "Singing upon the Book according to Vicente Lusitano," *EMH* 30 (2011), 55–103

Gabrielli, Giulia, *Il canto fratto nei manoscritti della Fondazione Biblioteca S. Bernardino di Trento*, Patrimonio storico e artistico del Trentino 28, Trento, 2005

Gozzi, Marco, "Il canto fratto: Prima classificazione dei fenomeni e primi esiti del progetto RAPHAEL," in *Il canto fratto: L'altro gregoriano*, ed. Gozzi and Luisi, 7–58

Le fonti liturgiche a stampa della Biblioteca musicale L. Feininger presso il Castello del Buonconsiglio di Trento, 2 vols., Patrimonio storico e artistico del Trentino 17, Trento, 1994

and Francesco Luisi, eds., *Il canto fratto: L'altro gregoriano. Atti del convegno internazionale di studi, Parma – Arezzo, 3–6 dicembre 2003*, Rome, 2005

Haggh, Barbara, "The Celebration of the 'Recollectio Festorum Beatae Mariae Virginis,' 1457–1987," *Studia Musicologica Academiae Scientiarum Hungaricae* 30 (1988), 361–73

Harrán, Don, *In Defense of Music: The Case for Music as Argued by a Singer and Scholar of the Late Fifteenth Century*, Lincoln, NE, 1989

Hughes, Andrew, "Late Medieval Plainchant for the Divine Office," in *Music as Concept and Practice in the Late Middle Ages*, ed. Reinhard Strohm and Bonnie J. Blackburn, The New Oxford History of Music, 3/1, Oxford, 2001, 31–96

Karp, Theodore, *An Introduction to the Post-Tridentine Mass Proper*, 2 vols., MSD 54, Middleton, WI, 2005

Kelly, Thomas, ed., *Plainsong in the Age of Polyphony*, Cambridge, 1992

Klaper, Michael, "'Verbindliches kirchenmusikalisches Gesetz' oder belanglose Augenblickseingebung? Zur Constitutio *Docta sanctorum patrum* Papst Johannes' XXII," *AfMW* 60 (2003), 69–95

Landwehr-Melnicki, Margareta, *Das einstimmige Kyrie des Lateinischen Mittelalters*, Regensburg, 1955

Llorens, José M., *Capellae Sixtinae Codices musicis notis instructi sive manu scripti sive praelo excussi*, Studi e testi 202, Vatican City, 1960

Long, Sarah, "The Chanted Mass in Parisian Ecclesiastical and Civic Communities, 1480–1540: Local Liturgical Practices in Manuscripts and Early Printed Service Books," Ph.D. diss., University of Illinois at Urbana-Champaign, 2008

Mannaerts, Pieter, "Observations on the Performance of Plainchant in the Low Countries (10th–18th Centuries)," *Trans: Revista Transcultural de Música* 13 (2009), www.sibetrans.com/trans/a60/observations-on-the-performance-of-plainchant-in-the-low-countries-10th-18th-centuries

Miazga, Tadeusz, *Die Melodien des einstimmigen Credo der Römisch-Katholischen Lateinischen Kirche*, Graz, 1976

Noone, Michael, and Graeme Skinner, "Toledo Cathedral's Collection of Manuscript Plainsong Choirbooks: A Preliminary Report and Checklist," *Notes*, Second Series 63 (2006), 289–328

Planchart, Alejandro Enrique, "Guillaume Du Fay's Benefices and his Relationship to the Court of Burgundy," *EMH* 8 (1988), 117–71

"Masses on Plainsong Cantus Firmi," in *The Josquin Companion*, ed. Richard Sherr, Oxford, 2000, 89–150

Progetto RAPHAEL (Rhythmic and Proportional Hidden or Actual Elements in Plainchant), www.cantusfractus.org

Ruini, Cesarino, *I manoscritti liturgici della Biblioteca musicale L. Feininger, presso il Castello del Buonconsiglio di Trento*, 2 vols., Patrimonio storico e artistico del Trentino, 21 and 25, Trento, 1998–2002

Sherr, Richard, "Music at the Cathedral of Bourges in the Time of Ockeghem," in *Johannes Ockeghem: Actes du XL<sup>e</sup> Colloque international d'études humanistes, Tours, 3–8 février 1997*, ed. Philippe Vendrix, Paris, 1998, 173–219

"The Performance of Chant in the Renaissance and its Interactions with Polyphony," in *Plainsong in the Age of Polyphony*, ed. Kelly, 178–208

"Two Hymns and Three Magnificats," in *The Josquin Companion*, ed. Richard Sherr, Oxford, 2000, 321–34

Stäblein, Bruno, *Schriftbild der einstimmigen Musik*, Musikgeschichte in Bildern 3/4, Leipzig, 1975

Talamo, Emilia, *Codices cantorum: Miniature e disegni nei codici della Cappella Sistina*, Florence, 1997

Tinctoris, Johannes, *The Art of Counterpoint*, trans. Albert Seay, MSD 5, n.p., 1961

*Opera Theoretica*, ed. Albert Seay, CSM 22, n.p., 1975

Wegman, Rob C., *The Crisis of Music in Early Modern Europe, 1470–1530*, New York and London, 2005

"From Maker to Composer: Improvisation and Musical Authorship in the Low Countries, 1450–1500," *JAMS* 49 (1996), 409–79

Wright, Craig, *Music and Ceremony at Notre Dame of Paris 500–1500*, Cambridge, 1989

· PART X RECEPTION ·

# 41

# The most popular songs of the fifteenth century

DAVID FALLOWS

In this chapter "songs" refers to written polyphonic songs, usually in two or three voices, a genre that stretches back to the beginning of the fourteenth century and exists in all the main European languages. For the years 1415–80 this amounts to about 2,000 pieces; for the entire century it is probably a bit over 3,000. Monophonic song also exists, though much more survives from the twelfth to fourteenth and early sixteenth centuries than from the fifteenth, but this too is plainly "high-style" music, not in any sense folksong or something aimed at the common people – a genre so rare that it is almost impossible to identify in the fifteenth century. So the popularity discussed here is within the genre often called "courtly," though it surely existed as much in university and ecclesiastical circles as it did in the court.

Obviously, "popular" is a tricky notion, not least because popularity need not equate with quality; but simply counting the manuscript sources for a piece can draw the attention to matters otherwise easily overlooked. Just as obviously, the number of surviving sources for a particular piece can be a function of many different matters: such a tiny proportion of the manuscripts survives that a lot of caution is needed in drawing any conclusions. Even so, to try to draw a path through fifteenth-century song in terms of the pieces that survive in the largest number of sources is instructive. Some of the directions in which the figures point seem only logical from other viewpoints; others are a touch surprising.

The lists below give the number of known sources for such songs from each decade from the 1410s to ca. 1480. That the pieces at the top of each list do indeed seem to have been largely among the most popular of their time is attested by other details added in parentheses, namely the number of later pieces and references based on the music, and, with the suffix "m," the number of mass cycles based on it.[1] Further evidence that broadly supports this picture comes from scattered details such as passing references in the theorists or account books, appearances among the poetry manuscripts, and so on, as detailed in my *Catalogue of Polyphonic Songs, 1415–1480* (Oxford, 1999).

---

1 The lists also appear, with further discussion, in Fallows, "John Bedyngham."

# Songs from the 1410s–1430s (four and more)

## *1410s*

Une foys avant que morir ANON. 13 [11 in tablature, of which 9 in the
  Buxheim Organ Book] (6)

A son plaisir FONTAINE 9 (1)

Je ne requier GRENON 6 (1)

J'ayme bien celui FONTAINE 5 (1)

Mon cuer pleure FONTAINE 4 (2)

La plus jolie GRENON 4

Se je vous ay GRENON 4

## *1420s*

Je loe amours BINCHOIS 12 [7 in tablature] (5)

Entrepris suis BROLLO 5 (2, 1m)

Adieu m'amour et ma maistresse BINCHOIS 4

Je me recomande BINCHOIS 4 (1)

Je ne suy plus DU FAY 4

Pouray je avoir DU FAY 4

## *1430s*

Se la face ay pale DU FAY 12 (2, 1m)

Dueil angoisseux BINCHOIS 10 (8, 1m)

Adieu mes tres belles amours BINCHOIS 7 (1)

Mille bonjours DU FAY 7

Adieu, adieu mon joyeux souvenir BINCHOIS 6

Esclave puist il devenir BINCHOIS 6 (3, 1m)

Craindre vous vueil DU FAY 6 (1)

Bon jour, bon mois, bon an DU FAY 4 (1)

C'est assez BINCHOIS 4

Je ne fay tousjours BINCHOIS 4 (1)

Adieu ma tres belle maistresse ?BINCHOIS 4

Liesse m'a mandé BINCHOIS/GROSSIN 4

First, for the three decades leading up to 1440, there are few enough songs that
survive in even four sources for them all to be listed. That is partly because
there are very few surviving songbooks from those years. Apart from the great
Oxford 213, which is an oddly individualistic personal collection of motets and
mass movements alongside the songs, there are really only two dedicated
songbooks, the northern Italian one in Paris 4917, and the one perhaps from

the Burgundian court now in the Escorial (V.III.24). Otherwise there are just fragments – oddly all but one apparently from northern Italy – or tiny selections of songs added to larger books mainly of sacred music, also from northern Italy, such as the two choirbooks in Bologna, Bologna Q 15 and Bologna 2216.

The relatively smaller numbers for those years have another reason, namely that there are very few songs from before about 1440 that continued to be copied later in the century (*Se la face ay pale*, *Je loe amours*, and *Entrepris suis* are among the few), whereas there are songs from the 1440s that were still being copied in the 1530s, printed in Formschneider's *Trium vocum carmina* (1538), included in lute tablatures, and so on. That is to say that the real growth in the number of surviving songbooks begins in about 1460, with the private collection of Hartmann Schedel, the Buxheim Organ Book, and the central chansonniers.

It must be true that when there are so few surviving manuscripts the difference between four and seven sources is of only marginal significance. Even so, the figures give a good outline of the main songs during those decades. In the 1410s, only Pierre Fontaine and Nicolas Grenon seem to have been widely followed: these were the main composers in the chapel of Duke John the Fearless of Burgundy, which had to be disbanded when he was murdered in 1419. At that point both composers traveled to Italy and joined the papal chapel for a short time, so perhaps that explains why their music is so well represented in the Italian manuscripts. All the same, most music historians would be inclined to think of that decade as the decade of Zacara da Teramo and Johannes Ciconia, partly because they are the composers from whom the most compositions survive. They are also the composers with the most distinctive music, works that have a deep fascination for us today. By contrast, Fontaine and Grenon are composers of immaculate taste and balance: their complete domination in the list above is a reminder that the best music is not necessarily the music that jumps to the eye or the ear. That, of course, is not special to the fifteenth century: many of what we now consider the greatest works of the nineteenth century yield up their riches only on repeated hearing and contemplation.

Besides, our main information about the music of that decade comes from large collections like Bologna Q 15 (with 323 pieces) and the Oxford manuscript just mentioned (with 325 pieces), sources copied in the north of Italy. Here Guillaume Du Fay is well represented by his early mass music, but we actually have very little idea of what Fontaine and Grenon composed: no sacred music by Fontaine survives, very little by Grenon. So it may well be that the songs listed above can at least prompt the imagination into realizing that the lack of northern French manuscripts from the early years of what we still call the "Burgundian era" may have skewed our view of the repertory. It would only be honest to report that we have absolutely no evidence that either Fontaine or Grenon composed lots of sacred music; but the figures at least force one to ponder the question.

Even more thought-provoking is the only anonymous piece, *Une foys avant que morir*: there are only two staff-notation sources, both of them messy and fragmentary: one is in a book prepared for instrumentalists on board ship (British Library, Cotton Titus A.xxvi); and the other is a tiny fragment in Paris (BnF n.a.f. 10660, fol. 47), so worn that the music can just be made out and the text (the only full text source) is all but illegible. But the song appears at the top of the list because it was intabulated no fewer than nine times in the Buxheim keyboard collection of ca. 1460. If that were the only witness of its reputation, one could put down its apparent prominence to the preference of a single intabulator. On the other hand, there are intabulations in two further sources, the Lochamer Liederbuch and a fragment in Munich (Bayerische Staatsbibliothek, clm 29775/6). There were also three dances with the same name, one in the famous Brussels basse danse manuscript perhaps of the 1470s (Brussels 9085), one in an English collection from around 1500 (Matlock, Derbyshire Record Office, D77 Box 38), and the other in an Italian single-leaf fragment (Turin, Archivio di Stato, Archivi Biscaretti, Mazzo 4, no. 14). Beyond these, the title turns up in two poetic lists of polyphonic song titles from the very end of the century, Jean Molinet's *Debat du vieil gendarme et du viel amoureux* and the anonymous ballade *Mon seul plaisir*, which is entirely made up of song titles. The relevant question is again: to what extent are the figures distorted by that circumstance? But the only possible answer is that these references, scattered across the century and across Europe, all seem to agree that *Une foys avant que morir* was a very popular song indeed, despite its unbelievably thin survival in song form – a survival so thin that the piece could easily have disappeared entirely.

For the 1420s and 1430s, the main surprise is that Binchois (Gilles de Bins), with ten appearances, seems to do so much better than Du Fay, with only six. Moreover, *Se la face ay pale* is the only Du Fay song that even begins to compete against the nine most successful songs of Binchois during those twenty years. That is hardly how they are seen today, with Du Fay normally being treated as the major figure, recorded and performed enormously more often than Binchois. But the witness of Martin Le Franc's *Le Champion des Dames* (ca. 1440) is that they were at the time considered equally important figures. Only later did Du Fay begin to occupy the foreground, with the compositions of the 1440s and 1450s. It is true that the difference between four sources and six could be put down largely to chance survival. On the other hand, the years when Binchois seems equally if not more copied are the years when Du Fay was mainly in Italy, where the vast majority of the surviving sources were copied, whereas Binchois was resident at the court of Burgundy, far away in the north of Europe. (The court of Burgundy in those years almost never visited the Duchy or the County of Burgundy, preferring to remain where their wealth was, namely in the Low Countries, based in Brussels and Lille.)

For listeners and particularly commentators today, Du Fay seems the more attractive song-writer, because each song can vividly evoke an occasion, a mood, a sound, whereas Binchois is far more withdrawn in his manner, far less inclined to portray unexpected moods, a composer who prefers to portray the "courtly" love in a restrained manner that was familiar to his listeners. What those figures would seem to say is that the cultivated music-lovers of the early fifteenth century really appreciated that gentle elegance. They may have enjoyed Du Fay's music too, but it was a stranger sound for them, and seems not to have been appreciated quite so soon. Once again, this is no particular surprise: many of what we think of as the canonic works of the nineteenth and twentieth centuries failed at their first performances and gained their canonic status only gradually.

Another important aspect of their songs is that their generation seems to have reacted strongly against the elaboration cultivated by the composers in what we now call the *ars subtilior*, the International Gothic of music in the work of Johannes Ciconia, Zacara da Teramo, Matteo da Perugia, Paolo Tenorista, Solage, and Jaquemin de Senleches. They surely knew all the techniques of these composers, not least because they were mentioned in the music theorists for several decades to come. But in their songs they cultivated simple phrases, syllabic texting, transparent textures, springy rhythms. This was an entirely new world. That Binchois cultivated those preferences in a way slightly different from Du Fay merely says that he was a different composer. Their broad aims, and their broad turning over of a new page in musical history, were shared. Losing track of Binchois's importance in that change is to lose an important dimension of the repertory.

One surprise here is obviously Bartolomeo Brollo, a Venetian composer whose French-texted song *Entrepris suis* had a career that spanned the entire century: it was copied, in various forms and adaptations, into the Glogauer Liederbuch (ca. 1480) and the Bologna manuscript Q 16, perhaps from the last decade of the century. There is room for asking whether its late popularity was fueled by the mass based on it in the 1460s by Vincenet (another composer who makes an unexpected appearance in our lists later on); but then that question could be turned on its head with the observation that it is most unusual indeed for a song so early to be used so late for a mass cycle.

The next detail to note about the 1420s is that the songs most lovers of that decade remember best would be the awesomely bleak *Triste plaisir* by Binchois to a text by Alain Chartier (unique in Oxford 213), the nostalgic *Adieu ces bons vin de Lannoys* by Du Fay (also unique in Oxford 213), and the loveliest and most memorable of all love songs, *De plus en plus* by Binchois (two sources only). But no. The songs that make it to the list include Binchois's *Adieu m'amour et ma maistresse*, famously dismissed by Gustave Reese as "a mere perfunctory stringing together of cadence formulas."[2] And the one that definitively tops the list is *Je loe amours*, a song that is hardly ever heard, partly perhaps because it is very hard to sing convincingly. You would expect to find that technical difficulty got in the way of a song's success, but apparently not in this case.

## Songs from the 1440s and 1450s

### 1440s ( five and more)

O Rosa bella BEDYNGHAM 18 (26, 3m)
Le serviteur DU FAY 17 (27, 4m)
Gentil madona BEDYNGHAM 16 (7, 1m)
Mon seul plaisir BEDYNGHAM 14 (11)
So ys emprentid BEDYNGHAM/FRYE 11 (6, 2m)
Puis que je vis ANON. 10 (3, 1m)
Myn hertis lust BEDYNGHAM 8 (2)
Pour prison ne pour BINCHOIS 7 (8)
Terriblement suis ANON. 5 (5, 1m)
Een vrauken edel ANON. 5

### 1450s (nine and more)

Ave regina celorum FRYE 23 (4, 1m)
Ma bouche rit OCKEGHEM 18 (11, 3m)
D'ung aultre amer OCKEGHEM 18 (20, 3m)
J'ay pris amours ANON. 17 (31, 3m)
Par le regart DU FAY 15 (7)
O gloriosa TOURONT 15 (1, 2m)
Comme femme BINCHOIS 11 (18, 2m)
Je ne vis oncques BINCHOIS/DU FAY 11 (12, 4m)
O pulcherrima mulierum ANON. 10 (2)
Quant ce viendra BUSNOYS 10 (1, 1m)
Tout a par moy FRYE/BINCHOIS 9 (9, 1m)

---

2 *Music in the Renaissance*, 88.

L'omme banny BARBINGANT 9 (7)
Elend du hast (B) [probably not by Morton] 9 (1)

With the 1440s, something entirely different comes across European song, namely the phenomenon of John Bedyngham.[3] To list the dozen or so more widely copied songs of that decade we still need to include songs that survive in only five sources. But the leaders now survive in numbers quite unknown to the previous decades: Bedyngham's *O Rosa bella* with eighteen sources, Du Fay's *Le serviteur* with seventeen, and Bedyngham's *Gentil madona* with sixteen. Certainly, the figures arise in part because the music continued to be copied for the next fifty years: that is why the numbers begin to be much greater. And part of the reason why they continued to be copied is that their notation was much simpler, with no major prolation and very little of the other details that would be strange to the growing bourgeois readership for this music in the second half of the century. But the picture is clear: an obscure Englishman about whom we still know almost nothing was writing songs that were not only copied many times over but also used for countless new pieces over the next years. Moreover, the musicians of the time too probably also knew nothing of Bedyngham: among the total of seventy-two copies of his eight known songs, only six come with a recognizable form of his name; another five copies have the name in garbled versions that can be identified with Bedyngham only by dint of stylistic comparison with the other pieces. He is also not named by any of the theorists and historians of the time. So, like the song *Une foys avant que morir*, Bedyngham is known to us by the thinnest sliver of evidence and could have disappeared completely from the record.

For the 1450s Johannes Ockeghem's name appears for the first time, and with pieces that should surprise nobody who knows the repertory, namely *Ma bouche rit* and *D'ung aultre amer*. But the list for this decade is headed by another piece by an obscure Englishman, Walter Frye's *Ave regina celorum*. Despite its evidently sacred Latin text this piece has a firm place in the list. It is there because almost all its known sources are vernacular songbooks, in several of which it is the first piece – as though a songbook, like a meal, should begin with a prayer. That is why in the same decade Johannes Touront's *O gloriosa* and the

---

3  It is no accident that the lists report most conflicting ascriptions but not the ascription of *O Rosa bella* to Dunstaple in a small songbook now in Rome, Vatican City, Biblioteca Apostolica Vaticana, Urb. lat. 1411, fols. 22v–23r. The fullest argument that it cannot possibly be aligned with any known work of Dunstaple and fits flawlessly into the work of Bedyngham is in Fallows, "Dunstaple, Bedyngham and *O rosa bella*," but the same views have been expressed more compactly by both Margaret Bent (*Dunstaple*, 85) and Reinhard Strohm (*The Rise of European Music*, 393); they are also accepted without any reservation in the fullest and most recent study of the song, Erhard, *Bedynghams O rosa bella*. Views that it may be by Dunstaple are based on an over-reverent attitude to great scholars writing long before much of the current research on the sources. I believe that associating *O Rosa bella* with Dunstaple seriously distorts our view of the topic.

anonymous *O pulcherrima mulierum* are also on the list. It is a reminder that the customary division of "sacred" from "secular" makes no sense in the music or the poetry of the fifteenth century: everything in life for the intelligent classes was informed by faith.

There is another historically important feature of those pieces by Bedyngham and Frye, namely that they were almost certainly composed to texts other than the ones they now carry. In 1955 Sylvia Kenney made the case beyond reasonable doubt for Frye's *Ave regina celorum*, showing that every detail of its music and its formal design argued that its original text must have been an English ballade;[4] but it is probably true to say that nobody took much notice of her flawless logic until Alexander Erhard made the same case for Bedyngham's *O Rosa bella* in 2010, using entirely different means, namely by showing that its musical lines do not match those of the Italian text in any way that would be recognized by a song composer of the fifteenth century.[5] That argument not only strengthens the case for *Ave regina celorum* being a contrafactum but does the same for many other songs by English composers in Continental sources. In particular it gives added support to hypothetical English texts already proposed for Bedyngham's *Mon seul plaisir* and *Gentil madona*.

Plainly most Continental musicians did not know English. Kenney's argument began from three attempts at writing English texts in the Neapolitan Mellon Chansonnier, not publicly known until 1939 – namely *Myn hertis lust, So ys emprentid*, and *Alas alas*. Of those three songs, the only one to show any hint of an English text otherwise is *So ys emprentid*, with the text cues "Soyez aprentiz" in the Laborde Chansonnier and "Suis aprentiz" in the Montecassino MS 871. Otherwise they appear only with texts in French or Latin, and it is fairly safe to conclude that neither the Laborde nor the Montecassino copyist was aware he was writing English. In the circumstances, then, it may not be so strange that there is no surviving hint of any original English text among the many surviving sources for *O rosa bella* and *Ave regina celorum*: not strange at all so much as horrifying, when one considers how many English sources must be lost. Of those six songs the only one surviving in any English manuscript is the first twenty-one notes of the discantus of *So ys emprentid*, copied without text in Oxford, Bodleian Library, Ashmole 191 (where it was identified by the great Manfred F. Bukofzer).[6]

One odd feature of these adaptations is that they very often made no attempt to match the form of the original: the 10-syllable lines of *So ys emprentid in my*

---

4 Kenney, "Contrafacta in the Works of Walter Frye." She reformulated and strengthened the case in her book *Walter Frye and the Contenance angloise*, 62–82.
5 Erhard, *Bedynghams O rosa bella.*    6 Bukofzer, *Studies in Medieval and Renaissance Music*, 94.

*remembrance* became the 8-syllable *Pour une suis desconforté*; the 10-syllable lines of *Myn hertis lust and sterre of my confort* became the 8-syllable *Grant temps ai eu et desiree*; the 10-syllable lines of *Mi verry joy and most parfit plesere* became the 8-syllable *Mon seul plaisir, ma doulce joye*. Given the care with which most poems are set to music in the fifteenth-century repertory, that is a most surprising circumstance, and it may reflect a slightly looser link between words and music in the middle decades of the century. For the works of the 1420s and 1430s that link was very close indeed, with much syllabic writing to go with the dancing rhythms and transparent part-writing. In the 1440s and 1450s the songs have much more melismatic writing, reflected too in the emphasis on elegance and flow.

A last feature of the songs of the 1450s is that we begin to see the regular use of the contratenor bassus. For the first half of the century the tenor and the contratenor were generally in the same range, the tenor making perfect counterpoint with the discantus and the contratenor contributing texture and rhythmic life. And that remains the case with several works from the 1450s, among them in this list *Ma bouche rit*, *D'ung aultre amer*, *Par le regart*, *Comme femme desconfortee*, and *Tout a par moy*. But in *Je ne vis oncques la pareille* (almost certainly from 1454), *L'omme banny*, *Quant ce viendra*, *O gloriosa*, and *Ave regina celorum* the contratenor is in a range well below the tenor. This is a slow transition: apart from *Quant ce viendra*, those pieces all include the old octave-leap cadence, for example. There is also the case of *J'ay pris amours*, which appears in some sources with a contratenor in the range of the tenor and in others with a contratenor bassus well below it. But in that respect this is perhaps among the most important decades in the entire recent history of music, the one when composers began cultivating a bass line as a fundament for musical thought, as it was to be for at least the next 450 years.

## Songs of the 1460s and 1470s

### *1460s (nine and more)*

De tous biens plaine HAYNE 30 (50, 4m)
Helas que pourra CARON 22 (3, 1m)
Le souvenir MORTON 16 (6, 1m)
N'aray je jamais MORTON 16 (3, 3m)
Fortune par ta cruaulté VINCENET 16 (2)
Cent mille escus CARON 15 (5)
La martinella MARTINI 13 (1, 3m)

Tart ara mon cueur MOLINET 12 (5, 1m)
Prenez sur moi OCKEGHEM 11
S'elle m'amera OCKEGHEM 10 (1m)
Vostre bruit DU FAY 9 (3)
Accueilly m'a la belle CARON 9 (1, 1m)

*1470s (ten and more)*

Allez regretz HAYNE 30 (6, 6m)
Je ne fay plus MUREAU 21 (3)
Nunca fue pena mayor WREEDE 19 (6, 2m)
Mon souvenir HAYNE 18 (2)
Amours amours trop HAYNE 17 (1)
Mes pensees COMPÈRE 15 (1, 1m)
Dictes moy toutes (A) COMPÈRE 10 (2m)
Le renvoy d'ung cuer COMPÈRE 10 (3, 1m)
Cela sans plus LANNOY 13 (7, 2m)
Le despourveu CARON 11 (1)
Malheur me bat MALCORT/MARTINI/OCKEGHEM 10 (2, 4m)

As we move to the 1460s it is worth stopping a moment on the stunning success of *De tous biens plaine* by Hayne van Ghizeghem, who was almost certainly a teenager when he composed it (he is described as a "jeusne filz" in a payment record of 1457). Not only does it survive in more sources than anything earlier, but it gave rise to an astonishing fifty-four later pieces, vastly more than any other musical work of the fifteenth century. It is a very puzzling piece indeed to have had such success. There are, to begin with, two contrapuntal blunders that are almost impossible to emend without complete re-writing.[7] Then there is the very odd circumstance that the text fits the tenor far more easily than the discantus, although not a single one of its thirty sources has its tenor texted (I have argued elsewhere that only the tenor should be texted; today I am not so sure, but will return to the topic below). Beyond that, it is one of the least obviously interesting songs of the century: the discantus line has no magical moment; the tenor, used for the majority of the later settings, is relatively staid; the text is one of the blandest possible poems of praise for a lady. Perhaps, once again, it was the very restraint of the musical expression that appealed to the refined tastes of the time rather more than it does today.

---

7 In measures 51 and 55 of the edition by Barton Hudson, Hayne van Ghizeghem, *Opera omnia*. The commentary reports no variants in either bar, though a few sources have a strikingly inelegant variant plainly devised to avoid the dissonance in measure 51.

The next interesting detail of the 1460s lies in two pieces that probably never had texts, *La martinella* and *Helas que pourra devenir*. The latter does actually appear in some sources with text (in fact two different texts in different forms: one a rondeau *quatrain*, the other a rondeau *cinquain*); but its intricate cross-rhythms make it unsuitable for singing to text, and more importantly it lacks any clear formal articulations. In almost all songs from the fifteenth century it is possible to predict the form even if there is no text; just at this juncture the situation changes and there is a growing repertory of apparently textless pieces. That of course matches the rise in the same years of "songbooks" without text, evidently intended for instrumental performance. One of the interesting details of these pieces is that they look on the surface just like normal rondeau settings, very often copied with a corona for the mid-point repetitions that the rondeau form needs. Only close analytical examination shows that there are no real line-divisions and that these pieces represent a new genre in the history of written polyphony. There are of course earlier pieces that were probably conceived for instrumental ensemble, but it is only in the 1460s that we see the emergence of a coherent genre that begins to grow across the years.

Other details of the 1460s may also surprise. One is the presence near the top of the list of two songs by yet another English composer, Robert Morton. These are truly glorious pieces, almost as compact as any song from the fifteenth century. In this case they probably did originate with the French texts that they now carry, not only because Morton was employed at the court of Burgundy (1457–77) but also because French remained a current language in fifteenth-century England. Even so, it is odd that his known output is of only eight pieces (four more are ascribed to him in a single manuscript, but all four give very good reason for thinking that they are not by him). Two other marginal figures appear to do well: Vincenet (recently revealed to be Vincent Bruecquet), a composer with a relatively small output, and Molinet, from whom no other music is known (whether this is the poet and chronicler Jean Molinet nobody knows, but the piece is remarkably skilled).

The 1470s are notable for the emergence of one of the loveliest song-writers of the century, Loyset Compère, the man who has perhaps benefited most in reputation from the recent redating of Josquin's birth: Compère was earlier thought a lesser contemporary of Josquin, whereas it now looks very much as though he pioneered many of the techniques – both musical and expressive – that drive Josquin's earlier works. It is hard to guess quite how far back his career reaches, though there is a good case for thinking that he was already a mature and polished composer at the time he wrote his motet *Omnium bonorum plena* (incidentally one of the earliest works based on Hayne's *De tous biens plaine*) in the early 1470s. So he may not have risen to sudden prominence like Hayne, but he injected a new elegiac tone into the last years of the *forme fixe* generation.

The most successful new songs of the 1470s begin to show the kind of expansion that led to the breakdown of the *formes fixes* (just as they would probably have broken down in the early years of the century but for the intervention of Binchois and Du Fay). Hayne's *Allez regretz* (fifty-three breves long before the last note) and *Amours amours* (sixty-four breves); Compère's *Mes pensees* (eighty-four breves), Firmin Caron's *Le despourveu* (fifty-eight breves). Marvelous though they are, in a full performance they risk collapsing under the strain of their length.

Also notable in the 1470s is the arrival of a song with Spanish text, *Nunca fue pena mayor* by Johannes Wreede of Bruges, who went to Spain and was known there under the name Juan Urreda. Only three songs by him are known today, but all three must count as the life-favourites for those who know them. Perhaps if we had more songbooks from fifteenth-century Spain (the only one is from Seville in the south, far from the areas where Urreda worked) there would be more songs from this wonderful composer. But this is the moment to recognize that almost all the songs on the lists have French texts, excepting only the works of John Bedyngham. We have had three in Latin, one in Flemish, one in German (the last two getting on to the lists by a hair). In the next decade we are to see an Italian text and two in Latin. But by and large the bulk of the successful repertory is French: among the 2,000 or so songs from 1415 to 1480, there are more than 1,300 with French text as against just over 400 with German or Flemish, 200 with Italian, sixty with Spanish, and fifty with English.

## Ca. 1480 (twelve and more)

Fortuna desperata FELICE/BUSNOYS 30 (33, 6m)
Si dedero AGRICOLA 28 (4, 3m)
Adieu mes amours JOSQUIN 25 (2, 4m)
Dulcis amica PRIORIS 22 (4, 1m)
Que vous madame JOSQUIN 17 (1)
Je n'ay dueil AGRICOLA 15 (2m)
Des biens d'amours MARTINI 12 (0)
Amours fait moult JAPART 12 (0)

The list of songs from around 1480 is rather more approximate than the others, partly because the dating of manuscripts in this decade is more disputed, but it is added to show the direction in which matters were progressing. First, and most significantly, is the arrival on the scene of Josquin des Prez with two songs that immediately made a massive impact, *Adieu mes amours* and *Que vous madame*. Second is the arrival of Alexander Agricola (described in 1475 as "honestus juvenis"), with his ubiquitous *Si dedero*. Third is the appearance of two highly successful songs almost certainly by composers of no other known music, namely Malcort's *Malheur me bat* and Felice's *Fortuna desperata*: both were used for masses by both Obrecht and Josquin, and both had substantial careers otherwise.

One remarkable detail of the entire repertory in those lists is that there are only three songs in four voices. While church and cathedral music had been routinely in four voices from about 1440, three-voice texture was to remain standard in the song repertory until some time around 1490 or perhaps even later. Quite a lot of the songs in these lists had a fourth voice added to them at some point in their history, but the only ones here that are genuinely in four voices are the three that belong to the genre known (uncomfortably but really unavoidably) as the "combinative chanson," with a *forme fixe* in the upper voice and different text material in the lower voices – namely Johannes Ockeghem's *S'elle m'amera*, Johannes Japart's *Amours fait moult*, and Josquin's *Adieu mes amours*. Certainly there were songs genuinely in four voices long before that, including some of what many consider the finest songs by Du Fay, Binchois, and Ockeghem. But these appear to have made less impact than the standard repertory in three voices.

Even so, the situation of those three combinative songs draws attention to one final important detail in the song repertory and its presentation. Anyone turning through the pages of the formal French songbooks, particularly the so-called "Central Chansonniers," will notice an absolutely standard pattern: that text is underlaid to only the discantus voice except when there is a combinative chanson, when quite suddenly all voices are texted because all have different texts. Among the thirty-three songs in the famous Copenhagen Chansonnier there is just one combinative chanson written in this way, for example; and among the sixty-six songs of the Nivelle de la Chaussée Chansonnier the lower voices are texted only for the three combinative chansons: Ockeghem's *S'elle m'amera*, Antoine Busnoys's *Vous marchez du bout du pié*, and Delahaye's *Tout au long de la grand couchette*. Many of the Italian songbooks from the first half of the century are less systematic in this respect, with bits of text underlaid to all three voices, as is the famous Cordiforme chansonnier of Jean de Montchenu, probably copied in Geneva in about 1475 – in which for the last twenty-one of its forty-three songs the scribe plainly attempted to underlay a full stanza of text to every voice (the manuscript contains no combinative chansons).

The second detail to strike the eye is that these formal French songbooks underlay only the first stanza of text to the discantus line. For later stanzas one must look to the bottom of the page; but that is in itself a lot harder than, say, singing the later stanzas of a modern hymn, because the music is elaborate and often florid. This is not music for sight-singing; nor is it music for amateurs to sing.

The third detail is that in the middle years of the century text underlay to the discantus line is invariably approximate and sometimes wildly inappropriate. Sensible texting requires the performer to know the music by heart and to have a clear analytic grasp of its design. Even for the first stanza that happens to be underlaid to the discantus, it would in most cases be easier to sing the text intelligently to the untexted tenor or contratenor.

This is to say that in these "choirbook-layout" songbooks the writing of text only under the discantus is by no means a statement that only the discantus should be texted: it is just a consequence of economy and elegance. Once partbooks are used for songs, all voices are equally underlaid (the odd exception here is in Petrucci's partbooks of mass music; but that's another story entirely and raises an entirely different set of questions).

That, in very brief outline,[8] is why most twenty-first-century editions of this music have all voices fully texted with three stanzas even though the source has only a single stanza under the discantus: this is the case for Jane Alden's edition of Delahaye; it is the case for Peter Woetmann Christoffersen's online editions of the four "central" chansonniers;[9] and it is the case for many pieces in my Musica Britannica edition of *Secular Polyphony 1380–1480*. Nobody is saying that all voices were always sung and always texted; but nobody is any more saying that because the text is underlaid only to the discantus only the discantus should be sung.

## Bibliography

Alden, Jane, ed., *Jean Delahaye: Chansons in Loire Valley Sources*, Paris, 2001

Bent, Margaret, *Dunstaple*, London, 1981

Bukofzer, Manfred F., *Studies in Medieval and Renaissance Music*, New York, 1950

*The Copenhagen Chansonnier and the "Loire Valley" Chansonniers: An Open Access Project*, http://chansonniers.pwch.dk

Erhard, Alexander, *Bedynghams O rosa bella und seine Cantus-Firmus Bearbeitungen in Cantilena-Form*, Tübinger Beiträge zur Musikwissenschaft 31, Tutzing, 2010

Fallows, David, *A Catalogue of Polyphonic Songs, 1415–1480*, Oxford, 1999

8  The fuller case is in Fallows, "Texting in the Chansonnier of Jean de Montchenu."
9  http://chansonniers.pwch.dk/index.html.

"Dunstable, Bedyngham and *O rosa bella*," *JM* 12 (1994), 287–305

"John Bedyngham and the Case of the Disappearing Composer," in *I codici musicali trentini del Quattrocento: Nuove scoperte, nuove edizioni e nuovi strumenti informatici. Atti del convegno internazionale di studi. Trento, Castello del Buonconsiglio 28–29 novembre 2009*, ed. Danilo Curti-Feininger and Marco Gozzi, Trento, 2013, 82–88

"Texting in the Chansonnier of Jean de Montchenu," in Fallows, *Songs and Musicians of the Fifteenth Century*, Aldershot, 1996, no. X

ed., *Secular Polyphony 1380–1480*, Musica Britannica 97, London, 2014

Hayne van Ghizeghem, *Opera omnia*, ed. Barton Hudson, CMM 74, n.p., 1977

Kenney, Sylvia W., "Contrafacta in the Works of Walter Frye," *JAMS* 8 (1955), 182–202

*Walter Frye and the Contenance angloise*, New Haven, 1964

Reese, Gustave, *Music in the Renaissance*, New York, 1954

Strohm, Reinhard, *The Rise of European Music 1380–1500*, Cambridge, 1993

# 42

# The nineteenth-century reception
# of fifteenth-century sacred music

ANDREW KIRKMAN

Though nascent in the eighteenth century, the rediscovery of fifteenth-century sacred music is really the achievement of the nineteenth.[1] Enlightenment conviction in the eternal value of the works of men was a powerful force in late eighteenth-century efforts to uncover the vestiges of early musics; yet the idea of a viable aesthetic appreciation of fifteenth-century compositions emerged only later, in the work of the towering music historian of the mid- to late nineteenth century, August Wilhelm Ambros. For Ambros, writing in 1864, the crucial awakening of Western musical art was the achievement of the generation of Du Fay:

> In the works of this School a fully developed art finally steps forth. It is no contradiction if in its details elementary and undeveloped [elements] can frequently be shown, and if this art described as completely developed appears only as the beginning of an almost two-hundred-year-long development. It is completely developed in the sense that its composers are no longer seeking – testing and experimenting – the rules of art, but, in fully conscious possession of art's rules, are capable of creating the art work corresponding to them. Here for the first time step forward musicians who are not scholastics, not acousticians, not mathematicians, not archeologists, but true artists. Thus they furnished also works that assume the rank of art works valid for all times. There is in these works – in still budding and undeveloped forms – something that evokes the rosy cheeks and blue eyes of blooming young girls.[2]

It is worth unpacking this passage to focus not just on the proclivities of Ambros's age, but also on its roots and the directions in which it was pointing. Engrained in the quotation at the deepest level is a conviction that art is subject to progress: while the works of Guillaume Du Fay's generation are susceptible to real aesthetic appreciation, they are nonetheless still a long way from full

---

1 For more detailed treatment of the topic presented here see Kirkman, "'Under Such Heavy Chains'" and "The Invention of the Cyclic Mass," from which the present essay derives.
2 Ambros, *Geschichte*, 2:453–54.

artistic fruition. Implicit here also is the notion that earlier composers were fumbling in the darkness – grappling with nitpicky rules and arid conventions – for (implicitly) eternal rules of art that Du Fay and his colleagues were newly "discovering."

However queasy such formulations may leave us today, this, in terms of sheer approbation, was a significant shift from what had come before. In a footnote to the above passage Ambros compares his position with that of Raphael Georg Kiesewetter, whose *Geschichte* of twenty years earlier represented the previous state of appreciation of this "First Netherlandish School." Kiesewetter's rather grudging statement that this music can "still today be heard without giving offense, and indeed even with pleasure," cited by Ambros as corroboration of his own assessment, nonetheless constitutes, for him, "a rather cool praise."[3]

The notion that Du Fay was representative of a "School" is expressive of another fundamental tenet of nineteenth-century music-historical formulations: the conviction that progress was effected in a series of stages, each headed by a representative genius. This model, baldly articulated in the 1852 *Geschichte der Musik* of Franz Brendel, was encapsulated most particularly in the principle, originating in Hegel and all-pervasive in mid-nineteenth-century German historical writing, of dialectics. For Hegel the dialectical principle bounded the passage of history in an all-encompassing progressive unfolding of a universal *Geist*. Thus history was in a perpetually recurring state of flux as the synthesis of each successive stage evolved, through conflict between the essence of the present on the one hand and a striving after innovation on the other, into a new thesis and antithesis to be resolved in a future stage.

For historians of culture the dialectical process revealed itself in more specific refractions in each of their respective fields. A recurring trope is the notion of a series of representative geniuses, at the same time optimal embodiments of the stage reached in their own time and harbingers of the next.[4] This, the substance of a formula that, in ever more embedded forms, persisted from that time on, will be the fundamental focus as I attempt to explain why the music of the fifteenth century achieved, in the nineteenth, the elevated status that it did.

Systematized by Hegel, the model of progress by incremental stages was inherent already in the Enlightenment project. For Enlightenment theorists,

---

3 Kiesewetter's history is available, as *History of the Modern Music of Western Europe*, in an English translation by Robert Müller. The cited judgment from Ambros appears in his *Geschichte*, 2:120.
4 Thus, in Eduard Krüger's words, the true artist had to be "mirror of his time, which he nonetheless at the same time animated and outshone." "Betrachtungen über Kritik und Philosophie der Kunst," *Neue Zeitschrift für Musik* 14 (1841), 148; quoted in Kümmel, *Geschichte und Musikgeschichte*, 205.

rediscovery of the past was shaped by a very particular view of humanity, one according to which people – of whatever cultural background – are essentially motivated by the same forces: those of self-discovery and self-fulfillment. Valued as the highest goal of the Enlightenment, revelation of the universality of humanity – or at least of the idealized humanity of late eighteenth-century Europe – thus became the guiding principle behind the newly rekindled interest in the past. Reinvented even as it was rediscovered in the image of the present, the past thus became a series of historical stages progressing via increments to the high point most recently attained, a stage that, in its turn, would also be superseded as the forward march of unending progress extended on into the future.[5] For an age in which one of the chief symbols of humanity had come to be the ability to produce works of art of intrinsic value whose principal *raison d'être* was as objects for the contemplation of beauty, that same ability was sought in the past as writers looked for ways to give their own particular world-view the stamp of historical legitimacy; and since that beauty was only conceivable as the unique creation of the individual genius,[6] the recognition of beautiful works from past cultures was inseparable – however those cultures had themselves perceived the status of the author – from the recognition of their authors.[7]

Propulsive in its forward drive, then, the notion of incremental progress was likewise dynamic in reverse. As increasingly early vestiges of Western musical history were rediscovered, so the phases already known acquired ever more elevated status as advances on those being unearthed. Thus the landmarks of the past became functions of those of the present, as the rediscovery of increasingly early vestiges of the Western tradition gave the self-image of the post-Enlightenment West ever greater historical depth. A consequence of this is that the earliest known generation (for Kiesewetter that of Du Fay) was characterized as relatively primitive when compared with the advances of its successor. As increasing knowledge pushed this conceptual frame further and further back into history, the status of Du Fay – followed in due course by that of the music of the Squarcialupi Codex and so on – rose as ever earlier repertories correspondingly assumed the role of *Vorstufe* (precursor). The

---

5  A process neatly summed up by Elisabeth Hegar in *Die Anfänge der neueren Musikgeschichtsschreibung*, 27. For Hegar's discussion of this principle as embodied in the late eighteenth-century historical perspective of Charles Burney, see 36–37.

6  The ultimate source for the notion of genius in the modern aesthetic sense was Shaftesbury (*Characteristics of Men, Manners, Opinions and Times*, 1711), a seminal influence, both directly and via such authors as Addison, D. Young, and Gerard, on Burney and Sir John Hawkins. See Hegar, *Die Anfänge*, 25–26.

7  Thus, for example, the limited invention perceived by Burney in chant was, for him, inseparably entwined with its anonymity. See Burney, *A General History of Music*, 423; discussed in Hegar, *Die Anfänge*, 43.

same development also had repercussions for later generations: while, for Kiesewetter, Johannes Ockeghem, with Du Fay following in his wake, was well on the way to assimilation into the canon, Josquin's status had by this stage risen to the point at which he "deserves to be classed, beyond doubt, among the greatest musical geniuses of any period."[8]

The operation of this process can be seen clearly in the writing of Ambros: offering the direct example of Kiesewetter quoting Charles Burney, he provides a clear instance of its progression during the eighty or so years leading up to his own *Geschichte*. For Burney, Palestrina's music reveals everywhere "the fire of genius ... in spite of the cramping limitations of cantus firmus, of canon, of fugue, of inversions which would be enough to freeze others or turn them to stone."[9] For Ambros, on the other hand, writing in a time by which the prevailing idioms of Palestrina's time had become much more familiar, "this remark would apply incomparably better to Josquin. With him – far more strongly than with Palestrina – one perceives beneath the limiting constraints of the contrapuntal style the powerfully driving fire of genius."[10]

A concomitant of the Hegelian notion of the forward incremental progress of history was that individual styles, composers, and art-works became – in common with all other manifestations of society – expressions of the prevailing Spirit of the Age. But the systematizing impact of the dialectical process extended a good deal further than this: relentless in its linkage of general and particular, the unity underlying the various expressions of the prevailing historical *Geist* was seen, particularly at the hands of such dedicated Hegelians as Franz Brendel, to reveal itself at the microcosmic level in the organic unity of its individual instances.[11] While the progression of history was a manifestation of dialectic played out in time, art-works revealed its workings on a logical plane. From a Hegelian perspective, then, a beautiful work of art must not only be expressive of the spirit of its time; it must also be organically unified.[12] This model received a powerful boost from the particular profile of

---

8 Kiesewetter, *Geschichte*, 140–41. For more on this process as exemplified by Ambros see Kirkman, "The Invention of the Cyclic Mass."

9 Ambros, *Geschichte*, 3:207–8.

10 Ibid., 208.

11 Observing the linkage between *particular* art-work and *general* universal system, Robert Wicks notes that "The principle of organic unity ... clearly exemplifies how a beautiful artwork renders perceivable Hegel's metaphysical vision of the total systematicity of the universe: the organic unity of the artwork visually represents the metaphysical interconnectedness of all things, perceptual and non-perceptual. The beautiful artwork is a microcosm and perceptually reveals one aspect of 'the divine' through its perceivable exemplification of organic structure. The most-beautiful artworks offer us a vision of what is perfect, what is 'divine,' by means of their perfected, idealized, systematically unified appearance" ("Hegel's Aesthetics," 368).

12 To quote Wicks again: "The principle of *organic unity* ... determines beauty as a mode of perfection. According to this well-known principle, the beauty of an artwork or natural object corresponds to its

the fifteenth-century repertory then known: by far its greatest concentration was in the genre of the cyclic mass, a genre that came to be characterized as the forum for compositional unity over an unprecedently large canvas.[13]

For Ambros, the repertory where true art first revealed itself comprised none other than Du Fay's late masses:

> works of refined and noble style, in which inner warmth of feeling and Du Fay's pure sense of beauty are expressed in the most attractive manner. The first Kyrie of the Mass *Se la face* already has something of the "seraphic" character which – albeit with far richer and much higher development of musical construction – Palestrina's compositions display. One could best describe particular moments, such as the end of the first Kyrie of the mass *L'homme armé*, as being [like] a smile through tears.[14]

The quality of Du Fay's masses, then, rests to a large degree on their perceived warmth and their ability, from his perspective, to portray emotion.[15]

Of much more lasting importance, though, is Ambros's judgment that these works are the first to possess not only true style but also Form, in the sense of Hegelian organic construction.[16] While he does not elaborate on this statement, his more specific observation on Guillaume Faugues's *Missa L'homme armé* gives at least a hint of the directions such ideas would take in the future. The transposition of the cantus firmus in the Kyrie of this work, he says, is "an indication that the master strove for musical architecture, and was already thinking further than just how to clothe a cantus firmus well or badly with counterpointing voices."[17]

Taking issue with Glareanus's condemnation of any chant-based composition that is more than the "decorative adjunct" ("schmückende Beigabe") of a chant melody, preserving the chant in its original sequence and integrity,

---

degree of organization or integration. In the ideal case, no elements of an artwork or natural object appear arbitrary, unplanned, accidental, or irrational. The best artworks have no 'dead spots.' Beauty thus becomes identified with systematicity, or an intense 'unity in diversity' in the field of appearance" (ibid., 367–68).

13 This was due fundamentally to the influence of Giuseppe Baini's *Memorie storico-critiche della vita e delle opere di Giovanni Pierluigi da Palestrina*. In discussing Palestrina's forebears Baini, a member of the papal chapel from the age of twenty and later its director and administrator of the college of papal singers, had privileged access to the large mass repertories of the San Pietro and Cappella Sistina manuscripts, at least the latter of which were entirely hidden from outside view at this time.

14 Ambros, *Geschichte*, 2:496–97. For Ambros's conception of Palestrina, rooted in nineteenth-century Catholic Palestrinianism and the composer's perceived association with the sublime, see Garratt, *Palestrina and the German Romantic Imagination*, 216–17. For Friedrich Ludwig's similar characterization of Palestrina as the culmination of an evolution beginning in earlier medieval music see Berger, *Medieval Music and the Art of Memory*, 21–22.

15 Ambros, *Geschichte*, 2:498.

16 Ibid., 496. It is worth noting in this context that for Kiesewetter, writing thirty years earlier, manifest design was only observable in compositions as far back as Ockeghem. Before that composers contented themselves with "mere premeditated submissions to the contrapunctic operation." (Kiesewetter, *Geschichte*, 128; for more on this see Kirkman, "'Under Such Heavy Chains'.")

17 Ambros, *Geschichte*, 2:500.

Ambros observes with approval that the true situation is quite different. Far from being constrained by veneration for ancient holy chants, composers

> rather manipulated [Gregorian chant] motifs with the most spirited freedom, and it is not difficult to recognize that their own contrapuntal inventions had an altogether different and higher meaning than that of an incidental, "into the bargain" decoration of the tenor, dispensable even in the best of cases ... The more richly and interestingly they formed their counterpoint, the more emphatically it emerges in its independent meaning.[18]

To Ambros, then, the chant was no more than the handmaiden of the polyphonic construct formed around it. No longer just the foundation for the sort of mechanical gloss that he perceived in the music of the earlier discantors (*Discantoren*), for the Netherlandish composers it served both to liberate the contrapuntal imagination and guarantee its consistency. Indeed, the source of the preexisting melody, or even whether it was sacred or secular, was to that extent immaterial: what mattered was that it could endow (in the eyes of a German author writing in the middle of the nineteenth century) the finished product with the desired attributes of organic perfection and inner unity:

> The most serious and cerebral work of this most especially important epoch for the development of music is founded on this premise: to develop, on the given foundations of Gregorian chant and folksong, polyphony arising out of the most varied conditions, in [the form of] art works encased in organic perfection and inner unity.[19]

Thus the unified art-work is one in which contrasting subject matter has been resolved in an ultimate unifying synthesis. Continuing on the same Hegelian track, Ambros turns to the notion of dialectic to explain the process whereby, in his view, the adaptation of a monophonic melody to a polyphonic context can lend coherence to the finished piece:

> The simple melody – as it breaks forth in monophonic song out of the innermost depth of the aroused spirit – now changes, in and through polyphony, to a new meaning, and here it places against itself now a second, now a third melody in counterpoint, so that out of the harmonic sounding together of these counterpoints a higher unity arises: thus may polyphony quite rightly be called a dialectical process.

If such perceived characteristics were to receive such high approbation in music generally, how much more impressive would their workings be seen in drawing together the parts of a five-movement multi-piece? Thus it is easy to

18 Ibid., 3:15.    19 Ibid., 9.

perceive how the advent of complete mass settings, with their perceived large-scale displays of coherence, organicism, and unity – attributes of such fundamental value in the post-Hegelian intellectual world to which Ambros belonged – came to be seen as a watershed of crucial importance to the advancement of Western music.

Driving forward the dialectical principle to the microcosmic level, Ambros focuses on imitation, the stylistic aspect of music beginning in the late fifteenth century that is probably most easily susceptible to a dialectical interpretation:

> Imitation builds the innermost core of polyphony. It emphasizes with clarity the inner cohesion of the tonal fabric; the voices, while answering one another, proceed under each other in direct interchange; at length the melody performs the dialectical process on itself and within itself, as its own elements become subject and counter-subject; what is otherwise temporally divided in it is allowed to sound together simultaneously, and brings to consciousness the multifaceted connections of its individual elements in a new, higher meaning.[20]

But the fact that the state of recovery of early repertories had arrived, by the time of Ambros, at the generation of Du Fay was propitious for still another reason. Just as for Hegel the fifteenth century had been "the dawn, the harbinger of a new fine day after the long, fateful, and terrible night of the Middle Ages,"[21] so for Ambros "The fifteenth century, at [one and] the same time the end of the Middle Ages and beginning of the new era, marks out intellectually a particularly exciting moment in history, and precisely in this century there also occurs a most noteworthy development in music."[22]

While Ambros never explicitly equated this new era with a musical Renaissance, he was certainly construed to have done so by later historians.[23] With the crystallization, in later historical writing, of the notion of a musical Renaissance beginning in the fifteenth century, the most characteristic expression of that era came to be seen to be the cyclic mass, and, in particular, the mass based on a cantus firmus. At least as far back as Brendel's *Geschichte* of 1852, the basis of the cyclic mass on a preexistent composition chosen apparently by the composer, rather than out of considerations of liturgical appropriateness, was seen as early evidence of the emancipation of the artist from the constraints of his working environment:

---

20 Ibid., 9–10.
21 Hegel, *Vorlesungen über die Philosophie der Geschichte*, 518. See Gombrich, "In Search of Cultural History," in *Ideals and Idols*, 33.
22 Ambros, *Geschichte*, 3:4.
23 For a detailed explanation of how this situation came to pass, see Kirkman, "The Invention of the Cyclic Mass," 31–36.

evidence, in other words, of what came to be seen as the Renaissance sensibility. That position was cemented by the fact that, as the earliest large-scale multipartite form in Western musical history, it was seen as the creative forum for the most sophisticated and ambitious structures and hence the greatest works of art of its era.

Such a characterization of fifteenth-century music, and of the cyclic mass in particular, is unlikely to come as much of a surprise to readers of this essay: it has become familiar via later refractions through the giants of twentieth-century scholarship on music of the era including Heinrich Besseler, Friedrich Blume, and especially Manfred Bukofzer. Though questioned increasingly in more recent years, it succeeded in creating a heuristically propitious model through which to comprehend and – most importantly – to appreciate the music anew for modern audiences. If we today are able to formulate new models of appreciation for our own era, it is nonetheless the case that we owe such a possibility to the work of our nineteenth-century forebears, and especially to August Wilhelm Ambros.

# Bibliography

Ambros, August Wilhelm, *Geschichte der Musik*, 2, Leipzig, 1864; 3rd edn., rev. Heinrich Riemann, 1891
  *Geschichte der Musik*, 3, Leipzig, 1868; 3rd edn., rev. Otto Kade, 1893
Baini, Giuseppe, *Memorie storico-critiche della vita e delle opere di Giovanni Pierluigi da Palestrina*, 2 vols., Rome, 1828; repr. Hildesheim, 1966
Berger, Anna Maria Busse, *Medieval Music and the Art of Memory*, Berkeley, 2005
Brendel, Franz, *Geschichte der Musik in Italien, Deutschland und Frankreich: Von den ersten christlichen Zeiten bis auf die Gegenwart*, Leipzig, 1852
Burney, Charles, *A General History of Music, from the Earliest Ages to the Present Period*, 2nd edn., London, 1789; repr. London, 1935
Garratt, James, *Palestrina and the German Romantic Imagination: Interpreting Historicism in Nineteenth-Century Music*, Cambridge, 2002
Gombrich, Ernst, *Ideals and Idols: Essays on Values in History and in Art*, Oxford, 1979; originally published 1969
Hegar, Elisabeth, *Die Anfänge der neueren Musikgeschichtsschreibung um 1770 bei Gerbert, Burney und Hawkins*, Strasbourg, [1932]; repr. Baden-Baden, 1974
Hegel, Georg Wilhelm Friedrich, *Vorlesungen über die Philosophie der Geschichte*, Sämtliche Werke 11, ed. Hermann Glockner, Stuttgart, 1928
Kiesewetter, Raphael Georg, *Geschichte der europäisch-abendländischen oder unserer heutigen Musik*, Leipzig, 1834; English translation by Robert Müller as *History of the Modern Music of Western Europe, from the First Century of the Christian Era to the Present Day*, London, 1848
Kirkman, Andrew, "The Invention of the Cyclic Mass," *JAMS* 54 (2001), 1–47

"'Under Such Heavy Chains': The Discovery and Evaluation of Late Medieval Music before Ambros," *19th-Century Music* 24 (2000), 89–112

Kümmel, Werner Friedrich, *Geschichte und Musikgeschichte: Die Musik der Neuzeit in Geschichtsschreibung und Geschichtsauffassung des deutschen Kulturbereichs*, Kassel, 1967

Wicks, Robert, "Hegel's Aesthetics: An Overview," in *The Cambridge Companion to Hegel*, ed. Frederick C. Beiser, Cambridge, 1993, 348–77

# 43

# The modern reception of the music of
# Jean d'Ockeghem

LAWRENCE F. BERNSTEIN

Jean d'Ockeghem's preeminence among the composers of his generation seems unassailable. Thirty years of service as chapel master to three successive kings of France and the adulation of Johannes Tinctoris, who ranks him in the dedication of his treatise on the modes among "the most famous and most celebrated teachers of the art of music," clearly place Ockeghem at the summit of any hierarchy of fifteenth-century composers. Even more telling are the words of his most serious challenger, Antoine Busnoys. Is there praise at a higher level than that of Busnoys's *In hydraulis*, which identifies Ockeghem in its *prima pars* as a supreme master of Pythagorean proportion and, in the *secunda pars*, as a melodist who reflects the "true image of Orpheus"? Busnoys presents his colleague, that is to say, as the *complete* composer.[1]

We would not expect this reputation to continue forever. The system by way of which Renaissance composers achieved fame was notoriously ephemeral, its spotlight shifting quickly from a current star to a newer one.[2] Even so, Ockeghem fared well, at least at first. Nicole Le Vestu's famous *chant royal* in praise of Ockeghem was composed in 1523, nearly a quarter-century after the composer's death.[3] And in 1567, Cosimo Bartoli likened Ockeghem to Donatello for having revived a music that was moribund, in much the way that Donatello was thought to have breathed new life into sculpture.

But Ockeghem could ride the crest of renown for only so long. And when he did fall from favor, his decline reflected a reception history that is surely unique among major composers for its precipitous reversal and the potency of the invective that was sometimes hurled his way. Thus, the composer who was lionized in the ways just described was later to be excoriated by Charles Burney for having composed music in which "learning and labour seem to have preceded taste and invention, [a music designed for] the eye of the performer, who was to solve canonical mysteries, and discover latent beauties of ingenuity

1 The text of *In hydraulis* is thought to be by Busnoys. See Busnoys, *Collected Works*, ed. Taruskin, 3:74–80.
2 Owens, "Music Historiography."   3 Plamenac, "Autour d'Ockeghem."

and contrivance, about which the hearers were indifferent."[4] And Ockeghem's famous triple canon, *Prenez sur moy*, was similarly vilified by Johann Forkel as "rigid and unsingable" for what he perceived to be the superficiality of its contrapuntal complexity.[5]

Even the later critics who championed Ockeghem's music often did so in ways that raise questions about the forces that influenced their specific appreciations of this composer. How could August Wilhelm Ambros, for example, characterize the very chanson that Forkel deemed unsingable as a work into which the composer breathed a "singing soul"?[6] And what motivated Heinrich Besseler and his followers, in the late 1920s, to perceive Ockeghem's polyphony as irrational music, designed to capture and reflect the feelings of pietistic devotion?[7]

As one surveys the trajectory of Ockeghem criticism just sampled, a central conundrum comes to the surface. In no way could this wide range of characterizations have resulted from a simple, objective assessment of the same music. Powerful variables must have contributed to accounts of Ockeghem's music so variegated and so contradictory. The pursuit of greater objectivity in representing our composer, therefore, demands a more refined understanding of the reception history surrounding his music.

Two decisive inflections were introduced into the Ockeghem reception around the middle of the sixteenth century. Both brought about significant change, but in very different ways. One reflects a very practical strain within the Ockeghem reception, affecting which music is available and how it is read; the other is a more subtle change within the forces that have an impact on how the music is appreciated.

The practical mutation occurred in 1563 with the publication of Ambrosius Wilphlingseder's *Erotemata musices practicae*, a treatise on mensural music mainly from the late fifteenth century that includes *Prenez sur moy*. Its presence in a treatise is, in and of itself, important, denoting a shift in the transmission of Ockeghem's music from practical to theoretical sources that had already begun as early as 1537.[8] Inevitably, this change highlights technical artifice simply because theorists are ever in pursuit of musical examples to illustrate theoretical complexities of one sort or another.[9] This contributed to the emerging view of Ockeghem as a composer preoccupied with technique. Beyond that, Wilphlingseder's treatment of *Prenez sur moy* distorted the chanson badly. He

4 Burney, *A General History of Music*, 1:731.    5 Forkel, *Allgemeine Geschichte der Musik*, 2:533.
6 Ambros, *Geschichte der Musik*, 3:173.    7 See nn. 30 and 31 below.
8 Other treatises that offered music by Ockeghem include Sebald Heyden (1537; the likely source for Wilphlingseder); Glareanus (1547); Gregor Faber (1553); Johann Zanger (1554); and Hermann Finck (1556).
9 Kirkman, "'Under Such Heavy Chains'," 96.

offered Ockeghem's puzzle canon *in resolutio* but mistakenly transcribed it in binary mensuration and botched the canon by arranging the imitative entries in descending fifths, where the canon reads "Fuga a trium vocum in Epidiatessaron," which calls for imitation at the upper fourth. The result is a contrapuntal travesty – one that could not have arisen in an environment in which Ockeghem's contrapuntal style was still understood.

The second of these two important shifts in the Ockeghem reception came in 1550 with the publication in Nuremberg of the *Compendium musices* by the Wittenberg music teacher, composer, and theorist Adrian Petit Coclico.[10] Early on in his treatise, Coclico introduces a quadripartite taxonomy of musicians, arranged in ascending order based on his criteria for musical quality. Pride of place belongs to the musicians of the fourth category, the *poetici*, unnamed but supreme masters of composing and extemporizing counterpoint, who honed their skill at the feet of the *musici*, an assemblage of composers of the Josquin and post-Josquin generation who populated the third category. The second category consists in the *mathematici*; they earn Coclico's scorn for defiling and obscuring the art of music by failing to honor the smoothness and sweetness of song and by cluttering their compositions with a sea of notational symbols. Among them are Guillaume Du Fay, Busnoys, Firmin Caron, and Johannes Tinctoris. In the first category we find a mixture of the biblical inventors of music and ancient and medieval writers: Tubal Cain, Orpheus, Guido d'Arezzo, and Boethius. To these, however, are added three composers: Alexander Agricola, Jacob Obrecht, and Ockeghem, about whom Coclico snarls, "These, however, were *only* theorists" (*hi autem tantum theorici fuerunt*).

Had the music of these composers disappeared from Coclico's orbit, we might regard his conclusion that they were theorists as a mistake, thereby ameliorating my sense of the hostility projected in this remark. However, not a year before the *Compendium musices* was published, the Nuremberg music printer and close friend of Coclico, Johannes Berg, published Erasmus Rotenbucher's *Diphona amoena et florida* (RISM 1549[16]), which contains music by all three of these masters.

Why did Coclico engage in this level of scurrility? Would it not have been sufficiently insulting to list Ockeghem among the *mathematici*? The level of invective reflects the intensity of Coclico's abhorrence of Ockeghem's predilection for such technical features as the proportional and notational systems that underlie a work like the *Missa Prolationum*. This repugnance must be seen against the backdrop of a battle then being waged across Germany, including in Wittenberg, where Coclico lived and worked. It was the raging conflict between the respective advocates of teaching music by way of its basis in

---

10 Coclico, *Compendium musices*. For an English translation, see Coclico, *Musical Compendium*, trans. Seay.

mathematics (*musica speculativa*) and the more practical route of studying counterpoint and singing (*musica practica*). No less influential a figure than Philipp Melanchthon, who taught at the University of Wittenberg, advocated transferring music from the quadrivium to the *humaniora*. Indeed, the thrust of Coclico's treatise is its staunch advocacy for *musica practica*.[11]

These two inflections in the Ockeghem reception shed light on the composer's reputation about a half-century after his death. More importantly, both remained viable sources of influence on the Ockeghem reception for a long time, rebounding over the centuries, as we shall see, to have a direct impact on the ways in which Enlightenment writers viewed our composer.

We have already quoted Burney's stinging indictment of the music of Ockeghem – made partly in reaction to *Prenez sur moy* – in his *General History of Music*. Of the three Enlightenment writers who treat Ockeghem's music in any detail – Sir John Hawkins and Johann Forkel are the other two – Burney's reaction is the easiest to understand. As Andrew Kirkman has demonstrated, the aesthetic outlook that emanated from the English rationalist-sensualist tradition – the milieu in which Burney and Hawkins worked – approached the writing of history from a progressive perspective. Current values like the privileging of beauty, nature, and order were perceived as a goal toward which the flow of history had been moving, and earlier attempts that fell short of this goal tended to be devalued.[12] To this equation must be added Burney's shameless anti-antiquarianism, which he sets out as a guiding force informing his historical outlook:

> If the second [volume, i.e., the one treating medieval and Renaissance music] confined the reader to antiquarian knowledge, and afforded him no information but of barbarous times and more barbarous Music; it is hoped that these final books will make him some amends, as they include all the simplicity and harmonical merit of the last century, and refinements of the present.[13]

A progressive view of history combined with a pungent antipathy toward early music were enough to predispose Burney to take a dim view of Ockeghem's music. His transcription of *Prenez sur moy* can only have reinforced this propensity, for it is seriously corrupt. It is, in fact, the Wilphlingseder travesty, but with the triple mensuration correctly restored.[14] It is easy to understand how

11 On the emergence of *musica practica* as a didactic alternative in the early sixteenth century, see Niemöller, "Zum Einfluss des Humanismus."
12 Kirkman, "'Under Such Heavy Chains'," 91–94.
13 Burney, *A General History of Music*, 2:1024.
14 In the second volume of his *General History*, which appeared some years after Hawkins's work, Burney seems to make an oblique reference to the Hawkins transcription (*General History of the Science and Practice of Music*, 1:338–39), which follows Wilphlingseder faithfully, by suggesting that "some have erroneously imagined it to be in common time."

Burney – working from a score that garbles the counterpoint as this one does and already inclined to disparage early music – would entertain serious doubts about the musicality of this chanson and its composer. In this way, blunders perpetrated in Nuremberg in 1563 came to roost in London two centuries later.

We might expect John Hawkins to approach Ockeghem's music as Burney did. Both of them were close to the English rationalist-sensualist tradition, which, as we have seen, favored a progressive view of history. But this was not Hawkins's approach to early music. On the contrary, the most extensive review of the Hawkins *History* by William Bewley lambasted the work for daring to suggest that some music of the sixteenth and seventeenth centuries compared favorably with the music of his own day.[15]

Actually, Hawkins struggled valiantly to understand early music in its own terms. As a writer steeped in the operatic traditions of his time, he could not help but be troubled by what he called the "narratory" character of the texts in Renaissance motets, "by which," he suggested, "no passion of the human mind can be either excited or allayed." And he criticized the music for its stylistic homogeneity, which, in his view, failed readily to distinguish compositions by different masters.[16] At first, such views seem consistent with the progressive approach of a writer like Burney. But Hawkins follows a very different histor-iographical approach when he suggests that it would be unfair to criticize the music of Ockeghem and Josquin for failing to reflect an ideal of contemporary opera that had not yet come into being – what he calls the pathetic "corre-spondence of sentiment between … music and the words to which it was adapted."[17] In advocating this approach, Hawkins adopts the posture of a relativist, which enables him to value such music as that of Ockeghem for its "fine modulation … close contexture and interchange of parts, different kinds of motion judiciously contrasted; artful syncopations, and binding concords with discords sweetly prepared and resolved."[18]

Thus, Hawkins mentions Ockeghem in the context of his relativist perspec-tive. He has nothing specific to say, however, about the one example he provides, *Prenez sur moy*, which, as mentioned, he took directly from Wilphlingseder. Apparently, Hawkins focused on Wilphlingseder's transcrip-tion in separate voices, taking note of the resolution alone. Otherwise, he

15 Bewley's review appeared in the *Monthly Review* 56 (February 1777), 137–44; 56 (April 1777), 270–78; and 57 (August 1777), 149–64. He traces his hostility to Hawkins to some remarks Sir John had published in 1760: "And, now I am upon this subject, I will tell the reader a secret; which is, That musick was, in its greatest perfection, in Europe, from about the middle of the sixteenth to the beginning of the seventeenth century." See Walton and Cotton, *The Complete Angler*, 287. For a detailed account of Bewley's review of the Hawkins history, see Lonsdale, *Dr. Charles Burney*, 209–19.
16 Hawkins, *General History*, 1:325.    17 Ibid.    18 Ibid.

would have noticed the theorist's specification that the canon was in epidia-tessaron, and known that this calls for canon at the upper fourth unambigu-ously. He must have been befuddled by this transcription, especially the abundance of structural fourths above the bass that resulted from Wilphlingseder's faulty resolution of the canon. One would be hard pressed to find in this transcription examples of the fine modulation and balance between consonance and dissonance that he esteems, more generally, in the music of the Ockeghem and Josquin generations. Nonetheless, we might expect that, in reacting to a less problematic example, he would surely have been ready to do so.

At first blush, Johann Forkel's treatment of Ockeghem appears to be a product of the same forces that gave rise to Burney's. Their conclusions and approaches seem very similar. Forkel's central example of Ockeghem's music is *Prenez sur moy*, which he dismisses as "rigid and unsingable" – one of the two most harshly deprecatory comments about Ockeghem in the literature. (Forkel is understandably so baffled by the notation of the *Missa Prolationum* as to remain beyond any meaningful appreciation of it.) A glance at the score he reproduces of the chanson shows that his transcription and Burney's offer essentially the same corruption of Ockeghem's counterpoint.[19] Moreover, the Göttingen school of cultural historians, of which Forkel was a member, adhered to the progressive view of history Burney favored, owing surely to the direct influence of the English rationalist-sensualist tradition. This was but one of many intellectual and cultural influences that arose from the free flow of ideas between Germany and England during the Enlightenment, beginning in 1714 when the first of five monarchs from the House of Hanover reigned over both Great Britain and the regions of Germany that included Göttingen.[20] A closer look, however, at Forkel's presentation of the musical text of *Prenez sur moy*, along with a more nuanced appreciation of the historiographical under-pinnings of his History, suggests that the forces that guided his appreciation of Ockeghem's music are more complex than what would result from a faulty transcription and a progressive view of history.

The score of *Prenez sur moy* Forkel prints is, indeed, virtually identical to Burney's, but Forkel realized its flaws, apparently too late in the production of the book to correct the music. In his text, however, he tells the reader exactly how the canon should be realized.[21] As to his historiographic methodology,

19 Forkel, *Allgemeine Geschichte der Musik*, 2:530–31.
20 Hegar, *Die Anfänge der neueren Musikgeschichtsschreibung*, 81–83; Kirkman, "'Under Such Heavy Chains'," 91–94.
21 Forkel, *Allgemeine Geschichte der Musik*, 2:533. This was first reported in Levitan, "Ockeghem's Clefless Compositions," 442.

Forkel certainly could assume a progressive stance in the course of evaluating the music of the past, as he did in criticizing the opening of *Sumer is icumen in* for its harmonic emptiness.[22] Indeed, Forkel outlines a markedly progressive outlook in the *Einleitung* to his History, in which he traces inexorable strides from the crudeness of the prehistory of music toward the achievement of its ultimate goal: modern harmony, with its unparalleled potential for the stimulation of sensation (*Empfindung*).

But this was not Forkel's only approach to history. Some thirteen years separated the publication of the first volume of the *Allgemeine Geschichte* in 1788 and the second in 1801. During that hiatus, Forkel rethought many aspects of his historiographical approach, absorbing, in the process, new ideas, including Johann Gottfried Herder's impassioned arguments for historical relativism.[23] Thus, in quoting an example of three-voice counterpoint from the *Practica musicae* of Gaffurius, Forkel strikes a relativist pose, suggesting that while "it is true that the example Gaffurius gives of this type is not excellent ... it shows what one held to be superbly beautiful in this time period .... "[24] He could even go the whole distance and find absolute value in Renaissance music, as he does in a three-voice *Parce Domine* by Obrecht, which he deems a work that can "be heard with pleasure even by modern ears when all three voices are sung with proper purity and equality."[25]

So, the Forkel who deprecated *Prenez sur moy* so harshly in 1801 is hardly mired in a progressive view of history, and, notwithstanding the corrupt score he published, he shows himself to have been the first modern writer addressing the piece who understood the canon. Yet he finds nothing to value in the music, going so far as to alert the reader to the weakness of the chanson, even after its canon has been properly resolved. Why? The answer to this question resides in a laudable aspect of Forkel's scholarship, albeit one that led him astray. Obviously aware of the dangers inherent in criticizing the music of the remote past, Forkel sought guidance in contemporaneous literature. His discussion of Renaissance music takes as its point of departure the taxonomy of composers offered by none other than Coclico. What is more, Forkel singles out Coclico as an exemplary theorist and underscores acceptingly the negative implications of his taxonomy – that is, its strongly derogatory posture with

---

22 Forkel, *Allgemeine Geschichte der Musik*, 2:501–2.
23 Herder's case for historical relativism may be read in *Kritische Wälder* (1769), *Vom Geist der ebräischen Poesie* (1782–83), *Ideen zur Philosophie der Geschichte der Menschheit* (1784), and *Kalligone* (1800) – copies of all of which Forkel owned.
24 Forkel, *Allgemeine Geschichte der Musik*, 2:513: "Die Probe, welche Gafor von dieser Art gibt, ist zwar nicht vortrefflich; ... sie aber zeigt, was man in dieser Zeitperiod für vorzüglich schön gehalten hat."
25 Ibid., 2:524: "noch von neuren Ohren mit Vergnügen angehört warden wenn er in allen drey Stimmen recht reinlich und gleich gesungen würde."

respect to *musica speculativa*. And he makes a point of quoting Coclico's odious characterization of Ockeghem as a "theorist." Having adopted Coclico's perspective, it is hardly surprising that Forkel seems predisposed to lambaste Ockeghem's music.

Like Wilphlingseder's faulty transcription, Coclico's strident denunciation of Ockeghem reverberated over the centuries, impacting upon the eighteenth-century view of our composer and inciting Forkel to a level of harshness in his critique of Ockeghem that is rivaled only by Coclico's own caustic aspersion. We may surmise why Forkel valued Coclico so much. In the German academy, the battle to situate the study of music in the humanities did not achieve the universal success it had in Wittenberg. The fight raged on in the eighteenth and nineteenth centuries, and, in Forkel's day, professors of music in Helmstedt, Jena, and Leipzig, for example, belonged to the Societät der musikalischen Wissenschaften, a society that espoused a distinctly mathematical orientation toward musical pedagogy. It is a mark of Forkel's stance regarding this conflict that his lectures at Göttingen were listed under *Schöne Wissenschaften und Künste*, as opposed to mathematics or *Wissenschaften* alone.[26] Thus, when Forkel needed a contemporaneous guide to the music of the fifteenth century, he followed the dictates of human nature in selecting a writer whose outlook on how best to teach music resonated sympathetically with his own.

The principal hero in early Ockeghem scholarship is August Wilhelm Ambros, whose command of musical sources expanded the available corpus of Ockeghem's works from the four pieces that were known in the eighteenth century to twenty-one. More importantly, he focused intensely on their musicality, rather than on their technique. Thus, when he addressed *Prenez sur moy*, Ambros suggested that what "elevates Ockeghem over his predecessors, however, is not the truly astounding sharpening of canonic and other structural artifice that we encounter in his music. It is by authority of an inherently musical spirit that Ockeghem breathes a singing soul into his music."[27]

Ambros's use of the metaphor of song cannot be accidental. Surely, he had Forkel in mind and offered this characterization as a corrective to the Enlightenment writer's fixation on Ockeghem's technique. The contrast between "unsingable" and a "singing soul" could not be more striking. Perhaps, though, it is a bit too striking. In highlighting the musicality of *Prenez sur moy*, Ambros underplays its counterpoint. He refers, in a general

---

26  Powers, "Johann Nikolaus Forkel's Philosophy of Music," 284–86, 323–24.
27  Ambros, *Geschichte der Musik*, 3:173: "Was nun aber Okeghem über seine Vorgänger erhebt, ist nicht die in der That erstaunliche Zuspitzung der canonischen und anderweitigen Satzkünste, der wir bei ihm begegnen. Kraft des ihm innewohnenden musikalischen Geistes haucht Okeghem seiner Musik die singende Seele ein …."

way, to its "astounding sharpening" but fails to note the extraordinary specifics of its complexity: how Ockeghem managed the canon at the irksome interval of a seventh in the outer voices, the relentless character of the canonic writing, or the constant elision at the ends of phrases.

This approach, moreover, extends to Ambros's broad view of Ockeghem's oeuvre, in which his emphasis is almost exclusively on the impressionistic qualities he detects in the music. His adjectives are revealing: *wondrous* and *strange*, *delicate* and *intimate*, *pleasing* and *tender*, *calm* and *melancholy*, *feminine* and *sentient*. This is hardly the vocabulary a fifteenth-century writer would use to characterize Ockeghem's music; it is the language of the co-founder of the Bohemian equivalent of the Davidsbund, the author of *Die Grenzen der Musik und Poesie*, and an avid reader of the works of Jean Paul. Ambros's shift in emphasis away from technique and toward musicality was undeniably needed, but its magnitude, obviously shaped by focusing on Ockeghem's music through the lenses of German Romanticism, seems to alter the symmetry inherent in one of the most trustworthy accounts of this music: that of Busnoys's *In hydraulis*, which, as we have seen, praises Ockeghem for his delicately balanced union of technique and song.

One of the most puzzling characterizations of Ockeghem's music is its portrayal as a mystical expression of pietism. Held to be irrational, the music is likened to the *docta ignorantia* of Nicholas of Cusa. Just as God can only be defined as what he is not, Ockeghem's polyphony is described in terms of the absence within it of the standard accoutrements of rational organization in music – cadences, imitation, profiled motives, and other sources of regularity. Two aspects of this argument are troublesome: there is no evidence linking Ockeghem to pietistic devotion, and his music conveys a sense of coherence that is suggestive of anything but irrationality.[28] Yet, despite these evidential flaws, the representation of Ockeghem's music as mystical enjoyed widespread acceptance for many years.

What gave rise to this interpretation? In October 1928, Heinrich Besseler published a survey of recent major editions of Renaissance music.[29] In it, he analyzed Du Fay's three-voice *Alma Redemptoris mater*, praising the work for its balance, clarity, and symmetry. When he assessed Ockeghem's motet on the same text, he characterized it only in terms of its failure to live up to the transparency of Du Fay's setting. A year later, when he edited Ockeghem's motet, he had to describe the work on its own, for which the negative analytical criteria of his prior characterization must have seemed awkward. Moreover,

---

28 On the sources of rational organization in Ockeghem's music, see the article "Jean d'Ockeghem" in the present volume, Ch. 6.
29 Besseler, "Von Dufay bis Josquin."

despite the failure of Ockeghem's motet to meet the Du Fay standard of clarity, Besseler perceived it as a work of genuine quality. In the absence, however, of the standard techniques he had described in connection with Du Fay, he was unable to explain how this quality came about. In addressing these problems, he tried to kill two birds with one stone by turning the deficit of the idealized lucidity in Ockeghem's motet into a unique quality: its capacity to project the mystical irrationality of pietistic spirituality.[30] Other writers were quick to jump on this bandwagon, including Besseler's students Wolfgang Stephan and Manfred Bukofzer, as well as Paul Henry Lang, also a student of musicology at Heidelberg in the early 1920s.[31]

It is not surprising that many sources of structural regularity in this music eluded writers in the 1920s, for the analysis of Renaissance music then was essentially descriptive. But, given the lack of any evidence for Ockeghem's contact with the institutions of pietism, turning to mysticism as an explanation for the nature of his music seems a bizarre stretch. Why mysticism? That all four early adherents to this view worked at Heidelberg provides a clue. In the 1920s, mysticism occupied a highly privileged place in the scholarly research conducted there. This can be seen in the writings of Raymond Klibansky and Ernst Hoffmann, who worked on Cusanus, the Brethren of the Common Life, and Flemish mysticism.[32] It even permeated the work of the Heidelberg art historian Carl Neumann, who demonstrated the affinity between Rembrandt and the mysticism of Jacob Boehme.[33] Concentration on mysticism was hardly unique to Heidelberg. It was a central interest of Martin Heidegger, with whom Besseler trained at Freiburg. And it permeated numerous areas of German thought in the 1920s, including the potent strain of anti-positivism that informed the ideology of National Socialism. Thus, when Besseler was hard pressed to find the words to account for the quality he sensed in a music whose structure his analytical tools could not explain, he turned to a central focus within his own intellectual milieu, the world of mysticism, a world that really had nothing to do with Ockeghem's music.

Ockeghem was a musical icon in his lifetime, but thereafter he was all too often the victim of an extraordinarily contorted reception. Many forces contributed to these distortions: faulty transcriptions, a skewed focus on technique in works transmitted by theorists, anti-antiquarianism, a progressive view of history, the disparagement of technical artifice by supporters of *musica*

---

30 Besseler, *Altniederländische Motetten*, 4; Besseler, *Die Musik des Mittelalters und der Renaissance*, 237–38.
31 For their expressions of this outlook, see Stephan, *Die burgundisch-niederländische Motette*, 80; Bukofzer, "*Caput*: A Liturgico-Musical Study," 291–92; Lang, *Music in Western Civilization*, 185–86.
32 See Cusanus, *Cusanus-Texte*, ed. Klibansky and Hoffmann. Many studies by these authors in this area of investigation could be cited.
33 Neumann, *Rembrandt*. The first edition appeared in 1902.

*practica*, and the extent to which mysticism permeated the German intellectual world of the 1920s. That so much went wrong in the reception of the greatest composer of his generation offers a sobering picture of how easy it is to misconstrue the music of the past as we view it through the inevitably inappropriate lenses of our own world-view.

# Bibliography

Ambros, August Wilhelm, *Geschichte der Musik*, 4 vols., Leipzig, 1862–68

Bernstein, Lawrence F., "Ockeghem the Mystic: A German Interpretation of the 1920s," in *Johannes Ockeghem: Actes du XL^e colloque international d'études humanistes, Tours, 3–8 février 1997*, ed. Philippe Vendrix, Paris, 1998, 811–41

"'Singende Seele' or 'unsingbar'? Forkel, Ambros, and the Forces behind the Ockeghem Reception during the Late 18th and 19th Centuries," *JM* 23 (2006), 3–61

Besseler, Heinrich, *Die Musik des Mittelalters und der Renaissance*, Handbuch der Musikwissenschaft 3, Potsdam, 1931

"Von Dufay bis Josquin: Ein Literaturbericht," *Zeitschrift für Musikwissenschaft* 11 (1928/29), 1–22

ed., *Altniederländische Motetten*, Kassel, 1929

Bukofzer, Manfred F., "*Caput*: A Liturgico-Musical Study," in *Studies in Medieval and Renaissance Music*, New York, 1950, 217–310

Burney, Charles, *A General History of Music from the Earliest Ages to the Present Period*, London, 1776–89; repr., ed. Frank Mercer, 2 vols., New York, 1935

Busnoys, Antoine, *Collected Works*, ed. Richard Taruskin, Masters and Monuments of the Renaissance 5, New York, 1990

Coclico, Adrianus Petit, *Compendium musices*, Nuremberg, 1552; facs. ed. Manfred Bukofzer, Documenta musicologica, Erste Reihe 9, Kassel, 1954

*Musical Compendium (Compendium musices)*, trans. Albert Seay, Colorado College Music Press Translations 5, Colorado Springs, CO, 1973

Cusanus, Nikolaus, *Cusanus-Texte: I. Predigten*, ed. Raymond Klibansky and Ernst Hoffmann, Sitzungsberichte der Heidelberger Akademie der Wissenschaften, Philosophisch-historiche Klasse, Jg. 1928/29, Heidelberg, 1929

Forkel, Johann Nikolaus, *Allgemeine Geschichte der Musik*, 2 vols., Leipzig, 1788–1801; repr. Die grossen Darstellungen der Musikgeschichte in Barock und Aufklärung 8, Graz, 1967

Hawkins, John, *A General History of the Science and Practice of Music*, London, 1776; repr. Die grossen Darstellungen der Musikgeschichte in Barock und Aufklärung 5, Graz, 1969

Hegar, Elisabeth, *Die Anfänge der neueren Musikgeschichtsschreibung um 1770 bei Gerbert, Burney und Hawkins*, Sammlung musikwissenschaftlicher Abhandlungen 7, Strasbourg, [1932]

Kirkman, Andrew, "'Under Such Heavy Chains': The Discovery and Evaluation of Late Medieval Music before Ambros," *19th-Century Music* 24 (2000), 89–112

Lang, Paul Henry, *Music in Western Civilization*, New York, 1941

Levitan, Joseph S., "Ockeghem's Clefless Compositions," *MQ* 23 (1937), 440–64

Lonsdale, Roger, *Dr. Charles Burney: A Literary Biography*, Oxford, 1965

Neumann, Carl, *Rembrandt*, 3rd edn., 2 vols., Munich, 1922

Niemöller, Klaus Wolfgang, "Zum Einfluss des Humanismus auf Position und Konzeption von Musik im deutschen Bildungssystem der ersten Hälfte des 16. Jahrhunderts," in *Musik in Humanismus und Renaissance*, Mitteilung der Kommission für Humanismusforschung 7, Weinheim, 1983, 77–97

Owens, Jessie Ann, "Music Historiography and the Definition of 'Renaissance'," *Notes* 47 (1990), 305–30

Plamenac, Dragan, "Autour d'Ockeghem," *La Revue musicale* 9 (1928), 26–47

Powers, Doris Bosworth, "Johann Nikolaus Forkel's Philosophy of Music in the *Einleitung* to Volume One of his *Allgemeine Geschichte der Musik* (1788): A Translation and Commentary with a Glossary of Eighteenth-Century Terms," Ph.D. diss., University of North Carolina at Chapel Hill, 1995

Stephan, Wolfgang, *Die burgundisch-niederländische Motette zur Zeit Ockeghems*, Würzburg-Aumühle, 1937

Walton, Isaac, and Charles Cotton, *The Complete Angler with Notes, Historical, Critical, Supplementary and Explanatory by Sir John Hawkins*, 7th edn., London, 1808; 1st edn., 1760

# Recordings of fifteenth-century music

HONEY MECONI

The fifteenth century was one of the last eras of Western art music to make it onto recordings. Record companies are businesses, dependent on the marketplace, and the audience for medieval and Renaissance music in general has always been considerably smaller than that for all later periods. Recordings of fifteenth-century music thus first appeared rather late in the game, in the 1930s.[1] Well into the 1950s the norm for these recordings was appearance as part of a larger historical survey of Western art music, of which the best known were the French *Anthologie sonore* series beginning in the 1930s (supervised by Curt Sachs) and the British *History of Music in Sound* from the 1950s, the latter spawned by a BBC broadcast series and intended to accompany *The New Oxford History of Music*.[2] A variety of artists and ensembles appeared in these and other series, but the most important for fifteenth-century music was arguably the Brussels-based Pro Musica Antiqua of Safford Cape (1906–73), which recorded music of John Dunstaple, Guillaume Du Fay, Gilles Binchois, Johannes Ockeghem, Antoine Busnoys, Johannes Brassart, Henricus Isaac, and Josquin des Prez over a period of some three decades.

Cape, an American who moved to Belgium in 1925 to study music, abruptly abandoned a promising career as a composer in 1932 to devote himself to the performance of medieval and Renaissance music.[3] That his father-in-law was noted Belgian musicologist Charles van den Borren was hardly a drawback in his new career, and, except for the period of World War II, his ensemble flourished, with international tours and a host of influential recordings.[4] The

---

1 For a short overview of early music recordings in general, see Haskell, *The Early Music Revival*, 112–20 and 127–30; see also Knighton, "Going Down on Record." Pre-1981 LP recordings of medieval and Renaissance music are documented in Coover and Colvig, *Medieval and Renaissance Music on Long-Playing Records* and the *Supplement*; and Croucher, *Early Music Discography*. To date, relatively little research examines recordings of early music, of which thousands exist; the Thomas Binkley Early Music Recordings Archive at Indiana University contains 5,394 medieval through Baroque items as of February 2012.

2 A brief synopsis of early series is found in Day, *A Century of Recorded Music*, 79–87; see also the discussion on 108–10 of Deutsche Grammophon Gesellschaft's Archiv series. Their "Research Period III: The Early Renaissance" included the fifteenth century.

3 On Cape, see Gagnepain, "Safford Cape et le 'miracle' Pro Musica Antiqua."

4 For recordings, see ibid., 212–14.

widely praised performances reflected Cape's concern with renditions that specifically observed the perceived rules at the time the music was created.

The LP "Guillaume Dufay: Secular Works," released in 1950, provides a good example of what those rules were then thought to be. That disc, EMS 206, was the sixth volume of the series "Anthology of Middle Age and Renaissance Music" and contained thirteen chansons, including eleven rondeaux. On the recording, formal structures were sometimes observed, sometimes not. Four works were performed on instruments alone, since, according to the liner notes, "Works of this type could either be sung, with or without accompaniment, or simply be done on instruments." Untexted parts were considered instrumental interludes. The performers played treble and tenor recorders, treble and tenor viols, and lute and "minstrel's harp." Instruments could double each other or a singer, and repeated sections could feature new instrumentation (the "Berlioz" approach to early performance). The solo voices all used vibrato.

Cape's performing choices were shared by his contemporaries and informed by early twentieth-century musicological thought. But the advantage of recordings is, of course, that one need not have in-person contact with a performing tradition to benefit from and be influenced by it. Thus, beginning with the generation after Cape, younger musicians could and did gain considerable exposure to early music – including that of the fifteenth century – through recordings; they did not have to be acolytes of figures such as Charles van den Borren. And recordings, more than live performances, began to shape the expectations of both listeners and performers.

The stylistic parameters fixed on recordings by Cape and his confrères remained largely unquestioned until the 1970s; virtually all important figures followed the basic "rules," with varying degrees of success. The most significant early music figure of the later 1950s and early 1960s, Noah Greenberg (1919–66), certainly did.[5] Greenberg, self-taught in early music and lacking any college education, formed what became known as the New York Pro Musica in 1953. The ensemble was professional; although its basic membership fluctuated, it eventually settled on a core of six singers and four instrumentalists, with members of the latter group normally adept at playing more than one instrument. The ensemble was founded quite specifically to make a recording, and live performance followed because of the need to generate record sales.

Greenberg was by all accounts a leader of manic energy and a talented showman; New York Pro Musica's sound was noticeably more robust than

---

5 On Greenberg see Gollin, *Pied Piper*, with discography on 404–10.

that of Cape's group, with crisper tempos and greater rhythmic drive. Greenberg had a talent for recognizing which repertory would grab an audience, and his free-standing recordings – not part of any series – proved that early music could thrive on its own, out of the shadow of an educational overview.

His recording of Obrecht's *Missa Fortuna desperata* on the disc "XV Century Netherlands Masters" (Decca DL 79413, released 1961) provides an example of his treatment of fifteenth-century sacred music. The musicians include four male soloists (countertenor, tenor, baritone, and bass), a separate sixteen-voice all-male choir (ditto the voice parts, with a 5/4/3/4 distribution), and a nine-voice boy choir. The texture shifts from solo to choir unexpectedly (i.e., within sections), as do tempos. Occasional instrumental doubling of vocal lines comes from a soprano cornetto, alto and tenor shawms, and alto, tenor, and bass sackbuts. Solo singing is marked by constant vibrato. Greenberg's liner notes include the notation for the tenor of the original song, references to use of the model, and identification of the editions used.

Greenberg's sudden death in 1966 did not signal the end of the New York Pro Musica, but the ensemble, though it continued to record and perform, could not sustain its preeminent position. Of the many early music groups started in the later 1960s, one in particular soared to the forefront of the performance scene: the Early Music Consort of London, founded in 1967. Its leader, David Munrow (1942–76), stood apart from Cape and Greenberg in one very significant component of his musical activity. Both the two older figures had conducted their ensembles, and while Munrow did conduct at times, his direction was more often from within the group as a performer, a virtuoso on seemingly every wind instrument used before 1750. He thus led by example, and his extroverted personality exploded in his music-making and on his recordings.

These discs were noteworthy not only for sheer verve and musical excitement, but also because of Munrow's consummate sense of programming. The recording "Music of Guillaume Dufay" (Seraphim S-60267, released 1974) provides a representative example. Prompted by the 500th anniversary of Du Fay's death, the collection opened with the charming *Gloria ad modum tube* and closed with the *Missa Se la face ay pale*. In between came the complete original three-voice chanson on which the mass was based, a four-voiced "instrumental" version attributed to Du Fay, and two keyboard arrangements from the Buxheim Organ Book. Thus Munrow, a born educator, prepared the listener for the full impact of the mass by ensuring that the model was first firmly in the ear (in contrast to Greenberg, who coupled his Obrecht mass with an unrelated group of compositions by Isaac). The recording's back cover outlined the layout of the cantus firmus (providing more information than Greenberg had with his mass) and a detailed insert included the expected translations, a modern transcription of the cantus-firmus model, and an extended essay by Munrow. As with Greenberg, sonic pleasure was thus coupled with intellectual nourishment.

Munrow broke new ground as well with a series of multi-disc ventures. Those that contained fifteenth-century music were "The Art of Courtly Love" (Seraphim SIC-6092, released 1973), whose third disc was devoted to the Court of Burgundy (Du Fay, Binchois, and anonymous works); and "The Art of the Netherlands" (Seraphim SIC-6104, released 1976), where six sides were divided into groupings of secular songs (French, Flemish, and Italian), instrumental music, motets, and a composite mass that included such previously unheard gems as the Kyrie from Johannes Tinctoris's three-voice mass, the Gloria from Antoine Brumel's twelve-voice *Missa Et ecce terre motus*, and the Sanctus from Pierre de La Rue's 6 ex 3 canonic *Missa Ave sanctissima Maria*. Numerous other composers, including many from the previous generation, appeared as well.

Munrow's multi-disc recordings, each with a relatively narrow focus, were bold and accomplished experiments, difficult to imagine in the preceding generation. Yet within half a dozen years after his death other ensembles had created three major boxed sets even more astonishing in their repertorial choice and success. All appeared on the niche label L'Oiseau-Lyre, founded in 1938 by the wealthy Australian music publisher and patron Louise Hanson-Dyer. The label's distinctive packaging for its Florilegium LPs – a largely white cover with a colorful center image, sober black lettering, and an intricate black and white border – was a canny marketing ploy that rapidly created an association in the buyer's mind with quality period-conscious performances of early repertory.[6]

Two of the three pathbreaking recordings were by the Medieval Ensemble of London, a small chamber ensemble led by two brothers, Peter and Timothy Davies. Though following in the tradition of Munrow and other predecessors, the group deviated from what had been the norm by concentrating on a much narrower repertory than usual. The name implies as much, but the ensemble went even further, recording only music from the fourteenth and fifteenth centuries. Munrow and Greenberg, by contrast, had explored music from medieval monophony to Handel. The Davies brothers further limited their choice of instruments to those actually cultivated before 1500, once again in

---

6 It is surely no accident that the later early music niche label Accent created a cover design so similar that on first glance their recordings appear to be from L'Oiseau-Lyre; see, for example, the advertisement in the May 1996 issue of *Early Music* on p. 334.

marked difference to earlier ensembles that often drew on instruments from the sixteenth century (or later).

One mammoth recording by the Medieval Ensemble was "Guillaume Dufay: Complete Secular Music" (L'Oiseau-Lyre Florilegium D237D 6, released 1981), a six-disc collection that covered everything in the secular volume of Du Fay's complete works edition in approximate chronological order. Another was "Johannes Ockeghem: Complete Secular Music" (L'Oiseau-Lyre Florilegium D254D 3, released 1982), correspondingly smaller at three discs. Listeners thus had, in two convenient sets, all the secular music of two of the most important composers of the fifteenth century.[7]

As impressive as this achievement was, it nonetheless represented an out-growth of previous recording practices (for all art music, even early music) that emphasized works by a named and usually well-known composer. In contrast, the remaining set was a radical break from that path: a four-disc recording by the Consort of Musicke (directed by Anthony Rooley) of "Le Chansonnier cordiforme" (L'Oiseau-Lyre Florilegium D186D 4, released 1980). Only nine-teen of the forty-three songs in the set were associated with composers, leaving twenty-four anonymous compositions, an unheard-of number for a recording at the time. L'Oiseau-Lyre counted on the audience for fifteenth-century recordings to be sufficiently sophisticated to support a recording inspired by the most beautiful of fifteenth-century chansonniers.

In addition to repertorial expansions, these recordings – and indeed, record-ings by Munrow's ensemble and some others as well – featured singers who eschewed vibrato, using instead a "straight" tone. The result was far greater clarity of musical line.

In barely fifty years, then, recordings of fifteenth-century music had expanded from those presenting short individual works to massive collections devoted to a single seemingly esoteric subject (esoteric in the grand scheme of recording, not in the eyes of scholars). Performers were ever more accom-plished on instruments; singers no longer sounded like refugees from the opera stage. But more and arguably greater change was afoot. In the eyes of some, the change represented heresy.

## Music in a time of heresy

In 1973, the year David Munrow's "Art of Courtly Love" was released, three new groups were formed in England: the Hilliard Ensemble (founded by Paul

---

7 Other recordings of fifteenth-century music by the Medieval Ensemble of London included an Isaac disc, one of Josquin masses, one of Josquin's three-voice secular music, and one of fifteenth-century English songs ("Mi verry joy").

Hillier, but named after the Elizabethan miniaturist), the Tallis Scholars (founded by Peter Phillips), and the Taverner Choir (founded by Andrew Parrott). Although it would be five years before any recordings by these groups appeared, the ensembles were radically different from other professional early music groups right from the start: they were composed of singers alone.

All-vocal performance of fifteenth-century music was not unknown before these groups began, but the assumption by earlier performers and almost all scholars was that instruments were widely used in both sacred and secular music and were indeed required for many lines.[8] All-vocal performance was seen as the exception rather than the norm. The main arguments in support of this view were derived from iconography (images of instruments were plentiful in art-works of the fifteenth century and earlier) and the manuscript sources, which most often provided full texting for only a single line. The melodic structure of many untexted lines was also thought to be especially unvocal in terms of range, disjunct motion, or rapid series of notes. Further, many ensembles (though by no means all) were run by gifted instrumentalists (e.g., Munrow, the Davies brothers, Rooley) who were naturally inclined to favor renditions that incorporated instruments.

Although the Hilliard Ensemble, Tallis Scholars, and Taverner Choir shared a commitment to vocal performance, the three developed distinctive profiles despite both some repertorial overlap and shared singers (for that matter, various members of these groups also recorded with the instrumentally-centered ensembles of Munrow and others). The Taverner Choir only rarely ventured before 1500, concentrating instead on music of the sixteenth century and beyond – sometimes far beyond (augmenting performances of later music with the instrumental Taverner Players when appropriate).[9] The Tallis Scholars likewise favored the sixteenth century, but still produced – to date – five discs of Josquin masses, recordings of Cornysh and music from the Eton Choirbook, and recordings of masses by Ockeghem, Brumel, Isaac, and Obrecht. In 1980, two years after starting their recording career, they created their own label, Gimell, which removed them from the need to please a record company before reaching an audience.

A small chamber choir, Tallis Scholars used women's in addition to men's voices, something never done for sacred music in the Renaissance. Reviewers who were also scholars routinely criticized their approach to accidentals

8 See Leech-Wilkinson, *The Modern Invention of Medieval Music*, for a detailed treatment of the changing performance expectations for early music across the twentieth century.
9 Fifteenth-century music is found on a Josquin disc and one of "Masterworks from Late-Medieval England and Scotland."

(especially avoidance of standard cadential *ficta*) as well as choices regarding tempo and proportional relationships. But only the cognoscenti were aware of these departures from musicological expectations, and the group's singing (ensemble, intonation, quality of vocal production) was quite simply of breathtaking beauty. They are easily the best-known pre-Baroque ensemble today, whose recordings and concerts have brought fifteenth- and sixteenth-century music to hundreds of thousands of listeners.

In contrast to the Tallis Scholars, the Hilliard Ensemble used male voices only, frequently with a single voice to a part. They also probed the fifteenth-century repertory far more deeply, and some recordings were landmarks for both repertory and rendition. Their output included discs of Du Fay, Ockeghem, Walter Frye, Isaac, La Rue, and Josquin, as well as explorations of specific sources: Oxford 213, the Speciálník Codex, and the Old Hall manuscript. Among their earliest recordings were discs devoted to Leonel Power and John Dunstaple, each of which marked the Ensemble as distinctive in its choice of repertory.

Members of the three all-vocal groups just mentioned, as well as numerous others to come, were often products of the choral traditions of Oxbridge and English cathedral choirs, two decades into a "golden age" when Peter Phillips provided an overview in 1980.[10] This tradition provided prodigious vocal experience and generated superlative sight-reading skills, but in fact offered little in the way of fifteenth-century repertory; in this respect new ensembles and recordings broke significantly with English choral practice.

Only to the most casual listener would the recordings of major *a cappella* groups sound alike, but in all of them the use of voices alone and preference for "straight" vocal production permitted a level of clarity and precision not previously heard on recording. The overall lighter vocal sound allowed an agility as well that belied earlier claims about the instrumentality of certain lines. Also noteworthy were the precision of intonation (enabled in part by uniformity of vowel sounds) and the fine choral blend. To the critic, the overall sound was uniform and boring, dynamically flat, underinflected, impassive, and repertorially indistinguishable.[11] To the fan, though, the sheer musicality of the performers generated carefully shaped melodic lines, gradual and expressive shifts in dynamics, and perfect synchronicity of entrances and releases. Slower tempos (prompted by cathedral acoustics?) permitted an unfolding of

10 See Phillips, "The Golden Age Regained." See also Page, "The English *a cappella* Renaissance," which provides appendices of reviews and recordings of major ensembles.
11 For example, fifteenth-century compositions with rapid-paced, nimble upper voices over slowly-moving foundations received the same full-bodied treatment as equal-voiced, rhythmically uniform polyphony of the sixteenth century. For a fascinating example of the implications of structure on performance, see the essay by Michael Long, "Hearing Josquin Hearing Busnoys," in this volume, Ch. 1.

the music that resulted in powerful performances whose every breve seemed to speak of a sonic truth captured through the most intimate knowledge of a composition. Recordings of neither European nor American choirs could touch the English for their technical proficiency and consequent expression in performance of this music when their discs first appeared, and as for one-on-a-part recordings, the singers equaled the finest string quartets in their musical ensemble. Vocal chamber music had never sounded so good.

At the same time that the earliest recordings of voices-only ensembles were appearing, scholars too were reexamining received notions of performance practice. Over a period of about fifteen years – from the late 1970s to the early 1990s – research on both secular and sacred music before 1500 led to the reversal of previously-held convictions. All-vocal performance of fifteenth-century music was now considered the norm – or at least the ideal – at the time the music was created, with instrumental use in composed polyphony not unknown but no longer thought standard.

One of the first and most important writers to argue for this new view was Christopher Page.[12] Ironically, Page himself was an instrumentalist, but the group he founded four years after he initially propounded voices-only performance – Gothic Voices (begun 1981) – championed all-vocal performance, as the group's name implies. Although their earliest recordings were firmly in the Middle Ages, Gothic Voices inched and then galloped into the fifteenth century, ultimately recording an entire CD of Pierre de la Rue.[13]

Page's recordings with Gothic Voices were of great importance, as they brought the voices-only aesthetic to the particularly thorny repertory of the French chanson (a major repertory of the fifteenth century, and one almost ignored by the all-vocal ensembles founded earlier). The skill and sensitivity of the musicians wrought exquisite performances that, to many listeners, served as proof for claims of all-vocal renditions. The recordings were also of value for experiments with textless vocalization as well as tuning adjustments (Pythagorean vs. just) according to the repertory (which was in itself adventurous, with recordings organized more often by political or cultural theme, e.g. "Lancaster and Valois," "The Garden of Zephirus," than by composer).

It was in a review of a Gothic Voices recording that Howard Mayer Brown, one of the world's foremost authorities on the Renaissance chanson, included the words "the new secular *a cappella* heresy" in 1987.[14] In the hands of others,

---

12 Many of the most important essays (by Page and others) concerning the evidence for all-vocal performance are collected in Meconi, ed., *Medieval Music* and Kreitner, ed., *Renaissance Music*; the introduction to the former provides a synopsis of the chronology in the debate. For detailed discussion, see again Leech-Wilkinson, *The Modern Invention of Medieval Music*.

13 An index of recordings through 1992 appears in *EM* 21 (1993), 292–95.

14 Brown, review of Gothic Voices' "The Castle of Fair Welcome," 278.

the phrase soon morphed into "the English *a cappella* heresy," used to represent all-vocal performance of both sacred and secular music. Today's recordings show that what was once heresy is now doctrine.

## Aftermath

Over the almost forty years since the founding of the first all-vocal early music groups, many practices they championed have become standard. Most noticeably, the use of instruments in recordings of fifteenth-century sacred music has largely disappeared, whether the ensemble is from England, America, or Europe. Recordings of secular music have been more resistant to all-vocal renditions, especially those from Continental groups; see, for example, Hesperion XX (e.g., their imaginatively orchestrated recordings of music from the Cancionero de la Colombina and the Cancionero de Palacio).

An explosion of high-quality ensembles has generated a wealth of recorded music, with multiple versions of many significant compositions. Some of the important results from a plethora of recording artists include the complete run of Ockeghem masses (Clerks' Group), five-CD coverage of the Eton Choirbook (The Sixteen), frequent presentation of polyphonic masses with historically accurate plainchant propers (e.g., Obrecht's *Missa de Sancto Donatiano* by Cappella Pratensis; the accompanying DVD recreates the service visually as well), and performances at the far end of written notation ("Extreme Singing" by Vox Early Music Ensemble). While scholarship and recording have always been intertwined, the directing of ensembles by Ph.D.-holding musicologists has generated CDs that incorporate the latest research or theories, e.g., the discs of The Binchois Consort (Andrew Kirkman), Pomerium Musices (Alexander Blachly), Capella Alamire (Peter Urquhart), Schola Discantus (Kevin Moll), and Cut Circle (Jesse Rodin). Other notable recordings in recent decades have come from Capilla Flamenca, the Orlando Consort, The Sound and the Fury, and Ensemble Organum, to name just a few. And with groups such as Ensemble Obsidienne, we now have performances that explore the unwritten music of the era through the kind of improvised counterpoint that was normal at the time but has been silent for centuries.

The extraordinarily high technical level of today's performing groups can make it easy for us to believe that we have at last "gotten it right." Yet such an assumption would be a huge mistake. Every age thinks that it is performing music (of any era) the way it should be done, but somehow styles of performance continue to change and evolve with each succeeding generation. Rather than coming ever closer to perfection, then, our performance choices surely reflect an ever-shifting hierarchy of values contingent upon an equally impermanent confluence of historical circumstance. The only constant is change.

Presenting this survey in such broad brush strokes means no consideration of many important recordings, such as the highly individual, folk-influenced work of Musica Reservata or the numerous musically fine productions of Bruno Turner and the Pro Cantione Antiqua, which were very frequently the first to capture many significant compositions on vinyl. It shows, though, that again and again a musically gifted and charismatic leader can make a dramatic difference in what is available for us to hear. Such leaders are needed as we face an uncertain future in terms of new economic models and changing technology, and, for the first time since recording began, a mode of transmission that is of diminishing rather than increasing audio quality. It is thus fitting to conclude with the words of Chichester Cathedral organist John Birch: "anything stands a good chance of survival while we have to fight for it."[15]

# Bibliography

Brown, Howard Mayer, Review of Gothic Voices' "The Castle of Fair Welcome," *EM* 15 (1987), 277–79

Coover, James, and Richard Colvig, *Medieval and Renaissance Music on Long-Playing Records*, Detroit Studies in Music Bibliography 6, Detroit, 1964

  *Medieval and Renaissance Music on Long-Playing Records: Supplement, 1962–1971*, Detroit Studies in Music Bibliography 26, Detroit, 1973

Croucher, Trevor, *Early Music Discography: From Plainsong to the Sons of Bach*, 2 vols., London, 1981

Day, Timothy, *A Century of Recorded Music: Listening to Musical History*, New Haven and London, 2000

Gagnepain, Bernard, "Safford Cape et le 'miracle' Pro Musica Antiqua," *Revue belge de musicologie/Belgisch Tijdschrift voor Muziekwetenschap* 34/35 (1980/1981), 204–19

Gollin, James, *Pied Piper: The Many Lives of Noah Greenberg*, Lives in Music Series 4, Hillsdale, NY, 2001

Haskell, Harry, *The Early Music Revival: A History*, London, 1988

Knighton, Tess, "Going Down on Record," in *Companion to Medieval and Renaissance Music*, ed. Tess Knighton and David Fallows, London, 1992, 30–35

Kreitner, Kenneth, ed., *Renaissance Music*, Farnham and Burlington, VT, 2011

Leech-Wilkinson, Daniel, *The Modern Invention of Medieval Music: Scholarship, Ideology, Performance*, Cambridge, 2002

Meconi, Honey, ed., *Medieval Music*, Farnham and Burlington, VT, 2011

Page, Christopher, "The English *a cappella* Renaissance," *EM* 21 (1993), 452–71

Phillips, Peter, "The Golden Age Regained," *EM* 8 (1980), 3–16; 178–98

---

15 Quoted in Phillips, "The Golden Age Regained," 16.

# Solidarity with the long-departed: fifteenth-century echoes in twentieth-century music

RICHARD TARUSKIN

We can still appreciate Bach and Handel or even Palestrina, but Dufay and Dunstable have little more than an historical interest for us now. But they were great men in their day and perhaps the time will come when Bach, Handel, Beethoven, and Wagner will drop out and have no message left for us.

Ralph Vaughan Williams[1]

–"Ja, mit solch einer Musik lässt's sich leben." –"Verflucht, dass die Musik dies' verloren hat"!

Paul Hindemith[2]

Isorhythmic motets are decisive testimony to the architectural value of rhythmic structures in relation to the strictly different sequences implied by the cadences. What better precedent could one invoke for modern research than a period when music was considered not just as an art, but also as a science?

Pierre Boulez[3]

The combination of early musics and contemporary musics in the same program might seem hazardous. But when one is dealing with composers who lived and worked before and after the great parentheses of romantic art . . . it is possible to find a certain analogy, if nowhere else than in the artistic conception and in the "modus operandi."

Domenico De Paoli[4]

These epigraphs prefigure the story this chapter will tell. The twentieth century was an age of sonic archeology. It made the music of the past available as never before to the musicians of the present, so that old music could influence new music directly. Ralph Vaughan Williams, steeped in nineteenth-century meliorism, saw the distant past only as a foreign country where they

---

1 Vaughan Williams, "Should Music Be National?," 8.
2 "– With such music one can cope with life. – Damn it, that music has lost this!" (exchange between the cellist Eckhart Richter and Paul Hindemith at a 1948 rehearsal by the Yale University Collegium Musicum of the Credo from Isaac's *Missa de Assumptione*); Richter, "Paul Hindemith as Director," 30.
3 Boulez, "Stravinsky demeure," 109.
4 De Paoli, Program note, 17; trans. Alana Mailes (to whom thanks are due for bringing it to the author's attention).

did things differently, and less well.[5] By the time Paul Hindemith made his
wistful remark about Henricus Isaac, fifteenth-century music had to an unprecedented degree already invaded the world of practical music-making, thanks
to the boom in research, publication, and amateur performance that attended
the growth of musicology – first in Hindemith's homeland, thence (and with
his help) in North America. Pierre Boulez and the Italian musicologist
Domenico De Paoli (1894–1984, author of biographies of Monteverdi and
Stravinsky) exemplify the Cold War avant-garde, whose most advanced members and spokespersons journeyed enthusiastically back to that foreign country
to justify their most radical ideas.

## Schoenberg, Webern, Krenek

Even Vaughan Williams sensed that the past might not be irrevocably dead –
indeed that, as William Faulkner would write, it might not even be past.[6]
Immediately after predicting that our own greats might join Guillaume Du
Fay and John Dunstaple in history's dustbin, he allowed that "[s]ometimes of
course the clock goes round full circle and the twentieth century compre-
hends what had ceased to have any meaning for the nineteenth."[7] We can
now look back on that circling clock, and the place to begin would be the
edition of the second volume of Isaac's *Choralis Constantinus*, that exquisite
early sixteenth-century distillation of fifteenth-century craft, in the series
Denkmäler der Tonkunst in Österreich. Isaac's first volume had been issued
in 1898 as vol. 10 (Jhg. V/1), edited by Emil Bezecný (1868–1930) and Walter
Rabl (1873–1940), two composers who had earned doctorates under Guido
Adler (1855–1941), the series editor, at the German University of Prague.
The editor of the second volume, issued in 1909 as vol. 32 (Jhg. XVI/1), was a
somewhat younger pupil of Adler's named Anton von Webern, who had
received his doctorate in 1906 at the University of Vienna. The edition had
been his dissertation. With Webern we encounter the confluence of musicology and advanced composition that made the twentieth century, the century
of modernism, as if paradoxically more sympathetic to the distant musical
past than any previous century had been. Webern's posthumous status as a
modernist icon has vouchsafed the wide dissemination of the preface to his
dissertation as an aesthetic testament. The peroration: "Ysaak uses canonic
devices very profusely ... [and] with the greatest insight, grasps the spirit of

5 "The past is a foreign country: they do things differently there" (opening sentence of Hartley, *The
Go-Between*).
6 "The past is never dead. It's not even past." *Requiem for a Nun*, 80.
7 Vaughan Williams, "Should Music Be National?," 8.

the [Gregorian] chant, so absorbing it into himself that the chant appears in the master's music not as something foreign to its nature but welded into the highest unity with it."[8]

This encomium powerfully conveys the Germanic Romantic spirit that suffused the aesthetics of the second Viennese school. Isaac's contrapuntal mastery, and his use of the paraphrase technique, are valued for the unity they lent his compositions. Integration of texture, preeminently realized by *die Niederländer*, was something that Webern and Schoenberg strove to emulate in their own work. Both saw the emancipation of dissonance and, later, the twelve-tone technique as keys to that integration, as Webern implied when he claimed of his Symphony, Op. 21, that "Greater unity is impossible. Even the Netherlanders didn't manage it."[9]

Arnold Schoenberg's acknowledgment of "Netherlandish" precedent may be found scattered throughout his writings. He included Josquin and his confrères among the elect creators of "New Music," writing that their secrets, "strictly denied to the uninitiated, were based on a complete recognition of the possible contrapuntal relations between the seven tones of the diatonic scale."[10] Schoenberg strove to match their achievement in a compositional essay of his own, labeled pseudo-archaically as *Eyn doppelt spiegel- und Schlüssel-Kanon for vier Stimen gesetzet auf niederlandsche Art* (A Double Mirror-and-Clef-Canon for Four Voices Composed in the Netherlandish Manner), a work coeval with the earliest twelve-tone experiments.[11] The bass, tenor, and treble form a mensuration canon, while the alto forms against the bass a canon at the twelfth by inversion. After four bars the alto and bass exchange roles with respect to inversion and the alto and tenor exchange rates of speed. And then, at what turns out to be the midpoint, the whole canon reproduces itself in retrograde, with the parts inverted and the clefs so arranged that if the whole score were turned upside down it would (but for the placement of the longer notes) look the same as it did right-side up. That Schoenberg was competing directly with Josquin is evident from a sketch that carries on its verso a multiple transcription, in various rhythmic reductions, of the famous three-voice mensuration canon from the Agnus Dei in Josquin's *Missa L'homme armé super voces musicales*.[12]

---

8 Adapted from Leo Black's translation in the English edition of *Die Reihe*, 2:24–25.
9 Webern, "The Path to Twelve-Note Composition," 56.
10 Schoenberg, "New Music, Outmoded Music," in *Style and Idea* (1946), 117.
11 Facsimile of the fair copy, dated Mödling, 16 February 1922, in *Arnold Schoenberg Gedenkausstellung*, ed. Hilmar, 148; *30 Kanons*, 8–9; *Sämtliche Werke*, Abteilung V, Reihe A, Band 3, 157 and critical report, Abteilung V, Reihe B, Band 3, 60–63.
12 *Sämtliche Werke*, Abteilung V, Reihe B, Band 3, 60.

For all its ingenuity, this opuscule is far from unimpeachable as counter-point; nor is it a serious attempt at pastiche. It retains a characteristically Schoenbergian touch of jesting, akin to the famous pseudocomplexities of "Der Mondfleck," the eighteenth melodrama in *Pierrot lunaire* (1913).[13] It nevertheless testifies to the huge importance Schoenberg and his followers attached to the principle of mirror-writing, an aspect of the Netherlandish legacy that had once given the "Franco-Flemish" school an equivocal reputa-tion in the eyes of posterity. Charles Burney's prejudiced but influential appreciation of "Okenheim" (Ockeghem) is quoted by Lawrence Bernstein in his contribution to this volume (Ch. 43). Compare Cecil Gray (obviously reliant on Burney), who called Ockeghem "a pure cerebralist," with "something of the mentality of Arnold Schoenberg to-day, the same ruthless disregard of merely sensuous beauty, the same unwearying and relentless pursuit of new technical means for their own sake."[14]

Where Gray disparaged, Ernst Krenek, one of the earliest twelve-tone composers beyond Schoenberg's immediate circle, identified strongly with the very same aspects of Ockeghem's style, and with the same comparison. In a handbook published in 1953, Krenek remarked that "[t]he objection of 'cerebralism' is so frequently leveled at many types of contemporary music that [when] a modern composer . . . notices that one of the venerable masters of the past is exposed to the same kind of attack, he feels a certain solidarity with his long-departed colleague."[15] Echoing Webern, Krenek went on to say that "[p]resent-day composers who practice the twelve-tone technique will be interested in the ways in which Ockeghem used his 'basic patterns,' the cantus firmi, to create structural unity in large musical areas."[16] Later composers in the "post-Webern" line have echoed this declaration, most recently György Ligeti, who cited Ockeghem as a model for the dense vocal "micropolyphony" in works from his Darmstadt period such as the *Requiem* (1963–65; rev. 1997) and *Lux Aeterna* (1966).[17] It was Ockeghem's "'varietas' principle, where the voices are similar without being identical" that Ligeti particularly sought to emulate in fashioning his "impenetrable textures of sound."[18] He maintained that "In order to perform [the 1967 orchestral piece] *Lontano* correctly, one must love Ockeghem very much."[19]

13 See Taruskin, "'Alte Musik' or 'Early Music'?"    14 Gray, *The History of Music*, 62.
15 Krenek, *Johannes Ockeghem*, 12.    16 Ibid., 80.
17 "I am more interested in Ockeghem than in Palestrina, because his music does not tend toward culminating points. Just as one voice approaches a climax another voice comes to counteract it, like waves in the sea." Ligeti, *György Ligeti in Conversation*, 26. For an impressionistic but comprehensive comparison of the two composers see Kievman, "Ockeghem and Ligeti."
18 Ligeti, *György Ligeti in Conversation*, 26 and 49.
19 Burde, *György Ligeti*, 166; quoted in Thein, "Zitat, Bearbeitung," 806.

The renewed interest in cantus-firmus treatment, where most of the mirror-writing in fifteenth-century music took place, is both reflected and urged in an article by R. Larry Todd (his first publication, written while a graduate student at Yale), which contained an annotated census of fifteenth-century compositions that employ either temporal or diastematic mirroring as a "structural" feature.[20] The article's title, by actually applying the language of twelve-tone analysis to the music of the "long fifteenth century," validates, in the name of the American academy, the affinity the early twelve-tone composers had previously asserted. (He lists works by Guillaume de Machaut, Richard Loqueville, Domenico da Ferrara, John Dunstaple, Guillaume Du Fay, Firmin Caron, Cornelius Heyns, Antoine Busnoys, Jacob Obrecht, Johannes Japart, Robert Fayrfax, Josquin des Prez, Mathurin Forestier, Johannes Mouton, Pierre de La Rue, Johannes Beausseron, Mathieu Gascongne, Isaac, Ludwig Senfl, and nine *anonymi*.[21]) In ascribing the impulse to vary the cantus firmus to a "serial" principle, and emphasizing artistic autonomy ("*the right of the composer* to predetermine rationally, or 'serialize,' ... various elements of the composition"), the article's summation reflects the preoccupations of its time.[22]

To others those preoccupations smacked of *Augenmusik*. Two decades before succumbing, like many quondam resisters, to the seductions of twelve-tone technique, Roger Sessions had complained that the Schoenbergians had elevated the *cancrizans*, "a technical curiosity which is admittedly inaccessible to the most attentive ear and which was used with the utmost rarity," into "a regular and essential technical procedure."[23] And Paul Hindemith asked, sarcastically:

> Is it not strange that the same composers who worship harmonic freedom – or what they mistake for freedom, which is only a dead end which they have not yet recognized as such – have been taken in as regards musical structure by a formalism that makes the artificialities of the early Netherland contrapuntists seem like child's play?[24]

## Stravinsky and Hindemith

In 1925, Guido Adler asked Webern to complete the edition of *Choralis Constantinus* for DTÖ by editing its third and last volume, "a task so time-consuming and financially unrewarding that Webern had to decline."[25] That

20 Todd, "Retrograde, Inversion."    21 Ibid., Table I, pp. 71–76; see also 52–55.
22 Ibid., 70. Italics added.    23 Sessions, "Music in Crisis," 75.
24 Hindemith, *The Craft of Musical Composition*, 154.
25 Moldenhauer and Moldenhauer, *Anton von Webern*, 285.

volume did not appear in a modern edition until 1950;[26] but when it did, it won for fifteenth-century music an important new friend. In December 1952, asked by a reporter from the *New York Herald Tribune* to name his favorite composer, Igor Stravinsky, who loved taking interviewers by surprise, began rhapsodizing about the music of Isaac:

> He is my hobby, my daily bread. I love him. I study him constantly. And between his musical thinking and writing and my own there is a very close connection … Here is the newly published volume of his "Choralis Constantinus," Book III: A great work. Not a home should be without it."[27]

By then, Stravinsky had been playing over the *Choralis Constantinus*, usually four-hands with his assistant Robert Craft, for about a year. In fact he was playing it in January 1952 at the same time that he was attending Craft's rehearsals of Schoenberg's Septet-Suite, Op. 29, and composing the *Cantata*, the first work in which he employed (in R. Larry Todd's sense) "serialized," if not yet twelve-tone, techniques ("*cancricans*" and "*riverse*," to use his terminology).[28] In 1956, Universal Edition sent Stravinsky a photocopy of Webern's edition of Volume 2, in which Stravinsky was by then, so to speak, doubly interested.[29] But Stravinsky's acquaintance with a wide variety of medieval and Renaissance music, and his creative appropriations from it, go back at least as far as 1939–40, the year he spent at Harvard University in the Charles Eliot Norton Chair of Poetry. There he met Prof. Archibald T. Davison, who, together with Willi Apel, a recent German refugee then employed at Harvard as a lecturer, was in the process of compiling the *Historical Anthology of Music*, a compendium of examples for music history classes. That Stravinsky had it, read it, and used it is evident to anyone else who ever had it, read it, and used it, because so many of the examples of early music to which he made archly knowing reference in his books of "conversation" with Craft can be found in this humble pedagogical source or others equally lowly.[30]

During his American years, Stravinsky collected all the standard textbooks on early music.[31] According to Craft, he owned "Reese (both *Music in the*

---

26  Isaac, *Heinrich Isaac's Choralis Constantinus*, ed. Cuyler.

27  Harrison, "Talk with Stravinsky," 21 December 1952; quoted in Joseph, *Stravinsky Inside Out*, 252.

28  Craft, *Stravinsky: Chronicle of a Friendship*, 72.

29  The photocopy is listed as no. 426 *in A Catalogue of Some Books and Music Inscribed to and/or Autographed and Annotated by Igor Stravinsky, and of Private Recordings and Test-Pressings Labelled by Him in the Estate of Vera Stravinsky* (typescript, 1983) prepared by Robert Craft with the assistance of Brett Shapiro to facilitate the sale of Stravinsky's library.

30  See, for example, Stravinsky and Craft, *Memories and Commentaries*, 100–1, 111.

31  When working in his archive, during the temporary custodianship of the New York Public Library in 1983, I found a letter from Faber and Faber to Stravinsky, dated 18 November 1960, confirming shipment of Carl Parrish's *A Treasury of Early Music*, another anthology that anyone who studied music in college or university in the 1950s or 1960s would have used.

*Middle Ages* and *Music in the Renaissance*), Apel and Davison, Parrish and Ohl
[*Masterpieces of Music Before 1750*], . . . and in fact every anthology of 'old'
music that he could find. Also every recording, from *Anthologie Sonore* down
or up and including private ones."[32] Beginning with *Orpheus* and the *Mass*,
both completed in 1948, almost every piece Stravinsky composed in America
bears some affinity to "early music" – that is to say, an earlier music than he had
drawn upon during his European "neoclassical" phase. "We are located in time
constantly in a tonal-system work," Stravinsky is quoted as saying, "but we
may only 'go through' a polyphonic work, whether Josquin's Duke Hercules
Mass or a serially composed non-tonal-system work."[33] He justified the barless
notation (resembling contemporaneous editions of fifteenth-century music) in
the *Diphonas* and *Elegias* from *Threni* (1958), his first fully twelve-tone composition, by noting that "there are no strong beats in these canons, . . . and the
conductor must merely count the music out as he counts out a motet by
Josquin."[34]

Stravinsky's knowledge of early music, acquired (the year at Harvard apart)
largely outside the academy, marks his case as exceptional. Hindemith's
considerable activity on its behalf was largely a by-product of academic
employment. For him, old music was an example of salubrious, socially integrative artistic activity, as revived in Weimar Germany by the so-called
*Jugendmusikbewegung*, or "movement for music for young people" (a.k.a.
*Singbewegung*), which was responsible for the revival of the recorder as a school
instrument, for one thing, and for the establishment of numerous *collegia
musica*, for another.[35] In contrast to the modernist attitudes discussed thus
far, Hindemith's involvement was a facet of his anti-modernist retrenchment,
strongly implied in a passage from *A Composer's World*, the lectures he gave
during his stint (a decade after Stravinsky's) as Harvard's Norton Professor of
Poetry, where he contrasts the debased artistic environment he and his audience shared with the vitality of "the period of Machaut, Dufay, and Josquin;

---

32  Robert Craft to Richard Taruskin, personal communication, 7 November 1984. In his most recent
volume of memoirs, Craft has added some interesting details: that Stravinsky received Helen Hewitt's then
brand-new edition of Petrucci's *Odhecaton* as a present from Nadia Boulanger in 1942, and that Manfred
Bukofzer introduced him not only to Dunstaple, as might have been expected, but also to Matteo da
Perugia, from whom "Stravinsky borrowed the concept of alternating instrumental and *a cappella* passages
in the Agnus Dei of his Mass" (Craft, *Stravinsky: Discoveries and Memories*, 68–69).
33  Stravinsky and Craft, *Conversations with Igor Stravinsky*, 23.      34  Ibid., 18–19.
35  See Jöde, ed., *Musikalische Jugendkultur* for a founding document, and, for a historical treatment, Scholz,
Jonas-Corrieri, *et al.*, eds., *Die deutsche Jugendmusikbewegung*. Most recent is Berger, "Spreading the Gospel
of *Singbewegung*." The extent of Hindemith's involvement with *Jugendmusik* is controversial, partly
because the movement picked up some unsavory political associations in retrospect, especially among
those who had been exiled from Germany during the run-up to World War II. Thus Krenek: "An unbroken
line leads from the activist *Wandervogel* (Boy Scout), by way of Hindemith's concerto grosso style, to the
Hitler Youth, of whom it is told that they give vent to their indomitable spirit of independence by secretly
performing Hindemith's *Spielmusik*" (*Music Here and Now*, trans. Fles, 75).

the time of Isaac, Senfl, Finck, Hofhaimer, and many other contributors to the art of the German Liederbücher in the sixteenth century," when "the art of ensemble activity with the emphasis on vocal participation flourished most noticeably."[36]

Hindemith's honor roll of worthies is strongly colored by the actual repertory of his own famous Collegium Musicum at Yale University, which he led in a series of annual concerts from 1945 to 1953 that served as a practical adjunct to a multi-year chronological survey of European theoretical treatises. The fifteenth-century year was 1947, and the program was as follows:

Compère: Missa l'homme armé – Kyrie
Finck: Missa in summis – Credo
Flordigal: Cui luna, sol et omnia
Agricola: D'ung aultre amer
Stockem: Brunette
Obrecht: Missa sub tuum praesidium confugimus – Sanctus and Benedictus
Tinctoris: Missa cunctorum plasmator [i.e., *L'homme armé*] – Agnus Dei
von Fulda: In decollatione S. Johannis Baptistae – Nuntius, celso
Anon.: Ich sachs eins mals
Anon.: In feuers hitz
Ockeghem: Ma bouche rit
de la Torre: Airado va el gentil hombre
Medina: No hay placer
Anon.: Noch weet ic een ionc vraukin fijn
Phillips: I love, I love, and whom love ye?
Cornish: Jolly Rutterkin
Barbireau: Der Pfobenschwancz
Rubinus: Der Bauernschwanz
Obrecht: Ic draghe de mutse clutse
Anon.: Hor oires une chanson
Obrecht: Tsat een meskin[37]

The 1948 Collegium program, designated "Early Sixteenth Century," contained several compositions by composers within the same age cohort: Pierre de La Rue, Isaac, Josquin, Heinrich Finck, and Paul Hofhaimer. Hindemith's repertory preferences were as revealing of his predilections as those of Schoenberg or Stravinsky. The emphasis on *Hofweisen* (or "Tenorlieder" as they are often called in modern scholarly literature) is both an aspect of Hindemith's somewhat nationalistic approach to early music and a souvenir of his own compositional past, since it was on three tenor-tunes from early

36 Hindemith, *A Composer's World*, 199.    37 http://hdl.handle.net/10079/fa/music.mss.0047.

sixteenth-century *Gesangbücher*, as typically appropriated by the *Singbewegung*, that he had based *Der Schwanendreher*, his viola concerto of 1935. Isaac's setting of *Zwischen Berg und tiefem Tal*, the main tune in the concerto's first movement, figured in the 1948 program. The first movement of Hindemith's Sonata for Alto Horn (1943) has as its middle section a long passage in isorhythm with a seventeen-beat talea; the finale is preceded by an intensely nostalgic German poem in the form of a dialogue between the soloist and the piano accompanist, which ends with the latter's advice to the former (as translated in the first edition): "Your task it is, amid confusion, rush, and noise / to grasp the lasting, calm, and meaningful, / and finding it anew, to hold and treasure it."

## The Cold War avant-garde

Hindemith's Collegium Musicum is often described as parent to the professional and collegiate early music ensembles that burgeoned in Europe and America in the 1950s; and indeed, the Yale group included a number of later American exponents of the repertory, including three members of Noah Greenberg's New York Pro Musica (the lutenist Joseph Iadone, the organist Paul Maynard, and the soprano Jean Hakes), as well as the recorder player Martha Bixler and the conductor Robert Hickok.[38] An equally characteristic venue for the performance of early music in the 1950s and 1960s was the programs of the new music ensembles that, in accordance with De Paoli's "parentheses" around the common practice, were also proliferating at the time. One of the early concerts given by Pierre Boulez's Domaine musical in Paris opened with isorhythmic motets by Du Fay and ended with madrigals by Claudio Monteverdi and Carlo Gesualdo – works that, by Boulez's explicit stipulation, had "a particular relevance for our time."[39] The Group for Contemporary Music, the first of countless American university-based new-music ensembles, formed by the composers Charles Wuorinen and Harvey

---

38  See Boatwright, "Paul Hindemith as a Teacher"; Richter, "Paul Hindemith as Director."

39  Watkins, *The Gesualdo Hex*, 122. In correspondence with Henri Pousseur, Boulez announced that he had purchased Guillaume de Van's editions of Machaut and Du Fay ("made by the American Institute of Musicology in Rome"), and averred that "these are the authors to whom, in historical position and tendency, we may feel the closest. We can go further yet in nurturing a way of organizing sounds that demands great severity and rigorousness of means. I would be inclined to call it scientific, were that not a rather grandiose way of describing rather modest discoveries" ("ce sont les auteurs dont, par la situation historique aussi bien que par la tendance, nous pouvons nous sentir les plus rapprochés. Nous pouvons nous advancer dans l'incubation d'un système sonore. Ce qui exige une grande sévérité, et l'emploi de moyens rigoureux. J'aurais tendance à dire scientifiques, si ce n'était pas bien grandiose pour nos découvertes du genre mineur") (letter dated "mid-September 1951" by Robert Piencikowski, who quotes it in "Boulez's *Rite*," 314–15 n. 30).

Sollberger at Columbia University, followed suit. The first program, on 22
October 1962, began with *Christes Crosse*, a formidable demonstration of
metric proportions from Thomas Morley's *Plaine and Easie Introduction to
Practicall Musick*. Thereafter, until 1968, the opening slot was always reserved
for old music with "a particular relevance for our time." At the second
concert it was "Music from the Mensural Codex of Nikolaus Apel (late 15th
century)" (the title taken directly from the modern edition in the series Das
Erbe deutscher Musik); at the third it was Wuorinen's *Bearbeitungen über das
Glogauer Liederbuch*, after another volume of Das Erbe deutscher Musik. At
the fourth and fifth concerts the opening pieces were what we would now call
*ars subtilior* chansons, by "Matheus de Perusio" and Anthonello de Caserta
(their names again copied from the modern editions in which the music was
found), including Matteo's *Le greygnour bien*, the redoubtable opening selection in Willi Apel's *French Secular Music of the Late Fourteenth Century*, published in 1950 by the Mediaeval Academy of America with a preface by
Hindemith. It was an inevitable choice at a time when academic composition
had itself become an *ars subtilior*, obsessed with rhythmic complication.
Elliott Carter, at the epitome of this tendency, credited "the rhythmic
procedures of late fourteenth-century French music, [as well as] music of
the fifteenth and sixteenth centuries that uses hemiola and other ways of
alternating meters, especially duple and triple," as important precursors
of, and inspirations for, the technique of "metric modulation" on which his
reputation as an innovator was based.[40]

Wuorinen attached particular significance to fifteenth-century music. He
enjoyed telling classes in his early days as a university teacher that "music
died in the middle ages and was reborn in the twentieth century."[41] His
Glogauer *Bearbeitungen* consisted of a suite of five items from the famous set
of partbooks, scored for four players (flute/piccolo, clarinet/bass clarinet,
violin, double bass) with a lot of color-changing in midstream, after the
manner of Webern's Bach orchestration. In a program note, Wuorinen
wrote that he was attracted to the style of this music by its fast and relatively
undirected harmonic rhythm, which offered a "pretonal" counterpart to the
"post-tonal" idiom of contemporary music.[42] His slightly older English

40  Edwards, *Flawed Words and Stubborn Sounds*, 91–92 n.
41  As told to the author, ca. 1969, by Peter Janovsky, a student in Wuorinen's introduction to music
("Music Humanities") class at Columbia College in New York. Compare Varèse's exultation, contemplating the postwar rise of electronic media, "that composers and physicists are at last working together, and
music is again linked with science, as it was in the Middle Ages" ("The Liberation of Sound," 33).
42  At least five of Wuorinen's compositions quote or arrange pieces by Josquin, or attributed to him,
beginning with his Third Symphony (1959), which ends with a pair of quotations from the *Déploration de
Jehan Okeghem*. *Ave Christe* (1994) is a transcription for piano solo of Josquin[?]'s four-voice motet;
*Josquiniana* for string quartet (2001) is an arrangement of six secular pieces, all of them early music

contemporaries of the so-called Manchester School made even more extensive and stylistically formative appropriations from fifteenth-century music. Alexander Goehr and Harrison Birtwistle have made use of the isorhythmic principle, the former in the scherzo from his String Quartet No. 2, Op. 23 (1967), the latter in a large number of important works. For them, as for Boulez, "the isorhythmic motets of Machaut and Dufay" provided the "starting-point" for advanced (or "total") serialism in its "detach[ment of] the polyphony from the rhythm."[43]

Both Birtwistle and Peter Maxwell Davies arranged fifteenth-century music for the concerts of their new music ensemble, founded as the Pierrot Players in 1965 and renamed The Fires of London in 1970.[44] Birtwistle's somewhat earlier *The World is Discovered: Six instrumental movements after Heinrich Isaak*, scored for double wind quintet, harp, and guitar (1960–61), is a much more thoroughgoing recomposition. The six *carmina* on which the movements are based, all taken from the volume of Isaac secular works in DTÖ,[45] are distorted in a manner Birtwistle attributed to the impression Picasso's studies after Velasquez's *Las Meninas* made on him at a Tate Gallery exhibition.

Davies's *Missa super L'Homme armé* for speaker or singer with flute, clarinet, keyboards, percussion, violin, and cello (1968; revised as music theater in 1971) "started as an exercise – a completion of incomplete sections of an anonymous fifteenth-century mass on the popular song 'L'homme armé' in fifteenth-century style."[46] The work in question was the Agnus Dei from the second of the six *L'Homme armé* masses in Naples MS VI.E.40, as published (with blank staves in place of the missing contratenors) by Laurence Feininger.[47] The distortions applied to the borrowed material are similar to Birtwistle's, although Davies attributed the idea to a literary rather than a painterly

chestnuts; *Ave Maria, Virgo Serena (on Josquin)* (2007) is a setting for clarinet, violin, cello, and piano of the mother of all "Renaissance" hits; and *Marian Tropes* for string quartet (2010) interweaves *fragmenta missarum* by Josquin and Du Fay with newly composed material in period style. (Another Du Fay arrangement, "Vergine bella of Guillermus Dufay," scored for mallet and keyboard instruments, furnishes an "entr'acte" before the middle movement of Wuorinen's *Percussion Symphony* of 1976.)

43 Boulez, *Stocktakings*, 120. The process might actually be more precisely described, conversely, as the detachment of rhythm from the polyphony.

44 Birtwistle's chief effort of this kind was an arrangement of Ockeghem's encomium to Busnoys, *Ut heremita solus*, for flute doubling piccolo and alto flute, clarinet doubling bass clarinet, viola, cello, piano and glockenspiel (1969).

45 Isaac, *Weltliche Werke*, v. 28: *Der Weld fundt* [title piece], *Tmeiskin uas iunch, Helogierons nous, Et ie boi d'autant, Maudit soit*.

46 Notes by the composer to a recording with The Fires of London and Vanessa Redgrave (Oiseau-Lyre DSLO 2 [1972]); repr. in Griffiths, *Peter Maxwell Davies*, 145–46; all quotations from the composer are from this source.

47 Feininger, ed., *Ordinarium Missae Tomus III-2: Anonymus, Missa II, super L'homme armé*. The Agnus Dei is on 33–36.

stimulus: Episode 12 ("Cyclops") from Joyce's *Ulysses*, wherein "a conversation in a tavern is interrupted by insertions which seize upon a small, passing idea in the main narrative, and amplify this, often out of all proportion, in a style which bears no relationship to the style of the germinal idea which sparked off the insertion." The anonymous mass is offset by "music which transforms the basic material into ever more distantly related statements," including some that clearly register as defacements (pseudo-Victorian hymns and faultily recorded popular music, performed by a player piano and by a gramophone). These defacements are juxtaposed with a speaker intoning the Passion narrative from the Vulgate Gospel of Luke. "Countercultural" provocation passes at this point from aesthetic vandalism into what plainly invites reading as blasphemy.

Luigi Nono made suitably veiled allusion to what he called a "version libre" of the chanson *Malor* [i.e. *Malheur*] *me bat* (which, following Petrucci's *Odhecaton*, he attributed to Ockeghem) in his string quartet *Fragmente-Stille, An Diotima* (1980). As with Stravinsky, interest in fifteenth- and sixteenth-century music induced Nono to correspond with leading scholars in the field, notably Edward Lowinsky.[48]

Interest in fifteenth-century music seems to have waned among composers of the early twenty-first century (with Fabrice Fitch, in his *Agricologies* of 2004–8, furnishing an exception). It does not figure prominently in the eclectic "polystylistic" mixtures of multicultural postmodernism. Today's eclecticism favors geographical diversity over temporal, and is more interested in synthesizing high and low genres than in appropriating or defacing aristocratic cultures of old. The Belgian musicologist Mark Delaere, recalling the bond between the musicians of his own age cohort and late medieval music, somewhat nostalgically associates the latter with the "soixante-huitard" politics of yesteryear. "The subversive potential of both early and contemporary music," he writes, "was acknowledged to the full extent during the 1960s, when they were partners in crime in the attempt to launch a counterculture."[49] The 1970s saw both the enhanced acceptance (also describable as commercial exploitation) of fifteenth-century music in the "mainstream" concert hall – emblematized by the performance of Du Fay's *Missa Se la face ay pale* at the London Proms by David Munrow and the Early Music Consort of London in August 1974 – and the flouting, by composers such as George Crumb, George Rochberg, or Wolfgang Rihm, of De Paoli's "parentheses," the quarantining

48 See Thein, "Zitat, Bearbeitung," 788–94. Correspondence between Nono and Lowinsky is preserved in both their archives: at the Fondazione archivio Luigi Nono in Venice and at the Regenstein Library of the University of Chicago, respectively.
49 Delaere, "Self-Portrait with Boulez and Machaut," 192.

of the music of the common practice (or what Steve Reich liked to call "the bourgeois classics"[50]) from the contemporary composerly purview. These cultural phenomena, often cited as portents of postmodernism, worked together to rob the music of the distant past of its alluring air of alterity.

# Bibliography

Berger, Anna Maria Busse, "Spreading the Gospel of *Singbewegung*: An Ethnomusicologist Missionary in Tanganyika of the 1930s," *JAMS* 66 (2013), 475–522

Black, Leo, trans., *Die Reihe: A Periodical Devoted to Developments in Contemporary Music*, Bryn Mawr, 1958

Boatwright, Howard, "Paul Hindemith as a Teacher," *MQ* 50 (1964), 279–89

Boulez, Pierre, *Stocktakings from an Apprenticeship*, trans. Stephen Walsh, New York, 1991

"Stravinsky demeure," in *Musique russe*, ed. Pierre Souvtchinsky, Paris, 1953, 1:151–224; repr. as "Stravinsky Remains," in Boulez, *Stocktakings*, 55–110

Burde, Wolfgang, *György Ligeti: Eine Monographie*, Zurich, 1993

Craft, Robert, *Stravinsky: Chronicle of a Friendship*, revised and expanded edn., Nashville, TN, 1994

*Stravinsky: Discoveries and Memories*, [Hong Kong, 2013]

and Brett Shapiro, *A Catalogue of Some Books and Music Inscribed to and/or Autographed and Annotated by Igor Stravinsky, and of Private Recordings and Test-Pressings Labelled by Him in the Estate of Vera Stravinsky* (typescript, 1983)

de Groot, Rokus, "Ockeghem and New Music in the Twentieth Century," *TVNM* 47 (1997), 201–23

De Paoli, Domenico, Program note in *La musica nel XX secolo: Convegno internazionale di musica contemporanea. Congresso di compositori, interpreti e critici musicali. Concorso internazionale per i "Premi dell'opera del xx secolo." Opera, concerti di musica sinfonica e da camera . . . Roma, 4–14 aprile 1954*, ed. Angiola Maria Bonisconti, Rome, 1954, 14–17

Delaere, Mark, "Self-Portrait with Boulez and Machaut (and Ligeti is there as well): Harrison Birtwistle's *Hoquetus Petrus*," in *The Modernist Legacy: Essays on New Music*, ed. Björn Heile, Farnham, 2009, 191–204

Edwards, Allen, *Flawed Words and Stubborn Sounds: A Conversation with Elliott Carter*, New York, 1971

Faulkner, William, *Requiem for a Nun*, 1951; New York, 1975

[Feininger, Laurence, ed.], *Ordinarium Missae Tomus III-2: Anonymus, Missa II, super L'homme armé*, Monumenta Polyphoniae Liturgicae Sanctae Ecclesiae Romanae, Rome, 1957

Frobenius, Wolf, "Krenek und Ockeghem," in *Ernst Krenek*, ed. Otto Kolleritsch, Vienna, 1982, 153–73

Gray, Cecil, *The History of Music*, London, 1928

---

50  Quoted in Taruskin, *Oxford History*, 5:368.

Griffiths, Paul, *Peter Maxwell Davies*, London, 1982

Harrison, Jay S., "Talk with Stravinsky: Composer Discusses his Music," *New York Herald Tribune*, 21 December 1952

Hartley, Leslie P., *The Go-Between*, London, [1953]

Hilmar, Ernst, ed., *Arnold Schoenberg Gedenkausstellung 1974*, Vienna, 1974

Hindemith, Paul, *A Composer's World: Horizons and Limitations* (Charles Eliot Norton Lectures 1949–50), Cambridge, 1952; repr. New York, 1961

*The Craft of Musical Composition*, trans. Arthur Mendel, New York, 1942

Isaac, Henricus, *Heinrich Isaac's Choralis Constantinus Book III Transcribed from the Formschneider First Edition (Nurnberg, 1555)*, ed. Louise Cuyler, Ann Arbor, 1950

*Weltliche Werke*, ed. Johannes Wolf, Denkmäler der Tonkunst in Österreich, 14/1 (28), Vienna, 1907

Jöde, Fritz, ed., *Musikalische Jugendkultur: Anregungen aus der Jugendbewegung*, Hamburg, 1918

Joseph, Charles M., *Stravinsky Inside Out*, New Haven, 2001

Kievman, Carson, "Ockeghem and Ligeti: The Music of Transcendence," Ph.D. diss., Princeton University, 2003

Krenek, Ernst, *Johannes Ockeghem*, London, 1953

*Music Here and Now*, trans. Barthold Fles, New York, 1939

Ligeti, György, *György Ligeti in Conversation with Péter Várnai, Josef Häusler, Claude Samuel, and Himself*, London, 1983

Moldenhauer, Hans and Rosaleen, *Anton von Webern: A Chronicle of his Life and Work*, New York, 1979

Piencikowski, Robert, "Boulez's Rite," in *Avatar of Modernity: The Rite of Spring Reconsidered*, ed. Hermann Danuser and Heidy Zimmermann, London, 2013, 306–15

Richter, Eckhart, "Paul Hindemith as Director of the Yale Collegium Musicum," *College Music Symposium* 18 (1978), 20–44

Schoenberg, Arnold, *30 Kanons*, ed. Josef Rufer, Kassel, 1963

*Sämtliche Werke*, ed. Tadeusz Okuljar and Martina Sichardt, Mainz and Vienna, 1980, 1991

*Style and Idea: Selected Writings of Arnold Schoenberg*, ed. Leonard Stein, trans. Leo Black, Berkeley, 1984

Scholz, Wilhelm, Waltraut Jonas-Corrieri, *et al.*, eds., *Die deutsche Jugendmusikbewegung in Dokumenten ihrer Zeit von den Anfängen bis 1933*, Wolfenbüttel and Zurich, 1980

Sessions, Roger, "Music in Crisis: Some Notes on Recent Musical History," *Modern Music* 10 (1932–33), 63–78

Stravinsky, Igor, and Robert Craft, *Conversations with Igor Stravinsky*, Garden City, NY, 1959

*Memories and Commentaries*, Garden City, NY, 1960

Taruskin, Richard, "'Alte Musik' or 'Early Music'?," *Twentieth-Century Music* 8 (2011), 3–28

*The Oxford History of Western Music*, New York, 2009

Thein, Wolfgang, "Zitat, Bearbeitung, Transformation: Spielarten der kompositorischen Auseinandersetzung mit Ockeghem in der Musik des 20. Jahrhunderts," in *Johannes Ockeghem: Actes du XL<sup>e</sup> Colloque international d'études humanistes*, ed. Philippe Vendrix, Paris, 1998, 787–809

Todd, R. Larry, "Retrograde, Inversion, Retrograde-Inversion and Related Techniques in the Masses of Obrecht," *MQ* 64 (1978), 50–78

Varèse, Edgard, "The Liberation of Sound," in *Perspectives on American Composers*, ed. Benjamin Boretz and Edward T. Cone, New York, 1971, 25–33

Vaughan Williams, Ralph, "Should Music Be National?" (1932), in *National Music and Other Essays*, London, 1963, 1–11

Watkins, Glenn, *The Gesualdo Hex: Music, Myth, and Memory*, New York, 2010

Webern, Anton von, "The Path to Twelve-Note Composition," trans. Leo Black, in *The Path to the New Music*, ed. Willi Reich, Bryn Mawr, 1963, 42–56

# Index

Italic indicates a music example or figure.

Printed in the USA
CPSIA information can be obtained
at www.ICGtesting.com
LVHW010011200923
758621LV00003B/223